CONTENTS

PART THREE. THE PRODUCT

PART FIVE. DISTRIBUTION STRUCTURE

16. DISTRIBUTION CHANNELS AND THE REAL MARKET   342

17. RETAILERS AND METHODS OF OPERATION   362

18. THE WHOLESALE MARKET AND WHOLESALING MIDDLEMEN   383

19. COMPETITIVE CONFLICTS AND COOPERATION IN DISTRIBUTION CHANNELS   404

20. DESIGNING AND MANAGING CHANNELS OF DISTRIBUTION   420

PART SIX. PROMOTIONAL ACTIVITIES

22. THE PROMOTIONAL PROGRAM   482

23. MANAGEMENT OF PERSONAL SELLING   504

24. MANAGEMENT OF ADVERTISING   522

PREFACE

Marketing is a dynamic segment of a dynamic field—business administration. The last half of the 1970s is posing new environmental challenges to business in general and to marketing in particular. A societal orientation and an awareness by executives of their social responsibilities are growing in marketing. Also, for the first time in over 30 years, several industries are faced with product shortages. A textbook in marketing should reflect these challenges and offer some strategic guides to marketing's executive leadership in its problem-solving and decision-making responsibilities. Consequently, several changes have been made in this revision of *Fundamentals of Marketing: Second Canadian Edition* in order to keep it up to date. However, those who are familiar with the first edition will find that the basic theme, approach, and organization have been retained. The central theme is that marketing is a *total system* of business action rather than a fragmented assortment of functions and institutions, as it has often been treated in marketing literature and in practice.

In this edition the material has been updated, and a number of chapters have been completely or extensively rewritten. Fourteen of the 24 cases are new. The chapter on consumerism and marketing's social responsibility has been greatly expanded. The emerging societal orientation in marketing is reflected in the broadened definition of marketing, the revised evolution of marketing management, the broadening of the marketing concept, and in other topics. "Marketing in an Era of Shortages" is introduced. The treatment of market segmentation is expanded to a complete chapter. Marketing information systems and marketing research are treated extensively. Other chapters have been partially rewritten to introduce recent developments and new concepts. There is a major expansion of materials on the French-Canadian market.

The sequence of some topics has been rearranged to effect a more logical order and to improve the teaching/learning experience. The sections on distribution structure and price systems have been reversed in order, reflecting the idea that a product typically is priced before it is distributed. The chapter on sociological influences on buying behavior is improved by bringing into that chapter the topics of diffusion of innovation (as part of small-reference-group theory) and family buying behavior. Perhaps a controversial shift is the relocation of marketing information systems and marketing research to Chapter 27 from its former spot as Chapter 3. The change is a response to the suggestion of several people over the years. Fortunately, the topic is sufficiently freestanding and flexible that it can be treated in either location, as an instructor prefers. (In our own teaching, two of us still prefer the earlier location because throughout the course we refer to this managerial aid in decision making.)

For those not acquainted with the first edition, this is a basic textbook in the dynamic, complex field of marketing. While more attention is directed to the role of marketing in our socioeconomic system, the book is written largely from the viewpoint of management *in an individual firm*—either a manufacturer or a middleman. Emphasis is placed on the marketing problem solving and decision making required of a firm's executives. For the most part, the coverage is analytical and evaluative. At the same time, descriptive material is certainly necessary in an introductory textbook. However, such material intentionally is limited to the amount needed by the student to undertake some intelligent analysis and evaluation.

Fundamentals of Marketing: Second Canadian Edition is intended for use in the introductory course in marketing. It is designed for students who plan to specialize in marketing and also for those who will be taking only one course in the field. Both of these groups are provided with a realistic treatment of marketing as it operates in Canadian business today. The book may also be used in management training programs or for general reading by business executives.

The "systems" idea of marketing has become more meaningful in recent years with the acceptance of the marketing concept—a philosophy which stresses the need for a marketing (rather than production) orientation which is compatible with society's long-run interests. A company's managerial planning and operations should be directed toward satisfying the customers' longrun wants, considering societal interests, and obtaining profitable sales volume. In short, marketing is becoming recognized as an all-pervasive part of the system of business management, and all managerial activity in a firm should be directed toward making the marketing process more effective.

This philosophy may be seen in the framework of the marketing process, which, to be effective, requires that a firm first identify, study, and measure its markets. Management then has four elements—its product, price system, channels of distribution structure, and promotional activities—which can be used to build a program to reach its markets. The firm is seeking to achieve the most effective marketing mix—that is, the best possible combination of the four ingredients. Throughout these four areas, especially in channel structure and promotion, management makes extensive use of another element—the human factor. Manpower considerations often are paramount in marketing decisions. At all stages in the marketing process, management should use marketing research as an aid.

This framework of the marketing process is reflected generally in the organization of the book's content. The text is divided into eight parts. Part 1 serves as an introduction and includes a chapter on the role of systems and the management process in marketing. Part 2 is devoted to an analysis of the consumer and the industrial markets. Population, income, and buyer behavior are analyzed as factors affecting the market for products.

Parts 3 through 6 deal with the development and operation of a marketing program, and each of these parts covers one of the above-mentioned four components of the marketing mix. In Part 3 various topics related to the product itself are discussed, including product planning and development, product-line policies and strategies, and several characteristics of a product such as branding and packaging. A firm's price system is the subject of Part 4, where we study pricing objectives, price determination in practice, and some major price policies and strategies. Part 5 covers the distribution structure. Retailing and wholesaling institutions are described and appraised. Consideration is given to the selection of channels of distribution, the selection of individual middlemen, and the ever-present conflict within and among marketing channels. The management of physical distribution, in which this activity is viewed as a system of product flow, is studied in a separate chapter. Part 6 is devoted to the total promotional program, including the advertising and the personal selling programs.

The major portion of the book pertains to the *domestic* marketing of *manufactured goods*. In the interest of completeness, however, Part 7 is devoted to marketing fundamentals as they are applied in the special fields of international marketing and the marketing of services.

Part 8 covers marketing information systems, marketing planning, and the evaluation of the marketing program. Included are such topics as marketing research, demand forecasting; and marketing cost analysis. Chapter 30 is devoted to consumerism and marketing's social responsibility. Chapter 31—the final chapter—is an appraisal of the role of marketing in the economy and a look to the future in this field.

Special attention has been devoted to the preparation of the discussion questions found at the end of each chapter. These questions generally cannot be answered "right out of the book." Instead, they are intended to be thought provoking and to serve as an aid in applying the material in the chapter. Some of the questions require outside fieldwork, and thus have the merit of introducing the students to practical business applications of the textbook fundamentals.

Another feature of *Fundamentals of Marketing: Second Canadian Edition* is the inclusion of short cases at the end of each of the eight parts in the text. Each one focuses on a specific issue related to topic covered in the text. These cases serve as both a teaching tool and study guide. In line with the managerial approach in this book, the cases provide an opportunity for problem analysis and decision making by the student.

Many people have contributed to this Second Canadian Edition. Many of these debts are acknowledged in footnotes and other references in the text. We particularly want to thank Jerry Byers of Humber College and Jacques Bourgeois of Carleton University for their useful comments and suggestions. Several of the cases were written by other professors and in each instance the authorship is identified. We are very pleased to be able to include their material. The assistance provided by David Warner and Sharon Harley of Memorial University and by David Courtney of Statistics Canada is very much appreciated.

WILLIAM J. STANTON

MONTROSE S. SOMMERS

JAMES G. BARNES

FUNDAMENTALS OF MARKETING

SECOND CANADIAN EDITION

MODERN MARKETING

MARKETING IN THE CANADIAN ECONOMY

Most of us probably consider ourselves rather well informed on the subject of marketing. After all, we watch television commercials and see how advertisers are trying to persuade us to buy. We purchase products on a self-service basis in a supermarket. We observe the quality of personal selling as we buy our clothes or gasoline. Some of us have friends who "can get it for us wholesale," or we ourselves may be shrewd shoppers who can ferret out bargains. Some of us have worked as salesclerks in retail stores. In short, everybody knows something about marketing. It is on this perilous base of a little knowledge that we begin our study.

NATURE AND SCOPE OF MARKETING

While most people probably do know a little something about marketing, the word itself has often been misunderstood and used loosely even by those in the field. When a salesman or sales manager speaks of marketing, he is actually talking about selling, an advertising account executive means advertising, and a department store manager means retailing or merchandising. Each of these people is talking about *one part* of the total marketing activity.

NARROW INTERPRETATION

The American Marketing Association (the professional association for marketers in Canada and the United States) says that marketing is "the performance of business activities that direct the flow of goods and services from producer to consumer or user."[1] In its comments, the committee suggests a somewhat broader meaning than this, and for the purpose of modern marketing, a broader definition is certainly needed. Marketing processes begin long before the goods go into production. Marketing decisions must be made regarding the product and its market, its pricing, and its promotion. Should the product even be made? How should it be packaged and labeled? What is the composition of its potential market? What will be the initial price? Just as marketing does not begin at the end of the production line, it does not end with the final sale. The customer must be satisfied if we expect his repeat business or if we want him to speak well of our company. Thus a product guarantee and considerable servicing may be required after the sale is made.

This narrow definition reflects the production orientation which has permeated so much of Canadian business. Products have been designed by engineers, manufactured by production men, priced by accountants, and then given to sales managers to sell. Just *building* a good product will not in itself result in a company's success, nor will it have much bearing on consumer welfare. The product must be *marketed* to consumers before its full value can be realized. Aggressive marketing practices have been largely responsible for the high material standard of living in Canada.

MARKETING AND THE STANDARD OF LIVING

Possibly the most expressive, all-encompassing, and yet short statement of modern marketing was made some years ago by Paul Mazur. He said that marketing is the delivery of a standard of living to society.[2] Malcolm McNair of Harvard added an important concept when he amended Mazur's fine definition to read that marketing is the *creation* and delivery of a standard of living to society.

SYSTEMS DEFINITION USED IN THIS BOOK

This broad concept of marketing gives us a feel for the "big picture," but it is not precise enough. Consequently, the following definition will be used in this text. *Marketing* is a total system of interacting business activities designed to plan, price, promote, and distribute want-satisfying products and services to present and potential customers.

Marketing is:
  A system: A system of business activities
  Designed to: plan, price, promote, and distribute (the action)
  Object of the action: want-satisfying goods and services
  Beneficiaries of the action: the market—present and potential household
        consumers or industrial users

---

1 Committee on Definitions, *Marketing Definitions: A Glossary of Marketing Terms,* American Marketing Association, Chicago, 1960, p. 15.

2 See Paul Mazur, "Does Distribution Cost Enough?" *Fortune,* November, 1947, p. 138.

This concrete definition has several important implications. First, it is a managerial definition rather than a legalistic or economic one. Second, the entire system of business action should be market- or customer-oriented. Customers' wants must be recognized and satisfied effectively. Third, the definition suggests that marketing is a dynamic business process—a total, integrated process—rather than a fragmented assortment of institutions and functions. Marketing is not any one activity, nor is it exactly the sum of several; rather, it is the result of the *interaction* of many activities. Fourth, the marketing program starts with the germ of a product idea and does not end until the customer's wants are completely satisfied, which may be some time after the sale is made. Furthermore, market programming should be done with a maximum of effectiveness and a minimum of cost. Finally, the definition implies that to be successful, marketing must maximize profitable sales *over the long run*. Thus, customers must be satisfied in order for a company to get the repeat business which ordinarily is so vital to success.

Marketing and related terms. Sometimes marketing is confused or misunderstood in relation to some other terms, especially selling, merchandising, and distribution. Marketing is the comprehensive concept. The others are each only one part—one activity—in the total marketing system.

Marketing is:	The total of what we are talking about.
Selling is:	One part of promotion and promotion is one part of the total marketing program.
Merchandising is:	Product planning—the internal company planning to get the right product or service to the market at the right time, and at the right price, and in the right colors and sizes.
Distribution is:	Market coverage—the retailing and wholesaling structure—the channels used to get the product to its market.
Physical distribution is:	Materials-flow activities such as transportation, warehousing, and inventory control.

BROADER, SOCIETAL DIMENSIONS OF MARKETING

The systems concept of marketing is essentially a management activity in business firms. Of course, it is true that the marketing system in a company is influenced by external factors—for instance, economic conditions, customers' behavior, technology, and legal forces. In fact, it is marketing's job to evaluate and capitalize on changes and opportunities in this external environment. Nevertheless, our systems definition is oriented mainly toward marketing *within* a business enterprise. And because this book deals with the management of marketing as a business activity in a firm, this systems definition is useful for our purposes.

However, marketing is not solely a business activity. We need also to recognize that marketing has a social dimension far broader than may be apparent in the above systems definition. In fact, a societal perspective is more meaningful and truly descriptive of marketing today. Any interpersonal or interorganizational relationship involving an exchange (a transaction) is marketing. That is, *the essence of marketing is a transaction.* Consequently, marketing occurs any time one social unit strives to exchange something of value with another social unit.[3]

Within this societal perspective then, (1) the marketers, and (2) what it is they are marketing, and (3) their potential markets all assume new and far broader dimensions. The category of *marketers* might include, in addition to business firms, such diverse social units as: *(a)* a political party trying to market its candidate to the public; *(b)* the director of an art museum providing new exhibits to generate greater attendance and financial support: *(c)* a labor union which markets its ideas or terms to its members and the company management; and *(d)* a Ministry in Ottawa attempting to convince a region or the population in general of the wisdom of a particular program. A professor is doing a marketing job when he attempts to make his course interesting and meaningful to his students. A young man is engaged in marketing when he tries to persuade a girl to date him or marry him.[4]

In addition to the range of items normally considered as products and services, in a broader sense *what* is being marketed might include: (a) ideas, such as reducing air pollution, stopping smoking, or contributing to the Red Cross drive; or, (b) people, such as a new hockey or football coach or a political candidate.

In a broad sense, *target markets* include more than the consumers of products, services, and ideas. Thus, a college's or university's market includes the local or provincial officials who provide funds, the citizens who live near the school who may be affected by student and school activities, and the alumni. A business firm's market may include government regulatory agencies, environmentalists, and municipal tax assessors.[5]

HISTORICAL DEVELOPMENT OF MARKETING

In this brief historical review, we shall see how marketing is born and grows as a society moves from a home handicraft economy of self-sufficiency into a socioeconomic system which involves a division of labor, factory industrialization, and urbanization of the population.

---

3 See Philip Kotler, "A Generic Concept of Marketing," *Journal of Marketing,* April, 1972, pp. 46-54; also see Philip Kotler and Sidney J. Levy, "Broadening the Concept of Marketing," *Journal of Marketing,* January, 1969, pp. 10-15; Philip Kotler and Gerald Zaltman, "Social Marketing: An Approach to Planned Social Change," *Journal of Marketing,* July 1971, pp. 3-12; Leslie Dawson, "Marketing Science in the Age of Aquarius," *Journal of Marketing,* July, 1971, pp. 66-72.

4 For a small sample of studies illustrating the broader view of marketing, see Adel I. El-Ansary and Oscar E. Kramer, Jr., "Social Marketing: The Family Planning Experience," *Journal of Marketing,* July, 1973, pp. 1-7; John U. Farley and Harold J. Leavitt, "Marketing and Population Problems," *Journal of Marketing,* July, 1971, pp. 28-33; William A. Mindak and H. Malcolm Bybee, "Marketing's Application to Fund Raising," *Journal of Marketing,* July, 1971, pp. 13-18; Steven A. Baumgarten, Santosh K. Choudhury, Tanniru R. Rao, and L. Winston Ring, "Study of Nursing Homes: The Patient as Consumer," in Fred C. Allvine (ed.), *Combined Proceedings: 1971 Spring and Fall Conferences,* Series No. 33, American Marketing Association, Chicago, 1972, pp. 452-456; and Benson Shapiro, "Marketing for Nonprofit Organizations," *Harvard Business Review,* September-October, 1973, pp. 123-132.

5 For an opposite point of view which questions the propriety of this broader meaning of marketing and which is concerned about the possible loss of marketing's identity, see David J. Luck, "Broadening the Concept of Marketing—Too Far," *Journal of Marketing,* July, 1969, pp. 53-55.

On the question of whether there is an identity crisis in marketing—are we stressing the management of the technology of marketing (product planning, promotion, etc.) rather than the social-process concept—see Daniel J. Sweeney, "Marketing: Management Technology or Social Process?" *Journal of Marketing,* October, 1972, pp. 3-10.

In an agrarian or backwoods economy, the people are largely self-sufficient. They grow their own food, make their own clothes, and build their own houses and tools. There is very little specialization of labor and very little need for trade of any sort. As time passes, however, the concept of division of labor begins to evolve, and craftsmen concentrate on the production of the item in which they excel. This results in each man producing more than he needs of some items and less than he needs of others. Whenever a person makes more than he wants or wants more than he makes, the foundation is laid for *trade,* and trade is the heart of marketing.

As exchange begins to develop in agrarian economies, it is on a simple basis. Most businesses are small-scale endeavors with no specialization in management. The emphasis is largely on production, and little or no attention is devoted to marketing. In fact, the general practice is to hand-make products to order.

In the next step in the historical evolution of marketing, small producers begin to manufacture their goods in larger quantities in anticipation of future orders. Further division of labor occurs as a type of businessman develops to help sell the increased output. This businessman—who acts as an intermediary between the producers and consumers—is the middleman. To facilitate communication and buying and selling, the various interested parties tend to assemble geographically. Trading centers are thus formed. There are nations or parts of nations in the world today going through these various stages of economic development. We may conclude that advancement and refinements in marketing generally go hand in hand with advancements in the society as a whole.

Modern marketing in Canada, as in other Western Countries, was born with the Industrial Revolution. Concurrent with, or as a by-product of, the Industrial Revolution there was a growth of urban centers and a decline in rural population. Home handicraft operations moved into factories, and people came to the cities to work in the factories. Service industries grew to supply the daily needs of factory workers, who were no longer self-sufficient. Marketing remained an infant during the last half of the nineteenth century and the first two decades of the twentieth. Emphasis was on the growth of manufacturing enterprises because the market demand generally exceeded the available supply of products.

Actually, mass marketing was a prerequisite for successful mass production. Only with a system of mass marketing could factories operate at optimum rates of output and thus enjoy the economies of scale. As the factory economy became more complex, the channels through which trade flowed became longer. Better methods had to be devised to market the industrial output. The growth of specialists in marketing was a natural step in this evolutionary development.

PRESENT-DAY IMPORTANCE OF MARKETING

Modern marketing came of age after World War I, when the words "surplus" and "overproduction" became increasingly common in our economics vocabulary. Since about 1920, with the exception of World War II and the immediate postwar periods, a strong buyers' market has existed in this country. That is, the available supply of products and services has far surpassed effective demand. There has been relatively little difficulty in producing most of these goods; the real problem has been in marketing them.

Ordinarily there cannot be a high level of economic activity without a correspondingly high level of marketing activity. During recession periods, people soon realize that it is a slowdown in marketing activity which is forcing cutbacks in production. (The deeper social, economic, and political factors which cause the slowdown in marketing activities are outside the scope of this book.) It becomes evident that in our economy "nothing happens until somebody sells something," and there are urgent requests for increased marketing not for increased production.

IMPORTANCE OF MARKETING IN OUR SOCIOECONOMIC SYSTEM

Some quantitative measures may help to point up the importance of marketing in our socioeconomic system. The gross national product—the measure of the total goods and services produced in Canada—rose from about $18 billion in 1950 to an estimated $184 billion in 1976 and a forecast $373 billion by 1985. It has been marketing's task to move the mountain of goods and nongovernmental services which constitute the bulk of the gross national product. There has been a tremendous increase in the volume of goods and services produced in Canada in the past 25 years, even after allowing for the inflation of prices. Also, there is every evidence that the economy will continue to grow despite short-run setbacks and will require even more effective marketing.

Another indication of the importance of marketing is the number of people employed in the field. It has been estimated that 20 percent of the Canadian labor force is directly engaged in distribution.[6] In the United States, the estimate for this type of occupation ranges from 25 to 33 percent. The Barger study in the United States pointed out that the number of people engaged in wholesaling and retailing activities there increased more than twelve times from 1870 to 1950, as contrasted with a threefold increase in the number of production workers during the same period.[7] This increase in the number of marketing workers in the U.S. is a reflection of marketing's expanded role in that economy. Our own experience would appear to be somewhat similar although not of the same relative magnitude.

A measure often used to indicate marketing's importance is its cost. On the average, about 50 cents out of the total retail dollar goes to cover marketing costs. Marketing *costs* should not be confused with marketing *profits*, however, nor should it be assumed that products and services would cost less if marketing activities were not performed.

An Economy of Abundance. A brief comparison of the Canadian economy with economies found elsewhere in the world further demonstrates the importance of marketing. The type of economy we have largely explains why marketing as we know it is so much a North American phenomenon, both in practice and as a field of study. Ours is not purely a raw-materials, "underdeveloped" economy, nor is it any longer a subsistence economy. It is not an economy of state capitalism, as is found in Russia, nor is it similar to the Western European economy of cartels and small businesses. It most certainly is not the static, perfectly competitive economy of classical economic theory.

Instead, ours is an economy of abundance. This means that as a nation we produce far beyond our subsistence needs. We have an adequate national disposable

---

6 M. S. Moyer and G. Snyder, *Trends in Canadian Marketing,* Dominion Bureau of Statistics, Ottawa, 1967, p. 5.

7 Harold Barger, *Distribution's Place in the American Economy since 1869,* Princeton University Press, Princeton, N.J., 1955, pp. 4-5.

income and considerable discretionary purchasing power. We are under no necessary compulsion to consume all that is produced, but unless we do, a severe economic decline can set in. While marketing exists in every type of modern economy, it is an especially important foundation stone for successful business performance in a highly competitive economy of abundance.

Marketing activity has the task of encouraging the consumption of the vast output of goods and services of our agriculture, business and industry. Although modern marketing has been successful to a reasonably high degree, it has not been greeted with equal joy in all quarters. There are still many scarce social and economic resources in our economy, and a number of respected students of our social, economic, and political systems have raised serious questions concerning the influence which marketing activities have on the allocation of these resources. The question they raise is whether too much marketing is leading to a misallocation of these resources—is marketing accepting its responsibility for guiding our economic abundance into socially desirable channels? Possibly we may have been so successful in promoting the consumption of automobiles, fashionable dresses, and outboard motors that we have overlooked other more basic issues such as education, savings, or municipal services to increase and improve housing, and the control and elimination of environmental pollution.

In *The Affluent Society,* Prof. John K. Galbraith raised the resource-allocation question in a slightly different fashion.[8] He said that we are investing too much in things and not enough in people, that we are producing too much of some things and not enough of others. Galbraith, in his book as well as in testimony before legislative committees in Canada and the U.S., has also suggested that we decrease our emphasis on production and devote greater attention to a more rational use of what we produce. (This suggestion, it seems, would have the unfortunate effect of forcing us to relinquish greater economic growth only because we have not learned to use our abundance wisely.)

David M. Potter, in his book *People of Plenty,* examined some of the influences which an economy of abundance has exerted upon the life and attitudes of the American people.[9] His analysis shows how the influence of abundance cuts across the fields of the behavioral sciences, history, and political science, how it has remade the American social structure, and how it has made democracy in America different from democracy anywhere else in the world. He also points out that Americans have made mistakes in trying to get the American way of life adopted in foreign countries, largely because of a lack of understanding of how economic abundance has influenced development. Truly the question of marketing and its influence on the allocation of resources in an economy of abundance is a very important one. The American experience in this regard allows us to better understand ourselves and our own priority problems as we deal with the question of defining a "Canadian way of life."

IMPORTANCE IN THE INDIVIDUAL FIRM

The vital importance of marketing in the successful operation of an individual firm was suggested in our definition of marketing. Marketing considerations are today

---

8 John K. Galbraith, *The Affluent Society,* Houghton Mifflin Company, Boston, 1958.

9 David M. Potter, *People of Plenty,* The University of Chicago Press, Chicago, 1954.

the most critical factors in business planning and decision making. In the United States, the National Association of Manufacturers put this cogently when it said:[10]

> In this exciting age of change, marketing is the beating heart of many operations. It must be considered a principal reason for corporate existence. The modern concept of marketing recognizes its role as a direct contributor to profits, as well as sales volume.
>
> No longer can a company just figure out how many widgets it can produce and then go ahead and turn them out. To endure in this highly competitive change-infested market, a company must first determine what it can sell, how much it can sell, and what approaches must be used to entice the wary customer. The president cannot plan; the production manager cannot manage; the purchasing agent cannot purchase; the chief financial officer cannot budget, and the engineer and designer cannot design until the basic market determinations have been made.

Many organizational departments in a company are essential to its growth, but marketing is still the sole revenue-producing activity. This fact sometimes seems to be taken for granted by other executives such as production managers who use these revenues, and financial executives who are responsible for managing them.

Several economic forces are pushing marketing to the fore in Canadian business and industry. Product lines are becoming more diversified. Stiffer competition is coming both from substitute products and from directly comparable goods. Production operations are growing more costly and complex. Foreign imports and the entry of foreign firms into the Canadian market further increase competition. Markets are ever growing and rapidly changing. More and more money is needed to develop and support marketing programs. Thus risks are increased, and the ability to make proper marketing decisions is at a premium.

MARKETING IN AN ERA OF SHORTAGES

In the early 1970s, advanced industries all over the world began to be faced rather abruptly with an economic situation which was quite new to management—there were shortages of materials with which to make their products and operate their factories, stores, and other institutions. Many students of the situation have been advancing the idea that North Americans in particular have reached the end of an era—characterized by economist Kenneth Boulding as a "cowboy economy"—an era which for Canadians reflected the frontier philosophy of unlimited resources where a person could use products and waste them as he pleased. After all, the Canadian North, the West, and other regions still held untapped resources.

The oil shortage in 1973 which triggered the so-called energy crisis generally epitomized the shortage situation. However, in the mid-1970s shortages seemed to occur suddenly not only in oil-based industries (plastics and other petrochemicals), but also in many other industries (wood, paper products, farm products, for example) where the shortages were not triggered by cutbacks in energy availability. This is not the place to argue the political and economic causes underlying the shortages, but we should recognize the impact they have on marketing in our economy as well as those of our major trading partners.

In preceding sections we made statements to the effect that for most products the real problem is marketing them, not producing them, and that marketing considerations are the most critical factors in business planning. In many industries

---

10 As quoted in "An Historic Marketing Paper," *Sales Management*, Mar. 20, 1950, p. 7.

today those statements must be modified. For the first time in about sixty years (with the exception of the World War II years) management is back to being worried about how to make the products.

At the same time in most of those industries, management still has to worry about how to market the output. Industries faced with shortages will not find their marketing task easier, even though some executives have the short-sighted idea of "why spend money on marketing when we can sell all we can produce." Most firms still face substantial challenges in marketing. Competition within industries and between industries is still intense in most cases. Essentially Canada is still an economy of abundance, and consumers still have considerable disposable income.

Today, when it seems that our priorities are changing, a company must be alert to adapt its marketing programs to new situations. In the 1950s and 1960s, for example, a guiding marketing strategy was to expand the product assortment—that is, to market a full line. In an abrupt about-face in the 1970s, companies have been slimming down their product mix by eliminating low-margin products and concentrating on the more profitable items. In the same vein, management should examine other parts of its marketing program with an eye toward pruning out unprofitable, wasteful segments. In advertising, for instance, total expenditures might be reduced, and a firm might shift from the direct-action type of ad (buy our product now) to the institutional and public-service type of advertising. Managing a sales force is different where the sales job is (1) to allocate a scarce supply among existing customers as contrasted with the job (2) of creative selling to develop new accounts. Management also might remember that shortages also create new marketing opportunities. Less building heat means more sweaters, and less gasoline means more bicycles. New products and services are needed to meet new conditions rather than a bigger effort put into "pushing" what made sense in the past.

Environmental forces such as inflation and shortages are changing the life style of Canadian consumers in many instances. Looking to the next few years, consumers may very well decide to live more simply, cut back on their buying, and generally conserve. These attitudes carry significant implications for the marketing programs in many firms. While it is still too early to predict detailed changes, we can rest assured that changes there will be and challenges there will be in marketing programs in Canada as well as other countries of the world.

THE MARKETING CONCEPT

As business administrators recognize that marketing is vitally important to the success of a firm and as they realize that a business is a marketing organization, an entirely new way of business thinking continues to evolve. It is called the marketing concept, and it has developed as production- and engineering-oriented firms have changed into market-oriented structures.

The marketing concept is based on three fundamental beliefs. First, all company planning, policies, and operations should be oriented toward the customer. Second, profitable sales volume should be the goal of a firm. Third, all marketing activities in a firm should be organizationally integrated and coordinated. In its fullest sense, the marketing concept is a philosophy of business which states that the customer's want-satisfaction is the economic and social justification of a company's existence. Consequently, all company activities in production, engineering, and finance, as well as in marketing, must be devoted first to determining what the customer's wants are and then to satisfying those wants while still making a reasonable profit.

A marketing executive at the parent of Canadian General Electric Company, one of the first companies formally to recognize and activate the marketing concept on a North American basis, expressed the philosophy nicely when he said:[11]

> We feel that marketing is a fundamental business philosophy. This definition recognizes marketing's functions and methods of organizational structuring as *only the implementation* of the philosophy. These things are not, in themselves, the philosophy.
>
> Fundamental to this philosophy is the recognition and acceptance of a customer-oriented way of doing business. Under marketing the customer becomes the fulcrum, the pivot point about which the business moves in operating for the balanced best interests of all concerned. . . .
>
> The second fundamental on which the marketing philosophy rests is that it is rooted in the profit concept, not the volume concept. (I am not eliminating the use of volume as a rewarding way of obtaining profits from the efficiency of the service rendered; rather, I am referring to the profitless volume or volume-for-the-sake-of-volume-alone concept.)

The marketing concept points up sharply the following contrasts between marketing and selling:

Selling	Marketing
1. Emphasis is on the product.	1. Emphasis is on customers' wants.
2. Company first makes the product and then figures out how to sell it profitably.	2. Company first determines what the customers want, and then the firm figures out how to profitably make and deliver a product to satisfy those wants.
3. Internal, company orientation.	3. External, market orientation.
4. Emphasizes company (seller's) needs.	4. Emphasizes market (buyers') needs.

The marketing concept calls for a management reorientation regarding what business a company is in. Typically, when an executive is asked, "What business are you in?" the answer is, "We make _____," or "We sell _____." These executives must start thinking in terms of what benefits they market—what needs (wants) are they satisfying.

In this vein, the National Film Board and the new Canadian film makers market entertainment and education rather than make movies. Canadian Pacific markets transportation rather than running a railroad. Bell Canada markets a communication system rather than operating a telephone company. The Lennox Company provides home comfort, instead of making furnaces and air conditioners.

We hope that management will not implement the marketing concept as did the company in Fig. 1-1.

DISTINCTION BETWEEN THE MARKETING CONCEPT AND MARKETING

The marketing concept is a philosophy, an attitude, or a course of business thinking, while marketing is a process or a course of business action. Naturally, the way of thinking determines the course of action.

---

11 Fred J. Borch, "The Marketing Philosophy as a Way of Business Life," *The Marketing Concept: Its Meaning to Management*, American Management Association, Marketing Series, no. 99, New York, 1957, pp. 3-5.

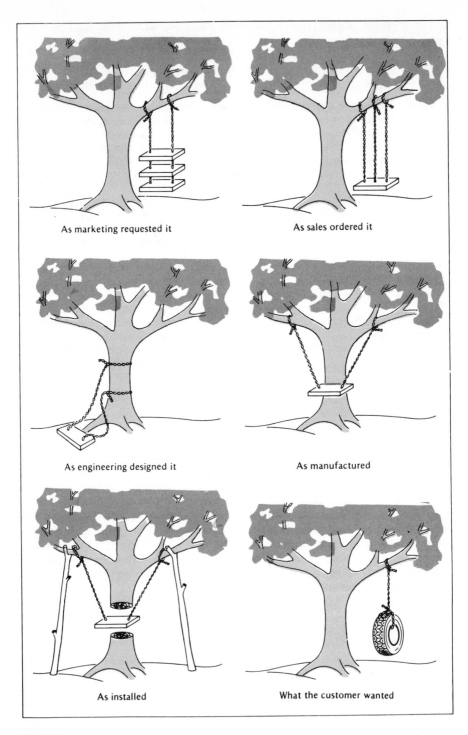

As marketing requested it

As sales ordered it

As engineering designed it

As manufactured

As installed

What the customer wanted

Figure 1-1

MARKETING MANAGEMENT: THE APPLICATION OF THE MARKETING CONCEPT

For a business enterprise to realize the full fruits of the marketing concept, the philosophy must be translated into practice. This means that (1) the marketing activities in a firm must be better organized, co-ordinated, and managed, and (2) the chief marketing executive must be accorded a more important role in total company planning and policy making than has been generally true in the past. As these two changes take place, we see emerging in Canadian business and elsewhere, the idea of marketing management. Marketing management is the marketing concept in action.

FOUR-STAGE EVOLUTION OF MARKETING MANAGEMENT

Marketing management has been evolving in North American business since the Industrial Revolution. Roughly, it has gone through three stages of development, and a fourth era is emerging. However, the managerial philosophies and practices of many companies are still in one of the earlier stages. This state of affairs is more pronounced in Canada than in the United States because of a different form of development during the early industrialization stages. Only a few Canadian firms as yet have the organization and philosophy which are characteristic of the most advanced developmental stage of marketing management.

Production stage. During the first stage, a company typically is production-oriented. The executives in production and engineering shape the company's objectives and planning. The operating philosophies emphasize mass production of simplified product lines at low unit costs. The function of the sales department is to sell this output at a price set by production and financial executives.

Early in this period of development the marketing activity is organized in a simple fashion. Manufacturers have sales departments headed by a sales manager whose major responsibility is to operate a sales force. Advertising, marketing research, and sales analysis are generally unknown. Production planning and sales budgeting are handled in other departments.

Later during this first period, expanding markets typically encourage a manufacturer to expand into specialized marketing activities. Thus, separate organizational divisions, each assigned to separate executives, may be established for advertising, marketing research, export sales, etc. The department responsible for selling the company's output is called the "sales department," and its chief executive typically has the title of sales manager or vice president of sales. This form of marketing organization, as shown in Fig. 1-2, predominated in Canadian organizations through the Great Depression in the 1930s and into World War II.

Sales Stage. The depression experienced both in Canada and the United States made it quite clear that the main problem in the North American economy no longer was one of being able to manufacture or grow enough products. Rather, the problem was in selling this output. Just producing a better mousetrap was no assurance of its market success; the product had to be sold. Thus, we entered a period during which selling and sales management were accorded new respect and responsibilities. Sales performance, however, still was measured primarily by the *sales volume* generated, and not by *marketing profits*.

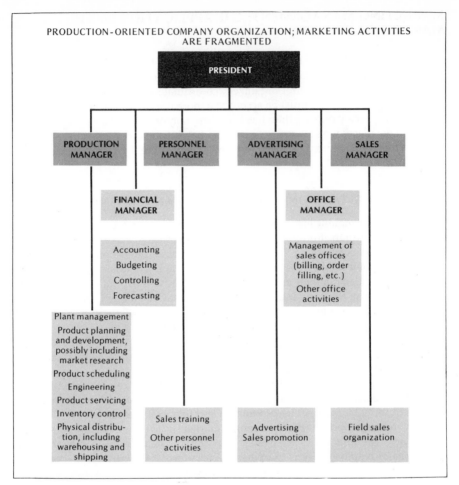

Figure 1-2: In the first stage of the evolution of marketing management, there is no marketing department, and sales management involves only operating a sales force. When managerial responsibility for marketing is fragmented, consider the problems in planning, coordinating, and directing such marketing activities as advertising, sales forecasting, product planning, and personal selling.

During this stage a better understanding of the scope of sales management results in two significant organizational changes in many firms. See Fig. 1-3. First, all marketing activities such as advertising and marketing research are grouped under one marketing executive, although he is still typically called *sales* manager or vice president of *sales*. Second, activities such as sales training, product servicing, and sales analysis, which were formerly carried out in departments outside sales or marketing, now are put under the marketing umbrella. While each of the several divisions (advertising, sales analysis, etc.) may have a separate manager, all report to the chief sales executive. This type of organization—and the sales era itself—generally extended from the 1940s well into the 1950s, although no specific dates

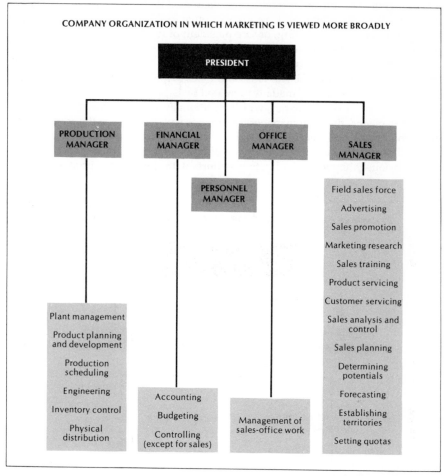

COMPANY ORGANIZATION IN WHICH MARKETING IS VIEWED MORE BROADLY

PRESIDENT

PRODUCTION MANAGER

FINANCIAL MANAGER

OFFICE MANAGER

SALES MANAGER

PERSONNEL MANAGER

Field sales force

Advertising

Sales promotion

Marketing research

Sales training

Product servicing

Customer servicing

Sales analysis and control

Sales planning

Determining potentials

Forecasting

Establishing territories

Setting quotas

Plant management

Product planning and development

Production scheduling

Engineering

Inventory control

Physical distribution

Accounting

Budgeting

Controlling (except for sales)

Management of sales-office work

Figure 1-3. In this stage of the evolution of marketing management, most marketing activities are under the control of the sales manager. The personnel manager no longer handles sales training. But note that the production manager is still in charge of production scheduling, inventory control, and physical distribution, while the office manager still controls management of sales-office work.

sharply define any of the four eras.[12] It was sustained by the backlog demand built up during the depression and war years. It can still be found all too frequently in Canada today.

Marketing stage. In the third stage of the evolutionary process, companies embrace the concept of integrated marketing management, directed toward the twin goals of

---

12 The conceptual foundations for scientific sales management and modern marketing management actually were laid in the literature of the 1920s and earlier, where we find a direct application of Frederick W. Taylor's scientific management concepts to early sales management. See Bernard J. La Londe and Edward J. Morrison, "Marketing Management Concepts Yesterday and Today," *Journal of Marketing,* January, 1967, pp. 9-13.

a customer orientation and *profitable* sales volume. Attention is focused on marketing rather than on selling, and the top executive in this area is called a marketing manager, director of marketing, or vice president of marketing. He is aligned organizationally with the top executives in production, finance, and personnel, to work with the president as the company's top planning and policy-making group. The increased competition of the late 1950s and 1960s helped push this concept along. A good deal of this push in Canada was created by U.S. subsidiaries based here.

In this stage, several activities which traditionally were the province of the production manager, financial manager, or other executives become the responsibility of the marketing manager (see Fig. 1-4). For instance, inventory control, warehousing, and aspects of product planning are often turned over to the marketing manager. Obviously he must coordinate his efforts with those of the production man-

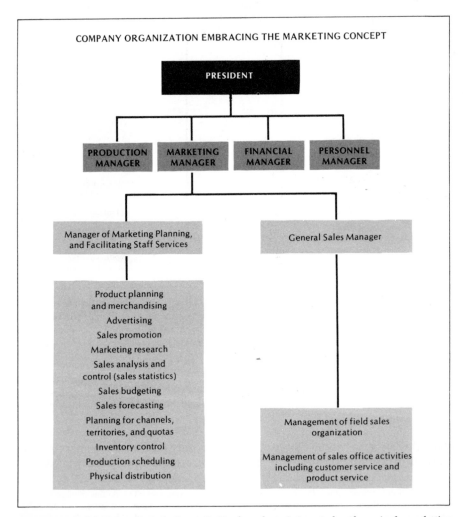

Figure 1-4. At this point all marketing activities have been integrated under a single marketing manager. Organizationally, the company has the "marketing concept."

ager and the top financial executive, but in the final analysis the marketing manager makes the decisions regarding packaging, design, color, and other product features. The position of the marketing manager is epitomized in Canadian General Electric's philosophy that he should be introduced at the *beginning* rather than at the *end* of the production cycle. In this way he can integrate marketing into each stage of the operations.

We are now living in this third stage in the evolution of marketing management. The marketing concept has generally been adopted by both large and medium-size companies in the United States, it is moving forward in Canadian firms and it can be seen in the aggressive multinationals based in countries all over the world. In large industrial firms, for example, one typical study concluded that (1) the marketing division is being used as a training ground for many top executives; (2) the marketing manager participates extensively in major policy decisions in virtually all companies studied; (3) the span of responsibilities of the marketing executive has greatly increased; and (4) his executive status and relative pay level have increased significantly.[13] Later studies show, however, that *(a)* consumer goods companies have tended to implement the marketing concept to a greater extent than have industrial goods manufacturers, and *(b)* large companies have tended to adopt and implement the marketing concept to a greater degree than is true in small and medium-size firms.[14]

In firms which have fully embraced the marketing concept, the entire company becomes a marketing organization. This position is reached when the attitudes of a company's executives change so that the entire company works to develop, manufacture, and sell a product from the marketing point of view. The president of the Burroughs Corporation caught the spirit of this when he said, "Any company is nothing but a marketing organization." Marketing becomes the basic motivating force for the entire firm, and marketing influences all short-term and long-range company policies. A top executive at Sylvania Electric Products observed: "Marketing faces the challenge of setting the leadership pace for the entire organization. . . . Marketing is charged with charting the future course a company must take,"[15] The president of the Pepsi-Cola Company said, "Our business is the business of marketing."

How well the many companies have actually implemented the concept, however, is still a moot question. We know that there are many forms and degrees of market orientation. Probably in many cases a company, while using the appropriately fashionable titles and other external trappings, is still paying little more than lip service to the concept. Management may believe in the concept and have adopted a marketing attitude, but may not have established a marketing structure and a formal marketing program. In a revealing study conducted among members of the New York Sales Executives Club—and this group includes many of the large com-

---

13 Stanford L. Johnson and John J. Tenge, Jr., "The Man behind the Marketing Concept," *Sales/Marketing Today,* June, 1967, pp. 14-17.

14 Carlton P. McNamara, "The Present Status of the Marketing Concept," *Journal of Marketing, January,* 1972, pp. 50-57. *For some examples of the marketing concept at work in specific companies, see "Why Philip Morris Thrives,"* Business Week, Jan. 27, 1973, p. 48; Don Korn, "The Best**?!≠z@ Sales Department in the Railroad Industry (Illinois Central Gulf R.R.)," *Sales Management,* Oct. 16, 1972, p. 21; "How Kodak Will Exploit Its New Instamatic," *Business Week,* Mar. 18, 1972, p. 46.

15 Alfred C. Veibranz, "Marketing's Role in Company Growth," *MSU Business Topics,* Autumn, 1967, p. 49.

panies operating both in Canada and the U.S.—the findings indicated that most of the firms had failed (1) to place all marketing functions under a single marketing executive and (2) to coordinate these activities to reach long- and short-range goals.[16] (Marketing functions as identified in this study were advertising, sales, product planning, marketing research, customer credit, inventory planning, and transportation.) Unfortunately, in too many cases the misunderstanding endures that "marketing" is just a fancy name for selling.

As one might expect, the full implementation of the marketing concept will not be accomplished overnight. The inflexibilities and conservatism of business, plus human opposition to change, will create some time spread between management's adoption of the concept and the fulfillment of all the consequent necessary organizational adjustments. General Electric executives have estimated that it took over five years to realign that corporation, once the decision was made to adopt the marketing concept. Once such a realignment has taken place in the head office of a multinational firm, in a short period of time it is more easily undertaken in Canadian and other foreign operations.

The key to implementing the marketing concept is a favourable attitude on the part of top management. As an executive of an aggressive bank stated, "Marketing begins with top management. Only top management can provide the climate, the discipline, and the leadership required for a successful marketing program. Top management must know the customers and the prospects; it must set the objectives, establish the policies, develop the plans, and create the organization."[17] It is apparent that when the Royal Bank or Bank of Commerce make the basic senior level commitments, the marketing efforts in banking in Canada become very contemporary and different from those to which we had been accustomed.

In summarizing the organizational implications in the concept, a top marketing executive at the International Minerals and Chemical Corporation warned:[18]

> But a company cannot become customer conscious by edict. Since all organizations tend to emulate their leader, it is most important that the head of the business be thoroughly customer conscious. There can only be one marketing head in any business and that must be the president. He can develop a mood, an atmosphere, and an *esprit de corps* reflecting the pre-eminence of the customer that permeates every nook and corner of the company.

Let it be clearly understood that we are *not* saying that marketing executives should hold the supreme position in a firm. In saying that marketing should be the foundation stone for company planning, we mean only that marketing must be fully integrated into a company's management. The marketing concept does *not* imply that the president of a firm must come up through the marketing department, but only that he must be marketing-oriented.

Consumerism and the social responsibility stage. Social and economic conditions in the 1970s have led to the fourth stage in the evolution of marketing manage-

---

16 Robert F. Vizza, Thomas F. Chambers, and Edward J. Cook, *Adoption of the Marketing Concept—Fact or Fiction?* Sales Executives Club of New York, New York, 1967. Also see B. Charles Ames, "Trappings vs. Substance in Industrial Marketing," *Harvard Business Review*, July-August, 1970, pp. 93-102.

17 "The Marketing Executive: Industry's New Crown Prince," *News Front*, August, 1963, p. 30.

18 Anthony E. Cascino, "Organizational Implications of the Marketing Concept," in Eugene J. Kelley and William Lazer (eds.), *Managerial Marketing Perspectives and Viewpoints*, 3rd ed., Richard D. Irwin, Inc., Homewood, Ill., 1967, p. 346.

ment—a period characterized by its societal orientation. It is becoming increasingly obvious that marketing executives must act in a socially responsible manner if they wish to succeed, or even survive, in this era. External pressures—consumer discontent rising from unfulfilled expectations, a concern for environmental and ecological problems, and political-legal forces—are influencing the marketing programs in countless firms.

Profit making will continue as a key goal in marketing management. However, in this fourth stage we can expect to see executives more concerned with long-run, rather than short-run, profit goals. Also, the concepts of social profit and social auditing will influence marketing managers.

Perhaps this fourth stage may be viewed more broadly as a human-orientation period—a time in which there will be a growing concern for the management of human resources in marketing. We sense a change in emphasis from materialism to humanism in our society. One mark of an affluent, economically well-developed society is a shift in consumption from products to services, and a shift in cultural emphasis from "things" to "people." In this fourth stage, marketing management must be concerned with creating and delivering a standard (a better quality) of *life*, rather than only a material standard of *living*.[19]

BROADENING THE MARKETING CONCEPT

The wave of consumer protests starting in the late 1960s—the rise of consumerism—is an indication to some people that there has been a failure to implement the marketing concept.[20] Others go so far as to suggest that the traditional marketing concept is an operational philosophy which conflicts with a firm's social responsibility.[21]

From one point of view, these charges are true. A firm may totally satisfy its customers (in line with the marketing concept), while at the same time adversely affect society. To illustrate, a steel company in Hamilton can be satisfying its customers in Winnipeg with the right product, reasonably priced, while at the same time this firm is polluting air and water in Ontario. Automobile manufacturers can satisfy consumers' short-run demand for cars, yet in the long run create urban traffic congestion and air pollution.

Nevertheless, it is to be kept in mind that the marketing concept and a company's social responsibility can be quite compatible; they need not conflict. The key to this compatibility lies in extending the breadth and time dimensions in the definition of the marketing concept.

Regarding breadth—if a company's customers who are to be satisfied include not only the buyers of the firm's products, but also the consumers of any elements

---

19 See Leslie M. Dawson, "The Human Concept: New Philosophy for Business," *Business Horizons*, December, 1969, pp. 29-38; Leonard L. Berry, "Marketing Challenges in the Age of People," *MSU Business Topics*, Winter, 1972, pp. 7-13; and George Schwartz, "Marketing: The Societal Concept," *University of Washington Business Review*, Autumn, 1971, pp. 31-38.

20 See Hiram C. Barksdale and Bill Darden, "Marketers' Attitudes toward the Marketing Concept," *Journal of Marketing*, October, 1971, pp. 29-36. Peter Drucker (a professor, management consultant, and certainly not unfriendly toward business) referred to consumerism as "the shame of the total marketing concept."

21 See Martin L. Bell and William Emory, "The Faltering Marketing Concept," *Journal of Marketing*, October, 1971, pp. 37-42; and Laurence P. Feldman, "Societal Adaptation: A New Challenge for Marketing," *Journal of Marketing*, July, 1971, pp. 54-60.

created by the firm, then the marketing concept and social responsibility in this firm can be compatible. Thus, in the preceding example, the Hamilton steel mill has several consumer groups to satisfy—(1) the Winnipeg customers of the steel shipments, (2) the consumers of the impure air elements given off by the mill, (3) the actual and potential users of the waterways affected by the mill waste matter, and (4) the community affected by employee traffic driving to and from work.

This broadening of the marketing concept is consistent with our previously developed broader, societal definition of marketing. There we recognized that a given marketer may have several different target markets.

Regarding the extended *time* dimension—we must view consumer satisfaction and profitable business as goals in the marketing concept to be achieved *over the long run*. If a company prospers in the long run, it must be doing a reasonably good job of satisfying its customers' current social and economic demands.

In conclusion, if the marketing concept and social responsibility are to be realistically compatible, management must strive for a balance over the long run among (1) satisfying the wants of product-buying customers, (2) satisfying the societal wants which are affected by the firm's activities, and (3) meeting the company's profit goals.

A more detailed discussion of consumers' protests and marketing's social responsibility is postponed until the final two chapters in this book. We can better evaluate these societal issues after we have an understanding of the marketing system and its institutions.

QUESTIONS AND PROBLEMS

1. "From one point of view marketing may be defined as the revenue-generating activity in a company. Production men use these revenues and financial executives manage them. However, the main job of the marketing man is to generate a satisfactory revenue over a long period of time." Discuss the meaning and implications of this quotation.
2. Marketing has been defined as the creation of time, place, and possession utilities. Explain the ideas involved in this definition.
3. What is the difference between marketing and selling?
4. For each of the following organizations, describe: (1) what is being marketed and (2) who is their target market.
   a. B.C. Lions professional football team.
   b. United Automobile Workers labor union.
   c. Professor teaching an introductory sociology course.
   d. Resort hotel in the Rockies.
   e. Police department in your city.
   f. Montreal Symphony Orchestra.
5. In line with the broader, societal concept of marketing, describe some of the ways in which nonbusiness organizations to which you belong are engaged in marketing activities.
6. One way of explaining the importance of marketing in our economy is to consider how we would live if there were no marketing facilities. Describe some of the ways in which your daily activities would be affected under such circumstances.

7. One writer has stated that any business has only two functions—marketing and innovation. How would you explain this statement to a student majoring in production management, accounting, finance, or personnel management?

8. How do you account for the fact that the number of workers engaged in wholesaling and retailing increased twelvefold between 1870 and 1950, as contrasted with only a threefold increase in the number of production workers during the same period?

9. Using a marketing approach (benefits provided or wants satisfied) for each of the following companies, answer the question: What business are you in?
   a. Polaroid (cameras)
   b. *Maclean's* magazine
   c. Bank of Montreal
   d. Esso
   e. CP Air

10. Distinguish between the sales era and the marketing era in the development of marketing management.

11. Name some companies which you believe are still in the production or sales stage.

12. A 65-year-old vice president of one of our national railroads was quoted as saying that in the railroad business, "marketing is just a new-fashioned idea of calling rates something different; really, marketing is nothing but determining rates," How would you answer him?

13. "The marketing concept does not imply that marketing executives will run the firm. The concept requires only that whoever is in top management be marketing-oriented." Give examples of how a production manager, company treasurer, or personnel manager can be marketing-oriented.

14. Name some companies or industries whose market position has declined considerably because of shifts in consumers' wants or behavioral patterns. What might these organizations have done to prevent their decline?

MARKETING SYSTEMS AND THE ROLE OF MANAGEMENT

In Chapter 1 we observed that the socioeconomic structure in Canada has evolved from an agrarian economy in a rural setting, through a production-oriented, subsistence-level economy in an urban society, and then through a sales-oriented economy into today's customer-oriented economy featuring an affluent society with discretionary purchasing power. In the current stage of this evolution, the marketing concept has emerged as a leading business philosophy. Marketing management, then, is the vehicle which business uses to activate the marketing concept. At the operational level the marketing concept—through marketing management—espouses the notion that an integrated, coordinated organization is essential as an efficient, profitable means of achieving the goal of customer want satisfaction.

This notion is consistent with our definition of marketing—it is a total *system* of business action, and not the fragmented assortment of institutions and activities which has passed as marketing in years gone by.

In this chapter we shall look a little more carefully at this systems concept of marketing. We shall observe that a firm operates its marketing systems within environmental constraints which are largely uncontrollable by it. It is management's role to develop, execute, and evaluate these systems. Finally, because management's responsibilities invariably involve problem solving and decision making, we shall briefly examine an orderly procedure in these activities.

SYSTEMS APPROACH TO MARKETING

An increasing number of companies are adopting the marketing concept and then implementing it with (1) a rational, fact-based approach to solving their marketing problems and (2) a coordinated effort in the management of their marketing programs. In effect, these companies are applying systems theory and analysis to their marketing activities.

WHAT IS A SYSTEM?

Webster's Seventh New Collegiate Dictionary defines a *system* as a "regularly interacting or interdependent group of items forming a unified whole." The concept of a system may be viewed in many contexts. The human body, for example, is a total organic system with digestive, circulatory, and muscular subsystems. We speak of a capitalistic or socialistic politico-economic system. In our natural environment we recognize the river systems and the solar system. While systems theory and analysis is a relatively new approach in the hands of marketing executives, the concept has been applied for many years by military men and engineers.

In the case of a marketing system, the "group of items" in the above definition includes such objects as products, price structures, channels of distribution, and promotional activities. The *systems approach* in marketing, then, is an orderly method of dealing with complex marketing problems under conditions of risk or uncertainty. Typically in these problems, multiple goals and alternative courses of action do exist.

SYNERGISM AND MARKETING SYSTEMS

Synergism is a related concept, useful in helping us to understand the systems approach in marketing. *Webster's* defines *synergism* as the "cooperative action of discrete agencies such that the total effect is greater than the sum of the effects taken independently." In other words, the effectiveness of managerial action in one area of a marketing program depends to a great extent upon decisions made with respect to related variables elsewhere in the program. Thus management cannot establish a price structure without considering the company's promotional program, and still expect to have optimum results in either area. The manufacturer's price of a product should be influenced by the nature of his advertising program, the extent to which retailers will be expected to promote the product, etc. The effectiveness of packaging and labeling is enhanced if a manufacturer's salesmen can persuade retailers to give the product a good display location. The degree to which a company achieves a synergistic result either in the firm as a whole or within its marketing program depends to a great extent upon the executives' ability to manage.

APPLICATIONS OF SYSTEMS CONCEPT OF MARKETING[1]

The systems approach is being applied, in both quantitative and qualitative ways, by companies in many parts of their marketing programs. Symbolic models have

---

1 The remaining part of this section on the systems approach is adapted from Lee Adler, "Systems Approach to Marketing," *Harvard Business Review*, May-June, 1967, pp. 105-118. See also Stanley F. Stasch, "Systems Analysis for Controlling and Improving Marketing Performance," *Journal of Marketing*, April, 1969, pp. 12-19.

been built to describe, quantify, and qualitatively evaluate alternative marketing strategies and programs. When a textile manufacturer in Quebec color-harmonizes its linens, bedspreads, and towels or when Canadian General Electric or Eaton's promotes a kitchen appliance center concept, the firm is dealing with a product system. Customers buy need satisfaction through product benefits; that is, they buy beauty, not cosmetics, or the removal and polishing of metal, not a grinding-wheel. By understanding this, a company can use the systems approach in product management to plan, develop, and market a related assortment of benefits rather than merely some products. In a later chapter we shall see that companies are using the systems approach in managing their marketing information, thus replacing the traditional notions of marketing research.

One of the first applications of systems theory in marketing was in the area of physical distribution management. Activities such as transportation, warehousing, order filling, inventory control, and materials handling were traditionally managed as separate activities. In many Canadian companies, given our geography and population distribution, these were high-cost functions. However, they were nicely adaptive to quantitative analysis, and innovative features (container ships, forklift trucks, piggyback express, etc.) began to appear. These factors led beautifully to the development of computer-based systems which coordinated these formerly fragmented activities in a very effective manner. Also in distribution management, companies are using the systems approach to better integrate the activities of all business units—manufacturer, wholesalers, retailers—in their distribution channels. The above few examples and several other subsystems in marketing will be examined in more detail throughout this book.

BENEFITS AND PROBLEMS IN USE OF SYSTEMS APPROACH

Adler identified several benefits stemming from the use of the systems concept in marketing. It is a methodical orientation to problem solving, encompassing all aspects of a problem. The approach coordinates all appropriate marketing tools, and it offers greater efficiency and economy in marketing operations. Impending problems can be identified more quickly because management can better understand the complex interplay of all pertinent variables. Finally, the results can be evaluated quantitatively. Many elements in the systems approach lend themselves nicely to a computer-based analysis, thus enabling management to process quickly the complex data involving many variables.

These features, in turn, should enable a company to broaden and deepen its market penetration by extending its product lines and being better able to cope with competition. The tourist industry, for example, attracted new winter customers by creating packaged skiing tours in the Rockies and Quebec (really product-service systems), which are more convenient and economical than those the consumer could assemble himself.

The systems approach is sufficiently new in marketing, on the other hand, so that it is still beset with problems. First, the approach can take considerable time and money to implement. One company, for instance, took over a year to develop the mathematical model of its physical distribution system, which was necessary before management could even begin to solve its problems. There are no standardized approaches; each company tailor-makes its own systems. Companies must be of considerable size (at least in resources) and experienced in order to use the potential of the systems approach. One would expect the subsidiaries of sophisticated foreign parents to be among the first to make use of such technology, as the advantages would be clear in such complex situations. Second, in marketing we must deal with social and psychological considerations in the behavior of people. In our study of consumer behavior, however, it is only in relatively recent years that we have been using mathematical models and other quantitative methods of analysis to any significant extent. Even then, this analysis often involves so many assumptions that it is of little practical value. Finally, and perhaps most troublesome of all, is the idea that the psychological nature of many marketing men is such that they are more like artists than scientists. They prefer to "fly by the seat of their pants," resisting the fact-based research, written plans, and other rigidities which are of necessity so much a part of the systems approach.

CONCLUSION

The notion of a systems approach to marketing should be useful as we continue through this book. This approach, however, should also be kept in proper perspective. We must not confuse the tool and its user, nor should we confuse the relative importance of the two. Systems analysis is only an *aid* to executive judgment and decision making; in no way is it a *substitute*. While the computer and quantitative analysis can help management to do a more effective job, we must remember that the output of this analysis is no better than the input. And the numerical input is usually a matter of executive judgment. But perhaps here we have the real key to the value of the systems approach—that is, it forces management to think formally about the right aspects of a problem.

EXTERNAL ENVIRONMENT OF MARKETING SYSTEMS

A company plans and operates its marketing system within a framework of forces which constitute the system's environment. Some of these forces are *external* variables generally *not* controllable by the executives in a firm. Other forces are *internal* to a company and thus are essentially controllable by management. An executive might paraphrase the words of one organization: "Grant me the strength to change the things I can change, the serenity to accept those I cannot, and the wisdom to know the difference." The ability of a decision-making executive may be measured by the skill with which he can (1) adjust to the external elements in his changing environment, (2) forecast the direction and intensity of these changes, and (3) use the controllable variables at his command in adapting to this external environment. Figure 2-1 illustrates the framework of major external, uncontrollable variables which influence a company's marketing system.

MARKET DEMAND: ECONOMIC AND BEHAVIORAL

The environmental factor of the market itself, as was stressed in Chapter 1, is the most significant external influence on the marketing decisions of a firm. This tremendously important force is the subject of Part 2 (Chapters 3 to 8) and is pointed up frequently throughout the text. Both economic and behavioral aspects of consumers affect a firm's marketing system.

In an economic sense, the key market influence is consumer income, along with the number and location of people with this buying power. Management needs to be aware of expenditure patterns of consumers at various income levels. A corollary influence is the general condition of the national economy. Macroeconomic influ-

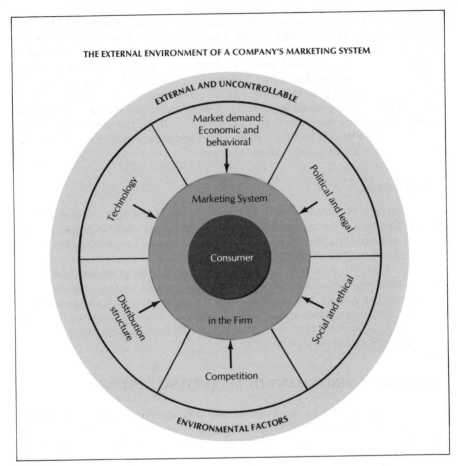

THE EXTERNAL ENVIRONMENT OF A COMPANY'S MARKETING SYSTEM

EXTERNAL AND UNCONTROLLABLE

Market demand:
Economic and
behavioral

Technology

Political and legal

Marketing System

Consumer

in the Firm

Distribution
structure

Social and ethical

Competition

ENVIRONMENTAL FACTORS

Figure 2-1

ences such as higher interest rates, inflationary pressures, price control strategies, federal and provincial tax policy, etc., can play major roles in determining the success of a company's marketing system. Export prices for raw and semi-processed materials must also be watched as they affect regional and local income and employment in various parts of the country.

The behavioral aspects of a market—sociological, psychological, and anthropological—become important environmental forces particularly as consumer's income increases. As a person's buying power allows him to rise above a subsistence level, he has increasing personal discretion as to how he spends this money. Consequently, marketing executives need to learn as much as they can regarding cultural traditions, consumer motivation, demographic patterns, group sociological behavior, and similar influences.

POLITICAL AND LEGAL FORCES

To an increasing extent a company's existence and conduct are being influenced by the political-legal framework and processes in our society. Legislation at the federal, provincial, and local levels exercises more influence on the *marketing* activities of a firm than on any other major areas of its operations. Anticombines laws, pricing legislation, and regulatory measures affecting advertising and distribution systems are just a few examples of these governmental forces which set legal guidelines and limits for business operations. Generally over the past half century, Canadians, through their elected representatives, have opted for more government planning and controls over society and the economy. Obviously this trend affects marketing management. Moreover, within this general trend, management must be alert to changes in the political attitudes or "climate," depending upon the philosophies of the administration in power at the time. Similarly, management must be alert to legal and fiscal developments in other countries as these are usually used as aids in the development of federal and provincial policies and laws.

SOCIAL AND ETHICAL INFLUENCES

Somewhat related to the environmental forces discussed above are the social and ethical influences on a company's marketing program. In fact, the failure of business to meet society's ethical expectations often leads to restrictive legal measures. The increasing political attention devoted to the consumer since the 1960s is continuing, and at a quickening pace.

Marketing executives are responding to social influences. Management realizes the value of a good corporate citizenship. Public disapproval of misleading advertising, poor product performance, hidden finance charges, and inadequate product information can indelibly hurt a business. In general, management knows that it must pay attention to its social responsibilities and that its decision making must be done within the framework of acceptable social practices if the company is to benefit in the long run and perform a useful social role.

COMPETITION

A firm usually faces competition from other firms within the same industry or from companies in other industries offering substitute products or services. Some of these competitors have access to the resources of foreign parents and other subsidiaries of the same parent. Various strategies may be tested in a European branch before being used in Canada, thus requiring a broad approach to the term "competition." Consequently, a marketing executive should understand a great deal about the economics of these industries and not just on a national basis. Regarding his own industry, he should understand its cost structure, pricing policies, general promotional practices, and any other competitive aspect which may influence his own planning and operation. For instance, in an industry where fixed costs are a large percentage of total costs, management may be willing to adopt flexible pricing practices so that it can cut its price below an announced level in order to make a sale. This willingness stems from the fact that in the short run management needs to cover only variable or out-of-pocket costs; any return above that level will help cover the huge fixed expense.

Management must also be alert constantly to the potential threat of industries marketing substitutable products or services of both domestic and foreign origin. Steel manufacturers are feeling inroads from aluminum and plastics producers. Interindustry competition between companies making aluminum foil, plastic wrap, tin cans, and other types of containers has been heightened by the revolution in packaging. As different countries around the world face differing domestic economic conditions, international competition increases and Canadian producers face new challenges in such industries as steel, television, and clothing.

DISTRIBUTION STRUCTURE

Several features of the distribution structure—the system by which goods flow physically and title is moved from producer to ultimate user—are beyond the control of executives who must use the structure. Facilities for handling and transporting the goods are largely external factors, for instance, as are the distribution institutions such as retailers and wholesalers.

TECHNOLOGY

In our zeal to have a customer orientation replace a production orientation in business management, we must not overlook the considerable impact which the work of scientists, engineers, and other technically oriented people has on a company's marketing system. The "knowledge explosion" which we have experienced in technology during the past several decades will undoubtedly continue, and probably at an accelerated pace. These advances have occurred not only in disciplines which we think of as being technical fields (the physical and biological sciences, for instance) but also in countless other areas of human endeavor. Additionally, the explosion is not just North American, it is world-wide and therefore much more difficult to monitor.

Technology is a major environmental influence on marketing because it has such an effect on consumers' life-styles and consumption patterns. Advances in medicine have lengthened the life-span and changed the activities within that span. Developments in transportation and communication have altered our way of living.

The relationship between technology and marketing is a two-way street, however, in that marketing has been (and should be) a major influence on technology. Technology must be marketed; it must be adjusted to consumers' wants. Just building a better mousetrap is not enough, as can be proved by reviewing the fantastic numbers of products which were engineering successes but market failures. Very early in a product's development—in the idea stage—we need to determine its potential market in terms of size, composition, customers' wants, etc.

CONTROLLABLE VARIABLES IN MARKETING SYSTEMS

A firm operates its marketing system within the constraints of the environment we just discussed. The goal of the system is to reach preselected market targets and to satisfy the consumers' needs in a manner profitable to the company. To reach these goals, management has at its disposal two sets of internal, controllable forces: (1) the company's resources in nonmarketing areas and (2) the components of the marketing mix—the product, the price structure, the promotional activities, and some features of the distribution system. Figure 2-2 illustrates this internal framework, and Fig. 2-3 reflects the marketing system as a combination framework of environmental and internal forces.

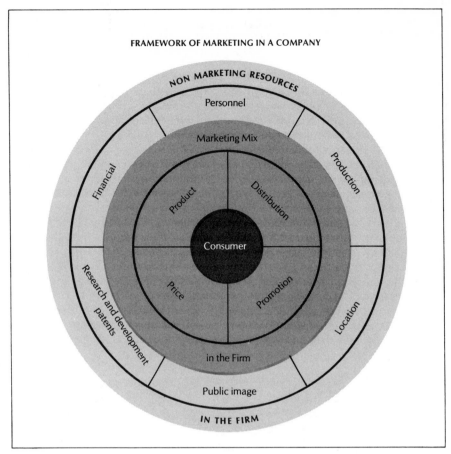

FRAMEWORK OF MARKETING IN A COMPANY

Figure 2-2

NONMARKETING RESOURCES

A company's marketing system is influenced by its production, financial, and personnel capability. If management is considering adding a new product to its present assortment, can existing facilities and expertise be used? If the new product requires a new plant or machinery, financial capability enters the picture. Some firms cannot enter new markets or market new products because of inadequate personnel.

Other nonmarketing forces which management must consider are the company's location, its engineering research and development strength as evidenced by its patents, and the overall image the firm projects to its public. Plant location often determines the geographic limits of a company's market, particularly if high transportation costs or perishable products are involved. The R & D factor may determine whether a company will lead or follow in the industry's technology and marketing.

THE MARKETING MIX

A marketing mix, effectively blended and properly attuned to customers' wants, competition, and the other environmental forces, can result in a successful market-

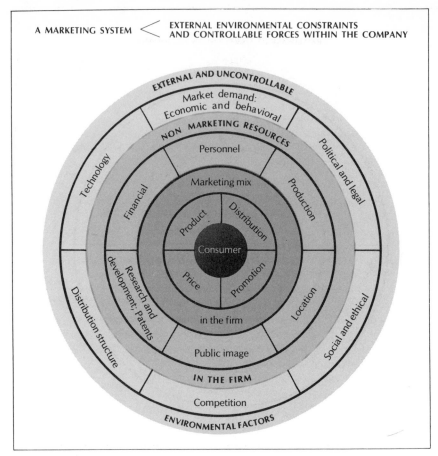

A MARKETING SYSTEM < EXTERNAL ENVIRONMENTAL CONSTRAINTS AND CONTROLLABLE FORCES WITHIN THE COMPANY

EXTERNAL AND UNCONTROLLABLE
Market demand: Economic and behavioral
NON MARKETING RESOURCES
Personnel
Marketing mix
Technology
Political and legal
Financial
Product
Distribution
Production
Consumer
Price
Promotion
Research and development; patents
Distribution structure
Location
in the firm
Public image
Social and ethical
IN THE FIRM
Competition
ENVIRONMENTAL FACTORS

Figure 2-3

ing system. *Marketing mix* is the term used to describe the combination of the four inputs which constitute the core of a company's marketing system: the product, the price structure, the promotional activities, and the distribution system.

The four "ingredients" in the mix are interrelated. Again we see the *systems* concept, as decisions in one area usually affect action in the others. Also, each of the four contains countless variables. A company may market one product or several—related or unrelated; they may be distributed through wholesalers or directly to retailers; etc. Ultimately, from the myriad of variables, management must select the combination which will be the most effective in profitably adapting to the environment. Relating to an earlier section in this chapter, management is seeking the mix which will lead to the optimum *synergistic* results.

The product. Managing the product component includes planning and developing the right products and/or services to be marketed by the company. Policy and strategy guidelines are needed for changing existing products, adding new ones, and taking other actions which affect the assortment of products carried. Decisions are also needed regarding branding, packaging, color, and other product features.

Price. In pricing, management must determine the right base price of its products and then establish policies for dealing with discounts, freight payments, and many other price-related situations.

Promotion. This is the component used to inform and persuade the market regarding a company's products. Advertising, personal selling, and sales promotion are the major promotional activities.

Distribution. Even though the distribution structure was noted earlier as a non-controllable environmental factor, a marketing executive has considerable working latitude within that framework. He has a choice of channels through which he will distribute his products, and the wisdom he uses in this selection may make the difference between a strong and a weak market position.

Management's responsibility is to select and manage the trade channels through which the products will reach the right market at the right time and to develop a distribution system for physically handling and transporting the products through these channels. Part of the distribution task is to select useful intermediaries (middlemen) in the channel and to develop effective working relationships with them.

In conclusion, a company's marketing effort should start and end with the customers. Management should select its market targets, analyze them carefully, and then develop a program to reach those markets. Permeating the planning and operation of this model is marketing research—a key activity intended to aid management in its decision making. See Fig. 2-4.

MANAGING THE MARKETING SYSTEM

If an effective marketing mix is influential in a firm's well-being, who determines the composition of this mix? The answer is the firm's *management*. The fundamental determinant of a company's success is the caliber of its management.

The "marketing" part of the term, "marketing management" was defined in Chapter 1, but what about the "management" part? *Management* or *administration* (the terms are used synonymously here) may be defined as the process of planning, organizing, directing, and evaluating the efforts of a group of people toward a common goal. As a result of management, the combined group output surpasses the sum of individual outputs. Here again is involved the important concept of synergism.

Management is a separate and distinct skill; it is an art in and of itself. As such, it should not be confused with technical operating skills. Managerial skills and operational abilities are not automatically interchangeable. A good salesman is not necessarily a good sales manager. Conversely, an outstanding administrator may have had only modest success as a technical operator in his field.

Because administrative ability is a distinct skill, it is adaptable to various jobs. The ability to plan, direct, organize, and evaluate human efforts is equally usable whether the executive is working for an automobile manufacturer or an appliance maker. Civil servants have become business executives; business executives have moved into college and university presidencies; university presidents have moved into administrative positions in other fields.

The management process, as applied to marketing, consists basically of the fol-

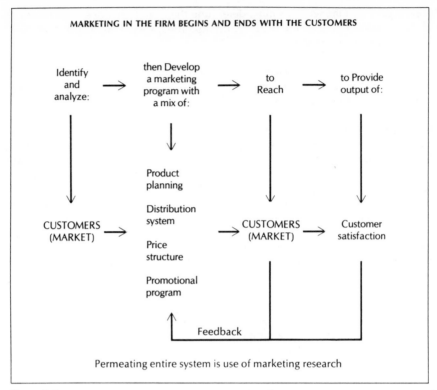

MARKETING IN THE FIRM BEGINS AND ENDS WITH THE CUSTOMERS

Figure 2-4

lowing activities: (1) developing a plan or program, (2) executing it, and (3) evaluating its results. The development stage includes setting the goals and planning how to reach them. Execution of the plan includes organizing, staffing the organization, and directing the actual operation of the plan. The evaluation stage is a good example of the interrelated, continuing nature of the management process in that evaluation is both a look back and a look ahead. Management looks back to analyze performance results in light of the goals. The findings from this evaluation of past performance then often influence the goals and plans for future periods. See Fig. 2-5. Now let us look briefly at some applications of these managerial activities in a marketing system.

DETERMINING OBJECTIVES

A firm's activity must be goal-directed to be effective. Since a firm's marketing objectives form the foundation of its marketing management, the first task of the marketing administrators is to determine their goals. These goals are an interpretation by management of its particular needs at a given time and place, and they guide the company's progress along the path to wherever management wishes the firm to be in the future.

Marketing goals should be set forth clearly in writing and then communicated downward in the organization. Otherwise, management runs the real risk that any

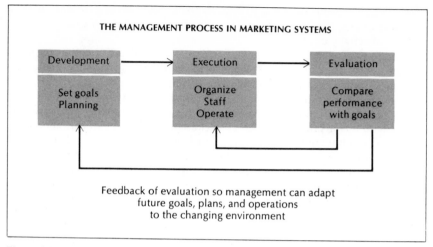

THE MANAGEMENT PROCESS IN MARKETING SYSTEMS

Development	Execution	Evaluation
Set goals Planning	Organize Staff Operate	Compare performance with goals

Feedback of evaluation so management can adapt
future goals, plans, and operations
to the changing environment

Figure 2-5

subsequent planning and operating will be done virtually in a vacuum. The firm is likely to experience misdirected marketing effort, inefficient use of resources, and low morale among the personnel.

Ordinarily a firm has different levels of marketing objectives, ranging from its ultimate long-range goals to its specific short-run operational ones. The broad objective may be to market a volume of goods at a level of profit over the long run that will satisfy the interests of the stockholders, consumers, and labor unions and still meet all governmental regulations. Broadly stated goals, however, such as "maximize profits" or "capture the tape-recorder market," are too vague to guide management effectively. A specific objective, such as "sign up 300 new dealers next year" or "increase the sales of product C by 20 percent," is a more useful tool for guiding executives in their activities. Viewed from another perspective, the levels of marketing goals range from total program objectives, down through goals for each marketing activity, to separate goals for each salesman, or middleman.

In marketing as in other types of group effort, the goals should be realistic and relevant. Moreover, the planning and operating decisions must be in line with the goals set up by management. For example, if the objective is to reach a mass market with a consumer product, the company must attempt to get distribution through the maximum number of retail outlets. A decision to use only one retail outlet in each city would not be consistent with the goal.

PLANNING

Once management has established its objectives, the next step in the administrative process is to determine the manner in which these goals will be reached. This managerial activity is called *planning*. Without planning, a company's operations have no meaning and no direction; there can be no orderly procedure in management's pursuit of its goals. One frequently finds that Canadian subsidiaries of foreign parents do a very detailed planning job because plans must be approved by the parent.

Planning may be classified according to the length of time for which it is done and the relative breadth of the activities planned. Short-term planning usually covers a year or less; long-term planning, one to five or ten years. Plans may cover many areas of activity or one area.

The general-management concept of planning has broad and countless applications in the field of marketing. Marketing executives are engaged in long-range and short-range planning regarding their markets, products, distribution systems, and promotional programs. The planning process may include laying plans for the introduction of a new car model or making sales forecasts. Marketing plans may be concerned with major programs, such as deciding when a large department store will open a new suburban branch, or with a specific situation, such as determining ways and means of promoting fresh produce in a supermarket on weekends.

"Strategy" and "tactics" are essentially military terms, but they have achieved wide application in nonmilitary activities. In marketing terms, a strategy is the overall plan of action to reach a predetermined marketing objective; tactics are the detailed methods and techniques employed to implement the strategy. Assume that a Montreal garment manufacturer's goal is to enter the prestige, high-income market for clothes. His strategy regarding channels of distribution would be to sell his product through one high-quality clothing store in each market. The tactics of the situation would involve selecting the specific store, such as Holt Renfrew in Montreal, Toronto, and Winnipeg. As promotional strategy, this manufacturer might plan an advertising campaign around a prestige appeal and nonprice competition. Promotional tactics would include using such media as *Maclean's* and/or *Saturday Night* magazines and never mentioning price in the advertisements.

Unless the objective in a given situation is specifically stated, there may be some confusion about what constitutes objectives, strategies, and tactics. In the above example of the garment manufacturer, some people might reason that the company's objective is to broaden its market. Then its strategy might be to capture the high-income market, and its tactics would consist of distribution in high-quality stores and a prestige-appeal promotional campaign. The issue here concerns the *level* of the objectives; the concepts of marketing strategies and tactics are meaningful only after the level of objectives is established.

ORGANIZING AND COORDINATING

Organizing is another major phase of the management process, and coordinating is a significant part of organizing. *Organizing* is the process of arranging activities and the people engaged in them in such a way as to achieve the maximum output with the highest possible degree of efficiency and coordination. The end structure of the process is an organization. In a good organization, the people involved produce more effectively as a group than they could individually.

Within the marketing department, activities in sales, advertising, marketing research, new-product development, customer service, and sales statistics all require careful coordination. Salesmen can help the advertising division, and the advertising people can be of direct benefit to the sales force. According to a top marketing executive with a manufacturer of dairy, grocery, and candy products, his company's biggest challenge was to achieve "more effective coordination of the marketing efforts of our scattered and diverse operating divisions, tying these more closely to the overall corporate program."[2]

---

2 "What's New in Marketing," *Sales Management*, Nov. 10, 1964, p. 159.

There are countless possible examples of *interdepartmental coordination*. Marketing can furnish sales estimates so that the production department can better plan its work, or it can push items which are overstocked. Production can help marketing by manufacturing the proper quantity and quality of products at the right time. Production can also provide product information for sales training and advertising programs.

Marketing executives must coordinate their activities with advertising agencies, transportation companies, and other *outside companies* which are helping the seller in his marketing program. Advertising agencies must plan their campaigns to coincide with the introduction of a new model. Transportation companies must have carrier facilities available when and where the product is to be loaded. The manufacturer can help by furnishing information regarding new products. Middlemen can help by giving the product adequate promotion and good display space. In many cases, Canadian firms with foreign parents and affiliates must allocate a good deal of effort to coordination so that information, product, technology and even personnel flows are well integrated.

The marketing concept implies the coordination of all company activities which impinge on the consumer.[3] Yet the organizational proposals and changes made to achieve this coordination can result in organizational conflicts between the marketing department and other local and international units of the organization. Conflict occurs (1) because each department wishes to stress the importance of its own tasks (just as marketing stresses the consumer point of view); (2) because each department defines its goals narrowly and in its own self-interest and (3) because foreign affiliates and parents (where they exist), have their own specific goals to attend to, and take a different view of the Canadian firm's needs. Thus engineering emphasizes functional features and few models with standard parts; marketing emphasizes sales features and many models with custom components. Finance wants set budgets and prices to cover costs; marketing wants flexible budgets and pricing to further market development. A parent wants to continue shipping assembled product to the Canadian subsidiary rather than approve a request for local manufacture and assembly. These conflicts will continue as long as each department or unit is judged by the efficient performance of its own tasks, and not by its overall company contribution. In this light, top management should reduce any narrow interest in departmental efficiency and, instead, work toward interdepartment policies designed to advance total company interest. Multinationals with Canadian operations are sometimes much maligned for doing exactly this.

STAFFING

The most important function of management is staffing the organization—assembling the human resources. If management is the key to successful business operations, then staffing is the key to successful management. Many will prefer to nominate planning, motivating, or some other activity as the critical function of management. However, proper personnel selection—both executive and nonexecutive—will eliminate or substantially reduce many management problems. A marketing manager's job is made easier if he hires an excellent advertising manager or sales-force manager. The sales-force manager, in turn, has fewer problems with training and compensation if excellent salespeople are hired.

---

3 This paragraph is adapted from Philip Kotler, "Diagnosing the Marketing Takeover," *Harvard Business Review*, November-December, 1965, pp. 70-72.

OPERATING

After the goals have been set, the planning accomplished, and the organization established and staffed, the program must be placed in operation. In the final analysis no plan is worth much unless it is carried out effectively. This is particularly important in marketing because success depends upon the way the business is operated. Management may develop excellent plans, but unless the sales force carries out its end of the task, success cannot be achieved. Here again we see the importance of personnel selection. Good people may bring about successful results even if the original planning was mediocre. The management function of operating and directing includes operating a sales force, directing an advertising campaign, and working with middlemen.

EVALUATING

The final stage of the management process consists of analyzing and evaluating the results of the company's operations to determine whether they met expectations. There are at least four major areas of application of this managerial function in the marketing program of a firm. First, the executive may analyze marketing costs by territories, products, or customer groups. In many firms the bulk of the sales volume and net profits comes from a small percentage of the customers, products, or territories. Management is often unaware of this situation. Consequently, it misdirects its marketing efforts by spreading them evenly over all territories or products even though these units do not produce equal returns to the company. Second, the performance of the individual salesmen may be evaluated. Third, both manufacturers and middlemen may evaluate the effectiveness of their advertising programs. Fourth, individual manufacturers may want to evaluate the performance of a middleman's volume in the light of his quota and customers' reactions.

THE ESTABLISHMENT OF MARKETING POLICIES

In order to guide executives in their decision making on recurring marketing problems, management should establish marketing policies covering every phase of its program. A *marketing policy* is a statement of a course of action followed under given circumstances. For example, after careful consideration the marketing executives in a manufacturing company may decide to pay half the cost of any retailer's advertisement which features the manufacturer's product. A retailer may decide to stay open until 9 P.M. on Monday, Wednesday, and Friday nights. Some policies are major ones, such as a manufacturer's decision to sell to only one retailer in a market or a retailer's decision to sell everything in the store at one price; others are less important. But they all serve the same essential purpose: They afford uniform executive action and uniform treatment of customers, and they save valuable executive time.

A policy is only as good as the research upon which it is based. Also, policies should be stable; if they are changed frequently, they cease to serve as guides. At the same time, a policy should be flexible; it should be reviewed periodically and revised when necessary. A flexible policy allows for some leeway in executive judgment and action. It is adaptable to a reasonable range of variations surrounding a given business situation.

PROBLEM SOLVING AND DECISION MAKING IN MARKETING SYSTEMS

Marketing management consists of a never-ending process of recognizing marketing problems, analyzing them, and making decisions. In fact, relative abilities in the combined art of problem solving and decision making are the features which differentiate high-caliber executives from the less able ones. One reason marketing executives generally receive higher-than-average earnings is that problem solving is more difficult in marketing than in many other fields. It is difficult because much of it involves abstract reasoning and subjective analysis.

One hallmark of a good executive is his ability to make decisions and to make them promptly. Some managers evade the responsibility of making decisions by enveloping themselves in a cloak of anonymity called a "committee." Some pass the buck to other executives. Many people find it difficult to make decisions. A student may ask his girl where she would like to go for the evening, rationalizing that he is being considerate. Actually he is refusing to make a decision.

Some decision-evading executives issue progress reports, but never a final decision saying that they need more information. This is often not a legitimate excuse. Ordinarily nobody has all the information needed or wanted, and yet the situation will not wait; a decision must be made. This is as true in other walks of life as it is in business. The quarterback must call a play and execute it in less than twenty-five seconds, even though he would like more information—for example, what defense is being set up against him. Often all information needed will not be available until after the decision is made. After the team runs the play, the quarterback finds out what kind of defense was set up against him. After a company locates a branch on a given corner, the executives find out whether a sufficient number of customers are attracted.

Management ordinarily will never know whether it made the best possible decision, even after it has been executed and the results are in. No matter how great the results are, an alternative decision might have turned out better. For example, if a quarterback with a ball on his own 15-yard line called a pass play and gained 60 yards, the move would be loudly acclaimed. But was that play the best one to call? No one knows; possibly an end run would have been good for a touchdown.

PROBLEM-SOLVING PROCESSES

The problem-solving responsibilities of today's marketing executives can be assisted considerably by the use of technological and other scientific advances in two general fields. The first is in the area of quantitative analytical tools where such aids as computers, mathematical models, and other quantitative methods are providing problem-solving capabilities of a speed, precision, and magnitude previously unimaginable. Market analysis, warehousing, evaluating middlemen's performance, forecasting sales, setting quotas and territories, and many other marketing tasks can be performed more easily and decisions are apt to be more sound if quantitative analytical tools are used.

The behavioral sciences are the other general area which can aid in marketing decision making. Management should capitalize on the potential contributions of psychology, sociology, and anthropology. These behavioral sciences can help in solving problems related to marketing organizational structures, branding and packaging, consumer behavior, and so on.

One procedure for solving marketing problems will be explained briefly. No single approach is better than any other; basically, all are variations of a scientific method applied to marketing management.

Five steps are involved in this approach. (It is assumed that the executives already have a thorough understanding of their industry, product, and market and of the other environmental forces which will influence their decision.)

1. Carefully and specifically define the problem.
2. Determine the reasonable courses of action.
3. Identify the major issues, factors, or subproblems bearing on the main problem.
4. Analyze each major issue and come to a decision on each in light of the alternative courses of action.
5. Make a decision; that is, select the best alternative.

Before an executive can solve a marketing problem, he must recognize that one exists, and then he must be able to identify it clearly. This is no easy task. Sometimes symptoms of a problem are mistaken for the problem itself. An analogy drawn from the medical field may sharpen this point. A person goes to a physician complaining of recurring headaches. Basically. the headaches are only symptoms. The real problem may be emotional tension, eyestrain, or any one of several other factors. In any event, the physician must identify and clearly define the problem before he can hope to remedy it.

In a marketing situation a symptom is often diagnosed as the basic problem. A marketing executive may say that his big problem is that his sales have declined steadily for two years. Actually declining sales are only a symptom. The real problem may be noncompetitive pricing, poor service to consumers, poorly packaged products, poor advertising, or a combination of several weaknesses. Truly it may take some careful investigating to pinpoint the real problem. Often a physician or a marketing executive will treat a symptom for some time before realizing that he has not yet found the real source of the trouble.

After an executive has decided what the main problem is, he should carefully define it in the form of a question. A question requires an answer. Instead of stating that the company's problem is its product packaging, the executive will ask: "From a marketing standpoint, what are the weaknesses in the product's packaging?" or "What packaging changes should be made to improve our product's marketability?" Questions should be specific. Broad questions, such as "What can the company do to increase its sales?" do not lend themselves to a good analysis.

The second step in the problem-solving process is to decide upon the alternative courses of action which seem reasonable under the circumstances. Normally this is not a difficult thing to do. Assume that a luggage manufacturer's problem is what channels of distribution he should use for his new line of airplane luggage. On the basis of his understanding of the product, company, market, and other environmental factors, he may decide that the following channels might be used:

Manufacturer—retailers (department stores, large luggage stores, discount houses)—consumers
Manufacturer—leather goods wholesalers—retailers—consumers
Manufacturer—manufacturers' agents—retailers—consumers

Other *possible* alternatives, such as door-to-door selling, are not always *reasonable* ones.

In some problems there may be only two reasonable alternatives. Assume that a manufacturer of business machines is trying to decide whether to add electric razors to its groups of products. About the only major alternative courses of action are to add or not to add.

The third, fourth, and fifth stages in problem solving are to identify the major issues which bear on the main problem, to analyze these issues, and finally to reach a decision on each one, The conclusions reached will have determining influences on the main decision. In the case of the business machine manufacturer who is trying to decide whether to add a line of electric razors, the major issues bearing on the problems are as follows:

1. Is there an adequate market demand for the proposed product?
2. From a marketing standpoint, can the proposed product be handled through the company's existing channels of distribution, middlemen, sales organization, and advertising program?
3. Does the product fit into the company's present production structure with respect to necessary labor skills, sources of materials, and product facilities?
4. What are the profit possibilities for the proposed product?
5. Does the new product pose any legal problems with respect to patent and packaging regulations?
6. Is the product in keeping with the company's overall image, self-concept, and objectives?

Thus, before it can make a sound decision on whether to add electric razors, management must first carefully analyze in great detail each of the above issues, or subproblems, and come to a decision on each one. Failure to recognize all the important issues may result in a very poor decision.

Management must consider the effect the subproblem decisions have on one another. Also, the major issues are not always equally important. An administrator cannot count up the number of "yes" and "no" decisions on the subproblems and from this make his final decision. In the above case, the decisions on issues 2 to 6 may have favored adding the product to the line, but the decision on issue 1 may have been negative. This one negative decision—that there is not an adequate market demand—should override all the others, and the firm should not add the product. On the other hand, if there were a substantial demand and the profit possibilities looked encouraging, the manufacturer might add the product even though it did not fit well into the existing marketing or production structure.

The final step is to make the decision regarding the main problem. This involves selecting the best alternative course of action in light of the analysis of the major issues or subproblems.

QUESTIONS AND PROBLEMS

1. How does the systems approach to marketing differ from the more traditional approaches?
2. Explain how the concept of synergism is related to the systems approach to marketing.
3. How can the systems approach benefit a company's marketing effort?
4. Explain, giving examples, how a firm's marketing system can be influenced by the environmental variable of technology; by political and legal forces.

5. If administrative ability is a distinct skill and is transferable among various jobs, why do so many more top marketing executives come up through the ranks of the sales force than through other divisions in marketing such as advertising or marketing research?

6. "The targets assigned to departmental operating executives should be consistent with company goals." Give some examples of sales department goals which might be in conflict with the goals assigned to production executives; to financial executives.

7. On the basis of your knowledge of their recent advertisements, what do you think are the current marketing objectives of the following companies?
   a. Ford Motor Company
   b. The manufacturer of Crest toothpaste (Proctor & Gamble)
   c. A leading department store in your city or in the nearest large city
   d. The telephone company
   e. An office machines manufacturer such as IBM, Burroughs, or National Cash Register

8. Interview a few small, local retailers (barbershop or beauty shop, restaurant, shoe repair shop, hardware store, clothing store, etc.) located near your campus to determine what, if any, specific marketing objectives they have consciously established.

9. Suggest some strategies and tactics which might reasonably be employed to reach the following marketing goals:
   a. A furniture manufacturer wishes to market patio furniture as an addition to his present group of products.
   b. A wholesaler of building materials wants to increase the average size of his sales; that is, he hopes to reduce the number of small orders.
   c. The cigar manufacturers' trade association wants to increase the market for cigars among college students.

10. How do you suggest that effective coordination might be secured between the department which includes the salespeople and each of the following departments?
    a. Advertising   c. Finance
    b. Production   d. Engineering

11. A manufacturer of small hand tools (hammers, saws, screwdrivers, etc.) frequently runs out of stock on some items, while holding a five-year supply of other articles. Who is at fault for this badly balanced inventory situation?

12. Suggest some specific ways that the salespeople and the advertising division within a marketing department can help each other.

13. "The evaluation stage may be considered both the final and also the first stage of the management process; that is, this stage involves both a look backward and a look forward in managing a company." Explain.

14. Give some examples from your everyday life which show the need for making decisions and the difficulty of doing so.

CASE FOR PART ONE

CASE 1: HARPER BANK

Applying the marketing concept

In early 1969, top management of Harper Bank was considering the failure of the introduction of the marketing concept in banking. Some members of management who had heard of excellent results from the introduction of the marketing concept in manufacturing firms were beginning to wonder whether different conditions were not required for the successful implementation of the marketing concept in the banking business. Harper Bank management began a self-analysis to determine where the bank went wrong and what could and should be done at this stage.

In 1968, Harper Bank was faced with the challenge of increasing competition from the other chartered banks and a dynamic thrust by the trust companies in the financial services market. A few of Harper's top executives who had come into contact with some marketing professors at a business conference were impressed with what they heard about the advantages of the marketing concept and brought back the idea to the bank. They thought if they were the first to truly introduce the marketing concept into banking in Canada, with the changes in the Bank Act (The Re-

Case prepared by Professor Lionel A. Mitchell, Acadia University.

vised Bank Act) which had been introduced, they should be able to anticipate and solve most of the problems which were likely to come to the fore—problems of customers and customers' demands and servicing, and problems arising out of the growth in foreign currency deposits and loans and real estate management. The top executives thought they could introduce the change on a test or experimental basis in a few of their branches in Montreal.

Harper was one of Canada's leading chartered banks, with head office in Montreal and branches throughout Canada and in many parts of the world. Most policy matters were initiated at head office; however, other matters were dealt with by divisional offices in the area where they arose. Divisional offices were located in Toronto, Winnipeg, Quebec City, Halifax, Edmonton and Vancouver. Each divisional vice-president had a lending limit of $500,000 with any loan exceeding this limit requiring the approval of the board of directors at head office.

Harper Bank was established more than a century ago and expanded through internal growth and mergers. Its growth was considered fairly substantial up to 1946 but even more so from 1946 to the mid-sixties when the number of branches tripled and profit growth, assets and foreign currency holdings more than doubled. The bank's main emphasis and target market were big business and large accounts. Not very much attention was given to attracting small depositors and investors. However, a wind of change was now blowing across the banking business and Harper predicted a struggle with its competitors to maintain their market share and perhaps to continue expansion of their operations. Management believed that a change in the bank's image and outlook was required. They thought a change in attitudes and approach was needed to cash in on increasing incomes and to stem the tides of greater and more intense competition from other banks and financial institutions. Moreover, they thought they would have to overcome the distorted and misunderstood image held by desired customers.

The responsibility for change would be placed in the Marketing Department under the marketing concept, the executives thought, if they understood the professors correctly. Consequently, a reorganization would have to take place. The Public Relations and Advertising Department could be enlarged into a Marketing Department with clearly defined functions but without in any way becoming too rigid. There would be, in addition, many undefined functions left for the department to undertake.

In the late 1940s, Harper Bank had begun to work on the idea of public relations, advertising and other promotion, and within ten years they had established a separate Public Relations and Advertising Department, headed by a manager who reported to the Secretary. This department supplied ink blotters and book-covers for students, posters which were displayed at branches, bus and train advertising cards, small informative folders for branch disposal, and many other similar items too numerous to mention. The common characteristic of each of these items was a message from Harper Bank; for instance, a message with descriptive pictures telling of the advantages of a savings account or a safety deposit box. This type of promotion may have been adequate for the period during which it was used, but the bank now found that it must do a lot more. This led to more intensive promotional activities, such as the establishment of student tours, sponsoring of prizes at regional fairs and exhibitions, student scholarships, and display booths at industrial fairs. Banking had become more complex and competitive, and the bank was outgrowing its Public Relations and Advertising Department.

John Morgan, who came to Harper from the marketing department of a leading

Canadian manufacturing firm, was appointed to head the new Marketing Department, with the title of Assistant General Manager of Marketing. John Morgan reported directly to Fred McKenzie, General Manager, who indicated to Morgan that he was in complete charge of the department and had "full rein" to implement any new marketing feature.

The new Marketing Department set as its first objective a major reorganization campaign designed to upgrade and modernize all services, to handle customer services more efficiently, and to listen to and act upon customers' suggestions and complaints.

The Public Relations and Advertising Department was to be subordinated to the new Marketing Department and, in time, completely absorbed by it. One of the first projects of the Marketing Department was the redesign of banking forms, using the new bank logo and maroon and gold color. The uniforms and outfits of porters, messengers, chauffeurs, mail and service staff were redesigned to reflect the new bank image. Banking hours were to be extended for customer convenience. It was suggested that Marketing Departments be established at divisional offices in Quebec City, Montreal, Halifax, Toronto, Winnipeg, Edmonton and Vancouver.

Within six months of its inception, the Marketing Department's staff numbered twenty-nine. Most of the projects had been initiated, and the Public Relations and Advertising Department was almost completely absorbed with most of its duties now performed by the Marketing Department. Extensive research had been in progress with a view to implementing marketing departments in the other regions. About this time, however, problems began to arise and conflicts developed. Doubts were raised about the many and frequent changes. Many of the changes did not transpire as well as the bank had expected. Mr. Morgan, who was inexperienced in banking matters, had plunged into his job of introducing a marketing orientation with little or no cooperation and assistance from the old staff members, that is, the experienced bank personnel. Morgan relied entirely on his previous marketing knowledge and experience, but some of his ideas were considered unorthodox by the banking public as well as many of the staff, including his subordinates and his superiors. Morgan secretly admitted that he did not care what the staff thought of the new concept, it was a good thing and it would be implemented. In the meantime, there was a clash with McKenzie and,in the weeks that followed, Morgan was unable to patch this relationship, which eventually led to his dismissal. A new Public Relations and Advertising Department was set up to perform the marketing function and Peter Forrest was installed as manager of the department.

QUESTIONS

1. Why did the introduction of the marketing concept fail?
2. What conditions are essential for the successful implementation of the marketing concept into banking?
3. Should the introduction of the marketing concept in a service industry be different from that in retailing, wholesaling and/or manufacturing?
4. If you were Peter Forrest what approach to your task would you adopt? Evaluate Peter Forrest's chance of success.

THE MARKET

MARKETS: HOW THEY CAN BE DEFINED

A sound marketing program should start with a careful quantitative and qualitative analysis of the market demand for the product or service. Adam Smith and other economists and philosophers both before and after him stated the fundamental importance of consumption—it is the only social and economic justification for production. Yet, because of the scarcity of goods, the difficulty of understanding the consumer, and the ease of measuring machine output, most economists devoted their attention to production rather than to consumption prior to the 1920s.

In North America, Western Europe and Japan, however, the output of the production system has been so great since the end of World War I that surpluses have developed. In these economies of abundance, the social and economic emphasis has shifted from production to consumption. For several years now it has been considered axiomatic that "the consumer is king." The consumer is the basic determinant of what goods and services will be produced and of where, when, and at what price they will be sold. Up to the limits imposed by income, the consumer today is free to choose the amount and kind of want-satisfying goods and services which he or she buys.

From a realistic standpoint there are considerable limitations to consumer sovereignty. Possibly the principal ones are the consumer's lack of organization, his lack of a voice to make his edicts known, and his general apathy. If he is king, he maintains a strange palace court in which the subjects have to spend huge sums to try to find out what the vacillating, disorganized, fickle king desires and to proclaim loudly that they, over all other courtiers, have just what he wants.

Import restrictions also limit the consumer. In many instances they keep him from getting fine foreign products at reasonable prices. From time to time, the efforts of government and farm, labor, and business interests take price control out of the hands of consumers. Determination of product quality by the consumer is often difficult, if not impossible.

WHAT IS A MARKET?

The concept of a market is sometimes confusing. There is a stock market and an automobile market, a retail and a wholesale market for furniture, and a local and a national market for building materials. One person may be going to the market; another may plan to market his product. Really, what is a market? Clearly, there are many usages of the term in economic theory, in business in general, and in marketing in particular. A market may be defined as a place where buyers and sellers meet and function, goods or services are offered for sale, and transfers of ownership of title occur. A market may also be defined as an aggregate demand by potential buyers of a product or service. For example, there is a farm market for petroleum products. In economic theory a market implies a set of conditions and forces which determine prices. That is, the meeting of buyers and sellers, price determination, and transfer of title are activities essential to the existence of a market. The concept of a market also implies a *demand* for a product or service. In fact, the terms "market" and "demand" are often used interchangeably, and they may also be used jointly as "market demand."

The above definitions of a market still may not be sufficiently usable by a marketing executive in an individual firm. Consequently, in this book a *market* will be defined as people with needs to satisfy, the money to spend, and the willingness to spend it. Thus in the market demand for any given product or service, there are three factors to consider—people with needs, their purchasing power, and their buying behavior. We shall employ the dictionary definition of *needs:* A need is the lack of anything that is required, desired, or useful. We do not limit needs to the narrow physiological requirements of food, clothing, and shelter essential for survival. The potentially limitless number of needs offers unbounded opportunities for market growth. Satisfying wants may be interpreted as the first step toward satisfying needs. We want something that will answer our needs.

MARKET SEGMENTATION

A company that is production-oriented is likely to treat its entire market as a single undifferentiated homogeneous unit. Under this concept—known as market aggregation—management will develop one product and one marketing program designed to reach as many customers as possible. The assumption which such a company makes about the market is that the needs, financial resources and buying behavior of people interested in the product are similar enough so that the various differences that exist between individuals and groups of people can be ignored or traded off against cost savings. Market aggregation enables a company to maximize its economies of scale in production, physical distribution, and promotion. Producing and marketing one product means longer production runs at lower unit costs. Inventory costs are minimized when there is no (or a very limited) variety of colors, styles, and sizes. Warehousing and transportation efforts are more efficient. Advertising costs per unit presumably are lower for one product than when several are being promoted. As long as competition is not severe, this strategy can be successful.

When competition becomes severe and management is forced to cut prices with the resultant drop in profits, a firm may try to differentiate its product from those of its competitors. Under this concept of *product differentiation,* a company will introduce some new feature—a package change (butter in a plastic squeeze tube), a new size (120 mm cigarettes), a new flavor (cinnamon-flavored toothpaste), or a new color. The new feature often is accompanied by heavy promotional expenditures in an effort to convey to the aggregate market that there are some actual or psychological differential benefits in the new product. But please note we still are dealing with the production-oriented philosophy of one market (market aggregation) and still ignoring differences that may exist.

When competition is vigorous or some competitors are market- rather than production-oriented, market aggregation may not be a very productive strategy. It is when such conditions exist that the real benefits of the heterogeneity of a given market can be put to work. Because of the differences that exist within a single product or service market, marketing managers are not easily able to derive maximum value from an analysis of it as a whole—they must disaggregate it. To speak of the market for vitamin pills, electric razors, or tractors is to ignore the fact that within the total market for each of these products there exist submarkets or segments which differ significantly from one another. This lack of homogeneity may be traced to differences in buying habits, ways in which the product is used, motives for buying, or other factors.

WHAT IS MARKET SEGMENTATION?

Market segmentation is the process of taking the total, heterogeneous market for a product and dividing it into several submarkets or segments, each of which tends to be homogeneous in all significant aspects. In terms familiar to an economist, we are developing several demand schedules—a separate one for each market segment—where only one schedule representing the total market existed previously. Thus, instead of speaking of a market for swimwear, we now segment this market into several submarkets—those for young men, young women, businessmen, housewives, and retired people. Still further segmentation might be based on geographic location or cultural background of the consumer. For example, we might speak of a Prairie Provinces market or of a Quebec youth market. A company may deal with a number of market segments. Rarely would it deal with all the segments that exist in a market. The industry in total, comprising all competitors, would likely deal with most if not all segments available.

Market segmentation is a customer-oriented philosphy. We first identify customers' needs in a submarket and then design a product and/or a marketing program to reach that submarket (segment) and satisfy those needs. Thus, in effect, each market segment calls for a separate marketing program which is different in some respect from the programs designed to reach other submarkets. Stated another way, in market segmentation we are employing a "rifle" approach (separate programs, pinpointed targets) in our marketing activities, as contrasted with the "shotgun" approach (one program, broad target) used in market aggregation.

As part of the strategy of segmenting its markets, a company frequently will develop for each segment a different variety of the basic product. Thus, auto producers and ski manufacturers, for example, have developed different models, each intended for a different market segment. On the other hand, market segmentation can be accomplished with no change in the product, but only with separate marketing programs each tailor-made for a given market segment. A producer of vitamin pills, for instance, can market the identical product to the youth market and also to the over sixty-five market, but in each case the promotional programs and probably the channels of distribution will be different. The same portable electric typewriters or the same airline or telephone service can be marketed effectively to different market segments by using different marketing programs. The promotional appeals, for instance, would stress different user benefits in each case.

Marketing practitioners and theoreticians have explored the concept of market segmentation at length in recent years.[1] Numerous attempts have been made to define distinctive market segments, primarily in the area of consumer products rather than industrial goods. These attempts have employed many different bases for segmentation, some of which will be reviewed in a later section of this chapter. Two distinct types of approaches to segmentation have been evident. The first begins with making use of observable differences among consumer groups and attempts to profile market segments based on these differences.[2] For example, most firms are easily able to segment their product or service market into heavy users and light users. An analysis of sales volume will show that a small percentage of buyers (perhaps 15-25) account for a very large percentage of sales (perhaps 75-80). Distinct marketing efforts can be created for each segment based on such observable usage data. More refined segmentation of heavy and light users can be conducted by gathering more data on each group and using such data to better focus efforts or to further segment, say, heavy users into two types or classes.

What amounts to an opposite approach is the gathering of consumer data on a large number of factors and then creating groups or types of consumers based on their similarities with respect to these consumer behavior factors. Each group can then be examined to determine if it can be a viable market segment for a product or service.[3] The first approach then starts with known characteristics of existing segments while the second starts with groups of consumers who have certain characteristics in common and assesses them for viability as market segments. The more

---

1 For reviews of the concept of market segmentation, the reader is referred to: James G. Barnes, "Market Segmentation," *The Canadian Marketer*, Spring, 1974, pp. 15-19; and to Ronald E. Frank, "Market Segmentation Research: Findings and Implications," in Frank M. Bass, Charles W. King, and Edgar A. Pessemier, eds., *Applications of the Sciences in Marketing Management*, John Wiley and Sons, Inc., New York, 1968, pp. 39-68.

2 See for example: Dik Warren Twedt, "Some Practical Applications of 'Heavy-Half' Theory," *Proceedings of the Tenth Annual Conference*, Advertising Research Foundation, New York, October, 1964.

3 See for example: John C. Bieda and Harold H. Kassarjian, "An Overview of Market Segmentation," in Bernard A. Morin, ed., *Marketing in a Changing World*, 1969 June Conference Proceedings, American Marketing Association, Chicago, 1969, pp. 249-253.

intense the competition within a potentially profitable market, the greater the gains to be derived from the latter approach of searching for segments.

BENEFITS OF MARKET SEGMENTATION

As suggested at the start of this chapter and also in the preceding chapter, a successful marketing program starts with a quantitative identification of the present and potential customers plus an understanding of their buying behavior and decision-making processes. A careful job of market segmentation supports this idea, and also can serve as a foundation stone for developing effective marketing strategies. By tailoring marketing programs to pinpointed market segments, management can do a better marketing job and make more efficient use of marketing resources. A small firm with limited resources might compete more effectively in one or two market niches, whereas the same firm would be buried if it tried to take on the total market.

More specifically, market segmentation can aid management in such ways as:[4]

1. Channeling money and effort to the potentially most profitable markets
2. Designing products that really match market demands
3. Determining what promotional appeals will be most effective for the company
4. Choosing advertising media more intelligently and determining how to allocate better the budget among the various media
5. Setting the timing of the promotional efforts so that they are heaviest during those times when response is likely to be at its peak

CONDITIONS FOR EFFECTIVE SEGMENTATION

The use of a market segmentation strategy may not be appropriate in all situations. There are certain conditions which must be met in order for the marketer to profitably develop unique marketing programs to appeal to particular groups. First, the bases for segmentation—the characteristics used to categorize customers— must be *measurable and data must be accessible.* To illustrate, fear of social disapproval or a desire for ecologically compatible products may be characteristics identifying a given segment of the market for a product, but data for these factors may not be readily accessible nor easily quantified.[5]

Second, each segment must be *large enough* to warrant a separate marketing effort. It is conceivable that a marketer could treat each individual consumer as a separate segment but it is unlikely that such a strategy could be employed profitably, with the possible exception of an industrial setting where customers may be sufficiently large and have such buying power that each is treated differently. In the consumer market it is unlikely that a company could go to the extreme of developing a very wide variety of styles, colors, sizes and prices in order to appeal to very

---

4 Daniel Yankelovich, "New Criteria for Market Segmentation," *Harvard Business Review,* March-April, 1964, pp. 83-84.

5 See Barnett A. Greenberg and Roy A. Herberger, "Is There an Ecology-Conscious Market Segment?" *Atlanta Economic Review,* March-April, 1973, pp. 42-44. For the contention that markets can be segmented on the basis of consumers' social consciousness, see W. Thomas Anderson Jr., and William H. Cunningham, "The Socially Conscious Consumer," *Journal of Marketing,* July, 1972, pp. 22-31; and Thomas C. Kinnear, James R. Taylor, and Sahrudin A. Ahmed, "Ecologically Concerned Consumers: Who Are They?" *Journal of Marketing,* April, 1974, pp. 20-24.

small market segments. The diseconomies of scale in production and inventory ordinarily will put reasonable limits on this type of expansion and proliferation.

Third, it is important that the *behavior of consumers be different from segment to segment.* For example, segments may vary in their average purchase rate of the product
or may exhibit different demand elasticities with respect to price and promotional
activities.[6] There is little rationale to treating two market segments with different
marketing programs if the members of each segment exhibit similar buying behavior or react in a similar manner to a particular marketing program.

Fourth, the bases on which markets are segmented should be *actionable.* It may
be possible to identify certain segments within a market which exhibit *interesting*
differences, but it may not be possible to translate these differences into marketing
programs which will appeal to the different segments.

Finally, market segments must be *accessible* through existing channels of distribution, salesmen, and advertising media.[7] To aid the marketer in this regard, a
number of national magazines such as *Maclean's, Time,* and *Readers' Digest* publish
separate regional editions. In the case of a marketer who is operating in only one
region of Canada, it is possible to purchase advertising space in a national magazine, thereby benefiting from the prestige associated with such a publication, but
have his advertisement appear only in that region of the country in which his business operates. In such a manner, wasted circulation is eliminated. Similarly, it is
possible to buy time on the broadcast media in such a manner that the advertising
message is directed only to that geographic market where the marketer's products
are available for sale.

The above conditions for effective segmentation are of particular importance to
Canadian subsidiaries. A segmentation strategy researched and developed abroad
could very likely flounder in Canada because the segment is not large enough here
or consumer behavior is not patterned in the same way as in a foreign locale. One
Canadian subsidiary with a U.K. parent (and a U.S. subsidiary) segmented a convenience food market into three for promotional purposes whereas in the United
States, the subsidiary had been able to profitably define five segments for the same
purposes. In this instance, the reduction in segments was simply a matter of scale
of total market.

BASES FOR MARKET SEGMENTATION

There are many different ways by which a company can segment its market. And
the methods will vary from one product to another. Moreover, the segmentation
process should be an ongoing activity for two reasons. First, markets are dynamic,
not static. They change continually as our attitudes, life-style, family situation, income, geographic patterns, etc., change. Second, the markets for a product change

---

6 Ronald E. Frank, "Market Segmentation Research: Findings and Implications," in Frank M. Bass,
Charles W. King, and Edgar A. Pessemier, eds., *Applications of the Sciences in Marketing Management,* John
Wiley and Sons, Inc., New York, 1968, p. 42.

7 See for example: John C. Bieda and Harold H. Kassarjian, "An Overview of Market Segmentation,"
in Bernard A. Morin, ed., *Marketing in a Changing World,* 1969 June Conference Proceedings, American Marketing Association, Chicago, 1969, p. 249; and James F. Engel, David T. Kollat, and Roger D. Blackwell,
"Personality Measures and Market Segmentation," *Business Horizons,* June, 1969, pp. 61-70.

as it goes through its life cycle (from its introduction, through its growth stage, to the period of sales decline).

Ultimate consumers and industrial users. One very important way of segmenting the entire Canadian market is to divide it into ultimate consumers and industrial users, the sole criterion being the reason for buying. *Ultimate consumers* buy and/or use products or services for their own personal or household use. They are satisfying strictly nonbusiness wants, and they constitute what is called the "consumer market." A mother who buys food and clothing and the family members who eat the food and wear the clothes are all ultimate consumers.

Industrial users are business, industrial, or institutional organizations who buy products or services to use in their own businesses or make other products. A manufacturer who buys chemicals with which to make fertilizer is an industrial user of these chemicals. The farmer who buys the fertilizer to use in commercial farming is an industrial user of the fertilizer. (If a homeowner buys fertilizer to use on his yard, he is an ultimate consumer because he buys it for household use.) A supermarket, hospital, bank, or paper manufacturer that buys accounting machines, pencils, and floor wax is an industrial user of these products because it uses them in a business or institution. Industrial users in total constitute the "industrial market."

The segmentation of all markets into two groups—consumer and industrial—is extremely significant from a marketing point of view because the two markets buy differently. Consequently, a seller's marketing program—his products, distribution, pricing, and promotion—will differ depending upon whether he is selling to the consumer or to the industrial market.

SEGMENTING CONSUMER MARKETS

Simply dividing the total market into consumer and industrial segments, while a worthwhile start, still leaves too broad and heterogeneous a grouping for most products. Consequently, we shall identify some of the widely used bases for further segmenting the consumer market. The discussion of the industrial market is left for Chapter 8.

Approaches to market segmentation have become more complex, more widely accepted, and more successful in accounting for the variability of consumer behavior. Marketers have sought to define the characteristics of heavy users, of brand loyal consumers, of socially conscious consumers, of frequent purchasers, of opinion leaders and innovators, and of the subscribers to various advertising media.[8]

The variables used as bases for market segmentation may be classified in a number of different ways. First, these variables may be general (age, income, and

---

8 Dik Warren Twedt, "Some Practical Applications of 'Heavy-Half' Theory," *Proceedings of the Tenth Annual Conference,* Advertising Research Foundation, New York, October, 1964; Ronald Frank, William F. Massy, and Thomas M. Lodahl, "Purchasing Behavior and Personal Attributes," *Journal of Advertising Research,* December, 1969, pp. 15-24; Thomas W. Anderson, Jr., and William H. Cunningham, "The Socially Conscious Consumer," *Journal of Marketing,* July, 1972, pp. 23-31; Douglas J. Tigert, "Psychometric Correlates of Opinion Leadership," working paper, University of Chicago, 1969; Elayn Bernay, "Life Style Analysis as a Basis for Media Selection," in Charles W. King and Douglas J. Tigert, eds., *Attitude Research Reaches New Heights,* American Marketing Association, 1970, pp. 189-195; and Douglas J. Tigert, "Are Television Audiences Really Different?" in Fred C. Allvine, ed., *Combined Proceedings,* 1971 Spring and Fall Conferences, American Marketing Association, Chicago, 1971, pp. 239-246.

other demographic variables) or may be specifically related to the situation and product under consideration (usage rates, consumption, or purchase behavior). Second, variables may be objective and observable (demographic, socioeconomic and purchase behavior variables) or they may be inferred (life style or attitude variables). Whereas early attempts at marketing segmentation relied on only one type of variable to explain differences among consumer segments, more recent attempts have employed several types of bases for segmentation with improved results.

Demographic, socioeconomic and personality bases for segmentation. One of the few publications dealing with market segmentation in Canada advocated that more attention be paid to segmenting the Canadian market, but discussed the potential for segmentation primarily in terms of a geographic breakdown of the country.[9] While markets have long been segmented on geographic bases, more recent attempts have sought to define meaningful market segments on demographic, socioeconomic and personality grounds.

Demographic bases for segmenting consumer markets have proven to be popular among marketers because of the ease of obtaining demographic data and because large, accessible segments were usually produced. But the success of demographic variables alone in explaining variations in consumer behavior has not been great. Generally, differences in purchase and consumption behavior among market segments may be attributed to other than demographic differences among the segments. Because of the inadequacy of segmenting consumer markets only on the basis of age, or sex, or education level, other bases for segmentation, incorporating socioeconomic and/or personality variables, have been proposed. But the addition of such bases have improved results only slightly. One major problem in the use of personality variables to segment markets has been that such attempts have generally relied on *clinical* measures of personality traits. None of these measures has been developed in a consumer behavior context. The use of personality measures in market segmentation implies that personality characteristics influence behavior equally strongly in all directions. Again, marketers generally prefer to regard the purchase decision as being influenced jointly by individual characteristics *and* the purchase situation. In general, either demographic, socioeconomic, or personality variables by themselves have not proven to be effective bases for the segmentation of consumer markets. Such characteristics of consumers "appear to have, at best, a relatively low degree of association with total household purchases of any particular grocery product."[10]

Product usage rates as bases for segmentation. Marketers are generally aware that possibly 80 percent of the purchases of a particular product are accounted for by 20 percent of the potential purchasers. One study showed that 17 percent of households buy 87 percent of all dog food sold, and that 33 percent of all households account for 83 percent of paper towel sales.[11] Such data have sparked an interest

---

9 Robert McGoldrick, "The Case for Market Segmentation in Canada," *The Marketer*, Spring, 1965, pp. 1-5.

10 Ronald E. Frank, "Market Segmentation Research: Findings and Implications," in Frank M. Bass, Charles W. King, and Edgar A. Pessemier, eds., *Applications of the Sciences in Marketing Management*, John Wiley and Sons, Inc., New York, 1968, p. 49.

11 Dik Warren Twedt, "How Important to Marketing Strategy is the 'Heavy User'?" *Journal of Marketing*, January, 1964, p. 72.

among marketers in what has come to be called the "heavy half," that is, that small percentage of consumers who purchase a product in large quantities. In just about any product category, there are *nonusers, light users,* and *heavy users.* It is obviously in the best interest of a marketer of beer, for example, if he can position his brand in the market in such a way that it appeals to the "heavy beer drinker," since he will likely be able to generate more sales with the same marketing effort than would be the case if the brand was positioned to appeal to the light user.

But how does one develop marketing programs to appeal to the heavy user? And, more importantly, how can such consumers be identified? The most practical approach would appear to be for the marketer to attempt to learn, through marketing research, as much as possible about consumers who may be considered heavy users. Information gathered about heavy users might include their media preferences, other interests and activities in which they engage, their attitudes toward certain general and product-specific topics, as well as their demographic and socioeconomic characteristics. Once the marketer has gathered such information about consumers who are heavy users of the product class in which he is interested, he is in a much better position to design a marketing program and to develop and position advertising material to appeal to this group.

For example, Tigert found the "heavy beer drinker" to exhibit the following characteristics:[12]

> The life-style findings suggest that the male heavy user of beer is a total hedonist: he exerts effort only when it results in his personal pleasure, or when it in some way furthers his fantasy-view of himself as the hard-drinking, swinging he-man. Being extremely self-indulgent (heavy eating, heavy smoking), he gives no indication that he is concerned with the everyday responsibilities of job, wife or family. In fact, he prefers to live dangerously, playing poker, betting at the races, taking chances, etc.
>
> While he is far from avant-garde, he does reject religious and "old-fashioned" values. He doesn't think movies should be censored and he doesn't think there is too much emphasis on sex today. Indeed, he seems to think that, "you only go around once in life, so you have to grab with all the gusto you can."
>
> The heavy beer drinker sees himself in a masculine role but it is masculinity in the sense of "one of the boys" rather than as a lady-killer. Although he is a girl watcher and unfolds the monthly playmate, masculinity to him is sports cars, bowling, poker and horse races. With the exception of bowling, his interest in sports seems to be limited to the role of the observer rather than the participant.
>
> Finally, drinking is a very important part of his masculine role: he sees himself as a *real beer drinker* and real beer drinkers as *real men.*

It should be obvious to the reader that such information on the life style of the heavy beer drinker would greatly assist marketers of this product in the development of marketing programs which would appeal to this group.

In addition to attempting to reach the lucrative heavy user segment with the objective of switching its members to his brand, the marketer should also be interested in appealing to the generally much larger segment of nonusers. Information on those consumers who do not now use the product might enable the marketer to develop a program, possibly involving some form of consumer promotion, which would induce trial of his brand.

---

12 Douglas J. Tigert, "A Research Project in Creative Advertising Through Life Style Analysis," in Charles W. King and Douglas J. Tigert, eds., *Attitude Research Reaches New Heights,* American Marketing Association, Chicago, 1970, pp. 224-225.

Attitudes as bases for segmentation. It may be argued that different segments of a market for a product may be characterized by the differing attitudes which the members of the various segments hold toward general issues and toward the product and its use. For example, it is likely that the consumer who is favorably disposed toward the use of convenience food products will hold quite different attitudes toward the role of the homemaker, the best way of feeding the family, and the value of one's time, than would a consumer who prefers to prepare meals from "scratch."

One author has advocated the identification of meaningful market segments through the collection of consumers' "spheres of attitudes" toward product, product class, and related items and concepts.[13] Such an approach would likely prove valuable in revealing gaps in the market and for suggesting advertising copy strategies.

Benefit segmentation. It may also be possible for marketers to segment consumer markets on the basis of the benefits which consumers seek to derive from the use of a product. Consumer research might indicate, for example, that different purchasers of color television sets may be interested in quite different benefits in purchasing that product. One consumer may be interested simply in the family entertainment value of the product, another may be primarily interested in the quality of sound and picture produced, while a third may be more interested in the ability of the product to contribute to the tasteful decor of the home. Each of these consumers may lie in a different market segment for color television sets. Consequently, we see that Zenith stresses the handcrafted quality of manufacture of that brand, while RCA indicates in its advertising that the quality of its picture is such that its brand is preferred by television directors as the set which they purchase for their homes, and Electrohome emphasizes the styling and eye-appeal of their Deilcraft cabinetry.

Research in the market for toothpastes has indicated that consumers of this product may be divided into four distinct segments.[14] These segments have been labelled the "sensory segment," the "sociables," the "worriers," and the "independent segment." Figure 3-1 indicates that each of these segments is interested in different product benefits and exhibits quite different brand preferences in the purchase of toothpaste. The "sensory segment" is primarily interested in the flavor and appearance of the product and tends to prefer brands like Colgate and Stripe. The "sociables," on the other hand, are concerned with their appearance and are interested in whiteness of teeth. They purchase brands like Macleans and Ultra Brite. The "worriers" exhibit a high level of health consciousness and wish to prevent tooth decay and are heavy users of Crest. Finally, the "independents" are more price-conscious and are likely not loyal to any of the major brands, preferring to purchase private label toothpastes and brands which are on sale.

Knowledge of the characteristics of each of these brand segments in terms of the factors listed in the first column of Figure 3-1 provides for the marketer of toothpaste considerable information which may then be used in the development of marketing programs. For example, new brands may be developed with particular

---

13 Harry E. Heller, "Defining Target Markets by their Attitude Profiles," in Lee Adler and Irving Crespi, eds., *Attitude Research on the Rocks,* American Marketing Association, Chicago, 1968, pp. 45-57.

14 Russell I. Haley, "Benefit Segmentation: A Decision-Oriented Research Tool," *Journal of Marketing,* July 1968, pp. 30-35.

Figure 3-1. Toothpaste Market Segment Description

Segment Name:	The Sensory Segment	The Sociables	The Worriers	The Independent Segment
Principal benefit sought:	Flavor, product appearance	Brightness of teeth	Decay prevention	Price
Demographic strengths:	Children	Teens, young people	Large families	Men
Special behavioral characteristics:	Users of spearmint flavored toothpaste	Smokers	Heavy users	Heavy users
Brands disproportionately favored:	Colgate, Stripe	Macleans, Plus White, Ultra Brite	Crest	Brands on sale
Personality characteristics:	High self-involvement	High sociability	High hypochondriasis	High autonomy
Life-style characteristics:	Hedonistic	Active	Conservative	Value-oriented

Source: Russell I. Haley, "Benefit Segmentation: A Decision-Oriented Research Tool," *Journal of Marketing*, July, 1968, p. 33.

flavor characteristics to appeal to a certain segment. Also, advertising programs may be prepared to appeal to particular segments. For example, the advertising for Crest toothpaste stresses decay prevention. This approach, with the endorsement of the Canadian Dental Association, holds obvious appeal for the "worrier" segment of the market. Similarly, other brands have stressed their ability to contribute to whiteness of teeth. An illustration of this latter approach to the "sociables" segment of the market has been extremely successful "sex appeal" campaign on behalf of Ultra Brite.

The application of benefit segmentation in marketing is not as simple as might first appear. The approach requires the gathering of considerable information, possibly through focussed group interviews, on those product benefits which are considered relevant to the consumer purchase decision. Once relevant benefits have been identified, the marketer must then determine the relative importance of each to consumers. Finally, the extent to which existing brands satisfy the benefits sought by consumers must be explored. Where market gaps are found to exist, it may be possible for a marketer to introduce a new brand which promises the consumer certain benefits which are not now being provided by existing brands.

Life-style segmentation. Possibly the most important recent development in market segmentation has taken place in the area of life-style analysis.[15] The benefits of this approach to segmentation may be stated as follows:[16] "So while demographics are descriptive information about who product buyers are, and behavioral product consumption data relate what they buy, psychographics expand our awareness to provide causal understanding of why they buy."

The purchase of a product should not be regarded as an isolated act, but as "part of a behavior pattern, a pattern that suggests an organized set of tastes and val-

15 See William D. Wells, *Life Style and Psychographics*, American Marketing Association, Chicago, 1974; Fred D. Reynolds, *Psychographics: A Conceptual Orientation*, research monograph number 6, College of Business Administration, University of Georgia, 1973; and William D. Wells, "Psychographics: A Critical Review," *Journal of Marketing Research*, May, 1975, pp. 196-213.

16 Alan Nelson, "Psyching Psychographics," in Charles W. King and Douglas J. Tigert, eds., *Attitude Research Reaches New Heights*, American Marketing Association, Chicago, 1970, p. 181.

ues."[17] The life-style approach to market segmentation is based on the premise that different groups of consumers exhibit quite different life styles, and that particular products and brands are more appropriate for some life styles than for others.

The marketer who employs this approach to segmentation will generally obtain considerable information from groups of consumers concerning their activities, interests and opinions, and concerning their use of the media and of certain products and brands. Such information is then used to develop detailed life-style profiles of the various segments of the market. Once the life-style profiles of the segments have been revealed, they may then be used by the marketer to pinpoint target market segments, to select media and to prepare advertising copy.

The applications of life-style segmentation have been many. One study developed a life-style profile of the regular user of bank charge cards such as Chargex and Mastercharge.[18] These persons were found to lead an active, urbane, and upper socioeconomic style of life congruent with higher income, position, and education. They tended to agree with such statements as: "we often serve wine at dinner"; "I do more things socially than most of my friends"; and "I like to think that I am a bit of a swinger." They expressed general disagreement with statements like: "I stay home most evenings"; and "my days seem to follow a definite routine." The male charge card user is aware of his appearance and spends more on fashionable clothing. He tends to subscribe to less conservative, less traditional values and is more willing to take risks. He tends also to belong to several organizations and is an active reader, particularly of business magazines.

Another interesting application of life-style segmentation lies in the provision of profiles of consumers who subscribe to certain magazines or who watch particular television programs. Such information on their audiences permits publishers and broadcasters to provide potential advertisers with detailed information on the types of consumers who will be reached if they advertise in these magazines or sponsor these programs.[19]

Summary. When using the above bases for segmenting markets, it is helpful to keep in mind two points. First, buying behavior is rarely traceable to only one segmentation factor. Useful segmentation is typically developed by including variables from several of the bases discussed above. Even looking at demographic variables, rarely is a useful market segment identified by a single market factor. To illustrate, rarely does the market for a product consist only of women, or of all of the people over sixty-five, or of all of the residents of the Atlantic Provinces. Instead, the segment is more likely to be narrowed down by combining several of these variables. A viable market segment might be women, who live in the Atlantic Provinces, who are married with young children, who are above a certain income level, and who exhibit a "young sophisticate" life style.

---

17 William D. Wells and Douglas J. Tigert, "Activities, Interests and Opinions," *Journal of Advertising Research,* August, 1971, pp. 27-35.

18 Joseph T. Plummer, "Life Style Patterns and Commercial Bank Credit Card Usage," *Journal of Marketing,* April, 1971, pp. 35-41.

19 Elayn Bernay, "Life Style Analysis as a Basis for Media Selection," in Charles W. King and Douglas J. Tigert, eds., *Attitude Research Reaches New Heights,* American Marketing Association, Chicago, 1970, pp. 189-195; and Douglas J. Tigert, "Are Television Audiences Really Different?" in Fred C. Allvine, ed., *Combined Proceedings,* 1971 Spring and Fall Conferences, American Marketing Association, Chicago, 1971, pp. 239-246.

The other point to remember concerns the interrelationships which exist among the various market segmentation factors. For example, age and stage of family life cycle are typically related. Income is generally tied to some degree to age, life cycle stage, education, and occupation. Similarly, the product benefits sought and the life style which one exhibits may be closely related to certain personality patterns or even some demographic characteristics of the individual.

QUESTIONS AND PROBLEMS

1. What is the definition of a market?
2. Distinguish between market aggregation and market segmentation.
3. What are some benefits a company can expect from segmenting its market?
4. What distinguishes an ultimate consumer from an industrial user?
5. Why has geographic segmentation been so popular in the past?
6. Personality variables have not proven to be generally successful in segmenting markets because personality is irrelevant in buyer decision making. Discuss.
7. What are the benefits of using product usage rate as a basis for segmentation?
8. What is benefit segmentation?
9. How does life-style segmentation "expand our awareness to provide causal understanding of why [people] buy"?

MARKETS: DEMOGRAPHIC SEGMENTATION VARIABLES

Having introduced the concepts of markets and the various bases available for market segmentation, we can now consider some of the detail that would allow us to begin to define markets and segments. In this chapter we examine such factors as regional population distribution, urban-suburban-rural mixes, age, sex, family life cycle and other demographic characteristics. We will also examine patterns of income distribution. Our purpose is to become more familiar with the details which aid in segmenting markets and programming for them.

As was pointed out in the previous chapter, it is unlikely that income or age or sex or being located in a suburb is, by itself, sufficient to identify a market segment. Rarely does a market consist of all women or all people living in British Columbia or all people over sixty-five. The segment is likely to be narrowed down by combining several variables. Thus a market segment might be women, living in British Columbia, married, with young children and above a certain income level.

POPULATION—ITS DISTRIBUTION AND COMPOSITION

Defining a market starts with people—potential and actual consumers. Every marketing person should study the geographic distribution and demographic composition of the population. In the following sections we shall consider only those population factors which affect the consumer market. The industrial market is discussed in Chapter 8. In analyzing population, a marketing executive should first find out which characteristics of the population—such as age, education, or family size—substantially affect the composition of the market for his product. Then he should get the current quantitative measurement of each of these characteristics. Finally, he should determine the trends in these data and understand the significance of these trends in terms of his marketing program.

TOTAL POPULATION

A logical place to begin an analysis of population is with an examination of the total population of Canada. Here, the existence of large absolute increases becomes apparent. The total population of the country rose from 7 million in 1911 to just over 10 million in 1931, but by 1976 had more than doubled to 23.0 million. Projections indicate, based on certain assumptions regarding fertility rates and levels of immigration, that the total population of Canada will number between 25 million and 28 million by 1986, and as many as 34 million by the end of this century.[1] These large increases in total population have important implications for marketing. Total consumer expenditures for food, clothing, recreational and sporting goods, services, houses and home furnishings, automobiles, snowmobiles, appliances, and all of the other products and services demanded by the population will increase by several billion dollars. The size and heterogeneity of the Canadian market make it necessary to analyse it in segments.

REGIONAL DISTRIBUTION

Figure 4-1 presents the distribution of the Canadian population in 1976 by province and the projected growth in provincial populations to 1986. The largest consumer markets are centered in Ontario and Quebec, which combined account for more than 63 percent of the Canadian population. The three Prairie Provinces together currently contain approximately 16.5 percent of the population, while the Atlantic Provinces account for 9.5 percent, and British Columbia for more than 10 percent. The projected rates of increase to 1986 indicate that the greatest growth in population will be experienced in Ontario and British Columbia. This growth pattern reflects two factors: the continued migration of Canadians to urban areas and to the more industrialized provinces; and the tendency for recent immigrants to Canada to settle in these provinces. An interesting projection concerns a predicted continued absolute decline in the population of Saskatchewan, reflecting a continuation of the movement of residents of that province to other regions of Canada.

The regional distribution of population is important to marketers because regional differences exist in the demand for many products. These differences are traceable to climate, religion, social mores and customs, and other factors. Per-capita consumption of soft drinks and cosmetics varies substantially among the regions of the country. Western Canadians prefer more casual clothing; French-speaking Canadians buy more patent medicines than English-speaking Canadians. In proportion to population, beauty parlors and barber shops do more business in

---

1 Statistics Canada, *Population Projections for Canada and the Provinces: 1972-2001,* Cat. No. 91-514, Information Canada, Ottawa, 1974, pp. 61-62.

Figure 4-1

DISTRIBUTION OF POPULATION BY PROVINCE, 1976, WITH PROJECTIONS TO 1986.

Province or Territory	1976 Population	% of Canada	PROJECTED POPULATION, 1986.			
			PROJECTION A[1]		PROJECTION C[2]	
			Population	% of Canada	Population	% of Canada
Newfoundland	557,725	2.4	660,800	2.38	610,100	2.40
Prince Edward Island	118,229	0.5	127,900	0.46	119,300	0.47
Nova Scotia	828,571	3.6	889,900	3.20	816,700	3.22
New Brunswick	677,250	2.9	720,000	2.59	674,800	2.66
Quebec	6,234,445	27.1	6,839,100	24.59	6,398,700	25.21
Ontario	8,264,465	35.9	10,935,500	39.33	9,747,200	38.40
Manitoba	1,021,506	4.4	1,119,300	4.02	1,006,100	3.96
Saskatchewan	921,323	4.0	757,600	2.72	775,700	3.06
Alberta	1,838,037	8.0	2,284,000	8.21	2,060,200	8.12
British Columbia	2,466,608	10.7	3,379,100	12.15	3,091,900	12.18
Yukon	21,836	0.1	31,200	0.11	26,600	0.10
NWT	42,609	0.2	66,500	0.24	55,800	0.22
Canada	22,992,604	100.0	27,810,900	100.00	25,382,900	100.00

Notes: [1] Projection A assumes a relatively high fertility rate and net immigration to Canada of 100,000 persons per year.
[2] Projection C assumes a relatively low fertility rate and net immigration to Canada of 60,000 persons per year.
Source: Statistics Canada, *Population Projections for Canada and the Provinces, 1972-2001*, Cat. No. 91-514, Information Canada, Ottawa, June, 1974, pp. 62-63, and *Statistics Canada Daily*, Cat. No. 11.001E, May 18, 1977.

Quebec than in any other province. Capital expenditures in the Atlantic Provinces are much lower than elsewhere in Canada. Fuel bills of British Columbians are lower than those of other Canadians, leaving them with more money to spend on other products.

Furthermore, one finds that the regions are systematically related to each other, as well as to regions in other countries in terms of adopting new products, fashions and ideas. British Columbians are very West-Coast-United-States-oriented whereas Ontarians look to New York, Detroit, and Chicago for some things, and to parts of Europe for others. Montreal, as a focus for Quebec, relies more on New York and Paris, than on, say, Toronto. Other Canadian regions tend to follow the Ontario lead in many cases, complemented by the adjacent American region. Regionalism means different styles of homes in different parts of the country, different fashions in furniture, different patterns of leisure activity, even different ways of caring for a lawn, using different equipment and supplies.

Shifts and trends in the regional distribution of population may also influence policies regarding channels of distribution. As regional markets for a company's products grow, the firm may establish sales branches or expand its own sales force to cover markets which had previously been assigned to wholesalers or manufacturers' agents.

URBAN, RURAL, SUBURBAN AND INTERURBAN DISTRIBUTION

For many years there has been a growing urbanization of the Canadian market. The population has been gradually moving from farms and very small towns into larger population centers. This has been marked by a rapid decline in the farm population in this country. In 1941 about one half of the Canadian population lived on farms; by 1951 this percentage had dropped to about 20 percent; and by 1971, only 6.6 percent of the total population lived on farms. This declining farm population is very much reflected in the declining population of Saskatchewan mentioned above. Indeed, the entire rural population of Canada has been dropping. In 1966, 27.6 percent of the population was considered rural; this percentage had dropped to 23.9 percent at the time of the 1971 census.

The declining rural population has led some marketers to underrate the rural market. Both as an industrial market for farm equipment and supplies and as a consumer market with increased buying power and a more urbanlike sophistication, the rural market is still very important. Sociological patterns (family size and customs) among rural people differ significantly from those of city dwellers, and these patterns have considerable influence on buying behavior. Per capita consumption of cosmetics and beauty aids, for example, is much lower in rural markets than in urban markets.

Evidence of the growing urbanization of the Canadian market is found in population data on the country's Census Metropolitan Areas. A Census Metropolitan Area (CMA) is defined by Statistics Canada as the main labor market of a continuous built-up area having a population of 100,000 or more. Figure 4-2 indicates the growth in the population of the twenty-three CMAs in Canada from 1971 to 1976. By 1976, these twenty-three population centres accounted for more than 55 percent of the total population of Canada. Obviously these areas present attractive, geographically concentrated market targets with considerable sales potential.

While it is true that the farm population has been declining and the metropolitan areas growing, something else is also going on *within* the metropolitan areas. The central cities are growing very slowly, and in some cases the older, established parts of the cities are actually losing population. The real growth is occurring in the fringe areas of the central cities or in the suburbs outside these cities. For the past thirty years, one of the most significant social and economic trends in Canada has been the shift of population to the suburbs. As middle-income families have moved to the suburbs, the economic and ethnic composition of many central cities (especially the core areas) has changed considerably, thus changing the nature of the markets in these areas.

The growth of the suburban population has some striking marketing implications. Since a great percentage of suburban people live in single-family residences, there is a vastly expanded market for lawn mowers, lawn furniture, home furnishings, and home repair supplies and equipment. The suburbanite is more likely to want two cars than is the city dweller. He is inclined to spend more of his leisure time at home, so there is a bigger market for items used for home entertainment and recreation.

Figure 4-2

POPULATION FOR CENSUS METROPOLITAN AREAS, SHOWING
PERCENTAGE CHANGE, 1971 and 1976

	1971(1)	1976	Percentage Change
Calgary, Alta.	403,343	469,917	16.5
Chicoutimi-Jonquière, Qué.	126,401	128,643	1.6
Edmonton, Alta.	496,000	554,228	11.7
Halifax, N.S.	250,581	267,991	6.9
Hamilton, Ont.	503,122	529,371	5.2
Kitchener, Ont.	238,574	272,158	14.1
London, Ont.	252,981	270,383	6.9
Montréal, Qué.	2,729,211	2,802,485	2.7
Oshawa(2), Ont.	120,318	135,196	12.4
Ottawa-Hull, Ont., Qué.	619,861	693,288	11.8
Ontario (part)	474,168	521,341	9.9
Québec (part)	145,693	171,947	18.0
Québec, Qué.	501,365	542,158	8.1
Regina, Sask.	140,734	151,191	7.4
St. Catharines-Niagara, Ont.	285,802	301,921	5.6
St. John's, Nfld.	131,814	143,390	8.8
Saint John, N.B.	106,744	112,974	5.8
Saskatoon, Sask.	126,449	133,750	5.8
Sudbury, Ont.	157,721	157,030	−0.4
Thunder Bay, Ont.	114,708	119,253	4.0
Toronto, Ont.	2,602,098	2,803,101	7.7
Vancouver, B.C.	1,082,352	1,166,348	7.8
Victoria, B.C.	195,800	218,250	11.5
Windsor, Ont.	248,718	247,582	-0.5
Winnipeg, Man.	549,808	578,217	5.2

(1) Based on 1976 Area.
(2) Not a Census Metropolitan Area in 1971.
Source: Statistics Canada Daily, Cat. No. 11-001E, May 18, 1977.

Marketers are now, however, watching a possible modest countertrend, that is a movement back to the central cities on the part of certain consumers. A number of large Canadian cities have undertaken the refurbishing of downtown neighborhoods. This, with the erection of downtown apartment complexes, has led to large numbers of residents moving back to the central core of the city. Many older people, whose families are grown, and mid- to upper-income young people find living in the downtown areas of the larger cities quite attractive since they do not have to contend with the problems of commuting from suburbia, and they have easy access to mass urban transit, theatres, and retail shopping facilities.

In several places in Canada the metropolitan areas have expanded to the point where there is virtually no rural space between them. This joining of metropolitan areas has been called "interurbia." Where two or more city markets once existed, there is today a single large urban market. For example, there is little rural space today along the northern shore of Lake Ontario from Kingston to Hamilton. We will soon see, through the growth of regional governments, one single continuous belt of urban population stretching from Montreal, along the St. Lawrence and Lake Ontario, to Niagara Falls.

AGE GROUPS

The size of various age groups has a substantial effect on the market for certain products. It is interesting, for example, to note the effect of declining fertility rates on the numbers of persons in the population aged 14 years and less. It is also interesting to watch the movement of the persons born during the late 1940s and the 1950s through the various age groupings. As Figure 4-3 indicates, the percentage of the Canadian population in the 0 to 14 age group is expected to grow very slowly or even to decline over the next ten years. At the same time, significant increases are expected in the percentage of the population in the 15 to 44 and over 65 age groups. These latter phenomena are a direct result of the large number of births during the post-war period and a gradual increase in the life expectancy of Canadians. The implications of such population trends are obvious. It is in the young adult age group, for example, that much growth is projected and it is during this period of the life cycle that people begin careers, start families, and spend money in a big way.

The youth market (roughly grade school ages five to thirteen) carries a three-way marketing impact. First, these children can influence parental purchases; second, billions of dollars are spent on this group by their parents; and third, these children themselves make purchases of goods and services for their own personal use and satisfaction.[2] Promotional programs are often geared to this segment of the market. Children's television shows, for example, have traditionally been sponsored by cereal manufacturers and other advertisers in an effort to develop brand awareness and preference at an early age. Recent developments in Canada, leading to the removal of all commercial advertising from television programming directed to children will have profound effects on the ability of such companies to reach this segment of the market and will likely lead to the development of new marketing techniques aimed at the youth market.

---

2 See James U. McNeal, "The Child Consumer: A New Market," *Journal of Retailing*, Summer, 1969, pp. 15-22ff; William D. Wells, "Children as Consumers," in Joseph W. Newman, ed., *On Knowing the Consumer*, John Wiley & Sons, Inc., New York, 1966, pp. 138-145; and Lewis A. Berry and Richard W. Pollay, "The Influencing Role of the Child in Family Decision Making," *Journal of Marketing Research*, February, 1968, pp. 70-72.

Figure 4-3

POPULATION PROJECTIONS, 1971-1986, BY AGE GROUPS (IN MILLIONS)

| AGE GROUP | POPULATION 1971 | PROJECTIONS TO 1986 | | | |
| | | PROJECTION A[1] | | PROJECTION C[2] | |
		Population	% Increase	Population	% Increase
0-14 years	6.4	6.9	7.8	5.6	-12.5
15-44 years	9.4	12.9	37.2	12.5	33.0
45-64 years	4.0	4.8	20.0	4.7	17.5
over 65 years	1.7	2.6	52.9	2.5	47.1
Total Population	21.6	27.8	28.7	25.4	17.6

Notes: [1] Projection A assumes a relatively high fertility rate and net immigration to Canada of 100,000 persons per year.
[2] Projection C assumes a relatively low fertility rate and net immigration to Canada of 60,000 persons per year.
Source: Statistics Canada, *Population Projections for Canada and The Provinces, 1972-2001*, Cat. No. 91-514, Information Canada, Ottawa, June 1974, p. 71, and Statistics Canada, *Age Groups*, Cat. No. 92-715, Information Canada, Ottawa, 1973, p. 1.

The teen-age market is recognized as an important one, and yet it has proved to be difficult to reach in some cases. While some companies (Levis, Thrifty's, Clairol, and 7-Up, for example) have had notable successes, other well-known firms have been considerably less successful in their attempts to reach the older end of the youth market. Possibly the mistake is to lump all teen-agers into one group, thus ignoring the many subgroups segmented by income, cultural background, political leanings, geographic location, etc. Certainly, the 13 to 16 age group is different from the 17 to 20 bracket.[3]

Yet, a manufacturer must understand the teen-age bracket, not only because of the size of this market, but also because its members have an increasing amount of money to spend. They are good customers for records, automobiles, cosmetics, clothes, jewelry, and other products. In order to tap this market, many manufacturers are adopting new product and distribution policies. For instance, some clothing manufacturers are now designing junior ready-to-wear dresses which reflect the age and not merely the size of the teen-age girl. Many department stores have conventional ready-to-wear departments labeled "college," "junior," or "miss," which handle similar styles but different sizes. Furthermore, items such as skirts, sweaters, and blouses are sold in separate departments. Some manufacturers feel this is "splintering" the market and consequently urge retailers to develop one "young adult" department which will carry all sizes and items necessary for the complete wardrobe of girls from 15 to 24 years old.

At the other end of the age spectrum are two market segments which should not be overlooked. One is the group of people in their 50's and early 60's. This mature market is large and financially well-off. They are at the peak of their earning power and typically no longer have financial responsibilities for their children. Thus this market segment is a good target for marketers of high-priced, high-quality products and services.

The other older age group are people over 65—a segment which is increasing both absolutely and as a percentage of the total population. Manufacturers and middlemen alike are beginning to recognize that people in this age group are logical prospects for small, low-cost housing units (trailers, as well as more conventional types of housing), cruises and foreign tours, health products, and cosmetics developed especially for older people. Many firms are also developing promotional programs to appeal to the buying motives of this group and to cater to their buying habits.[4]

The life-styles of the 1970s have had an interesting influence on the traditional segmentation by age groups. Marketers are finding that the youth market is not what it used to be. The youth market is no longer confined to the young in age, but should be redefined as the young in heart. The success of the Ford Mustang, with its marketing program aimed at persons who wished to appear young; the Pepsi campaign directed to "those who think young"; and the adoption of youth-oriented clothing styles by all age groups, are indications of the fact that the youth market can no longer be limited to those consumers in their teens and early twenties. The youth market needs to be treated as a state of mind, because it overflows all age boundaries. In a promotional program, for example, *youth-directed* advertis-

---

3 See Paul Gilkison, "Teen-Agers' Perceptions of Buying Frames of Reference: A Decade in Retrospect," *Journal of Retailing*, Summer, 1973, pp. 25-37. Repeating a study he had made 10 years earlier (*Journal of Retailing*, Fall, 1965, p. 33), the author discovered significant changes over a 10-year period in the buying frames of reference used by teen-agers.

4 *Business Week*, "The Power of the Aging in the Marketplace," November 20, 1971, p. 52.

ing (advertising targeted at the under-25 market) will be different from *youth-oriented* advertising which will be aimed at the entire 14 to 65 market.

SEX

Sex is probably an obvious basis for consumer market segmentation. In many product categories—automobiles, for example—women typically look for different product benefits than do men. Market segmentation by sex is also useful because many products have traditionally been purchased by one sex or another. However, some of these traditional buying patterns are breaking down, and marketers certainly should be alert to changes involving their products. Not too many years ago, for example, the wife did practically all the grocery shopping for her family, and the husband bought the products and services needed for the automobile. Today men are frequent food shoppers and women buy the gas. Marketing people also must be aware of product categories where women typically buy the products, but the goods are used by others in the family.

Although the ratio of males to females in any population is always close to 1:1, there are some interesting trends developing in the Canadian population, although the implications of such trends are not necessarily important for marketers. In Canada, in 1921, there were 106 males for every 100 females in the population. This number has declined to the point where, in the 1971 Census, the numbers of males and females in the population were almost exactly equal. Statistics Canada projections of Canadian population suggest, however, that by 1986 the number of females in the population could *exceed* the number of males by 175,000: a sex ratio of 98.7 males for every 100 females. This trend is possibly due to the cumulative effects of higher life expectancy among females than among males, and a more balanced sex distribution among immigrants to Canada in recent years.[5]

The changing role of women in the 1970s also has tremendous marketing implications. The increasing number of working women (married or single) has greatly expanded the markets for frozen foods, household appliances, and other laborsaving products and services. Products and activities considered limited to the male market not many years ago are today readily accepted by the women. Successful attempts to remove barriers of discrimination against women have generated many market opportunities. Interestingly enough, however, it has *not* been nearly so easy to get males to accept products traditionally considered feminine.[6] There are indications, however, supported by the success of such products as hair sprays, colognes, and hand-held hair dryers, that the female stereotyping of certain products is breaking down and that such products are gradually being accepted by the male market.

FAMILY LIFE CYCLE

The demographic factors of sex or age alone often do not adequately explain consumer buying behavior. Even when age and sex are combined into market segments such as young adult women or middle-aged men, we will find different buying behavior within the same segment. Frequently the factor accounting for the

---

5 Statistics Canada, *Population Projections for Canada and the Provinces: 1972-2001*, p. 77.

6 See John R. Stuteville, "Sexually Polarized Products and Advertising Strategy," *Journal of Retailing*, Summer, 1971, pp. 3-13.

difference in consumption patterns between two people is that each—while of the same age and sex—is in a different life cycle situation. The concept of a family life cycle refers to the important stages in the life of an ordinary family. A six-way classification of these stages is as follows:

1. Bachelor stage: young, single people
2. Young married couples with no children
3. Full next I: young married couples with children
4. Full next II: older married couples still with dependent children
5. Empty nest: older married couples with no children living with them
6. Older single people, still working or retired

Segmenting a market by life cycle stage recognizes the fact that life cycle position is a major determinant of buying behavior. A young couple with two children (the full-nest stage) has quite different product and service needs than does a couple in their mid-fifties with children no longer living at home (the empty-nest stage). Typical buying patterns found in each of the various stages are discussed in more detail in Chapter 6 in connection with family buying behavior.

A segmentation factor related to the life cycle is the *rate* of household and family formation. A *household* is defined by Statistics Canada as a person or group of persons occupying one dwelling. It usually consists of a family group, with or without lodgers, employees, etc. A *family* is defined as a husband and wife (with or without children who have never been married, regardless of age) or a parent with one or more children never married, living in the same dwelling. Every new household or family is potentially a market for a dwelling place, furniture, appliances, and other home furnishings. For manufacturers of appliances and furniture, the number of families is often more important than the size of the family. A manufacturer of refrigerators, for example, may hope to sell three refrigerators to three couples, whereas he would probably sell only one to a family with six members.

This latter point does not negate the fact that family size has important marketing implications. After steadily declining through the 1930s and 1940s, Canada's birth rate rose through the late 1940s and the 1950s to the point where, in 1959, an average Canadian woman would be expected to give birth to 3.9 children during her lifetime. The development of oral contraceptive and changing cultural influences have led to a rapid decline in the birth rate during the 1960s and early 1970s. By 1971, the number of births expected from the average Canadian woman during her lifetime had dropped to 2.19.[7] Even though there appears to be a definite trend toward smaller families, the number of family formations in Canada will continue to be large. The effect of the "post-war baby boom" of the late 1940s and the 1950s will be felt during the 1970s in the formation of new families, thereby adding pressure to the Canadian housing market and continuing demand for consumer durables.

An interesting trend from the marketing point of view lies in the difference between the rate of family formation and the rate of household formation in Canada through the 1960s. In the period from 1961 to 1971, the number of households in Canada increased by more than 33 percent, while the number of families increased by only 22 percent.[8] This difference reflects a growth in the number of persons liv-

---

7 Statistics Canada, *Population Projections for Canada and the Provinces: 1972-2001*, p. 35

8 Statistics Canada, *Summary Household and Family Characteristics*, Cat. No. 93-743, Information Canada, Ottawa, 1972, p. 2.

ing alone and in the number of unrelated persons living in the same dwelling. These two market segments—reflecting the changing lifestyles of the period—have been termed *singles* and *mingles*.[9]

Compared with the population as a whole, the singles segment is (1) more affluent, (2) more mobile, (3) oriented to immediate pleasures rather than long-term concerns, (4) fashion and appearance conscious, and (5) active in leisure pursuits.

The impact which singles of both sexes have on the market is demonstrated by such things as apartments for singles, social clubs for singles, special tours and cruises, and eating places seeking the patronage of singles. Truly, it is an interesting marketing challenge to isolate, reach, and then persuade the singles and mingles market segments.

OTHER POPULATION FACTORS AFFECTING SEGMENTATION

The market for some consumer products is influenced by such factors as education, occupation, race, national origin, and religion. With an increasing number of people attaining higher levels of education, for example, we can expect to see changes in product preferences and buyers with more discriminating taste and higher incomes. With an increasing number of married women working, we have already seen a great expansion of the market for frozen foods, home appliances, and other laborsaving products and services.

Geographically mobile consumers are a growing and perhaps unique market segment which is just beginning to receive attention. In view of the fact that some 7 percent of the Canadian people move each year, it is surprising that studies of the socioeconomic characteristics, life-styles, and buying behavior of this group have been relatively neglected until recently. Yet this segment of consumers presents a rather attractive market in that many of them have high incomes. Moreover, their moves force them to develop new shopping habits, seek new sources of products and services, and possibly develop new brand preferences.[10]

For some products it is quite useful to analyze the population on the basis of race, religion, or national origin. People of Italian descent in Southwestern Ontario have some product preferences that are quite different, say, from those consumers of Oriental descent living on the West Coast. There is a vast market for products (mainly food products) which can be associated with particular ethnic groups. Many of these groups tend to be geographically concentrated.

FRENCH CANADA: AN IMPORTANT MARKET SEGMENT

A rather obvious division of the Canadian consumer market is into English-Canadian and French-Canadian population segments. It is not so obvious, however,

---

9 See "Singles and Mingles—A Meaningful Marketing Explosion," *Grey Matter*, January, 1974.

10 See James E. Bell, Jr., *Selection of New Suppliers by the Mobile Family*, Michigan State University, Bureau of Business and Economic Research, East Lansing, 1969; John R. Thompson, "Perceived Risks and Learning Systems of Geographic Mobiles," *Southern Journal of Business*, July 1968, pp. 74-78; and Alan R. Andreasen, "Geographic Mobility and Market Segmentation," *Journal of Marketing Research*, November, 1966, pp. 341-349.

that Canadian companies have done an effective job in the past of marketing to the French-Canadian consumer. In many cases, marketing programs applied in French Canada have consisted of little more than literal translations of advertisements used in the English-Canadian media. The changing nature of the French-Canadian market now demands that marketers take more seriously the approaches they use in marketing their products to this important segment of the Canadian market. Let us now examine some of the demographic characteristics of the French-Canadian market.

HOW SHOULD THE FRENCH-CANADIAN MARKET BE DEFINED?

Possibly the best definition put forth of a French-Canadian consumer is one "whose mother tongue is French or whose language of adoption is likely to be French in the case of those having a mother tongue other than French or English."[11] Such a definition does not restrict the French-Canadian market to the geographic boundaries of the Province of Quebec. One study recommends that seven counties of New Brunswick and nine counties of Ontario should also be included in a definition of the French-Canadian market. These counties are included for the following reasons:

1. in all of them the percentage of the total population whose mother tongue is French exceeds 25%;
2. French-Canadian institutions are well organized and active in these areas;
3. the rate of assimilation of the French-Canadian group into English-Canadian society is far slower in these areas than in other parts of Canada outside Quebec;
4. these areas receive a considerable amount of overflow advertising from Quebec and, in some cases, are served by Quebec-based distributors;
5. some manufacturers already add these areas to the Province of Quebec in organizing their marketing effort.[12]

The absolute size of the French-Canadian market segment cannot be ignored. Figure 4-4 indicates that 25.7 percent of the population of Canada is French speaking and that these consumers are overwhelmingly concentrated in the Province of Quebec. More than 80 percent of the population of Quebec is French speaking and, if one eliminates the City of Montreal, virtually all of the remaining residents of the province speak French at home. Again, however, one cannot ignore the fact that large numbers of French-speaking consumers live in Ontario and New Brunswick, primarily in those contiguous counties mentioned above. Therefore, in Quebec and the 16 counties of Ontario and New Brunswick, there reside approximately 5½ million French-speaking consumers. Eighty-eight percent of all French-speaking Canadians are resident in Quebec. These data indicate the magnitude of the French-Canadian market. In many ways this market is unique, as French Canadians exhibit important differences in consumption behavior from English Canadians. Marketers must appreciate these differences and attempt to understand the factors which contribute to them if they are to market successfully in French Canada. We will return to a discussion of this market later in Chapter 6.

---

11 Pierre C. Lefrançois and Gilles Chatel, "The French-Canadian Consumer: Fact and Fancy," in W. H. Mahatoo, ed., *Marketing Research in Canada*, Thomas Nelson and Sons, Toronto, 1968, p. 80.
12 Pierre C. Lefrançois and Gilles Chatel, "The French-Canadian Consumer: Fact and Fancy," p. 81.

Figure 4-4

POPULATION OF CANADA AND SELECTED PROVINCES BY LANGUAGE MOST OFTEN SPOKEN AT HOME, 1971.

LANGUAGE MOST OFTEN SPOKEN AT HOME	CANADA		QUEBEC		NEW BRUNSWICK		ONTARIO	
	NUMBER	%	NUMBER	%	NUMBER	%	NUMBER	%
English	14,446,235	67.0	887,875	14.7	430,720	67.9	6,558,060	85.1
French	5,546,025	25.7	4,870,105	80.8	199,080	31.4	352,465	4.6
Total Population	21,568,310	100.0	6,027,765	100.0	634,560	100.0	7,703,105	100.0

Source: Statistics Canada, *Official Language and Language Most often Spoken at Home*, Cat. No. 92-726, Information Canada, Ottawa, 1973, p. 20-1.

Figure 4-5. Personal income and personal disposable income: 1950-1976 (in millions of dollars).

	1950	1960	1970	1976	% Increase 1950 to 1976	1960 to 1976
Total Personal Income	14,262	29,595	66,633	151,636	1,063%	512%
Total Personal Disposable Income	13,285	26,567	54,009	121,978	918%	459%

Source: Statistics Canada, *Systems of National Accounts—National Income and Expenditure Accounts*, Cat. No. 13-201, Annual; 13-533; 13-001.

CONSUMER INCOME AND ITS DISTRIBUTION

People alone do not make a market; they must have money to spend. Consequently, a detailed study of income, its distribution, and how it is spent is essential in any quantitative market analysis which an individual firm may make.

NATURE AND SCOPE OF INCOME

What is income? There are so many different concepts of income that it is well to review some definitions. The following outline is actually a mathematical equation:

National income: The total income from all sources including employee compensation, corporate profits, and other income

> **Less** corporate profits and social security contributions **Plus** dividends, government transfer payments to persons, and net interest paid by government, *equals*

Personal income: The income from wages, salaries, dividends, rent, interest, business and professions, social security, and farming.

> **Less** all personal federal, provincial, and local taxes and nontax payments, *equals*

Disposable personal income: The amount available for personal consumption, expenditures, and savings

> **Less** (1) essential expenditures for food, clothing, household utilities, and local transportation and (2) fixed expenditures for rent, house mortgage payments, insurance, and installment debt payments, *equals*

Discretionary purchasing power: The amount of disposable personal income over and above fixed commitments (debt repayments, homeowner taxes, tenant rent) and above that required for essential household needs. Consequently, as compared with personal income data, discretionary purchasing power is a better or more sensitive indicator of the consumer's ability to spend for nonessentials.

In addition, we shall hear the terms "money income," "real income," and "psychic income." *Money income* is the amount a person receives in actual cash or cheques for wages, salaries, rents, interest, and dividends. *Real income* is what the money income will buy in goods and services; it is purchasing power. If a person's money income rises 5 percent in one year but the cost of what he buys increases 8 percent on the average, then his real income decreases about 3 percent. *Psychic income* is an intangible but highly important income factor imputed to climate, a satisfying neighbourhood, enjoyment of one's job, etc. Some people prefer to take less real income in order to live in a pleasant suburb or in a part of the country which features a fine climate and recreational opportunities.

In terms of income, the Canadian market has grown rapidly in recent years. Total personal disposable income has grown from 13.3 billion, in 1950, to 26.6 billion in 1960, to 122 billion in 1976, almost a tenfold increase in twenty-six years. In the period 1950-1976, total personal income in Canada rose from 14.3 billion to 151.6 billion, (See Figure 4-5). The reason that personal disposable income has

Figure 4.6. Per capita personal income: 1961-1976 (in current dollars)

Year	Per Capita Personal Income	Year	Per Capita Personal Income	Year	Per Capita Personal Income
1961	$ 1,651	1966	2,303	1971	3,435
1962	1,764	1967	2,482	1972	3,839
1963	1,840	1968	2,690	1973	4,405
1964	1,933	1969	2,943	1974	5,116
1965	2,091	1970	3,129	1975	5,838
				1976	6,718

Source: Statistics Canada, *System of National Accounts—National Income and Expenditure Accounts,* Cat. No. 13-201, Annual. (Figure for 1976 is unpublished estimate from Statistics Canada sources.)

risen more slowly than has personal income is simply that the various governments are now taking a larger portion of personal income in the form of taxes.

Even after allowing for the rise in price levels and the growth in total population, the increases in personal income are still very impressive. Figure 4-6 shows personal per capita income for the period 1961 to 1976. In terms of current dollars, during that period per capita personal income in Canada rose by more than 400 percent.

INCOME DISTRIBUTION

To get full value from an analysis of income, a marketing executive should carefully study the variations and trends in the distribution of income among regions and among population groups. Regional income data are particularly helpful in pinpointing the particular market to which a firm wishes to appeal. Income data on cities and even sections within cities may indicate the best locations for shopping centers and suburban branches of downtown stores.

The income revolution which has been going on in Canada in recent decades may be seen in the changing profile of family income distribution, as shown in Figure 4-7. In 1961, the income distribution was skewed very much to the low-income end of the scale, with approximately 66 percent of Canadian families earning less than $6,000 per year and fewer than eight percent with incomes exceeding $10,000 per year. By 1971, only about 26 percent of families had annual incomes of less than $6,000, while about 43 percent of families earned more than $10,000. Projections suggest that by 1981, only 11 percent of Canadian families will have annual incomes of less than $6,000 while 30 percent of families will have an annual income of greater than $20,000. It should be noted that the data presented in Figure 4-7 represent incomes expressed in current dollars, but even after adjusting for inflation, it is clear that the real income of Canadian families is increasing. A major market development has been a tremendous growth of the middle-income market and a shrinking of low-income groups. We shall still have low-income families. However far fewer will be below the poverty level, even though that level (by definition) is moving upward in recognition of the inflationary factor and a more abundant society.

MARKETING SIGNIFICANCE OF INCOME DATA

The declining percentage of families in the poverty bracket, coupled with the sharp increases in the upper-income groups, presages an explosive growth in dis-

FIGURE 4-7
CHANGING SHAPE OF CANADIAN INCOME DISTRIBUTION

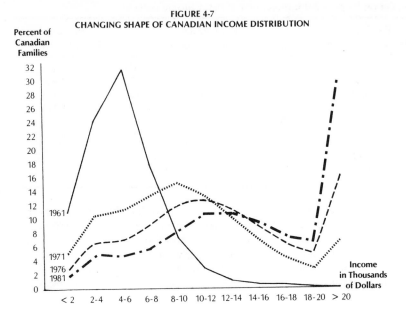

Source: John Kettle, "Footnotes on the Future: The Shapes of Poverty," *Executive*, November, 1973,
p. 54.

cretionary purchasing power. The level of discretionary income is of particular importance because as this type of income increases, so too does the demand for items which once were considered luxuries.

The middle-income market is a big market and a growing market, and it has forced many changes in marketing strategy. Manufacturers are seeking the widest possible distribution system which will appeal to the middle-income and not the low-income market. Many stores which once appealed to low-income groups are now "trading up" to the huge middle-income market by upgrading the quality of the products they carry and by offering additional services.

In spite of the considerable increase in disposable income and purchasing power in the past 25 years, many households are still in the low-income bracket or find their higher incomes inadequate to fulfill all their wants. Consequently, consumers give certain wants priority, and the sellers of many different products must compete for every consumer dollar. Furthermore, many customers are willing to forgo services in order to get lower prices. One consequence of this market feature has been the development of self-service retail outlets and discount houses.

The existence of a vast middle-income market should not blind a marketing person to the importance of the high-income market. Although the "luxury market" is small, its purchasing power is impressive. The highest income groups spend four times as much on food, five times as much on housing, and about eleven times as much on transportation and clothing as the lowest income groups. The high-income market is an excellent one for good jewelry, furs, better housing, automobiles, and boats.

EXPENDITURE PATTERNS

Statistics Canada periodically carries out detailed studies on the expenditure patterns of Canadian families. The latest data available covering the whole of Canada are from the study conducted in 1970 on family expenditure patterns in 1969. These data were collected from a total of over 15,000 Canadian families and are presented in Figures 4-8 to 4-10.

RELATION TO POPULATION DISTRIBUTION

In Figure 4-8, the expenditure patterns for families and unattached individuals are presented in actual dollars and in percentages for the five major geographic areas of Canada. In all regions the average percentage expenditure on shelter was approximately equal, ranging from 14.2 percent to 15.5 percent. On clothing, residents of Ontario and British Columbia spend, on average, a smaller percentage of family income. Expenditures on household operation and on transportation are relatively constant across the country in terms of the percentage of family income spent on these categories. A major exception to this consistent pattern is found in average expenditures on food. While families in the Atlantic Provinces spend fewer dollars on food each year than do residents of Ontario and Quebec, because of lower average family incomes in the Atlantic region, food accounts for a very large 22.4 percent of total family expenditures. This may be contrasted with 17.3 percent of family income spent on food in Ontario and 17.6 percent in British Columbia.

The key question at this point is: Why should a marketing person study the population in such detail if (at least at first glance) there is considerable homogeneity among the various segments? The reasons are several. In the first place, homogeneity is not complete. Even among the five regions examined in Figure 4-8, there are substantial differences in the food and clothing categories. Secondly, the simple percentages shown in Figure 4-8 can be misleading. A variance range of 1 or 2 percent may be quite substantial when the absolute percentage across regions for the expenditure category being examined is 5 or 6 percent. Based upon the absolute percentages, the variation becomes 20 or 40 percent. Thus for each product or service grouping, the variation is considerable if the variation in percentage terms between the regions with the highest and lowest figures is expressed as a percentage of the lowest region's figure. Thirdly, similarity exists only when we aggregate broad product categories. A detailed breakdown of each individual category shows large internal variations. Finally, differences exist among population segments with respect to buying motives and habits. Though families in Quebec and the Atlantic Provinces may spend approximately the same share of their annual income on clothing, the type of clothes they buy and the appeals to which they respond may be polar opposites. Hence a much deeper probing of various characteristics is demanded of the marketer.

RELATION TO STAGE OF FAMILY LIFE CYCLE

Family expenditure patterns will vary—and in substantial proportions for some products—according to the family's stage in its life cycle (see Figure 4-9). Young married couples with no children tend to spend large portions of their income on

Figure 4-8

Patterns of Expenditure By Region, 1969

	Atlantic Provinces	Quebec	Ontario	Prairie Provinces	British Columbia
			Region		
Number of families in sample	3,686	2,959	3,469	3,557	1,469
Estimated no. of families in population	493,792	1,546,385	2,197,856	1,008,500	635,288
Average					
Family size	3.71	3.54	3.18	3.09	2.93
No. of children under 5	.41	.31	.29	.30	.27
No. of children 5-15	1.03	.94	.78	.76	.68
No. of adults 16-17	.15	.14	.11	.13	.11
No. of adults 18-64	1.85	1.94	1.77	1.66	1.62
No. of adults 65 and over	.33	.25	.27	.29	.31
No. of full-time earners	.71	.82	.87	.77	.67
Age of head	48.0	46.4	46.8	48.1	48.4
Net income before taxes	6155.4	7789.6	8987.5	7190.6	8059.4
Other money receipts	132.0	146.0	221.3	208.0	257.5
Net change in assets and liabilities	6.6	41.4	211.3	89.5	296.3
Percentage					
Homeowners	67.3	44.5	61.7	65.3	60.1
Car or truck owners	66.2	63.3	74.6	76.5	76.6
With head Canadian born	95.2	88.4	67.4	71.4	62.8
With wife employed full-time	8.9	8.2	12.6	9.6	7.4
Average dollar expenditure					
Food	1425.0	1661.7	1573.4	1316.9	1418.7
Shelter	900.2	1196.0	1410.4	1096.2	1247.1
Rented living quarters	249.9	498.3	450.4	312.0	428.3
Owned living quarters	310.9	398.2	628.5	483.9	505.8
Other housing	39.1	57.9	78.0	53.2	55.7
Water, power and fuel	300.3	241.5	253.6	247.1	257.3
Household operation	274.1	313.9	379.2	283.5	327.2
Furnishings and equipment	264.6	326.3	430.7	351.8	401.3
Household appliances	80.6	90.4	103.6	93.3	98.7
Other	184.0	235.9	327.1	258.5	302.6
Clothing	577.7	710.0	707.7	596.7	574.8
Personal care	142.8	177.7	198.5	146.8	157.1
Medical and health care	162.9	279.5	323.9	240.1	235.5
Smoking and alcoholic beverages	268.2	353.3	322.6	243.7	282.1
Travel and transportation	887.2	963.8	1186.0	1031.9	1117.2
Automobile (and truck)	772.0	780.9	975.3	872.7	903.8
Purchase	362.6	355.0	459.3	412.5	408.0
Operation	409.4	425.9	516.0	460.2	495.8
Other	115.2	182.9	210.7	159.1	213.4
Recreation	188.3	219.6	331.9	277.7	331.1
Reading	34.9	52.8	55.4	43.3	54.0
Education	51.5	63.0	72.5	81.7	68.7
Miscellaneous expenses	91.1	116.8	136.9	121.5	151.6
Total current consumption	5268.6	6434.2	7129.1	5831.7	6366.6
Personal taxes	629.4	1007.3	1330.8	975.8	1129.3
Security	280.0	340.6	392.1	334.6	339.5
Gifts and contributions	178.5	155.6	260.1	236.5	223.4
Total expenditure	6356.6	7937.7	9112.2	7378.6	8058.8
Percentage distribution					
Food	22.4	20.9	17.3	17.8	17.6
Shelter	14.2	15.1	15.5	14.9	15.5
Rented living quarters	3.9	6.3	4.9	4.2	5.3
Owned living quarters	4.9	5.0	6.9	6.6	6.3
Other housing	.6	.7	.9	.7	.7
Water, power and fuel	4.7	3.0	2.8	3.3	3.2
Household operation	4.3	4.0	4.2	3.8	4.1
Furnishings and equipment	4.2	4.1	4.7	4.8	5.0
Household appliances	1.3	1.1	1.1	1.3	1.2
Other	2.9	3.0	3.6	3.5	3.8
Clothing	9.1	8.9	7.8	8.1	7.1
Personal care	2.2	2.2	2.2	2.0	1.9
Medical and health care	2.6	3.5	3.6	3.3	2.9
Smoking and alcoholic beverages	4.2	4.5	3.5	3.3	3.5

Travel and transportation	14.0	12.1	13.0	14.0	13.9
Automobile (and truck)	12.1	9.8	10.7	11.8	11.2
Purchase	5.7	4.5	5.0	5.6	5.1
Operation	6.4	5.4	5.7	6.2	6.2
Other	1.8	2.3	2.3	2.2	2.6
Recreation	3.0	2.8	3.6	3.8	4.1
Reading	.5	.7	.6	.6	.7
Education	.8	.8	.8	1.1	.9
Miscellaneous expenses	1.4	1.5	1.5	1.6	1.9
Total current consumption	82.9	81.1	78.2	79.0	79.0
Personal taxes	9.9	12.7	14.6	13.2	14.0
Security	4.4	4.3	4.3	4.5	4.2
Gifts and contributions	2.8	2.0	2.9	3.2	2.8
Total expenditure	100.0	100.0	100.0	100.0	100.0

Source: Statistics Canada, *Family Expenditure in Canada, Vol. 1. All Canada: Urban and Rural, 1969,* Cat. No. 62-535, Information Canada, Ottawa, 1972, p. 60.

automobiles, recreation and rented accommodation and relatively smaller percentages on food, medical and health care and household operation. When children begin to arrive, expenditure patterns shift as the young family often buys and furnishes a home. Families with older children find larger percentages of their annual income going to food, household operation, and clothing, and educational expenditures are shifted from courses taken by the parents to primary and secondary school education of the children (although, as a percentage of total family income, educational expenses do not vary much between families with no children and those with children between the ages of 4 and 16). Families in the "empty-nest" stage, especially when the head is between 50 and 65, are attractive to marketers because they typically have more discretionary purchasing power. The children are grown and on their own, and the house is paid for; yet the family earning power is generally at its peak.

RELATION TO INCOME DISTRIBUTION

Marketers can glean considerable information from an analysis of expenditure patterns of families in various income groups. For each income group, Figure 4-10 shows average dollar and percentages of family expenditures among the major categories of goods and services. Despite some general similarity of expenditure patterns, significant differences are observable in certain categories of goods and services and we can safely conclude that income distribution is a major determinant of these differences.

Some of the findings which might be observed from the data presented in Figure 4-10 are summarized below to suggest the type of information that an analysis of expenditure patterns by income groups might yield:

1. There was a high degree of uniformity in expenditure patterns of *middle-income* spending units. As we shall learn in Chapter 6, however, social-class structure is a much more meaningful criterion for determining expenditure patterns.
2. For each of the product categories shown in Figure 4-10, there was a considerable *absolute* increase in dollars spent as income rose (or, more correctly, as we compared one income group with a higher income group). In other words, people in a given income

Figure 4-9

Patterns of Expenditure By Stage of Family Life Cycle, 1969

	Unattached Individuals Under 45 Yrs	Unattached Individuals 45-64 Years	Unattached Individuals 65 and Over	(Married Couples Head Aged Under 45 Yrs.) (No Children)	(Children Under 16 Years) (1/More 0-4)	(Children Under 16 Years) (None 0-4)	(Married Couples Head 45-64) (No Children)	(Married Couples Head 45-64) (Children) (Under 16 Yrs)	Married Cpls Head 65 Yrs and Over	Other Families Incl Marr Cpls with Oth Rels
Number of families in sample	538	608	889	870	3,184	1,821	1,905	1,747	1,329	2,249
Estimated no. of families in population	375,726	320,693	451,767	356,627	1,110,119	687,432	712,561	620,654	460,040	786,202
Average										
Family size	1.00	1.00	1.00	2.08	4.44	4.83	2.68	5.19	2.32	3.72
No. of children under 5	.00	.00	.00	.00	1.36	.00	.00	.15	.00	.23
No. of children 5-15	.00	.00	.00	.00	1.15	2.51	.00	1.90	.05	.85
No. of adults 16-17	.01	.00	.00	.05	.04	.20	.17	.42	.03	.17
No. of adults 18-64	.99	1.00	.00	2.06	2.02	2.14	2.50	.00	.65	2.03
No. of adults 65 and over	.00	.00	1.00	.00	.00	.00	.03	.00	1.59	.55
No. of full-time earners	.68	.47	.08	1.27	.85	1.00	1.05	1.07	.31	.82
Age of head	28.2	56.1	74.2	29.8	31.8	37.9	55.7	50.6	72.0	50.0
Net income before taxes	5331.8	4224.3	2442.0	10512.9	8695.9	10385.2	9703.9	10508.2	5305.7	8051.2
Other money receipts	175.5	164.5	113.5	244.6	193.3	195.4	148.2	153.9	118.8	367.6
Net change in assets and liabilities	172.4-	110.8	17.3	619.2	74.0-	52.6	432.6	62.0	203.4	275.4
Percentage										
Homeowners	5.3	34.9	42.8	32.0	54.7	72.1	77.7	81.2	75.6	59.7
Car or truck owners	49.4	36.7	16.2	88.4	85.8	89.8	86.9	86.8	61.8	63.4
With head Canadian born	78.3	81.0	60.4	76.7	80.8	78.5	74.6	79.5	60.0	76.1
With wife employed full-time	.0	.0	.0	48.6	5.8	13.6	16.6	12.1	5.9	4.9
Average dollar expenditure										
Food	850.4	750.9	595.6	1425.0	1721.0	2024.0	1605.5	2157.1	1165.2	1656.6
Shelter	781.7	849.8	720.3	1489.4	1476.8	1572.8	1236.9	1409.4	940.1	1220.6
Rented living quarters	664.9	478.1	383.6	890.7	515.3	341.6	252.1	213.0	221.7	452.6
Owned living quarters	36.4	209.6	176.4	361.4	640.8	824.9	572.7	749.8	379.0	438.1
Other housing	39.9	32.4	10.2	71.6	42.0	80.8	106.2	102.3	63.1	54.9
Water, power and fuel	40.6	129.8	150.0	165.8	278.8	325.4	305.9	344.3	276.3	275.0
Household operation	198.5	190.5	139.8	333.7	429.1	437.0	329.4	379.3	233.5	350.9
Furnishings and equipment	147.5	140.4	70.0	601.5	509.7	525.1	389.1	458.7	231.9	317.4
Household appliances	20.6	30.9	15.5	147.1	145.7	130.8	93.4	118.4	63.2	84.2
Other	126.9	109.5	54.4	454.3	363.9	394.3	295.7	340.3	168.8	233.2
Clothing	430.4	250.9	126.2	735.4	694.3	968.2	726.3	1044.9	344.2	742.0
Personal care	119.2	90.6	50.4	207.3	184.0	232.2	204.1	235.6	114.9	191.6
Medical and health care	134.9	127.4	127.6	240.0	294.2	339.5	319.8	359.4	290.8	301.2
Smoking and alcoholic beverages	318.6	206.3	61.8	417.5	339.0	371.2	358.6	379.1	178.8	312.2
Travel and transportation	982.1	474.1	168.0	1598.6	1148.5	1334.0	1393.4	1368.4	624.2	1013.9
Automobile (and truck)	764.9	365.4	115.7	1333.8	978.2	1092.4	1173.1	1146.5	497.3	815.5
Purchase	416.5	180.0	62.5	665.7	422.7	487.4	567.6	534.2	202.9	380.8

Operation	348.4	185.4	53.2	668.0	555.5	605.1	605.5	612.3	294.3	434.8
Other	217.2	108.7	52.3	264.9	170.3	241.5	220.4	221.9	126.9	198.3
Recreation	247.6	145.0	68.8	402.5	301.4	386.2	314.5	365.5	163.8	269.5
Reading	46.1	36.4	21.5	65.7	53.0	63.7	53.8	59.9	40.2	50.5
Education	66.7	7.8	.5	81.8	56.8	101.2	88.8	141.8	15.7	76.5
Miscellaneous expenses	97.3	67.1	28.4	162.1	151.0	160.0	122.0	130.4	55.0	185.5
Total current consumption	4421.0	3337.2	2178.8	7760.5	7358.8	8515.2	7142.1	8489.6	4398.2	6688.4
Personal taxes	834.4	599.4	165.7	1728.3	1198.4	1484.2	1509.9	1495.4	484.1	916.6
Security	211.5	180.0	19.2	501.1	418.7	488.0	490.0	491.8	124.8	309.5
Gifts and contributions	256.9	167.6	186.4	223.2	165.7	213.4	290.0	222.2	229.8	236.4
Total expenditure	5723.9	4284.2	2550.0	10213.0	9141.6	10700.8	9432.1	10699.0	5236.9	8150.9

Percentage distribution

Food	14.9	17.5	23.4	14.0	18.8	18.9	17.0	20.2	22.2	20.3
Shelter	13.7	19.8	28.2	14.6	16.2	14.7	13.1	13.2	18.0	15.0
Rented living quarters	11.6	11.2	15.0	8.7	5.6	3.2	2.7	2.0	4.2	5.6
Owned living quarters	.6	4.9	6.9	3.5	7.0	7.7	6.1	7.0	7.2	5.4
Other housing	.7	.8	.4	.7	.5	.8	1.1	1.0	1.2	.7
Water, power and fuel	.7	3.0	5.9	1.6	3.0	3.0	3.2	3.2	5.3	3.4
Household operation	3.5	4.4	5.5	3.3	4.7	4.1	3.5	3.5	4.5	4.3
Furnishings and equipment	2.6	3.3	2.7	5.9	5.6	4.9	4.1	4.3	4.4	3.9
Household appliances	.4	.7	.6	1.4	1.6	1.2	1.0	1.1	1.2	1.0
Other	2.2	2.6	2.1	4.4	4.0	3.7	3.1	3.2	3.2	2.9
Clothing	7.5	5.9	5.0	7.2	7.6	9.0	7.7	9.8	6.6	9.1
Personal care	2.1	2.1	2.0	2.0	2.0	2.2	2.2	2.2	2.2	2.4
Medical and health care	2.4	3.0	5.0	2.3	3.2	3.2	3.4	3.4	5.6	3.7
Smoking and alcoholic beverages	5.6	4.8	2.4	4.1	3.7	3.5	3.8	3.5	3.4	3.8
Travel and transportation	17.2	11.1	6.6	15.7	12.6	12.5	14.8	12.8	11.9	12.4
Automobile (and truck)	13.4	8.5	4.5	13.1	10.7	10.2	12.4	10.7	9.5	10.0
Purchase	7.3	4.2	2.5	6.5	4.6	4.6	6.0	5.0	3.9	4.7
Operation	6.1	4.3	2.1	6.5	6.1	5.7	6.4	5.7	5.6	5.3
Other	3.8	2.5	2.1	2.6	1.9	2.3	2.3	2.1	2.4	2.4
Recreation	4.3	3.4	2.7	3.9	3.3	3.6	3.3	3.4	3.1	3.3
Reading	.8	.9	.8	.6	.6	.6	.6	.6	.8	.6
Education	1.2	.2	.0	.8	.6	.9	.9	1.3	.3	.9
Miscellaneous expenses	1.7	1.6	1.1	1.6	1.7	1.5	1.3	1.2	1.1	2.3
Total current consumption	77.2	77.9	85.4	76.0	80.5	79.6	75.7	79.3	84.0	82.1
Personal taxes	14.6	14.0	6.5	16.9	13.1	13.9	16.0	14.0	9.2	11.2
Security	3.7	4.2	.8	4.9	4.6	4.6	5.2	4.6	2.4	3.8
Gifts and contributions	4.5	3.9	7.3	2.2	1.8	2.0	3.1	2.1	4.4	2.9
Total expenditure	100.0	100.0	100.0	100.0	100.0	100.0	100.0	100.0	100.0	100.0

Source: Statistics Canada, Family Expenditure in Canada, Vol. I. All Canada: Urban and Rural, 1969. Cat. No. 62-535, Information Canada, Ottawa, 1972, pp. 56-57.

Figure 4-10
Patterns of Expenditure By Family Income Class, 1969

	All Classes	Under $3000	$3000-$3999	$4000-$4999	$5000-$5999	$6000-$6999	$7000-$7999	$8000-$8999	$9000-$9999	$10000-$10999	$11000-$11999	$12000-$14999	$15000 & Over
Number of Families in Sample	15,140	2,538	1,232	1,136	1,293	1,388	1,372	1,285	1,065	837	668	1,246	1,080
Estimated No. of Families in Population	5,881,821	979,153	416,822	403,585	469,370	521,133	509,183	498,715	431,377	330,902	271,219	545,359	505,003
Average													
Family Size	3.28	1.67	2.51	2.96	3.11	3.45	3.63	3.92	3.90	3.93	4.09	3.89	4.19
No. of Children Under 5	.30	.07	.19	.32	.37	.42	.48	.43	.38	.40	.33	.30	.21
No. of Children 5-15	.83	.17	.51	.71	.78	.94	1.00	1.19	1.15	1.12	1.12	.99	1.05
No. of Adults 16-17	.13	.04	.10	.11	.09	.12	.13	.14	.15	.18	.22	.17	.21
No. of Adults 18-64	1.79	.68	1.22	1.53	1.71	1.87	1.95	2.12	2.13	2.19	2.34	2.38	2.62
No. of Adults 65 and Over	.28	.73	.51	.34	.22	.15	.16	.10	.13	.10	.13	.11	.14
No. of Full-Time Earners	.80	.13	.35	.49	.67	.77	.87	.95	1.05	1.12	1.25	1.30	1.48
Age of Head	47.2	62.9	52.0	47.9	43.9	42.7	42.4	41.6	42.1	41.0	42.6	42.6	46.2
Net Income Before Taxes	8026.5	1857.6	3479.0	4488.3	5480.9	6489.8	7468.7	8470.0	9455.6	10464.0	11461.2	13264.9	20324.9
Other Money Receipts	195.7	258.2	220.0	202.4	153.1	131.5	190.0	132.8	138.7	266.9	125.6	194.0	263.8
Net Change in Assets and Liabilities	137.7	430.7-	285.2-	333.2-	245.5-	271.2-	55.3-	55.8-	173.7	303.9	256.5	855.9	2151.0
Percentage													
Homeowners	58.1	49.0	49.7	50.1	49.0	51.3	54.2	60.3	65.7	66.3	68.9	67.8	77.8
Car or Truck Owners	71.5	27.5	46.4	62.6	69.7	79.4	82.7	86.9	86.9	90.7	91.3	92.2	92.5
With Head Canadian Born	75.4	70.2	77.2	83.2	78.4	78.1	77.3	77.1	72.1	75.0	76.3	73.8	73.5
With Wife Employed Full-Time	10.0	.4	1.3	2.2	2.9	4.4	5.3	9.0	12.7	18.8	24.9	26.6	26.7
Average Dollar Expenditure													
Food	1523.5	719.3	1015.7	1209.6	1309.5	1470.2	1590.0	1721.4	1793.9	1866.4	2006.3	2040.6	2470.3
Shelter	1239.7	639.6	801.8	885.8	979.3	1106.4	1267.8	1347.0	1454.5	1549.6	1580.3	1686.4	2240.8
Rented Living Quarters	420.0	291.4	365.3	381.9	443.5	447.7	513.7	482.3	436.4	453.5	450.5	484.6	417.1
Owned Living Quarters	503.3	166.9	215.5	261.3	281.9	375.8	449.2	540.9	661.6	729.5	736.9	799.1	1212.2
Other Housing	62.8	7.4	15.5	27.1	30.8	39.5	47.5	47.8	70.2	70.6	91.2	101.5	252.6
Water, Power and Fuel	253.6	173.9	205.5	215.5	223.1	243.4	257.4	276.0	286.2	296.1	301.7	301.2	358.8
Household Operation	331.2	132.6	191.8	230.6	263.9	284.6	317.8	361.7	371.3	425.3	446.5	485.8	680.8
Furnishings and Equipment	372.6	95.3	172.9	216.4	255.5	308.4	340.7	407.8	438.5	530.8	551.2	608.1	862.2
Household Appliances	95.9	29.1	54.1	62.0	76.1	89.1	98.4	107.7	120.3	146.4	142.5	144.9	166.7
Other	276.7	66.3	118.9	154.3	179.4	219.2	242.3	300.1	318.3	384.4	408.7	463.2	695.6
Clothing	664.0	171.5	337.1	424.8	491.4	555.7	623.8	713.1	771.8	864.6	1005.7	1083.1	1484.5
Personal Care	175.0	59.3	99.7	114.5	138.4	160.5	175.6	198.7	209.8	228.4	259.9	263.3	329.6
Medical and Health Care	274.8	138.5	197.5	209.5	235.7	257.1	281.6	294.9	313.3	337.8	348.0	367.6	469.0
Smoking and Alcoholic Beverages	308.2	97.2	177.9	214.7	271.7	303.7	311.7	347.3	376.3	387.4	449.3	452.0	554.6
Travel and Transportation	1068.6	220.3	465.9	699.0	782.2	987.3	1083.8	1252.3	1231.6	1465.5	1600.7	1703.2	2289.3
Automobile (and Truck)	881.8	167.7	356.0	591.4	653.8	858.9	915.6	1044.6	1028.4	1230.0	1313.2	1425.6	1801.1
Purchase	410.2	74.4	161.0	271.1	283.9	382.9	417.4	467.0	438.7	572.7	637.7	672.9	923.8

Operation	471.6	195.1	320.3	369.9	476.0	577.6	498.2	589.7	657.3	675.5	752.7	877.3
Other	186.8	109.9	107.6	128.4	128.4	207.7	168.2	203.2	235.5	287.5	277.6	488.2
Recreation	280.9	117.1	156.4	192.5	208.2	288.3	243.6	342.7	374.8	395.1	473.7	749.3
Reading	50.7	28.7	31.6	37.5	42.8	53.9	48.7	59.3	69.5	68.1	76.5	105.5
Education	69.4	28.9	35.5	39.3	40.0	70.3	47.2	78.6	95.0	96.6	116.2	216.3
Miscellaneous Expenses	126.7	62.6	71.7	90.0	127.0	133.8	135.7	158.0	153.8	177.3	194.3	254.2
Total Current Consumption	6485.4	3697.6	4500.1	5087.0	5851.8	7190.6	6468.0	7599.7	8349.0	8985.0	9550.8	12706.5
Personal Taxes	1104.2	177.8	316.1	493.6	672.8	1043.6	851.7	1258.5	1493.1	1628.9	2107.8	4129.3
Security	353.6	82.2	142.4	216.1	293.5	383.4	334.7	438.3	477.1	529.0	627.0	1015.5
Gifts and Contributions	217.8	127.0	153.4	176.9	190.9	181.5	184.0	225.8	239.1	272.9	314.4	575.8
Total Expenditure	8161.1	4084.6	5112.1	5973.6	7009.0	8799.1	7838.4	9522.2	10558.4	11415.9	12599.9	18427.0
Percentage Distribution												
Food	18.7	24.9	23.7	21.9	21.0	19.6	20.3	18.8	17.7	17.6	16.2	13.4
Shelter	15.2	19.6	17.3	16.4	15.8	15.3	16.2	15.3	14.7	13.8	13.4	12.2
Rented Living Quarters	5.1	8.9	7.5	7.4	6.4	5.5	6.6	4.6	4.3	3.9	3.8	2.3
Owned Living Quarters	6.2	5.3	5.1	4.7	5.4	6.1	5.7	6.9	6.9	6.5	6.3	6.6
Other Housing	.8	.3	.5	.5	.6	.5	.6	.7	.7	.8	.8	1.4
Water, Power and Fuel	3.1	6.7	4.2	3.7	3.5	3.1	3.3	3.0	2.8	2.6	2.4	1.9
Household Operation	4.1	5.1	4.5	4.4	4.1	4.1	4.1	3.9	4.0	3.9	3.9	3.7
Furnishings and Equipment	4.6	3.7	4.2	4.3	4.4	4.6	4.3	4.6	5.0	4.8	4.8	4.7
Household Appliances	1.2	1.1	1.2	1.3	1.3	1.2	1.3	1.3	1.4	1.2	1.2	.9
Other	3.4	2.6	3.0	3.0	3.1	3.4	3.1	3.3	3.6	3.6	3.7	3.8
Clothing	8.1	6.7	8.3	8.2	7.9	8.1	8.0	8.1	8.2	8.8	8.6	8.1
Personal Care	2.1	2.3	2.2	2.3	2.3	2.2	2.2	2.2	2.2	2.3	2.1	1.8
Medical and Health Care	3.4	5.4	4.1	3.9	3.7	3.4	3.6	3.3	3.2	3.0	2.9	2.5
Smoking and Alcoholic Beverages	3.8	3.8	4.2	4.5	4.3	3.9	4.0	4.0	3.7	3.9	3.6	3.0
Travel and Transportation	13.1	11.4	13.7	13.1	14.1	14.2	13.8	12.9	13.9	14.0	13.5	12.4
Automobile (and Truck)	10.8	8.7	11.6	10.9	12.3	11.9	11.7	10.8	11.6	11.5	11.3	9.8
Purchase	5.0	3.9	5.3	4.8	5.5	5.3	5.3	4.6	5.4	5.6	5.3	5.0
Operation	5.8	4.8	6.3	6.2	6.8	6.6	6.4	6.2	6.2	5.9	6.0	4.8
Other	2.3	2.7	2.1	2.2	1.8	2.4	2.1	2.1	2.2	2.5	2.2	2.6
Recreation	3.4	2.9	3.1	3.2	3.0	3.3	3.1	3.6	3.5	3.5	3.8	4.1
Reading	.6	.7	.6	.6	.6	.6	.6	.6	.7	.6	.6	.6
Education	.9	.8	.7	.7	.6	.8	.6	.8	.9	.8	.9	1.2
Miscellaneous Expenses	1.6	1.5	1.4	1.5	1.8	1.5	1.7	1.7	1.5	1.6	1.5	1.4
Total Current Consumption	79.5	90.5	88.0	85.2	83.5	81.7	82.5	79.8	79.1	78.7	75.8	69.0
Personal Taxes	13.5	4.4	6.2	8.3	9.6	11.9	10.9	13.2	14.1	14.3	16.7	22.4
Security	4.3	2.0	2.8	3.6	4.2	4.4	4.3	4.6	4.5	4.6	5.0	5.5
Gifts and Contributions	2.7	3.1	3.0	3.0	2.7	2.1	2.3	2.4	2.3	2.4	2.5	3.1
Total Expenditure	100.0	100.0	100.0	100.0	100.0	100.0	100.0	100.0	100.0	100.0	100.0	100.0

Source: Statistics Canada, Family Expenditure in Canada, Vol. I, All Canada: Urban and Rural, 1969. Cat. No. 62-535. Information Canada, Ottawa, 1972, pp. 66-67.

bracket spent significantly more *dollars* in each product category than their less well-off neighbors, even though the lower-income households devoted a larger *percentage* of their total expenditures to the given product class. A marketing person is probably more concerned with the total dollars available from each income group than with the percentage share of total expenditures.

3. In each successively higher income group, the amount spent for food declined as a percentage of total expenditures.
4. The percentage of family expenditures devoted to the total of shelter and household operation remained reasonably stable in the middle-income brackets.
5. Amounts spent for personal, medical and health care gradually decreased as a percentage of total expenditures as incomes increased.
6. The share of expenditures going to automobile purchase and operation tended to increase as incomes increased in the low- and lower-middle-income groups. This percentage levelled off in the higher-middle- and higher-income groups.
7. Regarding clothing, with the exception of families with annual incomes below $3,000, the percentage of family expenditures going to this category remained quite constant until there was a marked increase among families earning more than $11,000 per year.

It is interesting to compare these generalizations on expenditure patterns with "Engel's laws." In 1857, Ernst Engel, a German statistician, published the results of his studies of spending patterns of workingmen's families. Later students of consumer spending behavior expanded on Engel's work, and the net result is a series of four statements regarding spending patterns in relation to various income levels. Engel's laws state that as family income increases:

1. A smaller percentage of expenditures goes for food.
2. Approximately the same percentage is devoted to clothing.
3. The proportion of total spending allotted to housing and house operation remains the same.
4. The share of total expenditures apportioned to other items (recreation, education, medical care, etc.) increases.

Engel's laws still stand up quite well more than one hundred years after their publication, although, on the basis of what we can learn from a detailed study of the data in Figure 4-10, certain of the laws may require some minor restatement. The first and third generalizations of Engel (regarding food and household operation and shelter) still hold true. The fourth is also relatively true, with the exception of personal care and medical expenditures which seem to decline as a percentage of total expenditures as incomes increase. The second generalization, regarding clothing, also holds true until one reaches the higher-income brackets where much larger percentages of expenditures are devoted to clothing.

Generalizations such as these provide a broad background against which a marketing executive can analyze the market for his particular product or service. People with needs to satisfy and money to spend, however, must be *willing* to spend before we can say a market exists. Consequently in the next two chapters we shall look into consumer buying patterns—the "willingness-to-buy" factor in our definition of a market.

QUESTIONS AND PROBLEMS

1. Why is the regional distribution of population said to be an important factor?

2. What is the marketing implication of declining birth rates?
3. What is the value of using family life cycle rather than age as a basis for segmenting markets?
4. How should the French-Canadian market be defined?
5. For each of the following population factors, give several examples of products whose market demand would be particularly affected by the individual population factor:
   a. Sex
   b. Age
   c. Urban, rural, and suburban distribution
6. Cite some regional differences in product preferences caused by factors other than climate.
7. Why are French Canadians an important market segment in this country?
8. The average level of formal education attained by people in Canada has risen substantially over the past few decades. What influence does this factor have on buying habits? In what ways might this trend affect the demand for particular products and services?
9. How is the marketing mix for automobiles likely to differ when marketing to each of the following market segments?
   a. High school students
   b. Husbands
   c. Bluecollar workers
   d. Housewives
   e. Young single adults
10. What users' benefits would you stress when advertising each of the following three products to each of the three markets?

Products	Markets
a. Stereo record player	a. School teachers
b. Toothpaste	b. Retired people
c. 10-day Caribbean cruise	c. Working women

11. Using the demographic and income segmentation bases discussed in this chapter, describe the segment which is likely to be the best market for:
    a. Snow skis
    b. Good French wines
    c. Power hand tools
    d. Birthday cards
    e. Outdoor barbecue grills
12. List four of the major trends in population noted in this chapter—for instance, a growing segment of the population is over sixty-five years of age. Then carefully explain how each of the following types of retail stores might be influenced by each of the trends:
    a. Supermarket
    b. Sporting goods store
    c. Drugstore
    d. Restaurant
14. Roger Carson, aged thirty-two, is married and has two children. The family net income is $750 a month. If the family expenditures are average, approximately how much will the Carson family spend on the following items?
    a. Food
    b. Clothing
    c. Automobile operation
    d. Recreation
15. Identify the major differences in expenditure patterns between residents of the Atlantic Provinces and those of Ontario.
16. What are Engel's laws? Are they still valid today? Why?

MARKETS: PSYCHOLOGICAL DETERMINANTS OF BUYER BEHAVIOR

In the course of doing her weekly family grocery shopping Friday afternoon at a local supermarket, a housewife selected a one kilogram can of Maxwell House drip-grind coffee. To the casual observer—and perhaps even to the housewife herself, by now—this may have been a simple, routine purchase. Yet this seemingly simple buying action was the result of decision making on several issues. Why did she buy Maxwell House instead of another brand? Why did she buy a one kilogram can instead of some other size? Why did she buy coffee instead of tea or some other drink? Why was drip-grind selected instead of the freeze-dried or regular instant coffee? Why did she shop at the particular supermarket, and why did she pick Friday instead of some other day?

IMPORTANCE AND DIFFICULTY OF UNDERSTANDING CONSUMER BEHAVIOR

We have reasonably good quantitative data on how many people live in each geographic region, how many are high school graduates, which language is spoken at home and so forth. We also have reasonably adequate market information about income and its distribution. For some products (snow shovel, oil filter), demographic and economic factors alone may explain why a consumer bought the product. Most consumer purchases, however, are also likely to be influenced by psychological or sociological factors. As indicated in the previous chapter, differences in demographic and economic factors alone do not satisfactorily account for some variations in personal behavior. These factors do not explain the differences between the woman who loves to cook and the one who does not, or the differences in brand preferences for soft drinks or cigarettes, when in blindfold tests consumers cannot tell one brand from another.

Consequently, to develop a successful marketing program, typically a company should learn as much as possible about its customers' motives, attitudes, beliefs, interests, values, personality, self-image, and other psychological variables.[1] If the patterning of such factors are closely related to demographic characteristics, well and good. If not, one must go beyond demographics. For the same reasons, we also need to study families and other groups—their internal relationships, their attitudes, and the diffusion of information among them—because these groups also influence buying behavior.

An understanding of the reasons *why* people buy a given product or shop at a certain store is critical. If the seller does not appeal to the right motive, he will probably lose the sale. Attempting to sell decorative outdoor lighting to a buyer in an industrial plant who wants lighting solely for security purposes will probably get a salesman nowhere. An understanding of the buying behavior of various market segments helps a seller to select the most effective product design, price, advertising appeals, channels of distribution, and the many other aspects of his marketing program.

However, we know very little about what goes on in a buyer's mind leading up to a purchase and following the purchasing action. In fact, the infinitely complex mechanism—the human mind—has frequently been referred to as a "black box" because we know so little about how it works.

Sometimes the explanation for his behavior is not even discernible to the buyer himself. To illustrate, buying motives may be grouped on different levels depending upon the consumer's awareness of them and his willingness to divulge them. In the first group, the buyer recognizes, and is quite willing to talk about, his motives for buying certain products. In the second, he is aware of his reasons for buying, but will not admit them to others. A man may buy a backyard swimming pool because he feels it adds to his social position in the neighborhood, or a woman may buy cosmetics to increase her attractiveness to men. But when questioned about their motives, they offer other reasons which they think will be more socially acceptable. The most difficult motives to uncover are those in the third group, where even the buyers themselves do not know the real factors motivating their buying actions. A purchase is rarely the result of a single motive. Furthermore, various motives may conflict with one another. In buying a new dress, a woman may want to please her husband, be admired (or possibly envied) as a fashion leader by other women in her social circle, and strive for economy. To do all this in one purchase is truly a difficult assignment. Buyer behavior also changes over a period of time because of changes in income, changes in life cycle stage, and other factors.

---

1 The term "psychographics" is currently being used by many marketing researchers as a collective synonym for these psychological variables, although as yet no universally agreeable definition has been developed for the term. See Ruth Ziff, "Psychographics for Market Segmentation," *Journal of Advertising Research*, April, 1971, pp. 3-9; and Fred D. Reynolds, *Psychographics: a Conceptual Orientation*, University of Georgia, College of Business Administration, Athens, Research Monograph No. 6, 1973.

If we add to this complexity the countless variations occuring because each consumer is a separate individual with a unique personality, then our task of understanding consumer behavior may seem an impossible dream. Yet try we must, because an understanding of buyer behavior is critical to the success of a marketing program. In the face of all the individuality and complexity, a seller must search for reasonably similar behavioral threads permeating a market segment so that he can appeal to a wide group with one marketing program. Fortunately marketers, working with behavioral scientists, have enjoyed some success in developing generalizations about individual and group factors as they influence consumer buying behavior.

THEORIES OF BUYER BEHAVIOR

Perhaps because we know relatively little about how the human mind works, there is still no comprehensive body of knowledge which is generally accepted as the "theory of buyer behavior." Instead, over the years several different theoretical models have been developed to explain buyer behavior. Each makes some interpretive contribution, and some are more useful than others in explaining the purchase behavior toward a given product. The economic model, for example, might best explain the purchase of expensive industrial equipment, while psychoanalytic theory might be used to explain the demand for cosmetics.[2]

We shall review briefly some of these theories, not only because they have some current validity and realism, but also because they are a part of the evolutionary development of present-day thinking. The first of these constructs was developed by economists. Later models emerged from the behavioral science fields of psychology and sociology.

MICROECONOMIC THEORY

One of the earlier theories of consumer behavior (which in modified form still has some usefulness today) was developed by classical economists in the course of their formulating a comprehensive theory of the individual firm (microeconomics). This behavioral theory first posed by Adam Smith and others, is based on the notion that man is an economic, rational being and that at all times he is acting in his self-interest. Later this theory was refined by the neoclassical economists, primarily Alfred Marshall of England.

The resultant concept—the marginal-utility theory of value—holds that a consumer will continue to buy units of a given product as long as the satisfaction he receives from the last unit consumed (marginal utility) equals or exceeds the marginal utility derived from the same expenditure for any other product.

This theory is based on some strong assumptions: (1) that the consumer is always trying to maximize his satisfactions (utilities) within the limits of his financial resources, (2) that he has complete knowledge of alternative sources for satisfying his wants, and (3) that he is always acting in a rational manner.

Some of the limitations in such a model should be obvious. First, it does not in-

---

2 For a review of five models of the buyer's "black box," along with their respective marketing applications, see Philip Kotler, "Behavioral Models for Analyzing Buyers," *Journal of Marketing*, October, 1965, pp. 37-45.

clude the psychological and sociological factors which influence behavior. Totally rational behavior is not typical among consumers. Nor is the theory sound when it implies that impulsive behavior is irrational. Finally, it is difficult to quantify the satisfactions received from a product. Research efforts over the years by scholars in such organizations as the Survey Research Center at the University of Michigan have done much to realistically modify the basic theory.[3]

While it is granted that the economic model cannot fully explain buyer behavior, nevertheless it does have some usefulness. Industrial buyers quite frequently base all or a good part of their buying decisions on the marginal-utility concept. Household consumers, when buying autos or other infrequently purchased, high-priced items, essentially act out the economic model as one significantly determining factor in their purchasing decision. Also, the theory can be particularly useful when it is treated as a *normative* rather than an *absolute* or *descriptive* model of behavior.[4] For instance, from the model we might hypothesize that the sales of a product will increase as its price decreases. For the model to be realistically useful, we must treat this sample hypothesis as a generalization. That is, sales will *usually* increase, or the hypothesis is applicable for most (not *all*) consumers. The fact that some consumers refrain from buying when the price goes down does not invalidate the hypothesis-generalization.

PSYCHOLOGICAL THEORIES

Psychologists are far from agreement about which of their constructs provides the best insights into the consumer's mind. Consequently, we shall summarize briefly some of the dominant theories as formulated by different schools of psychological thought.

Learning theories. Interpreting and predicting the consumer's learning process is a real key to understanding his buying behavior. Therefore, it is unfortunate that no simple learning theory has emerged as universally workable and acceptable. The three principal learning theories described here are (1) stimulus-response theories, (2) cognitive theories, and (3) gestalt and field theories.[5]

Stimulus-response theories. These were first formulated by psychologists such as Pavlov, Skinner, and Hull on the basis of their laboratory experiments with animals. This school of theorists hold that learning occurs as a person (or animal) responds to some stimulus and is rewarded (reinforced) with need satisfaction for a correct response or penalized for an incorrect one. When the same response is repeated in reaction to a given stimulus, habit-behavioral patterns are established.

An application of the S-R model is the *behaviorism* approach, expounded by Watson and still applied in advertising today.[6] He postulated the idea of repeating the

---

3 See for example, George Katona, *The Powerful Consumer*, McGraw-Hill Book Company, New York, 1960; G. Katona, "Rational Behavior and Economic Behavior," *Psychological Review*, September, 1953, pp. 307-318; G. Katona and Eva Mueller, "A Study of Purchase Decisions," in Lincoln H. Clark (ed.), *Consumer Behavior*, New York University Press, New York, 1954, pp. 30-87.

4 Kotler, *op. cit.*, p. 39.

5 See Ernest R. Hilgard and George H. Bower, *Theories of Learning*, Appleton-Century-Crofts, Inc., New York, 1966.

6 See John B. Watson, *Behaviorism*, The People's Institute Publishing Co., New York, 1925.

same stimuli over and over in order to solidify the response patterns. Out of this came the idea of constantly repeating an advertisement to firmly reinforce a given purchasing response. Applying this idea, for many years the advertising for Dominion Stores has featured the theme "mainly because of the meat" and recently Loblaws has featured "more than the price is right." For both supermarket chains, the basic theme is designed to build store loyalty. The concept of behaviorism by itself is probably too simplistic an approach, however, because we realize that perceptions, attitudes, and other cognitive factors (not just the mechanistic S-R concept) also can influence a consumer's response to repetitive advertising.

Cognitive theories. This set of learning theories rejects the S-R model as being too mechanistic. In S-R theory, behavior is the result of *only* the positive or negative reinforcement stemming from a response to some stimuli, and no other influencing variables are recognized as intervening in the S-R channel. Proponents of cognitive theory insist that learning is influenced by factors such as attitudes and beliefs, past experiences, and an insightful understanding of how to use the current situation to achieve a goal. Habitual behavioral patterns, then, are the result of perceptive thinking and goal orientation. In summary, cognitive theorists postulate that a person's brain processes and nervous system are significant in forming his behavioral patterns, while S-R theorists pay little attention to these intervening variables.

Gestalt and field theories. "Gestalt" is a German word for which there is no exact English counterpart. Roughly, the word means "configuration," "pattern," or "form." Gestalt psychologists are concerned with the "whole" of a thing—the total scene—rather than its component parts. They maintain that learning and behavior should be viewed as a total process, in contrast to the individual-element approach in the S-R model.[7]

In this behavioral theory, perception, past experiences, and goal orientation are key elements. (Note the similarity to the cognitive learning model.) Perception, which is discussed later, may be defined as the meaning we attach, on the basis of our past experiences, to stimuli as received through our five senses. According to gestalt theory, a person perceives and reacts to stimuli in light of his experiences. Furthermore, it is assumed that people behave in goal-oriented patterns. That is, some inner drive (tension) arises which demands satisfaction (the goal). Then in a more or less conscious, rational manner the person strives for this goal, solving problems and coping with this environment en route.

Field theory, as formulated by Kurt Lewin, is a useful refinement of gestalt psychology.[8] This theory holds that the only determining force accounting for a person's behavior at any given time is his psychological "field" as it exists at the time. The concept of a person's *field* or *life space,* which is a key element in the theory, may be defined as the totality of existing facts pertaining to the individual and his environment at the time of the behavior. Thus, to understand a consumer's goal-oriented behavior, we must understand him and his perception of his environment—all the complex forces, barriers, conflicts, etc., which influence him as he strives to satisfy the drive which initiated the goal-seeking process.

---

7 See K. Koffka, *Principles of Gestalt Psychology,* Harcourt, Brace, & World, Inc., New York, 1935; Wolfgang Kohler, *Gestalt Psychology,* Liveright Publishing Corporation, New York, 1947; and Willis D. Ellis (ed.), *Source Book of Gestalt Psychology,* Harcourt, Brace & World, Inc., New York, 1938.

8 See Kurt Lewin, *A Dynamic Theory of Personality* (1935) and *Principles of Topological Psychology* (1936), both McGraw Hill Book Company, New York.

Gestalt psychologists are concerned with man's perception and understanding of his total environment. They believe that man perceives the whole rather than its parts. They further postulate that a person's perception of the whole is quite different from what we might expect if each part were considered separately. Thus, looking at the following configuration, most people will perceive four sets of tracks, four pairs of lines, or four columns, but rarely do they perceive eight vertical lines.

Moreover, rather than perceiving the separate parts—the individual stimuli—a person will organize them (in his perception) into a whole which is meaningful to him in light of his past experiences. That is, it is the properties of the *total field* which influence his perceptions of the stimuli in that field. To illustrate, a distinguished-looking man in a white coat can speak in a serious tone in a TV commercial advertising a pain reliever or a brand of toothpaste. Many viewers will perceive him as a doctor and his message as a medical endorsement because that is how they interpret that total scene in light of their past experiences.

Several "field" principles which have applications in marketing have been developed by gestalt psychologists reflecting ways in which field properties of stimuli affect our perception of them.[9] The principle of *closure* postulates that we tend to produce a complete figure in a meaningful way. Thus "13 0" will be "closed" by the viewer to get the letters "BO." A change in spacing (illustrating the principle of *proximity*) can give different results—the number "130" rather than two letters. When the Kellogg Company (cereal manufacturers) ran billboard ads with the name so far to the right that the final "g" was cut off, viewers tended to add that final "g" to produce a complete figure. Incidentally, the attention-getting value of the ad is also increased. Of course, there is the danger that the reader will not take the time to close the gap or that the ad is so subtle that the closure point is missed.

Messages must be placed in a reasonable *context* (a smartly dressed debutante should not be shown painting her house). Also the ads should be *simple* in both structure and content. Because of locational properties, some items will *stand out* in the sea of similar-looking products. This principle places a premium on eye-level shelf position in a supermarket, for example. All parts of a marketing program—price, type of ads, product quality, retailers handling the product, etc.—must be in *harmony*, i.e., consistent with consumers' expectations. And each product marketed by a firm must fit in with the consumer's perception of the total field, i.e., the company and all its other products.

Psychoanalytic theories. The psychoanalytic school of thought, as founded by Sigmund Freud and later modified by his followers and critics, has had a tremendous impact on the study of human personality and behavior. Freud contended that there are three parts to our mind—the id, the ego, and the superego. The id houses the basic instinctive drives, many of which are antisocial. The superego is our con-

---

9 Adapted from James H. Myers and William H. Reynolds, *Consumer Behavior and Marketing Management*, Houghton Mifflin Company, Boston, 1967, pp. 21-34.

science, accepting moral standards and directing the instinctive drives into acceptable channels, thus avoiding feelings of guilt or shame. The id and the superego are sometimes in conflict. The ego is the conscious, rational control center which maintains a balance between the uninhibited instincts of the id and the socially oriented, constraining superego.

Freud's behavioral thesis was that a person enters this world with certain instinctive biological desires which cannot be satisfied in a socially acceptable fashion. As a person learns that he cannot gratify these needs in a direct manner, he develops other, more subtle means of seeking satisfaction. As the basic urges are being repressed, tensions and frustrations are developing. Also, feelings of guilt or shame about these drives cause a person to suppress and even sublimate them to the point where they become subconscious. Instead, he substitutes rationalizations and socially acceptable behavior. Yet the basic urges are always there. The net result is very complex behavior. Sometimes even the person himself does not understand why he feels or acts as he does.

Some of Freud's followers made refinements in his model when they introduced a cultural perspective to behavior, instead of adhering completely to the biologically determined foundation. Adler believed that man's basic drive is for power and superiority. Fromm felt that man is lonely; instead of freedom, he wants security and human companionship. Horney contended that man's behavioral patterns are influenced by his efforts to cope with his anxieties.[10]

One significant marketing implication in psychoanalytic theory is that a person's real motive for buying a given product, shopping at a certain store, or performing any other consumer buying act may well be hidden. The usual research techniques which are feasible for determining demographic and economic data normally will prove fruitless in uncovering the real reasons for a person's buying behavior. This situation has given rise to marketing's use of motivation research, a series of techniques originally developed for use in psychology. It is through motivation research that marketers concluded, for example, that a housewife who uses instant coffee is perceived as a lazy person who does a poor job caring for her husband and children, and that using household appliances gives a woman the guilt feeling that she is lazy. Manufacturers then promoted the idea that using such products would allow her to spend more time with her family.

In summary, it is out of psychoanalytic theory that marketers realized they must provide a buyer with socially acceptable rationalizations for his purchasing. Yet they also can appeal subconsciously to his dreams, hopes, and fears.

SOCIOLOGICAL THEORIES

The psychological theories which we have reviewed tend to concentrate on the individual, treating his social environment as a secondary consideration. In the behavioral theories developed by sociologists and cultural anthropologists, the primary focus is on interpersonal relations and influences. In the next chapter we shall examine some of these social influences as they relate to buyer behavior.

---

10 Alfred Adler, *The Science of Living*, Greenberg, Inc., New York, 1929; Erich Fromm, *Escape from Freedom*, Holt, Rinehart and Winston, Inc., New York, 1941; Karen Horney, *The Neurotic Personality of Our Time* (1937) and *Our Inner Conflicts* (1945), both by W. W. Norton & Company, Inc., New York.

SUMMARY OF THEORIES

We still have not developed a cohesive, comprehensive theory of buying behavior. We do, however, have some insights into the consumer's "black box" by virtue of contributions from various theoretical models. We see how the consumer balances prices and satisfactions within the limits of his income, although it is granted that the theory is weakened by some unrealistic assumptions. We see how repeated responses to given stimuli lead to habitual behavior. Cognitive theorists introduced the elements of thought, perception, and past experiences into the process. Gestalt and field theorists provided insight into human behavior in light of the total scene rather than the perception of individual elements in that psychological field. From Freudian thought we understand that behavior is influenced by repressed desires and hidden motives. Finally, sociologists and anthropologists have explained the interpersonal social influences on behavior.

The differences—sometimes quite great—in possible interpretations of the same behavior should remind us that the consumer's total psychological field is quite complex and that many forces—past and present, hidden and apparent, instinctive and learned, individual and environmental—all do influence behavior.[11]

PSYCHOLOGICAL DETERMINANTS OF BUYER BEHAVIOR

In discussing the psychological forces in the consumer's behavioral field, our model is as follows: one or more motives within a person will trigger behavior toward a goal which will bring satisfaction. This goal-oriented behavior is influenced by the person's perceptions. His perceptions, in turn, are influenced by his learning experiences, attitudes and beliefs, personality, and self-concept. See Fig. 5-1.

MOTIVATION

We are trying to understand why consumers act (behave) as they do. But first we might ask why a person acts at all. The answer is, "because he is motivated"; that is, all behavior starts with motivation. A *motive* (or drive) is a stimulated need which a goal-oriented individual seeks to satisfy (i.e., he seeks to reduce tension). Thus hunger, a need for security, and a desire for prestige are examples of motives.

It is important to note that a need must be aroused or stimulated before it can serve as a motive. It is possible and usual to have needs which are latent and thus do not serve as the instigator of behavior until they become sufficiently intense, that is, stimulated. The sources of this arousal may be internal (the person gets hungry) or environmental (he sees an ad for food); or just thinking about food may make him hungry.

There is no single generally acceptable classification of motives, simply because we do not know enough about human motivation. However, psychologists generally do agree that motives can be grouped into two broad categories—*biogenic* needs (such as the needs for food, drink, sex, and bodily comfort), which arise from phys-

---

11 For an examination of four additional contemporary theories of behavior, set in the context of marketing, see Charles D. Schewe, "Selected Social Psychological Models for Analyzing Buyers," *Journal of Marketing*, July, 1973, pp. 31-39. The four are: (1) the McClelland model, stressing the theory of achievement motivation, (2) the Goffman model of role theory, (3) the Festinger model of cognitive dissonance theory, and (4) the Riesman model of the inner-versus other-directed individual.

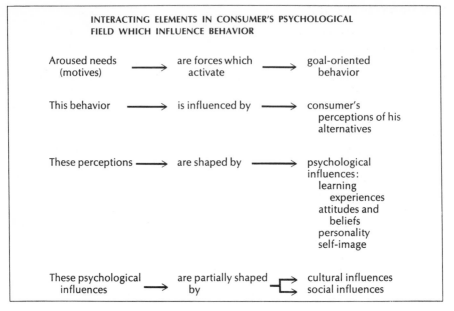

Figure 5-1

iological and psychogenic needs, which arise from psychological states of tension. Through the years marketers have used such dichotomous classifications of motives as instinctive-learned, product-patronage (why the consumer bought this *product* versus why she shopped at this *store*), and primary-selective (reasons for buying a *type* of product versus reasons for buying a certain *brand* of that product).

A. H. Maslow has formulated a useful theory of motivation. He calls it a "holistic-dynamic" theory in that it fuses the points of view of different schools of psychological thought and also conforms to known clinical, observational, and experimental facts.[12] Maslow identified a hierarchy of five levels of needs, arrayed in the order in which a person seeks to gratify them:

1. Physiological needs—for food, drink, sex, and shelter
2. Safety needs—for security, order, protection, and family stability
3. Belongingness and love needs—for affection, belonging to a group, and acceptance
4. Esteem needs—for self-respect, reputation, prestige, and status
5. Self-actualization needs—for self-fulfillment, for doing what one is best fitted for

For the relatively few people who move through the full array, even to fulfilling a need for self-actualization, Maslow identified two additional classes of cognitive needs:

1. The need to know and understand
2. The need for aesthetic satisfaction (beauty)

Maslow contended that a person theoretically remains at one level until all his needs at that level are satisfied. Then new needs emerge on the next higher level.

---

12 A. H. Maslow, *Motivation and Personality*, Harper & Row, Publishers, Inc., New York, 1954, pp. 80-106.

To illustrate, as long as a person is hungry, thirsty, etc., the physiological (biogenic) needs dominate. Once they are satisfied, the psychogenic needs in the safety category become important. When safety needs are largely gratified, new (and higher-level) needs arise, and so on.

In real life Maslow recognized that there is more flexibility than the rigid hierarchical model seems to imply. Actually a normal person is most likely to be working toward need satisfaction on several levels at the same time. And rarely are all needs on a given level ever fully satisfied.

While the Maslow construct has much to offer us, there are still some unanswered questions and disagreements. For one thing, there is no consideration of multiple motives for the same behavior. A teacher takes a ship's cruise to better her knowledge of foreign countries, to meet new people, and to rest her frazzled nerves. Other problems not fitting our model are (1) identical behavior by several people resulting from quite different motives and (2) quite different behavior resulting from identical motives.

PERCEPTION

Once a person is motivated, his goal-oriented behavior path will be influenced by his perceptions. Earlier we defined perception as the meaning we attribute, on the basis of past experiences, to stimuli as received through our five senses. A person's perceptions are shaped by three sets of influences: (1) the physical characteristics of the stimuli, (2) the relation of the stimuli to their surroundings (the gestalt field idea), and (3) conditions within the individual.

Our senses perceive the shape, color, sound, feel, and taste of stimuli, and our behavior is then influenced by these physical perceptions. Marketers must recognize that we are exposed to a tremendously large number of stimuli. Thus to gain a consumer's attention, a marketer must do something special. This is the principle behind the use of large ads, a novelty approach in advertising, and the use of color in a sea of black-and-white ads (or just the opposite—the use of a black-and-white ad in the midst of colored ads).

Each individual perceives a given stimulus within his own frame of reference. Factors within a person which influence his frame of reference include his learning experiences, attitudes, and personality and the way in which he views himself.

A continuous process of selectivity is going on as far as our perceptions are concerned. First, we are exposed only to a selective number of stimuli. We cannot read every magazine, visit all stores, or watch all TV programs. Then we perceive only part of what we are exposed to. We can read a newspaper and not notice a given ad, or we can watch a TV program and screen out the commercials. Then only part of what we selectively perceive do we retain. Finally, only part of what we selectively retain do we act upon.

There are many marketing implications in these selective processes.[13] From a marketing point of view, a product or service does not exist by itself, nor does it have any intrinsic meaning. A product exists in marketing only if a consumer perceives that it will satisfy his wants. Moreover, a given product will be perceived quite differently by different consumers. A child perceives a color TV set as a source of pleasurable entertainment; Mother views it as a baby-sitter, a source of informa-

---

13 Adapted in part from Harold H. Kassarjian and Thomas S. Robertson (eds.), *Perspectives in Consumer Behavior*, Scott, Foresman and Company, Glenview, Ill., 1968, pp. 58-59.

tion, and a teacher for her child; Father may view it as an overpriced luxury which prevented him from buying a new outboard motor (the old black-and-white set was perfectly OK as he perceived it); and to the retailer it is just another product carrying a lower gross margin than he thinks is reasonable. Then for countless other consumers this product simply does not exist; it has never entered their field of selective perception.

Marketers cannot afford unlimited advertising exposure, so they strive for the selective exposure which will fall within the target market range of selective perception. Then the message must be sufficiently meaningful and strong to survive the consumers' selective retention processes.

Learning experiences. As a factor influencing a person's perceptions, learning may be defined as changes in behavior resulting from previous experiences. However, also by definition, learning does *not* include behavior changes attributable to instinctive responses, growth, or temporary states of the organism such as hunger, fatigue, sleep, etc.[14]

The stimulus-response model, including reinforcement as an essential element, is an explanation of the learning process which is useful in marketing. Four factors—drive, cue, response, and reinforcement—are fundamental to the process.[15] A *drive* (or motive) is a strong stimulus for response action because it (the drive) requires satisfaction. A drive requires a response, but the *cues*—weaker stimuli—determine the pattern of this response—the "when" "where," and "how" of the behavior. For instance, a TV commercial, store hours, and a change in price are cues which might well shape a consumer's behavior as he seeks to satisfy an aroused need for some food item. Sometimes the cue itself serves to arouse a drive, as when a person passes an ice-cream shop and realizes he is thirsty or wants something sweet. His *response* is simply his behavioral reaction to the cues and the drive. *Reinforcement* is the result of a rewarding response-action.

If the response is gratifying, a connection between cue and response will be established; that is, a behavioral pattern will be learned. Learning, then, emerges from reinforcement. Continually rewarding responses lead to habit. Once a habitual pattern of behavior is established, it replaces conscious cognitive learning. The stronger the habit, i.e., the more set the reinforcement, the more difficult it is for a competitive product to enter a consumer's learning field. On the other hand, if the response-action is not appropriate (not rewarding), the consumer's mind is open to another set of cues leading to another response. For example, she will buy a substitute product type or switch to another brand.[16]

As we observed earlier, no general agreement exists regarding one basic learning process. Cognitive theorists would inject attitudes and beliefs into the learning model. They particularly would give weight to something other than past experience. They believe a person can use his insight or thinking abilities to understand a current problem situation even if there are no historical precedents.

---

14 For a discussion of other definitions of learning, see John F. Hall, *Psychology of Learning*, J. B. Lippincott Company, Philadelphia, 1966, pp. 3-6.

15 John Dollard and Neal E. Miller, *Personality and Psychotherapy*, McGraw-Hill Book Company, New York, 1950, chap. 3.

16 See Norman Kangun, "How Advertisers Can Use Learning Theory," *Business Horizons*, April, 1968, pp. 29-40; see also Sadaomi Oshikawa and John Wheatley, "Learning Theory, Attitudes, and Advertising," *University of Washington Business Review*, Summer, 1968, pp. 24-33.

Another approach holds that learning is a probabilistic process, under the assumption that the best predictor of future buying behavior is the sequence, rhythm, and frequency of past buying behavior.[17]

An interesting aspect of learning which has significant marketing implications is the question of whether learning can occur without awareness.[18] That is, can a person learn a new pattern of behavior without being aware that this behavior was influenced or changed? (Awareness is defined here as the conscious recognition of a behavioral stimulus. That is, a person consciously hears a TV commercial or is conscious of seeing a magazine ad. We should note that psychologists identify different levels of conscious and subconscious awareness of external stimuli.)

When awareness is defined in this manner, psychological theories and experimental findings both suggest that an individual may learn and behave without awareness. In other words, consumers perceive stimuli without being aware of them, and these unconsciously received stimuli might influence purchasing decisions. To illustrate, a person may buy a product, unaware that the real stimuli were some ads which he saw some time ago and which in his conscious mind he had forgotten about. Or during a TV commercial, he may engage in conversation, ignoring the commercial. Yet the message stimulus can make a subconscious impression which may lead to a purchase at some future time.

Attitudes and beliefs. Attitudes and beliefs are strong and direct forces affecting consumers' perceptions and buying behavior. They significantly influence a person's perceptions by selectively screening out any exposure of stimuli which conflict with his attitudes. Attitudes also can distort the perception of messages and affect the degree of their retention.

Beliefs may be categorized as knowledge, opinion, or faith, depending upon their verifiability.[19] To illustrate, if we believe that drinking milk is good for a growing child and we know on the basis of evidence that milk is beneficial, our belief has been verified. A belief is defined as knowledge if it can be, or has been, verified by personal experience or by outside-source research. An opinion is a belief which has not yet been verified. Faith is a belief which is unverifiable, and yet adhered to.

Attitudes may be defined as a person's enduring favorable or unfavorable cognitive evaluations, emotional feelings, or action tendencies toward some object or idea.[20] Attitudes thus involve thought processes as well as emotional feelings, and they vary in intensity. Attitudes influence beliefs, and beliefs influence attitudes. In fact, for the purposes of our generalized, introductory-level discussion of buying behavior, we shall use the two concepts interchangeably. They both reflect value judgments and positive or negative feelings toward a product, service, or brand.

Various studies uniformly report a very close relationship between consumers' attitudes and their buying decisions, as concerns both the type of product and the

---

17 Kassarjian and Robertson, *op. cit.*, p. 60; for a discussion and application of this approach, see Alfred A. Kuehn, "Consumer Brand Choice as a Learning Process,"*Journal of Advertising Research*, December, 1962, pp. 10-17.

18 This discussion is adapted from Sadaomi Oshikawa, "Learning and Behavior without Awareness: Their Implications to Consumer Behavior and Sovereignty," *California Management Review*, Summer, 1970, pp. 61-69.

19 This paragraph is adapted from Kassarjian and Robertson, *op. cit.*, pp. 60-61.

20 See David Krech, Richard S. Crutchfield, and Egerton L. Ballachey, *Individual in Society*, McGraw-Hill Book Company, New York, 1962, chap. 5; and Daniel Katz, "The Functional Approach to the Study of Attitudes," *Public Opinion Quarterly*, Summer, 1960, pp. 163-204.

brand selections. For many years the Survey Research Center at the University of Michigan has conducted studies of consumer buying intentions regarding *product types*. Consistently the results show that both buying intentions and actual purchases are influenced by consumers' attitudes; also, changes in buying are related to attitude change.[21] Studies of additional influence on *brand selection* show similar patterns. One study, for example, covering low-unit-price products (mostly food items), showed an extremely close relation between consumers' preferences (attitudes) and the brands they actually purchased.

Surely then it is in a marketer's best interests to understand how attitudes are formed, measured, and changed. They are formed, generally speaking, by the information a person acquires through (1) his past learning experiences with the product or idea, or (2) his relations with his reference groups (family, social and work groups, etc.). The perception of this information is influenced also by his personality traits.[22]

Attitude measurement is far from easy. In limited instances a researcher may simply employ the direct-question, survey research technique. Other studies lend themselves more to the projective technique, to be mentioned later in connection with motivation research. The most widely used techniques, however, have been some form of attitude scaling. Respondents may be asked, for instance, to rank their preferences when shown several models, designs, or materials. In another test the person might be shown several pairs of items, one at a time, and be asked to select which of the two she prefers (the paired-comparisons technique). Another technique is a rating scale where the respondent states her evaluation at some point, ranging from one extreme to another (extremely modern and extremely old-fashioned, for example).[23]

Given the hypothesis that attitudes strongly influence buying behavior, then the problem arises: how can a company bring its products and consumers' attitudes into a consonant state, that is, into a situation where a consumer perceives his need to be best satisfied by the given product or brand? A marketer has two choices— either he can change consumers' attitudes to be consonant with his product, or he can determine what consumers' attitudes are and then change his product to match those attitudes. Obviously, it is easier to change his product than to change consumers' attitudes. Nevertheless, attitudes sometimes can be modified, particularly in cases where this may be the only reasonable choice (as when a firm is introducing a truly new product or a quite unusual new use for an existing one).

Marketers should face the fact that it is *extremely* difficult to change consumers' attitudes, regardless of marketing critics' opinions to the contrary.[24] If there is to be a change, it is most likely to occur when a person is open-minded in his beliefs or

---

21 George Katona, *The Powerful Consumer*, McGraw-Hill Book Company, New York, 1960, especially pp. 52-53. For the suggestion that out of many possible attitudes, only a few really determine buying behavior, see James H. Myers and Mark I. Alpert, "Determinant Buying Attitudes: Meaning and Measurement," *Journal of Marketing*, October, 1968, pp. 13-20.

22 See Krech, Crutchfield, and Ballachey, *Op. cit.*, chap. 6.

23 For a discussion of some widely used scaling techniques, along with excellent footnote references, see James F. Engel, David T. Kollat, and Roger D. Blackwell, *Consumer Behavior*, 2d ed., Holt, Rinehart and Winston, Inc., New York, 1973, pp. 274-283; see also Myers and Reynolds, *op. cit.*, pp. 150-157, for a good discussion of attitude measurement.

24 This and the following paragraph are based on Engel, Kollat, and Blackwell, *op. cit.*, chaps. 10-11. These authors caution that much of the attitude-change theory and research so far does not have a lot of practical marketing applicability.

when an existing attitude is of weak intensity, that is, when there is little information to support the attitude or very little ego-involvement on the part of the individual. The stronger a person's brand loyalty is to a certain product, for example, the more difficult it is to change that attitude.

Highly persuasive communication is ordinarily needed if a seller is to have any hope of changing a buyer's attitude. The communication (advertisement, personal sales talk, etc.) should attempt to change one or more of the three dimensions in our definition of an attitude. By providing effective information about his brand, for example, a marketer might change the consumer's *cognitive evaluations* of that brand. With a strong, emotionally appealing ad, the seller might change the buyer's *emotional feelings.* The buyer's action *tendencies* toward a brand might be changed by getting him to do something which contradicts his current preferences. For instance, the use of coupons, free samples, or "cents-off" sales might induce the buyer to change his action patterns and try a new brand. Even then the buyer must be open-minded and willing to let his present brand preferences be challenged—no easy assignment for the seller.

Fear appeals. To induce a favorable consumer response (attitude change, decision to buy, etc.) typically a company will use a set of positive promotional appeals. These are appeals which stress the beneficial or desirable results from using the advertised item. However, management should recognize that negative, fear, anxiety-inducing appeals may very well be quite effective.[25] Negative or fear appeals warn the consumer about the bad consequences which will result from using (or *not* using, as the case may be) the advertised product or service. Thus the cancer society advertises the harm that can come from smoking. Insurance companies picture the terrible straits a family is left in when tragedy strikes and there is no insurance protection. People are warned about the dangers of combining drinking and driving. A person is pictured as a social outcast for not using the advertised brand of toothpaste, mouthwash, or deodorant.

Just how effective are these fear appeals in shaping consumers' attitudes and responses? One landmark study involving dental hygiene reported that a strong fear appeal was less effective than a mild or moderate fear appeal—that is, the stronger the fear appeal the less effective it was.[26] Other studies have concluded that fear appeals are likely to be more effective among nonusers and nonowners of a product than among users or owners.[27] Thus scare-advertising tactics regarding the harm from smoking have been more effective among nonsmokers or low-rate-of-use smokers than among heavy smokers. Possibly heavy users of a product become defensive and thus resist any appeal which suggests they are doing something wrong. One marketing implication in this situation is that fear motivation may be more effective in developing new markets than in selling to, or changing, entrenched ones.

---

25 See Michael L. Ray and William L. Wilkie, "Fear: The Potential of an Appeal Neglected by Marketing," *Journal of Marketing*, January, 1970, pp. 54-62.

26 Irving L. Janis and Seymour Feshbach, "Effects of Fear-Arousing Communications," *Journal of Abnormal and Social Psychology*, January, 1953, pp. 78-92.

27 For a report on the relative effectiveness of fear advertising on owners versus non-owners of life insurance, see John J. Wheatley, "Marketing and the Use of Fear- or Anxiety-Arousing Appeals," *Journal of Marketing*, April, 1971, pp. 62-64; also see John J. Wheatley and Sadaomi Oshikawa, "The Relationship between Anxiety and Positive and Negative Advertising Appeals," *Journal of Marketing Research*, February, 1970, pp. 85-89.

To reach users of a product, fear appeals may be effective in producing behavioral changes if "what is feared is damage to the *social image* of the self rather than to the physical self." Thus, in promoting safe driving, the appeal to "Watch out for that child" is more effective than "Watch out, or you'll be killed."[28]

On balance, the effectiveness of fear appeals seems limited. They have not resulted in any appreciable decrease in smoking, for instance. And traffic deaths did not decrease prior to the gas-shortage-induced lower speeds. But within its limits, fear appeals can be quite useful. It does seem unfortunate, however, that the ones who should respond the most to fear appeals (the heavy smokers or bad drivers) are likely to largely ignore or resist these appeals. And the people who need the admonition the least are the very ones likely to respond the strongest.

What are the ethical implications in the use of fear appeals? Is it a socially responsible approach? Again the answers are mixed, depending upon people's attitudes. Most people probably would agree that it is socially desirable to use fear appeals (or anything else) to discourage bad driving or the use of drugs. The nonsmoker market segment would agree it is appropriate to use fear appeals to discourage smoking. But when you get to the area of ads using fear appeals to sell personal grooming products, that is when the real arguments arise concerning the ethics of fear appeals.

Personality. The study of human personality has interested many (and sometimes widely divergent) schools of psychological thought for generations. Yet (and perhaps because of this multifaceted attention) we still lack even a consensus definition of the term. Attempts to inventory and classify personality traits have understandably produced many different structures. In this discussion *personality* is defined as an individual's pattern of inner and outer traits which are a determinant of his behavioral responses.

It is quite generally agreed that a consumer's personality traits will influence his perceptions and buying behavior. Unfortunately, however, in the present state of the art there is no agreement as to the nature of this relationship, i.e. *how* personality influences behavior. Two points of view prevail. One holds that personality traits are the dominant force in determining behavior, overpowering any external influences. The opposite contention, as advocated by many sociologists and social psychologists, is that the situational environment is the key determining factor; the individual (through his personality, perhaps) *adapts* to various external situations.

The empirical research support for each of these positions suggests they both have merit. Perhaps the answer lies in an approach which represents the *interaction* of the two, i.e., a blend of (1) the past-experience, individual-difference factor with (2) the external situational characteristics.[29]

Several research studies have been made in which the intent was to explain and predict buying behavior on the basis of personality traits as measured by standard personality testing systems. One group of these studies sought marketing applications for Riesman's social groupings of people. Riesman divided people into three groups: tradition-directed (oriented toward the past and resistant to change), inner-directed (guided by internal personal values), and other-directed (dependent

---

28 John R. Stuteville, "Psychic Defenses against High Fear Appeals: A Key Marketing Variable," *Journal of Marketing*, April, 1970, pp. 39-45, quote at p. 41.

29 Much of this discussion on personality is adapted from Engel, Kollat, and Blackwell, *op. cit.*, chap. 12.

upon other people for guidance).[30] Riesman hypothesized that other-directed people are susceptible to external social influences, and subsequent research supports this point. At this writing, however, the research is not sufficiently conclusive for marketers to apply Riesman's ideas in promotional or new-product marketing programs.

Another group of research studies tried to relate a person's personality traits and the ease with which he can be persuaded. Again the results were inconclusive. There is particularly an abundance of published research attempting to predict product, brand, and store choice on the basis of personality traits. Unfortunately, there are sufficient differences of opinions among the various results so as to make them inconclusive.

In summary, the situation regarding personality and buying behavior seems to be this—we are convinced that personality influences buying behavior, but we are not sure how. Current theory suggests that personality and environment interact to shape behavior. For each different environmental scene, a given set of personality traits will result in different behavior. Obviously, however, much additional research is needed.[31]

The self-concept. Another behavior determinant is a person's self-concept, or self-image. The self-image is the way a person sees himself, and at the same time it is the picture which he thinks others have of him. Some psychologists distinguish between a person's *actual* self-concept (the way a person really sees himself) and his *ideal* self-concept (the way a person wants to be or would like to see himself). To some extent, the self-image theory is a reflection of other psychological and sociological concepts already discussed. A person's self-image is influenced, for instance, by innate and learned physiological and psychological needs. It is conditioned also by economic factors, demographic factors, and social-group influences.

Studies of actual purchases show that people generally prefer brands and products which are more, rather than less, like their own self-concept.[32] There are mixed reports concerning the role of actual and ideal self-concept as an influence on brand and product preferences. Some psychologists contend that consumption preferences correspond to a person's actual self-image. Others hold that the ideal self-image is dominant in consumers' choices. Studies of prepurchase intentions report essentially the same results as in actual postpurchase reports. That is, when referring to intended future purchases, people still selected products and brands which matched either their actual or ideal self-concept.[33]

Consumers' self-images are not easy to identify, nor do they fall into sharply de-

---

30 David Riesman et al., *The Lonely Crowd,* Yale University Press, New Haven, Conn., 1950.

31 For a review of the state of the art in which we try to relate personality to buying behavior and other aspects of marketing, see Harold H. Kassarjian, "Personality and Consumer Behavior: A Review," *Journal of Marketing Research,* November, 1971, pp. 409-418. The author concludes that most studies show a weak relationship, or none at all, and then he suggests some reasons for these poor results.

32 See Ivan Ross, "Self-Concept and Brand Preference," *Journal of Business,* January, 1971, pp. 38-50. Also see Al E. Birdwell, "A Study of the Influence of Image Congruence on Consumer Choice," *Journal of Business,* January, 1968, pp. 76-88; Edward L. Grubb and Gregg Hupp, "Perception of Self, Generalized Stereotypes, and Brand Selection," *Journal of Marketing Research,* February, 1968, pp. 58-63; and Ira J. Dolich, "Congruence Relationships between Self Images and Brands," *Journal of Marketing Research,* February 1969, pp. 80-84.

33 See E. Laird Landon, Jr., "The Differential Role of Self-Concept and Ideal Self-Concept in Consumer Purchase Behavior," *Journal of Consumer Research,* Sept., 1974, pp. 44-51.

fined categories. A person's self-image is a complex thing and often consists of con-flicting elements. A secretary may see herself as a coolly efficient, highly effective, and valuable asset in a business organization, while at the same time considering herself a good mother, homemaker, and wife.

As marketing people, we want to be able to identify consumers' goals because they influence buying behavior. In many situations, we can determine these goals if we know what a person's self-image is. We must note, however, that a person's self-image tells us only what his goals are. This does not tell us *why* his self-image is as it is, nor does it explain why different people have different self-images. It is helpful just to understand that people do have different pictures of themselves. Our job is to determine what a person's self-image is. Then we can predict what his goals are and what his behavior is apt to be in the marketplace.

SUMMARY

Our model for discussing the determinants of buying behavior in the preceding sections is based on the assumption that this behavior is goal-oriented. The behav-ior is initiated when aroused needs (motives) create tensions which lead to activity designed to satisfy the needs and thus reduce the tensions. This goal-seeking be-havior is influenced by the individual's perceptions of the alternatives open to him. He is quite selective in the stimuli (ad, products, brands, stores) which he exposes himself to, retains, and acts upon. His perceptions, in turn, are influenced by his learning experiences, attitudes and beliefs, personality traits, and self-image and by environmental and social factors. These environmental and social forces are dis-cussed in the following chapter.

QUESTIONS AND PROBLEMS

1. Have your buying motives changed toward any products over a period of years? Name some products and trace the motivation changes, identifying the motives and explaining the reasons for the changes.
2. Explain how a company might apply the theory of marginal utility in the ad-vertising of:
   a. Children's blue jeans
   b. Automatic lawn-sprinkler systems for the home
   c. Vacation trip to Hawaii or the Caribbean.
3. Does the psychoanalytic theory of buyer behavior have any practical appli-cation in the marketing of:
   a. Eye shadow
   b. Electric dishwashers
   c. Outboard motor boats
   d. Portable, 9-inch-screen TV sets
      Explain your reasoning in each case.
4. Explain some of the "field" principles developed in gestalt psychology and describe some marketing applications of each of these principles.
5. Carefully distinguish between biogenic and psychogenic needs, and give examples of each.

6. Which needs in Maslow's hierarchy might be satisfied by each of the following products or services?
   a. Players cigarettes
   b. Travel agency located in your bank building
   c. *Webster's Intercollegiate Dictionary*
   d. Suntan lotion
   e. 1950 model Jaguar convertible selling for $100
   f. Services of a securities broker
   g. Portable cassette tape recorder
7. The following statements were taken from ads in magazines. Which, if any, of Maslow's needs are these products or services (as advertised) trying to satisfy?
   a. "That Maytag washer came to live with us over 14 years ago and it's only seen the repairman four times." (Clothes washing machine.)
   b. "Guaranteed to take from 1 to 3 inches off your waistline in just 3 days or your money refunded." (Sauna belt waistline reducer.)
   c. "How sweet it isn't." (Squirt—the semi-soft drink.)
   d. "Explore the marvelous mechanism that is THE BODY." (*Life* magazine's science library; book is entitled *The Body*.)
   e. "A diamond is forever." (DeBeers diamond mines; the company name is very obscure in this ad.)
8. Explain what is meant by the selectivity factors in perception.
9. Distinguish between *drives* and *cues* in the learning process.
10. Explain the relationship between consumers' attitudes and the brands they purchase.
11. What marketing strategies and tactics might be employed to change consumers' attitudes toward a product or a brand?
12. Is it ethical to use fear appeals in advertising?
13. Describe the differences you would expect to find in the self-images of an insurance salesman and a man working on a production line. Give some examples of resultant buying behavior. Assume that each has the same income.
14. Explain some practical marketing applications of the self-image theory.

MARKETS: CULTURAL AND SOCIAL-GROUP DETERMINANTS OF BUYER BEHAVIOR

The perceptual influences on behavior considered up to this point have focused primarily on the psychology of the individual. However, man is not an island unto himself. How he perceives things—how he thinks, believes, acts, etc.—is determined to a great extent by his cultural surroundings and by the various groups of people with whom he interrelates. In scope and numbers these social influences range from an entire culture down to the family or a close friend. See Fig. 6-1. For help in understanding these influences, marketing has drawn heavily from the fields of sociology and cultural anthropology.

CULTURE

Marketing practitioners and researchers have been predisposed to explain and predict buyer behavior generally on the bases of economic, psychological, and sociological influences. Unfortunately, we have made very little use of concepts in cultural anthropology, even though that field is concerned with man in his society.[1]

---

1 For a fine discussion of cultural value systems and their implications for marketing, see J. Allison Barnhill, "Marketing and Cultural Anthropology: A Conceptual Relationship," *University of Washington Business Review*, Autumn, 1967, pp. 73-84; see also Joseph F. Hair, Jr., and Rolph E. Anderson, "Culture, Accultura-

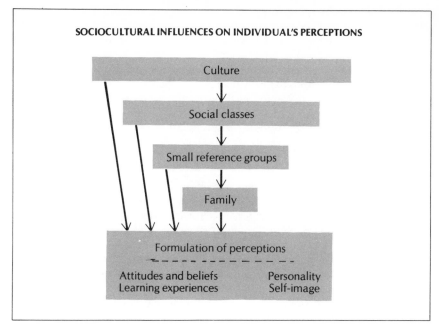

Figure 6-1.

DEFINITION AND CULTURAL INFLUENCE

Culture may be defined as the complex of symbols and artifacts created by man and handed down from generation to generation as determinants and regulators of human behavior in a given society. The symbols may be intangible (attitudes, ideas, beliefs, values, language, religion) or tangible (tools, housing, products, works of art). Culture is a totally learned and "handed-down" way of life. It does not include instinctive acts, although standards for performing instinctive biological acts (eating, bodily eliminations, sexual relationships) may be culturally established. Thus everybody gets hungry, but what we eat and how we act to satisfy the hunger drive will vary among cultures.

Actually much of our behavior is culturally determined. Our sociocultural institutions (family, schools, church, language, etc.) provide behavioral guidelines. Kluckhohn observed: "Culture . . . regulates our lives at every turn. From the moment we are born until we die there is constant conscious and unconscious pressure upon us to follow certain types of behavior that other men have created for us."[2]

Canadian culture is, as are the cultures of all "new" societies, an amalgam of the "old world". We have the two founding cultures or what have been termed charter groups—the French and the British.[3] These charter groups have throughout Cana-

tion and Consumer Behavior: An Empirical Study," in B. W. Becker and H. Becker (eds.), 1972 *Combined Proceedings*, American Marketing Association, Chicago, Series No. 34, 1973, pp. 423-428.

2 Clyde Kluckhohn, "The Concept of Culture," in Richard Kluckhohn (ed.), *Culture and Behavior*, The Free Press, New York, 1962, p. 26, as quoted in Barnhill, *op. cit.*, p. 84.

3 For a fuller discussion, see John Porter, *The Vertical Mosaic*, University of Toronto Press, Toronto, 1965, pp. 60-73.

dian history been contending over who should enter the country. The British charter group has usually been dominant and perhaps, of more importance, widely distributed throughout the country while the French have been concentrated. Thus outside the Province of Quebec but in an important part of Montreal, the pervasive ethic, established at an early period in terms of growth of the country, has been established by immigrants from the British Isles. It is the value system of this charter group that most immigrants coming to this country have encountered and which has shaped their adaptation and domestication. It was the behavior flowing from this ethic that was seen as appropriate for successful assimilation.

One component of Canadian culture, as well as of other modern Western societies, is a commitment to active mastery of the world to enhance standards of life.[4] There is a Canadian consensus for this and the means to this control are captured in such dictums as work harder to better yourself; idle hands are the devil's helpers; leisure is akin to laziness; be frugal. Hard work was rewarded with the obvious but not exclusive means to mastery—material well-being and wealth. The result for us has been a relatively high level of political, economic and social freedom. Immigrants of all types who have embraced and supported the standards of the dominant charter group have been rewarded with material and wealth.

There is a third charter group which we must consider, not because it founded the country and imposed its standards of culture but because we are importers of its culture by virtue of its proximity. American culture is as pervasive as that of the Canadian charter groups—perhaps more so over time. While Canadians value work, Americans prize activity in all spheres. Whereas Canadians believe in orderly change to achieve mastery, Americans value and encourage pragmatic change to the point where change becomes an end rather than a means to one. Within American society there is the espousal of equality and a facing of the problems such an espousal calls forth. In Canada we prize all these values as well, but in a characteristically Canadian muted manner. "The same values are valued but with much more hesitancy. This makes of excess itself a disvalue."[5] Yet while American values are reflected here but to a lesser degree, the American style of living provides a highly visible model for us—often at commuting distance or at least through the media. There are no great animosities that divide Americans and Canadians and the American style is easier, livelier, more daring, more outspoken and more varied than distant models from which our charter and other groups sprang. At the same time, the American model seems "unduly risky, precarious and unplanned."[6]

Marketing responds within the constraints of this cultural amalgam. Promotional appeals are geared to improving a person's material standard of living. When laborsaving devices are marketed, appeals stress getting hard work done but mechanically and thus freeing human energies for, say, the family. But some promotional appeals are too American—and they jangle us. Others are too muted, and although more congenial, they have no impact in our mixed cultural world. Still others are irrelevant in Quebec—be they too American or too Anglo-Canadian.

SUBCULTURES

Given the nature of Canadian culture, marketers should understand the concept of

---

4 Kaspar Naegele, "Canadian Society: Some Reflections" in Blishen, Jones, Naegele and Porter (Eds.), *Canadian Society*, The Macmillan Co. of Canada Ltd., Toronto, 1961, pp. 7-8.

5 *Ibid.*, pp. 26-27.
6 *Ibid.*, p. 36.

subcultures and analyze them as potentially profitable market segments. Any time there is a culture as heterogeneous as ours, there are bound to be significant subcultures based upon factors of race, nationality, religion, geographic location, age, urban-rural distribution, etc. Some of these were recognized in Chapter 4 when we analyzed the demographic market factors. Religion, for example, is a cultural factor which has significant marketing implications. Concentrations of Middle or Eastern Europeans in the Prairies provide a market for some products which would go unnoticed in Italian or French sections of Toronto or Montreal.

The sharpest subcultural differences are portrayed in behavioral differences between English- and French-Canadian communities on a country-wide basis, although to the urban dweller in Toronto or Montreal the acceptance (or ritual avoidance) of the obvious differences between a diversity of ethnic minorities is now a matter of course. As indicated in Chapter 4, marketing to French Canada involves considerably more than a cursory acknowledgement of ethnic differences.

THE CHANGING NATURE OF THE FRENCH-CANADIAN MARKET

French Canada, as a subculture, has been undergoing a revolution since the death of Maurice Duplessis in 1959. This cultural revolution—sometimes termed the 'Quiet Revolution'—has had a profound effect on the nature of the French-Canadian market. Prior to the political and social changes of the 'Quiet Revolution', Quebec had been:

> . . . a predominantly rural province with strong, nominally patriarchal, family units. The dominant overall institution was the Roman Catholic Church, which guided not only the educational system but, thanks to the power of its parish priests, much of the day-to-day life of the people. French Canada maintained and developed its traditional culture—of which the cornerstones were the Catholic religion and the French language—in relative isolation from the industrial and economic developments taking place in the United States, England, and English Canada. Ideologically it glorified its past, and spokesmen concerned themselves with the retour à la terre and la revanche des berceaux—the return to the land and the revenge of the cradle.
>
> English-French relationships, which have always been a basic dimension in French Canada, took a distinctive turn in the latter part of the nineteenth and twentieth centuries with the introduction of industry into Quebec by English-speaking outsiders. The symbiotic type relationship which developed did not displease the leaders of French Canada—the English needed workers and the French Canadians, with their high fertility rate and dwindling access to good farmland, welcomed the opportunities for more jobs. The French Canadians became the drawers of water and hewers of wood while the English controlled and managed industry and commerce. The language of communication between the two groups was English, with the bilingual French-Canadians serving as intermediaries."[7]

Since the beginnings of the Quiet Revolution, however, French-Canadians have taken major steps to preserve their cultural identity in the English-dominated North American society and to prevent the assimilation of French Canada into this society. The Quiet Revolution has been a modern, progressive movement which has been manifest in programs to preserve the French language, improved health

---

7. Frederick Elkin, *Rebels and Colleagues: Advertising and Social Change in French Canada*, McGill-Queen's University Press, Montreal, 1973, p. 3. Elkin's book is highly recommended as an excellent study of advertising as a vehicle for social change in French Canada before and during the Quiet Revolution.

and education programs, renewed interest in French-Canadian crafts and culture, and the confidence shown in Quebec's hosting of Expo '67 and the 1976 summer Olympics. As a movement, it has been exemplified in the slogan *Maîtres Chez Nous*—masters in our own house.

At the same time, there is evidence of other social change in French Canada which is of considerable interest to marketers. There is a suggestion of a diminishing role of the Church in French-Canadian life; a lesser role is being assigned to the family unit and women are playing a much larger role in the labor force; and there is a shift in the prestige attached to certain occupations. No longer do the traditional professions of the priesthood, law and medicine dominate the cultural hierarchy. A new middle class seems to be developing in French Canada which is less tradition-oriented, and more attuned to youth and business.[8]

One noticeable effect of the cultural change in French-Canada has been a marked decline in the fertility rate among Quebec women. The changing role of the women in French-Canadian society, increased education levels, reduced influence of the Church, and greater labor force participation on the part of women have caused the fertility rate (average number of births per woman) in Quebec to fall from 4.31 (the highest in Canada) in 1926, to 1.89 (by far the lowest in Canada) by 1971.[9]

DIFFERENCES IN CONSUMPTION BEHAVIOR

The differences in consumption behavior between English- and French-Canadians have been well documented. Certain products sell in much larger quantities in Quebec than in other provinces, while other products which sell well in English Canada are rarely purchased by French-Canadians. Some examples of differences in product preferences and buying behavior are:[10]

—there is a better acceptance in Quebec of premium priced products such as premium-grade gasoline and expensive liquors;

—French-Canadians spend more per capita on clothing, personal care items, tobacco and alcoholic beverages;

—the French-Canadian consumes more soft drinks, maple sugar, molasses, and candy per capita than does the English-Canadian;

—French-Canadians have much higher consumption rates for instant and decaffeinated coffee;

—French-Canadians watch more television and listen to radio more than do English-Canadians;

---

8 Bruce Mallen, "The French-Canadian Retail Customer: Changing? To What? So What?" *The Canadian Marketer*, Winter, 1975, p. 33.

9 Statistics Canada, *Population Projections for Canada and the Provinces: 1972-2001*, p. 37.

10 See Nariman K. Dhalla, *These Canadians: A Sourcebook of Marketing and Socio-economic Facts*, McGraw-Hill, Toronto, 1966, pp. 287-300; Frederick Elkin and Mary B. Hill, "Bicultural and Bilingual Adaptations in French Canada: The Example of Retail Advertising," *Canadian Review of Sociology and Anthropology*, August, 1965, pp. 132-148; M. Brisebois, "Marketing in Quebec," in W. H. Mahatoo, ed., *Marketing Research in Canada*, Thomas Nelson and Sons, Toronto, 1968, pp. 88-90; Bruce Mallen, "The Present State of Knowledge and Research in Marketing to the French-Canadian Market," in Donald N. Thompson and David S. R. Leighton, eds., *Canadian Marketing: Problems and Prospects*, Wiley, Toronto, 1973, pp. 100-101; and Jean-Charles Chebat and Georges Hénault, "The Cultural Behavior of Canadian Consumers," in Vishnu H. Kirpalani and Ronald H. Rotenberg, eds., *Cases and Readings in Marketing*, Holt, Rinehart & Winston of Canada Limited, Toronto, 1974, pp. 178-180.

—in Quebec, a much higher percentage of grocery sales is accounted for by independent grocers than in Ontario, where the retail food market is dominated by chain stores;

—French Canada's consumption of beer is 95 percent ale and 5 percent lager, as compared with 55 percent ale and 45 percent lager in Ontario;

—premiums and coupons are more popular in Quebec;

—French-Canadians buy more headache and cold remedies than do English-Canadians;

—in Quebec homes a full meal is generally served both at noon and in the evening.

In addition to examining these examples of specific product-related differences between English-Canadian and French-Canadian buying behavior, it might also be important for the marketer to get a more general overview of the differences in life style exhibited within the two cultures. An interesting study of life style differences between the two markets concluded that the French-Canadian female is:

—more oriented toward the home, the family, the children and the kitchen;
—more interested in baking and cooking and more negative toward convenience foods;
—more concerned about personal and home cleanliness, and more fashion and personal appearance conscious than her English counterpart;
—more price conscious;
—much more concerned about a number of social, political and consumer issues, including youth, liquor, drugs, big government, big business and the value of advertising;
—more religious, especially in feelings about the life hereafter;
—more security conscious and less prone to take risks;
—more positive toward television and less positive toward newspapers;
—more negative toward the use of credit in terms of bank borrowing and in terms of credit cards;
—able to be characterized by a set of values described as steady and consistent.[11]

FACTORS INFLUENCING FRENCH-ENGLISH CONSUMPTION DIFFERENCES

While it is relatively easy to determine where actual differences in consumption behavior exist between French- and English-Canadians, it is somewhat more difficult to identify reasons for the existence of such differences. And yet, it is important for marketers to have some understanding of the factors which contribute to these differences if they are to market effectively to both market segments.

A number of authors have pointed out that French-Canadians have a considerably lower per capita income than do English-Canadians, that they have lower average education levels, and that they are a much more rural population. These differences along income and other demographic lines might suggest that the differences in product purchase rates and shopping behavior between French-Canadians and English-Canadians may be attributable simply to demographic differences and that the consumption behavior of French-Canadians is really no different from that of English-Canadians of similar demographic characteristics. At least two studies have refuted this argument.

---

11 Douglas J. Tigert, "Can a Separate Marketing Strategy for French Canada be Justified: Profiling French Markets Through Life Style Analysis," in Thompson and Leighton, *Canadian Marketing: Problems and Prospects*, p. 128.

The first study indicated that consumption behavior was significantly different between Quebec and Ontario households when households of *similar size and income levels were compared.*[12] A more recent study found significant differences in household expenditure levels between English-Canadian and French-Canadian households for eight consumption expenditure categories after certain non-cultural differences (such as the rural-urban breakdown of the groups and stage of the family life cycle) between the two groups were controlled.[13] Such findings suggest that the consumption behavior differences between French- and English-Canadians are not attributable solely to demographic differences but, rather, are more likely explained by cultural differences.

Certain characteristics of the French-Canadian culture and directions in which that culture appears to be changing have been discussed earlier. The important message for the marketer is that French Canada is culturally distinctive from English Canada and that certain products, and other elements of the marketing mix, are perceived quite differently by the French-Canadian than they are by the English-Canadian. As has been suggested, the *function* and *meaning* of products sold to French Canada must be perceived by the French-Canadian culture as consistent with that culture.[14]

THE IMPACT OF CULTURAL DIFFERENCES ON MARKETING

The fact that French Canada represents a distinctively different culture from that found in English Canada requires that marketers who wish to be successful in the French-Canadian market develop unique marketing programs for this segment. There must be an appreciation of the fact that certain products will not be successful in French Canada simply because they are not appropriate to the French-Canadian life style and culture. In other cases, products which are successful in English Canada must be marketed differently in French Canada because the French-Canadian has a different perception of these products and the way in which they are used. It may be necessary for companies to develop new products or appropriate variations of existing products specifically for the French-Canadian market. Similarly, the retail buying behavior of French Canadians may necessitate the use of different channels of distribution in Quebec.

In the area of advertising, many national companies have encountered problems in reaching the French-Canadian market. Prior to and during the Quiet Revolution, the great majority of advertisements used by such companies in Quebec were first prepared in English and then translated into French, often with devastating results. Examples are numerous of advertisements containing English expressions and phrases which were translated literally into French only to find that the translated expression was meaningless or offensive to French Canadians. Prior to the late 1960s, much of the national advertising in Canada was prepared by English-Canadian advertising agencies (usually based in Toronto) which developed adver-

---

12 Kristian S. Palda, "A Comparison of Consumer Expenditures in Quebec and Ontario," *Canadian Journal of Economics and Political Science*, February, 1967, p. 26.

13 Dwight R. Thomas, "Culture and Consumption Behavior in English and French Canada," in Bent Stidsen, ed., *Marketing in the 1970s and Beyond*, Canadian Association of Administrative Sciences, Marketing Division, Edmonton, 1975, pp. 255-261.

14 C. R. McGoldrick, "The French-Canadian Consumer: The Past is Prologue," in M. D. Beckman and R. H. Evans, eds., *Marketing: A Canadian Perspective*, Prentice-Hall of Canada Limited, Scarborough, 1972, p. 91.

tisements for use in both English and French Canada. These agencies generally employed translators whose responsibility it was to translated the advertisements which had been developed by English Canadians for the English culture so that they might be used in the Quebec market. In many cases, literal translations were demanded and the end results were inappropriate for the French market.

The problems of advertising in French Canada go far beyond those of translating English to French. Even where the translation job is a good one and English expressions and slang are converted into expressions which are meaningful to French Canadians, the problem still remains that the basic approach to the advertisement is based in English-Canadian or even American culture. Many advertisements contain illustrations, themes, and representations of life styles which are quite appropriate in English Canada but quite inappropriate in Quebec. What is needed is that advertising which is to be directed to the French-Canadian market be planned from "scratch" with that market in mind. The advertising content must be consistent with the culture of the market and this requires that it be developed and written by French Canadians.

Recent years have seen a greater appreciation for this fact on the part of Canadian advertisers. During the 1960s, many large English-language advertising agencies in Canada established French departments which contained complete advertising staffs, rather than simply translators, and which developed advertising for French Canada. More importantly, since the early 1960s, there have been established in Quebec a number of highly successful French-language agencies. Many national advertisers now place their English-language advertising with an English-Canadian agency, but use a Montreal-based French-language agency to develop advertising for the French market.

In the packaging and labelling of consumer products there have also been recent developments which are important for marketing in French Canada. For many years, Canadian companies made no special effort to prepare product labels for use in French Canada, with the result that most of the products on the shelves of Quebec retail stores bore English labels. Since 1967, however, it has been a requirement of the Quebec government that all labels on food products sold in that province give at least equal prominence to the French language. Similarly, the federal government's Consumer Packaging and Labelling Act and its regulations now require that all label information on consumer products produced in Canada or imported into this country be conveyed in both English and French.

CULTURAL CHANGE

Contrary to what some young people may think, various aspects of culture do change over time as old patterns gradually give way to the new. Some of the new patterns come to us from those new to Canada. People newly arrived from Italy, Portugal, Trinidad, Hong Kong, Uganda, etc. all bring elements of culture, some of which are adapted into the larger society. Today the desire for more leisure time and the use of credit, for example, are increasingly accepted as cultural mores. Certainly the articulate younger generations in the 1970s are fostering cultural change. The 1970s have also seen the growth of the first mass market of affluent, educated adults in Canada. This factor is influencing consumer behavior and life styles in many ways.[15] Marketing executives must be alert to these changing patterns so that

---

15 See E. B. Weiss, "New Life Styles of 1975-1980 Will Throw Switch on Admen," *Advertising Age,* September 18, 1972, p. 61.

they can adjust their programs to be in step, or even a little ahead of the times.[16] We shall note a few of the changes which have significant marketing implications.

Changing role of women. One of the most dramatic occurrences in our society in recent years has been the changing role of women. The marketing impact of the growing number of working women was noted in Chapter 4. What is even more significant, however, are women's attempts to break from the traditional, and sometimes discriminatory, patterns which have stereotyped the male-female roles in families, jobs, recreation, social clubs, product use, and many other areas. Truly the "women's liberation movement" presents some real challenges to marketing in particular, as well as to business and society in general.[17]

Equally interesting and significant is the impact which the women's liberation movement has had on the blue-collar, working-class wives—a group which in general has been critical of women's liberation. A study conducted in the United States by the marketing research organization, Social Research, reported some dramatically changing attitudes among such American women.[18] The traditional triangle of husband-children-home has limited the blue-collar wives, but today these women are rejecting these limitations. Almost one-third of the women said they would not choose homemaking as a career if they could go back to being fifteen years old. The survey revealed a desire among the women for independence, fewer children, for a new interest in themselves as individuals, and a new interest in jobs and the community. The degree to which these changes have occurred in Canada is not clear but changes in this direction are apparent. It will be interesting to see how marketers react to the challenge and opportunities presented by the changing role of women in our society. What is apparent is that it is possible to go beyond unisex clothing.

Impulse buying. In recent years there has been a significant increase in impulse buying, that is, purchases made without much advance planning. A housewife may go to the grocery store with a mental note to buy meat and fruit. In the store she selects some fresh peaches because they look more appealing or are priced more attractively than the other kinds of fruit on display. She sees some cleansing tissue on the shelf and is reminded that she is running low on this item, so she buys two boxes. These are impulse purchases insofar as they were not necessarily preplanned at home.

In contrast to the patterns of many years ago, substantially more people embark on supermarket shopping trips today without a shopping list of specific items. Many items of clothing, drugs, cosmetics, toys, records, sports equipment, and other products are also bought on impulse.

Increases in disposable income and discretionary income have been major contributing factors to this trend. But when inflation is outstripping income increases, it can be expected that Canadian shoppers will resort more to preplanning in order to control their finances. The self-service method of retailing has also been both a cause and an effect of this behavior pattern.

---

16 See Lee Adler, "Cashing-in on the Cop-out: Cultural Change and Marketing Potential," *Business Horizons,* February, 1970, pp. 19-30.

17 See Andrew J. DuBrin and Eugene H. Fram, "Coping with Women's Lib," *Sales Management,* June 15, 1971, p. 20.

18 As reported in Rob Cuscaden, "Working-Class Wife Is 'Awakened Giant,' " *Denver Post,* Oct. 14, 1973, p. 35.

A key point to understand is that impulse buying is often done on a very rational basis.[19] Self-service, open-display selling has brought about a marketing situation wherein planning may be postponed until the buyer reaches the retail outlet.

Because of the trends in impulse buying, greater emphasis must be placed on promotional programs which get people into a store. Displays must be more appealing because the manufacturer's package must serve as a silent salesman. Manufacturers prefer distribution outlets which offer a consumer an opportunity to buy on impulse.[20] On the other hand, when consumers swing to more preplanning, products and brands should be promoted so that they are candidates for such planning.

Desire for conformity. Slowly but surely over the past century we have evolved from a nation of "rugged individualists" to one of conformists. This trend has been accelerated by the tremendous growth in suburban and high rise living, with its many look-alike housing and apartment developments. Another factor has been the rise of a managerial class working in lower and middle management for large- and medium-sized organizations. These executives often strive to follow the prescribed pattern of the "organization man" complete with "mod" clothing and hair styles. The fact that most families can afford national mass-communication media such as television and magazines is still another impetus toward conformity. Later in this chapter we shall consider some aspects of group influences on consumer buying behavior. In short, there is a strong drive to be accepted by the group and to be like others.

Importance of time. A frequently heard complaint in our society today is that "I don't have time" to do this or that. In our fast-paced way of living, time is becoming an increasingly precious commodity. This passion for time is coupled with an increasing consumer affluence which is taking some of the glitter from forms of ownership directed more to status than to use. The net result of this combination is a change in shopping patterns and the opening of vast new markets for personal services and products which conserve time and make it available for preferred uses—family outings, hobbies, etc. More use is being made of rentals and disposable or short-lived products to get jobs done and conserve time for other activities. The consumer's acceptance of time-oriented value systems is bound to have implications for many aspects of a company's marketing program.[21]

Increased leisure time. Canadian families are acquiring an increasing amount of leisure time from a shorter workweek, more and longer paid vacations, and laborsaving devices in the home. This trend has created a large market for goods and ser-

---

19 See Ronald P. Willett and David T. Kollat, "Customer Impulse Purchasing Behavior," *Journal of Marketing Research,* February, 1967, pp. 21-31.

20 For a discussion of the definitional and other problems which limit the practical usefulness of the concept of impulse buying, plus some recommendations to make the concept more useful in marketing decision making, see David T. Kollat and Ronald P. Willett, "Is Impulse Purchasing Really a Useful Concept for Marketing Decisions?" *Journal of Marketing,* January, 1969, pp. 79-83; also see Joseph S. D'Antoni, Jr., and Howard L. Shenson, "Impulse Buying Revisited: A Behavioral Typology," *Journal of Retailing,* Spring, 1973, pp. 63-76.

21 For a conceptual consideration of how time enters into consumers' product choices, see Philip B. Schary, "Consumption and the Problem of Time," *Journal of Marketing,* April, 1971, pp. 50-55.

vices such as travel, boating, photography, home swimming pools, musical instruments, outdoor furniture, commercial entertainment, and radio, television, and phonograph sets.

Leisure-market spending is an increasingly strong factor in total consumption. One note of alarm in this connection, however: In the Canadian economy it is not possible to continue increasing leisure time unless we have a corresponding increase in productivity. Otherwise there will be a decrease in disposable income and discretionary income which inflation will not be able to mask.

Leisure time is an influence on how, when, and where people buy. Some years ago the chairman of the board of one of the world's largest advertising agencies observed that leisure "is a dynamic influence in the character of today's living. It is not simply an attribute of modern life—it is a pervasive force in shaping it. Leisure is a cause." A five-day workweek, for example, permitted Canadians to move to the suburbs, and we have already noted some of the influence of this population shift. Now a developing trend toward the variable length of workday and workweek as well as fewer number of weeks worked can also be expected to have considerable impact on consumer life-styles and buying behavior. As a consequence of the increased leisure-time market, many companies have added greatly to the number and variety of their products. Product design and styling have been influenced by the "do-it-yourself" enthusiasts and by the expanded participation of amateurs in sports activities.[22]

Desire for convenience. As an outgrowth of the increase in discretionary purchasing power and the importance of time, there has been a substantial increase in the consumer's desire for convenience.[23] Several years ago, Charles G. Mortimer (then president and later chairman of the board of directors of the General Foods Corporation) pointed out the following ten kinds of convenience to be reckoned with in marketing.[24]

1. Form. Products must be available in a wide variety of forms. Thus drug products, for example, come in liquid, paste, syrup, powder, pill, or inhalant form.
2. Quantity or units. Goods must be offered in all sizes, quantities, or units desired by the consumer.
3. Time. Products must be available at any time the consumer wants them. This factor has stimulated the success of convenience stores (7-Eleven, Mac's Milk, Beckers, and others) which carry household necessities and which do most of their business when the supermarket is closed.
4. Place. Sellers must offer opportunities for consumers to shop in the most convenient locations possible. Historically, cities and other trading centers rose, in part at least, to satisfy this demand for convenience. Today the retail structure of cities is intertwined with consumer convenience. One student of the subject perceptibly sharpened the focus on place convenience by pointing out that when consumers make shopping de-

---

22 See A. H. Kizilbash and James E. Bell, "Workers' Life Styles and the Four Day Workweek: A Case Study," *Akron Business and Economic Review,* Spring, 1974, pp. 52-57; also see Milton Leontiades, "The Concept of Leisure," *Conference Board Record,* June, 1973, pp. 25-28.

23 See W. Thomas Anderson, Jr., "Identifying the Convenience-Oriented Consumer," *Journal of Marketing Research,* May, 1971, pp. 179-183; and same author, "Convenience Orientation and Consumption Behavior," *Journal of Retailing,* Fall, 1972, pp. 49-70.

24 Charles G. Mortimer, *The Creative Factor in Marketing,* General Foods Corporation, White Plains, N.Y., 1959, pp. 10-16. This is a reprint of the 1959 Parlin Memorial Lecture, an annual event sponsored by the Philadelphia chapter of the American Marketing Association.

cisions, they do so by balancing commodity costs and convenience costs.[25] *Commodity costs* are defined as the amount of money paid to the seller for the goods or services purchased. *Convenience costs* include expenditures of time, physical and nervous energy, and money (gasoline, parking, phone calls) necessary to obtain the goods or services. Furthermore, convenience costs are becoming an increasingly significant factor in determining where people will shop.

5. Packaging. Packages must be easy to find, open, use, and store.
6. Combination. Combination, or "packaging," convenience is also found in service industries. Insurance firms offer homeowners' combination policies, and the travel industry sells "packaged" tours.
7. Automation. Many consumers dream of a push-button home.
8. Credit. One of the most significant marketing developments in the past 30 years has been the tremendous increase in consumer credit. Years ago our heritage and the vivid memories of the Great Depression tended to place considerable emphasis on thrift. In recent years, during which incomes have risen and jobs have increased, a new psychology has enveloped the consumer. He wants to buy all kinds of products and services *now* and pay for them out of future income.
9. Selection. A seller must offer his products at convenient prices and in an assortment of colors, materials, or flavors.
10. Readiness. Virtually everything we buy today must be ready and easy to use.

Every major phase of a company's marketing program is affected by this craving for convenience. Product planning is influenced by the need for convenience in packaging, quantity, readiness, and selection. Pricing policies must be established in conformity with the demand for credit and with the costs of providing the various kinds of convenience. Advertising, display, and personal selling play a role in practically every phase.

Upgraded tastes and desire for elegance. For some years we have been in the midst of a cultural upgrading which is having a significant influence on marketing. This upgrading of living habits is being fostered by both economic forces (increased incomes) and social forces (improved education, extensive travel, and the influence of the mass-communications media). This new age of elegance, improved tastes, and gracious living is reflected in changing patterns of consumption and behavior on the part of consumers. There is a growing appreciation of art, music, literature, and drama; demand is increasing for gourmet foods, vintage wines, two homes, month-long vacations, period furniture, and art collections.

Concern for the environment. Our growing concern for our natural environment is a cultural factor significantly influencing business and marketing today. It seems that once a society acquires a reasonably high material standard of *living* they then turn to improving their standard of *life*. Consequently, our discontent with pollution and resource waste, coupled with resource shortages, has led to some significant changes in our life-styles. And, when our life-styles change, of course marketing is affected. Consumption patterns by both business and consumers changed rather abruptly when we encountered shortages in oil and some other commodities.

---

25 Eugene J. Kelley, "The Importance of Convenience in Consumer Purchasing," *Journal of Marketing*, July, 1958, pp. 34-38.

SOCIAL CLASS

Another determinant of a consumer's perceptions and buying behavior is the social class to which he belongs. Social classes do exist in Canada, and a person's buying behavior is more strongly influenced by the class to which he belongs, or to which he aspires, than by his income alone.[26] The idea of a social-class structure and the terms "upper," "middle," and "lower" class may cause some Canadians discomfort, but the sociologists who identified the class structure and the marketers who use it do not impute value judgments to it. We do not claim that the so-called upper class is superior to, or happier and better off than, the middle class. We do claim that Canadians at different class levels do live differently.

Some years ago W. Lloyd Warner and Paul Lunt directed a study in the United States which identified a six-class system within the social structure of a small town.[27] A person's placement in the structure was based on his type, not amount, of income and on his occupation, type of house, and area of residence within the community. Descriptions of the six classes and the estimated percentage of the Canadian population in each group are given below. The percentages are only approximations because they vary according to the city studied. The first three classes constitute the "quality market," and yet they include only about 12 percent of the population. Although we speak of Canada and the U.S. as middle-class societies, the real mass market (almost 75 percent) consists of the lower-middle and upper-lower groups.

1. The upper-upper class, about 1.5 percent, includes the "old families" in the community—the aristocracy of birth and inherited wealth. Usually they are second-or third-generation families, living graciously in large old homes in the best neighborhoods and displaying a sense of social responsibility.
2. The lower-upper class, about 2.0 percent, includes the "new rich" who are wealthy but who have not been accepted socially by the upper-upper families. See Fig. 6-2. This class includes the top executives, well-to-do doctors and lawyers, and owners of large businesses.
3. The upper-middle class, about 9 percent, is composed of the moderately successful business and professional men and owners of medium-sized companies. They are well educated and live well. Their strong drive for success is reflected in the husband's career, the wife's social participation, and their broad range of interests.
4. The lower-middle class, about 15 percent, is made up of the white-collar class of office workers, most salesmen, and owners of small businesses. This is the group striving for "respectability"—doing a good job, living in modest but well-cared-for homes, and saving for the children's college education. This class is the source of North America's moral code and aspirational system and is the most conforming, churchgoing part of the society.
5. The upper-lower class, about 55 percent, consists of the blue-collar class of factory workers, semiskilled workers, and the politicians and union leaders who would lose their power if they moved out of this class. Many earn good incomes, but they are oriented toward enjoying life on a day-to-day basis. They want to enjoy the comforts of life, but they are not striving to "keep up with the Joneses."

---

26 For a useful collection of papers on Canadian social class see J. E. Curtis and W. G. Scott, *Social Stratification: Canada* (Scarborough, Ont. Prentice-Hall Canada Ltd., 1973).

27 W. Lloyd Warner and Paul Lunt, *The Social Life of a Modern Community*, Yale University Press, New Haven, Conn., 1941; and W. Lloyd Warner, Marchia Meeker, and Kenneth Eels, *Social Class in America*, Science Research Associates, Inc., Chicago, 1949.

THE OLD RICH AND THE NEW RICH: SOME BEHAVIORAL DIFFERENCES

The new rich will carry a credit card; the old rich will use check or cash. The new rich will put their initials on their license plate; the old rich won't. The new rich—for example a lady on a trip down to the hair stylist—will sit in the back seat alone; the old rich will sit up front and chat with the chauffeur. The new rich will call the butler by his last name; the old rich by his first. The new rich will hole out all putts when golfing; the old rich will take anything under five feet. The new rich will wear wigs that look natural; the old rich, ones that are frankly false.

Figure 6-2. *Source:* Coleman McCarthy, "The Hard-core Rich," *The New Republic,* March 15, 1969, p. 14. Reprinted by permission of The New Republic, © 1969, Harrison-Blaine of New Jersey, Inc.

6. The lower-lower class, about 18 percent, includes unskilled workers, the chronically unemployed, unassimilated racial immigrants from other parts of the country, those frequently on welfare, and many inhabitants of slums. Classes above this one consider this group to be lazy, when often their only sin is being poor and uneducated.

In the U.S., the research division of the *Chicago Tribune* has conducted several studies of the relationships between social class, buying behavior, and consumers' perceptions of various products and types of stores. One of the *Tribune* studies in particular was a giant stride forward in this area. Done under Warner's guidance, the study was made in Chicago to determine whether his own analysis of social-class structure—developed from studies of small towns—also applied to a large metropolitan center.[28]

Three basic conclusions, highly significant for marketing, came out of the *Chicago Tribune* study. First, a social-class system is operative in large metropolitan markets and can be delineated. Substantial differences exist between classes with respect to their spending-saving behavior, the stores they patronize, the products they buy, and the brands they prefer. Furthermore, there is relatively little inter-class movement. Although our history is replete with examples of people rising to the heights from humble beginnings, and although hard-and-fast barriers between classes do not exist, the vast majority of people always remain within the boundaries of their own class tastes.

The second conclusion is that there are far-reaching psychological differences between classes. Some of the contrasting characteristics of middle and lower groups are listed in Fig. 6-3. The classes do not think in the same way. Thus they respond differently to a seller's marketing program, particularly his advertising. The supersophisticated, clever advertising in *Saturday Night, Toronto Calendar or Vancouver Life* is almost meaningless to lower-status people. This does not mean that they lack intelligence or wit, but only that they have different symbols of humor or art. Advertising must be believable by the class at which it is aimed. The reader must be able to identify himself with the people and the setting in the advertisement.

---

28 See Pierre D. Martineau, "Social Classes and Spending Behavior," *Journal of Marketing,* October, 1958, pp. 121-130.

The third conclusion is that consumption patterns are symbols of class membership, and class membership can be a more significant determinant of buyer behavior than is the amount of income. Traditionally, marketing people have relied on income as an index to buying behavior. With what we now know about social class,
however, we question the accuracy of this index. Today the bulk of the population
falls in the middle-income group. This group comprises not only white-collar
workers—traditional members of the middle class—but also skilled and semiskilled
blue-collar workers. These people are poles apart in their behavior, tastes, spending patterns, and aspirations. There is an old saying that a rich man is just a poor
man with money, and that given the same amount of money, a poor man would
behave exactly like a rich man. Studies of social-class structure have proved that
this statement is just not true.[29]

A word of caution, however—buying behavior may very well be different at the
various income levels within each social class or occupational group. A carpenter's
family with an income of $10,000 a year has consumption patterns different from
another carpenter's family where the annual income is $17,000. In this area of social
class and income perhaps a more useful basis for market segmentation is some
index which combines the two factors of occupation and income.[30]

Some of the points in the preceding paragraphs were illustrated by Coleman's
example of typical behavior in three families, each earning about $10,000 a year (in
1970 dollars), but each from a different social class.[31] There are quite significant
marketing implications in their differential behavior. An upper-middle-class family
in this income bracket—possibly a lawyer or college professor and his wife—is
likely to spend a relatively large share of its resources on a home in a prestige
neighborhood, expensive furniture, clothing from quality stores, and club member-
ships or cultural amusements. In comparison, a lower-middle-class family—that of
a salesman or diesel engineer, for example—probably has a better house, but not in
so fancy a neighborhood; more furniture and clothes, but not from name stores or
by top designers; and a much bigger savings account. Finally, the upper-lower
working-class family of a welder or truck driver has a smaller house in a less desirable neighborhood. However, this family will have a bigger, later-model car, more
kitchen appliances, and a bigger TV set. The man spends more on sports (hockey,
football, hunting, bowling, fishing).

The wives in these three families each have quite different goals, so there will be
differences in the stores they patronize, the magazines they read, the ads they notice, and the clothing and furniture they select. The upper-middle-class wife wants
to (1) shop in the "best" stores and (2) furnish her home as a testament to her fine
taste, paying attention to the dictates of the "best" magazines, interior decorators
in town, and the homes of other women in her class. The lower-middle-class wife
relies on medium-level shelter and service magazines and stores to furnish her

---

29 For the contention that ability to buy (income) is a better determinant of buyer behavior than is social
class (occupation), see James H. Myers, Roger R. Stanton, and Arne F. Haug, "Correlates of Buying Behavior: Social Class vs. Income," *Journal of Marketing*, October, 1971, pp. 8-15; and James H. Myers and John F.
Mount, "More on Social Class vs. Income as Correlates of Buying Behavior," *Journal of Marketing*, April,
1973, pp. 71-73; also see John W. Slocum, Jr., and H. Lee Mathews, "Social Class and Income as Indicators
of Consumer Credit Behavior," *Journal of Marketing*, April, 1970, pp. 69-74.

30 See William H. Peters, "Income and Occupation as Explanatory Variables: Their Power Combined vs.
Separate," *Journal of Business Research*, Summer, 1973, pp. 81-89.

31 Richard P. Coleman, "The Significance of Social Stratification in Selling," in Martin L. Bell (ed.), *Marketing: A Maturing Discipline*, American Marketing Association, Chicago, 1961, pp. 171-184.

PSYCHOLOGICAL DIFFERENCES BETWEEN TWO SOCIAL CLASSES

Middle class	Lower class
1. Pointed to the future	1. Pointed to the present and past
2. Viewpoint embraces a long expanse in time	2. Lives and thinks in a short expanse of time
3. More urban in identification	3. More rural in identification
4. Stresses rationality	4. Nonrational essentially
5. Has a well-structured sense of the universe	5. Has vague, unclear, and unstructured sense of the world
6. Horizons vastly extended or not limited	6. Horizons sharply defined and limited
7. Greater sense of choice making	7. Limited sense of choice making
8. Self-confident, willing to take risks	8. Very much concerned with security
9. Immaterial and abstract in his thinking	9. Concrete and perceptive in his thinking
10. Sees himself tied to national happenings	10. World revolves around family and self

Figure 6-3. There are many exceptions to this picture of class attitudes. For instance, can you think of a lower-class person (in terms of income and social status) who has middle-class attitudes? Are there enough exceptions to these patterns to render them invalid in planning marketing campaigns? Source: Pierre D. Martineau, "Social Classes and Spending Behavior," *Journal of Marketing,* October, 1958, p. 129.

home so that it is "pretty" enough to suit her and win praise from friends and neighbors. The upper-lower-class housewife first wants a kitchen full of appliances before she worries about any other room. In the coming years it will be interesting to see how much the changing role of women (as noted earlier in this chapter) will alter the behavior patterns discussed in this paragraph.

The concept of social class is most useful in interpreting buying behavior only when the concept is applied in a sophisticated, realistic, and sometimes subtle fashion. There is a risk that the concept may be misunderstood or oversimplified, and thus misused. It does not possess universal applicability. Consequently, a marketing executive needs to understand when and in what ways a social-class stratification is significant in marketing and, conversely, what its limitations of application are. Some products—air conditioners and children's playclothes, for instance—are classless. That is, social class is relevant only to the extent that it is correlated with income.

SMALL REFERENCE GROUPS

Small-group influence on buyer behavior introduces to marketing the concept of reference-group theory, which we borrowed from sociology. A *reference group* may be defined as a group of people who influence a person's attitudes, opinions, and values. A reference group's standards of behavior serve as guides or "frames of reference" for the individual. The reference-group concept may be applied to the full range of social influences from the total culture down to the family. However, the concept was originally developed in connection with small groups.

Reference-group theory is also related to the psychology of imitation.[32] Much of a person's learning is imitative learning, especially at early ages. A child, for example, learns by imitation the different vocational and occupational roles when he is given toy models which imitate the work done by his mother or father. As children grow up, they adopt by imitation certain models of behavior. How many of us have listened to parents saying, "Johnny, why can't you do this or that like the other kids do?" Or, Johnny wails, "All the other kids can do that, why can't I?"

When children observe the behavior in a model, the degree to which the model's behavior is imitated depends upon the response consequences to the model. That is, does the model's behavior meet with reward or punishment? If the children observe reward, they are more likely to imitate than is the case when the model is punished.

A consumer's behavior is influenced by the variety of small groups to which he belongs, or aspires to belong. These groups may include family, fraternal organizations, labor unions, church groups, athletic teams, or a circle of close friends or neighbors. Each group develops its own set of attitudes and beliefs which serve as norms for members' behavior. The members share these values and are expected to conform to the group's normative behavioral patterns.

A person may agree with all the standards set by the group or only part of them. A Conservative or NDP supporter may not agree with all the political views of his local riding organization. Also, a person does not have to belong to a group to be influenced by it. Youths frequently pattern their dress and other behavior after that of an older-aged group which the younger ones aspire to join. Another point is that some reference groups serve as negative influences on a person. He relates to them by doing the opposite of what they recommend. The seizing of certain magazines by police officers or X-rating a movie will often increase the magazine's sales or the movie's attendance.

The behavioral norms set by a reference group may or may not be enforced with penalties for nonconformity. In some instances the norms serve simply as informational guidelines, telling a consumer what is going on, but he can still "do his own thing." A person visits a ski slope and observes what kind of equipment and clothing is being used, but he may or may not buy what seem to be the popular styles. In other cases, failure to follow the norms can result in a penalty—a ticket for speeding or expulsion from the group, for example. In general, however, small groups do tend to exert pressure on their members to conform to the particular group's standards and behavioral patterns.

The type of social group which has the most direct influence on a consumer's buying behavior is the small group in which each member normally can interact with every other member on a face-to-face basis—a family, a circle of friends, a local fraternity chapter, neighbors, an athletic team, or a small garden club, for example. Studies have shown that informal personal advice in face-to-face groups is much more effective as a behavioral determinant than advertising in newspapers, TV, or

---

32 See Albert Bandura and Richard H. Walters, "The Role of Imitation," *Social Learning and Personality Development,* Holt, Rinehart and Winston, Inc., New York, 1963, chap. 2.

other mass media. That is, when it comes to selecting some products or changing brands, prospective buyers are more likely to be influenced by word-of-mouth advertising from satisfied customers in the group. This is true especially when the speaker is respected as an opinion leader regarding the particular product.[33]

Another useful finding pertained to the flow of information between and within groups. For years marketing men have operated in conformity with the "snob appeal" theory—the idea that if they could get social leaders and high-income groups to use their products, the mass market would also buy them. The assumption has been that influence follows a vertical path, starting at levels of high status or prestige and moving downward through successive levels of groups. Contrary to this popular assumption, studies by Katz and Lazarsfeld, and by others, have pointed up the *horizontal* nature of opinion leadership. Influence emerges on each level of the socioeconomic scale and permeates a given area wherein the opinion leader is dealing with his peers.[34]

The proved role of face-to-face groups as behavior determinants for some products, plus the concept of horizontal information flow, suggests that a marketing person is faced with two key problems: (1) that of identifying the relevant reference group likely to be used by consumers in a given buying situation and (2) that of measuring the extent of the group's influence on these consumers. Then the marketing strategy should focus on identifying and communicating with two key people in the group—the innovator (early buyer) and the influential person (opinion leader). (The adoption and diffusion of new products are discussed in the next section.) Each group has a leader—a tastemaker, or opinion leader—who influences the decision making of others in the group. The key here is for the seller to convince that person of the value of his product or service. The opinion leader in one group may be an opinion follower in another. The mother of a family may be influential in matters concerning food, whereas unmarried women are more apt to influence fashions in clothing and makeup.[35]

The effectiveness of small reference groups as behavioral influences will vary depending upon the product and the availability of information for the consumer. The less information or experience a person has concerning a given product, the stronger the reference-group influence will be for this product. As far as the product itself is concerned, reference-group influence is the strongest when the product is most conspicuous. There are two aspects of conspicuousness in this context: First, the product must be such that it can be seen and identified by others, and sec-

---

33 See John R. Stuteville, "The Buyer as a Salesman," *Journal of Marketing*, July, 1968, pp. 14-18; Ernest Dichter, "How Word-of-mouth Advertising Works," *Harvard Business Review*, November-December, 1966, pp. 147-166; and William H. Whyte, Jr., "The Web of Word of Mouth," *Fortune*, November, 1954, p. 140.

34 See Elihu Katz and Paul Lazarsfeld, *Personal Influence*, Free Press, New York, 1955, especially p. 325; see also Elihu Katz, "The Two-step Flow of Communictaions: An Up-to-date Report on an Hypothesis," *Public Opinion Quarterly*, Spring, 1957, pp. 61-78. For later empirical data supporting the horizontal-flow hypothesis ("trickle across"), see Charles W. King, "Fashion Adoption: A Rebuttal to the 'Trickle Down' Theory," in Stephen A. Greyser (ed.), *Toward Scientific Marketing*, American Marketing Association, Chicago, 1964, pp. 108-125.

35 See Charles W. King and John O. Summers, "Overlap of Opinion Leadership across Consumer Product Categories," *Journal of Marketing Research*, February, 1970, pp. 43-50; John O. Summers, "The Identity of Women's Clothing Fashion Opinion Leaders," *Journal of Marketing Research*, May, 1970, pp. 178-185; William R. Darden and Fred D. Reynolds, "Predicting Opinion Leadership for Men's Apparel Fashions," *Journal of Marketing Research*, August, 1972, pp. 324-328; and Reynolds and Darden, "Predicting Opinion Leadership for Women's Clothing Fashions," in B. W. Becker and H. Becker (eds.), 1972 *Combined Proceedings*, American Marketing Association, Chicago, Series No. 34, 1973, pp. 434-438.

REFERENCE-GROUP INFLUENCE ON BUYING DECISIONS

Weak —   Reference group influence relatively: Strong +

Strong +	Clothing Furniture Magazines	Cars* Cigarettes* Beer (premium vs. regular)	+
Reference group	Refrigerator (type) Toilet soap	Drugs*	Brand or
influence relatively:	Soap Canned peaches Laundry soap Refrigerator (brand)	Air conditioners* Instant coffee* TV (black & white)	Type
Weak —	Radios		
	—	Product	+

* Based on experimental evidence; other classifications are researchers' opinions.

Figure 6-4. Products and brands are classified by the extent to which reference groups influence their purchases. Reference groups influence the decision to buy an air conditioner, but the choice of brand is left up to the consumer. *Source: Group Influences in Marketing and Public Relations,* Foundation for Research on Human Behavior, Ann Arbor, Mich., 1956, p. 8, citing a research study by the Bureau of Applied Social Research, Columbia University.

ond, it must stand out and be noticed. If many people own the product, even though it can be seen and identified, it is not conspicuous in the second sense of the term.[36]

The possible susceptibility of products and brands to reference-group influence is illustrated in Fig. 6-4. According to this model, a particular item might be susceptible to group influence in three different ways, corresponding to three of the four cells. In the upper right-hand cell (product plus, brand plus) the reference-group influence is felt in both the product and the brand. Cars are socially conspicuous as to both product and brand. Cigarette brands cannot easily be differentiated, but advertising has created certain images with reference-group appeal.

In the lower right-hand cell (product plus, brand minus) the use of the product is socially conspicuous, but the particular brand is not important from a reference-group standpoint. In the upper left-hand cell (product minus, brand plus) we find that the product is not significant, but the brand is. That is, most people own the products (clothing, furniture, etc.), so they are not socially conspicuous. However, the styles, brands, and types of clothing or furniture are visible and quite susceptible to social influence. Purchasing behavior for items in the lower left-hand cell (product minus, brand minus) is influenced by product attributes, and usually not by any reference group.

Assuming that a product or brand can be placed in its proper cell, Bourne cites some practical marketing implications. When neither the product nor the brand seems subject to reference-group influence, the seller's advertising should stress

---

36 This paragraph and the remainder of the discussion on small groups is based on Francis S. Bourne, "Group Influence in Marketing and Public Relations," in Rensis Likert and Samuel P. Hayes, Jr., (eds.), *Some Applications of Behavioral Research,* UNESCO, Paris, 1957, chap. 6; or see the same report originally published by Foundation for Research on Human Behavior, Ann Arbor, Mich., 1956.

product attributes, price, quality, and competitive differential advantages. On the other hand, if reference-group influence does exist, the advertising should stress the kinds of people who buy and use the product or brand. Here it becomes important first to identify the appropriate reference group, and then to reinforce any existing stereotype of users in that group.

NEW-PRODUCT ADOPTION PROCESS AND THE DIFFUSION OF INNOVATION

The process by which a new product is adopted, and the diffusion of that innovation through a group of people, is a logical extension or application of reference-group theory. (By definition, an *innovation* is anything—product, service, idea—which is perceived by a person as being new; the *adoption process* is the decision-making activity of an *individual* involving his acceptance of an innovation; the *diffusion* of innovation is the process by which the innovation is communicated within social systems over time.)

An extensive bibliography exists on these processes, indicating something of the interest in the field.[37] Research activity in adoption and diffusion has extended through many academic disciplines—rural and medical sociology, economics, anthropology, education, and communication, to name just a few. Today the research is emerging in the fields of marketing and consumer behavior. A preponderance of diffusion research has been conducted by rural sociologists dealing with new farming practices and products. A great deal of it has also been carried out in developing countries with the aim of increasing crop yields. This is a reflection of (1) the financial support of various agencies around the world, (2) the ease of identifying and isolating the farmer as a market segment for controlled study, and (3) the socioeconomic importance of farming. Many of the findings and concepts developed in rural sociology research, however, are often applicable to other products and disciplines.[38]

STAGES IN DECISION-MAKING PROCESS

We can identify six separate mental stages which a prospective user goes through in the process of deciding whether or not to adopt something new. First is the *awareness* stage, in which the individual is exposed to the innovation, but knows very little about it. Next is the *interest-information* stage, in which the prospect becomes interested enough to actively seek considerable specific information about the new concept.

In the third stage—*evaluation*—the prospect mentally measures the relative merits of the innovation; this is sort of a mental "test market." Then in the next

---

37 For some foundations of diffusion theory, a review of landmark studies on diffusion of innovation, and extensive bibliographical references, see Everett M. Rogers and F. Floyd Shoemaker, *Communication of Innovations,* 2d ed., The Free Press, New York, 1971.

38 For some insights into the adoption and diffusion processes for industrial products, see Frederick E. Webster, Jr., "New Product Adoption in Industrial Markets: A Framework for Analysis," *Journal of Marketing,* July, 1969, pp. 35-39; Urban B. Ozanne and Gilbert A. Churchill, Jr., "Five Dimensions of the Industrial Adoption Process," *Journal of Marketing Research,* August, 1971, pp. 322-328; and John A. Martilla, "Word-of-Mouth Communications in the Industrial Adoption Process," *Journal of Marketing Research,* May, 1971, pp. 173-178.

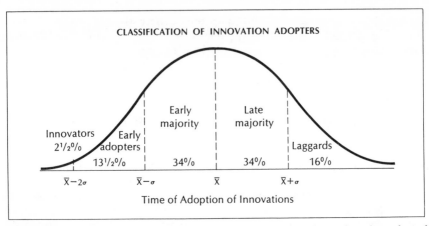

Figure 6-5. Studies show that the distribution of adopters (based on when they adopted the innovation) generally follows the normal curve. Thus, the area lying to the left of the arithmetic means ($\overline{X}$) minus one standard deviation (σ) includes 16 percent of the people adopting an innovation—the "innovators" and the "early adopters." *Source:* Everett M. Rogers and F. Floyd Shoemaker, *Communication of Innovations*, 2d ed., The Free Press, New York, 1971, p. 182.

step—the *trial* stage—the person actually adopts the innovation on a limited basis. Thus a consumer buys a small sample of a product, or a farmer tries a small can of weed killer in his garden before using it broad cast in a large field. If for some reason (cost or physical size, for example) an innovation cannot be sampled, the likelihood of its being adopted will decline.

The fifth stage is the *adoption* stage, in which the individual decides whether or not to use the innovation on a full-scale basis. If the innovation is adopted, the user goes through still another stage, that of *postadoption confirmation,* in which he continues to seek assurance that he made the right decision.

ADOPTER CATEGORIES

Some people will adopt an innovation quickly after it is introduced. Others will delay for some time before accepting the new product, while still others may never adopt it. Drawing from a number of studies in the diffusion of innovation, researchers have identified five categories of individuals, based on the relative time when they adopted a given innovation. Figure 6-5 illustrates the distribution of adopters. The categories are rather arbitrarily partitioned to represent unit standard deviations from the average time of adoption.[39]

Some of the key differences between the early and late half of the adopters are summarized in Fig. 6-6. Understanding these differences can be useful to marketing people when they are planning the advertising and personal selling programs for a new product.

---

39 Rogers and Shoemaker, *op. cit.*, chap. 5. Unfortunately, there are no general accepted standard criteria for classifying adopters into categories. Nor have researchers agreed upon one set of category titles. Also, nonadopters are excluded in our categorization.

DIFFERENCES IN CHARACTERISTICS OF EARLY- AND LATE-ADOPTER CATEGORIES		
	Adopters	
Categories with key feature	Early	Late
	Innovators: venturesome Early adopters: respected Early majority: deliberate	Late majority: skeptical Laggards: tradition- bound
Other characteristics		
Age	Younger	Older
Education	Well educated	Less educated
Income	Higher	Lower

Social relationships:
  Within or outside
  community
	Innovators: cosmopolites
	Others: more localites
		Totally local

Social status	Higher	Lower

Their information
  sources
	Wider variety; many
	  media
		Limited media expo-
		  sure; limited reliance
		  on outside media;
		  rely on local peer
		  groups

Figure 6-6.

Innovators. This *venturesome* group, which includes about 3 percent of the market, is the first to adopt an innovation and is most willing to accept the attendant risks. In relation to later adopters, the innovators are likely to be younger, have a higher social status, and be in a better financial position. Innovators also tend to have broader, more cosmopolitan social relationships. An innovator is likely to rely more on impersonal sources of information, including those external to his own social system, rather than using personal salesmen or other word-of-mouth sources.[40]

Early adopters. This group—about 13 percent of the market—tends to be a more integrated part of local social system; that is, whereas innovators are cosmopolites, early adopters are localites. Thus the early-adopter category includes more opinion leaders than any other adopter group. Early adopters are much *respected* in their social system. The "agents of change" who are seeking to speed up the diffusion of a given innovation will often try to work through the early adopters because they are not too far ahead of others in their peer group. Personal salesmen are probably used more by the early adopters than by any other category.

Early adopters, in contrast to later adopters, tend to be younger, better educated, more creative, and more mobile. They are involved in a range of community activities and tend to hold elected positions of leadership.

---

40 See Roman R. Andrus, John Knutsen, and Kenneth Uhl, "The Shopping Behavior of 'Innovators,'" *University of Washington Business Review*, Summer, 1971, pp. 71-75; and Louis E. Boone, "The Search for the Consumer Innovator," *Journal of Business*, April, 1970, pp. 135-40.

Business firms in both the innovator and the early-adopter categories are usually large and specialized in their operations.[41]

Early majority. This more *deliberate* group, representing about 34 percent of the market, tends to accept an innovation just before the "average" adopter in a social system. This group is a bit above average in social and economic measures. The members rely quite a bit on advertisements, salesmen, and contact with early adopters. Business firms in this category are average-sized operations.

Late majority. Representing about another 34 percent of the market, the late majority is a *skeptical* group. Usually they adopt an innovation in response to an economic necessity or to social pressure from their peers. They rely on their peers—late or early majority—for sources of information; advertising and personal selling are less effective.

This group is older, less well educated, and below average in social and economic status; it does not contain many opinion leaders. Business firms in this category tend to be small and nonspecialized.

Laggards. This *tradition-bound* group—16 percent of the market—includes those who are the last to adopt an innovation. Their point of reference is what was done in the past, and they tend to interact with those holding similar values. Laggards are suspicious of innovations and innovators. Much time elapses between the awareness stage and the final adoption of an idea. By the time laggards adopt something new, it may already have been discarded by the innovator group in favor of a newer idea. Laggards are older and are at the low end of the social and economic scales. Businesses in this group tend to be the smallest and have the lowest degree of specialization.[42]

CHARACTERISTICS OF INNOVATIONS AFFECTING ADOPTION RATE

The rate of adoption for a given innovation may range from a few weeks to several decades. There are five characteristics of an innovation, as perceived by individuals, which seem to influence the adoption rate.[43] One is *relative advantage*—the degree to which an innovation is superior to preceding ideas. Relative advantage may be reflected in lower costs, higher profitability, or some other measure. Another characteristic is *compatibility*—the degree to which an innovation is consistent with the cultural values and experiences of the adopters. Some electric appliances would find little market acceptance in some South American countries, not only because of widespread lack of electric power, but also because in terms of the value systems of the people, they would be rejected as an extravagance.

The degree *of complexity* of an innovation will affect its adoption rate. The fourth characteristic—*trialability*—is the degree to which the new idea may be sampled on

---

41 See David W. Cravens, James C. Cotham III, and James R. Felix, "Identifying Innovator and Non-Innovator Retail Firms," *Southern Journal of Business*, April, 1971, pp. 45-50; and Lyman C. Ostlund, "Identifying Early Buyers," *Journal of Advertising Research*, April, 1972, pp. 25-30.

42 See Kenneth Uhl, Roman Andrus, and Lance Poulsen, "How Are Laggards Different? An Empirical Inquiry," *Journal of Marketing Research*, February, 1970, pp. 51-54.

43 Rogers and Shoemaker, *op. cit.*, chap. 4.

some limited basis. On this point, a central home air-conditioning system is likely to have a slower adoption rate than some new seed or fertilizer, which may be tried on a small plot of ground. Finally, the *observability* of the innovation affects its adoption rate. A weed killer which works on existing weeds will be accepted sooner than a preemergent weed killer because in the latter case—even though it may be a superior product—there are no dead weeds to show to prospective adopters.

MARKETING IMPLICATIONS

From an understanding of diffusion theory an executive can develop many useful guidelines for his company's marketing effort. In its promotional program, for instance, it is important (while admittedly difficult) that a company be able to identify, and then communicate with, the early-adopter category of consumers. This market segment includes the greatest share of opinion leaders. Other consumers, in their respect for early adopters, look to them for information, advice, and assurance. Management probably should devote little, if any, promotional or other marketing effort to the laggard market segment because of the socioeconomic nature of the group and the fact that it looks to other laggards for information.

Looking at the product characteristics which affect the adoption rate, the product should be designed in divisible form so that it can be evaluated on a sample basis. If this is physically impossible, as with an automobile or an air conditioner, then the consumer should be able to use the product on a trial basis before having to make an adoption decision. Management should design products which minimize the complexity factor or which make obvious the product's compatibility or relative advantage. Then the advertising and personal selling effort should stress these features. Or if the product really is complex, the promotional program and product-servicing facilities must counteract this limitation.

FAMILY BUYING BEHAVIOR

Of all the small groups an individual belongs to through the years, ordinarily his family is the one which has the strongest and most enduring influence on his perceptions and behavior. For many products, the family, or at least the husband and wife, operates as a buying unit.

WHO DOES THE FAMILY BUYING?

A marketer should treat this question as four separate ones because each one may affect different segments of his marketing program and require different strategies and tactics: (1) Who influences the buying decision (this may be a member of the family, or the influence may come from an outside reference group)? (2) Who makes the buying decision? (3) Who makes the physical purchase? (4) Who uses the product? Four different people may be involved, only one member may do all four, or some other combination may be the case. Also, a user today may be the influencer, decider, and/or purchaser when the present product is used up.

For many years women have done most of the family buying. They still exert substantial influence in buying decisions and do a considerable amount of the actual purchasing, but men have increasingly entered the family buying picture. Self-service stores are especially appealing to men. Night openings and suburban shopping centers also encourage men to play a bigger role in family purchasing.

In recent years teen-agers and young children have become decision makers in family buying as well as actual purchasers. The amount of money teen-agers now have is substantial enough to be considered in the marketing plans of many manufacturers and middlemen. Even very young children are an influence in buying decisions today because they watch television programs or shop with their parents.

Purchasing decisions are often made jointly by husband and wife (sometimes even the children are included).[44] Young married people are much more apt to make buying decisions on a joint basis than older couples. Apparently the longer a husband and wife live together, the more they feel they can trust each other to act unilaterally. In many cases, decisions regarding savings, life insurance, vacations, housing, food, and the handling of money and bills are made jointly.

Who buys a product will influence a firm's marketing policies regarding its product, channels of distribution, and promotion. If children are the key decision makers, as is often the case in cereals, for instance, then the manufacturer may include some type of cutout toy or other premium with the product. In a department store—traditionally considered a woman's store—the men's furnishings department is often located on the street floor near a door. Then the man can enter, shop, and leave the store without having to wade through crowds of women shoppers. The entire advertising campaign—media, appeals, copy, radio and television programming, and so forth—is affected by whether the target is men, women, or children.

INFLUENCE OF FAMILY LIFE CYCLE

In Chapter 4 we observed that consumer expenditure patterns are influenced considerably by the stage of the life cycle the family is in at any given time. The life cycle concept can also serve as (1) an explanation for family buying behavior and (2) a guide to marketers in planning marketing programs which are consistent with that behavior. Figure 6-7 summarizes the behavioral influences and buying patterns for families in each stage of the cycle. Marketing people surely need to be aware of the striking contrasts in buyer behavior between, say, people in the full-nest stage with the youngest child under six and those in the empty-nest stages. Even significant differences exist between empty-nest stages I and II (depending upon whether the head of the house is working or retired).

OVERT BUYING PATTERNS AND THEIR MARKETING SIGNIFICANCE

In addition to understanding *why* consumers buy, manufacturers and middlemen must also understand *when, where,* and *how* they buy. We are talking now about consumers' buying habits, or, as they are often called, patterns of overt buying behavior.

When consumers buy. A marketing executive should be able to answer at least

---

44 See Robert F. Kelly and Michael B. Egan, "Husband and Wife Interaction in a Consumer Decision Process," in Philip R. McDonald (ed.), *Marketing Involvement in Society and the Economy,* American Marketing Association, Chicago, 1970, pp. 250-258; and William D. Perreault, Jr., and Frederick A. Russ, "Student Influence on Family Purchase Decisions," in Fred C. Allvine (ed.), *Combined Proceedings; 1971 Conferences,* American Marketing Association, Chicago, Series No. 33, 1972, pp. 386-389.

BEHAVIORAL INFLUENCES AND BUYING PATTERNS, BY LIFE-CYCLE STAGE

Bachelor stage: young single people not living at home	Newly married couples; young, no children	Full nest I, youngest child under six	Full nest II; youngest child six or over	Full nest III; older married couples with dependent children	Empty nest I, older married couples, no children living with them, head in labor force	Empty nest II, older married couples, no children living at home, head retired	Solitary survivor, in labor force	Solitary survivor, retired
Few financial burdens. Fashion opinion leaders. Recreation oriented. Buy: Basic kitchen equipment, basic furniture, cars, equipment for the mating game, vacations.	Better off financially than they will be in near future. Highest purchase rate and highest average purchase of durables. Buy: Cars, refrigerators, stoves, sensible and durable furniture, vacations.	Home purchasing at peak. Liquid assets low. Dissatisfied with financial position and amount of money saved. Interested in new products. Like advertised products. Buy: Washers, dryers, TV, baby food, chest rubs and cough medicine, vitamins, dolls, wagons, sleds, skates.	Financial position better. Some wives work. Less influenced by advertising. Buy larger sized packages, multiple-unit deals. Buy: Many foods, cleaning materials, bicycles, music lessons, pianos.	Financial position still better. More wives work. Some children get jobs. Hard to influence with advertising. High average purchase of durables. Buy: New, more tasteful furniture, auto travel, nonnecessary appliances, boats, dental services, magazines.	Home ownership at peak. Most satisfied with financial position and money saved. Interested in travel, recreation, self-education. Make gifts and contributions. Not interested in new products. Buy: Vacations, luxuries, home improvements.	Drastic cut in income. Keep home. Buy: Medical appliances, medical care, products which aid health, sleep, and digestion.	Income still good but likely to sell home.	Same medical and product needs as other retired group; drastic cut in income. Special need for attention, affection, and security.

Figure 6-7. *Source:* William D. Wells and George Gubar, "Life Cycle Concept in Marketing Research," *Journal of Marketing Research,* November, 1966, p. 362.

three questions about *when* people buy his products or service: During what season do they buy? On what day of the week do they buy? At what time of day do they buy? If seasonal buying patterns exist, he should try to extend the buying season. He may find that a change in his product or in his promotional program will smooth out seasonal fluctuations. There is obviously little opportunity for extending the season on Easter bunnies or Christmas tree ornaments, but the season for vacations has been shifted to such an extent that winter or other "off-season" vacations are now quite popular.

When people buy may influence the product-planning, pricing, or promotional phases of a firm's marketing program. After-shave lotion, cigarettes, and alcoholic beverages are distinctively packaged at Christmastime because they are purchased for gifts. In order to smooth the seasonal peaks and valleys in his production schedule, a doll manufacturer may want retailers to buy well in advance of the Christmas season, the season when the majority of dolls are sold. To get the retailers to do this, the manufacturer may offer them "seasonal datings," a pricing policy whereby retailers take delivery in September but do not have to pay until December.

Where consumers buy. A firm should consider two factors with respect to *where* people buy—where the buying decision is made and where the actual purchase occurs. For many products and services the decision to buy is made at home. On the other hand, the decision is often made in whole or in part right at the point of purchase. A person may be shopping in a sporting goods store for golf clubs when he sees some tennis balls on sale, knows he needs some, and decides on the spot to buy them. A husband may decide at home that he wants to buy a birthday gift for his wife, but he waits until he gets to the store before deciding whether it will be jewelry, candy, or lingerie.

A company's entire promotional program, and in many cases its product planning, must be geared to carry the greatest impact at the place where the buying decision is made. If the decision to buy is made in the store, then attention must be devoted to packaging and other point-of-purchase display materials, particularly if the store is operating on a self-service basis. A shopper may decide at home to buy some cold cereal, but the key decision regarding which type and which brand may be made at the store. Of course, some advertising effort must be directed to the consumer in his house because a totally unknown brand, no matter how attractively packaged, will usually be rejected in favor of a known brand.

How consumers buy. The *how* part of consumer's buying habits encompasses several areas of behavior, and it affects product and pricing policies, promotional programs, and other management decisions.

Long ago, for example, many firms found that consumers preferred to buy such products as pickles, cookies, and butter already packaged. The advantages of cleanliness and ease of handling offset the higher unit price. If consumers buy a manufacturer's product primarily in self-service stores, increased importance is placed on developing an attractive package and label. When deciding to use packages, manufacturers and middlemen should be aware of consumer preferences with respect to quantity. If a soap manufacturer packages all his soap in lots of three bars in an attempt to stimulate buying, much business will be lost if customers typically buy only one bar at a time.

The trend toward one-stop shopping has encouraged retailers to add related and even unrelated lines of merchandise to their basic groups of products. Self-service stores have found, however, that the addition of certain products to their lines does not materially increase sales. Many people prefer to buy groceries and drug items on a serve-yourself basis, but they will not buy clothing, carpets, or furniture this way.

Some people always pay cash, whereas others prefer to buy on credit. A firm may have to abandon its cash-and-carry policy if there is considerable demand for credit buying. Services such as delivery, installation, and even credit may be priced separately and offered on an optional basis.

QUESTIONS AND PROBLEMS

1. Give some examples of differences in the consumption patterns of French- and English-speaking Canadians.
2. How is the women's liberation movement likely to influence consumer buying patterns and consumption?
3. How do you account for the increase in impulse buying?
4. What effect is the four-day workweek likely to have on family consumption patterns?
5. What criteria did Lloyd Warner use as the bases for placing a person in Warner's social-class structure? Why is the *amount* of income not given more weight as an indicator of social class?
6. What were the major conclusions drawn from the *Chicago Tribune's* study of social-class structure in a large industrial city?
7. Which of the six social classes do you identify with each of the following products or activities? In some cases more than one class may be listed, but try to associate each item with only one of six classes.
   a. Debutante parties
   b. A cocktail before dinner
   c. Wine and liqueurs with dinner
   d. Beer with dinner
   e. A Cadillac
   f. *The New Yorker* magazine
   g. Boats
   h. Sitting on the front porch in warm weather in an undershirt
   i. Shopping at a credit jeweler
   j. Borrowing at a bank
   k. Borrowing from a pawnbroker
8. Discuss the concept of a reference group, explaining:
   a. The meaning of the concept
   b. Its use in marketing
   c. The relationship between reference groups and attitude formation (from Chapter 5)
9. "Reference groups stifle initiative, foster robotlike conformity among the members, and inflict severe penalties for failure to meet the group's standards of behavior." Discuss.
10. Using the product and brand, plus (+) and minus (−), system as modeled in Figure 6-4 for measuring-susceptibility to reference-group influence, rate each of the following products or brands. Explain your reasoning in each instance.
    a. Color television set, console model
    b. Perfume
    c. Electric kitchen range
    d. Fresh hamburger meat
    e. Wall-to-wall carpeting
    f. 35 mm. camera priced at $200
11. In the "trial" stage of deciding whether to adopt some innovation, the likelihood of adoption is reduced if the product cannot be sampled because of its

cost or size. What are some products which might have these drawbacks? How might these drawbacks be overcome?

12. Describe the people likely to be found in the innovator category of adopters. In the late-majority category.

13. Give some examples of innovations which meet the "compatibility" characteristic in new-product adoption and some which possess the "relative advantage" feature.

14. Cite examples of manufacturers or retailers who are recognizing the emergence of teen-agers as decision makers in family buying and as actual purchasers.

15. Cite a few examples of products where the same person normally makes the buying a decisions and the physical purchase and also uses the product. Then give some examples in which two or three different people are involved in these processes. Explain how a firm's marketing program may be affected by the number of people involved in the deciding, buying, and using processes.

16. Families in which stage of the life cycle are likely to be the best prospects for each of the following products or services?

    a. Braces on teeth   *e.* Refrigerators
    b. Suntan lotion   *f.* Life insurance
    c. Second car in the family   *g.* Snow skis
    d. Vitamin pills   *h.* 46-day Mediterranean cruise

17. Explain how the factors of *when* and *where* people buy might affect the marketing program for each of the following products:

    a. Water skis   *d.* Outboard motors
    b. House paint   *e.* Room air conditioners
    c. High-quality sunglasses

BUYING DECISION PROCESS AND CLASSIFICATION OF CONSUMER GOODS

In this concluding chapter on consumer buying behavior, we incorporate some of the material covered in the preceding three chapters. First we study the decision-making process in buying. Then there is a brief description of current significant efforts toward the statement of a comprehensive theory of buyer behavior. Next comes a consideration of what we call motivation research. In the final section we segment consumer goods, classifying them on the basis of buyer behavior and then considering the marketing implications of this classification.

DECISION-MAKING PROCESS IN BUYING

It is time now to tie together some of the points discussed in the preceding two chapters and to describe the process a consumer goes through when making a purchasing decision. The process is a problem-solving approach consisting of the following five steps (Fig. 7-1):

1. Recognition of an unsatisfied need
2. Identification of alternative ways of reducing tensions, i.e., achieving satisfaction
3. Evaluation of alternatives

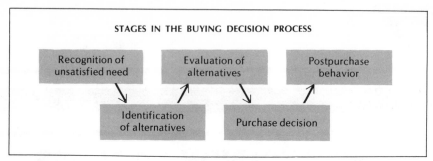

Figure 7-1.

4. Purchase decision
5. Postpurchase behavior

Once the process is started, a potential buyer can withdraw at any stage prior to the actual purchase. A total-stage approach is likely to be used only in certain buying situations—a first-time purchase of a product, for instance, or when buying high-priced, long-lived, infrequently purchased articles. For many products the purchasing behavior is a routine affair in which the aroused need is satisfied in a habitual manner by repurchasing the same brand. That is, past reinforcement in learning experiences leads directly to the buying response-act, and thus the second and third stages are bypassed. However, if something changes appreciably (price, product, services), the buyer may reopen the full decision process and consider alternative brands.

RECOGNITION OF UNSATISFIED NEED

The process starts when an unsatisfied need (motive) creates tension. It may be a biogenic need aroused internally (the person feels hungry), or the need may have been dormant until it was aroused by an external stimulus, such as an ad or the sight of the product. Perhaps dissatisfaction with the present product or brand created the tension.

Once the need is recognized, quite frequently the consumer or his family immediately becomes aware of conflicting motives or competitive uses for their scarce resources of time, manpower, or money. Let us say that a husband has a desire to install a swimming pool in his backyard at a cost of $6,000. His wife reminds him that she needs some new furniture for the living room and that funds would help their son get started in college next year. Or the man may fear that one of his key reference groups would not approve, or that the weather would be too cool for him to get enough use out of the pool to warrant the cost.

A person must resolve these conflicts before he can proceed. Otherwise, the buying process for the given product stops at this point.

IDENTIFICATION OF ALTERNATIVES

Once a need is recognized, then both product and brand alternatives must be identified. Let us say that a housewife wants to make her hands softer. Some alternative solutions include buying a new dishwasher, rubber gloves, a different detergent, or a new hand cream, or getting the kids to wash dishes and scrub floors. If one of the product alternatives is selected, there are several brands to choose from.

The search for alternatives, and the methods used in the search, are influenced by such factors as (1) what the time and money costs are (not much time is spent buying hamburger, as compared with buying a new winter coat), (2) how much information the consumer already has from past experiences and other sources, and (3) the amount of the perceived risk if a wrong selection is made.

For his sources of information the consumer may rely on his reference groups. He may also pay attention to advertisements, or make several shopping trips to various stores, seeking product demonstrations or help from salesclerks.[1]

EVALUATION OF ALTERNATIVES

Once all the reasonable alternatives are identified, the consumer must then evaluate each one preparatory to making the purchasing decision. Many of the same factors influence buyer activity in both the search and the evaluation stages. If the aroused need is urgent, less time is likely to be devoted to either of these stages. A buyer who likes to shop will spend more time evaluating than a person who does not have this propensity. People with more education and higher incomes are more likely to do a thorough evaluation job. The criteria a consumer uses in his evaluations should seem familiar by now. They include his past experiences and his attitudes toward various brands. He also uses the opinions of members of his family and other reference groups as guidelines in selection.

PURCHASE DECISION

After much searching and evaluating, the consumer at some point has to decide whether he is going to satisfy his aroused need or not, i.e., whether he is going to buy. Assuming that the answer is "yes," he is faced with a series of decisions as to the product type, brand, price, store, possible quantity and color, etc.

Anything a marketer can do to simplify decision making will be attractive to a buyer because most people find it very hard to make a decision or are not prepared to invest a lot of time and effort in the process. Perhaps in his advertising the seller can suggest what color is best for a given product use. Sometimes several decision situations can be combined and marketed as one package. A travel agency simplifies a traveler's decisions on transportation routes, hotels, local transportation, and which tours to take, by selling a packaged tour.

To do a better marketing job in this stage of the buying process, a seller needs to know answers to many questions regarding consumers' shopping behavior. For instance, how much effort is the consumer willing to spend in shopping for the product? What factors influence where a consumer will shop; i.e., what are her *patronage*-buying motives? Do stores each have an image? If so, is this important to a shopper when selecting a store? What factors determine the image of a given store? How does a retailer determine what is the image of his store? What are the differen-

---

1 See Terrence V. O'Brien, "Information Use in Consumer Decisions," paper presented at American Psychological Association, September, 1972; and "An Empirically Validated Model of Consumer Information Processing," Institute of Management Sciences, April, 1972.

tiating characteristics, if any, of impulse buyers? What influences do store layout and other physical store characteristics have on buyer behavior?[2]

Manufacturers and retailers, alike, are interested in knowing what motivates consumers to buy at certain stores. A producer who appeals to prestige and status motives in the sale of his product ordinarily would not want it distributed to retail stores which feature low-priced merchandise and no services. A consumer, of course, prefers to patronize stores where she perceives she is maximizing money, service, and product benefits while minimizing her risks as perceived in terms of product price, acceptability of product offerings, and required expenditure of time and effort.

Patronage motives, like product motives, are multiple and sometimes conflicting. Obviously a retailer cannot be all things to all people. He should not stress his many services and luxurious furnishings while trying to build up a low-priced economy-appeal image.

Some of the more important consumer patronage motives are as follows:

1. Convenience of location, rapidity of service, ease of locating merchandise, and uncrowded conditions
2. Price
3. Assortment of merchandise
4. Services offered
5. Attractive store appearance
6. Caliber of sales personnel

The several motives to which a store appeals can be used to describe the store's image or personality. Truly every store has an image, and the store's advertising is largely responsible for creating it. Women shoppers are acutely sensitive to cues in store advertising. They can accurately identify the characteristics of a store from its advertising alone. The findings from one study of a leading store illustrate this point (Fig. 7-2). Women in two cities were asked to evaluate the store's newspaper ads. The evaluations made by women who did not know the store's identity and who were judging solely by the physical appearance of the advertisements almost perfectly matched those made by shoppers who knew the store personally.

The marketing implications in this advertising-store image relationship make it imperative, from the beginning, that management plan its advertising program so as to accomplish the store's intended purposes. The store's image preselects its customers and thus determines the composition of its market. It is possible to change a store's image, but this can be done only gradually over a period of time.[3]

Patronage motives and choice of stores are related to the concept of social-class

---

2 For some research findings on several of these questions, see James F. Engel, David T. Kollat, and Roger D. Blackwell, *Consumer Behavior*, 2nd ed., Holt, Rinehart and Winston, Inc., New York, 1973, chaps. 19-21. See also Ben M. Enis and Gordon W. Paul, "Store Loyalty' as a Basis for Market Segmentation," *Journal of Retailing*, Fall, 1970, pp. 42-56; and Edward M. Tauber, "Why Do People Shop?" *Journal of Marketing*, October, 1972, pp. 46-59.

3 For a report on how downtown and suburban department stores differ in their respective images, see Stuart U. Rich and Bernard D. Portis, "The 'Imageries' of Departments Stores," *Journal of Marketing*, April, 1964, pp. 10-15. See also John H. Kunkel and Leonard L. Berry, "A Behavioral Conception of Retail Image," *Journal of Marketing*, October, 1968, pp. 21-27; Joseph Barry Mason and Morris L. Mayer, "Insights into the Image Determinants of Fashion Specialty Outlets," *Journal of Business Research*, Summer, 1973, pp. 73-80; and Dale L. Varble and Jim L. Grimm, "Image Assessment Can Be Administered by a Small Retailer," *Business Ideas and Facts*, Summer, 1972, pp. 15-21.

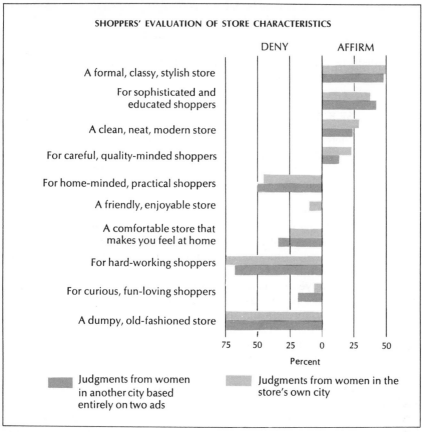

Figure 7-2. Shoppers often identify a store's "social status" without ever having been in the store, by reading its advertisements. The judgements of women who read a store's advertising but had never been inside it were almost identical to those of people who knew the store. For instance, nearly 50 percent of both groups agreed that the store in this study was for "sophisticated and educated shoppers." Almost everyone in both groups denied that the store was for "hardworking shoppers." *Source:* Pierre Martineau, *Motivation in Advertising,* McGraw-Hill Book Company, New York, 1957.

structure described in Chapter 6. The classic *Chicago Tribune* study of social class in Chicago showed definitely that people match their own values and expectations with the status of the store. Not all people want to shop at glamorous, high-status stores. A lower-status woman knows that she will be punished in subtle ways by the clerks and other customers if she goes into an exclusive department store. "The clerks treat you like a crumb," is one response. These types of reactions were also found as a result of conducting group interviews in Vancouver. Because social-class membership and choice of store are closely related, an important function of retail advertising today is to help a shopper make the necessary social-class identification. The shopper does not want to go to a store where she does not fit, and if she has any doubts she is apt to stay away from a store whose advertising appeal is not clear-cut. Usually a retailer must select his desired niche in the social structure and then set up his marketing and advertising accordingly. Normally, a store—even a large department store with a bargain basement as well as exclusive salon departments—cannot appeal strongly to all classes.[4] As mundane a store as a supermarket may project a certain image. Studies across Canada show that grocery chains offering essentially the same products, services, and prices in the same neighborhood still appeal to different social classes.

POSTPURCHASE BEHAVIOR

All the behavior determinants and the steps in the buying process up to this point are operative *before* or *during* the time a purchase is made. However, a buyer's feelings and evaluations *after* the sale are also significant for a marketer because they can influence repeat sales and also influence what the buyer tells others about the product or brand.

Typically a buyer experiences some postpurchase anxieties in all but routine purchases. Leon Festinger refers to this state of anxiety as *cognitive dissonance*.[5] Festinger theorizes that a person strives for internal harmony, consistency, or congruity among his "cognitions" (knowledge, attitudes, beliefs, values). Any inconsistency in these cognitions is called "dissonance."

Postpurchase cognitive dissonance occurs because each of the alternatives considered by the consumer usually has both advantages and limitations. Thus, when the purchase decision is finally made, the selected alternative has some drawbacks, while the rejected alternatives each possess some attractive features. That is, the negative aspects of the item selected and the positive qualities of the rejected products create cognitive dissonance in the consumer.

In the above explanation the consumer was aware of the dissonant elements before he made the purchase decision. Cognitive dissonance can also be aroused if disturbing information is received *after* the purchase is made. Currently we have some classic examples—consumers learn that the cholesterol in animal fats may lead to heart trouble; cigarette smokers learn that smoking apparently can lead to lung cancer; women are learning that the contraceptive pill can have negative side effects.

Festinger developed some hypotheses about the intensity of cognitive dissonance. Dissonance increases (1) as the dollar value of the purchase increases, (2) as the relative attractiveness of unselected alternatives increases, and (3) as the relative importance of the decision increases (buying a house or car potentially creates more dissonance than buying a candy bar).

To restore his internal harmony and minimize his discomfort, a person will try to reduce his postpurchase anxieties. Thus he is likely to avoid information (such as ads for the rejected products) which is likely to increase his dissonance. He may even change his behavior (cutting down on animal fats or quitting smoking, for example). He may change his opinions, or he may seek increased amounts of consonant information. Prior to making the purchase, he may shop around quite a bit,

---

4 See William Lazer and Robert G. Wyckham, "Perceptual Segmentation of Department Store Markets," *Journal of Retailing,* Summer, 1969, pp. 3-14; and John V. Petrof, "Race as a Factor of Store Preference," *Southern Journal of Business,* July, 1968, pp. 177-183.

5 Leon Festinger, *A Theory of Cognitive Dissonance,* Stanford University Press, Stanford, Calif., 1957; see also Jack W. Brehm and Arthur R. Cohen, *Explorations in Cognitive Dissonance,* John Wiley & Sons, Inc., New York, 1962.

especially for a high-priced, infrequently purchased article. He is seeking to avoid or minimize postdecision dissonance by spending more time in predecision evaluations. As was the case with personality theory, cognitive dissonance is a potentially useful concept. The marketing studies to date, however, have been somewhat conflicting or inconclusive.[6]

At the same time, some useful generalizations can be developed from the theory. For example, in his advertising or personal selling, anything a seller can do to reassure a buyer by stressing desirable features of a product can do much to reduce dissonance. The reduction will reinforce the consumer and increase his likelihood of repeat purchases. When the product in question is expensive and infrequently purchased, the seller's postsale service program can be a significant factor in reducing dissonance.

TOWARD A COMPREHENSIVE THEORY OF BUYER BEHAVIOR

The traditional approach to the study of buyer behavior has typically been a fragmented one. That is, research is done on attitudes or personality or social-group influence. This is perhaps a necessary approach when a new field is being developed. Certainly many of the theories and research findings on separate parts of buyer behavior have shed some light on the mental processes in the consumer's "black box." Also, many of the findings have been applied in a profitable manner by marketing practitioners.

In recent years, however, some notable attempts have been made to formulate a comprehensive theory of buyer behavior. Two of these models are described here in a *very* brief manner. Any more complete explanation is outside the scope of this book. Typically, any of the comprehensive models pose some problems. First, they are complicated and very difficult to explain, but then, consumer behavior is a complex activity. Second, the validity of the models still needs further empirical testing. Third, it is still difficult for a businessman to translate the theoretical abstractions into practical company research.

THE HOWARD-SHETH THEORY

One broad theory was developed by Howard and Sheth over a period of time which included a three-year validation test.[7] The model is based on the assumptions that (1) buying is a rational exercise in problem solving and (2) buyer behavior is systematic (not random) and thus is caused by inputs (stimuli) and results in outputs (buying behavior). The theory then attempts to describe what occurs between the inputs and outputs. This is reminiscent of the learning and cognitive theories discussed in Chapter 5.

The Howard-Sheth theoretical model is based on the idea that four sets of variables determine buyer behavior: (1) stimulus-input variables from the marketing

---

6 See Sadaomi Oshikawa, "Can Cognitive Dissonance Theory Explain Consumer Behavior?" *Journal of Marketing,* October, 1969, pp. 44-49.

7 Adapted from John A. Howard and Jagdish N. Sheth, "A Theory of Buyer Behavior," in Harold H. Kassarjian and Thomas S. Robertson (eds.), *Perspectives in Consumer Behavior,* Scott, Foresman and Company, Glenview, Ill., 1968, pp. 467-487. See also Howard and Sheth, *A Theory of Buyer Behavior,* John Wiley & Sons, Inc., New York, 1969.

program and social environment; (2) internal variables which together show the state of the buyer (his motives, attitudes, experiences, perceptions); (3) seven variables which affect the internal state of the buyer (these are called "exogenous" variables and include social class, culture, time pressure, and financial status); and (4) response-output variables (the buyer's behavior based on interactions of the first three sets of variables).

Summary of the theory. Much buying behavior is usually repetitive. When confronted with repetitive brand-choice decisions, a consumer tends to simplify his task by storing relevant information and establishing a routine in his decision process. The elements in this brand-choice decision are (1) a set of motives, (2) alternative choices of products and brands (called his *evoked set)*, and (3) decision mediators.

Decision mediators are a set of rules which the buyer uses to match his motive and the alternatives for satisfying these motives. These mediators rank-order the motives and then rank-order the brands on the basis of their potential for satisfying these motives. The rank ordering of the brands is based on learning experiences or outside information (ads, reference-group advice, etc.). From these influences a person develops his attitudes (H-S theory calls them "predispositions"). Inhibitors (price, availability, buyer's financial status) may interfere in the buying process.

When a buyer is considering a type of product which is new to him, he has no set of decision mediators, so he actively seeks information from his environment and will try to draw from experiences with similar types of products. It is important that a marketing executive try to determine the intensity of this information-seeking effort. If the buyer's brand choice is satisfactory, he tends to repeat that choice in future purchases. He is striving to develop a routine, thus reducing the complexity of buying. This is called the *psychology of simplification.* On the other hand, sometimes the same routine and the same brand become boring. When the buyer is satiated even with his preferred brand, he will complicate the situation by starting the search process all over again. This is called the *psychology of complication.*

The theory also explains how a given stimulus may result in different responses among buyers, depending on the person's "level of motivation." In the case of response to the stimulus of an advertisement, for example, one person may buy the brand, one may read the ad and store the information, and a third may ignore the ad. The concept of "predisposition toward a brand" is used to explain how two buyers may both need a product but why they buy two different brands.

THE ENGEL-KOLLAT-BLACKWELL THEORY

These three men have developed a comprehensive theoretical model which conceives of a person as being a system with outputs (behavior) which respond to inputs.[8] The model recognizes the existence of "intervening variables" between the initial inputs and ultimate outputs. We then try to understand how these variables affect the processes going on in the consumer's mind (called his *central control unit*). This theory holds that an individual's psychological makeup (personality, attitudes, stored information from learning experiences) affects the mental processes in his central control unit.

---

8 Engel, Kollat, and Blackwell, *op. cit.* The model serves as the conceptual framework for the book, but see pp. 49-67 for a brief description including two examples of using the model.

Inputs in the form of physical and social stimuli hit a person's sensory receptors and arouse some needs. How these stimuli are received and interpreted depends on the person's selective perceptions. These perceptions determine whether action will result. If so, problem recognition occurs, and the decision process goes into operation. This involves the search for, and evaluation of, alternatives; the purchasing act; and postpurchase evaluations.[9]

CLASSIFICATION OF PRODUCTS

Just as it is necessary to segment *markets* for meaningful programming in marketing, so also is it helpful to separate *products* into homogeneous classifications. First we shall divide all products into two groups—consumer goods and industrial goods—a classification that parallels our segmentation of the market. Then later we shall divide each of the major product categories still further.

CONSUMER GOODS AND INDUSTRIAL GOODS

Consumer goods include all products which are "destined for use by ultimate consumers or households and in such form that they can be used without (further) commercial processing." *Industrial goods* are those which are "destined to be sold primarily for use in producing other goods or rendering services as contrasted with goods destined to be sold primarily to the ultimate consumer."[10]

The fundamental basis for distinguishing between the two groups is the *ultimate use* for which the product is intended in its present form. A cash register purchased by a retailer for use in his store (the product renders a service in a business), a pair of overalls bought by a farmer to be worn while working (farming is his business), and materials or parts bought by a manufacturer for use in making his product—all are industrial goods.

A particular stage in a product's distribution has no effect upon its classification. Cornflakes or children's shoes would be classed as consumer products whether they were in the manufacturer's warehouse or on retailers' shelves because ultimately they will be used in their present form by household consumers. Cornflakes sold to restaurants and other institutions, however, are classed as industrial goods.

Often it is not possible to place a product definitely in one class or the other. A portable typewriter may be considered a consumer good if it is purchased by a student or a housewife for nonbusiness use. But if the typewriter is bought by a traveling salesman for use in his business, it is classed with industrial goods. The manufacturer of such a product recognizes that his product falls in both categories and therefore develops separate marketing programs for the different markets.

MARKETING SIGNIFICANCE OF PRODUCT CLASSIFICATION

The two-way product classification is a useful framework for programming marketing operations because each major class of products ultimately goes to a different

---

9 For two other comprehensive models, see Francesco M. Nicosia, *Consumer Decision Processes: Marketing and Advertising Implications,* Prentice-Hall, Inc., Englewood Cliffs, N.J., 1966; and Alan R. Andreasen, "Attitudes and Customer Behavior: A Decision Model," in Lee Preston (ed.), *New Research in Marketing,* University of California, Institute of Business and Economic Research, Berkeley, 1965, pp. 1-16.

10 Committee on Definitions, *Marketing Definitions: A Glossary of Marketing Terms,* American Marketing Association, Chicago, 1960, pp. 11, 14.

market and requires different marketing methods. In the field of product planning, for example, branding, packaging, and fashion are generally far more significant for a consumer product than for an industrial good. Since the channels of distribution for consumer products are typically longer and involve more middlemen than those for industrial goods, distribution policies would vary. Advertising policies, too, would be affected. Manufacturers of consumer goods ordinarily use much more advertising than do manufacturers of industrial products.

CLASSIFICATION OF CONSUMER PRODUCTS

Although the marketing differences between consumer and industrial goods make a two-part classification of products valuable, the category of consumer goods is still too broad for a marketing manager. Consequently, consumer products are further classified as convenience goods, shopping goods, and specialty goods (see Table 7-1). This is the traditional classification, and while it raises objections in some quarters, it is still better understood and more generally followed by businessmen than any of the alternatives yet suggested. It is important to note that this three-way subdivision is based on consumer *buying habits* rather than on consumer *products.* Specifically the two criteria used as bases for classifying consumer products are (1) the degree to which the consumer is aware of the exact nature of the product *before* he starts on his shopping trip and (2) the satisfaction received from searching for and comparing products, weighed against the time and effort required for this task.

Convenience goods. The significant characteristics of convenience goods are that the consumer has complete knowledge of the particular product (or its substitutes) which he wants *before* going out to buy it and that it is purchased with a minimum of effort on his part. Normally the gain resulting from shopping around to compare price and quality is not considered worth the extra time and effort required. The consumer is willing to accept any of several substitutes, and thus he will buy the one which is most accessible. For most buyers this subclass of goods includes groceries, tobacco products, inexpensive candy, drug sundries such as toothpaste and shaving accessories, and staple hardware items such as light bulbs and flashlight batteries. When the need for this type of goods arises, the consumer wants to make his purchase as rapidly and as easily as possible. Consequently, this type of product must be readily accessible in any shopping area.

Convenience goods typically have a low unit price, are not bulky, and are not greatly affected by fad and fashion. Among the well-known brands, one is not usually *strongly* preferred over another. Convenience goods are purchased frequently, although this is not a differentiating characteristic. Items such as Christmas tree lights or birthday cards are convenience goods for most people, even though they may be bought only once a year.

Marketing considerations. Since a product must be readily accessible when the consumer's demand arises, a manufacturer must secure wide distribution. But since most retail stores sell only a small volume of a manufacturer's output, it is not economical for him to sell directly to all retail outlets. Instead, he relies on wholesalers to reach part of the retail market.

The promotional policies of both the manufacturers and the middlemen, espe-

Table 7-1. Characteristics of classes of consumer goods and some marketing considerations.

Characteristics and marketing considerations	Type of product		
	Convenience	Shopping	Specialty
Characteristics:			
1. Time and effort devoted by consumer to shopping	Very little	Considerable	Cannot generalize. May go to nearby store and exert minimum effort, or may have to go to distant store and spend much time
2. Time spent planning the purchase	Very little	Considerable	Considerable
3. How soon want is satisfied after it arises	Immediately	Relatively long time	Relatively long time
4. Are price and quality compared?	No	Yes	No
5. Price	Low	High	High
6. Frequency of purchase	Usually frequent	Infrequent	Infrequent
7. Importance	Unimportant	Often very important	Cannot generalize
Marketing considerations:			
1. Length of channel	Long	Short	Short to very short
2. Importance of retailer	Any single store is relatively unimportant	Important	Very important
3. Number of outlets	As many as possible	Few	Few; often only one in market
4. Stock turnover	High	Lower	Lower
5. Gross margin	Low	High	High
6. Responsibility for advertising	Manufacturer's	Retailer's	Joint responsibility
7. Importance of point-of-purchase display	Very important	Less important	Less important
8. Advertising used	Manufacturer's	Retailer's	Both
9. Brand or store name important	Brand name	Store name	Both
10. Importance of packaging	Very important	Less important	Less important

cially the retailing middlemen, are involved here. A retailer typically carries several brands of a convenience item, so he is not able to promote any single brand. He is not interested in doing much advertising of these articles because many other stores carry them, and any advertising he does may help a competitor. Furthermore, quality and price of competitive products are reasonably similar, the product requires little or no explanation, and the retailer normally has no incentive to push one brand over another. Therefore, many retailers of convenience goods have adopted a self-service marketing technique. As a result, virtually the entire promotional burden is shifted to the manufacturer. He must advertise extensively to develop a recognition of, and preference for, his brand. Self-service in retailing places great importance on point-of-purchase displays and packaging because these tools have considerable influence on impulse buying.

Shopping goods. Shopping goods are products for which a customer usually wishes to compare quality, price, and style in several stores before purchasing. A key identifying characteristic, and the one which separates shopping goods from convenience goods, is that for shopping goods the consumer lacks full knowledge of pertinent product features before embarking upon the shopping trip. Thus, on the trip not only does he purchase the article, but he first must assess the relative suitability of alternative products. This search will continue only as long as the customer believes that the gain from comparing product features offsets the additional time and effort required. Examples of shopping goods typically include women's apparel, furniture and other durable goods, jewelry, piece goods, and, to some extent, men's ready-to-wear and shoes. In general, shopping goods are larger in unit value and are purchased less frequently than convenience goods.

Marketing considerations. The buying habits associated with shopping goods affect the distribution and promotional strategy of both manufacturers and middlemen. A manufacturer of a shopping good requires fewer retail outlets because the consumer is willing to look around a little for what he wants, purchases are usually made infrequently, and the need does not require immediate satisfaction. In order to increase the convenience of comparison shopping, a manufacturer tries to place his product in a store located near other stores carrying competing items. Similarly, department stores and other retailers who carry primarily shopping goods want to be bunched together.

Manufacturers usually work closely with retailers in the marketing of shopping goods. Since a manufacturer uses fewer retail outlets, he is more dependent upon those he selects. Retail stores typically buy shopping goods in large quantities. Thus there is less use of wholesalers than there is with convenience goods; distribution direct from manufacturer to retailer is common. Finally, the store name is often more important to the buyer of a shopping good than the manufacturer's name.

This last point carries significant promotional implications. The retailer is quite willing to assume a good part of the advertising, display, and selling costs, particularly for items such as wearing apparel, where the average customer does not know or care who made the product.

Some socioeconomic trends may be decreasing the scope and importance of the shopping goods category. Increased incomes, higher values placed on leisure time, and widespread exposure to mass-media advertising are forces which lessen a consumer's propensity to search and compare. Any significant decline in the search-shopping activity may influence future distribution policies, store locations, and retailing techniques.[11]

Specialty goods. Specialty goods have been defined as those with "unique characteristics and/or brand identification for which a significant group of buyers are habitually willing to make a special purchasing effort."[12] In the case of specialty goods, as with convenience goods but unlike shopping goods, the buyer has complete knowledge of the particular product he wants before going on his buying trip. The distinctive feature of specialty goods is that the buyer will accept only one brand. He is willing to forgo more accessible substitutes in order to procure the wanted brand, even though this may require a significant expenditure of time and effort. Examples of products usually classified as specialty goods include expensive men's ready-to-wear, fancy groceries, health foods, hi-fi components, photographic equipment, and, for many people, automobiles and certain home appliances. Ordinarily, only certain *brands* of these products fall into the specialty goods classification. For many men, a Shiffer-Hillman suit would be considered a specialty good—they insist on the brand and will accept no other—but men's suits in general would not be so classified.

The consumer's *insistence* on a certain brand is the key characteristic of specialty goods. Since the consumer insists on a certain brand, he is willing to expend considerable effort to find it. Consequently, manufacturers can afford to use fewer outlets. With the insistence on a given brand and with few outlets, the consumer *must* make a special effort. Thus the *willingness* to exert extra effort becomes a *need* to do so.

Marketing considerations. Usually only one outlet is used in a given area or market. Ordinarily, the manufacturer deals directly with his chosen retailers. The retailers are extremely important, particularly if the manufacturer is using only one in each area. Where the franchise to handle the product is a valuable one, the retailer may become quite dependent upon the producer. Actually they are interdependent; the success of one is closely tied to the success of the other.

Because brand is important and because only a few outlets are used, both the manufacturer and the retailer advertise the product extensively. Often the manufacturer pays some portion of the retailer's advertising costs, and the retailer's name frequently appears in the manufacturer's advertisements.

Criticism of product classification. Although we continue to use the convenience-shopping-specialty categorization, we cannot ignore its shortcomings. One of the quarrels with the traditional classification is that we really are not classifying consumer products at all. Instead, we are grouping consumer buying patterns. We are talking about convenience buying habits, not convenience products. The critics point out, and with justification, that buying habits may be categorized in this manner but that products cannot. When we attempt to establish the three-way classification, we find that given products shift in and out of one or more of the groups. Automobiles furnish a good illustration. When a person first buys a car, he may

---

11 William P. Dommermuth and Edward W. Cundiff, "Shopping Goods, Shopping Centers, and Selling Strategies," *Journal of Marketing*, October, 1967, pp. 32-36.

12 Committee on Definitions, *Marketing Definitions: A Glossary of Marketing Terms*, American Marketing Association, Chicago, 1960, p. 22.

shop extensively. He finally buys a Ford and is quite satisfied. When he needs a replacement, he goes straight to a Ford dealer without any shopping around. To him a car has shifted from a shopping to a specialty good. Later, for one reason or another, he becomes disenchanted with his Ford. Then when car-buying time comes around a third time, he will revert to shopping.

An adjunct to this first basic cricitism is that the attempt to classify products by systems that were really designed to sort out buying habits results in considerable overlapping of the product groups. Not all consumers react in the same way to a given product. In fact, some items may fall in all three classes, depending upon the consumers.

A second objection to the classification is that it suggests sharp, rigid demarcations, when in fact none exist. Actually this criticism should not worry a marketing man. He should have long since realized that marketing does not lend itself to sharply demarcated categorizations. Instead, he deals constantly with gray areas and twilight zones where imperceptible shadings often occur. In reality, the classification of goods is better depicted as a continuum representing degrees of effort expended, with convenience goods clustered at one end and specialty products occupying positions near the other end.

Another criticism concerns the confusion surrounding the concept of specialty goods. The term "specialty" itself is used in conjunction with several other aspects of marketing—specialty salesmen and specialty stores, for example—and these have no connection with specialty products. In fact, many specialty stores carry shopping goods, and many specialty salesmen sell convenience products.[13]

Classification extended to retail stores.[14] Bucklin proposes that the system for classifying consumer goods can be extended to retailing, with a resultant classification of consumer patronage motives and retail stores. That is, we have convenience stores, shopping stores, and specialty stores. The category in which a given store is placed depends upon whether consumers shop there because it is accessible or because they prefer that store regardless of its accessibility.

By cross-classifying product and patronage motives we get a nine cell matrix as follows:

Goods:	Stores:		
	Convenience	Shopping	Specialty
Convenience			
Shopping			
Specialty			

---

13 For a proposal that we draw from the theory of cognitive dissonance to develop a fresh set of behavioral criteria for classifying consumer goods, see Stanley Kaish, "Cognitive Dissonance and the Classification of Consumer Goods," *Journal of Marketing*, October, 1967, pp. 28-31. See also John E. Mertes, "Taste, Variety, and Change: Yesterday and Today," *Business Perspectives*, Fall, 1968, pp. 4-11, for the suggestion that we incorporate the concept of fashion goods into the classification.

14 This section is adapted from Louis P. Bucklin, "Retail Strategy and the Classification of Consumer Goods," *Journal of Marketing*, January, 1963, pp. 50-55. For a conceptual extension of Bucklin's classification, adding the dimension of retail strategies, see Morris L. Mayer, Joseph Barry Mason, and Morris Gee, "A Reconceptualization of Store Classification as Related to Retail Strategy Formulation," *Journal of Retailing*, Fall, 1971, 27-36.

The nine possible types of buying behavior represented by this matrix are as follows.[15]

1. Convenience Store—Convenience Good: The consumer, represented by this category, prefers to buy the most readily available brand of product at the most accessible store.
2. Convenience Store—Shopping Good: The consumer selects his purchase from among the assortment carried by the most accessible store.
3. Convenience Store— Specialty Good: The consumer purchases his favored brand from the most accessible store which has the item in stock.
4. Shopping Store—Convenience Good: The consumer is indifferent to the brand of product he buys, but shops among different stores in order to secure better retail service and/or lower retail price.
5. Shopping Store—Shopping Good: The consumer makes comparisons among both retailer controlled factors and factors associated with the product (brand).
6. Shopping Store—Specialty Good: The consumer has a strong preference with respect to the brand of the product, but shops among a number of stores in order to secure the best retail service and/or price for this brand.
7. Specialty Store—Convenience Good: The consumer prefers to trade at a specific store, but is indifferent to the brand of product purchased.
8. Specialty Store—Shopping Good: The consumer prefers to trade at a certain store, but is uncertain as to which product he wishes to buy, and examines the store's assortment for the best purchase.
9. Specialty Store—Specialty Good: The consumer has both a preference for a particular store and a specific brand.

This matrix is a realistic representation of how people buy. Supermarkets (convenience stores) do carry some exotic specialty foods, and we can buy common brands of after-shave lotion (convenience goods) in exclusive men's shops. Normally, however, consumer behavior toward a given product can be represented by only three or four of the categories. With this cross-classification system to guide him, a retailer can first select his market targets and then develop appropriate strategies to reach those segments. To illustrate, to appeal to the convenience store-specialty good segment, two important elements in the retailer's marketing mix would be (1) a highly accessible location, and (2) a good selection of widely accepted brands. Depth of assortment, price, and personal selling are less important. Store promotion facilities probably are also of little importance.

QUESTIONS AND PROBLEMS

1. What patronage motives influence your choice of the following?
   a. Restaurant   *d.* Sporting goods store
   b. Movie theater   *e.* Shoe store
   c. Department store
2. Following is a series of headlines or slogans taken from advertisements of various retailers. To what patronage motive does each appeal?
   a. "Factory trained mechanics at your service."
   b. 'We never close."
   c. "We never have missed paying a semiannual dividend since we opened."
   d. "One dollar down, no payments until the steel strike is over."

---

15 Bucklin, *op. cit.,* pp. 53–54.

3. In what ways can retail stores make profitable use of the findings on social-class structure? If possible, use specific stores to illustrate your points.

4. Explain the concept of cognitive dissonance as it operates in the buying decision process.

5. What causes cognitive dissonance to increase in a buying situation? What can a seller do to decrease the level of dissonance in a given purchase of the seller's brand?

6. Give some examples of products, other than those cited in this chapter, which are both consumer and industrial goods. What determines the category in which a product will be placed?

7. What are some brands or types of products which are specialty goods so far as your personal buying patterns are concerned? In each instance do you believe that most consumers would classify the article as a specialty product? If not, how do you explain your own rating?

8. "As brand preferences are established by women with regard to women's shoes and ready-to-wear, these items, which traditionally have been considered shopping goods, will move into the specialty goods category. At the same time, women's clothing is moving into supermarkets and variety stores, thus indicating that some articles are convenience goods." Explain the reasoning involved here. Do you agree that women's clothing is shifting away from the shopping goods classification? Explain.

9. In what way is the responsibility for advertising a convenience good distributed between the manufacturer and the retailers? A shopping good? A specialty good?

10. Compare a manufacturer's marketing mix for a convenience good with the mix for a specialty good.

11. To what extent is the marketing mix for a shopping good similar to the mix for a specialty good?

THE INDUSTRIAL MARKET

Besides the consumer market there is another market—a big, rich, and widely diversified one, requiring the efforts of hundreds of thousands of workers in thousands of different jobs. This market is not criticized for extreme claims in selling or advertising; it is not accused of costing too much, of offering duplicate brands, or of paying middlemen exorbitant profits. It is not a target for widespread complaint because it is largely unknown to the public. The market of which we speak is the industrial market.

NATURE AND IMPORTANCE OF THE INDUSTRIAL MARKET

In Chapter 3 *industrial users* were defined as business or institutional organizations that buy products and services either to use in making other goods and services or to use in their own business. *Industrial goods* were differentiated from consumer goods on the basis of their ultimate use. Industrial goods are those intended for use in making other products or for rendering a service in the operation of a business or institutional enterprise. *Industrial marketing,* then, is the marketing of industrial goods and services to industrial users.

Because the industrial market is largely an unknown quantity to the average consumer, he is apt to underrate its significance. Actually this market is a huge one in terms of its total sales volume and the number of firms involved in it. It is estimated that about 50 percent of all goods manufactured in Canada are sold to the industrial market. In 1971, manufacturing companies in Canada purchased materials and supplies valued at $27.7 billion from other businesses.[1] In addition to manufactured products, about 80 percent of all farm products and virtually all minerals and forest and sea products are industrial goods. They are sold to firms for further processing. Industrial farm products and minerals alone would add another $18 billion to the volume of industrial goods marketed.[2]

The magnitude and complexity of the industrial market may also be shown by the many transactions required in producing and marketing a product. Consider the number of industrial marketing transactions and the total sales volume involved in getting a pair of cowhide work shoes to a consumer. First, the cattle must go through one or two middlemen before reaching a meatpacker. Then the hides are sold to a tanner, who in turn sells the leather to a shoe manufacturer: The shoe manufacturer may sell to a shoe wholesaler, who will market his products to factories which supply shoes for their workers. Each time the cow, leather, and shoes are sold, it is an industrial marketing transaction.

In addition to the leather, the manufacturer must buy metal eyelets, laces, thread, steel safety toe plates, rubber or composition heels and/or soles, and shoe polish. He does not make any of these products himself. Although he may buy shoestring material in large quantities, cut it to the desired length, and add the metal tips, other industrial firms must first buy the raw cotton and then spin, weave, dye, and cut it so that it becomes shoestring material. All the manufacturers involved have plants and offices with furniture, machinery, and other equipment—industrial goods which have their own marketing patterns and problems. The factories themselves are industrial products, as are the heating and maintenance equipment and supplies. In short, a myriad of industrial products and industrial marketing situations come into play before almost any product, whether it is a consumer or industrial good, reaches its final destination.

Another indication of the scope and importance of the industrial market may be seen in the following industry classifications which make up this market:

1. Agriculture, forestry, and fishing
2. Mining and quarrying
3. Contract construction
4. Manufacturing
5. Transportation, communication, and other public utilities
6. Wholesale trade
7. Retail trade
8. Finance, insurance, and real estate
9. Services
10. Government—federal, provincial, and local

Every retail store and wholesaling establishment is an industrial user. Every bus company, airline, and railroad is part of this market, as is every hotel, restau-

---

1 Statistics Canada, *Manufacturing Industries of Canada: Type of Organization and Size of Establishments, 1971.* Cat. No. 31-210, Information Canada, Ottawa, 1975, p. 18.

2 Sales value of minerals produced in Canada in 1974 was $11.6 billion (Statistics Canada, *Canada's Mineral Production, Preliminary Estimate, 1974.* Cat. No. 26-202, Information Canada, Ottawa, 1975). Cash farm income in 1974 was $8.4 billion: 80 percent of which is $6.7 billion (Statistics Canada, *Quarterly Bulletin of Agricultural Statistics, October-December, 1974.* Cat. No. 21-003, Information Canada, Ottawa, 1975, p. 225).

rant, bank, insurance company, hospital, theater, garage and so on. In total there are approximately half a million industrial users in Canada. While this is far short of the approximately 22 million consumers, the total sales volume in the industrial market far surpasses total sales to consumers. This differential occurs because so very many industrial marketing transactions are involved before a final product is sold to its ultimate user.

THE FARM MARKET AND THE GOVERNMENT MARKET

Two large segments of the industrial market—the agricultural market and the government market—deserve an expanded discussion at this point because they often are underrated and overlooked, as so much attention is typically devoted to the manufacturing segment. The high level of cash receipts—$8.4 billion in 1974—from the sales of farm products gives farmers as a group a level of purchasing power which makes them a highly attractive market. Moreover, the world population forecasts and the continued existence of diet deficiencies in many countries undoubtedly will keep pressure on farmers to increase their output. Manufacturers and middlemen hoping to sell to this farm market must analyze it carefully and be aware of significant trends. Both the farmers' share of total population and the number of farms have been decreasing and probably will continue to decline. Counterbalancing this has been the increase in large corporate farms, and even the surviving "family farms" are tending to increase in size. Farming is becoming more automated and mechanized. This means, of course, that capital investment in farming is increasing. Truly, agribusiness is becoming big business in every sense of the word. As a buyer, the farmer is becoming increasingly sophisticated and well informed. As farm customers become fewer and larger, manufacturers must change the distribution and promotional strategies to reach this market effectively.

The fantastically large government market includes thousands of federal, provincial and local units buying for countless government institutions such as schools, offices, hospitals, and the military. Spending by the federal government alone accounts for about 20 percent of our gross national product; the spending at the provincial and municipal levels accounts for another 20 percent.[3] The government as a buyer is so big, however, that it is difficult to comprehend and difficult to reach key buying influences. Certainly government procurement processes are different from those found in the private sector of the industrial market.

A unique feature of government buying is the bidding system. Much government procurement must be done on a bid basis. That is, the government advertises for bids, stating the product specifications. Then it usually must accept the lowest bid which meets these specifications. In other buying situations the government negotiates a purchase contract with an individual supplier. This marketing practice might occur when the Department of National Defense wants someone to develop and build a new weapons system, and there are no existing comparable products for the effective bidding purposes.

Many companies make no real effort to sell to the government, preferring not to contend with the red tape. Yet government business can be quite profitable. To deal with the government to any significant extent, however, usually requires specialized marketing skills, techniques, and information.

---

3 Statistics Canada, *National Income and Expenditure Accounts, Fourth Quarter and Preliminary Annual, 1974.* Cat. No. 13-001, Information Canada, Ottawa, 1975, pp. 24-29.

CLASSIFICATION OF INDUSTRIAL PRODUCTS

Separating all products into consumer and industrial goods is a valuable aid to marketing executives. The general category of industrial products is still too broad however, because marketing practices for various products are different. Consequently, some subdivision is necessary. The classification used here separates industrial goods into five categories: raw materials, fabricating materials and parts, installations, accessory equipment, and operating supplies. This classification is based on the broad *uses* of the product, in contrast to the classification of consumer products on the basis of buying habits. (See Figure 8-1).

Parenthetically, it may be noted that the consumer goods classification of convenience-shopping-specialty products is also applicable in part to industrial goods. Items such as scratch pads, light bulbs, and dust mops are the "convenience goods" of the industrial market. They are purchased with a minimum of effort and searching time. For other products, such as office machines or replacement motors for production machines, a purchasing agent for a manufacturer will shop carefully. He will compare price, quality, product features, and service given by the sellers, thus placing these products in the shopping goods category. Industrial products fall into the specialty goods category when, for example, a coal mining firm insists on Goodyear conveyor belts or a steel mill insists on safety goggles made by Imperial Optical.

RAW MATERIALS

Raw materials are industrial goods which will become a part of another physical product and which have received no processing at all other than that necessary for economy or protection in physical handling. Raw materials include (1) goods found in their natural state, such as minerals, land, and products of the forests and the seas, and (2) agricultural products, such as wheat, corn, cotton, tobacco, fruits, vegetables, livestock, and animal products—eggs and raw milk. These two groups of raw materials are marketed quite differently.

Marketing considerations. The marketing of raw materials found in their natural state is influenced by several factors. The supply of these products is limited and cannot be substantially increased. Usually only a few large producers are involved. The product must be carefully graded and, consequently, is highly standardized. Because of their great bulk, their low unit value, and the long distance between producer and industrial user, transportation is an important consideration.

These factors necessitate short channels of distribution and a minimum of physical handling. Frequently, marketing is direct from producer to industrial user; at most, one middleman may be used. The limited supply forces users to assure themselves of adequate quantities. Often this is done either by contracting in advance to buy a season's supply of the product or by vertical integration. Advertising and other forms of demand stimulation are used very little. Because there is little brand or other product differentiation, competition is built around price and the assurance that a producer can deliver the prescribed quality of the product in the exact quantity specified.

Agricultural products used as industrial raw materials are supplied by many small producers located some distance from the markets. The supply is largely

Figure 8-1. Classes of industrial products—some characteristics and marketing considerations.

Characteristics and marketing considerations	Type of Product				
	Raw materials	Fabricating parts and materials	Installations	Accessory equipment	Operating supplies
Characteristics:					
1. Unit Price	Very low	Low	Very high	Medium	Low
2. Length of life	Very short	Depends on final product	Very long	Long	Short
3. Quantities purchased	Large	Large	Very small	Small	Small
4. Frequency of purchase	Frequent delivery; long-term purchase contract	Infrequent purchase, but frequent delivery	Very infrequently	Medium	Frequent
5. Standardization of competitive products	Very high; grading is important	Very high	Very low; custom-made	Low	High
6. Limits on supply	Limited; cannot be increased quickly or at all	Usually no problem	No problem	Usually no problem	Usually no problem
Marketing considerations:					
1. Nature of channel	Short; no middlemen	Short; middlemen only for small buyers	Short; no middlemen	Middlemen used	Middlemen used
2. Negotiation period	Hard to generalize	Medium	Long	Medium	Short
3. Price competition	Important	Important	Not important	Not main factor	Important
4. Presale/postsale service	Not important	Not important	Very important	Important	Very little
5. Demand stimulation	Very little	Moderate	Salesmen very important	Important	Not too important
6. Brand preference	None	Generally unimportant, but some sellers try	High	High	Low
7. Advance buying contract	Important; use of long-term contracts	Important; use of long-term contracts	Not usually	Not usually	Not usually

controllable by man, but it cannot be increased or decreased rapidly. The product is perishable and is not produced at a uniform rate throughout the year. Close attention must be given to transportation and warehousing. Transportation costs are high relative to unit value, and standardization and grading are very important.

Because producers are small and numerous, many middlemen and long channels of distribution are needed. Very little promotional or demand-creation activity is involved, and branding is unimportant.

FABRICATING MATERIALS AND PARTS

Fabricating materials and parts are industrial goods which become an actual part of the finished product. They have already been processed to some extent (in contrast to raw materials). Fabricating *materials* will undergo further processing. Examples include pig iron going into steel, gray goods becoming a part of finished printed cloth, yarn being woven into cloth, and flour becoming a part of bread. Fabricating *parts* will be assembled with no further change in form. They include such products as spark plugs and fan belts in an automobile, the barrel and stock of a rifle, and the buttons on a dress.

Marketing considerations. Fabricating materials and parts are usually purchased in large quantities. To ensure an adequate, timely supply, a buyer may place his order a year or more in advance, with the guarantee that he will be given the advantage of price reductions. Because of these buying habits, most fabricating products are marketed on a direct-sale basis between producer and user. Individual industries, such as textiles, may provide exceptions to this rule.

Middlemen are used most often where the buyers are small or are placing small fill-in orders on rapid-delivery basis. Normally, buying decisions are based on price and service provided by the seller. Branding is generally unimportant, although some firms have made successful attempts to pull their products out of obscurity by identifying them with a brand. Canadian Industries Limited (CIL), Dominion Textile Limited (Tex-Made), and MacMillan Bloedel Limited are notable examples.

INSTALLATIONS

Installations are manufactured industrial products—the long-lived, expensive, major equipment of an industrial user. Examples, would include large generators in a dam, a factory building, diesel engines for a railroad, coke ovens and blast furnaces for steel mill, computers for a missile manufacturer, and jet airplanes for an airline. The differentiating characteristic of installations is that they set the scale of operation in a firm. Adding twelve new typewriters will not affect the scale of operation at Air Canada, but adding twelve new jet airplanes certainly will.

Marketing considerations. Marketing of installations presents a real challenge to management because every single sale is important. Usually no middlemen are involved; the channel is direct from producer to industrial user. Typically the unit sale is large, and often the product is made to detailed specifications. There may be a long negotiation period before the transaction is consummated. Much presale and postsale servicing is needed. High-caliber salesmen are needed to market installations, and often sales engineers are used. Promotional emphasis is on personal selling rather than advertising, although some advertising is used.

While direct sale is most common, middlemen agents or wholesalers are often used to sell less expensive, standardized installations. Middlemen are also relied upon to reach small buyers, and to sell supplies and replacement parts used with large installations.

ACCESSORY EQUIPMENT

Accessory equipment is a class of industrial products used to aid and implement the production operations of an industrial user, but it does not have a significant influence on the scale of operations in a firm. Accessory equipment does not become an actual part of the finished product. The life of accessory equipment is shorter than that of installations and longer than that of operating supplies. Examples would include office equipment, cash registers in a retail store, small power tools, and forklift trucks.

Marketing considerations. It is difficult to generalize on the distribution policies of firms marketing accessory equipment. In some cases direct sale is used, particularly where the order is for several units of the product or where the product is of relatively high unit value. A firm like Hyster Canada Limited, manufacturing forklift trucks, may sell directly because the price of a single unit is large enough to make this distribution policy profitable. In the main, however, manufacturers of accessory equipment use middlemen because the market is geographically dispersed, there are many different types of potential users, and individual orders may be relatively small.

Accessory equipment is not generally made to specification, so the products of a given manufacturer are ordinarily standardized. Also, the goods are not highly technical. For these reasons, manufacturers can use advertising effectively in a promotional program.

OPERATING SUPPLIES

Operating supplies are the "convenience goods" of the industrial field; they are short-lived, low-priced items usually purchased with a minimum of effort. They aid in a firm's operations, but do not become a part of the finished product. Illustrations are floor wax, lubricating oils, pencils and stationery, registration supplies in a university, heating fuel, and washroom supplies.

Marketing considerations. As with consumer convenience products, industrial operating supplies necessitate broad distribution. A firm will make extensive use of wholesaling middlemen because the product is low in unit value, is bought in small quantities, and goes to many users. Price competition is heavy because competitive products are quite standardized and brand insistence is low.

CHARACTERISTICS OF INDUSTRIAL MARKET DEMAND

Four general demand characteristics help to differentiate the industrial market from the consumer market.

DEMAND IS DERIVED

Since industry has no purpose except to supply the wants of the consumer market, the volume of goods which can be sold to an industrial user is dependent upon the behavior of the ultimate consumer. That is, the demand for industrial goods is derived from the demand for consumer products which the industrial items play a part in making. The demand for steel is partially dependent upon the consumer demand for automobiles and refrigerators, for example. The demand for steel is also dependent upon the demand for butter, baseball gloves, and bongo drums because the tools, machines, and other equipment involved in making these items are made of steel. Thus as the demand for baseball gloves increases, the glove manufacturers may buy more steel sewing machines, steel filing cabinets, or adding machines.

We should note, however, that the factor of derived demand is often operative only over the long run. In the short run, the derived demand is most noticeable in those products which are used directly in the production of consumer goods, for instance, steel used to make automobiles. This would exclude the large number of goods (often called "producers' durables") whose demand is so indirectly dependent on consumer demand that it is hardly amenable to treatment as derived demand at all. Their demand is dependent largely on other variables, such as changes in the cost of labor, in technology, and in the availability of capital.

There are several important marketing implications in the fact that industrial market demand is a derived demand. The producer of an industrial product may direct a considerable share of his promotional program to the ultimate consumer. Thus steel manufacturers, through consumer media such as television and magazines, have urged consumers to have a "white Christmas" by buying new refrigerators and stoves or by furnishing their kitchens with all-steel cabinets. Du Pont of Canada has advertised to the consumer the advantages of clothing made of Dacron (a Du Pont-branded fiber).

Accurate long-range market planning and forecasting of consumers' needs are of vital importance to producers of industrial goods. Telephone, gas, and electric companies must forecast consumer population movements years in advance so that pipelines, cables, and other equipment can be installed underground.

DEMAND IS INELASTIC

Another significant characteristic of the industrial market, and one related to the derived-demand feature, is that the demand for many industrial products is inelastic. That is, the demand for the product will respond very little to changes in its price. If the price of buttons for men's shirts and jackets should suddenly rise or fall considerably, there would probably be no appreciable change in demand. If there were a radical increase in price, manufacturers might put fewer buttons on coat sleeves; or if prices were to drop substantially, some firms might stockpile a supply. On balance, however, there would be very little shift in demand.

A basic reason for the general inelasticity of demand for industrial goods is that the cost of a single part or material is ordinarily an inconsequential portion of the total cost of the finished product. The cost of the chemicals in paint is a small part of the price that a consumer pays for a gallon of enamel; the cost of enamel on a refrigerator is a small part of the price of the product to the consumer. Even the cost of expensive capital equipment (installations), when distributed over thousands of units of a product, becomes a very small part of the total unit cost. As a result, when the price of the industrial product shifts, there is very little change in demand for the ultimate consumer product, even when the effect of the price shift is passed on to the consumer. If there is no appreciable shift in the demand for the consumer good, then by virtue of the derived- demand feature, there is no change in the demand for the industrial product going into the consumer good.

From a marketing point of view, there are the three factors to consider regarding the inelasticity of industrial market demand. The first is the position of an entire industry as contrasted with that of an individual firm. An industry-wide cut in the price of steel belts used in tires will have a negligible effect on the demand for automobile tires, and consequently there will be a negligible change in the total demand for steel belts. The pricing policy of an individual firm, however, can substantially alter the demand schedule facing this firm. If one supplier significantly cuts the price of steel belts, he may draw a great deal of business away from his competitors. His advantage, of course, will be temporary because his competitors will undoubtedly retaliate in some way in order to recapture their lost business. Nevertheless, in the short run, the demand curve facing a single firm is much more elastic than the industry's curve.

Another marketing factor involved here is time. Much of what has been said refers to short-run situations. Over the long run, the demand for a given industrial product is more elastic. If the price of cloth for men's suits is raised, there probably will be no immediate shift in the price of the finished garment or in the demand for it. The increase in cost of materials may be reflected in a $10 rise in suit prices for next year and may influence the demand for suits, and thus for cloth, over a period of a year or more.

One further aspect of this point is the relative importance of a specific industrial product in the cost structure of a finished good. We may generalize to this extent: the more significant the cost of an industrial product as a percentage of the total price of the finished good, the greater the elasticity of demand for this industrial item.

DEMAND IS WIDELY FLUCTUATING

The market demand for most classes of industrial goods fluctuates considerably more than the demand for consumer products. Fluctuations in the demand for installations—major plant equipment, factories, large generators, etc.—are especially great. Substantial fluctuations also exist in the market for accessory equipment—office furniture and machinery, minor plant equipment, delivery trucks, and similar products. These are reflected in, and tend to accentuate the swings in, the demand for industrial raw materials, such as metals and other minerals. One exception to this generalization is found in agricultural products intended for processing. There is a reasonably consistent demand for animals intended for meat products, for fruits and vegetables which will be canned or frozen, and for grains and dairy products.

Fluctuations in market demand for industrial products can influence all aspects of a firm's marketing program. In product planning, they may stimulate a firm to diversify—to go into other product lines, even into consumer products—in order to ease production and marketing problems. Distribution policies may be affected. Rather than use a sales force, which must be either trimmed back or maintained at full strength (but at a loss) when demand declines, a seller may decide to make greater use of manufacturers' agents or wholesalers to reach his market. Pricing policies and practices may be involved; management may attempt to stem a decline in sales by cutting prices and thus attracting the business of competing firms. Marketing management is hard pressed to know how to budget for its advertising program. When demand declines, the inclination is to cut back in advertising. Yet at the same time, a firm wants to keep its name before its potential market and also be in there promoting when the market starts to pick up again.

MARKET IS KNOWLEDGEABLE

Unlike the ultimate consumer, the typical industrial buyer is usually well informed about what he is buying. He knows the relative merits of alternative sources of supply and competitive products. A purchasing agent's advancement in the firm, often his very job, depends upon how well he performs. Naturally he will do all he can to ensure that what he orders is a combination of the lowest cost, best quality, and most service from the seller.

In marketing its product, an industrial goods firm places greater importance on its personal selling program than does a firm selling consumer goods. Industrial salespeople must be carefully selected, properly trained, and adequately compensated. They must give the most effective sales presentation possible and furnish satisfactory service both before and after the sale is made.

DETERMINANTS OF INDUSTRIAL MARKET DEMAND

To make a detailed analysis of market demand, a firm selling to *consumer* markets would make a quantitative analysis of the distribution and composition of population and income and a qualitative analysis of consumer motivation and buying patterns. Essentially the same basis of analysis can be used by a firm selling to the *industrial* market. The factors affecting the market for industrial products are the number of potential industrial users and their purchasing power, buying motives, and buying habits. Since the quantitative and qualitative aspects of the industrial market are examined from the point of view of an individual seller, it will be possible to bring out additional differentiating characteristics of this market and to observe specific differences between consumers and industrial users.

NUMBER AND TYPES OF INDUSTRIAL USERS

Total market. Analysis of the industrial market shows that it contains relatively few buying units when compared with the consumer market—approximately one-half million users, in contrast with 22 million consumers in about six million households. The industrial market will seem particularly limited to most companies because they sell to only a segment of the total. A firm which sells to meat processing plants in 1972, for example, would find only 468 potential customers in Canada. Similarly, there were only 223 plants engaged in metal stamping and pressing which employed more than 20 employees in 1972, and only 27 companies manufacturing batteries in Canada in that year.[4] Consequently, marketing executives

---

4 Statistics Canada, *Slaughtering and Meat Processing, 1972.* Cat. No. 32-221, Information Canada, Ottawa, 1974, p. 4: *Metal Stamping, Pressing and Coating Industry, 1972.* Cat. No. 41-227, Information Canada, Ottawa, 1974, p. 13: *Battery Manufacturers, 1973.* Cat. No. 43-208. Information Canada, Ottawa, 1975, p. 5.

should try to pinpoint their market carefully by type of industry and geographic location. A firm marketing mining equipment is not interested in the total industrial market or even in all of the many companies engaged in mining in this country. This seller is interested in information which will help him identify the market for his particular products.

One very useful source of information is the Standard Industrial Classification system (SIC) which enables a company to identify relatively small segments of its industrial market.[5] All types of businesses in Canada are divided into twelve groups as follows.

1. Agriculture
2. Forestry
3. Fishing and trapping
4. Mines, quarries and oil wells
5. Manufacturing industries (20 major groups)
6. Construction industry
7. Transportation, communication and other utilities
8. Trade
9. Finance, insurance and real estate
10. Community, business and personal service industries (8 major groups)
11. Public administration and defence
12. Industry unspecified or undefined

A separate number is assigned to each major industry within each of the above groups, then, three- and four-digit classification numbers are used to subdivide each major category into finer segments. To illustrate, in division 5 (manufacturing) major group 4 (leather) contains:

SIC code	Industrial Group
172	Leather tanneries
174	Shoe factories
175	Leather glove factories
179	Luggage, handbag, and small leather goods manufacturers

Size of industrial users. While the market may be limited in the total number of buyers, it is large in purchasing power. As one might expect, industrial users range in size from very small companies with fewer than 5 employees to firms with over 1,000 workers. A relatively small percentage of firms account for the greatest share of the value added by a given industry. As an example from a recent Statistics Canada report (Figure 8-2), 1.4 percent of the firms—those with 500 or more employees—accounted for about 38 percent of the total dollar value added by manufacturing and for 32 percent of the total employment in manufacturing. The firms with fewer than 50 employees accounted for 81 percent of all manufacturing establishments, but produced only 14 percent of the value added by manufacturing.

The marketing significance in these facts is that the buying power in the industrial market is highly concentrated in a relatively few firms. This market concentration has considerable influence on a seller's policies regarding his channels of dis-

---

5 Statistics Canada, *Standard Industrial Classification Manual.* Cat. No. 12-501, Information Canada, Ottawa, 1970.

Figure 8-2. Size distribution of manufacturing establishments in Canada, 1971, by number of employees.

This table shows that buying power in the industrial market is highly concentrated in relatively few firms. 4.8 percent of the companies, those with 200 or more employees, accounted for 60 percent of the value added by manufacturing. How might this concentration affect a seller's marketing program?

Number of Employees	Number of Establishments	Total Number of Employees	Value Added	Percentage of Firms	Percentage of Employees	Percentage of Value Added
1-4	10,159	14,788	185,446	31.8	1.0	0.9
5-9	5,327	34,132	334,385	16.7	2.2	1.5
10-19	5,126	71,226	749,231	16.1	4.6	3.4
20-49	5,229	162,022	1,854,111	16.4	10.4	8.5
50-99	2,729	190,542	2,346,736	8.6	12.3	10.8
100-199	1,810	256,390	3,358,634	5.7	16.5	15.5
200-499	1,085	327,893	4,598,242	3.4	21.1	21.2
500-999	316	220,449	3,483,023	1.0	14.2	16.0
1000 +	127	274,163	4,827,707	0.4	17.7	22.2
Total	31,908	1,551,605	21,737,514	100.0	100.0	100.0

Source: Statistics Canada, *Manufacturing Industries of Canada: Type of Organization and Size of Establishments, 1971.* Cat. No. 31-210, Information Canada, Ottawa, 1975, pp. 18-19.

tribution. He has greater opportunity to deal directly with the industrial users. Middlemen are not so essential as in the consumer market.

Regional concentration of industrial users. There is a substantial regional concentration in many of the major industries and among industrial users as a whole. A firm selling products usable in oil fields will find the bulk of its market in Alberta, in the Northwest Territories, and in the U.S. and abroad. Rubber products manufacturers are located mostly in Ontario, shoes are produced chiefly in Quebec and almost all of the nation's garment manufactuers are located in Southern Ontario and Quebec. There is a similar regional concentration in the farm market.

Four-fifth of all manufacturing plants are located in Ontario and Quebec. Five census metropolitan areas had manufacturing shipments of more than one billion dollars each in 1967. In descending order of importance, these were: Toronto, Montreal, Hamilton, Vancouver and Windsor. Together they accounted for about 47 percent of all Canadian manufacturing industries. If Winnipeg and Kitchener are added, these seven centers account for over 55 percent of all goods produced by manufacturers in Canada.

While a large part of a firm's market may be concentrated in limited geographic areas, a good portion may lie outside these areas. Consequently, a distribution policy must be developed which will enable a firm to deal directly with the concentrated market and also to employ middlemen (or a company sales force at great expense) to reach the outlying markets.

Vertical and horizontal industrial markets. A marketing executive who is analyzing his industrial market should determine whether this market is vertical or horizontal. If his product is usable by virtually all firms in only one or two industries he has a *vertical* market. Some precision instruments are intended only for the marine market, but every boatbuilder or shipbuilder is a potential customer. Many types of agricultural equipment may have no market outside the farm market, but every operating farm is a potential user. If his product is usable by many industries, his market is said to be broad, or *horizontal*. Industrial supplies, such as lubricating oils and greases, small tools, small motors, and some paper products, may be sold to a wide variety of industries.

This analysis of the market will influence a firm's marketing policies. In a vertical market a product can be tailor-made to meet the specific needs of one industry. In a horizontal market the product must be developed as an all-purpose item. Middlemen are more apt to be used in the marketing program for horizontal markets, although some vertical markets do employ middlemen simply because the orders are too small to warrant the cost of using company salesmen. Advertising and personal selling programs can be more pinpointed in vertical marketing situations, and trade journals in specific fields can be used as an advertising medium.

BUYING POWER OF INDUSTRIAL USERS

Another determinant of industrial market demand is the purchasing power of industrial users. This can be measured either by the expenditures of industrial users or by their sales volume. Many times, however, expenditures or sales volume data are not available or are very difficult to estimate. In such cases it is more feasible to use an activity indicator, or market factor, which is related to income generation and expenditure. Sometimes an activity indicator is a combined indicator of purchasing power and the number of industrial users. Following are examples of activity indicators which might be used to estimate the purchasing power of industrial users.

Measured by manufacturing actvity. Firms selling to manufacturers might use as market indicators such factors as the number of employees, the number of plants, and the dollar value added by manufacturing. A firm selling work gloves used the number of employees in manufacturing establishments to determine the relative values of various geographic markets. A company which sold a product to control stream pollution used two indicators—the number of firms processing wood products (paper mills, wood pulp processors, plywood mills, and so forth) and the manufacturing value added by these firms.

Measured by mining activity. The number of mines operating, the volume of their output, and the dollar value of the product as it leaves the mine all may indicate purchasing power of mines and thus may be used by any firm marketing industrial products to mine operators.

Measured by agricultural activity. A company marketing fertilizer, feed, or agricultural equipment can estimate the buying power of its market by studying such indicators as cash farm income, acreage plants, or crop estimates and yields. The chemical producer who sells to a fertilizer manufacturer might study the same indices because the demand for chemicals in this case is derived from the demand for fertilizer.

Measured by construction activity. If an enterprise is marketing building materials, such as lumber, plywood, brick, gypsum products, or builders' hardware, its market is dependent upon construction activity. This may be indicated by the number and value of building permits issued or by the number of construction starts by type of housing (single-family residence, apartment, commercial). A seller must select the appropriate indicator. A firm producing residential builders' hardware (door locks, window catches, and kitchen cabinet hardware) should not use an index which includes industrial and commercial construction.

BUYING MOTIVES OF INDUSTRIAL USERS

Industrial buying behavior, like consumer buying behavior, is initiated when an aroused need (a motive) is recognized. This leads to goal-oriented activity designed to satisfy the need. Once again marketing practitioners must try to determine what motivates the buyer.

Industrial buying motives, for the most part, are presumed to be rational, and an industrial purchase normally is a methodical, objective undertaking. The industrial buyer is motivated primarily by a desire to maximize his firm's profit. More specifically, his buying goal is to get the optimum combination of price, quality, and service in the products he buys. On the other hand, salespeople would maintain that some industrial buyers seem to be motivated more toward personal goals (moving up in the firm, or even lining their own pockets) which are in conflict with their employers' goals.

Actually, the industrial buyer does have two goals—to improve his position in the firm (personal self-interest) and to further his company's position (in profits, competition, acceptance by society, etc.) Sometimes these goals are mutually consistent, and sometimes they are in conflict. Obviously, the greater the degree of similarity, the better for both the organization and the individual. That is, he sees the mutuality of his and the company's goals, and he is more susceptible to rational promotional appeals from sellers. When very little mutuality of goals prevails, the situation is poor. Probably the more usual situation is to find some overlap of interests, but also to find a significant area where the buyer's goals do not coincide with those of the firm. In these cases a seller might appeal to the buyer on a rational, "what's-good-for-the-firm" basis and also on an ego-building basis. Promotional efforts attuned to the buyer's ego are particularly useful when two or more competing sellers are offering essentially the same products, prices, and services.[6]

INDUSTRIAL BUYING PROCESS

Competition and the complexity of industrial marketing are encouraging companies to focus attention on the *total* buying process and to treat it as an ongoing relationship of mutual interest to both buyer and seller. As one example of this approach, researchers in a Marketing Science Institute study developed a framework to explain different types of industrial buying situations.[7] The grid-type model for

---

6 For the notion that industrial buying behavior often is motivated by noneconomic influences such as buyers' personality, personal needs, and emotions, see David T. Wilson, "Industrial Buyers' Decision-Making Styles," *Journal of Marketing Research*, November, 1971, pp. 433-436; Jack Schiff, "Why Pros Buy Like Amateurs," *Sales Management*, October 15, 1970, p. 50; Ernest Dichter, "Industrial Buying Is Based on Same 'Only Human' Emotional Factors that Motivate Consumer Market's Housewife," *Industrial Marketing*, February, 1973, p. 14; and Wallace Feldman and Richard Cardozo, "The Industrial Revolution and Models of Buyer Behavior," *Journal of Purchasing*, November, 1969, pp. 77-88.

7 Patrick J. Robinson, Charles W. Faris, and Yoram Wind, *Industrial Buying and Creative Marketing*, Allyn and Bacon, Inc., Boston, 1967; in the same vein, see Frederick E. Webster, Jr., and Yoram Wind, "A General Model for Understanding Organizational Buying Behavior," *Journal of Marketing*, April, 1972, pp. 12-19. For a more complete conceptual study of the topic, see Webster and Wind, *Organizational Buying Behavior*, Prentice-Hall, Inc., Englewood Cliffs, N.J., 1972.

this framework is illustrated in Fig. 8-3. The model reflects two major aspects of the industrial buying process—(1) the classes of typical buying situations and (2) the sequential steps in the buying process.

THE BUY-GRID FRAMEWORK

BUY PHASES	BUY CLASSES		
	New task	Modified rebuy	Straight rebuy
1. Anticipation or recognition of a problem (need) and a general solution			
2. Determination of characteristics and quantity of needed item			
3. Description of characteristics and quantity of needed item			
4. Search for and qualification of potential sources			
5. Acquisition and analysis of proposals			
6. Evaluation of proposals and selection of supplier(s)			
7. Selection of an order routine			
8. Performance of feedback and evaluation			

Figure 8-3. The most complex buying situations occur in the upper left-hand portion of the "buy grid" framework when the largest number of decision makers and buying influences are involved. The initial phases of a new task generally represent the greatest difficulty for management. *Source:* Patrick J. Robinson, Charles W. Faris, and Yoram Wind, *Industrial Buying and Creative Marketing,* Allyn and Bacon, Inc., Boston, 1967, p. 14.

Three typical buying situations (called *buy classes*) were identified as follows: new tasks, modified rebuys, and straight rebuys. The *new task* is the most difficult and complex of the three, and it usually involves more buying influences than the other two. The problem is new, information needs are high, and evaluation of alternatives is critical. The seller has his greatest opportunity to be heard and to display his creative salesmanship in identifying and satisfying the buyer's needs.

Straight rebuys—a routine purchase with minimal information needs and no real consideration of alternatives—is at the other extreme. Buying decisions are made in the purchasing department, usually working from a list of acceptable suppliers. Suppliers, especially those from new firms not on the "list," have difficulty getting an audience with the buyer. *Modified rebuys* are somewhere between the other two in terms of time required, information needed, alternatives considered, etc.

The other major element in the buy grid reflects the idea that the industrial buying process is a sequence of eight stages, called *buy phases*. The process starts with the recognition of a problem; ranges through the determination and description of product specifications, the search for and evaluation of alternatives, and the buying act; and ends with postpurchase performance feedback and evaluation. (This surely is reminiscent of the consumer's buying decision process outlined in the preceding chapter.)

BUYING PATTERNS OF INDUSTRIAL USERS

Overt patterns of buyer behavior in the industrial market differ significantly from consumer behavior patterns on several points.

Length of negotiation period. The period of negotiation in an industrial sale is usually much longer than that in a consumer market sale. Some of the usual reasons for the extended negotiations are (1) several executives are involved in the buying decision; (2) the size of the sale is often large; (3) the industrial product is made to order, and considerable discussion is involved in establishing the exact specifications; and (4) bids are often involved (as in construction work), and the seller needs time to prepare careful estimates.

Frequency of purchase. In the industrial market, firms buy certain products very infrequently. Large installations are purchased only once in many years. Smaller parts and materials to be used in the manufacture of a product may be ordered on long-term contracts, so that an actual selling opportunity exists only once every year. Even standardized operating supplies, such as office supplies or cleaning products, may be bought only once a month.

Because of this buying pattern, a great burden is placed on the advertising and personal selling programs of industrial sellers. Their advertising must keep the company's name constantly before the market so that when a buyer is in the market, he will be acquainted with the selling firm. The salespeople must call on potential customers often enough to know when a customer is considering a purchase. In this instance, patterns of infrequent sales and lengthy negotiation periods are closely related. A salesperson for National Cash Register may find out, through a regular call, that a hospital is considering the installation of a machine accounting system. The sale may not be consummated for a year or more. Nevertheless, the seller would have lost all opportunity for the sale if his representative had not called when the prospective customer was first contemplating the changeover.

Size of order. The average industrial order is considerably larger than its counterpart in the consumer market. This fact, coupled with the infrequency of purchase, means that an industrial seller cannot afford to lose sales because of weaknesses such as poor salesmanship, noncompetitive pricing, uncertain delivery, or imperfect products.

Many sellers in the industrial market are plagued by firms that buy in small, hand-to-mouth quantities. A small order is unprofitable for most sellers, who are constantly combating this problem through buyer education and changes in their pricing and distribution policies.

Direct purchase. Direct sale from the producer to the ultimate consumer is rare. In the industrial market, however, direct marketing from the producer to the industrial user is quite common, especially when the order is large and much technical assistance is needed by the buyer both before and after the sale is made. From a seller's point of view, also, direct marketing is reasonable because there are relatively few potential buyers, these are big buyers, and they are geographically concentrated. Nevertheless, some products, such as hand tools, office supplies, and many manufacturing supplies, are marketed through middlemen, as are most industrial agricultural products.

When a seller deals directly with industrial users, he must organize and operate a high-caliber sales force. If a firm cannot build up a topnotch sales force, middlemen may have to be used in spite of the advantages of direct selling.

Multiple influences on purchases. In the industrial market, the purchasing decision is frequently influenced by more than one person, particularly in medium-sized and large firms. Even in small firms where the owner-manager makes all major decisions, he will probably consult with someone in the office or factory before making certain purchases. In firms large enough to have a separate purchasing department, a seller may be misled into thinking that the real purchasing power in the firm lies in one man or one department. We must distinguish between (1) initiating a purchasing project, (2) determining product specifications, and (3) selecting a supplier. Typically, the purchasing department places the orders. In many instances the purchasing agent also selects the individual supplier, but he must select one who carries the item or brand agreed upon by others in the firm.[8]

This buying pattern tends to lengthen the negotiation period, and it requires salesmen who are capable of determining who influences the buying decisions. Very often a salesperson will call on the wrong executive. Even after he finds out who the decision makers are in the buying firm, it may be very difficult to reach them.

Reciprocity arrangements. A highly controversial industrial buying habit is the practice of reciprocity, the policy of "I'll buy from you if you'll buy from me." Traditionally, reciprocity has been common among firms marketing homogeneous basic industrial products (oil, steel, rubber, paper products, chemicals) where price competition generally does not exist and one of the firms is a major supplier to the other. Today, however, reciprocal selling is found in a wide range of industries. Several companies have established a "trade relations" department. This unit, aided by the computer, can quickly collect the sales records and purchasing data needed to make the most effective use of this powerful selling tool.[9]

Some reasons are suggested for the increased use of reciprocity arrangements. First, a tightening in economic conditions may stimulate some firms to adopt reciprocity as a countermeasure to declining sales volume. Then after these conditions improve, the companies are hesitant to give up their new policy. Second, the trend toward product diversification opens additional avenues and opportunities for reciprocity dealings. Also, increased competition encourages sellers to try to control markets through reciprocity. Finally, many products today are of such acceptable

---

8 For a comprehensive study of purchasing procedures, indicating which departmental executives are involved in each stage of the process, see *How Industry Buys: 1970*, Research Department of *Scientific American*, New York, 1970. This study reported on the purchase of materials, component parts, and equipment by industry as a whole and by separate major industries. Also see, Steve Blickstein, "How to Find the Key Buying Influence," *Sales Management*, Sept. 20, 1971, p. 51.

9 For a discussion of the trade relations director—his rise, his responsibilities, and the typical services he performs—see Velma A. Adams, "The Rise of the Trade Relations Directors," *Dun's Review*, December, 1964, p. 35; Edward McCreary, Jr., and Walter Guzzardi, Jr., "A Customer is a Company's Best Friend," *Fortune*, June, 1965, p. 180; and "Trade Relations Men Walk Shaky Tightrope," *Business Week*, Oct. 5, 1968, p. 96.

quality that a given item made by any one of several manufacturers normally will satisfy a buyer's need for that type of product.

On the other hand, there are a number of dangers inherent in the practice of reciprocity. There is evidence that the Federal Department of Consumer and Corporate Affairs will take a closer look at reciprocal arrangements in the future, especially where such arrangements are engaged in on a formalized basis. There is a possibility that such arrangements will be considered in restraint of trade where they result in other potential suppliers not being able to deal with customers to whom they would normally be permitted to sell. Recent amendments to the Combines Investigation Act prohibit "tied selling" arrangements in which a company would agree to purchase from a supplier only if that supplier agrees in turn to buy the company's products. Under such legal pressures, some companies have abolished their trade relations departments, and have stopped generating information relating to a supplier's status as a customer. A firm engaging in reciprocity runs the risk of serious loss of morale in its sales force. Similarly, unless a clear policy statement is written regarding the practice, the morale and efficiency of the purchasing department may suffer. Under any circumstances it is difficult to justify purchasing from customers unless the purchases are voluntary acts and unless the buyer is getting competitive prices, quality, and service from the reciprocating seller.[10]

Catalogue buying and selling. Catalogue buying is quite prevalent among industrial users, particularly in connection with standardized, short-lived, and relatively low-priced products. Many wholesalers depend heavily upon their catalogue when selling to retailers.

From a marketing standpoint, catalogue buying relieves a sales force of some pressure but adds considerable importance to the preparation of the printed sales messages. In some cases, printed aids do virtually the entire selling job; salesmen call infrequently or not at all. In other instances, a salesman always calls but depends heavily on his catalogue. A firm selling to catalogue buyers has two general choices regarding the distribution of its printed materials: It may send its own catalogue to each buyer, or it may contribute its printed information to a common catalogue which will include material furnished by competitive firms and firms selling related products. *Thomas's Register of Manufacturers* or the *Canadian Trade Index* are examples of widely used common catalogues.

Demand for product servicing. The user's desire for excellent service is a strong industrial buying motive and may determine buying patterns. Consequently, sellers appeal for sales on the basis that they furnish better service than competitors. Frequently a firm's only attraction is its service, because the product itself is so standardized that it can be purchased from any number of companies.

Sellers must stand ready to furnish services both in advance and after the sale. A manufacturer of office machines may study a firm's accounting operation and suggest a more effective, lower-cost system which, incidentally, involves using the

---

10 For a report on reciprocity and the conditions of market structure and corporate organization which may draw government censure of reciprocal setting arrangements, see F. Robert Finney, *We Like to Do Business with Our Friends,* Marketing Science Institute, Cambridge, Mass., 1969. See also Reed Moyer, "Reciprocity: Retrospect and Prospect," *Journal of Marketing,* October, 1970, pp. 47-54; and "Reciprocity Is Dead," *Sales Management,* Oct. 15, 1970, p. 27.

seller's machines. He will also arrange to retrain the present office staff. He may even assume the responsibility of selecting and training additional machine operators. After the machines are installed, other services, such as repairs, may be necessary; buyers want to know that the seller will handle these matters promptly.

Quality and supply requirements. Another industrial buying motive which is reflected in buying patterns is the industrial user's insistence upon an adequate quantity of uniform-quality products. Variations in the quality of materials going into his finished product can cause considerable trouble for a manufacturer. He may be faced with costly disruptions in his production processes if the imperfections exceed quality-control limits. Adequate quantities are as important as good quality. A work stoppage caused by an insufficient quantity of material is just as costly as one caused by an inferior quality of material.

Meeting these supply requirements is in large part the responsibility of the seller's production department. But the marketing people are not completely absolved of responsibility, because they must furnish forecasts of what quantity and quality will be needed and when it must be available.

Adequacy of supply is an especially big problem for sellers and users of industrial raw materials such as agricultural products, metal ores, or forest products. Climatic conditions may disrupt the normal flow of goods, for example, when logging camps or mining operations become snowbound or when agricultural products fluctuate in quality and quantity from one growing season to another. These "acts of God" create additional managerial problems for both buyers and sellers with respect to their warehousing, standardization, and grading activities.

Leasing instead of buying. A growing behavioral pattern among firms in the industrial market is that of leasing industrial products instead of buying them outright. In the past, this practice was limited to large equipment, such as shoe manufacturing equipment (The United Shoe Machinery Company), data-processing machines (IBM), packaging equipment (American Can Company), postage meters, heavy construction equipment, and textile machinery. Even some freight cars and locomotives are owned by life insurance companies and leased to railroads. Today, industrial suppliers and users are expanding leasing arrangements to include delivery trucks, salesmen's automobiles, machine tools, agricultural feed mills, storage bins, and other items generally less expensive than big installations.[11]

Leasing has several merits. For the firm leasing out its equipment, total net income, after charging off pertinent repair and maintenance expenses, is often higher than it would be if the unit were sold outright. Also, the market may be expanded to include users who could not afford to buy the product, especially if it is large installation type of equipment, such as that leased by IBM and the can manufacturers. Leasing offers an effective method of getting distribution for a new product. Potential users may be more willing to rent a product than to buy it. If they are not satisfied, their expenditures are limited to a few monthly payments. Another advantage to the lessor is that he may be able to sell supplies for use with the machine (although he can no longer *require* the renter to buy his supplies).

From the lessee's point of view, some of the benefits may be summarized as follows:

---

11 See Leonard L. Berry and Kenneth E. Maricle, "Consumption without Ownership: Marketing Opportunity for Today and Tomorrow," *MSU Business Topics*, Spring, 1973, pp. 33-41.

1. Leasing allows the user to keep his investment capital free for other purposes.
2. There may be significant tax advantages; rental payments are totally tax-deductible, and they are usually larger than corresponding depreciation charges on owned products.
3. The advantages of using the equipment can be enjoyed sooner, and the disadvantages of major capital expenses avoided, if the equipment is rented rather than purchased.
4. New firms can enter a business with less capital outlay than would be necessary if they had to buy the equipment outright. This may not be an unmixed blessing, however. While ease of entry increases competition, it can also lead to an overcrowding of the field.
5. The user has available to him the newest products developed by the lessor.
6. Rented products are usually serviced by the lessor; this eliminates one headache associated with ownership.
7. Leasing is particularly attractive to users who need the equipment seasonally or sporadically, as in food canning or construction.

On the foundation of a careful market analysis an industrial goods manufacturer or middleman can develop strategies with respect to various parts of his marketing mix. In the following three chapters we shall consider some of the programming done in connection with one ingredient in the marketing mix—the product.

QUESTIONS AND PROBLEMS

1. "About 80 percent of all farm products are industrial goods." Give some examples of farm products which are *consumer* goods.
2. In which of the five subclassifications of industrial goods should each of the following be included? Which products may belong in more than one category?
   a. Typewriters
   b. Central air conditioners
   c. Nuts and bolts
   d. Dental chairs
   e. Automobile wax
   f. Land
   g. Cotton cloth
   h. Printing presses
   i. Copper wire
   j. Trucks
3. Give some examples of industrial products where the factor of derived demand is operative mainly in the long run. In the short run. From a marketing standpoint, what difference does it make whether the derived-demand characteristic is effective in the long run or the short run?
4. If the demand for most industrial goods is inelastic, why is it that sellers do not raise their prices to maximize their revenues?
5. Why do industrial goods usually fluctuate more widely in demand than consumer goods?
6. What are some marketing implications in the fact that the demand for industrial goods:
   a. Fluctuates widely.
   b. Is inelastic
   c. Is derived
7. "Economic recessions decrease the market demand for industrial goods more than for consumer goods." Do you agree? Explain.
8. What are the marketing implications for a seller in the fact that his customers are geographically concentrated and limited in number?
9. What differences would you expect to find between the marketing program

of a company selling to horizontal industrial markets and that of a company selling to vertical industrial markets?

10. In the industrial buying process we identified eight stages, called "buy phases." Yet the consumer buying decision process had only five steps, according to our discussion in Chapter 7. How do you addount for this difference? Are some of the required steps in the industrial buying process not necessary when a household consumer is making a buying decision?

11. Select four of the "buy phases" in the industrial buying process and explain how the relative importance of each one changes depending upon whether the buying situation is a new task or a straight rebuy.

12. Select three advertisements of industrial products and identify the buying motives stressed in the ads.

13. National Cash Register, IBM, Burroughs, and other manufacturers of office machines make a substantial proportion of their sales directly to industrial users. At the same time, wholesalers of office equipment are thriving. Are these two market situations inconsistent? Explain.

14. What suggestions do you have for industrial sellers to help them determine who influences the buying decision among industrial users?

15. What are the marketing implications for both buyers and sellers in the fact that a multiple purchasing influence often exists in industrial marketing?

CASES FOR PART TWO

CASE 2: JACK TURNER—PHOTOGRAPHER*

Analysis of a consumer market

Jack Turner had worked for many years for a professional portrait photographer in Vancouver. Jack was a capable photographer and, while gaining experience, he had saved enough money to buy the necessary equipment to establish his own portrait studio. He decided that he wanted to begin his own business somewhere in the Maritime Provinces, since both he and his wife had lived there for a number of years as children. Jack was especially good at portraits of young children and teenagers and he thought that he might specialize in the taking of portraits of younger people when he established his own business.

Jack had visited both Charlottetown and Fredericton some years earlier and thought that one of these cities would be his choice for the location of his business. His final choice depended upon which city provided a better opportunity for his line of work. His major problem was that he would have a difficult time choosing, since he was located many miles away in Vancouver. To begin his investigation,

*Case prepared by David K. Warner, Executive Assistant, School of Business Administration and Commerce, Memorial University of Newfoundland.

Jack went to the local Statistics Canada office to find some information on Charlottetown and Fredericton from the 1971 Census data.

Jack found that there were three portrait photographers located in each of the two cities. In 1971, the three portrait photographers in Fredericton shared a total income of approximately $60,000.00. Among them they employed a total of five employees. In the same year, the three portrait photographers in Charlottetown shared a total income of $56,000.00, and employed three employees.

Jack was also curious about the size of his potential market in the two cities. He found the following data concerning the size of the age groups in which he was interested.

TABLE 1

Age Composition of Population, 1971

	Total	Age Group			
		0-4	5-9	10-14	15-19
CHARLOTTETOWN					
TOTAL	19,130	1,330	1,605	1,855	1,975
MALE	8,880	705	820	950	940
FEMALE	10,250	620	790	910	1,030
FREDERICTON					
TOTAL	24,255	1,855	2,080	2,070	2,365
MALE	11,730	960	1,060	1,075	1,150
FEMALE	12,525	925	1,020	995	1,215

Source: Statistics Canada, Catalogue No. 92-715, Vol. I-Part 2, Table 10.

These accumulated statistics showed some close similarities between the two cities, such as the composition of the population in age groups and sex ratios. Jack felt that he needed some additional information, such as average income levels for the two cities. Using Statistics Canada Labour Census data he found the information in Table 2.

Jack Turner felt that his future would be more secure if he were to locate where incomes were relatively high. He reasoned that since his services as a portrait photographer were certainly not a necessity for the average family, there may be a relationship between higher incomes and the amount spent on portraits. He noticed from the data in Table 2 that average male earnings were about 11% higher in Fredericton and average female earnings were about 13% higher in that city. He also noted that there were more than twice as many people earning $10,000 or more per year in Fredericton as in Charlottetown.

Jack felt that he needed more information on family incomes so he went back to the Statistics Canada office to look for information on family income levels. He located the information presented in Table 3.

Jack felt that the decision to have portraits taken was a family decision and thus family income would be considered. He found that family income in Fredericton was 12% higher than in Charlottetown. He also found that the number of families earning over $12,000.00 a year was much higher in Fredericton than in Charlottetown.

TABLE 2

Individual Income Levels, 1971

CITY	Total Wage-Earners		Average Earnings	
	Male	Female	Male	Female
Charlottetown	5,835	4,020	$5,784	$2,816
Fredericton	10,075	6,025	$6,441	$3,185

Wage-earners reporting earnings by amount of earnings (partial breakdown)

	$5,000-6,999		$7,000-9,999		$10,000+	
	Male	Female	Male	Female	Male	Female
Charlottetown	1,035	375	990	145	770	15
Fredericton	2,200	720	2,025	275	1,670	95

Source: Statistics Canada, Catalogue No. 94-714, Vol. III-Part 1, Table 42.

TABLE 3

Family Income Levels, 1971

City	Families	Average Income
Charlottetown	4085	$ 9,287
Fredericton	5805	$10,478

	Family income (partial breakdown)		
	$5,000-7,999	$ 8,000-11,999	$12,000+
Charlottetown	1030	1030	915
Fredericton	1330	1640	1785

Source: Statistics Canada, Catalogue No. 93-724, Vol. II-Part 2, Table 87.

Jack realized that the Statistics Canada Census data were not current but they did provide him with some interesting facts. While he was certainly a long way from making up his mind, these data provided him a good starting point from which to begin his study of the city in which he was to relocate. Now he is planning to visit the two cities to obtain additional information.

QUESTIONS:

1. When Jack visits the two cities, where should he go to locate more information concerning the potential market for portrait photography?

2. Could he find out additional information on the potential of these markets without visiting the two cities?
3. Should Jack be using data that are five years or more old? Why might he want to obtain more recent data?
4. Does Jack have enough information at this moment to make a decision about where to locate his business? If not, what additional types of information does he need?

CASE 3. MARTIN BROTHERS*

Analysis of consumer market

The Martin brothers, John and Frank, were troubled because the sales in the paint department in their new retail hardware store were substantially below the levels—both in dollar volume and as a share of total store sales—which had been attained in the store which they had owned a few years ago. Because the paint department had constituted a major part of their business in earlier years, the two brothers were determined to identify and rectify the reasons for the currently poor performance.

In 1969 John and Frank were the owner-managers of a chain of three full-line retail hardware stores in a western city of 750,000 people. The stores had a combined annual sales volume of about $800,000. At that point in time, the brothers sold the stores, and John returned to school to work for a master's degree in business administration.

In 1972 the brothers decided to reenter the hardware business, so they purchased a store located in a suburban shopping center in an area called Forest View. The store also happened to be one of the units which they had previously owned and operated. John had received his M.B.A. degree and was teaching accounting at a university nearby. Frank worked at the store full time.

The Forest View store had 2,500 square feet of floor space, and the total store offering was classified for control purposes into the following nine departments:

1. Toys
2. Sporting goods
3. Lawn and garden
4. Tools
5. Builders' hardware
6. Fasteners (screws, bolts, etc.)
7. Plumbing and electrical supplies
8. Paint and paint sundries
9. Housewares

As this was the same departmental breakdown which they had used previously, the Martins were able to compare present performance with past results. When the Forest View store was re-acquired, it was not a continuing business. The store had been closed because of bankruptcy in 1971. Initially, the Martins were concerned about this situation, but by 1973 they realized that most of the departments were falling back into line. By 1974, all of the departments had reached or exceeded previous sales levels with the exception of the paint department. This troubled the

---

* Adapted from case prepared by Michael D. Hutt and Roger W. Hutt, Michigan State University. Reproduced with permission.

Martins because paint had constituted a major part of their business in 1969 and earlier years. (See Table 1.)

During the last half of 1974, the Martins purchased two additional hardware stores in the local area and hence had little time to devote to the paint problem at the Forest View store. Early in 1975, however, John again began to concentrate his efforts on the paint department problem and reflect on the past. "Before we sold out in 1969, we were doing $800,000 in sales for the three stores. The paint department contributed $160,000 of this total." This volume had enabled Martins to sell their own private brand of paint. The private label paint was made by a local manufacturer and sold under the label Martin Brothers. The private label paint accounted for 13 percent of the paint sales volume in the three stores in 1968. The bulk of the remainder came from Glidden interior house paint. Custom-mixed paint had accounted for a very small portion of sales in 1968. John had liked the private label because it "got the Martin name into homes and tied people to our brand of paint." The Martins however, felt they did *not* have the sales volume in 1974 to justify having a private label. Private brand paint had to be purchased in truck load lots at a cost of $5,000 per load.

When the Martins sold out in 1969, the nearest competition was Fairfax paint store, located in the same shopping center. When the Forest View store was re-acquired in 1972, there was new competition—Bargain Paint Center and Plaza Discount Store. Bargain Paint Center carried several national brands such as Pittsburgh and CIL in addition to their own private label. John described Bargain Paint Center's strategy in this manner: "They advertise national brands but they don't have much depth in them. Just a sampling. Also, they emphasize price and then try to switch you to their own brand." Plaza carried Moore paint and the Martins were not sure of the effect of their competition.

John could not pinpoint the exact cause of the decline, but he believed at least three factors contributed to it. First, wall paneling became more important and there was a re-birth of interest in wallpaper. Since interior paint constituted the major portion of total paint sales, this would naturally have an impact on the paint sales. Second, from discussions with salesmen, John thought that mixed colors were possibly more important in 1974 than they had been in 1969. Martins had used a mixing system before they sold out. However, because custom-mixed paint accounted for only a very small portion of sales, they had not used it since re-acquiring the Forest View store. Moreover, the equipment needed for the mixing system cost $1,200 and it required some experience and time on the part of the employees. Martins had no one who specialized in paint because they had a low overhead operation with no more than one full-time employee and one part-time employee working in the store.

Third, John was not convinced that potential paint customers were brand conscious. He did, however, believe that Bargain Paint Center had been successful in attracting customers by advertising national brands and then selling their private label at discount prices. Since the re-opening of the Forest View store, the Martins had been selling Glidden paint at discount prices. They also had been carrying specialty paint (spray paint and touch-up paint) and also paint supplies.

In the way of corrective measures, John believed that there were at least three alternative courses of action worthy of consideration: (1) purchase a paint-mixing system and train the employees to use it; (2) sell a private label paint; (3) follow Bargain Paint Center's strategy and offer two or three national brands in addition to a private brand.

Table 1. Forest View Store

Year	Total sales	Paint dept. sales	Paint dept. sales as % total sales
1968	$100,000	$19,000	19
1969	100,000	20,000	20
1973	107,000	5,350	5
1974	145,000	7,250	5

Before making any decision involving product or promotional policies, John thought they ought to find out more about the buying motives and habits of their present and potential paint customers. To gather this information that would aid in their decision making, the Martins retained the services of Mr. Paul Carillo, a marketing instructor at a nearby university. Mr. Carillo discussed the problem with the Martins and personally evaluated the competition. He then developed a questionnaire that was passed out to customers in the store by Martin's employees. Of the 600 questionnaires distributed, 430 were returned and the findings were tabulated for analysis. The highlights of these results are shown in the Appendix.

QUESTIONS

1. Analyze Martins' market for its paint products, and describe the characteristics of this market.
2. What course of action should the Martins take to improve the sales performance of their paint department?

APPENDIX: HIGHLIGHTS OF MARTIN BROTHERS' PAINT QUESTIONNAIRE
(Based on 430 Respondents)

1. Have you purchased any paint within the past year?

	Yes	No	Total
	79%	21%	100%

2. Factors which are most important, somewhat important, and unimportant when making a paint purchase.

	Most important	Somewhat important	Unimportant	Total
Famous brand name	24%	50%	26%	100%
Number of famous brands available	11%	50%	39%	100%
Number of colors available	74%	26%	0	100%
Discount prices	42%	55%	3%	100%
Assistance of experienced salesperson	72%	25%	5%	100%
Availability of credit terms	5%	6%	89%	100%

3. Name the store (or stores) that provides the best combination of those factors which are most important to you when making a paint purchase.

Bargain Paint Center	38%
Martins	19%

Sears	19%
Fairfax Paint Store	16%
Plaza discount store	3%
Midtown department store	3%
Any paint store	2%
Total	100%

4. Who purchases most of the paint for your home?

	Percentage of Responses
Wife only	21%
Husband only	63%
Husband and wife	11%
Painting contractor	5%
Total	100%

5. Who performs the major painting jobs in your home?

	Percentage of Responses
Wife only	8%
Husband only	55%
Husband and wife	32%
Painting contractor	5%
Total	100%

CASE 4: PAUL FINNEY TAKES UP TENNIS*

Social and Psychological Determinants of Behavior

When Paul Finney started his new job teaching Economics at Fanshawe College of Applied Arts and Technology, he vowed to himself that he was going to make more time available for sports and other recreational activities. Paul, who was 25, viewed himself as a person who had always been interested in sports and for many years had participated actively in various kinds of athletics. As an undergraduate at Queen's University, he had been a member of the varsity basketball team as well as playing on intramural squads in volleyball, water polo, and touch football. After graduating from Queen's, Paul had spent two years studying for a Master's degree at the University of Chicago. There, the pressure of studies had been too intense to allow much free time. Consequently, he had done almost nothing in the way of sports activities. He often complained to his wife of feeling lethargic through lack of exercise. However, Paul now had a new job in a new city. To him, it was clearly time to resume active participation in sports.

During the fall and winter months, Paul Finney lived up to his self-made promise. He took up badminton—a game that he used to play before going to Chicago. Quite a few of the faculty at Fanshawe played badminton at noon in the gym, and there was never any trouble in finding a partner for a game. True, Paul did not play as often as he had intended but, after all, it was his first year of teaching in a new environment. Besides, it was a substantial improvement over doing nothing at all.

Around February, Paul began to think ahead to the coming summer months. Badminton was best played indoors. Paul suspected that most of his associates at the College gave up the game over the summer in favour of outdoor activities. He

---

* Copyright University of Western Ontario, School of Business Administration, 1968. This case was written by Robert E. Nourse and was prepared as a basis for class discussion.

often had heard his friends express their interest in the arrival of warm weather. By the way they spoke, most of these people seemed to be looking forward to the opportunity to play one of two sports: golf or tennis.

Paul had played golf before, but he had never joined a golf club or played with any degree of regularity. Four years previously, while still a student at Queen's, he and several classmates had taken summer jobs with the Department of Industry in Ottawa. Using borrowed or rented clubs, they would occasionally drive to the Chaudière Club in nearby Hull and play nine holes in the early evening. Paul probably played golf a dozen times that summer but had played on only three or four other scattered occasions during his life. Both of his parents were avid golfers and had encouraged him to take up the game so frequently and forcefully that Paul sometimes wondered if he hadn't rebelled against the whole idea. Golf just didn't seem to be his "cup of tea." For one thing, he reasoned, it was far too time-consuming—at least three hours to play a decent round. He had never "broken 50" for nine holes and had been told by someone, he couldn't remember who, that the only way to improve was to play at least three times a week. At the same time, Paul had the impression that golf courses were always crowded and he invariably had the feeling of being rushed.

Tennis might well be different. Paul had never played a game of tennis, but he had watched Davis Cup matches on television. He reasoned that he could surely play a recreational game of tennis in an hour or less. This would allow lots of time in the day for other work. Furthermore, there were several tennis courts right on the campus at Fanshawe. Quite a few of his associates at the College seemed to be tennis players and, given his experiences with badminton, there would probably be no trouble in lining up a game at any time on a moment's notice. Paul began to think seriously about taking up tennis in the coming summer.

One night in March, he was sitting in his living room after supper checking through the day's mail. A sale catalogue had arrived from a local department store. Paul picked it up to browse through. He enjoyed looking through mail order catalogues—particularly those advertising a sale—even if he had no specific purchase in mind. By habit, he always started at the back page and worked toward the front. The kind of things he might like to buy always seemed to be in the back half of the book while the front was always full of women's dresses and lingerie. Sure enough, just a couple of pages from the back, he spotted a tennis racket. It seemed to be a pretty good bargain—a Dunlop, regularly $17.95, on sale for $10.95. He decided to keep it in mind.

It was early April before the issue of a tennis racket arose again. Paul was visiting the home of Dave Babcock, a fellow teacher at Fanshawe, and recalled having heard that Dave was an active tennis player. He decided to ask Dave about the racket in the catalogue. "I've been meaning to ask you about something," he led off. "I've been thinking about taking up tennis this summer, but I've never played before and haven't the foggiest idea of what kind of racket to get. I saw one on sale the other day in Sears' catalogue, but I just haven't any basis for evaluating whether the thing's any good or not. Have you any suggestions as to what I should be looking for in a racket?"

"It's really been some years since I bought a racket," David replied. "I'm not so sure that I'm the right person to ask. I don't really know what to tell you. The man you'd be best to ask is Bill Englander in the Math Department. He's played a lot of tennis and was the Junior Champion of British Columbia a few years ago.'"

The next day Paul attended a faculty meeting at Fanshawe. Arriving a little early, he noticed Bill Englander and thought to ask about the tennis racket. Paul had met Bill before and had spoken with him on numerous occasions during the year. It was not difficult, therefore, to broach the tennis racket question in much the same manner as he had with Dave Babcock the night before.

"I have to admit that I'm not too keen on Dunlop rackets," Bill offered. "I've seen a lot of people break them too easily. So I probably wouldn't be too enthusiastic about the racket you saw in the catalogue. That is, not unless it happened to be a Dunlop Max-Ply. For some reason, the May-Ply is way ahead of the other rackets Dunlop puts out and, in fact, is really a first-class racket. I rather doubt, however, that the one you saw was a Max-Ply. I think they run somewhat more expensive than $17.95 and aren't the kind of racket that's likely to go on sale."

Bill's remark came as somewhat of a disappointment to Paul because he had become quite interested in the Dunlop racket in the catalogue. Then, the thought crossed his mind that the racket was reduced to almost half price at a time when the tennis season was just coming up. "Why," he asked himself, "would there be such a large price reduction unless something was wrong with it?"

"A lot of people I know use Slazengers," Bill continued, "but I personally don't like them too well." He proceeded to explain what he didn't like about Slazenger rackets, but Paul was beginning to lose track of the conversation. He wondered to himself if Bill wasn't leading up to recommending a racket that would suit his own needs more than those of a beginner. At the same time, Paul sensed a definite tone of authority and expertise in Bill's remarks. There was little doubt that the fellow could be trusted to recommend a good racket—the only problem was that it might be *too* good.

Although nothing was said, Bill seemed suddenly to sense the hesitations that were running through Paul's mind. He paused for a moment, then began to speak again in a slower and more deliberate voice. "There are several good rackets on the market, but my choice for someone starting to play for the first time would be a Spalding. The reason I say this is that Spalding started making their rackets in Belgium about two years ago. At that time, they really lowered their prices. I think that you'd get better value in a Spalding racket than in anything else. After you've been playing for a while, you'll find that you develop fairly distinct ideas about what you want in a racket—a certain type of grip, the weight, or any one of a number of things. But you have to play for some time before you find this out. If you're starting, I don't think you could go far wrong with a Spalding."

Paul had begun to listen intently again. "If I bought a Spalding," he asked, "what would be a reasonable price to pay for it?"

"Well, I would think that somewhere between $12 and $15 would buy you a decent racket. Of course, you'd also have to pay to have it strung. That would cost anywhere from $5 to $15, depending on what kind of stringing you get."

"Do you have any advice on that? I don't know the first thing about having a racket strung."

"For a starter, you should probably get braided nylon. Don't get the plain nylon—it's the cheapest and won't last very long before it breaks. The braided nylon is made up of a lot of strands of thin nylon fibre braided together. That gives it a lot of strength, but at the same time isn't too expensive. They'll probably also ask you what tension you want it strung at—the more tension you have, the more 'zip' there is to the racket when you hit the ball. I'd say about 50 pounds would be fine. If you get the tension much higher than that, it becomes quite difficult to control the ball when you hit it."

When he got home that night, Paul checked the sale catalogue again. As Bill had suspected, the Dunlop racket that was on sale was not a Max-Ply.

For the next three or four weeks, Paul made no further move to buy a tennis racket, but he did think about it a lot. He mentioned to Bob Foulkes, a frequent badminton partner, that he was going to take up the game of tennis and was in the market for a racket. He also followed closely the newspaper accounts of upcoming Davis Cup matches between Canada and Mexico. Canada was supposed to have a good chance of winning but someone must have been too optimistic because they lost ignominiously in five straight matches.

In a casual conversation with a neighbour, Tom Norton, Paul discovered that Tom was also a tennis player. Tom mentioned that he had bought a new Dunlop Max-Ply the previous summer. He offered to sell Paul his old racket, which was not a Max-Ply, at a good price. Paul didn't encourage the idea and the matter of buying a used racket never developed further. Paul frequently met Bill Englander in the course of his work at Fanshawe, and Bill never failed to ask if Paul had bought a tennis racket yet. Each time, Paul replied negatively, always adding that he certainly was going to in the near future.

On the morning of April 28, Paul slept in. He had no classes to teach until 11:30 that morning; so he decided to visit Tom Munro Sports on his way into work. Munro's was one of two sporting goods stores in the city. Of the two, it seemed to be the one that most of Paul's friends talked about patronizing. Paul himself had bought badminton shuttles at Munro's on several occasions. Knowing the approximate layout of the store, he quickly spotted the tennis racket section upon entering and started to walk toward it. He was the only customer in Munro's at the time and was intercepted by a youthful-looking sales clerk even before reaching the tennis rackets.

"May I help you, sir?" asked the clerk.

"Yes, I'm interested in buying a tennis racket," Paul began. "I particularly like the Spalding—you do string them right here in the store, I assume?"

"Uh . . . yes sir, we do, but . . ."

"Good. You have the braided nylon?"

"Yes indeed. But I'm sorry to say that we don't have any Spaldings. We dropped their line about a year ago."

"Oh . . . why did you do that?"

The clerk slowly began to walk the remaining short distance tward the tennis racket section. Paul followed as the young man continued to talk. "Well, about two years ago, they dropped the prices on all of their rackets by a really significant amount. They started making their rackets overseas somewhere—Formosa, I think—they're not made in North America anymore, you know."

"No, they're made in Belgium."

"Is that it? . . . Well, anyhow, what happened to us, is that one day we were selling a Spalding racket for, say, $17.95. All of a sudden, we had the same racket being sold for about $7.95. Pretty soon, some of the people who had paid $17.95 began to notice this. Needless to say, they didn't like it one bit. We'd explain that it was Spalding who had reduced the price, but people were still pretty hostile. Eventually, we found that the only way to avoid this kind of situation was to drop the line altogether."

"No kidding!"

"That's exactly what happened . . . Do you mind me asking if you're new to the city, sir?"

"Well, yes I am—I just moved here last summer."

"I thought so because I was really surprised when you asked specifically for a Spalding. I don't recall ever having anyone ask me for a Spalding before. They just aren't that popular with tennis players around here . . . Did it have to be a Spalding, or could I show you something else?"

"Well, I'm not sure. I certainly had planned to buy a Spalding. What other lines do you carry?"

"Well, here in London, all the good tennis players use Dunlop Max-Ply. It's truly an excellent racket. The good players all swear by it."

"What does it run?"

"It's $26.95. Terrific value for a racket of that quality." The clerk removed a Max-Ply from the rack and held it loosely in his hand. Paul did not move to take it from him.

"I'd like to think about it for a while. I don't need the racket right away. What I really came in for was a pair of white shorts, size 36."

"By all means." Without looking further at tennis rackets, the two walked to a nearby counter containing the shorts. There was only one style of white shorts available. They were wrapped in a clear polyethylene bag.

Paul noted the price of $4.95 marked on the outside of the bag, but did not bother to remove the shorts. "I'll take a pair in size 36," he said. Immediately after paying for the shorts, he left the store.

During the next week, Paul was out of town on business. Soon after returning he happened to pass by College Sports, the only other sporting goods store of significant size in the city. He went in and walked over to the selection of tennis rackets. College Sports carried Slazenger, Wilson, and Dunlop rackets, but there were no Spaldings. Paul didn't bother to examine the rackets closely or to remove any from the rack. He left the store almost immediately, before a sales clerk had a chance to approach him.

Later in the week, Paul was shopping in Wellington Square Mall, an indoor shopping centre in the downtown area. Remembering that he had seen a small sporting goods department on the main floor of the Eaton's store there, he decided to see if they had any tennis rackets. There was only a limited selection. All except one of the rackets were pre-strung and there were no Spaldings. Again, he didn't bother to examine any closely and left the store quickly.

At about this time, Paul began to wonder if the whole business of buying a tennis racket wasn't taking up too much of his time. He tried to think of any other store in London that might have a large selection of rackets, but none came to his mind. He had visited three stores and had not found a Spalding racket in any of them. Paul began to think that he'd have to settle for some other kind of racket, but wasn't at all sure what it would be. He could feel himself getting quite confused.

On June 1st, Paul took his young son to Simpson's department store to buy a new pair of running shoes. On entering the store, he realized that it would be relatively convenient to walk by the sporting goods department on the way toward getting his son's shoes. "They probably don't have any more of a selection than Eaton's," he thought to himself, "but there's nothing to lose by taking a look anyhow."

While still some distance away from the sporting goods department, Paul could see quite a large number of tennis rackets displayed on a vertical rack sitting upright on an island counter. This rather surprised him. He walked up to the rack and looked more closely. All of the rackets were of a single brand, Jelinek, which

Paul had never heard mentioned before. Altogether, there were about 25 rackets displayed in various models of the Jelinek line; they ranged in price from $3.95 to $10.95. Looking more closely, Paul noticed from the label on one racket that the Jelinek brand was manufactured in Japan.

Paul walked slowly around to the other side of the island counter. There, he discovered a display of about two dozen additional rackets that he had not been able to see from his previous position. Most of them were Spaldings, although there were a few Dunlop Max-Ply rackets at one end. All were prestrung except the Max-Ply. Stapled beneath each racket's position on the rack was a small white card indicating the name of the racket, its price, and the kind of material with which it was strung. Paul read each of the cards carefully, noticing at the same time that most of the rackets were not hung in the correct position corresponding to their card. One card identified the Max-Ply at $26.95, unstrung. Another indicated a Wilson racket at $16.95, but the store was apparently out of stock because Paul couldn't see any Wilson rackets at all. Of the remaining four cards, all identified various Spalding models. Three of the four were identified as being strung with twisted nylon; they were priced at $7.95, $9.95, and $12.95. The remaining Spalding racket was a Fred Stolle model at $15.95, strung with braided nylon.

Removing the Fred Stolle racket from the rack, Paul was surprised to note how heavy and clumsy it felt in comparison to a badminton racket. The grip was much thicker and the whole racket much heavier. He swung it through the air a couple of times.

Holding the Fred Stolle racket in his hand, Paul looked over the remaining ones still hanging on the rack. He re-read the white cards beneath each one and, as he was doing so, a sales clerk approached him. The clerk said nothing. Finally, Paul pointed to the cards on the rack and asked the clerk to explain the difference between twisted nylon and braided nylon.

"I'm sorry sir, but I don't know very much about tennis rackets," the clerk replied.

" . . . Well, that's all right . . . I'm pretty sure this is what I'm looking for anyhow." Paul handed the clerk the Spalding Fred Stolle racket that he'd been holding.

While the clerk rang up the sale, Paul decided to look at tennis balls. The majority of the tennis balls stocked by Simpson's were various price lines of the Jelinek brand. Somehow Paul decided that he didn't want to start out by buying Japanese tennis balls. The only alternative was a large cellophane bag of twelve tennis balls for about $1.99. It was apparent to Paul that these were real "cheapies." Not only were they priced far below the other tennis balls, but they were also not packed in a vacuum cannister. Paul wasn't sure why tennis balls should be packed in a vacuum cannister, but the only ones he could ever recollect seeing had been in a container of that kind. He decided not to buy any tennis balls at this time.

However, after looking at the tennis balls, Paul remembered that he had intended to get a cover for his racket. No one had specifically suggested that he should have a cover. In fact, he had never kept his badminton racket in a cover. But Paul recalled having seen players walking to or from tennis courts at various times in the past. Most of them had a wooden press or cloth cover protecting the racket when it was not in use. Paul had ruled out the idea of a press, saying to himself that a press was heavy and that he'd never bother to put the thing on and take it off each time he played. Simpson's had several covers displayed on a counter near the tennis rackets. The first to catch Paul's eye was a white simulated leather cover with black trim and the word "Spalding" boldly emblazoned across each side. It was

$3.95. a less expensive cover at $2.95 was available in several different colours, but it had "Wilson" written across each side. Finally, there was a plain blue nylon cover priced at $1.49 with nothing written on each side. He picked up the Spalding cover and the plain blue one, examining each. A small label sewn inside the blue cover indicated that it was made in Japan. After a moment's hesitation, he decided to buy the plain blue cover.

A couple of days after buying the racket, Paul had commented on its purchase to Jack Bailey, a fellow member of the teaching staff at Fanshawe.

"Have you used it yet?" asked Jack

"Hell no—I just bought it and haven't played a game of tennis in my life."

"Then it's about time you started. What are you doing right now?"

"Not a great deal. But are you willing to waste your time with a duffer like me?"

"Sure—I'll show you what little I know of the game. The only problem is that I don't have any tennis balls with me."

"I haven't bought any yet myself, but I'm willing to do so right now."

"Good enough. We can drive down to Munro's and pick some up. Then we'll drop back here and have a game."

The two drove to Munro's in Paul's Car. There were no convenient parking places near the store, so Paul double-parked while Jack went into the store. He bought a cannister of three Slazenger balls for $2.59 on Paul's behalf.

Paul enjoyed his first game of tennis, although it was hardly a game in the true sense of the word. Paul quickly realized that he had a lot to learn yet and felt rather awkward at his seeming inability to hit the ball with any degree of accuracy. He noticed that Jack also had a Spalding racket, although not a Fred Stolle model.

During the weeks that followed, Paul noticed that he came to think and talk about tennis quite a bit. For example, he told John Lowery, a teacher of Economics at Fanshawe, of his initial experience at Tom Munro Sports. Paul raised the question as to whether the store's logic in dropping the Spalding line was sound business practice and whether Spalding's own decision to reduce prices on its rackets so drastically was a good one.

Paul had dinner with a former Queen's classmate, Peter Doubless, and learned that Peter was thinking about taking up tennis. Peter said that he thought he'd invest about $5.00 in a racket. Paul then explained how carefully he'd considered the matter of a tennis racket purchase and why he decided to start out by spending around $15.00. Peter's response was that he hadn't really thought about it that way, but that he probably should reconsider and spend more than he had initially planned.

Paul also showed his new racket to his neighbour, Tom Norton, and explained the difficulty he had encountered in finding a local merchant who stocked the Spalding line. Tom replied that he wished he had known Paul was looking for a Spalding because he knew that Sayvette, a local discount house, carried that brand. Paul didn't say anything, but the next time he was near Sayvette he went into the store and looked at their tennis rackets. He noted that there were two Spalding models, but that they were cheaper rackets priced at $3.95 and $5.95.

One one occasion, Paul showed his new racket to Bob Foulkes. Bob apparently played very little tennis, but was very keen on badminton. During the winter months, it had been Bob with whom Paul had played badminton most frequently. Noting that Paul's tennis racket was a Spalding, Bob asked if his badminton racket was also a Spalding.

"I really don't know," Paul replied. "Let me think for a moment . . . about all I can remember is that it's called a 'Viceroy.' But I don't think that's a manufacturer's name. It's just the name given to my particular model of badminton racket. I don't remember ever looking to see who the manufacturer was. I've had the racket for about six years now. It was given to me second-hand by an old fellow named Gord who used to run the locker room at the gym at Queen's."

Paul's curiosity was sufficiently aroused by this question that, later the same day, he made a point of looking closely at his badminton racket. The model name was not "Viceroy," as he had previously reported to Bob Foulkes. Rather, it was a "Varsity" model. The racket had been manufactured by Spalding.

QUESTION

1. What are the psychological and sociological determinants of Paul Finney's behavior?
2. To which of these should a tennis equipment manufacturer pay close attention?

CASE 5: PARK MANOR CONDOMINIUM*

Analysis of social and psychological market factors

Park Manor is a condominium apartment community located twenty-five minutes from downtown Winnipeg. (A condonimium is a building in which individuals own separate apartments, but share the ownership and maintenance of common facilities such as halls, roofs, heating systems, and outdoor area.) Park Manor was developed especially for individuals who have passed their forty-eighth birthday. In the first five years of its development, the 200-acre development has sold nearly four hundred apartments priced from $18,000 to $27,000, with an aggregate value of some $9 million.

Park Manor differs from other retirement communities which have been so successful in that it tries to attract both retired and working individuals. It has succeeded in this attempt, and over two-thirds of the residents are regularly employed. Further, Park Manor has been designed to serve and draw from a local, rather than a national, market. It also differs from the "family" condominiums which have sprouted in most large cities and which abound with children. No one with children under sixteen may live at Park Manor. In other respects, however, Park Manor is similar to the other types of condominium communities. It is attractive, well built, and located on spacious grounds with rapid access to the central city. Numerous recreational and personal-achievement activity opportunities are available. The chief rationale for Park Manor is that it provides "elegant but economical living in a maintenance-free, parklike atmosphere."

Troubled by a significant decline in sales in recent months, the developers, Herbert Klein, Hilton Howard, and Lloyd Franklin, have debated whether they have curtailed the market too severely by their age and no-children barriers. Mr. Howard believes they have already exhausted the "over-forty-eight" market and should lower the minimum age limit. Most present residents, however, view the peaceful, childless atmosphere as a major advantage and would fight such a change. Mr.

---

* Adapted from case written by Prof. John M. Hess, University of Colorado.

Franklin contends that the market is hardly touched but that they have drawn too heavily on retired individuals and have not spent enough of their energies attracting working people whose children have left home and who no longer desire a large house with its attendant maintenance problems. Mr. Klein thinks that they have taken the wrong tack entirely in terms of their geographic market. Rather than limiting their efforts to the local area, he suggests that Park Manor should attempt to draw retirees from a regional market. He points out that other prairie cities and towns have plenty of retirees, and that these people would like to stay in the region close to their families rather than go south or to the West Coast.

A recent market study conducted for Park Manor has revealed some public misconceptions and prejudices. There has been a tendency to shift promotional emphasis entirely each time one of the three partners perceives a new market segment which might be approached. This, in turn, has contributed to the public's confusion. A summary statement from the market study report reads as follows:

In review, the chief objections to Park Manor are:

1. Age. Most respondents view Park Manor as an old-people's home: It is clearly identified with the retirement, perhaps even the nursing-home market. Most people, regardless of their age, just do not think they are old enough to move there yet.
2. Income. The majority of the respondents identify Park Manor as an expensive high-income, high-cost place to live. They frequently parroted words from Park Manor's advertising such as "exclusive", "luxurious," and "country-club atmosphere." Another group has taken the economy advertising seriously and sees Park Manor as low-cost housing.
3. Institutionalization. People feel that they would lose their freedom if they moved to Park Manor. They associate the many activities and facilities with regimentation and institutionalism.
4. Not quite respectable. Many respondents perceive Park Manor as being not quite respectable. They suggested that the residents were probably rather shiftless and hedonistic. Words such as "playground," "leisure living," "pleasure," and "fun" were apparently drawn directly from advertising copy by such respondents.
5. Apartment living. Homeowners do not like the idea of living in an apartment, and apartment dwellers do not wish to invest or tie up funds in their residence.

It appears that each segment of the market reads or hears that portion of the advertising which confirms the feeling that Park Manor is for someone else.

The development company has learned that buying a home and moving are emotion-laden activities, and that each segment of the market has substantially different motives for changing residences. Unfortunately, it also appears that the motives of various segments are often at cross-purposes, so appeals to one segment may well alienate other segments. Park Manor, however, can no longer prosper by appealing to one segment of the market, so it must identify and select those market elements which are most compatible.

QUESTIONS
1. Which market should be the prime target for Park Manor?
2. Identify other logical submarkets for Park Manor and indicate which might be approached without alienating other submarkets.
3. What psychological or sociological factors are at work in limiting the market for Park Manor condominium apartments?

PART

3

THE PRODUCT

9

PRODUCT PLANNING AND DEVELOPMENT

After carefully analyzing his market, a marketing manager is in a position to develop a total marketing program designed to capture his desired share of that market. He has the four components of the marketing mix with which to work: the product, the price structure, the distribution system, and promotional activities. Each of Parts 3 to 6 is devoted to one of these components.

MEANING OF THE "PRODUCT"

In a very *narrow* sense, a product is simply a set of tangible physical and chemical attributes assembled in an identifiable form. Each different product category carries a commonly understood descriptive name, such as apples, steel, shoes, or baseball bats. Product attributes appealing to consumer motivation or buying patterns play no part in the definition. A Sunbeam Shavemaster and a Schick Flexamatic are one and the same product—an electric shaver.

A *broader* interpretation recognizes each brand as a separate product. In this sense an Eaton's man's suit and a Tip Top Tailors' man's suit are two different products. So too are two brands of an ethical drug, even though the consumer may perceive no difference except the imprint of the brand name on the pill. The brand name suggests a product difference to the consumer. Thus the concept of consumer want satisfaction begins to enter the picture.

Any change in a physical feature (design, color, size, packaging, etc.), however minor it may be, creates, in effect, another product. The seller has an opportunity to use a new set of appeals to reach what may be essentially a new market. When a manufacturer of cigarettes comes out with a flip-top box, this packaging change creates a new product. Mennen's shave cream, Rise, became three products when ingredients in the basic item were modified to create Rise with Lanolin, Rise with Menthol, and Rise Regular.

Carrying the analogy further, we can see that an Electrohome television set bought in a discount house on a cash-and-carry basis is a different product from the identical model purchased in a department store, where the customer buys the set for a higher price but gets it on credit, has it delivered free of extra charge, and avails himself of other store services. Again the interpretation of "product" is broadened, and we came nearer to a definition valuable to marketing people.

Our definition is as follows: A *product* is a complex of tangible and intangible attributes, including packaging, color, price, manufacturer's prestige, retailer's prestige, and manufacturer's and retailer's services, which the buyer may accept as offering satisfaction of wants or needs.

The key idea in this definition is that the consumer is buying more than a set of chemical and physical attributes. Fundamentally he is buying want satisfaction. A wise firm sells product *benefits* rather than just the product. As Elmer Wheeler, an author and well-known sales training consultant, said, "Don't sell the steak, sell the sizzle." A travel agency should not sell a two-week Caribbean cruise; rather, it should sell romance, glamour, rest, a chance to meet people, and the opportunity for education.

Manufacturers sell symbols as well as products. "People buy things not only for what they can do, but also for what they mean."[1] Goods are psychological symbols of personal attributes, goals, and social patterns. As was suggested in Chapter 5, we buy products which reinforce our self-image or self-concept, and people are shrewd judges of symbols.

WHAT IS A "NEW" PRODUCT?

We have been talking about the importance of *new*-product planning and development. But just what is a new product? Are the new models that auto manufacturers introduce each autumn new products? If a firm adds men's after-shave cologne to its product mix of toiletries and drug sundries, is this a new product? Or must an item be a totally new concept before we can class it as a *new* product?

Probably it is not important to seek a very limited definition; instead we may recognize several possible categories of new products. What is important for marketing executives to understand, however, is that each separate category may very well require quite different marketing programs to ensure a reasonable probability of market success.

Three recognizable categories of new products are as follows:

1. Products which are *really* innovative—truly unique. These are items such as a hair restorer or a cancer cure—products for which there is a real need but for which there are

---

1 Sidney J. Levy, "Symbols for Sale," *Harvard Business Review*, July-August, 1959, p. 118.

no existing substitutes generally considered satisfactory. In this first category we can also include those products which are quite different replacements for existing goods serving existing markets. Thus television to a great extent replaced radio and movies, plastics compete with wood and metals, and atomic power competes with other energy sources.

2. Adaptive replacements of existing products involving a *significant* differentiation in the existing article. Instant coffee replaced ground coffee and coffee beans in many markets; then freeze-dried instant replaced older-style instant coffee. Soup and dry cereal manufacturers introduce new types of these products and often discontinue existing ones which no longer fulfill company sales and profit expectations. Annual model changes in autos and new fashions in clothing also belong in this second category.

3. Imitative products which are new to your company but not new to the market. Your firm simply wants to enter that existing market with essentially a "me-too" product.

Perhaps the key criterion as to whether a given product is new is how the intended market perceives it. If buyers perceive that a given item is significantly different (from competitive goods being replaced) in some characteristic (appearance, performance, construction, etc.), then this is a new product.

RELATED TERMS

In addition to "product" and "product policies," you will hear such terms as "product planning," "product development," and "merchandising" and may wonder what they mean and how they are related.

Product planning and product development. *Product planning* embraces all activities which enable producers and middlemen to determine what should constitute a company's line of products. Ideally, product planning will ensure that the full complement of a firm's products is designed to strengthen the company's profit position. *Product development*, a more limited term, encompasses the technical activities of product research, engineering, and design. Here we are concerned with product innovation or improvement and are working with production, research, and engineering departments.

More specifically, the scope of product-planning and product-development activities includes decision making in the following areas:

1. Which products should the firm make and which should it buy?
2. Should the company expand or simplify its line?
3. What new uses are there for each item?
4. What brand, package, and label should be used for each product?
5. How should the product be styled and designed, and in what sizes, colors, and materials should it be produced?
6. In what quantities should each item be produced?
7. How should the product be priced? (Part 4 is devoted entirely to pricing.)

Merchandising. "Merchandising" is probably one of the two most loosely used terms in the marketing vocabulary. (The other, "sales promotion," is discussed in Part 6.) Merchandising means many things to many people. To some it is synonymous with marketing. To others it is the all-inclusive term, and marketing is only part of merchandising. Retailers make particularly heavy use of the word as a verb, noun, or adjective. A clothing buyer may be complimented for have "merchandised" a new sports shirt very well this season. Another executive may claim that sound "merchandising" is the foundation of a store's success. A third may note that the "merchandising" plans for next season are completed. One of the high-level executives in a department store is merchandising manager, and normally retail stores have no one with the title "marketing manager" or "sales manager."

In this book, *merchandising* is synonymous with product planning. That is, merchandising includes all planning activities of manufacturers and middlemen designed to adjust their products to the market demand.

Merchandising by manufacturers versus merchandising by middlemen. While it is true that most manufacturers are concerned with what to *make* and most middlemen are concerned with what to *buy*, one thing that is even more fundamental is that both groups are concerned with what to *sell*. The goals of product planning by manufacturers and middlemen are similar. Both want their merchandising to be market-oriented—to please a consumer by satisfying his wants. In fact, manufacturers and middlemen often work jointly to reach this goal. For instance, some high-quality furniture stores take a customer's order for a sofa covered with individually selected fabrics and then relay the order to a prearranged manufacturer. Very often retailers or wholesalers provide ideas which result in new mass-produced articles or refinements of established products.

IMPORTANCE OF PRODUCT INNOVATION

Most new products are marketing failures! Even large, usually successful companies have had products which did not meet their marketing goals and which were dropped. Ford had its Edsel and General Motors its Firenza. Estimates of product failure rates have run as high as 80 percent. Even among a group of prominent, well-managed companies, the success rate for products which reached the market was still only two of three.[2] These sobering facts should point up the importance of a good program for planning and developing new products.

JUSTIFICATION OF A FIRM'S EXISTENCE

Fundamentally, the social and economic justification for the existence of a business is its ability to satisfy its customers, whether they are industrial users or ultimate household consumers. A company meets its basic responsibility to society through the medium of its product (using the terms broadly here to include nontangible "goods," usually called "services"). Unless it fulfills this mission, a firm should not exist, and normally the competitive forces in our socioeconomic system do not permit its continuation, at least not for long.

Here an implicit and corollary social responsibility of business is to make effective use of its resources—particularly to minimize the waste of scarce human resources such as scientific and technical talent. Yet even in leading industrial firms, it is estimated that about 70 percent of new-product expenditures are for products that never become commercial successes. Of the money spent in the scientific and

---

2 *Management of New Products*, Booz, Allen & Hamilton, Inc., New York, 1968, pp. 2, 11-12. Failure-rate estimates vary because of different definitions of what constitutes failure in the market.

engineering development stage, 80 percent goes into the development of products that fail.[3]

In an even broader context, business management has the responsibility for interpreting correctly the emerging environment so as to identify new needs of various consumer groups. Then business must manage our increasingly sophisticated scientific technology so as to make available the goods and services to fulfill these new needs. As Professor Pessemier observed: "Perhaps the real challenge of product development will be to bridge the gap between the emerging and the fully developed societies. *We need suitable products to improve the present life style of all men, giving the citizens of less-developed nations the means and incentives to join rapidly the more advanced technical societies.*"[4]

MARKETING PROGRAMMING STARTS WITH THE PRODUCT

It has been said that nothing happens until somebody sells something. This is not entirely true. First, there must be something to sell—a product, a service, or an idea. From inside or outside the firm must come the germ of a product idea. In the latter case, an express demand may come from the market. That is, the question may be asked: Why don't they make a ____? The next step is to get the firm's marketing department to determine whether there is an adequate market for the product and to decide how the product should be planned.

PRODUCT IS BASIC PROFIT DETERMINANT

Good executive judgement elsewhere cannot offset weaknesses in product planning. A company cannot successfully sell a poor product over the long run. Often it is easy to create a demand for initial sales, but a company needs a good product to get repeat sales, and repeat sales are needed to stay in business. Problems with channels of distribution are magnified by a poor product.

New-product planning is essential for sustaining a company's expected rate of profit. Figure 9-1 illustrates a typical relationship between the sales volume curve and the profit margin curve through the life cycle of new products. While similar in shape, the two curves have different timing. The profit curve starts to decline while the volume sales curve is still ascending. Often the sales curve has been the basis for the marketing planning. The action of the profit curve, however, suggests that management should gear its product strategy to this curve rather than to the sales curve.

HIGH COST OF PRODUCT FAILURES

New complexities in the business environment have increased both the risks and penalties for product failure.[5] Investment requirements for new products continue to climb, thus generating higher break-even points. The net result here is to increase the time period required for a company to pay back its new-product costs. Government environmental controls affecting pollution, product safety, warran-

---

3 *Ibid.*, pp. 10-11, 24.

4 Edgar A. Pessemier, "New-Product Ventures," *Business Horizons,* August, 1968, p. 19.

5 Adapted from Thomas A. Staudt, "Higher Management Risks in Product Strategy," *Journal of Marketing,* January, 1973, pp. 4-9.

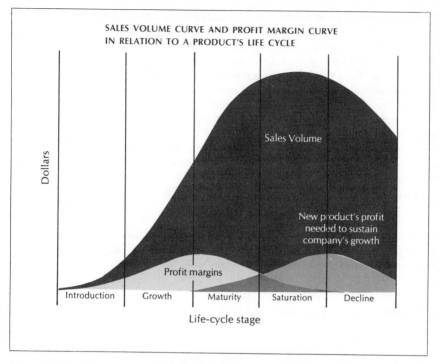

SALES VOLUME CURVE AND PROFIT MARGIN CURVE
IN RELATION TO A PRODUCT'S LIFE CYCLE

Dollars

Sales Volume

New product's profit
needed to sustain
company's growth

Profit margins

| Introduction | Growth | Maturity | Saturation | Decline |

Life-cycle stage

Figure 9-1. Profit margin usually starts to decline while a product's sales volume is still increasing. How does the relationship between these curves influence the time at which additional new products should be introduced? *Source:* Booz, Allen & Hamilton, Inc.

ties, etc., are new cost factors to contend with. A consequence of these risk factors is to increase the lead time between product idea and market entry. On balance, the pace of innovation may well be slowed down, but the cost of each individual innovation will increase.

The costs associated with new product failure have been revealed in a recent study which reported on the new product development activities of 150 Canadian companies engaged in industrial marketing.[6] Of the 150 companies, almost 60% rated their product development activities "moderately successful" or worse. The same study estimated that if the product successes which were examined had, in fact, been failures, the median losses would have been almost $100,000 per venture. In a number of cases, new product failures had resulted in corporate bankruptcy. Several other firms had been forced to refinance with new owners because of substantial losses from failures of new products.

NEW PRODUCTS ARE ESSENTIAL TO GROWTH

The watchword for management must often be "innovate or die," and this innovating attitude can become a philosophy almost paralleling that of the marketing con-

---

6 Robert G. Cooper and Blair Little, "Reducing the Risk of Industrial New Product Development," *The Canadian Marketer*, Fall, 1974, p. 8.

cept. Peter Drucker recognized the coimportance of the two concepts when he said, "Because it is its purpose to create a customer, any business enterprise has two—and only these two—basic functions: marketing and innovation."[7]

Many companies will get a substantial percentage of their sales volume and net profits this year from products which did not exist five or ten years ago, and this situation will undoubtedly continue. One study has estimated that 75 percent of sales growth in certain industries comes from new products.[8]

There can be little doubt that growth industries are new-product-oriented. Generally, those industries which spend the most on new-product development have enjoyed the greatest rates of growth. When one examines the levels of expenditure on research and development in Canadian, as compared with American, companies, it is evident that in most industries the U.S. firms outspend the Canadian.[9] It must be concluded from such data that Canadian firms spend less on new product development, preferring to allow the responsibility for such development to rest with their American parent companies. Many product innovations enter the Canadian market through the United States. Exceptions seem to be the case in the wood products, paper and allied products, and primary metals industries, where Canada has natural advantages in terms of resource bases and appears to capitalize upon them.

INCREASED CONSUMER SELECTIVITY

As the years go by, consumers become more selective in their choice of products. As disposable income in the hands of consumers has increased since World War II and as an abundance of products has become available, consumers have fulfilled many of their wants. The big middle-income market is reasonably well fed, clothed, housed, transported, and equipped. In our economy today, one of Thorstein Veblen's theories may be found in practice. His theory was that as members of a social class attain means to accumulate wealth, they pass through a period of conspicuous consumption, during which they acquire worldly goods to impress their neighbors. When they have proved to themselves that they can pay for a large house or a second car, these people switch to a practice of conspicuous *underconsumption.* They buy small foreign cars or compact North American cars. They need not continue to buy additional mountains of goods to impress people because people are already impressed.

If market satiation—in terms of quantity—does exist to some extent, it follows that the consumer may be more critical in his appraisal of a product, more aware of quality differentials, and more responsive to improved labeling. While the consumer is being increasingly selective, the market is being surfeited with products which are imitations or which offer only marginal competitive advantages. This situation in the economy may be leading to "product indigestion," the cure for which is to develop *really* new products and to create *really* new markets. A company's product-planning efforts should be designed to *innovate* and not just *imitate;* these efforts should place emphasis on *leading,* not just *meeting,* competition.[10]

---

7 Peter Drucker, *The Practice of Management,* Harper & Row, Publishers, Inc., New York, 1954, p. 37.

8 *Management of New Products, op. cit.,* p. 6.

9 A. J. Cordell, "The Multinational Firm, Foreign Direct Investment and Canadian Science Policy," Special Science Council of Canada Study #22, December, 1971, p. 83.

10 *Grey Matter,* March, 1968, p. 4.

UNIQUE CANADIAN FACTORS

One author has concluded that there exist a number of factors which are unique to the Canadian situation which influence the development of new products in this country.[11] These factors which should be considered in choosing new products in Canada may be summarized in the following guidelines for marketers:

1. *Avoid* highly scale-sensitive manufactured products and ancillary products; avoid products applicable to human beings in quantity. The big market blocs have basic advantages in mass consumer products, pharmaceuticals, mass transit vehicles, automobiles, large fleet aircraft, large computers, etc. etc. Canada might have a share of some of these manufactures but we cannot get as big a return from innovation in these fields as others can.
   Exceptions: products linked to industries which are very large in Canada by world standards, e.g. mining, pulp and paper; also products for which special export arrangements have been made; also specialized components for scale-sensitive products if made for world use by special arrangement in Canada, e.g. by participation in multi-government consortia.
2. *Avoid* products which rely excessively on export sales for viability and success.
   Exceptions: products which are linked to existing large and successful exports from Canada—export packages for food would be an example; products for which special export arrangements have been made, e.g. via foreign parents, partners or governments, or via allocation by parent company of a world business to the Canadian subsidiary company.
3. *Choose* products less sensitive to scale, e.g. for which total world need is not large, preferably with a greater than average need in Canada, e.g. airport 'carousels', flight training devices, navigation aids, etc.; products for which the need is not large and is variable due to custom requirements, seasonality, fashion etc. e.g. custom machine shop work, engineering design and consultancy, contract test laboratory work.
   Exceptions: note that clothing fashions tend to be tied to the world tourist trade which establishes the buying circuit.
4. *Choose* products based on special Canadian needs and strengths and exploit them on a world scale, e.g. geophysics instruments for mineral and engineering surveys, resources surveillance (forests, pests, pollution, resources satellites) navigation aids, search and rescue devices for remote places including under the sea, underground tunnelling techniques for mines, expressways, etc., ground gear for aircraft, off-terrain vehicles, ground gear and track for high-speed bulk freight trains, snow and ice controls, etc.
   Avoid mainstream pollution control technologies for standard industries, urban centres (except for Arctic and low temperature problems); mainstream transportation technologies for mass transit of people, (large fleet aircraft, high speed passenger trains, linear electric motors, mono rails, ferries, etc.)
5. *Campaign* for a wider association of Canada with other like-minded nations. It will do more to enlarge new product opportunities than anything else.

DEVELOPMENT OF NEW PRODUCTS

THE DECISION TO MAKE OR BUY

One of the first product problems calling for a decision is whether to make a product or buy it. All manufacturers must wrestle with this problem, while most re-

---

11 S. S. Grimley, "Canadian Factors in the Generation and Evaluation of New Product Ideas," *The Business Quarterly*, Summer, 1974, pp. 32-39.

tailers and wholesalers automatically think in terms of buying. Some large retail food chains, variety chains, and department stores, however, do make their own bakery goods and candy. Other firms, such as Sears and Eatons establish such rigid product specifications, work so closely with the product department of a manufacturer, and take such a large percentage of the firm's output that for all practical purposes they are making rather than buying.

A firm may solve its make-or-buy problem at some in-between point. For example, it may decide simply to assemble a series of premanufactured parts. Other firms may decide to make some parts and buy others and then assemble them. Furniture manufacturers usually follow this approach. In still another situation, an enterprise may assemble premanufactured parts and then paint or otherwise finish the end product. Automobiles, generally, are a case in point. Often many of the final parts, such as engines, call for make-or-buy decisions with respect to the components of the part. That is, an automobile manufacturer must decide whether to make or buy spark plugs, gaskets, valves, engine blocks, and other units making up the complete engines.

There are no pat solutions. As in so many other phases of marketing, the answer is: "It depends." Whether to make or buy a product depends upon the outcome of management's analysis of several issues, such as the following:

1. Relative costs of making or buying.
2. Extent to which specialized machinery, techniques, and production resources are needed.
3. Availability of production capacity.
4. Managerial time and talents required—the amount of production supervision needed.
5. Secrecy of design, style, and materials—the extent to which the company wants its processing methods kept secret. Because of a patent situation, what the firm wants may be available only through buying.
6. Attractiveness of the investment necessary to make a product.
7. Willingness to accept seasonal and other market risks. If a company decides to buy, the supplier can still shift some of these risks to the purchaser by requiring a contract guaranteeing acceptance of a certain quantity.
8. Risk of depending upon outside sources—will they raise the price, cut off relationships, etc.?
9. Extent of reciprocity present—is the supplier of the item also a customer for the buyer's other products?

STEPS IN DEVELOPMENT PROCESS

As a new product is developed, it progresses from the idea stage to the production and marketing stage. Although there may seem to be no particular pattern, we can say that in general, it follows the steps outlined below. In each stage management must decide whether (1) to move on to the next stage, (2) to abandon the product, or (3) to seek additional information.

1. Generation of new-product ideas. New-product development starts with an idea. Excellent ideas may come from salesmen or servicemen, nonmarketing employees, consumers or industrial users, middlemen, governmental agencies, competitive products, trade associations, private research organizations, and inventors. The particular source of ideas is not nearly so important as the company's system for stimulating new ideas and then acknowledging and reviewing them promptly.

2. Screening of ideas to determine which ones warrant further study. This is only the first of several screening reviews the product will receive.
3. Business analysis. The idea is expanded into a concrete business proposal in which management (1) identifies product features, (2) estimates market demand and the product's profitability, (3) establishes a program to develop the product, and (4) assigns responsibility for further study of the product's feasibility. The second and third stages embody what is referred to as "concept testing," that is, pretesting the product *idea*, as contrasted to the later pretesting of the product itself and its market.[12]
4. Product development. The idea-on-paper is converted into a physical product. Pilot models or small quantities are manufactured to designated specifications, and laboratory tests and other technical evaluations necessary to determine the production feasibility of the article are made.
5. Test marketing. Market tests, in-use tests, and other commercial experiments in limited geographic areas are conducted in order to ascertain the feasibility of the full marketing program. In this stage, design and production factors may have to be adjusted as a result of test findings. At this point management must make a final decision regarding whether to market the product commercially. Two major problems often encountered in this stage result because (*a*) competitors can devise ways of disrupting or countering the research and (*b*) they may take advantage of the time lag caused by test marketing and introduce their own version of the new product without pretesting it.
6. Commercialization. Full-scale programs are planned, and then the product is launched. Up to this point in the development process, management has virtually complete control over the product. Once the product is "born," however, and enters its life cycle (as discussed later), the external competitive environment becomes a major determinant of its destiny.

In reviewing the six-step evolution, the first three stages—the idea or concept stages—are the critical ones. Not only are they less expensive—each stage becomes progressively more expensive in dollars and scarce manpower—but, more importantly, experience indicates that most products fail because either the idea or the timing was wrong, and not because the company lacked the production or marketing know-how. Studies also indicate, fortunately, that companies in general are doing a better job of eliminating product ideas of limited potential before they reach the more expensive stages of development.

It is encouraging to note that manufacturers of *industrial* products are giving more attention to the development and marketing of new products and to the mortality rates of these products. These firms are seeking ways to minimize the risks of new-product marketing by improving their programs for new-product planning and development.[13] Often in the past these activities seemed to be almost entirely the concern of marketers of *consumer* goods.

Companies are increasingly using mathematical models and other quantitative techniques in various stages of new-product development, and also as evaluative follow-up once the product is being commercially marketed. To illustrate, PERT (Program Evaluation and Review Technique) and CPM (Critical Path Method) are two similar managerial tools used to aid in planning and controlling programs. It is

---

12 To avoid overestimating a new product's potential during concept testing, management should recognize that consumers may be favorably disposed toward the new product, yet have no need for it, according to Edward M. Tauber, "Reduce New Product Failures: Measure Needs as Well as Purchase Interest," *Journal of Marketing*, July, 1973, pp. 61-64.

13 See *Appraising the Market for New Industrial Products*, National Industrial Conference Board, Studies in Business Policy, #23, New York, 1967; and Robert G. Cooper and Blair Little, "Reducing the Risk in Industrial New Product Development," *The Canadian Marketer*, Fall, 1974, pp. 7-12.

the successful application of such techniques as PERT that has been credited with enabling such major projects as Expo '67 and the 1976 Olympics—despite some interesting problems—to be completed on schedule. The use of PERT can aid tremendously in coordinating, timing, and scheduling the many activities in the new-product-development process.[14]

MANUFACTURER'S CRITERIA FOR NEW PRODUCTS

Insofar as possible, a manufacturer should establish objective benchmarks against which he can measure a prospective addition to his product line.

1. There should be an adequate *market demand*. This is the first and by far the most important criterion to apply to a proposed product. Too often management begins with a question such as, "Can we use our present sales force?" or "Will the new item fit into our production system?" The basic question is: Do enough people really want our product? Administrators should try to get quantitative measures of the size and location of the potential market.

2. A company must consider the factor of *social and environmental compatibility* when evaluating a new product.[15] Do the manufacturing processes heavily pollute air or water? (Steel or paper mills.) Will the use of the finished product be harmful to the user or the environment? (Automobiles.) After being used, is the product harmful to the environment? (DDT and some detergents.) Does the product have recycling potential? Early in the developmental process (idea stage, for example) admittedly it may be difficult to assess the socioenvironmental consequences of the new product.

3. The product should fit into the company's present *marketing* structure. The general marketing experience of the company is important here. The Sunbeam Corporation would probably find it easy to add another kitchen appliance to its line, whereas a paint manufacturer would find it quite difficult to add margarine to his. Sometimes the general marketing relationship may not be apparent at first. Many people questioned the wisdom of Procter & Gamble's move in adding Gleem toothpaste to its list of products. On closer observation, however, it can be seen that the marketing of Gleem is similar in many respects to the marketing of Tide, Ivory, and other Procter & Gamble soap products. Gleem is a consumer convenience product which will be distributed, priced, and promoted in much the same manner as consumer soaps and detergents.

   More specific questions may also be asked regarding the marketing fit of new products: Can the existing sales force be used? Do the salespeople have the time and ability to sell the new product? Can the present channels of distribution be used? If the company has a service organization, can it handle the new product?

4. A new-product idea will be more favorably received if the item fits in with existing *production* facilities, manpower, and management.

5. The product should fit from a *financial* standpoint. At least three questions should be asked: Is adequate financing available? Will the new item increase seasonal and cyclical

14 See Edgar A. Pessemier and H. Paul Root, "The Dimensions of New Product Planning," *Journal of Marketing,* January, 1973, pp. 10-18; Warren Dusenberry, "CPM for New Product Introductions," *Harvard Business Review,* July-August, 1967, pp. 124-139; H. B. Sullivan, "Using PERT/CPM to Manage the Introduction of New Products," *Marketing Forum,* July-August, 1967, pp. 31-35; Morris Hamburg and Robert J. Atkins, "Computer Model for New Product Demand," *Harvard Business Review,* March-April 1967, pp. 107-115; A. Charnes, W. W. Cooper, J. K. Devoe, and D. B. Learner, "DEMON (Decision Mapping via Optimum Go-no Networks): A Management Model for Marketing New Products," *California Management Review,* Fall, 1968, pp. 31-46, and Donald S. Tull, "The Relationship of Actual and Predicted Sales and Profits in New-product Introduction," *Journal of Business,* July, 1967, pp. 233-250.

15 Dale L. Varble, "Social and Environmental Considerations in New Product Development," *Journal of Marketing,* October, 1972, pp. 11-15.

stability in the firm? Are the profit possibilities worthwhile? Here again some objective criteria are needed to decide what a "worthwhile" profit is. Some products must cover their total costs, while others may be considered satisfactory if they cover only their variable costs and contribute something to overhead. The latter type may be acceptable when they are added only to satisfy middlemen who want a full line from a manufacturer.

6. Before accepting a new product, management should make certain that there are no *legal* objections. Patents must be registered or applied for, labeling and packaging must observe all pertinent regulations, and so on.

7. *Management* of adequate ability should be available. It is important that the executives in the company have the necessary time and ability to handle the proposed new product.

8. The product should be in keeping with the *company's image*, self-concept, and objectives. The proposed product should not run counter to the company's goals. A firm stressing low-priced, high-turnover products normally should not add an item which shouts prestige or status.

MIDDLEMAN'S CRITERIA FOR NEW PRODUCTS

A middleman who is trying to determine whether to add a new product to his line must consider all the criteria that a manufacturer would, except those related to production. He has, in addition, two further points to consider:

1. Relations with the manufacturer. A middleman in wholesaling or retailing should consider the reputation of the manufacturer. A middleman should examine the possibility of acquiring exclusive sales rights in a given geographic territory. He must be sure that he can get an adequate supply. In the ready-to-wear fields, a retailer often will not place an original order unless he is guaranteed delivery of reorders within a certain number of days after placing them. A retailer should also consider the nature and amount of promotional help given by the manufacturer.

2. In-store policies and practices. A retailer has to study the type of selling effort a new product will require. He must consider how the proposed product fits with in-store policies and practices regarding mechanical service, clothing alteration, credit, and delivery. Stores using self-service ordinarily do not want to add items requiring extensive demonstration and personal selling. For this reason, food retailers have in the past tended to avoid carrying clothing and appliances. Recently, however, supermarkets have moved in the direction of carrying broader varieties of non-food items, including clothing, garden furniture and equipment, and hardware. The relatively high margins on such products are important in offsetting the traditionally low margins on food items.

IMPORTANCE OF TIMING

An analysis of case histories will show that new-product development is considerably more time-consuming than many marketing executives realize. As a result of underestimating the time needed for orderly development, management may take shortcuts in some of the developmental stages, the result frequently being product failure. In many cases, 10 or more years have elapsed between the time the new-product development was started, and the date the product was introduced in test markets. This means that a company should have several new products in the development hopper at any given time.

Proper timing is of the utmost importance in every stage leading to the introduction of a new product. Managerial decisions involving time generally start with a determination of when to offer the product for sale. If the product has an annual model change or if it is intended primarily for a special season, the decision is reasonably easy. If the product is to be sold to the industrial market or if it affects the use of other products now in the hands of retailers and wholesalers, timing can create many problems for management.

After deciding when the product will be offered for sale to the ultimate consumer or industrial user, the producer must determine when the product will be sold to the wholesalers and retailers. Arrangements must be made to reduce inventories of the old product and build up stocks of the new. The physical distribution of the product must be dovetailed with the promotional program so that supplies will be on hand when advertising is released and the personal salesmen start selling.

ORGANIZING FOR PRODUCT INNOVATION

Product innovation should be a responsibility of top management. Moreover, the extent of the top executives' active involvement in new-product programs is a vital determinant of a company's success with new products. These conclusions have been reached in several studies of programs for product planning and development. To be effectively managed, these programs must be effectively organized and controlled. In one study of major problems encountered in new-product programs, more than four out of five (81 percent) of the companies—and these were experienced, well-managed firms with relative success in new products—identified some kind of problem relating to organization. Organizational problems constituted over one-half (55 percent) of all those mentioned by reporting firms.[16]

NEED FOR CONSTRUCTIVE, INNOVATING ATTITUDE

While it is helpful to have a well-designed organizational framework, a more important key to success is the *attitude* which the entire company has toward planning and developing products. The right attitude must permeate all levels of managerial thinking. This "right" attitude is one that constructively encourages—in fact, thrives on—innovation.

Management should have a critical attitude, but its criticism must be constructive. When management reacts to new-product ideas with the philosophy, "We have been doing it this way for twenty years, why do you want to change it?" management is an impediment to growth. Some managers can test a new product to death. They are forever wanting to run another product or market test, with the result that the item never does reach the stage of a full-scale marketing program.

POTENTIAL PROBLEMS IN ORGANIZATION

In some organizations—the Jell-O division of General Foods, for example—the responsibility for new-product development is separated from product-planning activities (such as finding new uses for a product or making package changes) which

---

16 *Management of New Products, op. cit.*, pp. 16-17; see also Philip R. McDonald and Joseph O. Eastlack, Jr., "Top Management Involvement with New Products," *Business Horizons*, December, 1971, pp. 23-31.

are related to the modification of established products. This kind of situation, where the division of responsibility is not always sharply demarcated, can create real managerial problems, and careful administrative coordination is an absolute requirement. Effectiveness is greatly reduced if the two separate organizational units disagree over whether a given item is a brand-new product, and thus should be developed by department A, or whether it is an improvement on an already existing product and thus should be assigned to department B.

Regardless of the organizational setup, there may be a shift in responsibility as the product moves through the various stages from the inception of the idea to a full-scale marketing program. A new-product-development manager may be responsible for the initial development and market testing. Then at an appropriate time, responsibility may be handed over to a product manager, who carries the product to its fulfillment as a nationally marketed item. If the product manager is already satisfied with the growth rate and profit results in his department, however, he may not want to take on a new, untried product which may cause a disruption in his scheduled routine.

TYPES OF ORGANIZATION

At the outset, it should be emphasized that there is no "one best type" of organizational structure for new-product planning and development, nor does any one type seem to be selected by a large majority of manufacturers. The type which is most effective for any given firm will depend upon the company's size, products, managerial abilities, and other circumstances.

As one criterion, an organizational structure should enable management to implement effectively the processes of specialization and coordination. While these are basic processes in any organization, they are especially key ingredients in a company's organizational mix pertaining to new-product planning and development. As specialists in the research, production, and sales area all work on product innovation, they typically develop different viewpoints and work better in separate organizational structures. While these specializations and differences may improve the innovative research and development, they may also contribute to disagreements which can impede product innovation. At this point in the innovative process, a company must depend upon its organizational structure to provide a counterbalancing provision for coordination so that the executives with diverse points of view can resolve their differences of opinion, and progress with a unity of effort.[17]

In large and medium-sized companies which have enjoyed relative success in new-product marketing, apparently the popular trend is to locate the organizational responsibility for product planning and development in one of the following: (1) a product-planning committee, (2) a new-product department, (3) product managers, or (4) a venture team. Another alternative is that of using outside new-product-specialist firms alone or in some combination with any of the other types of structures.

Product-planning committee. Today the most widely used organizational structure for new-product planning and development is probably the committee, with heavy

---

17 Jay W. Lorsch and Paul R. Lawrence, "Organizing for Product Innovation," *Harvard Business Review*, January-February, 1965, pp. 109-122.

representation from top management. The firm's president and men from the marketing, production, engineering, research, and finance departments usually are involved.

In a committee, the ideas and wisdom of several executives can be pooled. Any new product which results is likely to win the approval of the administrators who took part in its development. On the other hand, committee activity takes much valuable executive time and slows the decision-making process. Also, the committee structure makes it difficult to place responsibility for managerial actions and may even serve as a "buck-passing" device.

Many companies which use a new-product-development committee also have a product manager who is responsibile for marketing the item after it has successfully passed through the necessary testing and other introductory stages of development. In other instances, a new-product department has evolved as the next step beyond a product-planning committee, but the company will still retain the committee as an advisory group to evaluate new-product ideas and development plans.

New-product department. In recent years a separate department devoted to new-product planning and development has been created in an increasing number of manufacturing firms. As suggested earlier, these departments have often evolved as the next logical step beyond a product-planning committee. Although there are some exceptions, generally the departments are relatively small, containing no more than four or five people, and frequently these are one-man departments. Usually the head of this department reports to the president, or the department may be one part of a staff unit directly serving the president. Typically these departments have administrative responsibility for such new-product tasks as determining objectives and programs, recommending new projects, planning the activities, generating and screening ideas, guiding the new products through the various developmental stages, and coordinating the new-product activities involving other departments. When a product is ready for full-scale commercial marketing, it is turned over to the appropriate operating department.

This organizational pattern has the advantage of making new-product development a full-time activity, so there is less risk that it will become a stepchild in a department which is more concerned with day-to-day operating problems. The Booz, Allen & Hamilton studies identify two operating weaknesses sometimes found in new-product departments. One is the failure to plan thoroughly just how the department will operate. The other is the failure to staff the department with a person who has the prestige to gain from other executives the support necessary for success.

Product manager. The structure which activates the concept of the product manager is another widely used form of organization for product planning and development. Normally, however, a product manager's responsibility is *not* limited to new products. This executive—sometimes called a "brand manager" or a "merchandise manager"—is ordinarily an administrator in the marketing department, reporting to a top marketing executive. In business and professional journals the wealth of discussion regarding the product-manager system is some indication of management's interest.[18]

---

18 See, for example, B. Charles Ames, "Payoff from Product Management," *Harvard Business Review*, November-December, 1963, pp. 141-152; B. Charles Ames, "Dilemma of Product/Market Management," *Har-*

The scope of a product manager's responsibilities varies widely among different companies, thus reflecting differences in their product and market requirements. In companies at one end of the spectrum, the product manager's activities may be limited essentially to selling and sales-promotional work.[19]

Other firms—Pillsbury, Kimberly-Clark (Kleenex), Colgate-Palmolive, and Procter & Gamble, for example—view the product manager's job as involving a much broader group of activities. In such cases, this executive is responsible for planning the complete marketing program for his brand or group of products. Thus he may be concerned with new-product development as well as the improvement of existing goods. His responsibilities encompass such activities as setting marketing goals and planning marketing strategies, pricing, developing advertising and sales-promotional plans, preparing budgets, and helping field salesmen to do a more effective selling job. However, this executive has no line authority over the field sales force; he can only advise them.

As an organizational concept, the product-manager system is not new. It has been used for years in retailing, especially in department stores, where the department buyer system exists and each merchandise manager has complete product-planning responsibilities for a limited line of goods. In manufacturing, Procter & Gamble and Johnson and Johnson have used the brand-manager system successfully for half a century. For most firms, however, the product manager is a relatively new specialist in marketing organizations; yet his value is being questioned less and less. He brings the benefits of specialization and organizational decentralization to each product line.

Probably the biggest single problem most companies face in the use of a product manager is that they saddle him with great responsibility and yet refuse to give him the corresponding authority. Outside his own department, the product manager has no line authority in the classical organizational sense. He cannot, for example, order the salespeople to do something. Even though advertising may be critical to the success of his plans, the product manager does not select the advertising agency. Perhaps the most burdensome aspect of the product manager's responsibility is that he is made accountable for the profitability of his brand and yet is often denied any control over product costs, the setting of prices, or the determination of advertising budgets.[20]

---

vard Business Review, March-April, 1971, pp. 66-74; Robert M. Fulmer, "Product Management: Panacea or Pandora's Box?" California Management Review, Summer, 1965, pp. 63-74; The Product Manager System, National Industrial Conference Board, Experiences in Marketing Management, no. 8, New York, 1965; and "The Brand Manager: No Longer King," Business Week, June 9, 1973, p. 58.

19 For an excellent review of the application of the product or brand manager concept in Canadian packaged goods companies and of the responsibilities assigned to brand managers in these companies see: A. M. Ragab and A. W. Babcok, "An Investigation into the Practice of the Product Manager Concept by Selected Canadian Companies," in Bent Stidsen, ed., Marketing in the 1970s and Beyond, Canadian Association of Administrative Sciences, Marketing Division, Edmonton, 1975, pp. 217-237.

20 For suggestions to improve the effectiveness of this type of organization, see Stephens Dietz, "Get More Out of Your Brand Management," Harvard Business Review, July-August, 1973, pp. 127-136; and David J. Luck and Theodore Nowak, "Product Management: Vision Unfulfilled," Harvard Business Review, May-June, 1965, pp. 143-154.

For illustrations of how various forms of interpersonal influence are exerted by product managers in the absence of formal authority, see Gary R. Gemmill and David L. Wilemon, "The Product Manager as an Influence Agent," Journal of Marketing, January, 1972, pp. 26-30. Also see David J. Luck, "Interfaces of a Product Manager," Journal of Marketing, October, 1969, pp. 32-36.

Venture team. The venture team is a relatively new, rapidly growing organizational concept for managing product innovation from idea stage to full-scale marketing.[21] A venture team is a small, multidisciplinary group, organizationally segregated from the rest of the firm. It is comprised of representatives from engineering-production, finance, and marketing research. A team operates in an entrepreneurial environment, in effect being a separate small business. Typically the group reports directly to top management and has one goal—to enter a new market profitably.

Once the new product reaches the stage of being commercially viable, typically it is turned over to another division—an existing unit, a new division, or even a new subsidiary company. The given venture team is then disbanded. However, in some cases it may continue on as the management nucleus when a company is established.

A venture team is designed to avoid the product-development problems found in traditional organizational structures—problems of bureaucratic operation, reluctance to change, a "don't-rock-the-boat" attitude, inability to get decisions made quickly, and lack of authority to move a product through the developmental stages.

Use of outside new-product specialists. To speed up the innovation process and *to sell off their unused new products and technology,* several major manufacturers are relying on a combination of (1) a special type of new-product department plus (2) outside firms which specialize in finding or developing new products. In this rather radical organizational departure from tradition, management is bypassing its research and development department for two reasons. First, R & D's traditional approach to new-product development is too slow for today's competitive environment, and second, often the products are dictated by the technical abilities of the R & D people, rather than reflecting consumer market demands.

An innovative variation of a new-product department has developed in some firms—General Electric and National Cash Register, for example. This department is responsible for generating new products *quickly* by such means as (1) reviving old patents, (2) contracting with outside product brokers who can match other companies' products with the firm's needs, or (3) farming out ideas to firms specializing in new-product development. This new-style department has another unusual job—that of selling off products, inventions, and technology which the manufacturer has developed but which he cannot market right now for one reason or another. Rather than "sit on" the product for several years, management gets some immediate payoff for its research and development investment.

Two types of outside new-product specialists are being used to varying degrees by many major manufactuers. One type is a firm which will completely develop a new product—from the idea stage to the commercial marketing stage. In effect, this type of specialist enables a manufacturer to buy, rather than make, a new product. Using an outside firm gives a manufacturer considerable flexibility and objectivity. The manufacturer is not limited by its own company attitudes or executives' ego. The outsider brings the benefits of experience and expertise. His use also enables a manufacturer to better control product-development costs.[22]

---

21 Adapted from Richard M. Hill and James D. Hlavacek, "The Venture Team: A New Concept in Marketing Organization," *Journal of Marketing,* July, 1972, pp. 44-50. Also see Mack Hanan, "Corporate Growth through Venture Management," *Harvard Business Review,* January-February, 1969, pp. 43-61.

22 For an analysis of this "outside" new-product development specialist—its services, relative merits, and track record, see Edward M. Tauber, "The Emerging New Product Development Industry," *Business Horizons,* April, 1973, pp. 5-10.

The other specialist is a product broker who will find a seller of products wanted by a manufacturer, or will help the manufacturer sell off his unused products or technology.

WHY NEW PRODUCTS FAIL: A SUMMARY

As a conclusion to this chapter, we shall summarize the results of one study on why new products fail and then consider some final points for corrective action. The Conference Board surveyed 125 companies which were considered successful product innovators. Even these firms experienced a failure rate of slightly more than 20 percent among products which had been introduced to the market during the preceding five years.[23] The major reasons given for the failure of the new products or services, in order of frequency of mention, are as follows:

1. Inadequate market analysis. This includes overestimating potential sales of the new product, inability to determine buying motives and habits, and misjudgments on what products the market wanted.
2. Product deficiencies. Poor quality and performance, too complicated, and especially the product did not offer any significant advantage over competitive products already on the market.
3. Lack of effective marketing effort. Failure to provide sufficient follow-through effort after introductory program, and failure to train marketing personnel for new products and new markets.
4. Higher costs than anticipated. This led to higher prices which in turn led to lower sales volume than anticipated.
5. Competitive strength or reaction. Speed and ease of copying an innovation soon overcrowded the market.
6. Poor timing of introduction. Usual mistake here was to introduce a product too late, although in a few cases the problem was premature market entry.
7. Technical or production problems. Could not produce sufficient quantities to meet demand, so competition gained an unanticipated share of market.

After analysing the above factors, two points become quite clear. First, the factors which lead to product failures are typically within the control of the company itself. Second, an extremely large percentage of the causes of failure are marketing-related.

Cooper and Little, in their study of 150 Canadian companies, have concluded that inadequate market knowledge and inadequate assessment of the market are the foremost reasons for product failure. In order to overcome such deficiencies, these authors have proposed the application of the stage-wise approach to product development presented in Figure 9-2. The application of such a stage-wise approach is seen to offer a number of inherent advantages:[24]

a) The need for a balance between R & D work and market assessment activities is clearly demonstrated.

---

23 David S. Hopkins and Earl L. Bailey, "New-Product Pressures," *Conference Board Record,* June, 1971, pp. 16-24. Here it is important to note that the failure rate represents products which failed in some important respect to meet management's original goals. Only about 5 percent of the new products were actually withdrawn from the market.

24 Cooper and Little, *op cit,* pp. 10-11.

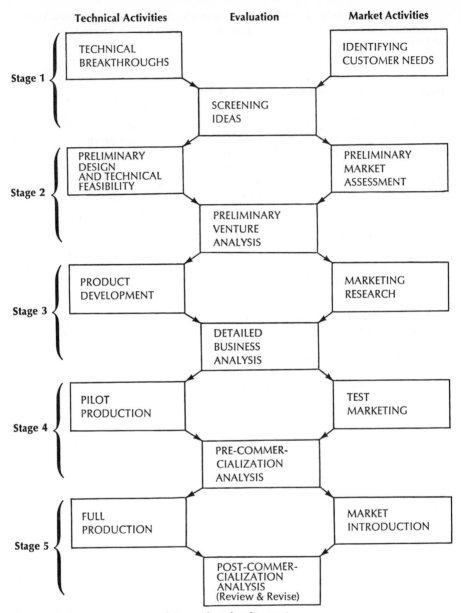

Figure 9-2: A stage-wise approach to product development.

Source: Robert G. Cooper and Blair Little, "Reducing the Risk of Industrial New Product Development," *The Canadian Marketer,* Fall, 1974, p. 11.

b) Each evaluation stage requires inputs from both the technical and the marketing groups. Market assessment and marketing research become vital ingredients in the development process.

c) At each stage and prior to each major commitment of funds, the viability and profitability of the project is reviewed. This evaluation provides for the cancellation of unfruitful ventures, or can point to the need to secure additional information before proceeding.

d) As the cumulative expenditures on the project increase at each stage of the process, so the uncertainties—both technical and market—are reduced. Risk is maintained at an acceptable level.

It is the market-related activities presented on the right side of Figure 9-2 that are most often overlooked. A closer examination of these activities is important to the successful development of new products. If the first commandment of marketing is to "Know thy customer," then the second is "Know thy product." The products or services sold by a firm are prime determinants of the company's rate of growth, rate of profit, and total marketing program. Policies and strategies with respect to the full complement of a firm's products are considered in the following chapter.

QUESTIONS AND PROBLEMS

1. In what respects are the products different in each of the following cases?
    a. An Arrow shirt sold by a local men's clothing store and a similar shirt sold by Sears under the retailer's brand name. Assume that the same manufacturer makes both shirts.
    b. A Sunbeam Mixmaster sold by a leading department store and the same model sold by a discount house.
2. Explain the various interpretations of the term "new product." Give some examples, other than those stated in this chapter, of products in each new-product category.
3. Bring to class three advertisements which stress product benefits. Bring three which stress some part of the product rather than the benefits to be derived from this product.
4. Compare the product-planning activities of a manufacturer and a retailer.
5. Why is it important for a company to plan for the introduction of new products?
6. What are some of the questions which management is likely to want answered during the "business-analysis" stage of new-product development?
7. Assume that the following additions to their product lines are being considered by the stated companies. What is your initial recommendation, based upon general information which you may already have relating to the criteria set forth in this chapter?
    a. Automobile manufacturer—outboard motors
    b. Firm such as National Cash Register—office dictating machines
    c. Supermarket—wallpaper
    d. Manufacturer of electronic parts and equipment—automatic garage-door opener
    e. Department store—well-known brand of compact cars
8. List the factors which influence the type of organizational structure selected for new-product development. Explain how each of these factors might affect the choice of structure.
9. Under what conditions might a firm profitably use a separate department for new-product development?
10. What are some of the problems typically connected with the "product-manager" type of organizational structure for new-product development?
11. Why do so many new products turn out to be market failures?

PRODUCT-LINE POLICIES AND STRATEGIES

An appliance manufacturer eliminates a number of models of refrigerators, kitchen ranges and air conditioners. Ford drops the Edsel and later adds the Maverick and Pinto. General Motors drops the Corvair and the Firenza and adds the Chevette. A large cigarette manufacturer diversifies into food products, and a paper manufacturer into retail stores specializing in home decorating products. Bombardier moves from producing logging equipment to manufacturing snowmobiles, trail bikes, and other recreational products. A number of large department stores regularly shop for the latest European fashion creations and adapt them to the mass North American market. All of these cases have one thing in common. They all involve managerial strategies and policy making with respect to the firm's line of products and services.

PRODUCT LINE AND PRODUCT MIX

A broad group of products, intended for essentially similar uses and possessing reasonably similar physical characteristics, constitutes a *product line*. Wearing apparel is one example of a product line. But in a different context, say, in a small specialty shop, men's furnishings (shirts, ties, and underwear) and men's ready-to-wear (suits, sport jackets, topcoats, and slacks) would each constitute a line. In another context, men's apparel is one line, as contrasted with women's apparel, furniture, or sporting goods.

The *product mix* is the full list of all products offered for sale by a company. The structure of the product mix has dimensions of both breadth and depth. Its *breadth* is measured by the number of product lines carried; its *depth*, by the assortment of sizes, colors, and models offered within each product line. See Fig. 10-1.

MAJOR PRODUCT-LINE STRATEGIES

Several major product-line strategies are used by manufacturers and middlemen in marketing their products. Most of these strategies involve a change in the product mix. However, some involve an expansion of the market by means of new uses for the existing product, but with no alterations in the mix. A discussion of planned obsolescence as a product strategy, and of fashion as an influence on the product mix, is deferred until later in the chapter.

EXPANSION OF PRODUCT MIX

A firm may elect to expand its present product mix by increasing the number of lines and/or by increasing the depth within a line. The Campbell Soup Company added food items, including V-8 juice, Swanson frozen TV dinners, and Pepperidge Farm frozen desserts. McCain has similarly expanded its food line from frozen vegetables to include frozen pizza and desserts. The Molson organization has moved into the retailing of hardware and building supplies through its Beaver Lumber stores. IBM has developed a line of office copiers at the same time that Xerox was moving into the computer field. The 3M Company, which manufactures Scotch tape, has broadened its tape line to include strapping tape and recording tape. Eaton's has added such services as a travel agency and investment management. A company may expand in both depth and breadth. For example, Dominion Stores has added lines of clothing, hardware, and housewares in some of its stores (breadth), while at the same time increasing its variety of dry cereals, cake mixes and cleaning products (depth).

CONTRACTION OF PRODUCT MIX

A product strategy trend in the 1970s is to thin out product lines, either by eliminating an entire line or by simplifying the assortment within a line. The shift from fat and long lines to thin and short lines is designed to eliminate low-profit products and to get more profit from fewer products. RCA and General Electric both dropped their line of computers. B. F. Goodrich no longer markets rubber footware. Motorola thinned its line by deleting portable radios, record players, and tape players.

This practice of slimming the product mix has long been recognized as an important product-line strategy. However, in the 1970s it has *really* been pushed to the forefront by raw-materials scarcities, price controls, and the energy shortage. A wide variety of industries has been forced to retreat from (1) the full-line product concept with its emphasis on growth and total sales volume to (2) a product position which emphasizes profits and efficient use of materials and energy.

PART OF A SKI RETAILER'S PRODUCT MIX, ILLUSTRATING BREADTH AND DEPTH OF LINE		
Breadth (Different lines)	Depth (Assortment)	
Skis	Slalom, cross-country, GLM (short skis)	
Ski boots	Foam, nonfoam, after-ski	Each in several brands and sizes
Ski pants	Men's and women's, ski and after-ski, under- and over-the-boot styles	

Figure 10-1.

ALTERATION OF EXISTING PRODUCTS

As an alternative to developing a new product, management should take a fresh look at the company's existing products. Often improving an established product can be more profitable and less risky than developing a new one. This alternative strategy should be followed regardless of the breadth and depth of the product mix and regardless of whether management is committed to a policy of expansion or contraction of the mix.

For industrial goods, especially, *redesigning* is often the key to the product's renaissance.[1] Not only did a redesigned pressure switch cost 52 percent less than the model it replaced, but the new one was also easier to install and performed better. The market for a hospital centrifuge was expanded by redesigning it so that it harmonized architecturally with modern cabinetry. *Packaging* has been a very popular area for product alteration, particularly in consumer products. Even something as mundane as thread, glue, or cheesecloth can be made more attractive by creative packaging and display. The *use of new materials* has also been popular. In place of cotton and wool, clothing manufacturers have substituted materials of synthetic fibers.

Sometimes the alteration is only in the advertising appeal—the product remains unchanged—as when the advertising for Welch's grape juice ceased to be against fat and *in favor of* refreshment and energy production. It should also be beneficial if management would analyze the qualities which have contributed to the long-lived, seemingly indestructible success of such products as Kellogg's Corn Flakes, Hershey chocolate, Sunlight Soap, Vaseline petroleum jelly, and Cow Brand baking soda.

DEVELOPMENT OF NEW USES FOR EXISTING PRODUCTS

Another major product strategy is to search for new uses for products. Although a company probably cannot rely on this strategy alone to increase volume and profits, we should not underestimate its effectiveness in tapping new markets. The 3M Company has followed this approach successfully with its product Scotch

---

1 Kenneth Van Dyck, "New Products from Old: Short-cut to Profits." *Industrial Marketing*, November, 1965, pp. 85-87.

tape. General Foods has advertised the use of Jell-O in salads and the manufacturers of Cow Brand Baking Soda have promoted their product as a deodorizer in refrigerators.

POSITIONING THE PRODUCT

Management's ability to position a product appropriately in the market is a major determinant of company profits. A product's *position* is the image which that product projects in relation to images projected (1) by competitive products and (2) by other products marketed by the company in question.[2] Thus, Avis positioned itself as only No. 2 in rental cars and so must try harder. The Pinto and Vega autos are positioned to compete head on with foreign imports. Canadian Club whiskey has been positioned, through its advertising, to appeal to adventure-seekers. The goal here is to position a new or modified product so as to maximize profits; that is, without "cannibalizing" sales and profits from the company's other products. The operational problem is to position correctly and not make positioning errors.

For some products (North American subcompact cars, for example) the best position is a head-on stance against competition. For other companies that is exactly what *not* to do. Avis became successful only after it stopped positioning itself directly against Hertz and readily admitted it was No. 2. General Electric and RCA abandoned their computer lines after years of unsuccessfully positioning themselves directly against IBM, a firm with a strong position in the field.[3]

Sometimes a strong position can be established by moving into a previously unoccupied niche in the market. This is what Ford did with its Mustang. Also, 7-Up moved ahead on its claim as an Un-Cola, rather than continuing to fight Coca-Cola and Pepsi-Cola directly. Typically a weak position is a "me-too" stance where a product really has no differentiating features from its entrenched competitors. In some markets (gasolines, toilet soaps, cigarettes, floor waxes) real differences are virtually impossible to establish. In these cases special attention to positioning is essential because the task is so difficult. The task is doubly difficult in the cigarette industry in Canada owing to the voluntary removal of cigarette advertising from the broadcast media.

TRADING UP AND TRADING DOWN

As product strategies, trading up and trading down are intentional attempts to reposition a product, and they also involve an expansion of product line. Normally, a firm will trade up or down, but not both.

Trading up means that a manufacturer or middleman adds a higher-priced, prestige product to his line in the hope of increasing his sales of an existing lower-priced product. In the automobile industry, Ford Motor Company introduced the Thunderbird, and Chevrolet marketed the Corvette. In a similar move, Volkswa-

---

2 John H. Holmes, "Profitable Product Positioning," *MSU Business Topics*, Spring, 1973, pp. 27-32. Unfortunately, the term "product positioning" has no generally accepted definition, so this important concept in product strategy remains loosely used and difficult to measure,

3 See Jack Trout, "Positioning Revisited: Why Didn't GE and RCA Listen?" *Industrial Marketing*, November, 1971, p. 116.

gen introduced Audi to the North American market. The manufacturers in these cases expected their lower-priced cars to benefit from the reflected prestige of the new ones.

When a company embarks upon a policy of trading up, at least two avenues are open with respect to promotional emphasis: (1) Usually the seller continues to depend upon the older, lower-priced product for the bulk of the sales volume, or (2) eventually he may shift the promotional emphasis to the new product and expect it to produce the major share of volume. In fact, the lower-priced line may be dropped altogether after a transition period. Many department stores have followed this policy as they have traded up from their former target of the low-income market to a new, larger middle-income market.

A company is said to be *trading down* when it adds a lower-priced item to its line of prestige products in the hope that people who cannot afford the original product will want to buy the new one, because it carries some of the status of the higher-priced good. Several years ago Buick attempted to broaden its market by introducing four series of cars in an attempt to compete at all price levels.

Trading up and trading down are perilous strategies because the intended goal may not materialize. The new product may simply confuse buyers, so that the net gain is negligible. Nor is any useful purpose served if sales in the new line are generated at the expense of the older product. Trading up or trading down cannot be considered successful unless sales increase in total or the company retains business that would otherwise go to competitive products.

When trading down, the new article may permanently hurt the firm's reputation and its established high-quality product. This situation may be avoided by using differentiating brands, channels of distribution, promotional programs, or product design.

When trading up, the seller's major problem is to change his image enough so that the market will accept his new, higher-priced, higher-quality product. To illustrate, many women will never believe that they can buy good-quality, high-fashion clothing in women's ready-to-wear chain stores. Through the years these stores have projected a corporate image or personality which connotes low-priced merchandise. In recent years, Woolco Department Stores have utilized fashion advertising for women's ready-to-wear on television. Such advertising might be viewed as an attempt to alter store image and to trade the consumer up to higher-fashion and higher-priced clothing items.

PRODUCT DIFFERENTIATION AND MARKET SEGMENTATION

These two concepts were introduced in Chapter 3 in connection with identifying and analyzing markets. Product differentiation and market segmentation also are two related *product strategies* which may be employed by firms who wish to engage in nonprice competition in markets characterized by imperfect or monopolistic competition.[4] These strategies usually require a considerable amount of advertising and other kinds of promotional effort. Consequently, they are often regarded as both promotional and product-planning strategies.

As a product strategy, *product differentiation* involves developing and promoting

---

4 Much of this section is based on a penetrating analysis of these strategies by Wendell R. Smith. See his "Product Differentiation and Market Segmentation as Alternative Marketing Strategies," *Journal of Marketing,* July, 1956, pp. 3-8.

an awareness of differences between the advertiser's product and the products of competitors. The strategy is used to enable a business to remove itself from price competition so that it can compete on the nonprice basis that its product is different from, and better than, competitive models. Sometimes a company will differentiate the quality or design of the product, or the only differentiation may be in the brand or packaging. Frequently two products are virtually identical in a physical and chemical sense. The difference between them is trivial and sometimes only psychological. This strategy is frequently used by companies selling reasonably standardized products, such as soaps, cigarettes, and gasoline, to a broad horizontal market which is fairly homogeneous in its wants for the given item.

In terms familiar in economic theory, the seller assumes in a general sense that there is a single demand curve for his product. Any variations in the wants of individual consumers will be minimized by extensive advertising and sales promotion emphasizing the product's broad market appeal. Essentially, as Wendell R. Smith has said, ". . . product *differentiation* is concerned with the bending of demand to the will of supply."

Inexorable market pressures are working against the seller who attempts to expand his market by using the strategy of product differentiation. The broader the market, the more difficult it becomes to fit all consumers' wants to the single product. Competition is felt to an increasing extent. Any one of these alternative products is apt to satisfy more precisely the wants of some group in this broadening range of consumers. Our seller must resort to increased promotional expenditures or reduced prices, or both, in his attempts to offset the variations in consumer preference, that is, in his attempts to fit more consumers in that single demand curve.[5]

In employing the strategy of *market segmentation,* a seller recognizes that his total heterogeneous market is made up of many, smaller homogeneous units. Each of these smaller units has a different set of wants, motivations, and other characteristics. He sees his market as a *series* of demand curves rather than the *single* curve considered above in product differentiation. The seller then attempts to develop different products, each one specifically for one or more of these market units. Tailor-made products are extreme examples of this strategy in action. As one marketing executive said, "Proper market segmentation represents the ultimate extension of the marketing concept. It not only starts with consumers and what they want, but it recognizes the fact that not all people are alike and that one man's *mousse au chocolat* is another man's plain chocolate pudding."[6]

Market segmentation has been employed for years in the field of industrial products, where it is quite common to make products according to buyers' specifications. The strategy is also being used to an increasing extent in the consumer market. Some of the specific benefits derived from market segmentation were discussed in Chapter 3. In that same discussion we recognized the problems of (1) identifying measurable market segments, which (2) are large enough to be poten-

---

5 For an analysis of the issue of whether product differentiation in the auto industry, through annual style changes and heavy promotion, has transformed a competitive industry into a noncompetitive oligopoly, see H. Paul Root, "Should Product Differentiation Be Restricted?" *Journal of Marketing,* July, 1972, pp. 3-9.

6 Russell I. Haley, "The Implications of Market Segmentation," *Conference Board Record,* March, 1969, pp. 43-47; quotation on p. 43.

For a report on how some firms treat a market segment of over twenty million consumers—namely, left-handed people—see "Left-handed Compliment," *Sales Management,* Sept. 1, 1969, pp. 34-36.

tially profitable, and which (3) are accessible within reasonable limits of promotion and distribution selectivity. Some useful bases (demographic, life style, psychological, and sociological) for segmenting a market also were identified in Chapters 3, 4, and 5.

Market segmentation attempts to penetrate a limited market in *depth,* whereas product differentiation seeks *breadth* in a more generalized market. Smith says, "The differentiator seeks to secure a layer of the market cake, whereas one who employs market segmentation strives to secure one or more wedge-shaped pieces."

A firm may first employ the strategy of market segmentation, but soon be forced by competition to combine it with product differentiation. A firm that makes electric razors may divide the market into two groups—men and women—and then develop separate products to meet the specific wants of each group. Eventually the women's market will be recognized as a separate market by many firms, each of which will bring out an electric razor for women. Soon all these sellers will resort to differentiation to maintain a separate identity. Thus any given segmentation of markets is a transitory phenomenon, and competitive conditions force a seller constantly to seek new ways of segmenting his market.[7]

Some of the reasons for the emergence of market segmentation as a formally recognized strategy follow:

1. There has been a decrease in the minimum size of the efficient manufacturing unit for many products; thus production runs of identical items need not be so long as in the past.
2. Self-service and similar cost-cutting techniques require that products be better adjusted to demand.
3. Increases in discretionary purchasing power result in more careful shopping; the customer is willing to pay a little more to get just what he wants.
4. A marketer of multiple products fears that one of his brands may draw sales from another of his products, if they are both aimed at the same market.
5. Market segmentation becomes necessary for growth after promotion on a generalized basis to a broad market reaches a point of diminishing returns; that is, a broad-based promotional appeal to a wide market has a weaker effect than a narrower appeal zeroed in on one market segment.

FACTORS INFLUENCING CHANGES IN PRODUCT MIX

A marketing executive who wishes to use his product mix strategically in the market should understand the main factors underlying a company's desire to expand or simplify its line.

CHANGES IN MARKET DEMAND

Consumer population and industrial users. A major change in a component of population may induce a firm to change its product mix. As birthrates declined in the 1960s, the Gerber Products Company—producer of baby foods—added a line of other baby products (bibs, crib sheets, socks, shirts, and waterproof pants) for distribution through supermarkets, along with its food lines. The growth in suburban population led furniture manufacturers to expand into patio and lawn furniture

---

7 See Walter P. Margulies, "Creative Ways of Segmenting Markets to Divide and Conquer," *Marketing Insights,* Oct. 21, 1968, pp. 20-21.

and encouraged makers of power tools, such as Black and Decker, and home appliances, such as Sunbeam, to bring power lawn mowers onto the market.

In the industrial market, the mobility of customers may force a manufacturer or wholesaler to drop some lines and add others to take up the slack.

An interesting phenomenon often occurs when a major U.S. company decides to open or acquire a subsidiary in Canada to serve the Canadian market. When the company is large enough or important enough to its suppliers, the suppliers also enter the Canadian market by new investment in or the acquisition of their own subsidiaries. Suppliers cannot continue to supply from the U.S. because Canadian tariffs and the costs of freight often put them at a cost disadvantage. When they move into Canada, they may (and often do) look for other customers to expand their markets.

Alternatively, the entry of major U.S. corporations into the Canadian market provides ample opportunity for smaller Canadian manufacturers to adapt their capabilities and expand their sales by becoming their suppliers. The entry of U.S. firms into the Canadian market also provides opportunities for Canadian distributors and merchandisers in expanding their business.

Buying power. Increases in purchasing power have played a significant role in leading several firms to raise the quality of their merchandise. No doubt this is one reason why manufacturers of outboard motors and snowmobiles have added larger motors to their lines.

Oddly enough, products are sometimes dropped because of an increase in purchasing power. In the past two decades, people have become able to afford better merchandise, and the market for low-priced, low-quality goods has declined considerably.

Customer behavior. Several situations involving customer motivation, attitudes, preferences, and buying habits will encourage a marketing executive to expand or contract his product mix. In the first place, he will add products in order to satisfy ultimate consumers or industrial users who want a more complete line. As household consumers have made it evident that they prefer the convenience of one-stop shopping, supermarkets have broadened their mix by adding magazines, health and beauty aids, small housewares, staple clothing, and many other nonfood lines.

Sometimes the impetus for a change in product mix comes from middlemen who prefer a more complete line, for competitive, cost, or promotional reasons. A manufacturer of a glass-cleaning compound found that when he added other cleaning and polishing products to his line, wholesalers were much more eager to work with him.

The increase in the leisure-time market was undoubtedly a major factor in prompting Bombardier and other companies to enter the trail bike market. The consumer's demand for convenience helped to spark the market for battery-powered, cordless electric appliances such as razors, carving knives, mixers, and vacuum cleaners.

COMPETITIVE ACTIONS AND REACTIONS

In order to meet competition more effectively, a firm may want to differentiate its product line so that price comparisons will not be possible. In other instances a manufacturer may want to diversify his product line so as to free himself somewhat from a bitterly competitive situation in which his profit margins are dangerously low. The plywood industry is a good example of one in which price competition is prevalent and differentiation of the basic product is difficult. Some of the larger firms—MacMillan Bloedel, for example—have added other products to their mix, such as a variety of finished interior paneling, shingles and shakes. The same company is also further diversified outside their immediate industry and into folding cartons and paper and packaging specialty products.

A "follow-the-leader" policy often seems to prevail in industry. It is difficult to know whether this "me-tooism" is based on sound marketing analysis or whether it stems from a belief that "if those other fellows are doing it, maybe we should try it too; they usually know what they are doing." Of course, if one firm enters a market with a new product that holds promise of being successful, other companies are almost forced to meet his competition. After the success enjoyed by early manufacturers of metal skis, many competitive firms felt they had to add this product to their lines. Later, similar experiences were observed with respect to fiberglass skis.

MARKETING INFLUENCES

Two major reasons for adding products are (1) to increase sales by tapping new markets or expanding present ones and (2) to use the firm's marketing capacity more efficiently by a better use of salesmen or warehouses. Adding 10 percent more products usually results in less than a 10 percent increase in salesmen's salaries and traveling expenses, marketing research expenses, and other marketing costs.

Of course, in some cases a firm can increase its marketing effectiveness by simplifying its line. The salesmen may be spreading themselves too thinly over the market, or warehouse space may be taken up slow-moving items. With the elimination of some products, salesmen can concentrate on fewer items and sell them properly.

PRODUCTION INFLUENCES

A manufacturer often wishes to change his product mix in order to use his manufacturing capacity more effectively and thus lower his net production costs. Here it is assumed that the firm is producing at a level of output such that if there were an increase in output, using the present facilities, the result would be a reduction in unit cost. Product additions also occur when a firm wishes to use an item whose manufacture elsewhere has been discontinued.

Product mix may be expanded in order to put by-products to better use. A classic example is found in the meat-packing industry, where by-products have resulted in the production of fertilizer, glue, soap, leather products, and many other items. Several firms have developed new products by using wood scraps.

FINANCIAL INFLUENCES

There are several financial reasons why a business enterprise may wish to change its product mix. One is to enable the firm to generally diversify its financial risks. Any one of several factors, such as a new competitive product or a change in a component of demand, can obsolete a given product. Hence from a financial standpoint, it is wise to spread risks among several products.

Expanding the product mix can help to increase a firm's profitable sales volume. Supermarkets, for example, have added several nonfood items to their lines; these items ordinarily bring a significantly higher margin than the 15 to 18 percent gross margin typical for the store as a whole. A full line can also help smooth out the seasonal fluctuations in sales volume. The classic example in days gone by was the iceman who added coal to his product mix in the winter.

A full line of products can make a manufacturer's product-servicing organization financially feasible. It is not economical to maintain a service organization, as many appliance manufacturers do, unless there are several products over which the costs can be spread.

A firm may hope to cushion recessions by product diversification. A company with one major product or market is like a town with one industry. Manufacturers who sell virtually all their output to the government, or to a firm with government contracts, are particularly susceptible to losses caused by unrenewed contracts.

Financial considerations may encourage a company to *simplify* its line. Sometimes a few items require so much capital investment in production or inventory facilities that the value of these products to the company can be questioned. By dropping slow-moving items, such as extremely large or extremely small shoe sizes, a manufacturer or middleman may experience a small decline in sales but a substantial decrease in cost. Such a change might result in longer and thus lower-cost production runs, less chance of mistakes in filing and shipping orders, lower insurance and investment costs on inventory, and curtailed losses from obsolescence.

DESIRE TO CHANGE COMPANY IMAGE

Changing the product mix in an attempt to alter the firm's image is related to the strategy of trading up or trading down. Variety chains have added so many higher-quality, higher-priced, non-variety-store items to their mix that today they often are small department stores, a far cry from the "five-and-ten-cent store." Of course, the desire to upgrade a store's image involves more than the emotional factor of management's own self-concept. There are sound, rational business reasons at play: The low-income market is not as big today as it was twenty-five years ago, but the middle-income group is a prime target.

CONCEPT OF THE PRODUCT LIFE CYCLE

Products, like people, have life cycles. From its birth to its death, a product exists in different stages and in different competitive environments. Its adjustment to these environments determines to a great degree just how successful its life will be. One set of product strategies employed by many firms is built around the understanding and management of the life cycles of their products. To better manage the cycle, it is useful to divide a product's life into six stages—introduction, growth, maturity, saturation, decline, and abandonment.

The length of the life cycle varies among products, ranging from a few weeks or a short season (a fad or an apparel fashion) to several decades (autos, telephones). The shape of the sales and profit curves may vary somewhat among products, although the basic shape and the relationship between the two curves are usually about the same as pictured in Fig. 9-1. Even the duration of each stage may be different among products; some take years to pass through the introductory stage, while others are accepted in a few weeks.[8] Certainly not all companies' products go through all stages. Some may fail in the introductory stage, and other firms may not enter with their brand until the market is in the growth or maturity stage. In virtually all cases, however, decline and possible abandonment are inevitable because (1) the need for the product disappears (as when frozen orange juice generally replaced juice squeezers); (2) a better or less expensive product is developed to fill the same need (plastics are replacing wood, metal, and paper in many products); or (3) a competitor does a superior marketing job.

MARKETING AND ENVIRONMENTAL CHARACTERISTICS OF EACH STAGE

It is quite important that management recognize what part of the life cycle its product is in at any given time because the competitive environment and the resultant marketing programs will ordinarily differ depending upon the stage. A brief summary of the competitive environment and some of the marketing reactions which typify each stage may be useful here.

Introduction. During the first stage of a product's life cycle, it is launched into the market in a full-scale production and marketing program. It has gone through the embryonic stages of idea screening, pilot models, and test marketing. The entire product may be new, as in the case of a machine which cleans clothes electronically without using any water. Or the basic product may be well known, but a new feature or accessory is in the introductory stage—a gas turbine engine in an automobile, for example. In still another situation, a product may be well accepted in some market segments, but be in the pioneering stage in other markets. Introductory promotion was needed (and in many cases still is) to sell automatic dishwashers to housewives, air travel to old folks, and home freezers to consumers long after these products and services were well accepted in some markets.

In many respects, the pioneering stage is the most risky and expensive one, as witness the high percentage of product failures in this period, even among firms with a reasonably successful history of new-product introductions. Operations in the introductory period are characterized by high costs, low sales volume, and limited distribution. For really new products, there is very little direct competition. The promotional program stimulates primary, rather than secondary, demand. That is, the type of product rather than the seller's brand is emphasized.

Growth. In the growth, or market-acceptance, stage, both the sales and the profit curves rise, often at a rapid rate. Competitors enter the market, and in large numbers if the profit outlook is particularly attractive. Sellers shift to "buy-my-brand" rather than "try-my-product" promotional strategy. The number of distribution outlets increases, economies of scale are introduced, and prices may come down a bit.

---

8 For the quantitative measurement of product life cycles, see William E. Cox, Jr., "Product Life Cycles as Marketing Models," *Journal of Business,* October, 1967, pp. 375-384; and Rolando Polli and Victor Cook, "Validity of the Product Life Cycle," *Journal of Business,* October, 1969, pp. 385-400.

Maturity and saturation. Sometimes it is difficult ot tell whether we are dealing with two separate stages or simply separate parts of one stage. During the first part of the period, we see sales still increasing but at a decreasing rate. While the sales curve is leveling off, the profits of both the manufacturer and the retailers are starting to decline. Marginal producers are forced to drop out of the market. Price competition becomes increasingly severe, and the producer assumes a greater share of the total promotional effort as he fights to retain his dealers and the shelf space in their stores. New models are introduced as manufacturers broaden their lines, and trade-in sales become significant.

As the market reaches the saturation stage, each of the characteristics described in the preceding paragraph is intensified. Replacement sales become a major factor, and the sales curve will react to changes in economic conditions. Good middlemen become particularly important.

Decline and possible abandonment. For virtually all products, obsolescence sets in inevitably as new products start their own life cycles and replace the old ones. Cost control becomes increasingly important as demand drops. Advertising declines, and a number of competitors withdraw from the market. Whether the product has to be abandoned or the surviving sellers can continue on a profitable basis in a specialized, limited market often depends upon management's abilities.[9]

MANAGEMENT OF THE PRODUCT LIFE CYCLE

The shape of a product's sales and profit curves is not inevitable in a company; to a surprising extent, the shape can be controlled.[10] One key to life cycle management is to forecast the profile of the proposed product's cycle even before it is introduced. Then at each stage management should anticipate the marketing requirements of the following stage. The introductory period, for instance, may be shortened by concentrating on broadening the distribution or by increasing the promotional effort. A product's life can be extended in the maturity and saturation stages by revitalizing it through new packaging, repricing, or product modifications. The makers of nylon, Jell-O, and Scotch tape—as an illustration—all have employed four different strategies to expand sales: (1) increase frequency of the product's use, (2) develop more varied use of the product, (3) attract new users, and (4) find new uses for the product. Bicycle manufacturers capitalized on a fitness trend and encouraged the use of their products by all family members. The makers of Johnson's Baby Shampoo have extended the life cycle of their product by promoting its use by adults.

Perhaps it is the sales-decline stage that a company finds its greatest challenges in life cycle management. At some point in the product's life, management may have to consider whether to abandon it. The costs of carrying profitless products go

---

9 For the idea that within the decline stage of some products there is a *product petrification stage* during which sales level off, costs are low, and profits actually increase, see George C. Michael, "Product Petrification: A New Stage in the Life Cycle Theory," *California Management Review*, Fall, 1971, pp. 88-91.

10 See, for example, Theodore Levitt, "Exploit the Product Life Cycle," *Harvard Business Review*, November-December, 1965, pp. 81-94; also see Harry H. Elwell, Jr., "Exploiting the Product Life Cycle—Revisited," *Southern Journal of Business*, January, 1971, pp. 54-63; and John E. Smallwood, "The Product Life Cycle: A Key to Strategic Marketing Planning," *MSU Business Topics*, Winter, 1973, pp. 29-35.

beyond the uncovered direct or indirect expenses which are found on financial statements. The real burdens are the insidious costs accruing from the managerial time and effort which are diverted to sick products instead of being applied to the healthy ones. Unfortunately, management often seems reluctant to discard a product, either for emotional and sentimental reasons or because they rationalize that they need the item to round out the product line, or that the decline is temporary and they will soon hit the jackpot.

When sales are declining, management has these alternatives:

1. Improve the product in a functional sense or revitalize it in some manner.
2. Review the marketing and production programs to make sure they are as efficient as possible.
3. Streamline the product assortment by pruning out unprofitable sizes, colors, and models. Frequently, this tactic will *decrease* sales and *increase* profits.
4. "Run out" the product; that is, cut all costs to the bare-minimum level that will optimize profitability over the limited remaining life of the product.
5. Abandon the product.

Knowing when and how to abandon products successfully may be as important as knowing when and how to introduce new ones. Certainly management should develop a systematic procedure for phasing out its weak products.[11]

PLANNED OBSOLESCENCE AND FASHION

As a marketing device, obsolescence has not lost its place in our economy. Apparently the roots of our quest for the "new" are deep: our desire to escape boredom, the psychology of a highly mobile population, our love of the frontier, and our belief in progress. Changes cannot be radical, however. The market wants newness, but still it wants to be moved gently out of its habitual patterns, not shocked out of them. Consequently, many manufacturers have developed the product strategy of planned obsolescence.

NATURE OF PLANNED OBSOLESCENCE

The economic and social aspects of planned obsolescence have been discussed at length and usually with much emotion. Although often there is no clear agreement on what planned obsolescence involves or how it should be defined, there does seem to be general agreement on its object. It is intended to make a product out-of-date and thus to increase the replacement market.

Planned obsolescence has been interpreted in a number of ways:

1. Technological, or functional, obsolescence. Under this interpretation, significant improvements as measured by technical standards have been made. When an automobile

---

11 For approaches to the pruning-out process, see R. S. Alexander, "The Death and Burial of 'Sick' Products," *Journal of Marketing,* April, 1964, pp. 1-7; Conrad Berenson, "Pruning the Product Line," *Business Horizons,* Summer, 1963, pp. 63-70; and Philip Kotler, "Phasing out Weak Products," *Harvard Business Review,* March-April, 1965, pp. 107-118; also see James T. Rothe, "The Product Elimination Decision," *MSU Business Topics,* Autumn, 1970, pp. 45-52; and Paul W. Hamelman and Edward M. Mazze, "Improving Product Abandonment Decisions," *Journal of Marketing,* April, 1972, pp. 20-26.

manufacturer installed power steering and automatic transmissions, these changes created functional, or technological, obsolescence with respect to earlier models.

2. Postponed obsolescence. Technological improvements are not introduced until the market demand for present models decreases, and a new market stimulus is needed. A good example of this strategy is found in the activities of the Polaroid Corporation which has released new, improved models of their Polaroid Land Camera at strategic points during the life of their patent.

3. Intentionally designed physical obsolescence. A product is designed to wear out physically within a reasonably short period of time. Obviously this is a dangerous strategy because a firm may acquire a reputation for shoddy merchandise. Durability is still a significant buying motive.

4. Style obsolescence. This is sometimes called "psychological" or "fashion" obsolescence. The intent is to make a person feel out-of-date if he continues to use an old model. Superficial characteristics of the product are altered so that the new model is easily differentiated from last year's model.

When a person criticizes planned obsolescence, he is usually referring to this last interpretation—style obsolescence. In our discussion, planned obsolescence will mean style obsolescence only, unless otherwise stated.

NATURE OF STYLE AND FASHION

Although style and fashion are often used interchangeably with respect to planned obsolescence, there is a clear distinction between the two. *Webster's* defines a *style* as a "distinctive or characteristic mode of presentation, construction, or execution in any art, employment, or product, especially in any fine art; also distinctive manner or mode of singing, playing, behaving, etc." Thus we can have several styles in many different products. There are styles in automobiles (sedans, convertibles, station wagons) and in bathing suits (one-piece suits, swimming trunks, bikinis). Scandinavian and French Provincial are furniture styles, and Gothic and Italian Renaissance are architectural styles.

A *fashion* is any style which is popularly accepted and purchased by several successive groups of people over a reasonably long period of time. "A fashion is always based on some particular style. But not every style is a fashion. . . . A style does not become a fashion until it gains some popular use, and it remains a fashion only so long as it is so accepted."[12]

A *fad* normally does not remain popular as long as a fashion, and it is based on some novelty feature.

A student of fashion should recognize its separate identify, its importance, and its pervasiveness in all societies. Fashion is really a field by itself. It is not simply a factor affecting buying patterns in the consumer market, and it is not merely a product strategy. Fashion is the pursuit of the "new" for its own sake. While basic styles never change, fashion is always changing. Fashion is the behavioral complex underlying all stylistic innovations, that is, all design changes which are not purely the result of engineering advances. In its broad sense fashion is the means used by society to innovate, select or reject, and progress.[13]

Style obsolescence is not limited to the fields of women's ready-to-wear and au-

---

12 Paul H. Nystrom, *Fashion Merchandising*, The Ronald Press Company, New York, 1932, p. 33.

13 John E. Mertes, "Fashion: A Prod toward Progress," *Dimensions*, June, 1970, pp. 12-18.

tomobiles. It is found in countless commodities, including appliances, motor boats, and bathroom scales. It is also apparent in such different fields as architecture, pedigreed dogs, and music. Fashion is found in all societies, whether they are primitive groups, the great Oriental cultures, or the societies of ancient and medieval Europe.

However, fashions do change more rapidly in our society. The Industrial Revolution and the rise of the common people account for this accelerated rate of change. Industrialization increased the ease with which fashions could be produced and distributed, and the rise of the common people increased the size of the potential market. The power behind fashion shifted from "the aristocracy of rank to the aristocracy of wealth."[14]

ORIGIN OF FASHION

Sapir has said that "fashion is emphatically a historical concept." A fashion must be studied within its historical context and related to prevailing cultures and social norms.

Fashion is also rooted in sociological and psychological factors. Basically, people are conformists. They follow rather strictly the patterns and standards established by the opinion leaders, or tastemakers, in their groups. At the same time, people yearn to look, act, and be a little different from others. They are not in revolt against custom. They simply wish to deviate a bit and still not be accused of bad taste or insensitivity to the code. Fashion discreetly furnishes them the opportunity for self-expression because "fashion is custom in the guise of departure from custom."

Stanley Marcus, president of Neiman-Marcus, the high-fashion women's store in Dallas, Texas, observed[15]

> If, for example, a dictator decreed feminine clothes to be illegal and that all women should wear barrels, it would not result in an era of uniformity, in my opinion. Very shortly, I think you'd find that one ingenious woman would color her barrel with a lipstick, another would pin paper lace doilies on the front of hers, and still another would decorate hers with thumb-tacks. Other women would emulate the examples they liked the best until a bare barrel would be unique. *This is a strange human urge toward conformity, but a dislike for complete uniformity.* [Italics supplied.]

Another socio-psychological factor underlying the growth of fashion in sophisticated societies such as ours is boredom. This is fostered by leisure time and highly specialized forms of activity, and it leads to restlessness and curiosity. In an attempt to break the monotony, people seek change.

Along with the desire to break a little from a regularized conforming existence, there is a corollary factor involving a person's ego. Most people want to add to their personal attractiveness, or to any object of their love or friendship. This ego-building consideration is also expressed in the desire to attract favorable attention and in the desire for prestige or even notoriety.

---

14 Edward Sapir, "Fashion," *The Encyclopedia of Social Sciences,* The Macmillan Company, New York, 1931, vol. VI, pp. 139-144. Much of the following section on the origin of fashion is drawn from this article.

15 Stanley Marcus, "Fashion Merchandising," A Tobe lecture on retail distribution delivered at the Harvard Graduate School of Business Administration, Cambridge, Mass., Mar. 10, 1959, pp. 4-5.

WHY YOU WEAR WHAT YOU DO:
UNDERSTANDING THE PSYCHOLOGY OF FASHION

On blue Monday, Linda wore a pale yellow mini dress to work. Tuesday, the 23-year-old management trainee showed up at the departmental meeting with a knee-length, gray, pin-striped shirtwaist with white cuffs and collar. She'd planned to wear another dress on Wednesday, but the rain made her change to a denim smock top and cotton slacks. On the way home, Linda stopped at the dry cleaners to pick up the flowered silk palazzo outfit she planned to wear to the theater on Saturday; and later, she changed into a pair of comfortable jeans, tank top, and floppy suede hat for an informal supper party. Linda doesn't know it, but her clothes are talking—about her.

"Linda obviously has a rich personality and a good self-image," says Jean Rosenbaum, M.D., a Colorado psychiatrist. "She's flexible and has options in her social situations. She takes advantage of the dress options available to her."

Clothes say a lot about Linda—just as they do of everyone. Clothes are a deeply felt, deeply needed, strongly motivated psychological statement—an expression of self. In what people wear and don't wear, in how they wear what they do, in what they do to make their clothes seem unique while still remaining safely part of the group, people are telling the world what they think of themselves.

"We have an image of ourselves, of our bodies. Our clothing is an extension of this image." . . .

The clothes hog—the lady with 60 pairs of shoes in her closet, the man who throws out his old wardrobe and buys everything new when a fashion change is announced—thinks his or her individual personality is worthless, says the doctor. The person has to depend on others for a sense of identity, and could be suffering from hidden depression. "But no matter what this person does, no matter how many hats or purses or suits he or she buys, the bad self-feeling remains." The opposite, on the other hand, is not necessarily the sign of a good self-image. The person who refuses to buy new clothes and continues to wear the noticeably out-of-date, tattered clothing of years back is demonstrating a personal rigidity and inflexibility.

Source: Liz Smith, "Why You Wear What You Do," *Today's Health* (published by the American Medical Association), October, 1973, pp. 36, 38.

FASHION-ADOPTION PROCESS

The concepts of (1) large-group and small-group influences on consumer buying behavior and (2) of the diffusion of innovation, as discussed in Chapter 6 may be applied to the fashion-adoption process. We observed that people usually seek to emulate others in the same social or economic stratum, or those on the next higher level. Consequently, in fashion adoption the scene is set for successive waves of purchases, as a given style is popularly accepted throughout a group until it finally falls out of fashion. This wavelike movement, representing the introduction, rise, popular culmination, and decline of the market's acceptance of a style, is referred to as the "fashion cycle."[16] Like an ocean wave, the fashion cycle builds up slowly, but declines rapidly once its crest is reached.

Somewhat conflicting theories exist regarding whether a given fashion cycle flows *vertically* through several socioeconomic strata, or moves *horizontally* and *simultaneously* within several strata. These theories of fashion adoption have been called, respectively, the "trickle-down" and the "trickle-across" processes.

Traditionally, the trickle-down theory has been used as the basic model to explain the fashion-adoption process. For example, designers of women's apparel first introduce a style to the leaders in a group—the tastemakers. Usually these people are social leaders and are in the upper-income brackets. If they accept the style, it will quickly appear in leading fashion stores. Soon the middle-income and then the lower-income markets will want to emulate the leaders, and the product will be mass-marketed. As its popularity wanes, the style will appear in bargain-price stores and finally will no longer be considered fashionable.

To illustrate the trickle-across process, let us again use the example of women's apparel. Within a few days or a few weeks at the most, at the beginning of the fall season, the same style of dresses will appear (1) in small, exclusive dress shops appealing to the upper social class, (2) in large department stores appealing to the middle social class, and (3) in discount houses and low-priced women's ready-to-wear chain stores, where the appeal is to the upper-lower social class. Price, quality, and materials mark the differences in the dresses sold on the three levels—the style is basically the same. *Within each class* the dresses are purchased early in the season by the opinion leaders—the innovators. If the style is accepted, its sales curve will rise as it becomes popular with the early adopters, and then with the late adopters. Eventually the sales decline as the style ceases to be popular. This cycle or flow is a horizontal movement occuring virtually simultaneously within each of several social strata.

In a series of research studies conducted in the Toronto retail market, it has been found that a high level of "fashion consciousness" is not related to a consumer's age or family income. It would appear, therefore, that persons who are likely to be influential in the adoption of new fashions are not concentrated in the upper social classes, but are spread throughout society. Fashion leaders are present at all social class levels.[17]

Other authors have also begun to question whether the trickle-down theory accurately reflects the contemporary adoption process.[18] While granting the existence of some vertical flow, they hypothesize that several market factors today would seem to impede the trickle-down adoption process while at the same time fostering a horizontal flow. Today a much larger segment of the total population can afford to purchase fashion merchandise. By means of modern production processes, com-

---

16 As Nystrom observed, "The popular use of the term [fashion cycle] unfortunately may be both confusing and misleading. Cycle literally means circle and as applied to fashion suggests starting with some style, moving away from it and finally coming back to the same style again. Nothing like this is meant by the term 'fashion cycle' here. . . . The fashion cycle is simply the forward wavelike movement completed and involves no necessary repetition of the style." *Economics of Fashion*, The Ronald Press Company, New York, 1928, p. 18.

17 Douglas J. Tigert and Jacques C. Bourgeois, "Retail Fashion Segmentation: A Lifestyle Application," in Bent Stidsen, ed., *Marketing in the 1970s and Beyond*, Canadian Association of Administrative Sciences, Marketing Division, Edmonton, 1975, pp. 133-142.

18 See, for example, Charles W. King, "Fashion Adoption: A Rebuttal to the 'Trickle Down' Theory," in Stephen A. Greyser (ed.), *Toward Scientific Marketing*, American Marketing Association, Chicago, 1964, pp. 108-125. The trickle-across theory is also compatible with the small-group research findings of Katz and Lazarsfeld, as noted in Chap. 6, where the *horizontal* nature of opinion leadership was identified.

munications systems, and transportation methods, we can disseminate style information and products so rapidly that all social strata can be reached at about the same time. In the apparel field, particularly, the fashion industry's manufacturing and marketing programs also tend to foster the horizontal movement of the fashion cycle. Manufacturers produce a wide *variety* of essentially one style. They also produce various *qualities* of the same basic style so as to appeal to different income groups simultaneously. Retailers, in turn, introduce that same basic style at different price levels, thus reaching several social strata concurrently. When an entire cycle may last only one short season, a seller cannot afford to wait for the style acceptance to trickle down; he must introduce it into many social levels as soon as possible.

The length of the fashion-adoption cycle may vary considerably from one product to another, although in general the cycle for any given product is shorter today than it was years ago. A style in houses or furniture may remain fashionable for many years, whereas styles in women's hats or shoes may be in fashion for only one season. This does not mean that all parts of the national market accept a style with the same rapidity and eagerness. It may reach a given point in its fashion cycle a year later in Moncton than in Montreal, and it may never be accepted as a fashion in rural communities.

Three basic elements in fashion theory may help to explain why fashions move as they do.[19] First, all styles build up to a point of excess. The overriding responsibility of a fashion designer is the unending provision of novelty. He must keep adding various frills to a basic style in order to give it a continuing semblance of newness so that it will appeal to the market. Thus in the Victorian era so much gingerbread was added to houses and furniture that they became style monstrosities, and the market rebelled. The styles which took over were noted for their stark, functional simplicity. In the 1960s there were indications that some people were preferring a little more decoration and adornment on their furniture and houses. Thus the currently fashionable styles in housing and furniture are already moving from the stage of simplicity toward their inevitable end of complexity end excess.

The second consideration is that the designer must shift the consumers' attention from one feature of a style to another as the style is running its fashion course. Thus as the women's clothing style epitomized by the miniskirt (the "young look") progressed through its fashion cycle, attention was drawn at one time to hemlines, while at other times emphasis shifted to hosiery, shoes, and jewelry.

The third principle of fashion concerns the rapid demise of a given cycle. "A fashion can never retreat gradually and in good order. Like a dictator it must always expand its aggressions—or collapse. Old fashions never just fade away—they die suddenly and arbitrarily."[20] Once a style is sold in large quantities (the economic emulation stage of the fashion cycle), it no longer appeals to fashion leaders who desire distinctiveness. Once the tastemakers begin to seek another style, the emulators rebel against the first, and it collapses as a fashion.

MARKETING CONSIDERATIONS IN FASHION

Management must recognize the stage a fashion cycle is in at any particular time. They must decide at what market they are aiming, at what point they want to get

---

19 Dwight E. Robinson, "Fashion Theory and Product Design," *Harvard Business Review*, November-December, 1958, pp. 121-138.

20 *Ibid.*, p. 128.

into the cycle, and when they should get out. Ordinarily, a retailer cannot success-fully participate in all stages of the fashion cycle at the same time. A high-grade specialty store in women's apparel—whose stocks are displayed discreetly in limited numbers without price tags—will want to get in at the start of a fashion trend. A department store appealing to the middle-income market will plan to enter the cycle in time to mass-market the style as it is climbing to its peak of popu-larity.

A seller—manufacturer or retailer—who typically enters a fashion cycle at its be-ginning will find that his ability to identify and communicate with the early buyers in any group is one major key to successful fashion marketing. These innovators are often quite influential, serving as opinion leaders, in their social structure. As indicated in Chapter 6, these acceptors of newness do constitute a unique market segment which can be differentiated from other segments.

A manufacturer's product and distribution policies will also be related to the fashion cycle. If he wishes to project an image of distinctiveness, he will produce only a few units of each model. They will be relatively expensive and will be dis-tributed through a limited number of high-grade stores. If he produces low-cost products with inexpensive materials, he must market them through low-quality stores acitve in the declining stage of the cycle.

To a great extent, success in fashion merchandising lies in the seller's sense of timing. He must not enter the cycle too early or leave it too late. For example, in a mass fashion market, a manufacturer or a middleman who waits until the style reaches its peak of popularity and then produces or stocks it is apt to be left with a large quantity on hand after the downswing starts.

Accurate forecasting is, therefore, of inestimable value in achieving success in fashion merchandising. This is an extremely difficult task, however, because the forecaster is often dealing with complex sociological and psychological factors. Fre-quently a retailer or a manufacturer operates largely on intuition and inspiration, tempered by considerable experience. Of course, the earlier the stage of the fashion cycle in which a firm participates, the tougher the forecasting job.[21]

Tigert and Bourgeois have observed that, given that fashion conscious con-sumers can be found in approximately equal proportions across broad socio-eco-nomic strata, a specific fashion retailer cannot simultaneously attempt to appeal to the fashion conscious segment and to a particular soci-economic segment. This would suggest that retailers should develop separate fashion departments to attract the fashion conscious consumers from the various socio-economic and demogra-phic groups in society: a youth fashion department, an upper-class fashion depart-ment, etc.[22]

FUTURE OF PLANNED OBSOLESCENCE

If someone asks whether obsolescence of any kind is losing its hold on the North American market, the answer is a definite "no." Our interest in something new is still strong, and the economy thrives on replacement demand. If the question is

---

21 For the suggestion that fashion trends are easy to detect, see William H. Reynolds, "Cars and Cloth-ing: Understanding Fashion Trends," *Journal of Marketing*, July, 1968, pp. 44-49. For a similar suggestion that a framework built on known aspects of individual and social psychology already exists for predicting the timing and direction of movements in a fashion example, see Chester R. Wasson, "How Predictable Are Fashions and Other Product Life Cycles?" *Journal of Marketing*, July, 1968, pp. 36-43.

22 Tigert and Bourgeois, "Retail Fashion Segmentation: A Lifestyle Application," p. 138.

ANOTHER "LAW OF FASHION"

The same dress is indecent 10 years before its time, daring 1 year before its time, chic in its time, dowdy 3 years after its time, hideous 20 years after its time, amusing 30 years after its time, romantic 100 years after its time, and beautiful 150 years after its time.

Source: James Laver, British costume historian, in *Today's Health,* October, 1973, p. 69.

whether planned or style obsolescence is diminishing in favor, however, the answer is a qualified "yes." For instance, planned obsolescence seems to be decreasing in popularity in both the automobile and major appliance industries. On several makes of automobiles, major design changes are no longer introduced every year or even every second or third year.

If planned obsolescence is declining in some fields, then what will take its place? The answer seems to be that technological change will become increasingly important. Increased leisure time, higher discretionary income, and improved communications have opened up new fields to consumers. They still want newness, and they still have the psychological drives that lead to fashion changes. The difference is that they now seek new kinds of products rather than model variations of the same product. They can better satisfy their egoistic demands with a new boat or swimming pool (new product) than with a new car (new model of an old product). The consumer is also more discriminating. Finally, people have accumulated considerable quantities of tangible goods, thus socially establishing their ability to buy. As former status symbols lose their prestige, consumers find it fashionable to spend money for travel and other educational and cultural pursuits.

Of course, as technological obsolescence supersedes the emphasis on style and fashion, several marketing problems will arise. Technological obsolescence is expensive and difficult to plan. Product-development costs will increase, and greater burdens will be thrust on marketing research to ensure that the company is making sound marketing decisions. Designers cannot be ordered to "invent on schedule." This means that there may be years when a firm has nothing really new to sell. Technological change may require more advertising than style change does. Technological improvements often are difficult to explain, and they will require new thinking in the advertising and personal selling fields.

EVALUATION OF PLANNED OBSOLESCENCE

Style obsolescence is one of the most controversial aspects of modern marketing. As is true of most social complaints against marketing, much of the criticism of style obsolescence is neither all true nor all false. One criticism is that fashion designers are dictators (especially in women's ready-to-wear) and people voluntarily follow like sheep to buy whatever the designers decree will be fashionable. This is true only in a very superficial sense. The designers themselves obey many masters. First and foremost, the designs must be profitable to the manufacturers. Thus, behind the psychological determinants of fashion, there is the necessity of considering manufacturing processes and the cost of materials. Also, the designer is controlled by established custom; he cannot depart too far from it. Actually, what he tries to do is to anticipate intuitively what the customers want even before they themselves know. That is, rather than impose fashion, the designer seeks to coax people into accepting what they themselves have unconsciously suggested. Furthermore, a designer just cannot combat a fashion trend established by the social psychology factors noted earlier. No matter how aesthetically pleasing a style may be in the abstract, if it does not fit in with a trend it will be a failure.

Sapir, along with other writers, has noted that throughout history there has been both a social and economic criticism of fashion. Social critics object to fashion—particularly women's ready-to-wear—because it calls attention to the human body. Actually, the criticism is valid. Women's apparel generally is intended to draw attention to the human form. This fits in with human psychology. People want to be as expressive—even as immodest, perhaps—as society will allow. Fashion helps them to achieve this objective. Regarding the factor of economic waste, whether the criticism is justified or not seems to be somewhat beside the point. "Waste seems to be of no concern where values are to be considered, particularly when these values are both egoistic and unconscious.[23]

Supporters of the strategy of style obsolescence and annual model changes point out that it satisfies the consumers' desire to have something new. It also maintains our economy at a higher level than would be possible if consumers used a product until it wore out physically. Furthermore, people who cannot afford to buy new automobiles or appliances have an opportunity to satisfy their wants for these products by purchasing used models. These would not be available if other consumers had not traded in their older models in order to acquire the latest ones.

Frequently it is difficult to distinguish between technological obsolescence and style obsolescence. Small functional improvements each year may add up to a substantial change over a period of years, but no single change might be said to have created technological obsolescence.

Planned obsolescence—both functional and style—is a characteristic of a free and expanding economy. In any economy which is controlled by the state or by cartels, product obsolescence and innovation are apt to take place slowly. In a free economy, in the long run, the consumers' marketplace vote is the controlling factor which determines whether a product stays on the market. As consumers continue to desire new products and can afford them, and as manufacturers are free to supply them, the result is a flow of new products, which inevitably tends to make obsolete many existing goods.

No matter how marketing people try to answer the social and economic criticisms—and some of the typical answers have been noted above—many people, including businessmen, have a nagging conscience about style obsolescence, and these answers are not sufficiently quieting. Two basic issues seem to keep arising. First, does our prevailing system of style obsolescence make sensible use of our resources and productive capacity? Certainly, antifunctionalism is materialism at its worst. When management is engaged in a policy of style obsolescence, often it has no choice but to make slight model change in order to make the differentiation apparent to the consumer, even though this is done at the cost of a postponed technological innovation. Frequent model changes increase the manufacturer's production costs and the middlemen's investment in inventory. The second, and related, issue concerns whether the system of planned obsolescence results in an artificially short life for the products which are produced, thus creating some sort of disutility. One cannot help asking why marketing men cannot be just as aggressive with

---

23 Sapir, *op. cit.*, p. 143.

worthwhile appeals and functional innovation as they are with superficial styling and prestige appeals.

After basic decisions have been made concerning the product line and product mix in a company, management may turn its attention to questions of branding, packaging, labeling, color, sizes, and other attributes or characteristics of the products. These topics are covered in the following chapter.

QUESTIONS AND PROBLEMS

1. "It is inconsistent for management to follow concurrently the product-line strategies of *expanding* its product mix and *contracting* its product mix." Discuss.
2. Cite examples of firms that have simplified their product mix in recent years.
3. "Trading up and trading down are product strategies closely related to the business cycle. Firms trade up during periods of prosperity and trade down during depressions or recessions." Do you agree?
4. How might the manufacturers of each of the following articles implement the product strategy of market segmentation? Of product differentiation?
   a. Shoes
   b. Paint
   c. Tape recorders
   d. Typewriters
5. Select two of the population trends discussed in Chapter 4 and describe how these two might influence the product mix of consumer goods manufacturers.
6. Identify those factors which might lead a manufacturer to alter his product mix.
7. Name some products which you believe are in the introductory stage of their life cycles. Be sure to identify the market which considers your examples to be new products.
8. Give examples of products which are in the stage of market decline. In each case, point out whether you think the decline is permanent. What recommendations do you have for rejuvenating the demand for the article?
9. How might a company's pricing strategies differ depending upon whether a product is in the pioneering stage or maturity stage of its life cycle?
10. What advertising strategies are apt to be used when a product is in the growth stage?
11. Carefully distinguish between "style" and "fashion," using examples other than the ones (automobiles, swimsuits, furniture, and architecture) cited in this chapter.
12. What products, other than wearing apparel and automobiles, stress fashion and style in marketing? Do styles exist among industrial products?
13. Select a product and trace its marketing as it moves through a complete fashion cycle. Particularly note and explain the changes in the distribution, pricing, and promotion of the product in the various stages of the cycle.
14. What is the relation between fashion and the small-group influence on buying behavior explained in Chapter 6?

15. Is the trickle-across theory applicable in describing the fashion-adoption process in product lines other than women's apparel? Explain, using examples.

16. Planned obsolescence is criticized as a social and economic waste because we are urged to buy things we do not like and do not need. What is your opinion in this matter? If you object to planned obsolescence, what are your recommendations for correcting the situation?

11

BRANDS, PACKAGING, AND OTHER PRODUCT FEATURES

Have you ever stopped to think why you selected some of the products which you are now using? Many industrial users of lubricating products insist upon Esso oils and greases, while others might prefer lubricants made by Gulf. Some homemakers prefer Aylmer canned peaches, while others buy Del Monte. Yet many people contend that there are no significant differences among the well-known brands of lubricants or canned peaches. The buyer's choice may have been influenced by the guarantee offered or by an attractive package. Frequently the brand, the package, the color and design, and other product characteristics combine to project an image of the product to the prospective consumer.

INFLUENCES OF PRODUCT FEATURES ON BUSINESS FUNCTIONS

Branding, packaging, and the other product features analyzed in this chapter are interrelated with the production and financial functions of a firm as well as with other marketing activities. Production runs will be shorter and thus more costly if goods are manufactured in six colors instead of one. A product made in small units and packaged in an attractive wrapper is ordinarily more costly than one put up in large, bulk-packaged units.

Financial risks increase as the variety of sizes and colors is increased. Packaging products in special Christmas containers exposes a company to a financial loss on merchandise unsold on December 26. A business which offers a generous warranty—double your money back if not entirely satisfied or free servicing for one year—has greater financial risks than a firm which says "all sales are final" and gives no allowances for servicing.

A multitude of interrelationships exist among the various product features and the marketing policies regarding distribution, pricing, and promotion. A few examples will illustrate this point. A firm manufacturing products which will be sold by retailers on a self-service basis must devote special attention to packaging and labeling in order to attract the customer at the point of purchase. Normally, branding increases price rigidity. At the same time, however, well-known brands are most likely to have their prices cut below the usual level to attract customers to the seller's establishment. In some cases a product's label has been redesigned for more effective display on television.

BRANDS

The word "brand" is a comprehensive term, and in one way or another it includes other, more particularized terms. A *brand* is "a name, term, symbol, or design, or a combination of them which is intended to identify the goods or services of one seller or group of sellers and to differentiate them from those of competitors."[1] A brand *name* consists of words, letters, and/or numbers which may be *vocalized*. A brand *mark* is the part of the brand which appears in the form of a symbol, design, or distinctive coloring or lettering. It is recognized by sight but is not expressed when a person pronounces the brand. Ski-Doo, Du Maurier and Labatt's 50 are brand names. The distinctive signature of Coca-Cola and the stylized CN logo of Canadian National are brand marks.

A trademark may be defined as a brand which is given legal protection because under the law it has been appropriated exclusively by one seller. Thus "trademark" is essentially a legal term. All trademarks are brands and thus include the words, letters, or numbers which may be pronounced. They may also include a pictorial design (brand mark). Some people erroneously believe that the trademark is only the pictorial part of the brand.

One major method of classifying brands is on the basis of who owns them—producers or middlemen. IBM, Arrow, Bick's and York are producers' brands, while Domino, Viking, Pride of Arabia, Kenmore, Coldspot, Birkdale, and Ann Page are middlemen's brands.

Although the terms "national" and "private" brands have been used to describe producer and middleman ownership, respectively, marketing people prefer the producer-middleman terminology. To say that the brand of a small manufacturer of poultry feed who markets his products in two or three provinces is a national brand, while the brands of Eaton's, Loblaws, The Bay, Woodward's and Dominion Stores are private brands, seems to be stretching the meaning of the terms "national" and "private."[2]

---

1 Committee on Definitions, *Marketing Definitions: A Glossary of Marketing Terms,* American Marketing Association, Chicago, 1960, p. 8.

2 For a proposed new branding language, eliminating the confusion in terminology which has led to communications problems among marketers and to distortion in measurement of trends in manufacturer-owned and distributor-owned brands, see Thomas A. Schutte, "The Semantics of Branding," *Journal of Marketing,* April, 1969, pp. 5-11.

IMPORTANCE TO THE CUSTOMER

Brands are an easy way for a purchaser to identify the product or service he desires. Furthermore, the individual units of a branded item maintain a consistency of quality that buyers can depend upon. A brand also offers some protection to the consumer: it identifies the firm behind the product. A customer may have purchased a fan belt or a few yards of woolen plaid piece goods with which he was greatly pleased. When replacement parts or additional material is needed and the customer wants to get the same product, he can be assured of doing so only if the item is branded. Branding is an insurance of merchandise comparability when the buyer uses more than one source of supply. Westinghouse light bulbs are Westinghouse light bulbs, regardless of where purchased.

Branded products tend to improve in quality over the years. Competition forces this improvement, for brand owners are constantly seeking new ways to differentiate their products in order to secure a stronger market position. In the constant search for more profitable sales volume, product improvements have frequently been the key to success. Improvements may not be perceptible on a year-to-year basis, but a 1977 General Electric fluorescent light bulb is noticeably better than one made in 1960.

IMPORTANCE TO THE SELLER

Branding can be used to achieve several of the typical marketing objectives of both manufacturers and middlemen.

To aid in advertising and display programs. Having a brand gives a seller something to advertise—something around which to build a company image. The brand is often of greater help in demand stimulation than the company name or the technical aspects of the product. Not only can brand names or marks denote more to a customer than several lines of advertising copy, but the brand itself can also do it more rapidly. In the case of many manufacturers' brands, the consumer probably does not even know the name of the producer. A firm whose product is sold on a self-service basis ordinarily must rely heavily on brand appeal. The product must be presold through advertising so that it will be recognized and selected by the customer as he walks by the mass of products displayed on shelves.

To help increase control and share of market. A firm which sells unbranded canned tomato juice and advertises and promotes the generic product is helping the whole industry, but is not necessarily increasing its share of the market. By the same token, a retailer who advertises a manufacturer's brand, such as CIL paints, may stimulate a customer to buy this brand but to buy it in a competitive outlet. Only when a manufacturer or middleman puts his own brand on a product can he be assured of some control over the market. Branding also helps the brand owner to stimulate repeat sales and to protect himself from product substitution. Unless the product has a brand identification, company A has no assurance that a retailer will not substitute a product made by another firm and tell the customer it was made by company A.

To reduce price comparisons and help stabilize prices. A brand in itself differentiates a product and enables the brand owner to establish a price which cannot easily be compared with prices for competing goods. The mere act of branding may create a marketing difference between two items. At the retail level, a store can prevent customers from price-comparison shopping by the expedient of putting its own brand on products instead of using manufacturers' brands. A customer can compare prices on Electrohome television sets at several department and appliance stores. Eaton's avoids this type of competition by placing its Viking brand on its television sets.

There is little doubt that branding increases a firm's independence in pricing activities. The less desirable alternative for the individual firm is to expose itself to the unrelenting mercies of the market for the determination of its prices. Competition on the basis of price alone may be desirable from a consumer's standpoint, but a seller usually prefers to compete on a nonprice basis. Branding enables the seller to do this to some extent. Price competition is never completely eliminated, of course.

Branding also reduces price flexibility. Several studies have shown that prices of well-known brands tend to fluctuate less than those of nonbranded items or obscure brands. Whether price rigidity is desirable for society in general or for the individual firms involved is open to question.

To facilitate expansion of product mix. If a firm has one or more lines of branded goods, it can add a new item to its product mix much more easily than a company selling unbranded merchandise. If the new item is similar to established products and the same brand can be attached, introduction of the new item is facilitated. Even when a different brand must be affixed, however, it certainly helps to be able to say, "The new product, brand A, is made by the ABC Company, manufacturers of brand Z and other fine products for over fifty years."

REASONS FOR NOT BRANDING

Many firms do not brand their products because they are either unable or unwilling to assume the two major responsibilities inherent in brand ownership: (1) the responsibility for demand stimulation through advertising, personal selling, and other forms of promotion and (2) the responsibility for maintaining an adequate quality of output.

Company considerations. Customer dissatisfaction with the quality of the product purchased will reflect unfavorably on the brand owner. If it is a manufacturer's brand, the customer may seek an immediate remedy from the middleman who sold the item, but the long-run harmful effects are felt by the manufacturer-owner. The customer will hesitate to repurchase not only the item that once proved unsatisfactory but any other product carrying the same brand.

Nature of the product. Some items are not branded because of the difficulty of differentiating the products of one firm from those of another. Clothespins, safety pins, nails, and industrial raw materials (coal, cotton, wheat) are examples of goods for which product differentiation is generally unknown. The physical nature of some items, such as fresh fruits and vegetables, may discourage branding, although now that producers or middlemen are packaging these goods in typically purchased quantities, the brand can be applied to the package. Producers frequently do not brand that part of their output which is below their regular quality. Products graded as seconds or imperfects are sold at a cut price and are often distributed through channels different from those used for the regular goods.

SELECTING A GOOD BRAND

Selecting a good brand name is one of the most difficult tasks facing marketing management. In spite of the acknowledged importance of a brand, it is surprising how few really good brand names there are. In a study made many years ago, it was found that only 12 percent of the names helped sell the product; 36 percent actually hurt sales, and 52 percent were "nonentities—contributing nothing to the sales appeal of the product." There is no reason to believe that the situation has improved materially since this study was made.

Characteristics of a good brand. Most marketers would agree that a good brand should possess as many of the characteristics noted below as possible. It is extremely difficult, however, to find a brand which possesses all of them.

In the first place, a brand should suggest something about a product's benefits— its use, characteristics, quality, and action. Furthermore, the name must achieve these objectives without legally being considered descriptive (unfairly appropriating ordinary English words) or deceptive. Examples of names suggesting desirable benefits include Wear-Ever (cookware), Easy-Off (oven cleaner), Mor-Power (batteries), Frigidaire (refrigerators and home freezers), and Beautyrest (mattresses). Product action is suggested by Spic and Span, Klear, Minute Maid, Pop-Tarts, and Ultra Brite. The name should be easy to pronounce, spell and remember. Simple, short, one-syllable names are helpful such as Tide, Gleem, Crest, Ban, and Raid. A brand name should also be distinctive. Many brands with names like Presto, National, Star, Acme, and Standard, fail on this point.

A brand should be sufficiently versatile to be applicable to new products added to the product line. An innocuous name, such as those common in the sporting goods market (Spalding, Jelinek, Cooper and Adidas) may serve the purpose better than a highly distinctive name suggestive of product benefits. Coldspot is an excellent name for a refrigerator, but Sears does not use that name on its other major appliances, preferring to use the Kenmore name. Management should select a brand name and a mark which are adaptable to any advertising medium. Companies are constantly redesigning their brands and logos in order to make their advertising more affective. Finally, the brand should be capable of being registered and legally protected under the Trade Marks Act and other laws.

Generic usage of brand names. Over a period of years some trademarks become so accepted that the brand name is substituted for the generic or descriptive name of the particular product. People associate the name with the product and not with the producer-owner of the brand. A number of product names such as shredded wheat and linoleum were originally trademarks limited to use by the owner, but they have long since lost their distinctiveness and any firm may use them.

A company may lose the right to exclusive use of a brand name for a number of reasons. Under protection of a patent, a manufacturer's brand name may become so closely associated with the product that, upon expiration of the patent, that brand name is used by the public to describe all brands of the product, regardless of manufacturer. There is simply no better name available to the public to describe the product class.

More often, trademark protection is lost simply because a company has done an outstanding job of marketing its product. In these cases, a product becomes so successful that its brand name becomes synonymous with the type of product. Where the brand name falls into such common usage that it ceases to be distinctive or to distinguish the product of one manufacturer from those of others, then the original owner of the brand name is in danger of losing the legal right to exclusive use of the brand. A number of brand names would appear to be in danger of becoming generic. These might include such brands as Band-Aid, Ski-Doo, Kleenex and Xerox. All of these are extremely successful brand names but have been promoted so well that consumers tend to use them generically. Ideally, a firm wants its brand to be preferred and even insisted upon by consumers, but it does not want its brand name to become generic.[3]

It is the responsibility of the trademark owner to assert his rights in order to prevent the loss of the distinctive character of his trademark. A number of strategies are employed to prevent the brand name from falling into generic usage. The most common strategy is to ensure that the words "trade mark" or the letters "TM"® appear adjacent to the brand name wherever it appears. Coca-Cola Limited often uses the following phrase in its advertising: "Coca-Cola is a registered trade mark which identifies only the product of Coca-Cola Limited." Such phrases give evidence to the public and to competitors that the brand name has been registered.

A second strategy is to use two names—the brand name together with either the company's name or the generic name of the product. An example of this is the name "Thermos Vacuum Bottle," which is designed to suggest to the public that "Thermos" is but one brand of vacuum bottle and that the name "Thermos" should not be applied to all products in that product category.

A third strategy for protecting a trademark involves the incorporation into the trademark of a distinctive signature or logo. Many companies have adopted distinctive ways of presenting the brand name of their products so that the consumer is able to identify their products whenever they encounter the particular brand written in a certain script or typeface. Some examples of such signatures and logos are presented in Figure 11-1.

Finally, the owner of a registered trademark must be willing to prosecute any other companies which attempt to market products under a brand name which is identical to or similar to the brand name which is registered. By prosecuting such infringements of the trademark protection, the owner is demonstrating to the courts that he is actively protecting his right to use of the brand and is guarding against its falling into generic usage. If the owner fails to prosecute infringements, even if he decides to prosecute at a later date after other companies have adopted his brand, the distinctive character of his trademark will be lost and the courts are likely to rule that the original owner no longer has exclusive right to use of the brand name, as it is in the public domain. Some companies seek to show competitors or others who wish to make use of registered trademarks that they are willing to take legal action to protect their trademarks. An example of advertising which is designed to achieve this purpose is presented in Figure 11-2.

BRAND POLICIES AND STRATEGIES

Manufacturers' strategies. A manufacturer's decision must be based on a recognition of the values of branding and the responsibilities of brand ownership. He must

---

3 For a detailed discussion of the law as it applies to trademarks, the reader is referred to: Frederick R. Hume, (ed.), *Anger's Digest of Canadian Law*, 19th. ed., Canada Law Book Company Ltd., Toronto, 1967, chap. 25; and to: Harold G. Fox, *The Canadian Law of Trade Marks and Unfair Competition*, 3rd. ed., The Carswell Company Limited, Toronto, 1972.

Figure 11-1: Examples of Corporate and Product Symbols.

decide whether to brand his product and whether to sell any or all of his output under a middleman's brand.

Market entire output under manufacturer's own brand. Companies which follow this brand policy typically are very large, well financed, and well managed. Polaroid, Maytag, and IBM are some examples. They typically have broad product lines, well-established distribution systems, and large shares of the market. Probably only a small percentage of manufacturers follow this policy, and their number seems to be decreasing.

Many of the reasons for adopting this policy have already been covered in the section on the importance of branding to the seller. In addition, middlemen often prefer to handle manufacturers' brands, especially when the brands have high consumer acceptance. Of course, manufacturers' brands are virtually imperative for middlemen who are unable to establish their own.

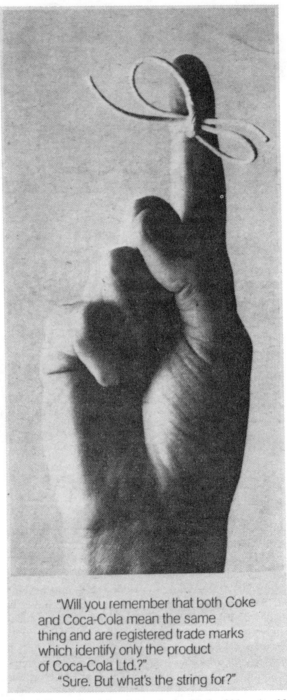

Figure 11-2: Trademark Protection Advertising. *Source: Weekend Magazine,* November 15, 1975, p. 26.

Besides the earlier-mentioned responsibilities of brand ownerships—the need to promote the brand and stand behind the product's quality—manufacturers face other problems when they use brands. Large retailers who want to use their own brands often will not buy products which carry the producer's brand. Also, many retailers chronically complain that manufacturers' brands provide inadequate gross margins and too little middleman control over the pricing.

Branding of fabricating parts and materials. A corollary to the above strategy is one in which producers of industrial fabricating materials and parts (products used in the further manufacturing of other goods) decide to brand their products. This strategy is used in the case of Domtar building materials, Goodyear's Neolite soles and heels, DuPont's Teflon resins and Dacron fibres, and in marketing many automotive parts, such as Purolator oil filters and Champion spark plugs.

Underlying this strategy is the seller's desire to develop a market preference for his branded part or material. He wants consumers and industrial users to specify that they want his item in the finished product. For instance, the Du Pont Company wants to build a market situation where customers will insist on a shirt made with Dacron. In addition, the parts manufacturer wants to persuade the producer of the ultimate finished item that using the branded materials will help sell the end product. That is, the Du Pont Company hopes to convince the manufacturers of Forsyth shirts that their sales will increase if their shirts are made with Dacron (the Du Pont Company's branded material).

From the standpoint of a purchaser, this can be an effective strategy for a manufacturer who wishes to capitalize on the reputation of these brands when he is selling his finished product. By building in highly promotable components and materials during the earliest phases of product planning, the seller may be able to keep customer interest alive long after the new-product promotional activities have ceased to be effective.

Certain product characteristics are particularly conducive to the effective employment of this strategy. First, it helps if the product is also a consumer good bought for replacement purposes. If the customer must replace the oil filter or spark plugs in his car, this encourages the branding of Champion spark plugs and Fram oil filters. The seller's situation is improved in a second way if the part is of high unit value and is a major part of the finished product—a television picture tube, for example. In the third place, if the material or part is easily distinguished or frequently replaceable, it is apt to be branded. Here an interesting comparison arises between parts in the hard goods industries and materials in soft goods. Hard goods parts—in automobiles, for example—are not replaced often, but they stand out clearly. In textiles, the material may not be easily distinguished or visibly labeled, but the brand is brought to the fore because the item is replaced more often.

Marketing under a middleman's brand. Manufacturers may elect the strategy of selling part or all of their output under the brands of one or more middlemen. A comprehensive study of brand policy, conducted by the Marketing Science Institute, has contributed much to our understanding of brand management.[4] This study shed light especially on the problems of a manufacturer who sells under a mixed-

---

4 Victor J. Cook and Thomas F. Schutte, *Brand Policy Determination,* Allyn and Bacon, Inc., Boston, 1967.

brand policy, that is, who produces goods under his own label as well as under middlemen's brands. The study indicated that an increasing majority of producers are adopting a mixed-brand policy, and this trend is likely to continue.

Financial considerations are a major reason for this trend. This business generates additional sales volume and profit dollars. Orders typically are large, payment is prompt, and a manufacturer's working-capital position is improved. Also, a manufacturer may utilize his production resources more effectively, including his plant capacity. Furthermore, refusing to sell under a retailer's brand will not eliminate competition from this source. Many middlemen want to market under their own brands, and if one firm refuses their business, they will go to another. In terms of marketing strategy, a manufacturer can get, from the middlemen whom he is supplying, information regarding consumer behavior, the middlemen's operations, and even competitors' programs. Marketing overhead can be spread over more accounts, and a manufacturer enjoys greater flexibility in his pricing.

Probably the most serious limitation to marketing under a middleman's brand is that the manufacturer is at the mercy of the middleman. This disadvantage increases as the proportion of his output going to the middleman's brand increases. Furthermore, the manufacturer has no assurance of continuity of orders, and often the unit profit is lower on volume sold under the middleman's brand. Another drawback is that the manufacturer's goodwill may suffer if the public becomes aware of his dual role of selling under his own brand and a middleman's brand, particularly if the latter is priced significantly lower than his own.

A declining number of manufacturers market their *entire* output under middlemen's brands. These producers typically are too small, are inadequately financed, or lack the marketing resources and know-how to warrant the use of their own brands.

Middlemen's strategies. The question of whether "to brand or not to brand" must also be answered by middlemen.

Carry only manufacturers' brands. Most retailers and wholesalers follow this policy because they are in no position to take on the dual burdens of promoting a brand and being responsible for maintaining its quality. Manufacturers' products afford a more ready source of supply. Even though they usually carry lower gross margins, manufacturers' brands often have a higher rate of turnover and a better profit possibility.

Carry middlemen's brands in conjunction with manufacturers' brands. Many large retailers and some large wholesalers have their own brands. To establish and market his own brand successfully, a retailer must have earned the confidence of his customers, and he must carefully maintain a high level of quality control over the items which he selects to sell under this brand. He should also have a very large sales volume because no other firm will help him sell this brand. Some retailers have been extremely successful in marketing their private label products. As part of Loblaw's recent revitalization of their operations in the Ontario market, that chain has placed considerable emphasis on the development of a strong line of private label products. By late 1974, there were over 400 items in the Loblaws private label line and these items accounted for seventeen percent of the chain's grocery sales and this percentage was expected to increase.[5] Other chains, most notably Eaton's

---

5 "Loblaw Private Labels 17% of Grocery Sales," *Canadian Grocer*, August, 1974, p. 1.

and Sears, have enjoyed such success with their private label products that their middlemen's brands such as Viking, Kenmore and Allstate have achieved the status of national brands.

Large middlemen, retailers particularly, may incur the ill will of manufacturers if they decide to use their own brands in direct competition with strong, established manufacturers' brands. For many reasons, however, a middleman may feel that it is advantageous to market his own brand. In the first place, it increases his control over his market. If a customer prefers a middleman's brand, he can get it only at the middleman's store. By using his own brand a middleman can reap the full benefit of his promotional efforts and any customer goodwill attached to the brand. Salesclerks in the store can even use the sales argument that "our brand is the same as the widely advertised brand A, which is selling for a 20 percent higher price."

If a middleman decides to adopt his own brand, he can usually sell it at a price below that of the manufacturers' brands and still get a higher gross margin. This is possible because he can buy at a lower cost. The cost may be lower because the manufacturer does not include a share of his advertising and selling costs in the price, or because he is anxious to get the extra business in order to keep his plant running in slack seasons.

Middlemen have more freedom and flexibility in pricing products sold under their own labels. Some manufacturers give a retailer no price flexibility, even to meet local competition. At the other extreme, some manufacturers' brands are used as a price football. The price is cut indiscriminately by competing stores to a point where a retailer may lose money on every sale. When a middleman has his own brand, it becomes a differentiated product, and this hinders price comparisons which might be unfavorable to the store.

Middlemen may be able to control their own branded product and its supply more than they can a manufacturer's brand. A middleman who has his own brand need not fear that manufacturers will either withdraw their brand or not sell to him in the first place. Also, a retailer or wholesaler who decides to use his own brand can establish specifications under which it is to be produced.

Strategies common to manufacturers and middlemen. Manufacturers and middlemen alike must adopt some strategy with respect to branding a line of products and also with respect to branding for market saturation.

Branding a line of products. At least four different strategies are widely used by firms which have more than one product: (1) the same "family" or "blanket" brand may be placed on all products. This policy is followed by Heinz, Campbell, Aylmer, and Del Monte and others in the food field, as well as by Westinghouse and General Electric. (2) A separate name may be used for each product. This strategy is employed by General Foods, Procter & Gamble, and Lever Brothers. (3) A separate family brand may be applied to each grade of product or to each group of similar products. Sears, for example, groups its major home appliances under the name Kenmore, its paints and home furnishings under Harmony House, its tools under Craftsman, and its tires and automotive accessories under Allstate. (4) The company's trade name may be combined with an individual name for the product. Thus, there is Kraft Velveeta and Kraft Cracker Barrel, and Molson's Canadian and Molson's Export.

When used wisely, a family-brand strategy has considerable merit. It is much simpler and less expensive to introduce new related products to a line. Also, the general prestige of a brand can be spread more easily if it appears on several products rather than on one. A family brand is best suited for a marketing situation where the products are related in quality, in use, or in some other manner. Canada Packers does not associate its Maple Leaf and York brands of food products with its Shur-Gain brand of livestock and poultry feeds.

On the other hand, the use of family brands places a greater burden on the owner to maintain consistent quality among all products. One bad item can reflect unfavorably, and conceivably even disastrously, on all other goods carrying the same brand. Another drawback to family brands is that each individual item under the brand usually gets less aggressive promotional effort than it would if each product were separately distinguished.

Branding for market saturation. Frequently, in order to achieve a greater degree of market saturation, a firm will employ a multiple-brand strategy. Often one type of sales appeal is built around a given brand. To reach another segment of the market, the company must use other appeals. Procter & Gamble's two detergents, Tide and Ivory Snow, illustrate this point. Some consumers are likely to feel that if Tide is strong enough to clean dirty, greasy work clothes, it is not sufficiently gentle to use on lingerie or baby clothing or on dishes. For these consumers, Procter & Gamble has marketed Ivory Snow, still a detergent, but one whose image is considerably more gentle than that of Tide.

Sometimes a producer wants to expand the number of retail outlets in a given geographic market. Possibly he has granted an exclusive territory to one retailer, and now that the market has enlarged enough to support two or three retailers, the original store does not want to have the brand distributed to its competitors. Rather than antagonize his original dealer, the manufacturer may market the identical product in other outlets but under another brand.

The use of multiple brands on the same or similar products affords the seller some flexibility in his pricing. A competitor may have an attractively priced item, and rather than cut the price on his known brand, a manufacturer may come out with another "fighting brand" priced to beat that of the competitor and still leave the price image of the original brand unscathed.

As a rule, it is a sound strategy to use separate brands on different qualities of the same general type of product. Obviously, to run counter to this policy—that is, to market different qualities under the same brand—is risky. It violates a fundamental thesis in branding, namely, that all units of a given brand should be reasonably consistent in quality. Several manufacturers of sheets, towels, and pillowcases do market various levels of quality under the same general brand, but with additional differentiating labels.

THE BATTLE OF THE BRANDS

Middlemen's brands have proved to be eminently successful in competing with manufacturer's brands. However, neither group has demonstrated a convincing competitive superiority over the other in the marketplace. Consequently, the "battle of the brands," which has been one of the significant marketing developments of the past decades, shows every indication of continuing and becoming more intense. According to the Marketing Science Institute study referred to above, the market impact of middlemen's brands varies considerably among product lines.

The share of total industry sales held by middlemen's brands ranged from 7 percent for portable appliances to 52 percent for shoes. In between, the middleman-brand market share was 13 percent in grocery products, 15 percent in gasoline, 33 percent in major appliances, and 36 percent in replacement tires. *Trends* in market share also vary quite a bit. Manufacturers' brands may be declining in importance in some product lines and enjoying increasing market shares in others.

Historically, middlemen's brands emerged generally in the 1920s, became of some significance during the Depression of the 1930s, and with a few exceptions almost disappeared during World War II. Several factors have accounted for the highly successful resurgence of these brands. The thin profit margins on manufacturers' brands in particular, and on total volume in general, have encouraged retailers to establish their own labels. Consumers have become more sophisticated in their buying, and their brand loyalty has declined, so that they will consider many alternative brands. The improved quality of retailers' brands has boosted their sales. It is quite generally known that middlemen's brands are usually produced by large, well-known manufacturers. Large retailers such as Eaton's, Sears and Woolco have recently begun to make extensive and very effective use of media advertising (particularly on television) to promote their own brands.

In this battle, the manufacturers are vocal in their point of view. A few—not many—refuse to produce store-branded merchandise. Manufacturers charge retailers with accepting funds for cooperative advertising of manufacturers' products and then diverting these funds for the advertising of the stores' brands. Furthermore, retailers generally have not contributed much to product innovation. Certainly store brands would be apt to suffer considerably if they did not have manufacturers' advertised brands to use for price and quality comparisons.

Manufacturers do have some effective responses they can use to combat the inroads of retailers' brands.[6] Producers can devote top priority to product innovation and packaging, an area where retailers are not as strong. Manufacturers' research and development capacity enables them to enter the early stages of a product's life cycle, whereas retailer brands typically enter after a product is well established. For example, in recent years retailer brands did not appear in paper diapers until well after several producers' brands had been introduced. Another area where manufacturers are ahead of retailers is in their use of research techniques to position new products, reposition old ones, and generally use shrewd market segmentation. Canada Dry, for instance, improved its market situation considerably when it switched from a mixer-only position to soft-drink status. Manufacturers need to communicate product advantages and a value image more effectively in their advertising. They also must employ increased automation and productivity to reduce the price gap between their brands and store brands. Manufacturers must place more stress on servicing their products so as to compete with large retailers who have achieved a strong market position because of their service capabilities. Finally, when selling to retailers, the manufacturers can stress the strength of well-known brands as "traffic-pullers" for the store.

PACKAGING

Packaging may be defined as the general group of activities in product planning which involve designing and producing the container or wrapper for a product.

---

6 See *Grey Matter*, July, 1973, and December, 1970.

Packaging obviously is closely related to labeling and branding because the label often appears on the package and the brand is typically on the label.

There are three reasons for packaging:

1. A utilitarian as well as a marketing reason for packaging a product is to protect it on its route from the manufacturer to the consumer or industrial user, and in some cases even during its life with the customer. Compared with bulk items, packaged goods generally are more convenient, cleaner, and less susceptible to losses from evaporation, spilling, and spoilage. Packaging helps to identify a product and thus may prevent substitution of competitive goods.

2. Packaging also may implement a company's marketing program. A package may be the only significant way in which a firm can differentiate its product. In the case of convenience goods or industrial operating supplies, for example, most buyers feel that one well-known brand is about as good as another. Also, changing a package is an inexpensive way to give the impression that the product itself has been changed. Packaging can be used effectively to help introduce a new product or to help increase or maintain the market for existing products.

   In a distribution system, wholesalers derive cost benefits from protective packaging of manufacturers' products. Also, retailers recognize that effective protection and promotion features in a package can cut their costs and increase sales.

   The utilitarian reasons for packaging—protection, identification, and convenience—may in themselves be exploited in selling. Some features of the package may serve as a sales appeal, for example, a no-drip spout, a self-applicator, an aerosol spray dispenser, or a reusable jar. Furthermore, the package advertising copy will last as long as the product is being used in its packaged form. Every time the housewife takes down a jar of peanut butter, she is exposed to the message on the label. At the point of purchase, the package serves as a silent salesman encouraging impulse buying.

3. Management may package its product in such a way as to increase profit possibilities. A package may be so attractive that customers will pay more just to get the special package—even though the increase in price exceeds the additional cost of the package. Also, an increase in ease of handling or a reduction in damage losses will cut marketing costs.

GROWING IMPORTANCE OF PACKAGING

Packaging is in the socioeconomic forefront today because of its relation to environmental pollution issues. Perhaps the biggest challenge facing packagers is how to dispose of their product after it has done its job of marketing, product protection and consumer convenience. Used packaging is a major contributor to the problem of solid-waste disposal. The consumer's desire for convenience in the form of throwaway containers conflicts with a generally held desire for a clean environment. There is here a real challenge to our technology, but perhaps even more difficult is the marketing challenge to influence consumer attitudes favorably toward recycling waste and toward the more efficient use of packaging.[7]

Most companies recognize that packaging is important for purposes of protection and convenience. The activity has been production-oriented in most firms, however, and marketing values have been ignored. But this attitude is changing, and the marketing significance of packaging is being recognized.

---

7 See Tom Alexander, "The Packaging Problem Is a Can of Worms," *Fortune,* June, 1972, p. 105; William N. Gunn, "Packagers and the Environmental Challenge," *Harvard Business Review,* July-August, 1972, pp. 103-111; and William G. Zikmund and William J. Stanton, "Recycling Solid Waste: A Channels-of-Distribution Problem," *Journal of Marketing,* July, 1971, pp. 34-39.

The increased use of branding and the public's rising standards of health and sanitation have contributed to the growth of packaging. The major factor, however, is the importance of packaging as a real competitive force in today's struggle for markets. The widespread use of self-service, automatic vending, and other self-selection methods of retail selling means that the package must do the selling job at the point of purchase. It is no simple task for a manufacturer even to get his product placed on display in a retail outlet. Shelf space is at a premium, and retailers are inclined to cater to producers who have used effective packaging.

The pace of packaging development has left industry the victim of unplanned obsolescence. These new developments, occurring rapidly and in a seemingly endless flow, require management's constant attention to packaging research and design in order that the marketing opportunities presented by these features can be optimized. We see new packaging materials replacing the traditional ones, exotic new shapes and sizes, new closures (flip-top, pull-tab, rip-cap), and other new features (measured portions, fractional packages, metered flow)—all making for increased convenience for consumers and additional selling points for marketers. In many cases the consumers perceive that the package is part of the product. To illustrate, when shoe polish is sold in a can with an applicator and polishing cloth or when cheese spread comes in an aerosol can, an executive asks, "Which is the product and which is the package? We are selling the combination and it's getting harder to tell the difference."

Because of the growing importance of packaging, the responsibility for this activity should rest with top management. Packaging decisions are being centralized at the vice-presidential and even the presidential level in some companies. Several major companies have even established separate corporate packaging staffs to oversee the packaging area.

While marketers have come to appreciate the importance of packaging in the product design decision, consumers have often been quite critical of packaging innovation. In addition to the problems associated with the ecological effects of packaging, consumers have often accused marketers of overpackaging their products.[8] This charge relates to two specific issues, the proliferation of package sizes and the unnecessarily heavy expenditure on packaging materials. It has long been a criticism of consumers that many products are packaged in too broad a range of package sizes. This not only suggests a reduction in packaging efficiency, in that production runs are likely shorter when a large number of package sizes are being used, but also makes it considerably more difficult for consumers to compare brands on a price per unit basis.

In 1974, it was estimated that Canadian marketers spent more than two and one-quarter billion dollars on packaging materials.[9] Many consumer groups have suggested that it is a waste of money to package products in elaborate packages which are discarded once the product is used. In some cases it has been shown that the package costs the manufacturer more than does the product which it contains.

POLICIES AND STRATEGIES OF PACKAGING

Changing the package. Whether to change a package and, if so, when to make the change are related problems. The trend today is in favor of change, and this trend is

8 "Of Consuming Interest," *Chatelaine,* Spetember, 1973, p. 20.

9 "Packaging Market to Advance 10% in '75," *Marketing,* March 24, 1975, p. 13.

gaining momentum. In general, management has two reasons for considering package innovation: a decrease in sales or a desire to expand a market by attracting new groups of customers.

More specifically, a firm may want to correct a bad feature in the existing container. The box may leak after being opened, or it may not be sufficiently airtight. A company may want to take advantage of new materials. Some companies change their containers to aid in the firm's promotional program. The new package may be used as a major appeal in the advertising copy, or the old containers may not show up well in advertisements.

In Canada, manufacturers of many packaged consumer products have had to initiate changes in package design in recent years in order to conform with the requirements of the Consumer Packaging and Labelling Act relating to metrication. Since Canada has adopted the metric system of measurement, it is now a requirement of this Act that since March 1, 1976, all food products must be labelled in metric units. Some companies have changed the labels on their existing packages and containers so that the labels bear both the metric and imperial units of measure. Other manufacturers have gone the route of "hard conversion" in which the container is actually redesigned to a rounded metric capacity. For example, most soft drink bottlers have replaced their 10-ounce bottles with new 300 millilitre bottles.[10]

Packaging the product line. A company must decide whether to develop a family resemblance in the packaging of its several products. *Family packaging* involves making the package identical for all products or using some common feature on all the packages. For example, Heinz and Campbell soups each uses virtually identical packaging on their condensed soup products. Management's evaluation of family packaging parallels its evaluation of family branding. When new products are added to a line, promotional values associated with old products extend to the new ones. On the other hand, this strategy should be used only when the products are related in use and are of similar quality.

Reuse packaging. Another strategy to be considered is reuse packaging. Should the company design and promote a package which can serve other purposes after the original contents are consumed? Glasses containing cheese can later be used for fruit juices. Peanut butter, jelly, and pickle jars make good containers for leftovers or can be used for home canning purposes. Reuse packaging should stimulate repeat purchases. If a person purchases a certain brand of peanut butter in order to collect a set of drinking glasses and, once he has them, switches to another brand, the dual-use packaging strategy has been of little help to the peanut butter manufacturer.

Multiple packaging. For many years there has been a trend toward *multiple packaging,* or the practice of placing several units in one container. Dehydrated soups, motor oil, beer, golf balls, soap, building hardware, candy bars, towels, and countless other products are packaged in multiple units. Test after test has proved that multiple packaging increases total sales of a product. Multiple packaging can also help introduce new products and win consumer acceptance of a new concept.

---

10 For an example of how one company handled the conversion from imperial to metric units see: "*Metric Conversion and Coca-Cola Limited,*" Coca-Cola Limited, Toronto, 1974.

Although a user may not particularly like the different taste of a new product the first time he tries it, by the time he has finished the third box that came in the multiple package he may be impressed favorably. In other instances, multiple packaging is convenient for special price offers and for the sale of small items. Retailers like this method of packaging because it cuts unit-handling and price-marking costs. On the other hand, if a product is used infrequently or if it lasts a long time, quantity packaging is not advantageous.

LABELING

Labeling is another product feature which requires managerial attention. The *label* is that part of a product which carries verbal information about the product or the seller. A label may be part of the package, or it may be a tag attached directly to the product. Obviously, there is a close relationship between labeling and packaging and between labeling and branding.

Labeling also has considerable social significance. Several of the public's criticisms of marketing have centered around charges of false, deceptive, or misleading packaging and labeling. In the textile field, this has led to federal legislation dealing with the labeling of textile products. The requirement that consumers be provided with informative and accurate labels has also led to the passage of a number of sections of the Food and Drugs Act dealing with labeling and to the proclamation in 1974 of the Consumer Packaging and Labelling Act.

Although there has been considerable improvement in labeling practices over the past twenty-five years, legislation alone cannot do the job. Further improvement is needed, and it will come as additional firms realize the marketing advantages of good labeling. Nevertheless, it will not be easy to develop a labeling system which will enable consumers to determine quality and compare products. Standards must be developed so that comparisons can be made. Then consumers will have to be educated regarding the meaning of the standards and the importance of reading the information on the labels.

TYPES OF LABELS

Typically, labels are classed as brand, grade, descriptive, and informative. A *brand label* is simply the manufacturer's brand name applied to the product or to the package. A *grade label* identifies the quality of the product by a letter, number or word. For example, in Canada, beef is grade-labeled A, B, or C, and each grade is subdivided by numbers from 1 to 4, indicating an increasing fat content. The letters indicate the age of the animal, with A and B indicating young beef. In this book, *descriptive labels* and *informative labels* are used synonymously. These are labels which provide objective written or illustrative information about the use, construction, care, performance, or other features of the product. On a descriptive-informative label for a canned food product there may be statements concerning the type of product, its style (for example, sliced, diced, or whole), the can size, the number of servings, and a list of ingredients. Descriptive-informative labels are very much influenced by government regulations which require that certain information be conveyed through the label on a product. These types of regulations will be discussed in the section which follows.

Relative merit. Brand labeling creates very little stir among critics. While it is an acceptable form of labeling, its severe limitation is that it does not supply sufficient information to a buyer. The real fight centers around grade versus descriptive labeling, and whether grade labeling should be made mandatory. Historically, consumer organizations have been in favor of grade labeling, and businessmen have advocated descriptive-informative labeling. Some of the arguments on both sides are noted here, but on balance it seems that no one type of labeling is best for all products.

The proponents of grade labeling argue that it is simple, definite, and easy to use. They also point out that if grade labels were used, prices would be more related to quality, although grade labeling would not stifle competition. In fact, they believe that grade labeling might increase competition because consumers would be able to judge products on the basis of both price and known quality. The cost of grade labeling is very low, so it would not place a great burden on the manufacturer. Grade labeling would in no way do away with brand names. Many firms already using grade labeling have tied in the grade with their promotional programs.

Those who object to grade labeling point out that it is not possible to grade differences in flavor and taste, or in style and fashion. A very low score on one grading characteristic can be offset by very high scores on other factors. Companies selling products which score high *within* a given quality bracket would be hurt by grade labeling. It would not be possible for these companies to justify a higher price than that charged for another Grade A product which scored very low in the Grade A quality range. Some people feel that grades are an inaccurate guide for consumer buying because the characteristics selected for grading, the weights assigned to them, and the means of measuring them are all established on an arbitrary basis.

STATUTORY LABELING REQUIREMENTS

The importance of packaging and labeling in terms of its potential for influencing the consumer's purchasing decision is reflected in the large number of federal and provincial laws which exist to regulate this marketing activity. At the federal level, the Combines Investigation Act has for a number of years regulated the area of misleading advertising and a number of companies have been convicted of misleading advertising for false or deceptive statements which have appeared on their packages. In this case, the information which appears on a package or label has been considered to constitute an advertisement.

The Hazardous Products Act was passed in 1969, giving the federal government the power to regulate the sale, distribution, advertising, and labeling of certain consumer products which are considered dangerous. A number of products have been banned from sale under this Act and since 1971 all hazardous products, such as cleaning substances, chemicals, and aerosol products, must carry on their labels a series of symbols which indicate the danger associated with the product and the precautions which should be taken with its use. The symbols illustrate that the product is poisonous, inflammable, explosive, or corrosive in nature.

Similarly the federal Food and Drugs Act regulates the sale of foods, drugs, cosmetics, and medical devices. Under this Act, regulations exist which deal with the manufacture, sale, advertising, packaging, and labeling of such products. Certain misleading and deceptive packaging and labeling practices are specifically prohibited.

The Textile Labelling Act requires that manufacturers label their products, including wearing apparel, yard goods, and household textiles, according to the fiber content of the product. In the past, more than seven hundred fabric names have appeared on products, but most of these were the brand names of individual companies. For example, the fiber known generically as polyester has been labeled as Terylene, Trevira, Dacron, Kodel, Fortrel, Tergal, Tetoron, and Crimplene, all of which are manufacturers' brand names for polyester. In order to reduce confusion among the buying public, products now have to be labeled according to the generic fiber content, with the percentage of each fiber in excess of five percent listed.[11]

There also exist in Canada, two government sponsored consumer product labeling schemes which are informative in nature. These programs are the Canada Standard Size program and the Textile Care Labelling program. The Textile Care Labelling program involves the labeling of all textile products with symbols which indicate instructions for washing and dry cleaning the product. Figure 11-3 shows the various symbols and what they mean.

The Consumer Packaging and Labelling Act came into effect in 1974 and regulates all aspects of the packaging and labeling of consumer products in this country. The regulations which have been passed under this Act require that most products which are sold in Canada must bear bilingual labels. The net quantity of the product must appear on the label in both metric and imperial units. If the quantity of a food product is expressed in terms of a certain number of servings, the size of the servings must also be stated. Where artificial flavorings are used in the manufacture of a food product, the label must contain the information that the flavor is imitation or simulated. The Act also makes provision for the standardization of container sizes. The first set of regulations to be passed under the Act set down the standard package sizes for toothpaste, shampoo, and skin cream products and it is in contravention of the regulations to manufacture these products in other than the package sizes approved. It is likely that this program of standardization of package sizes will be extended to other product categories in the future.

The requirements of the Consumer Packaging and Labelling Act have caused many manufacturers of consumer products, especially in the food industry, to undertake the redesign of their product's packages and labels. Since the passage of the packaging and labeling regulations in 1974, manufacturers have had to incorporate the bilingual and metric requirements into the design of their labels. At the same time, most manufacturers added the Canadian Grocery Product Code to the design of their labels. The adoption of this code is part of the process of automating the checkout process in supermarkets and will be discussed in Chapter 17.

The provinces have also moved into the field of regulating packaging and labeling. A number of provinces have passed legislation regarding misleading advertising and any information which appears on a package or label is considered an advertisement. In Quebec, that province's Official Language Act requries that all labels be written in French or in French and another language. If both English and French appear on the label, at least equal prominence must be given to the French.

The federal government also has plans to become considerably more involved in the field of informative labeling. The Department of Consumer and Corporate Affairs has been planning the introduction of the CANTAG program which would be designed to provide consumers with considerably more information about major purchases at the point of sale. This program will involve the provision of somewhat

---

11 "Of Consuming Interest," *Chatelaine*, January, 1973, p. 25.

This is what the symbols mean:

Figure 11-3: Textile Care Labeling Symbols and their Meaning. The colour of each column from left to right is: grey, yellow, green.

more technical information than the consumer normally receives from advertising. The program would apply primarily to major appliances and home entertainment products. For refrigerators, for example, there would be provided such information as the cubic capacity, the space needed for the location of the appliance, the energy consumption and temperature ranges of the cooling and freezing compartments. This program is patterned after similar informative labeling programs which have been in existence in European countries for a number of years.[12]

OTHER IMAGE-BUILDING FEATURES

A company cannot assert that it has a well-rounded program for product planning and development until it has instituted a company policy on several additional product attributes: product design, color, sizes, product quality, and guarantee and servicing.

PRODUCT DESIGN

One way to build an image of a product is through its design. In fact, a distinctive design may be the only significantly differentiating feature of a product. Many firms feel that there is considerable glamour and general promotional appeal in product design and the designer's name. In the field of industrial products, engineering design has long been recognized as extremely important, but today there is a realization of the marketing value of appearance design as well. Office machines and office furniture are examples of industrial products where conscious attention has been given to product design, and often with good sales results. The marketing significance of design has been recognized for years in the field of consumer products, whether they are big items like automobiles and refrigerators or small products like fountain pens and apparel.

Product materials and performance are related to design. New developments in plastics, synthetic fibers, lightweight metals, and other materials have broadened the designer's horizon considerably. Of course, the marketing opportunities presented by new materials must not obscure production and financial considerations. Regarding product performance, the designer must know the answers to the following questions: What will the product be used for? What does the buyer expect? What is the cost of building in the various levels of performance?

Good design can improve the marketability of a product in many ways. It can make the product easier to operate; it can upgrade the product's quality or durability; it can improve product appearance and lower manufacturing costs. Good design can also generate new uses for a product or make it adaptable for initial use by new customers.

COLOR

People seem to be more conscious of color today than in the past. It is often the determining factor in a customer's acceptance or rejection of a product, whether it is a

---

12 Tom Messer, "Ottawa Pushes for More Informative Labeling Practices," *Marketing*, March 31, 1975, p. 10. and Department of Consumer and Corporate Affairs, *European Informative Labelling*, Consumer Research Report No. 5, Ottawa, 1973.

dress, a table, or an automobile. Even in industrial products, color is an important aspect of design.

Color by itself, however, is no selling advantage because many competing firms offer color products. The marketing advantage comes in knowing the right color, how many colors to use, and when to change colors. If a garment manufacturer or a retail store's fashion coordinator guesses wrong on what will be the fashionable color in women's clothing, it can be disastrous. There is an increasing need for thorough research and expert help on the subject. Many firms employ the services of color stylists today.

Marketers must reckon with color as both a psychological and sociological force. Its careful use can increase sales, increase worker productivity, reduce eyestrain, and generally affect emotional reactions. Some colors have different meanings to various ethnic groups, and there are geographic preferences in colors.

SIZES

The assortment of sizes in which goods are produced by a manufacturer or stocked by middlemen can have a substantial bearing on the marketing success of a firm. It is simply lost business when an industrial distributor does not have a desired size of valve or rubber belting in stock, or when a clothing store does not have the right shirt or blouse size.

Manufacturers and middlemen alike are pressured to increase the number of sizes they market and to carry something for everybody. On the other hand, middlemen know that their shelf space is at a premium and that the little-called-for sizes often end up being sold at a considerable markdown. Manufacturers may fight the pressure because they too fear economic losses inherent in slow-moving sizes.

It is difficult to detect whether there is a trend toward larger or smaller package sizes. Possibly there is a significant movement in both directions. Coca-Cola and Pepsi-Cola added larger bottles to their product lines, including a 60-ounce size. Jell-O jelly powders are also now available in a larger package size. At the same time, however, both Coke and Pepsi have reintroduced their 10-ounce bottles and Sun-Maid raisins are now available in small 2-ounce packages as a children's snack product. Campbell's Soup introduced their products in smaller cans containing one individual serving. Large packages offer economy and small ones offer convenience.

PRODUCT QUALITY

The quality of a product is extremely important, but probably the most difficult of all the image-building features to define. Users frequently disagree on what constitutes quality in an item, whether it is a cut of meat, a piece of music, or an article of clothing. Personal tastes are deeply involved. Nevertheless, a marketing executive must make several decisions about product quality. First, the product should reach only a level of quality compatible with the intended use of the item; it need not be any better. In fact, "good" and "poor" are misleading terms. "Correct" and "incorrect" would be much more appropriate. If a housewife is making a peach cobbler, Grade B or C peaches are the correct quality. They are not necessarily the best quality, but they are right for the intended use. It is not necessary to pay Grade A prices for large, well-formed peaches when these features will not be seen in the cobbler.

Next, units of output must maintain as consistent a degree of quality as is reasonably possible. Furthermore, all the components of a given product should be similar in quality. Like the parts of the "one-hoss shay," ideally all parts will perform equally well and cease performing simultaneously.

PRODUCT WARRANTY

The general purpose of a warranty is to give the buyer some assurance that he will be compensated in case the product is not up to reasonable expectations. In years past, courts seemed generally to recognize only *express* warranties—those stated in written or spoken words. Usually these were quite limited in what they covered and seemed intended only to protect the seller from buyers' claims.

But times have changed! Consumer complaints have led to a governmental campaign to protect the consumer in many areas, one of which is product liability. Today, courts and government agencies are broadening the scope of warranty coverage by recognizing the concept of *implied* warranty—that is, the idea that warranty was intended by the seller, although not actually stated. Manufacturers are being held responsible, even when the sales contract is between the retailer and the consumer. Warranties are considered to "run with the product." Manufacturers are held liable for product-caused injury, whether or not they are to blame for negligence in manufacturing. It all adds up to "let the seller beware."[13]

Manufacturers are responding by broadening and simplifying their warranties, and they are using them as a promotional device to stimulate purchases by reducing the consumer's risks. As a dimension of competitive strategy, a promotional warranty policy will probably be most effective when:

1. The unit price of the product is high.
2. The product is purchased infrequently.
3. The product is perceived by consumers as being complex.
4. The buyer does not have much knowledge of the product; he cannot judge the product's quality by inspecting it; or, as in mail-order selling, the purchasing decision (and maybe the payment) must be made in advance of seeing the product.
5. The seller's share of market is small or the product is not well known.[14]

The Hazardous Products Act indicates how the law has changed regarding product liability and injurious products. This law prohibits the sale of certain dangerous products and requires that other products which may be potentially dangerous carry an indication on their labels of the dangers inherent in their use. As further indication of the growing interest on the part of consumer groups and governments in the protection which existing forms of warranties offer the con-

---

13 See Lynn J. Loudenback and John W. Goebel, "Marketing in the Age of Strict Liability," *Journal of Marketing*, January, 1974, pp. 62-66; Conrad Berenson, "The Product Liability Revolution," *Business Horizons*, October, 1972, pp. 71-80; John S. Berens, "Consumer Costs in Product Failure," *MSU Business Topics*, Spring, 1971, pp. 27-30; David L. Rados, "Product Liability: Tougher Ground Rules," *Harvard Business Review*, July—August, 1969, pp. 144-152; and Alfred A. Cox, "Product Liability," *Southern Journal of Business*, April, 1969, pp. 80-86.

14 Jon G. Udell and Evan E. Anderson, "The Product Warranty as an Element of Competitive Strategy," *Journal of Marketing*, October, 1968, pp. 1-8.

sumer, the Ontario Law Reform Commission in 1972 issued their Report on Consumer Warranties and Guarantees in the Sale of Goods. This report recommended broad and sweeping changes in the law respecting warranties and guarantees which would provide the consumer with greater protection. This report has formed the basis for the drafting of new legislation regarding product warranties in a number of provinces.[15]

PRODUCT SERVICING

A related problem is that of adequately providing the services guaranteed by the warranty. One writer has proposed the following four guidelines to help management meet its social responsibilities in these areas, as well as to ensure customer satisfaction.[16]

1. Ensure the integrity and credibility of the warranty.
2. Institute a meaningful education program regarding use of the product.
3. Strengthen the company program for quality control in manufacturing.
4. Provide high-quality maintenance and repair service.

Product servicing requires management's attention as products become more complex, service facilities seem unable to keep pace, and consumers grow increasingly dissatisfied and vocal. To cope with the problems, management can consider several courses of action. For instance, a producer can establish several geographically dispersed factory service centers, staff them with well-trained company employees, and strive to make servicing a separate profit-generating activity. Or a manufacturer can shift the main burden to his middlemen, compensate them for their efforts, and possibly even train their service employees. As a promotional strategy, management may stress its high-quality service. Conversely, a company can view servicing as a costly penance for the sin of engineering or production mistakes, try to minimize this cost, and then spend money to eradicate the mistakes which brought about the need for repairs.

QUESTIONS AND PROBLEMS

1. What is the difference between a brand and a trademark?
2. List five brand names which you think are good ones and five which are poor.
   Explain the reasoning behind your choices.
3. Evaluate each of the following brand names in light of the characteristics of a good brand, indicating the strong and weak points of each name:
   a. Xerox (office copier)
   b. IBM (business machines)
   c. Mustang (automobiles)
   d. Hush Puppies (shoes)
   e. A-1 (steak sauce)
   f. Hotpoint (appliances)
4. What arguments can you put forth for labeling certain products only under their generic names? What products do you feel should be sold only under their generic names? Why?

---

15 See for example: Saskatchewan Department of Consumer Affairs, "White Paper on Consumer Product Warranties, 1975," Regina, 1975; and Ontario Ministry of Consumer and Commercial Relations, "Green Paper on Consumer Product Warranties in Ontario," Toronto, 1973.

16 George Fisk, "Guidelines for Warranty Service after Sale," *Journal of Marketing*, January, 1970, pp. 63-67.

5. Suggest some brands which are on the verge of becoming generic. What course of action should a company take to protect the separate identity of its brand?

6. Under what conditions would you recommend that a manufacturer brand a product which will be used as a part or material in the production of another article?

7. In which of the following cases should the company adopt the strategy of family branding?

   a. A manufacturer of men's electric razors introduces a model for women.

   b. A manufacturer of women's cologne and deodorants adds men's after-shave lotion to the product lines.

   c. An automobile manufacturer adds a line of outboard motors to his product mix.

   d. A producer of mattresses introduces a line of electric blankets.

8. Some camera manufacturers follow a strategy of using the same brand name on all their cameras regardless of price and quality and regardless of the type of camera. Evaluate this branding strategy.

9. Why do some firms sell an identical product under more than one of their own brands?

10. Assume that a large department store chain proposed to the manufacturers of Maytag washing machines that Maytag supply the department store with machines carrying the store's brand. What factors should Maytag's management consider in making a decision? If the product were General Foods' Jell-O, to what extent would the situation be different?

11. Why are some consumers critical of packaging?

12. What changes would you recommend in the typical packaging of:

   a. Cornflakes   *c.* Pepsi-Cola

   b. Toothpaste   *d.* Typing paper

13. What are the implications of metric packaging for consumers?

14. Identify at least four factors which have forced changes in label design in Canada in recent years.

15. Distinguish among: brand labels

                              grade labels

                              informative labels.

16. Summarize the legislation and government programs which have affected packaging and labeling in Canada in recent years.

17. Give examples of products in which the careful use of color has increased sales. Can you cite examples to show that poor use of color may hurt a company's marketing program?

18. Explain the relationship between a product warranty on small electric appliances and the manufacturer's distribution system for these products.

19. How would the warranty policies set by a manufacturer of skis differ from those adopted by an automobile manufacturer?

CASES FOR PART THREE

CASE 6. DEL MAR JEWELRY MANUFACTURING COMPANY, INC.*
Addition of new product to manufacturer's line

Del Mar Jewelry Manufacturing Company, Inc., located in Miami, Florida, produced costume jewelry and distributed it through manufacturer's agents to retailers throughout the country. As there was very little manufacturing of jewelry items in the South, the company held a rather unusual position with its retail accounts, especially in Florida. Del Mar's competitive strength decreased, however, as the distance to its retail accounts increased. Its greatest volume of sales was generated by its agents in Florida and the Gulf States.

Some advantages in the sale of Del Mar products was attributed to a natural preference by retailers for high-quality gift merchandise produced in Florida for sale during the tourist seasons. To exploit this advantage further, all of the manufacturer's agents who represented Del Mar noted the local requirements of their retail accounts, and made considerable effort to point out that Del Mar could offer services which were unobtainable from northern suppliers. In accord with this policy, Mr. Phillip Johnson, the Del Mar representative in the lucrative Florida Gold

*Case prepared by Prof. Barry J. Hersker, Florida Atlantic University. Reproduced with permission.

Coast area (Palm Beach to Key West), reported a possible opportunity to add several new items to the line of necklaces, bracelets, and earrings—a product group called "Del Mar Jewels."

Mr. Johnson had called upon Mr. Jim Kay, owner of Kay's Accessories Stores of Ft. Lauderdale, Florida. During their conversation Mr. Kay remarked that he was pleased to see that the new items of Del Mar Jewels included Aurora Borealis crystals. (These were imported, cut crystal beads with an iridescent coating that refracted light in many colors.) Mr. Kay stated further that products made with this type of crystal beads were selling very well in all three of his stores. In fact, Aurora-crystal goods were in short supply, and back-orders from New York suppliers were not uncommon.

Mr. Kay placed sample orders for several of the Aurora crystal items from the Del Mar Jewels line, as well as for several other items which did not contain these crystal beads. Mr. Johnson knew that if these sample items moved well, Mr. Kay would reorder in larger quantities.

When producing necklaces, bracelets, or earrings, one styling technique used by Del Mar was to create products that were different from those available from northern suppliers. Thus, direct price comparisons were difficult to make. While the finished products were distinctive, they did compare favorably with merchandise produced by "middle" or "high-end" manufacturing firms in New York City.

Occasionally a large jewelry manufacturer would obtain an "exclusive" on a certain style of bead by purchasing the entire output of that bead from a European factory. Then the bead itself, being only one of a kind, could provide a distinctive look in a piece of jewelry. Del Mar's output was too limited to obtain such exclusive control of particular beads. Almost all of Del Mar's component parts were purchased through import agents or from American manufacturers.

As he was preparing to leave the Kay's Accessories store, Mr. Johnson noticed a recently-arrived shipment of Aurora crystal merchandise which consisted of single-strand necklaces of six-, eight-, and ten-millimeter, tin-cut Aurora crystal beads of the same high quality used by Del Mar. Mr. Kay commented that these items sold so well that he was frequently out of stock. His northern supplier had been slow filling Kay's reorders, primarily because of shortages in the supply of Aurora crystal beads. Mr. Johnson immediately commented that Del Mar could make these items, since they stocked these millimeter sizes of Aurora crystals to use as components of their other items.

Mr. Kay thought this was a fine idea, and promised to reorder all this merchandise from Del Mar if they would supply it locally at the same price as he was buying out of New York. He gave a sample of each style of the necklace to Mr. Johnson to take back to the Del Mar factory to see if they could copy the items.

On his return trip to Miami, several other retail accounts advised Mr. Johnson that they also would be interested in obtaining these items from Del Mar, since they were selling quite well and delivery was slow from New York. Mr. Johnson informed the Del Mar owners about what he had learned and turned the samples over to them for possible duplication. They promised to "price out" the merchandise to see what they could sell it for. Their analysis of the direct cost (labor and materials) of the single-strand, 12-1/2" necklaces using six-, eight-, and ten-millimeter Aurora crystal beads, was as follows:

6 mm Necklace

63 6 mm Aurora @ .012 ea $.756

Assorted metal parts	.030
Labor	.200
Total direct costs	$.986

8 mm Necklace

31 8 mm Aurora @ .020	$ .620
6 6 mm Aurora @ .012	.072
1 7 mm Aurora @ .015	.015
30 5 mm Spurs @ .007	.210
Assorted metal parts	.030
Labor	.200
Total direct costs	$1.147

10 mm Necklace

26 10 mm Aurora @ .028	$ .736
1 8 mm Aurora @ .020	.020
6 6 mm Aurora @ .012	.072
25 5 mm Spurs @ .007	.175
Assorted metal parts	.030
Labor	.200
Total direct costs	$1.233

The management of Del Mar advised Mr. Johnson that they would be willing to sell the six-millimeter necklace for $36 per dozen, the eight-millimeter necklace for $42 per dozen, and the ten-millimeter necklace for $48 per dozen. Their usual pricing formula called for a markup of three times direct cost, with the resulting price altered to correspond to the nearest price line. Thus, on the eight-millimeter necklace, three times $1.147 = $3.441 each, times 12 = $41.292 per dozen. The nearest customary price line to this would be $42 per dozen. (In the costume jewelry trade, wholesale price lines per dozen were $6.75, $13.50, $18, $24, $30, $36, $42, $48, etc. Corresponding *unit* retail prices were $1, $2, $3, $4, $5, $6, $7, $8.)

Mr. Johnson pointed out that these prices were totally unacceptable. The necklaces supplied by Mr. Kay had wholesaled for $13.50 per dozen for the six-millimeter, and $18 per dozen for both the eight- and ten-millimeter necklaces. "If a northern supplier is selling at these prices, then these are the competitive prices that we must meet."

A Del Mar executive replied, "Even if we apply our minimum markup formula (two times cost) we would have to get $24 a dozen on the six-millimeter and $30 for both the eight- and ten-millimeter necklaces. And this would require our selling for less than the normal markup that we take on the Del Mar Jewels line." "Look," Mr. Johnson argued, "you can still afford to sell for the competitive price, even if it is way below your average markup. There is no telling how much volume we might do on these items. Mr. Kay and my other accounts report that the six-millimeter, Aurora necklace is a terrific seller at $2 retail; and at $3, the eight- and ten-millimeter sell even faster!"

"You salesmen always want to cut price!" exclaimed one of the members of the Del Mar management team. "Where do you think those prices would leave us after we pay you your 12-1/2 percent commission and give the 3 percent cash discount?" (Common terms of sale extended by manufacturers and jobbers in the costume jewelry trade are 3%, 10 days, End of Month.)

"And what about bad-debt expense? Last year that ran 2 percent. Even though we exceeded our average minimum markup percentage last year on the Del Mar Jewels line, the way I figure it, we didn't even cover our overhead on these items."

"But those expenses you must contend with in any event," replied Mr. Johnson.

"On the other hand," another member of the firm commented, "maybe our prices are restricting our volume. Are we or aren't we competitive?—that's what we should be asking."

"You are competitive," Mr. Johnson replied, "but you are speaking of your current line of high-end goods. I'm not arguing about those prices. I'm talking about this one new series of items, on which you might do real volume."

"But the more we sell, the more we'll lower our average markup for our whole line, Johnson. And I don't think we're making any money on Del Mar Jewels the way things are. The reason we've tried not to design this type of item was to avoid the kind of price competition that is bound to exist on something like this. These less elaborate styles are the ones most likely to get kicked around price-wise. And any time we're undersold, our whole reputation suffers and suddenly our accounts will assume we're overpriced on everything."

Another member of the firm added, "I agree we should give our accounts what they want, but they should pay our prices for these items, or we shouldn't be producing them."

QUESTION

1. Should Del Mar add the Aurora crystal necklaces to its line?

CASE 7: McGREGOR LIMITED

Organization for new-product planning and development

In his long-range planning activities, Mr. Rodney Bruning, the president of McGregor, forecasts the continuation of changing consumer buying patterns in the luggage industry over the next several years. He also recognizes that the prospects for growth in the industry are very favorable. At the same time, these changes in consumer behavior and the potential growth market will probably be accompanied by an increasing severity of competition. As a consequence of these and other factors, Mr. Bruning doubts whether the company's present program for planning and developing new products can meet the market challenges of the future. He is convinced of the importance of product planning and thinks possibly that his company needs to formalize, or at least to strengthen, the organization and management of this function. He is concerned particularly with two aspects of product planning and development. One is the procedure for generating new-product ideas, and the other is the organizational structure needed to implement the planning and development of new products.

Established around the turn of the century, McGregor today markets three seemingly unrelated lines of merchandise. Its general offices and production facilities are in Montreal. Soon after World War II, McGregor acquired a furniture company in Toronto, producing mainly folding tables and chairs. Recently McGregor added a line of desk accessories—calendar pads, penholders, leather and plastic desk blotters, etc. McGregor manufactures some of these accessories and purchases others, but all are marketed under the McGregor brand. The luggage line accounts for roughly 60 percent of the company's annual sales volume, the furniture represents 35 percent, and the accessories 5 percent.

Some competition has developed through the opening of Canadian subsidiaries of U.S. parents. In addition, a trend toward concentration has characterized this industry, thus lending further support to Mr. Bruning's forecast of increasing competition. Ten years ago, there were about twice as many luggage firms in Canada as there are today. The largest company has possibly 25 percent of the market, and the second largest around 10 percent.

In luggage, McGregor manufactures and markets a complete line of men's and women's nonleather cases. Most of the products are vinyl-covered, over aluminum or magnesium frames, and are lined with a good quality of rayon cloth. The products are sold nationwide directly to retailers. In addition, the company is becoming increasingly involved in foreign marketing. Management has franchised companies in the United States, Western Europe, South America, and Japan to produce McGregor luggage. This involvement in international marketing is another factor which has stimulated Mr. Bruning's concern about product planning and development.

In the Canadian and American markets, Mr. Bruning sees changes in consumer behavior insofar as these people view luggage. It is no longer considered a once-in-a-lifetime type of purchase to be used until it is physically worn out. It is no longer just a utilitarian, heavy suitcase—a necessary burden for carrying clothes and other personal belongings. Mr. Bruning recognizes that today the element of fashion has been introduced in luggage. Manufacturers and consumers are increasingly concerned with the factors of style and design. The increase in leisure time plus the higher disposable income have resulted in more time spent in pleasure traveling. This means more of a market for luggage. While luggage is still a popular item for special gift-giving occasions such as graduation, retirement, weddings, and birthdays, sales are no longer so concentrated on these occasions. New items are being added to the traditional suitcase-type product. Attaché cases, for example, have enjoyed increasingly widespread market acceptance, whereas the traditional briefcase has declined in popularity.

At the present time, there is no formal system for generating ideas for new products at McGregor, nor does the company have any systematized arrangement for processing new-product ideas from their inception through to the commercial marketing stage. McGregor utilizes a small, wholly owned subsidiary company for purposes of new-product research and for the styling and design of McGregor products. The subsidiary company's management is autonomous and independent—a state which Mr. Bruning insists must be maintained if the company is to fulfill usefully its unique function. Ideas are also filtered out of customer complaints as relayed to the company through its retail dealers. Any executive, of course, can make suggestions. The company has not adopted the commonly used "employee suggestion box" system—that is, a system of financial awards for worthwhile suggestions and ideas from employees. Sometimes new-product ideas come as a by-product of marketing research among consumers, as done by an independent marketing research firm.

As far as organizational or procedural arrangements are concerned, the style and design subsidiary company informally feeds information (new-product ideas or even models of new products) to one of the McGregor executives. Sometimes the executive vice-president or even the president gets involved in the initial stages of decision making as to the disposition—acceptance, test market, rejection, etc.—of the new-product idea or model.

To bring about more effective management of product planning and development, Mr. Bruning is considering establishing a new-product committee, consisting of himself, the president of the subsidiary company, the vice-president of manufacturing, the vice-president of sales and marketing, and the product manager (a staff executive) of the luggage division. This committee would have responsibility for evaluating all ideas and new-product models as presented by the subsidiary style and design company. If the pilot model received the tentative approval of the committee, a short production run would be authorized so that the product could be test-marketed by the research firm retained by McGregor. If the test-market result were satisfactory, the new product committee would authorize full-scale production and marketing. By including all key executives on the committee, Mr. Bruning feels that a new product would be well received by manufacturing and marketing departments because the vice-president at the head of each of these departments would have already approved the product.

The vice-president of sales and marketing feels that the usual managerial drawbacks of committee action would render a new-product committee ineffective as an organizational and administrative unit for product planning and development. Instead, he recommends that the company establish a new product-development department. In this way, the product-planning function would be recognized for the full-time activity that it really is. Such a department would devote an appropriate amount of time and effort to product planning over the long run.

The product manager, who reports to the vice-president of sales and marketing, has suggested that his domain of activity be enlarged to include the planning and development of new products. He argues that such an assignment is a logical extension of his present responsibilities. He could take a new-product idea or model and carry it through all the development and testing stages. If the product were to be marketed on a commercial basis, it could be turned over to the appropriate department.

QUESTIONS

1. What organizational structure should McGregor establish for the planning and development of new products?
2. What sources should the company use in order to generate ideas for new products?

CASE 8: CANADIAN-WESTERN PAINT COMPANY LTD.

Brand policy in company merger

Now that Canadian-Western Paint has acquired 100 percent control of Hawkins Paint, the executives of Canadian-Western must decide what brand and labeling policies will be established for the existing product lines of the two firms. Currently, there are varying degrees of duplication in the two companies' product lines, geographic markets, and advertising media. By using one brand and one company name, Canadian-Western could possibly effect economies in television and newspaper advertising, stationery, packaging, labeling, and other operational areas of the marketing program.

Canadian-Western Paint, established in 1910, has its main offices and manufacturing plant in Vancouver, British Columbia. The firm produces a complete line of paints, lacquers, and varnishes under its Lion Gate brand. A line of brushes and other painting equipment and supplies is purchased from other manufacturers, but is marketed by Canadian-Western under the Lion Gate brand. Annual sales volume is now approximately $15 million. The company's geographic market covers the three westernmost provinces, from British Columbia eastward through Alberta into Saskatchewan. Sales branches are maintained in Victoria, Calgary, Edmonton, and Saskatoon. Company salesmen sell to about 450 retail and wholesale accounts including paint, lacquer, and varnish wholesalers and retail paint stores, hardware stores, lumber and building materials dealers, and department stores. The Lion Gate brand has a high degree of consumer recognition and acceptance. The company advertises extensively, using television primarily, but also relying heavily on newspapers and outdoor poster panels as promotional media.

When it was purchased by Canadian-Western Paint, Hawkins Paint had been operating for over seventy years. The manufacturing plant and general offices are located in Winnipeg, with a sales branch in Calgary. The company's paint, lacquer, and varnish products are sold under the Hawkins brand, and these products pretty well duplicate the Canadian-Western line. Hawkins' annual sales volume is approximately $4 million. Company salesmen have around two hundred retail and wholesale accounts in Manitoba, Saskatchewan, and Alberta. Among these accounts, particularly among the older ones and especially in Manitoba, surveys have shown that there is a strong dealer loyalty to the Hawkins brand. Furthermore, this brand is well accepted among painting contractors and household consumers. This brand loyalty and acceptance decline, however, the further west we get from Manitoba.

Until about ten years prior to the merger, Hawkins had been extremely successful. During the past decade, however, its profit performance has declined, even though the sales volume has held steady. At the time of the merger, Hawkins was operating at a loss, and the morale of its employees was low. Clarence Bullen, the vice-president of marketing at Canadian-Western, feels that Hawkins' profit decline was caused by its poor management. As an example, too often "deals" or "concessions" were made to existing accounts in order to keep their business. Some customers who would normally be considered retailers were reclassified as distributors (wholesalers) and thus were granted larger discounts. Also, the company has become quite inactive lately in its advertising program, and there is concern that its image may be changing unfavorably.

The paint, lacquer, and varnish industry in western Canada is highly competitive. Already, competitors of Canadian-Western have contacted most of the Hawkins accounts, stating that Canadian-Western was absorbing Hawkins and that all dealer and distributor relations would be changed. Because of the internal turmoil that has existed in the Hawkins operation in recent years, Canadian-Western cannot counter this type of competition, as it normally could.

At this point, the Canadian-Western executives are debating what the brand policy of their company should be, in light of the recent acquisition of Hawkins.

The advertising manager, Harry Foster, believes that the best course would be to carry on as before. That is, both the Lion Gate and the Hawkins brands would continue to be used, and the two separate company product lines would be marketed. Mr. Foster points out that it is important to keep in mind the geographical market coverage of the two firms. Between them, they cover the four western provinces in Canada. Canadian-Western markets in British Columbia, Alberta, and Saskatchewan; Hawkins sells in Alberta, Saskatchewan, and Manitoba. Thus, Hawkins does not market in British Columbia, and Canadian-Western is unknown in Manitoba, but there is a territorial overlap and conflict among existing accounts in Alberta and Saskatchewan.

Clarence Bullen has advocated a different alternative. He would drop the Hawkins brand now and concentrate all efforts on the Lion Gate label. In this way the company would be promoting only one name, and this would result in cost-saving efficiencies such as one set of television commercials, billboards, newspaper advertisements, labels, and packages.

He does realize that his recommendation poses some problems in that it might be difficult to convince the existing Hawkins dealers regarding the advantages of a one-brand program. Also, by dropping the Hawkins brand, the company would risk losing the dealer brand loyalty attached to the Hawkins name and the consumer recognition of, and preference for, that label. Furthermore, the Lion Gate label is unknown in Manitoba.

The president thinks that both the Foster and the Bullen recommendations leave much to be desired. Neither of them, for example, solves the problem of what to do about the conflicting accounts and duplication of effort in Alberta and Saskatchewan. The president is considering the possibility of either a totally new name or a name that will combine the two existing ones—a name such as Lion Gate-Hawkins, for instance. He also raises this question: Must our course of action involve an immediate major change, or could we possibly initiate a series of small moves which would constitute a major change over a period of two to four years?

QUESTION

1. What brand policy should Canadian-Western adopt now that it has acquired Hawkins?

THE PRICE SYSTEM

12

PRICING OBJECTIVES AND PRICE DETERMINATION

"How much do you think we ought to sell it for?" This is a question frequently asked by executives who have the responsibility for pricing the products or services they are marketing. The question would be more accurately worded if they asked, "How much do you think we can get for this item?" or "How much should we ask for it?" The question would then be in accord with the generalization that *prices are always on trial*. A price is simply an offer or an experiment to test the pulse of the market. If the customers accept the offer, this is fine. If they reject it, the price usually will be changed quickly, or the product may even be withdrawn from the market. Before being concerned with actual price determination, however, an executive should understand the meaning and importance of price, and he should decide on his pricing goals.

IMPORTANCE OF PRICE

IN THE ECONOMY

Pricing is considered by many to be the key activity within the capitalistic system of free enterprise. Price becomes a hub around which the system revolves. It is the balance wheel which keeps the system operating on an even keel. Imperfections in pricing are an indication of imperfections in the system.

The market price of a product influences wages, rents, interest, and profits. That is, the price of a product influences the price paid for the factors of production—labor, land, capital, and entrepreneurship. In this way, price becomes a basic regulator of the entire economic system because it influences the allocation of these resources. High wages attract labor, high interest rates attract capital, and so on. Conversely, low wages, low rent, or low profits reduce the availability of labor, land and risk takers.

Criticism of the North American system of reasonably free enterprise and the public's demand for further restraints on them are often triggered by reactions to prices, price level changes or pricing policies.

IN THE INDIVIDUAL FIRM

A company's pricing structure, more than any other segment of its marketing program, is influenced by legislation. We have restraining laws affecting packaging, labeling, distribution policies, and promotional activities, but the key legislative regulations in marketing apply to pricing, as our experience with the Anti-Inflation Board indicates. Because of the normal legal considerations, executives are hesitant to disclose information about their companies' pricing practices although under A.I.B. legislation substantial disclosure has taken place.

The price of a product or service is a major determinant of the market demand for the item. Price will affect the firm's competitive position and its share of the market. As a result, price has a considerable bearing on the company's revenue and net profit. The revenue is equal to unit price times the volume of units sold. The profit is equal to revenue minus costs. To some extent, costs are a function of volume, and costs themselves are measured by their price. Price also affects the market segment that will be reached by a firm.

The price of a product also affects the firm's marketing program. In product planning, for example, if management wants to improve the quality of its product or add differentiating features, this decision can be implemented only if the market will accept a price high enough to cover the costs of these changes. The pricing structure will determine whether the manufacturer or his retailers will be expected to finance the bulk of the promotional program.

At the same time, there usually are countervailing forces limiting the importance of pricing in a company's marketing program. Differentiated product features or a persuasive advertising campaign may be more important to a consumer than price. Thus, these forces may engender rigidities or a "stickiness" in the pricing mechanism, so that it does not respond so quickly to changes in demand or supply. Thus, the traditional, theoretical role of price as an allocator of scarce resources is modified somewhat in today's economic system.

To put the role of pricing in a company's marketing program in its proper perspective, then, let us say this—price is important, but not all-important, in explaining marketing success. One study among manufacturing companies, for example, identified product-related activities and sales effort as the most important factors contributing to marketing success in a firm. One-half of the respondents did not even list price as one of the top five factors.[1] Three situations may account for this relatively low ranking of pricing: (1) Because supply generally exceeds demand, most sellers must be highly competitive (or collusive) in their pricing; (2) today's

---

1 Jon G. Udell, "How Important Is Pricing in Competitive Strategy?" *Journal of Marketing,* January, 1964, pp. 44-48.

relatively affluent consumer is interested in more than just price; and (3) a seller may achieve some pricing freedom through successful product differentiation.

PRICE AND PRODUCT-QUALITY RELATIONSHIP

Some of the psychological aspects of pricing should also be understood by a marketing executive. For instance, consumers rely heavily on price as an indicator of a product's quality, especially when they must make purchase decisions with incomplete information. Studies have consistently shown that consumers' perceptions of product quality vary directly with price.[2] Thus, the higher the price, the better the quality is perceived to be. Consumers make this judgment particularly when no other clues as to product quality are available, or when they are judging the quality of products sold by the same retailer or made by the same manufacturer. Consumers' quality perceptions can, of course, also be influenced by store reputation, advertising, and other variables.

MEANING OF PRICE

Undoubtedly many of the difficulties associated with pricing start with the rather simple fact that often we do not really know what we are talking about. That is, we do not know the meaning of the word "price," even though it is true that the concept is quite easy to define in familiar terms.

In economic theory, we learn that price, value, and utility are related concepts. *Utility* is the attribute of an item that makes it capable of want satisfaction. *Value* is the quantitative expression of the power a product has to attract other products in exchange. We may say the value of a certain hat is three baseball bats, a box of Red Delicious apples, or 30 litres of gasoline. Because our economy is not geared to a slow, ponderous barter system, we use money as a common denominator of value and use the term "price" to describe the money value of an item. *Price* is value expressed in terms of dollars and cents, or whatever the monetary medium may be in the country where the exchange occurs.

Practical problems connected with a definition of price arise, however, when we try to state simply what is the price of a pint of fresh strawberries or an office desk. Harry paid 85 cents for a pint of strawberries, while Bill paid only 40 cents and was allowed to eat all the strawberries he wanted at the seller's location. The 40-cent price was what he paid for the strawberries he took home with him. The price quoted to Harry for an office desk was $325, while Bill paid only $175.

---

2 For a summary of several of these studies, see Kent B. Monroe, "Buyers' Subjective Perceptions of Price," *Journal of Marketing Research,* February, 1973, pp. 70-80; Arthur G. Bedeian, "Consumer Perception of Price as an Indicator of Product Quality," *MSU Business Topics,* Summer, 1971, pp. 59-65; and Benson P. Shapiro, "The Psychology of Pricing," *Harvard Business Review,* July-August, 1968, pp. 14-16ff. Also see David M. Gardner, "Is There a Generalized Price-Quality Relationship?" *Journal of Marketing Research,* May, 1971, pp. 241-243; Robert A. Peterson, "The Price-Perceived Quality Relationship: Experimental Evidence," *Journal of Marketing Research,* November, 1970, pp. 525-528; and Norman D. French, John J. Williams, and William A. Chance, "A Shopping Experiment on Price-Quality Relationships," *Journal of Retailing,* Fall, 1972, pp. 3-16ff.

For the contention that price often is *not* a good indicator of product quality, see Ruby T. Morris and Claire S. Bronson, "The Chaos of Competition Indicated by Consumer Reports," *Journal of Marketing,* July, 1969, pp. 26-34.

At first glance it looks as if Bill got the better deal in each example. Yet when we get all the facts, we may change our opinion. Harry bought his strawberries at the local supermarket. Bill responded to a strawberry grower's advertisement which stated that if one came out to the farm and picked the berries himself, they would cost 40 cents a box. The grower furnished the pint-sized boxes and allowed Bill to eat all he wanted while he was berry picking. Harry's desk was delivered to his office, he had a year to pay for it, and it was all beautifully finished. Bill bought a partially assembled job with no finish on it. (He was a do-it-yourself fan.) He had to assemble the drawers and legs and then painstakingly stain, varnish, and handrub the entire desk. He arranged for the delivery himself, and he paid cash in full at the time of purchase. Now let us ask the question of who paid the higher price in each case. The answer is not as easy as it seemed at first glance.

These examples illustrate how difficult it is to define price in an everyday business situation. Many variables are involved. The definition hinges around the problem of determining exactly what it is that a person is buying. This relates to the problem posed in Chapter 9, that of trying to define a product. In pricing we must consider more than the physical product alone. A seller usually is pricing a combination of the physical product plus several other services and want-satisfying benefits. Sometimes it is difficult even to define the price of the physical product alone. On one model of automobile a stated price may include radio, power steering, and power brakes. For another model of the same make of car these three items may be priced separately. In another situation the price may be defined as that which the buyer pays or the seller nets, with the difference being the freight charges. Some sellers quote a price that includes various services (alterations, installation, credit, delivery), while others price these individual services separately.

In summary, *price* is the amount of money (plus possibly some goods) which is needed to acquire in exchange some combined assortment of a product and its accompanying services. Obviously there are many possible combinations of a product and the various services which may accompany it.

PRICING OBJECTIVES

We have observed that before a company can do a marketing job properly, management needs a goal. Pricing is no exception. Management should decide upon the objectives of pricing before determining the price itself. Very few firms, however, consciously establish pricing objectives or clearly state their specific price policies. Even fewer have written statements of their pricing goals.

In a landmark study, the Brookings Institution in the U.S. reported on the price policies and the methods of price determination used by a group of twenty large firms. Many of the findings are also applicable to Canadian firms, particularly subsidiaries with U.S. parents and those who compete against them. We can gain considerable insight into pricing goals from this study and a related article by one of the principal investigators. Much of the material in this section is drawn from the original study and the subsequent article.[3] See Figure 12-1.

The main goals in pricing may be classified as follows:

---

3 A. D. H. Kaplan, Joel B. Dirlam, and Robert F. Lanzillotti, *Pricing in Big Business,* The Brookings Institution, Washington, D.C., 1958; Robert F. Lanzillotti, "Pricing Objectives in Large Companies," *American Economic Review,* December, 1958, pp. 921-940.

1. Achieve target return on investment or on net sales.
2. Stabilize prices.
3. Maintain or improve a share of the market.
4. Meet or prevent competition.
5. Maximize profits.

ACHIEVE TARGET RETURN ON INVESTMENT OR NET SALES

Many firms seek to achieve a certain percentage return on investment or on net sales. This goal was the one most frequently mentioned by the subjects of the Brookings Institution study. Target-return pricing may be defined as building a price structure to provide enough return on capital used for specific products or groups of products so that the sales revenue will yield a predetermined average return for the entire company. Target return may be a short-run (one year) or a long-run goal, but it is mostly the latter. If an estimate is made of return expected over the long run, fluctuations will occur in short-run volume, but they will average out.

Many retailers and wholesalers use target return on net sales as a pricing objective for short-run periods. They set a percentage markup on sales which is large enough to cover anticipated operating costs plus a desired profit for the year. In such cases the *percentage* of profit may remain constant, but the *dollar* profit will vary according to the number of units sold.

Target return on investment was typically selected as a goal only when one or both of two conditions were present. First, ordinarily the firms were leaders in their industry, or they sold in protected markets. For example, target return on investment was a stated goal of General Motors, International Harvester, Aluminum Corporation of America, the Du Pont Company, Johns-Manville Corporation, and Union Carbide Corporation. Second, this goal was typical in connection with new products and low-unit-price, high-volume, standardized items.

Some of the reasons most frequently stated by companies for selecting a particular level of return were as follows:

1. It is a fair or reasonable rate. The concept of "fair and reasonable" is important to these companies because most of them are very much in the public eye. Their pricing structure is of great interest to the government, the labor unions, and the public in general. To avoid charges of monopoly or restraint of trade, they must set "fair and reasonable" prices.
2. It is traditional in the industry.
3. Management wants to reach or improve a corporation's average return over a recent period.
4. It was what the company felt it could get in the long run.

The Brookings Institution study discovered a trend toward the adoption of some form of target return as pricing objective either for particular products or for the entire company. Some of the major reasons for this trend are:

1. An increasing awareness of the interrelationship of profit, capital, and investment and a realization of the importance of budgeting for this triumvirate.

Figure 12-1. Pricing goals of twenty large industrial corporations.

Company	Principal pricing goal	Collateral pricing goals
Alcoa	20% on investment (before taxes); higher on new products (about 10% effective rate after taxes)	"Promotive" policy on new products Price stabilization
American Can	Maintaining market share	"Meeting competition" Price stabilization
A & P	Increasing market share	Promotive
Du Pont	Target return on investment—no specific figure given	Charging what traffic will bear over long run Maximum return for new products—"life cycle" pricing
Exxon (Standard Oil of N.J.)	"Fair-return" target—no specific figure given	Maintaining market share Price stabilization
General Electric	20% on investment (after taxes); 7% on sales (after taxes)	Promotive policy on new products Price stabilization on nationally advertised products
General Foods	33-1/3% gross margin ("1/3 to make, 1/3 to sell, and 1/3 for profit"); expectation of realizing target only on new products	Maintaining market share
General Motors	20% on investment (after taxes)	Maintaining market share
Goodyear	"Meeting competitors"	Maintaining "position" Price stabilization
Gulf	Following price of most important marketer in each area	Maintaining market share Price stabilization
International Harvester	10% on investment (after taxes)	Market share: ceiling of "less than a dominant share of any market"
Johns-Manville	Return on investment	Market share not greater than 20% Stabilization of prices
Kennecott	Stabilization of prices	
Kroger	Maintaining market share	Target return to 20% on investment before taxes
National Steel	Matching the market—price follower	Increasing market share
Sears	Increasing market share (8-10% regarded as satisfactory share)	Traditional return on investment of 10-15% (after taxes) Promotive (low-margin) policy
Standard Oil (Indiana)	Maintaining market share	Stabilizing prices Target return on investment (nonspecified)
Swift	Maintaining market share in meat-packing	
Union Carbide	Target return on investment	Promotive policy on new products; "life cycle" pricing on chemicals generally
U.S. Steel	8% on investment (after taxes)	Target market share of 30% Stable price and margin

Source: Adapted from Robert F. Lanzillotti, "Pricing Objectives in Large Companies," *American Economic Review*, December, 1958, pp. 924-927.

2. The desire for a common basis for evaluating performance of products and divisions in the company.
3. The fact that government contracts focus attention on rate of return.
4. The tendency to copy large, successful firms which have been using target return as a pricing goal for some time.

STABILIZE PRICES

The goal of stabilizing prices is often found in industries that have a price leader. In industries where demand can fluctuate frequently and sometimes violently, large companies, especially, will try to maintain stability in their pricing. In the Brookings Institution study, United States Steel and Kennecott Copper were pointed out as two firms which apparently sought this goal, but often with considerably less than total success. American Can, The Aluminum Corporation of America, and some of the chemical companies seemed to have achieved a greater degree of price stability.[4]

Price leadership does not necessarily mean that the goal of stability is reached by having all firms in the industry charge the same price as that set by the leader. Price leadership means only that some regular relationship exists between the leader's prices and those charged by other firms. Some companies may regularly sell at a level above or below that set by the leader. In a given geographic market, "minor" oil companies frequently price their gasoline at 1 or 2 cents a gallon under the level charged by the "majors."

Companies seeking stability in their pricing are very anxious to avert price wars, even when demand is declining. Price leaders tend to take a long-run point of view in achieving stability. Their goal, in a sense, is to "live and let live." The companies are willing to forgo maximizing profits in times of prosperity or short supply if they have the opportunity to earn a reasonable profit during less prosperous periods.

Many retailers and manufacturers of consumer products have attempted to stabilize prices throughout a market by resorting to suggested list prices.

MAINTAIN OR IMPROVE SHARE OF MARKET

In some companies, both large and small, the major pricing objective is to maintain or increase the share of the market held by the firm. One factor that makes market share a workable goal is that a company can usually determine what share of the market it enjoys. In some respects, market share is a better indicator of corporate health than target return on investment, especially in times of increasing markets. A firm might be earning what management considers a reasonable return. However, unless management keeps fully abreast of conditions in an expanding market, this "reasonable" profit may be too small. The company may be getting a decreasing share of the market. In the Brookings Institution study, market share seemed to be almost as important as a target return on investment. A & P, for example, constantly reported that it sought to increase its share of the market through continuous low pricing.

---

4 For a challenge to the traditional economic theory that prices in some industries are controlled or "administered" by a few large firms, see Gilbert Burck, "The Myths and Realities of Corporate Pricing," *Fortune*, April, 1972, p. 85.

Large firms may try to limit their share of the market for some reason. In some cases they fear government intervention or restraint if they get too large. General Motors, with approximately 50 percent of the automobile market, has been in this situation for years. Certainly some adjustments are needed either in a company or in an economic system when companies must consciously hesitate to do the most complete, aggressive, and consumer-satisfying marketing job of which they are capable. Some companies—Johns-Manville, for example—said that they preferred to have a *relatively* small market share, say, 20 percent rather than 50 percent, because they would rather work to *expand* a smaller share than to *defend* a larger share.

MEET OR PREVENT COMPETITION

Countless firms, regardless of size, consciously price their products to meet or sometimes even prevent competition. When a company seeks simply through trial and error to find a price at which its output can be sold, we can almost say that it has no pricing objective. At least it has no control over the goal and the means used to reach it.

Larger rubber companies, such as Goodyear Tire, reported that generally they felt that they could exercise very little influence over the market-determined price. In an industry where there is a price leader and where the product is highly standardized, most firms have a "follow-the-leader" policy. National Steel and Kroger said they pursued this policy as a rule. Gasoline companies professed that they simply set their prices to meet competition, particularly during a price war. The major firms usually wait until they have proof that the price in a market has broken. Then they cut their prices in order to meet the competition.

Some firms consciously price to prevent competition. Normally this goal or practice is not publicly admitted, but it has been brought to light in court cases involving manufacturers and retailers in the food field. When introducing a new product, a company will frequently set a low price in order to discourage competition. Usually this policy is unsuccessful. If the new item is popular enough, other producers will be attracted into the field regardless of the pricing policy of the innovator.

MAXIMIZE PROFITS

The pricing objective of making as much money as possible is probably followed by a larger total number of companies than any other policy yet mentioned. The trouble with this goal is that the term "profit maximization" has an ugly connotation. It is connected in the public mind with profiteering, high prices, and monopoly. In economic theory or business practice, however, there is nothing wrong with profit maximization. Theoretically, if profits become unduly high because supply is short in relation to demand, new capital will be attracted into a field to better balance demand and supply. In the marketplace, it is difficult to find many situations where a monopolistic situation has existed over an extended period of time. Substitute products are available, purchases are postponable, or competition increases, and prices are thus kept at a reasonable level. Where prices may be unduly high and entry into the field is severely limited, public outrage soon balances the scales. If market conditions and public opinion do not do the job directly, government restraints which represent the feeling of the public will soon bring about moderation.

A profit maximization policy is apt to be far more beneficial to a company and to the public if practiced over the long run. Pricing by companies who cannot see beyond the end of their next month's profit and loss statement often results in repercussions which may be detrimental to the firms. Practiced over the long run, profit maximization should result in a socially desirable allocation of resources. Efficient firms are rewarded and inefficient firms disappear. Profits attract new capital into a field. Prices are kept at a reasonable level, and supply is sufficient to satisfy market demands.

To maximize profits over the long run, firms may have to accept short-run losses. A firm entering a new geographic market or introducing a new product frequently finds it advantageous to use relatively low prices in order to build a large clientele. Such companies often do not expect to show a profit for the first few years, but they are laying a solid foundation for adequate profits over the long run.

The goal should be to maximize profits on total output rather than on each single item. A manufacturer may maximize total profits by practically giving away some articles which will attract the buyer's attention or will stimulate sales of other goods. Through its sponsored broadcasts and telecasts of athletic events in the U.S., the Gillette Company frequently promotes razors at very low, profitless prices. Management hopes that once a customer acquires a Gillette razor, he will become a long-term profitable customer for Gillette blades. In this way the company maximizes profits in total but not on each product in its line. A retailer often finds that the best way to maximize profits over his entire store is to offer well-known items as "leaders." They are sold at a very small profit or even at a loss, but they attract so many customers to the store—customers who stay to buy other items—that the overall profit picture of the store is enhanced considerably.

PROCEDURE FOR PRICE DETERMINATION

The first step in establishing a price system is consciously to formulate an objective and state it clearly in writing. Once the pricing objective is agreed upon, the executives can move to the heart of price management—the actual determination of the base price of the products or services. No one procedure, generally acceptable by all companies, has yet been developed for determining base prices. One critical reason for the lack of exact pricing models or formulas is the fact that sufficiently detailed information on costs at various volumes and on demand at various prices is not available.

The price-determination procedure used here can be divided into six steps:

1. Estimate the demand for the product.
2. Anticipate the competitive reaction.
3. Establish the expected share of the market.
4. Select the price strategy to be used to reach the market target.
5. Consider company policies regarding products, channels, and promotion.
6. Select the specific price.[5]

5 For other procedures, see Alfred R. Oxenfeldt, "A Decision-Making Structure for Price Decisions," *Journal of Marketing*, January, 1973, pp. 48-53; Gerald Albaum, "Price Formulation," in J. Howard Westing and Gerald Albaum (eds.), *Modern Market-Thought*, 2d ed., The Macmillan Company, New York, 1969, pp. 346-359; Bill R. Darden, "An Operational Approach to Product Pricing," *Journal of Marketing*, April, 1968, pp. 29-33.

At this point we are concerned with determining only the basic or list price of the product or service. Later we shall deal with specific policies regarding discounts, freight allowances, price lines, and other factors which may alter this basic price somewhat. Ordinarily the original price setter is a producer, although sometimes a large middleman sets or strongly influences the original price.

The same general steps are followed in pricing a product, whether it is a new article or an established one. Pricing an established product often offers very little challenge because the exact price or a very narrow range of prices may be dictated by the market. At the same time, some stages in the pricing procedure are particularly important and difficult for a new article. Consequently, any special conditions involved in pricing new products will be woven into the discussion.

ESTIMATE DEMAND FOR PRODUCT

The first stage in pricing a product is to estimate the total demand for it. This is easier to do for an established product than for a new one. The seller is not certain that a new product will have any demand at all. Two practical steps in demand estimation are, first, to determine whether there is a price which the market expects and, second, to estimate the sales volume at different prices.

The "expected" price. The expected price for a product is the price at which customers consciously or unconsciously value it. It is what they think the product is worth. Often, rather than being one specific dollar amount, the expected price can be determined within a range. It might be "between $250 and $300" or "not over $10."

It is sometimes surprising how shrewd customers can be in evaluating a product. In the case of a new product, however, direct competition and price comparison are often slight during its early life, so the manufacturer has considerably more latitude in setting his price than is the case with older products. The seller may set a higher initial price on the product than would be possible if it were an established item subject to comparison. Then, after the market has developed an image of a high-priced article, the seller can lower the price and the market may think it is getting a bargain.

A producer must also think of middlemen's reaction to the price. Middlemen are more likely to give an article favorable treatment in their stores if they approve of its price. Because of their extensive experience, retail or wholesale buyers can frequently examine an item and make an accurate estimate of the selling price that the market will accept.

Research may uncover the fact that the expected price is below the level at which the firm can make or buy the product. Unless adjustments can be made in production costs, the relatively low expected price may preclude the production or purchase of the item. However, a manufacturer should not feel that it is impossible to change the expected price, particularly on a new product. This may be done:

1. By adding product features which increase the apparent value of the article by more than the actual cost of the added features, or
2. By selecting distribution channels which reach customers who will see the article in comparison with more expensive items, or
3. By using an advertising program to increase the value of the product in the customer's eye.

It is possible to set a price too low. If the price is much lower than that which the market expects, often sales will be lost. For example, it would probably be a mistake for a well-known cosmetics manufacturer to put a 19-cent price tag on lipstick or to price its imported perfume at $1.29 an ounce. Either customers will be suspicious of the quality of the product, or their self-concepts will not let them use such low-priced merchandise. More than one seller has raised the price of his product and experienced a considerable increase in sales. In terms of market-demand curves, the situation is referred to as "inverse demand"—the higher the price, the greater the unit sales.[6]

How does a seller determine the expected price? He may submit the article to an experienced retailer or wholesaler for appraisal. Manufacturers of industrial products sometimes approach engineers working for prospective customers. By showing models or blueprints, the manufacturer can solicit informed judgments on what the price "ought to be." Another possibility is to observe prices of comparable competitive products. A third alternative is to survey the potential consumers. They may be shown the article and asked what they would pay for it. This approach can bring misleading answers because there is often a considerable difference between what a person *says* the product is worth and what he will actually pay. A much more effective approach is to market the product in a few limited test areas. By trying different prices under controlled research conditions, the seller can determine at least a reasonable range of prices. When it is not practical to produce a sufficient quantity to test the market, the seller may have to rely on some form of depth interviewing of potential customers.

Estimates of sales at various prices. It is extremely helpful in price determination to estimate what the sales volume will be at several different prices. These estimates involve a consideration of the demand elasticity of the product. A product with an elastic market demand should usually be priced lower than an item with an inelastic demand. By estimating the demand for its product at different prices, management, in effect, is determining the demand curve for the item. These volume estimates at different prices are important also in relation to determining break-even points, which are discussed in the next chapter.

ANTICIPATE COMPETITIVE REACTION

Present and potential competition is an important influence on price determination. Even with a new product, any possible distinctiveness is limited in that it is ordinarily only a matter of time until some form of competition will be felt strongly. The threat of *potential* competition is greatest when the field is easy to enter and the profit prospects are encouraging.

Competition can come from three *existing* sources. First, from directly similar products: the manufacturer of Wheaties must consider the price set on Kellogg's Corn Flakes or General Foods' Post Toasties. Second, from available substitutes: for many years steel companies considered only directly similar competitors such as other steel companies in Canada and abroad. Now steel producers must be alert to prices on aluminum and plastics because for many end products steel is no longer

6 See Zarrel V. Lambert, "Product Perception: An Important Variable in Price Strategy," *Journal of Marketing,* October, 1970, pp. 68-71; and by same author, "Price and Choice Behavior," *Journal of Marketing Research,* February, 1972, pp. 35-40.

the only reasonable alternative material. Third, competition may come from unrelated items seeking the same consumer dollar.

ESTABLISH EXPECTED SHARE OF MARKET

The next step in price determination, and one which tends to narrow still further the range of the probable pricing decisions, is to determine what share of the market the company expects. An aggressive firm seeking a larger share of the market ordinarily will price differently from a company which is content with its present share. Sometimes the drive for a certain market share is characterized by advertising and other forms of nonprice competition rather than by price appeals.

The expected share of the market will be influenced by present production capacity, costs of plant expansion, and ease of competitive entry. It would be a mistake for a firm to aim for a larger share of the market than its plant capacity can sustain. If a new product is priced low in an attempt to gain a broad market, and if the market response is extremely favorable, the company may not be able to fill its orders. If management is not interested in expanding its plant because ease of competitive entry undoubtedly will drive down future profits, the initial price should be set relatively high.

SELECT PRICING STRATEGY TO REACH MARKET TARGET

Any one of several pricing strategies might be employed by management to achieve the predetermined share of the market. By focusing attention on two alternatives which are polar extremes, we can highlight many of the pertinent issues. These alternatives are popularly referred to as "skim-the-cream" pricing and "penetration" pricing. They are most appropriate to the pricing of new products.[7]

Skim-the-cream pricing. The cream-skimming strategy involves setting a price which is high in the range of expected prices. The seller may continue with this strategy for an indefinite period, or he may later lower the price in order to tap other segments of the market. Cream skimming is probably most effective with a highly distinctive article which is aggressively promoted in the early stages of its life cycle.

There are at least five reasons why skim-the-cream pricing may be particularly suitable for new products. First, demand is likely to be less elastic in the early stages of a product's life cycle. In the early stages, price is less important, competition is at a minimum, and the product's distinctiveness lends itself to real salesmanship. Second, this strategy can effectively segment the market on an income basis. The appeal at first is to that segment of the demand curve which responds to distinctiveness and exclusiveness in a product and is relatively insensitive to price. Later on, the seller can lower his price and appeal to segments of the market which are highly sensitive to price.

A third advantage of cream skimming is that it acts as a strong hedge against a possible mistake in setting the price. If the original price is too high and the market

---

7 These opposite strategies are discussed in Joel Dean, *How to Price a New Product,* Small Business Administration, Management Aids for Small Manufacturers, no. 62, Washington, D.C., April, 1955; see also Joel Dean, "Pricing Policies for New Products," *Harvard Business Review,* November, 1950, pp. 45-53. Much of the discussion in this section is adapted from these two sources.

does not respond, management can easily lower it, but it is very difficult to raise a price which proves to be too low to cover costs. Fourth, high initial prices can often generate more revenues and profits than can low prices in the early stages of market development. Finally, high initial prices can be used to keep demand within the limits of a company's productive capacity.

Penetration pricing. In this strategy, a low initial price is set in order to reach the mass market immediately. This strategy can also be employed at a later stage in the product's life cycle. Many a firm has saved its product from a premature old age or death simply by switching to penetration pricing from skimming.

Compared with skimming, penetration pricing is a more aggressive competitive strategy and is likely to be more satisfactory when the following conditions exist: (1) the quantity sold is highly sensitive to price; that is, the product has a highly elastic demand; (2) substantial reductions in unit production and marketing costs can be achieved through large-scale operations; (3) the product faces very strong competition soon after it is introduced to the market; and (4) there is an inadequate high-income market to sustain a skim-the-cream price.

The nature of potential competition will critically influence management's choice between the two pricing strategies. If competitors can enter a market easily and quickly and if the market potential for the product is very promising, management probably should adopt a policy of penetration pricing. Low initial pricing may do two things. First, it may discourage other firms from entering the field because the investment needed in production and marketing facilities will be too great in light of the anticipated low profit margin. Second, low prices may give the innovator such a strong hold on his share of the market that future competitors cannot cut into it. On the other hand, skimming may be more feasible where market potential is not large enough to attract the big competitors. While percentage margins per unit of sale may be attractive, the total dollar profits will be too small to attract large firms.

CONSIDER COMPANY MARKETING POLICIES

Another major stage in the pricing procedure is to consider the company's marketing policies with respect to the product itself, the distribution system, and the promotional program.

Product policies. We have already observed that the price of a product is influenced substantially by whether it is a new item or an older, established one. Other aspects of the product must be considered. For example, product perishability influences a firm's pricing policy. The importance of a product in its end use must also be considered. To illustrate, price competition is largely absent and a stable price structure exists among manufacturers of packaging materials, industrial gases, and aluminum fabrications. These products are only an incidental part of the final product.

Whether the article will be sold under a middleman's brand or under the manufacturer's own brand will affect the price established by the manufacturer. The interdependence of the product mix is another consideration. Where products are related, the price set on any one item affects all others in the line. Thus General Motors cannot establish the price for a Chevrolet without considering the prices of other General Motors cars. On the other hand, a firm such as Union Carbide, which sells both Prestone and industrial oxygen, has greater flexibility in pricing.

Channels of distribution. The channels selected, the types of middlemen used, and the gross-margin requirements of these middlemen will influence a manufacturer's price. A firm selling through wholesalers and also directly to retailers often sets a different factory price for each of these two classes of customers.

Promotional methods. The promotional methods used and the extent to which the job is done by the manufacturer or the middlemen are still other factors to consider in pricing. If the bulk of the promotional responsibility is placed upon retailers, they ordinarily will require a larger margin than if the product is heavily advertised by the manufacturer. Even when a manufacturer promotes heavily, he may want his middlemen to use local advertising, store display, and other types of promotion to tie in with his national advertising. Such a decision must be reflected in the dealer's margin and, consequently, in the manufacturer's price.

QUESTIONS AND PROBLEMS

1. Two students paid 69 cents for identical tubes of toothpaste at a leading department store. Yet one student complained that he paid a much higher price than the other. What might be the basis for this complaint?
2. "Watching television commercials is too high a *price* to pay to see a hockey game." "Having to put up with Mr. ___ [a sports analyst with a syndicated column in many newspapers] is part of the high *price* we pay for freedom of the press." Are these correct interpretations of the concept of price?
3. Explain how the chosen pricing objective may influence a firm's promotional program. Which goal will involve the largest, most aggressive promotional campaign?
4. "The goal of price stabilization is marked by nonaggressive marketing strategies and is usually found only in mature companies." Discuss.
5. Are the principal and collateral pricing goals compatible in each of the following companies? (Refer to Table 12-1.)
   a. The American Can Company
   b. The Gulf Oil Company
   c. The National Steel Company
6. Evaluate target return on investment or net sales as a pricing goal for a manufacturer. Consider the merits and limitations from both a business-competitive and a social point of view.
7. What marketing conditions might logically lead a company to set "meeting competition" as a pricing objective?
8. Is profit maximization compatible with each of the other major pricing goals?
9. What marketing conditions have served to reduce the importance of the price-setting function in many companies today?
10. What is the expected price for each of the following articles? How did you arrive at your estimate in each instance?
    a. A new type of carbonated cola beverage which holds its original carbonation long after it has been opened; packaged in 8-ounce and 32-ounce bottles
    b. A nuclear-powered, 21-inch, table-model television set guaranteed to run for ten years without replacement of the original power-generating component; requires no battery or electric wires

    c. An automatic garage-door opener for residential housing

11. Name some products for which you think an inverse demand exists. Within which price range does this demand exist for each product on your list?

12. Give some examples of products which have an elastic demand. An inelastic demand.

13. For each of the following products, do you recommend that the seller adopt a skimming or a penetration pricing strategy? Support your decision in each instance.
    a. Original models of women's dresses styled and manufactured by Dior
    b. A new wonder drug
    c. An exterior house paint which wears twice as long as any competitive brand
    d. A cigarette really totally free of tars and nicotine
    e. Instant beer
    f. An atomic-powered motor boat, family-sized

14. Discuss the following propositions:
    a. Skim-the-cream pricing is feasible only when the seller employs an exclusive or a highly selective distribution policy.
    b. Penetration pricing is practical only when a firm engages in intensive distribution.

BASIC METHODS OF SETTING PRICE

In the pricing procedure outlined in the preceding chapter, the final step was to narrow the range of expected prices to the point where a specific selling price is established. Over the years many different methods have been used by individual companies to accomplish this task. Most of these approaches to price setting, however, are based on one of the following major methods:

1. Prices may be based on total cost plus a desired profit.
2. Prices may be based on a balance between estimates of market demand and costs of production and marketing.
3. Prices may be set by competitive market conditions.

PRICES BASED ON COSTS

In its simplest form, the cost-plus approach means that the selling price for a unit of a product is equal to the unit's total cost plus an amount to cover the anticipated profit on the unit. As an example, a contractor figures that the labor and materials required to build and sell ten houses will cost $300,000 and that his other expenses (office rent, depreciation on equipment, wages of management, etc.) will equal $100,000. On this total cost of $400,000, he anticipates a profit of 10 percent of cost.

Cost plus profit amounts to $440,000. Therefore, each of the ten houses will sell for $44,000.

While this is a very simple, easily understood, and easily applied pricing method, it has one serious limitation. It disregards the fact that there are different types of costs and that not all of them act alike as output increases or decreases. Referring to our housing example, if the contractor sold only eight houses, his total sales would be $352,000. His labour and materials chargeable to eight houses would total $240,000 ($30,000 per house). He would still incur the full $100,000 in overhead expenses, however, so his total cost would be $340,000, leaving a profit of only $12,000, or about $1500 per house instead of the anticipated $4,000.

DIFFERENT COST CONCEPTS

A more sophisticated approach to cost-plus pricing takes into consideration the several types of costs and their different reactions to changes in level of output. That is, the total unit cost of a product will change as output expands or contracts. The following classification of cost concepts is important for our purposes:

1. Total fixed costs
2. Total variable costs
3. Total cost
4. Average fixed costs

5. Average variable costs
6. Average total costs
7. Marginal costs

Three of these concepts may require some elaboration. *Total fixed costs* are elements, such as rent, executives' salaries, and property taxes, which remain constant regardless of level of output. Even if production ceases entirely, these costs continue. We shall, however, implicitly assume here that we are dealing with a fixed plant capacity and a short-run period of time. Over the long run, *all* costs tend to be variable.

With respect to *average variable costs,* we shall, under a simplified assumption, keep these constant. In such a case the *total* variable costs will increase with each additional unit of output. The direct labor and material costs *per unit,* however, will remain the same. In a more typical production operation, unit variable costs are relatively high for the first few units of output. Then, as total output increases, the average variable costs come down because of quantity discounts on material, more efficient use of manpower, etc. Beyond some optimum point, average variable costs will increase as expanded output results in overtime pay, overuse and crowding of plant facilities, and generally less efficient use of labor and materials resources.

Marginal cost is the cost of producing and selling one more unit, that is, the cost of the most recent or last unit. If it costs $500 to produce sixty units and $527 to produce sixty-one units, the marginal cost is $27.

These seven cost concepts and their interrelationships may be studied in Table 13-1 and in Figs. 13-1 and 13-2, which are based on the table. Figure 13-1 shows the relationship among the curves representing the *totals* of (1) all costs, (2) fixed costs, and (3) variable costs, respectively. Here we can see that total fixed costs are represented by a straight line because they are constant within a short-run period. As output increases, total costs increase by the amount of variable cost incurred by each unit. Thus the total cost curve is a line which rises to the right. In Fig. 13-1, however, variable costs are not constant per unit. Therefore, the total cost line is curved. If variable costs were constant, the total cost line would be straight.

Table 13-1. Costs for individual firm.

Total fixed costs never change, despite increases in quantity. These costs are incurred for land rent, executives' salaries, and other items which remain constant no matter what quantity is being produced. Variable costs represent increasing costs for input of materials, labor, power, etc., as production quantity rises. Total cost is the sum of all fixed and variable costs. The other measures in the table are simply methods of looking at costs per unit and always involve dividing costs by number of units produced according to the formulas at the tops of the columns.

Quantity output, Q	Total fixed costs, TFC	Total variable costs, TVC	Total costs, TC = TFC + TVC	Marginal costs per unit, MC	Average fixed costs, AFC = TFC ÷ Q	Average variable costs, AVC = TVC ÷ Q	Average costs per unit, ATC = TC ÷ Q
0	$256	$ 0	$256		Infinity	$ 0	Infinity
1	256	64	320	$ 64	$256.00	64	$320.00
2	256	84	340	20	128.00	42	170.00
3	256	99	355	15	85.33	33	118.33
4	256	112	368	13	64.00	28	92.00
5	256	125	381	13	51.20	25	76.20
6	256	144	400	19	42.67	24	66.67
7	256	175	431	31	36.57	25	61.57
8	256	224	480	49	32.00	28	60.00
9	256	297	553	73	28.44	33	61.44
10	256	400	656	103	25.60	40	65.60

Source: Adapted from Paul Samuelson, *Economics*, McGraw-Hill Book Company, New York, 1961.

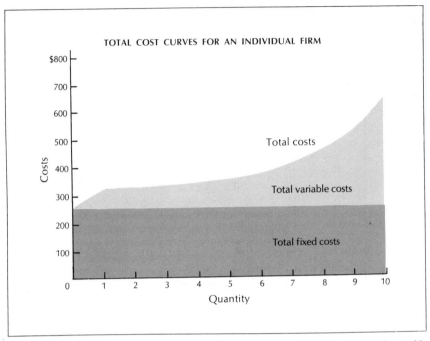

Figure 13-1. This graph shows the relationships among total fixed costs, total variable costs, and total cost so that their significance in pricing can be seen. The effect of total variable costs in this simplified example is to make total cost a slowly ascending curved line.

Figure 13-2 graphically displays the interrelationships among the various *average unit* costs. The average variable cost curve (AVC) would be horizontal if the average variable costs were constant. In our example, it curves downward until the sixth unit is passed, then diminishing returns set in. The average total cost curve (ATC) will slope downward as long as marginal costs are less than average unit costs. Even though the marginal costs are up after the fifth unit, the average cost curve continues to slope downward until after the eighth unit. This is because marginal costs, even though going up, are still less than average costs. The marginal cost (MC) and the average total cost curves intersect at the lowest point of the average total cost curve. Beyond that point (the eighth unit in the example) the cost of producing and selling the last unit is higher than the average of all units. Therefore, from then on the average total cost will rise. The reason for this is that the average variable costs are increasing faster than the average fixed costs are decreasing. Producing the ninth unit reduced average fixed costs from $32 to $28.44, but average variable costs rose $5. The average total cost curve will slope downward as long as average variable costs increase less than average fixed costs decrease.

The marginal cost, as shown by the marginal cost curve in Fig. 13-2 and in column (5) of Table 13-1, is a critical figure to keep in mind. This represents the cost of producing and selling the last unit. Later in the analysis we shall see that to maximize profits, a firm theoretically will continue producing and selling as long as the sales revenue from this last unit (called "marginal revenue") exceeds the cost of the unit.

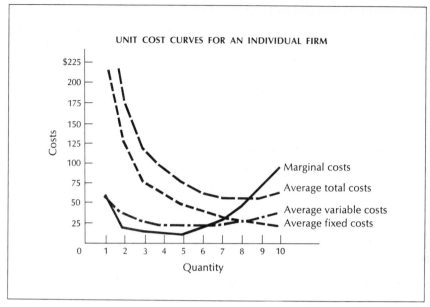

Figure 13-2. Here we see how unit costs change as quantity increases. The average total cost per unit is generally U-shaped. It starts quite high because total fixed cost is spread over so few units. As quantity increases, average fixed cost declines, thus pulling down the average total cost line. But the total cost per unit will start to slope upward when the quantity produced begins to put a strain on the productive capacity of the plant, which shows in increasing average variable costs. The increase in costs is also reflected by the acute U shape of the marginal cost line. The cost of producing one more unit goes up as workers are crowded, machines are overburdened, and other troubles are encountered. What is the most logical solution to this problem for a manufacturer who has a profitable product but encounters rising unit costs as a result of high quantity produced?

REFINEMENTS IN COST-PLUS PRICING

Once management understands that not all costs behave the same as output increases or decreases, refinements are possible in price setting based on the cost-plus approach. If we assume that the desired profit is included either in the fixed costs or in the variable costs schedules, then management can refer to its table or graphs and find the appropriate price, once a decision is made regarding intended output. If the executives decide to produce six units in our above example, the selling price will be $66.67 per unit. A production run of eight units would be priced at $60 per unit.

This pricing method assumes that all the output will be sold. Also, if fewer units are produced, each must sell for a higher price in order to cover all costs and show a profit. Obviously, if business is slack and output is cut, it will not be wise to raise the unit price. The difficulty is that no attention has been paid to market demand in this pricing approach. For this reason the method has limited application by producers. It may be used by a company which enjoys a spatial monopoly because high freight rates will check the number of potential competitors. Cost-plus pricing may also be used by firms in an industry or market where all competitors follow the same approach.

PRICES BASED ON MARGINAL COSTS ONLY

Another approach to cost-plus pricing is to set a price which will cover only the marginal costs, not the total costs. Let us refer again to the cost schedules shown in Table 13-1 and Fig. 13-2 and assume that the firm is operating at an output level of six units. Under marginal cost pricing, the firm will accept an order for one unit at $31 instead of at the full cost of $66.67 because it is trying to cover only its variable or out-of-pocket costs. If the firm can sell for any price over $31, say, $33 or $35, the excess will be considered a contribution to payment of fixed costs. Obviously, not all orders can be priced to cover only variable costs. Marginal cost pricing may be feasible, however, if management wants to keep its labor force employed during a slack season rather than face costly plant shutdowns and start-ups. Marginal cost pricing may also be used in an introductory campaign for a new product or when one product is expected to attract business for another. As an example of the last point, a department store may price meals in its tearoom at a level which covers only the marginal costs, reasoning that this facility will bring shoppers to the store, where they will buy other merchandise.

COST-PLUS PRICING BY MIDDLEMEN

Cost-plus pricing is widely used by retailing and wholesaling middlemen. At least it seems this way upon first glance. A retailer, for example, pays a given amount to buy a product and have it delivered to his store. Then he will add to the acquisition cost an amount (markup) which he estimates is necessary to cover his expenses and still leave a reasonable profit. To simplify his pricing and accounting, he may add the same percentage markup to all his products. This is an average markup which he has determined through experience will be large enough to cover the costs and profit for his entire business. If a clothing store buys a garment for $30, including freight, the item will be priced to sell at 66-2/3 percent over cost, or $50. (Store policy will probably result in this price being set at $49.95; pricing at odd amounts is discussed in Chapter 15.) The price of $50 will give the retailer a markup of 40 percent of his selling price or 66-2/3 percent based on his merchandise cost. Different types of retailers will require different percentage markups because of the nature of the products handled, services offered, etc. A self-service supermarket has lower costs and thus a lower average markup than a full-service delicatessen. Furniture and jewelry stores have higher markups than drugstores. The topic of markups is discussed in more detail in the Appendix.

To what extent is cost-plus pricing truly used by middlemen? At least three significant indications suggest that what seems to be cost-plus pricing is really market-inspired pricing. In the first place, most retail prices which are set by applying average percentage markups are really only price *offers*. If the merchandise does not sell at the original price, that figure will be lowered until it reaches a level at which the merchandise will sell. The second indication of market influences is the fact that many retailers do not use the same markup on all the products they carry. A supermarket will have a markup of 6 to 8 percent on sugar and soap products, 15 to 18 percent on canned fruit and vegetables, and 25 to 30 percent on fresh meats and produce. These different markups for different products definitely reflect competitive considerations and other aspects of the market demand. Some items are slower-moving than others, and some face stiffer competition. In other cases, store location will influence the initial markup. Middlemen find, perhaps through trial and error, what percentage markup will bring in the greatest dollar volume and profit margin from the market. Then this market-reflecting markup is expressed as if it were a cost-plus approach.

The third consideration here is that the middleman usually does not set the basic price. The manufacturer's price is set so as to allow each middleman to add his customary markup and still sell at a retail price circumscribed by the competitive market. That is, the *key* price is set by the manufacturer with an eye on the market.

EVALUATION OF COST-PLUS PRICING

This book has emphasized that a firm must be market-oriented and must cater to consumers' wants. Why, then, are we now considering cost-plus pricing? Actually, it provides a good point of departure in the discussion of price determination. Also, it is spoken of so widely in business that we must understand it. Adherents of cost-plus pricing point to its simplicity and its ease of determination. They say that costs are a known quantity, whereas attempts to estimate demand are fraught with guess work.

This opinion is questionable on two counts. First, it is doubtful whether adequate, accurate cost data are available. We know a fair amount about cost-volume relationships with respect to production costs, but what we know is still insufficient. Furthermore, our information regarding marketing costs is woefully inadequate. Certainly there is a dearth of information about costs of new products because sales volume is still an unknown quantity. Really, when we consider costs in relation to pricing, we are, at best, usually dealing with approximations. The second point concerns the inexactitude of demand estimations. The difficulty of constructing a demand schedule estimating sales volume at various prices is great. Nevertheless, sales forecasting and other research tools can do a surprisingly helpful job in this area.

Critics of cost-plus pricing do not say that costs should be disregarded in pricing. Costs should be a determining influence, they maintain, but not the only one. Costs are a floor under a firm's prices. If prices stay under this floor for a long period of time, the firm will be forced out of business. Ordinarily a company will not sell its products below cost, but it may sell particular items at or below cost if they are needed to round out the line or to generate market acceptance and customer traffic for other profitable items. At the other end of the scale, costs plus a reasonable profit should not act as a ceiling price. The market should set the upper level of prices.

Some students of pricing claim that the cost-plus method is normally used to set the price of over one-half of all our products. This conclusion exaggerates the incidence of cost-plus pricing. Many firms say that they use cost-plus as the method of setting their basic prices, but really they are using some form of market-inspired pricing.

Costs furnish a good point from which to start computing price. Management can determine a tentative price on a cost-plus basis but then make adjustments in the cost-plus price when it is able to measure demand factors. When used by itself, cost-plus is a weak and unrealistic method of pricing because it completely ignores the influences of competition and market demand.

BREAK-EVEN ANALYSIS

One way to use market demand as a basis for price determination and still consider costs is to approach pricing through a break-even analysis. A break-even analysis involves developing tables and/or charts which will help a company determine at what level of output the revenues will equal the costs, *assuming a certain selling price*. Sales at levels above the break-even point will result in a profit on each unit, and the further above the break-even point a firm goes, the higher will be the total and unit profit. Output at any stage below the break-even point will result in a loss to the seller. Break-even analysis is also a valuable pricing tool if the company's pricing objective is to maximize profits.

DETERMINATION OF BREAK-EVEN POINT

The method of determining the break-even point is illustrated in Table 13-2 and Figs. 13-3 and 13-4. In our hypothetical situation, the company's fixed costs are $250 and its variable costs are constant at $30 a unit. Thus the total cost of one unit is $280. For five units the total costs are $400 ($30 multiplied by 5, plus $250). In Fig. 12-3 the selling price is $80 a unit. Consequently, every time a unit is sold, $50 is contributed to overhead. That is, the variable costs or the out-of-pocket costs are $30 per unit, and these expenses are incurred in producing each unit. But any revenue over $30 can be used to help cover the fixed costs. At a selling price of $80 the company will break even if five units are sold. Stated another way, the variable costs for five units are $150 and the fixed costs are $250, for a total cost of $400. This is equal to the revenue from five units sold at $80 each. Stated as a formula:

$$\text{Break-even point in units} = \frac{\text{total fixed costs}}{\text{unit contribution to overhead}}$$

It is important to note the assumptions and limitations underlying the computations in the preceding paragraph and in Fig. 13-3. First, we assume that total fixed costs are constant. This is true only over a short period of time and within a limited

Table 13-2. Computation of break-even point.
>At each of several prices, we wish to find out how many units must be sold to cover all variable costs plus total fixed costs. At a unit price of $100, the sale of each unit contributes $70 to cover the overhead expenses. We must sell about 3.6 units to cover the $250 fixed cost. See Figs. 13-3 and 13-4 for a visual portrayal of data in this table.

(1) Unit price	(2) Unit variable costs, AVC	(3) Contribution to overhead, (1) − (2)	(4) Overhead (total fixed costs)	(5) Break-even point (4) ÷ (3)
$ 60	$30	$ 30	$250	8.3 units
80	30	50	250	5.0 units
100	30	70	250	3.6 units
150	30	120	250	2.1 units

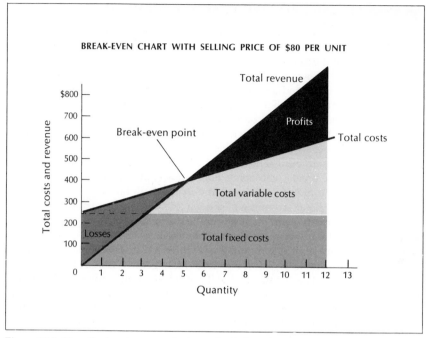

BREAK-EVEN CHART WITH SELLING PRICE OF $80 PER UNIT

Figure 13-3. Here the break-even point is reached when the company sells five units. Fixed costs, regardless of quantity produced and sold, are $250. The variable cost per unit is $30. If this company sells five units, total costs are five times $30, or $150, plus $250, or $400. At a selling price of $80, the sale of five units will yield $400 revenue, and costs and revenue will equal each other. At the same price, the sale of each unit above five yields profit.

range of output. It is reasonably easy, however, to develop a break-even chart wherein the fixed costs, and consequently the total costs, are stepped up at several intervals. This is what happens in actual practice. A good example may be found in the case of the size of the sales force. A static level of fixed costs assumes a given number of salespeople. When demand reaches a higher level, it will be necessary to add one or more salespeople. This involves a sudden increase in fixed marketing costs to cover the additional salaries, expenses, and supervision. A second assumption in our example is that the variable costs remain constant per unit of output. In the earlier discussion of the cost structure of the firm, it was noted that the average variable costs in a firm usually fluctuate. Thus the total costs were shown as a curved line in Fig. 13-1, and the average variable cost line in Fig. 12-2 was curved and sloped rather than straight and horizontal. It is also possible to develop a break-even chart for a company with a fluctuating average variable cost.

Another limitation of Fig. 13-3 is that it shows a break-even point only if the unit price is $80. It is possible and highly desirable to compute the break-even points for several different selling prices. Therefore, in Fig. 13-4 the break-even point is determined for four prices—$60, $80, $100, and $150. Figure 13-4 is also based on Table 13-2. If the price is $60, it will take sales of approximately 8.3 units to break even; at $150, only about 2.1 units. Every different selling price will result in a different break-even point.

BREAK-EVEN ANALYSIS RELATED TO MARKET DEMAND

Up to this point in our discussion of break-even analysis, we have found that its major limitation as a realistic pricing tool is that it ignores the market demand at the various prices. It is still essentially a tool for cost-plus pricing. The revenue curves in Figs. 13-3 and 13-4 show only what the revenue will be at the various prices *if* (and it is a big if) an unlimited amount can be sold at these prices. The curve *presumes* that the company can sell any output at the given price. Actually this presumption smacks considerably of a perfectly competitive market, an unrealistic situation in practice. So far, our break-even charts show only the amount which must be sold at the stated price in order to break even. The chart does not tell us whether we *can* actually sell this amount. The amount which the market will buy at a given price may be below the break-even point. For instance, at a selling price of $80 per unit, the break-even point is five units. If the market will buy only three or four units, the firm will not break even; it will show a loss.

This deficiency in break-even analysis can be remedied by estimating the total demand which actually exists at several different selling prices. Then this market information can be superimposed on the predetermined break-even data. This procedure is illustrated in Table 13-3 and Fig. 13-5. Management first constructs a demand schedule, that is, its estimate of what it can sell at various prices. Columns (1) and (2) of Table 13-3 show this information. From these figures, total revenue at each price is determined—column (3)—and this information is plotted on a graph. The DD curve in Fig. 13-5 is the resulting total demand curve. Students may be more familiar with the traditional demand curves which slope downward to the

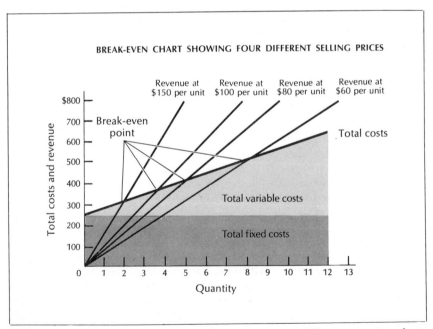

Figure 13-4. Here the company is experimenting with several different prices in order to determine which is the most appropriate. There are four different prices and four break-even points. At a price of $60, the company will start making a profit after it has sold 8.3 units. At the opposite extreme, the break-even point for a price of $150 is about 2.1 units.

right. The difference is that the usual demand curve shows *average* revenues, while the DD curve in Fig. 13-5 represents *total* revenues. Basically the curves are developed from the same demand schedule. In fact, a traditional demand curve could be plotted from the figures in columns (1) and (2) of Table 13-3.

After the total DD curve is drawn, it is placed on the break-even chart, which already shows several revenue lines representing different unit selling prices. To maximize profits, management finds the point on the demand curve which is the greatest vertical distance above the total cost curve. The specific selling price selected is the one represented by the revenue line which intersects this point on the DD curve. The optimum level of output is also determined by this intersection. In our example, $100 is the selling price, and five units is the output which will maximize profits at $100. An $80 price will sell six units and bring profits of $50. The other two prices, $60 and $150, however, will result in losses of $40 and $10, respectively, because demand at these prices is less than the output needed to break even.

EVALUATION OF BREAK-EVEN ANALYSIS

Certainly no one should claim that break-even analysis is the perfect pricing tool. Some of its limitations have already been touched upon. For example, many of the underlying assumptions are unrealistic in a practical business operation. It assumes that costs are static, and it requires an empirical determination of the company's cost curve. Break-even analysis has a very limited value as a pricing tool in firms whose costs fluctuate frequently and widely and whose product mixes vary considerably. On the revenue side, break-even analysis often oversimplifies or assumes as static a revenue activity which is really highly volatile. It also assumes that one can accurately estimate demand at different prices.

These limitations should not lead management to dismiss break-even analysis as a pricing tool. While it is not perfect, it is extremely valuable, especially when used

Table 13-3. Relations between break-even analysis, total revenue from market demand, and profits.

By comparing market demand and break-even point at each unit price, we find which price will maximize profits. Note that at a $60 price the break-even point is 8.3 units. Yet the market will buy only seven units at the price, so a loss would result. Explain why there is a $50 profit at the $80 price. This is shown graphically in Fig. 13.5.

(1) Unit price	(2) Market demand at the price, in units	(3) Total revenue TR = (1) × (2)	(4) Break-even point	(5) Total cost (TC) of units sold*	(6) Total profits (spread between TR and TC at number of units sold) (3) − (5)
$ 60	7	$420	8.3	$460	$−40
80	6	480	5.0	430	50
100	5	500	3.6	400	100
150	2	300	2.1	310	−10

* Computed from cost data in Table 13-2. (Unit variable costs are $30, and total fixed costs are $250.)

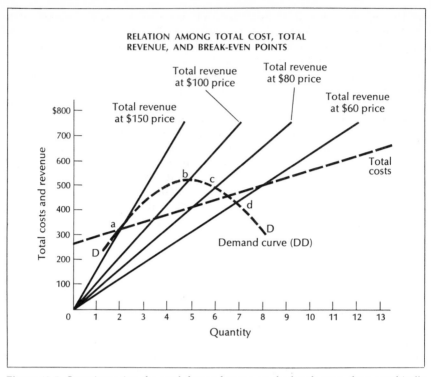

Figure 13-5. Superimposing the total demand curve on the break-even chart graphically shows which price will maximize profits. We seek the point at which the demand curve is the greatest vertical distance above the total cost line (point b in this case). Then we determine which price is represented by the total revenue line intersecting the demand curve at this point. $100 is our price. Note that the lower price of $60 would result in a loss of $40 (point d is below the total cost line).

in conjunction with an analysis of total demand. Refinements and flexibility can be introduced into a break-even analysis through the use of mathematical models. Even in its simplest form, break-even analysis is very helpful because in the short run many firms are faced with reasonably stable costs and demand structures.

PRICES BASED ON BALANCE BETWEEN SUPPLY AND DEMAND

Another major method of price setting involves balancing unit demand with unit costs in order to determine the best unit price for profit maximization. Firms that do not have profit maximization as their pricing goal should understand this method, and possibly they can use it for setting their basic list prices. This pricing method parallels the marginal analysis of demand and supply which was developed by classical and neoclassical economists. The analytical approach has been updated by the pioneering contributions of Edward H. Chamberlain and Joan Robinson, who developed the theory of monopolistic, or imperfect, competition.

In our discussion of demand, we must be careful to distinguish between the demand curve or schedule facing an individual seller and the one facing the industry as a whole. Theoretically, when a firm operates in a market of perfect competition, its demand curve is horizontal at the market price. That is, the single seller has no control over the price, and he can sell his entire output at the market price. Even in a perfectly competitive market, however, the industry has a downward-sloping curve. That is, for the industry as a whole, more units can be sold at lower prices than at higher prices.

The market situation facing most firms in Canada today is one of monopolistic, or imperfect, competition, characterized by product differentiation and nonprice competition. By differentiating his products, an individual seller has some control over his prices. In effect, each seller becomes a separate "industry"; his product is to some extent unlike any other. An individual seller in monopolistic competition has a downward-sloping demand curve. That is, he will attract some buyers at a high price, but to broaden his market and to sell to more people, he must lower the price.

If the price is to be set by balancing demand and supply, the price setter must understand the concepts of average and marginal revenue in addition to those of average and marginal cost. Marginal revenue is the income derived from the sale of the last unit—the marginal unit. Average revenue is the unit price at a given level of unit sales. It is total revenue divided by the number of units sold. Referring to the hypothetical demand schedule in Table 13-4, we see that the company received an additional $70 (marginal revenue) from the sale of two units instead of one. The fifth unit brought a marginal revenue of $53. After the sixth unit, however, the total revenue declined each time an additional unit was sold. Hence there was a negative marginal revenue.

The downward-sloping demand curve which faces most firms is an average revenue curve. It shows how many units will be sold at various unit (average) prices.

Table 13-4. Demand schedule for individual firm.

At each market price, a definite quantity of the product will be demanded at any given time. Thus changing the unit price upward or downward will result in a differing number of units sold and a differing amount of total revenue. Marginal revenue is simply the amount of additional money gained by selling one more unit. In this example, the company no longer gains marginal revenue after it has sold the sixth unit at a price of $60.

Units sold	Unit price (average revenue)	Total revenue	Marginal revenue
1	$80	$ 80	
2	75	150	$70
3	72	216	66
4	68	272	56
5	65	325	53
6	60	360	35
7	50	350	−10
8	40	320	−30

To make an average revenue curve slope downward, the marginal revenue must always be less than the average revenue. That is, as unit sales increase, the revenue from the last unit becomes progressively smaller (see the revenue curves in Fig. 13-6). The firm's average unit cost curve (average fixed costs plus average variable costs) and its marginal cost curve have been placed in Fig. 13-6, along with the revenue curves, in order to depict graphically the price-setting process.

The firm will continue to sell as long as the revenue from the last unit sold exceeds the cost of producing this last unit. That is, output continues as long as marginal revenue exceeds marginal costs. At the point where they meet, output theoretically should cease. Certainly management will not want to sell a unit at a price less than the out-of-pocket (variable) costs of production. Thus the *point of production* is where marginal costs equal marginal revenue. This is quantity OE in Fig. 13-6. The *price* is determined by locating the point on the average revenue curve which represents OE output. Remember that average revenue represents the unit price. Thus the unit price at OE output is EC. This is the same as OB on the main vertical axis. At price EC the average unit cost is DE. Thus the company enjoys a unit profit of DC. Total profit is OE times DC (quantity times unit profit). This is the area bounded by ABCD.

Supply and demand analysis as a basis for price setting has enjoyed only limited use. Businessmen usually claim that the analysis does not take into consideration

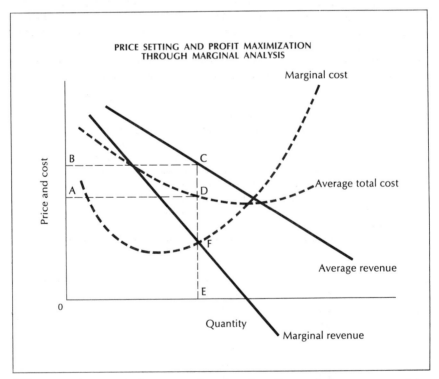

Figure 13-6. Maximum profit occurs at the point where the marginal revenue curve intersects the marginal cost curve. In most situations, the company will not produce one more unit if the revenue derived from selling that unit would be less than the cost of producing and selling it.

important variables that exist in the dynamic, real-life market situation. They feel that more and better data are needed for plotting the curves exactly. Demand and supply analysis can be used, they feel, to study past price movements, but it cannot serve as a practical basis for setting prices.

Those who are skeptical of the practical values of supply and demand analysis at the present time should take heart: management's knowledge of costs and demand is improving. Better methods of forecasting have been a boon in this area. Data-processing equipment is bringing more complete and detailed information to management's attention all the time. In the preceding chapter it was pointed out that management usually can estimate demand within broad limits, and this is helpful. Also, experienced management in many firms can do a surprisingly accurate job of estimating marginal and average costs and revenue.

PRICES SET IN RELATION TO MARKET ALONE

Cost-plus pricing is one extreme among pricing methods. At the other end of the scale is a method whereby an individual firm's prices are set in relation *only* to the competitive market price. Cost in no way determines the price. In fact, usually it is the other way around—price determines the firm's costs. The seller's price may be set right at the market price level in order to meet competition, or it may be set either above or below the competitive market level, and still be related to this level.

PRICING TO MEET COMPETITION

Management may decide to price a product right at the competitive level when any one of several situations exists. A firm is most likely to use this pricing method when the market is highly competitive and the product is not differentiated significantly from competitive models. To some extent, this method of price reflects market conditions which parallel those found under perfect competition. That is, effective product differentiation is absent, buyers and sellers are well informed about the market price and market conditions, and the seller has no discernible control over the selling price. Most producers of agricultural products must set their prices to meet competitive market levels. Even when farmers act as a group, as in an agricultural cooperative, they have very little, if any, real influence over the selling price, at least not in the short run. Manufacturers of gray goods in the textile industry, most manufacturers of automobile tires, and small firms producing well-known, standardized products all ordinarily use the market-based method of pricing.

The market-based method of pricing is also used when a traditional or "customary" price level exists. Candy bars, soft drinks, and chewing gum, for example, were traditionally priced at a nickel or a dime. In the face of rising costs, most sellers, rather than trying to change the price of a candy bar from 10 cents to 12 or 13 cents, accepted the dime price and then tailored their costs to the market price by reducing the quantity or the quality of the bar. (Today in most markets inexorable cost pressures have forced the "customary" price to rise to 25 cents.) The sharp drop in revenue which occurs when the price is raised above the customary level gives an indication that the individual seller faces a kinked demand (see Fig. 13-7). The customary price is at P, the location of the kink in the curve. If the seller tries to go above that level (OA), the demand for the product drops sharply, as indicated

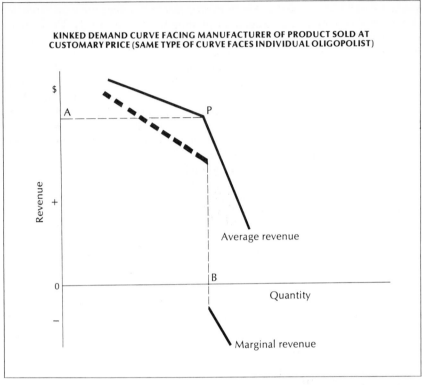

KINKED DEMAND CURVE FACING MANUFACTURER OF PRODUCT SOLD AT
CUSTOMARY PRICE (SAME TYPE OF CURVE FACES INDIVIDUAL OLIGOPOLIST)

Figure 13-7. The kink occurs at the point of the customary price (OA). Above OA, demand declines rapidly. A price set below OA will result in very little increase in volume, and consequently the marginal revenue is negative. Which part of the average revenue line reflects an elastic demand, and which segment shows inelastic demand?

by the flat average revenue curve above point P. At any price above OA, the demand is highly elastic. Below price OA, the demand is highly inelastic, as represented by the steeply sloping average revenue curve and the negative marginal revenue curve. That is, the total revenue decreases each time the price is reduced to a level below P. The customary price is so strong that a reduction in price by one firm will not increase the firm's unit sales very much, certainly not enough to offset the loss in average revenue.

Up to this point in our discussion of pricing to meet competition, we have observed market situations which involve many sellers. Oddly enough, the same pricing method is often used when the market is dominated by only a few sellers. This type of market is called an *oligopoly*. The products of all manufacturers are reasonably similar, and the demand is usually inelastic. The demand curve facing an individual seller in an oligopoly is a kinked one, as in Fig.13-7. An oligopolist must price at the market level in order to maximize profits. Selling above market price will result in a drastic reduction in total revenue because the average revenue curve is so elastic above point P. If an oligopolist cuts below the market price, all other members of the oligopoly must respond immediately. Otherwise the price-cutter will enjoy a substantial increase in business. Therefore, the competitors retaliate with comparable price cuts, and the net result is that a new market price is established at a lower level. Each member of the oligopoly gets about the same share of the market that he had before, but his unit revenue is reduced by the amount of the price cut. Theoretically, an oligopolist gains no advantage by cutting his price. For his own good, he will simply set his price at a competitive level and let it stay there. In reality, price wars are often touched off in an oligopoly because it is not possible to fully control all sellers of the product. Assuming the absence of collusion, every so often some firm will enter the market with a price reduction, and all others usually must follow in order to maintain their respective shares of the market.

The market-equated method of pricing is rather simple to apply. A firm ascertains what the going price is, and after allowing for customary markups for middlemen, it arrives at its own selling price. To illustrate, a manufacturer of men's dress shoes is aware that his retailers want to sell the shoes for $19.95 a pair. He sells directly to the retailers, and they want an average markup of 40 percent of their selling price. Consequently, after allowing $7.98 for the retailers' markup, the manufacturer's top price is about $12. He then decides whether $12 is enough to cover his production and marketing expenses and still leave him a reasonable profit. Sometimes he faces a real squeeze in this matter, particularly when his costs are rising but the market price is holding firm.

PRICING BELOW COMPETITIVE LEVEL

A variation of market-based pricing is to set a price at some point below that which is considered the competitive level. This method of pricing is usually found at the retail level of distribution, although it is not unknown among manufacturers. In recent years, the most talked-about example of this kind of pricing has been discount-house pricing. Discount houses typically price well-known, nationally advertised brands 10 to 30 percent below the suggested retail list price or the price actually being charged by most other retailers. They operate on the principle of low markup and high volume. The manufacturer's reputation for quality merchandise usually offsets customer concern about the reputation of the retailer.

Often firms prefer to operate on the basis of fewer services but lower prices. Pricing below competition is also a good way for a company to penetrate a new market. It is a method particularly adaptable to products with an elastic demand. That is, in general, the type of product upon which the discount houses have built such huge volume. At the manufacturing level, pricing below market is a strategy employed by small fringe firms attempting to compete with much larger organizations.

PRICING ABOVE COMPETITIVE LEVEL

Manufacturers or retailers sometimes set their prices above the market level. This may be done by a producer who follows a temporary or even a permanent strategy of cream skimming. Usually above-market pricing can be done only when the product is distinctive or when the seller has acquired prestige in his field. An outstanding women's specialty clothing store is able to price an article above the market level just because the article carries the store's label. Most cities have a prestige clothing, jewelry, or furniture store where price tags are noticeably above the competitive level set by other stores which handle similar types of products.

CONCLUSION

In view of the importance of pricing, it is unfortunate that so much mystery, tradition, and fuzzy thinking seem to pervade businesspeople's approach to this marketing activity. Many pricing concepts are based on the models of classical economic theory, in that setting the emphasis was on production (not consumption) and an agrarian-subsistence economy. We assumed the existence of perfect competition and rational buying behavior in the economy. Now we must identify more realistically the type of economy in which business operates, and also understand the socio-psychological aspects of buyers' perceptions of prices.

Figure 13-8 outlines 16 criteria which executives can use as practical guidelines in their price determination. Many of these generalizations were discussed in the past two chapters, so Fig. 13-8 also can serve as a meaningful summary.

QUESTIONS AND PROBLEMS

1. Explain the difference between variable costs and marginal costs.
2. Referring to Fig. 13-2, at what point does the marginal cost curve (MC) intersect the average total cost curve (ATC)? Explain why the ATC curve is declining up to the intersection point and rising beyond it. Explain how the MC curve can be rising while the ATC curve is still declining.

SUMMARY OF CRITERIA FOR SETTING PRICES

Low price when	Pricing criteria	High price when
Little	1. Promotion	Much
Commodity	2. Product type	Propietary
Mass-produced	3. Manufacture	Custom-made
Intensive	4. Market coverage	Selective
Long-lived	5. Product obsolescence	Short-lived
Slow	6. Technological change	Rapid
Capital-intensive	7. Production	Labor-intensive
Large	8. Market share	Small
Short	9. Channels of distribution	Long
Mature	10. Stage of market	New
Long-term	11. Profit perspective	Short-term
Single-use	12. Product versatility	Multiple-use
Much	13. Promotional contribution to line	Little
Few or none	14. Ancillary services	Many
Short	15. Product life in use	Long
Fast	16. Turnover	Slow

Figure 13-8. Custom-made products are priced higher than mass-produced ones (No. 3). Long-lived products can be priced lower, because costs can be amortized over a longer period (No. 5). Price low if you want a large market share (No. 8). Prices will be higher for new products (No. 10) with multiple uses (No. 12) and requiring much presale and postsale service (No. 14). *Source:* William J. E. Crissy and Robert Boewadt, "Pricing in Perspective," *Sales Management*, June 15, 1971, p. 44.

3. In Table 13-1, what is the marginal cost of the seventh unit produced?
4. "Without exception, the marginal cost is always equal to the variable cost of the marginal unit." Do you agree?
5. What are the merits and limitations of the cost-plus method of setting a basic price?
6. In a break-even chart, is the total *fixed* cost line always horizontal? Is the total *variable* cost line always straight? Explain.
7. Referring to Table 13-2 and Fig.13-4, what are the break-even points at prices of $50 and $90, if the variable costs are $40 a unit and the fixed costs remain at $250?
8. Referring to Table 13-2 and Fig. 13-4, find the break-even point for selling prices of $60 and $100 if the fixed cost totals $400.
9. A small manufacturer of ball-point pens sold his product to retailers at $8.40 per dozen. His manufacturing cost was 50 cents on each pen. His expenses, including all selling and administrative costs except advertising, were $19,200. How many dozen must he sell to cover these expenses and pay for an advertising campaign costing $6,000?
10. "Beyond the break-even point, all revenue from sales is pure profit. Consequently, once the break-even point is achieved, it behooves the seller to increase his advertising and personal selling efforts in order to get more of these profitable, above-break-even-point sales." Discuss.
11. Does supply and demand analysis in relation to pricing have any practical value for the businessman?
12. Referring to Fig. 13-6, why would the firm normally stop producing at quantity OE? Why is the price set at EC (same as OB) and not at EF or ED?
13. Are there any stores in your community which generally price above the competitive level? How are they able to do this?
14. A soft drink manufacturer has been pricing his 10-ounce bottled drink to sell for 15 cents at retail. The product has strong market acceptance in its regional market, competing favorably with Coca-Cola, Pepsi-Cola, 7-Up, and other well-known brands. For some time, production and marketing costs have been increasing, and management must now take some action. Which of the following courses of action should the company follow? Can you propose a better alternative?
    a. Raise the price to 18 cents or two bottles for 35 cents.
    b. Reduce the quality of the beverage.
    c. Reduce the quantity to 8 ounces.
    d. Curtail the advertising.

PRICE POLICIES AND STRATEGIES

After setting the basic or list price for a product, management must examine the many facets of its price structure which require specific policies. What kind of quantity discount schedule will it adopt? Will it insist upon f.o.b. pricing, or will it occasionally absorb freight?

In this chapter and the next, we shall discuss eleven problem areas in pricing, listed below, which call for executive policy making. We shall also consider the more important legal aspects of some of the price policies.

1. Discounts and allowances
2. Geographic price policies
3. One price versus variable price
4. Unit pricing
5. Pricing multiple products
6. Price lining
7. Resale price maintenance
8. "Leader" pricing
9. Guarantee against price decline
10. Psychological pricing
11. Price competition versus nonprice competition

DISCOUNTS AND ALLOWANCES

Discounts and allowances result in a deduction from the list price. The deduction may be in the form of cash or some other concession, such as a free case of merchandise. The philosophy underlying discounts and allowances is that the customer will in return perform some marketing activities whose value to the seller will be equivalent to the amount of the discount or allowance. Commonly used forms include quantity, trade, cash, and seasonal discounts and promotional, brokerage, and freight allowances.

QUANTITY DISCOUNTS

Quantity discounts are deductions offered from list prices by a seller in order to encourage a customer to buy in larger amounts or to concentrate his purchases with this seller. The discounts may be based on a dollar or unit purchases.

Cumulative and noncumulative quantity discounts. A *noncumulative* discount is based upon an individual order of one or more products. Thus a retailer may sell golf balls at $1 each or at three for $2.50. A manufacturer or a wholesaler may set up a quantity discount schedule such as the following, which was used by a manufacturer of industrial adhesives. Noncumulative quantity discounts are expected to encourage large orders. Many expenses, such as billing, order filling, shipping, and salesmen's salaries, are about the same whether the seller receives an order totaling $10 or $500. Consequently, selling expense as a percentage of sales decreases as the order becomes larger.

Boxes purchased on single order	Percentage discount from list price
1-5	0.0
6-12	2.0
13-25	3.5
Over 25	5.0

A *cumulative* discount is based on the total volume purchased over a period of time. These discounts are an advantage to a seller because they tie customers more closely to him. They are really patronage discounts in that the more total business a buyer gives a seller, the greater is the discount. They are especially applicable to the sale of perishable products. The seller wants to encourage a customer to buy fresh supplies frequently so that the merchandise will not grow stale. Thus the discount is based on total purchases over a month, rather than on each separate order.

Either type of quantity discount can be used nicely by a company producing several related or even nonrelated products which are apt to be purchased by a single buyer. Often the sales of a slow-moving item can be stimulated if it is offered in an attractive discount package with more popular items. Finally quantity discounts can help a manufacturer effect real economies in the production end of the business as well as in selling. Large orders can result in lower-cost production runs. A cumulative discount based on total orders from all units in a retail chain may enable a producer to make much more effective use of his production capacity, even though orders are shipped in small amounts with no savings in marketing costs.

Discount schedules can create ill will between buyers and sellers. The buyer whose purchases are just below the next bracket often pressures the seller to give him the higher discount. A salesman may be tempted to overload his customers by urging them to buy larger quantities than they need in order to get higher discounts. Management faces a real problem in the task of constructing the discount schedule. Cost studies and analyses of customer buying habits are usually necessary in order to set up the proper discount percentages and quantity brackets. A drawback to cumulative discounts is that they are in no way related to the size of individual orders. Hence there is no premium attached to buying in large, economical units.

TRADE DISCOUNTS

Trade discounts, sometimes called "functional" discounts, are a reduction from the list price offered to buyers in payment for marketing functions which they will presumably perform. A manufacturer may quote a retail list price of $400 with trade discounts of 40 percent and 10 percent. The retailer pays $240 ($400 less 40 percent), and the wholesaler pays the manufacturer $216 ($240 less 10 percent). The wholesaler is given the 40 and 10 percent. He is expected to keep the 10 percent to cover the costs of his wholesaling functions and to pass on the 40 percent to the retailers. It should be noted that the 40 and 10 percent do not constitute a total discount of 50 percent off the list price. Each discount percentage in the "chain" is computed on the amount remaining after the preceding percentage has been deducted. Trade discounts vary considerably from one industry to another because of differences in the normal markups required by various types of middlemen and differences in the customary channels used.

In addition to allowing a middleman his usual markup in payment for functions he performs, trade discounts serve other purposes. They are usually high enough to cover high-cost middlemen, who otherwise would not be interested in handling the product. A large discount, however, may offer retailers an opportunity to sell below list. They can show the list price to the customer and make him feel he is getting a bargain. In another situation, many companies publish catalogues with list prices. The net price can be varied simply by changing the amount of the trade discount. Therefore, if prices change, the seller does not have to print a new catalogue. He just changes the trade discount on the particular item.

Trade discounts originated in the traditional channel relationships which existed within each industry. A wholesaler was a wholesaler, and his functions were easy to distinguish from those of a retailer. Today, however, channel structures are far more complex, and price differentials occasioned by trade discounts are much more difficult to justify on a cost basis. Unless management makes a detailed marketing cost analysis by classes of customers, it can hardly prove that the discounts are equivalent to the cost differentials incurred in dealing with these different classes of customers.

CASH DISCOUNTS

A *cash discount* is a deduction granted to the buyer for paying his bill within a specified period of time. The discount is computed on the net amount due after first deducting trade and quantity discounts from the initial price. If a buyer owes $360 after the other discounts have been granted and he is offered terms of say, 2/10, n/30 on an invoice dated November 8, he may deduct a discount of 2 percent ($7.20) if he pays his bill within 10 days after the date of invoice (by November 18). Otherwise he must pay the entire bill of $360 in 30 days (December 8). In a cash discount, two elements are present—the percentage reduction itself and the time period within which the bill must be paid. There are many different terms of sale because practically every industry has its own combination of these two elements. For example, one may see 2/10, n/30; 2/10 e.o.m. (2 percent discount if paid within 10 days after the end of the month); 3/10, n/60 r.o.g. (the ten-day discount period starts upon receipt of the goods).

Most buyers are extremely eager to pay the bills in time to earn the cash discounts. The discount in a 2/10, n/30 situation may not seem like very much. But management must realize that this 2 percent is earned just for paying 20 days in advance of when the entire bill is due. If a buyer fails to take the cash discount in a 2/10, n/30 situation, he is, in effect, borrowing money at a 36 percent annual rate of interest. (Figuring a 360-day year, there are eighteen periods of 20 days each in the year. Eighteen periods at 2 percent each equal 36 percent.)

SEASONAL DISCOUNTS AND FORWARD DATING

If a firm producing an article, such as air conditioners or lawn mowers, which is purchased on a seasonal basis, management may want to consider the strategy of granting a *seasonal discount*. This is a discount of, say, 5, 10, or 20 percent which is given to a customer who places an order during the slack season. Off-season orders enable the manufacturer to make better use of his production facilities.

Forward dating is a variation of both a seasonal discount and a cash discount. A manufacturer of fishing tackle will seek orders from wholesalers and retailers during the winter months. The bill will be dated, say, April 1, and terms of 2/10, n/30 may be offered as of that date. Thus the seller can get orders in December and January which help him to level out his production. The wholesale or retail buyers do not have to pay their bills, however, until after the season starts.

PROMOTIONAL ALLOWANCES

Promotional allowances are price reductions granted by sellers to buyers in payment for promotional services performed by the buyer. These allowances may also be in the form of promotional material supplied by the seller. To illustrate, a manufacturer of builders' hardware gives a certain quantity of "free goods" to dealers who prominently display his line. A clothing manufacturer pays one-half the space charge of a retailer's advertisement which features the manufacturer's product. A luggage manufacturer provides advertising display materials for his retailers. The use of promotional allowances as a promotional strategy rather than a price strategy is discussed in Chapter 22.

BROKERAGE ALLOWANCES

When the services of a broker as a wholesaling middleman are employed in the producer's channel of distribution, the broker is paid a certain percentage of the sales volume he generates. This payment is called a *brokerage allowance* and is really just another form of trade discount. Because of the legal implications in certain types of brokerage arrangements, these allowances are noted separately instead of being included with trade discounts. Many times in the past, the commission which the seller normally paid a broker was *instead* paid to large-scale buyers who performed the services usually ascribed to brokers.

LEGAL REGULATION OF DISCOUNTS AND ALLOWANCES

The discounts and allowances discussed in this section may result in different prices for different customers. Whenever price differentials exist, there is price discrimination; the terms are synonymous. In certain situations, price discrimination is prohibited under the Combines Investigation Act. This is one of the most important federal laws affecting a company's marketing program.

Background of the act. Anti-combines legislation in Canada was first introduced in 1888. Small businessmen who suffered from the monopolistic and collusive practices in restraint of trade by large manufacturers pressured Parliament into setting up a Combines Investigation Commission. Investigators attempting to verify the allegations of the small tradesmen unearthed a widespread range of restrictive practices and measures.

The results of the investigation led Parliament in 1889 to pass an Act for the Prevention and Suppression of Combinations Formed in Restraint of Trade. The intent of the Act was to declare illegal monopolies and combinations in restraint of trade. Although the Act was incorporated into the Criminal Code as Section 520 in 1892, it proved ineffectual, because to break the law an individual would have to commit an illegal act within the meaning of the "common law". In 1900 the Act was amended to remove this loophole and undue restriction of competition became, in itself, a criminal offence.

Additional legislation was passed in 1910 after a rash of mergers involving some fifty-eight business firms, to complement the Criminal Code and assist in the application of the Act. In 1919 the Combines and Fair Prices Act was passed which prohibited undue stockpiling of the "necessities of life" and also prohibited the realization of exaggerated profits through "unreasonable" prices.

In 1923, Canadian combines legislation was finally consolidated. The most important sections of the Combines Investigation Act of 1923 are still operative. Following the presentation of a report by the Economic Council of Canada in 1969,[1] the Government of Canada introduced into Parliament in 1971, Bill C-256 (The Competition Bill) which contained a number of important amendments to the Combines Investigation Act and which was to form the basis for a new competition policy for Canada. First Stage amendments to the Combines Investigation Act were finally passed by Parliament in December 1975 and became law on January 1, 1976.[2]

---

1 Economic Council of Canada, *Interim Report on Competition Policy*, (Ottawa: Queen's Printer, July 1969).

2 The materials presented in this section are adapted from the Act itself, from selected portions of presented papers by D. H. W. Henry (The Director of Investigation and Research under the Act) as reproduced in M. D. Beckman and R. H. Evans, (eds.), *Marketing: A Canadian Perspective* (Scarborough, Ont.: Prentice-Hall Canada Ltd., 1972), pp. 102-125 and from D. H. W. Henry, "The Combines Investigation Act", as reproduced in B. Mallen and I. A. Litvak (eds.), *Marketing: Canada*, Second Edition (Toronto: McGraw-Hill Book Co., 1968), pp. 184-211.

A detailed examination of the proposed amendments to the Combines Investigation Act and of the Competition Bill in general is contained in: Department of Consumer and Corporate Affairs, *Proposals for a New Competition Policy for Canada*, (Ottawa: Information Canada, November, 1973).

Predatory pricing as an office. The provisions respecting predatory pricing are contained in paragraph 34(1) (c) of the Combines Investigation Act, which states:

> 34.(1) Every one engaged in a business who (c) engages in a policy of selling products at prices unreasonably low, having the effect or tendency of substantially lessening competition or eliminating a competitor, or designed to have such effect, is guilty of an indictable offence and is liable to imprisonment for two years.

In order for a conviction to result under paragraph 34(1)(c), it must be shown that prices are unreasonably low and that such prices have the effect of reducing competition. Such conditions are difficult to prove and, as a result, very few predatory pricing charges have been laid. The amendments to the Combines Investigation Act which were passed in December 1975 extended the predatory pricing provisions to the sale of both articles and services. The word "products" is now defined in the Combines Investigation Act to include articles *and* services.

Price discrimination as an offence. At present, price discrimination is regulated under paragraph 34(1)(a) of the Combines Investigation Act, which states:

> **34.**(1) Every one engaged in a business who
> (a) is a party or privy to, or assists in, any sale that discriminates to his knowledge, directly or indirectly, against competitors of a purchaser of articles from him in that any discount, rebate, allowance, price concession or other advantage is granted to the purchaser over and above any discount, rebate, allowance, price concession or other advantage that, at the time the articles are sold to such purchaser, is available to such competitors in respect of a sale of articles of like quality and quantity;
> is guilty of an indictable offence and is liable to imprisonment for two years.

This section goes on to state in paragraph 34(2):

> (2) It is not an offence under paragraph (1)(a) to be a party or privy to, or assist in any sale mentioned therein unless the discount, rebate, allowance, price concession or other advantage was granted as part of a practice of discriminating as described in that paragraph.

The following conditions must, therefore, be met in order for a conviction to be registered for price discrimination: (1) a discount, rebate, allowance, price concession or other advantage must be granted to one customer and not to another; (2) the two customers concerned must be *competitors*; (3) the price discrimination must occur in respect of *articles* of like quality and quantity; (4) the act of discrimination must be part of a *practice* of discrimination.

Not all price discrimination is, per se, an offence. It is lawful to discriminate in price on the basis of quantities of goods purchased. The cost justification defence—that of a seller differentiating his price to a favored competitor because of a difference in the costs of supplying that customer—is not viewed as an acceptable basis for discrimination. On the other hand, a seller does not have to demonstrate a cost difference in order to support a quantity discount structure. Rather, the basis for such price discrimination is accepted only on a quantity of goods purchased basis. Establishing volume discount pricing structures which are available to competing buyers who purchase in comparable quantities is a major basis for discriminating under the provision.

It is also of note that the buyer is seen as being as liable as the seller in cases of discrimination. The legislation applies to those who are party to a sale and this includes both buyer and seller. This wording was intended to restrain large-scale buyers from demanding discriminatory prices. In addition, the buyer (as well as the seller) must know that the price involved is discriminatory. From a practical standpoint, it is difficult for the Crown to prove that a buyer "knowingly" received a discriminatory price. While the intent of the legislation is to prevent price discrimination, the difficulty involved in proving that the various provisions of paragraphs 34(1)(a) and 34(2) have been met has contributed to the fact that there has never been a conviction for price discrimination in Canadian courts.

Granting promotional allowances as an offence. The Combines Investigation Act in section 35 requires that promotional allowances be granted proportionately to all competing customers. This section states:

> **35.** (1) In this section "allowance" means any discount, rebate, price concession or other advantage that is or purports to be offered or granted for advertising or display purposes and is collateral to a sale or sales of products but is not applied directly to the selling price.
>
> (2) Every one engaged in a business who is a party or privy to the granting of an allowance to any purchaser that is not offered on proportionate terms to other purchasers in competition with the first-mentioned purchaser, (which other purchasers are in this section called "competing purchasers"), is guilty of an indictable offence and is liable to imprisonment for two years.
>
> (3) For the purposes of this section, an allowance is offered on proportionate terms only if
>
> (a) the allowance offered to a purchaser is in approximately the same proportion to the value of sales to him as the allowance offered to each competing purchaser is to the total value of sales to such competing purchaser,
>
> (b) in any case where advertising or other expenditures or services are exacted in return therefor, the cost thereof required to be incurred by a purchaser is in approximately the same proportion to the value of sales to him as the cost of such advertising or other expenditures or services required to be incurred by each competing purchaser is to the total value of sales to such competing purchaser, and
>
> (c) in any case where services are exacted in return therefor, the requirements thereof have regard to the kinds of services that competing purchasers at the same or different levels of distribution are ordinarily able to perform or cause to be performed.

The Competition Bill Amendments, passed in December 1975, extended the provisions of section 35 to the sale of both articles and services. This amendment is not likely to alter the fact that price discrimination through the use of promotional allowances is difficult to prove. While discrimination in the granting of promotional allowances is a *per se* offence, not requiring proof of the existence of either a practice of discrimination or a lessening of competition, there have been no convictions under section 35. A marketer who wishes to discriminate among his customers may do so through the legal practice of granting quantity discounts.

GEOGRAPHIC PRICE POLICIES

In pricing, a seller must consider the factor of freight costs involved in shipping the product to the buyer. This consideration grows in importance as freight becomes a larger part of total variable costs. Pricing policies may be established whereby the buyer pays all the freight, the seller bears the entire costs, or the two parties share the expense. The decision can have an important bearing on the geographic limits of a firm's market, the location of its production facilities, the source of its raw materials, and its competitive strength in various market areas.

F.O.B. POINT-OF-PRODUCTION PRICING

In one widely used geographic pricing system, the seller quotes the selling price at the factory or other point of production and the buyer pays the entire cost of transportation. This is usually referred to as *f.o.b. mill* or *f.o.b. factory* pricing. Of the five systems discussed in this section, this is the only one in which the seller does not pay *any* of the freight costs. The seller pays the costs of loading the shipment aboard the carrier—hence the term "f.o.b.," or "free on board." The title to the merchandise passes to the buyer at that point, and he assumes all costs and responsibilities for shipping. Even though this policy is usually thought of as a manufacturer's pricing policy and therefore is labeled f.o.b. factory or some other point of production, it is used by many middlemen. Cash-and-carry wholesalers price their merchandise f.o.b. warehouse. Many retailers sell on an f.o.b. store basis, and the consumer pays the delivery costs.

Under the f.o.b. factory price policy, the seller nets the same amount on each sale of similar quantities. The delivered price to the buyers varies according to the freight charges and such a policy has important economic and marketing implications. In effect, f.o.b. pricing tends to establish a geographic monopoly for a given seller. Freight rates prevent distant competitors from entering his market. He in turn is increasingly priced out of markets that are far from his factory. At the same time, buyers located some distance from the seller pay heavy freight bills. If freight is a significant part of the total cost of the seller's product, it can have considerable influence on the size of his market.

UNIFORM DELIVERED PRICING

Under a uniform delivered pricing system, the same delivered price is quoted to all buyers, regardless of their locations. This policy is sometimes referred to as "postage stamp pricing" because of the similarities of the pricing of mail service. Actually, the seller is pricing f.o.b. at the buyer's location. The seller receives varying factory net prices on each sale depending upon the amount of his shipping costs.

A uniform delivered price is typically used where transportation costs are a minor item in the seller's total cost structure. The policy is also used by many retailers who feel that "free" delivery is an additional service which will strengthen their market position.

It has been generally assumed that a uniform delivered price is legal when it is truly maintained over the seller's entire geographic market. A uniform delivered price does mean, however, that the seller is absorbing freight on shipments to distant customers and overcharging on freight (called "phantom" freight) in sales to buyers located near the shipping point.

Under a uniform delivered price system, buyers located near the seller's factory are paying for some of the costs of shipping to more distant locations. The counterargument is that an f.o.b. *factory* system gives an undue advantage to buyers located near the factory. Critics of f.o.b. factory price are usually in favor of a uniform delivered price. They feel that the freight expense should not be isolated and charged to individual customers any more than any other single marketing or production expense. From a marketing standpoint, a uniform delivered price is a convenient method of quoting a price. It also lends itself to national advertising.

ZONE DELIVERED PRICING

Under a zone price policy, a seller's market is divided into a limited number of broad geographic zones, and a uniform delivered price is set within each zone. Zone delivered pricing is similar to the system used in pricing long-distance telephone service. A firm which quotes a price and then says "slightly higher west of the Rockies" is using a two-zone pricing system.

Whether the company uses a single-zone pricing system (uniform delivered price) or a multizone system, the freight charge built into the delivered price is approximately an average of the charges at all points within a zone area. Therefore, a seller either absorbs some of the freight costs or includes phantom freight in sales to all points, with one exception. This exception is sales made to buyers who are located at the point in the zone where the actual freight costs are equal to the arbitrary freight figure included in the selling price.

When a zone delivered price system is employed, the seller must walk a neat tightrope to avoid charges of illegal price discrimination among buyers or among customers of the buyers. This means that the zone lines must be drawn so that all competing buyers are in the same zone.

FREIGHT ABSORPTION PRICING

A freight absorption price policy may be adopted to offset some of the competitive disadvantages of f.o.b. factory pricing. With an f.o.b. factory price, a firm is at a price disadvantage when it tries to sell to buyers located in markets nearer to competitors' plants. In order to penetrate more deeply into these markets, a seller may be willing to absorb some of the freight costs. As a policy, freight absorption usually means that seller A will quote to the customer a delivered price which is equal to A's factory price plus the freight costs which would be charged by the competitive seller located nearest the customer.

Our seller can continue to expand the geographic limits of his market as long as his mill net after freight absorption is larger than the marginal costs on the units sold. Freight absorption is particularly adaptable to a firm whose fixed costs per unit of product are high and whose variable costs are low. In these cases, management must constantly seek ways to cover fixed costs, and freight absorption is one answer.

The legality of freight absorption is reasonably clear. The policy is legal if it is done independently and not in collusion with other firms. Also it must be done only to meet competition. In fact, if practiced properly, freight absorption can have the effect of strengthening competition, because it can break down spatial monopolies and barriers around protected markets. Predatory freight absorption with the intent of destroying competition obviously would be unlawful.

BASING-POINT PRICING

Even though it is not so widely used as it once was, and even though its legality is questioned, the basing-point system still is important. Under this system the delivered price of a product is equal to (1) the price at the point of production plus (2) published freight charges between the basing point nearest the buyer and the buyer's locations. The actual shipping point has no bearing on the computation of the delivered price. A basing point itself is simply an arbitrary location from which delivered prices are computed by all competing sellers in an industry. Usually all basing points used by an industry are also important production points for the commodity, but not all production locations are basing points. Thus there are fewer basing points than production centers.

To illustrate basing-point pricing, let us assume that a buyer is located in Regina and that Hamilton is the nearest basing point. The established freight rates between Hamilton and Regina for the product in question are $15 a unit. Manufacturers are located in Montreal, Hamilton and Regina. Freight charges between Montreal and Regina are $25 a unit. Let us assume also that all three manufacturers can produce and sell the product for $100 a unit at their factories. The delivered price in this example is $115—the price at point of production plus freight from the basing point closest to the buyer, regardless of the actual shipping point. The Hamilton seller would have a mill net of $100; he just breaks even in this transaction. The Montreal manufacturer would have to absorb $10 of freight and would net only $90 at his factory. The Regina manufacturer would have a mill net of $115 because he would receive $15 in nonincurred, or phantom, freight.

Characteristics of industries using basing-point system. In addition to the steel industry, such industries as cement, sugar, gypsum products, plate glass, heavy chemicals, lumber products, and corn products have used the basing-point system. These industries have several common characteristics which are conducive to the use of basing-point pricing. In the first place, the product in each case is a standard, nondifferentiated item. Sugar is sugar, and window glass is window glass. Price is all-important, and brands are not significant. Another point is that freight constitutes a substantial cost element. Furthermore, fixed expenses constitute a large part of total costs, and excess capacity typically exists in basing-point industries. Thus, there is a constant thread of price-cutting by firms willing to accept orders at any price above variable costs. Even though total costs are not covered, any return over variable costs is a contribution to overhead. Finally, there are relatively few firms in the industry, and it is rather easy to get agreement on the use of the system and to enforce the agreement.

Evaluation of basing-point system. Several rather strong objections are typically raised against the basing-point pricing system. One is that it is not possible to justify the phantom freight. This is an unearned element, and it results in price discrimination. Another incriminating objection is that collusion is required to make the basing-point system work. The use of a freight rate book, published by the industry's trade association and rigidly followed when quoting prices, is considered evidence of collusion by many people.

Another criticism of basing-point pricing is that it eliminates price competition and makes for rigidity in the pricing structure. All sellers quote the same delivered price at any one location. Usually any attempt to cut below the "proper" price is met with swift retaliation from competitive sellers. One seller cannot effectively take advantage of the fact that he is located nearer to buyers than other sellers are. Without a basing-point system, new plant development might be encouraged in markets where present demand exceeds supply and where there are good growth prospects. These new sellers could use their locational advantage to serve as the basis of a price advantage. Finally, there is a considerable amount of transportation crosshauling, which results in duplicate use of transportation facilities and resources. Because the delivered price is the same regardless of shipping point, a Sault Ste. Marie firm, for example, may buy from a Hamilton seller, and a Hamilton firm may buy from a Sault Ste. Marie seller.

A number of advantages are stated in support of basing-point pricing, but they have some fundamental weaknesses. A frequently mentioned merit is that basing-point systems prevent the growth of spatial, or geographic, monopolies. Without this sytem, buyers would be at the mercy of the nearest seller. Consequently, many buyers are said to prefer basing-point pricing. This argument is weak on at least three points. First, if a seller were really prospering in his geographic area because outsiders could not overcome the freight barriers, other sellers would soon build competitive plants in the area. Second, distant sellers could still enter the market by absorbing freight on an independent basis. Finally, the buyers who are located near the sellers and who are paying phantom freight are certainly not in favor of basing-point pricing.

Legal regulation of geographic pricing policies. Certain geographic pricing policies are considered illegal in Canada. As a special case of predatory pricing, paragraph 34(1)(b) states:

> 34. (1) Every one engaged in a business who
>   (b) engages in a policy of selling products in any area of Canada at prices lower than those exacted by him elsewhere in Canada, having the effect or tendency of substantially lessening competition or eliminating a competitor in such part of Canada, or designed to have such effect;
> is guilty of an indictable offence and is liable to imprisonment for two years.

As with other sections of the Combines Investigation Act, the Competition Bill Amendments, passed in December 1975, extended the provisions of paragraph 34(1)(b) to include the sale of both articles and services.

The intent of paragraph 34(1)(b) is to control the situation where a large national company might be able to reduce its prices in a local market in order to cause smaller local companies, which would not likely be able to sustain low prices for as long a period as could the national firm, to go out of business. Unlike other paragraphs in Section 34, there have been court proceedings under paragraph 34(1)(b).

In a recent case, it was found that prior to and for some time after a new firm entered the film processing field in Guelph, Ontario, other firms had lowered their prices on color prints in the Guelph area while maintaining regular prices elsewhere. It was alleged that the existing firms had reduced their prices in an effort to eliminate the new entrant to the Guelph market. On May 29, 1972, a Federal Court issued an order of prohibition which prohibited the offending companies and their personnel from engaging in a policy of selling color prints in the Guelph area at lower prices than they charged elsewhere, except where lower prices reflect lower costs or are granted to meet the lower prices of competitors.[3]

There is no law in Canada against basing-point pricing *per se*. However, in that the basing-point system used by firms involves phantom freight it may be construed as being discriminatory, and thus illegal. In the U.S., it has been inferred

---

3 Department of Consumer and Corporate Affairs, *Report of the Director of Investigation and Research, Combines Investigation Act, for the year ended March 31, 1973*, (Ottawa: Information Canada, 1973), p. 61.

that a basing-point system is inherently discriminatory (because of the phantom freight) and thus unlawful under the Robinson-Patman Act.

QUESTIONS AND PROBLEMS

1. Carefully distinguish between cumulative and noncumulative quantity discounts. Which of these two types of quantity discounts has the greater economic and social justification? Explain your position, disregarding the legal considerations for the time being.

2. A manufacturer of appliances quotes a list price of $500 a unit for a certain model of refrigerator. He then grants trade discounts of 35, 20, and 5 percent. What is his selling price? Who might get these various discounts?

3. Interview a few different types of local retailers (restaurant, clothing store, sporting goods store, furniture store, etc.) and determine what terms of sale are customarily applied to their purchases. What accounts for the variations among the different types of retailers?

4. Two families living in the same apartment house each purchased a set of dining-room furniture from the same retailer. One family was charged $25 more than the other family. Is this a violation of the Combines Investigation Act?

5. The Combines Investigation Act prohibits price discrimination, and yet manufacturers and wholesalers often charge different customers different prices. Is this illegal?

6. Company A sells to all its customers at the same published price. A sales executive finds that company B is offering to sell to one of A's customers at a lower price. Company A then cuts its price to this customer, but maintains the original price to all other customers. Is this a violation of the Combines Investigation Act?

7. Explain the provisions of those sections of the Combines Investigation Act dealing with predatory pricing.

8. Explain the "proportionate terms" provisions of that section of the Combines Investigation Act which deals with promotional allowances.

9. Name some products which logically might be sold under a uniform delivered price system.

10. "An f.o.b. point-of-production price system is the only geographic price system which is fair to all buyers." Discuss.

11. Distinguish between a uniform delivered pricing system and a zone delivered system.

12. Explain how the basing-point system of pricing enables a seller to expand his market.

13. "The pricing system based on freight absorption has all the desirable features but none of the undesirable features of the basing-point system." Discuss.

14. If an Eastern manufacturer wants to compete in Western markets, where he is at a significant disadvantage with respect to freight costs, what pricing alternatives are open to this firm to help it overcome the freight differential?

15. "Adopting a multiple basing-point system eliminates the inherent undesirable features of basing-point pricing." Discuss.

16. Which geographic pricing policies might be considered illegal in Canada.?

PRICE POLICIES AND STRATEGIES (CONT.)

ONE-PRICE VERSUS VARIABLE-PRICE POLICY

Rather early in its pricing consideration, management should decide whether the company will follow a one-price policy or a variable-price policy. While adopting one will not necessarily preclude the use of the other, normally it is not strategic to waver back and forth.

Under a *one-price* policy the company charges the same price to all similar types of customers who purchase similar quantities of the product under essentially the same terms of sale. Discounts and allowances may be granted under this policy if they are offered on equal terms to all comparable customers.

When a *variable-price* policy is used, the company will sell similar quantities to similar buyers at different prices. Sometimes variable prices are offered when the buyer and seller are friends. In other cases, sellers want the business of certain customers and will offer them favorable differential prices. Usually, however, under this policy the price is set as a result of bargaining.

In Canada, the one-price policy has been used more than variable pricing, particularly at the retail level. This is in contrast to many foreign countries where the final price is customarily determined by bargaining and haggling. A one-price policy is by no means the rule in Canada, however. In the marketing of any product where a trade-in is involved, variable pricing abounds. Thus a one-price policy is virtually unknown in automobile retailing, even though posted factory list prices may suggest that the same price is offered to all.

A one-price policy builds customer confidence in a seller, whether at the manufacturing, wholesaling, or retailing level. Weak bargainers need not feel they are at a competitive disadvantage. The policy is also a great time-saver. Finally, this policy can be adopted whether personal salesmen are used or not. It lends itself nicely to self-service retailing, mail-order selling, and automatic vending.

A variable-price policy also has some advantages. It offers the seller flexibility in his dealings with different customers. The seller may wish to make price concessions to woo a buyer away from a competitor, or he may want to give a buyer a better deal because the customer shows promise of becoming a large-scale buyer in the future.

On balance, however, a variable-price policy is generally less desirable than a one-price policy. In sales to business firms, not to consumers, variable pricing could be considered a violation of the Combines Investigation Act. As we have seen in the preceding chapter, a supplier must charge the same price to competitors who purchase the same quantities of a product. Also, a variable price policy could generate considerable ill will when the word gets around that some buyers acquired the product at lower prices. Variable pricing can trigger a price war and bring strong retaliation in some industries. In most retail stores, variable pricing would result in chaotic selling conditions and a virtual absence of managerial control.

UNIT PRICING

Unit pricing is a retail price-information-reporting policy which to date has been employed largely by supermarket chains, although the same method is adaptable to other types of stores and products. The policy is a business response to consumer protests that the proliferation of packages sizes (especially in grocery stores) has made it virtually impossible to compare prices of similar products. In canned beans, for example, is 15½ avoirdupois ounces for 19 cents a better deal than 1-pound 1-ounce (482 grams) at 2 cans for 45 cents? How does the price of 41 cents for a 1-pound 4-ounce box of Tide detergent compare with 83 cents for the 3-pound 1-ounce box of Cheer brand of detergent?

Under a policy of unit pricing, for each separate product and package size there is a shelf label which states (1) the price of the package and (2) this price expressed in dollars and cents per ounce, pound, pint, kilogram, litre or some other standard quantity measure.

Several studies have been conducted on unit pricing to measure consumers' response, the impact on the retailer, and the possible repercussions on manufacturers.[1] Because unit pricing was generally instituted only recently (1970s), it is a little too early to get complete information on its effect. The hope is that consumers will make more informed purchase decisions. Undoubtedly, there will be some con-

---

1 See Lawrence M. Lamont and James T. Rothe, "The Impact of Unit Pricing on Channels Systems," in Fred C. Allvine (ed.), *Combined Proceedings: 1971 Spring and Fall Conferences,* American Marketing Association, series no. 33, Chicago, 1972, pp. 653-658; Kent B. Monroe and Peter J. LaPlaca, "What Are the Benefits of Unit Pricing?" *Journal of Marketing,* July, 1972 pp. 16-22; Michael J. Houston, "The Effect of Unit-Pricing on Choices of Brand and Size in Economic Shopping," *Journal of Marketing,* July, 1972, pp. 51-69; and James M. Carman, "A Summary of Empirical Research on Unit Pricing in Supermarkets," *Journal of Retailing,* Winter, 1973; pp. 63-70.

sumer switching of sizes, brands, and even stores. Installing and maintaining unit pricing is an added retailer cost, hopefully offset by societal benefits. Unit pricing will force manufacturers to change packages and labels. Brand loyalties may decline as price competition increases. Middlemen's brands may become stronger. All in all, unit pricing will pose several challenges to a manufacturer's marketing program.

PRICING MULTIPLE PRODUCTS

Most firms market several lines of products or offer a breadth of products within one line. As the number of products increases, the pricing problems become more complex. No article produced or carried by a company is an island unto itself. It is related to the company's other products through market demand, through cost, or through both. Management must consider these interrelationships when pricing the company's full complement of products.

On the cost side of the pricing equation, it can be seen that some products present joint cost situations. In the product lines of a meat-packer, for example, many items are derived from one beef carcass. In pricing related products, management may decide that each article must recoup its full cost plus a profit or that each must cover only variable costs, with any return above that level considered a contribution to overhead.

On the *demand* side, the products may differ but be related in quality, uses, or sizes. These interrelationships reduce management's flexibility in pricing because the executives must consider the effect which the price of one item will have on the prices of other products. A manufacturer of outboard motors sells a line of products in which one of the relative differences is the size of each model as measured by its horsepower. Thus when pricing a 15-horsepower motor, the executive must consider this price in relation to the prices set for motors of 7.5, 10, and 25 horsepower.

A key consideration in the pricing of multiple products is the degree to which the market for each size, quality level, brand, etc., can be isolated from the market for other sizes, brands, and quality levels. In the above example, if various sizes of outboard motors were sold to separate markets, isolated from one another, then each size could be priced without reference to the others. These markets usually are not isolated, however; they overlap and actually represent a continuum.

Another key consideration in pricing multiple products is that the firm should be trying to achieve a pricing goal on its total output or for a related group of products but not necessarily for each individual item. If a company can increase its total profits by pricing certain articles below total costs, then this is sound marketing strategy.

PRICE LINING

Price lining is found more commonly among retailers than among wholesalers or producers. It consists of selecting a limited number of prices at which the store will sell its merchandise. A shoe store may sell several styles of shoes at $14.95 a pair, another group at $19.95, and a third assortment at $24.95. Price lining is used extensively in the retailing of all types of apparel. Many years ago, Woolworth's and other variety stores got the nickname "five-and-ten-cent-stores" because of their policies of price lining everything at one of these two levels.

For the consumer, the main benefit of price lining is that it simplifies buying decisions. From the retailer's point of view, the policy is advantageous because it helps the store owner to plan his purchases. A dress buyer, for example, can go into a market looking for dresses which may be retailed for $19.95, $29.95, or $39.95.

On the surface, price lining may seem to ease management's pricing decisions because the retail price is already set. Initially, however, the company had to decide how many lines to have and at what level each price line should be. Furthermore, every time the retailer wants to make a purchase, he has fundamentally the same pricing decisions to make that an executive in any non-price-lining company has. The only difference is that a price-lining company, the cost must fit into the price. The retailer still has the alternative of equating marginal cost and marginal revenue or of using cost-plus pricing in the form of his usual markup. The decision is made with respect to the price paid for the merchandise rather than the price at which it will be sold.

Two big problems in price lining center around the task of setting the initial price lines and the difficulties encountered when the costs are increasing. In determining the price lines, management does not want too many or too few, and care must be taken that they are not too close together or too far apart. If they are too close together, the consumer may not be able to see why one item is x dollars higher than another. If they are too far apart, sales may be lost because some consumers want an article at a price in between the two levels.

Rising costs can put a real squeeze on price lines, because a company hesitates to change its price line every time costs go up. But if costs increase and prices remain stationary, profit margins are compressed, and the retailer may be forced to seek products with lower costs. Where longtime relationships exist between manufacturers and retailers, or where price lines are traditional, as in 5- and 10-cent candy bars, manufacturers may reduce the product's size or quality (and thus its costs) and enable retailers to hold prices at existing levels.

RESALE PRICE MAINTENANCE

It is often in the interests of manufacturers to exert some control over the prices at which retailers will resell their products. This is most commonly done in Canada through the use of suggested retail prices. The practice of *requiring* that retailers sell a product at a particular price is known as resale price maintenance and such a practice is illegal in Canada. In certain of the states of the United States, however, "fair trade" laws permit resale price maintenance for certain types of products. It may be interesting to examine why manufacturers may wish to control resale prices and how consumers would likely react.

EVALUATION OF RESALE PRICE MAINTENANCE

Manufacturer's viewpoint. A manufacturer may want to maintain the price of his product in order to be able to advertise its price or to prevent its being used as a loss leader. He may fear that price cuts will damage his product's prestige. If price reductions are permanent, as they would be in the hands of some large retailers, consumers may feel that the regular list price is an inflated indication of the product's value. Also, if the product becomes a price football, dealers who sell at the regular list price may discontinue the product or push substitute brands.

A manufacturer may want to protect his small dealers from the price competition of large-scale retailers, because he feels that he needs small dealers. A price-cutting retailer may not be willing to provide the selling effort and in-store promotion desired.

On the other hand, the competitive limitations of resale price maintenance far outweigh any advantages which this policy may seem to have for manufacturers. It is doubtful that the absence of a price maintenance policy really can hurt the prestige of a product. Consumers are used to paying different prices at different outlets. If the product is a good one and is properly promoted by the manufacturer, many retailers will continue to carry it because of consumer demand.

Retailer's viewpoint. Some retailers, particularly smaller operations and high cost, large retailers, have traditionally favoured resale price maintenance. This has been the case because these retailers are unable to match the price cuts offered by large, low cost stores.

Another disadvantage of resale price maintenance is that it eliminates price competition at the retail level. Price maintenance protects the high cost, inefficient operator who wishes to maintain high unit margins even though he sells only a relatively small number of units. On the other hand, resale price maintenance penalizes the retailer who prefers to earn a small profit per unit of sale and depend upon huge volume to reach his total profit goal. Price maintenance also penalizes the low cost retailer who is not able to use his competitive advantage by passing on to consumers the lower prices resulting from the efficiency of his operation. Resale price maintenance works particularly to the advantage of the full-service retailer and to the disadvantage of the retailer whose costs are low because he offers few services.

Consumer's viewpoint. From the point of view of the consumer it is difficult to build a case in support of resale price maintenance. The proponents of resale price maintenance, particularly in the United States, claim that fair trade laws tend to keep prices on all products at a reasonable level. Without resale price maintenance, it is claimed, prices would be cut on a few items but raised on articles whose prices are not so well known to consumers. The practice of resale price maintenance ensures wide distribution of products and makes it possible for consumers to buy items at conveniently located stores.

On balance, these arguments are weak. The biggest objection to resale price maintenance from the consumer's viewpoint is that, as various studies have shown, prices are higher on an item when it is price maintained than when it is not. Also, if consumers are willing to forego services and instead enjoy lower prices, this alternative is not open to them if resale price maintenance is practised.

LEGAL ASPECTS OF RESALE PRICE MAINTENANCE

Resale price maintenance has been illegal in Canada since 1951.[2] In this country, attempts on the part of manufacturers to control or to influence upward the prices at

---

2 For excellent background information on the regulation of resale price maintenance in Canada, the reader is referred to *Restrictive Trade Practices in Canada,* edited by L. A. Skeoch, Toronto: McClelland and Stewart, Limited, 1966, pp. 156-157.

which their products are sold by retailers have been considered akin to price fixing.

Section 38 of the Combines Investigation Act prohibits a manufacturer or supplier from requiring or inducing a retailer to sell a product at a particular price or not below a particular price. On occasion, a supplier may attempt to control retail prices through the use of a "suggested retail price." Under Section 38, the use of "suggested retail prices" is permitted *only* if the supplier makes it clear to the retailer that the product *may* be sold at a price below the suggested price and that the retailer will not in any way be discriminated against if the product is sold at a lower price. Also, where a manufacturer advertises a product, and in the advertisement mentions a certain price, the manufacturer must make it clear in the advertisement that the product *may* be sold at a lower price.

Prior to 1975 it was legal in Canada for a manufacturer to refuse to supply a product to a retailer if that retailer was selling that product as a loss leader or was using the product in "bait advertising" to attract people to his store. The 1975 amendments to the Combines Investigation Act eliminated this provision and it is now illegal for a manufacturer to refuse to supply a product to a retailer or to otherwise discriminate against that retailer because of the pricing policies of the retailer. In other words, a retailer is free to sell a product at whatever price he deems appropriate, and the manufacturer of that product is not permitted to exert any pressure on the retailer to sell at a particular price.

In recent years, Canadian courts have dealt with a large number of cases involving alleged efforts on the part of suppliers to influence resale prices. In these cases, convictions have resulted in the imposition of fines as large as $15,000. There is, however, some question concerning the effectiveness of the legislation and this activity in the courts in reducing the incidence of resale price maintenance. Cases involving this practice do not reach the courts unless a retailer is willing to register a complaint against a supplier. There is some evidence that, despite the provisions of Section 38, some suppliers still employ certain measures which ensure that prices are maintained at the retail level.

LEADER PRICING AND UNFAIR-PRACTICES ACTS

Many firms, primarily retailers, cut prices temporarily on a few items in order to attract customers. This price and promotional strategy, involving the use of loss leaders, is called *leader pricing*. Leader items are, or should be, well-known, heavily advertised articles which are purchased frequently. Actually, the term "loss leaders" is a misnomer; "profit leaders" would be more descriptive of the goal of the policy. The idea is that customers will come to the store to buy the advertised leader items and then stay to buy other regularly priced merchandise. The net result, the firm hopes, will be an increase in total volume and total profits.

Three provinces, B.C., Alberta and Manitoba, have had legislation dealing with loss leader selling. The approach has been to prohibit a reseller from selling an item below invoice cost, including freight, plus a stated markup which is usually 5 percent at retail. No prosecutions had taken place under these provincial statutes up to time of writing.[3]

The general intent of these laws is commendable. They eliminate much of the

3 See L. A. Skeoch, "Canada" in B. S. Yamey (ed.), *Resale Price Maintenance* (London: Weiderfeld and Nicolson, 1966), pp. 62-63.

predatory type of price-cutting; however, they permit firms to use loss leaders as a price and promotional strategy. That is, a retailer can offer an article below full cost but still sell above cost plus 5 percent markup. Under such acts low-cost, efficient businessmen are not penalized, nor are high-cost operators protected. Differentials in retailers' purchase prices can be reflected in their selling prices, and savings resulting from the absence of services can be passed on to the customers.

On the other hand, the acts have some glaring weaknesses. In the first place, the provinces do not establish provisions or agencies for enforcement. It is the responsibility and burden of the injured party to seek satisfaction from the offender in a civil suit. Another limitation is that it is difficult or even impossible to determine the cost of doing business for each individual product. The third weakness is that the laws seem to disregard the fundamental idea that the purpose of a business is to make a profit on the total operation, and not necessarily on each sale of each product.

GUARANTEE AGAINST PRICE DECLINE

A producer must decide whether he will make a refund to his middlemen in case he reduces his price within a stated period of time after filling their orders. Some sellers guarantee the price until orders are delivered or received. Others protect the price well into the season when the merchandise is being sold by the middlemen. If a manufacturer must reduce his price, he simply credits each middleman's account with an amount equal to the unit price cut times the number of units the middlemen has on hand.

Wisely used, a price-guarantee policy is especially worthwhile for firms producing goods subject to seasonal fluctuations in demand. This policy should encourage middlemen to place large orders well in advance of the season. Then the manufacturer can keep his plant operating in what would otherwise be a slack season. During periods of falling prices a middleman can order in large amounts and have no fear of taking a loss if prices decline still further.

This policy has some limitations from the standpoint of the manufacturer. If he has sold huge quantities of merchandise and the price drops, he may be faced with a heavy financial loss. The cost of policing the policy is an important factor, especially if the manufacturer guarantees the price until the merchandise is resold. Middlemen might inflate their inventory figures, and bad customer relations might be created, if the manufacturer used his salesmen to check the middlemen's stocks. Price guarantees encourage inventory speculation by middlemen. They take no risk at all. If prices go up, they gain; if prices drop, the guarantee protects them. Also, price guarantees may lead to price rigidity. Even when market conditions call for a price cut, manufacturers may hesitate to reduce their prices because they dislike having to give a rebate.

PSYCHOLOGICAL PRICING—ODD PRICING

Several price policies can be grouped under the general heading of psychological price policies. We have already touched upon three of these: price lining, prestige pricing above competitive market levels, and the use of customary prices at the market level. We also pointed out that if a price is set below the expected level, sales will suffer. Actually, volume can be increased by raising the price.

At the retail level, another psychological pricing policy is commonly used. Prices are set at odd amounts, such as 19 cents, 49 cents, $19.95, etc. Automobiles are priced at $3,995 rather than $4,000, and houses sell for $46,950 instead of $47,000. The practice originally developed as a control measure over theft by retail sales-clerks. Odd pricing usually forces a clerk to make change, and this in turn forces him to ring up the sale on the cash register.

In general, retailers believe that pricing items at odd amounts will result in larger sales. Thus 49 cents or 98 cents will bring greater revenue than 50 cents or $1. Furthermore, retailers believe that buying psychology is such that odd prices will bring more sales volume than the next *lower* even-numbered price. That is, at 49 cents or 98 cents, a firm will sell more units than at 48 cents or 96 cents. In this situation the seller's average revenue curve would have a zigzag shape, as shown in Fig. 15-1.

There is little concrete evidence to support retailers' belief in the value of odd prices. Various studies have reported inconclusive results.[4] Odd pricing is often avoided in prestige stores or on higher-priced items. Thus expensive men's suits are priced at $250, not $249.95.

PRICE COMPETITION VERSUS NONPRICE COMPETITION

In the course of developing its marketing program, management has a choice of emphasizing price competition or nonprice competition. Rarely is one of these strategies employed to the exclusion of the other, but one can be intentionally stressed more than the other.

PRICE COMPETITION

With monopolistic competition and product differentiation so prevalent in the economy today, we may overlook the fact that there is still a considerable amount of price competition. Management may decide to engage in price competition by regularly offering prices which are as low as possible. Often when this is done the seller also offers a minimum of services. In their early years, discount houses and chain stores competed in this way. Two other situations involving price competition which we should examine are (1) price changes made by our company and (2) our reaction to price changes made by a competitor.

Price changes by our firm. Any one of several situations may prompt a change in price. As costs increase, for instance, management may decide that the best course of action is to raise the price, rather than to cut quality or aggressively promote the product and still maintain the price. If our company's share of the market is declining because of strong competition, we may react initially by reducing our price. We should, of course, try to determine what accounted for the improvement in our competitor's position—an improved product or aggressive advertising, for example. In the long run, our best alternative may be to improve aspects of our own marketing program, rather than to rely on the price cut.

Temporary price adjustments may be necessary to correct an imbalance in inventory. Temporary price cuts may also be used as a promotional tactic when introduc-

---

4 For example, see David M. Georgoff, "Price Illusion and the Effect of Odd-Even Retail Pricing," *Southern Journal of Business*, April, 1969, pp. 95-103.

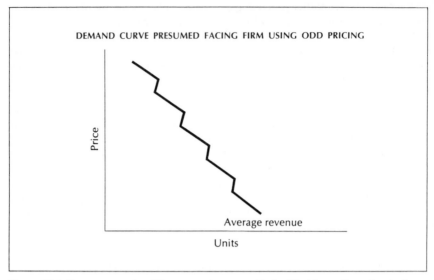

Figure 15-1. Some segments of the curve slope negatively. That is, as the price declines, volume also decreases. The zigzag shape reflects the idea that a familiar odd price will bring more sales volume than the prices immediately below these figures. Thus by pricing an article at 49 cents or 98 cents, the company will sell more units than at 48 cents or 96 cents. Do you agree? What types of stores use odd pricing? What products lend themselves to odd pricing?

ing a new product or in an effort to stimulate sales of an existing product. One study of temporary price reductions on three consumer items (regular coffee, cleansing tissue, and frozen dinners) established some useful guidelines for management. Professor Hinkle concluded:[5]

1. Off-season reductions are more profitable than equal or even greater reductions during high-volume seasons.
2. Frequent price cuts on the same brand bring successively smaller gains in market share.
3. Temporary price reductions seldom prevent new brands from gaining a foothold in the market.
4. Price cuts on new brands are more effective than price cuts on established products.
5. Price reductions seem to have little power to reverse a declining sales trend.

Before changing a price, management should consider several factors. Price-cutting may be advisable, for example, only when the seller is faced with an elastic demand curve. By reducing its price, management hopes that the volume will be increased sufficiently to increase total revenue. If demand is inelastic, a price cut will serve only to reduce total revenue.[6]

---

5 *Marketing Science Institute,* July 1965, p. 1; see also Charles L. Hinkle, "The Strategy of Price Deals," *Harvard Business Review,* July-August 1965, pp. 75-85; and Alfred Gross, "Cents-off: A Critical Promotion Tactic," *MSU Business Topics,* Spring, 1971, pp. 13-20.

6 For a new concept of price sensitivity—one which suggests that the pricing decision should rest on a better rationale than elasticity, because often there are identifiable desensitizing factors (such as eccentricities in consumer behavior, unequal ability of salesmen, and difficulty in comparing different products)—

A seller should also determine what percentage of sales increases will be necessary to offset any given percentage cut in unit price. For example, if unit prices are cut 20 percent, sales must increase 25 percent to give the same dollar sales volume as before the cut. The formula is

$$X = \frac{C}{1 \text{ minus } C}$$

where C is the percentage price cut and X is the percentage by which sales must increase to give the same dollar sales volume as before the cut.

Management should also determine what effect a given price cut will have on *gross margin,* and what sales increase (in units or dollars) will be needed to offset this reduction. To determine the increase in *dollar* sales volume needed to earn the same dollar gross margin as before a price cut, the formula

$$X = \frac{M(1-C)}{M-C} - 1$$

where C is the percentage price reduction, M is the gross-margin percentage, and X is the percentage increase in *dollar* sales volume needed to earn as many gross-margin dollars as before the cut. This formula assumes that unit production costs remain constant. Thus if a firm has a 30 percent gross margin and cuts prices 10 percent, it needs a 35 percent increase in *dollar* sales volume.[7]

From the seller's standpoint the big threat in price-cutting is that competitors will retaliate, especially in oligopolistic market situations. The net result can be a price war, and the price may even settle permanently at a lower level. Price-cutting is most likely to be found in markets where there are several sellers and the products or services are reasonably similar. In such a situation, a cut below market price will probably bring a large increase in volume.

We should note that an oligopoly is not necessarily found only among large firms. The term "oligopoly" means "a few sellers." Thus, a group of small neighborhood merchants can constitute an oligopoly. For instance, the barbers in a community may try to avoid price competition because if one reduces his price, all must follow.

Reaction to competitors' price changes. We can assume that our competitors will change their prices. We may not know when the change will occur, what its magnitude will be, or whether it will be an increase or a decrease. But change they will. Consequently, we should at least be ready with some policy guidelines or, better yet, have a plan of reaction established. Advance planning is particularly necessary in the case of a competitive price reduction, since time will then be of the essence. If a competitor boosts his prices, a reasonable delay in reacting will probably not be perilous. In fact, it may turn out to be this wise thing to do if his increase was a mis-

---

see Richard T. Sampson, "Sense and Sensitivity in Pricing," *Harvard Business Review,* November-December, 1964, pp. 99-105.

For a challenge to conventional wisdom when deciding on price changes for *industrial* goods, see Reed Moyer and Robert J. Boewadt, "The Pricing of Industrial Goods," *Business Horizons,* June, 1971, pp. 27-34.

7 To determine the increase in unit sales volume needed to maintain the same dollar gross margin in face of a price cut, the formula is $X = \dfrac{M}{M-C} - 1$. In the above example, the unit sales increase needed is 50 percent.

take. Our decision on what to do in the face of a price cut by a competitor will depend upon answers to such questions as: (1) Why did he cut his prices—is it a temporary move, or do we gauge it to be a long-run strategy? (2) *Can* we meet the price cut—that is, do we forecast that our cost-price-volume relationships permit a cut, or should we try to counter in nonprice fashion? (3) *Must* we meet the reduction—how important is this product or market to us, and how sensitive is the market to price competition?

NONPRICE COMPETITION

In nonprice competition, a seller maintains a stable, constant price and attempts to improve his market position by emphasizing his product, distribution system, promotional program, or services. Of course, management still has the task of setting the price, and competitive prices still must be taken into consideration. Furthermore, the price may change over a period of time. Nevertheless, in a nonprice competitive situation the emphasis definitely is on something other than price.

By using terms familiar in economic theory, we can differentiate nonprice competition from price competition. In price competition a seller attempts to move up or down his demand curve by changing the price. In nonprice competition a seller attempts to *shift* his demand curve to the right by means of product differentiation, promotional activities, or some other device. This point is illustrated in Fig. 15-2. At $150 the producer of a given model of metal skis can sell 35,000 pairs a year in the western region of his market. On the basis of price competition alone, he can increase his sales to 55,000 if he is willing to reduce his price to $130. The demand curve facing him is still *DD*. However, he is interested in boosting his sales without any decrease in selling price. Consequently, he embarks upon a promotional program—a form of nonprice competition—and he is able to inform and persuade enough new customers to buy at the original $150 price so that his unit sales increase to 55,000 pairs a year. In effect, his entire demand curve has shifted to position *D'D'*.

There is an increasing use of nonprice competition in marketing. Companies want, at least to some extent, to be the masters of their own destiny. In nonprice competition, a seller's entire advantage is not removed when a competitor undersells him. Furthermore, customer loyalty is fleeting when price competition is relied upon exclusively. Buyers will stick only as long as a seller offers the lowest price. Patronage built upon nonprice factors is less susceptible to a competitor's price appeal. Many sellers dread the price wars which can result from price competition.

Nonprice competition has become extremely important in Canada since the imposition of wage and price controls in late 1975. When prices are controlled to a certain extent by government regulation, marketers must turn to elements of the marketing mix other than price in order to remain competitive.

When used by a manufacturer, the strategy of nonprice competition is often accompanied by a policy of price control which prevents middlemen from using price as a direct competitive weapon. Producers accomplish this control by (1) circumventing middlemen entirely and selling directly to ultimate consumers or industrial users, (2) leasing or selling on consignment, (3) using suggested resale prices along with a carefully policed exclusive distribution.

Methods of nonprice competition. One of the major forms of nonprice competition is *product* differentiation, a concept inherent in monopolistic, or imperfect, competi-

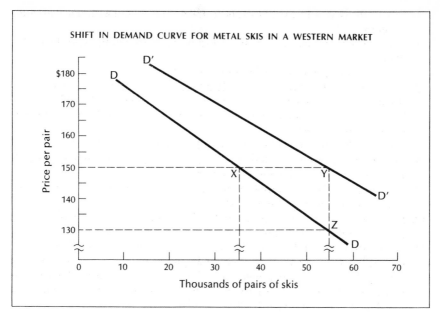

Figure 15-2. Use of nonprice competition can shift the demand curve for a product. A company selling metal skis in a Western market used a promotional program to sell more skis at the same price, thus shifting *DD* to *D'D'*. Volume increased from 35,000 to 55,000 units at $150 (point *X* to point *Y*). Besides advertising, what other devices might this firm use to shift is demand curve? If price competition were used, at what price could the company sell 55,000 pairs?

tion. The seller attempts to avoid direct price comparisons with competitive products, so he makes his product actually or seemingly different from others. This concept was discussed in Chapter 10 in connection with product planning.

Some firms emphasize the *variety and quality of services* they offer to middlemen and final customers. Liberal credit terms, free delivery, unlimited returns, free installations, and product warranties are offered by many firms. Sometimes *convenience of location* can be used as the basis for nonprice competition. Suburban shopping centers stress this factor when competing with downtown shopping districts. At the manufacturing level, a firm may open sales branches in order to serve its market better.

Possibly the most important method of nonprice competition is *promotion*. In fact, along with product differentiation, promotion is a hallmark of nonprice competition and monopolistic competition. The topic of promotion is treated later, in Part 6.

QUESTIONS AND PROBLEMS

1. Under what marketing conditions is a company likely to use a variable-price policy? Can you name some firms which employ this policy, other than when a trade-in is involved?

2. What effects is unit pricing likely to have on a manufacturer's marketing program?

3. Are retailers ever faced with the problem of pricing multiple products? Explain.

4. Why might a retailer engage in price lining?

5. What are the advantages and disadvantages to manufacturers, retailers, and consumers of a law which makes resale price maintenance illegal?

6. Why are fewer manufacturers now printing a suggested list price on their products' packages?

7. Distinguish between leader pricing and predatory price-cutting.

8. Explain the reasoning underlying the zigzag shape of the demand curve in Fig. 15-1. Does this demand phenomenon actually exist in real life?

9. "The use of periodic, temporary price cuts to stimulate consumer demand is not a wise marketing strategy." Discuss.

10. How should a manufacturer of prefinished plywood interior wall paneling react if a competitor cuts his price?

11. What factors account for the increased use of nonprice competition?

12. On the basis of the topics covered in Chapters 14 and 15, establish a set of price policies for the manufacturer of a new glass cleaner which is sold through a broker to supermarkets. The manufacturer sells the product for $4.90 for a case of a dozen 16-ounce bottles.

CASES FOR PART FOUR

CASE 9. HILLCREST PRODUCTS LTD.

Pricing a new product

The executives of Hillcrest Products were trying to decide what the retail price should be for their new product—a glass cleaner—which was ready for marketing on a full-scale basis. Hillcrest Products was a new company, and the glass cleaner was its first product to be marketed commercially, although it had developed and market-tested several other cleaning products. Plans called for the introduction of the other products as soon as they could be given adequate attention by management. Since the company was small, the executives wisely did not wish to spread their efforts over too many products at one time.

The new glass cleaner was liquid in form and golden in color. It was competititve with such brands as Windex, Bon-Ami, Glass Wax, and Easy-Off. Windex was easily the leading brand in sales. Surveys of consumer brand preferences had shown that Windex was the brand purchased in about 70 percent of the households using commercial glass cleaners. No other brand reached over 10 percent of this market.

Management in the Hillcrest company felt that its product was demonstrably superior to anything on the market. Market tests had shown that once consumers tried this product, they strongly favored it over anything they had used previously. The product's main differential advantage was that it did not leave a film. The Hillcrest people felt that all other brands, regardless of their advertising claims, left a film. Also, the Hillcrest product was nontoxic, a distinct advantage in households where there were small children.

The product came in two attractively labeled packages—a Duo-Pak and a 16-ounce glass refill bottle. The Duo-Pak consisted of a 16-ounce bottle plus an 8-ounce empty clear plastic bottle with a plunger-type spray dispenser top. The intent was that the consumer would fill the plastic bottle and use it, rather than the glass bottle, for actual cleaning work. The fact that the plastic was unbreakable was another favorable differentiating product feature. Both the Duo-Paks and the refills were packed twelve to a case.

Hillcrest marketed through supermarket chains in the Atlantic provinces. The company used a separate food broker to reach the chains in each brokerage area.

Hillcrest had no desire to sell its product at uniform prices. In setting its own selling price, however, the company had to have some intended retail price in mind in order to allow for the necessary broker's fee and retailer's margin. The company planned to allow retailers a margin of 25 percent of their selling price, and the brokers a fee of 10 percent of Hillcrest's selling price.

The unit variable costs for Hillcrest's product packed in case lots were 33 cents for the Duo-Pak and 14 cents for the refill. These costs included the glass and plastic packages, the cardboard holder for the Duo-Pak, the liquid cleaner itself, the shipping carton, freight, and direct labor for filling the packages and preparing the cartons for shipment. Actually, the largest single direct costs were the glass and plastic packages. If the company could order these packages in lots of 10,000 or more, the unit cost could be reduced 2 cents.

The company conservatively expected to sell 100,000 16-ounce bottles during the first year in a 1:2 ratio of Duo-Paks to refills. It was difficult to estimate overhead very accurately at this stage. Administrative and office salaries would be about $7,000. Other overhead costs, including travel expense but excluding advertising, were figured at $5,000. Of course, the largest single indirect expense was advertising. The company expected to plow all available funds into advertising and display. If necessary, the company would operate at a loss for a few years rather than skimp on advertising. The advertising budget for the first year was set at $10,000.

The usual retail selling prices of competitive products in supermarkets were as follows:

Brand	Product	Price, in cents
Windex	20-oz bottle	40-45
Windex	14-oz aerosol can	59
Windex	8-oz bottle	24
Windex	Plunger-type spray dispenser	15
Easy-Off	15-oz aerosol can	49
Bon-Ami	15-oz aerosol can	65
Glass Wax	16-oz bottle	59

QUESTIONS

1. What unit retail prices do you recommend for the Duo-Pak and for the refill?
2. What should be Hillcrest's selling prices per case for Duo-Paks and for refills?
3. What is the break-even point in sales volume and in units, assuming that Duo-Paks and refills sell in a 1:2 ratio?

CASE 10: NOVA GREENHOUSES LIMITED*

Pricing policies and marketing plans

Nova Greenhouses is a florist producer-wholesaler which does business in Nova Scotia, New Brunswick, Prince Edward Island and Quebec. The head office and production houses are located in Kings County. The product mix for Nova can be classified as perishables, florist supplies, and certain vegetables.

Perishables are the natural flowers grown in the greenhouses; they include potted plants such as lilies, hydrageas, pot mums and azaleas; cut flowers such as poms, carnations, roses, gladioli, cymbidiums, tulips and iris; and greens (grown out-of-doors) which are used to complement flower arrangements. Samples of these perishables are not carried by the salesmen when they call upon customers. Therefore customers do not see what they are getting until their orders arrive. Florist supplies include artificial flowers, dried grasses, and all types of containers and materials used by the florist.

In 1972, the chief competitors of Nova Greenhouses in order of largest market share are Bains, Verdale, Gellineau and Lator in the Atlantic Provinces, and Verdale, Gellineau, Bernie's, Solace, Cultide and Bains in Quebec. Nova Greenhouses' distribution channel is very short and runs through to retailers, then to the consumer.

Nova Greenhouses distributes its products to 500 retailers, 260 of whom are in the Atlantic Provinces and 240 in Quebec. Nova Greenhouses does not distribute its products through chains. The company has both inside and field sales representatives totalling seven. Salesmen are paid on a straight salary and selling expenses are reimbursed. Three of the seven people joined the company less than three years ago while the oldest salesman had been with the company for twenty years. There are no specific territories assigned to salesmen, although the company has five men to cover the Atlantic region and two men for the Quebec region. The company does not promote its products through advertising. Thus the sales force plays a major role in marketing. To assist the salespeople, catalogues listing the company's florist supply products are mailed to present and prospective retailers. Most accounts are contacted by the company's salesmen on a weekly basis; however, the key accounts are called upon even more frequently. Recently the sales manager, son of the president, resigned.

Early in 1972 at a somewhat heated meeting of the Board of Directors, Felton Merlo, the president, was informed by the Board that they were not happy with the latest performance of Nova Greenhouses. The performance referred to is the move-

---

*Case prepared by Professor Lionel A. Mitchell, Acadia University.

ment of the company from recording yearly profits to the recording of a loss in 1969 and 1971 as shown in Table 1. Felton Merlo was told to reestablish the company on a profitable basis.

Felton Merlo was the founder of the company thirty-seven years ago. At that time, the company's objective was to serve the Nova Scotia market at a profitable rate of return. During the years from 1935 to 1972 inclusive the company had broadened its equity base in the process of growth and expansion. However, the period of accelerated growth in sales was the decade 1962 to 1971 inclusive as shown in Table 1.

The objectives of the company in 1962 according to Felton Merlo were "to earn a profit and reinvest in capital expansion any balances from depreciation fund and some profits." At the end of 1962, net fixed assets were $137,000; sales were $362,000; and net profit after taxes was $22,000 from 175 major customers, half of whom were in Nova Scotia, one quarter in New Brunswick, and the remainder in Newfoundland, Prince Edward Island and Quebec. Nova had approximately 44% of the market in 1962 and the chief competitors in order of market positions were Bains, P. Feathers, B. Feathers, Gellineau, Solace, Cultide, and Bernie's. Of the original thirteen including Nova, there are only nine operating today. Three of the nine have increased their volume and capacity, two are operating at decreased volume and capacity and the remainder are operating at about the same level. Bains sales in 1962 were $250,000 while the total of the rest was about $200,000.

In 1971, Verdale, which was selling east and west of Ontario and to a lesser extent in the Atlantic Provinces, had sales of almost $6,000,000. However, Nova had about half of the market in the Atlantic Provinces where the total sales by wholesalers, is $3,500,000. Nova's net fixed assets at the end of 1971 were $800,000; sales were $1,984,000; and net loss was $43,000.

In Felton Merlo's opinion, although the pattern of distribution for flowers and florists supplies has been changing, especially in the last decade as a result of the growth of shopping centres, the company has tried some new outlets in the past three years that did not prove successful. Nevertheless, the company increased production in 1968 and 1969. It moved into Quebec in more force in 1968 when a warehouse-sales outlet was opened there and it did seem to be holding its own there after some initial problems, but a lot of work remains to be done in that region.

Table 1. Nova Sales for the Period 1962-1971.

Year	Sales	Profit (loss) after taxes
1962	$ 362,000	$22,000
1963	420,000	5,000
1964	560,000	14,000
1965	723,000	11,000
1966	851,000	9,000
1967	1,010,000	47,000
1968	1,203,000	15,000
1969	1,520,000	(37,000)
1970	1,828,000	78,000
1971	1,984,000	(43,000)

Many problems confronted Nova. One such problem began when one of their key executives retired two years ago. He was an extremely knowledgeable man in the greenhouse business and, naturally, when such experts retire it takes some time for the replacement to adjust. Another type of problem arises from lack of pricing policy and control over pricing at the retail level. For example, pot mums sold to retailers at $2.00 each were in turn sold by the retailer to the consumer at $6.00 each; azaleas sold to the retailer at $4.75 were in turn sold the consumer at $16.00; roses sold to the retailer at $4.50 per dozen were sold by the retailer to the consumer at $16.00 per dozen. In other words, retailers were putting a markup of up to 300 percent on the prices shown in Exhibits 1 to 5.

Exhibit 1   Potted Plants—Price List

Lilies	9 per Carton	20 cartons & over @	$2.00
		12-19 cartons	2.10
		6-11 cartons	2.20
		1- 5 cartons	2.25
Hydrangeas	6 per Carton		3.50
			4.25
			5.00
Pot Mums			
4″	15 per Carton		.75
5″	6 per Carton		1.65
6″	6 per Carton		2.00
8″	4 per Carton		3.75
Azaleas	9″		4.25
	11″		4.75
	13″		5.25

Exhibit 2   Cut Flowers—Price List

Poms—White, Yellow, Mauve, Bronze	15 Bunches per Ctn. @	$1.90
	Other than Ctn. lot	2.00
Disbuds—White, Yellow, Mauve, Bronze	12 per Ctn.	1.90
	Other than Ctn. lot	2.00
Commercials—White, Yellow	32/ctn. #1	.50
	Other than Ctn. lot	.55
	40/ctn. #2	.40
	Other than Ctn. lot	.45
Carnations	#1	3.25
	#2	2.75
Miniature Carnations	Bunch	2.75

Roses   24″   21″   18″   15″   12″   9″
  dozen 6.00   5.25   4.50   3.75   3.00   2.25

Gladiolus		2.75
Cymbidiums		1.90
Tulips	Dozen	2.35
Iris	Dozen	2.75

Exhibit 3   Artificial Flowers Price List

#		Pack	Price Box
1	Carnation	50	$2.25
2	Rose	50	2.25
5	Peony	25	2.50
6	Aster	50	2.50
13 Georgine	50		2.75
17 Cherry Rose	100		3.00
20 Mum	50		5.00
21 Dahlia	50		2.75
24 Carnation	50		3.00
	Cloth Valley	1 gross	2.10

Exhibit 4   Artificial Flowers Price List

		Per Doz.	Per Gross
CH	8328 Spanish Daisy	$1.60	$17.50
MK	13102 Carnation	.80	8.60
WQ	12812 Rose	.95	10.40
KC	5064 Rose	.80	8.70
DE	17841 Dahlia	.85	9.40
ND	5555 Poppy	.85	9.40
WS	149041 Dahlia/Spray	1.60	17.40
SR	20602 Tulip	.95	10.00
FA	4729 Daisy	.85	9.20
YA	136 Straw Flower	.45	4.60
FL	3918 Rose Pick	.50	4.75/100
DE	17824 Rose Pick	.50	5.20/gross, not illus.
DA	7114 Lily Pick	.70	7.50
KN	15801 Carnation Pick	.65	7.50
MK	13164 Lily of the Valley	.85	9.40
WK	7824 Hibiscus Pick	.90	9.90
VB	4919 Pin Mum Bush	3.30	
WA	2055 Peach Blossom	1.70	18.75
DD	12902 Baby Orchid	.65	7.50
KR	17449 Pansy Cluster	1.25	13.40

Exhibit 5   Florist Supplies—GREENS Price List

Asparagus	$1.50
Leather Leaf	1.50
Boxwood	1.70
Huckleberry	1.70
Salal	1.70

Scotch Broom	1.70
B.C. Cedar	1.70
Eucalyptus	3.00
Emerald Short	1.50
Emerald Long	2.00
Laurel	2.50
Heather	2.75
Cedar	1.80
Acacia	3.60

Still on the subject of pricing, it seems that some of Nova Greenhouses' key personnel were confused about costs and pricing as evidence by the comments of two of its personnel.

"We should adopt a policy of pricing in such a manner that we make a certain percentage return above our costs of producing the products," stated Sam Mann, the recently appointed sales manager.

"But we do not know and have never known in the five odd years I have been here what our costs of each product are," said one of the directors of the company.

"That is not true! We know what it costs us to produce the products. For example, take pot mums, here is what it costs us," said Nathan Hanna, the production manager, showing the costing sheet attached as Exhibit 6.

"I am not sure that cost and pricing is our main problem although I agree that it is a problem. I think that the very nature of our product and the manner in which we market them is more of a problem," was the opinion of Nelson Random, the controller. He continued: "For example, roses are a five-year crop. We get some in the first year but the peak production is around the third year. Thus once we have planted them we will leave the bushes in the ground for five years. On the other hand, poms are a 90-day crop; then again there are some products that we produce for a special season such as Easter and Christmas.

"To give another example, using another of our product lines, we must remember that florists sell everything from flowers to strictly foliage plants such as rubber trees, and what we call florist supplies, which include flower boxes, flower arrangement containers, ornaments, stuffed animals, pottery, wooden tubs, wrapping paper, and many more items. We cannot put different flowers together in the same greenhouse. Under these circumstances, what must we do to get the greatest efficiency from our employed resources?

"In general, it should be noted that most flower sales are to florists but some sales are made to Simpsons, K-Mart, Stedmans and other department stores and hardware stores. On the other hand florist supplies, although sold mainly to florists, have a high potential for sales to other retailers depending upon the type of supplies one is talking about," Nelson Random concluded.

"Are you saying that we should place more emphasis on florist supplies?" Jean Marcott, the salesman for the Quebec region enquired of the controller.

"It seems to me that the ability to increase cut flower sales is limited unless the public is educated to a greater degree to 'say it with flowers' rather than with a box of candy. Couple this with additional advertising and cut flower sales will increase, but only to a point. Nova Greenhouses would have to consider building more greenhouses that may or may not be required year round depending upon the demand for year-round flowers as against possibly increased special days' produc-

Exhibit 6   *A Grower's Cost of Production for*
                             a six (6) inch Pot Mum

I. PLANT COSTS AND TRANSPORTATION
   5 cuttings @ 6¢ =   .30
   (cutting cost ranges between 5 + 7¢ each according to volume,
   including royalty @ 6/10th of a cent)
   Transportation (air, rail, truck, etc.) @ approximately 4/10th of
   a cent per cutting × 5 =   .02
                                                           Total   .32

II. POTTING COSTS
    Container: 6" clay pot   .12
               (6" plastic pot)   (.07)
    Soil + Potting   .05
                                                                        .17 (.12)
                                               Sub Total   .49 (.44)

III. GROWING COSTS
    All costs incurred in bringing plant to maturity for sale.
    Includes: labor, administration, water, fertilizers, insecticide
    chemicals, growth retardants, heat, lights, shade cloth, CO_2,
    taxes, depreciation, insurance, interest, etc. (to calculate divide
    total sq. ft. bench area into total overhead costs.)
    7¢ per week per sq. ft. of bench area approximate production
    cost for pot plants to cover above growing costs.
    Approximately 11 weeks total crop time (ranges between 10-14
    weeks, depending upon time of year + varieties). One 6" pot
    occupying 1.4 sq. ft. of bench area at 14" × 14" spacing costs
    9.8¢ per week @ 11 weeks + (for every additional week on the
    bench add 9.8¢)   1.08
                                               Sub Total   1.57

IV. LOST FACTOR (Disease, culls, breakage, etc.)
    COST   approximately 5%   .08
                                                                            1.65

V. MARKETING COSTS (Selling, advertising, sleeving
                    packaging, handling, transportation and
                    delivery) @ 25¢   .41
                                                                            2.06

VI. PROFIT (5-10%)   @ 5%   .11
    Take your pick   @ 10%   *or*   .21
                                      Total Cost 2.14 or $2.27
                                      Minimum wholesale price   2.17

tion. This is important as it relates to the fact some houses would be closed down
for part of the year and you know what that does to fixed costs. Therefore, it seems
possible that perhaps Nova should get more deeply involved with the 'florist supply' area. Is it not a fact that more florists are selling items that do not necessarily

relate to flower sales? Compare a florist in a small town with one in a large shopping centre and the difference in the type of goods sold is extremely large. Caution is required in this area to minimize the possibility of large inventory buildup. Perhaps it is unwise to get too involved here because Nova Greenhouses really does not have the expertise necessary to maintain this properly."

"I think our pricing is too rigid, coupled with the fact that we do not pay enough attention to our small customers when there is scarcity of supply but expect them to respond favourably when there is abundance of supply. There should be some relationship established between the products in the lines and the pricing, as well as some policy as to how we are going to deal with certain customers. All in all, we should be aiming to increase our sales by a target amount," suggested Jean Marcott.

"Looking at some problem areas involving customers, we have some small customers who buy in two and three box lots and some of these will never become large," said one of the senior salespeople.

"There are others who may grow," said another salesman, in defense of the small customer.

"We have some customers to whom we ship C.O.D. because the amount owing by them is very large and we are having difficulty collecting from them. Moreover, there are some customers who return to us our competitors' goods," stated the inside sales manager.

"Alright, gentlemen, before proceeding further with listing more problems faced by this company, suppose we look briefly at some facts about our company," said Felton Merlo, the president. "In spite of the problems enumerated, we have set as our objectives for 1972 retaining dominant market share of 55% in the Maritimes and, of course, bringing back the business to a profitable footing. As longer term objectives, that is, within the next five years, we want to increase our Nova Scotia market from 60% to 70%, our Prince Edward Island market from 10% to 20%, our New Brunswick market from 25% to 50%, and our Quebec market share from 15% to 30%. To achieve our objectives we intend to (a) improve the quality standard of our products, (b) give better service to the 'better paying' customers. This means that we will be more critical of sales to customers who provide little contribution to profits as well as those who are difficult to sell and those who are slow in paying their accounts.

"The market mix elements will show that in the case of our products these can be grouped into four categories (1) perishable flowers, (2) florist supplies, (3) vegetables, and (4) import perishables. In 1971, the sales for the four categories were $1,031,500 for category No. 1; $468,000 for No. 2; $22,600 for No. 3; and $461,900 for No. 4. Product lines profits are in proportion to sales. Our prices are based on cost-plus pricing which takes into consideration supply, demand and competitors' pricing. The low sales months are July, August, and September, while the peak months are December, February, March, April (Easter) and May. The area over which we can effectively compete is limited by our distribution system which has certain constraints such as time and shipping costs.

"In the promotional mix, heavy emphasis is placed on selling with very little emphasis on direct advertising. In spite of my earlier remark to the effect that I thought that patterns of distribution for flowers and florist supplies have been changing, we are still using the same channel that we used more than a decade ago.

"Then, from what you have all said here today, it would seem pretty obvious that we need to review our pricing policies and practices.

"Now gentlemen, some of you are the products of well-known universities and agricultural colleges and have been with us for many years while others have joined us recently. Nevertheless, you all have had experience in business and are capable, intelligent men. You are all aware of what is happening in this company. Therefore, let us pool our knowledge and resources and decide: What do we do now? Where do we go from here? What plans can we come up with for marketing in 1972 and beyond?"

CASE 11: CENTRAL OPTICAL COMPANY

Action to meet strong price competition

The two Plachy brothers, Homer and Ted, who owned and managed the Central Optical Company, were trying to determine what would be the most effective pricing strategy for meeting the increasing competition from chain budget opticians who sold their products at a much lower price than did Central Optical.

The Central Optical Company, which sold high-quality eyeglasses, was the largest optician in a western Ontario city. The company had its main store in the downtown area, plus a branch in each of two nearby shopping centers. Homer and Ted's father, Mr. Conrad Plachy, started the company in 1937 and turned it over to his sons upon his retirement in 1960. Homer supervised all sales activities in the main store as well as the manufacturing of lenses. Ted managed all other business activities, in addition to supervising sales and service in the two branch stores.

Central Optical did its own lens grinding, using the newest and most efficient grinding equipment available. Other companies the size of Central Optical generally would send their lenses out to be ground rather than doing it themselves. The Plachy brothers believed they were one of the most automated retail optician firms in Canada.

Since its inception the company has had a steady growth, and financially Central Optical has been quite successful. Management attributed the firm's success to the rapid growth of their city and the somewhat necessary nature of their product, as well as to their high-quality service and eyeglasses.

Last year the company's sales exceeded $400,000. Although this was an increase of $25,000 over the previous year's sales, the net profit last year was $10,000 *under* expectations. The two brothers attributed the lower-than-expected profits to the rising cost of goods sold. Plastic and glass lenses plus the eyeglass frames were continuing to increase in price.

At the same time, Central Optical had not raised the retail price on its finished eyeglasses in more than five years. Homer and Ted were reluctant to raise prices, because already their prices were higher than most other opticians in the city. Central Optical felt it was unethical to advertise, because of the professional nature of the business. Consequently, the company depended upon strong customer loyalty, word-of-mouth advertising, and doctors' recommendations for its continued growth and success. A price increase might jeopardize those promotional stimulants, reasoned Homer and Ted.

While eyeglasses were the company's main product, Central Optical also sold contact lenses, sunglasses, eyeglass cleaner and tissue, and other related products. Of all the products carried by the company, eyeglass frames provided the highest gross margin—40 per cent. While the price range was $10 to $20 for men's frames and $10 to $30 on frames for women, the frames most frequently selected sold at retail for about $14. The frames usually amounted to about 65 per cent of the total price of the eyelgasses. Most of the completed spectacles (frame and lenses) cost the customer from $20 to $30.

Because Central Optical had a much higher investment in lens-grinding equipment, the company earned a slightly lower net profit on lens sales than do most opticians. The owners felt, however, that the added expense was justified by the fact that they could fill customers' orders within one day. Most other opticians sent lenses away to be ground, and this usually took five to six days. The company purchased all its glass from nationally known manufacturers. Moreover, Central Optical bought only the highest quality orthogon glass, which cost about two dollars per blank unground lens. The retail customer's price for these lenses after grinding was usually in the neighborhood of $10 to $12. The company bought lenses in lots as large as $20,000, in an attempt to earn maximum quantity discounts and thus offset some of the high costs involved in the grinding operations.

During the past five years, Central Optical's share of market had been reduced significantly by an influx of low-priced, "budget" opticians into the city. Prior to that time Central Optical had the market virtually to itself. Two of the largest new competitors were separate subsidiary divisions of a national chain of jewelry stores. These two new firms sold eyeglasses for as low as $12. These chain opticians and other similar low-price firms were able to sell at such prices for three reasons. First they had their own central manufacturing plant for making frames and grinding lenses. Second, they often imported frames and unground lenses from Japan. Japanese lenses could be purchased preground for as little as 68 cents each. Japanese frames, which looked to be identical to $18 Canadian frames, cost about one dollar. Third, these companies used a much lower quality of plastic and glass in their frames and lenses. Yet upon looking at these glasses, the normal customer could not tell the difference between the high-quality and lower-quality glasses.

These low-price firms sold a large quantity of eyeglasses, partially because they advertised so heavily. Last year the two chain subsidiaries spent about $40,000 in local advertising in Central Optical's market alone. The Plachy brothers thought this advertising had also helped to increase primary demand, because Central Optical's sales also increased so much ($25,000) last year. The fact still remained, however, that Central Optical's management was convinced that the success of the four low-priced opticians now in town was likely to intensify the competition, and thus further cut into Central's declining share of market.

Central Optical thus was faced with increasing competition from low-price firms at the same time that Central's costs of materials were steadily increasing. Smaller optical companies in a similar position had either raised their prices or been forced to use cheaper materials. Through the years, Central Optical had been proud of its reputation for providing the very highest quality of service and eyewear. Now, however, management in Central Optical was very reluctant to raise their already high prices. Yet their alternatives seemed equally unattractive. The brothers realized they could increase their gross margin only by (1) raising prices, (2) maintaining existing price levels and cutting the cost (and thus the quality) of goods sold, or (3) cutting prices and also reducing cost of goods sold, thus appealing to the low-price segment of the market.

QUESTION

1. What action should Central Optical take to improve its profits and competitive position?

CASE 12: TARTAN DRUG STORES*

Using price/quantity relationships to evaluate pricing policy

Winter of 1975 found Miss Lorie Atfelter, an employee of Tartan Drug Stores Ltd. of Toronto, engaged in a special project for Mr. Walter Reginald, Marketing Vice-President of Tartan Drug Stores Ltd. Mr. Reginald sought to review the pricing policies of Tartan Drug Stores for their vitamin products, and so commissioned Miss Atfelter, a B.Comm. graduate of the University of Toronto, to prepare a special report. Vitamin E was chosen as the specific vitamin product to be studied.

Miss Atfelter decided to concentrate upon sales in one store. During the study period (January 9 to February 20, 1976, inclusive), Miss Atfelter descended upon one of the company's stores, where she worked as a clerk and kept careful watch over the sales of Vitamin E. At the end of February 1976, Miss Atfelter submitted the following report, and returned to her usual job of executive secretary and assistant to the Vice-President of Marketing.

March 1, 1976

INTERNAL MEMORANDUM

TO: Mr. W. J. Reginald

FROM: Miss L. Atfelter

SUBJECT: Analysis of Pricing of Vitamin E
200 I.U. and 400 I.U. for Four
Different Brands at Different Prices.

I collected data for 100 capsule size only in the 200 I.U. and 400 I.U. strengths. Table 1 presents the basic data on amounts sold each week by brand. Table 2 presents the quantity and percent per week and total for 200 I.U. according to price. Table 3 presents data on the 400 I.U. strength.

Table 1. Amounts of Vitamin E Sold Each Week in Locking Plaza Store.

Brand	Strength	Week 1 (Jan.9-16)	Week 2	Week 3	Week 4	Week 5	Week 6
Tartan	200	12	15	9	11	15	12
	400	14	10	12	15	12	16
Wampole	200	12	9	7	11	10	12
	400	10	13	11	14	15	13
Abbott	200	7	8	6	7	9	9
	400	19	18	12	16	18	15
Webber	200	2	1	2	0	2	3
	400	3	4	2	5	3	4

---

* Case prepared by Prof. G. H. Haines, Jr., Professor, and C. A. Rees, student in the B.Comm. programme, University of Toronto.

Table 2. Quantity and percent per week and total for 200 I.U. According to Price, Locking Plaza Store.

Tartan price	—	$3.79
Wampole price	—	$3.96
Abbott Price	—	$5.99
Webber price	—	$8.39

Brand	Week 1 Quantity	Week 1 Percent	Week 2 Q	Week 2 %	Week 3 Q	Week 3 %	Week 4 Q	Week 4 %	Week 5 Q	Week 5 %	Week 6 Q	Week 6 %
Webber	2	6.0	1	3.0	2	8	0	0	2	6	3	.84
Abbott	7	21.2	8	24.2	6	25	7	24	9	25	9	25.0
Wampole	12	36.4	9	27.3	7	29	11	38	10	28	12	33.3
Tartan	12	36.4	15	45.5	9	38	11	38	15	41	12	33.3
Total	33		33		24		29		36		36	

TOTALS

Brand	Quantity	Percent
Webber	10	5.25
Abbott	46	24.08
Wampole	61	31.94
Tartan	74	38.74
Total	191	

As you can see from the percentages in Table 2, the 200 I.U. Vitamin E shows a definite downward sloping demand. That is, a higher percentage is sold of the cheapest brand than of any other brand. The most expensive brand sells the least.

Unlike the 200 I.U. strength, the 400 I.U. does not have a downward sloping demand curve. If we examine the percent of total sales each week the least two expensive brands sell about the same percent of the total sales. The next most expensive brand, Abbott, sells the largest percent of total sales, while the most expensive brand sells the smallest amount for the entire six weeks. Why do the demand curves differ for the two strengths? Why do people buy the more expensive brand when the cheaper brands are exactly the same?

Analysis. The data were recorded for a six-week period in the relatively small Locking Plaza drug store where I worked. I recorded the sales of the four brands of Vitamin E we carry for the 200 I.U. and 400 I.U. gel strengths only. Webber and Tartan have strengths from 75 I.U. to 800 I.U., but to be consistent, I recorded only the data for the two most popular strengths. All brands contain natural Vitamin E, so the contents of the products are exactly the same. Only the brand name and price are different.

Vitamin E was first discovered by a laboratory that was sponsored by Webber Pharmaceuticals, hence Webber is automatically associated with Vitamin E. While

Table 3. Quantity and percent per week and total for 400 I.U. According to Price, Locking Plaza Store

	Tartan price	—	$ 5.69
	Wampole price	—	$ 6.34
	Abbott price	—	$ 8.99
	Webber price	—	$16.19

Brand	Week 1 Quantity	Week 1 Percent	Week 2 Q	Week 2 %	Week 3 Q	Week 3 %	Week 4 Q	Week 4 %	Week 5 Q	Week 5 %	Week 6 Q	Week 6 %
Webber	3	6.53	4	8.9	2	5.41	5	10	3	6.25	4	8.33
Abbott	19	41.30	18	40.0	12	32.43	16	32	18	37.50	15	31.25
Wampole	10	21.74	13	28.9	11	29.73	14	28	15	31.25	13	27.08
Tartan	14	30.43	10	22.2	12	32.43	15	30	12	25.00	16	33.34
Total	46		45		37		50		48		48	

TOTALS

Brand	Quantity	Percent
Webber	21	7.66
Abbott	98	35.77
Wampole	76	27.74
Tartan	79	28.83
Total	274	

some research has been done on Vitamin E, there are still a lot of varied opinions as to its value. While different grades of the vitamin are all available in Canada, the companies all have to put the same International Units of Vitamin E in each capsule. If a company uses a poorer grade, it must use more to get the same I.U. content as a company that uses the best grade oil.

Most pharmaceutical companies advertise to the doctors and pharmacists rather than to the general public. The feeling is that these are the people who will be recommending their products. Webber is perhaps the best advertised and tells the physician a little about the drug. Most doctors usually recommend the 400 I.U. for therapeutic use, and often tend to recommend the more expensive, well established, pharmaceutical companies' brands.

The largest percentage of sales for the data collected for the 200 I.U. strength is from the cheapest brand. If we analyze the price to quantity ratio, we see that price varies inversely with the quantity sold. This produces, for the 200 I.U. strength, a perfect downward sloping demand curve. We may conclude from this that people buy more of the cheapest brand, and that makes or brands do not have as much to do with the sale as the price does.

The above analysis fails, however, for the 400 I.U. strength. The largest percentage sold in this strength is of the second most expensive brand, Abbott, a well known pharmaceutical company. We see that for the 400 I.U. strength we have a downward sloping demand curve to a point. Then it slopes upward. This, we can conclude, means that people would rather buy the slightly more expensive brand than the cheapest brand. This strange phenomenon may be accounted for in a number of ways.

Firstly, since a lot of people who take this strength take it for therapeutic use, they may believe that the more expensive brand is better than the cheapest. Whereas, those who take the 200 I.U. just take it because they think they need to take something, and so feel the cheapest brand is good enough.

Secondly, most of the doctors recommend the 400 I.U. and usually recommend a brand name of a well known pharmaceutical company. The popular brands are more expensive than the other brands and this could account for the strange shaped demand curve. Most people also demand the same brand as what the doctor recommends to them as they believe the others not to be so active.

Thirdly, people act in strange ways. They may believe that to get the best quality they have to pay a higher price. While this may be true in some cases, it is not so in all. The analysis of the 400 I.U. strength of Vitamin E is one such case. The quality is the same for each brand and only the price differs.

Conclusions. Since the data were only collected for a relatively short period of time, the above analyses may not hold true for the long run. We find that the 200 I.U. strength has an inverse relationship of quantity sold to price. The 400 I.U., however, sells more of the slightly more expensive brand than it does of the cheapest brands.

QUESTIONS

1. Should the report be accepted?
2. What are the implications for pricing Tartan Brand Vitamin E—should the price of 400 I.U. Vitamin E be changed?

DISTRIBUTION STRUCTURE

DISTRIBUTION CHANNELS AND THE RETAIL MARKET

Our product is now ready for its market. The next general step in the marketing process is to determine what methods and routes will be used to bring the product to the market. This involves establishing distribution strategies, including selecting channels of distribution and providing for physical handling and distribution. First, however, we should make certain that management understands something of the concepts underlying the distribution system.

CHANNELS OF DISTRIBUTION

A *middleman* is an independent business concern standing between the producer and the ultimate household consumer or industrial user. A middleman renders services in connection with the purchase and/or sale of products as they move from producer to consumer. Either he takes title to the merchandise as it flows between producer and consumer or he actively negotiates the transfer of title.

The essence of a middleman's operation is his active and prominent role in negotiations involving the buying and selling of goods. His income arises directly from the proceeds of these transactions. It is his part in the transfer of ownership which differentiates a middleman from other institutions, such as banks, insurance companies, and transportation firms, which help in the marketing process but do not take title and are not actively involved in purchase and sales negotiations. Whether a firm actually handles the products is not relevant to the definition of a middleman. Some middlemen warehouse and transport merchandise, while others do not physically handle it at all.

A common method of classifying middlemen is on the basis of whether they take title to the products involved. *Merchant* middlemen actually take ownership title to the goods they are helping to market. *Agent* middlemen do not take title, but they do actively assist in the transfer of title. Brokers and manufacturers' agents are examples of agent middlemen. The two major groups of merchant middlemen are wholesalers and retailers. It should be noted particularly that retailers are merchant middlemen.

A *channel of distribution* (sometimes called a *trade channel*) for a product is the route taken by the *title* to the goods as they move from the producer to the ultimate consumer or industrial user. A channel always includes both the producer and the final customer for the product, as well as all agent and merchant middlemen involved in the title transfer. The channel does *not* include firms such as railroads, banks and other nonmiddlemen institutions which render a marketing service but play no major role in negotiating purchases and sales. If a consumer buys apples from the grower at his roadside stand, or if a manufacturer sells a shirt by mail direct to a college student, the channel is from producer to consumer. If the shirt manufacturer sold to a department store which in turn sold to the college student, the channel would be producer—retailer—consumer.

The channel for a product extends to the last person who buys it without making any significant change in its form. When its form is altered and another product emerges, a new channel is started. When lumber is milled and made into furniture, there are separate channels for the lumber and the furniture. The channel for lumber may be lumber mill—broker—furniture manufacturer. The channel for the finished furniture might be furniture manufacturer—furniture wholesaler—retail furniture store—consumer.

CONCEPT OF CHANNEL STRUCTURE

To understand a channel of distribution, we should first recognize that it is a structure. A structure is organized and evolves in order to do a job. As related to channels of distribution, a structure may represent a choice among alternative channels, or it may involve a description of the different marketing situations faced by the various firms (retailers, wholesalers, producers) within the structure. It may be considered as a series of functions which must be performed in order to market products effectively. Any structure may be evaluated from a socioeconomic point of view.

The distribution structure is a highly complex organism. Its constantly changing nature makes thoughtful analysis difficult and renders a description of it quickly out of date. Another factor obscuring a careful study of the distribution structure is the oversimplified treatment it receives in marketing literature and Statistics Canada data. In the census, each separate establishment is placed in a traditional, single category depending upon which category represented over 50 percent of the firm's annual sales volume. Thus if a company does 60 percent of its business at retail and the rest at wholesale, it is classed as a retailer. This system of classification suggests a more orderly structure than actually exists. It effectively reduces the number of categories into which firms are sorted and avoids hybrid, nondescript classifications. However, hybridity is too common among marketing firms to be ignored.[1]

A CHANNEL AS A TOTAL SYSTEM

To maximize benefits to all groups concerned (producers, middlemen, and consumers), a channel of distribution should be treated as a unit—a total system of action. Within this systems concept, a channel would include the marketing organizational units of a manufacturer as well as the organizations of the middlemen used by this manufacturer. Consequently, there is a real need to coordinate the manufacturer's activities with those of the middlemen used in the distribution of the given product. A distribution system properly operated then becomes a significant competitive differential advantage for a company.

Unfortunately, a trade channel all too often is treated as a fragmented assortment of competing, independently operating organizations. A manufacturer may view his own retailers as his competition, or a middleman may be in conflict with his supplier, rather than recognizing that the real threat is other middlemen or the distribution systems of other manufacturers. That is, the real competition is between distribution systems of different producers, rather than between the organizational units within one producer's system.[2]

It is true that power structures do exist in trade channels simply by virtue of the fact that a distribution system is comprised of separate, independent companies. Power struggles may also exist between groups *within* a company. Two marketing units—the advertising department and the field sales force, for instance—may look upon each other as competitors, which is quite contrary to the philosophy of total marketing underlying the market concept.

A CHANNEL AS AN INVESTMENT

Management should also recognize that a channel represents a financial investment in the same sense that the plant, equipment, or any other asset is an investment. If profit maximization is a company goal, then the selection of a marketing channel should be based on the estimated rate of return to be earned on the capital investment in the channels. Thus "the process of channel selection should be considered as an investment decision by a manufacturing firm."[3]

---

1 Philip McVey, "Are Channels of Distribution What the Textbooks Say?" *Journal of Marketing,* January, 1960, p. 61.

2 For the notion that treating a channel as a system of marketing functions rather than as a sequence of institutions is more useful in understanding marketing channels, see William P. Dommermuth and R. Clifton Andersen, "Distribution Systems: Firms, Functions, and Efficiencies," *MSU Business Topics,* Spring, 1969, pp. 51-56.

3 Eugene W. Lambert, Jr. "Financial Considerations in Choosing a Marketing Channel," *Business Topics,* Winter, 1966, p. 25. This author suggests that channel choice is determined primarily by financial considerations rather than what are generally thought of as marketing factors.

IMPORTANCE OF MIDDLEMEN

In any economy except a very primitive one, it is often not economically feasible for a producer to deal directly with an ultimate consumer. Think for a moment how inconvenient our daily existence would be if there were no retail middlemen—no drugstores, newspaper stands, supermarkets, or gasoline stations. If we live in a large city, we might think that we could buy things wholesale, but if there were *no* middlemen, there would be no wholesalers.

Concentration, equalization, dispersion. Frequently the quantity and assortment of goods produced by a firm are out of balance with the variety and amounts wanted by consumers or industrial users. A businessman needs paper, pencils, typewriters, and desks. A homeowner wants grass seed, topsoil, fertilizer, a rake, and a roller, and eventually he hopes to need a lawn mower. No single firm produces all the items either of these users want, and no producer may sell any of them in the small quantity the user desires. Obviously there is a need for someone to perform the function of balancing or equalizing what various producers turn out with what the final customers want. This is part of the task of marketing.

The job to be done involves (1) collecting or concentrating the output of various producers, (2) subdividing these quantities into amounts desired by the customers and gathering the various items together in the assortment wanted, and (3) dispersing this assortment to consumers or industrial buyers. In a few cases, the task of concentrating, equalizing, and dispersing is simple enough to be done by the producer and final customer working closely together. A copper miner may sell directly to the smelter firm; iron-ore producers may sell directly to the steel mill. In most cases, however, the producer and consumer are not able to work out the proper quantity and assortment. A specialist in concentration, equalization, and dispersion is needed, and this is the role of the middleman.

Creation of utility. Middlemen aid in the creation of time, place, and possession utilities. In classical economic theory, production is defined as the creation of utility, and several types of utility are recognized. One is form utility, in which something is added in a chemical or physical manner to a product to make it more valuable. Lumber is made into furniture and flour into bread, thus creating form utility. Other utilities are equally valuable to the user. Furniture located in Montreal or Hamilton in April is of little value to people in Victoria or Halifax who want the furniture to give as Christmas presents. Transporting the furniture from Montreal to Halifax increases its value: place utility is added. Storing it from April to December adds another value—time utility. The final value of possession utility is created when the Victoria and Halifax families buy the items.[4]

PROBLEMS IN MANAGEMENT OF DISTRIBUTION CHANNELS

To establish the channels of distribution for a firm, a marketing executive must undertake the following tasks:

---

4 For a summary of the concepts and theories which have been developed to explain marketing channels, see Edwin H. Lewis, *Marketing Channels: Structure and Strategy*, McGraw-Hill Book Company, New York, 1968, chap. 7; see also Louis P. Bucklin, *A Theory of Distribution Channel Structure*, University of California, Institute of Business and Economic Research, Berkeley, 1966.

Managerial tasks	Discussed in Chapter
1. Understand the retail and wholesale markets and the types of middlemen institutions available in each.	16-18
2. Understand the conflicts which typically exist between and within channels.	19
3. Decide what channels to use and what type of middlemen (if any) to use at each stage.	20
4. Determine the number of outlets desired in each stage.	20
5. Select the individual middlemen.	20
6. Establish a system for physical distribution of the product.	21

NATURE OF RETAIL MARKET

If a supermarket sells some floor wax to a gift shop operator who wants to polish the floor tiles in his store, is this a retail sale? Can a wholesaler or a manufacturer engage in retailing? When a gas station runs a big sale on tires and advertises that the products are being sold at the wholesale price, is this retailing? "Retailing," "retail store," "retail sales," and "retailers" are terms that should be defined not only to clarify their legal implications but also to avoid any possible misunderstanding in later discussions.

Retailing includes all activities directly related to the sale of goods or services to the ultimate consumer for personal, nonbusiness use. While most retailing is done through retail stores, it may be done by any institution. A manufacturer selling brushes or cosmetics door-to-door is engaged in retailing, as is a farmer selling strawberries at a roadside stand. Any firm—manufacturer, wholesaler, or retail store—which sells something to the ultimate consumer for his nonbusiness use, regardless of *how* it is sold (by person, telephone, mail, or vending machine) or *where* it is sold (in a store or at the consumer's home), is making a *retail sale*.

A *retailer* or a *retail store* is a business enterprise which sells *primarily* to ultimate consumers for nonbusiness use. A key word in the last definition is "primarily." A retailer may sell items infrequently to industrial users, but these are wholesale transactions, not retail sales. If over one-half of his dollar volume of business comes from sales to ultimate consumers, that is, sales at retail, he is classed as a retailer. The word "dealer" is used frequently in business and generally is synonymous with "retailer." In contrast, a distributor is a wholesaling middleman.

EASE OF ENTRY INTO RETAILING

It is easier to go into retailing than virtually any other trade, profession, or line of business. To practice medicine or law, one must pass provincial licensing examinations. To start a manufacturing or wholesaling firm, one must have a substantial sum of money to acquire a plant, equipment, and merchandise. To enter a laboring trade in many parts of the country, one must acquire union membership, and some unions have strict apprenticeship provisions. But to operate a retail store there are no examinations, and the necessary business licenses are easy to acquire. Furthermore, many people entering retailing have the idea that no real training or special experience is needed.

There are important economic and social implications in the ease with which people may enter retailing. Often, underfinanced, poorly qualified people come into the field. Soon they fail, thus causing economic waste and inefficient use of human and economic resources. Mortality is higher among retail establishments than in any other classification of business and industry.

On the bright side, ease of entry results in fierce competition and added value for the consumer. Except perhaps in a small town, it is rather difficult to establish an unregulated, monopolistic position in retailing. Certainly, large-scale enterprises exist in retailing, and in some markets there is substantial concentration of business among a relatively small percentage of firms. In a study recently completed for the Food Prices Review Board, Dr. Bruce Mallen concluded that concentration in the Canadian retail food industry led to excessive market power and a decline in competition. The result of such power can be that in certain markets food prices are higher than they would be under a more competitive structure. Mallen found that in some Canadian cities, the four major food chains (Safeway, Loblaws, Dominion, and Steinbergs) account for more than 90% of total retail food sales, while in four markets (St. John's, Kitchener, Calgary and Edmonton) one chain holds more than 50% of the retail food market.[5]

SIZE OF RETAIL MARKET

There are about 160,000 retail stores in Canada, and their total annual sales volume in 1974 was almost $45 billion (see Table 16-1). In contrast, there are about 122,000 service trade establishments, about 44,000 wholesaler locations, and about 31,000 manufacturers. The figures in Table 16-1 show that there has been a remarkable stability over the past fifteen years in the total number of retail stores in Canada. In spite of the population increase and rising consumer income over the past twenty to twenty-five years, there were not many more retail establishments in 1974 than in 1961. In absolute amounts, total retail sales volume today is almost three times that at the beginning of the 1960s. Of course, the figures in Table 16-1 do not take into consideration two factors influencing the rise in total dollar volume. One is the big rise in the price level during the period covered in the table, and the other is the increase in population. Nevertheless, even after allowing for

Table 16-1. Total retail trade in Canada, selected years. Retail sales have almost tripled since 1961. Even after allowing for the increase in population and the rise in price levels, we find a huge increase in physical volume of merchandise sold. In contrast, note the remarkable stability in the number of retail establishments since 1961.

	1974	1971	1969	1967	1961
Number of stores (000)	160.0	158.2	154.0	153.7	152.6
Total Sales ($000,000)	$ 44,569	$ 32,080	$ 27,065	$ 23,890	$ 16,072
Average sales per store	$278,556	$202,758	$175,325	$155,500	$105,504

Source: Statistics Canada.

5 Canadian Grocer, March, 1976, p. 26.

these two factors, the retail sales per capita as measured in 1974 dollars were still considerably higher in 1974 than in 1961. That is, there has simply been a huge increase in the physical volume of merchandise sold at retail.

COSTS AND PROFITS OF RETAILERS

Information regarding the costs of retailing is very meager. By gleaning data from several sources, however, we can make some rough generalizations.

Total costs and profits. As nearly as can be estimated, the total average operating expense for all retailers combined is about 25 to 27 percent of retail sales. Wholesaling expenses are estimated at about 8 percent of the *retail* dollar or about 10 to 11 percent of *wholesaling* sales. Thus retailing expenses in total are about 2½ times the total of the costs of wholesaling when the expenses are stated as a percentage of sales of the middlemen in question. See Fig. 16-1.

The proportionately higher retailing costs are generally related to the expense of dealing directly with the consumer. In comparison with wholesalers' customers, consumers demand more services. Also, the average retail sale is smaller, the rate of merchandise turnover is lower, buying is done in smaller lots, rent is higher, expenses for furniture and fixtures are greater, and salespeople cannot be used efficiently because the customers do not come in at a steady rate.

Costs and profits by kind of business. Studying the expenses of retailers in total is not nearly as meaningful as studying the expenses of one classification of retailers, because the expense ratios vary from one type of store to another. Table 16-2 shows expenses as a percentage of sales when stores are classified by the nature and extent of product lines handled. Total operating expenses and profit range from 13.5 percent of net sales for motor vehicle dealers through 19.3 percent for food stores, and 31.6 percent for drug stores, to 37 percent for men's clothing stores. Table 16-2 also shows the average net operating profit after income taxes for selected kinds of business in 1971.

ECONOMIC BASES OF RETAILING

To get into retailing is easy. To be forced out is just as easy. Consequently, the social and economic justification for the retailer's existence must be based upon the services he offers. He exists only because he does a better job than his competitors in his primary responsibility—catering to the consumer—and in his secondary job—serving producers and wholesalers.

IMPORTANCE TO CONSUMERS

The function of the retailer is to make the consumer's buying job as easy and convenient as possible. Essentially, the retailer acts as the consumer's purchasing agent; this task involves anticipating his wants. Then the retailer has the responsibility of supplying the right kind of goods at a reasonable price. The retailer also performs the service of *bulk breaking,* that is, dividing large quantities into smaller units, such as individual cans or boxes, appropriate for consumer use. The retailers offer a large

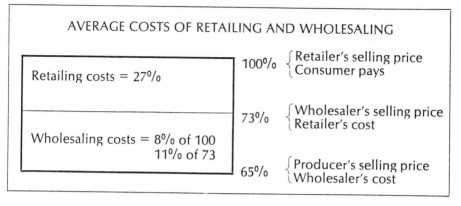

Figure 16-1.

Table 16-2. **Gross margin and net profit, as percentage of net sales, for selected types of retailers, 1971.**
Wide differences exist in the operating expenses of various types of retailers. Automobile dealers' gross margin is 13.5 percent of net sales, while men's clothing stores need a margin of 37 percent to cover expenses and net profit. How do you account for these differences? Note that net profit percentages are very low.

Line of Business	Gross Margin %	Net profit % after income taxes
Food Stores	19.3	0.96
Department Stores	32.3	1.31
Variety Stores	32.3	3.00
General Merchandise Stores	22.6	1.63
Accessory and Parts Stores	30.1	1.69
Service Stations	24.0	1.72
Motor Vehicle Dealers	13.5	0.87
Motor Vehicle Repair Shops	45.4	3.51
Shoe Stores	37.9	2.11
Men's Clothing Stores	37.0	2.53
Women's Clothing Stores	35.9	1.24
Dry Goods Stores	33.4	2.14
Hardware Stores	32.4	3.28
Furniture Stores	31.9	1.84
Electrical Supplies Stores	38.5	1.83
Drug Stores	31.6	3.52
Book and Stationery Stores	43.2	2.84
Florists Shops	54.0	1.68
Fuel Dealers	30.5	2.76
Jewellery Stores	45.4	5.22
Tobacco Stores	17.9	1.28

Source: Statistics Canada, *Market Research Handbook,* Cat. No. 63-224, 1975, pp. 188-196.

assortment of merchandise, including appropriate sizes, colors, styles, and seasonal items.

Retailers perform the function of transporting and storing the goods so that they will be readily available when and where the consumer wants them. Thus, time and place utilities are created. Retailers usually assume certain consumer risks in that they guarantee the goods they sell. Often retailers provide an installation and repair service.

Financing is another important function of retailers. They offer consumers open-book charge accounts payable once a month, revolving credit plans, and long-term installment programs. Retailers also add to the convenience and ease of consumer purchasing. They offer convenient shopping locations, considerable market information, personal salesmen, and other services, such as ample parking space, clothing alterations, and lessons on product use.

IMPORTANCE TO PRODUCERS AND WHOLESALERS

For the producers and wholesalers, the retailer acts as a specialist in selling. He offers physical facilities and manpower so that the producers and wholesaling middleman can have a point of contact with consumers near the consumers' homes. He also uses advertising, display, and personal selling to aid in moving the producers' products. In determining the needs and wants of the consumer, the retailer can act as an interpreter of consumer demand and relay vital information back through the channel of distribution.

By dividing large unit quantities into consumer-sized amounts, the retailer is performing a service to manufacturers as well as to consumers. It would be highly uneconomical for manufacturers to package and ship their goods in the quantities demanded by consumers. Retailers' storage activities also help both producers and consumers. By ordering and accepting delivery in advance of the season, the retailer removes some of the risk burden from the manufacturer.

CLASSIFICATION OF RETAILING MIDDLEMEN

To better understand the role that retailing middlemen play in the channel structure, we shall classify them on the following bases:

1. Size of store
2. Extent of product lines handled
3. Geographic location

4. Form of ownership
5. Method of operation

Any given store may be classed according to any one of the above five bases, as we have done below using Simpsons-Sears and a neighborhood paint store as examples.

Simpsons-Sears	Classification base	Paint Store
Large	1. Size of store	Small
General merchandise	2. Product-lines carried	Single line
Variety of locations	3. Geographic location	Variety of possible locations
Corporate chain	4. Form of ownership	Independent

Both in-store and mail order; supermarket method and full service depending on product department.	5. Method of operation	In-store selling; full service

SIZE OF STORE

Classifying retailing institutions according to their sales volume recognizes the fact that stores of different sizes present different management problems. Buying, promotion, financing, personnel relations, and expense control are influenced significantly by the volume size of the store. When we discuss retailing on the basis of store size, we find that a dichotomous situation exists. Retailing is at one and the same time both a small-scale and a large-scale operation.

Quantitative measurement. Most establishments are very small. In 1971, about 63 per cent of the retail stores in Canada had an annual sales volume of less than $100,000, but these stores accounted for only 13.2 per cent of all retail sales (see Table 16-3). Retailing is probably the best example of small business in Canada, particularly when we include retailers of services such as restaurants, hair stylists and garages.

Although most retailers are small, at the same time there is a high degree of concentration in retailing: a small number of establishments account for a substantial share of retail trade. In Table 16-3, we see that stores with an annual sales volume of over $1 million accounted for only 3.2 per cent of all establishments, but for over 45 per cent of total retail sales.

As impressive as the figures in Table 16-3 may seem, they still do not tell the full story of large-scale retailing because they represent a tabulation of individual *store* sales and not individual *company* volume. A single company may own many establishments, as in the case of chain stores. When retail sales are analyzed by companies, the high degree of concentration becomes even more evident. Table 16-4 shows the sales of the ten largest retailers in Canada as well as their net profit. The small size of the average net profit as a percentage of sales (1.45%) might surprise some people who may feel that retailing is a highly profitable business. Sales of

Table 16-3. Retail trade in Canada, 1971: by sales size of establishment

Annual Sales	Stores			Sales		
	Number	Percent	Cumulative Percent	Sales in $Millions	Percent	Cumulative Percent
Less than $10,000	12,137	7.8	7.8	62.3	0.2	0.2
$ 10,000—$ 29,999	27,066	17.3	25.1	538.0	1.7	1.9
$ 30,000—$ 49,999	27,723	14.5	39.6	900.7	2.9	4.8
$ 50,000—$ 99,999	36,364	23.2	62.8	2,633.1	8.4	13.2
$ 100,000—$199,999	30,216	19.3	82.1	4,250.5	13.5	26.7
$ 200,000—$499,999	17,927	11.5	93.6	5,340.2	17.0	43.7
$ 500,000—$999,999	5,072	3.2	96.8	3,523.0	11.2	54.9
$1,000,000 and over	5,027	3.2	100.0	14,142.4	45.1	100.00
Total	156,532			31,390.1		

Source: 1971 Census of Canada, Retail Trade by Annual Sales Size, by Kind of Business. Cat. No. 97-705.

Table 16-4: Ten largest retailers in Canada, 1974: by sales volume.
The sales of these giant retailers (plus Eaton's, which does not publish public statements) represents approximately one third of total retail sales in Canada, and yet their average profit was only 1.45 percent of sales. What are some of the marketing implications of this concentration for a manufacturer of department store merchandise?

Company	1974 sales ($ million)	Net profit after taxes as % of sales
1. George Weston Ltd.	4,733	0.8
2. Dominion Stores Ltd.	1,650	1.0
3. Canada Safeway Ltd.	1,547	1.9
4. Simpson-Sears Ltd.	1,341	2.6
5. Steinberg's Ltd.	1,197	1.4
6. Hudson's Bay Co.	1,014	1.8
7. M. Loeb Ltd.	898	0.4
8. Oshawa Group Ltd.	867	0.8
9. F. W. Woolworth Co.	842	1.8
10. Woodward Stores	504	2.0

Source: The Financial Post, July 26, 1975, p. 13.

these ten firms plus Eaton's, which is privately held and does not publish financial statements, are approximately one third of the total value of retail trade in Canada in 1974.

Competitive positions of large and small retailers. The relative competitive positions of large-scale and small-scale retailers may be evaluated in the light of several factors.

Division of labor. The opportunity to enjoy the advantages of division of labor both at the executive level and in the manpower ranks is one of the strongest factors favoring large-scale retailers. Large retailers can afford to hire managerial specialists for each major function, such as buying, promotion, and accounting. The small store usually cannot pay enough money or offer enough future opportunity to attract a high-caliber full-time person to perform these functions. The owner-manager may be a good executive, but he has to divide his time among too many activities to be effective in all of them.[6]

Flexibility of operations. Small stores generally are more flexible in their management practices than large units. Small retailers can stock merchandise to suit specific local needs, and they can adopt a flexible policy regarding services.

Buying power. Large-scale institutions have a buying power advantage. They can buy in bigger quantities than small stores and secure higher discounts. They can achieve additional economies by purchasing from manufacturers. Sometimes this buying power is instrumental in acquiring other benefits, such as allowances for

6 For a study of the way in which a small retailer's personality can affect the success of his daily operations, see L. S. Tarpey and James L. Gibson, "Dogmatism as a Factor in Small Business Retail Management," Journal of Retailing, Winter, 1969-1970, pp. 45-55.

advertising, preferential treatment in case of shortages, and sole dealership rights in a given market.

Use of advertising. Large stores can make effective use of advertising. It is not economically feasible for a corner grocery store to advertise in a metropolitan daily paper or on television. A large department store or a grocery chain with several stores blanketing a city can make good use of these media because the media match the market. There is little waste circulation.

Retailer's own brand. Large retail institutions are in a good position to develop and promote their own brands. For the small store, the potential sales volume from its own brand is more than offset by the funds required to promote the brand and guarantee its quality.

Financial strength. Underlying many of the points noted here is the fact that large retailers are usually in a better financial position. When they need money, they can attract investors or borrow from lending institutions much more easily than small retailers can. A strong financial position enables a store to take advantage of all cash discounts offered, and these are extremely important in retailing because of the low net profit margins. A good financial position also enables a store to attract valuable franchises and attention from leading brand manufacturers. The financial strength of a retailer is a key point in a manufacturer's selection of individual middlemen.

Integration—horizontal and vertical. Large retailers handle a sufficient volume of merchandise to make it worth their while to take over wholesaling functions and sometimes even manufacturing operations. A large grocery chain may buy or set up a bakery just to supply its own stores.

Cost of operations. There is a lack of precise information regarding the effect which size has on operating expenses. Generally, large stores have higher operating expense ratios than small stores. The expenses in large organizations, however, also include the wholesaling activities conducted by these firms. Certainly, large stores have higher overhead expenses than small ones. Part of the advantage of management and labor specialization is offset by the higher cost attendant upon the division of labor. Large stores also have a greater percentage of total employees in non-selling jobs.

Experimentation, innovation, and marketing research. With their specialized executive manpower and great financial strength, large retailers are in a good position to conduct all kinds of needed marketing research. They can experiment with new ideas. They can afford to risk more on innovative features, such as a daring new style of clothing or a new selling method (self-service in housewares or automatic vending of staple clothing items). A multistore organization can test something in one store before committing all units to the new practice.

Legal considerations. Large-scale retailers have often been a major target of legislators. This is more especially so since the dramatic growth of the consumerism movement in North America during the 1960s and 1970s. Certainly the misleading advertising provisions of the Combines Investigation Act and many aspects of legislation affecting retail pricing have a dramatic impact on the way in which retailers are now beginning to conduct their business. Some of this legislation has been discussed in greater detail in Chapters 14 and 15.

Improved position of small retailer. The competitive position of some small retailers in many fields has improved over the years by virtue of developments among both the large and the small firms. One such development has been the voluntary association of retailers into a chainlike form of organization which gives the individual members of these associations the features of specialized management, buying power, and other advantages of scale discussed above. A second development has been the expansion of franchising operations in many fields of products and services (Holiday Inn, Hertz and Avis, McDonald's hamburgers, for instance). In these stores, small-scale businessmen are able to operate their own small business under the name and guidance of a large company, thus giving these small entrepreneurs sort of the best of both worlds. Franchising and voluntary associations are discussed in more detail in the next chapter.

Changes in the consumer market is another factor working to the advantage of a small retailer. At the same time that huge supermarket-type stores carrying a wide variety of merchandise are catering to consumers' wants, we find also that small boutiques and other specialty shops are growing in number and apparently thriving in response to another facet of consumer buying behavior. A small retailer who takes advantage of his flexibility can adapt not only his merchandise lines to his market, but also he can establish his own store's personality through unusual store layout and design. The relative position of small stores also is improved because large retailers suffer from operating problems seemingly inherent in large-scale operations—retailing or otherwise. High overhead costs, problems of unionized sales forces, difficulty in motivating salesclerks, and organizational inflexibilities all combine to limit the competitive position of the large-scale retailer.

EXTENT OF PRODUCT LINES HANDLED

Retail stores may be classified according to the extent of the product lines they carry. In this classification, stores are grouped as general merchandise stores, single-line stores, and specialty stores. Subdivisions within these three groups are recognized by names which consumers typically use in identifying retail stores. That is, we speak of department stores, hardware stores, gas stations, and so on.

This basis of classification is still useful for some types of stores—apparel, furniture, building materials, for instance. For other types such as food stores and drugstores, however, the store's sales figures are becoming less meaningful as accurate indicators of the relative sales volume of the different commodities. The reason for this is that there has been a pronounced trend toward scrambled merchandising, that is, the practice of adding new, unrelated lines to the products customarily sold in a particular type of store. It is a mistake, for example, to interpret food store sales as being equal to total sales of food products. Supermarkets carry many nonfood lines, and food products, in turn, are sold in drugstores, gas stations, department stores, etc.

General merchandise stores. Institutions which offer a large variety of lines, usually with some depth of assortment in each line, fall into the classification of general merchandise stores. The classification includes department stores, dry goods stores, variety stores, and general stores. As a group, these retailers account for 18.4 per cent of the total retail trade. Department stores—usually considered a major segment of the retailing structure—represent almost 12 per cent of all retail sales, and variety stores contribute less than 2 percent of the total.

Department stores: importance and relative merits. To be considered a department store for the Statistics Canada classification, an institution must meet the following requirements:

> **Department store**—A retail outlet that sells the following general lines for merchandise:
>
> (1) family clothing and apparel;
> (2) furniture, appliances and home furnishings; and
> (3) all other (miscellaneous). At least 20% of the outlet's total sales must be derived from (1); 10% from (2); and 10% from (3).
>
> In the family clothing and apparel category the outlet must sell men's and boys' clothing or furnishings and at least five of the following commodity lines: women's and misses' dresses, housedresses, aprons and uniforms; women's and misses' coats and suits'; women's and misses' sportswear; furs; infants' and children's wear; girls' and teenage wear; lingerie, and women's sleepwear; intimate apparel; millinery; women's and girls' hoisery; women's and girls' gloves, mitts and accessories and women's, misses' and children's footwear.
>
> In the furniture, appliances and home furnishings category the outlet must sell furniture (wooden and upholstered goods for dining-room and/or living room and/or bedroom) and at least three of the following commodity lines: linens and domestics; china and glassware; home furnishings; major appliances; TV, radio and music; and hardware and housewares.
>
> In the all other (miscellaneous) category the outlet must sell at least three of the following commodity lines (with not one of these lines representing more than 50% of the total sales): toiletries, cosmetics and drugs; photographic equipment and supplies; piece goods; notions and smallwares; jewelery; sporting goods and luggage; stationery, books and magazines; and food.[7]

Department stores are highly organized business enterprises. Merchandising or product planning, headed by a general merchandising manager, is usually the key to a store's success. Under the merchandising manager are the department buyers. In effect, each department is a business in itself, and the buyer has considerable autonomy.

Another department store feature is the common use of leased departments. The store leases a department to an outside firm which will establish and operate it. To all external appearances, a leased department is operated by the store itself. Beauty shops, restaurants, and departments handling hearing aids, optical goods, millinery, and groceries are frequently leased.

Leased departments offer several advantages to a department store. They help to round out a store's line with no risk to the store. This is especially advantageous in fields where fashion risks are high. Leased departments may bring to the store a highly qualified specialist in a given product field and thus relieve the store's own managerial burden. Stores can also gain financially by leasing out a department whose establishment would require considerable capital outlay.

The lessee is in a favorable position because his rent is often based on a percent-

---

7 *Market Research Handbook*, Statistics Canada, Cat. #63-224, 1975, pp. 95-96.

age of his sales volume. In such cases, the rent is a variable expense, and the store assumes a significant part of the risk of poor sales. Also, the lessee enjoys the prestige of the store, and he can make use of other store services, such as delivery and credit.

In addition to the general merits of large-scale retail operation (specialized management, buying power, etc.), other advantages accrue to department stores in particular. Department stores offer a wider variety of products and services than any other type of retail institution where the customer comes to the store. (A form of nonstore retailing—the mail-order house—may carry more lines than a department store.) The opportunity for one-stop shopping is almost unlimited.

Department stores suffer from several specific limitations, as well as from those generally associated with large-scale activity. Operating costs are considerably higher than for most other kinds of retail business, running about 35 percent of sales. One of the features of department stores—their many services—also contributes significantly to the high operating expense.

A substantial problem confronting department stores has been their location— typically in the heart of the downtown shopping district. The population exodus to the suburbs and the traffic problems downtown have combined to force many department stores to open branches in the suburbs. The big downtown store, with its large investment, high-tax location, and high-cost operations, must be maintained, but it reaps a decreasing share of the total business in the area. Department stores are running into strong competition on other fronts as well. In the late 1940s and 1950s the high gross margin of department stores gave impetus to the development of discount selling.

Besides building branches in suburban shopping centers, department stores are making other concerted efforts to meet the new competition. Working with other downtown merchants, the stores are spearheading movements to revitalize downtown areas. Possibly the best example of this revitalization is the massive Eaton Centre in downtown Toronto. Stores have been modernized and redecorated, and better municipal transit systems and expanded parking facilities are being developed.[8] To meet the competition from discount sellers, perhaps the best alternative for department stores is a compromise—that is, to upgrade merchandise lines and stress fashion, while at the same time offering on a limited basis some of the discounters' features.

Today's innovative competitive strategies of department stores reflect an attitude of "Get aggressive or go out of business." Stores are building "out-of-store" specialty shops to attract young shoppers. Bargain basements are being revitalized to counter the lower prices in discount stores. Eaton's has recently expanded into the discount business with the opening of their Horizon stores. Some department stores now accept Chargex and Master Charge cards as well as their own credit cards. Most major department stores operate warehouse outlets, sell certain items through the mail, and Simpsons-Sears continues to operate its mail order catalogue division. In order to counter the trend established by Consumers Distributing, both Woolco and the Hudson's Bay Company have opened catalogue stores. Eaton's and Simpsons, in order to offer a broader range of services to their customers, have

---

8 For some case examples of what various organizations are doing to revitalize the downtown areas, see "Suburban Malls Go Downtown," *Business Week*, Nov. 10, 1973, p. 90; see also E. B. Weiss, "Reversing the Trend: Downtown Areas, the Original Shopping Centers, To Become New Mecca of Retail," *Marketing Insights*, Feb. 27, 1967, p. 16.

added travel agencies, income-tax counseling, insurance and mutual funds departments. In the United States, some department stores are experimenting with hybrid outlets which combine the traditional department store, a discount store and a food outlet under one roof. Management in many stores is using more marketing research and is trying to upgrade the effectiveness of its salesclerks.

Single-line stores. This category of retailing institutions includes stores which carry a considerable assortment of a related group of products. Thus we find stores identified by the names of the individual line of products featured: grocery stores, appliance stores, furniture stores, building materials stores, hardware stores, and sporting goods stores. In some cases, stores of this type carry two related lines, such as men's and women's clothing.

Specialty stores. Specialty stores constitute that class of retail institution which carries a limited variety of products. Typically they handle only part of a single line of convenience or shopping goods. Examples of this type of store include dairy stores, tobacco shops, bakeries, meat markets, men's shoe stores, millinery shops, and furriers. Specialty stores should not be confused with specialty goods. Actually, specialty shops often do not carry specialty goods. The term "specialty" in relation to the store implies a limited line of merchandise, rather than the well-known, branded products which people are willing to expend considerable effort to purchase. Although there is some chain-store activity in this field, the majority of the business is done by independent small-scale retailers.

Because specialty stores handle a limited line of merchandise, they usually have an excellent assortment. In the apparel field, they often feature the newest fashions. Frequently they are the exclusive dealers for certain brands in a given market. Successful specialty stores usually have highly capable buyers who are expert judges of what will sell. Because they limit their merchandise to a narrow field, these stores can often buy reasonably large quantities and thus secure favorable prices.

GEOGRAPHIC LOCATION

Classifying retail stores according to their geographic location tells us something about consumer buying patterns. It also brings out the general conclusion that retail trade is concentrated in relation to population and reflects the buying power of various regions of the country. For example, Table 16-5 indicates that the Atlantic Provinces accounted for 9.4 percent of the Canadian population in 1974, but because of a lower average per capita income in this region, these four provinces accounted for only 8.1 percent of total Canadian retail sales for that year. Conversely, the higher than average per capita incomes of Ontario, Alberta, and British Columbia explain the fact that these provinces accounted for a larger share of retail sales than would be warranted by population alone. Thus an analysis of the geographic location of retail trade can be used to evaluate regional market potential for many products.

Urban-rural distribution. As we might expect, the great bulk of retail sales and retail stores is concentrated in the very small land mass which constitutes the Census Metropolitan Areas. In Canada, Statistics Canada has defined a total of 23 Census Metropolitan Areas. In 1974, these urban areas contained 54.8 percent of the Cana-

Table 16.5: Provincial Shares of Population and Retail Sales.
These data reflect the buying power of the various regions and provinces of Canada. Note that the lower income areas of Canada, most notably the Atlantic region, account for a proportionately lower share of retail sales, while Ontario, Alberta and British Columbia account for larger shares of retail sales than would be warranted by population.

Province	% of Canadian population 1974	% of total retail sales
Newfoundland	2.4	1.8
Prince Edward Island	0.5	0.4
Nova Scotia	3.6	3.3
New Brunswick	2.9	2.6
ATLANTIC PROVINCES	9.4	8.1
Quebec	27.2	24.8
Ontario	36.1	37.5
Manitoba	4.5	4.4
Saskatchewan	4.0	4.0
Alberta	7.6	8.5
PRAIRIE PROVINCES	16.1	16.9
British Columbia	10.8	12.4

Source: "Survey of Buying Power," *Sales Management*, July 21, 1975, p. E-12.

dian population, but accounted for 58.2 percent of total retail trade in Canada during that year.[9]

The buying power of urban markets is also influenced by the extent to which these markets attract sales from nonresidents and from persons who live in rural areas but who come into the "city" to shop. *Sales Management* has calculated an index to measure this buying power. The Sales Activity Index of a city is obtained by dividing its percentage of Canadian retail sales by its percentage of Canadian population. Because the total retail sales represents all sales made in the market, it reflects the buying of nonresident as well as resident shoppers. On the other hand, the population percentage includes only residents of the market. An index above 1.0 indicates a strong influx of nonresident shoppers, heavy buying by business concerns, heavy buying by residents, or all three. An index below 1.0 indicates that residents have below average incomes or that business and residents go outside the area in which they are located to make retail purchases. In 1974, most of the Census Metropolitan Areas of Canada produced Sales Activity Indices larger than 1.0, with Toronto and Montreal producing the largest indices at 13.5 and 12.0 respectively, indicating very heavy nonresident and business buying in these cities as well as higher per capita incomes.[10]

Distribution within urban parts of metropolitan areas. Within the central city and its adjacent cities and suburbs in a metropolitan area, there are several discernible types of shopping districts. Together these constitute a retailing structure which

9 *"Survey of Buying Power,"* Sales Management, July 21, 1975, p. E-16.

10 *"Survey of Buying Power,"* Sales Management, July 21, 1975, pp. A-17 and E-16.

should be recognized by marketers. The hub of the retailing activity traditionally has been the central downtown shopping district—the location of the main units of department stores, major apparel specialty stores, and single-line jewelry and furniture stores. This district is the heart of shopping goods stores, although convenience goods are also readily available. The downtown area draws customers from a wide market, in some cases from over 100 miles.

In the older, larger cities of Central Canada, we often find a secondary shopping district.[11] This may be located in the main city about 5 to 8 miles from the downtown area; it may also be found in the "downtown" areas of older suburbs, such as Port Credit, Ontario. These districts are not planned or controlled for marketing purposes and thus are differentiated from the modern, planned suburban shopping centers. Secondary districts often contain a branch of a downtown department store and branches of specialty or limited-line stores. Shopping goods are available, but not in as wide an assortment as in downtown areas.

A third type of shopping district found in cities is a string-street development or a small cluster of neighborhood stores. Most of the retailers are small, and convenience goods stores predominate, although some small furniture or apparel stores also locate in these districts. The trading area in a neighborhood district is quite small compared with that in a secondary or downtown district.

Since World War II, another significant type of shopping district has arisen in metropolitan areas—the planned, controlled suburban shopping center. Such a center differs from all other shopping districts in that is is planned, developed, and controlled by one organization. The developer may be a major downtown department store or an individual promoter-investor-developer. These planned centers evolved from (1) *neighborhood* centers built around a supermarket, through (2) *community* centers featuring a discount store or junior department store, to (3) the earlier-built *regional* centers anchored by a branch of one or two downtown department stores. In the regional centers, ideally there is at least one specialty or limited-line store to compete with each department in the department store.

In recent years, there has been a trend to develop giant-sized regional centers—in effect, they are miniature downtowns. Such centers would include Yorkdale, Square One, Bramalea City Centre, and Scarborough Town Centre in the Toronto area; Carrefour Laval, Place Vertu, and St. John's Square in Montreal; Northgate Mall and Golden Mile in Regina; and Park Royal in Vancouver. These supercenters have as many as four department stores and supermarkets, plus many small stores and service operations. They also might include hotels, banks, office buildings, and theatres. These comprehensive centers integrate retail, cultural, and commercial activities all enclosed under one roof and with a climate-controlled mall featuring fountains, sculptures, and floral displays.

Another trend in the establishment of shopping centers in Canada has involved the revitalization of downtown areas through the building of enclosed shopping malls in the heart of the downtown commercial district. Such malls in Canada include Scotia Square in Halifax; Place Ville Marie in Montreal; Toronto-Dominion Centre and Commerce Court in Toronto; and the Pacific Centre in Vancouver. These centers have contributed significantly to the reversal of the trend which saw much of the retail trade of metropolitan areas moving to the more suburban regional shopping centers.

---

11 With a few exceptions, Western cities do not have secondary shopping districts because most of these cities did not become large enough to support such a district until after World War II. By that time, retailing developments were taking place in planned suburban shopping centers.

Statistics Canada defines a shopping center as follows:

A group of stores which are planned, developed and designed as a unit, containing a minimum of five retail establishments (or four retail establishments and a restaurant) in operation during any part of the year. The centre must have a minimum of 20,000 square feet of usable parking area adjacent to it, and the parking facilities must be free of charge to customers. For shopping centres with paved parking areas of 20,000-50,000 square feet, the ratio of parking area to gross floor area must be 1.5 to 1 or better. The merchandising development must contain either a grocery and combination store, (i.e., a grocery store with sales of fresh meat accounting for 20 to 40%, of total sales), a department store, or a chain variety store. While a shopping centre is usually designed as a single project, all establishments do not necessarily have to be leased from a single (private or collective) ownership. A retail establishment may own the building and the land on which it is situated and still be fully integrated with the centre. A shopping centre usually bears a name and, as a rule, matters of common interest to the tenants, such as children's playgrounds, community activities, parking, etc., originate from one authority.

This definition excludes most downtown malls and a number of planned multi-store, multi-level shopping plazas because they do not allow free parking (even though parking may be conditionally free, i.e., contingent upon a minimum purchase), or fail to meet the requirements of the foregoing definition in some other way.[12]

In Canada in 1973, a total of 664 shopping centers met this definition. Of these, 266 were located in Ontario and 154 in Quebec. Retail sales of stores located in the 664 shopping centers represented 17.6 percent of all retail sales in Canada in 1973 and this percentage is expected to increase dramatically as more centers are built during the 1970s.[13] The success of suburban shopping centers lies essentially in their appeal to, or conformity with, consumer buying patterns. A wide selection of merchandise is available; stores are open evenings; an informal atmosphere encourages mothers to dress informally and bring the children; plenty of free parking space is available. The success of these centers is enhanced by the group effort of the member stores. By coordinating their promotional efforts, all stores benefit; one builds traffic for another. Many stores in these centers are too small to do effective, economical advertising on their own, but they can make good use of major media by tying in with overall shopping center advertising and promotion. They also cash in on the general prestige and reputation of the center.

QUESTIONS AND PROBLEMS

1. "You can eliminate the middleman, but you cannot eliminate his functions." Discuss.
2. Which of the following institutions are middlemen? Explain.

   a. Food broker   g. Chain supermarket
   b. Stockbroker   h. Bank
   c. Real estate broker   i. Grain elevator
   d. Department store   j. Hardware wholesaler
   e. Railroad   k. Fuller Brush salesman
   f. Advertising agency   l. Radio station

---

12 *Market Research Handbook*, Statistics Canada, Cat. No. 63-224, 1975, pp. 90-91.

13 *Market Research Handbook*, Statistics Canada, Cat. No. 63-224, 1975, pp. 55, 60.

3. What is a channel of distribution; and how is it related to the physical distribution of the product?
4. Explain how time, place, and possession utility may be created in the marketing of the following products. What business institutions might be involved in creating these utilities?
   a. Sewing machines
   b. Fresh peaches
   c. Hydraulic grease racks used in garages and service stations
5. Define the terms "retailing," a "retail sale," and a "retailer." Explain the three concepts in light of the following situations:
   a. Avon cosmetics saleslady selling door-to-door
   b. Farmer selling his produce door-to-door
   c. Farmer selling his produce at his roadside stand
   d. Sporting goods store selling uniforms to a professional baseball team
6. How do you account for the wide differences in operating expenses between the various types of retail stores shown in Table 16-2?
7. Why is retailing more expensive than wholesaling? Why is retailing inherently less efficient than manufacturing?
8. The mortality rate among retail stores is one of the highest among all types of business institutions. How do you account for this?
9. "Retailing is typically small-scale business." "There is a high degree of concentration in retailing today; the giants control the field." Reconcile these two statements, using facts and figures where appropriate.
10. Referring to the ten criteria given in this chapter for evaluating competitive positions of large-scale and small-scale retailers, on which counts are small stores in a stronger competitive position than large-scale retailers? In light of your final score, how do you account for the numerical preponderance of small retailers?
11. What courses of action might a small retailer follow to improve his competitive position?
12. What can department stores do to offset their competitive disadvantages?
13. What can single-line and specialty stores do to compete effectively with department stores?
14. Identify the various types of shopping districts in a nearby city. Relate this structure to the one described in this chapter.
15. What is the relationship between the growth and successful development of planned suburban shopping centers and the material studied in Chapters 3 to 7 regarding the consumer?
16. Comment on the changing geographic pattern of retailing in Canada.

RETAILERS AND METHODS OF OPERATION

In the preceding chapter, retailing institutions were analyzed on three bases: the size of the store as measured by sales volume, the extent of the product lines handled, and the geographic location. In this chapter, we will discuss forms of ownership and methods of operation.

RETAILERS CLASSIFIED BY FORM OF OWNERSHIP

Classified according to the form of ownership, retail institutions fall into two major groups: independent stores and corporate chain stores. A third group, which we shall consider here, consists of voluntary associations of independents who band together in chainlike fashion in order to compete more effectively with the corporate chain-store organization. Other less important ownership categories, such as leased departments, company stores, consumers' cooperatives, and government commissaries, account for a negligible percentage of total retail trade.

CORPORATE CHAIN STORE

A *chain store organization* is, according to the Statistics Canada definition, an organization consisting of four or more stores centrally owned and managed, and handling generally the same lines of products on the same level in the distribution structure. Technically, four or more units may constitute a chain, although today many merchants who consider themselves small-scale independents have more than four units which they have opened up in shopping centers and newly populated areas. These retailers ordinarily do not think of themselves as a chain. Consequently, it might be more meaningful to consider a larger number of units to be a reasonable minimum when categorizing a store as a chain. For Census purposes, Statistics Canada defines a chain store organization as one which operates four or more retail outlets in the same kind of business under the same legal ownership. Those operating two or three stores are termed multiples, and, together with the single stores, are referred to as independent stores. All department stores are considered chain store organizations regardless of whether they own one or more outlets.

Central ownership is the key factor which differentiates corporate chains from voluntary associations of independent wholesalers or retailers. The third element in our definition of a chain-store system is central management. Individual units in a chain have very little autonomy. Buying is highly centralized with respect to both the physical purchasing and the determination of what will be bought. Centralized management also leads to considerable standardization in operating policies among the units in the chain.

Many chains are also vertically integrated, but this feature is not essential for definitional purposes. Dominion Stores, the large grocery chain, maintains large distribution centers where they buy from producers, do their own warehousing, and then distribute to their own stores in their own trucks. Some chain organizations, such as Eaton's, actually own and operate manufacturing plants to supply some of their needs. Another form of vertical integration has resulted in *manufacturer-owned* retail chains, such as shoe stores (Bata Shoe), sewing machines (Singer), and gasoline outlets (Imperial Oil).

Importance. In number of stores and total sales, independent single unit stores constitute by far the largest segment of retail trade when institutions are classed by ownership. In fact, in 1974, Statistics Canada showed that about 88% of all stores were independents and that they accounted for about 59% of all retail sales. Of course, the other side of these statistics suggests the degree of concentration in retailing. Organizations with four or more stores did 41% of total retail business with only about 10% of total stores.

The importance of chains varies considerably from one type of commodity to another (see Table 17-1). Chains account for more than 80% of total sales in the general merchandise and variety stores categories. Among hardware stores and furniture stores, however, chains account for less than 20% of total retail sales. In the food field, there are several giant chain firms, yet chains still account for less than 60% of total food store sales.

Chain store companies have increased their share of the total retail market since the early 1960s, but the growth has not been uniform in all fields. In the food store category, for example, since 1966 chain stores have increased their share of total food sales from 44.9% to 57.5% since 1966. On the other hand the share of variety store sales accounted for by chains has in fact decreased since 1966. The growth of chains in the drug store field reflects the way these stores have expanded into a wide variety of products. Further growth in drug chains is likely as they capitalize on potential government-sponsored business and the fact that the over-sixty-five market is increasing in size and in buying power.

Table 17-1. Chains' share of total sales volume, by kind of business, 1966 and 1974.

Kind of Business	Percent of Sales 1966	Percent of Sales 1974
Total Retail Sales	33.4	41.1
Grocery & Combination Stores	44.9	57.5
Other Food Stores	8.7	8.1
Department Stores*	100.0	100.0
General Merchandise	74.7	80.4
Variety Stores	86.7	83.2
Men's Clothing	13.2	18.6
Women's Clothing	26.5	40.9
Family Clothing	21.9	28.5
Shoe Stores	45.0	51.8
Hardware Stores	15.5	19.0
Furniture Stores	19.2	19.2
Drug Stores	13.4	18.5
Jewelry Stores	33.7	39.4

* All Department Stores are considered chains by Statistics Canada.
Source: Statistics Canada, *Market Research Handbook*, 1975, Cat. No. 63-224, pp. 66-67.

The importance and concentration of chain stores in Canada is also reflected in the fact that in 1973, 834 chains operated a total of 18,555 stores which generated sales of $11,338 million. What is particularly interesting is the fact that of these 834 chains, a total of 34 operated more than 100 stores each. These 34 chains operated a total of 7,670 stores (41.3% of all chain outlets) and sold $6,901 million worth of merchandise (60.9% of all chain store sales).

Competitive advantages. Chain-store organizations are large-scale retailing institutions and, as such, enjoy the general competitive advantages of large-scale retailing discussed in Chapter 16. In addition, chain stores per se have some particular merits.

Lower selling prices. Chain stores have traditionally been credited with selling at lower prices than independents. This is an image chains have projected to the public, but the claim of lower prices needs careful scrutiny because it can be misleading. It was probably more justified in the past than it is today. Many independents have improved their operating methods and thus have reduced their costs. They have also pooled their buying power so that in many instances they can buy products at the same prices as the chains.

It is very difficult to compare prices of chains with those of independents. The merchandise is often not exactly comparable because many chains sell items under their own brands. It is difficult to compare the price of Del Monte peaches with Loblaws peaches. Also, it is not accurate to compare the price of a product sold in a cash-and-carry, no-customer-service store with the price of an indentically branded product in a full-service store. The value of services should be included in the comparison.

When the chains do have a price advantage, it is traceable to one or more of three factors. First, chain-store operating costs may be lower than those of independents. Chains usually offer fewer "free" services. They reduce costs by careful buying and careful inventory controls which maximize their rate of turnover and minimize the number of slow-moving items in stock. Chains further reduce operating costs by doing their own wholesaling and, in some instances, their own manufacturing.

The second factor holding prices down is that chains normally are satisfied with a lower percentage of net profit. They depend upon huge sales volume to maximize their dollar profit. Some of the large food chains, for example, show net profits of 1 to 2 percent of net sales, and this is *before* income taxes.

The third factor is the buying ability of the chains. The quantities in which they buy—carloads and even trainloads—and their ability to contract often a year in advance for the output of a farm or factory enable them to secure a favorable price. Chain-store buyers typically are very skilled specialists in their business.

Opportunity to use advertising. Chain organizations are in a much better position to make effective use of advertising than even large independents. This competitive advantage is more a result of the multitude of chain outlets than of the total volume size of the corporation. That is, a grocery chain may have 25 medium-sized stores blanketing a city, and an independent competitor may have one huge supermarket doing three to four times the business of any single unit of the chain. Yet the chain can use the metropolitan daily newspaper as an advertising medium with much less waste circulation than the independent can. Many chains also make effective use of national advertising media.

Ability to spread risks. Chain stores do not have all their eggs in one basket or in one store. Even large-scale independent department stores or supermarkets cannot match this advantage of the chain. A multiunit operation automatically has spread its risks among many members. If one store is located in a declining market, that store can be closed and any loss absorbed by other, still healthy outlets.

Flexibility for experimentation. In many respects a chain is bogged down in administrative inflexibility solely because the multiunit operation requires standardization. This same multiunit operation, however, offers a number of opportunities for flexibility. As a case in point, one outlet's slow-moving merchandise can be moved to another outlet whose customers might view it more favorably. The company can experiment with layouts, different store fronts, or new types of merchandise by introducing any of these features into a few stores before committing itself to a full-scale introduction.

Competitive disadvantages. Chain stores suffer the limitations of all large-scale retailing institutions, as well as a few additional ones.

Standardization and inflexibility. The feature of standardization, the hallmark of a chain-store system and a major factor in its success, is a mixed blessing. Chains have not always been able to adjust rapidly to local competition or to take full advantage of local market opportunities because store managers could not act without first getting approval from a central office.

Chains are well aware of these limitations and have instituted several measures designed to give store managers greater freedom and to lessen the rigidities of merchandising policies. Chain-store executives, however, are also aware that in decreasing the amount of standardization, they run the risk of increasing their operating costs. Consequently, the single-unit store undoubtedly will continue to enjoy the advantage of flexibility in competition with a chain.

Personnel problems. Chain stores are particularly susceptible to the personnel problems associated with large-scale businesses. Store managers are shifted from one store to another, thus making it difficult for them to establish real rapport with other employees or with a particular community.

Poor public image. In the 1940s, the chains were generally held in very low regard and high suspicion by many consumers. Some common criticisms were that chains are run by absentee ownership; that they do not pay their fair share of taxes; that they have miserable personnel policies, such as long hours and low pay; and that they are monopolistic and engage in unfair competition. Many of these charges were half-truths, and others were not true at all. Nevertheless, this poor image undoubtedly presented substantial obstacles to chain development. Changing social and economic considerations, along with more enlightened, socially responsible chain-store management, have improved the situation, but chains will probably never enjoy the degree of public sympathy and support that local, independent merchants do.

FRANCHISE SYSTEMS INVOLVING SMALL, INDEPENDENT RETAILERS

One of the strongest competitive limitations facing corporate chains in the past 30 years has been the increased effectiveness of independent retailers and wholesalers who have copied chain-store marketing methods. Independents have adopted self-service methods in many types of stores; they have improved store appearance and layout; they have sought better locations, including suburban shopping centers; they have improved their merchandising practices by eliminating some slow-moving items and keeping fresh stock; and they have improved their accounting and inventory control systems.

Probably the most effective measure adopted by small independents has been their practice of voluntarily associating with wholesalers, manufacturers, or other retailers in some form of contractual franchise system. In some instances these associations resemble a corporate chain so closely that about the only significant difference is that the retail stores are not centrally owned. These voluntary affiliations coupled with the limitations of large, corporate chain forms of retailing and changing nature of the consumer market are resulting in a revitalization of the small, independent retailer.[1]

Nature of franchise systems. The concept of franchising is blurred sometimes by the broad, loose usage of the term and by the many variations in the scope of franchise agreements. Historically in marketing, a franchise was defined narrowly as "a system under which a manufacturer granted to certain dealers the right to sell his product or service, in generally defined areas, in exchange for a promise to promote and merchandise the product in a specific manner."[2]

---

1 See Alton F. Doody and William R. Davidson, "Growing Strength in Small Retailing," *Harvard Business Review,* July-August, 1964, pp. 69-79.

2 Charles M. Hewitt, "The Furor over Dealer Franchises," *Business Horizons,* November, 1958, p. 81.

Perhaps at this point it will be more useful if we broaden our interpretation of franchising to include any contractual arrangement between a franchiser (a supplier, who may be a manufacturer or a wholesaler) and a series of independent franchisees (either wholesalers or retailers). The franchiser grants the right to sell certain goods or services in generally defined markets. He usually provides equipment, the products or services for sale, and managerial services. In return the franchisee agrees to market the product or service in a manner established by the supplier. Within the broader definition we find two main types of franchising systems—one is a voluntary association of retailers and/or wholesalers; the other is a retailer network initiated and sponsored by a manufacturer.[3]

Associations of independent retailers. These associations may take any of several forms, but the two most important are wholesaler-sponsored groups and retailer-sponsored groups, also known, respectively, as voluntary chains and retailer cooperative chains. A *voluntary chain* is an association of independent retailers, initiated and sponsored by a wholesaler for the primary purpose of assuring the wholesaler of a series of profitable retail outlets for his products. The connecting link between the wholesaler and the retailer is a contract. In some instances, the wholesaler who sponsors a group of independent stores also belongs to a federation or association of similar group-sponsoring wholesalers. An example in the food field is the Independent Grocers Alliance (IGA), which grants a franchise to a wholesaler, who in turn licenses his member retailers as IGA stores.

The essence of the contract in a wholesaler-sponsored chain is that the wholesaler will furnish various services to member retailers, who in turn will buy all or almost all their merchandise from this wholesaler. Through the tremendous buying power of the combined retail units, wholesalers are able to buy at prices competitive with those of corporate chain organizations. Wholesalers offer various marketing and management services, such as proposals for store layout, effective display methods, advertising aids, accounting and stock control systems, reasonable credit, and field supervisors. Sales volumes of voluntary chains, particularly the combined organizations such as IGA, are big enough to enable them to market under their own brand. This practice provides lower-cost buying opportunities, offers promotional advantages, and prevents consumers from making direct price comparisons with merchandise offered by corporate chains.

A *retailer cooperative chain* is an organization instituted and sponsored by a group of independent retailers who jointly buy and operate a wholesale warehouse. The formal tie is stock ownership in the cooperative warehouse. The retailer members usually maintain their separate identities.

Retailer-sponsored chains have the same basic purpose as wholesaler-sponsored chains—to enable independent wholesalers and retailers to meet more effectively the competition from corporate chain stores. These associations of independents differ from each other in the following respects: (a) sponsorship of the association—retailer or wholesaler, (2) ownership of the wholesale house—retailer or wholesaler, (3) the connecting link between wholesaler and retailer—stock ownership or contract, and (4) the nature of services provided by the wholesaler.

---

3 For the point of view that these two systems are sufficiently different that they should be identified as separate concepts and that the term "franchise selling" should be limited to the manufacturer-sponsored system, see Leonard J. Konopa, "What Is meant by Franchise Selling?" *Journal of Marketing,* April, 1963, pp. 35-37.

Manufacturer-sponsored systems. This type of franchise system follows the narrow definition stated earlier. That is, a manufacturer sets up a network of retail outlets by contracting with new or established independent operators. The contract may cover (1) a single department in a store, (2) only one brand within a department (Magnavox or Maytag appliances), or (3) the entire retail outlet (dealerships for autos, farm equipment, or petroleum products; McDonald's or Dairy Queen drive-ins; Holiday Inns and Howard Johnson restaurants; Fred Astaire dance studios; Hertz or Avis auto rentals; Office Overload part-time help).

We can distinguish between two concepts in producer-sponsored franchise systems. One features franchising as a form of exclusive distribution. This type has existed for years and often involves a large-scale retailer. The other concept is the rise of entrepreneurship franchising. The practice is relatively new, and it typically has involved small-scale retailers. Enterprise franchising has especially proliferated in (1) the fast-foods industry (Kentucky Fried Chicken, Baskin-Robbins ice cream, McDonald's hamburgers) and in (2) service industries (recreation, auto rentals, motels, auto repairs).[4]

Extent of franchising systems. Wholesaler-sponsored chains, such as IGA, are more prevalent in the grocery field than in other lines of retailing, although these chains do exist in the fields of hardware (Home Hardware, Buildall), variety stores, auto supplies (Canadian Tire, Western Auto), and drugs (Shoppers' Drug). Retailer-sponsored chains are also quite significant in the grocery field, but otherwise they are not very important in the total retailing picture. Group affiliations of independent retailers have been growing rapidly since World War II. In 1972, for example, total Canadian retail sales of grocery and combination stores was $7,890 million and of that total voluntary group stores accounted for $2,050 million or 26%. In comparison, in 1963 voluntary group stores accounted for just over 23% of total retail sales of grocery and combination stores. The importance of food voluntary groups differs in various provinces. For example, in 1972, food voluntary groups accounted for 36.9% of total grocery and combination store sales in Quebec, but for only 18% of corresponding sales in Ontario.

Among manufacturer-sponsored systems, the concept of franchising an entire retail outlet (as contrasted with a single department or one brand within a department) is not new—oil companies and automobile manufacturers have done this for years. What is new, however, is its substantial growth since about 1950 and its spreading into many new fields. In addition to a huge volume in fast-food and refreshment services, today producer-sponsored franchise selling also embraces a variety of other products and services including auto mufflers, putting greens, paint, part-time office help, hearing aids, motels, and dance studios.

Competitive advantages. Franchising has many economic and social factors encouraging its growth. In voluntary groups a manufacturer may reach hundreds of independents simply by contacting one wholesaler. A manufacturer-sponsored system offers a manufacturer an opportunity for greater control and supervision over the pricing, advertising, and selling of his product—a sharp contrast with the

---

4 For a comprehensive study of fast-food franchising, see Urban B. Ozanne and Shelby D. Hunt, *The Economic Effects of Franchising*, U.S. Government Printing Office, Washington, 1971; see also Jack M. Starling. "Franchising," *Business Studies* (North Texas State University), Fall, 1970, pp. 10-16; and *Journal of Retailing*, Winter, 1968-1969, special issue devoted to franchising.

situation he faces when distributing through giant retailers. Franchising also provides a supplier with the means for rapid market expansion and a wide distribution system at a relatively low cost. The franchisee typically puts up some of the money. With his own money at stake, a franchisee has more incentive and is apt to be a more dedicated entrepreneur than a store manager hired by the manufacturer.

In both types of franchise systems, retailers are identified as a group. Thus a manufacturer can make effective use of cooperative advertising programs, display materials, and other promotional features. The group buying power enables the independent retailer-members to obtain lower-cost merchandise and a better selection of the latest products. Furthermore, the retailers are able to do a better job of retail store management because of the administrative services furnished by the wholesaler, particularly in voluntary chains. Finally, the opportunity to use group advertising enhances the competitive position of these retailers.

In a manufacturer-sponsored network particularly, franchising enables a person to realize a dream that many people have—the opportunity to own his own business. This goal now can be reached, and with the added security that the business has been tested. Also, the franchisee's investment is relatively small, and it is easier for him to borrow the necessary funds now that a big national firm is behind him. He may be an independent, small-scale retailer, and yet he is backed by the buying power, promotional programs, and management know-how of a big company.

Limitations. In the authors' opinion, the biggest single competitive weakness of all independent retailers, whether affiliated or not, is their assumption that the sole advantage of the chain is its buying power. Through the years many retailers have come to the conclusion that this assumption is false. But too many still fail to realize that the real strength of a large-scale institution lies in its superior management personnel and specialized management practices.

Ignorance or disregard of this fact today places major limitations on voluntary associations of independents. Too often these retailers reject the management advice given by field supervisors. Many retailers still think of the association as a buying aid only and make little use of advertising, display, accounting, and other association services. In general, the problem is simply that these retailers are independent in every sense of the word. They want to be in business for themselves, and they do not take kindly to outside supervision.

The rapid expansion of producer-sponsored franchising systems during the past 20 years also brought the industry its share of problems.[5] One is the charge that franchising agreements are terribly one-sided—all in favor of the franchisor. To the extent that this charge is true, any imbalance can be minimized if both parties will carefully analyze all appropriate criteria when selecting a franchising partner.[6] The problem of one-sidedness also can be minimized by carefully designing the contract, and by the franchisor's intelligent handling of conflict situations.[7]

Another problem is that franchisors sometimes engage in deceptive practices

---

5 For an evaluation of the favorable and unfavorable consequences of franchising, see Shelby D. Hunt, "The Socioeconomic Consequences of the Franchise System of Distribution," *Journal of Marketing*, July, 1972, pp. 32-38.

6 See Ronald L. Tatham, Ronald F. Bush, and Robert Douglas, "An Analysis of Decision Criteria in Franchisor/Franchisee Selection Process," *Journal of Retailing*, Spring, 1972, pp. 16-21ff.

7 See P. Ronald Stephenson and Robert G. House, "A Perspective on Franchising," *Business Horizons*, August, 1971, pp. 35-42.

when selling franchises and negotiating franchise agreements. While unethical techniques do exist. Hunt concluded that there was no widespread, systematic misrepresentation.[8]

Perhaps the major threat to continued successful expansion of franchising is the practice whereby the producer-sponsor takes over the ownership of successful units in his franchise system. This, in effect, turns the independent units into a corporate chain system. One unfortunate aspect of this trend is to reduce the numbers of successful, small, independent entrepreneurs.[9]

RETAILERS CLASSIFIED BY METHOD OF OPERATION

Manufacturers and wholesalers will find some value in analyzing retail middlemen according to their methods of operation. The two broad categories observed here are in-store retailing and nonstore, or outside-of-the-store, retailing. Major methods of in-store retailing which should be considered are full-service retailing, supermarket retailing, and discount retailing. Major forms of nonstore retailing are mail-order selling, automatic vending, and personal selling on a door-to-door basis.

FULL-SERVICE RETAILING

This is the traditional form of in-store, across-the-counter-retailing where the customer comes to the store, is waited on by salesman, and may avail himself of other store services. It is no secret that this form of retail selling has declined considerably over the past thirty years or so. It is still prevalent, however, and probably will remain so in product lines where high-fashion goods are involved or where a salesman's demonstration, explanation, or fitting is needed.

SUPERMARKET RETAILING

It is somewhat difficult to analyze supermarket retailing because there is no universally accepted definition of the term. To some people it is a *type* of retail institution found in the grocery business. To others, the term describes a *method* of retailing and may be used in connection with stores in any field.

In this discussion, a *supermarket* will be defined as a large-scale, departmentized retailing institution offering a wide variety of merchandise (including groceries, meats, produce, and dairy products), operating largely on a self-service basis with a minimum of customer services, and featuring a price appeal and usually ample parking space. No minimum sales volume is established as a criterion in this definition. It is believed that in selecting a channel of distribution, a manufacturer is more concerned with the marketing methods of a type of retailing institution than with its precise volume.

---

8 Hunt, *op. cit.*, pp. 37-38. See also Shelby D.Hunt, "Full Disclosure and the Franchise System of Distribution," in Becker and Becker (eds.), 1972 *Combined Proceedings*, American Marketing Association, series no. 34, Chicago, 1973, pp. 301-304.

9 See Shelby D. Hunt, "The Trend toward Company-Operated Units in Franchise Chains," *Journal of Retailing*, Summer, 1973, pp. 3-12; see also Alfred R. Oxenfeldt and Anthony O. Kelly, "Will Successful Franchise Systems Ultimately Become Wholly-Owned Chains?" *Journal of Retailing*, Winter, 1968-1969, pp. 69-83.

The major marketing policies and strategies of a supermarket are stated or implied in the above definition. First, these stores operate largely or entirely on a self-service basis, and they characteristically offer very few services, such as credit or delivery. Second, the limited service feature, combined with the large buying power and willingness to take low percentage profit margins, means that supermarkets can sell at low prices. A third marketing characteristic of supermarkets is that they offer a wide variety of merchandise, and it looks as if the trend toward product diversification will continue.

Development of supermarkets. Supermarkets, as we know them today, had their start in the Depression days of the early 1930s. They were owned and operated by *independents* attempting to compete with the chain stores. Those "pine-board" operations were a far cry from the supermarkets of today. As large-scale retailers, supermarkets enjoy the general advantages attributable to scale, and they also may escape one of the serious problems of bigness, namely, the impersonal relations that exist between store and customer. Because most consumers who shop in supermarkets prefer to be left alone, the big store's lack of friendly, sociable salesclerks may be no limitation.

Supermarkets are overwhelmingly the dominant institution in food retailing today. Yet in the 1960s several factors combined to level off the expansion rate of conventional supermarkets. As the market share held by the full-service food stores became very small, there was less of an area to expand into. Thus the demand for large, self-service stores became well saturated.

Consequently, the large retailers resorted to competing fiercely with one another, because a new supermarket had to attract much of its business from existing large stores. At first the struggle was in the form of price competition. When store profits were reduced to dangerously low levels, companies shifted to nonprice competition by offering trading stamps, contests, longer store hours, and other services. These forms of nonprice competition did, of course, increase operating costs and selling prices, but unfortunately not profits.

Discount supermarkets. The inviting vacancy at the bottom of the supermarket pricing structure enticed innovative competitive institutions to fill the voids. A move toward discount selling in food products started when discount department stores established discount-food departments in their stores. The next evolutionary development in food retailing was the establishment of separate, "free-standing" discount supermarkets. Both types of these discount-food retailers operate with fewer services, lower gross margins, no trading stamps, and lower prices compared with conventional supermarkets. In fact, competition from discount food retailers has become so intense that many food chains have converted some or all of their stores to discount operations.[10]

"Convenience stores." Another innovative competitor of conventional supermarkets has been the "convenience stores," which interestingly enough have higher prices and a more limited product assortment and are smaller in size. But they do have longer shopping hours, convenient locations, and the ability to provide fill-in type of purchases when other food stores are closed. In some ways they are a

---

10 "Discounting: A Food Chain Reaction," *Business Week*, Sept. 26, 1970, p. 44; see also Robert J. Minichiello, "The Real Challenge of Food Discounters," *Journal of Marketing*, April, 1967, pp. 37-42.

throwback to the corner grocery store of years past.[11] These chains are often known as "jug milk" stores and include such chains as Green Gables, Perrette, Mac's Milk, Beckers, and 7-Eleven. Such stores have enjoyed a high growth rate in recent years and accounted for 2.3 per cent of retail food store sales in Canada in 1974. In some areas, conventional supermarkets are attempting to meet convenience store competition by extending their store hours into nights and Sundays.

In 1975, the Food Prices Review Board undertook a study to determine the cost to Canadian consumers of dealing with convenience stores. The Board compared the prices of a 32-item basket of food items at convenience stores and at conventional supermarkets in five Canadian cities, and concluded that the consumer pays from 5 to 24 percent more in convenience stores. These stores are generally able to charge higher prices because of the convenience of time and place which they offer the consumer. The Food Prices Review Board found that convenience stores' gross margins average 25.5 percent as compared with 21 percent for food distributors generally. But the higher operating expenses of the convenience stores result in a pre-tax profit percentage which is almost identical to that of other food distributors.[12]

The superstore. The newest and possibly the toughest competitor of the supermarket is the superstore—also called a hypermarché. By the late 1970s, this new breed of supermarket—a huge combination grocery and general merchandise store—is expected by some observers to capture a large portion of food sales. But the hypermarché concept has not caught on in North America as well as it did in Europe—where it was first developed.

The first Canadian hypermarché was opened in 1973 in Laval, a suburb of Montreal. This store is, at 240,000 square feet, about four times as large as the largest of conventional supermarkets. In addition to the food items carried by supermarkets, the hypermarché carries a large volume of general merchandise, including clothing, hardware, housewares, toys, linens, electrical appliances, and home entertainment products. The breadth of product line and its sheer size are the major differences between the hypermarché and the supermarket.[13]

A number of food retailers have rejected the hypermarché concept in favor of building very large supermarkets with larger than normal general merchandise sections. Some reasons for this decision include: 1. The high cost of the large amount of land needed for the free-standing hypermarché; 2. The apparent reluctance of Canadians to buy food and clothing to the same store; 3. The tendency for hypermarchés to produce a very high percentage of sales from low-margin food items; 4. The sheer size of the hypermarché which may intimidate some shoppers and which leads to a reluctance on the part of shoppers to "retrace their steps" to search for an

---

11 See "The Threat to Southland's (7-11 stores) Growth," *Business Week*, Oct. 28, 1972, p. 60; and Philip D. Cooper, "Will Success Produce Problems for the Convenience Store?" *MSU Business Topics*, Winter, 1972, pp. 39-43.

12 Food Prices Review Board, "Convenience Food Stores Survey," Ottawa: Information Canada, November, 1975.

13 Walter J. Salmon, Robert D. Buzzell, and Stanton G. Cort, *The Super-Store—Strategic Implications for the Seventies*, Marketing Science Institute, Cambridge, Mass., study commissioned by *Family Circle* magazine, 1972. This study was later summarized by same authors in "Today the Shopping Center, Tomorrow the Superstore," *Harvard Business Review*, January-February, 1974, pp. 89-98.

item which may have been missed or forgotten during the initial trip through the store.[14]

But despite the slow growth of the hypermarché in the North American market, it remains a concept to be watched and one which could have considerable impact on retailing in the future.

In conclusion, executives in the conventional supermarket chain organizations are faced with substantial competitive challenges designed to meet the heterogeneous demands of the market. How they meet these threats in the late 1970s and 1980s will determine their rate of survival and degree of success.[15]

DISCOUNT RETAILING AND THE DISCOUNT HOUSE

The development of the modern discount house in the decade following World War II is quite significant. This institution or method of selling entered the retailing field as a brash innovator and forced a re-examination of traditional pricing structures and operating margins, costs, and methods.

What is a discount house? Is it a retailing *institution* which is separately discernible and which is capable of being defined so as to differentiate it, or are we really talking about a *method* of retail pricing and sales promotion which is applicable to almost any type of store? Actually there is nothing new about discount selling—the practice of selling below the list price or the regular advertised price. There is also nothing new about discount houses. They have existed in some form for many years. If this is the case, one may wonder why suddenly in the late 1940s and early 1950s there was so much excitement about them. The reason is that the earlier discount houses were of a different type. Many were small establishments which displayed no merchandise, instead, customers selected from manufacturers' catalogues and placed orders by model or style number. Generally, access to these stores was restricted in some fashion.

The discount houses which emerged after World War II, however, and which caused so much consternation in the ranks of traditional retailers are different. They are large stores, freely open to the public, advertising widely, carrying a reasonably complete selection of well-known brands of hard goods (appliances, home furnishings, sporting goods, jewelry), consistently selling below nationally advertised list prices, operating in heavily traveled but low-rent districts, and offering a minimum of customer services.

Growth of discount retailing. To understand the early success of the discount house, let us examine the reasons why some retailers were able to sell at low prices, and then analyze the market to see why consumers were so receptive to a low-price-no-service appeal. First, what factors led to the traditional retail markup on appliances and other products that are typically discounted? In the 1930s, electric home appliances were relatively new products and were generally classed as luxuries. Consequently, manufacturers had to offer retailers large markups—30 to 40 percent—to encourage them to stock the products and perform the necessary ser-

---

14 Susan Goldenberg, "Are hypermarches feasible here?" *The Financial Post*, May 17, 1975.

15 See Rom J. Markin, "The Supermarket Today and Tomorrow!" *Atlanta Economic Review*, October, 1972, pp. 20-24; and Fred C. Allvine, "The Supermarket Challenged!" *Business Horizons*, October, 1968, pp. 61-70.

vices. Personal selling was required to demonstrate, explain, and truly *sell* these items. Retailers had to advertise the products in the local market, and the dealers had to service them.

By the end of World War II, product and market considerations had changed substantially. Products were presold to consumers through national advertising by the manufacturers. The products were of better quality, so the manufacturer's guarantee on parts was sufficient for the consumer.

After the war a new consumer market emerged—a vast middle-income market—composed in large part of people who had been in low-income groups. These people were price-conscious. They were the people with whom supermarket methods of selling had been so successful. The supermarkets conditioned these consumers for discount selling—low prices and few services. Also, this market had a pent-up demand from the war years. With so many wants and limited income, people were forced to place importance on price when buying.

The situation was ripe from major changes in retailing. Most retailers, however, either failed to grasp the significance of the situation or paid no heed. Instead, they maintained their traditional markup policies. On the other hand, the discount sellers saw the tremendous possibilities in a low-margin, high-turnover type of operation, with few services but big price reductions. Their operating methods enabled them to limit expenses to 12 to 18 percent of sales, as compared with the 30 to 40 percent found in department and limited-line stores.

Recent developments in discount retailing. Discount selling has led to a revision of traditional retailing margins. Manufacturers have altered their channels of distribution to include discounting retailers. Small-scale retailers have been forced to drop discounted products or else meet the discount-house price by offering fewer services and adopting more efficient methods. Large-scale retailers, such as department stores, have responded in several ways. In selling appliances, some stores conduct almost a continual warehouse sale. Others have realistically lowered their markups on discounted products.

The discount stores themselves are changing. Some, such as Woolco and K-Mart, are upgrading their image to that of a "promotional department store," and many have opened stores in suburban shopping centers. In general, all discounters are trading up in products and services. In the early 1950s, discount sellers ordinarily did not carry food products or soft goods. Today many have added soft goods, including a line of wearing apparel. In fact, reasonably expensive, high-fashion women's ready-to-wear is carried in a number of large discount houses and some are even using national television advertising to promote fashion sales. Separate discount department stores have been established by "conventional" retailers such as Woolworth (Woolco), Kresge (K-Mart) and Eaton's (Horizon).

The discount sellers' risks and operating costs are, of course, being increased as they add more expensive merchandise, broaden their assortments, move into fancier buildings and locations, and add more services. Vastly intensified competition is also causing real financial problems for many discounters, and there are signs of a slowdown in the rate of entry into the field.

A recent analysis of the problems faced by the discounters has observed that there has been very little real growth in the discount field since the late 1960s as discounters' sales per square foot in real dollars have been declining. The slowdown in the growth of discounters is partially linked to overexpansion, declining inventory turnover, and high costs of carrying inventory, but is more fundamentally linked to the discounters' reaction to changing consumer needs. As consumers have become more affluent, their demands have changed from looking for the lowest prices to looking for the best value for their money. As the discounters have continued to emphasize price, consumers have tended to move back to the conventional department stores where merchandise is generally of better quality and where prices are not much higher, if higher at all, than those charged by the discount stores.[16]

As discount houses and conventional retailers adopt each other's strong points, we can see discount sellers losing their identity as a distinctive form of retailing institution. Perhaps price will cease to be their principal appeal for consumer patronage. Instead, mature discount houses will have to rely more on the forms of nonprice competition (services, quality products, good location, believable promotion, ethical standards, etc.) used by older types of retailers.

NONSTORE PERSONAL SELLING

One of the oldest retailing methods in history is to have buyer and seller transact their business at the buyer's home or at some other nonstore location. This is called *door-to-door* or *house-to-house* selling. Unfortunately, these terms are a poor description of nonstore personal selling. They suggest a cold canvass, wherein the salesman literally goes from door to door, without advance selection of prospects. Actually, relatively little selling is done in this haphazard way.

Nonstore sales may be made by either producers or retailers selling directly to consumers. Bakery and dairy products are frequently distributed in this fashion. Many manufacturers also use this method, including makers of cosmetics (Avon), brushes (the Fuller Brush Company), costume jewelery (Sarah Coventry), housewares (Stanley Home Products), reference books (World Book Encyclopedia), and vacuum cleaners (Electrolux). At the retailer level, automobile dealers do some door-to-door selling. Also, rugs, draperies, and home heating departments in department stores often have their salesmen call directly on people at home.

The oldest and most common way for a "direct-to-home" salesman to reach his prospects is simply to make a door-to-door canvass of a neighborhood. Another way is "party-plan" selling where one customer acts as the hostess of a party to which she invites several friends. Stanley Home Products and Tupperware are two major users of the "party-plan" approach. The salesman, who is at the party and actually stages it, has a larger prospective market under more advantageous conditions than if he had approached each of the "guests" individually on a house-to-house basis. Another house-to-house approach is to make the initial contact in a store, by telephone, or by having the prospect mail in a coupon. Then the salesman follows up by calling at the prospect's home.

Statistics Canada estimates that direct or door-to-door selling accounts for only about four percent of equivalent retail sales—that is after sales of merchandise not normally sold door-to-door are deducted. While this is obviously not a substantial part of the total retailing picture (direct sales in 1974 were $1,227 million), there are indications that an increasing number of companies are using this method to sell a growing variety of products.[17]

---

16 Douglas J. Tigert and George H. Haines, Jr., "The Death of the Discount Store: An Analysis of the Changing Structure of Retailing in Canada," a paper presented at the Second Triennial Marketing Conference, York University, Toronto, May, 1975.

17 See "The Awesome Potential of In-Home Selling or Look Who's at the Door," *Sales Management*, Apr. 15, 1971, p. 27.

In-house selling is attractive to consumers because it offers the convenience of buying at home, plus personalized service. From the company's point of view, door-to-door selling provides an opportunity for the most aggressive forms of retail selling, plus the chance to demonstrate a product in the customer's home. A sales talk can be prepared in detail, with the assurance that this talk is more apt to reach prospective customers if it is given by a door-to-door salesman than if it is passed through retailers' salesmen.

It is questionable whether the cost and profit factors of door-to-door selling are an advantage or a limitation. By eliminating the middleman, consumers may think they are saving money. Yet products sold door-to-door are probably higher-priced than those sold in stores, although price comparisons are difficult because the products are not identical. Sellers, in turn, are attracted by the seemingly high profit margins. Retail prices are easy to maintain at the producer's suggested level. The biggest single selling expense—salesmen's commissions and expenses—is a variable one because salesmen usually are paid a straight commission on sales and they pay their own expenses out of their commissions. Higher net profits are hardly possible, however, unless the producer can perform all wholesaling and retailing functions at a lower total cost than would be possible if separate middlemen were used. On balance, the presence of higher profits is frequently a mirage.

The problems inherent in door-to-door selling explain why it will probably remain a minor form of modern retailing. First, while offering some conveniences to a consumer, it also runs counter to other buying habits, such as the desire to select from a wide assortment of merchandise or to shop and compare price and quality.[18] This method of selling has acquired a poor reputation because many door-to-door salesmen have been nuisances or even unscrupulous, fraudulent operators. All provinces have passed legislation designed to protect the consumer against fraudulent direct sellers. These laws give the consumer a "cooling off period" of from three to ten days after a door-to-door purchase is made, during which time the consumer may cancel the purchase and be entitled to full reimbursements of any payments made. Another limitation is that managing a door-to-door sales force poses tremendous problems. Good salesmen are extremely hard to find, and the turnover rate is high. Often they are poorly selected, inadequately trained, and insufficiently supervised. On top of everything else, door-to-door selling is the most expensive form of retailing. Salesmen's commissions alone run as high as 40 to 50 percent of retail price. When we add to this the costs of managing the sales force, plus freight on the merchandise, we often get total margin requirements which are higher than a corresponding total of wholesalers' and in-store retailers' margins.[19]

NONSTORE, NONPERSONAL SELLING

Two other forms of nonstore retailing that involve no personal contact between buyer and seller are mail-order selling and automatic vending.

Mail-order selling. In mail-order selling, a consumer may (1) buy out of a catalogue, (2) mail in an order form appearing in an advertisement, or (3) use an order

---

18 See Peter L. Gillett, "A Profile of Urban In-Home Shoppers," *Journal of Marketing,* July, 1970, pp. 40-45; and William H. Peters and Neil M. Ford, "A Profile of Urban In-Home Shoppers: The Other Half," *Journal of Marketing,* January, 1972, pp. 62-64.

19 See Marvin A. Jolson, "Direct Selling: Consumer vs. Salesman—Is Conflict Inevitable?" *Business Horizons,* October, 1972, pp. 87-95.

form received from the seller directly through the mail. Some of the mail-order houses (such as Simpsons-Sears) are *general merchandise* houses offering an exceptionally wide variety of product lines with much depth of assortment in each line. Other institutions might be termed *specialty* houses in that they limit the number of lines they carry—books, records, garden supplies, or food, for example.

Mail-order retailing enjoys some competitive advantages. Operating costs are lower than for in-store retailing. Labor costs per dollar sales are low. Mail-order houses are in low-rent locations, and they do not need elaborate store fixtures. Mail-order retailing also fits in with some consumer buying habits. A wide variety of merchandise is offered by general merchandise houses. Also, the consumer can leisurely shop the catalogue and then place an order without the inconvenience of going to a store. Stated prices seem lower because they usually are quoted f.o.b. warehouse, that is, without the freight charges which the consumer must pay.

Mail-order retailing has some drawbacks both for the consumer and for the seller. Except where items are displayed at catalogue stores, customers must place their orders without actually seeing the merchandise they are buying. This limitation is counteracted to some extent by liberal return privileges, guarantees, and excellent catalogue presentations. Customers must plan their purchases well in advance in order to allow time for delivery. Mail-order houses have attempted to speed delivery by establishing branch warehouses and transmitting orders by teletype. Mail-order houses have little flexibility. Catalogues are costly and must be prepared long in advance of the season. Price changes and new merchandise offerings can be announced only through the issuance of supplementary catalogues, and these are a weak selling tool.

Several of the factors which accounted for the early growth of mail-order retailing no longer exist. Automobiles and good rural roads have made city stores easily accessible to farmers, and rural retailing generally has improved. Far from being in a state of decline, however, catalogue buying by mail and telephone is resurging. The convenience of in-home, "one-stop" shopping appeals to a large group of consumers who are showing signs of revolting against standing in line, getting no help from salesclerks, and fighting the traffic and parking problem.

Automatic vending. Today an amazingly wide variety of products is sold through coin-operated machines which automatically vend merchandise (or services) without the aid or presence of a salesclerk. Usually the machines are owned by a vending machine operating company which rents the space needed for desirable locations. In 1974, according to Statistics Canada, there were 106,278 vending machines in Canada. The total volume of sales through these machines was $227.4 million, of which $105.4 million were cigarette sales. Vending machines account for only about one-half of one percent of total retail sales, with the bulk coming from cigarettes, soft drinks, candy, and hot beverages. The remainder was spread over a wide field of such diverse goods as hosiery, cosmetics, film, sandwiches, T-shirts and fishing worms, and such services as laundering and insurance policies.

Vending machines can expand a firm's market by reaching customers where and when it is not feasible for stores to do so. Products sold through vending machines typically have low unit values and low markups, so they are relatively expensive to sell through regular retail stores. Many stores use vending machines as a complementary form of retailing. Some have placed a bank of machines outside the store to get nighttime business. Another major expanding market for automatic vending lies in the field of in-plant feeding, that is, the feeding of employees of factories, offices, and other places where large numbers of workers must be fed in a short period of time. The outlook for "robot retailing" is promising. Even department stores are experimenting with vending machines.

Automatic vending still faces major problems, however. In the first place, operating costs are high, and there is a continual need for machine maintenance and repair. New machines make former expensive models obsolete before they are depreciated. The prices of automatically vended products are frequently higher than store prices of the same products. A second significant problem is that products which can be sold successfully by machine must be well-known, presold brands with a high rate of turnover. They must be reasonably low in unit value, small and uniform in size and weight, and generally of a convenience goods nature. Only a limited amount of processing can be accomplished. A related set of problems concerns the extent to which automatic vending is compatible with consumer buying habits. Normally, consumers like to feel or see a product before buying. Also, the machine offers no opportunity to return unwanted merchandise.

TRENDS AND PROSPECTS

Producers and wholesalers of consumer goods, and marketing men who work with them, must understand the retail market before they can intelligently develop distribution strategies. In this and the preceding chapter we have noted many current developments and trends in particular retailing institutions.

The retailing structure is not static; rather, it is complex, dynamic organism, with stress particularly on the word "dynamic." Three major forces causing change are (1) the changing consumer markets served by retailers, (2) the retailers' own constant search for more effective and profitable methods, and (3) the manufacturers' realization that they need mass-marketing methods to keep up with the mass production of goods. These forces underlie several broad, significant trends in the retailing structure.[20]

One of these trends is the continuing move toward *scrambled merchandising*—the practice of product diversification which results in an intensification of competition among traditionally different types of stores now carrying the same products. In the constant search for higher-margin items, one type of store will add products which traditionally were handled by other types of outlets. Consequently, wholesalers and manufacturers must change their channel systems, and retailers must adjust their marketing programs to meet this challenge of scrambled merchandising.

Out of dangerously low and shrinking profit margins is coming an intensified drive for *better management and increased productivity* in retailing. Through sophisticated applications of computer technology, retailers' information systems—accounting, inventory control, marketing research, etc.—are becoming more effective.[21] Automated materials-handling systems are helping to cut physical distribution costs. Operations research techniques are starting to be used to aid

---

20 For the trends on some 60 specific issues in retailing as forecasted by a sample of top executives from large retail firms, see Leo Bogart, "The Future in Retailing," *Harvard Business Review*, November-December, 1973, pp. 16-18ff.

21 See M. S. Moyer, "Market Intelligence for Modern Merchants," *California Management Review*, Summer, 1972, pp. 63-69.

management decision making in areas such as product selection and pricing, store location and layout, and advertising and sales-force activities.[22] Regarding credit plans for consumers, stores are expected to move from their own credit cards (or bank credit cards) to a centralized system which someday will be part of a checqueless, cashless society. Even top management in retailing is changing. Traditionally store presidents came up through the merchandising ranks and were "good merchants." Today accountants and lawyers are moving into the top spots.[23]

The move by retailers to adopt the *computerized checkout* is linked to a need to reduce the growing labor costs associated with retailing and to provide management with better information. The computerized equipment which is designed to read the Canadian Grocery Product Code will mean savings of up to 50 percent in checkout and other personnel costs, better inventory and pilferage control, and instant information for management on a day-to-day basis about movement of merchandise by size, brand, and price.[24]

There is a trend toward *concentration of retail trade* among a relatively small number of large-scale institutions. No matter how we classify retailers, it is obvious that fewer stores are doing a steadily increasing share of the retail business. Concentration has developed through mergers of corporate chains, voluntary associations of independents, and the expansion of chains into new geographic markets. An important by-product of concentration in retailing has been the increasing power of large retailers in the marketing system. No longer are these retailers at the mercy of manufacturers and wholesalers. Some retailers have integrated backward to take over wholesaling and manufacturing activities. Others have established their own brands in effective competition with manufacturers' brands.

An interesting *polarity in store size and merchandise assortment* is developing in retailing. At one pole are the mass-merchandising operations of superstores, discount stores, and department stores with their huge stores and their tremendously wide variety of products. At the other end of the spectrum is the small specialty shop—the boutique-type store. Even large stores (department stores, for example) are setting up separate specialty stores featuring a deep assortment of products, but in one very limited line such as women's sportswear or home furnishings.

The growing polarity of retailing, with the mass merchandisers at one end and the specialty stores on the other, is linked to two other concepts which merit watching. These are *classification dominance* and the application of *warehouse technology* to retailing.[25] Many retailers have clearly defined their target markets and have decided to attempt to dominate a small number of categories of merchandise rather than carrying only adequate inventories in a large number of categories. These retailers generally carry a complete variety of types and styles of product in their product classes. Examples of retailers who have achieved classification dominance are Consumers Distributing in small appliances, Canadian Tire in garden supplies, and Thrifty's in leisureware.

Several mass merchandisers have also applied warehouse technology to retailing with considerable success. Under this concept greater use is made of the vertical space in the retail store as merchandise is often palletized and stacked almost to

---

22 M. S. Moyer, "Management Science in Retailing," *Journal of Marketing*, January, 1972, pp. 3-9.

23 The New Breed that Runs the Big Stores," *Business Week*, June 26, 1971, p. 54.

24 See *Grey Matter*, vol. 45, no. 2, October, 1974, and "Bringing Home the 33900-10020," *Time*, December 30, 1974.

25 Tigert and Haines, *op cit.*, pp. 6-8.

ceiling height. The store often becomes the warehouse and the result is much higher sales per square foot than is realized in a conventional store.

We can anticipate a considerable increase in *nonstore retailing* in the coming years, to the point where some executives forecast that as much as one-third of all general merchandise business will be done outside the store by the end of this century.[26] Mail-order sales, in some cases tied in with catalogue showrooms, and telephone sales are expected to increase. On the horizon is buying through television-tele-phone (phonovision) systems coupled with computer systems. Consumers will be able to do much of their buying at home, using a telephone, seeing the merchan-dise on a television screen, and ordering through a computerized system which will deliver the products and arrange for automatic payment from the customer's bank account.[27]

In the institutional structure in retailing there is a real *breaking away from the tradi-tional store classifications*. The variations are proliferating. Already we have noted such changes as department stores developing small branches as specialty shops, rather than the usual full-line branch. F. W. Woolworth branched into discounting with its Woolco chain, and now Woolco has opened a chain of catalogue showrooms. We have already mentioned the growth in warehouse retailing, and the trend toward catalogue shopping in showrooms such as those pioneered by Consumers Distributing shows little sign of abating. "Free-form" corporations are evolving from former department stores.[28] In these organizations there is no spe-cialization by channel level or by kind-of-business classification. Eaton's, for exam-ple, operates urban department stores, auto services centres, drugstore depart-ments, a life insurance and financial services department, travel agencies, commercial photographic studios, a contract sales division, Horizon discount stores, and, until recently, a mail order catalogue division. Simpsons-Sears con-tinues to operate its department stores and its catalogue division.

Through the years, many of the evolutionary changes in retailing have followed a cyclical pattern which we call the *wheel of retailing*. As Professor McNair has so succinctly explained it:[29]

The cycle frequently begins with the bold new concept, the innovation. The innovator has an idea for a new kind of distributive enterprise. At the outset he is ridiculed, condemned as "illegitimate." Bankers and investors are leery of him. But he attracts the public on the basis of a price appeal made possible by the low operating costs inherent in his innovation. As he goes along he trades up, improves the quality of his merchandise, improves the ap-

26 Bogart, *op. cit.*, p. 26.

27 See William G. Nickels, "Central Distribution Facilities Challenge Traditional Retailers," *Journal of Re-tailing*, Spring, 1973, pp. 45-50.

28 William R. Davidson, "Changes in Distributive Institutions," *Journal of Marketing*, January, 1970, pp. 7-10. Also see Rollie Tillman, "Rise of the Conglomerchant," *Harvard Business Review*, November-De-cember, 1971, pp. 44-51.

29 Quoted in *Sales Management*, Nov. 21, 1958, p. 9. See also M. P. McNair, "Significant Trends and De-velopments in the Postwar Period," in A. B. Smith (ed.), *Competitive Distribution in a Free, High-level Econ-omy and Its Implications for the University*, The University of Pittsburgh Press, Pittsburgh, Pa., 1958, pp. 17-18. For an excellent critical analysis and refinement of McNair's "wheel of retailing" hypothesis, see Stanley C. Hollander, "The Wheel of Retailing," *Journal of Marketing*, July, 1960, pp. 37-42. For an interesting anal-ogy in which (1) channels of distribution are regarded as social and ecological systems, and (2) a retailer's chances for survival and success within this ecological system are explained in terms of the ecological con-cepts of *requirements, tolerances,* and *adaptation,* see Rom J. Markin, "The Retailer in the Vertical Marketing Network," *University of Washington Business Review*, Autumn, 1971, pp. 39-44.

pearance and standing of his store, attains greater respectability. Then, if he is successful, comes the period of growth, the period when he is taking business away from the established distribution channels that have clung to the old methods. Repeatedly something like this has happened in American distribution . . .

The maturity phase soon tends to be followed by top-heaviness, too great conservatism, a decline in the rate of return on investment, and eventual vulnerability. Vulnerability to what? Vulnerability to the next revolution of the wheel, to the next fellow who has the bright idea and who starts his business on a low-cost basis, slipping in under the umbrella that the old-line institutions have hoisted.

This familiar cycle can be observed in several instances in the past 100 years. First the department stores supplanted small retailers in the cities during the late 1800s and early 1900s. In the 1920s mail-order houses hit their peak.In that same decade the chain stores grew at the expense of independents, particularly in the grocery store field. In the 1930s the independents retaliated with supermarkets, which proved so successful that the chain stores copied the method. In the 1950s the discount houses—young innovators—placed tremendous pressure on department stores, which had become staid, mature institutions. By the early years of the 1960s the discount houses had passed the youthful stage, and discounters in soft goods and foods were appearing. Now we wait to see what new institution or method will be the innovator in the 1970s and 1980s—perhaps it will be automated retailing. By the same token, manufacturers must keep abreast of the inevitable changes in the retailing institutional scene and be ready to appraise the potential of any retailing innovators. Also, established retailers must be alert to meet the challenge with innovations of their own. Truly, a retailer must be ready, willing, and able to innovate, for the alternative is to die.

QUESTIONS AND PROBLEMS

1. "High-price, high-quality, high-fashion merchandise lines ordinarily do not lend themselves to chain-store operation." Why?
2. Do chains sell at lower prices than independents? Compare prices on several items carried by both chain stores and independents in your community.
3. The growing concentration of retail sales in the hands of a small number of chains will eventually lead to the disappearance of small, independent retail stores. Comment.
4. Carefully distinguish between a retailer cooperative chain and a voluntary chain. Are there examples of either type in your community?
5. In what ways does a corporate chain (Eaton's, Loblaws, or Sears) differ from a voluntary chain such as IGA?
6. With all the advantages attributed to voluntary associations of independents, why do you suppose some retailers are still unaffiliated?
7. "The only significant competitive advantage which chains have over independents is greater buying power. If buying power can be equalized through antichain legislation or by having the independents join some voluntary association, then independents can compete equally with the chains." Discuss.

8. "The supermarket, with its operating expense ratio of 20 percent, is the most efficient institution in retailing today." Do you agree? In what ways might supermarkets reduce their operating expenses?

9. Why do consumers continue to patronize small, independent, neighbourhood stores when prices at these stores are usually higher than those charged by supermarkets?

10. How have discount stores changed their methods of operation in recent years?

11. Name some discount houses in your community or in a large nearby city. Is there a distinction between "discount selling" and a "discount house"?

12. How have department stores met the challenge of the discount house?

13. "House-to-house selling is the most efficient form of retail selling because it eliminates both the wholesalers and the retail stores." Discuss.

14. "The factors which accounted for the early growth of mail-order retailing no longer exist, so we may expect a substantial decline in this form of selling." Discuss.

15. Why would a retailer install vending machines to sell products that he already carries in his store?

16. What are the conditions which will limit the growth of in-home buying? Of automatic vending?

17. The ease of entry into retailing undoubtedly contributes to the high mortality rate among retailers, with the resultant economic waste. Should entry into retailing be restricted? If so, how could this be done?

18. What recommendations do you have for reducing the costs of retailing?

19. Looking to the future, what retailing institutions or methods will decline and which ones will increase in importance? Explain.

THE WHOLESALE MARKET AND WHOLESALING MIDDLEMEN

"Let's eliminate the middleman" and "The middleman makes all the profit" are cries which have been echoed by many consumers, businesspeople, and legislators through the years. Typically these people are focusing their complaints on the wholesaling segment of the distribution structure. Historically, the wholesaler has been a truly powerful figure in marketing. During the past 25 to 50 years, however, many manufacturers and retailers have made successful attempts to eliminate the wholesaler from their trade channels. Yet wholesaling middlemen continue to be an important force, and in many cases a dominant figure, in the distribution system.

NATURE AND IMPORTANCE OF WHOLESALING

For several marketing and legal reasons, the wholesaling concepts discussed here should be defined precisely and distinguished carefully from the corresponding retailing terms. For example, when manufacturers are establishing their pricing structures, they often must allow wholesalers and retailers different discounts, because the two groups perform different services and thus have different operating costs to cover.

WHOLESALING BROADLY DEFINED

Wholesaling or wholesale trade includes the sale, and all activities directly incident to the sale, of products or services to those who are buying for purposes of resale or for business use. Thus, broadly viewed, sales made by one manufacturer to another are wholesale transactions, and the selling manufacturer is engaged in wholesaling. A retail variety store is engaged in wholesaling if it sells pencils or envelopes to a restaurant. That is, wholesaling includes sales of any firm to any customer except an ultimate consumer who is buying for personal, nonbusiness use. As in defining retailing, the only real criterion in identifying wholesaling and wholesale sales is the purchaser's purpose for buying.

THE NARROWER DEFINITION OF WHOLESALING

While the above general definition of wholesaling is accurate, it is too broad to be of practical value for our purposes of (1) understanding the role of wholesaling middlemen and (2) establishing channels of distribution policies. For analytical convenience, the definition must be limited. Therefore we shall be concerned with companies which are engaged *primarily* in wholesaling. We shall exclude retailers who occasionally make a wholesale sale. We shall also exclude sales of manufacturers and farmers because their major activity is not wholesaling. Primarily, they are engaged in creating form utility rather than time, place, and possession utilities. If a manufacturer operates a physically separate establishment, such as a sales branch where the main function is wholesaling and not manufacturing, however, this establishment will be included as a wholesaling middleman. Thus ownership of the establishment does not determine its classification. It may be owned by a manufacturer (a sales branch), a retailer (a retailer cooperative warehouse), or a farmer (a cooperative grain elevator) and still be considered a wholesaling establishment.

WHOLESALERS AND WHOLESALING MIDDLEMEN

The term "wholesaler" applies only to a *merchant* middleman engaged in wholesaling activities; that is, he takes title to the goods he handles. "Wholesaling middlemen" is the all-inclusive term, covering wholesalers and other wholesaling middlemen, such as agents and brokers, who do not take title to the merchandise. Thus a food broker or a manufacturers' agent is not a wholesaler, but he is a wholesaling middleman. Sometimes one hears the terms "jobber" and "distributor." Although usage varies from trade to trade, in this book these terms are considered synonymous with "wholesaler."

DEVELOPMENT AND ECONOMIC JUSTIFICATION OF WHOLESALING

Up to the end of World War I, the merchant wholesaler remained the kingpin in the channel structure. In general, manufacturers were small and poorly financed. They had no knowledge of the market, and it was not economically feasible for them to establish their own sales forces to go directly to the retailers, or even to deal directly with other manufacturers. At the same time, the retailers were also small, geographically scattered, and financially weak.

Even though large-scale activity in manufacturing developed in the late 1800s and the early 1900s, manufacturers still had to rely largely on wholesalers to reach the retailers. After World War I, however, large-scale retailers, such as corporate chains, began to expand. Thus the existence of large-scale businesses in manufacturing and in retailing set the scene for a shift in the balance of power. While the wholesaler has remained remarkably healthy and has continued to grow over the last 40 years, it is true, however, that he does not enjoy his old-time, almost monopolistic position in most channels of distribution.

Most manufacturing companies in Canada are still small and specialized. They have inadequate capital with which to maintain the sales force necessary to contact many scattered small retailers. Even among manufacturers who have sufficient capital, output is too small to justify the necessary sales force. Conversely, the typical retailer buys in small quantities and has a limited knowledge of the market and source of supply. Wholesalers can pool the orders of many retailers and so furnish a market for a small manufacturer, and at the same time perform a buying service for retailers.

Looking at wholesaling from a macro point of view, it brings to the total distribution system the economies of skill, scale, and transactions. Wholesaling middlemen are marketing specialists. Wholesaling *skills* can be effectively concentrated in a relatively few hands, thus saving the waste and duplication of effort which would occur if the many producers, now using these middlemen, were to take on the wholesaling functions themselves. Economies of *scale* are effected because, by using existing wholesaling middlemen, rather than duplicating them, there is an effective use of manpower resources. Also, wholesalers, typically can perform the physical handling and other wholesaling functions at an operating expense percentage lower than that at which most manufacturers can do the job. *Transaction* economies come into play when wholesaling middlemen are introduced between producers and their customers. Assume nine manufacturers want to sell to nine retailers. Without a wholesaling middleman there are 81 transactions. By using one wholesaler the number of transactions is cut to 18—9 occurring when the producers all sell to the wholesaler, and another 9 when the wholesaler sells to all the retailers.

SIZE OF TOTAL WHOLESALE MARKET

In 1971 there were about 44,000 wholesaling establishments in Canada, and they had a total annual sales volume of $42.3 billion. Table 18-1 shows that in each Census since 1941, the number of establishments increased substantially over the

Table 18-1. Total Wholesale Sales in Canada compared with Retail Sales

Year	Number of Wholesaling Establishments	Wholesale Sales (million)	Retail Sales (million)
1971	43,951	$42,293	$32,080
1961	30,855	19,453	16,073
1951	26,157	14,376	10,694
1941	18,576	3,141	3,415

Source: Summary Statistics, Census of Retail Trade, 1971; Retail Trade, 1961-1966, Statistics Canada Summary Statistics, Census of Wholesale Trade, 1971

preceding census year. The 1971 total wholesale trade represented an increase of over 100 percent since 1961 and over a twelvefold increase since 1941. Of course a substantial part of this increase is traceable to the rise in the price level. Even if each year's wholesale trade were expressed in constant dollars, however, we would still see a major increase.

CLASSIFICATION OF WHOLESALING MIDDLEMEN

Any attempt to classify wholesaling middlemen in a meaningful way is a precarious project. It is easy to get lost in a maze of categories, because in real life these middlemen vary all over the place in (1) the products they carry, (2) the markets they sell to, and (3) their methods of operation. In an attempt to minimize students' (a) yawns about this whole topic and (b) complaints that "we gotta memorize a bunch of wholesalers," we will set up a classification based on the KISS (Keep it simple, stupid!) system. See Fig. 18-1.

All wholesaling middlemen are grouped into only three broad categories—merchant wholesalers, manufacturers' sales branches and offices, and agents and brokers. These three groups basically are tied to the classification used in the Census, because the Census is the major source of quantitative data covering wholesaling institutions and markets.

Merchant wholesalers. These are the firms we usually refer to as wholesalers, jobbers, or industrial distributors. They typically are independently owned and they take title to the merchandise they handle. They are the largest single segment of wholesaling institutions when measured either by sales or number of establishments. Merchant wholesalers accounted for 56 percent of the total wholesale trade in 1969. We will report separately on petroleum bulk plants and assemblers of farm products, since data on these have been collected separately in the past.

Manufacturers' sales branches and offices. These establishments are owned and operated by manufacturers, but they are physically separated from the manufacturing plants. The distinction between a sales branch and a sales office is that a branch carries merchandise stock and an office does not. In 1969 sales branches and offices accounted for 8 percent of the total wholesale trade.

Agents and brokers. These middlemen do *not* take title to the merchandise they handle, but they do actively negotiate the purchase or sale of products for their principals. The main types of agent middlemen are manufacturers' agents, commission men (in the marketing of agricultural products), brokers, and selling agents. As a group their sales represented 15 percent of total wholesale trade in 1969.

While we have included petroleum bulk plants and assemblers of farm products in the merchant wholesaler category represented in Figure 18-1, the specialized nature of their operations as well as some differences in ownership patterns (fewer independents in bulk plant operation as well as in farm product assembly) and government interest makes it useful to review their scale.

Petroleum bulk plants and terminals. Basically these are merchant wholesalers or manufacturers' sales branches. That is, they are owned by independent whole-

TYPES OF WHOLESALING INSTITUTIONS

Merchant Wholesalers
{ Independently owned
Take title to their merchandise
May be called jobbers, distributors, mill supply houses
Specialization by product line:

Full-service:
    General-line wholesaler (drugs, hardware)
    Specialty wholesaler (frozen foods, product)

Special types:
  Rack jobber
  Petroleum bulk plants
  Assemblers of farm products

Limited service:
  Drop shipper
  Truck jobber

Manufacturers' sales branches (with merchandise)
                   offices (without merchandise stocks) } Owned and operated by manufacturer

Agents and Brokers:
{ Independently owned
Do not take title to merchandise, but actively help in negotiating the transfer of title

Manufacturers' agents
Commission men
Brokers
Selling agents

Figure 18-1.

salers and perform all the usual wholesaling services, or they are owned and operated by petroleum refiners. They are separately noted because of their special physical plant facilities and their somewhat different operations. These middlemen are engaged in the buying, storing, and wholesale selling of gasoline, oil, gases, and other bulk petroleum products. In 1969 there were 4,500 such establishments, with a total sales volume of $3.3 billion, which was 10 percent of all wholesale trade.

Assemblers of farm products. This census classification includes various boards, co-operatives and firms engaged in buying raw farm products from agricultural producers, or fish and seafood products from fishermen. In contrast to other types of wholesaling middlemen tabulated in the census, assemblers buy in *small* quantities from *many* producers and sell in *large* quantities to *fewer* customers. After the products are concentrated in large, economical quantities, they are sold to other wholesaling middlemen in central wholesale markets or to industrial users, such as food processors. Assemblers are tabulated separately because their methods of operation, their physical facilities, and the products they handle all pose a different set of problems. In terms of ownership of goods or ownership of establishment, however, assemblers are similar to some of the middlemen already mentioned. For instance, assemblers are similar to merchant wholesalers in that they take title to the products and usually perform many marketing services, such as storage, delivery and dissemination of market information. In 1969 there were 1,200 assemblers' establishments, with annual sales of $3 billion. This was 9 percent of the total wholesale trade.

Some of the subcategories widely used in the wholesaling business are reflected in Fig. 18-1. This model actually cuts across several different classification bases often used in describing the wholesaling structure. For example, it cuts across:

Ownership of products—merchant wholesalers versus agent middlemen
Ownership of establishment—manufacturers' sales branches versus independent merchants and agents
Range of services offered—full-service wholesalers versus limited service firms
Depth and breadth of line carried—general-line wholesalers (drugs, hardware) versus specialty firms (frozen foods, dairy products)

The quantitative measures in Table 18-2 for the groups of wholesaling middlemen reflect their current status and sales trends. There has been some shifting among the five groups over the past 20 to 25 years. Manufacturers' sales offices and branches and agents and brokers have declined in importance while merchant wholesalers have increased, indicating the inability of more specialized operations to handle the costs of widely separated markets.

CUSTOMERS OF WHOLESALING MIDDLEMEN

One might expect that total retail sales would be considerably higher than total wholesale trade, because retail prices on a given product are higher than the wholesale price and because many products sold at retail never pass through a wholesaler's establishment and so are excluded from total wholesale sales. Total sales figures belie this particular line of reasoning (see Table 18-1). In 3 of the 4 census years since 1941, the volume of wholesale trade is higher than total retail sales.

Table 18-2. Total Wholesale Trade and Percentage of Total Sales By Type of Operation

Type of Operation	Number of Establishments (000)	1966 Sales (millions)	Percentage of Total Sales		
			1966	1961	1951
Canada, Total	30,900	$31,172	100	100	100
Primary Product Dealers	1,274	2,687	8.6	9.2	10.6
Wholesale Merchants	24,124	18,922	60.7	57.7	37.9
Agents and Brokers	2,216	3,731	12.0	15.3	17.3
Manufacturer's Sales Branches	499	2,638	8.5	7.2	26.5
Petroleum Bulk Tank Plants and Truck Distributors	2,787	3,194	10.2	10.6	7.1
Others	—	—	—	—	0.6

Source: Wholesale Trade Establishments, 1966. Statistics Canada Census of Canada, 1951 and 1961, Statistics Canada.

The explanation for this seemingly upside-down situation may be found in an analysis of the customers of wholesaling middlemen (Table 18-3). A smaller percentage of merchant wholesalers' sales are made to retailers for resale today than before 1951. Primary product operations sell more heavily to industrial users and other wholesalers than in the past. This is also the case for agents and brokers. Petroleum bulk plant operations sell more both to industrial users and directly to consumers. What is indicated is a greater development of industrial infrastructure and markets compared with reasonable stability for retail markets.

OPERATING EXPENSES AND PROFITS OF WHOLESALING MIDDLEMEN

The average total operating expenses for all wholesaling middlemen combined has been estimated at about 11 percent of *wholesale* sales.[1] It has also been estimated that operating expenses of retailers average about 27 percent of *retail* sales (omitting bars and restaurants, which do some processing of products). Therefore, on a broad average, the expenses of wholesaling middlemen take about 8 percent of the consumer's dollar.

Expenses by type of operation. Table 18-4 shows operating expenses as a percentage of net sales for selected categories of wholesale merchants as classified in Statistics Canada. Wholesalers of electronic equipment and supplies have the highest average operating expenses (36%). Faster moving, low-margin products such as frozen foods and dairy products produce much lower levels of operating expenses as a percentage of net sales.

Care should be exercised when interpreting these figures. For instance, we should not conclude that wholesalers of tobacco and dairy products are highly efficient because their operating expenses are low and that wholesalers of electronic equipment and office furniture are inefficient. The cost differentials are attributable to the differences in the nature of the products handled and to the nature of the services provided by the various wholesalers. Were more data available, we would

---

[1] Harold Barger, *Distribution's Place in the American Economy since 1869*, Princeton University Press, Princeton, N.J., 1955, p. 60.

Table 18-3. Percentage Distribution of Sales of Wholesale Establishments: By Class of Customer

Type of Operation	Retailers for Resale		Industrial or Other Large Users		Other Wholesalers for Resale		Household Consumers		Export		Total	
	1951	1961	1951	1961	1951	1961	1951	1961	1951	1961	1951	1961
Primary Product Dealers	15.5	6.8	26.9	29.3	43.4	52.4	2.5	0.5	11.7	11.0	100%	100%
Wholesale Merchants	48.9	41.5	32.5	31.9	10.5	15.7	2.0	3.0	6.1	7.9	100	100
Agents and Brokers	12.7	14.9	20.8	29.1	32.8	41.4	0.1	0.2	33.6	14.4	100	100
Manufacturer's Sales Branches	30.8	30.7	37.2	34.4	17.3	17.6	0.2	1.7	14.5	15.6	100	100
Petroleum Bulk Tank Plants and Truck Distributors	31.8	24.6	34.4	46.0	25.5	16.9	6.9	12.3	1.4	0.2	100	100

Source: Census of Canada, 1951 and 1961, Statistics Canada

Table 18-4. Operating expenses as percentage of net sales of Incorporated Wholesale Merchants, 1971: Wholesalers of stationery, electronic equipment and office furniture have highest operating costs. Are they less efficient? How could you explain the differences between the low cost and high cost wholesalers?

Type of Operation	Operating Expenses, percentage of net sales
Wholesale Merchants (total)	14%
Electronic Equipment and Supplies	36
Office Furniture	33
Stationery and Office Supplies	32
Hardware	20
Petroleum Products	17
Drugs	14
Electrical Appliances and Supplies	14
Household Furniture	10
Frozen Foods	7
Tobacco Products	6
Dairy Products	5

Source: 1971 Census of Canada, *Wholesale Trade,* Cat. No. 97-725 pp. 64-66.

likely find that agents and brokers have much lower levels of operating expenses than do wholesale merchants. Similarly, we generally find that manufacturers' sales branches and offices have lower operating expenses as a percentage of sales. Even when merchant wholesalers in given product lines (paper products, machinery) are compared with manufacturers' sales branches in the same line, the branch ordinarily shows a lower operating cost ratio. Careful analysis shows that the comparison is often "loaded" in favor of the manufacturers' branch operations. Branches and sales offices are located only in the markets offering the highest potential sales and profits. Thus the manufacturers' operations would get more sales per dollar of effort. Often, too, a branch is not allocated its full share of costs. Many indirect administrative expenses are charged in full to the home office, even though the branches share in the benefit. Finally, costs of manufacturers' sales branches and merchant wholesalers are not always comparable because of differences in services provided.

Expenses by kinds of goods handled. Expense analyses based on broad categories of wholesaling establishments, as shown in Table 18-5, give a general picture of wholesaling costs. An executive in a given company, however, is probably interested in more detailed cost data. There are tremendous variations in the wholesaling costs of different products. Product considerations such as perishability, value in relation to bulk, rate of turnover, special storage and handling requirements, and technical selling needs influence the operating cost ratio.

Net Profits. Net operating profits expressed as a percentage of net sales are modest for wholesaling middlemen and are considerably lower than those for retailing

Table 18-5. Average net operating profit of selected wholesale merchants, 1971. It is surprising to find such differences between the pretax profits of drug wholesalers and food wholesalers, for example. How can such differences be explained?

	Net Sales ($'000)	Net Operating Profit as Percentage of Net Sales
Drugs	269,051	13
Automotive Parts, Accessories and Supplies	1,509,986	12
Paint, Glass and Wallpaper	103,598	12
Petroleum Products	3,434,530	11
Electronic Equipment and Supplies	139,697	11
Amusement and Sporting Goods	139,174	10
Stationery and Office Supplies	117,838	10
Household Furniture	59,994	7
Household Electrical Appliances and Supplies	121,292	5
Farm Machinery and Equipment	703,999	4
Office Furniture, Machinery and Equipment	283,721	4
Men's and Boy's Clothing	79,168	4
Lumber, Plywood and Millwork	1,556,300	3
Hardware	523,927	2
Frozen Foods	287,152	2
Tobacco Products	627,478	1
Dairy Products	204,378	1

Source: 1971 Census of Canada, Wholesale Trade, Cat. No. 97-725 pp. 64-66.

reported by Statistics Canada. Note that this table presents net *operating* profits. Most types of wholesale merchants have a net operating profit which is less than ten percent of net sales. The average net operating profit for those types of wholesale merchants reported in Table 18-5 ranges from a low of one percent of net sales for wholesalers of dairy and tobacco products to a high of 13 percent for wholesalers of ethical drugs.

REGULAR, OR FULL-SERVICE, WHOLESALERS

A regular, or full-service, wholesaler is an independent merchant wholesaling middleman who generally performs a full range of wholesaling functions. This is the firm which fits the layman's image or stereotype of a wholesaler. He may be called simply a "wholesaler," or he may go under the name of "distributor," "mill supply house," "industrial distributor," or "jobber," depending upon the usage in his line of business. He may handle consumer and/or industrial products, and these goods may be manufactured or nonmanufactured, and imported or exported. Most of our discussion in this section, however, revolves around the *full-service* wholesalers of *manufactured* goods in the *domestic* market.

Merchant wholesalers (of manufactured products or farm products) have accounted for close to one-half of total wholesale trade. Thus the regular wholesaler has held his own in the competitive struggles within the distribution system. Maintaining their market-share percentage means, of course, that the regular wholesalers' dollar sales have increased substantially over the years, even in the face of competition from agents and brokers as well as from direct-selling manufacturers and their sales offices and branches, and from direct-buying customers.

This picture of stability in the regular wholesalers' share of market, when viewed in the aggregate of total wholesale trade, may be a bit misleading in that it hides the volatility and shifting competitive positions within various industries. Wholesalers have increased their market share in some industries and have declined in other areas where they once dominated. Certainly the aggregate market-share figures are misleading in industries where wholesalers are, and always have been, used very little.

SERVICES RENDERED TO CUSTOMERS AND SUPPLIERS

Growth among service wholesalers has occurred in the face of strong competition from other wholesaling middlemen and from large manufacturers and retailers who are attempting to bypass the wholesaler. In light of the fact that nobody is subsidizing the wholesaler, the presumption is that his existence is maintained by the socioeconomic services which he renders. This will be clearer if we examine briefly the services that wholesalers render to their customers and to manufacturers.

Buying. Wholesalers act as purchasing agents for their customers whether they are small retailers or industrial users. The wholesaler determines in advance what his customers will want, and then he has the merchandise on hand when the customers are ready for it. Wholesalers have a broad knowledge of sources of supply and are able to assemble in one place the products from these different sources. A good wholesaler has trained buyers constantly in touch with the appropriate markets, who seek out new and better products and acquire other types of market information. Through the use of wholesalers, the retailer can talk to a few salesmen—the wholesalers'—and thus have access to all these manufacturers. Essentially the same situation prevails among industrial users. These users often prefer to buy from industrial distributors rather than from manufacturers, especially when the product is not technical, has a small unit value, and is purchased infrequently and in small quantities.

In serving as the purchasing agent for retailers and industrial users, the wholesaler also indirectly but significantly aids manufacturers. By ordering enough of a given item to take care of the needs of several retailers, the wholesaler is able to submit a larger order than any of his individual customers could place. Many operating costs, such as order filling, billing, and shipping, are therefore lower per dollar of sales.

Selling. As has been noted before, most manufacturers are small and have limited financial resources. They can build a good product, but they need someone to sell it. The wholesalers perform this service.

The key to an appreciation of the selling activity of wholesalers is a recognition of the nature of the retail market. Of the 160,000 stores, about 88 percent are independent, single-unit operations. Most of these are small, and many are located in small towns. A wholesaler can afford to sell to these small scattered retailers because he represents many manufacturers and can carry many items. Consequently, he can usually get orders large enough to justify his widespread operations.

The cost of direct selling from manufacturer to retailer would be prohibitive, and even is a manufacturer attempted direct distribution, retailers would often reject it. In many cases the retailers know and trust the wholesaler as a result of past business dealings. The manufacturer is a stranger and would not be accorded the same welcome.

For industrial products, the industrial distributor offers a manufacturer essentially the same selling services as a wholesaler of consumer goods. The distributor provides a manufacturer who has no marketing facilities, or who is manufacturing a narrow line and cannot support a sales force, with an excellent means of reaching the market. He is frequently in a good position to know who influences a customer's buying decisions. The prestige which an established industrial distributor enjoys makes him an excellent middleman for introducing a new product.

A firm using a wholesaler to help distribute its products is faced with certain problems in the selling area. Since the wholesaler is not an employee of the firm, it has little control over his selling methods. The wholesaler represents many firms and can provide only part-time selling effort for the products of any of them.

Dividing, or bulk breaking. One service provided by wholesalers—dividing, or bulk breaking—is probably of equal value to their customers and to manufacturers. The wholesaler buys in carload or truckload lots from a manufacturer and resells in case lots or less. Because of transportation costs alone, manufacturers find it economically unjustifiable to sell in small quantities directly to retailers. When carload or truckload quantities are shipped, the transportation costs are computed at the carload or truckload rate. If the manufacturer had to ship in smaller quantities to the retailer, a much higher freight rate would be charged. Furthermore, many manufacturers refuse to sell in the less-than-carload or less-than-truckload quantities, and many retailers will not buy in the larger quantities.

Transportation. In addition to buying in such quantities that the transportation costs are minimized for both manufacturer and customer, a wholesaler furnishes other transportation services to his customers. Since he usually provides quick and frequently delivery, retailers and industrial users need not carry large inventories. Consequently, their costs are reduced because their investments in inventory, insurance, and storage costs are lower. For the retailer, there is less risk that the merchandise will spoil or become obsolete and require markdowns.

Warehousing. Wholesalers create both place and time utility through their warehousing activities. The customer's opportunity to order frequently and in small quantities implies that the wholesaler has the desired merchandise on hand where and when the retailer wants it. Furthermore, wholesalers ordinarily have better storage facilities and can make more effective use of a given amount of space than their customers.

Manufacturers also benefit from this efficiency of storage, particularly manufacturers of seasonal items. Consider the warehousing problems of two manufacturers, one making snow skis and the other producing baseball equipment. A wholesaler can store these two alternate seasonal items in a single unit of space. As the space is emptied of skis during the fall and winter, it can be filled with baseballs and gloves.

Financing. In general, wholesalers aid their customers financially through open-book credit. They usually offer a cash discount if the customer pays his bill within a given period of time after the date of invoice or the receipt of goods. If the customer does not pay within that cash discount period, however, he still has several weeks or months, depending upon the practices in the trade, before the bill falls due. In many cases wholesalers have carried retailers for extended periods of time when the retailers were unable to collect on their customers' accounts.

The financing activities of a wholesaler tend to reduce a retailer's capital requirements. We have already mentioned the advantage of being able to maintain a low inventory. In addition, on seasonal merchandise, such as fishing tackle or Christmas items, wholesalers often deliver the merchandise in advance of the season but do not require payment until after the season is under way. Thus the retailer actually pays for his goods with the money he receives for selling them. This is very close to consignment selling or grubstaking.

In most cases, manufacturers either could not or would not offer comparable aid. They are too far removed from the retailers and industrial users to risk granting credit, and they are not nearly so able to get current and accurate credit information as the wholesaler is.

By granting credit to retailers, the wholesaler is indirectly providing financial help to manufacturers. In addition, wholesalers often supply a more direct form of financial aid to producers. Wholesalers will buy in advance of a season or will accept and store several shipments, paying for them well in advance of the time they will be resold to retailers. Wholesalers also help by generally paying their bills promptly, thus further reducing a manufacturer's capital requirements.

Risk bearing. Several of the points already mentioned suggest ways in which wholesalers reduce risks for their customers and for manufacturers. In addition, wholesalers usually guarantee the merchandise they sell, and the retailer can thus get immediate satisfaction on claims involving defective merchandise.

Simply by taking title to the merchandise, a wholesaler reduces a manufacturer's risk. If the product deteriorates, goes out of fashion, or for some other reason does not sell, the wholesaler usually bears the burden. Also, a manufacturer's credit loss is reduced by dealing with wholesalers because the wholesaler is absorbing the higher-risk venture of granting credit to retailers.

Management services and advice. By furnishing managerial services and advice, especially to retailer customers, wholesalers have significantly strengthened their own position in the market. The existence of a full-function wholesaler is dependent upon the economic health and well-being of small retailers. Therefore, by helping the retailer, the wholesaler really helps himself. Some of the managerial services provided by wholesalers today include training of retail salesclerks; advising on, and helping with, store displays and store layout; and establishing better systems for inventory control and accounting. Wholesalers can supply information regarding new products, competitors' prices, special sales by manufacturers, and other data regarding market conditions.

SPECIAL TYPES OF MERCHANT WHOLESALERS

Within the broad category of merchant wholesalers there are a few subclassifications worth observing because of the special nature of their operations. Their titles reflect either the specialized nature of their job or the limited range of wholesaling services they offer. (Recall Fig. 18-1.)

Rack jobber. The rack jobber, called a "rack merchandiser" in the Census, emerged after World War II as supermarkets added nonfood items. The rack jobber has expanded to serve drugstores, hardware stores, variety stores, and other stores which have instituted the self-service method of retailing. The general-line grocery wholesalers in these nonfood lines could not easily sell to supermarkets for at least three reasons. First, the wholesalers' regular customers, such as drugstores or hardware stores, would complain loudly and probably withdraw their business. Second, too many different wholesalers would have to call on the supermarket to fill all the nonfood lines, and the retailer would object to so many wholesalers. Third, a single supermarket ordinarily would have too small an order in any one nonfood line to make it profitable for the wholesaler in that line.

One rack jobber (or a very few) can furnish all the nonfood items in a supermarket. The rack jobber furnishes the rack or shelves upon which to display the merchandise, and he stocks only the fastest-moving brands on these racks. He is responsible for maintaining fully stocked racks, building attractive displays, and price-marking the merchandise. In essence, the retailer merely furnishes floor or shelf space and then collects the money as the customer goes through the checkout stand.

With the expansion of nonfood items in supermarkets, the position of rack jobbers should become stronger and more attractive. The only significant threat to his position is the possibility that the nonfood business in supermarkets will grow so large that retailers will want to deal directly with the manufacturers.

Limited-function wholesalers. A small group of merchant wholesalers who have received attention in marketing literature through the years, possibly more attention than their numerical importance merits, are the limited-function wholesalers. These are merchant middlemen who do not perform all the usual wholesaling functions. The activities of most of these wholesalers are concentrated in a few product lines. In general, operating costs are lower for limited-function wholesalers than for full-service wholesalers, but this is to be expected because of the differential in services performed. The major types of limited-function wholesalers are truck jobbers, drop shippers, and retail cooperative warehouses. The retailer cooperative warehouse was discussed in the preceding chapter.

A *truck distributor* or jobber (sometimes still called a "wagon jobber" in memory of the days when he used a horse and wagon) is a specialty wholesaler, chiefly in the food field. He carries nationally advertised, fast-moving, and perishable or semi-perishable goods, such as candies, dairy products, potato chips, and tobacco products. The unique feature of his method of operation is that he sells and delivers merchandise during his call. His competitive advantage lies in his ability to furnish fresh products so frequently that the retailer can buy perishable goods in small amounts and have a minimum risk of loss. The major limitation of a truck jobber is his high operating cost ratio, which is caused primarily by the small size of his orders and the inefficient use of delivery equipment. A truck is an expensive warehouse.

The *drop shipper,* sometimes called a "desk jobber," gets his name from the fact that the merchandise he sells is delivered directly from the manufacturer to the customer and is called a "drop shipment." Drop shippers take title to the products, but they do not physically handle the goods. They operate almost entirely in coal and coke and in lumber and building materials. These products are typically sold in carload quantities, and freight is high in comparison with unit value. Thus it is desirable to minimize the physical handling of the product.

AGENT WHOLESALING MIDDLEMEN

Another important group of wholesaling middlemen consists of agents and brokers. These middlemen are distinguished from merchant wholesalers in two important respects: Agent middlemen do *not* take title to the merchandise, and they typically perform fewer services for their clients and principals. (See Table 18-6.) For these reasons, the average operating expenses for agents and brokers are generally less than those for full service wholesalers. There were 2,200 establishments of agents and brokers in Canada in 1967, and they transacted 5 percent of the total volume of wholesale trade (Table 18-2). Based on sales volume, the major types of agent middlemen are manufacturer's agents, selling agents, brokers, and commission men.

All agent middlemen have some characteristics in common which help to explain the role they play. One such similarity relates to their customers. Industrial users constitute the major customer group, and together with retailer customers the two groups account for over 60 percent of the agents' total sales (Review Table 18-3.)

A second common characteristic of agent middlemen is that they are usually compensated by a percentage commission based on the volume of sales or purchases they negotiate. The third point is that agent middlemen generally either act as a substitute for a manufacturer's sales force or serve as an addition to the sales force, thus enabling a manufacturer to sell in markets located beyond the limits of his own salesmen. A final common characteristic, and one which sometimes creates a problem, is that although most agent middlemen ostensibly are working for a seller (they are paid by a seller), they often act in the best interests of the buyer. Apparently their idea is that they can always get another supplier, but customers are hard to find and hold.

Table 18-6. Services provided by agent wholesaling middlemen.

Services	Manu-facturers' agents	Selling agents	Brokers	Commission men
Provides buying services	Yes	Yes	Some	Yes
Provides selling services	Yes	Yes	Yes	Yes
Carries inventory stocks	Sometimes	No	No	Yes
Delivers the products	Sometimes	No	No	Yes
Provides market information	Yes	Yes	Yes	Yes
Sets prices and terms of sale	No	Yes	No	No
Grants credit to customers	No	Sometimes	No	Sometimes
Reduces producers' credit risks	No	Yes	No	No
Sells producers' full line	Sometimes	Yes	Sometimes	No
Manufacturer uses his own sales force along with agents	Sometimes	No	No	No
Continuing relationship with producer throughout the year	Yes	Yes	No	No
Manufacturer uses same agent for entire market	No	Yes	No	No

MANUFACTURERS' AGENTS

A *manufacturers' agent* (frequently called a manufacturers' representative) is an agent commissioned by a manufacturer to sell part or all of the producer's products in a restricted territory. The agent, however, is independent and is in no way an employee of the manufacturer. He has little or no control over the price and terms of a sale; these are established by the manufacturer. Because a manufacturers' agent sells in a restricted territory, a producer typically uses several agents. The size of an agent's territory usually depends upon the density of its potential. One territory may be limited to the Vancouver metropolitan area; another may cover interior British Columbia, yet another Alberta, Saskatchewan and Manitoba. Unlike a broker, a manufacturers' agent has a continuing, year-round relationship with his principal. He usually represents several noncompeting manufacturers of related products and can pool into one profitable sale the small orders which otherwise would go to several individual manufacturers. For this reason, he can operate in markets that none of his principals could individually afford to enter. Besides, buyers may prefer to deal with one representative rather than with direct salesmen from several manufacturers.

Manufacturers' agents are used extensively in the distribution of many types of consumer products and industrial products. The main service offered to manufacturers by this agent middleman is selling. He seeks out and serves markets which the manufacturer himself cannot profitably reach. Furthermore, because a manufacturers' agent does not carry nearly so many lines as a regular wholesaler, the agent can offer a higher-caliber, more aggressive form of selling service. Operating expenses depend upon the product sold and whether the merchandise is stocked. Some representatives operate on a commission as low as 2 percent, while others charge as much as 20 percent. These commissions cover operating expenses and net profit. On an overall basis, the operating expense ratio is about 6 percent for agents.

There are some limitations which a manufacturer may face if he decides to use manufacturers' agents. If the agent does not carry merchandise stocks, the manufacturer may be at a competitive disadvantage because he cannot fill orders quickly. Most agents cannot furnish customers adequate technical advice and repair service, nor are they equipped to install major products. While the agent's commission may be reasonably low, the additional cost of services that the manufacturer must perform himself may result in a total marketing cost which is higher than it would be if another type of middleman were used.

Manufacturers' agents may be used in three characteristic situations:

1. In a small firm, usually a new one, with a limited number of products and no salesmen, manufacturers' agents may do all the selling.
2. In a firm which wants to add a new and possibly unrelated line of products to the existing product mix, where the present salesmen either are not experienced in a new line or cannot reach the new market, the new line may be given to manufacturers' agents. Thus a company may have both salesmen and agents covering the same geographic market.
3. In a firm wishing to enter a new geographic market which is not yet sufficiently developed to warrant sending salesmen, manufacturers' agents familiar with that market may be used. If a company has been selling from Atlantic Provinces to the Prairies and now wishes to extend into British Columbia, it can employ agents who know potential customers and may already be calling on them with other products.

SELLING AGENTS

A selling agent is an independent middleman who is used essentially in place of a manufacturer's entire marketing department. This agent typically performs more marketing services than any other type of agent middleman, and he also has more control and authority with respect to the marketing program of his client-principal. A manufacturer will employ one selling agent to market the full output of the firm over its entire market. Selling agents are used most in the marketing of textiles and coal, although they are also found to some extent in the distribution of apparel and of food, lumber, and metal products. Their operating expenses average about 4 percent of sales.

Agents usually have considerable authority in establishing prices and terms of sale, and they frequently supply financial aid to manufacturers. Because of their critical position in a manufacturer's operations, selling agents sometimes really run their clients' companies—a sort of "tail wagging the dog" situation in which manufacturers are pretty much at the agents' mercy.

Despite the apparent similarity between a selling agent and a manufacturers' agent, there are some fundamental differences between the two. First, a manufacturer uses only one selling agent, whereas he would use several manufacturers' representatives if he took this alternative. Manufacturers' agents have restricted territories; selling agents do not. Second, if a selling agent is used, a manufacturer will have no salesmen; if manufacturers' representatives are used, a seller will often have a sales force of his own. Third, selling agents have far more control over prices and terms of sales. Fourth, selling agents always sell the entire output of a firm; manufacturers' agents usually sell only part of the product line in all the market, or all the product line in only part of the market.

BROKERS

Brokers are agent middlemen whose prime responsibility is to bring buyers and sellers together. They furnish considerable market information regarding prices, products, and general market conditions. Brokers do not physically handle the goods. Also, they do not work on a continuing basis with their principals. Most brokers work for sellers, although about 10 percent represent buyers. A broker has no authority to set prices. He simply negotiates a sale and leaves it up to the seller to accept or reject the buyer's offer. Because of the limited services provided, brokers operate on a very low cost ratio—about 3 percent of net sales.

Brokers are most prevalent in the food field. Their operation is typified by a seafood broker handling the pack from a salmon cannery. For possibly three months out of the year, the cannery is in operation. The canner employs a broker (the same one each year if relationships are mutually satisfactory) to find buyers for the salmon pack. The broker provides information regarding market prices and conditions, and the canner then informs him of the price he desires. The broker seeks potential buyers among chain stores, wholesalers, and others. When a transaction is completed, the broker receives his commission—usually 2 percent of the total sale. When the entire pack is sold, the agent-principal relationship is discontinued until possibly the following year.

An evolutionary development in the food brokerage field should be noted. Through the years many brokers have established permanent relationships with some principals and are performing activities which more accurately would classify these middlemen as manufacturers' agents. They still call themselves "food brokers," however, and they are classed as brokers in the Census of Canada— Wholesale Trade.

COMMISSION MEN

In the marketing of many agricultural products such as fresh fruits and vegetables, grains, and livestock, a widely used middleman in the large central markets is a *commission merchant*, also called a *commission man* or a *commission house*. (The term "commission merchant" is actually a misnomer. This handler is really an agent middleman. In many transactions today, he does not take title to the commodities he handles.)

The commission method of operation in central markets may be described briefly as follows: An assembler in a local market (possibly a local resident produce buyer or a grain elevator) consigns a shipment to a commission merchant in a central market. These firms usually have established working relationships over a period of years. The commission man meets a train or truck and takes charge of the shipment. It is his responsibility to handle and sell the goods. He arranges for any necessary storage, grading, and other services prior to the sale. He finds a buyer at the best possible price, makes the sale, and arranges for transfer of shipment. He deducts his commission, freight charges, and other marketing expenses and remits the balance as soon as possible to the local market shipper. In some cases, commission men extend credit to local shippers or make advance payments on carloads consigned to them.

During the past thirty years, commission dealings in fresh produce have declined. To an increasing extent, commission men are taking outright title to the goods they handle. Today it is not at all uncommon to find wholesale carlot receivers who act as commission men (agent middlemen) in some transactions and as merchant wholesalers in others. Three reasons underlie the decline in commission selling of fresh fruits and vegetables. First, many shippers lost faith in the system: some commission men abused their trust and shortchanged the shippers, taking advantage of the fact that shippers were far away and knew little about market conditions. Second, facilities for physical handling, storing, and shipping have improved, so that losses from perishability are reduced. Finally, improved dissemination of market information means better data, and thus less risk, on demand and supply in a given market.

Commission selling is still widespread in such commodities as grain and livestock. These products are not so perishable, and there is always a market for them. The key to the continued success of a commission merchant is his ability to sell at prices satisfactory to the shipper, to move the commodities quickly with minimum losses due to perishability, and to manage the commodities properly and in good faith. The organized systems of trading on commodity exchanges and the improved dissemination of information have reduced the likelihood of abuses.

WHOLESALING SERVICES PROVIDED BY NONMIDDLEMEN

There are several types of firms which are not middlemen but which do provide important services for manufacturers and middlemen alike.

FAIRS, TRADE SHOWS, AND EXHIBITIONS

Many industries periodically hold trade shows, fairs, or exhibitions of products. Some hold these affairs annually in one city, while others have three or four shows a year, each in a different city. For example, there is an annual furniture show in Toronto. Such shows are not permanent exhibitions; they last for a few days or a week. They offer an opportunity for a manufacturer to display his wares and make contacts with wholesalers and retailers. Middlemen in turn can contact suppliers and customers.

MERCHANDISE MARTS

Several cities have central market facilities where manufacturers or wholesaling middlemen rent space and exhibit their products on a reasonably permanent basis. Showrooms usually are not open to consumers, but the exhibits offer retailers and wholesalers an opportunity to see what is available and to place orders.

PUBLIC WAREHOUSES

Bonded public warehouses are independently owned storage facilities which provide warehousing and other wholesaling functions. Many specialized types are available, such as cold-storage warehouses and grain elevators. These institutions may be used by manufacturers or wholesaling middlemen in lieu of maintaining their own storage facilities. A manufacturer may rent space in several public warehouses located throughout his market, thus maintaining stocks of merchandise at strategic locations near his wholesalers or other customers. Upon notice from the manufacturer, the warehouseman will fill an order and make arrangements for shipping it. Public warehouses are discussed in more detail when we consider the management of physical distribution.

FREIGHT FORWARDERS AND TRANSPORTATION COMPANIES

Railroads, truckers, and other common carriers, as well as freight forwarders, which typically provide some wholesaling services, are discussed in Chapter 21.

Our survey of the major types of wholesaling middlemen and of the services they render, their costs, and typical situations in which they might best be used gives some insight into the way a firm establishes a channel structure for its products. Wholesaling middlemen are specialists in marketing. A producer must decide which wholesaling services he needs and then select the right institutional specialist to perform these services. When a manufacturer criticizes the high cost of a given wholesaler, he may be using the wrong type of wholesaler, or he may be paying for services which he is not using.

QUESTIONS AND PROBLEMS

1. A large furniture warehouse is located in a major western city. The following conditions exist with respect to this firm:
   a. All merchandise is purchased directly from manufacturers.

    b. The warehouse is located in the low-rent, wholesaling district.

    c. Merchandise remains in original crates; customers use catalogues and swatch books to see what the articles look like and what fabrics are used.

    d. about 90 percent of the customers are ultimate consumers, and they account for 85 percent of the sales volume.

    e. The firm does quite a bit of advertising, pointing out that consumers are buying at wholesale prices.

    f. Crates are not price-marked. Salesmen bargain with customers.

    g. Some 10 percent of sales volume comes from sales to furniture stores.
    Is this firm a wholesaler? Explain.

2. Which of the following are wholesaling transactions?

    a. A farmer sells fresh produce to a restaurant.

    b. A chemical manufacturer sells chemicals to a fertilizer manufacturer.

    c. A drug wholesaler sells drugs to a hospital; to a drug retailer.

    d. A retail lumberyard sells plywood to a building contractor; to a homeowner for his "do-it-yourself" project.

3. Carefully distinguish between the following: wholesaler, wholesaling, jobber, wholesaling middleman, distributor.

4. Historically, what have been the economic justifications for the existence of wholesaling middlemen? Which of these still exist?

5. What conditions account for the fact that manufacturers' sales offices and branches have maintained a steadily increasing share of total wholesale trade, while the agents' and brokers' share has declined?

6. How do you account for the substantial variation in operating expenses among the major types of wholesalers shown in Table 18-4?

7. In comparing the operating expense ratio for retailers and for wholesalers, we see that wholesalers typically have lower operating expenses. How do you account for this?

8. What activities could regular wholesalers discontinue in an effort to reduce operating costs?

9. What service does a full-function wholesaler provide for a manufacturer?

10. What types of retailers, other than supermarkets, offer reasonable fields for entry by the rack jobber? Explain.

11. Carefully distinguish between a selling agent and a manufacturers' agent.

12. Why would a manufacturing firm prefer to use manufacturers' agents instead of its own company sales force?

13. Why is it that manufacturers' agents often can penetrate a market faster and at a lower cost than a manufacturer's sales force?

14. What is the economic justification for the existence of the broker, especially in light of the few functions he performs?

15. Which type of agent middleman, if any, is most likely to be used by each of the following? Explain your choice in each instance.

    a. A small manufacturer of a liquid glass cleaner to be sold through supermarkets

    b. A small manufacturer of knives used for hunting, fishing, and camping

    c. A salmon canner in B.C. packing a high-quality, unbranded product

    d. A small-tools manufacturer who has his own sales force selling to the industrial market and who wishes to add backyard barbecue equipment to his line

e. A Quebec textile mill producing unbranded towels, sheets, pillowcases and blankets.

16. Looking into the future, which types of wholesaling middlemen do you think will increase in importance, and which ones will decline? Explain.

CHAPTER
19

COMPETITIVE CONFLICTS AND COOPERATION IN DISTRIBUTION CHANNELS

In Chapter 16 we set forth the idea that a company's trade channel should be regarded as a total system of distribution, rather than as a fragmented assortment of independent institutions operating in an uncoordinated fashion. Manufacturers and middlemen alike should understand that the middlemen used by a manufacturer are only a logical component of a systematic organization which starts with the manufacturer and is designed to maximize marketing effectiveness in the sale to the final customer. The systems concept of distribution suggests then a need for cooperation and coordination among channel members. Yet power structures do exist in trade channels, and a struggle does go on continuously among channel members.

At the root of this struggle is institutional change, several examples of which were observed in our study of retailing and wholesaling institutions. This change, in turn, is caused first by the shifting nature of market demand and second by the economic growth and competitive activity among the institutions. It is axiomatic that change begets conflict and that, conflict very often results in change.[1]

While pressures for institutional change have mounted over the years, at the

---

1 For an approach to anticipating changes in distribution structures before such changes develop into obvious trends, see Bruce Mallen, "Functional Spin-Off: A Key to Anticipating Change in Distribution Structure," *Journal of Marketing*, July 1973, pp. 18-25.

same time strong psychological and sociological barriers stand in the path of this change. These barriers often persist in the face of economic analyses showing that the change may result in channels which will offer economic advantages and that resistance to change may extend the life of uneconomic channels.

Several of these noneconomic barriers may be identified.[2] One is the presence of group solidarity and collective action among resellers of common backgrounds—retail druggists, for example. Sometimes entrepreneurial values—particularly those of small retailers—place higher ratings on stability than on growth, and this of course tends to restrict innovation. Even in larger organizations, change may be resisted because it "violates group norms, creates uncertainty, and results in loss of status." Finally, a firm's position in the channel may be correlated to its acceptance of, or resistance to, change. That is, the "insiders" in the dominant channel, the "strivers" who want to become part of that system, and the "complementors" who assist the first two groups are all emotionally and economically committed to the dominant channel. They endeavor to maintain the status quo against the minor intrusions of "transients" and the major threats from "outside innovators" who would realign the existing structure.[3]

NATURE OF THE CONFLICTS

Three separate forms of competitive conflicts within channels of distribution may be identified. Two of these occur on the horizontal level of distribution: the first is competition between middlemen of the same type—hardware store versus hardware store, or industrial distributor versus industrial distributor; the second is competition between different types of middlemen, but still on the same level—hardware store versus paint store, or industrial distributor versus manufacturers' agent. The third type of confict if vertical in nature, involving institutions on different levels of distribution—manufacturer versus wholesaler, for example.

COMPETITION ON THE SAME LEVEL OF DISTRIBUTION

On the same level of distribution, perhaps the main form of conflict has been the competition engendered by "scrambled merchandising"—that is, the practice whereby a middleman diversifies his product assortment by adding merchandise lines not traditionally carried by that type of institution. This practice, which started before World War II, has spread throughout the fields of retailing and wholesaling. Today it continues to show signs of increasing, rather than decreasing in intensity.

We have seen grocery supermarkets, as an illustration, add toiletries, drugs, clothing, magazines, small appliances, records, alcoholic beverages, and other non-food lines. The retailers who traditionally sold these lines become irritated both at

2 Bert C. McCammon, Jr., "Alternative Explanations of Institutional Change and Channel Evolution," in Stephen A. Greyser (ed.), *Toward Scientific Marketing*, American Marketing Association, Chicago, 1964, pp. 477-490.

3 For a conceptual model of conflict in channels of distribution and its effect on the efficiency of channel performance, see Bert Rosenbloom, "Conflict and Channel Efficiency: Some Conceptual Models for the Decision Maker," *Journal of Marketing*, July, 1973, pp. 26-30; and Larry J. Rosenberg and Louis W. Stern, "Toward the Analysis of Conflict in Distribution Channels: A Descriptive Model," *Journal of Marketing*, October, 1970, pp. 40-46.

the grocery stores for diversifying and also at the manufacturers for using these "unorthodox" channels. The stimulus for product proliferation among middlemen and the crossing of traditional channel lines may come from three general sources—the market, the middleman, or the manufacturer.

Market-inspired. Preference for one-stop shopping and the trend toward self-service selling are two changes in consumer buying behavior which have encouraged the development of scrambled merchandising. Consumers want convenience in their shopping. They prefer to go to one store and buy food, toothpaste, and a couple of inexpensive cooking pans, for example, rather than having to visit three different retailers. Also, the consumer acceptance of—even preference for—self-selection of merchandise has acted as an incentive for many stores to add new product lines which lend themselves to self-service selling.

Middleman-inspired. The middleman's constant search for more profitable marketing methods has furnished an impetus to the growth of scrambled merchandising. A retailer, such as a food supermarket, operating on a gross margin of 18 to 20 percent is bound to be attracted to items such as drug sundries or housewares, where the margin may be about 30 percent.

Some retailers seek to increase their store traffic by adding new merchandise lines. Furniture stores have added small appliances, and jewelry stores have added records and gift items for this purpose. In other situations, any really new product is usually very attractive to all types of retailers who consider the item even remotely marketable in their store. Consequently, product innovation will continue as a big factor in the further scrambling of traditional product assortments.

A substantial segment of a middleman's total costs are fixed, and furthermore they are common to all products sold. That is, they cannot be identified directly with any given product, nor do they vary with sales volume in the short run. This cost factor is a real incentive for a retailer or wholesaler to add new product lines to broaden the base over which he can spread his fixed costs. This proliferation intensifies the degree of channel conflict.

Manufacturer-inspired. Sometimes the stimulus for scrambled merchandising comes from the manufacturer. Consider the manufacturers who have taken over the responsibility for repair service on their products. Appliance manufacturers used to be limited in the type and number of retailers they could use because it was essential that the dealer be prepared to service the appliances. Once the manufacturer assumes that responsibility, he can sell through many new types of retailers who formerly were not qualified.

In another situation, a manufacturer may add new products to his line and want new types of outlets so as not to antagonize his existing middlemen. Thus he keeps harmony in his present channels, but creates conflict in the new, nontraditional outlets. Finally, improvements in production technology may change the shape and location of a manufacturer's cost curve. His break-even point may be higher, or he may be in a position to decrease his unit costs considerably by increasing his output. In any event, the marketing department must find new markets (and thus possibly new types of middlemen) for the potential increase in output.

CONFLICT BETWEEN DIFFERENT LEVELS OF COMPETITION

Perhaps the most severe competitive conflicts in distribution systems today are of a vertical nature—that is, between retailer and wholesaler, between manufacturer and retailer, or between manufacturer and wholesaler. Retailers may make some sales to institutions and other industrial users, thus competing with wholesaling middlemen, as when stationery stores sell office supplies to other retail stores, for example. Producers compete with retailers by selling house-to-house, by selling through the manufacturers' own retail stores, or by selling at the point of production—at the factory or farm. Conflicts frequently develop between manufacturers and agent middlemen when manufacturers place their own sales forces in territories which were developed and heretofore covered by the agents. The remainder of this chapter is devoted to the vertical types of conflict.

WHO CONTROLS THE CHANNELS?

In marketing literature, authors have generally taken a manufacturer-oriented approach to channels of distribution. The implication is that the manufacturer is the one who makes the decisions regarding type of outlet, number of outlets, and even the selection of individual outlets. This is a one-sided point of view. Actually, the middleman has considerable freedom to make his own choices in establishing channels. "The selection of a multi-stage channel is not the prerogative of a manufacturer unless his franchise is coveted by the middlemen he seeks, as being more valuable to them than their franchise would be to him."[4] Certainly the name of Dominion, Eaton's, Sears, and other strong retailers means more to the consumers than most of the brands sold in these stores. Large retailers today are challenging manufacturers for channel control, just as the manufacturers challenged the wholesaler fifty years ago. Even a small retailer may be influential in a local market, and his prestige may become greater than that of his suppliers. McVey observed: "In some instances his local strength is so great that a manufacturer is virtually unable to tap that market, except through him. In such a case the manufacturer can have no channel policy with respect to that market."

Actually, the questions of who is the channel leader and who *should* be remain largely unsettled.[5] The position supporting leadership by the manufacturer is production-oriented. He creates the new products, and he needs the increasing sales volume to derive the benefits of large-scale operations. A large retailer may use the same arguments, especially if he provides new-product ideas or specifications. Also, one can argue that the retailer is the natural leader under the marketing concept—standing closest to the consumer, knowing his wants, and being his purchas-

---

4 Phillip McVey, "Are Channels of Distribution What the Textbooks Say?" *Journal of Marketing*, January, 1960, pp. 61-65; see also Robert W. Little, "The Marketing Channel: Who Should Lead This Extra-corporate Organization?" *Journal of Marketing*, January, 1970, pp. 31-38.

5 This paragraph is adapted from Bruce Mallen, "Conflict and Cooperation in Marketing Channels," in L. George Smith (ed.), *Reflections on Progress in Marketing*, American Marketing Association, Chicago, 1965, pp. 74-77; see also Louis P. Bucklin, "A Theory of Channel Control," *Journal of Marketing*, January, 1973, pp. 39-47; David L. Wilemon, "Power and Negotiation Strategies in Marketing Channels," *Southern Journal of Business*, February, 1972, pp. 71-82; and Adel I. El-Ansary and Louis W. Stern, "Power Measurement in the Distribution Channel," *Journal of Marketing Research*, February, 1972, pp. 47-52.

ing agent. Perhaps the best answer to the channel-control questions is a compromise—a balance of power should exist rather than a domination by any one level in the distribution channels.

MANUFACTURER VERSUS WHOLESALER

A significant channel conflict during the past half-century has been between the manufacturer and the wholesaler, as manufacturers have tried to bypass wholesalers and deal directly with retailers. Ordinarily, the battle is between the producers and wholesalers of manufactured *consumer* products. As a rule, it does not involve wholesaling middlemen for industrial products. There is a tradition of direct sale in the industrial field, and where middlemen are used, the need for their services has long been recognized. Nor does this conflict involve agent middlemen for consumer goods to any great extent. The relationships between a manufacturer and his agent middlemen are relatively peaceful for two reasons. First, these relationships are established on a temporary basis. Brokers work with a manufacturer only part of the year. Manufacturers' agents know in advance that they may lose their franchises as soon as the territory can support the manufacturer's sales force. Second, agent middlemen offer fewer services than wholesalers. This means that there are fewer areas of possible conflict with manufacturers.

HISTORICAL BACKGROUND OF THE CONFLICT

The clash of interests between wholesalers and manufacturers in the marketing of manufactured consumer products can be best understood by reviewing (1) the position of the wholesaler before 1920, (2) the changing position of the manufacturer over the years, (3) the changing position of the retailer since 1920, and (4) the net effect these changes have had on the wholesalers and manufacturers.

Historically, the wholesaler occupied a position of major importance in distribution systems. Before 1920, he was dominant because both manufacturers and retailers were small and poorly financed. In addition, retailers were widely dispersed over the entire country. In effect, the wholesaler served as the sales force of the manufacturer and as the purchasing agent for the retailer. In so doing, he granted credit to the retailers, an especially important service in the days when our economy was largely agricultural and cash was available only at harvest time. He carried a wide assortment of products, even from competing manufacturers. Essentially he was an order taker; he did no aggressive selling, nor did he consider this his function.

As a result of the risks he took and the broad scale of his services, the wholesaler had high operating costs. To cover these costs he needed a wide margin of profit. Through the nineteenth century and the early part of the twentieth, wholesaler institutions suffered increasingly from inertia, a low caliber of management, and a lack of flexibility in management. The firms did not adjust to changing economic and social conditions. Thus we see the familiar picture of an organization which reaches a stage of maturity and faces little competition.

During the last half of the nineteenth century and the first part of the twentieth, the position of the manufacturer changed substantially. Manufacturing was becoming more efficient and production management was of a higher caliber. Furthermore, manufacturers were beginning to realize that it was better to make a small profit on the sale of many units than a wide margin on the sale of a few units. Manufacturers were quick to learn that the best means of achieving increased volume was through a change in marketing methods. Aggressive selling effort, lower prices, product identification through branding, and advertising were recognized as keys to mass markets. Once the manufacturer embarked upon these programs, he disliked giving wholesalers the customary wide margin on sales which his policies were stimulating.

After World War I, the position of the retailer changed considerably. Large-scale retailing institutions developed in great numbers, and retail markets became concentrated in geographic areas in and around metropolitan centers. New organizational forms, particularly the corporate chains, were developing. Large-scale operations entailed large buying power, well-financed retailers, and better-managed firms. Large-scale retailers also were economically able to assume many wholesaling functions. All these factors encouraged retailers to go directly to the manufacturers to purchase their merchandise.

Wholesalers were caught between large-scale, integrated retailers on the one hand and large-scale, direct-selling, integrated manufacturers on the other. The wholesaler saw his prestige being reduced, yet he realized that he could not afford to promote aggressively the products of any one manufacturer, and he resented any cut in his discount margin. By refusing to cooperate in the manufacturer's efforts to promote products to retailers and by installing his own brands of merchandise, the wholesaler further increased the conflict between himself and the manufacturer.

MANUFACTURERS' SIDE OF THE CONFLICT

Reasons for bypassing wholesalers. Basically, either because they are dissatisfied with the wholesalers' services or because of market conditions, manufacturers favor direct sale from manufacturer to retailer or to consumer.

Wholesalers' failure to promote products aggressively. Manufacturers charge that the wholesalers ordinarily will not aggressively promote the products of individual producers—that wholesalers are essentially order takers, not salesmen. To really sell a product, manufacturers say, wholesalers demand special incentives, such as larger discounts or exclusive territorial franchises.

Wholesalers agree that these charges leveled by the manufacturers are largely true. Generally speaking, all products are the same to the wholesaler, and he does not feel that it is his responsibility to promote those of one manufacturer over those of another. With the thousands of items typically carried by wholesalers, it is not possible for their salesmen even to *mention* each item to prospective customers, much less try to sell each one.

Wholesalers' failure to perform storage function. In some cases, manufacturers have eliminated wholesalers because they failed to provide the traditional storage services that producers were used to. Manufacturers have been forced to carry larger stocks and to bear a greater share of the market risk. Several factors have encouraged wholesalers to reduce their storage services and to buy on a hand-to-mouth basis. Improved transportation and communication services, for example, make it possible for wholesalers to get necessary merchandise much more quickly today than in years gone by.

Development of wholesalers' own brands. Also adding to manufacturers' desire to bypass the wholesaler is the fact that many middlemen are aggressively promoting their own brands in direct competition with manufacturers' brands.

Manufacturers' desire for close market contact. Manufacturers sometimes bypass wholesalers in an attempt to control their products over a greater proportion of the distance from producer to ultimate consumer or industrial user. This interest on the part of the manufacturer is particularly evident where installing, servicing, and repairing the product play a significant role in the product's sales success. Furthermore, by eliminating the wholesaler, the manufacturer can better learn how his product is moving in the market and what the consumer's reaction to it is.

Need for rapid physical distribution. If products are subject to physical perishability or fashion obsolescence, it may be essential to reduce the channels to the shortest length possible. Where fashion obsolescence is concerned, it is far too slow and risky to distribute through wholesalers. For products such as women's ready-to-wear or millinery, orders are frequently placed by telephone and shipped by airplane.

Cost of wholesalers' services. One of the biggest pitfalls in the marketing process is the assumption that manufacturers can perform the traditional wholesaling functions at a lower cost. Many producers have learned the hard way that bypassing the wholesaler may actually increase the cost of marketing or result in poor market coverage. Eliminating the wholesaler results in economy only if the manufacturer and/or the retailer can perform the wholesaler's functions more effectively. Even when his research shows that costs will be lowered by eliminating wholesalers, the producer should still investigate further to determine whether the wholesaling services will be performed adequately and whether his long-range market and profit position will be improved.

Preference of retailers for buying directly. Many retailers believe that they can get lower prices on merchandise, more advertising allowances, and better service and merchandise selection if they deal directly with manufacturers. Usually the retailers who prefer to buy directly are large-scale enterprises. Consequently, manufacturers seek their business and try to meet their needs.

Courses of action open to manufacturers. If a manufacturer wishes to bypass wholesalers, he has three major alternative channels: He may sell directly to the retailer, he may establish sales offices or branches and sell directly through them to the retailer, or he may bypass the retailer as well as the wholesaler and sell directly to the ultimate consumer. If a manufacturer prefers to use a wholesaler but needs more aggressive selling, he may employ a group of missionary salesmen.

Whatever alternative channel of distribution is used in lieu of wholesalers, direct selling inevitably places a greater financial burden on the manufacturer and adds immeasurably to his management problems. He must operate a sales force, handle the physical distribution of the product, and operate a credit system. Direct selling does not normally result in as intensive a market coverage as wholesalers can provide. Manufacturers are also faced with small-order problems. Finally, once a manufacturer embarks upon a program of direct selling, he must be ready to face competition from his former wholesalers who are now pushing competitive products.

Sell directly to retailers. A decision to sell directly to retailers without the use of sales offices or branches should be based on the situation surrounding five factors. The first is the *market*. An ideal retail market for direct selling is one made up of large-scale retailers who are geographically concentrated, who buy in large quantities, and who maintain central buying offices. Thus we find such retail organizations as corporate chains, mail-order houses, and voluntary chains buying directly from manufacturers. In addition, a manufacturer may establish profitable direct-sale arrangements with specialty stores. While the volume of a specialty store may not be so great as that of a department store or supermarket, the specialty store nevertheless presents an attractive volume outlet in its limited product line. Frequently a shoe store, a clothing store, or a retailer of photographic equipment and supplies will have a sales volume greater than that of a corresponding department in a department store.

The *product* considerations which make direct sale possible or in some cases even necessary are (1) physical or fashion perishability, (2) high unit value or high gross margin, (3) demand for custom-made or specially constructed products, (4) importance of mechanical servicing or installation, (5) manufacturer's output consisting of a full line of related products, and (6) large total order.

Adequately qualified marketing executives are usually a prerequisite for a successful direct-selling program. When circumventing a wholesaler, a manufacturer creates countless managerial problems with respect to operating a sales force.

In direct selling, preferably both the manufacturer and the retailer should have *financial strength*. If the manufacturer employs a field selling force, the financial requirements will be especially heavy. Also, someone must take over the credit risks and responsibilities previously assumed by the wholesalers.

Sometimes a manufacturer can eliminate a wholesaler only if there are excellent *physical distribution facilities* for the product. The existence of public warehouses, for instance, may enable a manufacturer to perform the storage function normally handled by wholesalers.

Open sales offices or branches. Salesmen working out of sales offices or branches under decentralized management may be desirable when:

1. There is a concentrated market for the product.
2. The manufacturer has a large sales force and needs to supervise it closely.
3. The company places greater emphasis on personal selling than on advertising in its promotional program.
4. There is a need to install, service, and repair the product.
5. Customers demand rapid, economic delivery, and the company does not want to use public warehouses.

Executives in a manufacturing establishment should recognize that branch organizational structures raise major financial and operating problems. Not only are operating costs higher because of duplication of manpower and effort, but there is also the fixed cost attendant upon the investment in the branch plant and equipment. Operating decisions must be made regarding which functions will be decentralized and which will be handled in the home office. For instance, who is to have the authority and responsibility for hiring, training, promoting, and firing salesmen? Who is to have the authority to grant credit and to change prices?

On balance, the statement made by Professor Tosdal many years ago still seems pertinent. He said, "If there is any general rule to be applied to the establishment of branch organizations, it is to the effect that the burden of proof is upon those who advocate establishment of branches rather than upon those who oppose such extensions.[6]

Sell directly to consumer. Various distribution methods may be used to make this short channel effective (see Chapter 17). The producer may employ personal non-store selling (house-to-house) or mail-order selling. He may establish retail stores, or he may sell directly to the consumer at the point of production—the factory, farm, boat dock, or some other location.

Use missionary salesmen. When a manufacturer wants to use a wholesaler but also wants to have the advantages of aggressive selling, he may employ missionary salesmen. Also known as promotional salesmen, detail men, or factory representatives, they perform a number of services and may be used under several different conditions. Typically, missionary salesmen call upon a retailer and aggressively promote the product of the manufacturer. If the salesman secures any orders, he passes them on to the jobber, and the jobber receives his normal commission. Missionary salesmen may be used to install point-of-purchase displays in retail stores or to introduce new items to retailers. Sometimes these salesmen are called in to close difficult sales which wholesalers have not been able to handle themselves. These factory representatives may train retail salesmen, particularly when technical product information is necessary. They may also seek new accounts and stand ready to handle complaints. Because using this sales force is a step short of establishing a sales office or branch, it is less expensive and presents fewer management problems.

WHOLESALERS' SIDE OF THE CONFLICT

The wholesaler in his turn is often dissatisfied with the actions of the manufacturer. Marketing administrators should understand the wholesaler's complaints and evaluate the alternatives open to wholesalers who want to meet the competitive threat of being bypassed.

Reasons for wholesalers' dissatisfaction. Some of the reasons wholesalers are unhappy with manufacturers are implicit in our earlier discussion. The sample of grievances stated here should establish the tenor of the wholesalers' objections.

Manufacturers fail to understand true role of wholesalers. From the wholesaler's point of view, probably the main irritant is the manufacturer's failure to understand or accept the fact that the primary obligation of the wholesaler is to serve his customers. The wholesaler's responsibility as a service agent for the manufacturer is only secondary.

Manufacturers expect too much. Wholesalers often feel that manufacturers' expectations with regard to warehousing and other services are far greater than the wholesalers' discounts justify. As explained earlier, the wholesaler is in no position to

---

6 Harry R. Tosdal, *Introduction to Sales Management,* 4th ed., McGraw-Hill Book Company, New York, 1957, p. 513.

promote individual products aggressively, nor can he push point-of-purchase displays and other promotional material.

Manufacturers skim cream off market. Wholesalers note that often they are used only in the early stages of territorial development. Then, when the market is intensively cultivated, the manufacturers bypass them and deal directly. Wholesalers also note that manufacturers often use middlemen only in the least profitable segments of the market. In the concentrated, fertile segments, producers sell directly to retailers or industrial users. While this observation is accurate, the wholesaler should understand that his real worth lies in being able to reach markets which the manufacturer himself cannot penetrate profitably.

Manufacturers sell to retailers who use their own brands. Manufacturers often sell products to retailers who place their private brands on the product. Wholesalers object to this practice because these products compete with the manufacturers' own brands carried by the wholesaler. Here perhaps the wholesalers are tilting at windmills. Retailers who sell under their own brand names are large-scale organizations. If one manufacturer refuses to sell them, they will get the merchandise from another. And in any event, their brands will still be in the market competing with those carried by the wholesaler.

Courses of action open to wholesalers. Wholesalers have taken several measures to improve their competitive position and to meet the threat of being eliminated. All these measures attempt (1) to improve efficiency to such an extent that neither suppliers nor customers can find more desirable means of accomplishing marketing tasks and (2) to tie retailers to the wholesaler in one way or another.

Improve internal management. Many wholesalers have modernized their establishments and upgraded the caliber of their management. These have been refreshing changes. New, functional single-story warehouses have been built outside the congested downtown areas, and mechanized physical-handling equipment has been installed. In the office, computers and machine accounting systems have streamlined the inventory and accounting controls and have thus reduced losses from obsolete, slow-moving items.

Many wholesalers have added limited-function departments and have otherwise increased the flexibility of their operations. Another cost-cutting, efficiency-inducing factor has been the adoption of selective selling. That is, less profitable accounts are visited less frequently, and really low-profit accounts may be solicited only by mail or telephone.

These and other innovations have generally had the effect of lowering operating costs or of giving the retailer far better service for the same money. Much remains to be done, of course. Activities related to managing the sales force, for instance, have not kept pace with improvements in clerical operations and in the physical handling of products.

Provide management assistance for retailers. Wholesalers are coming to realize that their success is totally dependent upon the success of their small, independent retail customers. Therefore, anything the wholesalers do to improve the retailers' operations is really in their own self-interest. Management guidance for retailers may take several forms. Using their own salesmen or other field employees as management advisers, wholesalers can help retailers choose store locations, improve their store layouts, and install better accounting and inventory processes. They can help retail store operators do a better job of selecting, displaying, and promoting their merchandise.

Form voluntary chains. Voluntary chains of retailers formed by wholesalers have proved to be an effective device for meeting the competitive challenges in channels of distribution. This structure was discussed in Chapter 17. In a voluntary chain, a wholesalers enters into a contract with several retailers, agreeing to furnish them with management services and large-volume buying advantages. In turn, the retailers agree to do all or almost all their buying from the wholesaler.

Develop and promote own brands. Many large wholesalers have successfully established their own brands. If a wholesaler is connected with a voluntary chain of retailers, the chain provides the wholesaler's brand with a built-in market. Private brands help the retailers, too, because consumers cannot easily compare private-brand prices with those of manufacturers' brands carried in other stores.

Seek legislative aid. A final method used by wholesalers to meet the competition of other institutions is to seek legislative aid at the provincial or federal level. While the authors do not recommend this method as a long-run salvation of the wholesaler, it seems to be a favorite choice of many wholesalers. Wholesaler organizations fought vigorously for unfair-practices protection. One intent of such protection was to neutralize the large-scale buying power of giant retailers, such as corporate chains and large, independent department stores. As noted in the discussion of retailing institutions, a fundamental error made by many middlemen—wholesalers and retailers alike—is to believe that the only advantage corporate chains have over small independents is large buying power. Even if all stores bought merchandise at the same price, the other advantages of large-scale enterprises would clearly enable them to out-compete the smaller merchants.

In the author's opinion, legislative aid can help the wholesaler only temporarily. It obscures his basic problems and therefore postpones their effective long-range solution. The wholesaler's real salvation and opportunity for growth lie in his ability to improve the internal management of his establishment and to help the small-scale retailer become a more effective institution.

FUTURE OF THE WHOLESALER

In the 1930's, it was frequently forecast that the full-function merchant wholesaler was a dying institution. Statistics in Chapter 18 and elsewhere, however, show that the merchant wholesaler enjoyed a resurgent growth rate during the past 35 years—a growth rate quite comparable to that in the gross national product. While shifts will continue to occur within the wholesaling structure, the full-function wholesaler today holds a strong and significant position in the economy.

There are two basic reasons for the comeback of the merchant wholesaler. One is a fuller realizaton of the true economic worth of his services. The other is the general improvement of his management methods and operations. The bandwagon to eliminate the wholesaler proved to be a blessing in disguise. Innumerable firms tried to bypass the wholesaler and came to realize that the net result was unsatisfactory. They could not perform some of the wholesaling functions at all, or they found the cost prohibitive. In many cases, it became evident that the wholesaler was able to provide the manufacturers and retailers with better services, and to provide them at a lower cost, than these firms themselves could.

Wholesalers are still the controlling force in the channels used by many firms. We must not conclude, however, that only low-cost wholesalers can survive in the competitive market. Even seemingly high-cost wholesalers are thriving. A high operating cost ratio is not necessarily a result of inefficiency. Instead, it is usually a result of more and better service. Many wholesalers' costs are high only because they offer an established distribution system (granted, it may be nonaggressive) and many other services which ease the producers' marketing and financial burdens.

Growth in the wholesaling sector also reflects the emergence of new industrial and institutional markets where the demand for wholesaling services is high. There also has been a shift in the wholesaler's traditional role as a middleman for standardized products to one who participates in the marketing of complex products requiring extensive inventories and selling effort. At the same time, mass-marketing practices have not proved as applicable in wholesaling as in retailing. Possibly the future for small-scale middlemen lies more in wholesaling than in retailing.[7]

Wholesalers, admittedly slow to adopt modern business methods and attitudes, are striving to catch up in this respect. Moreover, the already evident trends shaping the future of wholesale distribution suggest that (1) the wholesaler is responsive to his environment and (2) he can effectively adapt to pressures from both suppliers and customers for lower-cost distribution. Indications are that wholesalers will continue to interpret and respond to these pressures.[8]

MANUFACTURER VERSUS RETAILER

Today, perhaps even more significant than the conflict between manufacturers and wholesalers is the struggle for channel control which goes on between manufacturers and retailers. A very basic reason for the conflict is this: *"The people who manufacture the goods and the people who move the goods into the hands of the ultimate consumer do not share the same business philosophy and do not talk essentially the same language."*[9] In manufacturing corporations, an executive's point of view is typically characterized as a psychology of *growth*. His goals are essentially dynamic and evolving. He is forever climbing to the top and is not content to rest on past accomplishments. In sharp contrast, the psychology of the small and medium-sized retailer is essentially *static* in nature. His goals are well defined and are far more circumscribed than those of the manufacturing corporation executive. At some point the retailer levels off into a continuously satisfying plateau.

---

7 This paragraph is adapted from Louis P. Bucklin, "National Income Accounting and Distributive Trade Cost," *Journal of Marketing,* April, 1970, pp. 14-22, especially pp. 21-22.

8 See Richard S. Lopata, "Faster Pace in Wholesaling," *Harvard Business Review,* July-August, 1969, pp. 130-143.

9 Warren J. Wittreich, "Misunderstanding the Retailer," *Harvard Business Review,* May-June, 1962, p. 147. The balance of the paragraph is drawn from this article.

DOMINATION VERSUS COOPERATION

In the struggle each group has weapons it can use in its efforts to dominate. A manufacturer can use his promotional program to build a strong consumer preference for his product. Legal weapons are available to him in the form of franchise contracts, consignment selling, or outright ownership of the retail store. As a negative method of dominating, the manufacturer may choose not to deal with uncooperative retailers. Suggestive devices such as premarking the price on products or advertising the suggested resale price are weaker control methods.

.Retailers are not necessarily unarmed in this situation. By effective advertising programs or by establishing their own brands, they can develop consumer preferences for their stores. A retailer can either concentrate his purchases with one supplier or spread his buying among many sources, depending upon the number of manufacturers involved and which strategy is most effective for him.

On the other side of the coin, fortunately, channel members seem to realize that the returns from cooperating with one another do outweigh any reasons for conflict. Perhaps manufacturers and retailers alike understand that it is in their own best interests to treat a distribution channel as a total system—to consider a channel an extension (forward or backward, as the case may be) of their own internal organizations.[10] To implement this concept, a manufacturer should do the sort of thing for a retailer that he does for his own marketing organization. That is, the manufacturer can provide advertising aids, training for dealer salesmen, managerial assistance, etc. Retailers can reciprocate by carrying adequate inventories, promoting the product, and building consumer goodwill. (These methods of mutual cooperation are elaborated on in the following chapter.)

Dual distribution. The increased use of one form of dual distribution is another real source of conflict between manufacturers and retailers. Broadly defined, *dual distribution* is the practice whereby a supplier uses more than one type of channel or marketing organization to distribute his product. We are concerned here with the type of dual distribution in which a manufacturer sells the same brand, or two brands of basically the same product, to the same market through *competing* channel networks. A paint manufacturer, for instance, may distribute through a series of retail stores which he owns, at the same time using conventional channels of independent paint wholesalers and retailers—all aiming at the same market. The general practice is not new. For years it has been carried on by oil companies, tire manufacturers, and paint companies. But what is new is the surge in its growth and its adoption in industries heretofore generally untouched.[11]

The impetus for this growth is coming from several sources. In many industries, increasing competition has spurred manufacturers to open their own stores in markets where no satisfactory outlet is available. Some manufacturers establish their own stores as testing grounds for new products and marketing techniques. In suburban markets, small retailers often do not have the financial resources to open a store in shopping centers. Consequently, many large manufacturers must open their own stores in these centers if they want suitable outlets.

---

10 For additional insight on this point, see Valentine F. Ridgeway, "Administration of Manufacturer-Dealer Systems," *Administrative Science Quarterly*, March, 1957, pp. 464-483; and Peter Drucker, "The Economy's Dark Continent," *Fortune*, April, 1962, p. 103.

11 See Lee E. Preston and Arthur E. Schramm, Jr., "Dual Distribution and Its Impact on Marketing Organization," *California Management Review*, Winter, 1965, pp. 59-70.

VERTICAL MARKETING SYSTEMS

The traditional marketing channel structure hardly deserved to be called a system. The channels for many products were dominated by small and medium-sized firms, each operating independently as profit-seeking, short-run—oriented units. Manufacturers, wholesalers, and retailers frequently competed and conflicted with each other. The net result often was an inefficient, effort-duplicating situation.

Institutional changes in distribution during the past 20 to 30 years have led to the development of vertical marketing systems.[12] In contrast with the traditional individualistic structures, the newer vertical marketing systems offer significant economies of scale and increased coordination in distribution. They also eliminate the duplication of marketing services, providing instead for the singular performance of any given marketing activity at the most advantageous position in the system.

Vertical marketing systems are characterized as corporate, administered, or contractual (see Fig. 19-1). In *corporate vertical marketing systems* the production and marketing facilities are owned by the same company. As a manufacturer, for example, the Sherwin-Williams paint company operates a number of their own retail stores. Many large food chains own some processing facilities. Sears has ownership interests in manufacturing firms which supply Sears. In these integrated systems, to refer to the corporate owner as a manufacturer or a retailer oversimplifies the realities of the situation.

In *administered vertical marketing systems* the necessary coordination of production and marketing activities is achieved essentially through the domination of one powerful channel member. This type of distribution is exemplified by Samsonite in luggage, Canadian General Electric, and General Foods. The manufacturer's brand and market position are strong enough to get the voluntary administrative cooperation of retailers in matters of advertising, pricing, and store display.

In *contractual vertical marketing systems,* independent institutions—producers, wholesalers, and retailers—are banded together by contracts to achieve the necessary economic size and coordination of effort. Three types of contractual systems can be identified: wholesaler-sponsored voluntary chains, retailers-owned cooperatives, and franchise systems. All three were discussed in Chapter 17.

Among the major types of vertical marketing systems—corporate, administered, and contractual—the most rapid rate of growth during the past 20 to 30 years has been in the contractually integrated networks.

To conclude, in this chapter we have taken a macro point of view as we studied the constantly evolving, dynamic competitive conflict and cooperation occurring in distribution systems. In the next chapter we shall return to our microanalysis and examine the process by which marketing executives select a channel of distribution and establish working relationships with individual middlemen.

QUESTIONS AND PROBLEMS

1. There is an increase in "scrambled merchandising" on the retail level of distribution. What effect will this trend have on wholesaling middlemen?
2. "Large manufacturers always control the channels used to reach local mar-

---

12 Much in this section is drawn from the works of Prof. Bert C. McCammon, Jr., of the University of Oklahoma.

Type of network	Control maintained by	Examples
Corporate	Ownership	Hart, Schaffner & Marx clothes Sherwin-Williams paints
Administered	Economic power	Coors beer, Scott lawn products, Samsonite luggage, General Electric
Contractual { Wholesaler-sponsored voluntary chain	Contract	IGA, Super Valu (food stores) Ace Hardware
Retailer-owned cooperative	Stock ownership by retailers	Associated Grocers Auto dealers
Franchise systems { Manufacturer-sponsored retailers, Manufacturer-sponsored wholesalers, Marketers of services	Contract	Soft-drink bottlers McDonald's, Hertz, Avis, Fred Astaire, Howard Johnson, Holiday Inn

Figure 19-1. Types of vertical marketing systems.

kets." Do you agree? In your community, are there big manufacturers who are unable to tap the market except through local independent retailers?

3. Explain the role played by each of the following factors in the conflict between manufacturers and wholesalers, particularly in the marketing of consumer products:

   a. Traditional position of the wholesaler before 1920

   b. Changing position of the manufacturer since the late 1800s

   c. Changing position of the retailer since 1920

4. Why is there considerably less friction between manufacturers and wholesalers in the industrial goods field than in the consumer goods field?

5. Explain the reasons why the manufacturer is dissatisfied with the performance of the wholesaler. Do you agree with the manufacturer's point of view?

6. What can a manufacturer do to stimulate wholesalers into performing a more aggressive, effective job of promoting the manufacturer's products?

7. Use examples to explain how bypassing a wholesaler will sometimes *increase* the cost of marketing.

8. Why are regular wholesalers relatively unimportant in the marketing of women's high-fashion wearing apparel, furniture, and large electrical equipment?

9. "The use of missionary salesmen is a compromise between the use of a wholesaler and the elimination of the wholesaler." Discuss this idea, showing how missionary salesmen may offset manufacturers' objections to wholesalers.

10. In the channel conflict, what are the wholesaler's reasons for being dissatisfied with the manufacturer? Assuming you are the manufacturer, what would be your rebuttal to these points?

11. In one region of the country, a general merchandise wholesaler had been supplying small, independent variety stores for years. Recently, two of the national limited-price variety chains entered the area and are giving the independents some stiff competition. Should this general merchandise wholesaler establish his own voluntary chain, signing up as members his present independent retail accounts? Would your recommendation be the same if the field were hardware stores? Stores selling low-priced shoes for the entire family?

12. "The future of the wholesaler depends upon his ability to increase his own efficiency and to furnish managerial aids to his retailers." Discuss, pointing out the alternatives if the wholesaler fails to meet this challenge.

13. What marketing conditions might encourage a manufacturer to adopt a policy of dual distribution at the retail level?

14. What are some of the problems a manufacturer is likely to encounter if he decides to set up his own retail stores?

15. What penalties can a manufacturer level at a retailer who is not living up to this manufacturer's expectations?

CHAPTER
20

DESIGNING AND MANAGING CHANNELS OF DISTRIBUTION

Marketing executives frequently find that designing channels for their products and solving the problems connected with channel management are among their most difficult tasks. In part this difficulty is traceable to the dynamic nature of the distribution structure and its propensity for change. Competitive conflicts constantly call for attention and sometimes force channel adjustments. Long channels compound a producer's problem because he is far from his ultimate consumers or users. Also, frequently he has little or no control over his middlemen and cannot get from them necessary market information regarding his markets and products.

Three steps are involved in this decision-making phase of the marketing process. First, a manufacturer must select the general channel to be used, keeping in mind the goals of the company's marketing program and the job to be done by means of the distribution system. Second, assuming he is going to use middlemen, he must make a decision regarding the *number* of middlemen or the intensity of distribution to be used at each level and in each market. Finally, again assuming he will use middlemen, he must select the specific firms which will handle his product, and then manage the day-to-day working relationships with them.

Only infrequently—as when a new company is started or when an established firm introduces a new product or enters a new market—will a marketing manager establish a distribution system from the ground up. The more usual task of channel management involves a continuing evaluation, and possibly a reorganization, of the existing structure.

You may have noted that the task of establishing channels is approached from the manufacturer's or producer's point of view. Middlemen also face channel problems similar to those of a producer. Furthermore, the control of the channels used by manufacturers and the freedom of choice regarding these channels may actually rest with middlemen. Simply as a framework for analysis in this chapter, however, channel policies and strategies will be studied from the vantage point of the producer.

MAJOR CHANNELS OF DISTRIBUTION

Actually there are several alternative channels, and in most industries each alternative is used by at least a few firms. Even to describe the major channels used for consumer products and for industrial goods is risky because it may suggest an orthodoxy which does not exist. Nevertheless, that risk is taken in the following section, which outlines the most frequently used channels for the two major classes of products. These channels are illustrated in Fig. 20-1.

DISTRIBUTION OF CONSUMER GOODS

Five channels are widely used in the marketing of consumer products. In each, the manufacturer also has the alternative of using sales branches or sales offices. Some students will justifiably conclude that consideration of these institutions triples the number of alternatives. Furthermore, whenever wholesalers are used, goods may be distributed from one large wholesaler to several subjobbers and then to retailers, thus placing two wholesaling links in the chain. Obviously, our suggestion that there are only five major channels is an oversimplification, but one which seems necessary if we are going to discuss this unwieldy subject in a few paragraphs.

Producer—consumer. The shortest, simplest channel of distribution for consumer products is from the producer to the consumer, with no middlemen involved. The producer may sell from house to house, as many dairies and some agricultural producers do, or he may sell by mail.

Producer—retailer—consumer. Many large retailers buy directly from manufacturers and agricultural producers. Also, some manufacturers—the Sherwin-Williams Paint Company, and the Florsheim division of the International Shoe Company, for example—have established their own retail stores, although this is not a common practice.

Producer—wholesaler—retailer—consumer. If there is a "traditional" channel for consumer goods, this is it. As was noted in preceding chapters, small retailers and small manufacturers by the thousands find this channel the only economically feasible choice.

Producer—agent—retailer—consumer. Instead of using wholesalers, many producers prefer to use a manufacturers' agent, selling agent, broker, or another agent middleman to reach the retail market, especially *large scale* retailers. A manufacturer

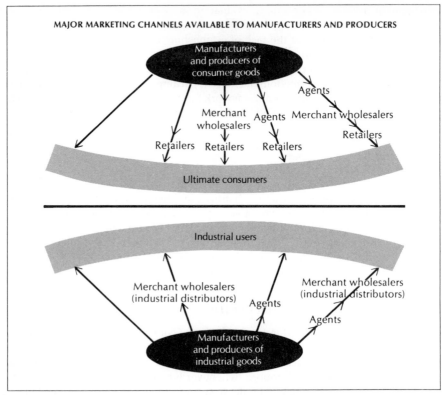

Figure 20-1. In each channel, a manufacturer or producer may use his own sales branches or personnel to reach the next institution. The channel leading directly from producer to consumer at the upper left of the diagram represents door-to-door selling and direct mail. In any channel, two levels of merchant wholesalers may be involved—one wholesaler sells the product to another wholesaler.

of a glass cleaner selected a food broker to reach the grocery store market, including the large chains. A manufacturer of a line of fishing lures used manufacturers' agents to reach sporting goods stores, hardware stores, and other retailing institutions.

Producer—agent—wholesaler—retailer—consumer. When trying to reach *small* retailers, the producers mentioned in the preceding paragraph often use agent middlemen, who in turn go to wholesalers who sell to small stores.

DISTRIBUTION OF INDUSTRIAL PRODUCTS

Four types of channels are widely used in reaching industrial users. Again, a manufacturer may use a sales branch or a sales office to reach the next institution in the channel, or two levels of wholesalers may be used in some cases (see Fig. 20-1).

Producer—industrial user. This direct channel accounts for a greater *dollar* volume of industrial products than any other distribution structure. Manufacturers of large installations, such as locomotives, generators, and heating plants, usually sell directly to the users.

Producer—industrial distributor—user. Producers of operating supplies and small accessory equipment frequently use industrial distributors to reach their markets. Manufacturers of building materials, construction equipment, and air-conditioning equipment are only a few examples of firms which make heavy use of the industrial distributor.

Producer—agent—user. Firms without their own marketing departments find this a desirable channel. Also, a company which wants to introduce a new product or enter a new market may prefer to use agents rather than its own sales force.

Producer—agent—industrial distributor—user. This channel is similar to the preceding one, except that for some reason it is not feasible to go through agents directly to the industrial user. Probably the unit sale is too small to sell directly, or perhaps decentralized inventories are needed to supply the users rapidly. In such cases, the storage services of the industrial distributor are required.

SOME GENERALIZATIONS ABOUT DISTRIBUTION CHANNELS

A few broad generalizations may serve as a guide to management in its task of developing channels of distribution. First, channel analysis should begin with the final customer and work backward to the producer because, essentially, channels of distribution are determined by consumer buying habits. This point, of course, is in complete alignment with the philosophy of the marketing concept. Thus if a significant percentage of the potential customers wish to buy on credit or prefer to shop in the evenings, the manufacturer should see to it that the retail section of the channels includes the appropriate outlets.

A second generalization is that the channels finally established must be totally appropriate to the basic objectives of the firm's marketing program. If the company's goal is to render the best possible servicing for its complex industrial product, then a short channel should be used. If management sees as its goal the widest possible distribution of its product line, then obviously an exclusive franchise policy at the retail level is *not* appropriate.

Third, the channels should provide a firm with access to a predetermined share of the market. A manufacturer of golfing equipment seeking as broad a market as possible made a mistake in establishing channels which included only department stores and sporting goods stores at the retail level. The executives should also have considered a channel which would reach discount houses and the professional shops at country clubs.

Fourth, the channels must be adequately flexible so that the use of one channel will not permanently close off another. A manufacturer of small appliances (irons, toasters, etc.) distributed only through appliance wholesalers and then to appliance retailers. The company had an offer from a drug chain to buy the products directly from the manufacturer. The appliance retailers threatened to discontinue the line if the manufacturer placed it in drugstores, and the producer decided to turn down the drug chain's offer. Subsequently, a competitive manufacturer accepted a similar offer and profited considerably.

A fifth point to keep in mind is that there is a high degree of interdependence among all firms in the channel for any given product. There can be no weak link in the chain if it is to be successful. In effect, each firm in the channel becomes his brother's keeper. Manufacturers using wholesalers are only as good as the wholesalers. Wholesalers, in turn, are successful only if their retailers do well.

A sixth observation is that evolutionary changes are constantly occurring. Channels of distribution and middlemen are always on trial. Sometimes in the course of categorizing institutional middlemen a person may succumb to the notion that markets are segmented or otherwise protected so that the different types of middlemen do not compete with one another. Actually, there is considerable competition, and this is one of the economic forces making for constant change.

Two other generalizations are corollaries of the preceding one. Middlemen survive only when their existence is economically sound and socially desirable. Nobody subsidizes a middleman if he does not serve well. Furthermore, new middlemen and channels arise to do new jobs or to do those which are not being done well.

FACTORS AFFECTING CHOICE OF CHANNELS OF DISTRIBUTION

In the course of making decisions with respect to its channels of distribution, management should carefully analyze its market, its products, its middlemen, and the company itself.

MARKET CONSIDERATIONS

Because channels of distribution should be determined by customer buying patterns, the nature of the market is the key factor influencing choice of channels.

Consumer or industrial market. The most obvious point to consider is whether the product is intended for the consumer or the industrial market. If it is going to the industrial market, retailers will not be included in the channel. If it is going to both markets, the company will want to use more than one channel.

Number of potential customers. A large potential market is likely to necessitate the use of middlemen. If the market is relatively small in numbers of customers, the company may be able to use its own sales force to sell direct. A related consideration is the number of different industries to which the company sells. A firm selling drilling equipment and supplies only to the oil industry used its own sales force and sold directly to the users. One reason for this channel choice was the relative narrowness of the market. (Incidentally, this company also maintained a few sales branches in order to have the centralized stocks or parts and supplies readily available for its customers.) For a paper products manufacturer, this aspect of the market led to an opposite decision. The company's products were ultimately sold to many different industries and to many firms in each industry. Consequently, the manufacturer made extensive use of industrial distributors.

Geographic concentration of market. Firms selling to the textile or the garment industry will find that a large proportion of the buyers are concentrated in a few geographic areas. Direct sale is more feasible than it would be if the market were spread over the entire nation. Even when a market is truly national, some segments have a higher density rate than others. There are more potential customers for office machines in Montreal than in Moncton. In densely populated markets, a seller may establish sales offices or branches, but he will decide to use middlemen in markets where the numbers of potential customers are less heavily concentrated. A company selling hard-rock mining equipment has a geographically concentrated market, and direct sale is feasible. On the other hand, the same company may sell drills, compressors, and other construction equipment to contractors all over the country. Here the lack of a geographically concentrated market, or of market segments with high density rates, forces the company to use industrial distributors.

Order size. The volume of sales to individual firms will influence the channels used to reach these companies. A food products manufacturer will sell directly to large grocery chains because the total volume of business makes this channel economically desirable. The same manufacturer cannot sell to small grocery stores in sufficient quantities to warrant direct sale, so wholesalers will be used because they afford a larger volume potential. One reason industrial operating supplies are typically sold through industrial distributors is that the volume purchased by most individual users is too small to justify direct sales.

Customer buying habits. The buying habits of ultimate consumers and industrial users—the amount of effort the consumer is willing to expend, the desire for credit, the preference for one-stop shopping, and the desire for the services of a personal salesman—all significantly affect channel policies.

PRODUCT CONSIDERATIONS

Unit value. The unit value of a product influences the amount of funds available for distribution. Usually, the lower the unit value, the longer the channels of distribution. In contrast, if the product is of high unit value, more funds are derived from each unit sold, and the company is more apt to use shorter, more costly channels. This is one reason why installation-type industrial products are sold direct, while small accessory equipment usually goes through industrial distributors or agents. However, when products of low unit value are sold in large quantities or are combined with other goods so that the total unit *sale* is large, shorter channels may be feasible.

Bulk and weight. Management must consider the cost of freight and handling in relation to the total value of the product. A producer of a heavy, bulky item, where freight is a significant part of the total value, will seek to minimize the physical handling of the product and will prefer to ship in carload or truckload quantities. This is one reason drop shippers are used in the marketing of coal and building materials. Although the title may go through middlemen, the physical product is shipped directly to the industrial user or retailer.

Perishability. Products subject to physical or fashion perishability must be speeded through their channels. Typically the channels are short. If middlemen are used for physically perishable products, they may be selected because of their special storage facilities. Manufacturers of nonperishables have wider choices in channel selection. They can offer better guarantees to middlemen and normally will find more middlemen willing to carry their goods.

Technical nature of a product and servicing required. An industrial product which is highly technical often will be distributed directly to the industrial user. The manufacturer must have salesmen and servicemen who can explain the product to potential customers and who can provide considerable presale and postsale service. Wholesalers normally cannot do this. Consumer products of a technical nature provide a real distribution challenge for the manufacturer. Ordinarily he cannot sell the goods directly to the consumer. As much as possible, he will try to sell directly to retailers, and even then the servicing of the product often poses problems.

Custom-made versus standardized products. This factor is somewhat related to the preceding one. If a product is custom-made, it will probably be distributed directly from producer to ultimate consumer or industrial user. One important exception is found in tailor-made consumer products, such as home furnishings, where retailers are widely used. In these instances, the retailers do not carry merchandise stock. They have samples and catalogues from which consumers may order.

Extent of product line. A manufacturer's channel choice is influenced appreciably by the *extent* of his product line. In the field of home appliances, for example, a firm is almost required to produce a full line of products if it wishes to secure desirable wholesalers and retailers. In other instances, the broader the line, the shorter may be the channel. The manufacturer with only one item may have to use wholesaling middlemen, whereas he could go directly to retailers if he had several products which could be combined in one large sale. Again using the appliance field as an example, a retailer ordinarily cannot buy a carload of washing machines alone, but he might buy a carload of mixed appliances.

COMPANY CONSIDERATIONS

Probably the one factor which tells most about a company and has the greatest influence on channel policies is its size. The company that has been successful enough to become large is almost certain to have financial strength, capable management, the ability to provide services for middlemen, and a desire to control the channel for its product. Given comparable market and product considerations, a large firm is more apt to have shorter channels than a small enterprise.

Financial resources. A financially strong company needs middlemen less than one which is financially weak. A business with adequate finances can establish its own sales force. It can also grant credit or warehouse its own products, whereas a weak firm would have to use middlemen to obtain these services.

A financially weak firm may deal directly with retailers or industrial users if they can take the entire output of the plant. Some large chains have such working agreements with manufacturers. Usually the product is sold under the retailer's brand. The obvious disadvantage of this arrangement is that the producer is completely at the mercy of its one large customer.

Experience and ability of management. Channel decisions are affected by the marketing experience and ability of the management. Many companies lacking marketing know-how prefer to turn the job over to middlemen. New companies, built upon the engineering and production abilities of management, often rely heavily on middlemen to do the marketing job. An established company planning to sell a new product or enter a new market is likely to use middlemen until it acquires experience in the new field.

Desire for control of channel. A manufacturer may establish a short channel simply because he wants to control the distribution of his product, even though the cost of the more direct channel is higher. The producer may feel that he can give his product more aggressive promotion by controlling the channel. Also, he can better control the freshness of merchandise stocks and the retail prices of the goods.

Services provided by seller. Often a producer's channel decision is influenced by the quantity and quality of marketing services he can provide in relation to those demanded by the middlemen. Frequently manufacturers can sell their products to retail chains only if the goods are presold through heavy advertising. Other middlemen may demand that the manufacturer build in-store displays or send missionary salesmen to call on retailers and industrial users.

MIDDLEMEN CONSIDERATIONS

Services provided by middlemen. A producer should select middlemen who will provide the marketing services he himself either is unable to provide or cannot economically perform. If a product needs aggressive promotion to enter a new market, a manufacturers' agent can usually provide the service better than a full-function wholesaler. If a product requires special storage facilities, a wholesaler may provide these facilities best. In these examples we can see the relationships between the nature of the product and the services provided by middlemen.

Availability of desired middlemen. The middlemen which a producer desires may not be available. They may be carrying competitive products and may not wish to add another line. In any event, the manufacturer may have to alter his entire channel. One producer of industrial machinery who could not secure desirable distributors in a metropolitan market opened a sales office in that city. It proved so successful that eventually he opened branches or offices in several other markets and discontinued his use of industrial distributors in those cities.

Attitude of middlemen toward manufacturer's policies. Sometimes a manufacturer's choice of channels is limited because his marketing policies are not acceptable to certain types of middlemen. The producer's unwillingness to guarantee the product against a price decline will eliminate many middlemen from consideration. Some types of retailers and wholesaling middlemen are interested in carrying a line only if they can get an exclusive franchise in a territory.

Sales volume possibilities. All other factors being equal, a producer will select a channel offering the greatest potential volume over the long run. There are two problems inherent in that statement, however, the first is the difficulty of forecasting which channel will generate the largest volume. The second is that realistically all other things are not equal. A high-volume channel may also be a high-cost channel, or a firm may secure maximum volume but lose all control over its distribution.

Cost requirements. The final point to consider is the cost of selling through alternative channels. Expenses should be equated with functions performed by the middlemen. As noted in preceding chapters, a high-cost middleman is not to be excluded automatically from consideration. This cost may be high only because he provides so many services. When analyzing these costs, a firm should study the *total* channel expense rather than the expense of *separate* types of middlemen.

Analysis of cost by channels of distribution is a difficult task. (See Chapter 29 for a discussion of this topic.) If such an analysis is not made, however, management has no sound foundation for judging channel expenses. Furthermore, even after a cost analysis shows which is the lowest-cost channel, then the products, the market, or other considerations may indicate that this channel is not the best choice.

SELECTION OF CHANNELS FOR NEW PRODUCTS OR NEW COMPANIES

Special channel problems are faced by an established company adding a new, unrelated product to its line, or by a new company starting out with either a new product or an established product. Three important considerations will influence the decision making in these situations. The first concerns the newness of the product and the extent to which consumers realize they want it. A manufacturer of men's suits who adds shirts to his line faces different channel problems from those of an appliance manufacturer who adds electronic clothes washers which require no water. In the latter case a primary demand must be created, and provisions must be made in the channel to educate consumers regarding the new product.

Second, for any new product or company the promotion requirements are particularly high. Aggressive selling is needed. We have seen that wholesalers do not perform this service. Yet they may be needed to reach retailers or industrial users. The manufacturer, faced with the need to spend huge sums on advertising and to establish a missionary sales force, has some alternatives. Instead of using wholesalers, he may develop his own sales force to call directly on retailers or industrial users. Or he may compromise by employing a manufacturers' agent and giving him a commission large enough to encourage him to sell the product aggressively.

The third point is that the company may find it difficult to establish the channels it wants simply because the middlemen are not eager to take on an unknown company or product. In this case the manufacturer may have to use any channel which will accept the product and hope that in time he can change to more appropriate channels.

USE OF MULTIPLE CHANNELS OF DISTRIBUTION

A manufacturer may use multiple channels either to reach different markets or to sell the same market.

A firm selling the same products to consumer and industrial markets would usually establish separate channel structures. In like manner, differences in the size of the buyers or the market densities often result in the use of more than one channel. A manufacturer of food products will sell directly to large grocery chains, but to reach smaller stores he will use another channel which includes grocery whole-salers. A producer may establish sales branches in a concentrated market and from these branches send out a sales force to reach wholesalers or retailers. In more sparsely populated markets, the same producer will use manufacturers' agents in-stead of his own sales force.

Sometimes a producer is reaching different markets, and thus is using multiple channels, because he is selling unrelated products. Firms producing margarine and paint, or rubber products and plastics, illustrate the point. These firms may also have organized their sales forces into separate divisions according to the various customer groups or product lines.

As we noted in the preceding chapter, a significant development in dual distri-bution (and a source of channel conflict) has been the increased use of *competing* channel systems by manufacturers to sell the same brand to the same market.

DETERMINING INTENSITY OF DISTRIBUTION

After a manufacturer has decided upon the general channels he will use, he then should determine the number of middlemen—the intensity of distribution—to be employed at the wholesaling and retailing levels. In this respect, a manufacturer has three major alternative courses of action. These are not neatly compartmenta-lized alternatives. Instead, the degrees of intensity of distribution form a contin-uum, or points on a scale. At one end is *intensive* distribution, in which the manu-facturer tries to get maximum exposure for his product by having it sold in every outlet where final customers might possibly look for it. The second alternative is *se-lective* distribution, in which the producer selects a limited number of wholesalers and/or retailers in a given geographic area. The third possibility is *exclusive* distribu-tion, which involves the use of only one wholesaling middleman or retailer in a specified geographic market.

INTENSIVE DISTRIBUTION

Ordinarily the policy of intensive distribution is adopted by the manufacturers of consumer convenience goods. Consumers demand immediate satisfaction for this class of product and will not defer a purchase in order to get a particular brand. In the field of industrial products, intensive distribution is usually limited to operating supplies or other highly standardized items, such as small tools and some lubri-cants. Retailers often control the extent to which the policy of intensive distribution can be implemented. For example, a new manufacturer of toothpaste may want distribution in all supermarkets, but these retailers may limit their assortment to the four fastest-selling brands. Intensive distribution also places most of the burden of advertising and promotion on the shoulders of the manufacturer. Retailers are not going to pay to advertise a product which all competitors are selling.

SELECTIVE DISTRIBUTION

Selective distribution covers a wide range of distribution intensity. A business which adopts this policy may have only a few outlets in a particular market, or it may have a large number but still have something short of intensive distribution. The policy of selective distribution lends itself especially well to manufacturers of consumer shopping or specialty goods and industrial accessory equipment, for which most customers have a brand preference. Even makers of convenience goods often limit the number of their outlets to some extent because it simply is not profitable to sell to every existing outlet.

When a firm adopts a selective distribution policy at the retail level, there will normally be a reduction in the number of wholesalers used. Conversely, a firm may limit the number of retail outlets by the simple expedient of first limiting the number of wholesalers to whom it sells. Adopting a selective distribution policy at the retail level may make it possible for the manufacturer to bypass wholesalers.

Many companies have switched to selective distribution in order to achieve higher profit levels. Although they forecast a decline in sales volume, many of them actually increased their volume substantially because they were able to do a more thorough selling job with the smaller number of accounts.

A company may decide to adopt a selective distribution policy after some experience with intensive distribution. The reasons for the change usually hinge upon the high cost of intensive distribution or the unsatisfactory performance of middlemen. Some customers perennially order in small, unprofitable amounts. Others may be poor credit risks. Still others may be chronic complainers, frequently returning goods they orderd or demanding extraordinary services. Some retailers may be eliminated because they are not providing adequate repair and maintenance facilities to service the products.

Once the executives in a firm decide to follow a selective distribution policy, special requirements ordinarily fall upon the chosen outlets. The fewer the number of outlets, the heavier the requirements. For example, if there is a limited number of middlemen, they are expected to display the products more prominently and to promote them more aggressively than if distribution were unlimited.

EXCLUSIVE DISTRIBUTION

Under an exclusive distribution policy the supplier enters into an agreement with a particular wholesaling middleman or retailer whereby the supplier will sell only to that wholesaler or retailer in the given market. Under these exclusive distributorships (with a wholesaler) or exclusive dealerships (with retailers) the middlemen are sometimes prohibited from handling a directly competitive line of product.[1]

When used. A new firm having difficulty establishing a distribution system or an established firm trying to market a new product may attract outlets by offering exclusive franchises. Some risk is involved in using exclusive selling agreements to

---

1 In technical language, a contract wherein the middleman agrees not to handle competitive products is known as an "exclusive dealing" agreement. On the other hand, the terms "exclusive selling," "exclusive dealerships," "exclusive distributorships," and "exclusive distribution" refer only to arrangements whereby the seller agrees not to sell to other retailers or wholesalers in the particular market. These arrangements have nothing to do with other products.

Frequently the term "exclusive agency" is used to describe exclusive dealerships, and the retailer is referred to as the "exclusive agent" for the product. No agency relationship exists in a legal sense. The retailer buys the product outright and legally performs in his own interest. He is not the legal agent of a manufacturer-principal. Because he is an independent retailer, the term "exclusive franchise" would more appropriately describe his relationship with the manufacturer.

secure initial distribution because if the manufacturer later wants to terminate the exclusive arrangement, considerable ill will may be engendered. Exclusive dealerships are frequently used in the marketing of consumer specialty products. Expensive men's suits, sold under heavily advertised brands, fall into this category. When department stores or very large specialty stores are granted these franchises, a manufacturer often gets a bonus in the form of several outlets in the one market because the retailers open branch stores in suburban shopping centers.

Management often adopts an exclusive distribution policy when it is essential that the retailer carry a large inventory in order to ensure customers an adequate choice. This form of distribution is also desirable when the dealer or distributor must furnish installation and repair service. Manufacturers of farm machinery, large construction equipment, and commercial heating and air-conditioning equipment frequently use exclusive distributorships for this reason.

Evaluation from manufacturer's standpoint. An exclusive distribution policy helps the manufacturer control the retail segment of his channel. He is better able to determine what the retail price of his product will be, and he is in a position to approve advertisements featuring his product. A dealer is more likely to be cooperative and to promote the product aggressively because he realizes that his future is tied to the success of the manufacturer. With fewer accounts, the manufacturer is able to reduce credit losses and marketing costs. His billing, shipping, and order-filling functions are simplified. The dealer will probably carry a complete stock and be more willing to service the products than he would be if there were broader distribution.

On the other hand, there are a few serious competitive limitations to this distribution policy. Probably the most significant is that the manufacturer substantially limits the number of his sales outlets. He may lose the business of some customers who would normally buy his brand if it were available at more convenient locations. Also, the manufacturer will suffer if his exclusive dealer incurs customer ill will. Essentially, the manufacturer has all his eggs in one basket, and he is pretty much dependent upon the retailer. Another problem is the difficulty of getting good dealers. Often the best ones in a market are already taken on by competitors.

Evaluation from retailer's standpoint. A significant advantage of being an exclusive dealer is that such a retailer reaps all the benefits of the manufacturer's marketing and advertising activities in the particular market and gets all repeat sales. He finds it easier to maintain the margin on the product because he is protected from price-cutting competitors. If he does not carry competitive lines, he may increase his rate of stock turnover in the exclusive product line and also reduce his investment in inventory. Because he is important to the manufacturer, the lone retailer probably gets better treatment from him.

For a retailer, the main drawback to an exclusive dealership is that he becomes wedded to the manufacturer. If the manufacturer does a good job with the product, the dealer prospers. But if the manufacturer fails, the dealer is powerless to do anything but sink with him.

Dealership agreements often require the retailer to invest a considerable sum of money in equipment and facilities. If the agreement is then canceled, he stands to lose a major investment. Having cut himself off from other suppliers, he may have virtually no opportunity to acquire a product line of another firm. Another hazard is that once the volume is built up in a market, the manufacturer may add other dealers. The retailer is often at the mercy of the manufacturer. It is a one-sided arrangement in this respect, particularly if the brand is strong and the franchise is valuable. High quotas and other demands set by the manufacturer may put a heavy strain on the retailer. To keep the valuable franchise, the middleman may have to give up his independence and operate almost as a sales branch.

Legal considerations. Although exclusive distribution is not illegal, federal laws and judicial interpretations have imposed restrictions on three major aspects of its use. One aspect is *exclusive dealing contracts,* the arrangement whereby the franchise holder is prohibited from carrying similar product lines from competing manufacturers. A second involves *tying contracts,* under which the exclusive dealer or distributor is required to carry a manufacturer's full line if this supplier so desires. The third arrangement is the *closed sales territory* or *market restriction* wherein the manufacturer limits each franchise holder to selling only to buyers located within the assigned territory.[2]

None of the three arrangements is automatically illegal. Section 31.4 of the Combines Investigation Act specifically states, however, that such contracts are unlawful if their effect is "to substantially lessen competition". It is under this provision that unreasonably restrictive exclusive dealing contracts and tying contracts may be ruled illegal. Questions on the legality of closed sales territories usually involve Section 31.4 of the Combines Investigation Act, which prohibits unfair competition that may result in reduced competition.

Exclusive dealing contracts have been declared unlawful if the manufacturer's sales volume is a substantial part of the total volume in a market or if the volume done by the exclusive dealers is a significant percentage of the total business in an area. That is, the law is violated when the competitors of a manufacturer are essentially shut out from a substantial part of the market because of this manufacturer's exclusive dealing contract.

By inference, it is clear that exclusive dealing is not illegal in all situations. In fact, where the seller is just getting started in a market or where his share of the total market is so small as to be negligible, his negotiation of exclusive dealing agreements may not only improve his competitive position but also strengthen competition in general.

Ordinarily there is no question of legality when a manufacturer agrees to sell to only one retailer or wholesaler in a given territory, provided there are no limitations on competitive products. Also, a manufacturer can sell to dealers who do not carry competitors' products, as long as this is a voluntary decision on the part of the franchise holder.

With regard to tying contracts, apparently a dealer can be required to carry a manufacturer's full line as long as this does not impede competition in the market. The arrangement may be questionable, however, if a supplier forces a dealer or a distributor to take slow-moving, less attractive items in order to acquire the really desirable products.

---

2 For an economic analysis of the impact which these three types of distribution restrictions may have on market competition and of the development of standards for determining whether a company's restrictive distribution arrangements are compatible with governmental policy concerning maintenance of competition, see Lee E. Preston, "Restrictive Distribution Arrangements: Economic Analysis and Public Policy Standards," *Law and Contemporary Problems,* Summer, 1965, pp. 506-529.

Closed sales territories may be illegal because they restrict competition. They may also tend to create a monopoly for a product in a given territory in that buyers cannot play exclusive dealers in different territories against one another. Perhaps the safest policy is to assign each reseller a geographic area of primary responsibility rather than a closed sales territory.

The situation regarding contractual channel relationships was summed up nicely by Professor Dixon when he observed: "The future importance of contractual integration in marketing will depend in part upon the extent to which the restraints in these contractual arrangements present problems under the antitrust laws."[3]

SELECTING AND WORKING WITH INDIVIDUAL MIDDLEMEN

When all is said and done, middlemen can often make or break a manufacturer. They are the ones who personally contact the final customer, whether he is an ultimate consumer or an industrial user. Consequently, a manufacturer's entire channel effort is designed to reach one goal—that of maximizing the marketing effectiveness at the point of final sale. This generalization supports the systems concept of a channel of distribution. That is, to maximize the effectiveness of a distribution channel, it must be treated as a complete system and not as a series of independent, competing links. Thus the success of a manufacturer's distribution effort depends ultimately upon how well he selects his individual middlemen and then administers the action system involving these distributors and dealers.

The final step in establishing channels is particularly important at the *wholesaling* level because a manufacturer uses fewer wholesalers than retailers. Furthermore, the choice of wholesaling middlemen preempts to a considerable extent the manufacturer's choice of retailers. At the *retail* level, the choice of individual middlemen is particularly important when the producer has decided upon a policy of selective or exclusive distribution.

FACTORS AFFECTING CHOICE OF MIDDLEMEN

Several factors may contribute to a middleman's success in his business operation. Some, such as business conditions and competition, are external to the firm's operation and generally are not controllable by the wholesaler or retailer. Other points which are controllable by middlemen include the caliber of their executives, their ability to advertise, and the soundness of their product planning.

The manufacturer should establish qualifying standards for each factor so that he will know what he is looking for. Then he must find the available middlemen who meet these predetermined standards. Here we again observe that channel research is one of the most difficult types of marketing research. Getting the desired information regarding potential middlemen will undoubtedly involve some kind of field research. When the manufacturer has a prospective retailer in mind for a selective or exclusive dealership, he probably should talk with the retailer's suppliers

3 Donald F. Dixon, "The Impact of Recent Antitrust Decisions upon Franchise Marketing," *MSU Business Topics,* Spring, 1969, pp. 68-79.

and competitors. If possible, the manufacturer should find out what the retailer's customers are like and what they think of his store. It is important to make certain that all information is currently accurate. A store that was doing an outstanding job in promotion last year may have lost the key executive who was the guiding force behind this success.

Access to desired market. In the selection of an individual wholesaler or retailer, by far the most important factor to consider is: Does he sell to the market I want to reach? This really is the *sine qua non* of middleman selection. If he does not now reach the manufacturer's desired market, it is doubtful that the manufacturer's products will induce him to change his customer list substantially.

Location. A good location is particularly important at the retail level, but it must also be considered in selecting wholesaling middlemen because a firm's location is often closely related to its ability to reach a desired market.

A retailer's location must be considered with respect to competitive outlets and trading areas. A manufacturer who wants to select a specialty store in a shopping center will first want to determine whether the shopping center is the most desirable one in the market. In one case, a shopping center had no leading department store, and therefore a specialty store was not selected in this center. Even the location of the retail store within the shopping center may be an important consideration. Manufacturers of shopping goods will try to select retailers who are located close to competitors and are in an area where there is heavy customer traffic.

Product-planning policies. A manufacturer should carefully consider the product policies of prospective wholesalers or retailers. To illustrate, a manufacturer ordinarily seeks stores where his line will complement rather than compete with the store's other products. If he refuses to sell to middlemen who carry a competing line, then he must seek outlets which have no such line or which are willing to drop their present lines. A garment manufacturer had such a policy, and his products were so attractive to retailers that many stores discontinued their previously handled brands in order to get his line.

The assortment typically carried by a dealer within a product line may influence a manufacturer's choice of outlet. A manufacturer of health and beauty aids produced a wide line of products in several sizes, types of packaging, and colors. Department stores and large drugstores would carry the full assortment, but supermarkets wanted only one or two sizes of a few fast-moving items. This manufacturer could not rely only on supermarkets for his retail distribution. He had to use other stores which were willing to carry a larger proportion of his assortment.

A manufacturer must consider the comparative quality and price of other lines in a store. Even if the retailer were willing, a manufacturer should not be interested in selling his line of dresses which start at $79.95 to stores whose highest-priced lines of other dresses sell for $29.95.

The pricing policies and practices followed by middlemen should influence a manufacturer. If the manufacturer wants to maintain a suggested retail price, he must avoid dealers who are well-known price-cutters or who might use the brand as a price football.

Promotion policies. If a manufacturer must rely on middlemen to do the bulk of the promotion, he will select them differently from the way he would if he himself planned to advertise and otherwise promote the product heavily. Some manufacturers have been forced to shun large retailers who were otherwise desirable because these dealers demanded promotional allowances, displays, or product demonstrators. The manufacturers either could not afford these promotional devices or preferred to use other methods.

For producers of many types of goods, the nature of the middleman's personal selling activities is important. A manufacturer of earth-moving equipment made it a point to ascertain the technical abilities of salesmen of industrial distributors before granting a franchise in a territory. If a product does not lend itself to the self-service method of retail selling, then obviously the many stores employing this method are eliminated from further consideration.

Services available to customers. The consumer's acceptance of discount selling, with its limited services but low prices, has changed managerial thinking with regard to the necessity of services. However, this does not mean that manufacturers and middlemen can consider customer service a thing of the past. Where service is important, a manufacturer should judge the potential middlemen on the basis of the services they normally offer to their customers. Manufacturers and wholesalers of big-ticket consumer products, such as furniture and appliances, usually prefer retailers who supply credit and delivery services for their customers. Middlemen for many industrial products must be able to provide their customers with good mechanical service and rapid delivery of parts and supplies.

Financial ability. A manufacturer should investigate a middleman's financial condition and the financing services he provides for his customers and suppliers. Naturally a manufacturer will prefer middlemen who pay their bills regularly and promptly. In some cases a manufacturer will select an individual retailer who is small and financially insecure because he holds great promise for the future.

Quality of management. An overall factor for a manufacturer to consider is the caliber of executives in a middleman's business. Their capacity to manage—that is, their ability to perform all aspects of the management process, such as planning, organizing, and staffing—is crucial to the success of the firm. The quality of management is reflected in all aspects of the middleman's business.

THE WORKING RELATIONSHIP

In the administration of a channel system (as we saw in the preceding chapter), some institutions assume the role of *primary* (controlling) organizations, while others occupy secondary roles.[4] Regardless of whether the manufacturer or the middlemen holds the controlling position, a real interdependence exists between the two groups. Unless the manufacturer is successful, the welfare of the dealer is in jeopardy, and, conversely, the manufacturer has a vital interest in his dealer's success. The greater the share of his total business that a dealer derives from the sale of a given manufacturer's product, the greater is his dependence on that supplier.

---

4 Ideas in this and the following paragraph are adapted from Valentine F. Ridgeway, "Administration of Manufacturer-Dealer Systems," *Administrative Science Quarterly,* March, 1957, pp. 464–483.

There is also a community of interests in what each organization—manufacturer and middleman—expects from the other in terms of support of an effective total marketing program. A series of rewards and penalties may be instituted by either party in order to encourage the other to perform as expected. The major reward for either party is in the form of increased profits. A manufacturer can also use programs of recognition or financial incentives to further reward a dealer. Probably the most powerful penalty which a manufacturer can impose is to terminate his sales agreement with a dealer. A middleman, in turn, can penalize a manufacturer by not promoting his products adequately, by pushing a competitor's products, or ultimately by dropping the manufacturer's line entirely.

A middleman has a right to expect the manufacturer to provide well-designed, properly priced, salable products for which consumer demand has been built by a good advertising program. A manufacturer may also grant territorial protection in the form of an exclusive franchise.

On a day-to-day basis, a manufacturer can furnish promotional and managerial assistance in many forms. Preparing sales manuals and conducting sales training programs for dealer or distributor salesmen are only two examples. A manufacturer's in-store promotional aids may be useful, and his missionary salesmen are often welcomed because they can check stock, build displays, and work with salesclerks. Middlemen should be notified about price changes and stock conditions, and they should be completely informed about new products. Manufacturers can offer managerial assistance in accounting systems, buying activities, and advertising. Managerial advice should be available for a middleman when he selects a location for a new store, arranges a store layout, or modernizes an existing store.

Day-to-day working relationships between manufacturers and their middlemen determine the ultimate success of the arrangement. Friction can develop easily if there is not a real spirit of cooperation. The communication system which provides for information interchange in such categories as physical inventory, promotion, product features, pricing, and market conditions seems essential for the coordination of intrachannel activities. See Fig. 20-2.

In return for the products and services which he supplies, the manufacturer has a right to expect certain assistance from middlemen in day-to-day relationships. Some of these points have been developed at greater length in the preceding chapters on the distribution system. A retailer or wholesaler may be expected to carry adequate stocks of merchandise, undertake some advertising and sales promotion, grant credit to customers, and possibly service the product. The amount of help to be provided in each of these activities depends upon the product itself and the nature of the middleman's franchise. More is expected from holders of exclusive franchises than from middlemen used in intensive distribution.

ANALYSIS AND EVALUATION OF CHANNELS OF DISTRIBUTION

In the face of changing conditions in the market and among middlemen, constant appraisal of channel activity is mandatory. Yet a surprisingly large number of companies assume that the channel job is completed once their channels are established. Executives who regularly sponsor product innovation and who insist on a new advertising campaign twice a year often seem perfectly content with an archaic distribution structure.

Several types of quantitative and qualitative marketing research may be under-

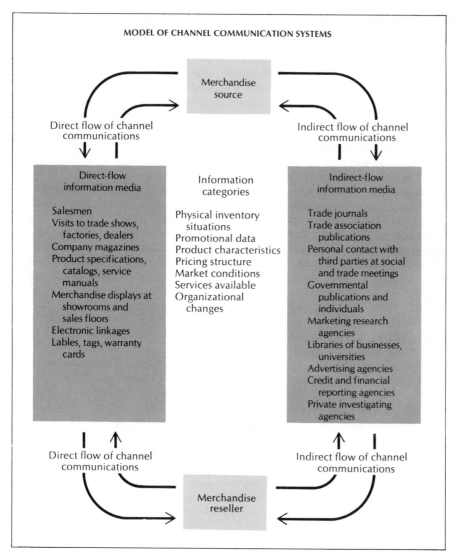

MODEL OF CHANNEL COMMUNICATION SYSTEMS

Merchandise source

Direct flow of channel communications

Indirect flow of channel communications

Direct-flow information media	Information categories	Indirect-flow information media
Salesmen Visits to trade shows, factories, dealers Company magazines Product specifications, catalogs, service manuals Merchandise displays at showrooms and sales floors Electronic linkages Lables, tags, warranty cards	Physical inventory situations Promotional data Product characteristics Pricing structure Market conditions Services available Organizational changes	Trade journals Trade association publications Personal contact with third parties at social and trade meetings Governmental publications and individuals Marketing research agencies Libraries of businesses, universities Advertising agencies Credit and financial reporting agencies Private investigating agencies

Direct flow of channel communications

Indirect flow of channel communications

Merchandise reseller

Figure 20-2.

taken to aid a business in appraising its channels. In a quantitative sense, a company may analyze the sales volume performance of each of its middlemen to determine whether they are getting an adequate volume from each territory, product line, and customer group. The need for a cost analysis by channels of distribution has already been mentioned. These kinds of quantitative analyses are discussed in more detail in Chapter 29.

To do a proper job of evaluating a middleman's performance, a manufacturer must establish standards and then develop methods for measuring the middleman's performance against these predetermined criteria. A commonly used standard of performance is a sales quota. The manufacturer sets the number of units or the dollar volume of each of his products which a middleman must sell in a given time period. Other bases for appraising performance include the total amount of advertising the middleman devoted to the manufacturer's products, his treatment of competitive lines which he handles, his promptness in paying bills, and the number of complaints which the manufacturer receives from his customers. External factors, such as new competitors and general business conditions in a market, should often be taken into consideration when measuring performance.

Another type of valuable research involves determining the attitudes of middlemen and even final customers toward the manufacturer, his products, and his marketing policies. Essentially, the manufacturer is trying to get some "feedback" from his middlemen and final customers. Middlemen's attitudes may be uncovered by a formal questionnaire survey conducted either by the manufacturer himself or by an outside research agency. A few years ago, a major home appliance manufacturer employed a research firm to determine what the appliance dealers' attitudes were toward the manufacturer's salesmen, distribution system, and advertising program. The main findings were that dealers wanted the products to be presold through advertising and to be of high quality, and they wanted the manufacturer's service facilities close by. Additional findings regarding what the dealers expected from the manufacturer's salesmen were incorporated into the latter's sales training program.

QUESTIONS AND PROBLEMS

1. Which of the channels illustrated in Fig. 20-1 is most apt to be used for each of the following products? Defend your choice in each case.
   a. Life insurance   f. Iron ore
   b. Single-family residence   g. Toothpaste
   c. Farm tractor   h. Women's shoes
   d. Newspaper printing press   i. Men's shoes
   e. Office furniture   j. Refrigerators

2. "The great majority of industrial sales are made directly from the producer to the industrial user." Explain the reason for this in terms of the nature of the market. In terms of the nature of the product.

3. A small manufacturer of fishing lures is faced with the problem of selecting his channel of distribution. What reasonable alternatives does he have? Consider particularly the nature of his product and the nature of his market.

4. What special channel problems are involved with new products and new companies? How would you overcome each of the problems?

5. Is a policy of intensive distribution consistent with buying habits for convenience goods? Shopping goods? Is intensive distribution normally used in the marketing of any type of industrial goods?

6. Why would a manufacturer ever want to abandon intensive distribution in favor of selective distribution?

7. Assume that a manufacturer of builders' hardware wanted to move to a selective distribution system. How would he go about determining which accounts to keep and which to eliminate?

8. From the manufacturer's viewpoint, what are the competitive advantages of exclusive distribution?

9. What are the drawbacks to exclusive selling from the retailer's point of view? To what extent are these alleviated if the retailer controls the channel for the particular brand?

10. What is a tying contract? Is it illegal under the Combines Investigation Act?

11. Identify a few retailers near your school who have exclusive franchises for particular products. Study these retailers and determine to what extent they meet the standards discussed in this chapter in connection with selecting individual middlemen.

12. How can a manufacturer determine whether an individual retailer or wholesaler sells to the market the manufacturer wants to reach?

13. A manufacturer of a well-known brand of men's clothing has been selling directly to one dealer in a Western city for many years. For some time, the market has been large enough to support two retailers very profitably, and yet the present holder of the franchise objects strongly when the manufacturer suggests adding another outlet. What alternatives does the manufacturer have in this situation? What course of action do you recommend that he take?

14. "A manufacturer should always strive to select the lowest-cost channel of distribution." Do you agree? Should he always try to use the middlemen with the lowest operating costs? Explain.

MANAGEMENT OF PHYSICAL DISTRIBUTION

After the channels of distribution have been established, a firm can turn its attention to the physical distribution of its product through these channels. *Physical distribution* is the term used to describe the range of activities concerned with the movement of the right amount of the right products to the right place at the right time.

TOTAL SYSTEM CONCEPT OF PHYSICAL DISTRIBUTION

Physical distribution in marketing is essentially a problem in logistics. An army cannot afford to have one of its units in a position where it has guns but no ammunition, or trucks but no gasoline. By the same token, a private business is in a weak position when it has orders but no merchandise to ship, or when it has a good supply of machinery in Winnipeg but an urgent customer in Red Deer. These situations indicate the importance of *location* in marketing, whether it is the location of a store, warehouse, or stock of merchandise. The appropriate assortment of products must be in the right place at the right time in order to maximize the opportunity for profitable sales volume.

Physical distribution, then, is the management of the physical flow of products and the development and operation of efficient flow systems. In its full scope, physical distribution for a manufacturer would involve not only the movement of *finished goods* from the end of the production line to the final customer but also the flow of *raw materials* from their source of supply to the beginning of the production line. Similarly, a middleman would manage the flow of goods *onto* his shelves as well as *from* his shelves to the customer's home or store.

The task of physical distribution may be divided into the five parts listed below. What is done in one area, however, very definitely affects decision making in others. A decision on the location of a warehouse may influence the selection of the

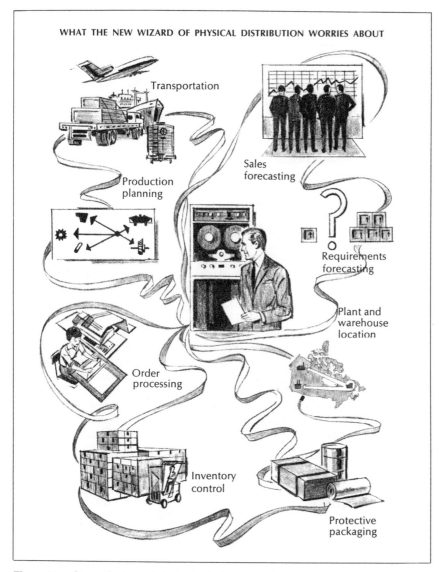

WHAT THE NEW WIZARD OF PHYSICAL DISTRIBUTION WORRIES ABOUT

Transportation

Production planning

Sales forecasting

Requirements forecasting

Plant and warehouse location

Order processing

Inventory control

Protective packaging

Figure 21-1. *Source: Business Week,* Sept. 24, 1966, p. 113.

transportation carrier. The decision on the carrier influences the optimum size of the shipment. See Fig. 21-1.

1. Determine the inventory locations and establish a warehousing system.
2. Establish a materials-handling system.
3. Maintain an inventory control system.
4. Establish procedures to process the orders.
5. Select a method of transportation.

From time to time in this book, it has been pointed out that marketing is a total system of business action and not a fragmented series of operations. Nowhere is this idea seen more clearly than in the matter of physical distribution. But it has not always been this way. Traditionally—and unfortunately this is still true in too many firms—the activities involved in physical distribution have been fragmented, and managerial responsibility for them has been compartmentalized into units which often have conflicting, and even diametrically opposite, goals. The production department, for instance, sets the production schedule and is interested in long production runs so as to minimize the unit manufacturing costs, even though the result may be abnormally high inventory costs. The traffic department looks at the freight rates rather than at the total cost of physical distribution. Thus carriers with low ton-mile charges are often selected, even though this may mean undue time spent in transit and require larger inventories to fill the long pipelines. The finance department wants to minimize funds tied up in inventories, while the sales department wants to have a wide assortment of products available at locations near the customers. Under managerial conditions such as these, it is not possible to optimize the flow of products. Applying the systems approach to physical distribution, however, should result in more effective linkage and coordination of these various functional activities. See Fig. 21-2.

In physical distribution, management is dealing with a large number of variables which are readily measurable. Problems in this situation lend themselves nicely to solution by statistical and mathematical techniques. For instance, operations research—a technique involving the use of statistical probability theory, mathematical models, and other quantitative methods—has been particularly helpful in such problems as determining the number and location of warehouses, the optimum size of inventories, and transportation routes and methods. Improvements in computers and other electronic data-processing equipment have made it possible to process rapidly the large quantities of data used in these quantitative analyses. In our survey treatment in this chapter, however, we shall be concerned with the fundamentals and the conceptual aspects of physical distribution management rather than with the methods of quantitative analysis used in solving problems in this field.[1]

---

1 For a more complete textual treatment of physical distribution as an integrated systems concept, see Donald J. Bowersox, Edward W. Smykay, and Bernard J. LaLonde, *Physical Distribution Management*, rev. ed., The Macmillan Company, New York, 1968; J. L. Heskett, Robert M. Ivie, and Nicholas A. Glaskowsky, Jr., *Business Logistics*, 2d ed., The Ronald Press Company, New York, 1973; or James A. Constantin, *Principles of Logistics Management*, Appleton-Century-Crofts, Inc., New York, 1966.

For an appraisal of existing physical distribution planning models and the development of an improved model for long-range planning, see Donald J. Bowersox, "Planning Physical Distribution Operations with Dynamic Simulation," *Journal of Marketing*, January, 1972, pp. 17-25.

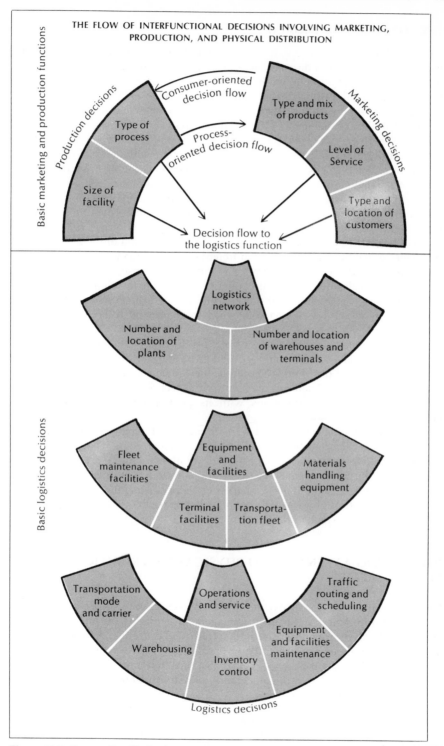

Figure 21-2. *Source: Alan H. Gepfert, "Business Logistics for Better Profit Performance," Harvard Business Review,* November-December, 1968, p. 78.

THE TOTAL COST APPROACH

As part of the systems concept, executives should apply the *total cost approach* to the management of physical distribution. A firm has alternative methods of physically handling and distributing its products. The administrators should try to optimize the cost-profit relationship of these various choices after analyzing the total cost of physical distribution, rather than considering separately the costs of shipping storage, handling, or some other fragmented activity.

Too often an executive looks at the cost of only one aspect of physical distribution—transportation, for example—and tries to minimize this single cost. Possibly he frowns on the high cost of shipment by air freight or shipping in small units. He does not see that efforts to reduce transportation expenses may result in increases in warehousing expenses, which more than offset the saving in freight costs.

The airlines particularly have been conscious of the total-cost concept because unit freight rates are appreciably higher for air transportation than for land or sea shipment. The Armour Pharmaceutical Company (a division of the Armour Company) found that the higher costs of air freight were more than offset by the savings in lower inventory costs, less insurance and interest expenses, lower crating costs, and fewer lost sales due to depletion of stock. The company eliminated all except one warehouse, cut inventories by 50 percent, boosted the rate of stock turnover, and found it could supply markets which had previously been inadequately served.

The point made here is *not* that air freight is the best method of transportation. (In fact, Armour later substantially reduced its business with airlines.) Rather, the idea is that physical distribution should be viewed as a total process and its costs analyzed accordingly. Then management can expect to get a better picture of its operations, better communications with its field activities, and consequently greater control over its distribution system.[2]

Implicit in the total cost concept is the thought that management should strive for an optimum balance between total cost and customer utility. That is, rather than seeking *only* to minimize the total costs of physical distribution, executives should also consider customer want satisfaction in connection with this segment of the firm's marketing program. It may be necessary to incur something above the lowest possible total costs of physical distribution in order to achieve something nearer an optimum level of customer utility.

INCREASING ATTENTION TO PHYSICAL DISTRIBUTION MANAGEMENT

Fortunately, in recent years we have witnessed a significant increase in the emphasis which North American business management is placing on physical distribution. Happily, there are no signs at all that this trend is abating. A major reason for the increased attention is the fact that physical distribution expenses are a substantial cost factor in many industries. To cite just one study, these costs ranged from about 10 percent of sales in the machinery industry to 30 percent in the food in-

---

2 For further examples of companies which have improved their performance by treating physical distribution as a total system, see "What You Should Know about Physical Distribution Management," *Sales Management,* Jan. 1, 1971, p. 28. See also Raymond LeKashman and John F. Stolle, "The Total Cost Approach to Distribution," *Business Horizons,* Winter, 1965, pp. 33-46.

dustry.[3] For many products, the largest single operating expenses are those involved in physical distribution. For other products, costs equal to as much as one-half of the wholesale price are incurred in performing transportation and warehousing activities. Not only do these costs already loom large, but they are increasing.

Through the years, management has made substantial progress toward optimizing the costs of production activities. Cost reductions have also been effected in many areas of marketing. This leaves physical distribution as a prime target. It is the new (and perhaps the last) major frontier for cost cutting. By treating this activity as a total system, rather than as a set of fragmented parts, business can take a significant stride toward greater efficiency.

By focusing attention on such a substantial expense item as physical distribution costs, management may recognize the considerable "leverage" effect which cost savings in this area can have on profits. In a supermarket operation, for instance, where the net profit on sales may be one percent, every dollar of savings in physical distribution costs has the same effect on profits as does an increase of $100 in sales volume.

In addition to cost considerations, other factors also account for the increased attention being devoted to physical distribution management.[4] Improvements in inventory control and advances in computer capabilities have resulted in a trend toward more frequent ordering of small quantities. Sellers catering to these customers are finding that their existing methods of distributing products do not give the required levels of service. Another factor forcing a review of distribution systems is the dramatic break in recent years from traditional institutional patterns. (These changes were observed earlier in Chapters 16 to 19.) Governmental enforcement of price legislation can encourage companies to base their discounts and other price differentials on cost differences, so these firms would be forced to study their distribution systems carefully to determine their actual costs. Finally, where competitive marketing strategies were at one time centered largely around price and product features, now we are recognizing that effective physical distribution services can constitute a significant competitive differential.

A FIRM'S STRATEGIC USE OF PHYSICAL DISTRIBUTION

The strategic use of business logistics may enable a company to strengthen its market position by providing more customer satisfaction and by reducing total operating costs. The management of this activity can also affect a firm's marketing mix—particularly its product-planning, pricing, and channels of distribution policies.

IMPROVE CUSTOMER SERVICE

A sophisticated logistics system can improve the distribution service a firm gives its customers—be they middlemen or ultimate users. The manufacturer of Norge

3 Richard E. Snyder, "Physical Distribution Costs," *Distribution Age*, December, 1963, pp. 35-42; see also Robert P. Neuschel, "Physical Distribution—Forgotten Frontier," *Harvard Business Review*, March-April, 1967, pp. 125-134.

4 Wendell M. Stewart, "Physical Distribution: Key to Improved Volume and Profits," *Journal of Marketing*, January, 1965, pp. 65-70.

kitchen appliances found that the way to increase profits was to raise its own warehousing costs—this led to more-than-offsetting sales increases as well as allowing the dealers to maintain lower inventories. The level of customer service directly affects demand. So management must strive for the optimum balance between the distribution services given to customers and the cost of this service. In establishing service levels, generally speaking the physical distribution models have stressed spatial considerations (warehouse location, for example). We are beginning to realize that a temporal perspective may be equally useful—that buyers are influenced by service-time differentials among suppliers.[5]

REDUCE DISTRIBUTION COSTS

Many avenues to cost reductions may be opened by the effective management of a company's physical distribution activities. Effectively systematizing these activities may result in a simplification, such as the elimination of warehouses, which will cut costs. Inventories—and their attendant carrying costs and capital investment—may be reduced by consolidating stocks at fewer locations and by shortening the replenishment cycle in warehouses. Sometimes a redesigned package permits more efficient transportation and warehousing.

GENERATE ADDITIONAL SALES VOLUME

A properly designed logistics system can also help to generate additional sales volume. Such a system will minimize out-of-stock conditions, the result being an increase in both sales and customer satisfaction. A responsive system can shorten the order cycle and thus reduce inventory requirements. Cost savings can be passed on to customers in the form of larger discounts. Increased efficiencies in physical distribution often enable a seller to expand his geographic market.

ADJUST TO RATE, TIME, AND PLACE DIFFERENCES IN PRODUCTION AND CONSUMPTION: CREATION OF TIME AND PLACE UTILITIES

There are several conditions under which management can make profitable use of both transportation and warehousing facilities in adjusting its rate, time, and place of production to meet the market demand for the firm's product. To illustrate, there may be a market situation of year-round consumption but only seasonal production, as in the case of agricultural products. Proper use of warehousing facilities will enable a producer to store the seasonal surplus so that it can be marketed long after the harvest has ended.

In other instances warehousing helps to adjust conditions of seasonal consumption but year-round production, as in the case of skis. A manufacturer likes to produce on a year-round basis in order to operate his plant efficiently. Consequently, enough surplus stocks are warehoused during the off-season so that the peak-season demand may be met without the need for overtime operation or additional plant capacity. In an economic sense, the main function of the transportation sub-

---

5 Ronald P. Willett and P. Ronald Stephenson, "Determinants of Buyers Response to Physical Distribution Service," *Journal of Marketing Research,* August, 1969, pp. 279-283; see also J. L. Heskett, "A Missing Link in Physical Distribution System Design," *Journal of Marketing,* October, 1966, pp. 37-41.

system in physical distribution is to add value to products through the creation of *place utility*. A fine suit hanging on a garment manufacturer's rack in Montreal has less value to a retailer or consumer in Halifax than a similar suit displayed in the retailer's store. Transporting the suit from Montreal to the retailer in Halifax creates place utility and adds value to the product. Also, speed in transportation may prevent loss of orders and create place utility more rapidly.

The economic value of storage (as a key part of warehousing) is the fact that it creates *time utility*. A product may be properly located with respect to its market, but the timing may be such that there is no present demand for it. Precious value is added to this item simply by holding and properly preserving it in storage until the demand rises. Time utility is created and value added when bananas are picked green and allowed to ripen in storage, or when meat is aged and tobacco cured in storage. Storage is essential when there is an imbalance in the timing of production and consumption.

In this discussion a careful distinction is made between warehousing and storage. *Storage* is the marketing activity which involves holding and properly preserving products from the time of their production until their final sale. *Warehousing* embraces storage plus a broad range of action-oriented functions, such as assembling, dividing (bulk breaking), and preparing products for reshipping. In many respects, warehousing is related both to transportation and to storage.

STABILIZE PRICES

Careful management of warehousing and transportation facilities can help to stabilize prices for an individual firm or for an entire industry. If a market is temporarily glutted with a certain product, sellers can warehouse the product until supply and demand conditions are more favorable. This managerial use of warehousing facilities is commonly found in the marketing programs for agricultural products and other seasonally produced goods. The judicious movement of products from one market to another may relieve gluts in one area, enable a seller to avoid a market with depressed prices, or allow a seller to take advantage of a market which has a shorter supply and higher prices.

DETERMINE CHOICE OF CHANNELS AND LOCATION OF MIDDLEMEN

Administrative decisions regarding the management of inventory—its location, handling, transporting, and control—have an important bearing on a manufacturer's selection of his trade channels and the location of his middlemen. Logistics considerations may become paramount, for example, when a company has decided to decentralize its inventory, and now must determine how many sites to establish and whether to use wholesalers, its own branch warehouses, or public warehouses. One manufacturer may select merchant wholesalers who perform storage and other warehousing services, while another may prefer to use a combination of manufacturers' agents and public warehouses. The agents can solicit orders, provide aggressive selling, and do the necessary promotional work, while the orders can be physically distributed through and from the public warehouses.

Logistics facilities may influence a manufacturer's decision on where to locate his branches or in what cities he will seek wholesalers. Sometimes a company wants to locate a branch in a small town or a suburban community, but finds that the additional freight and handling costs from the nearest transportation center are prohibitive. Physical distribution facilities thus force the company to establish its branch in the central city.

A note of caution should be sounded at this point. Rarely are channels selected primarily on the basis of physical distribution considerations. Instead, logistics is only one factor to consider. We can recall from the preceding chapter that the nature of the market and other factors heavily influence channel decisions.

USE TRAFFIC MANAGEMENT TO ENSURE LOWEST COSTS

Effective traffic management can aid a company's total marketing program and improve its profit picture. A good traffic manager will see to it that his company is enjoying the fastest routes and the lowest possible rates on whatever method of transportation the administrator has decided upon. The pricing of transportation services is one of the most complicated parts of the North American business scene. To read a rate or tariff schedule properly (this is the carrier's "price list") is a real art and requires considerable practice.

Another service which a traffic manager can render his company is the auditing of freight bills. This job is necessary because carriers sometimes charge a higher rate than the one which should apply. They are not intentionally trying to defraud the shipper. They are simply misinterpreting the complex rate schedule.

A good traffic manager can also negotiate with carriers in order to get his products reclassified or to get a special rate. A company may offer to ship larger quantities on a given carrier if lower rates are granted. The traffic manager should investigate the possibility of having his company operate its own private carriers, especially its own trucking system. If this possibility seems reasonable for a shipper, it can be an effective bargaining tool in getting reduced rates from common carriers.

DETERMINE INVENTORY LOCATIONS (ESTABLISH WAREHOUSING SYSTEM)

The name of the game in logistics is inventory management in the fullest sense of the term. Executive judgment must be exercised regarding the size, location, handling, and transporting of the inventories. Decision making in these four areas is interrelated. Decisions on the number and locations of inventory sites, for example, will influence decisions on inventory size and transportation methods. These interrelationships are often quite complex; they rarely occur in simple, consecutive, straight-line order. The problem of what should be decided first or where management should start in the logistics planning process resembles the "chicken or the egg" proposition.

One place where planning can begin is with a determination of the number and location of inventory sites. Final judgments will depend greatly on the nature of the market (its size, density, and location), the nature of the product, and the seller's financial position. (These considerations were discussed in the preceding two chapters in connection with the selection of channels and the company-branch-versus-the-wholesaler controversy.)

Perhaps basic to the inventory location problem is the company's intended strategy regarding inventory deployment—is it to be heavily concentrated or dispersed throughout the market? Each strategy has its merits and limitations. Centralizing the inventory means that it can be reduced in total size, can be better controlled, and is more responsive to unusual requests. Efficiency in warehousing and materials handling should be increased. On the other hand, centralizing the stocks of products will probably mean higher total transportation charges and slower delivery service to some segments of the market. Dispersing the inventory presents the other side of the coin on any of the points just noted.

To make a decision on the number and location of inventory centers requires consideration of many variables—transportation methods, freight rates, transit times, warehousing costs, customer buying patterns, and production costs and schedules, to mention just a few of the factors involved. Fortunately, with the aid of operations research techniques, a company can simulate the operations and predict the results of several plans of action.[6]

THE DISTRIBUTION CENTER CONCEPT

Perhaps an effective compromise in the concentration-dispersion inventory deployment controversy is for a company to establish one or more *distribution centers*. Planned around markets rather than transportation facilities, the basic thought behind the distribution-center concept is to develop under one roof an efficient, fully integrated system for the flow of products—taking orders, filling them, and delivering them to customers. The distribution center is a "new look" in warehousing, having achieved prominence only since the 1950s, but the concept is rapidly being adopted by many well-known firms.[7] In the United States, such companies as Borden planned to cut from 136 warehouses down to 16 to 18 distribution centers. After a three-year study, Libby, McNeill & Libby eliminated 214 warehouses and in their place established 5 distribution centers. Similar patterns have been followed by the Raytheon Co. (electronics), the Whirlpool Corp. (appliances), the Bigelow-Sanford Co. (carpeting), and many other firms. In Canada, the concept is appropriate where markets are concentrated, such as in the Quebec City-Montreal-Toronto-Windsor corridor. In smaller market areas the distribution center concept can take a different form. One example is a Vancouver distribution center which is shared by a number of non-competing firms rather than being operated by a single one.

Aided by the use of the latest techniques in data processing, materials handling, and inventory control, firms are able to process orders rapidly. This new distribution system has lowered distribution costs by reducing the number of warehouses, cutting excessive inventories, and eliminating out-of-stock conditions. Storage time and delivery time have been cut to a minimum thus putting into practice the adage that companies are in business to sell goods, not to store them.

OWNERSHIP AND TYPES OF WAREHOUSES

A firm (manufacturer, wholesaler, or retailer) has the option of operating its own private warehouse or using the services of a public warehouse. A private ware-

---

6 See Ronald H. Ballou, "Dynamic Warehouse Location Analysis," *Journal of Marketing Research*, August, 1968, pp. 271-276.

7 "The New Nerve Centers of Distribution," *Dun's Review*, June 1963, p. S-104. See also *Chain Store Age*, executive edition, June, 1969, for several articles on the topic "Push-button Warehousing, Automation, Computers Help Run Distribution Centers of Future, Today."

house is more likely to be used if a company moves a large volume of products through it and there is very little, if any, seasonal fluctuation in this materials flow. A competitive limitation to private warehousing is that it represents a relatively inflexible expense item. Also, it requires an expenditure of managerial time and talent.

Public warehouses offer storage and handling facilities to any interested individual or company. The users pay only for the cubic space occupied by their goods, and they pay only for the time during which this space is occupied. Several types of public warehouses are in wide use today. Probably the most common is the *general merchandise* warehouse, which stores practically any kind of manufactured or nonmanufactured product needing protection from the weather but having no special temperature, humidity, or handling requirements. Various types of *special commodity* warehouses are used for particular agricultural products, such as grains, wool, fruits, and tobacco. Ordinarily each of these warehouses handles one kind of product and offers special services particularly required for that product. Another widely used type of public warehousing facility is the *cold-storage* warehouse.

A particular type of general merchandise warehouse or special commodity warehouse is the *bonded* warehouse. This is used to store products on which a federal tax must be paid before they can be sold. Some imported goods, alcoholic beverages, and tobacco products are typically stored in these facilities. In bonded warehouses the import duty or excise tax need not be paid until the merchandise is sold.

SERVICES OFFERED BY PUBLIC WAREHOUSES

The best-known and most widely used service offered by public warehouses is storage. Products can be stockpiled in appropriate physical condition and in strategic locations until the seller wishes to distribute them to customers. In addition to storage, public warehouses offer other services.

Dividing bulk shipment and reshipping. Public warehouses receive large-quantity shipments, such as carload units, and bulk break, or divide, them into smaller units and then reship the smaller quantities to predetermined customers. In this way a seller can combine several less-than-carload orders into one carload shipment and consign the car to a warehouse located near the several buyers. The shipper enjoys the lower carload rate from his shipping points to the warehouse location. Actually, the warehouseman may be acting as a freight forwarder, since products are not actually stored but simply handled and reassembled for final delivery. Some public warehouses accept products shipped in bulk and then package the goods according to the seller's specifications.

Specialized management and labor. Because they are specialists in the activities which they perform, public warehouses can offer the advantages of specialization in management, labor, and facilities. They can provide management advice with respect to physical distribution. Also, they have the latest equipment required for efficient handling of products.

Financing. Public warehouses can aid the owner of goods financially by issuing a warehouse receipt and providing a field (custodian) warehousing service. A warehouse receipt may be used as collateral to secure a loan from a bank. When the goods are sold, the loan may be paid off and the ownership receipt redeemed so that the merchandise may be released from the warehouse.

Field warehousing (also called custodian warehousing) works in the following manner. Assume that some products are stored in the owner's private warehousing facilities and that he wants to get a bank loan on the merchandise without having the expense of moving it to a public warehouse. The owner calls in a public warehouseman and leases to him a section of the warehouse which contains the merchandise in question. A field warehouse is not limited to a portion of a regular private warehouse. It may be an office cabinet, locked desk drawer, office safe, open yard, grain elevator, or some other storage facility. The products may even be shipped from a manufacturer to his wholesaler's warehouse and then placed under a field warehousing plan. The warehouseman issues a receipt for the goods, and this receipt again serves as collateral for a bank loan. The leased area, in effect, becomes a public warehouse, and the goods cannot be removed until the receipt is redeemed.

Substitute for company branch warehouse or wholesalers. A very significant advantage of public warehouses is that they may be substituted both for a company branch warehouse system and for wholesalers. In addition to the bulkbreaking and reshipping services mentioned above, public warehouses will provide office and display space for sellers. These storage firms will also accept and fill orders for vendors. A manufacturer can ship in carload quantities to a public warehouse, just as he can ship to his own branches or wholesalers. Public warehouses enable him to maintain decentralized stocks of merchandise so that he can satisfy hand-to-mouth buyers and fill orders rapidly. Public warehousing costs are variable expenses requiring no capital investment. A firm does not pay for unused capacity, as it often must with a branch warehouse. Furthermore, public warehouses afford greater flexibility in the location of merchandise stocks. If a seller wishes to change or add inventory locations, he can easily change public warehouses.

ESTABLISH A MATERIALS-HANDLING SYSTEM

The selection of the proper equipment to handle products is an important aspect of the management of physical distribution. Too often insufficient administrative attention is devoted to this activity. This careless attitude is surprising in light of the fact that the cost of handling products is a substantial part of the total cost of physical distribution.

In this discussion of materials-handling equipment, we include the warehouse building itself. Historically, warehouses have been multistory buildings located in congested, run-down parts of town. Their operation has been characterized by elevators, chutes, and other highly expensive vertical methods of moving products. Modern warehouses are huge, sprawling, one-story affairs located in outlying parts of town where land is less expensive and loading platforms are easily accessible to motor trucks as well as railroad spurs. Forklift trucks, conveyor belts, motor scooters, and other mechanized equipment are used to move merchandise. In some warehouses the order fillers are even equipped with roller skates.[8]

With respect to materials-handling equipment, many firms have found that "palletization" (the use of pallets to aid in mechanical handling of merchandise)

---

8 See Ronald H. Ballou, "Improving the Physical Layout of Merchandise in Warehouses," *Journal of Marketing*, July, 1967, pp. 60-64.

makes physical handling more economical. On the other hand, products which are oddly shaped or are handled in small quantities may not lend themselves to the use of pallets.

"Containerization" is a cargo-handling system which is gaining increasing acceptance in the physical distribution system. The system involves enclosing a shipment of products in containers of metal, wood, or some other material and then transporting them by rail, truck, and/or ship unopened from the time they leave the shipper until they reach their destination. The bright future of containerization is not without its roadblocks, however. Shippers and carriers are seeking to solve the problems of lack of standardization of containers, labor's unenthusiastic reaction to the system, and the need for revisions in transportation rate schedules.

MAINTAIN INVENTORY CONTROL SYSTEM

A key activity in a firm's physical distribution system is the maintenance of effective control over the size and composition of the inventories. Inventory represents a sizable investment in many companies. The goal of inventory control is to minimize the investment and fluctuations in inventories, while at the same time providing prompt order-filling services for customers.

Perhaps the greatest boon to inventory control in recent years has been the improvements in computer technology. This factor has enabled management to shorten the order-delivery cycle and to reduce substantially the size of inventories. Through use of the computer, a greater variety of more accurate information is more speedily available than was heretofore considered possible.

Inventory size may be determined by balancing the market needs and cost factors. Market demands on inventory can be anticipated by analyzing the sales forecast. Thus, the more accurate the forecast, the greater is the probability of optimizing inventory size. The cost factors to consider are (1) acquisition costs, i.e., the costs of making or buying the products to put in inventory and (2) carrying or holding costs—warehousing expenses, interest on investment, losses due to spoilage and pilferage, inventory taxes, etc.

The inventory's upper limit will also be influenced considerably by the desired level of customer satisfaction, that is, what percentage of orders the company should be able to fill promptly from inventory on hand. Out-of-stock conditions result in lost sales, loss of goodwill, and maybe even a loss of customers. Yet to be able to fill 100 percent of the orders promptly may require an excessively costly inventory. One authority estimates that about 80 percent *more* inventory is required to fill 95 percent of the orders than to fill only 80 percent.[9]

Related to the size question is the need to establish the optimum quantity to reorder (make or buy) when it is time to replenish inventory stocks. The determination of this "economic order quantity" (EOQ) for a manufacturer moves us back into the production-scheduling process. Once again we see the total-system aspect of physical distribution. Decisions on the size of the EOQ will be made by balancing acquisition costs, carrying costs, and the desired level of satisfaction in filling customers' orders.

Closely related to the inventory control system and every bit as valuable to management are merchandise planning systems. Two commonly used systems are basic stock lists and model stock plans. Both planning systems are based essentially on an analysis of past sales.

---

9 John F. Magee, "The Logistics of Distribution," *Harvard Business Review*, July-August, 1960, p. 92.

The *basic stock list* is widely used in the distribution of staple goods where identical or closely related items are carried year after year. Under this system, reasonably detailed information is maintained for every item the company keeps in stock. That is, separate records are maintained for each size, color, or other significant feature of a given product. The information includes sales of the item, minimum limits when reordering is necessary, and the quantity to be reordered.

For fashion merchandise the most widely used merchandise planning system is called a *model stock plan*. The same items are not carried year in and year out in product lines subject to fashion changes, so a basic stock list is not feasible. A certain style of women's dress or shoes may be carried for only one fashion season, but there are other factors in the area of fashion merchandise which do remain reasonably constant and thus lend themselves to planning. For example, a dress manufacturer or the dress department in a department store will find that the percentage of total unit dress sales in each size remains about the same over a period of years. Perhaps size 12 dresses account for 16 percent of total sales, size 14 dresses represent 24 percent, etc. Also, the manufacturer or retailer may find that each price line accounts for about the same share of unit sales each year. Consequently, a firm can plan what it considers an ideal, or model, stock on the basis of size, price line, or any other product characteristic which remains reasonably constant for several seasons.

ESTABLISH PROCEDURES TO PROCESS ORDERS

As another step in a physical distribution system, management needs to establish a procedure for handling and filling orders. This should also include provision for credit-granting decisions, invoice preparation, and collections on past-due accounts. A considerable amount of consumer ill will can be generated if a company makes mistakes or is slow in filling orders. From the company's standpoint, the activities connected with handling and filling orders offer opportunities for a substantial reduction in marketing expenses. Processing orders includes activities in two areas—the pertinent office work and the physical task of assembling and shipping.

SELECT METHOD OF TRANSPORTATION

A major decision involving the logistics system of a company is that of determining which agencies will be used to ship the products from the manufacturer to the middlemen or final customers, or from one middlemen to another. (At this point, we are concerned primarily with *intercity* shipments.) The transportation routes and the freight rate structure are important determinants of the geographic limits of a company's market, the outline of its sales territories, and the location of its inventory stocks. When the decision is made regarding the method of transportation to be used, the company may establish its own facilities, such as its own truck, rail, or barge line, or it may employ common carriers.[10]

---

10 Transportation carriers are often divided into three types: common, contract, and private. A *common* carrier is one which is granted operating rights by a government regulatory agency. The carrier operates on announced schedules and rates and is expected to handle merchandise from any shipper. *Contract* carriers operate in a less regulated manner. They enter into contracts with individual shippers and agree to move specified shipments for specified periods of time. *Private* carriers are owned and operated by individual firms for the shipment of their own goods only.

Before making the decision, however, management should understand the relative merits, costs, special features, and services of each of the five major forms of transportation: railroads, trucks, water, pipelines, and airplanes. The relative importance of each in Canada and the United States, along with some trends in its use, is shown in Table 21-1. For the United States, the figures reflect intercity freight traffic only. Ocean coastal traffic between United States ports is not included. Virtually all farm-to-farm and intracity freight movements are made by motor truck. Consequently, the figures for water and truck carriers really understate the importance of these methods of transportation by a considerable margin. Nevertheless, Table 21-1 is illuminating. It shows that railroads are still the major intercity freight carrier although their relative position has declined steadily. The information also shows that the distribution networks vary between Canada and the United States and indicates the varying degrees of importance of carriers.

RAILROADS

Railroads are particularly well adapted for long hauls of carload quantities of bulk products which are low in value in relation to their weight and the freight charges. Thus these carriers are low-cost agencies for the shipment of items such as autos, coal, sand, gravel, minerals, and agricultural and forest products. On the other hand, railroads are limited by their inflexibility—they can go only where the track is laid. Railroads have been hurt and trucks have been helped by the growth of markets, including suburban markets, not located on rail lines.

In spite of the many services that railroads have instituted, the nature of the market is such that other carriers will probably make further inroads on the railroads. Marketing executives, however, should be aware of the various services offered by railroads because for many products and in many marketing situations, railroads are still the lowest-cost, most efficient method of transportation.

Table 21-1. Estimated distribution of freight traffic in Canada and United States: in millions of ton miles.

Railroads are still the major carrier for intercity freight. While the physical volume of rail freight had increased substantially, the railroads' share of the market has declined considerably.

Carrier	Ton-miles		Percent of Total			
	Canada 1968	U.S. 1969	Canada 1968	U.S. 1969	Canada 1949	U.S. 1950
Railroads	95,000	780,000	37.3	41.2	72.0	56.2
Great Lakes	59,000	111,000	23.1	5.8	21.0	10.5
Rivers and Canals	8,800	185,000	3.4	9.8	3.0	4.9
Motor trucks	22,000	404,000	8.7	21.3	3.8	16.3
Oil pipeline	70,000	411,000	27.5	21.7	0.2	12.1
Air carriers	200	3,200	0.1	0.2	—	—
Total	255,000	1,894,200	100.0	100.0	100.0	100.0

Source: Statistics Canada, Canada Yearbook, 1970-71. Reproduced by permission of Information Canada. Yearbook of Railroad Facts, Association of American Railroads, Washington, D.C., 1970, p. 42.

Carload versus less-than-carload freight rates. Railroads offer substantial savings to firms which can ship in carload (c.l.) quantities as compared with less-than-carload (l.c.l.) shipments. For many items the c.l. freight rate is as much as 50 percent less than the l.c.l. rate. This is a tremendous incentive to shippers of large quantities of products, especially to shippers of minerals, agricultural products, and similar goods where freight expenses are a significant percentage of total value.

Combined shipments. Long ago the railroads realized that they were vulnerable to competition from other types of carriers when it came to handling l.c.l. shipments. Consequently, the railroads have developed several measures designed to reduce the cost of l.c.l. shipments, to speed them up, and generally to make the railroads a more attractive carrier for firms wishing to ship in smaller quantities. These measures provide for combining into a c.l. quantity the freight from one or more companies who are shipping products to customers located in one area. The pooled freight can go at c.l. rates and can be delivered much more rapidly than if its component parts were sent separately in l.c.l. units. Sometimes the initiative in pooled shipments is taken by a group of retailers who arrange to buy a carload of some item, have it loaded at the shipping point, and then provide for the distribution of the individual orders when the car reaches its destination.

In-transit privileges. Two in-transit privileges offered by railroads are (1) diversion in transit and (2) the opportunity to process some products en route. *Diversion in transit* allows a seller to start a shipment moving in one general direction and to establish or change destination while the car is en route, just as long as the new destination involves a forward movement of the car and no backtracking. The charges are computed on the basis of the through rate or long-haul rate from the point of origin to the ultimate destination, plus a small charge for diversion. This is a valuable service to shippers of perishable products which are subject to frequent price fluctuations and to variations in price from one city to another on any given day. To illustrate, B.C. Tree Fruits may want to ship MacIntosh apples to Eastern markets. Several carloads will be shipped from Kelowna to Toronto, or they may be shipped eastward with the specific destination to be determined some time after the shipment leaves Kelowna. Before the shipment reaches Toronto, the shipper may receive word that prices in the Toronto market are temporarily depressed because of a heavy supply in relation to the demand but that there is a good market in Montreal. Consequently, at the appropriate "diversion point" (probably Toronto in this case) the cars will be rerouted to Montreal. The freight charges will be based on the through rate from Kelowna to Montreal. A shipment may be diverted several times before reaching its final destination.

Under the privilege of *processing in transit,* a shipper may have his product unloaded, graded, manufactured, or otherwise processed in some manner while en route, and then have it shipped on to its final destination. As an example, livestock may be shipped from Alberta to Toronto. En route the animals may be unloaded, watered, and fattened in feedlots, but the through rate to Toronto will apply. Wheat may be shipped from Saskatchewan to Winnipeg where it may be made into flour shipped to Toronto. Again, the shipper has the privilege of processing in transit. The through rate is usually substantially less than the combined rates from origin to processing point and from processing point to destination.

Piggyback and fishyback services. In recent years the railroads have attempted to meet competition from trucks by offering a "piggyback" service to shippers. Under this arrangement truck trailers are carried on railroad flatcars. The goods can be loaded on trucks at the seller's shipping dock and need not be handled again until they are unloaded at the buyer's receiving station. This combination of truck and rail transportation offers more flexibility than railroads alone can offer. Also, less handling of the goods tends to decrease damage and pilferage.

"Fishyback" service involves transporting loaded trailers on barges or ships. The trailers may be carried piggyback fashion by railroad to the ship's dock, and then at the other end they can be loaded back onto the trains for the completion of the rail haul. In an alternative use of the fishyback service, railroads are not used at all. Merchandise is trucked directly to ports, where the trailer vans are loaded on barges. At the end of the water journey the vans are trucked to the receiving station.

Freight rate structure. A few comments on the railroad rate structure may give some indication of the enormous complexity of transportation rates. Railroads are used as examples because they frequently set standards for rates on other types of carriers. Also, railroad rates are often used as a basis for comparison when analyzing shipping costs on trucks, airlines, or barges. Most products shipped by railroad go under a class rate or a commodity rate, although bargaining and competition from other carriers have led to the establishment of special rates for particular products in certain parts of the country.

Class rates have been established in an attempt to simplify the problem of determining shipping rates for thousands of items shipped between countless points of origin and destination. Many classes have been set up, and each has its own rate per 100 pounds shipped over a given distance. Products which are reasonably similar in size, value, perishability, or some other distinguishing feature are grouped into one class. Several thousand manufactured products are classed in this manner, and their shipping costs are figured accordingly. Within each class, the rates may vary according to distance, but the ton-mile charges are less as the length of the haul increases. Also, there are regional differences in class rates for the same distance. Further complications enter the picture in at least three ways. First, thousands of new rates are filed each year with the Canadian Transport Commission. Second, attempts are always being made to have products changed to a lower class. Third, a slight change in the description of what is being shipped may move a product from one class to another.

Commodity rates have been established for the shipment of bulky, low-value products, such as sand, gravel, iron ore, lumber, coal, grains, and other agricultural products. A separate rate is set for each product going between two specific points.

TRUCKS

The tremendously increased use of highway transportation noted in the discussion of Table 21-1 is traceable largely to three factors: an improved system of highways, new developments in equipment for trucking and materials handling, and the competitive advantages of this method of transportation. Trucks have proved to be a very effective transportation medium for short hauls of high-value merchandise. Highway carriers have the advantages of speed and flexibility of movement. Once the merchandise is loaded at the shipper's dock, it can be sent directly to the buyer without any loading or unloading in between. Truck shipments receive less handling and therefore less careful and expensive packaging than rail shipments.

Another factor favoring highway transportation is its lower total freight cost for many products. This is not because of lower freight rates for trucks. Actually many rail and truck freight rates are similar for shipping many products in many parts of the country. The difference is due largely to the fact that trucks go from the seller's loading dock to the buyer's receiving platform. Railroads go from terminal to terminal, and there are added costs in moving products to and from the terminals.

WATERWAYS

A considerably amount of freight is transported by ships and barges on the Great Lakes system, the St. Lawrence Seaway and coastal waterways. These waterways are especially good for shipping bulky, low-value, nonperishable products, such as petroleum, sand, gravel, coal, grain, and metallic ores. Water transportation is the cheapest and also the slowest of all major methods of shipping. Its use is sometimes limited by climatic conditions.

PIPELINES

Pipelines are a rather special method of transportation in that they are limited largely to carrying petroleum products, especially crude oil and natural gas. While pipelines are technically common carriers open to use by any shipper, most of them are used to ship the products of the companies who own the lines. They are obviously limited in use because of their inflexibility. Pipeline shipping of crude oil costs less than rail transportation, but more than water transportation.

AIRLINES

Although the newest of the major methods of transporting products, the airlines have undoubtedly done more than any other type of carrier to spearhead the systems approach and total cost concept in physical distribution. Obviously unable to compete on the basis of rates or ton-mile costs alone, the airlines had to demonstrate that the use of air freight would result in savings in other distribution elements (smaller inventory, faster delivery, fewer warehouses, less expensive packaging, etc.), which would tend to offset the higher air transportation costs. Even though air freight rates have been reduced considerably over the years, and are expected to go still lower as the Boeing 747 (jumbo jet) comes into more general use, these rates are still substantially higher than truck or rail freight rates.

Air express (door-to-door shipment) and air freight (terminal-to-terminal shipment) together account for only a small part of total intercity freight shipments, although the tonnage has increased steadily and appreciably over the past several years. Low shipment figures, however, conceal the wide use of air freight, and the important role it plays, in certain marketing situations. To an increasing extent, the use of air freight as a transportation method is being dictated by management's customer-oriented sales thinking, and not only by its orientation toward total cost savings.

The strongest selling point for air freight is its speed. This factor has enabled many industries and firms to expand their market limits and to open new markets. Products subject to physical deterioration (fresh-cut flowers, biologicals, fresh seafood, radioisotopes) can be delivered to many more markets by air than by any other carrier.

FREIGHT FORWARDERS

The freight forwarder is a specialized marketing institution which has developed through the years to serve firms who ship in l.c.l. quantities. Freight forwarders do not own their own transportation equipment, but they do provide a valuable service in physical distribution. Their main function is to consolidate l.c.l. shipments or less-than-truckload shipments from several shippers into carload and truckload quantities. Their operating margin is generally the spread between c.l. and l.c.l. rates. That is, the shipper pays l.c.l. rates, and the freight forwarder transports the products at c.l. rates. The freight forwarder also picks up the merchandise at the shipper's place of business and arranges for delivery at the buyer's door. In addition to this pick-up and delivery service, an l.c.l. shipper enjoys all the advantages of speed and minimum handling associated with c.l. shipments, even though he pays l.c.l. rates. Also, freight forwarders provide the small shipper with traffic management services. They select the best transportation methods and routes.

ORGANIZATIONAL RESPONSIBILITY FOR PHYSICAL DISTRIBUTION

A significant question which may be asked is: Who is in charge of physical distribution? All too often, the answer is "no one." We observed earlier that activities within the system often are not coordinated and that managerial responsibility is consequently compartmentalized into units which may even have conflicting goals. There are many examples of firms which have developed the ability to analyze their total distribution effort, have identified substantial cost-savings opportunities, and yet have been unable to capture these dollars because they were not organized to do a total physical distribution job.[11]

It is encouraging to note, however, that there is a trend toward the establishment of a separate formal department responsible for the management of all physical distribution activities.[12]

One study suggested that a prospective physical distribution department passes through four stages: (1) shipping—total organizational fragmentation; (2) traffic—a managerial specialist in transportation is used; (3) movement—the dawn of a systems viewpoint; and (4) physical distribution—the activities are planned and operated as a system in the full sense of the word.[13]

Assuming that a company has a physical distribution department, the next organizational question is: To whom should the head of this department report? At the risk of charges of "empire building by the marketing people," current enlightened managerial thinking suggests that physical distribution should be the respon-

---

11 John F. Stolle, "How to Manage Physical Distribution," *Harvard Business Review*, July-August, 1967, pp. 93-100. See also Robert P. Neuschel, "Physical Distribution: Forgotten Frontier," *Harvard Business Review*, March-April, 1967, pp. 125-134, for a study in which only five out of twenty-six large, profitable companies in a wide variety of industries were ranked "good" (in contrast to "average" or "poor") in all criteria used in this study to evaluate their physical distribution management.

12 See Donald J. Bowersox, "Emerging Patterns of Physical Distribution Organization," *Transportation and Distribution Management*, May, 1968, pp 53-56

13 J. L. Heskett, "Ferment in Marketing's Oldest Area," *Journal of Marketing*, October, 1962, pp. 40-45; see also Robert E. Weigand, "The Management of Physical Distribution: A Dilemma," *Business Topics*, Summer, 1962, pp. 67-72.

sibility of either the chief marketing executive or a separate department whose head reports directly to the president of the company. In any event, logistics management should be viewed by top management as one of its prime responsibilities.[14]

QUESTIONS AND PROBLEMS

1. In some companies, activities such as processing and shipping orders, maintaining an inventory control system, and locating warehouse stocks throughout the market are treated as separate, fragmented tasks. What are some of the administrative and operational problems which are likely to occur in this type of arrangement?

2. "The goal of a modern physical distribution system in a firm should be to operate at the lowest possible *total* costs," Do you agree?

3. Name some products for which the costs of physical distribution constitute at least one-half of the total price of the goods at the wholesale level. Can you suggest ways of decreasing the physical distribution costs of these products?

4. "Storage adds value to products in that it creates time utility. At the same time, the value of a product may be totally destroyed by storing it too long." Explain.

5. Explain how a marketing manager can use transportation and warehousing facilities to stabilize the prices of his products.

6. "Inventory size will be smaller but transportation expenses will be larger if a manufacturer follows an inventory-location strategy of concentration rather than dispersion." Do you agree? Explain.

7. "The use of public warehouse facilities makes it possible for a manufacturer to bypass wholesalers in his channels of distribution." Explain.

8. If a public warehouse can provide so many wholesaling services, why have these warehouses not largely eliminated full-function wholesalers and manufacturers' sales branches?

9. What is the relationship between inventory management and the "economic order quantity" in production scheduling?

10. How are transportation decisions related to packaging policies?

11. Why are l.c.l. shipments so much slower and more costly than c.l. shipments?

12. What alternatives does a manufacturer have if he must ship in l.c.l. quantities, but the competitive price structure for his product is such that he cannot afford to pay the high l.c.l. freight rates?

13. As traffic manager of a large department store in the big city nearest your campus, you are asked to determine the best transportation method and route for the shipment of each of the following items to your store. In each case your store is to pay full freight charges. Unless specifically noted, there is no time urgency involved.

    a. Fresh salmon from Prince Rupert. Total shipment weighs 200 pounds.

    b. An assortment of various types of large appliances from Montreal. Total weight is 20,000 pounds.

---

14 For an excellent summary of the "where it has been," "where it is now," and "where it is going" aspects of physical distribution, see Donald J. Bowersox, "Physical Distribution Development, Current Status, and Potential," *Journal of Marketing*, January, 1969, pp. 63-70

   c. A refill order of 200 dresses from Toronto. This is a "hot" fashion item, so speed is of essence.

   d. Sheets, pillowcases, and towels from a mill in Sherbrooke. Total weight is 100 pounds.

   e. Ten sets of dining-room furniture from Kitchener, Ont.

14. Under what conditions is a company apt to select air freight as its main method of transporting its finished goods?

15. The Belden Wholesale Company has been considering a new ordering system for its salesmen. Under the present system the salesmen write and mail their orders at the end of the day. A new system has been suggested which would have the salesmen phone the home office once a day and dictate the orders into a tape recorder. The clerical staff could then transfer the taped orders onto IBM cards. The main advantages of such a system would be the following:

   a. Faster receipt of orders

   b. Increased ease and speed of order filling in the stockroom owing to the systematic compilation of orders which the computer would provide.

   c. Faster billing.

   Following is a comparison of the old and proposed new systems, showing the number of days required from receipt of order to shipment of goods from the warehouse:

	Old	New
Time from order to transmission of order:	½ day	½ day
Time from transmission of order to writing up of order:	3 days	½ day
Time to fill out order:	1 day	½ day
Time to pack, label and move goods to warehouse exit:	½ day	½ day
	5 days	2 days

   Customers expect delivery within five days, therefore, Belden has had to stock an almost complete line. Since Belden would have three days' grace and have time to react to stockouts (under the proposed system), it was estimated that with the reduction in order-processing time, the inventory of $1,500,000 would be reduced by 30 percent. Under the new system it would also be possible to attach the bills to the orders rather than sending out the bills three days after the order as previously. The billings for the year are $50,000,000. You are asked to:

   a. Calculate the savings from (1) the smaller inventory and (2) the faster billing, given that the imputed holding cost of inventory is 18 percent and the prime interest rate is 8 percent. Assume 250 billing days per year.

   b. Suggest other costs which will decrease and any which will increase.

CASES FOR PART FIVE

CASE 13: THE BONNIE LASS COMPANY*
Distribution Implications of Demographic Changes

The Bonnie Lass Company had its head office and manufacturing plant in Winnipeg and had been a manufacturer of ladies' apparel for more than thirty years. In 1975, the company moved into expanded production facilities. Although Bonnie Lass had experienced a slow increase in the demand for its products in recent years, there was still considerable excess plant capacity owing to the company's expanded facilities. Realizing that the company's manufacturing machinery was versatile, and that an adequate supply of raw materials and trained manpower was available, Mr. Angus McGregor, president of Bonnie Lass, decided that the company could produce and sell children's and infants' wear.

In talking with officials of Statistics Canada at the local Winnipeg office, Mr. McGregor learned that the Canadian population was expected to grow at approximately 2% per year. Mr. McGregor was most interested in finding out information on the existing sales of children's and infants' wear in Canada. A little digging through Statistics Canada reports produced the information contained in Table 1.

---

* Case prepared by David K. Warner, Executive Assistant, School of Business Administration and Commerce, Memorial University of Newfoundland.

Table 1. Retail Sales, 1968 and 1974, Children's and Infants' wear

	1968	1974
Newfoundland	$ 2,491,200.	$ 4,710,400.
Prince Edward Island	903,500.	1,423,100.
Nova Scotia	6,577,700.	7,969,400.
New Brunswick	7,671,200.	6,754,900.
Quebec	61,156,700.	58,757,700.
Ontario	82,532,800.	80,804,000.
Manitoba	7,408,800.	9,712,500.
Saskatchewan	6,353,400.	6,834,000.
Alberta	13,579,800.	18,535,800.
British Columbia	15,377,600.	22,745,100.
TOTAL: CANADA	$204,052,700.	$219,467,900.

Source: Statistics Canada, Catalogue Nos. 63-518 and 63-526.

The increased sales of children's and infants' wear from 1968 to 1974 interested Mr. McGregor very much. He felt that demand would continue to increase as the Canadian population grows and as disposable incomes increase. Mr. McGregor had asked his marketing department to determine the competitive price structure at the retail and wholesale levels for the proposed product line. The marketing staff was unable to obtain precise information on where the Canadian consumer is now buying children's and infants' wear and was unable to recommend the type of store where the Bonnie Lass line of children's and infants' wear should be distributed.

At the present time, Bonnie Lass marketed its regular line of ladies' wear through a number of regional wholesalers across Canada. Consequently, the company employed a small sales force of only three salesmen. It was decided to add an additional wholesaler to carry the new line of children's and infants' wear. Mr. McGregor had held a number of meetings with his marketing staff in recent weeks and had finally decided to use Kiddytogs Limited of Montreal as a wholesaler for the new line. Kiddytogs was a company which distributed the lines of a number of manufacturers across Canada and appeared to be very knowledgeable in the distribution of children's and infants' wear. From their new wholesaler, Bonnie Lass was able to obtain the information contained in Table 2 on the distribution of sales of children's and infants' wear in Canada.

The wholesaler also had data on the number of each type of retail store located in each province and in certain large cities, and miscellaneous information on the number of employees, annual sales, inventory levels, and payrolls. The Bonnie Lass Company and the wholesaler were now ready to plan a promotion and advertising program for the new line of children's and infants' wear. Mr. McGregor felt that they were in a good position to direct the campaign to the area where it would be most effective and to the type of retail store that offered the most potential.

In addition to the information that it had obtained from Statistics Canada (Table 2), Kiddytogs Limited had studied copies of monthly reports on retail trade. These reports were quite current and confirmed the impression that trends indicated continued increases in retail sales in Canada. Some of the additional information obtained by Kiddytogs Ltd. is presented in Table 3.

Table 2. Distribution of Retail Sales of Children's and Infants' Wear, Canada, 1968 and 1974

	1968	1974
Department Stores	$80,894,600.	$120,245,300.
Children's and Infants' Wear Stores[1]	46,261,700.	
Variety Stores	33,373,800.	25,208,400.
Family Clothing and Furnishing Stores	18,974,500.	31,072,800.
General Merchandise Stores	4,113,300.	22,742,100.
Women's and Misses' Clothing Stores	3,260,400.	10,416,700.
Combination Stores[2]		4,460,700.
All Other Stores	17,174,400.	5,321,900.

Source: Statistics Canada, Catalogue Nos. 63-518 and 63-526.
[1] Not reported separately in 1974, included with family clothing and furnishing stores.
[2] New category in 1974.

Table 3. Percentage Changes in Retail Trade—By Provinces and Kind of Business
January to December, 1974 (partial list)

KIND OF BUSINESS	CANADA	NFLD.	P.E.I.	N.S.	N.B.	QUE.-
Combination Stores	+17.4	+28.6	+14.5	+20.7	+18.8	+15.5
Department Stores	+17.2	+24.0	+49.6	+21.4	+15.0	+17.8
General Merchandise Stores	+13.2	+12.5	—	+19.4	+13.0	+10.1
Variety Stores	+ 9.3	+27.6	—	+13.5	+12.9	+ 7.3
Women's Clothing Stores	+13.2	—	—	+13.9	—	+ 6.0
Family Clothing Stores	+13.9	+ 9.9	—	+10.2	+11.7	+14.6
TOTAL—All Stores	+14.6	+17.7	+16.7	+16.2	+15.0	+13.7

	ONT.	MAN.	SASK.	ALTA.	B.C.
Combination Stores	+17.2	+17.9	+16.1	+18.4	+19.1
Department Stores	+15.7	+13.6	+25.9	+20.4	+16.2
General Merchandise Stores	+12.0	+14.4	—	+15.8	+15.0
Variety Stores	+ 7.5	—	+16.9	+13.4	+ 8.8
Women's Clothing Stores	+13.4	+18.5	+11.4	+29.6	+16.9
Family Clothing Stores	+13.5	+16.3	+13.4	—	+13.4
TOTAL—All Stores	+13.0	+15.5	+21.0	+18.3	+15.9

Source: Statistics Canada, Catalogue No. 63-005.

On a cold day in mid-January 1976, Mr. McGregor was having lunch in a downtown Winnipeg hotel with an old college roommate, John McPherson, who was now a successful Winnipeg chartered accountant. John McPherson expressed some concern over the fact that Mr. McGregor's company was considering the expansion into children's and infants' wear at a time when the Canadian population among the younger age groups was likely to fall. He advised McGregor to obtain some additional information on population projections for the next twenty years or so before making the move into children's and infants' wear. Immediately after lunch, before returning to his office, Angus McGregor paid another visit to the Winnipeg office of Statistics Canada. This visit proved quite fruitful, as McGregor obtained the information contained in Table 4. In helping McGregor locate the information, Jane Morgan of the Statistics Canada office pointed out to him that the population figures for 1968 and 1972 were actual figures while the projections for 1980, 1985, and 1990 were based on an assumption that Canada would continue to experience a low fertility rate and normal levels of immigration.

This new information provided Mr. McGregor with some food for thought. On the one hand, he had excess production capacity and the technology and market expertise to support expansion into the children's and infants' wear market. On the other hand the population projections which he had just obtained from Statistics Canada indicated that expansion into this market might not be advisable at this time.

Table 4. Population Estimates and Projections by Province for Ages 0-14.

PROVINCE	YEAR				
	1968	1972	1980	1985	1990
NFLD.	198,500	194,300	174,100	176,500	187,600
P.E.I.	36,900	35,000	28,800	29,200	31,000
N.S.	248,700	236,900	193,200	188,100	188,600
N.B.	215,300	201,200	166,600	163,800	162,100
QUE.	1,902,900	1,727,300	1,308,400	1,254,100	1,282,300
ONT.	2,219,600	2,192,600	2,044,900	2,141,600	2,265,300
MAN.	298,100	282,000	233,300	226,100	223,600
SASK.	311,400	269,900	188,700	169,700	158,500
ALTA.	514,000	509,900	466,400	481,100	507,100
B.C.	593,900	612,400	619,800	672,900	729,500
CANADA	6,559,000	6,283,200	5,448,700	5,528,700	5,764,700

Source: Statistics Canada, Catalogue Nos. 91-203 and 91-514.

QUESTIONS:

1. Should Mr. McGregor consider regional differences in deciding to market his product from coast to coast in Canada?
2. Does Mr. McGregor need any additional information before making a decision on whether or not to expand into the children's and infants' wear market? If so, what information does he need and where should he look for it?
3. What changes are likely to occur in the pattern of Canadian retail trade in light of the changing population projections indicated in Table 4?

CASE 14: KEN & RAY'S*

Using survey data for retail strategy

Neil Walker and Peter Hill, owners of Ken & Ray's supermarket chain in Kingston,
Ontario, were concerned. Ten months had passed since their acquisition of Ken &
Ray's in January, 1974. Meat sales in particular were falling and the total figures
were nothing like what they thought possible when they bought the chain. Something was wrong and required action.

The retail food industry. If only one word could be used to describe the retail food
industry, it would be the word "dynamic." Perhaps it was because of the perishable nature of the product in this business, but whatever the reason, changes were
always taking place. Dominion Stores Limited, for example, adopted a discount
pricing policy in October 1969 and permanently altered the pricing practices of the
industry.

In 1972, Loblaw Companies Limited began a major revitalization and overhaul.
Upper management levels were completely revamped, a number of older and
smaller stores shut down, other stores redesigned and modernized, advertising
took on the dimensions of professionalism and skill, and the warehousing and merchandising activities were completely modernized.

In 1973, Oshawa Wholesalers Limited opened in Montreal their Hyper Marché,
a huge store of five to ten times the size of other supermarkets.

On the technological side, the retail food chains were beginning to experiment
with new and computerized equipment. One innovation, for example, was the
magic wand which could read price and product information directly off the
printed label. The recorded information would then be available for immediate inventory and sales analysis.

At the more immediate operating level, the dynamic nature of the retail food industry was also apparent. Marketing programs were developed and changed on a
weekly basis. Ordering, inventory taking, and sales analysis also followed this
weekly cycle. One result was that owners and managers were required to act
quickly in order to meet competitive measures. Taking chances was an often-
repeated behavior.

It was in this dynamic Ontario market that there operated several large chains as
well as a number of independents. Dominion and Loblaws were the major chains
and each accounted for about one fifth of total sales (Exhibit 1): A&P, Miracle Food
Mart (Steinberg's), and Food City (Oshawa Wholesalers) were the next largest
chains. IGA, an affiliated group of independently owned stores, also accounted for
a large proportion of the sales. Canada Safeway was making a steady but sure in-
trusion into the Ontario market while both the Becker and Mac's Milk seven-day-a-
week convenience outlets were also adding new stores to each market.

Kingston, Ontario. Kingston was an old Ontario city whose origins dated back to
Frontenac's early explorations into Upper Canada. Situated at the end of Lake Ontario and the beginning of the St. Lawrence River, Kingston was within a two- to
three-hour drive of the large metropolitan areas of Toronto, Ottawa, and Montreal.
While Alcan and Du Pont each operated major manufacturing plants in Kingston,
the largest proportion of the city population was employed in any one of several

*Case prepared by Professor Stephen J. Arnold, School of Business, Queen's University.

government-operated organizations in the area. For example, there were five penal institutions in the Kingston area, a training school for prison officers, the Canadian Forces Staff College, Royal Military College, Canadian Forces Hospital, and Canadian Forces Base, Kingston. Queen's University and St. Lawrence College were also important elements in the Kingston community.

According to the 1971 census figures, the population of the city of Kingston was 59,065. On the west end of the city was Kingston Township, another urban area with a population of 17,395, and beyond that Amherstview, another community with a population numbering approximately 2,000. On the east end of the city of Kingston was Pittsburgh Township with a population of 9,455. In total, it was estimated that the population of the Kingston metropolitan area was close to 90,000.

The growth that the Kingston metropolitan area was experiencing was mostly in Kingston Township where at least one new subdivision was appearing each year. Growth in the City and in Pittsburgh Township was evident but not as high as in Kingston Township.

Exhibit 2 is a small scale map of Kingston and indicates the location of the supermarkets in the Kingston metropolitan area. Dominion Stores Limited had two older stores in the City and a newer one in the Frontenac Mall in Kingston Township. Loblaws also had three stores, but only one was in the City, in the Kingston Shopping Centre. The other two stores were in Kingston Township. A & P had two stores, one on the boundary between Kingston and Kingston Township and the other one in the city. Oshawa Wholesalers' only store, Food City, was in Kingston Township. Bennett's was an old, established independent operation and was located in the City. Like Food City, Ken & Ray's had no stores in the City. One store was located in Reddendale on the southern end of Kingston Township, one in Collins Bay at approximately the center of the Township, and the third in Amherstview.

Ken & Ray's. The origin of Ken & Ray's went back to the 1940s when the Collins Bay store was first built and was known as Wiser's Grocery. Over a period of years, the store had been continually modified and enlarged to its present-day size of 10,000 square feet. Its most recent modification was a brick front which was added in 1968. The Reddendale store was built in 1952 and contained 10,000 square feet. The Amherstview store was the most recent addition to the chain and was built in 1970. This store also contained 10,000 square feet.

Until its recent purchase by the two partners, Ken & Ray's was owned and operated by J. Earl McEwen, a well-known individual in the area. Food retailing was not the only interest of Mr. McEwen and he had demonstrated interest and proficiency in real estate development, horse breeding, cattle raising, and Kingston Township politics. Over the past twenty years, for example, he had served as councillor, deputy reeve and reeve.

It was in 1973 when Mr. McEwen first indicated he was interested in selling the supermarket chain. It was not long before the business opportunity came to the attention of M. Loeb Limited, a major wholesaler in both Canada and the United States, and, in particular, to the attention of two of its employees. These employees were Neil Walker, a chartered accountant, and Peter Hill, a long-time Kingston resident who also had considerable experience in the food retail business with Dominion Stores, as well as with Loeb.

After a series of negotiations, agreement was finally reached and the change of ownership of Ken & Ray's took place on January 21st, 1974. In this transaction, Mr.

McEwen sold the equipment and inventory but only leased the buildings to the two partners. The funds for the purchase were provided by Loeb under the conditions that Loeb would be the wholesaler to Ken & Ray's.

Management. Overall operation of the three Ken & Ray's stores was shared by the two partners although each individual tended to assume responsibility for his own particular area of expertise. Mr. Walker, for example, looked after accounting, record keeping, payments, and grocery selection, while Mr. Hill tended to concern himself with the advertising. Each partner had an office in one of the stores: Mr. Walker in the Reddendale store and Mr. Hill in the Collins Bay store.

Staff. In addition to the presence of two owners, each store had its own full-time manager. The remainder of the staff tended to be drawn from part-time help, with many being high school students. No one on the staff belonged to a union and most were paid the minimum provincial wage. An average employee package was available and contained such benefits as group life insurance and drug insurance.

Employee productivity at Ken & Ray's tended to amount to approximately fifty dollars of sales per man hour. Although this figure was lower than the estimated Loblaw average of ninety-five dollars of sales per man hour, the partners believed the lower productivity was more than compensated by the lower costs attributable to employee wages.

Record-keeping. Careful records were kept of sales and inventories. Meat and produce were inventoried every week while an exhaustive inventory was completed four times each year. Sales were analyzed on a weekly basis.

Store maintenance. Store maintenance occupied a fair proportion of the attention of the new owners. When Mr. Hill and Mr. Walker originally took over the operation, they found that maintenance appeared to have been neglected. The new owners spent some time cleaning up each store in addition to engaging in much painting and brightening. The Reddendale store was completely repainted as was the trim at the Collins Bay store.

Changes in layout also took place in the Reddendale store. For example, the produce area was originally characterized by two large parallel shelvings which tended to leave the fruit and vegetables under lower lighting levels. One shelf was consequently moved alongside the wall and replaced by a table.

Meat. A typical product sales mix in modern day supermarkets was twenty percent meat, seventy to seventy-two percent groceries, and eight to ten percent produce. When the new partners took over Ken & Ray's, they were surprised to find that meat sales accounted for thirty-five percent of the sales. It appeared that the previous ownership tended to cater to the freezer business in addition to offering the full range of A, B, C and D meat grades. Meat processing also tended to be done at the store level.

The new owners of Ken & Ray's moved quickly to bring the product mix in line with conventional practices. They dropped the grade D meats and adopted Loeb's "Cryovac" vacuum packaging. Adoption of this practice reduced the labor requirements at the store level and moved it back to the wholesaler level. In order to attempt to maintain their volume of the meat business, the partners asked Loeb to vacuum pack grade C meat as well as grades A and B.

By the summer of 1974, it was apparent that their new policy was not working.

Meat sales simply dropped by about seventeen percent and were not compensated by sales increases in groceries and produce.

Produce. Produce was always difficult to maintain and it required expensive equipment. At this point in time, only the Reddendale store had been equipped with new produce shelves.

Assortment and variety. The new owners were certainly aware of the distribution of sales by product types. For example, one estimate was that three percent of the items in a supermarket accounted for fifty to sixty percent of sales. As a consequence, products and brands were always carefully scrutinized by buyer committees in the big chains before they were allowed to take up valuable shelf space. Despite the industry practice, the new partners believed that their local ownership gave them more flexibility and that they could offer consumers a wider choice. One consequence was that minor experiments were continually taking place with consumers being offered a variety of new and different products. Pina Colada soft drink turned out to be an interesting seller at the Reddendale store as did some unusual varieties of Bulgarian jam.

Customer service. In contrast to the city stores, but like the other supermarkets in Kingston Township, Ken & Ray's remained open each evening until ten o'clock. Unlike all other supermarkets, the Collins Bay store was also open on Sundays. During the week, a reasonable amount of front-end service was offered although it dropped to the very minimum on Sundays as a consequence of a reduced staff. Customer service tended to be emphasized by the owners because they felt this was an area where they might be able to differentiate themselves from their competitors.

Pricing. Pricing was considered to be an important element of the merchandizing activities and was given close attention by the new owners. In meat and produce, the owners set their own store prices after careful consideration of their costs and competitors' actions. On the remainder of the items, they followed the Loeb's "zone pricing" system. Zone pricing meant that certain grocery brands were designated as competitive items and had to have a price that was at least the same as or lower than any competitor's price. On these items, margins were close to zero and sometimes even negative.

During the initial months of 1974, the Zone 1 prices were followed, which meant that between three hundred to four hundred items were designated as competitive items. For Ken & Ray's, it meant that they offered the lowest prices in Kingston. In order to make their required nineteen to twenty percent overall gross margin, Ken & Ray's tended to rely on the sale on high margin items such as health and beauty aids and confectionery.

Sales. The owners of Ken & Ray's observed that their chain had sales characteristics unlike those of similar size supermarkets. Milk sales, for example, accounted for a high proportion of their sales. In addition, there tended to be a low average sale per customer with the lowest figure at the Reddendale store and highest at the Amherstview store.

An individual familiar with the food retailing business in Kingston made the following estimate of dollar sales per week by each of the major chains. Dominion was doing approximately two hundred and fifty thousand dollars in sales a week, of which one hundred and fifty thousand dollars was being accounted for by the Kingston Township store. Loblaws was probably accounting for about two hundred and forty-five thousand dollars, of which seventy thousand dollars was being generated by each of the Kingston Township stores. Bennett's was probably doing one hundred and sixty thousand dollars of business, A & P twenty thousand dollars, Food City sixty thousand dollars and finally Ken & Ray's one hundred thousand dollars. Broken down by stores it was estimated that the Reddendale store was doing about thirty thousand dollars, Collins Bay thirty thousand dollars, and the Amherstview store forty thousand dollars.

A marketing research firm made the following market share estimates: September, 1973—Dominion, 27.1 percent; Loblaws, 21.4 percent; Bennett's 17.2 percent; Ken & Ray's 12 percent; A & P, 6.5 percent; Food City 7.5 percent; and, all others, 8.3 percent.

A useful figure to use in rationalizing these two estimates of market share was that there was a potential of $11.38 in sales per person per week in a market (industry rule of thumb).

Survey of consumer attitudes. In October 1974, a survey was made of Kingston retail food shoppers using a questionnaire, parts of which follow as Exhibit 3. In the first part of the questionnaire, the shoppers were asked to identify the food store which they rated the highest on each of thirteen patronage factors as well as the food store which they used on their last major shopping trip. In the second part of the questionnaire, the shoppers were asked to rate each factor on a 10-point scale of importance. Finally, in the last part of the questionnaire, the respondents were asked to indicate their social-economic and demographic status.

The three parts of the questionnaire were administered by students at the School of Business, Queen's University, as part of a class project in Marketing Research. In order to meet the requirements of this project, approximately 30% of the households were contacted by personal interview, 30% by telephone interview, and 40% by mail.

The Kingston City Directory was used to define the Kingston metropolitan population. Approximately 200 respondents were selected from this population using random number tables. In the case of the telephone and personal interviews, each student was asked to make at least two call-backs. Of the respondents contacted in the survey, 129 provided completed questionnaires. These questionnaires represented a 53% response rate among those contacted by mail, 73% among those contacted by telephone, and 74% among those contacted by personal interview.

The results of the survey are found in Exhibits 4 and 5.

QUESTION:

1. What adjustments, if any, should the owners of Ken and Ray's make in their retail operations?

Exhibit 1
RETAIL GROCERY SALES IN CANADA
Estimated Sales in 1969—By Province and By Chain Affiliation

(millions)

Corporate Chains	B.C.	Prairies	Ontario	Quebec	Atlantic	Total
Dominion Stores	$ —	$ 16	$ 422	$ 149	$ 65	$ 652
Loblaw Group	—	85	415	15	25	540
Canada Safeway	201	260	20	—	—	481*
Steinberg's	—	—	150	370	—	520
A & P	—	7	203	50	—	260
Weston Group	105	35	8	—	—	148
Sobey's Stores	—	—	—	—	55	55
Overwaitea (Neonex)	55	—	—	—	—	55
Food City (Oshawa)	—	—	88	—	—	88
Marche Union	—	—	—	30	—	30
Provigo Group	—	—	—	20	—	20
M. Loeb	—	—	25	—	—	25
Becker Milk	—	—	50	—	—	50
Mac's Milk	—	—	40	—	—	40
Other	8	2	85	—	5	100
Sub-Total	$369	$405	$1,506	$634	$150	$3,064

Independents						
IGA	$ 30	$ 90	$ 285	$ 133	$ 30	$ 568
Much More	4	62	6	3	—	75
Loblaw Group	—	—	290	—	60	350
Weston Group	240	155	10	—	—	405
Provigo Group	—	—	—	260	—	260
Canada Safeway	10	60	—	—	—	70
Other Independent.	—	78	225	763	230	1,296
Sub-Total	$284	$445	$816	$1,159	$320	$3,024
GRAND TOTAL	$653	$850	$2,322	$1,793	$470	$6,088

Source: Estimates by BURNS BROS. AND DENTON LIMITED, based on company annual reports, and information contained in trade magazines.

   * Safeway's chain store sales exclude $70 million of estimated wholesale volume, which is classified under "Independents".

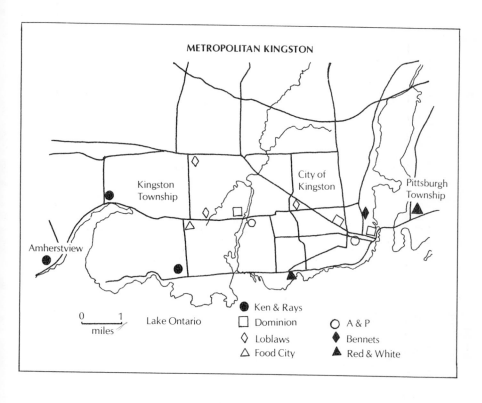

METROPOLITAN KINGSTON

Kingston
Township

City of
Kingston

Pittsburgh
Township

Amherstview

0   1
miles

Lake Ontario

● Ken & Rays
□ Dominion
◊ Loblaws
△ Food City

○ A & P
♦ Bennets
▲ Red & White

Exhibit 3
Questionnaire

Thank you. I would like to ask you some questions about the supermarkets in Kingston such as A&P, Bennett's, Dominion, Food City, Ken & Ray's, Loblaws, Red & White, etc. For each question, please tell me the *one* supermarket which you think best answers the question.

	A&P	Ben-nett's	Domin-ion	Food City	Ken & Ray's	Lob-laws	Red & White	Other
Which supermarket is the easiest one to get to from your home?	1	2	3	4	5	6	7	0
Has the lowest prices?	1	2	3	4	5	6	7	0
Has the best quality meat?	1	2	3	4	5	6	7	0
Has the best customer service?	1	2	3	4	5	6	7	0
On your last major food shopping trip which store did you use?	1	2	3	4	5	6	7	0
Which supermarket has the highest prices?	1	2	3	4	5	6	7	0
Has the best quality produce such as fresh fruits and vegetables?	1	2	3	4	5	6	7	0
Has the cleanest stores?	1	2	3	4	5	6	7	0
Has the best weekly "specials" that are usually advertised in the newspaper?	1	2	3	4	5	6	7	0
Gives you the best value for the money in their own private label or store brands?	1	2	3	4	5	6	7	0
Has the best overall assortment or variety of merchandise?	1	2	3	4	5	6	7	0
Has the best store layout?	1	2	3	4	5	6	7	0
Has the best overall advertising	1	2	3	4	5	6	7	0

Some reasons are probably more important to you than others in selecting a supermarket. Would you please rate each of the following reasons from 1 to 10 where 1 means "not at all important" and 10 means "very important."

	Not at all important							Very important		
Easiest to get to	1	2	3	4	5	6	7	8	9	10
Lowest prices	1	2	3	4	5	6	7	8	9	10
Best quality meat	1	2	3	4	5	6	7	8	9	10
Best customer service	1	2	3	4	5	6	7	8	9	10
Best quality produce	1	2	3	4	5	6	7	8	9	10
Cleanest stores	1	2	3	4	5	6	7	8	9	10
Best weekly specials	1	2	3	4	5	6	7	8	9	10
Best value for the money in private label or store brands	1	2	3	4	5	6	7	8	9	10
Best overall assortment or variety of merchandise	1	2	3	4	5	6	7	8	9	10
Best store layout	1	2	3	4	5	6	7	8	9	10
Best overall advertising	1	2	3	4	5	6	7	8	9	10

Exhibit 4
Percentage of Respondents
Selecting Each Store

STORE	Easiest to get to	Lowest Prices	Best Quality Meat	Best Customer Service	Store Last Shopped	Highest Prices	Best Quality Produce	Cleanest Stores	Best Specials	Best Value in Private Brands	Best Assortment	Best Store Layout	Best Advertising
A & P	15.4*	6.9	8.8	9.2	9.0	12.9	6.5	8.2	4.3	9.8	2.8	12.6	3.1
Bennetts	13.8	23.8	18.4	22.0	21.3	5.0	15.7	8.2	30.4	6.5	15.7	15.3	25.0
Dominion	25.2	28.7	35.1	31.2	36.1	18.8	29.6	36.1	29.3	34.8	36.1	32.4	25.0
Food City	5.7	11.9	4.4	6.4	4.9	1.0	9.3	—	9.8	3.3	0.9	0.9	3.1
Ken & Ray's	12.2	5.0	1.8	2.8	1.6	4.0	—	—	—	1.1	—	—	—
Loblaws	24.4	21.8	23.7	26.6	25.4	49.5	38.9	44.3	25.0	43.5	42.6	37.8	43.8
Red & White	2.4	—	2.6	0.9	—	7.9	—	2.1	—	—	—	—	—
Other	0.8	2.0	5.3	0.9	1.6	1.0	—	1.0	1.0	1.1	1.9	—	—
TOTAL	100.0	100.0	100.0	100.0	100.0	100.0	100.0	100.0	100.0	100.0	100.0	100.0	100.0

* Read: 15.4 percent of respondents said that A & P was the easiest store to reach from their home.

Exhibit 5
Relative Importance Scores
for Patronage Factors

FACTOR	AVERAGE IMPORTANCE SCORE
Easy to get to	6.920*
Lowest Prices	7.833
Meat Quality	8.107
Customer Service	7.159
Product Quality	7.770
Store Cleanliness	7.295
Specials	6.350
Value of Private Labels	6.330
Assortment of Merchandise	7.286
Store Layout	5.934
Advertising	4.504

* Read: on a scale from 1 to 10 (1 = Not at all important: 10 = very important), respondents assigned an average score of 6.920 to the ease of reaching a store.

CASE 15: CROCKETT ELECTRIC COMPANY LTD.

Selection of channels of distribution

The vice-president in charge of production and engineering at Crockett Electric saw
an automatic garage-door opener at a home show and became interested in the
possibilities of adding a similar article to his company's line. He has approached the
marketing department executives with the product idea, and they were interested
enough to do some preliminary marketing research. Studies have shown that a
large market potential exists and that only a minute part of this potential has been
tapped. Many competitive models exist, but none had had any degree of market acceptance or success. In brief, here is a product with a terrific potential, but as yet no
firm has been able to capitalize on these opportunities.

Crockett's engineers have now developed a patentable electronic door opener.
The product is fairly simple. It consists of two units, one of which is to be installed
inside the garage. The other is a portable unit which can be mounted in some convenient location within the car or placed in the glove compartment. The user simply
pushes a button on the portable unit in the car to open or close the garage door.
Once the car is in the garage, the door can also be closed by turning off the garage
light. Additional automobile units can be purchased for families with more than
one car. The entire product is transistorized. Crockett's model would retail for
about $225, which is well within the range of competitive prices. The product can
be installed easily and inexpensively by the homeowner, according to simple and
clear instructions.

So far, one important product weakness has been discovered. The unit in one person's car sometimes opens garage doors in other homes having a similar product. This weakness would become increasingly critical as more units of the product were sold. The executives have horrible visions of what might happen in a row of surburban houses, all with garages equipped with Crockett door openers: one person driving down the street and pushing the button in his car unit might open all the garage doors in the block, one by one. The engineers are hard at work on this problem, and have just about perfected a mechanism which would make it possible to set different electronic signals for each door opener produced.

Crockett Electric is a manufacturer of industrial and consumer electrical products, including industrial switching and timing equipment, radio and television components, and portable public-address systems. Annual sales are approximately $5 million. The company has a small sales force operating out of three sales offices (the Hamilton home office and the Montreal and Vancouver offices). Salesmen sell directly to large industrial users, to government agencies, and also to industrial distributors and manufacturers' agents.

Currently, the executives are trying to determine what channels to use for the door opener. Part of their decision stems from the fact that they do not know whether they are dealing with an industrial or a consumer market. Mr. Shannon, the marketing vice-president, feels that the door opener is a consumer product. He is not, however, certain whether it should be sold through wholesalers and retailers of building materials, whether it should go through channels for home appliances or whether it should be treated like power lawn mowers and other patio and garden equipment. Mr. Moyer, the sales manager, definitely feels that the door opener is an industrial product. He thinks that once a house is built and sold, the resident consumer will not add the door opener and that Crockett should reach the people who are building the homes. Consequently, he thinks that the product should be sold directly to architects and to building contractors engaged in large suburban housing developments. Mr. Moyer also feels that there is a substantial market among all sorts of industrial users, such as manufacturing plants, retail stores, gasoline service stations, automobile repair garages, parking garages, warehouses, and any other type of company with large overhead doors for loading docks.

A related question facing these executives is whether to use the company's present sales force and, if so, to what extent. The product itself presents no problems in this respect. The salesmen are qualified to sell it. None of the proposed channels, however, involves middlemen on whom the sales force is presently calling. Thus an entirely new customer list must be developed. Also, the salesmen would have only one product to sell to these newly added middlemen. It is questionable whether it would be profitable for Crockett's present salesmen to sell the door opener. The executives are considering the feasibility of using manufacturers' agents to reach the appropriate parties.

QUESTIONS

1. Do better market opportunities lie in treating the door opener as a consumer or an industrial product?
2. Which channels should be used to reach your recommended market?
3. Should the company use its present sales force to sell the door opener, should it establish a separate sales force, or should manufacturers' agents be used?
4. Should Crockett select one distributor in each geographic market and offer him an exclusive franchise?

CASE 16. KELSEY MANUFACTURING COMPANY LTD.

Getting middlemen to promote manufacturer's products

The Kelsey Manufacturing Company Ltd. was one of the large manufacturers of repair materials for automobile tires and tubes in Canada. One of the major objectives set by management was for the company to show a continuous growth in sales and profits at a rate of 10 percent a year. In view of this goal, management was greatly concerned by the fact that Kelsey's annual sales volume had remained at about the same level for eight years. Some executives labeled the sales volume as "stable," while others referred to it as "stagnant." Whatever description was given to this sales situation, management believed it would be improved considerably if the company's wholesalers and retailers could be persuaded to promote Kelsey's products more aggressively. Consequently, management was trying to figure out how to "spread the word"—i.e., disseminate its product and promotional messages—through the company's rather lengthy channels-of-distribution system, so that the ultimate customer—the retail service station operator—effectively received these messages.

The Kelsey Company was founded in the early 1920s as a small, family-owned company to manufacture cold patches for repairing innertubes. Within a few years hot-patch material was introduced, marking the beginning of a period of great growth. Tire repair was a service in much demand during the years of the 1930s depression and World War II. During that war the government took about 90 percent of the production. In 1972 the Kelsey Company was acquired by a large, diversified conglomerate and was operated as a division of one of that corporation's subsidiary firms.

One key official said, "Once we were just a nice-size family. Now we're really in the mainstream of corporate life. We used to be able to communicate with each other and with our customers on an informal party-line basis. Now we have to pay close attention to the proper channels. As the prison warden said in the movie *Cool Hand Luke,* 'What we've got here is a problem in communication!' "

Kelsey manufactured tire and tube repair materials under three brand names: Lion, which accounted for 54 percent of the sales; Topps, 10 percent of sales; and Air Float, 36 percent. Under the Lion brand the company produced the following products: Chembond patches (a chemical application), rubber cement, liquid buffer and cleaner, Perma Strip patches (outside tire repair), hot vulcanizing patches, clamps, repair gun, cold patches, unitized patches, boot cement, tubeless sealant, tire talc, and rattle stops. In addition, a number of other items were purchased for resale under the Lion name. As a result of the merger with the chemical corporation, Kelsey Manufacturing added a new product line consisting of some 280 items in the category of tire valves and accessories.

As the number of products increased, the problem of communicating with the customers was intensified. The sales manager Mr. Ralph Knott summed up the problem by saying, "In the old days our sales representatives could carry the entire line in a small briefcase. Now, we'd be hard pressed to get everything in a station wagon. We just aren't able to let the customers know what we really can do for them."

Top executives in Kelsey believed that the firm held about 15 percent of the total tire and tube repair market. The major competitors were H. B. Egan Ltd., Bowes Seal Fast, Monkey Grip Sales, Remaco, and Kex Products. Kelsey, however, marketed the most complete line of products in their field.

Kelsey's annual net sales for the years 1965-1973 were as follows:

1965	—$1,589,000
1966	— 1,136,000
1967	— 1,028,000
1968	— 1,284,000
1969	— 1,208,000
1970	— 1,058,000
1971	— 1,151,000
1972	— 1,205,000
1973	— 1,998,000

During the above period there were no significant fluctuations in the company's gross margin (30-40 percent of sales) or the net profit before taxes (10 percent of sales). While most of Kelsey's sales were to wholesalers who in turn sold to retail service stations, the company also sold in the export market, and under private brands to major oil companies and to chain stores.

In recent years there was an increasing demand for the chemical (Chembond) patch at the expense of hot patches. This change in product popularity had enabled competition to make some inroads in the market, since the Kelsey company did not have the advantages productionwise in chemical patches that they had in hot patches.

Looking to the future, Kelsey's management recognized that it faced two problems which were created by technological improvements in other areas: (1) tires are continually being improved, mainly through creation of better rubber and fabric and (2) the highway system is continually being upgraded. These factors tend to produce less tire trouble per mile traveled with less use of repair materials per mile traveled.

However, these points may be offset by the increase in the number of vehicles on the road and the number of miles traveled per vehicle. Also, the two-ply tire, which is standard on most new cars, is more susceptible to punctures than is the four-ply tire. Still another positive factor in this repair-products industry is the large increase in the number of motorbikes, pneumatic industrial tires, and other inflatable rubber and/or plastic items.

Kelsey, like most of its competitors in the industry, distributed its products through manufacturers' representatives (agents) who sold to automotive-parts warehouse distributors. These distributors sold to smaller automotive-parts jobbers who, in turn, sold to service stations. In a sense the service station sells the product to the individual automobile owner, but by the very nature of the tire repair business, the ultimate consumer seldom knows what kind of products have been used to repair his tire or tube.

Because of this lengthy channel of distribution, Kelsey was having trouble getting its product story down to the service station. Obviously, no *real* sale occurred until the service station bought the product. Unless the retailers bought, the jobbers and warehouse distributors, in turn, would not reorder.

In the past, most of Kelsey's manufacturers' agents had handled Kelsey products exclusively. With the increasing difficulty in realizing growth in sales, however, all the representatives now handled other automotive lines, thus dividing their loyalty and decreasing the time available to communicate to the customer about the Kelsey products. Part of the reasoning behind the addition of the new product line of tire valves and accessories was the hope of rebuilding the agents' loyalty to Kelsey.

As Charles Bronson, the Kelsey vice president, said: "Our real problem right now is getting our story told. We've got to have better contacts with the customers. In the past our reps had to tell the story effectively or they didn't eat. Now, they're handling so many other customers that our story gets lost in the shuffle. As we have traveled across the country and talked with service station operators, we find that they have very little knowledge about the benefits or use of our tire repair materials."

On the other hand, Ray Levine, the manufacturers' representative covering the Prairie Provinces saw the problem this way: "The product line is now so large that you can't possibly do justice to the Kelsey products. I'd have to spend a week with each customer to tell him what the company wants told about each product. There just isn't enough time or money to do what they want."

QUESTION

1. What should the Kelsey Company do to get its middlemen to promote the company's products more informatively and aggressively?

PROMOTIONAL ACTIVITIES

THE PROMOTIONAL
PROGRAM

Having studied the product planning, price structure, and distribution system in a firm, we now examine the final operational area in a company's marketing system—the promotional activities. Chapters 22 to 24 are devoted to the management of the *promotional* mix, that is, the most strategic combination of advertising, personal selling, sales promotion, and other promotional tools that can be devised to reach the goals of the sales program.

When a home handicraft economy exists and a man makes a good product, his neighbors probably know about it. The "better mousetrap" theory is not realistic, however, in our modern economy. The present situation is more accurately described by the statement "Nothing happens until somebody sells something." This statement expresses rather succinctly the place of promotional activities in today's business scene. Promotional activities are probably the most criticized part of the entire marketing program. For this reason, we should remember one thing; not to confuse a tool with its user. Without question, many advertisements are misleading, and many salesmen act in poor taste. This is no fault of the tool of advertising, but simply indicates that it has been used poorly. Yet it is human nature to blame the tool itself: a person will hammer a nail crooked and blame the poor quality of the nail, he will hit his finger and blame the hammer.

NATURE AND IMPORTANCE OF PROMOTION

Many people consider that "selling" and "marketing" are synonymous terms, but actually selling is only one of the many components of marketing. Selling is defined by the American Marketing Association as "the personal or impersonal process of assisting and/or persuading a prospective customer to buy a commodity or a service or to act favorably upon an idea that has commercial significance to the seller."[1]

In this book, "selling" and "promotion" are used synonymously, although "promotion" is the preferred term. This preference is based on the belief of some people that selling suggests only the transfer of title or the use of personal salesmen and does not include advertising or other methods of stimulating demand. We are saying that promotion includes advertising, personal selling, sales promotion, and other selling tools. While the two words may be unfortunately similar, it should be noted particularly that "promotion" and "sales promotion" are different. "Promotion" is the all-inclusive term representing the broad field under discussion here, and "sales promotion" is only one part of it.

In line with the systems approach, a company should treat all its promotional efforts as a complete subsystem within the total marketing system. This means coordinating the sales-force activities, the advertising programs, and other promotional efforts. Unfortunately, today in many firms these activities still are fragmented, and management in the advertising and sales-force areas often conflict and compete with one another.[2]

In economic theory terms, the essential purpose of promotion is to change the location and shape of the demand (revenue) curve for a company's product. (See Fig. 22-1 and recall the discussion of nonprice competition in Chapter 15.) Through the use of promotion, a company hopes to increase a product's sales volume at any given price. It also hopes that promotion will affect the demand elasticity for the product, making the demand inelastic in the face of a price increase and elastic when the price goes down.

Basically, promotion is an exercise in information, persuasion, and influence. These three are related in that to inform is to persuade, and conversely, if a person is persuaded, he is probably also being informed. Many years ago, Prof. Neil Borden, of Harvard University, pointed up the pervasive nature of persuasion and influence when he said that "the use of influence in commercial relations is one of the attributes of a free society, just as persuasion and counterpersuasion are exercised freely in many walks of life in our free society—in the home, in the press, in the

---

1 Committee on Definitions, *Marketing Definitions: A Glossary of Marketing Terms*, American Marketing Association, Chicago, 1960, p. 21.

2 One helpful contervailing trend is the growing number of books which treat promotion as a total subsystem in marketing. See, for example, James F. Engel, Hugh G. Wales, and Martin R. Warshaw, *Promotional Strategy*, Richard D. Irwin, Inc., Homewood, Ill., 1971; Jerome B. Kernan, William P. Dommermuth, and Montrose S. Sommers, *Promotion: An Introductory Analysis*, McGraw-Hill Book Co., New York, 1970; Rollie Tillman and C. A. Kirkpatrick, *Promotion: Persuasive Communication in Marketing*, Richard D. Irwin, Inc., Homewood, Ill., 1968; Frederick E. Webster, Jr., *Marketing Communication: Modern Promotional Strategy*, The Ronald Press Company, New York, 1971, and M. Wayne DeLozier, *The Marketing Communications Process*, McGraw-Hill Book Co., New York, 1976.

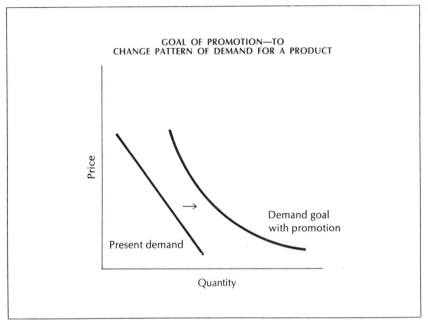

**GOAL OF PROMOTION—TO
CHANGE PATTERN OF DEMAND FOR A PRODUCT**

Price

→

Demand goal
with promotion

Present demand

Quantity

Figure 22-1.

classroom, in the pulpit, in the courts, in the political forum, in legislative halls, and in government agencies for information."[3]

PROMOTIONAL METHODS

The two most widely used methods of promotion are personal selling and advertising. Another is sales promotion, which is designed to supplement and coordinate personal selling and advertising efforts and which includes such activities as setting up store displays, holding trade shows and exhibitions, and using samples or premiums. In addition, there is a group of marketing strategies, discussed in earlier chapters, which are in part promotional. Such strategies as product differentiation, market segmentation, trading up, trading down, and branding belong in this group.

IMPORTANCE OF PROMOTION IN MODERN MARKETING

In the realistic marketplace, perfect competition does not exist. Under conditions of imperfect competition, with product differentiation, nonrational behavior, and less-than-complete market information, promotional activities are essential. Promotion is an adjunct of imperfect competition. In one study of almost five hundred successful products, promotion was perceived by management as being the most important facet of marketing strategy leading to this success.[4]

---

3 Neil H. Borden, *The Economic Effects of Advertising*, Richard D. Irwin, Inc., Homewood, Ill., 1942, p. 802.

4 John G. Udell, "The Perceived Importance of the Elements of Strategy," *Journal of Marketing*, January, 1968, pp. 34-40.

Several factors point up the need for promotion today. In the first place, as the physical distance between producers and consumers increases, and as the number of potential customers grows, the problem of market communication becomes a significant one. Furthermore, improvements in physical distribution facilities are expanding the geographic limits of markets.

Once middlemen are introduced into a marketing pattern, it is not enough for a producer to communicate only with the ultimate consumers or industrial users. It becomes essential that middlemen be informed about products. Wholesalers, in turn, must promote the products to retailers, and retailers must communicate with consumers.

The intensification of competition between different industries, as well as between individual firms within given industries, has placed tremendous pressures on the promotional programs of individual sellers. In our economy of abundance, want satisfaction has replaced, to a great extent, the mere necessity of fulfilling basic physiological requirements. As consumers engage in the satisfactions of wants rather than needs, they become more selective in their choices of alternative expenditures. To attract customers, a firm must have a good promotional program. Customer demand is largely dormant; it must be awakened and stimulated.

Promotional effort looms important in the overall operations of a business. It is usually the largest part of the total marketing expenses. All promotional expenses together often constitute the largest single cost in a firm—even larger than its total production costs.

Any type of an economic decline quickly points up the importance of selling. During such a period, there are no major problems in product planning. Channels remain essentially the same, and the pricing structure is basically unchanged. The key problem is selling. Promotion is needed to maintain the high material standard of living and the high level of employment which we enjoy in this country.

THE COMMUNICATIONS PROCESS

In any society, the nature of interpersonal relations depends in large measure upon the effectiveness of interpersonal communications. Certainly in business in general, and in marketing in particular, the effectiveness of the system is related to the effectiveness of the communications. To go one step further, within the marketing system the promotional activity is basically an exercise in communications. If an executive understands something of the theory of communications, he should be able to better manage a promotional program in his firm.[5]

The word "communication" is derived from the Latin word *communis,* meaning "common." Thus, when you communicate, you are trying to establish a "commonness" with someone. Through the use of verbal or nonverbal symbols, you as the source send a message through a channel to a receiver in an effort to share an idea, attitude, or some other kind of information. Fundamentally, a communications process requires only three elements—a *message,* a *source* of this message, and a *receiver.* However, to refine the process into a workable form—one which recognizes environmental practicalities—additional elements come into play. The information

---

5 See Jerome B. Kernan and Montrose S. Sommers, "Meaning, Value, and the Theory of Promotion," *Journal of Communications,* June, 1967, pp. 109-135; and Michael L. Ray, "A Decision Sequence Analysis of Developments in Marketing Communication," *Journal of Marketing,* January, 1973, pp. 29-38.

which the sending source wants to share must first be *encoded* into transmittable form and then later *decoded* by the receiver at the destination. Another element to be reckoned with is *noise* which may interfere at any stage with the transmission or reception of the message. The final element in the process—feedback—tells the sender whether the message was received and how it was perceived by the destination target. The feedback element is also the basis for planning ahead. The sender learns how he might improve his communications by using different channels, encoding, or messages.

These elements constituting a general communications system may be conceptualized in a model as diagramed in Fig. 22-2.[6] This same model, as adapted to the promotional activities in a company's marketing program, is illustrated in Fig. 22-3. The information source may be a person with an idea to communicate. He will encode it into a transmittable form by putting it into written or spoken words, or perhaps even into a gesture of some sort (wave of his arms, dim his bright lights). The coded message is then carried by print media, sound waves or light waves to the destination—an individual, a church audience, or a university class, for example. Each receiver decodes (interprets) the message in light of his individual experiences or frames of reference. The closer the decoded message is to its encoded form (as-

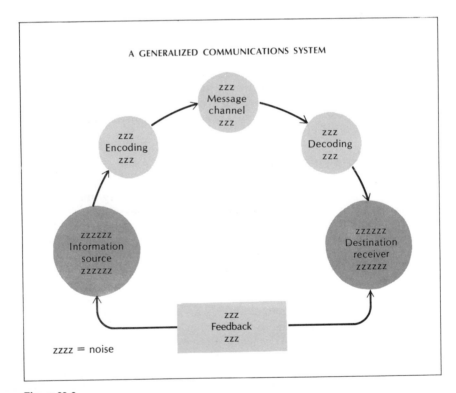

Figure 22-2.

6 Adapted from David K. Berlo, *The Process of Communication,* Holt, Rinehart and Winston, Inc., New York, 1960, pp. 30-32. See also the model in Claude E. Shannon and Warren Weaver, *The Mathematical Theory of Communication,* The University of Illinois Press, Urbana, 1949, p. 5.

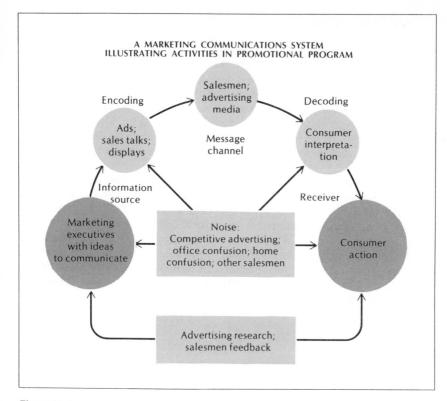

A MARKETING COMMUNICATIONS SYSTEM
ILLUSTRATING ACTIVITIES IN PROMOTIONAL PROGRAM

Figure 22-3.

suming it was encoded fully and accurately), the more effective the communication is. By the receiver's words or actions (feedback) the sender can judge the extent to which his message got through.

Let us illustrate the process with a marketing example. An executive wants to communicate a selling message to a consumer. The message is encoded into a radio commercial and carried to the consumer via a radio program and a receiving set. The consumer hears the commercial and interprets it. Through marketing research feedback the sender will try to determine how effectively the message came through and how much it moved the consumer to action. At any point in the process, interfering noise may reduce the effectiveness of the system. While the radio commercial is on, the children may be making noise in the house, or someone may ring the doorbell. Competitive advertisements, salespeople, or displays are also forms of noise. The sender can counteract the noise by preparing an especially good commercial or by running it at a time when doorbells and children are apt to be quiet.

In effect, the marketing executive uses his previous analysis of consumer characteristics and behavior to provide him with encoded symbols which can be used to communicate the merits of his product and the reasons for buying it. An analysis of the market for carbonated beverages, for instance, might show that one major market is made up of people who serve soft drinks at parties. The seller can then encode his message in an advertisement which pictures the use of his product in an entertainment setting.

THE CAMPAIGN CONCEPT

When planning the total promotional program in a firm, management must ordinarily make use of the campaign concept. A *campaign* is a planned, coordinated series of promotional efforts built around a single theme or idea and designed to reach a predetermined goal. Although the term "campaign" is probably thought of most often in connection with advertising, it seems more appropriate to apply the concept of a campaign first to the entire promotional program. Then the total promotional campaign can be subdivided into its advertising, personal selling, and sales promotion components, and the subcampaigns can be planned in more detail.

Many types of promotional campaigns may be conducted by a company, and several may be run concurrently. Geographically, a firm may have a local, regional, or national campaign, depending upon the available funds, objectives, and market scope. One campaign may be aimed at consumers, and another at wholesalers and retailers. The stage of a product's life cycle may determine whether a pioneering or a competitive campaign will be conducted. Sometimes a firm is most concerned with building an image of promoting its services through an institutional campaign. A campaign may run for a week, a month, a year, or even longer. Three to six months is quite common.

Perhaps the first step in developing a promotional campaign should be to establish the campaign goals and determine the campaign strategy. One writer has suggested some areas which should be considered in the course of setting this strategy.[7]

1. What is the relative emphasis to be placed on primary versus secondary demand stimulation?
2. What balance is desired between the immediacy of the action-response and the duration of the response?
3. Do we wish to influence everyone a little bit or a few people intensively?
4. At what point are we targeting our emphasis on the spectrum between brand awareness and brand insistence?
5. What issues or product features (both ours and our competitors) shall we stress?

Early in the course of planning the campaign, management should decide what selling appeals will be stressed. This decision will be based to a large extent upon the specific objectives of the campaign and the research findings concerning the buying motives and habits of the customers. If the goal of a promotional campaign put on by Alberta's new airline is to introduce its new jumbo jet service, the appeals might be to the customers' desire for speed, a quiet and restful trip, or fine food and courteous service. If the same airline wants to increase its plane loadings of air freight, however, the ads and the personal selling presentation might stress low total cost of air freight, reduction in losses due to spoilage and handling, advantages of savings in packaging, or convenient schedules.

A campaign revolves around a central idea or focal point. This "theme" permeates all promotional efforts and tends to unify the campaign. A theme is simply the appeals dressed up in a distinctive, attention-getting form. As such, it is related to the campaign's objectives and the customers' behavior. It expresses the product's

---

7 Dodds I. Buchanan, "A New Look at 'Old' Advertising Strategy," *Business Horizons*, Winter, 1965, pp. 85-96.

benefits. Frequently the theme takes the form of a slogan, such as Coutts Hall-mark's "when you care enough to send the very best" or Loblaws' "more than the price is right" or DeBeers' "a diamond is forever." Some companies use the same theme for several campaigns; others develop a different theme for each new campaign.

In a successfully operated campaign, the efforts of all groups concerned will be meshed effectively. The *advertising program* will consist of a series of related, well-timed, carefully placed ads. The *personal selling effort* can be tied in by having the salesmen explain and demonstrate the product benefits stressed in the ads. Also, the salesmen will be fully informed about the advertising part of the campaign—the theme, media used, schedule of appearance of ads, appeals used, etc. The salesmen, in turn, should carry this information to wholesalers and retailers so that they can become effective participants in the campaign. *Sales-promotional devices* such as point-of-purchase display materials need to be coordinated with the other aspects of the campaign. For each campaign, new display materials must be prepared, reflecting the ads and appeals used in the current campaign, in order to maximize the campaign's impact at the point of sale. Personnel responsible for the *physical distribution activities* must ensure that adequate stocks of the product are available in all outlets prior to the start of the campaign.

DETERMINATION OF PROMOTIONAL MIX

Determining the most effective promotional *mix* is another of the difficult tasks in marketing management. Several different promotional tools or combinations thereof may be used. The underlying difficulty is that management does not know the exact extent to which advertising, personal selling, or any other promotional tool will help achieve the goals of the sales program. The executives do not know how much should be spent on each promotional activity, nor do they know what to expect from the expenditure. Guideposts to aid management in its decision regarding the promotional mix will be examined in the following section.

FACTORS INFLUENCING PROMOTIONAL MIX

Four factors which should influence management's decision making with respect to the promotional mix are (1) the amount of money available for promotion, (2) the nature of the market, (3) the nature of the product, and (4) the stage of the product's life cycle.

Funds available. Regardless of what may be the most desirable promotional mix, the amount of money available for promotion is the real determinant of the mix. Businesses with ample funds can make more effective use of advertising than enterprises with limited financial resources. Small or financially weak companies are likely to rely on personal selling, dealier displays, or joint manufacturer-retailer advertising. The use of personal salesmen may be inefficient compared with advertising in magazines or newspapers. Either of these advertising media can carry at least part of the promotional message to far more people at a much lower cost per person than personal salesmen. To do an effective promotional job in advertising, however, may take a considerable sum of money.

Nature of the market. As is true in most problem areas in marketing, management's decision on the promotional mix will be influenced to a great extent by the nature of the company's market. This influence is felt in at least three ways.

Geographic scope of the market. Businesses selling only in local markets will often use promotional ingredients quite different from those used by firms which have national markets. Personal selling may be adequate in a small local market, but as the market broadens geographically, greater reliance must frequently be placed on advertising.

Concentration of the market. Market concentration influences a firm's promotional strategy in three basic ways. First, the total number of prospective customers is a consideration. The fewer potential buyers there are, the more apt a seller is to stress personal selling rather than advertising.

The second consideration is the number of different types of potential customers. A market that is concentrated in one type of customer or industry will call for a different promotional mix from that required when a firm sells to many different customer groups. A firm selling large power saws and other cutting equipment used only by lumber manufacturers may be able to use personal selling effectively, and there will be very little advertising in its mix. In contrast, a company selling hand tools used by thousands of consumers and virtually all types of industrial users probably will include liberal portions of advertising in its mix because personal selling would be prohibitively expensive in reaching the final customers.

Finally, even though a firm sells nationally, it may find its market concentrated in relatively few spots. In this type of market concentration, emphasis on personal selling may be feasible, whereas it would be unrealistic if the potential customers were widely distributed all over the country.

Type of customers. The promotional strategy is influenced by whether the business is aiming its sales campaign at industrial users, household consumers, or middlemen. To illustrate, a promotional campaign aimed at retailers will probably contain a greater percentage of personal selling than will a program designed to attract household consumers. In many situations the middlemen may strongly influence the promotional strategy used by a manufacturer. Often a retail store will not even stock a product unless the manufacturer agrees to do a certain amount of advertising.

Nature of the product. Consumer products and industrial goods frequently require different strategies. Within the category of consumer goods, a promotional mix is influenced by whether the product is generally considered a convenience, shopping, or specialty item. In industrial goods, installations are not promoted in the same way that operating supplies or raw materials are.

Firms marketing convenience goods will normally rely heavily on manufacturers' advertising plus emphasis on dealer displays. Personal selling plays a relatively minor role. This mix is best because a convenience product is widely distributed, needs no special demonstration or explanation, and is competing with many brands that have reasonably equal acceptance. Furthermore, buying decisions are often made at the point of purchase.

In the field of industrial goods, the promotional strategy behind installations usually features heavy emphasis on personal selling. The market for such products is more easily pinpointed than the market for other types of industrial products. Also, the unit sales are typically large, products are often made to specification, and considerable presale and postsale personal service is necessary. Raw-materials sellers also rely on personal selling, often to the total exclusion of advertising. Many raw materials are unbranded, and the products of any one of several firms will fill a buyer's need. Personal services and persuasion from salesmen may be the only differentiating features offered by one seller over another.

Stage of the product's life cycle. In Chapter 10, we observed that products go through a life cycle, starting with the introductory period; then progressing through the stages of growth, maturity, and saturation; and finally ending in decline and possible abandonment. Strategy decisions for promoting a product should be influenced considerably by the phase of its life cycle which it is in at any given time.

In the pioneering, or introductory, stage a seller must stimulate *primary* demand—the demand for a type of product—as contrasted with *selective* demand—the demand for a particular brand. Thus manufacturers first had to sell the consumers on the value of microwave kitchen ovens in general before it was feasible to promote Tappan, Thermador, or some other brand.

When a product is in the pioneering stage (as far as a prospective customer is concerned), the customer does not recognize that he wants the commodity. He does not immediately understand how it will benefit him. Therefore, the promotional strategy is to inform and educate the potential customer. He must be told that the product exists, how it may be used, and what want-satisfying benefits it provides.

Normally, heavy emphasis must be placed on personal selling when a firm is promoting a new product or is pioneering a new market. Trade shows and fairs also may play a major role in the promotional mix, particularly in the case of industrial goods which go directly from producer to customer. Rather than call on each customer or each industrial plant individually, the company can promote its new product at a home show, automobile show, or some other type of trade show where the prospective customers will come to the seller's exhibit. Manufacturers rely heavily on personal selling in attracting middlemen to handle a new product. The middlemen in turn often use more personal selling in their promotional mix than they will after the item gains broader market acceptance.

During the middle stages of a product's life, the promotional mix calls for increased emphasis upon advertising. Customers are aware of the want-satisfying benefits of the product, so advertising can perform whatever informational and educational tasks remain to be done. As a product moves through the middle stages and attracts stiff competition, more and more attention is devoted to advertising as a tool of persuasion rather than of information only. Intense competition forces sellers to devote larger sums to advertising and thus contributes to the declining profits experienced in the maturity and saturation stages.

Most products eventually reach the final stages of their life cycle—decline and possible abandonment. New and better products are taking their place. Manufacturers are discontinuing the production of the older goods, the profit rates are declining, and even promotional effort is substantially cut back.

QUESTIONS OF BASIC PROMOTIONAL STRATEGY

By asking and then analyzing some seven questions regarding promotional strategy, we can set some guidelines to aid management in determining its promotional mix. At the same time, we are relating back to the four basic influencing factors we just discussed.[8]

When should personal selling be main ingredient? Personal selling will ordinarily carry the bulk of the promotional load (1) when the company is small or has insufficient funds with which to carry on an adequate advertising program, (2) when the market is concentrated, or (3) when the personality of the salesman is needed to establish rapport or create confidence. Personal selling will also be emphasized when the product (4) has a higher unit value, (5) requires demonstration, (6) must be fitted to the individual customer's needs, as in the case of securities or insurance, (7) is purchased infrequently, or (8) involves a trade-in.

When should advertising be main ingredient? If the market for the product is widespread, as in the case of a national consumer market, advertising should receive heavy emphasis. Advertising also works best when the seller wishes to inform many people quickly, as in the case of an announcement of new store hours, a special sale, or a new credit policy.

Certainly not every product lends itself to advertising. Many years ago Prof. Neil H. Borden identified five criteria which may serve as guides for management in determining the "advertisability" of its product.[9] If all five of these criteria are met, normally there is an excellent opportunity to advertise. However, this ideal condition rarely exists. Ordinarily a firm has a product which meets some, but not all, of these conditions. Then the decision on whether to advertise becomes more difficult.

The five criteria are as follows:

1. The primary demand trend for the product should be favorable. Advertising works best when the market demand for a product is on the upswing. In spite of the layman's opinion, advertising cannot successfully sell a product that people do not want, nor can advertising reverse a declining primary demand trend.
2. There should be considerable opportunity to differentiate the product. When this condition exists, it is easier to advertise because the company has something to say. For this reason, automobiles or cosmetics are easier to advertise than salt or sugar. Products which are not easily differentiated by brand may still be advertised by a trade association. Products advertised by the Canadian Dairy Foods Service Bureau, the Canadian Cotton Council, or the Canadian Cooperative Wool Growers are cases in point. A retailer who cannot easily differentiate his product lines from those of his competitors may try to differentiate his services, such as credit or location, which are an adjunct to the sale of the product.
3. The product should have hidden qualities. This condition affords the seller grounds for educating the market through advertising. On this point, a sofa or a mechanical device is easier to advertise than greeting cards. Where hidden qualities are important, consumers learn to rely on the dependability of a certain brand. Thus brand preference can be developed.

---

8 This question approach to promotional strategy was first noted in the writings of Prof. James D. Scott, University of Michigan.

9 Borden, *op. cit.*, pp. 424-428.

4. Powerful emotional buying motives should exist for the product. Then buying action can be stimulated by appeal to these motives. It is easier to build an effective advertising campaign for Weight Watchers or some other balanced diet for weight reduction than for an article such as clotheslines, hammers, or sheets. Prestige products or stores have achieved their status largely through advertising which appeals to emotional motives.
5. The company must have sufficient funds to support an advertising program adequately.

When should promotional efforts by retailer be stressed? If the product has important qualities which can be judged at the point of purchase, or if it is a highly standardized item, it lends itself to dealer display. So do products which are purchased on impulse. A product with a limited market, which makes advertising unreasonable, may also be promoted through the dealers. Dealer promotion is particularly important when the retailer is better known in the market than the manufacturer.

When should manufacturer-retailer cooperative advertising be used? There are really three questions involved here. First, when should a manufacturer list his dealers' names and addresses in his advertisements? Second, under what conditions should the manufacturer pay the retailer to mention the manufacturer's product in the retailer's advertisement? Finally, when should a retailer emphasize the manufacturer's product in the store's advertising and display?

In answer to the first of these questions, the retailers' names should be mentioned particularly when the manufacturer employs selective or exclusive distribution policies. It then becomes important to tell the market where the product may be obtained. Concerning the second question, the manufacturer may have to pay the retailer to promote the product in order to get the retailer even to carry the commodity. Also, the retailer may be in a position to demand payment when his name has better selling power than the manufacturer's. In answer to the third question, a retailer should emphasize the manufacturer's products in the store advertising and display when the manufacturer's name is very important.

Is retailer promotion needed when manufacturer emphasizes advertising or personal selling? The answer to this question is "yes." Personal selling, advertising, and merchandise display work done by the retailer can be quite effective. No matter how much advertising the manufacturer does, he can always benefit from high-caliber selling at the retail level. Promotional effort by a well-known, respected store can be the final impetus needed to penetrate a local market and to stimulate consumer buying power. When a retail store operates on a self-service basis, dealer display is almost imperative to move the product, regardless of how good a job the manufacturer has done in his national advertising. Displays serve as an excellent reminder to the customer, reinforcing what he has seen in the national advertising.

If a retailer emphasizes personal selling, does he need to advertise? Under certain conditions the answer to this question is "yes." In the first place, advertising will help to attract the customer to the store. Regardless of the quality of personal selling, it is largely wasted if the retailer cannot first attract an adequate number of potential customers. Furthermore, the advertising can support the efforts of the personal salesmen. If the product is high-price, or is purchased infrequently, again some promotional device is needed to attract the customers to the store. Discretionary purchases are very easy to put off indefinitely.

Should promotional activity be continued when the demand is heavy or exceeds capacity? The answer is a definite "yes." It is important that the manufacturer keep his name before the public. Boom conditions may pass, or the seller may acquire new plant capacity. A market is a dynamic institution, and customer loyalty is a "sometime thing;" old customers leave and new customers must be won. If conditions of high demand persist, they are certain to attract competitors. If they are temporary, the seller's heavy advertising may discourage competitors from coming in. In any event, the nature of the advertising message may change. When demand is heavy in relation to supply, the company will probably switch to institutional or indirect-action advertising.

EXAMPLES OF PROMOTIONAL MIX

The business applications of some of the points developed in this section are reflected in Tables 22-1 and 22-2. These tables summarize some of the findings made in a study of marketing expenditures in relation to company sales. Forty-six of the firms sell consumer goods (Table 22-1), and twenty-nine sell industrial products (Table 22-2); some of the firms market both types of commodities. The amount spent for three promotional activities—advertising, sales promotion, and personal selling—is shown as a percentage of net sales. It should be noted particularly that

Table 22-1. Promotional costs as percentage of sales of consumer goods: by individual companies.
Note the wide variations in the promotional mixes used by different firms. Compare the cosmetics firm (No. 3) and the insurance company (No. 40). Also note the variations in total promotional appropriations. A paint company (No. 9) devoted 27 percent of sales to promotion, while the promotion budget of an appliance company (No. 28) was only 8 percent of sales. How do you account for these differences?

Number	Type of product	Advertising budget[a]	Advertising	Sales promotion	Sales force
1.	Toiletries and proprietaries	A	30.0	4.0	10.0
2.	Package goods	AA	25.0	8.0	8.0
3.	Cosmetics	AAA	22.0	2.0	10.0
4.	Drug sundries	A	14.0	3.0	5.0
5.	Drugs	A	12.0	8.0	7.0
6.	Books	A	11.0	6.0	5.0
7.	Food	AAA	11.0	6.0	—
8.	Mail order	AAA	10.5	0.2	0.3
9.	Paints	B	10.0	2.0	15.0
10.	Housewares	B	10.0	2.0	6.0
11.	Food	AAA	7.0	5.0	3.0
12.	Appliances	AAA	5.0	1.0	—
13.	Soft drinks	B	5.0	3.0	1.0
14.	Soft goods	C	5.0	6.0	12.0

Table 22-1. (cont'd)

Number	Type of product	Advertising budget[a]	Advertising	Sales promotion	Sales force
15.	Salt	C	5.0^b	—^{b}	—
16.	Tool manufacturing	C	4.0^b	—^{b}	10.0
17.	Paper converting	C	4.0	4.0	—
18.	Tires, foam rubber	A	4.0	4.0	—
19.	Pianos	C	4.0	0.3	5.0
20.	Chemicals	D	3.5	1.0	—
21.	Automotive parts	C	3.5	—	10.3
22.	Textiles	B	3.0	0.7	3.6
23.	Marketing cooperative— fresh produce	C	3.0^b	—^{b}	10.0
24.	Baby foods	A	2.7	2.6	6.0
25.	Hand tools	B	2.5	0.9	7.1
26.	Home furnishings	B	2.5	2.0	6.0
27.	Power tools	C	2.5	—	—
28.	Appliances	A	2.5	1.5	4.0
29.	Airline	AA	2.2	0.7	—
30.	Liquors	A	2.0	—	—
31.	Heating and air conditioning	A	2.0	0.5	4.5
32.	Soft goods	C	2.0	2.5	4.5
33.	Floor coverings	A	2.0^b	—^{b}	—
34.	Shoe manufacturing	D	2.0^b	—^{b}	5.3
35.	Transportation	AA	1.8	0.2	6.0
36.	Building materials	AA	1.5	0.7	8.0
37.	Automotive	D	1.5	—	3.0
38.	Rubber products	C	1.3	1.0	—
39.	Photographic equipment	B	1.3	0.7	3.0
40.	Insurance	A	1.0	0.5	17.5
41.	Textiles	B	1.0	1.0	0.5
42.	Retail food chain	AAA	1.0^b	—^{b}	—
43.	Petroleum	A	0.6	0.3	—
44.	Domestic pumps and water systems	C	0.6	1.0	—
45.	Glass manufacturing	A	0.5	0.2	—
46.	Aluminum	B	0.1	0.1	—

Note: Dash (—) indicates data not given.

^{a} AAA—$10,000,000 and over; AA—$5,000,000-9,999,999; A—$1,000,000-4,999,999; B—$500,000-999,999; C—$100,000-499,999; D—under $100,000.

^{b} Advertising and sales promotion combined.

Source: Adapted from Dale Houghton, "Marketing Costs: What Ratio to Sales?" *Printers' Ink,* Feb. 1, 1957, pp. 54-55.

Table 22-2. Promotional costs as percentage of sales of industrial goods: by individual companies.

Sales-force expenditures are typically much higher than advertising appropriations. In the promotional mix, marketers of industrial goods usually emphasize personal selling to a much greater degree than firms selling consumer products. Why? Compare this table and Table 22-1. Note that the total promotional budget for industrial products is typically a smaller percentage of sales than that for consumer goods.

Number	Type of product	Advertising budget[a]	Advertising	Sales promotion	Sales force
1.	Paint	D	10.0	—	—
2.	Road construction and agricultural	D	4.0[b]	—[b]	7.0
3.	Office equipment	C	2.5[c]	—[c]	—
4.	Instrument	C	2.0	0.9	9.0
5.	Tool manufacturing	C	2.0[c]	—[c]	10.0
6.	Paper converting	C	2.0	2.0	—
7.	Instruments and controls	C	2.0[b]	—[b]	15.0
8.	Electrical control	C	1.8	3.8	—
9.	Graphic arts	C	1.5	0.5	16.0
10.	Metalworking	C	1.5[c]	—[c]	5.0
11.	Metal-cutting tools	C	1.2	—	5.6
12.	Industrial machinery	D	1.0	2.0	7.0
13.	Automotive parts	C	1.0	0.5	4.5
14.	Nonferrous metals	A	1.0[c]	—[c]	—
15.	Die cutting	D	1.0	—	10.0
16.	Basic metals	AA	1.0	—	—
17.	Aluminum	A	0.8	0.4	—
18.	Chemicals and plastics	A	0.8	—	—
19.	Hand tools	C	0.5	0.2	2.4
20.	Materials handling	B	0.5	0.5	—
21.	Soft goods—textile	C	0.5	—	12.0
22.	Automotive	D	0.5	—	0.5
23.	Plate steel fabrication	D	0.4	0.5	0.5
24.	Foundry	C	0.3	—	—
25.	Rubber products	D	0.3	—	—
26.	Chemicals	B	0.1	—	—
27.	Glass manufacturing	D	0.1	—	—
28.	Oil	C	0.1	—	—
29.	Aircraft	C	0.1	—	—

Note: Dash (—) indicates data not given.

[a] AAA—$10,000,000 and over; AA—$5,000,000-9,999,999; A—$1,000,000-4,999,999; B—$500,000-999,999; C—$100,000-499,999; D—under $100,000.

[b] Advertising, sales promotion, and marketing research combined.

[c] Advertising and sales promotion combined.

Source: Adapted from Dale Houghton, "Marketing Costs: What Ratio to Sales?" *Printers' Ink,* Feb. 1, 1957, p. 24.

the "—" symbol indicates that data were not reported, not that there were no expenditures for the activity. In this study, sales promotion was defined as those marketing efforts which are neither advertising nor personal selling but which coordinate advertising and personal selling and make them more effective. Expenditures for catalogues, price lists, display materials, and promotional booklets are examples of sales-promotion costs.

One main point which can be gleaned from the tables is the amount of the total promotional appropriation in relation to sales. Among consumer goods firms, the toiletries and cosmetics manufacturers devote as much as 35 to 45 percent of net sales to promotion. At the other extreme, firms producing steel or aluminum spend almost nothing (as a percentage of sales) to promote their consumer products. In general, the proportion of sales revenue expended on the promotion of industrial goods is much smaller than that spent on the promotion of consumer goods.

From the tables it is obvious that several of the firms did not delineate expenditures for the separate marketing activities. Nevertheless, the study does show the differences in the promotional mixes used by the various companies. In the consumer goods fields (Table 22-1), most of the cosmetics and toiletries manufacturers relied much more on advertising than on sales promotion or personal selling. These firms need to develop brand acceptance in a highly competitive national market. The cost of personal selling in these industries probably stems mainly from the heavy use of manufacturer-financed demonstrator salesmen in retail stores. As might be expected, in a mail-order firm (No. 8), the ratio of advertising to all other promotional activities is about 20:1. On the other hand, a tool manufacturer (No. 16), and an automotive parts firm (No. 21) emphasizes personal selling. In these firms, the product requires more explanation, the market is more concentrated as a rule, and manufacturers' brands are not usually important.

Among firms selling industrial products (Table 22-2), more reliance was placed on a sales force than on an advertising program. Some of the firms reported a very high ratio of personal selling to advertising. For example, a textile manufacturer (No.21) stated a 24:1 ratio, and a die-cutting firm (No.15) had a 10:1 ratio.

DETERMINATION OF TOTAL PROMOTIONAL APPROPRIATION

It is extremely difficult to establish promotional appropriations. Management lacks reliable standards for determining how much to spend on advertising or personal selling in total, or how much to spend on specific activities within each area. An even more serious problem is that management normally cannot assess the results of its promotional expenditures. A firm may add ten salesmen or increase its trade-show budget by $20,000 a year, but no one can determine what increase in sales or profits is to be expected, nor can anyone measure the relative values of the two expenditures. The growing number of companies using mathematical methods and a long-range budgeting approach in advertising budgets may be presaging a breakthrough in this problem area.[10] Promotional activities usually are budgeted as current operating expenses, implying that their benefits are used up immediately.

---

10 For a review of past, current, and future mathematical approaches to the budgeting of advertisng, see Paul E. Green, Patrick J. Robinson, and Peter T. FitzRoy, "Advertising Expenditure Models: State of the Art and Prospects." *Business Horizons*, Summer, 1966, pp. 72-80; see also Robert M. Fulmer, "How Should Advertising and Sales Promotion Funds Be Allocated?" *Journal of Marketing*, October, 1967, pp. 8-11; and Donald C. Marschner, "Theory versus Practice in Allocating Advertising Money," *Journal of Business*, July, 1967, pp. 286-302.

Joel Dean and others have proposed that advertising (and presumably other promotional efforts) should perhaps be treated as a capital investment. This change in point of view would have an impact on the evaluation of promotion's effectiveness, on test marketing, and on decision making in other areas.

In determining how much money should be appropriated for the entire promotional program, management should consider promotional costs in light of the influence the program will have on production costs. Here is another instance where it is better to employ the total cost approach instead of basing decisions on a fragmented cost analysis of individual activities. To illustrate, assume that a firm is operating in the declining stage of its cost curve. That is, as output increases the unit costs of production decrease. By increasing its promotional appropriation, the company may be able to increase its total sales to the point where the reduction in unit production costs more than offsets the increased promotional expenditures.

METHODS OF DETERMINING APPROPRIATION

There are four basic methods of determining the budget allocation for promotion. They are frequently discussed in connection with the advertising appropriation alone, but they may also be applied to the total promotional appropriation.

Relation to income. The promotional appropriation may be related in some way to company income. First, the expenditures may be set as a percentage of past or anticipated *sales*. Second, the appropriation may be based on a percentage of net or gross *profit*. Third, some businesses prefer to budget a fixed amount of money per *unit* of past or expected future sales. Manufacturers of products which have a high unit value and a low rate of turnover (automobiles or appliances, for example) frequently use this last method. Fruit growers' cooperative associations assess member growers a certain amount per case of fruit sold through the cooperative.

The percentage-of-sales method is probably the most widely used of all those discussed here. It has achieved broad acceptance because it is simple to calculate. It also sets the cost in relation to sales income and thus tends to act as a variable expense rather than as a noncontrollable fixed expenditure. Actually the method is unsound and logically inconsistent. By setting promotional expenditures for one year on the basis of sales in the preceding year, management is saying that promotion is a *result* of sales, when, in fact, it is a *cause* of sales. Even when promotion is set as a percentage of future sales, this method is logically indefensible. By forecasting future sales and the setting the promotional appropriation, management is still considering advertising and personal selling to be a result of sales. If sales depend upon promotion, as is truly the case, then they cannot be forecast until the promotional appropriation is determined. Another undesirable result of this method is that promotional expenditures will be reduced just when sales are declining. If the reasons for a sales decline are not clear, management can compound its difficulties by withdrawing promotional support at that time. Experience shows that a better course of action is to maintain the level of promotional activity, even if profits drop temporarily, until the basic causes of the sales decline can be determined and corrected.[11]

---

11 For some research findings illustrating this point, see A. C. Neilsen, Jr., "Many Measurements Available to Increase Advertising Effectivness," *Media/scope*, September, 1965, p. 72.

Task or objective. A much sounder basis for determining the promotional budget is first to decide what tasks the promotional program is intended to accomplish and then to determine what the cost of promotion must be. Various forms of this method are widely used today.[12] The task method forces management to define realistically and in detail the goals of its promotional program. This method also involves management in long-run, rather than year-to-year, planning. Sometimes this approach is called the "buildup method" because of the way it operates. For example, a company may set as one goal the entry into a new geographic market. The executives decide that this venture will require ten additional salesmen. Compensation and expenses of these salesmen will cost a total of $170,000 per year. Salary for an additional sales supervisor and expenses for extra office and administrative needs will cost $20,000. Thus in the personal selling part of the promotional mix, an extra $190,000 must be appropriated. Similar estimates may be made for the anticipated cost of advertising, sales promotion, and other promotional tools to be used in connection with the goal of entering a new territory.

Use of all funds available. A new company frequently plows all possible available funds into its promotional program. Management may expect to wait one to five years before it will earn a profit and be able to budget for its sales program in a different manner.

Follow competition. A weak method of determining the promotional appropriation, but one which is used enough to be noted here, is to match the promotional expenditures of competitors. Sometimes only one competitor is followed. In other cases management will have access to industry averages through its trade association, and these will become company bench marks. The system is weak on two counts at least. First, a firm's competitors may be just as much in the dark as the firm itself, and second, the firm's needs and goals may be quite different from those of its competition.

SALES PROMOTION

In Chapter 9, "merchandising" and "sales promotion" were called the two most loosely used terms in the marketing vocabulary. In fact, the sales promotion manager of a major oil company once referred to sales promotion as "muddled, misused, and misunderstood."[13] Many businessmen use the terms synonymously with "advertising" or "promotion" in total. Today in the field of marketing, how-

---

12 In the study referred to in the preceding footnote, most respondents stated that "the job to be done" was the single most important determinant of their advertising budgets. Yet in practice most of the firms began building their budgets with a set figure—usually either a percentage increase over last year's budget or a percentage of next year's sales forecast. Few companies actually first determined their advertising objectives, then planned the program to reach these goals, and finally calculated the cost of this program.

13 See William R. Kelly, "Muddled . . . Misused . . . Misunderstood . . . That's Sales Promotion!" *Sales Management,* Jan. 15, 1954, p. 36. Sixteen years later the same author conducted a comparative survey and found (1) that the role of the sales promotion manager has changed markedly, but (2) that the field of sales promotion as a marketing activity is still vaguely defined and organized. See "Sales Promotion: Super Success Is Still To Come." *Sales Management,* June 1, 1970, p. 25.

ever, we are beginning to get agreement that sales promotion is a separately distinguishable field.[14]

What then is sales promotion? The American Marketing Association says its preferred definition is, "those marketing activities, other than personal selling, advertising, and publicity, that stimulate consumer purchasing and dealer effectiveness, such as displays, shows and expositions, demonstrations, and various nonrecurrent selling efforts not in the ordinary routine."[15]

In what ways are sales promotion and advertising different? First, except for direct mail, advertising deals with media owned and controlled by others, while sales promotion tries to inform and persuade groups through tools and methods controlled by the company itself. Sales promotion deals with nonrecurring and nonroutine matters, in contrast to advertising or personal selling. Finally, while most companies could not exist profitably without advertising or personal selling, they could do without sales promotion. Frey called sales promotion the "plus" ingredient in the marketing mix.

In effect, a major function of sales promotion is to serve as a bridge between advertising and personal selling—to supplement and coordinate efforts in these two areas. Not only are we seeing an increase in the stature of sales promotion, but also the trend is to integrate it as a part of the total marketing strategy. Often, for example, it is being introduced at the inception of a campaign, and not tacked on afterward.

IMPORTANCE OF SALES PROMOTION

There is a saying in retailing that "it is the final three feet which count." This refers specifically to the distance from the retail salesclerk to the consumer, but the meaning can be broadened to suggest the importance of all activities at the point of purchase, whether it is a purchase by an ultimate consumer, middleman, or industrial user. Firms "have spent millions on determining the most effective techniques and appeals for luring the prospect into the dealer's place of business . . . but they have failed to follow through by studying how to get him to buy—and to buy *their* products—once he is inside the store."[16]

Today much consumer dissatisfaction with respect to retail selling could be alleviated by a good sales-promotional program. The growing use of self-service, automatic vending, and other sales methods where salesmen are not used also points up the need for sales promotion. Sales-promotional devices are often the only promotional materials available at the point of purchase. Advertising media reach potential customers at their homes, at their places of business, or in their travels. When the time for buying arrives, the impact of the advertisements may have worn

---

14 For a more detailed treatment of sales promotion, see John F. Luick and William L. Ziegler, *Sales Promotion and Modern Merchandising*, McGraw-Hill Book Company, New York, 1968.

15 Committee on Definitions, *Marketing Definitions: A Glossary of Marketing Terms*, American Marketing Association, Chicago, 1960, p. 20. In this set of definitions, however, the American Marketing Association also observes that in retailing, sales promotion is interpreted to cover "all methods of stimulating customer purchasing, including personal selling, advertising, and publicity." Thus in retailing, "sales promotion" is used in a broad sense and is virtually synonymous with "promotion," as the term is used in this book and also by most manufacturers.

16 Robert N. McMurry "How to Win or Lose Sales at the Point of Purchase," *Journal of Marketing*, July, 1959, p. 41.

off (or the prospect may not even have seen the advertisement), but sales-promotional devices at the point of purchase inform, remind, or otherwise stimulate the buyer. People who see the promotional devices are excellent prospects. They are usually in a buying frame of mind, or they would not be there.[17]

SERVICES RENDERED BY SALES PROMOTION

The sales promotion department of a manufacturer may work with many different groups—consumers, dealers and distributors, or other sections of the marketing department. Similarly, retailers engage in sales-promotional activities aimed at consumers. A manufacturer's sales-promotional program which is directed toward the consumer may be divided into two groups—activities intended to *educate* or *inform* the consumer and those intended to *stimulate* him. To inform consumers, companies will prepare booklets, give demonstrations, and offer free consulting services. To stimulate consumers, many firms give away samples and premiums or distribute cents-off coupons.[18] Others conduct contests, offering prizes for the best statement which tells in 25 words or less why the consumer likes the given product. These various activities are intended to get the consumer to use the product or (as in a contest) to get him to think of all the possible reasons why he likes it.

Services rendered to dealers and distributors include such things as conducting training programs for the middlemen's salesmen, giving managerial advice, and installing displays. In summary, a manufacturer tries to increase the dealers' interest in the product and to enhance their effectiveness as merchants.

Within the manufacturer's marketing department, the sales promotion division can perform services for the personal selling, advertising, and marketing research groups. Sales promotion people can prepare sales manuals, demonstration kits, and other selling aids used by the salesmen. Also, in the field, the sales force can concentrate on product selling while the sales promotion men do all the missionary work with dealers. The marketing research department can get help in field survey work. The sales promotion department can aid the advertising people by preparing displays and other point-of-purchase advertising materials.

In conclusion, a marketing manager should consider the role which sales promotion can play in a marketing mix. This activity should not be submerged in departments which are concerned primarily with advertising or the personal sales force. Once marketing executives become aware of the value of sales promotion work, they will undoubtedly use this tool more effectively to supplement the work of the marketing division. At the present time, unfortunately, much remains to be done to determine the most effective use of sales promotion in a company's marketing program and to measure the results of using these promotional tools.[19]

---

[17] See "A P.O.P. (point-of-purchase) Art Form that Turns Shoppers On," *Business Week,* Jan. 8, 1972, p. 36.

[18] There has been a recent resurgence in the use of coupons by Canadian manufacturers. For more on this topic, see "Coupons Gaining Ground, says Neilsen," *Marketing,* August 4, 1975, p. 5.

[19] For conflicting points of view regarding whether we can quantitatively measure the effect which sales promotion has on sales, see John H. Weber, "Can Results of Sales Promotion Be Predicted?" *Journal of Marketing,* January, 1963, pp. 15-19; Milton J. Margolis, "How to Evaluate Field Sales Promotion," *Journal of Marketing,* July, 1963, pp. 42-46; and Lee Adler, "Sales Promotion Effectiveness *Can* Be Measured," *Journal of Marketing,* October, 1963, pp. 69-70.

QUESTIONS AND PROBLEMS

1. What is the difference between selling and marketing?
2. What are the relationships and differences between the following?
   a. Promotion   c. Sales promotion
   b. Advertising   d. Personal selling
3. Explain and illustrate a communications system using the following situations:
   a. A teen-age girl trying to sell her father on the idea that she should get contact lenses instead of glasses
   b. A salesman talking to a prospect about buying a small electric automobile as a second car in the family
4. Identify the central idea—the theme—in some current promotional campaigns.
5. Explain how the *nature of the market* would affect the promotional mix for the following products:
   a. Oil-well drilling equipment   c. Golf clubs
   b. Plywood   d. Cigarettes
6. Explain how the promotional mix is likely to be affected by the life cycle stage in which each of the following products is situated.
   a. Portable electric typewriters   c. Freeze-dried coffee
   b. Telephoto telephones
7. Using Borden's criteria, evaluate the advertisability of each of the following products. Assume that sufficient funds are available in each case.
   a. Car batteries   c. Wall mirrors
   b. Mattresses   d. Small power tools
8. Can you name any products which are advertised heavily but which do not meet the criterion of having hidden qualities?
9. Explain why personal selling is, or is not, likely to be the main ingredient in the promotional mix for each of the following products:
   a. Life insurance being considered by a young, newly married couple
   b. Living-room furniture
   c. Burglar alarm system for industrial plant
   d. Metal tennis rackets
10. Explain why retailer promotional efforts should or should not be stressed in the promotional mix for the following:
    a. Expensive men's suits sold through exclusive distribution
    b. Chiquita-brand bananas
    c. A line of expensive cosmetics for women
    d. Steel-belted radial tires
11. If a manufacturer heavily emphasizes advertising to the consumer, is dealer promotion still needed for:
    a. Car batteries   c. Alka-Seltzer
    b. Skis   d. Expensive men's suits
12. Why is the percentage-of-sales method so widely used to determine the promotional appropriation when, in fact, most authorities recognize the task or objective method as the most desirable one?
13. Visit a supermarket, clothing store, and hardware store, and then make a list of all the sales-promotional tools or devices which you observed in each store. Which of these devices do you feel are particularly effective?

14. Is sales promotion effective for selling expensive consumer products such as houses, automobiles, or backyard swimming pools? Is your answer the same for expensive industrial products?
15. Explain how sales promotion can be used to offset weaknesses in retail salesmanship.

MANAGEMENT OF PERSONAL SELLING

Salesmen have long been featured in song and story; they have been alternately praised and ridiculed. Selling is essential to the health and well-being of our economic system, and it probably offers more job opportunities than any other single vocation today. Yet personal selling is frequently criticized, and it is very hard to attract qualified young people into selling jobs.

NATURE AND IMPORTANCE OF PERSONAL SELLING

The goal of all marketing efforts is to increase profitable sales by offering want satisfaction to the market over the long run. Personal selling is by far the major promotional method used to reach this goal. The number of people employed in all aspects of advertising in Canada is approximately 50,000. In personal selling, the number is more than a million. In many companies personal selling is the largest single operating expense, often equaling 8 to 15 percent of net sales. Advertising costs average 1 to 3 percent of sales. Expenditures for salespeople's salaries, commissions, and travel expenses; the costs of operating sales branches; and the expenses of managing these salespeople all add up to a tidy sum.

Personal selling is the most important element in the marketing mix, according to a survey among the top executives (not the marketing executives) in some four hundred large and successful firms. These people also reported that the number and importance of sales jobs were increasing in their firms. Most of the companies (63 percent) had increased the share of the marketing budget allocated to personal selling since 1960. Furthermore, about one-half of the companies expected to increase this proportion still more in future years.[1]

RELATIVE MERITS

Personal selling consists of individual, personal communication, in contrast to the mass, impersonal communication of advertising, sales promotion, and the other promotional tools. Consequently, compared with these other tools, personal selling has the advantage of being more flexible in operation. Salespeople can tailor their sales presentations to fit the needs, motives, and behavior of individual customers. Also, salespeople can see the customer's reaction to a particular sales approach and then make the necessary adjustments right on the spot. A second merit of personal selling is that it permits a minimum of wasted effort. In advertising, much of the cost is devoted to sending the message to people who are in no way real prospects. In personal selling, a company has an opportunity to pinpoint its market target far more effectively than can be done with any other promotional device.

In most situations, personal selling can be used to make the actual sale. Advertisements can attract attention and arouse desire, but usually they do not get buying action and complete the transfer of title. Finally, salespeople can perform for management many other services which are not strictly selling jobs. They can collect credit information, reflect customer attitudes, and relay complaints to management. Some firms use their sales representatives to handle adjustments, perform major repair services, and act as fieldmen for marketing research projects.

If personal selling has a major limitation, it is its high cost. Even though the use of salesmen enables a business to reach its market with a minimum of wasted effort, the cost of developing and operating a sales force is high. Another disadvantage is that personal selling is often limited by the company's inability to get the caliber of people needed to do the job. At the retail level many firms have abandoned their sales forces and shifted to self-service for this very reason.

NATURE OF THE SALES JOB

The sales job of today is quite different from that of years gone by. The old type of salesman—the cigar-smoking, back-slapping, joke-telling person epitomized by Harold Hill in *The Music Man* and Willy Loman in *Death of a Salesman*—generally has disappeared, and his talents are not especially desired in today's economy.[2]

True, high-pressure selling still exists and may always have a role in some fields, but it is no longer typical. Instead, as part of the implementation of the marketing

---

1 *Penetration*, vol. 5, no. 2, 1966 (publication of Klein Institute for Aptitude Testing, the sponsor of this study, which was conducted by Prof. D. J. Duncan). Findings also were reported in "Top Executives Rank Salesmanship Tops, Study Shows," *Sales Management*, Mar. 18, 1966, p. 120.

2 See Donald L. Thompson, "Stereotype of the Salesman," *Harvard Business Review*, January-February, 1972, pp. 20 ff; then by way of contrast, see "The New Supersalesman: Wired for Success," *Business Week*, Jan. 6, 1973, p. 44; Carl Rieser, "The Salesman Isn't Dead—He's Different," *Fortune*, November, 1962, p. 124; and J. N. Bauman, "Rebirth of a Salesman," *Dun's Review*, March, 1968, p. 45.

concept in a firm, we see a new type of salesperson—a territorial marketing manager. Rather than just pushing whatever the factory has to sell, our new breed of salesperson interprets customers' wants and relays them back to the firm so that appropriate products may be developed. They engage in a *total* selling job—missionary selling, servicing customers, selling the full line of products, being territorial profit managers, and acting as a mirror of the market as they feed back marketing information.

In this new position, the salesperson occupies many roles with many divergent role partners, which makes heavy emotional demands on him.[3] Among other roles he is a persuader, service person, information gatherer, expediter, coordinator, problem definer, traveler, display arranger, and customer ego builder. His operations are socially, psychologically, and physically independent of the usual worker-boss relationship. In this performance, the salesperson faces role conflicts of identification and advocacy. He must identify in shifting fashion first with his company and then with the customer. In do doing, there are conflicts regarding whose position—the company's or the customer's—he is advocating. The several groups with whom the salesperson interacts often have differing and conflicting expectations.

The salesperson's job, then, involves a wide range of behaviors, flexibility in behavior, and fluctuating intensity of social contact. The emotional and interactional demands on a salesperson are great because of the high level of role conflict and because he must handle the behavioral ambiguities pretty much on his own. If management can determine the temperamental dimensions—that is, the emotional and interactional demands—of a given sales job and then weave these into the existing job requirements and selection devices, the results of the total selection effort certainly should be more successful than in the past.

SALES JOBS ARE DIFFERENT FROM OTHER JOBS

We dwell on the nature of a sales job not only because it is so important to the economic health of a firm, but also because it is quite different from other jobs. Salespersons represent their company to the outside world. Consequently, opinions of a company and its products often are formed from impressions left by the sales force. The public ordinarily will not judge a firm by its office or factory workers. In fact salespersons often are blamed for mistakes made elsewhere in the firm only because these people are so visible and available.

Other employees usually work under close and constant supervisory control, whereas salespersons typically operate with little or no direct supervision of their activities. As another differentiating feature, most nonselling employees can perform well with relatively less stimulation. To be successful in many selling tasks, however, salespersons must work hard physically and mentally, be creative, persistent, and show great initiative—and all this requires a high degree of motivation.

Salespersons probably need more tact, diplomacy, and social poise than other employees in the organization. Many sales jobs require the person to mix socially with customers, who frequently are people of high rank. The salesperson must display considerable social intelligence in dealing with buyers.

---

3 This paragraph and the following one are adapted from James A. Belasco, "The Salesman's Role Revisited," *Journal of Marketing,* April, 1966, pp. 6-11; see also Richard T. Hise, "Conflict in the Salesman's Role," *University of Washington Business Review,* Winter, 1968. pp. 52-61.

Salespersons are among the few employees authorized to spend company funds. They have the responsibility for proper use of money for entertainment, room, food, transportation, and other business expenses. Their effectiveness in discharging this responsibility can have a significant influence on marketing costs and profits.

Sales jobs frequently require a considerable amount of traveling and much time spent away from home and family. Being in the field puts a salesperson in enemy territory, where he deals with an apparently endless stream of customers who seem determined not to buy his products. These mental stresses and disappointments coupled with the physical demands of long hours, much traveling, strange beds and food, and perhaps heavy sample cases, all combine to require a degree of mental toughness and physical stamina rarely demanded in other types of jobs. Selling is hard work!

WIDE VARIETY OF SALES JOBS

No two selling jobs are alike. Even when sales jobs are grouped or classified on some basis, we find that the types of jobs and the requirements needed to fill them cover a very wide spectrum. The job of a soft drink driver salesperson who calls in routine fashion on a group of retail stores is in a different world from that of a computer salesperson who sells to an automobile manufacturer a system for retrieving and disseminating information. A salesperson for a cosmetics manufacturer selling door-to-door has a job only remotely related to that of an airplane manufacturer selling a fleet of executive-type aircraft to large firms.

Perhaps one useful way to classify the many different types of sales jobs is to array them on the basis of the creative skills required in the job, moving from the very simple to the highly complex, as, for example, the following:[4]

1. Positions in which the job is primarily to deliver the product—e.g., driver salesman for soft drinks, milk, or fuel oil. The selling responsibilities are secondary. Good service and a pleasant personality may lead to more sales, but few of these people originate many sales.
2. Positions in which the salesperson is primarily an *inside* order taker—e.g., the retail clerk standing behind a counter. The customer comes to the salesclerk. Most of the customers have already decided to buy; the salesclerk only serves them. He or she may use suggestion selling, but ordinarily cannot do much more.
3. Positions in which the salesperson is primarily an *outside* order taker, going to the customer in the field—e.g., packinghouse, soap, or spice salesperson who calls on retail food stores. In his contacts with chain-store personnel, he actually may be discouraged from doing any hard selling. That task is left to executives higher in the organization. Although good service and a pleasant personality may help him, he does little creative selling.
4. Positions in which the salesperson is not expected or permitted to solicit an order. His job is to build goodwill, perform promotional activities, or provide services for the customers. This is the missionary salesperson for a distiller, for example, or the detail salesperson for an ethical pharmaceutical manufacturer.
5. Positions in which the major emphasis is placed on the salesperson's technical product knowledge—e.g., the sales engineer.
6. Positions that demand creative selling of *tangible* products, such as vacuum cleaners, airplanes, encyclopedias, or oil-well drilling equipment. Here the salesperson's job is

---

4 Adpated from Robert N. McMurry, "The Mystique of Super-salesmanship," *Harvard Business Review,* March-April, 1961, p. 114.

often more difficult because the customer may not be aware of his need for the product, or he may not realize how the new product can satisfy his wants better than the product he is now using. When the product is of a technical nature, this category may overlap that of the sales engineer.

7. Positions that require creative selling of *intangibles,* such as insurance, advertising services, consulting services, or communications systems. Intangibles are typically more difficult to sell because they are less readily demonstrated.

DEVELOPMENT AND OPERATION OF A SALES FORCE

SELECTING THE SALES FORCE

As explained in Chapter 2, it is the authors' contention that staffing is the most important of all managerial activities. In a promotional program the value of good selection is seen in several ways. First, since it is very difficult to find good salespeople, it is essential that the selection program maximize the opportunity of getting the type of person needed. Second, sales managers are no better than salespeople. No matter how well managed a sales force may be, if it is distinctly inferior in quality to that of a competitor, the competitor will win out. Third, if a sales force is well selected, many other tasks in sales management such as training and supervision are made easier. Also, selling costs will be reduced because turnover rates will be lower. In addition to its many other advantages, a well-selected sales force should be more productive and should build better customer relations than a poorly chosen group.

Scope of selection task. The three major steps in sales-force selection are:

1. Determine the number and type of people wanted. This step includes the preparation of a written job description. Management must also determine specifically what qualifications are needed to fill the job as it is described.
2. Recruit an adequate number of applicants.
3. Select the qualified persons from among the applicants.

What makes a good salesperson? The key to success in the first step is to establish the proper hiring specifications, just as if the company were purchasing equipment or supplies instead of manpower. To establish these specifications, management must first know what the particular sales job entails. This calls for a detailed job analysis and a written description. It should include specific statements regarding the title of the job, organizational relationships, job duties, and applicant qualifications. This written description will later be invaluable in training, compensation, and supervision.

Determining the qualifications needed to fill the job is the most difficult part of the selection function. We still really do not know all the characteristics that make a good salesperson. We do not know to what quantitative degree each should be possessed, nor to what extent an abundance of one can offset the lack of another.[5]

Over the years many myths have arisen regarding what traits lead to success in selling. A good sales representative was supposed to be aggressive, extroverted, ar-

---

5 A very good review of the characteristics that have been associated with a high level of success in sales positions may be found in Jacques C. Bourgeois, "Sales Force Personnel Selection: A Review," unpublished paper, School of Commerce, Carleton University, Ottawa, 1975.

ticulate, well-groomed, and endowed with a great physique. Yet in actual fact many outstanding salespeople have been mild-mannered and introverted. Other good ones have been somewhat inarticulate and carelessly dressed. Many good salespeople are of average or even small size.

While the search for what makes a good salesperson may be an impossible dream, still the quest continues. As one approach to the problem, some companies have analyzed the personal histories of their past sales representatives to determine traits common to the successful or unsuccessful performers. Sometimes it helps to interview people when they leave the company to see whether meaningful patterns can be uncovered.

One psychologist who has worked extensively in sales management concluded that people who are outstanding sales successes inevitably possess these traits:[6]

1. A high level of energy
2. Abounding self-confidence
3. A chronic hunger for money, status, and the good things in life
4. A well-established habit of industry
5. The habit of perseverance—each objection or resistance is a challenge
6. A natural tendency to be competitive

Moreover, McMurry maintains that the *sine qua non* of sales success is an intangible, largely intuitive, sensitivity to people. These supersalespeople are, in effect, constant and habitual "wooers." They have an inherent flair for winning the acceptance of others.

Unfortunately, many of these wooers have what psychologists would call "infantile" or even "pathological" personalities. Their wooing is a compulsive need to win and hold the acceptance and affections of others. Often these salespeople are basically passive and dependent persons, craving love and acceptance and continually battling to prove themselves. They may feel worthless and rejected. Then the hostility in them motivates them to get even by selling. The need to win love and respect combined with the hostility results in an ambivalent love-hate attitude toward customers and managerial authority. The salesmen need these other people, but at the same time they resent them. Supersalespeople frequently are difficult to supervise and control.

In another approach to the question of what makes a good salesperson, Mayer and Greenberg concluded after some years of research that two personality traits are basic to sales success:[7]

1. Empathy—the ability to identify with the customer and his feelings
2. Ego-drive—the personal need to make a sale, as a measure of self-fulfillment and not just for the money

Recruiting applicants. A planned system for recruiting a sufficient number of applicants is the next step in selection. A good recruiting system has these characteristics:

---

6 *Ibid.*, pp. 117-118. See also Robert N. McMurry and James S. Arnold, *How to Build a Dynamic Sales Organization*, McGraw-Hill Book Company, New York, 1968, pp. 2-9.

7 David Mayer and Herbert M. Greenberg, "What Makes a Good Salesman?" *Harvard Business Review*, July-August, 1964, pp. 119-125.

1. It is operating continuously, not just when there are vacancies on the sales force.
2. It is systematic, reaching and exploiting all appropriate sources of applicants.
3. It provides a continuous flow of qualified applicants in greater numbers than the company can use.
4. It is phased so that mechanical, initial steps can be delegated and will not require a high-level executive's time.

Matching applicants with hiring specifications. The third step involves two tasks. First management must establish a system of measuring applicants against predetermined standards. Then it must activate the system so as to select the necessary number of people who have the proper qualifications. Sales managers should use all available selection tools in their effort to determine which applicants possess the desired qualifications. These tools include application blanks, interviews, references, credit reports, psychological tests, and physical examinations. Probably all companies use application blanks. They serve as records of personal histories and may be used to implement interviewing. Some companies assign scores to various answers on a blank and total the applicant's score. If this score is below a predetermined level, the applicant will usually be eliminated.

The interview is the other most widely used selection device. Virtually no salesperson is hired without one personal interview, and it is desirable to have several. Ideally these should be conducted in different physical settings and by different people. This should help to reduce the effect of one person's possible bias, to get other people's opinions, and to see how the recruit acts under different conditions. Usually an interview can help an employer to determine how badly the applicant wants the job, whether the company can assure him the success he wants, and whether he will work to his fullest capacity. Patterned or preplanned interviews are usually considered most desirable because they overcome many weaknesses found in the typical interviewing process.

Many companies now make use of psychological testing in the recruitment of salespersons and some research effort has been devoted to determining which specific personality traits are good predictors of sales success. One recent study showed that successful salespersons scored higher than persons in non-sales occupations on such personality scales as extraversion, dogmatism, need for affiliation, dominance, exhibitionism, social recognition, aggression, and opinion leadership. The salespersons scored significantly lower, however, on such traits as abasement, succorance, and social responsibility. This same study hypothesized that successful salespersons also would score higher on a scale designed to measure outgoingness or willingness to engage in interpersonal communication. A scale to measure this personality trait was developed and the results of the study showed that salespersons indeed exhibit a greater propensity to communicate.[8]

ASSIMILATING NEW SALESPEOPLE INTO THE ORGANIZATION

When salespeople are hired, management should pay close attention to the task of integrating them into the company family. Often this step is overlooked entirely. The people are carefully selected and wined and dined to recruit them into the firm.

---

8 K. B. Wong and J. G. Barnes, "Development of a Scale to Measure Propensity to Communicate: Application to Recruitment of Salespersons," *Proceedings*, Canadian Association of Administrative Sciences, Edmonton, 1975.

Then as soon as they are hired, the honeymoon is over, and they are left to shift for themselves. In such cases people often become discouraged and may even quit. A wise sales manager will recognize that the new people know very little about the details of the job, their fellow workers, or their status in the firm. A vital need exists to maintain open two-way channels of communication between new sales personnel and management.

TRAINING THE SALES FORCE

Another major aspect of operating a sales force includes developing and conducting a training program. All salespeople, even experienced ones, need some training periodically. Training involves the following problem areas; in each instance, decisions will be based to a considerable extent upon the kind of training program involved—whether it is an indoctrination program, a refresher course, or some other type.

1. What are the goals of the program? In general, the aim of the program is to increase productivity and stimulate the sales force. In addition, executives must determine what specific ends they wish to accomplish. For instance, the goal may be to increase sales of high-margin items, to improve prospecting methods to develop new accounts, or to introduce the new season's line of products.

2. Who should do the training? The training program may be conducted by the line sales executives, by a company staff training department, or by outside training specialists.

3. What should be the content of the program? A well-rounded sales training program should cover three general topics: product knowledge, information about company policies, and selling techniques. Salespeople must know everything possible about their own products and about competitive goods. Usually these subjects are covered in initial training programs, and information regarding new products is included in refresher courses and continuous training programs. The job description will provide an excellent guide to the content of the program.

   A sales force should also know the company history, the executives, and the policies concerning pricing, discounts, returns, delivery, guarantees, minimum orders, etc. Finally, new salesmen especially need to be instructed in whatever selling techniques are required for the particular product.

4. When and where should training be done? Some companies believe in fully training people before they go into the field. Others let people prove that they have some desire and ability to sell and then bring them back into the office for intensive training. Both points of view have merit.

   Firms may employ either centralized or decentralized training programs. A centralized program may involve a periodic meeting which all salespeople attend, or the company may employ an organized school conducted on a continuing or periodic basis. A decentralized program may be held in branch offices, in traveling sales clinics, or during on-the-job training. Decentralized programs generally cost less than centralized programs. They do not take people away from their work for long and do not disrupt home office routine. The trainees can learn right in the environment where they work and where their problems occur. The big problem with decentralized programs is that the quality of instruction is often inferior.

5. What instructional methods should be used? The lecture method can be employed to inform trainees about company history and practices. Demonstrations may be used to impart product knowledge or selling techniques. Round-table discussions are often employed to analyze problems encountered by the sales force in their work. Role playing is an excellent device for training a person in proper selling techniques. On-the-job training can be used in almost any phase of the program.

COMPENSATING SALESPEOPLE

To compensate their sales force, companies may offer both financial and non-financial rewards. The nonfinancial rewards involve giving people an opportunity for advancement, satisfying their need for recognition of their efforts, and giving them a feeling of belonging. Financial rewards may take the form of direct monetary payment or of indirect monetary payment (paid vacations, pensions, and insurance plans).

Before designing a specific plan, management should understand the broad goals of a sound pay arrangement. It should enable a company to attract, keep, and develop desirable people. It should correlate a person's rewards with his efforts and results, particularly results. A sound plan should enable management to control the activities of the sales force. It should ensure proper treatment of customers. To reach these general goals, the specific plan should (1) provide for a steady income as well as an incentive income, (2) be flexible and yet easy to understand, (3) be economical to administer, and (4) be competitive and still be fair to management and the salespeople. In designing a compensation plan, management should, by referring to the job description, relate the pay plan to the sales job. As much as possible—and this is difficult—the plan should be based upon job elements which are controllable by the salespeople and are also quantitatively measurable.

Establishing a compensation system really involves making decisions on two general problems—the *level* of compensation and the *method* of compensation. The level refers to the total dollar income which a salesperson earns over a period of time. The method of compensation refers to the system or plan by which the salesperson will reach the intended level. The level is influenced by the type of person required for the job and the competitive rate of pay for similar positions.

There are three widely used methods of compensating a sales force: straight salary, straight commission, and a combination plan. Today, well over one-half of the firms in the country use some kind of combination plan.

The straight-salary plan offers a maximum of security and stability of earnings for a salesperson. Management is in a better position to control and direct the activities of the salespeople because they are paid the same amount each month regardless of what tasks they perform. Turnover is usually minimized. Under this arrangement salespeople can consider the customers' best interests. A commonly stated drawback of the plan is that it does not offer adequate incentive. Also, it is a fixed cost unrelated to sales revenue. Determining the proper salary level is often a problem. Moreover, unless management provides a high quality of supervision and control, the company wastes the advantage of being able to direct people under this plan. Straight-salary systems are typically used for compensating new salespeople and missionary salespeople, when opening new territories, or when the sale involves a technical product and a lengthy period of negotiations.

A straight commission tends to have just the opposite merits and limitations. It provides tremendous incentive for the salespeople, and the commission costs can be related directly to sales or gross margin. Sales representatives have more freedom in their work, and their level of income is determined largely by their own efforts. On the other hand, it is difficult to control the people and to get them to do a fully balanced sales job. It is particularly difficult to get them to perform tasks for which no commission is paid. There is always the danger that they will oversell a customer or otherwise incur his ill will. Straight-commission plans may work well if:

1. Great incentive is needed to get the sales.
2. Very little nonselling missionary work is required.
3. The company is financially weak and must relate its compensation expenses directly to sales or gross margin.
4. The sales force prefers the plan, or it is quite common in the industry.
5. The company is unable to supervise the sales force.

The ideal way to develop a combination plan is to balance the best features of both the straight-salary and the straight-commission plans with as few of their drawbacks as possible.

An important element in a sales force's financial affairs is the reimbursement for business expenses which they incur in traveling or selling. The importance of salespeople's expense control is difficult to overrate. With shrinking profit margins and higher break-even points in a company's operations, many administrators are justly concerned over the expense items incurred by the sales force. It is essential that sales executives develop a plan to control these costs and reimburse the salespeople for them. In principle, a salesperson should not make or lose money because of his expense account, nor should he forgo any beneficial sales activities because he will not be adequately reimbursed for the attendant expenses. Most firms pay salespeople for these expenses under an expense account arrangement. Ordinarily, arrangements for reimbursing salespeople for these expenses should be separated from the compensation plan. A substantial number of companies, however, let the salespeople pay all their own expenses from their total salaries or commissions.

SUPERVISING SALESPEOPLE

Another management responsibility involved in operating a sales force is to provide adequate supervision. This activity can serve both as a method of continuation training and as a device to ensure that company policies and practices are being carried out. One of the values of supervision is that it affords a vertical two-way channel of communication between management and the sales force. Executives must determine how much supervision is needed to avoid either over- or under-supervising. There is probably little doubt that personal supervision is most effective. This may be done by field supervisors, branch managers, or home office sales executives. Other methods of supervision include the use of correspondence, reports, and sales meetings.

EVALUATION OF SALESPEOPLE'S PERFORMANCE

Part of the task of managing a field selling force should include the job of establishing and operating an orderly procedure for evaluating the efforts of the salespeople. Until an executive knows what his sales force is doing, he is in no position to make constructive proposals for improvement. By studying salespeople's activities and by establishing standards for what constitutes good performance, management should be able to upgrade the sales force's efforts in general.

By analyzing the characteristic activities of good and poor salespeople, management may be able to identify the factors that lead to sales success. Management may find, for example, that the top ten salespeople average 20 percent more calls per week than the poorest ten. It may find that the successful ones spend more time giving managerial advice to retailers and training retail clerks.

Performance analysis can help the salespeople improve their own efforts. Salespeople with a poor sales record may have known for a long time that they are doing something wrong but be unable to determine what it is because they have no objective standards by which to measure their performances.

Performance evaluation can be an aid in determining what should be included in a training program, and it can help in sales supervision. A supervisor who knows some of the specific strengths and weaknesses of each salesperson can do a better job of directing and training. Performance evaluation can also help management determine salary increases and promotion for the sales force.

BASES FOR EVALUATION

Both quantitative and qualitative factors should be used as the bases for performance evaluation. The quantitative bases generally have the advantage of, or capacity for, being more specific and objective. Qualitative factors, unfortunately, must rely too much on the subjective judgment of the evaluators. For either of the two types of appraisal factors, however, management has the difficult task of setting the standards against which performance can be measured.

Quantitative bases. Sales performance should be evaluated on the basis of both input (or efforts) and output (or results). A person's productive effectiveness is a concept that involves the relationship between the two—output as measured by sales volume, gross margin, etc., and input as indicated by call rate, expenses incurred, nonselling activities, etc.

In a performance evaluation, the importance of output factors is readily recognized. Sometimes, however, the value of input factors is underestimated. Actually, the input factors usually are critical in locating trouble spots. If a person's output performance (average order size, gross margin, etc.) is unsatisfactory, very often the cause lies in the handling of the various input factors over which the salesperson has control.

Some *output* factors which are ordinarily quite useful as evaluation bases are as follows:

1. Sales volume—by products, customer groups, mail, telephone, etc.
2. Sales volume as a percentage of quota or territorial potential
3. Gross margin by product line, customer group, and order size
4. Orders:
   a. Number of orders
   b. Average size (dollar volume) of order
   c. Batting average (orders divided by calls)
5. Accounts:
   a. Percentage of accounts sold
   b. Number of new accounts
   c. Number of lost accounts

Some useful *input* factors to measure are:

1. Calls per day (call rate)
2. Days worked

3. Direct selling expense, in total and as a percentage of sales volume or expense quota
4. Nonselling activities:
   a. Advertising displays set up
   b. Number of service calls made
   c. Number of meetings held with dealers and/or distributors

One key to a successful evaluation program is to appraise a salesperson's performance on as many different bases as possible. Otherwise, management may be misled. A person may have a low ratio of selling expenses to sales volume and be commended for thrifty management of company funds. Yet that low expense ratio may have occurred because the person failed to prospect for new accounts or to cover the territory adequately. A high daily call rate may look good, but it tells us nothing about how many orders per call are being written up. A high batting average (orders divided by calls) may be camouflaging a low average order size or a high sales volume on low-profit items.

Qualitative bases. It would be nice if the entire performance evaluation could be based only on quantitative factors, thus minimizing the subjectivity and personal biases of the evaluators. Unfortunately, this cannot be done. Too many qualitative factors—outlined below—must be considered because they influence a salesperson's performance.

1. The salesperson's knowledge of the product, company policies, and competition
2. The management of his own time and his preparation for calls
3. Customer relations
4. His personal appearance and health
5. Personality and attitudinal factors, such as:
   a. Cooperativeness
   b. Resourcefulness
   c. Ability to analyze logically and make decisions

The evaluator assumes a key role because the success of a qualitative evaluation depends to a great extent upon the salesperson's ability to be objective and impartial. Merit rating forms are useful at this stage in an evaluation. These forms permit the judgments of the several evaluators to appear in a standardized manner. This uniformity aids in comparing one salesperson with another. Rating forms also provide a written report for company records. What is more important, however, use of rating forms should result in an evaluator's being more thorough in his work, since his appraisals now appear on record for others to see and, perhaps, for him to defend.

THE PERSONAL SELLING PROCESS

If marketing executives understand the fundamentals of salesmanship—that is, the theories underlying the interaction between buyer and seller—they are in a better position to develop an effective selling procedure for their sales force to follow. For the most part these "theories" are based upon research in the behavioral sciences or upon knowledge gained from years of selling experience in practical market settings.[9] The basic concepts explaining buyer-seller interactions were developed in earlier chapters in our discussions of customer motivation and behavior.

Coupling their marketing knowledge with others' research findings in interaction theory, Robertson and Chase derived the following set of predictions relative to the sales process.[10] Salespeople and executives alike should find it useful to incorporate these generalizations into their personal selling programs.

1. The more closely matched the physical, social, and personality characteristics of customer and salesperson are, the more likely a sale is to result.[11]
2. The more believable and trustworthy the customer perceives a salesperson to be, the more likely a sale is to result.
3. The more persuasible a customer is, the more likely it is that a sale will result.
4. The more a salesperson can make prospective buyers view themselves favorably, the more likely it is that a sale will result.
5. The second salesperson to call on a prospect will generally have an advantage over the first one.

At this point we shall summarize briefly one procedure which can be used in personal selling.

PRESALE PREPARATION

In the chain of events which it is hoped will lead to a sale, the first step is to make certain that the salesperson is prepared. This means that he must be well acquainted with the product, the market, and the techniques of selling. Before salespeople make their first call, they should know as much as possible about the motivation and behavior of the market segment to which they will sell. They should be informed on the nature of the competition, the business conditions prevailing in their territories, etc.

LOCATING OR PROSPECTING FOR POTENTIAL BUYERS

The sales person is now ready to locate customers. This second step toward a sale involves drawing up a profile of the ideal prospect. The salesperson can examine records of past and present customers in his effort to determine the characteristics of such a prospect. From this profile he may develop a list of people or companies who are logical potential buyers of the product.

There are other ways salespersons can acquire a list of prospects. Their sales manager usually prepares a list for them; present customers can suggest new leads;

---

9 For a summary of the theoretical aspects of salesmanship with excellent source references, see Richard R. Still and Edward W. Cundiff, *Sales Management,* 2d ed., Prentice-Hall, Inc., Englewood Cliffs, N.J., 1969, pp. 46-56; see also Robert F. Gwinner, "Base Theory in the Formulation of Sales Strategy." *MSU Business Topics, Autumn,* 1968, pp. 37-44; and Harry L. Davis and Alvin J. Silk, *Behavioral Research of Personal Selling: A Review of Some Recent Studies of Interaction and Influence Processes in Sales Situations,* Marketing Science Institute, Cambridge, Mass., 1971.

10 Thomas S. Robertson and Richard B. Chase, "The Sales Process: An Open Systems Approach," *MSU Business Topics,* Autumn, 1968, pp. 49-50. The systems approach was used to conceptualize the sales process, framing it in an input-output model. That is, inputs (human, technological, and organizational) were transformed by the sales process into the hoped-for output of satisfied customers.

11 See Franklin B. Evans, "Selling as a Dyadic Relationship: A New Approach," *American Behavioral Scientist,* May, 1963, pp. 76-79.

present users may want later or different models of the product. The salesperson might build a list of users of competitors' products. A little thought will often suggest logical prospects. For instance, salespeople of home furnishings, insurance, light fixtures, or telephone equipment find prospects in the regularly published lists of building permits issued. Salespeople of many products find leads among birth or engagement announcements in newspapers.

PREAPPROACH TO INDIVIDUAL PROSPECTS

Before calling on prospects, the salesperson should learn all he can about the person or company to whom he hopes to sell. He might want to know what products or brands the prospect is now using and what the reaction to them is. A salesperson should try to find out the personal habits, likes, dislikes, etc., of the prospect. In general, the salesperson should try to get all the information he can so that he will be able to tailor his presentation to the individual buyer.

SALES PRESENTATION

The actual presentation of the salesperson will start with an attempt to attract the prospect's attention, and then try to hold the customer's interest while building a desire for the product. Then the salesperson will try to close the sale. All through the presentation, the salesperson must be ready to meet any hidden or expressed objections which the prospect may have.[12]

Attract attention—the approach. Several approaches are frequently used to attract the prospect's attention and start the presentation. The simplest approach is merely to greet the prospect, introduce oneself, and state what one is selling. While this is direct, in many selling situations it is not so effective as other approaches. If the salesperson was referred to the prospect by a customer, the right approach might be to start out with a reference to this common acquaintance. Sometimes this is called the "Joe sent me" approach. The salesperson might suggest the product benefits by making some startling statement. One sales training consultant often greets a prospect with the question, "If I can cut your selling costs in half, and at the same time double your sales volume, are you interested?" This approach parallels the strong, attention-getting headlines often used in advertisements. A fourth approach, which can be effective if the salesperson has a new product, is simply to walk in and hand the product to the prospect. While the prospect looks it over, the salesperson can start the sales presentation.

Hold interest and arouse desire. When the salesperson has attracted the prospect's attention, he can hold his interest and stimulate his desire for the product by means of the sales talk itself. There is no common pattern here. Usually, however, a product demonstration is invaluable. Also, if it has not been possible to determine a prospect's specific needs during the preapproach, certainly this must be done in the course of the presentation. Whatever pattern is followed in the talk, the salesperson must always show the prospect how the product will benefit him.

---

12 *Sales Management* magazine has devoted an entire issue to each of three steps in the sales presentation process. See "Opening the Sale," Oct. 30, 1972; "The Presentation," Oct. 1, 1973; and "Closing the Sale," June 1, 1971.

Many companies insist that their salespeople use a "canned" sales talk. That is, all representatives must give identical presentations verbatim or with very minor changes. Although many people may feel that this is a poor practice, it has been proved time and time again that a canned sales talk can be effective. Salespeople can still project their own individual personalities, even though they all say essentially the same thing. These presentations ensure that all points are covered, they employ tested techniques, and they facilitate the sales training job considerably.[13]

Meet objections and close the sale. After explaining the product and its benefits, the salesperson should try to close the sale and write up an order. As part of the presentation, the salesperson may periodically venture a trial close in order to sense the prospect's willingness to buy. By posing some "either-or" questions, a salesperson can start to bring the presentation to a head. That is, he may ask, "Do you prefer the gray or the green model?" "How soon would you want this delivered?" or "Would you plan to charge this or pay cash?"

The trial close is important because it gives the salesperson an indication of how near the prospect is to a decision. A salesperson may lose a sale by talking too much The prospect may be ready to buy at the beginning and then change his mind if the salesperson insists on a full presentation. Sometimes sales are lost simply because the representative fails to ask for the order.

The trial close also tends to bring out the buyer's objections. A salesperson should encourage a buyer to state his objections. Then the salesperson has an opportunity to answer them and to bring out additional product benefits or re-emphasize previously stated points.

The toughest objections to answer are those which are unspoken. A salesperson must uncover the real objections before hoping to make a sale. Another difficult situation occurs when the prospect says he wants to "think it over." A generalization on this point is that the salesperson must close the sale then and there, or the chances are that it will be lost.

Textbooks on salesmanship discuss different types of final closing techniques. The assumptive close is probably used as much as any other, and it can be used in a wide variety of selling situations. In this closing technique, the salesperson assumes that the customer is going to buy, so it is just a case of settling the details. He will ask such questions as, "When do you want this delivered?" "Is this a charge sale?" "Do you want this gift-wrapped?" or "What color have you decided upon?"

POSTSALE ACTIVITIES

An effective selling job does not end when the order is written up. Normally, sales success depends upon repeat business. Also, a satisfied customer will furnish leads to other prospects. Consequently, the final stage of our selling process is a series of postsale services which can build customer goodwill and lay the groundwork for many years of profitable business relations. If mechanical installation is necessary, the representative should make certain the job is done properly. It is necessary to make sure that all points in the sales contract and the guarantee are clearly under-

---

13 For a new look at the different types of canned sales presentations, and the importance of relating the *method* of presentation to the *objective* of the presentation, see Marvin A. Jolson, "Should the Sales Presentation Be 'Fresh' or 'Canned'?" *Business Horizons*, October, 1973, pp. 81-88.

stood. In the case of large industrial products, the salesperson will often spend weeks or months in the customer's establishment, training operators and checking to be sure that the product is working smoothly within the buyer's system.

In general, all these activities by the salesperson serve to reduce the customer's postdecision anxiety—his cognitive dissonance. The theory of cognitive dissonance (as we can recall from Chapter 7) holds that after a person has made a decision, anxiety (dissonance) will usually occur because he knows the alternative he selected has some disagreeable features, as well as advantages. Consequently, the person seeks support and reassurance that he made the correct choice, and conversely he wants to avoid anything which suggests that one of his discarded choices really would have been better. (Sometimes this anxiety will set in before the buying decision is made, and the net result may be no sale because the customer cannot make a decision.)

In this final stage of the selling process, it is the salesperson's job to minimize the customer's dissonance. In addition to other postsale services, the salesperson should reassure the customer that he made the right decision by (1) summarizing the product's benefits, (2) repeating why it is better than the discarded alternative choices, and (3) pointing out how satisfied he will be with the product's performance.

REASONS FOR SHORTAGE OF QUALIFIED SALESPEOPLE

In spite of the many job opportunities and the high levels of compensation in selling, there is an acute shortage of qualified people entering this field. Management is often forced to accept submarginal people. For several reasons, talented prospects will consider a selling career only when they cannot qualify for any other job. Selling usually involves considerable traveling, and this is often a deterrent to people with families. The career lacks social prestige and status. Also, many people have a poor image of the salesperson owing to the abundance of traveling-salesman jokes and the fact that the only sales activities most people ever see are retail clerking and door-to-door selling. Most sales jobs in no way resemble these two activities. The majority of people are totally unaware of the many really good sales jobs which involve selling to manufacturers, retailers, or wholesalers.

One writer, in analyzing the problem, points out that selling is considered a white-collar job, salespeople receive a relatively high income, and the job offers freedom of action—all three factors being characteristic of high-prestige occupations. At the same time, selling's prestige is lowered because (1) no formalized education and training are required and (2) power and authority are lacking both in the job and in dealing with customers.[14]

Possibly a fundamental reason why people stay away from selling jobs is that they are just not talented enough to become salespeople. Consciously or unconsciously, people may recognize that sales work is one kind of activity that requires grasping the naked sword and coming to grips with reality in a situation stripped of all possibilities for excuse making. It is a virile activity that puts a person's mettle to

---

14 John L. Mason, "The Low Prestige of Personal Selling," *Journal of Marketing,* October, 1965, pp. 7-10; see also John L. Mason, "The Salesman's Prestige: A Re-examination," *Business Topics,* Autumn, 1962, pp. 73-77; and Gerhard W. Ditz, "Status Problems of the Salesman," *MSU Business Topics,* Winter, 1967, pp. 68-80.

the test every day. In a sense, sales work reduces the relationship between two people to a very simple test of power: Can I get you to buy? Most other jobs modify this relationship, allowing workers to operate in a protected environment where they may affect sales indirectly and impersonally, without exposing themselves to the possibility of failure and a recognition of their personal inadequacies.

QUESTIONS AND PROBLEMS

1. A double-page, full-color advertisement in one issue of a national magazine may cost much more than the compensation and expenses needed to maintain one salesperson for one full year. A sales-force executive is urging his company to eliminate a few of these ads and instead hire a few more salespeople. This executive believes that one good salesperson working for an entire year can sell more than one ad in one issue of the magazine. How would you answer this executive?

2. "The salesperson occupies many roles with many divergent role partners, which places heavy emotional demands on him." Explain.

3. Refer to the seven-way classification of sales jobs found early in this chapter and answer the following questions:
   a. In which types of jobs is the salesperson most free from close supervision?
   b. Which types are likely to be the highest paid?
   c. Which are likely to involve the most traveling?
   d. For which groups is a high degree of motivation necessary?

4. "Salespeople are born, not made" Do you agree? If so, why does a firm need a good training program? If not—that is, if you believe that salespeople are made, not born—why does a firm need a good selection program?

5. "A good selection program is desirable but not essential. Improper selection of salespeople can be counterbalanced by a good training program, by a good compensation system, or by fine supervision." Discuss.

6. What sources should be used for recruiting sales applicants in each of the following firms? Explain your reasoning in each instance.
   a. A company selling executive airplanes to a manufacturer of paper products
   b. A firm selling cosmetics door-to-door
   c. A dress manufacturer selling high-fashion dresses to department stores and exclusive specialty shops
   d. A grocery products wholesaler selling to retailers and institutions in northern British Columbia and Alberta.

7. "It is best to hire experienced salespeople because they do not require any training." Discuss.

8. What factors should be considered when determining the level of sales compensation?

9. Compare the merits of a straight-salary plan and a straight-commission plan of sales compensation. Name some types of sales jobs in which each plan might be desirable.

10. What measure might be used to determine whether a salesperson is using high-pressure selling tactics which may injure customer relations?

11. In this chapter, many of the bases for evaluating salespeople's performance seemed to apply more to "outside" salespeople—those who go to the customers. What bases might be used to evaluate the performance of in-store retail salespeople?

12. How can a sales manager evaluate the ability of his salespeople to get new business?

13. What are some of the sources you might use to acquire a list of prospects for the following products?
    a. Automobiles   c. Life insurance
    b. Baby furniture

14. What can a salesperson do when customers object that the price of his product is too high?

15. What can be done to make selling more attractive as a career?

MANAGEMENT OF ADVERTISING

A hunter ordinarily does not use a rifle to hunt ducks. He needs a device which will enable him to hit more ducks with the same amount of effort expended in using a rifle. Thus he will use a shotgun. By the same token, mass communication is needed to reach mass markets at a reasonable cost. Advertising and sales promotion are just the tools for this job. It is too costly and time-consuming to try to do the job with salespeople alone.

NATURE AND IMPORTANCE OF ADVERTISING

Advertising consists of all the activities involved in presenting to a group a nonpersonal, oral or visual, openly sponsored message regarding a product, service, or idea; this message, called an *advertisement,* is disseminated through one or more media and is paid for by the identified sponsor.

Some important considerations should be noted in connection with this definition. First, there is a significant distinction between advertising and an advertisement. The advertisement is simply the message itself. Advertising is a process—it is a program or a series of activities necessary to prepare the message and get it to the intended market. Another point is that the public knows who is behind the advertising because the sponsor is openly identified in the advertisement itself. Also, payment is made by the sponsor to the media which carry the message. These last two considerations differentiate advertising from propaganda and publicity.

TYPES OF ADVERTISING

Understanding the various ways in which advertising can be classified should be useful to an executive, because different types of advertising will be called for depending upon the company's objectives in its advertising program.

Product and institutional. All advertising may be classed as product or institutional. In product advertising, the advertiser is informing or stimulating the market about his products or services. Product advertising is often further subdivided into direct-action and indirect-action advertising. With *direct-action* advertising, the seller is seeking a quick response to his advertisement. An advertisement with a coupon may urge the reader to send in immediately for a free sample. Thursday-night and Friday-morning advertisements run by supermarkets list products featured in weekend sales. *Indirect-action* advertising is designed to stimulate demand over a longer period of time. Advertisements are intended to inform the customers that the product exists and to point out its benefits so that when they are in the market for the product, they will look favorably upon the seller's brand. Product advertising may also be subclassed as *primary-demand* and *selective-demand* advertising to correspond with the stages of the product's demand or life cycle. (This topic was discussed in Chapter 22.)

Institutional advertising is designed to create a proper attitude toward the seller and to build goodwill, rather than to sell a specific product or service. Institutional advertising may be further subdivided into three areas: patronage, public relations, and public service institutional advertising. In *patronage* institutional advertising, a seller is trying to attract customers by appealing to patronage-buying motives rather than product-buying motives. To illustrate, a retailer may inform his market about new store hours or a change in his delivery policy. A manufacturer may stress new credit and returned-goods policies when advertising in trade journals to attract wholesalers. *Public relations* institutional advertising is used to create a favorable image of the firm among employees, stockholders, or the general public. A manufacturer may run some ads telling what he is doing to reduce stream pollution caused by his plant's operations. *Public service* institutional advertising is illustrated by ads urging the public to support the fund-raising efforts of the Salvation Army or the Canadian Cancer Association. McGuinness Distillers has for a number of years leased the entire Toronto transit system for New Year's Eve and allowed Torontonians to travel free. This service and McGuinness' corresponding advertising which urges people to use the transit system rather than drive on New Year's Eve might be considered an example of public service advertising.

National and local. National (general) advertising is that sponsored by manufacturers or other producers. Local (retail) advertising is just that—advertising placed by retailers. Although the terms "national" and "local" are used synonymously with "general" and "retail" in the advertising business, this is an unfortunate and inexact comparison. It is true that most manufacturers sell in more than one local market, and it is also true that a retailer's market is usually confined to one locality. As currently used in the trade, however, the term "national" advertising refers only to the level of the advertiser and has no relation at all to geographic coverage. If a manufacturer places a single ad in only one city, this is still referred to as national advertising.

Another purposeful distinction may be drawn between a manufacturer's and a retailer's advertising. A manufacturer's advertising is designed to build a demand for his product. He does not care where the item is purchased, as long as the customer buys his brand. In retailer's advertising, the stress is on the store. A retailer does not care what product or brand you buy, as long as you buy it at his establishment. Therefore, his advertisements often feature appeals to patronage motives, showing you what services he offers and why it is to your advantage to buy at his store.

Nature of market. Several classifications of advertising are based upon subdivisions of the market. Advertising differs depending upon whether the market target is the consumer, middleman, industrial user, or professional man. Consumer advertising is aimed at ultimate consumers who purchase for nonbusiness, personal use. In trade advertising, the target may be retailers, where the appeal is, "Buy this product to resell in your store at a profit." In industrial advertising, an industrial user is urged, "Buy this product to use in your business." The professional market is approached with advertising which says, "Specify this product for use by your patients or clients."

IMPORTANCE OF ADVERTISING

Advertising in one form or another is used by virtually all manufacturers and retailers in the country. The importance of advertising may also be expressed by various quantitative measures.

Advertising expenditures in total and by media. One quantitative indication of the importance of advertising is the total amount spent on advertising in Canada. In 1975, the total revenues of Canadian advertising media were 1.8 billion dollars—more than double the revenues of 1966. Table 24-1 shows the dollar revenues and the percentage of the total accounted for by each of the major media. For years, newspapers have been the most widely used medium, based upon total advertising dollars invested. About 81 percent of the expenditures for advertising in Canadian daily newspapers goes for local and classified advertising rather than for national advertising. While the revenues generated by television networks and stations have been increasing in recent years, television still remains in third place behind newspapers and direct mail in terms of total advertising revenues generated.

Another perspective on advertising expenditures can be obtained by comparing Canadian and United States outlays in dollar terms, on a per capita basis, and as a proportion of Gross National Product. Table 24-2 shows these comparisons. In 1974, expenditures on advertising in the United States totalled 26.55 billion dollars, as compared with 1.65 billion in Canada. When these amounts are translated into ratio terms, an interesting picture develops. Although some Canadians have been critical of the volume of advertising in this country, when Canadian and American advertising expenditures are compared, we find that in Canada only $73.51 was spent per capita on advertising in 1974, as compared with $125.30 per capita in the United States. In Canada, slightly more than one percent of G.N.P. is devoted to advertising expenditures as compared with almost two percent in the United States.

Advertising revenues as a percentage of company sales. When gauging the importance of advertising, it is often more meaningful to measure expenditures against a bench mark rather than simply to look at the total in an isolated position. Frequently, advertising expenses are expressed as a percentage of a company's sales. Table 24-3 shows the fifty largest advertisers in Canada for 1974. Some of these advertisers which spend a large dollar amount on advertising actually devote a *very* small percentage of sales to advertising. Table 24-4 presents data which permits a comparison of various industries in terms of the percentage of sales devoted to advertising expenses. The data for 1965 (the last year for which Statistics Canada has produced figures) show that the heaviest expenditures, on a ratio basis, are by the toilet preparations (No. 29) and the soap and cleaning compounds manufacturers (No. 25). At the other extreme, are the sugar refiners (No. 28) at 0.19 percent of sales and pulp and paper mills (No. 23) with 0.24 percent. It is clear from the table that, in general, the consumer goods industries are spending more per sales dollar than are industrial goods manufacturers. It is also interesting to note the change in ratios from 1954 to 1965. Pharmaceutical and medicines manufacturers (No. 22) have increased their spending ratio; the manufacturers of toys and games (No. 30) have increased spending substantially; industries such as agricultural implements have moved in the opposite direction. Within each industry, of course, a variance exists with some firms spending quite heavily compared to the industry average and others relying on non-advertising forms of promotional variables and spending a small amount compared to the industry average.

Sometimes it may seem as if the public is bombarded on all sides by advertising; however, the total amount spent is usually small in relation to sales volume.

One representative study showed that manufacturers of consumer products spend about 3 percent of sales for advertising purposes, while manufacturers of industrial goods spend less than 1 percent (see Tables 22-1 and 22-2). In a summary report, The Conference Board showed advertising as a percentage of sales for various types of manufacturers, retailers, and service industries. In the majority of these industries, advertising was less than 2 percent of sales.

Cost of advertising versus cost of personal selling. While we do not have accurate totals for costs of personal selling, we do know they far surpass advertising expenditures. In manufacturing, only a few industries, such as drugs, toiletries, cleaning products, tobacco, and beverages, have advertising expenditures which are higher than those for personal selling. In countless companies, advertising runs 1 to 3 percent of net sales, while in many firms the expenses of managing and operating a sales force run from 8 to 15 percent of sales.

At the wholesaling level, advertising costs are very low. Personal selling costs may run ten to fifteen times as high. Even among retailers in total, and this includes those with self-service operations, the cost of personal selling runs substantially higher than the cost of advertising.

OBJECTIVES OF ADVERTISING

Fundamentally, the only purpose of advertising is to sell something—a product, a service, or an idea. The intent may be to generate a sale immediately or at some time in the future. Nevertheless, the basic objective is to sell. Stated another way, the real goal of advertising is effective communication. That is, the ultimate effect of advertising should be to modify the attitudes and/or behavior of the receiver of the

Table 24-1. Net advertising revenues of Canadian media 1971-1975 (thousands of dollars).

	1971 $	1971 % of Total	1972 $	1972 % of Total	1973 $	1973 % of Total	1974 $	1974 % of Total	1975 $	1975 % of Total
BROADCAST										
Radio—Total	124,688	10.9	144,703	11.1	160,300	10.8	182,740	11.1	203,000	11.2
National	45,860		50,730		51,419		54,190		61,000	
Local	78,828		93,973		108,881		128,550		142,000	
Television—Total	147,671	12.9	166,025	12.7	198,517	13.4	218,810	13.3	245,000	13.5
National*	119,000		130,000		154,778		167,650		185,000	
Local	28,671		36,025		43,739		51,160		60,000	
NEWSPAPERS										
Dailies—Total	327,887	28.7	374,465	28.7	428,134	28.9	483,000	29.3	526,900	29.1
National	70,838		77,299		86,602		93,500		100,100	
Local	176,797		203,452		228,486		251,000		278,600	
Classified	80,253		93,714		113,046		138,500		148,200	
Weekend Supplements—Total	23,131	2.0	25,938	2.0	23,348	1.6	23,550	1.4	22,800	1.3
National	20,279		23,044		20,650		20,850		20,100	
Local	2,852		2,894		2,698		2,700		2,700	
Weeklies, semi, tri, etc. (including controlled distribution)—Total	55,565	4.9	63,848	4.9	75,328	5.1	85,000	5.2	93,500	5.2
National	10,770		11,600		13,567		15,000		16,500	
Local	44,795		52,248		61,761		70,000		77,000	
PERIODICALS—Total	128,697	11.2	147,650	11.5	172,609	11.7	194,200	11.8	215,000	11.9
Magazines, general	26,307		31,431		35,808		40,000		43,000	

Business papers	29,732		31,899		36,136		39,000		41,800
Farm papers	5,441		7,216		6,975		7,900		8,800
Directories, phone, city	62,378		71,390		86,502		99,500		113,000
Religious, school & other	4,839		5,714		7,188		7,800		8,500
OTHER PRINT—Total	238,555	20.8	270,999	20.8	304,327	20.6	335,764	20.3	368,000	20.3
Catalogues	51,439		59,842		63,806		67,000		73,000
Other printed advertising	114,437		128,004		144,838		160,000		176,000
Imported advtg. matter	16,429		19,153		21,683		24,764		27,000
Postage cost**	56,250		64,000		74,000		84,000		92,000
OUTDOOR—Total	98,033	8.6	109,277	8.4	116,858	7.9	127,000	7.7	137,000	7.6
Factory shipments of signs (electric & non-electric) incl. advtg. displays, stands and fixtures	68,033		77,277		81,858		87,000		94,000
Other outdoor (1)	30,000		32,000		35,000		40,000		43,000
TOTAL ALL MEDIA	1,144,227	100.0	1,302,905	100.0	1,479,421	100.0	1,650,064	100.0	1,811,700	100.0

* Includes M-H Research Bureau estimates of CTV network revenue 1970-72 inclusive to make comparable with Statistics Canada 1973 actuals.

(1) Firms in other outdoor advertising business (renting space, putting up billboards, or other displays, placing advertising matter on streetcars, buses and other transit systems, and so forth); advertising revenue of other sign producers, show card writers, sign painters, etc.

Source: Canadian Advertising Rates and Data, May 1976, inside front cover.

** Postage: 75% of third class mail.

Table 24-2. Total per capita advertising expenditures, U.S.A. and Canada, 1961-1975*.

	Total Advertising Expenditures ($ millions)		Per Capita Expenditures		Ad. Expenditures Percent of GNP	
	USA	Canada	USA	Canada	USA	Canada
1961	$11,845	$ 609	$64.46	33.39	2.28%	1.56%
1962	12,380	643	66.33	34.60	2.21	1.52
1963	13,107	674	69.20	35.60	2.22	1.48
1964	14,155	724	73.68	37.53	2.23	1.45
1965	15,255	798	78.39	40.62	2.23	1.45
1966	16,670	873	84.66	43.62	2.22	1.42
1967	16,866	941	84.70	46.12	2.13	1.43
1968	18,127	983	90.10	47.39	2.09	1.38
1969	19,482	1,081	95.87	51.33	2.10	1.38
1970	19,600	1,134	95.56	53.05	2.01	1.34
1971	20,840	1,144	100.65	53.04	1.97	1.22
1972	23,130	1,303	110.75	59.69	2.00	1.25
1973	25,140	1,479	119.48	66.94	1.95	1.23
1974	26,550	1,650	125.30	73.51	1.90	1.17
1975	N/A	1,812	N/A	79.54	N/A	1.12

* Expenditures quoted in national currencies.   N/A: not available

Sources: U.S. data: McCann-Erickson Inc.; Canadian data: Maclean-Hunter Research Bureau.

Table 24-3. Fifty Largest Advertisers in Canada, 1974.

	1974 Advertising Expenditures*
1. Procter and Gamble	$10,774,993
2. General Foods	9,498,063
3. Government of Canada	9,446,988
4. General Motors	8,424,146
5. Colgate-Palmolive	6,855,119
6. Warner Lambert	6,493,428
7. Bristol-Myers	6,018,599
8. Kraft Foods	5,875,432
9. The Molson Companies	5,693,759
10. Ford Motor	4,413,352
11. Carling O'Keefe	4,280,486
12. Sterling Drug	4,209,761
13. Imasco	4,149,987
14. Canadian Pacific	3,940,204

Table 24-3. (cont'd)

	1974 Advertising Expenditures*
15. Quebec Government	3,913,133
16. S. C. Johnson & Son	3,894,008
17. Whitehall Laboratories	3,815,189
18. Air Canada	3,800,935
19. K-Tel International	3,701,434
20. Labatt Breweries	3,639,047
21. Olympics 76	3,554,831
22. Seagram	3,330,158
23. Benson and Hedges	3,139,569
24. Lever Bros.	3,117,030
25. Gillette	3,081,694
26. Imperial Oil	3,070,061
27. Coca-Cola	3,016,716
28. Chrysler	2,984,074
29. Canada Packers	2,928,764
30. Gulf Oil	2,927,253
31. Kellogg	2,919,081
32. Bell Canada	2,840,516
33. Rothmans of Pall Mall	2,838,732
34. Eaton's	2,815,706
35. Royal Bank	2,631,168
36. Ontario Government	2,629,265
37. Gilbey	2,579,018
38. Campbell Soup	2,524,795
39. Johnson & Johnson	2,504,171
40. Nestlé	2,433,719
41. Standard Brands	2,332,470
42. Macdonald Tobacco	2,278,163
43. Oshawa Group	2,277,679
44. Nissan Automobile	2,179,762
45. Candian Motor Industries	2,175,679
46. Dominion Stores	2,137,875
47. McDonalds Restaurants	2,135,706
48. Canadian National Railways	2,125,936
49. Shell	1,957,648
50. Nabisco	1,930,355

*All figures represent space and time costs only in six major media measured by Elliott Research and do not represent the total advertising budgets of the advertisers concerned, nor do they include production costs or advertising expenditures in other media.
Source: *Marketing,* September 15, 1975, p. 1.

Table 24-4. Selected Advertising Ratios, 1954 and 1965.

Industry	Ratio of Advertising to Sales	
	1954	1965
	(%)	
1. Agricultural implement	1.20	0.98
2. Artificial ice manufacturers	0.96	0.15
3. Battery manufacturers	2.34	1.20
4. Boiler and plate works	0.91	0.36
5. Breweries	2.19	6.56
6. Broom, brush and mop industry	2.01	2.65
7. Button, buckle and fastener industry	0.94	1.36
8. Carpet, mat and rug	0.87	1.11
9. Clock and watch manufacturers	3.88	6.70
10. Confectionery manufacturers	2.68	4.78
11. Distilleries	3.50	2.74
12. Electric lamp and shade	1.14	0.31
13. Flour mills	1.14	2.11
14. Foundation garments	6.38	5.42
15. Fur goods	2.55	0.26
16. Hardware, tool and cutlery manufacturers	1.20	3.41
17. Heating equipment manufacturers	2.23	0.81
18. Hosiery mills	1.63	2.01
19. Linoleum and coated fabrics	3.26	1.27
20. Pen and pencil manufacturers	6.24	7.35
21. Petroleum refining	0.88	1.17
22. Pharmaceuticals and medicines manufacturers	6.07	8.65
23. Pulp and paper mills	0.10	0.24
24. Scientific and professional equipment manufacturers	1.32	2.06
25. Soap and cleaning compounds manufacturers	11.26	10.85
26. Sporting goods	1.80	1.37
27. Statuary, art goods, regalia, etc.	1.62	0.86
28. Sugar refineries	0.07	0.19
29. Toilet preparations manufacturers	15.86	15.22
30. Toys and games	0.95	6.50
31. Umbrella manufacturers	0.28	0.98
32. Wineries	2.89	3.99
33. Wire and wire products	0.51	0.21
34. Women's clothing factories	0.30	0.45

Source: Advertising Expenditures in Canada, 1965, *Cat. No. 63-216, Table 19.*
Reproduced by permission of Information Canada.

message. Sometimes the public, and even an advertising businessperson, over-looks this fact. The businessperson is not interested in awarding a prize to his salesperson who is best liked by everybody. Instead, he wants to reward the salesperson who has the best sales record. At the same time, he may be trying to earn awards for having the best copy or use of color in his advertisements, forget-ting that his real aim is, or should be, to build an ad that will sell the most merchan-dise.

Specific objectives. The general goal of advertising is to increase profitable sales, but this goal is too broad to be implemented effectively in an advertising program. It is necessary to establish more specific objectives which can be worked into the program. A few examples of these more limited aims are listed below:

1. Support personal selling program. Advertising may be used to open customers' doors for salespeople and to acquaint the prospect with the seller's company. Advertising can also reduce selling costs by doing some of the sales prospecting. It permits the salesper-son to make fewer calls and enables the company to maintain contact with the custom-ers between salespeople's calls. See Fig. 24-1.
2. Reach people inaccessible to salespeople. A salesperson may be unable to reach top business executives and professionals, or he may not be certain who makes the buying decisions in a company. In either case, there is a good chance that all these executives will read a journal which carries the ads.
3. Improve dealer relations. The goal of an advertising campaign may be to attract new dealers by showing them how profitable it is to carry the manufacturer's line. The pur-pose of the other advertisements may be to give the names and addresses of retailers who carry the product.
4. Enter a new geographic market or attract a new group of customers.
5. Introduce a new product.
6. Increase sales of the product. An advertising campaign may be designed to lengthen the season for the product (as has been done in the case of soft drinks), increase the fre-quency of replacement (as is done in campaigns for spark plugs and light bulbs), in-crease the variety of product uses, or increase the units of purchase.
7. Expand the industry's sales.
8. Counteract prejudice or substitution.
9. Build good will for the company and improve its reputation by rendering a public ser-vice through advertising or by telling of the organization behind the product.

DEVELOPMENT OF AN ADVERTISING CAMPAIGN

Up to this point in our analysis of advertising, it has been tacitly assumed that the firm is going to advertise. Actually, the first decision management must make in this area is whether or not it should advertise its products. Some guideposts to use in answering this question of basic promotional strategy have already been ana-lyzed.

Once the decision is made to advertise, management can get on with the job of developing an advertising campaign. In Chapter 22, a campaign was defined as a planned, coordinated series of promotional efforts built around a central theme and designed to reach a specific goal. The series of ads used in the campaign must be integrated with the sales-promotional efforts and with the activities of the sales force.

"I don't know who you are.

I don't know your company.

I don't know your company's product.

I don't know what your company stands for.

I don't know your company's customers.

I don't know your company's record.

I don't know your company's reputation.

Now—what was it you wanted to sell me?"

MORAL: Sales start **before** your salesman calls—with business publication advertising.

McGRAW-HILL MAGAZINES
BUSINESS • PROFESSIONAL • TECHNICAL

Figure 24-1. *Source:* McGraw-Hill publications.

INITIAL PLANNING

In the course of planning the total promotional campaign, presumably management has already established its specific goals.[1] It has decided what the central

---

1 For a report, accompanied by case histories, describing how companies put management-by-objective techniques to work in planning advertising, see *Setting Advertising Objectives*, The Conference Board, Studies in Business Policy no. 118, New York, 1966.

theme will be and what appeals will be stressed in light of consumer buying motives and habits. The total promotional appropriation has been determined and has been allocated among the various promotional tools, including advertising. Management can now concern itself with the selection of the advertising media and the creation and production of individual advertisements.

SELECTING THE MEDIA

Three levels of decision making are required in the selection of advertising media. First, management must determine what general types of media to use. Will newspapers, television, or magazines be used? If magazines are to be used, will they be general consumer magazines such as *Maclean's*, women's magazines such as *Chatelaine*, or business magazines or papers such as *The Financial Post*? If television is selected, will it be local, national network, or spot telecasting? Finally, the specific vehicle within the medium must be chosen. The company which decides first on radio and then on local stations now must decide whether to use station CKEY or CHUM in Toronto.

Several factors should be considered in making media decisions. Some of these factors affect all three levels of media decision making, whereas others relate more specifically to only one or two levels.

Objective of the advertisement. Media choices are influenced both by the purpose of a specific advertisement and by the goal of an entire campaign. For example, if the goal of the advertising is to make appointments for salespeople who are going to call on industrial users, the advertising company will probably use direct mail. If an advertiser wants to make last-minute changes in an advertisement, or if he wishes to place an ad inducing action within a day or two, he may use newspapers or radio. Magazines are not so good for this purpose because the ad must be placed weeks before the date of publication.

Media circulation. Media circulation must match the distribution patterns of the product. Consequently, the *geographic* scope of the market will influence the choice of media considerably. Furthermore, media should be selected which will reach the desired *type* of market with a minimum of waste circulation. A firm manufacturing shotguns, for example, will advertise in a magazine which appeals primarily to hunters. Media used to reach a teen-age market will be different from those used to reach mothers with young children.

Requirements of the message. Management should consider the media which are most suitable for the presentation of the message to the market. Meat products, floor coverings, and apparel are ordinarily best presented in pictorial form. Thus, radio is not a good medium for these lines. If a product, such as insurance, calls for a lengthy message, outdoor advertising is poor. If the advertiser can use a very brief message, however, as in the case of salt, beer, or sugar, then billboards may be the best choice.

Time and location of buying decision. The advertiser should select the medium which will reach the prospective customer at or near the time he makes his buying decision and the place where he makes it. For this reason, outdoor advertising is often good for gasoline products. Grocery store ads are placed in newspapers on Thursday nights or Friday mornings in anticipation of heavy weekend buying.

Cost of media. The cost of the advertising media should be considered in relation to (1) the amount of funds available and (2) the circulation of the media. In the first instance, the amount of funds available may rule out television as a choice, or possibly the advertiser can afford local television but not a national network. On the second count, the advertiser should try to develop some relationships between the cost of the medium and its circulation.

Cooperation and promotional aids offered by media. A manufacturer may want to tie in his advertising with that of his dealers. Consequently, he will look favorably upon media such as magazines which offer reprints for use in counter or window displays. Another firm may want some research done on local markets. Management may select the individual medium which can provide this service.

Characteristics of major types of media. In the process of selecting the media to use in a campaign, a marketing executive must consider the advertising characteristics of newspapers, magazines, and the other main classes of media. The term "characteristics" is carefully chosen instead of "advantages and disadvantages." To illustrate, one characteristic of radio as an advertising medium is that it makes its impression through the ear. For many products this feature is an advantage. For those which benefit from a colored photograph, this characteristic of radio is a drawback.

Newspapers. As an advertising medium, newspapers are flexible and timely. They can be used to cover one city or several urban centers. Ads can be canceled on a few days' notice or inserted on one day's notice. Newspapers also give an advertiser an intense coverage of a local market because almost everybody reads newspapers. The local feature also helps in that the ads may be adapted to local social and economic conditions. Many newspapers offer promotional assistance, and they are an excellent source of market information. This medium offers an opportunity to use a fair quality of color, and circulation costs per prospect are low. Newspapers are also helpful if the advertiser wishes to present his message to the market frequently. On the other hand, the life of a newspaper advertisement is very short.

Magazines. Magazines are an excellent medium when a high quality of printing and color is desired in an advertisement. Magazines can be used to reach a national market at a relatively low cost per prospect. Through the use of class magazines, an advertiser is able to reach a selective audience with a minimum of waste circulation. Magazines are usually read in a leisurely fashion, in contrast to the haste with which other print media are read. This is a particularly valuable point for the advertiser who must present his message at some length. Many magazines now also cater to the needs of regional advertisers. A number of magazines have been founded in recent years to serve large urban markets. The "calendar" magazines such as *Montreal Calendar, Toronto Calendar,* and *Vancouver Calendar* are examples of this type of magazine, as are *Toronto Life, Toronto Month* and *Montreal Ce Mois-Ci.* Another service to regional advertisers is provided through the regional editions which are published by most national consumer magazines. For example, *Chatelaine* is published in a total of thirteen different regional market editions. By advertising only in the Prairie Provinces English edition, for example, a company which does business only in this region can channel its advertising only to its market area, and still obtain the benefits of advertising in a national magazine without incurring the costs and wasted circulation which would be involved had its advertising appeared in all editions of *Chatelaine*, coast to coast.[2] Some of the less favorable characteristics of magazines are their inflexibility and the infrequency with which they reach the market, as compared with other media.

Direct Mail. Direct mail is probably the most personal and selective of all the media. Because it reaches only the market which the advertiser wishes to contact, there is a minimum of waste circulation. The personal feature and the aspect of selectivity also mean that the copy itself can be extremely flexible. Direct mail is not accompanied by articles or other editorial matter, however, unless the advertiser provides it. As a result, the direct-mail advertisement itself creates its own circulation and attracts its own readership. Direct mail is quite costly in terms of prospects reached when compared with other media, but other media reach many people who are not real prospects. A severe limitation is posed by the difficulty of getting and maintaining good mailing lists.

Television. Television, the newest and fastest growing of all major media, is also probably the most versatile. It makes its appeal through both the eye and the ear; products can be demonstrated as well as explained. It offers considerable flexibility in terms of the geographic market covered and in terms of the time the message is presented. By making its impression through the ear, it can take advantage of the personal, dramatic impact of the spoken word. On the other hand, television is an extremely expensive medium. The message is not permanently recorded. Thus if the prospect is not reached the first time, he is lost forever as far as that particular message is concerned. Television does not lend itself to long advertising copy, nor does it present pictures so clearly as magazines do. As in direct mail and radio, television advertisers must create their own audiences.

Outdoor. Outdoor advertising is a highly flexible, low-cost medium. Because it reaches virtually the entire population, it lends itself nicely to widely used consumer products which require only a brief selling statement. It is excellent for the reminder type of advertising, and it carries the impact of large size and color. There is complete flexibility in geographic coverage and in the intensity of market coverage within the area. These advantageous features, however, carry with them some inherent drawbacks. Unless the product is a widely used consumer good, considerable waste circulation will occur. While the cost is low in terms of reaching an individual prospect, the total cost of a national campaign is quite high. There is no opportunity to present lengthy copy, and it is not possible to show much detail in the pictures.

CREATION OF ADVERTISEMENTS

The advertisements are the heart of the entire advertising program. All the other steps in the campaign are designed to aid in delivering the sales message to the

---

2 Information on the regional editions of national consumer magazines may be obtained from *Canadian Advertising Rates and Data,* a monthly publication of Maclean-Hunter.

market target in the most effective manner. Obviously, the message itself is of considerable importance, so its creation constitutes a major phase in a campaign.

Before creating the advertisement, the people concerned should remember that the main purpose of advertising is to sell something and that the ad itself is a sales talk. The ad may be a high-pressure sales talk, as in a hard-hitting direct-action ad. Or it may be a very long-range, low-pressure message, as in an institutional ad. In any case it is trying to sell something. Consequently, it involves the same kind of selling procedure as a sales talk delivered by personal salespeople. That is, the ad must first attract attention and then hold interest long enough to stimulate a desire for the product, service, or idea. Finally, the ad must move the prospect to some kind of action. The desired action may lie anywhere within a virtually unlimited scope of possibilities, ranging from an immediate change in overt behavior to a slowly changing thought process.

Creating an advertisement involves the tasks of writing the copy—including the headline—selecting illustrations which may be used, preparing the layout, and arranging to have the advertisement reproduced for the selected media.

The *copy* in an advertisement is defined as all the written or spoken material in it, including the headline, coupons, and advertiser's name and address, as well as the main body of the message. The *illustration*—whether it is a photograph, drawing, reproduction of a painting, cartoon, or something else—is a powerful feature in an advertisement. Probably the main points to consider with respect to illustrations are (1) whether they are the best alternative use of the space and (2) whether they are appropriate in all respects to the ad itself. The *layout* is the physical arrangement of all the elements in an advertisement. Within the given amount of space or time, the layout man must place the headline, copy, and illustrations. Decisions are made regarding the relative amount of white space and the kinds of type to be used. A good layout can be an interest-holding device as well as an attention getter. It should lead the reader in an orderly fashion throughout the entire advertisement.

EVALUATION OF ADVERTISING PROGRAM

At several stages in the course of the advertising program, management should carefully evaluate the effectiveness of what has been done or what is planned for the future. Executives may wish to evaluate an entire advertising campaign, a single advertisement, or some part of an individual advertisement. They may wish to appraise various aspects of the advertising media.

IMPORTANCE

Advertising typically is one of the most highly criticized segments of our marketing system. While great strides may have been made to improve advertising through the years, much still remains to be done. We need to increase the effectiveness of advertising, and we also must find better ways to evaluate this effectiveness. Management needs to test advertising in order to know not only *which* ads are better than others, but also *why* they are better.

Shrinking profit margins and increasing competition, both foreign and domestic, are forcing management to appraise all its expenditures carefully. Top executives want more proof than they now have that advertising really does pay. They want to know whether dollars spent on advertising are resulting in proportionately as many sales as dollars spent on other activities. Unfortunately, it seems that a very small proportion (educated guesses say less than 1 percent) of total advertising dollars is being spent to measure advertising's effectiveness.[3]

> "I know that about half of my advertising is wasted, but I don't know which half."
> "I spent $2 million for advertising, and I don't know if that is half enough or twice too much."
>
> —John Wanamaker

DIFFICULTY

Many limitations confront a company in its efforts to measure the effectiveness of its advertising. This is one of the least-developed areas of marketing research. One problem is our inability to identify the effectiveness of any given advertisement or even an entire campaign. Except in the case of mail-order advertising, we cannot attribute a given unit of sales to any specific advertisement or campaign. By the very nature of the marketing mix, all elements—including advertising—are so intertwined, and there are so many variables, that measurement of any one by itself is impossible. Many factors besides advertising influence sales success.

Even in evaluating a particular advertisement, management is likely to run into difficulty because one part of an ad may be more easily appraised, and thus given more emphasis, than another.[4] Essentially there are only two parts of an advertisement—*what* is said and *how* it is said. One part deals with product attributes to be explained, and the other comprises the headlines, illustrations, and layouts. Over the years, a great deal has been done to improve the manner of presentation (the "how") because research has been able to establish criteria to measure its effectiveness. Most of the widely used measurement methods have emphasized the use of attention-getting devices in advertisements and the number of people who note, read, and remember the advertisements and the claims in them. Little has been done to aid management in its evaluation of the "what" part of an ad, and at the present time the effectiveness of this part is difficult to judge.

Many individual advertisements, and even entire campaigns, do not aim primarily at immediate sales results. Consequently, it is difficult to measure their effectiveness. Some advertisements simply announce new store hours, new service policies, or a new product. Probably the most difficult type of advertising to evaluate is that which is intended to build good will, create a company image, or influence attitudes. Institutional advertising falls in this category.

Presently used evaluative methods tell us simply which ad is the best among those being appraised. There are no standards for determining what must be included in an ad to ensure success. Furthermore, even though we test several advertisements in advance in order to select the one that is best, we still have no guarantee that sales results will be successful.[5]

---

3 For a report on interviews with advertisers, agencies, and media to determine why so little is being spent on this measurement task, see "Advertising Really Pays—What's Your Proof?" *Media/Scope*, June, 1969, p. 35.

4 Clarence E. Eldridge, "Advertising Effectiveness: How Can It Be Measured?" *Journal of Marketing*, January, 1958, pp. 242-243.

5 For encouraging reports from some of the companies which are making advances in measuring the effectiveness of their advertising, see Gail Smith, "How GM Measures Ad Effectiveness," *Printers' Ink*, May 14, 1965, p. 19; and "Who Says Ad Impact Can't Be Measured?" (DuPont's story), *Sales Management*, Apr. 19, 1963, p. 37.

METHODS USED TO MEASURE EFFECTIVENESS

When evaluating the effectiveness of its advertising, a company should not rely solely on the opinions of professional advertising people. They have been proved time and again to be poor judges of which ads will elicit favorable consumer response. Often they are too concerned with the manner in which the message is presented—the "how" part of advertising. If possible, management should plan to use some testing technique which will sample customer reaction.

The effectiveness of an advertisement may be tested before the advertisement is presented to the public, while it is being presented or after it has completed its run. The "sales results test" attempts to measure the sales volume stemming directly from the advertisement or series of advertisements being tested.

Most other types of tests are indirect measurements of advertising's effectiveness. One group, called "readership," "recognition," or "recall" tests, involves showing respondents part or all of the previously run advertisement to determine whether it was read, what parts in it were remembered, and whether the respondent knows who sponsored it. The theory underlying these tests is that the greater number of people who see, read, and remember an advertisement, the greater will be the number who do as the advertisement urges them.[6] Another type of test involves measuring the number of coupons or other forms of inquiries which were received from certain advertisements.

Sometimes marketing people use a consumer panel or consumer jury to appraise a group of advertisements. With respect to radio and television advertisements, several techniques are used to measure the quantity and quality of program audiences. The theory is that the number of people who will buy the sponsor's products varies proportionately with the number who watch or hear the program.

Many of these various measurement devices have enjoyed some degree of success. In general, however, there is still a long way to go before really effective evaluation tools and techniques will be developed for advertising. Possibly our hope for the future lies in the more effective use of psychological and sociological testing methods and in the use of mathematical models and operations research.[7]

We should remember, however, that the basic goal of advertising is to sell something—to modify consumer attitudes or behavior. Therefore, when we deal with the evaluation of advertising's effectiveness, we should be more concerned with measuring advertising's ability to influence these attitudes and behavior than with measuring the extent to which consumers recall given advertisements.

ORGANIZING FOR ADVERTISING

There are four widely used organizational arrangements employed to facilitate the work done in an advertising program. Within a company, the job may be done by a separate advertising department, or it may be handled by another department, possibly a general sales department, as only one part of its departmental responsi-

---

6 For research findings which refute the idea that a recall of advertised facts about a given product is a significant measure of the effectiveness of these ads, see Jack B. Haskins, "Factual Recall as a Measure of Advertising Effectiveness," *Journal of Advertising Research*, March, 1964, pp. 2-7.

7 For some of the problems encountered in the use of standard econometric models, see Richard E. Quandt, "Estimating the Effectiveness of Advertising: Some Pitfalls in Econometric Models," *Journal of Marketing Research*, May, 1964, pp. 51-60.

bility. A third arrangement involves turning the entire task over to an advertising agency, and the fourth combines the use of an advertising agency and the company's own department.

ADVERTISING MANAGEMENT WITHIN THE COMPANY

Advertising activities are sometimes administered by the department which operates the sales force. This arrangement is most common when advertising is a relatively unimportant part of the promotional mix or when the firm is small.

In larger businesses or in those where advertising is a substantial part of the promotional mix, advertising activities are usually administered by a separate department. Under these circumstances the head of the department should report to the marketing manager if the company is to implement the marketing concept. In some companies the advertising manager still reports directly to the president. It is considered a better arrangement, however, if all marketing activities are coordinated at an executive level below the president.[8]

Large retailers often have their own advertising departments and do not use an advertising agency. The advertising department performs all the tasks involved in planning and executing the campaign. Many manufacturers have their own departments but also use an advertising agency. The question then arises of why a department is needed if the company has a good agency. In the first place, the department acts as a liaison between the agency and the company. The department approves the agency's plans and advertisements and has the responsibility of preparing and administering the advertising budget. Finally, direct-mail advertisements, dealer displays, and other activities ordinarily not performed by the agency are handled by the company department.

ADVERTISING AGENCY

An advertising agency is an independent company set up to render specialized services in advertising in particular and in marketing in general. Today the term "agency" is a legal misnomer. These firms are not agents in the legal sense, but instead are independent companies. Advertising agencies started as space brokers for handling advertisements placed in newspapers. Through the years, however, the function of the agencies has changed. Their main job today is not to aid media but to serve advertisers.

Services rendered. Many agencies offer a broad range of marketing and advertising services. In the field of advertising alone, they plan and execute entire advertising campaigns. In radio and television, they are responsible for producing the entertainment as well as the commercials. Many of these firms are becoming *marketing* agencies, offering services which heretofore were performed either by another type of outside specialist or by the advertiser himself. A company's decision to involve its advertising agency in performing marketing (but nonadvertising) services for the firm will depend upon the extent to which management perceives that (1) its competitive environment is rapidly changing (as contrasted with a stable environment), (2) the agency is knowledgeable about the products and the industry, and

---

8 See Lois Stolzman, "The Ad Manager: Where Has He Been? Where Is He Today? Where Is He Going?" *Industrial Marketing*, May, 1970, p. 29.

(3) the costs of agency services are lower than the costs of those provided by alternative sources.[9]

In recent years a series of limited-service, advertising-specialist firms has evolved. These newer institutions provide flexible, cafeteria-style services (media space and time buying, various creative services, for example) in contrast to the traditional full-service agencies. These specialists claim to provide faster service at lower costs, because clients pay only for the services they use.[10]

Reasons for using when a company has own department. Even when a company has a good advertising department, there are several reasons why it may be interested in using an agency. In the first place, the company normally does not have as many types of specialists as a large or medium-sized advertising agency would have. Because an agency can spread the costs of its staff over many accounts, it can do more for the same amount of money.

The company can also get an objective, outside viewpoint from an agency, assuming that the agency representatives are not acting as "yes-men" in order to keep the advertiser's account. A related point is that the company can benefit from the agency's experiences with its many other products and clients. Another advantage is that an agency feels a greater pressure than does the company's own department to produce effective results. Relations between an agency and a client are very easy to terminate, but it is difficult to get rid of an ineffective advertising department. Finally, because of the manner in which agencies are compensated, the use of an agency may cost the advertiser very little.

Agency compensation. There are two major methods of compensating advertising agencies: the commission method and the fee method. Under the typical commission system, an agency receives an amount equal to 15 percent of the cost of the media time or space. The commission is paid by the media, who bill the agencies for the stated rate, less 15 percent. Then the advertiser pays the full rate to the agency. Thus if an agency prepares and places an advertisement in magazine space worth $40,000, the media will bill the agency for $34,000 ($40,000 less 15 percent). The agency in turn bills the client for the full $40,000. It is with this income of $6,000 that the agency performs its services. Most retailers deal directly with the local media and pay lower rates. No agency commission is paid on these rates. If a local advertiser uses an agency, he usually pays a fee.

In the preceding section it was stated that agency services may cost the advertiser very little. In the example, the company could have used its own department to prepare and place the advertisement, but the space would still have cost the company $40,000. In addition, the company would have had the expense of preparing the advertisement.

For many years there has been considerable dissatisfaction with the straight-commission system. Profits of the agencies declined because they were forced by competition to perform more and more services without additional compensation. Large advertisers who bought much media time and space felt they were paying too much. Agencies received the same compensation whether they placed the same advertisement in ten different magazines or had the extra expense of creating ten

---

9 Derek A. Newton, "Advertising Agency Services: Make or Buy?" *Harvard Business Review*, July-August, 1965, pp. 111-118.

10 See "Advertising that Comes à la Carte," *Business Week*, May 1, 1971, p. 44.

different advertisements. Furthermore, only accredited agencies were eligible to receive the commission.

Today there is a definite trend toward the use of the fee system or toward a combination of commission and fee, although the straight-commission method is still probably the most widely used. Many agencies are able to supplement their commission income by providing their clients with related marketing services such as package and label design, preparation of trade show displays and direct mail materials. Compensation for such services is generally on a fee basis.

REGULATION OF PROMOTIONAL ACTIVITIES

Because the primary objective of promotion is to sell something by means of informing, persuading, or otherwise communicating with a market, promotional activities attract attention. Consequently, abuses of the activities by individual firms are easily and quickly noted by the public. This situation in turn soon leads to public demand for correction of the abuses, assurances that they will not be repeated, and general restraints on promotional activities. To answer this demand, regulations and other safeguards have been established by the federal government and by most provincial governments. In addition, many private business organizations, both profit and nonprofit in nature, have attempted to establish voluntary guideposts for the direction of promotional activities.

For the most part, these regulatory measures have been applied far more to advertising than to personal selling or any other promotional tool. The probable reason for this unbalanced emphasis is that advertising is more centralized and is easier to control. There are far fewer media through which advertising messages may be carried than there are personal salespeople. Also, advertising messages are recorded, whereas usually there is no certain evidence of what a salesperson said.

THE FEDERAL ROLE

A number of departments of the Federal government administer acts which are aimed at controlling various aspects of promotion, particularly advertising. The Broadcasting Act, which established the Canadian Radio-Television and Telecommunications Commission (C.R.T.C.) in 1968, provides for sweeping powers of advertising regulation. Under Section 16 of the Act, the C.R.T.C. may make regulations concerning the character of broadcast advertising and the amount of time which may be devoted to it. While the potential for substantial control exists, the Commission does not in reality pass on each commercial message. What it has done is to delegate authority in certain fields to other agencies such as the Health Protection Branch of the Department of National Health and Welfare and the Combines Investigation Branch of the Department of Consumer and Corporate Affairs.

The Health Protection Branch deals with advertising in the fields of drugs, cosmetics and devices (officialese for birth-control products), and it has sweeping powers to limit, control, rewrite or ban promotion for the products under its authority. The authority itself is embodied in such acts, and regulations associated with them, as the Health and Welfare Department Act, the Proprietary or Patent Medicine Act, the Food and Drug Act, the Criminal Code of Canada and the Broadcast Act. The various acts and regulations result in general types of prohibition aimed at preventing the treatment, processing, packaging, labeling, advertising and selling of foods, drugs and devices in such a manner as to mislead or deceive, or even be "likely to create an erroneous impression as to their character, value, quantity, composition, merit or safety."[11]

The Branch also prevents the advertising of whole classes of drugs. It has developed a list of diseases or conditions for which a cure may not be advertised under any circumstance. This prohibition stands even if a professionally accepted cure exists. The logic for the prohibition of advertising, in spite of the existence of a cure, is that the Branch does not wish members of the general public to engage in self-diagnosis of the condition which can be treated.

By virtue of the powers delegated to it by the C.R.T.C., the Branch has absolute control over radio and television advertisements for the products under its jurisdiction. All such advertisements must be submitted to it at least fifteen days prior to airing, and no medium can air an ad without its having been approved by the Branch and, thereby, the C.R.T.C. In practical terms, the Health Protection Branch, even though an appeal routine to C.R.T.C. is available, has complete authority and advertisers have no recourse of any consequence.

In contrast to the delegated review powers the Health Protection Branch has over advertisements using the broadcast media, its position with reference to the print media is weak. Its formal control is in terms of alleged Food and Drug violations which must be prosecuted in court. Given the lack of jurisprudence in this area, the Branch is loath to go to court in case it loses and thus sets a precedent or in case its regulations (many of which have not been tested in court) are found to be illegal. What the Branch does is advise advertisers of its opinion of advertisements which are prepared for the print media. This opinion is not a ruling and ads submitted as well as those that are not are still subject to the regulations for which the Branch has responsibility. This does not mean that the Branch does not monitor the print media. Newspapers and magazines are sampled and advertisements examined.

The Department of Consumer and Corporate Affairs has substantial and major responsibility in the area of regulating promotion. The Combines Investigation Branch of the Department carries the major burden of promotional regulation. The acts administered include: (1) Hazardous Products Act (concerning poisonous compounds for household use); (2) the Precious Metals Marketing Act (i.e., definitions of sterling and carat weight); (3) the Trade Marks Act; (4) the Consumer Packaging and Labelling Act and (5), of greatest significance, the Combines Investigation Act. Within the Combines Investigation Act, a number of sections pertain directly to the regulation of advertising and promotional activities. Section 35, for example, requires that manufacturers or wholesalers who offer promotional allowances to retailers must offer such allowances on proportionate terms to all competing purchasers. Section 36 of the Act regulates misleading advertising in general, while Section 37 pertains specifically to "bait and switch" advertising.[12]

Section 36 of the Combines Investigation Act makes it illegal for an advertiser to make any false or misleading statement to the public in advertising or promotional

---

11 *Report of the Special Senate Committee on Mass Media*, vol. II, Ottawa, 1970, p. 155.

12 For a review of court decisions in misleading advertising cases in Canada, the reader is referred to James G. Barnes, "Advertising and the Courts," *The Canadian Business Review*, Autumn, 1975, pp. 51-54. The Misleading Advertising Division of the Department of Consumer and Corporate Affairs also publishes a quarterly review of misleading advertising cases entitled the *Misleading Advertising Bulletin*. Persons interested in receiving this bulletin can have their names placed on the mailing list simply by writing to the Department of Consumer and Corporate Affairs.

materials or with respect to warranties. This section also regulates the use of false statements regarding the expected performance or length of life of a product and the use of testimonials in advertising. Section 36.2 of the Act regulates the use of "double ticketing" in retail selling and requires that, where a retailer promotes a product at two different prices or where two prices appear on a product or at the point of sale, the retailer must sell the product at the lower of the prices. Businesses or individuals who are convicted of violating Section 36 are subject to fines as large as $25,000 or to imprisonment for up to one year.

Paragraph 36(1)(d) of the Combines Investigation Act regulates "sale" advertising and would apply particularly to retail advertisers. Section 37 requires that an advertiser who promotes a product at a "sale" price have sufficient quantities of the product on hand to satisfy reasonable market demand. Section 37.1 prohibits an advertiser from selling a "sale" item at a price higher than the advertised "sale" price. Finally, Section 37.2 regulates the conduct of contests, lotteries and games of chance. This section requires that advertisers who promote such contests disclose the number and value of prizes and the areas in which prizes are to be distributed, and further requires that prizes be distributed on a basis of skill or on a basis of random selection.

The provisions of the Combines Investigation Act relating to misleading advertising do not apply to publishers and broadcasters who actually distribute the advertising in question to the general public, provided that these publishers have accepted the contents of the advertising in good faith. In essence, this means that a newspaper can not be prosecuted for misleading advertising if it accepted the advertising on the assumption that its contents were not misleading. Although no newspaper cannot be prosecuted for misleading advertising if it accepted the advertising on the assumption that its contents were not misleading. Although no some question concerning whether media production departments and advertising agencies, which actually participate with the advertiser in the production of misleading advertising, might not in the future be considered jointly responsible with the advertiser for the contents of the offending advertisement. This is a question with which the Canadian courts may deal in the future.

THE PROVINCIAL ROLE

In each of the provinces, a considerable variety of legislation exists which is aimed at controlling various promotional practices. For instance, in Ontario, various degrees of control are exercised by the Liquor Control Board of Ontario, the Ontario Board of Film Censors, the Ontario Superintendent of Insurance, the Ontario Human Rights Commission, the Ontario Securities Commission, the Ontario Police Commission, the Ontario Racing Commission, various Ministries of the Ontario Government responsible for financial, commercial, consumer and transportation functions and services and yet more. Most of the provinces have similar sets of legislation, regulatory bodies and provincial departments. While much of the Federal regulation must in the end result in argument and prosecution in a courtroom, the provincial machinery would appear to be much more flexible and potentially regulatory in nature and if pursued, may have more substantial effect on undesirable practices.

The powers of provincial governments in relation to the regulation of misleading advertising have been increased considerably in recent years. Since 1974 a number of provinces have passed new legislation dealing with unfair and unconscionable trade practices. The "trade practices" acts passed by British Columbia, Alberta, and

Ontario contain "shopping lists" of practices which are made illegal by these acts. In reality, these pieces of legislation write into law practices which have been considered illegal by federal prosecutors for a number of years. Relating to advertising, these acts prohibit such practices as advertising a product as new when it is in fact used; advertising which fails to state a material fact, thereby deceiving the consumer; and advertising which gives greater prominence to low down payments or monthly payments rather than to the actual price of the product. The Alberta Unfair Trade Practices Act also contains a provision for corrective advertising. This provision means that a court, upon convicting an advertiser for misleading advertising, can order that advertiser to devote some or all of his advertising for a certain period to informing his customers that he had been advertising falsely in the past and to correcting the misleading information which had been communicated in the offending advertisements.

The Province of Quebec has within its Consumer Protection Act a section which regulates quite stringently advertising directed at children. This section forbids the use of exaggeration, endorsements, cartoon characters, and statements which urge children to buy. Quebec's Official Language Act also contains a number of sections which govern the use of French and English in advertising in that province.

REGULATION BY PRIVATE ORGANIZATIONS

Several kinds of private organizations also exert considerable control over promotional practices of businesses. Magazines, newspapers, and radio and television stations regularly refuse to accept advertisements which they feel are false, misleading, or generally in bad taste, and in so doing they are being "reasonable" in the ordinary course of doing business. Some trade associations have established a "code of ethics" which includes points pertaining to sales-force and advertising activities. Some trade associations regularly censor advertising appearing in their trade or professional journals. Better Business Bureaus located in major cities all over the country are working to control some very difficult situations. The Canadian Advertising Advisory Board administers the Canadian Code of Advertising Standards and also administers, through the Advertising Standards Council, a number of other advertising codes, including the Broadcast Code for Advertising to Children (on behalf of the Canadian Association of Broadcasters) and a code regulating the advertising of over-the-counter drugs which was developed by the CAAB in cooperation with the Proprietary Association and Health and Welfare Canada.

QUESTIONS AND PROBLEMS:

1. How do you account for the fact that more advertising dollars are spent on newspaper space than for time on television?
2. What might explain the lower per capita expenditure on advertising in Canada as compared with the United States?
3. How do you account for the variations in advertising expenditures as a percentage of sales among the different types of companies listed in Table 24-4?
4. Several specific objectives of advertising were outlined early in this chapter. Bring to class some advertisements which illustrate at least six of these

goals, or be prepared to describe a current radio or television advertisement which is attempting to achieve these objectives.

5. In what respects does the advertising of an automobile manufacturer differ from that of a large department store? Consider the objectives, nature, and scope of the advertising as well as the nature of the products and markets of these two firms.

6. Which advertising medium is best for advertising the following products?

   a. Life insurance
   b. Plastic clothespins
   c. Auto seat covers
   d. Suntan lotion
   e. Women's hosiery
   f. Industrial valves and gauges

7. Many grocery products manufacturers and candy producers earmark a good portion of their advertising appropriations for use in magazines. Is this a wise choice of media for these firms?

8. Why do department stores use newspapers so much more than local radio as an advertising medium?

9. Why is it worthwhile to pretest advertisements before they appear in the media? Suggest a procedure for pretesting a magazine ad.

10. What procedures can a firm use to determine how many sales dollars resulted from a given ad or from an entire campaign?

11. Many advertisers on television use program ratings to determine whether to continue the sponsorship of a program. These ratings reflect the number of families who watch the program. Are program ratings a good criterion for evaluating the effectiveness of advertising? Does a high rating indicate that sales volume will also be high? Discuss.

12. If a manufacturer has a good advertising agency, should he discontinue using his own advertising department?

13. Many manufacturers use an advertising agency to help with the company's advertising program, while most retailers do not use an agency. How do you account for this difference?

14. Explain how an advertiser may actually save money by using an agency. In your analysis, consider the factor of agency compensation.

15. In your opinion, should the media be held responsible along with the advertiser in a case where a company is charged with misleading advertising?

16. What are the benefits to the consumer of "corrective advertising"?

17. Do you think we need additional legislation to regulate advertising? Personal selling? If so, explain what you would recommend.

CASES FOR PART SIX

CASE 17: CROWN SPECIALTY STEEL COMPANY LTD.

Promotional program in expanding industrial market

Mr. Oscar Meade, president of Crown Specialty Steel of Hamilton, Ontario, realized that potential sales in the Hamilton area far exceeded the area's supply of specialty steel products and services. Moreover, the market was showing signs of expansion. Consequently, Mr. Meade was wondering what kind of a program his firm should develop (1) to take advantage of the growing market opportunities and (2) to minimize the effects of competition, which were sure to intensify.

Crown Specialty Steel's sole line of business was to provide Hamilton-area industries with custom-made, alloyed steel products capable of withstanding heavy, excessive abuse in specialized use situations. Basically, Crown was a service organization. The company did not produce any of the products it sold; instead, it acted as a liaison between steel users and steel producers. During regular calls on prospective customers, Crown salesmen would seek to identify problem situations calling for specialty steel products. Or when a user—even a large concern such as Ford or General Motors—encountered a problem which might feasibly be solved by the use of high-strength, alloyed steel, that company would initiate the contact with a specialty steel company like Crown. A Crown representative would analyze the problem and recommend the particular type of steel needed in the situation.

An order was then forwarded to a steel manufacturer. There the mill's metallurgists formulated the processes and components which would yield the desired products. Typically some material (tungsten, silicon, manganese, or nickel) was mixed with the molten steel to form an alloy which would give the desired hardness, toughness, tensile strength, or ability to withstand temperature extremes.

Extra-high-strength steel is most useful in heavy-wear areas in a factory or in situations requiring materials which can withstand heavy blows and stresses over long periods of time. Alloyed steel is commonly used in conveyor systems, blast furnaces, and certain machine parts. For example, the conveyor hooks which attach to a car body during automobile assembly must be small, but extremely strong, to provide adequate life while not impairing assembly. These small conveyor hooks are made from a special nickel-alloy, high-strength steel. Conveyors carrying gravel are subject to heavy wear and are also constructed of special steel alloys. Machine parts typically produced with specialty steels include gears, bearings, shafts, connecting rods, blades, springs, pins, and cutting units.

Through the years there have been increasing industrial needs for specialized, high-strength steel products. Two specific reasons, however, explain why the specialty steel suppliers developed to satisfy these needs, rather than the major users' going directly to large steel producers to get these products. First, the major users of special steel found that they did not use this type of product often enough to warrant having a separate facility for its procurement. But when the users *did* need the specialty product, determining its specifications and procuring it were complex tasks. Second, the greatly expanded list of steel alloys available meant that considerable expertise was needed to ensure correct product choice.

Crown's primary market was the heavily industrialized area within a 60-mile radius of Hamilton. This included the Toronto area. However, the company did consider that its total market extended out 200 miles from Hamilton. The company held 22 percent of the specialty steel market within that 200-mile limit, according to Mr. Meade. Crown faced three competitors in this market. The competitors' market shares and number of salespeople were as follows:

	Market Share (percent)	Number of Salespeople
Company A	30	11
Company B	28	9
Company C	20	8
Crown	22	8

Competition in the specialty steel industry was usually on a non-price basis because steel-mill suppliers maintained comparable prices. An important part of the product-service mix of a specialty steel firm was the ability of its salespeople to analyze a user's problem and to recommend a steel alloy which would provide the required service at a reasonable cost to the user. However, all Crown's competitors could provide this service. Competition was also affected by the personal relations which salespeople built with their customers and by other promotional efforts designed to strengthen the company image and customer loyalty.

In its relatively short life Crown had experienced some significant ups and downs in its sales history. From its beginning in 1952 until the late 1950s the company showed gradually increasing sales and profits. In the early 1960s, however, Crown's sales leveled off and even declined during four consecutive years. The reason for the decline was Crown's failure to provide fast, reliable delivery on its orders. A steel mill may receive ten to fifty orders a week from the specialty steel companies, and often will delay production of a certain order for weeks or even months. Crown's former president, Mr. Michael Latrobe, ordered from several different suppliers. Consequently, he did not enjoy a favored position with any one, nor did he maintain adequate contact with them so as to ensure prompt production of his orders.

In 1965 Mr. Meade took over as president of Crown, since when sales increased annually to the present level of about $1 million. Net operating profit increased to 7 percent of net sales. Mr. Meade credited much of this successful turnaround to his methods of working with suppliers. He selected only one mill supplier—Dofasco—and he maintained intensive written and personal contact with the manufacturer. The result was that Dofasco filled Crown's orders promptly; and consequently, Mr. Meade was usually able to provide faster service than any of his competitors.

Crown's market position had progressed to the point where Mr. Meade estimated that the four specialty steel companies could handle only 80 percent of the potential business in the Hamilton area, and furthermore the market was expanding rapidly. Crown had built a clientele of steady customers in the automotive, cement, and gravel industries. The account list included Ford, General Motors, Oxford Gravel Works, and some smaller cement companies. In addition, new users and new uses of specialty steel offered opportunities for market expansion. Local chemical companies and machine parts makers, for instance, were potential customers.

Crown's main promotional efforts were through the company's eight salespeople. Sometimes Mr. Meade made the initial contact with a customer, but from then on a salesperson handled Crown's work with that customer. Further promotion consisted of customer entertainment. No advertising was done at all. In fact, only one of Crown's three competitors used any advertising, and then only in a very small amount.

With demand outrunning supply in the specialty steel market, Crown's market prospects looked good. Mr. Meade was smart enough to realize, however, that the current market situation could very well be a short-lived phenomenon. Such a market was bound to attract additional competitors and to draw more aggressive, better-trained selling effort from existing firms. Consequently, he was wondering how he might improve and intensify Crown's promotional efforts in order to capture a satisfactory share of the expanding market.

As one alternative, Mr. Meade considered budgeting $45,000 to $50,000 for an advertising program during the coming year. He consulted a Toronto advertising agency who indicated that a program of direct-mail advertising, plus placing advertisements in selected trade journals and Southern Ontario newspapers, would have several advantages, some of which were:

1. It would make salespeople's efforts more efficient by using advertising to make the initial customer contact.
2. It would establish company identity and image.
3. It would reach customer personnel now inaccessible to the sales force.

Another alternative was to use the same amount of money to hire, train, and compensate three additional salespeople. The total cost per person would be about

$16,000, depending on the amount of training they needed—which in turn would depend to some extent upon whether experienced people were hired, thus reducing training costs. Any unallocated funds could be used (1) to further train the present salespeople and (2) to equip the sales force with better sales tools (catalogues, samples, etc.)

An informal market investigation, which Mr. Meade conducted, revealed the following interesting facts about the purchase decision for specialty steel products:

1. The initial purchase idea comes from a first level of management—a foreperson or general foreperson—which is in closes contact with a company's problems.
2. Buying decisions for specialty steels are made quickly when a need arises, and then the buyer seeks the assistance of a specialty steel company; the purchase is not a long-range, planned affair.

QUESTION

1. What promotional program should the Crown Company use to expand its sales effectively and profitably?

CASE 18: THE CANADIAN BANK SERVICE PACKAGE*

Analysis of service package market and promotional program design

Throughout the 1970s, there has been increased competition among Canadian chartered banks for a larger share of the market for banking services. This competition has led to the introduction by Canadian banks of a number of different banking services. One of the most innovative of these services has been the Bank Service Package. Within the past few years, most major Canadian banks have introduced Service Packages. These are: the Canadian Imperial Bank of Commerce's Key Account; the Royal Bank of Canada's Certified Service; the Bank of Montreal's Full-Service Package; the Bank of Nova Scotia's Scotiaclub; and the Toronto-Dominion Bank's Personal Service Plan.

The Bank Service Package has been heralded as a new dimension in personal banking. Typically the Package contains all banking services which the individual customer is likely to need. For a fixed monthly fee, which varies from $2 to $3 depending on the particular bank, the holder of the Bank Service Package is exempt from service charges on the following items: (1) the writing of cheques; (2) the provision of personalized cheques; (3) safety deposit boxes; (4) the purchase of money orders and drafts; and (5) the purchase of traveler's cheques. In addition, the holder of a Bank Service Package is allowed the following privileges and conveniences: (1) payment of utility bills at a branch of his/her bank; (2) ability to cash cheques at other branches; (3) a reduced personal loan rate; and (4) overdraft protection.

The Bank Service Package idea originated with the Wells Fargo Bank of San Francisco in early 1973. During the Spring of 1973, Wells Fargo revealed its new package in a series of information seminars which were attended by representatives of all Canadian chartered banks.

---

* Case prepared by Professor James G. Barnes, School of Business Administration and Commerce, Memorial University of Newfoundland.

Following the revealing of this new banking concept by Wells Fargo, most Canadian banks adopted this innovation and introduced to the market their own versions of the Bank Service Package. The Canadian Imperial Bank of Commerce was the first Canadian bank to offer its customers a Service Package. The Bank of Commerce's Key Account Package came on the Canadian market in December, 1973. Within the following four months, four other Canadian banks had offered their customers similar bank service packages. In January, 1974, the Royal Bank of Canada introduced its Royal Certified Service. During February, 1974, the Bank of Nova Scotia introduced its Scotiaclub and the Toronto-Dominion Bank introduced its Personal Service Plan. By April, 1974, the Bank of Montreal had introduced its FullService Package to the Canadian market.

The research study. In early 1975, by which time the Canadian Bank Service Packages had been available to the public for approximately one year, one of the largest Canadian chartered banks decided to undertake a research study which would provide their Marketing Department with a profile of Canadian consumers who had taken advantage of a Bank Service Package as compared with consumers who had not applied. The decision to undertake such a research study was based on the knowledge that the Bank Service Packages had been rather hastily introduced in Canada and that the Canadian chartered banks had little knowledge of the characteristics of the holders of their Bank Service Packages as compared with those customers who had not decided to apply for such a package. It was felt that knowledge of the demographic and "life style" characteristics of Bank Service Package holders would be beneficial to the Bank's Marketing Department in several ways. This information would enable a meaningful market segmentation strategy to be formulated for the new product. In addition, advertising campaigns could be designed to complement the activities, interests and opinions of Bank Service Package holders. Finally, there were rather obvious implications for media selection and scheduling.

Accordingly, a research study was undertaken utilizing the services of a professional marketing research company. The study was designed to provide information on those persons who had subscribed to a Bank Service Package. Comparisons could then be drawn to indicate how Service Package holders differed from average bank customers. It was decided that information could be obtained on customers' attitudes towards banks and bank service costs; attitudes towards credit and toward financial risk generally. In addition, questions were added to the questionnaire concerning customers' attitudes toward retail shopping, since a requirement of the Bank Service Packages was that the holder of the package also be a holder of a Chargex or Master Charge card. In addition, the questionnaire contained a number of questions relating to the customers' actual use of banking facilities and other financial institutions as well as a number of general demographic and socioeconomic questions.

Part 1 of the questionnaire used in the study contained 112 statements relating to banking and financial matters. Respondents to the questionnaire were asked to indicate their level of agreement or disagreement with each of these statements. Part 2 of the questionnaire contained 17 questions relating to the respondents' use of banking and other financial services and a number of specific questions relating to Bank Service Packages. Finally, Part 3 of the questionnaire contained certain demographic and socioeconomic questions.

Copies of the questionnaire, along with a covering letter and a stamped self-ad-dressed envelope, were mailed by the Marketing Research Company to 800 adult residents of a medium-sized Ontario city. Members of the sample were selected at random from the City Directory and the covering letter which accompanied the questionnaire assured respondents of their anonymity and provided them with a definition of Bank Service Packages. It was considered necessary to clarify this point to ensure that no misunderstanding arose with regard to certain questions in Part 2 of the questionnaire.

Results. The total of 240 individuals returned the questionnaire. Of those returned, a number were discarded because respondents had failed to answer a large number of questions or because answers were submitted in an unacceptable form. Of the 210 usable questionnaires, 172 were returned by respondents who were not holders of a Bank Service Package, while 38 respondents were holders of one of these packages.

Responses to the statements in Part 1 of the questionnaire could range from a high of 6 to a low of 1. A response of 1 would indicate that the respondent completely disagreed with the particular statement, while an answer of 6 would indicate complete agreement. Respondents' answers on the 112 statements in Part 1 of the questionnaire were analysed using a computer program known as Factor Analysis. This program has the effect of grouping together similar statements from the list of 112 statements. Each group of statements formed may be interpreted as a "scale" which represents an attitude toward a particular concept or idea. For example, one of the scales contains statements relating to the use of credit. By calculating a respondent's score on this scale, it is possible to determine whether he or she has a positive or negative attitude toward the use of credit. A list of the scales formed and the average scores of package holders and non-holders on each scale are presented in Table 1. This table indicates the manner in which a high score on each scale should be interpreted. For example, on the first scale, a high average score would indicate a positive attitude toward banks in general.

Table 1. Average Scores for Holders and Non-holders on "Life Style" Scales.**

Scale: a higher score indicates	Average Score Holders	Average Score Non-holders
1. positive attitude toward banks	1.91	2.02
2. positive attitude toward use of credit	3.84	3.04*
3. greater use of the mass media	3.73	3.82
4. more liberal outlook, less conservative	3.63	3.63
5. greater self-confidence	4.61	4.29*
6. positive attitude toward in-bank service	2.82	2.49
7. greater enjoyment of retail shopping	3.78	4.12
8. greater willingness to take risks	4.50	4.52
9. negative attitude toward in-bank delays	3.67	2.90*

* indicates that the difference between holders' and non-holders' average scores is statistically significant.

** average scores can range from a low of 1 to a high of 6.

Table 2 contains a list of selected statements from Part 1 of the questionnaire on which holders and non-holders produced significantly different average scores. This table contains average scores for each statement. The higher the score, the greater the level of agreement with the statement.

Table 3 contains information on the extent to which holders and non-holders make use of banking and other financial services. Table 4 contains comparative demographic and socioeconomic information on holders and non-holders.

Table 2. Average scores for holders and non-holders on selected "life style" statements.

Statement	Average Score Holders	Average Score Non-Holders
1. I would like to own and fly my own airplane.[1]	3.50	2.56
2. I prefer to make installment payments on large purchases than to pay cash.	3.37	2.65
3. The security I get from keeping my money in a bank is worth paying for.	3.11	4.05
4. Personalized cheques are a waste of good money.	2.42	3.34
5. A woman's place is in the home.	2.00	3.24
6. We will probably move at least once in the next three years.	3.37	2.26

[1] Statements should be interpreted as: "service package holders agree more that they would like to own and fly their own airplane."

Note: The higher the score, the more the person agrees with the statement. A score of 6 indicates total agreement with the statement. A score of 1 would indicate total disagreement with the statement.

Table 3. Usage of banking services by holders and non-holders.

Variable	Holders	Non-Holders
1. Percentage with chequing account	89.5%	67.9%
2. Percentage with oil company credit card	73.7%	61.4%
3. Percentage with department store credit card	78.9%	61.4%
4. Percentage who have borrowed from bank or finance company in last 24 months	70.6%	51.3%
5. Average number of bank visits per month	4.78	3.39

Table 4. Demographic and socioeconomic characteristics of holders and non-holders.

Variable	Holders	Non-Holders
1. Percentage married	82.6%	100.0%
2. Average number of children if married	2.3	1.5
3. Occupation:		
Professional	47.1%	19.8%
Manager/owner	5.9%	18.6%
Skilled laborer	11.8%	23.3%
Clerical	29.4%	9.5%
4. Spouse's Occupation:		
Professional/Supervisory	36.8%	11.6%
Housewife	26.3%	46.5%
Clerical	26.3%	8.1%
5. Family income greater than $15,000 per year	83.3%	47.7%
6. Age 35 years or less	55.6%	19.3%
7. Education:		
Some university	11.1%	8.3%
University graduate	38.9%	26.2%
8. Spouse's Education:		
Some university	22.2%	8.2%
University graduate	11.1%	15.1%

QUESTION

1. What should the bank do in terms of promoting the service package?

CASE 19: SUPERIOR TIRE AND RUBBER COMPANY LIMITED

Advertising program among franchised retailers

What is known today as the Superior Tire and Rubber Company Ltd. was founded in 1934 in a small town in Southern Ontario, when Mr. Roger Atkins developed a piece of equipment which he called a "rubber welder." This machine was able to join two pieces of rubber together in such a way that they would remain attached even while being used under extreme environmental conditions. With the help of a few employees, Mr. Atkins manufactured the machine in his garage. He also served as the sales force, traveling throughout the area and calling upon service stations, tire repair shops, and garages. The rubber welder found an eagerly waiting market among tire repair shops and garages in Ontario and Quebec. In fact, many of the customers called upon by Mr. Atkins were so favorably impressed with the capabilities and potentialities of the rubber welder that these repairmen wanted to have exclusive rights to the use of the machine in their markets. It was from these requests that Mr. Atkins developed the franchising arrangements used by Superior Tire and Rubber today.

Later in the 1930s, Mr. Atkins, using the same basic rubber-welding principles, designed and manufactured a machine which would put a complete new tread on a tire casing. This retreading machine was also well accepted by the garages and tire repair shops. When new tires were not available during World War II, the tire retreading business boomed, and Superior Tire and Rubber expanded its operations considerably. After the war, as new tires once more became plentiful, the market for tire retreading machines slumped. To offset the decline in his business, Mr. Atkins signed an agreement with the B. F. Goodrich Company. Under the agreement, Superior's franchised retail dealers were provided with B. F. Goodrich's well-known national brand of tires and tubes to sell along with their other products and services.

Today the Superior Tire and Rubber Company Ltd. remains as it has always been—a manufacturer and supplier; it is not a retailer. The company does, however, serve as the "parent" company for approximately one hundred retailers from coast to coast who operate as franchised dealers. Virtually all these franchise holders are either tire repair and retread shops or auto repair garages specializing in tire maintenance and front-end service. Under the terms of the franchise agreement, Superior grants each dealer the right to sell Superior products and services and to use the Superior name in a territory protected from encroachment by any other Superior franchise holder. The retailer owns his own building and equipment and handles his own advertising.

Superior manufactures the tire retreading and repairing equipment used by its franchised dealers. In addition to manufacturing the tread rubber and the various tread matrices which are used in the retreading machines, Superior also produces wheel alignment equipment, wheel balancing equipment, and automotive truing machines for servicing the front-end mechanisms in automobiles. All these pieces of equipment are sold directly to the franchised retailers.

A few years ago, Superior discontinued carrying the B. F. Goodrich brand of tires and tubes and started selling under the Superior name a line of tires and tubes purchased from another large manufacturer. Also under its own brand, Superior supplies to its franchise holders a line of batteries, shock absorbers, brake linings, and front-end repair parts. Annual sales of Superior have reached $10 million, and the largest part of this volume is from the sale of new tires.

At the present time, Superior itself does no advertising. The only advertising of Superior products and services is done at the local level by the franchised retailers. The parent company provides the dealers with point-of-purchase advertising materials and grants them an advertising allowance of 1½ percent of their purchases. From time to time, several dealers will group together and advertise jointly in their immediate market area. For example, some years ago, three stores in the Halifax market started a joint advertising program by sharing the cost of a $50-a-month advertising program in local newspapers. This has grown, until today eighteen stores in the Atlantic Provinces cooperate in a $40,000-a-year local advertising effort.

Mr. Atkins has become increasingly concerned that his company's promotional efforts are inadequate to meet the stiffening competition his company is facing in its bid for tire and parts replacement business. All his major competitors—Eaton's, Simpsons-Sears, Canadian Tire, the major tire companies, the major petroleum companies, discount houses, and other department stores—are advertising heavily. In view of this competitive promotion, Mr. Atkins is considering the use of national advertising by his company to support the local promotional efforts of the franchised dealers. Also, strong requests have been received from many dealers, urging Superior to do some advertising on television and in national magazines.

Mr. Atkins envisions an annual appropriation of about $200,000 for this advertising. He wants to use spot commercials on television and periodic advertisements in *Macleans* and other magazines. He would use both product and institutional advertising and would contract with an advertising agency to do the work.

By embarking upon a national advertising campaign, Mr. Atkins believes the company would increase its prestige and upgrade its image among consumers. This type of promotion would help to attract new franchise holders. It would also pave the way for expansion of product lines. For some time, Mr. Atkins has hoped that the Superior Tire and Rubber stores could be patterned after the retail outlets of the Firestone and the Goodyear companies, where a wide variety of merchandise is carried.

The vice-president of sales, Mr. R. K. Llewellyn, is not in favor of the national advertising idea. Instead, he believes Superior should increase its support to the dealers in their local promotional programs. He fears that the cost of national advertising would be prohibitive. He would prefer to do no advertising rather than waste money on an inadequate program. In his view, the money could be better spent by increasing the dealers' advertising allowance to 5 percent of purchases and by furnishing more and better point-of-purchase advertising materials. To stimulate the dealers to do more newspaper advertising, Mr. Llewellyn would have Superior provide, at no cost to these dealers, all the necessary mats for the ads. The only cost to the dealer would be the space charges.

Regardless of the direction taken in their promotional programs, both Mr. Atkins and Mr. Llewellyn are wondering what the main appeal should be in these programs. On one hand, the company could emphasize the quality of its products. The idea would be to build brand recognition for the Superior name and to stress product benefits of the tires, tubes, and other items sold to consumers. On the other hand, both executives realize that "quality of service" is a very effective advertising appeal. For example, a few years ago, the two largest Superior dealers handled the B.F. Goodrich tire. They have since switched to the new Superior private-branded tire; these firms are still the two top dealers, and their volume on new tires has increased. This would seem to indicate that consumers are more interested in the dealer and his services than in the brand name of the products he sells. Furthermore, by using the "service-center concept" as an appeal, the company might better attract new retailers and increase the market for its retreading equipment and front-end alignment equipment.

QUESTIONS

1. Should Superior engage in national advertising, or should it only give more support to retailer advertising at the local level?
2. Should the company's main promotional appeal stress "quality of service" or "quality of product"?

PART
7

MARKETING IN SPECIAL FIELDS

MARKETING OF SERVICES

As we developed a marketing program for an individual company in Parts 3 to 6, our thoughts were focused largely on the domestic marketing of manufactured goods. The marketing programs in two additional fields will be considered separately, although briefly, in this chapter and the next one. The areas to be discussed are the marketing of services and the marketing of commodities and products in foreign countries. In each case, we are still concerned with building a marketing program around the constituent parts of the marketing mix—the product, the price structure, the distribution system, and the promotional program.

In the first chapter of this book, we defined marketing as a system designed to plan, price, promote, and distribute goods and *services* to markets. Then we promptly devoted the intervening twenty-four chapters largely to the marketing of *products,* dealing with such things as credit, delivery, and management advice only when they were associated with, and incidental to, the sale of goods. Now we shall rectify that imbalance a bit.

Some students may question the usefulness of a separate chapter on the marketing of services, however, believing that *fundamentally* there is no difference between product marketing and service marketing. In bare-bone outline, it is true, the two are the same in that marketing research is used to develop a marketing mix which will profitably reach a predetermined market. Moreover, often there are substantial similarities in the flesh put on these bones. At the same time, however, significant differences do exist between product marketing and service marketing. Consequently, the marketing planning—the strategies and tactics—often must be substantially different, so the marketing of services does well deserve separate attention.[1]

NATURE AND IMPORTANCE

Out of every dollar that we as consumers spend, about 40 cents goes for services, and services provide more than half of all private, nongovernmental jobs. Furthermore, the forecast is that these figures will increase, rather than decrease. Yet relatively little has been published in the way of a conceptual, all-encompassing study to guide marketing executives in service concerns.[2]

DEFINITION AND SCOPE OF FIELD

No common boundaries have been set to delimit the field of services. The American Marketing Association defines service as "activities, benefits, or satisfactions which are offered for sale, or are provided in connection with the sale of goods."[3] Under this interpretation, we would include (1) intangible benefits offered for sale independently of other goods or services (insurance, legal service); (2) intangible activities which require the use of tangible goods (amusement, house rentals, transportation service); and (3) intangible activities purchased jointly with products or other intangible activities (credit, training dealer salespeople). This definition is too broad for useful marketing analysis. Particularly, we should separate out those services which exist *only* in connection with the *sale* of a product or another service. Thus, when we talk about the marketing of services, using the above three-way classification, we are talking only about those activities in parts (1) and (2).

Consequently, in this chapter we shall define *services* as separately identifiable, intangible activities which provide want satisfaction when marketed to consumers and/or industrial users and which are not necessarily tied to the sale of a product or another service. Therefore, we include such services as insurance, repair service (but not the repair parts purchased), and entertainment; we exclude credit, delivery, and packaging services which exist only when there is a sale of an article or another service.

The definitional problem will continue and some statistics on services may be misleading because it is becoming more difficult to separate products and services in our economy. Actually, we rarely find situations (as in legal services) where we market services with no product involvement whatsoever. "Most goods, whether consumer or industrial, require supporting services in order to be useful; most ser-

---

1 See Robert C. Judd, "Similarities or Differences in Product and Service Retailing," *Journal of Retailing,* Winter, 1968, pp. 1-9.

2 For two noteworthy exceptions to this statement, see Donald D. Parker, *The Marketing of Consumer Services,* University of Washington, Business Study Series, no. 1, Seattle, 1960; Eugene M. Johnson, *An Introduction to the Problems of Service Marketing Management,* University of Delaware, Bureau of Economic and Business Research, Newark, 1964.

3 Committee on Definitions, *Marketing Definitions: A Glossary of Marketing Terms,* American Marketing Association, Chicago, 1960, p. 21.

vices require supporting goods to be useful."[4] It is this product-service mix which really is growing in importance in our economy.

We are concerned primarily with the services sold by some business or professional firm with profit-making motives—commercial services—in contrast to those sold by nonbusiness organizations such as churches, public schools, and the government. One useful classification of commercial services is given below. No attempt is made to separate these services according to whether they are sold to household consumers or industrial users. In fact, most are purchased by both market groups.

1. Housing (includes rentals of hotels, motels, apartments, houses, and farms)
2. Household operations (includes utilities, house repairs, repairs of equipment in the house, landscaping, and household cleaning)
3. Recreation (includes rental and repairs of equipment used in participating in recreation and entertainment activities; also admission to all entertainment, recreation, and amusement events)
4. Personal care (includes laundry, dry cleaning, beauty care)
5. Medical and other health care (includes all medical service, dental, nursing, hospitalization, optometry, and other health care)
6. Private education
7. Business and other professional services (includes legal, accounting, management consulting, and marketing consulting services)
8. Insurance and financial (includes personal and property insurance, credit and loan service, investment counseling, and tax service)
9. Transportation and communications (includes freight and passenger service on public carriers, automobile repairs and rentals, and telephone service)

THE IMPORTANCE OF SERVICE CONSUMPTION

The statistics on consumer services tell an interesting story. While expenditures for services have increased in absolute dollar terms every year as a proportion of personal consumption expenditures (see Table 25-1), the consumer allocation to total services remains essentially the same with the most current allocation being approximately 38 cents out of every dollar of personal expenditure. Service expenditures as a percent of gross national product for the 1966-73 period show a reasonably consistent downward trend in the later years. In aggregate terms, personal financing of consumer services seems to be becoming less important. This is in contrast to the American experience which shows growth in the importance of services over the same period both in terms of service expenditures as a percentage of personal consumption expenditures and as a percentage of gross national product. As a percentage of U.S. gross national product, in 1965 services were 25.8 percent and by 1973, 26.1 percent.

Care must be taken in interpreting statistics on service expenditures. Inflation has had a greater impact on service costs than on costs for goods. The federal and provincial governments now finance and supply more services than in the past and consumers do not pay for these out of their disposable income but rather through various forms of taxation. Medical care and education are prime examples of services which have grown rapidly in terms of expenditures but for which individuals do not pay directly. Although expenditure patterns for goods and services remain

---

4 John M. Rathmell, "What Is Meant by Services?" *Journal of Marketing*, October, 1966, p. 33.

Table 25-1. Expenditures for Personal Services as a Percentage of the Gross National Product and Total Personal Consumption Expenditures, 1966-1973 (in millions of current dollars).

Year	Services	Personal Consumption Expenditures (in millions of current dollars)	Gross National Product	Service Expenditure as percentage of:	
				Personal Consumption Expenditures	Gross National Product
1966	13,982	36,890	61,828	37.90	22.61
1967	15,299	39,972	66,409	38.27	23.04
1968	17,238	43,704	72,586	39.44	23.75
1969	19,018	47,492	79,815	40.04	23.83
1970	20,697	50,327	85,685	41.13	24.15
1971	21,858	54,468	93,462	40.28	23.39
1972	23,780	60,580	103,952	39.41	22.88
1973	26,351	69,367	120,438	38.14	21.88

Source: Statistics Canada, Market Research Handbook, 1975, p. 10 and 147.

reasonably stable, as indicated in Table 25-2, the categories of goods and services acquired and made use of changes over the time period. This is particularly the case with services, as governments finance more and more of those becoming defined as social in nature, and individuals increase their financing of other personal services such as travel, entertainment and household utilities. As personal incomes increase and life styles change, the demand for some services which must be purchased by individuals increases and for others, declines. Thus the shift in preference for services is to be carefully examined by those engaged in various parts of the service industries.

When we say that close to 40 percent of the average consumer's income is spent for services, we still grossly understate the economic importance of services. These figures do not include the vast amounts spent for business and industrial services. By all indications, spending for business services has increased even more rapidly than that for consumer services. The truth of the matter is that we do not have accurate measurements reflecting total sales of services. This lack of complete statistical data is traceable, in part at least, to definitional problems. Nonetheless, it is quite clear that the market for services is an exceedingly large one.

In the business field, services have grown in importance. Business has become increasingly complex, specialized, and competitive, and as a result management has been forced to call in experts to provide services in research, taxation, advertising, labor relations, and a host of other areas.

One theory of economic growth holds that there are three observable stages of development.[5] In the primary stage (low-level economies), agriculture, forestry, hunting, and fishing occupy the population's attention. In the secondary stage, the major emphasis is on manufacturing. In the tertiary stage, the important activities involve trade, transportation, finance, communication, construction, and professional and governmental fields. Since most of these activities are services, an econ-

5 Colin Clark, The Conditions of Economic Progress, 3d ed., Macmillan & Co., Ltd., London, 1957, p. 491, as cited in William J. Regan, "The Service Revolution," Journal of Marketing, July, 1963, pp. 57-62.

Table 25-2. Expenditure Trends for Goods and Services as a Percent of Personal Consumption Expenditures, 1966-73 (Based on Current Dollar Expenditures in Millions).

Year	Percent Durables	Percent Semi-Durables	Percent Non-Durables	Percent Service	Total Annual
1966	14.88	13.70	33.52	37.90	36,890
1967	14.80	13.86	33.07	38.27	39,972
1968	14.86	13.62	32.08	39.44	43,704
1969	14.69	13.53	31.74	40.04	47,492
1970	13.51	13.20	32.16	41.13	50,327
1971	14.34	13.31	32.07	40.28	54,266
1972	15.02	13.44	32.13	39.41	60,337
1973	15.51	13.75	32.60	38.14	69,094

Source: Calculated from Data in Market Research Handbook, 1975.

omy in the third stage of development should experience an increasing share of expenditures in the services sector, whether they are financed publicly or privately.

CHARACTERISTICS OF SERVICES

Services possess distinctive characteristics which create marketing problems and result in marketing programs which are often substantially different from those found in the marketing of products.

INTANGIBILITY

Services are intangible. The impossibility of a customer's tasting, feeling, seeing, hearing, or smelling a service before he buys it places some strain on the marketing organization. This burden falls mainly on a company's promotional program, where the salespeople and advertising department must concentrate on the benefits to be derived from the service, rather than emphasizing the service itself. An insurance company will promote service benefits such as guaranteed payment of the children's educational expenses, protection against losing one's life's savings in a damage suit resulting from an auto accident, or a retirement income of so many dollars a month. The telephone companies in their advertising tell us how companies can cut selling and inventory costs, and often save a sale, by using long-distance calls.

On the other hand, the factor of intangibility offers some competitive advantages to a firm. Problems of physical distribution are eliminated. There is nothing to store or handle. There is no inventory to control, and a company will never be faced with losses from a decline in inventory values.

INSEPARABILITY

Services often cannot be separated from the person of the seller. A corollary to this point is that some services are often created and marketed simultaneously. For example, a hair stylist is creating the service of a haircut and dispensing the service at the same time. Of course, preparation and training may be done in advance.

From a marketing standpoint, inseparability means that frequently direct sale is the only possible channel of distribution, and a seller's services cannot be sold in very many markets. This characteristic also limits the scale of operation in a firm. One person can repair only so many autos in a day or treat only so many medical patients. Also, because each person—that is, each "service institution"—is a specialist, the service company often cannot add a variety of other services to its line, the way a department store or supermarket can.

As a modification of the inseparability feature, there may be a tangible representation of the service by someone other than the creator-seller. A travel agent, insurance broker, or rental agent, for instance, may represent and help promote the service which will be sold by the institution producing it.

HETEROGENEITY

It is impossible to standardize output among several sellers of presumably the same service. As a matter of fact, it is not possible to standardize completely even the output of one seller. A railroad does not give the same quality of service on each trip. All repair jobs a mechanic does on automobiles are not of equal quality. Complicating this characteristic is the fact that often it is difficult to judge the quality of a service. (Of course, we can say the same for some products.) It is particularly difficult to forecast the quality in advance of buying a service. A person pays to see a sporting event without knowing whether it will turn out to be an exciting one, well worth the price if admission, or a low-quality, dull performance.

In light of these problems of standardization and quality evaluation, the service company should pay particular attention to the "product-planning" stage of its marketing program. Management must do all it can to ensure consistent and high-quality performance. In this way, the company can build the customer confidence and good reputation that are so vital to repeat business and to favorable word-of-mouth advertising.

PERISHABILITY AND FLUCTUATING DEMAND

Services are highly perishable, and they cannot be stored. Unused electrical power, empty seats in a stadium, and idle repairmen in a garage all represent business which is lost forever. Furthermore, the market for services fluctuates considerably by seasons, by days of the week, and by hours of the day. Many ski lifts lie idle all summer, and golf courses in some areas go unused in the winter. Football stadia are used mainly in the fall, and then only one day a week. Use of city buses fluctuates within a day.

The combination of perishability and fluctuating demand offers product-planning, pricing, and promotion challenges to executives in a service company. They might look for new uses for idle plant capacity in off-seasons. Through advertising, they can show consumers the advantages of using city transportation facilities during nonpeak hours. In an attempt to level demand, telephone companies price at lower rates on nights and weekends.

THE MARKETING CONCEPT AND SERVICE MARKETING

The growth in services has generally been attributed to the maturation of our economy and the rising standards of living in our affluent society, but not to marketing developments in the service industries. Traditionally, executives in service comanies have not been marketing-oriented. They have lagged behind sellers of products in accepting the marketing concept. Service organizations have also generally been slow in adopting promotional methods, "product" strategies, and other marketing techniques. With a few notable exceptions, such as the insurance industry and, more recently, the telephone companies, marketing management in service firms has not been especially creative. Innovation has come typically from product-associated companies.

To illustrate, the major impetus for the increased use of electrical power has come from appliance manufacturers, not electric utilities.[6] The laundry and dry-cleaning industry stood still, despite increased competition from home laundry equipment and coin-operated dry-cleaning establishments, and despite the development of wash-and-wear and permanently pressed fabrics. The repair industry has left a trail of dissatisfied and even irate customers for years.

Perhaps we can identify the reasons for this lack of a marketing orientation. No doubt the intangibility of services poses more difficult marketing problems than those which product sellers face. In many service industries—particularly professional services—the sellers think of themselves as producers or creators, and not as marketers, of the service. They are proud of their ability to repair a car, diagnose an illness, fly a plane, sing a concert, or give a good haircut. They do not think of themselves as businessmen. It is not "ethical," for example, for a doctor or a lawyer to advertise. Failure of management to recognize that competition existed may account for lack of interest in marketing in some industries—banking, railroads, and public utilities, for instance.

The all-encompassing reason, however, seems to be that top management has yet to recognize how important marketing is to the success of a firm. This failure is reflected in three areas of weakness.[7] First, these executives have a limited view of the marketing function and of the business they are in. They equate marketing with selling and fail to consider other parts of the system. Movie producers thought of themselves as being in the business of making movies; instead, they were really marketing entertainment. Railroad executives saw their task as running a railroad, instead of marketing a transportation system or a total materials-handling system. The second point—a consequence of the first—is that management fails to recognize that many of its problems are marketing problems. And once this fact is recognized, management may still not act quickly. Finally, there has been insufficient coordination of all marketing activities in service firms. Many service firms lack an executive whose sole responsibility is marketing—the counterpart of the vice president of marketing in a goods-producing company.

---

6 An appreciation of the marketing concept in gas-electric companies would affect their budgeting, promotional spending, and organizational structure, according to William E. Reif and William A. Knoke, "The Marketing Concept for Combination Gas and Electric Companies," *Public Utilities Fortnightly*, Oct. 22, 1970, pp. 33-39. This article also considers some common misconceptions about the utility industry (e.g., lack of competition, nature of demand, concept of product, engineering approach to pricing) which impede the adoption of the marketing concept.

7 Eugene M. Johnson, "Marketing Is Key to Success in Service Busines," *Sales/Marketing Today*, November, 1964, pp. 8-11.

Fortunately, this total situation seems to have improved markedly over the past decade.[8] While there may still be a long way to go in some service fields (perhaps in repair services, personal grooming, and others where small businesses predominate), the overall future prospects look good for the recognition and acceptance of the marketing concept in service industries.

The banking industry provides an interesting example of a service industry which in the past has been very much *non*marketing oriented, but which is struggling to make the transition to modern times. For years commercial banks made a customer feel as if they were doing him a big favor by holding his money in a chequing account with no interest but with a service charge, or in a savings account at very low interest rates. Loans were granted grudgingly to consumers. Banks were marble mausoleums; tellers were faceless people behind protective bars, and the banker was a "black hat," stereotyped in song and story.

In recent years, however, many banks have been striving to change those images, because the market situation in banking has changed appreciably. Competition both from within and also from outside the industry has intensified. Bankers are beginning to realize that money is a highly standardized, nondifferentiated product. One bank's money is no crisper or greener than another's. Large industrial and commercial customers are diverting idle cash funds into various types of notes and other high-yield investments, rather than leaving these funds in banks at low interest rates. Today the problem facing banks is more likely to be how to *acquire* funds, rather than how to lend or otherwise *employ* them. So banks increasingly are looking to the consumer market (called the "retail" market in banking) as a source of funds.

To meet these challenges, many banks finally are starting to do a little marketing. In fact, some banks are trying to shorten the transition period by pirating marketing executives from consumer-product companies.[9] Banks are establishing marketing departments, conducting sales training programs, engaging in marketing research, shifting from institutional advertising to hard-sell "product" ads, expanding their services (product) mix, and sending their people to bank-marketing executive development programs.

Banks are making concentrated efforts to attract retail (consumer) business. Buildings and internal layouts are designed to project an image of warmth, friendliness, and informality. Cash card and credit card systems have been added for consumer convenience (and incidentally, additional revenues). Other new services include insurance, no-charge chequing accounts, travel service, personal financial counseling, payment of customers' utility bills, and 24-hour outside-wall depositories and cash dispensers.

Admittedly most banks have quite a way to go before anyone would call them a full-fledged marketing company, but the progress is encouraging. Perhaps soon some banks may even abolish "bankers' hours" and introduce "customers' hours" by staying open and providing full services during the evenings and on Saturdays

---

8 For some examples, see David L. Bickelhaupt, "Trends and Innovations in the Marketing of Insurance," *Journal of Marketing*, July, 1967, pp. 17-22; Thomas R. Wotruba, "The Role of Marketing in a Gas or Electric Utility: A Perspective," *Southern Journal of Business*, October, 1968, pp. 26-34; "United Charts a New Flight Plan," *Business Week*, Aug. 14, 1965, p. 128; and " 'A Hell of a Way to Run a Railroad,' " *Sales Management*, Mar. 4, 1966, p. 28.

9 "Now Banks are Turning to the Hard Sell," *Business Week*, June 24, 1972, p. 78; see also "Tyros in the Marketing Game," *Business Week*, Sept. 15, 1973, p. 129; and Martin Everett, "See the Bankers Selling," *Sales Management*, July 9, 1973, p. 16.

just like other retailers intent on serving their customers. The cashless, chequeless economy is anticipated by many bankers, although consumer resistance to the unknown and the consumer's inability to fully control his payments may delay the full implementation of that innovation. When a cashless, chequeless system is in effect, however, it will provide banks with a vast fund of information for use in planning, evaluating, and controlling marketing activities in both consumer and industrial markets.[10]

A PROGRAM FOR MARKETING OF SERVICES

Because we are dealing with intangibles, the task of determining the marketing-mix ingredients for a total marketing program in a service industry is perhaps more difficult and thus requires more skill than is true in product-marketing firms.

MARKET ANALYSIS AND MARKET PLANNING

Procedural considerations involved in market analysis and planning are essentially the same whether a firm is selling a product or a service. A marketer of services should understand the components of population and income as they affect the market for his services. In addition, he must carefully analyze his customers' motivation for buying his services—that is, *why* do they want his services, and does each segment of his market have the same or different motives? Also, the seller must determine the buying patterns for his services—when, where, and how do customers buy, who does the buying, and who makes the buying decisions? Essentially the same determinants of buying behavior—attitudes, perceptions, personality, etc.—are as pertinent in the marketing of services as in product marketing. In like manner, the sociological factors of social-class structure and small-group influences are market determinants for services. The fundamentals of the adoption and diffusion of product innovation are also relevant in the marketing of services.[11]

Some of the trends pointed up in Chapters 4 to 8 are particularly worth watching because they carry considerable influence in the marketing of services. As an example, increases in disposable income and discretionary buying power mean that consumers can buy more than basic personal and household necessities. Consequently, they become a growing market for more insurance, or transportation service. The increasing number of working women means greater markets for many services. Women will now pay for services such as laundry or household repairs which formerly they performed themselves. Shorter working hours have resulted in increases in leisure time. More leisure time plus greater income means increased markets for recreation and entertainment services.

A service industry may be able to segment its market on some basis and then use an appropriate marketing strategy to reach each segment more effectively. The airlines, for instance, identified the youth market (ages twelve to twenty-two) as a

---

10 For examples of marketing activities which banks could then engage in, see Robert H. Myers, "Profiles of the Future: Marketing Opportunities," *Business Horizons*, Feb., 1972, pp. 12-14.

11 For a study of the diffusion of three life insurance innovations through the industry, see Robert A. Peterson, William Rudelius, and Glenn L. Wood, "Spread of Marketing Innovations in a Service Industry," *Journal of Business*, October, 1972, pp. 485-496.

separate unit and then established a youth fare (half price with a membership card or on a space-available basis) to reach that market segment.[12]

PLANNING AND DEVELOPING THE SERVICE

Product planning and development should have its counterpart in the marketing program of a service industry. Management should use an organized, systematic procedure to determine (1) what services will be offered, (2) what the company's policies will be with respect to the length and breadth of the service line offered, and (3) what, if anything, needs to be done in the way of service attributes such as branding or providing guarantees.

Unfortunately, planning and developing the service has been a neglected activity in most service firms until very recent years, and it is still ignored in too many cases. The basic reason for this neglect goes back to the lack of a marketing orientation in service industries and their narrow view of what business they are in. A motion picture firm which thinks its job is to "make movies" (instead of marketing entertainment) is not apt to get involved in creating and marketing a filmed comedy series for television. By taking the broad view of its service offerings, a company may stay in business long after narrower firms have disappeared. An electric utility which thinks of its business as marketing energy (instead of producing electricity) will not be dismayed when solar radiation or atomic energy is used as a source of power.

New services are just as important to a service company as new products are to a product-marketing firm, even though service companies may not face the problem of obsolescence to as great an extent. Similarly, improving existing services is every bit as important as improving existing products. Certainly much of the procedure for developing new products and many of the criteria for selecting new products (as discussed in Chapter 9) are equally applicable in a service firm.

A service industry can expand or contract its "product line," alter existing services, and trade up or down—in the same way that a product-marketing organization does. Dry cleaners, for instance, have expanded into laundry services, mothproofing, storage, dyeing, and clothing alterations and repairs. Auto insurance firms have added life and fire insurance. The reasons for these line expansions are familiar—the company wants to increase its total volume, reduce seasonal fluctuations in volume, cater to changing buying patterns such as the desire for one-stop shopping, etc. Railroads have simplified their line by dropping passenger service or by abolishing freight stations at some small, unprofitable locations. Some service firms have effectively expanded their line by working jointly with companies selling related services. Automobile rental firms have working arrangements with airlines and hotels, so that when a customer flies to his destination, a car will be ready for his use at that point, and he will have a hotel room reserved. Travel agencies combine many transportation and recreation services in one package.

In some respects, policy making is easier for services than for products. Tasks related to packaging, color, labeling, and style are virtually nonexistent in marketing services. However, in other areas—branding and standardization of quality, for instance—the job in service industries poses greater problems. Branding is difficult

---

12 See Kit G. Narodick, "What Motivates the Consumer's Choice of an Airline?" *Journal of Retailing*, Spring, 1972, pp. 30-38ff; also see William R. Darden and Warren A. French, "Selected Personal Services: Consumer Reactions," *Journal of Retailing*, Fall, 1972, pp. 42-48.

because consistency of quality is hard to maintain and because the brand cannot be physically attached to a service.

Standardization of quality in a service is an extremely important goal to strive for. In some fields such as beauty care, medical care, and some of the recreation industries, no attempt is made to mass-produce a service. Instead, the sellers often offer custom-tailored service for each customer. Even in this case, however, the customer wants consistency of quality, and this consistency is very difficult to achieve because the service is produced and sold in individual units—one haircut, one appendectomy, or one dance lesson.

PRICING OF SERVICES

Perhaps nowhere in the marketing of services is there greater opportunity for managerial creativity, skill, and imagination than in the area of pricing. Price determination is critically important here because of the discretionary nature of customer buying. In the case of most services, personal or business, the customer may postpone his purchase or even perform the service himself. Only rarely does a buyer face the situation where he needs a service immediately and the number of sellers is quite limited. Another factor to consider is that markdowns are not possible in many cases. If there are empty seats at a given concert or athletic contest, it is not possible to hold them over and offer them at a lower price later.

These considerations suggest that the elasticity of demand for a service should influence the price set by the seller. Interestingly enough, sellers often recognize an inelastic demand. Then they charge higher prices. But they fail to act in opposite fashion when faced with an elastic demand, even though a lower price would increase unit sales, total revenue, utilization of facilities, and probably net profit.

The basic methods of price determination for services are generally the same as those for products. Cost-plus pricing is used for various kinds of repair service where the main ingredient is direct labor and the customer is charged on an hourly basis. The price equals the repairperson's wages plus an amount to cover overhead and profit. For other services (rentals, entertainment, management counsulting) the prices are determined primarily by market demand and competition. It is pretty much a case of what the traffic will bear.

Certainly perfect competition does not exist to any extent, if at all, in the pricing of services. Because of the inability to standardize quality, services are highly differentiated, and it is virtually impossible to have complete market information. Also, in any given market, such as a neighborhood, there are geographic limits within which a buyer will seek a service, and consequently there is not a large number of sellers. The heavy capital investment required to produce many services (transportation, communications, medical care) limits the freedom of entry considerably.

In some service industries, the private seller will establish a price, but it must be approved by a regulatory agency of the provincial or federal government. This public regulation of prices, however, need not stifle the opportunity for imaginative, skillful pricing designed to stimulate sales. Lower rates for long-distance telephoning on nights and Sundays and different prices which benefit large or small volume users of electricity are examples of creative pricing to increase market penetration or shift demand.

Sometimes a trade or professional association is a price setter within an industry. Barber unions set the price on haircuts, and a laundry and dry-cleaning as-

sociation sets the price on cleaning a suit of clothes. Fees charged by doctors, architects, accountants, and advertising agencies are frequently influenced strongly by
professional associations.

Many of the areas of pricing policies discussed in Chapters 14 and 15 must also
be considered by executives in a service firm. Thus we see quantity discounts in the
pricing of electrical power, and cash discounts are offered if you pay your auto insurance premium once a year instead of quarterly or semiannually. Doctors and
management consultants use a variable-price policy, whereas a movie theater has a
one-price policy at any given time of day. A motel or apartment owner offers multiple services (one bedroom, two bedrooms, suites), and he must price one service
in relation to another. Geographic pricing policies may be involved, although the
variable here is time, not freight charges. A repairman will charge more if he must
go out of town, and a doctor will charge more for house calls than office calls.

CHANNELS OF DISTRIBUTION FOR SERVICES

When developing a distribution system for his services, a seller is concerned only
with the transfer of ownership. No problems of physical distribution such as bulk
breaking, transportation, or warehousing are involved. Most services are sold directly from producer to consumer or industrial user. No middlemen are used because the service cannot be separated from the person of the seller, nor is it feasible
to use a tangible representative of the service. Public utilities, medical care, repair
service, and others are typically sold without middlemen. The only other channel
frequently used involves one agent middleman. We see this channel used in the
sale of securities, transportation, housing rentals, labor, and entertainment. Sometimes dealers are trained in the production of the service and then are franchised to
sell it, as is the case with the Sanitone dry-cleaning process, Fred Astaire dance studios, Kelly Girl part-time office help, and Holiday Inn motels.

Whether the seller markets directly or uses an agent to reach his customers, the
seller's or agent's *location* with respect to the potential market is all-important. Services cannot be delivered to a customer, so the seller should select a convenient, accessible location where there is maximum customer traffic. Many motels and restaurants have gone out of business because a new highway drew away traffic when
it bypassed their formerly good locations.

The inability to use middlemen to any great extent limits the geographic market
that a service seller can reach. On the other hand, it gives this seller a chance to
serve his customers better. It also provides him with a golden opportunity to get
customer feedback quickly and in sufficient detail so that he can improve his marketing program.

PROMOTING THE SERVICE

Management's task is especially difficult when the company must build a promotional program around intangible service benefits. It is so much easier to sell something which can be seen, felt, and demonstrated. In the marketing of services, we
find that personal selling, advertising, and indirect forms of promotion are all used
extensively.

Personal selling is important because of the close relationship between the buyer
and the seller. Brands are not used extensively, so brand preferences and loyalties

often cannot be depended upon. Also, self-service or automatic vending has limited application. Whether selling consumer or industrial services, the salesperson can often build or destroy customer goodwill toward the firm. Consequently, it is imperative that management do a careful job in selecting, training, and otherwise managing the sales force. In most service industries where personal selling is the main promotional tool used, high-caliber salespeople are usually required.

Not much more needs to be said here about advertising because the principles and procedures are generally the same as those developed in Chapter 24. Small firms can often make effective use of local advertising. Also, a group of small local firms can participate in joint advertising ventures. National trade associations (laundry, dry cleaning, and others) have done considerable national advertising to stimulate primary demand for their services. Even though a service is intangible, store displays that show the results of using the service can be effective.

Many service firms, especially in the recreation-entertainment field, benefit considerably from free publicity. Sports coverage by newspapers, radio, and televison media helps in this matter, as do newspaper reviews of movies, plays, and concerts. Travel sections in newspapers have helped sell transportation, housing, and other services related to the travel industry.

As an indirect means of promotion, doctors, lawyers, and insurance men may participate actively in community affairs as a means of getting their names before the public. Other service firms (banks, utilities, railroads) may advertise to attract new industry or more population, knowing that anything which helps the community grow will automatically mean an expanded market for them.

A promotional program in a service company should have two major goals. One is to portray the service benefits in as appealing a manner as possible. The other is to build a good reputation. Because the firm is marketing intangibles, a good reputation is perhaps even more important in a service company than in a product-marketing business. Advertising campaigns can stress dependability of the service—its consistent, high quality. Ads can also emphasize the courteous, friendly, efficient service.

A service firm's promotional effort can be even more effective if the seller can tie in with something tangible—a distinctive color, as used by Howard Johnson or Holiday Inn, or a personal symbol like Smokey the Bear or Reddy Kilowatt.

FUTURE OUTLOOK IN SERVICE MARKETING

NEED FOR INCREASED PRODUCTIVITY

In recent years the boom in the services market has been accompanied by a deterioration in the quality of many services. In general, service industries have been plagued by poor management, inefficiency, and low productivity.[13]

This inefficiency—and the need to increase productivity—is probably the biggest problem facing service industries in general. The productivity problem also has significant implications for the health of the total economy. Because service industries are very labor-intensive compared with manufacturing, wage increases in the service sector of the economy have a significant impact on price levels and inflation. While wage increases in service industries have kept pace with, or even surpassed,

---

13 See "Services Grow while the Quality Shrinks," *Business Week*, Oct. 30, 1971, p. 50.

those in manufacturing, productivity increases in service industries have lagged behind manufacturing.

Perhaps the key to increasing efficiency in service industries is for the management to adopt a "manufacturing attitude."[14] The concept of "providing a service" traditionally conjures visions of personal ministration and attendance on others. To improve performance meant simply to try harder, but essentially to continue performing a task in the same old way. In contrast, the concept of manufacturing (or efficiently producing) benefits or results enables us to focus on new performance methods, and to apply manufacturing technology, planning, and organization changes to the task at hand—but all this at a price of less humanism.

Four manufacturing concepts being applied in service industries to increase productivity are mechanization, assembly-line standardization, specialization, and organizational consolidation. The use of *mechanization* to implement hand labor has increased per-man output in laundry and dry cleaning, for example. Machines have increased service output in commercial dishwashing and floor sanding. Machines help auto repairpeople to do more effective work. *Assembly-line* technology has proven fruitful in such diverse service fields as fast-food retailing (Kentucky Fried Chicken and McDonald's hamburgers) and mass physical examinations for corporations and labor unions, using mobile health units and automated test equipment.

Several service firms have made labor more productive by *specialization* of effort. The medical field abounds with specialists. Auto repair firms specialize in brakes, transmissions, or mufflers. Even management consultants and firms in the advertising field have started to break their work forces into specialized elements in order to cut costs and increase efficiency. *Consolidation* as a means of improving productivity is being practiced when Canadian Pacific adds hotels to its service mix, or when Manpower, Inc. (temporary workers) branches into travel agencies, home care for the elderly, income-tax preparation, day-care centers, and distribution of new-product samples. The development of chain organizations is another useful form of consolidation in service firms. Finally, the advent of large product firms into service fields is a type of organizational consolidation which should make for more efficient service performance.

PROSPECTS FOR GROWTH

There is every reason to believe that services will continue to take an important share of the consumer dollar, just as they have done generally over the past 25 years. This forecast seems reasonable even if we should experience periods of economic decline, for history shows that the demand for services is less sensitive to economic fluctuations than the demand for products. It also seems reasonable to expect that the demand for business services will continue to expand as business and industry become even more complex and as management increasingly recognizes its need for business-service specialists.

We should temper these optimistic forecasts with some caution, however, because there are forces both external and internal to service industries which potentially could limit growth in these fields.[15] Perhaps the most obvious external com-

---

14 Theodore Levitt, "Production-line Approach to Service," *Harvard Business Review*, September-October, 1972, pp. 41-52.

15 See Eugene M. Johnson, *Our Service Economy: Trends and Implications*, working paper published by Marketing Science Institute, Cambridge, Mass., 1968, pp. 38-57.

petitive factor is the customer's alternative of performing the services himself. Another growth deterrent comes from product manufacturers who produce (1) goods with built-in features replacing former reliance on service industries— wash-and-wear shirts instead of commercial laundry service, for example, or televisions sets which substitute for commercial entertainment—or (2) goods which help the consumer to perform the service himself, as in the case of home appliances, home hair permanent sets, etc. The significant role of government services is always an external force to consider.

Internal barriers to future growth in service industries ae (1) the small size of the average service firm; (2) the shortage of people with specialized skills—doctors, for instance; and (3) the limited competition in many service industries—transportation, medicine, communication, education. These barriers limit internal price competition and sometimes limit entry into the field. Perhaps the overriding internal growth deterrent is managerial deficiencies—the lack of creativity and marketing innovation, the little emphasis on research and development in many service fields, and the general failure to recognize the importance of marketing in any business.

One student of service marketing has posed the following series of five propositions supporting the forecasts for growth.[16]

1. We have exhausted much of the growth potential in domestic markets for goods, so manufacturers are turning to markets which are more difficult to serve but which have higher rates of return. These are markets where commodity-associated services provide utilitarian satisfactions to business and functional satisfactions to household consumers. Also, higher incomes and higher consumption levels will provide bigger markets for service industries such as education, travel, and research.

2. Mass-production techniques are being developed which will routinize services so they can be provided faster, more conveniently, and at lower unit costs for the mass markets. In this respect, we have seen how data-processing systems have been developed successfully for communications and information services. Language laboratories, teaching machines, and programmed learning systems are mechanizing the field of education services.

3. As a wider market is reached by means of technologies in service systems, we can expect a growing impersonalization of these services.

4. The impersonalized attention and substitution of manufactured equipment will encourage a reduction in the extrinsic values of a service, even though the intrinsic values may be the same or higher. In the medical field, for instance, technology may improve the accuracy of the diagnosis and the quality of the remedy (intrinsic essentials). The delivery of these services to more and more people will probably result in a decrease in the extrinsic elements such as abundant personal attention from the family doctor.

5. In the long run, however, we can expect a proliferation of services which are adaptable to a wide variety of tastes, just as the mass production of commodities has led to a diversity in product choice today.

QUESTIONS AND PROBLEMS

1. When defining services, from a marketing standpoint why is it useful to exclude the group of services (credit, delivery, training dealer salesperson; etc.) which exist only in connection with the sale of a product or another service?

---

16 Regan, "The Service Revolution," *op. cit.*, pp. 60-62.

2. How do you account for the substantial increase in expenditures for services relative to expenditures for products since the end of World War II?
3. What are some of the marketing implications in the fact that services possess the characteristic of intangibility?
4. Why are middlemen rarely used in the marketing programs of service firms?
5. Services are highly perishable and are often subject to fluctuations in demand. In marketing its services, how can a company offset these factors?
6. Cite some examples of service marketers who seem to be customer-oriented and describe what these firms have done in this vein.
7. "Traditionally, marketers of services have *not* been marketing-oriented." Do you agree? If so, how do you account for this deficiency?
8. Present a brief analysis of the market for each of the following services. Make use of the components of a market as discussed in Chapters 4 to 8.
   a. Laundry and dry-cleaning firm located in a shopping center near your campus
   b. Four-bedroom house for rent at a major seashore resort
   c. Bowling alley
   d. Nursing home
9. What are some of the ways in which each of the following service firms might expand its line?
   a. Advertising agency
   b. Telephone company
   c. Automobile repair garage
10. Explain the importance of demand elasticity in the pricing of services.
11. "Personal selling should be the main ingredient in the promotional mix for a marketer of services." Do you agree? Discuss.
12. When athletic contests are televised, the area within 50 miles of the event is sometimes "blacked out." When there is a sellout on seats for the event, should the blackout restriction be removed?
13. In what ways does the marketing of services differ from the marketing of products?

INTERNATIONAL MARKETING

Canadians have long known that their welfare depended to an important degree on their success in world markets. For many years our exports have ranged from 20 to 25 percent of gross domestic product (similar to the U.K.) compared with a 4 to 6 percent range for the United States. International marketing's role in trade is a substantial one, and it is the progress which we will make in international marketing that will substantially affect our future economic welfare. While some people may believe that this is an overstatement of the position of international marketing, we cannot deny the fact that multinational companies are rapidly evolving all over the world and firms are creating new units as well as integrating their domestic and foreign operations into world enterprises. Americans, who are at the forefront of this movement, feel that "more than ever before, the economic future of the United States is vested in the marketing process—and future American progress will be determined largely by marketing management's success on the new frontier—the world market."[1] If this is true for the U.S. with such a small percentage of their gross domestic product involved in foreign trade, it is undeniably true for Canada with 4 to 5 times greater reliance on international markets and international marketing.

---

1 Ray R. Eppert, "Passport for Marketing Overseas," *Journal of Marketing,* April, 1965, p. 6.

Basically, marketing fundamentals are universally applicable. Whether a firm sells in Timmins or Timbuktu, its marketing program should be built around a good product or service properly priced, promoted, and distributed to a market which has been carefully analyzed. We devote a separate chapter to international marketing, however, because there are considerable differences in the strategic and tactical implementation of marketing programs for foreign as against domestic markets. These modifications become necessary because of the environmental differences which exist between and within the many nations.

A company operates its marketing program within the economic, political, and cultural environment of each of its markets—foreign and domestic—and none of these environments is controllable by the firm. Consequently, an executive should try to understand this environment and anticipate its effect on his marketing program. What complicates this task in international marketing is the fact that the environment—particularly the cultural environment—often consists of elements very unfamiliar to, and perhaps not even recognized by, the marketing executives. Further complicating the situation is the tendency for a person unconsciously to use his own cultural values as a frame of reference for solving problems centered in a foreign environment. This "self-reference criterion" has been called the root cause of many international business problems.[2] One need only point to the problems Anglophone firms operating in Quebec have had in the past to underscore the point.

IMPORTANCE OF INTERNATIONAL MARKETING

Among companies in Canada, there seems to be a growing awareness of international marketing opportunities and an increasing willingness to enter foreign markets. As domestic markets become saturated, Canadian producers—even those with no previous international experience—now look to foreign markets as outlets for their productive capacity and sometimes as sources of wider profit margins and higher returns on investments. Naturally, many firms look to the U.S. for a market and tend not to consider it as foreign.

The world market outside of North America often offers greater growth and profit opportunities than the domestic market. The indication of continued increases in buying power, gross national product, and capital investment in many foreign nations makes it almost inevitable that these countries will constitute profitable growth markets (as well as strong competition) for many consumer and industrial products. During the decade of the 1960s, as just one example, the population of Western Europe increased only about 10 percent, while the overall gross national product went up 70 percent. The net result has been a rising standard of living and a larger potential market. The great increases in purchasing power accruing to the OPEC countries open up new capital goods and services markets.

Canada's position in international markets and its requirements for international marketing are interesting both in terms of our pattern of goods marketed and in terms of our access to markets. The United States is our largest customer by far, taking nearly 70 percent of our total exports. Our exports to the U.S. as a percent of

---

2 James A. Lee, "Cultural Analysis in Overseas Operations," *Harvard Business Review*, March-April, 1966, pp. 106-114. This article proposes a systematic four-step framework designed to reduce the influence of the self-reference criterion.

trade have increased from 54% in 1961 to 66% in 1974. Our second largest international customer, the United Kingdom, took 15.8 percent of our trade in 1961 compared with 6.0 percent in 1974. Our trade with other Commonwealth and preferential tariff countries has also decreased slightly from 5.7 percent in 1961 to 3.5 in 1974. All other countries accounted for 24.6 percent in 1974, compared with 24.5 percent in 1961. Thus, our reliance is on the United States and non-Commonwealth countries with Japan and the Federal Republic of Germany rapidly becoming important international markets for us.[3]

Our major problem as a trading nation is evident from Table 26-1, which shows crude material exports and manufactured goods exports with the latter broken into fabricated materials (which in the main are semi-crude materials such as lumber, wood pulp, newsprint and metals and alloys) and end products. In Canada's situation, the end product category contains most of the truly manufactured product in international marketing. Much of the increase in end product from 1966 on is a result of the Canada-U.S. Automotive Agreement of 1965. While the agreement has resulted in an increase of manufacturing exports, most of these have been parent-subsidiary transfers negotiated without any international marketing efforts. What Table 26-1 does demonstrate then is that vigorous international marketing efforts

Table 26-1. Canada's exports by percentages in each stage of fabrication—selected years

| Stages of Fabrication | Percent based on current $ | | | | | |
	1956	1961	1966	1971	1973	1974
(1) Crude materials	34.5	37.0	33.7	27.1	29.3	34.3
(2) Manufactured goods:	65.5	63.0	66.3	72.9	70.7	65.7
fabricated materials	(54.7)	(50.7)	(41.9)	(34.7)	(34.5)	(34.8)
end products	(10.8)	(12.3)	(24.4)	(38.2)	(36.2)	(30.9)
Total	100.0	100.0	100.0	100.0	100.0	100.0

Source: Calculated from data in Statistics Canada, *Canada Year Book,* 1975.

are required in Canada to increase sales of end products so that jobs can be created. In addition, because of our great reliance on crude material sales and semi-crudes in the form of modestly processed fabricated materials, care and attention must be paid to the marketing of these products. Since competition is world-wide, more international marketing efforts can result both in the penetration of markets other than the U.S. as well as in helping to maintain the stability of existing and newly developed markets.

International marketing is a two-way street, however. The same foreign markets which offer growth opportunities for Canadian firms also have their own producers who, in turn, are providing substantial and intensive competition both in Canada

3 Statistics Canada, *Canada Year Book 1975.*

and abroad. See Table 26-2. Canadian consumers have responded favorably, for example, to a great array of American products, to Japanese radio-TV products (Sony) and motorcycles (Honda), to Italian clothes and sewing machines (Necchi), to German cameras (Leica) and autos (Volkswagen), and to Dutch petroleum products (Shell) and electric razors (Philips). Especially strong competition is coming from Japan and the countries in the European Economic Community (EEC), more popularly known as the European Common Market. Ultimately, tariffs and other trade barriers will be erected around it. Competitive challenges are also being encountered from the member units of other multinational economic organizations such as the Latin American Free Trade Association (LAFTA), and even the Council for Mutual Economic Assistance (COMECON—Russia and other Communist European nations).

ALTERNATIVE ORIENTATIONS TOWARD INTERNATIONAL OPERATIONS

Four separate stages may be identified in the evolution of international operations in a firm, and each phase has its own set of managerial attitudes and philosophies.[4] These stages and their accompanying attitudes form a conceptual framework which may serve as a starting point for guiding a company in developing its market strategies. The four stages are: ethnocentrism (home-country orientation), polycentrism (host-country orientation), regiocentrism (a regional orientation), and geocentrism (a world orientation).

In the *ethnocentric* stage, foreign operations are treated as secondary to domestic operations. Planning for foreign markets is done in the home office, using the same procedures as for domestic markets. Marketing personnel are primarily home-country nationals. The marketing mix follows domestic patterns. No major changes are made in the products sold abroad. In pricing, overseas distribution costs are simply added to home prices. Promotion and distribution strategies are essentially the same as at home. The sales force is hired and trained at home, and operates from a home-country base.

The ethnocentric position is likely to be adopted by a small company just entering the international market, or by a larger firm whose foreign sales are insignificant. For these companies, the cost of extensive foreign marketing research or the cost of tailoring products and marketing programs to specific foreign market requirements simply is not justified in terms of anticipated revenue.

In the *polycentric* stage, each foreign country is treated as a separate entity with its own autonomous subsidiary organization. Each of these foreign subsidiaries does its own marketing planning and research. Products are changed to meet local needs. Each subsidiary does its own pricing and promotion. Distribution is through channels and a sales force native to the country in question.

Today most international executives probably view the polycentric position as

---

4 This section is adapted from Yoram Wind, Susan P. Douglas, and Howard V. Perlmutter, "Guidelines for Developing International Marketing Strategies," *Journal of Marketing,* April, 1973, pp. 14-23; see also Howard V. Perlmutter, "The Tortuous Evolution of the Multinational Company," *Columbia Journal of World Business,* January-February, 1969, pp. 9-18.

the most desirable one. In marketing, even more so than in finance or production, it is so important to adapt to country-by-country differences, and to use local nationals of the country in doing a marketing job. Polycentrism, however, is likely to lead to problems of coordinating and controlling the marketing activities among the several countries.

Table 26-2. **The 20 largest industrial companies outside North America, ranked by sales, 1973.** Lux soap, Shell gasoline, Mercedes and Datsun autos, and other names familiar to North American consumers are in this list.

Rank Company	Country	Industry
1. Royal Dutch/Shell Group	Netherlands-Britain	Petroleum products, natural gas, chemicals
2. Unilever	Britain-Netherlands	Food, detergents, toiletries, feed
3. Philips Gloeilampenfabrieken	Netherlands	Electronics, electrical equipment, chemicals
4. British Petroleum	Britain	Petroleum products, chemicals
5. Nippon Steel	Japan	Iron, steel
6. Volkswagenwerk	Germany	Automobiles
7. Hitachi	Japan	Electrical equip., appliances, machinery
8. Farbwerke Hoechst	Germany	Chemicals, pharmaceuticals
9. Daimler-Benz	Germany	Automobiles
10. Toyota Motor	Japan	Automobiles
11. Siemens	Germany	Electrical equipment, electronics
12. BASF	Germany	Chemicals
13. ICI (Imperial Chemical Indus.)	Britain	Chemicals
14. Mitsubishi Heavy Industries	Japan	Machinery, shipbuilding, aircraft, autos
15. Nestlé	Switzerland	Food products
16. Nissan Motor	Japan	Automobiles, trucks
17. Renault	France	Automobiles, tractors, machine tools
18. Bayer	Germany	Chemicals
19. Montedison	Italy	Chem., syn. fibers, pharmaceuticals
20. Matsushita Electric Industrial	Japan	Electrical & electronic equip, appliances

Source: Fortune, August, 1974, p. 176.

In the *regiocentric* and *geocentric* stages, a given region or the entire world is treated as a single market, regardless of national boundaries. Marketing plans and programs are set for the entire region, or the world. Personnel can come from anywhere. Standardized products are used throughout the entire market—region or world. Channels and promotion are developed on a regional or global basis to project a uniform image of the company and its products.

A regiocentric approach is probably more economical and manageable than a worldwide program. From a practical point of view, however, national environmental constraints (laws, currencies, culture, life-styles, etc.) may severely limit either one of these broad marketing approaches.

STRUCTURE FOR OPERATING IN FOREIGN MARKETS

Once a company has decided to market in foreign countries, management must select a method or organizational structure for operating in those markets. There are four separately identifiable methods of marketing entry, each successively representing an increased international involvement, leading ultimately to a truly multinational firm. These alternatives reflect, and parallel to some extent, the philosophies expressed in the conceptual framework discussed in the preceding section.

A company may progress from one method to another, or management may bypass some stages. The same firm may be using several operating methods at the same time. To illustrate: depending upon a company's familiarity with a given foreign market, the maturity of economic development in the foreign nation, and the country's political stability, this company may export products to one country, establish a licensing arrangement in another, and build a manufacturing plant in a third.

The simplest way of operating in foreign markets is by *exporting through foreign trade agent middlemen.* Management's effort in the exporting venture may be somewhat sporadic—up when there are excess inventory stocks to be marketed, and down when the domestic market can assimilate the manufacturing output. The company may establish the position of export manager, and he will use various export-import middlemen to reach the foreign markets; or the domestic sales manager may be assigned the responsibility of contacting these foreign trade middlemen. At this point, very little risk or investment is required. Also, little time or effort is required on the part of the exporting producer. On the other hand, the exporter must pay tariffs, and he has little or no control over his agent middlemen. Furthermore, these middlemen are generally not aggressive marketers, and normally they do not generate a large sales volume.

To counteract some of these deficiencies, management will move to the second stage—*exporting through company sales branches* or other sales subsidiaries located in foreign markets. Bypassing the export-import agent middlemen enables a company to promote its products more aggressively, to develop its foreign markets more effectively, and to control its sales effort more completely. Of course, the firm is still exporting, with the attendant drawbacks. Also, management now has the time- and money-consuming task of selecting, training, and otherwise managing a sales force of (1) foreign nationals unfamiliar with the product and the company's marketing practices or (2) Canadian middlemen unfamiliar with the market.

As foreign markets expand and as our company gains experience in international marketing, management may enter *licensing* arrangements, whereby foreign manufacturers are authorized to produce the articles. To distribute this foreign-produced output, the company may still rely on foreign trade middlemen, or the company's own sales branches may be established in major foreign markets.

Licensing offers a manufacturer a flexible arrangement with a minimum investment whereby he can still enjoy the advantages of his patents, research, and know-how. Through licensing, he can enter a market which might otherwise be closed to him as an exporter because of exchange restrictions, import quotas, or prohibitive tariffs. At the same time, by licensing, a manufacturer may be building a future competitor who will learn all he can from the manufacturer and then proceed independently when the licensing agreement expires.

In the fourth method, the company builds or otherwise acquires its own production facilities in foreign countries. The structure may be a *joint venture or a wholly owned foreign subsidiary*. A joint venture is a partnership arrangement where the foreign manufacturing or marketing operation is owned in part by the Canadian company and in part by the local nationals (company or individuals) of the foreign country involved. Share of foreign ownership may be any percentage—more than, less than, or exactly 50 percent. Obviously, when controlling interest in a joint venture is owned by the foreign nationals, the Canadian firm has no real control over any of the marketing or production activities. Decision-making authority accompanies ownership control. At the same time, a joint venture may be the only structure (other than licensing) through which a firm can enter a given foreign market. Nationalistic tendencies in the form of exchange restrictions, tariffs, or plain political exclusion of foreign-owned companies may preclude any operation other than a joint venture or one in which there is a licensing arrangement.

Wholly owned manufacturing and marketing subsidiaries in foreign markets are commonly found in companies which have evolved to an advanced stage of international business. Even then, however, this international division is typically still separate from, and second in importance to, the domestic operations. With a wholly owned foreign subsidiary, a company has maximum control over its marketing program and production operations. This type of international structure, however, requires a substantial investment of money, manpower, and managerial attention. Thus, a large-volume operation is usually needed to justify the investment. As noted earlier, nationalistic tendencies on the part of foreign governments may preclude this type of structure. Also, organizational problems may arise when there is an attempt to coordinate the international and domestic divisions.

This leads us to the final evolutionary stage—and one reached by very few companies as yet—the emergence of the truly *world enterprise*. Massey-Ferguson is the prime Canadian example of this type of organization. Both foreign and domestic operations are integrated and no longer separately identified. In this type of multinational venture, one plant may be in Bombay, a second in Brussels, a third in Boston. The regional sales office in Toronto is basically the same as the one in Athens.

PROBLEMS IN DEVELOPING AN INTERNATIONAL COMPANY

A purely Canadian company faces significantly greater risks when it sets up an international marketing organization than it does when this task is performed at home. In the domestic market, company management is usually more familiar with the environment—and politically and economically this environment is usually more stable. Executives are acquainted with the institutional structure for distribution. Their experience is an aid in forecasting competitive strategies. And their marketing intelligence provides a relatively high level of knowledge concerning consumer motives and habits.

Canadian subsidiaries with foreign parents who have other subsidiaries scattered around the world do not have the same types of problems if they are involved in multinational marketing in a real sense. In such cases, the Canadian operation can call for help from a number of corporate sources to obtain information and reduce risks in planning and decision making.

EXTERNAL PROBLEM CONDITIONS

Aspects of *exchange controls* and *other currency regulations* constitute a major problem to consider when expanding into a foreign market. Many nations set limits on the amount of earned or invested funds which may be withdrawn from the country. These exchange controls may be established because the country has a balance-of-payments problem or a shortage of foreign exchange. Limits may also be set in order to prevent the flight of domestic capital, to protect local industry, or to aid in the socialization of the economy.

Tariffs, import quotas, and other import restrictions are another problem area hindering international business. While these limits are established to stimulate national self-sufficiency and to encourage the development of domestic enterprise, the net result is still a significant obstacle to transnational operations. In some countries, the *political uncertainty* occasioned by social unrest, forthcoming elections, recent or impending independence, extreme programs, and even armed conflict is a deterrent. Sometimes high tax levels, tax discrimination, or other *unsatisfactory tax conditions* in a country will discourage foreign business activity. Another impediment is some form of *restriction on foreign companies and/or personnel*. Perhaps a nation requires that executives and other personnel of a foreign firm operating within the country be local citizens or that majority ownership be held by nationals of the country. *Labor problems*—strong unions, shortages of qualified personnel, required profit sharing, limits on a firm's authority to reduce the work force by layoffs—all act as an obstacle to foreign expansion.

Counterfeiting of products is a hazard faced by firms in some countries. Pirated copies of Levi's jeans are produced in more than 25 foreign countries. In Asia, Colgate toothpaste competes with Coalgate, Goalgate, Goldkey, and Goldcat brands.[5] *Archaic distribution systems* plague marketing programs in many foreign markets. Even in Japan, for example, where the manufacturing system has achieved high levels of efficiency, some Japanese businessmen admit that some of their distribution systems have changed very little over several centuries.[6]

INTERNAL MANAGEMENT PROBLEMS

Notwithstanding these substantial external roadblocks, companies may experience a greater incidence of *internal,* rather than external, problems in the management of an international business. One major internal problem is *orientation,* that is, the problem of getting the top executives to manage the firm as a single, integrated world enterprise rather than thinking in terms of a domestic company with a sepa-

---

5 "Why a Global Market Doesn't Exist," *Business Week,* Dec. 19, 1970, p. 144.

6 "Japan's Remarkable Industrial Machine," *Business Week,* Mar. 7, 1970, p. 73.

rate international division. *Organization* is a second, and perhaps corollary, problem area. Organizational difficulties arise when the international division is appended to the domestic operations, instead of the two being integrated. When established separately, the international operation tends to be isolated, and top management accords it stepchild status. This leads to another problem—*staffing.* Failure to organize as an integrated world company leads to a failure to develop truly international executives. To an important extent, the success of an international company will depend upon the type of people selected as marketing executives.[7] Another staffing consideration is the difficulty of selecting and training foreign nationals for executive and lower-level jobs. Finally, in the area of managerial control, questions arise as to whether *control* of operations should be centralized in corporate headquarters or whether, and to what extent, it should be vested in decentralized foreign locations. Perhaps the best course is an "interactive" approach to marketing planning, rather than either an ethnocentric or polycentric stance.[8] In an interactive approach, foreign subsidiaries would be responsibile for marketing, production, and personnel activities related to unique factors in each national market. Headquarters staff at regional or world levels would be responsible for strategic planning, financial control, and the coordination of product, pricing, and promotional programs.

DEVELOPING AN INTERNATIONAL MARKETING PROGRAM

Firms which have been eminently successful in marketing in Canada have no assurance whatsoever that the same pattern will be duplicated in foreign markets. A key to satisfactory performance overseas lies in gauging which aspects of domestic marketing techniques should be retained, which ones adapted, and which ones abandoned in foreign markets.

One analysis of the experiences of American firms successful in multinational marketing identified some basic concepts around which these companies built their marketing programs.[9] First, outstanding marketers have learned to export their approach to decision making—their analytical marketing techniques—rather than their domestic marketing practices. The ability to identify a problem, analyze it, and select the best alternative is the firm's differential advantage. A specific marketing practice may be useless abroad, but the analytical technique for developing this practice is universally exportable. The successful marketer also realizes that foreign countries, and even sections within a country, usually have environmental and cultural differences which can affect virtually every aspect of his marketing program. Finally, a successful company is sensitive to the differences in its competitive position at home and abroad, and will change its marketing strategies accordingly. A company which enjoys 30 percent of the Canadian market for a product will need a different marketing program in a foreign country where it is fighting for a 3 percent share of the market.

---

7 For a report showing that, except for the president, the marketing executive is the most influential man in today's European firm, see *European Top Management Comparison Report,* American Management Association, New York, 1969, as reported in *Sales Management,* Oct. 1, 1969, p. 36.

8 Warren J. Keegan, "Multinational Marketing: The Headquarters Role." *Columbia Journal of World Business,* January-February, 1971, pp. 85-90.

9 *Inernational Enterprise: A New Dimension of American Business,* McKinsey & Company, Inc., New York, 1962, pp. 18-19.

INTERNATIONAL MARKETING RESEARCH

As important as a marketing information system may be in the domestic market, it would seem to be even more essential in foreign markets because the risks are so much greater. Actual practice is to the contrary, however. Only limited facilities and modest funds are invested in marketing research in foreign countries as compared with expenditures at home. The several reasons advanced to account for this disparity can perhaps be distilled into one basic point. Because of the differences in the problems encountered in foreign as against domestic marketing research, the costs relative to the value received are greater abroad than at home. Consider just two illustrations of this point. Each of the many heterogeneous foreign markets is usually quite a bit smaller than the domestic market. Yet, when conducting a research study which involves sampling in these smaller markets, the sample size needed to ensure statistical validity and reliability does not decrease in proportion to the market size. Consequently, the cost of the research project, relative to market size, is greater for the smaller markets. As another example, consider the many types of market information (population, buying power, weather data, etc.) which are readily and inexpensively available in Canada, but which must be collected at some cost in each foreign market.

The extent of use of foreign marketing research and the nature of the facilities seem to vary somewhat in relation to the level of economic development achieved in the country. Apparently, marketing research is used very little in underdeveloped countries, whereas considerable and sometimes very sophisticated use is made of this tool in countries with advanced economies.[10]

To understand the problems of research in international marketing, an executive should try to understand how the environmental conditions in each foreign market affect the following four basic elements of research: systematic analysis, customer information, statistical data, and operational economy.[11] Fundamental to marketing research is the idea that problems should be solved in a *systematic, analytical manner*. In many parts of the world, the cultural personality—tempered by aspects of religion and education—is such that people are guided by intuition, emotional reaction, or tradition. None of these is particularly conducive to the scientific approach. A second and related element in marketing research—*customer information*—is dependent upon the ability and willingness of people to respond accurately and completely when researchers pose questions involving attitudes, buying habits, motives, etc. In many foreign societies, the suspicion of strangers, the distrust of government, and the individualistic personality which believes these things are "none of your business" all serve to compound the problems of gathering information.

---

10 For some of the difficulties in applying research techniques in less-developed countries, see Roman R. Andrus, "Marketing Research in a Developing Nation—Taiwan: A Case Example," *University of Washington Business Review*, Spring, 1969, pp. 40-44; and Harper W. Boyd, Jr., Ronald E. Frank, William F. Massy, and Mostafa Zoheir, "On the Use of Marketing Research in the Emerging Economies," *Journal of Marketing Research*, November, 1964, pp. 20-23. See Reed Moyer, "International Market Analysis," *Journal of Marketing Research*, November, 1968, pp. 353-360, for some quantitative techniques for estimating present and future market demand in underdeveloped countries.

For a picture at the other end of the scale, see Edward L. Brink, "The State of Marketing Intelligence in the United Kingdom," in Peter D. Bennett (ed.), *Marketing and Economic Development*, American Marketing Association, Chicago, 1965, pp. 72-78.

11 John Fayerweather, *International Marketing*, 2d ed., Prentice-Hall, Inc., Englewood Cliffs, N.J., 1970, pp. 90-93.

The scarcity of *reliable statistical data* may be the single biggest problem in some foreign markets.[12] Figures on population, personal income, and production may be only crude estimates. Few studies have been made on such things as buying habits or media coverage. In the design of a research project, the lack of reliable data makes it very difficult to set up a meaningful sample. Lack of uniformity makes intercountry comparisons very unreliable. The element of *operational economy* was mentioned earlier as a partial explanation of why less money is spent on foreign than domestic marketing research.[13]

ANALYSIS OF FOREIGN MARKETS

Nowhere in a company's total marketing program is the influence of the cultural and economic environment seen more clearly than in the analysis of consumer and industrial market demand. Market demand in all countries is determined by population, economic ability to buy, and buying behavior—motives and habits. Also, human wants and needs have a basic universal similarity. People need food, clothing, and shelter. They seek a better life in terms of lighter work loads, more leisure time, social recognition and acceptance, etc. But at about this point, the similarities in foreign and domestic markets end. Furthermore, significant differences exist between and within foreign countries, thus forcing us to segment and define each market carefully.

A cosmetics firm selling in a Latin-American country, for example, may segment its market by upper-, lower-, and middle-income groups and by urban and rural areas. The same marketing program will not reach each segment because these markets have different potentials and characteristics. The upper-income class wants high-grade products sold through exclusive stores and advertised in high-quality newspapers. In rural markets, the products must be inexpensive. There may even be a need to promote primary demand because cosmetics are not fully accepted in this market.

When analyzing the economic ability to buy on the part of consumers in a given foreign market, management may first study the broad measures such as gross national product or per capita national income. Three other economic factors which perhaps are more meaningful in each market are (1) distribution of income, (2) rate of growth of buying power, and (3) extent of available consumer financing. Large portions of the population in the emerging economies have very low incomes. A much different income-distribution pattern—with resulting differences in marketing programs—is found in the industrialized markets of Western Europe, where there are large groups of working classes and a burgeoning middle-income market. Thus, many of the products commonly in demand in Belgium or the Netherlands would find very small markets in some African or Asian countries. See Fig. 26-1. Japan, of course, is an exception in Asia. Rising incomes in Japan have generated

---

12 For sources of secondary data on foreign markets, see Cateora and Hess, *op. cit.*, pp. 653-657; and Gordon E. Miracle and Gerald Albaum, *International Marketing Management*, Richard D. Irwin, Inc., Homewood, Ill., 1970, pp. 225-234.

13 For a model of a proposed international business information system, see J. Alex Murray, "An Inquiry into International Business Intelligence Systems," in Boris W. Becker and Helmut Becker (eds.), 1972 *Combined Proceedings*, American Marketing Association, series no. 34, Chicago, 1973, pp. 249-256; also see J. S. Downham, "Marketing Research in a Multinational Corporation (Unilever)," in Becker and Becker (eds.), *ibid.*, pp. 179-182.

huge markets in pursuit of travel, bowling, skiing, golf, and other leisure-time activities. In response, shops in London, Paris, and Rome display window signs indicating that "Japanese is spoken here."[14]

An understanding of the cultural environment in a given market will, in turn, help in understanding the buying motives and habits of consumers in that market. Some of the cultural elements to identify and to analyze for their effect on a firm's marketing program include (1) the family system, (2) other social groups and institutions, (3) the educational system, (4) the language, and (5) the religious system.[15] A country where the *family* is a close-knit unit will attract a different type of advertising campaign from the one appropriate in a society where the family members more frequently come and go independently, and it will constitute a market for different products. In India and other cultures where parents often arrange the marriages of their children, marketing programs are different from those in Canada and other countries where youths are free to find and select their own mates. Examples of the cultural differences in *social groups and institutions* in Japan and other countries are shown in Fig. 26-2 and 26-3.

The *educational system* affects the literacy rate, which in turn influences advertising, branding, and labeling. The brand may become all-important if the potential consumers cannot read and so must recognize the article by the picture on the label.

EUROPE'S SPENDING SPREE

In the 1960s and 1970s Western Europeans were spending like Americans did in the late 1940s and 1950s. Some of the results (in percentage of family ownership):

Household appliances: electric irons (81%), refrigerators (72%), washing machines (57%).

Leisure time increased; so did television sets (75%).

Buying power brought mobility: autos (47%) and portable radios (54%).

Households in the original Common Market countries spent more heavily on laborsaving devices, while families in places like Austria, Portugal, Sweden, Norway, and Switzerland showed higher ownership of products linked with affluence and leisure time.

About half the families own their own home in Sweden, Denmark, Luxembourg, France, and Norway.

Buying power is not evenly distributed among the nations; median family income in Scandinavia and Switzerland is six times greater than in Portugal.

Figure 26-1. *Source:* Based on "A Survey of Europe Today" by *Reader's Digest* magazine as reported in *Sales Management,* Mar. 15, 1971, p. 28.

---

14 See "The Frantic Race for a Leisurely Life," *Business Week,* Aug. 1, 1970, p. 28.

15 See Maneck S. Wadia, "The Concept of Culture," *Journal of Retailing,* Spring, 1965, pp. 21-29ff.; Montrose Sommers and Jerome Kernan, "Why Some Products Flourish Here, Fizzle There." *Columbia Journal of World Business,* March-April 1967, pp. 89-97; Yoram Wind, "Cross-cultural Analysis of Consumer Behavior," in Reed Moyer (ed.), *Changing Marketing Systems,* American Marketing Association, Chicago, 1968, pp. 183-185; and Cateora and Hess, *op. cit.,* chap. 4, "Cultural Dynamics in Assessing World Markets."

FOR THE TRAVELING EXECUTIVE—
THOSE UNWRITTEN SOCIAL RULES REGARDING:

TIME

South Africans expect on-the-dot promptness; the unawareness of time in some tropical countries is legendary.

Japanese may excuse tardiness for a business meeting but expect promptness at a social event; Swedish executives expect you to show up on time for either business or social meetings.

Businessmen in Yugoslavia routinely schedule appointments at 7 A.M.; in Mexico City a foreign visitor may be received at 10 P.M.

SPACE

Arabs, when relaxed and confidential, get very close to the persons they are talking to; Japanese prefer to keep more distance between themselves and visitors.

Handshakes are not customary in some foreign countries, especially with women.

MANNERS

A Swedish executive likes plenty of notice (about 3 weeks) when a visit is forthcoming.

In Southeast Asia it is a mark of disrespect to sit with legs crossed so the bottom of a foot is showing.

The U.S. custom of having family photos on the desk is rarely practiced in foreign countries.

Figure 26-2. *Source: Fortune,* January, 1971, p. 52.

JAPANESE BEHAVIORAL CHARACTERISTICS THAT INFLUENCE
NEGOTIATIONS WITH U.S. EXECUTIVES

THE JAPANESE:

1. Possess greater emotional sensitivity than do Americans.
2. Hide their emotions, but their feelings about a person are important in business dealings.
3. Dislike the bold use of raw power; they are more discreet.
4. Trait of *amaeru* (longing to be looked after and protected), and the resultant lifetime employment system, affects personnel relations.
5. Prefer to work as members of a group, not individually.
6. May take a long time to make a decision.
7. Believe very much in "saving face."
8. Go out of their way to avoid directly saying "no" to a person.
9. Place great value on friendship.
10. Are very reluctant to argue or retort when challenged, even when they feel they are right.

Figure 26-3. *Source:* Howard F. VanLandt, "How to Negotiate in Japan," *Harvard Business Review,* November-December, 1970, pp. 45-56.

Language differences, too, pose problems. Literal translations of advertising copy or brand names may result in ridicule of, or even enmity toward, Canadian products. Even some English words have different meanings in England, Australia, and the United States. See Fig. 26-4. The *religion* in a country has a tremendous influence on the value systems and behavioral patterns of consumers. In countries where the Protestant ethic (hard work and frugal living) is prevalent, we find less of a market for laborsaving devices and prepared cake mixes. Moslems disapprove of liquor, and Hindus de-emphasize material goods.

A few examples may illustrate how buying habits are influenced by cultural elements. One-stop shopping is unknown in most parts of the world. In many foreign markets people buy in small units, sometimes literally on a meal-to-meal basis. Also, they buy in small specialty stores. To buy food for a weekend, a housewife in West Germany will visit the chocolate store, the dairy store, the meat market, the fish market, a dry grocery store, the greengrocer, the bakery, the coffee market, and possibly some other specialty food stores. While this may seem to be an inefficient use of time, we must recognize that a shopping trip to that housewife is more than just a chore to be done as quickly as possible. To her it is a major part of her social life. She will visit with her friends and neighbors in these shops. Shopping in this fashion is simply a foreign version of the Canadian woman's bridge club or neighborhood coffee break. Only in recent years in some Western European countries have we seen the advent of the supermarket. Another buying habit to contend with in many foreign markets is the absence of the one-price system. Consumers

---

MARKETING PROBLEMS ARE CREATED
BY CULTURAL DIFFERENCES IN:

LANGUAGE

Is Chevrolet's Nova a good brand name? In Spanish, *no va* means "it doesn't go."

In German, 3M's "Scotch" tape becomes "Scotch" schmuck.

In Japanese, General Motors' "Body by Fisher" translates as "Corpse by Fisher," and 3M's slogan "Sticks like Crazy" comes out "Sticks Foolishly."

COLOR

In Malaysia, a green-colored product suggested illness.

Blue is considered feminine and warm in Holland, but in Sweden that color is associated with masculinity and coldness.

In Germany, consumers said a new menthol cigarette in a brown package tasted much better than the same product in a blue package.

White indicates mourning in China and Korea.

Red is popular in China, but not in some African countries.

DESIGN PREFERENCES

In Britain, products like Jell-O are preferred in solid-wafer or cake form.

Germans usually buy salad dressing in tubes.

Most of the industrialized countries outside the United Sates employ the metric system for measurements.

Figure 26-4.

expect to haggle and bargain over each purchase. It is a way of life which must be acknowledged in a marketing program.

Often the question of "who buys" is related to the cultural factors in a market. In many Moslem countries, wives are kept in seclusion, and yet they play a major role in managing the family's economic life. In other countries where women enjoy freedom and liberties not available to Moslem women, the men of the house may make the buying decisions. In still other foreign markets the buying is done by servants. Each situation requires a different approach to the person who buys.

In this chapter, we have stressed the point that significant environmental differences exist between and within foreign countries. Perhaps we have overstressed this point or at least have neglected to note a countervailing development. On the horizon we can see a trend toward standardization of tastes, wants, and habits, especially in the Western European countries. Travel, television, and trade are proving to be effective homogenizers of European culture. Signs indicate that European consumers are developing into a mass market. Now let us be sure we understand this situation. A German is still a German, a Swede knows he is still a Swede, etc. In Europe's uncommon market, there is no such thing as a Mr. and Mrs. European—yet. The *Reader's Digest* survey (see Fig. 26-1) showed that the British watch more TV, buy more life insurance, eat more canned food, and use more soap than any other Europeans. German teen-agers drink more Coca-Cola than any other country's teen-agers. People from Sweden and Luxembourg go abroad for their holidays, while most Britons stay home.

However, while the cultural differences are still very much present, the old order is changing, and we can see increasingly cosmopolitan demands. Pizzerias do business in Germany, lasagna is sold in a Stockholm supermarket, British fish-and-chips are wanted on the Continent, and whiskey sales are large in France. People from many countries have a common demand for better housing, cars, appliances, and opportunities to travel.[16]

PRODUCT PLANNING FOR INTERNATIONAL MARKETS

Most companies would not think of entering a domestic market without careful and often extensive product planning. Yet typically a Canadian firm enters a foreign market with essentially the same product it sells in Canada. Even when a product is changed expressly for an international market, the modification is apt to be minor—converting an appliance to 220-volt electrical systems, or painting and packaging the product to protect it against the destructive tropical climate and insects, for example.[17]

One key to success in product planning has a familiar ring—that is, adapt to the cultural tastes and economic characteristics of the particular foreign market, rather than try to sell the Canadian product abroad. In Europe, a 6-cubic-foot refrigerator

---

16 For a brief report on the "Westernizing" of two Eastern European countries—Yugoslavia and Romania, see Arthur A. Benson, "Letter from Eastern Europe," *Sales Management*, Sept. 1, 1971, p. 42; in this context "Westernizing" means more consumer goods, improved channels of distribution, and modernized retailing.

17 For a promising approach to international trade which is closely related to the product-life-cycle concept, see Louis T. Wells, Jr., "A Product Life Cycle for International Trade?" *Journal of Marketing*, July, 1968, pp. 1-6.

is the most popular size, in contrast to the larger units preferred in North America. While the cost difference is a factor, the basic reasons for the Europeans' choice lie in the cultural behavior patterns of the consumers. As noted earlier, to many European housewives a food-shopping trip is a social event. They go daily and thus do not buy large quantitites which must be stored for a few days in a refrigerator. Also, if they have no car, they walk to the store and cannot carry large quantities. As yet, frozen foods are not purchased to any extent, so large freezer space for storage is not needed.

Warren Keegan has identified five alternative strategies for adapting a product and its related marketing communications to a foreign market.[18] The first of these strategies is *one product, one message—world wide*. Pepsi-Cola and Coca-Cola have used this alternative successfully, but on balance there probably are more market failures than successes with this approach. When Campbell's tried to market its U.S. tomato soup to the British, this introduction was not successful because the English prefer a soup with a more bitter taste. Problems with consumer preferences can also occur when entering the U.S. market. When Corn Products Company introduced Knorr dry soups (popular in Europe) into the U.S., the move was a failure because Americans did not want to take the 15 to 20 minutes to cook the soup.[19]

The second strategy, *same product, but modified communications*, is practical when the same product can be used to fill different needs in foreign markets. The same outboard motors used for recreation in Canada may be used for commercial fishing or transportation abroad. In this instance, the advertising copy would be quite different in the various countries, depending upon the product use being promoted.

Under the third strategy, *product adaptation-communications extension*, the marketer uses essentially the same promotional messages abroad as at home, but the product is changed to meet local conditions. To illustrate, a soap formula is changed to adapt to local water conditions. Chemical fertilizers are altered to fit soil conditions. Voltage requirements alter appliances, and climatic factors make for packaging changes.

The fourth strategy, *dual adaptation*, involves changes in both the product and the message—in effect a combination of the second and third alternatives.

The fifth strategy is *product invention* wherein a company develops a new product in response to foreign market demands. For markets with low buying power, one firm "invented backwards" by developing an inexpensive, hand-operated washing machine with the tumbling action of an automatic machine.

Often in a foreign-market product-planning situation, a company is faced with this problem: Can we afford to modify the design, quality, or some other feature of our product? That is, will the demand offset the additional costs of producing and marketing the modified products? Answers to these questions are not easy to come by. Sometimes management can compromise by making a relatively inexpensive change, such as selling pharmaceuticals by the individual capsule or packaging razor blades singly rather than in multiple units.

Branding is especially important in foreign marketing. As suggested above, the brand picture may be the only part of the product that a consumer can recognize.

---

18 The discussion of these strategies is adapted from Warren J. Keegan, "Multinational Product Planning: Strategic Alternatives," *Journal of Marketing*, January, 1969, pp. 58-62.

19 For a report on U.S. consumers' reactions to another set of imported products, see Ralph Gaedeke, "Consumer Attitudes toward Products 'Made In' Developing Countries," *Journal of Retailing*, Summer, 1973, pp. 13-24.

Foreign consumers' preference for well-known North-American products often overcomes their nationalistic feelings, so in many instances a company can use the same brand that is used in the domestic market. The legal aspects of brand registration and ownership in foreign countries may create problems. In some nations, a local firm or person may "pirate" a brand name and thus block its use by the Canadian company in that foreign country.

PRICING IN INTERNATIONAL MARKETS

In earlier chapters, we recognized that determining a basic price and establishing various pricing policies are complex tasks, often involving trial-and-error decision making. These tasks become even more complex in international marketing because management must contend with additional variables such as currency conversion problems, a myriad of possible bases for price quotations, and often a lack of knowledge or control of middlemen's pricing. The principles and methods of price determination in multinational marketing are quite similar to those discussed in Chapters 12 to 15.

Cost-plus pricing is probably used to a greater extent in export marketing than at home. The cost-plus approach, coupled with additional cost factors not found in the domestic market (tariffs, shipping costs, larger margins for middlemen, etc.), can result in some startling differences between foreign and domestic prices on the same article. An example of this "price escalation" is shown in Table 26-3. Some manufacturers try to reduce these differentials by (1) accepting a lower net price on exported goods, (2) establishing overseas manufacturing operations to escape tariffs, (3) modifying the product to get it into a lower tariff classification, or (4) eliminating some of the middlemen in the trade channels.[20]

Sometimes a firm's foreign price may be *lower* than its domestic price. The price may be lowered in order to meet foreign competition, to dispose of outmoded products, or to remove supply from the home market and thus preserve the home-market structure. Sometimes governments engage in the practice of "dumping." That is, government action supports the domestic price at a level above the international market price. Then when these products are exported, they are sold below the domestic price. Through the years the surplus production of several raw materials has led to government control of world market prices. Individual governments have tried to stabilize the prices of coffee, nitrates, sugar, and rubber. Also, governments of several countries have established joint agreements covering the price of such commodities as tin, potash, cocoa, and wheat.

Foreign middlemen often are not aggressive in their pricing policies and strategies. They prefer to maintain high unit margins at the expense of low sales volume, rather than develop large sales volume by means of lower prices and smaller margins per unit sold. In fact, there is considerable rigidity in price structures in many foreign markets. In some cases, inflexibility stems from the combinations of firms which tend to restrain independent action in pricing and other marketing activities. The rigidity is sometimes engendered by price-control legislation which prevents retailers from cutting prices substantially and at their own discretion. Canadian producers should be aware that combinations among manufacturers and middlemen are tolerated to a far greater extent in many foreign countries than in Canada, even when the avowed purpose of the combinations is to restrain trade and reduce

---

20 Cateora and Hess, *op. cit.*, pp. 679-680.

Table 26-3. Causes and effects of price escalation.

The price paid by the foreign consumer at retail can greatly exceed the manufacturer's net when we use cost-plus pricing and include the many extra costs to be covered in international marketing. Why is the retail price in example 4 ($4.79) so much higher than the $2.58 price in example 1?

	Domestic example	Foreign example 1: assuming the same channels with wholesaler importing directly	Foreign example 2: importer and same margins and channels	Foreign example 3: same as 2, but with 10 percent cumulative turnover tax	Foreign example 4: long channels, larger retail margins, no turnover tax
Mfg. net	$ .95	$ .95	$ .95	$ .95	$ .95
Transport, c.i.f.	x	.15	.15	.15	.15
Tariff (20%)	x	.19	.19	.19	.19
Importer pays	x	x	1.29	1.29	1.29
Importer margin when sold to wholesaler (25% on cost)	x	x	.32	.32	.32
				+.13 turnover tax	
Wholesaler pays landed cost	.95	1.29	1.61	1.74	1.61
Wholesaler margin (33-1/3% on cost)	.32	.43	.54	.58	.54
				+.17 turnover tax	
Local foreign jobber pays jobber	x	x	x	x	2.15
Jobber margin (33-1/3% on cost)	x	x	x	x	.72
Retailer pays	1.27	1.72	2.15	2.49	2.87
Retail margin (50% on cost)	.63	.86	1.08	1.25	1.92 (66-2/3% on cost)
				+.25 turnover tax	
Retail price	$1.90	$2.58	$3.23	$3.99	$4.79

Note: (1) All figures in Canadian dollars; (2) x means this cost is not applicable in this example; (3) the exhibit assumes that all domestic transportation is absorbed by the middlemen; (4) transportation, tariffs, and middleman margins vary from country to country, but for purposes of comparison only a few of the possible variations are shown.

Source: Philip R. Cateora and John M. Hess, *International Marketing*, rev. ed., Richard D. Irwin, Inc., Homewood, Ill., 1971, p. 678.

competition. Probably the best known of international marketing combinations is the cartel. A *cartel* is a group of companies which produce similar products and which have combined to restrain competition in manufacturing and marketing. Cartels exist to varying degrees in steel, aluminum, fertilizers, electrical products, petroleum products, rayon, dyes, and sulfur. Originally they were formed to regulate competition in industries faced with conditions of chronic overproduction. Later they expanded their activities to include maintaining prices, setting up sales territories, establishing uniform documents, and even doing centralized selling.

Another area of pricing practices peculiar to foreign trade relates to aspects of price quotations. With respect to shipping, insurance, and related export charges, three bases of price quotations used extensively in foreign trade are f.o.b., f.a.s., and c.i.f. When a shipment is priced f.o.b. (free on board), the f.o.b. point is usually the inland point of departure of the port of shipment. When a shipment is priced f.a.s. (free alongside ship, at port of export), the seller pays all charges to deliver the goods to the dock within reach of the ship's tackle, but not on board. All shipping activities, costs, and risks from that point are the responsibility of the buyer. Under a price quotation of c.i.f. (cost, insurance, freight) at a given point of destination, the seller pays all costs up to the arrival of the shipment at the foreign port.

Prices may be quoted in Canadian or U.S. dollars or in the currency of the foreign buyer. Here we become involved in problems of foreign exchange and conversion of currencies. When prices are quoted in Canadian or American dollars, exchange controls by foreign governments may impede the conversion of foreign currency to dollars, thus delaying the collection of invoices. As a general rule, a firm engaged in foreign trade—whether it is buying or selling, exporting or importing—prefers to have the price quoted in its own national currency. Risks from fluctuations in foreign exchange—that is, devaluation of the currency of the other country—then are shifted to the other party in the transaction. In addition, an importer can readily determine his resale price, compute his profits, and compare offerings from sellers in different countries. Sometimes a foreign importer will prefer to have the price quoted in the currency of the exporting nation if he sees an opportunity to speculate profitably in exchange fluctuations, or if he thinks that he can buy at a lower price by assuming the risks of fluctuations. The decision on whether to quote prices in the national currency of the importer or the exporter depends on the bargaining power of each and on how badly each wants the sale to be made.

INTERNATIONAL DISTRIBUTION SYSTEMS

Perhaps nowhere else in the marketing program do we find it as difficult to categorize international marketing patterns as in the area of distribution systems. The conglomerate nature of *domestic* middlemen and their functions is found to an even greater degree when we examine *international* distribution patterns.

Understanding the environment in a foreign market helps in understanding the middlemen and the distribution system because these marketing institutions are a product of their environment. In foreign markets, just as in Canada, consumer buying habits are a major factor in shaping distribution channels and middlemen's activities. The perceptive, and thus usually successful, retailers, for example, will capitalize on environmental change by introducing innovations which anticipate trends in the environment. Thus, when supermarkets were introduced in some Western European countries, they were accepted enthusiastically because enough of the market was ready to change from the practice of shopping at several small, limited-line stores. In fact, several European retailers have done a good job of innovating. Within a relatively few years they have moved from the stage of "mom and pop" stores to a variety of retailing concepts as advanced as anything in Canada. In so doing, these innovative retailers simply telescoped time and leapfrogged several stages of institutional development.[21] In mass retailing, the *hypermarché* in France and the *verbrauchermarkt* in Germany are huge self-service combination superstores operating very profitably and at much lower gross margins than similar Canadian stores. At the other end of the size scale, Europeans also have been innovative in small specialty shops retailing shoes, clothing, and other products.

Environmental changes in Japan—rising incomes and industrialization, for instance—are having an impact on Japanese department stores. They are employing sales training and better inventory control, and broadening their lines of products and services. At the same time they must contend with rising costs, in-store congestion, and other new problems.[22] An increasing number of both North American and foreign-based retailers are responding to growth opportunities by crossing national boundaries. These international retailers are increasing their own profits and also changing the competitive structures of the countries they enter.[23]

Middlemen used in foreign marketing. Four groups of middlemen to be recognized in foreign trade include (1) Canadian foreign trade middlemen, (2) foreign trade middlemen located abroad, (3) wholesalers and retailers operating within foreign markets, and (4) manufacturers' sales branches and offices located in foreign countries.

Canadian foreign trade middlemen. Many foreign trade middlemen located in Canada engage in such a wide variety of activities today that they defy accurate titling or meaningful classification. They are simply Canadian middlemen engaged in foreign marketing. Any narrower descriptive title may be misleading or erroneous. One company may do both importing and exporting as an independent merchant and at the same time act as a manufacturers' export agent. Another importer-exporter may also own and operate sugar plantations, manufacturing plants, a bank, or a steamship line.

The "export house" is probably the most popular term used to describe all foreign trade middlemen, with the possible exception of brokers. The term is even used to include those firms which *import* products into Canada. The operations of "export and import brokers" are much the same as those of brokers in domestic marketing. In foreign trade these middlemen are especially active in the marketing of staple commodities.

---

21 Ralph Z. Sorenson II, "U.S. Marketers Can Learn from European Innovators," *Harvard Business Review*, September-October, 1972, pp. 89-99; also see Eugene D. Jaffe, "The Growth and Performance of Self-service Food Shops in Israel: A Study of an Adoption of an American Innovation in a Developing Country," *University of Washington Business Review*, Summer, 1968, pp. 60-66.

22 Paul O. Grokë, "How Japanese Department Stores Are Meeting the Challenge of a Rapidly Changing Environment," *Journal of Retailing*, Fall, 1972, pp. 72-80. Also see "Spaniards Say 'Si' to Department Stores," *Business Week*, May 28, 1966, p. 176.

23 See Stanley C. Hollander, *Multinational Retailing*, Michigan State University, East Lansing, International Business and Economic Studies, 1970; Bruce J. Walker and Michael J. Etzel, "The Internationalization of U.S. Franchise Systems: Progress and Procedures," *Journal of Marketing*, April, 1973, pp. 38-46; "Britain's Retail Champ (Marks and Spencer) Takes on the World," *Business Week*, Nov. 3, 1973, p. 88; and "Carrefour: A Superdiscounter Eyes the U.S.," *Business Week*, Dec. 15, 1973, p. 78.

Foreign trade middlemen located abroad. In most foreign countries there are independent middlemen (importers, exporters, brokers, and some wholesalers) who are engaged in foreign trade and who operate in essentially the same way that Canadian-based foreign trade firms do. For a Canadian producer, however, the main outlets abroad for manufactured goods are *agents and distributors.* These are firms which act as sales representatives for the Canadian firms in foreign markets. Agents and distributors differ primarily in two respects: Agents do not take title to the goods and normally do not carry inventory stocks. These two types of middlemen are so important in the distribution system that often a manufacturer will grant them exclusive territorial rights. They perform a wide variety of services, including personal selling, advertising, providing market and credit information, making repairs, billing, settling disputes, and collecting invoices. In addition, distributors perform the functions of warehousing and bulk breaking.

Channels of distribution. When selecting the channel of distribution to be used in foreign marketing, an executive probably will use one of the following five alternatives. Two of these are indirect, involving the use of middlemen all the way, and the other three involve direct selling to some extent, along with the establishment of foreign sales offices or branches by the manufacturer.

1. Manufacturer—foreign trade middlemen (exporters) in Canada—foreign trade middlemen (importers) abroad—wholesalers and/or retailers in foreign countries—consumers or industrial users.
2. Manufacturer—foreign trade middlemen in Canada—wholesalers and/or retailers in foreign countries—consumers or industrial users
3. Manufacturer—foreign trade middlemen in foreign countries—wholesalers and/or retailers—consumers or industrial users
4. Manufacturer—wholesalers and/or retailers abroad—consumers or industrial users
5. Manufacturer—consumers or industrial users

The main problem at this point is to decide whether to engage in direct selling and, if so, to what extent. Middlemen operating *within* foreign countries are, in general, less aggressive and perform fewer marketing services than their Canadian counterparts. The foreign marketing situation, however, usually argues against by-passing foreign middlemen. Often the demand is too small to warrant the establishment of a sales office or branch. Also, the wage structure and selling methods tend to give foreign middlemen an advantage. Government controls frequently preclude the use of a Canadian sales organization abroad. Thus, middlemen in foreign countries ordinarily are used in the channel structure, whether the Canadian seller exports directly to sales offices abroad or uses Canadian exporting middlemen.

When foreign middlemen are used, the seller usually advertises extensively and furnishes point-of-purchase display materials to strengthen the efforts of the middlemen. Missionary salespeople are sometimes employed. If the product requires mechanical servicing or installation, the Canadian manufacturer must provide reliable repair service. This means training local middlemen, sending in service representatives, or both. Local middlemen often require financial assistance. If retailers cannot get bank credit, the manufacturer must meet this need.

Physical distribution. In foreign marketing, various aspects of physical distribution are quite different from anything found on the domestic scene. In general, the total cost of physical distribution is a much larger share of the final selling price in foreign markets than in domestic markets. Packing requirements, for example, are more exacting for foreign shipment. Problems caused by humidity, pilferage, breakage, and inadequate marking of shipments must be considered. Requirements of commercial shipping documents and governmental documents complicate the paper work in foreign shipping. Marine insurance and the traffic management of international shipments are specialized fields involving facilitating agencies ordinarily not used in domestic marketing. In conclusion, the new capabilities in logistics control plus the faster rates of change in international marketing point up the need for an enlarged, higher-level physical distribution activity.

ADVERTISING IN FOREIGN MARKETS

Any analysis of international promotional programs should encompass the management of international sales forces, sales-promotional techniques, and advertising programs. Because of space limitations, however, our brief discussion is confined only to advertising as illustrative of the managerial problems in international promotion. Advertising is selected because it is probably used by more firms in international marketing than either a company sales force or some of the sales-promotional techniques. Many companies without their own international sales force—they use foreign trade middlemen—will advertise internationally.

In international advertising, one controversial issue is the extent to which advertising can be standardized in foreign markets. In years gone by, the consensus was that a separate program (copy, appeals, media, etc.) had to be tailored for each country or even regions within a country. While nobody is recommending complete uniformity, today we are finding much support for the idea that a commonality can exist successfully in international compaigns. Many companies are using basically the same appeals, theme, slogan, colors, copy, layout, etc., in all their international advertising—particularly in the Western European countries. Certainly standardization of advertising is spurred by the fact that (1) hordes of Europeans travel from one country to another while on vacation; (2) many radio and TV broadcasts from one country reach audiences in another country; and (3) the circulation of many European magazines and newspapers crosses national borders.

Perhaps the issue comes down to this point: The goal of advertising is essentially the same at home and abroad, namely, to communicate information and persuasive appeals effectively. The basic approach to developing an advertising campaign can be the same in every country. It is only the media strategy and specific messages which must be attuned to each country's cultural, economic, and political environment.[24] For some products the appeals are sufficiently universal and the market sufficiently homogeneous so as to permit the use of uniform advertising in several countries. Standardization undoubtedly will increase, being propelled by such factors as increasing international communications and rising standards of living.[25]

Attitude of foreign markets and governments toward advertising. In many countries the traditionally negative attitude toward marketing in general and toward advertising in particular is a hardship for Canadian firms. The "build a better mouse-

---

24 Gordon E. Miracle, "International Advertising Principles and Strategies," *MSU Business Topics,* Autumn, 1968, pp. 29-36.

25 For an exchange of views on the standardization of international advertising, see Arthur C. Fatt, "The Danger of 'Local' International Advertising," *Journal of Marketing,* January, 1967, pp. 60-62; and James H. Donnelly, Jr., and John K. Ryans, Jr., "Standardized Global Advertising: A Call as yet Unanswered," *Journal of Marketing,* April, 1969, pp. 57-60.

trap" theory still prevails to a great extent throughout Europe and the rest of the world. Some foreign consumers feel that a product is of dubious value if it has to be advertised. People in many foreign countries object particularly to blatant or "hard sell" advertising. Many countries have stringent laws regulating advertising copy and media. In West Germany, for example, a seller cannot make product comparisons in his advertising. As a general rule, advertising must be factual and must employ a "soft sell" approach. On the other hand, some markets—Latin America, for example—treat and accept advertising much as we in Canada do. Where the government regulates the use of radio and television for advertising and where newspapers are government-controlled, this too affects their use as advertising media.

Choice of media. Essentially the same types of advertising media are available in foreign countries as here, with the exception of television in some markets. Some print media, such as *Time* and *Reader's Digest*, which are published in Canada are also published abroad in foreign languages.

In foreign markets Canadian exporters encounter problems related to media selection which are not normally met at home. One factor peculiar to foreign marketing is the low rate of literacy in many areas. A seller might ordinarily prefer print media to show a colored picture of his product and explain its merits. If he is selling in a market where 90 percent of the people cannot read and do not buy magazines or newspapers, however, he may be forced to use radio, which on other counts may be a far less effective medium for his product. Another major problem is the unavailability of accurate information regarding the quantitative and qualitative nature of media circulation. Sometimes the rates paid for media space are determined on a bargaining basis. Sometimes the rates for Canadian sellers are higher than those for native firms. Political and religious considerations are more important determinants of newspaper readership in many foreign markets than in Canada.

Preparation of advertisements. Most of the mistakes in writing copy and preparing individual advertisements may be traced to lack of intimate knowledge of the foreign market. As we have said, the wrong use of color or a poor choice of words can completely nullify an otherwise good ad. Illustrations are of prime importance in many markets because of the illiteracy factor. They are, of course, effective in all markets, but they must be accurate, believable, and in accord with local cultures. If agencies and advertisers could have qualified people from the individual foreign markets check every advertisement before it reaches the public, many mistakes could be prevented. The translation of the advertising copy into the appropriate foreign language is a major problem. Here the advertiser especially needs someone both adept and current (an expatriate often will not do) in the idioms, dialects, and other nuances of the foreign language.

Management of foreign advertising. The advertising program in foreign markets can be coordinated in three general ways: Control may be centralized in the home office of the Canadian seller; it may be exercised jointly by the home office and the foreign representatives; or it may be delegated entirely to the seller's foreign representatives. On balance, the best arrangement seems to be centralized control. It is difficult to exert budgetary control over an internationally decentralized operation. Often better advertising talent and more advertising specialists ae available in the home office than in any single foreign market. The home office can work with advertising agencies that have foreign offices. Thus it can have some of the advantages of local market contacts but still retain basic control. Economies can be realized through centralized creation and production of the individual advertisements. Also when international media are used, some centralized control is necessary. Finally, centralized management of the advertising program makes it easier to coordinate advertising with other aspects of the company's promotional and marketing programs. Of course, centralized management means that the Canadian seller loses the tremendous advantage of having personnel closely acquainted with local cultures, languages, and buying habits. The more these latter factors differ from Canadian ones, the greater the hazards of centralization.

GOVERNMENT SUPPORT FOR INTERNATIONAL MARKETING

In most of the decision-making areas in international marketing, the Federal government, as well as many provincial governments, provide contacts, information, guidance and even financing for Canadian firms. For example, international marketing efforts are aided by the Department of Industry, Trade and Commerce and the Export Development Corporation. The Department attempts to assist firms from the research and development stage through to the international marketing of finished products. The Export Development Corporation provides insurance, guarantees, loans and other financial facilities to help Canadian exporters.

Within the Federal Department a number of units exist which work on specific problems associated with international marketing. The Office of General Relations is responsible for advance planning of Canada's external trade policies and general policy affecting primary and secondary industry. The Office of Area Relations protects and improves the access of Canadian goods to export markets. The Industry, Trade and Traffic Services Branch deals with shipping problems and trade control, and provides information on Canadian products and companies. The Fairs and Missions Branch coordinates all departmental activities designed to promote the sale of Canadian products and services abroad. The International Defence Programs Branch promotes defence and export trade. The Trade Commissioners Service, with 76 offices in 55 countries, promotes export trade, and protects commercial interests abroad. The Publicity Branch supports foreign trade promotion programs. The operational branches within the Department (Aerospace; Marine and Rail; Agriculture; Fisheries and Food Products; Apparel and Textiles; Chemicals; Electrical and Electronics; Machinery, Materials; Mechanical Transport and, Wood Products) each works to promote the sales of products and services in international markets.

THE FUTURE: A WORLD MARKETING ENTERPRISE

For countless companies, the marketing opportunities and challenges of the future lie in international marketing. This conclusion seems inevitable as management views its home markets being saturated, its excess productive capacity, its shrinking profit margins, and the intensified competition in Canada coming from both domestic and foreign firms. This broadening of marketing horizons, however, will be a new experience in most cases. Many companies in Canada have never realized that export markets provide them with an opportunity to increase sales volume and profits significantly. Even the increasing competition from foreign imports has usually served only to intensify Canadian sellers' competitive efforts at home, rather than turning their interest to international markets.

But the winds of change are awakening executives to the opportunities in multinational marketing. To make the most of these opportunities a company is urged to think big and plan ahead—clichés, yes, and perhaps trite, but useful admonitions nevertheless. A country-by-country market analysis is becoming increasingly common and is certainly better than going abroad with a one-shot, unplanned approach because some random opportunity has presented itself. Better than a country-by-country analysis, however, is a global planning approach. A company that takes a total global system approach is not apt to be blocked later on by some decision made earlier in another country.[26]

This chapter has stressed the notion that a separate marketing plan is needed for each country because of environmental differences. While it is true that differences between foreign markets are still great, the experiences of a growing number of multinational firms suggest that real benefits can be derived from standardizing some elements of the marketing programs used in different countries.[27]

It is commonly alleged that products manufactured in Canada are being priced out of world markets because of our high cost structure. While this cannot be denied, our labour costs and prices are often offered as excuses, when the truth of the matter is that we have failed to apply our know-how of modern marketing management in foreign countries.[28] While marketing skills and aggressiveness are increasing among foreign firms, Canadian firms do not have a market orientation in their export business. In the past, much emphasis has been placed on production and financial problems in foreign markets.

Let us move for a moment from the micro level of the individual firm to the macro level of the total economy. It is becoming increasingly apparent that the rate of economic growth in less-developed nations will depend largely upon how effective the marketing systems established in these countries are. Typically in these countries (as true earlier in Canada) the economic development effort has been concentrated in production. Now these governments are beginning to recognize the role which marketing can play in their national economic growth. This enlightened attitude offers countless marketing opportunities (but not without attendant problems) to the internationally oriented business firm. Particularly, a marketing executive must understand the government's role in business in each country.[29]

---

26 For a step-by-step case example of how one firm went about global planning, plus an evaluation of this approach, see *International Enterprise: A New Dimension of American Business*, McKinsey & Company, Inc., New York, 1962, pp. 21-24.

27 Robert D. Buzzell, "Can You Standardize Multinational Marketing?" *Harvard Business Review*, November-December, 1968, pp. 102-113.

28 Laurence P. Dowd, "Is the United States Being Priced out of World Markets?" *Journal of Marketing*, July, 1960, pp. 1-8.

29 For discussions of the increased attention being paid to marketing and economic growth in emerging economies, see, for example, Charles C. Slater, "Marketing Processes in Developing Latin American Societies," *Journal of Marketing*, July, 1968, pp. 50-55; James E. Littlefield, "The Relationship of Marketing to Economic Development in Peru." *Southern Journal of Business*, July, 1968, pp. 1-14; Harry A. Lipson and Douglas F. Lamont, "Marketing Policy Decisions Facing International Marketers in Less-developed Countries," *Journal of Marketing*, October, 1969, pp. 24-31; in Reed Moyer (ed.), *Changing Marketing Systems*, American Marketing Association, Chicago, 1968, see Lee E. Preston, "Market Development and Market Control" pp. 223-227, and Peter D. Bennett, "Marketing and Public Policy in Latin America," pp. 233-238; and Reed Moyer and Stanley C. Hollander (eds.), *Markets and Marketing in Developing Economies*, American Marketing Association, Chicago, 1968.

Permeating this chapter has been the theme that marketing management in Canadian firms must become more internationally minded. We conclude with a statement made by the same executive who was quoted at the beginning of the chapter. He notes the following five reasons why it is mandatory to be successful in world marketing.[30]

1. We cannot adequately expand our economy at home without meeting competition abroad.
2. We cannot eliminate large-scale unemployment in this country unless we do smaller-scale employing in other countries.
3. To achieve a higher tide of prosperity here, we must be willing to develop trade with those whose prosperity is still at a very low ebb.
4. Balancing our international payment books at home requires filling many more order books abroad.
5. If we are to remain dominant and competitive in our home market, we must compete successfully in the world market.

QUESTIONS AND PROBLEMS

1. In what fundamental respects is international marketing different from domestic marketing?
2. Report on *export* marketing activities of companies in the province where your school is located. Consider such topics as the following: What products are exported? How many jobs are created by export marketing? What is the dollar value of exports? How does this figure compare with the value of foreign-made goods imported into the province?
3. A luggage manufacturer with annual sales over $5 million has decided to market his products in Western Europe. Evaluate the alternative organizational structures which this company should consider.
4. Select three countries—one in Europe, one in South America, and one in Africa—and assume that a Canadian subsidiary of a U.S. manufacturer of auto and truck tires plans to have the Canadian plant market products in these countries. What problems will this manufacturer face in each of the following areas?
   a. Exchange controls
   b. Tariffs on tires
   c. Restrictions on foreign companies or personnel
5. From a management standpoint, what are the differences between a company organized and operating truly as a world enterprise and a firm in which the international division is separate from the domestic organization?
6. Select one product—manufactured or nonmanufactured—for export and the country to which you would like to export it. Then prepare an analysis of the market for this product in the selected country. Be sure to include the sources of information which you used.
7. Many countries unfortunately have a low literacy rate. In what ways might a company adjust aspects of its marketing program to overcome this problem?

---

30 Ray R. Eppert, "Passport for Marketing Overseas," *Journal of Marketing*, April, 1965, p. 6 .

8. Why should special attention be devoted to labeling and branding when selling Canadian products in foreign markets?
9. Describe the role of the export house in foreign marketing.
10. If a Canadian manufacturer uses foreign middlemen, he must usually stand ready to supply them with additional financial, technical, and promotional help. If this is the case, why is it not customary to bypass these middlemen and deal directly with foreign buyers?
11. Why does a Canadian exporter prefer to have prices quoted in Canadian dollars? Why should the foreign importer prefer that the quotation be in the currency of his country?
12. "Prices of products are always higher in foreign countries than at home because of the additional risk, expenses of physical distribution, and extra middlemen involved." Discuss.
13. Carefully distinguish between f.o.b., f.a.s., and c.i.f. as bases for price quotations in foreign marketing.
14. Study the advertisements in the foreign newspapers and magazines available in your college or city library. Particularly note the advertisements for Canadian type products and compare these with the advertisements for the same products in local newspapers and magazines. In what respect do the foreign ads differ from the domestic ads? Are there significant similarities?

CASES FOR PART SEVEN

CASE 20 MEDICAL-DENTAL FINANCIAL PLANNING, INC.

Pricing and promoting a new service

Mr. Donald Heaton, the president of Medical-Dental Financial Planning, Inc., believed that his company offered a service which so far was being marketed by very few companies in the United States. At the same time he believed that there was a huge potential market for his company's service, and that only a minute portion of that market as yet had been tapped. Consequently, Mr. Heaton was wondering what type of promotional program would be most effective in (1) reaching additional portions of this large market and (2) strengthening his firm's competitive position in the market. He also was uncertain about how to price some segments of his company's financial planning service.

The service being marketed by Medical-Dental Financial Planning, Inc., was a relatively new concept—it was a total financial management program for physicians and dentists. Mr. Heaton established this "financial clinic" in 1968 after observing that doctors needed help in planning and managing their financial affairs. Heaton said, "Nine out of ten doctors are in deep financial trouble. They earn good money, but nobody misuses his funds like a physician or a dentist. They make lousy businessmen."

Currently Medical-Dental had two offices in California (Los Angeles and San Francisco), two in Canada (Toronto and Montreal), and one each in Denver, Colorado; Hartford, Connecticut; New York City; and Washington, D.C. The company managed the total financial affairs of about 1,200 clients and provided more limited, specific financial services for about 4,000 other clients. The company was in sound financial condition and it enjoyed fairly high profits. The board of directors of the company included physicians, accountants, attorneys, and experts in the fields of insurance, banking, mutual funds, and real estate.

The operational manner in which Medical-Dental produced its financial service was relatively simple. One of its sales representatives lined up a prospect, and then reported on the prospect's financial situation, ambitions, and personality to the company's home office. There a six-man advisory committee, which included specialists in taxation, insurance, real estate, mutual funds, and banking, worked out a program suited to the client's needs. In many cases it obtained for the client unsecured bank loans for capital or personal investments. When the client had saved funds or had large cash values in his insurance policies, the money was put into mutual funds or real estate investments. The firm, in turn, made its money from commissions and fees, plus a share of the profits from its real estate dealings.

"We're not interested in making our clients into millionaires," said Heaton. "Our goal is to take care of many of the financial things they don't have the time or the talent for, to solve their tax problems, and help them accumulate a small amount of wealth. We custom design a complete financial program suited to the professional man's particular needs. We feature one-stop shopping with expert advice. We're interested in increasing an individual's total net worth. Usually a doctor has several financial advisors (insurance men, real estate brokers, bankers), each of whom is competing for his funds. We use the systems concept."

Because the concept of total financial planning for doctors was relatively new, Medical-Dental had very little direct competition from similar types of organizations. However, the company did have considerable competition from the insurance, mutual fund, real estate, and "estate planning" industries.

The firm felt it had a natural advantage over all these competitors because of its comprehensive approach versus their limited-service approaches. It fully expected, however, to face stiff competition, beginning in the near future, from enterprises such as itself. As one company executive said, "Our approach is the coming thing. We've got to expect competition soon." He went on to explain the pioneering work the company had done to firmly establish itself and to prepare for coming competition. He was especially pleased with Medical-Dental's success in lining up banks which were willing to make large (up to $30,000), unsecured loans to doctors.

Mr. Heaton viewed his company's potential market as including virtually all the physicians and dentists in Canada and the United States—in effect, an almost unlimited market with a great geographic dispersion. Medical-Dental's major problem with respect to that market was how to gain access to the doctors. As a general rule, doctors were extremely busy and sheltered from business contacts. It was hard to reach them through advertising, and contacts through personal selling usually were difficult to make because of the doctors' inaccessibility and the newness of Medical-Dental's service.

Mr. Heaton and some of his top executives were trying to figure out the best way to promote their company's financial management services. They believed they had better than a 50-50 chance to sell a doctor on their total service package if they could get the prospective client to sit down seriously with a Medical-Dental representative for a period of time and listen attentively and without interruption to the representative's message. Medical-Dental had salespeople working out of each of the company's offices. The people were paid a salary and a commission. They called on doctors in the doctors' offices, and they tried to make contacts with the doctors at country clubs, downtown athletic clubs, and similar places.

Some of the Medical-Dental executives felt the company should do some advertising, but they were not certain as to what media to use, how much to spend, or what type of sales message to use in the ads.

The executives were also wrestling with the problem of whether to charge a fee for working up a financial program as part of the company's initial contact with a prospective client. Presently, the company worked up a comprehensive program for each prospective client who showed enough interest to provide the salesperson with the basic information. There was no charge for this service, and the doctor could become a client, use the advice on his own or with the help of others, or forget the whole thing. If he became a client, the firm charged commissions and fees for the transactions it conducted in his behalf, and shared in any real estate profits.

Some members of the firm believed it would be a better marketing strategy to charge a fee for the initial professional advice and services rendered. The sales manager, Mr. Clark Irwin, felt that professionals recognize the value of professional advice and would prefer to pay a fee for it. This would be more in keeping with the practices they themselves employ. He also pointed out that if a fee were charged to all those who requested that a program be worked up for them, then the ones who became clients would not feel they were subsidizing the ones who do not buy bearing all the costs of this service. "I think it would help separate us as professional financial managers from the quacks and piece-meal estate planners who are trying to compete with us," Irwin added. "Our professional image would be strengthened if we charged a fee."

Other executives argued that many prospective clients would be turned away by this initial fee. They pointed out that the new physician or dentist trying to set up private practice needs financial advice and might make an excellent client in the long run, but at the moment he can ill afford to pay the fee. Therefore, he would be discouraged from ever becoming a client and would probably wind up with a piece-meal financial program worked up by competing bankers, brokers, insurance salespeople, and the like. They thought that the "free service, with no obligation" approach allowed the company to explain its services to many more prospective clients than would be possible if a fee were charged for the initial advice.

The cost of working up the initial program normally ranged from $250 to $500 for time, materials, and professional services. Between 60 and 80 percent of all doctors who have programs worked up for them did become clients. The company normally earned between $1,000 and $5,000 in commissions and fees during a client's first year with Medical-Dental.

Mr. Irwin believed that the *principle* of the fee was more important than the *amount*. He suggested that the fee could be based on actual costs to the company for each individual program prepared; it could be a standard fee for all, based on average costs; or, it could be only a token fee, not intended to cover the costs of the service. If the doctor became a client, the company could apply the amount of the fee against the commissions it normally charged, if this practice was deemed desirable.

Mr. Heaton was anxious that his company employ the best marketing strategy possible, in order to become as strong as it can and to corner as large a share of the market as it can before competition becomes severe.

QUESTIONS

1. Design a promotional program for Medical-Dental to reach and attract new clients.
2. Should Medical-Dental charge a fee for its initial advisory service?
   a. If so, what should be the price?
   b. If charged, should the fee be reimbursed to those who become clients?

CASE 21: PIONEER INDUSTRIES LTD.

Strategy in Foreign Markets

While his more immediate task in March 1973 was to prepare for negotiations with a Japanese distributor interested in marketing the company's new lockset in the Far East, Steve Corbin, Marketing Vice-President of Pioneer Industries Ltd., was also anxious to review his company's policies and performance in foreign markets to date. He believed that these markets offered a substantial potential for Pioneer's lockset—a potential which had remained largely unexploited. Corbin felt that high priority should now be given to developing a more effective policy to tap this potential, particularly in view of the low sales volume achieved in the Canadian market and the recent appearance of a competing product.

The Techno Lockset. Pioneer was formed as a private company in 1967, with a capital of $100,000, to produce and market its revolutionary lockset "Techno" which had been invented and developed by Jim MacMillan—now a director in charge of the company's Research and Development.

Techno was radically different from conventional locksets. Made entirely of thermoplastic, Techno was an injection-moulded lock which had only 16 parts instead of about 75 parts in conventional locks. It required no maintenance, was easy to assemble, was static-electricity free, was adaptable to any style of handle, and could be used for a passage door (not requiring a lock) or for a door where privacy was required. The new lock operated in exactly the reverse manner of conventional sets. In a conventional lock, a complex metal mechanism of many moving parts, and placed in the door itself, was required to retract the bolt. But in the new lock, the latchbolt was on the jamb, and all that was required to operate the lock was a simple spring together with two other moving parts. Closure and forced-entry tests by an independent testing laboratory showed Techno to be highly durable—a fact which enabled the company to issue a 25-year warranty for its lockset.

Production arrangements for the new lock involved no major capital outlays. The company had a set of dies made to the exact specifications of the lockset. The dies were the only equipment owned and controlled by Pioneer. Company policy was to sub-contract actual production to one or more of the injection moulding firms with reputation for strict adherence to quality specifications. A set of dies was estimated to produce 800,000 locksets before it needed replacement, and to cost $15,000 in early 1973.

This case was written by T. Abdel-Malek and was made possible by the co-operation of a company which wishes to remain anonymous. Names and figures were disguised. The case was prepared as a basis for class discussion and is not designed to illustrate correct or incorrect handling of business situations.

The Canadian market. Initially, management was highly optimistic about the sales prospects in the Canadian market. Techno's unique features and apparent superiority to conventional sets in terms of design and durability, low production costs, and the very favorable comments made by the few architectural offices and hardware dealers who were shown samples of the new lock tempted management to press ahead with production arrangements without undertaking a more comprehensive testing of the market. This optimism, however, was gradually dampened by the emergence of three problems. First, the booming building industry was placing contractors under heavy time pressure which made them reluctant to make the necessary adjustments in the door's standard routing pockets (and incur the extra costs) to fit the new lock which differed in shape and size from conventional locks. Second, appreciable temperature variability caused a change in the size of the gap between the door and its jamb and, as a result, the new lock was found capable of locking people in when that gap narrowed significantly. Third, Techno lockset were meant for use on interior doors only. The company had no key lock to offer, and it was not technically feasible to develop such a lock in the near future. Although Pioneer had not anticipated any significant problems, most building contractors and particularly apartment builders expressed a preference for using matching locks for interior and main doors. This limited the company's ability to attract sizeable orders from residential building contractors.

Although Jim MacMillan was soon able to solve the lock-in problem caused by temperature variability, by making certain adjustments in the lockset, Pioneer had to find ways of overcoming the other two problems. Thus, instead of selling to building contractors only—a policy that was adopted during the first two years but which failed to produce a satisfactory sales volume—the company sought wider distribution by selling also to retail outlets through regional hardware distributors. There were approximately 12 such distributors who serviced over 3,000 retail hardware stores in Canada.

Pioneer initially established a suggested retail price of $4.39 for a passage set and $5.39 for a privacy set. These were in line with prices of good-quality conventional sets. Because Techno's production costs (including packaging) were significantly lower, amounting to about $1.20 per set for a production run of 25,000 sets, the company offered attractive markups of over 35% and 50% to distributors and retailers respectively, by selling to distributors at $2.15. This price applied to sales to contractors and door manufacturers also. The resulting markups were 5% to 10% higher than could be made on conventional sets. However, toward the end of 1972 another plastic lock appeared in the market and was selling to distributors and contractors at $1.35. Although Pioneer believed its lock to have a better quality and a more attractive design, the new lock represented a real threat and the company lowered its distributor's price to $1.59 in February 1973.

Pioneer relied primarily on free publicity articles in local papers and on a brochure sent to potential buyers to promote Techno. In addition, the president and marketing vice-president occasionally paid visits to some of the larger construction firms and distributors. Mr. Corbin felt that the company should reach the ultimate user also, but the tight financial position it was experiencing presently made this difficult to accomplish.

Pioneer's sales force consisted of 4 salaried salespeople covering various provinces. Except for large orders, personal selling was considered very expensive since several calls were often necessary to close a sale which typically ranged between 300 and 600 sets.

Total sales of Techno in Canada amounted to $50,000 in 1971 (its second full year in the market) and $65,000 in 1972. This compared with an estimated $5 million sales of locks to the residential segment in the latter year.

Foreign markets. From the outset, management believed that an appreciable market potential existed for Techno in many foreign markets, because of its perceived unique advantages. The question was how to go about tapping such potential most effectively in order to gain a share of the estimated $250 million world lockset market. As a preliminary measure, Pioneer obtained patents in 24 countries in 1970, including the U.S.A., most West European countries, Japan, India, Australia, New Zealand, Turkey, and the Philippines at a cost of $18,000. In many of these countries, annual fees approximately equal to those paid initially to obtain the patents had to be paid to keep them valid. But this was viewed as a necessary expense to protect Pioneer's future business.

Mr. Corbin pointed out that the world market was dominated by few large lock manufacturers such as Weiser, Dexter, Yale, Union, and Beaver. These firms not only dominated their home markets but often did an appreciable amount of foreign business also, either through exports or manufacturing and assembly operations abroad.

(a) *United States.* Soon after Techno was launched into the Canadian market, Pioneer attempted to enter the California market, and appointed a salesperson who operated from Los Angeles. But by the end of 1971 little results were achieved. Consequently, the company withdrew the salesperson and engaged commission agents in California and five other States. They were paid a commission of 7% on Pioneer's selling price.

Although Pioneer had expected to sell 50,000 sets during 1972 through agents, actual sales amounted to a few hundred sets only. Mr. Corbin indicated that a 17% import duty, a high price-consciousness on the part of U.S. buyers, and inadequate marketing effort by Pioneer due to its limited resources, were responsible for poor sales.

(b) *Australia.* The company's interest in the Australian market was enhanced by the favourable appraisal which Techno received from a number of major Australian buyers of locks who had been sent samples of the new lock early in 1970. In view of Australia's import duty of 22½%, Pioneer decided to experiment with a licensing arrangement as a means of gaining a firm position in that market. In June 1970, an agreement was successfully negotiated by the president and marketing vice-president with an Australian injection moulding firm during their trip there. Under the agreement, Pioneer received an initial lump sum of $2,000 and became entitled to a royalty of 8% on Techno sales made by the licensee. Sales were expected to reach 30,000 to 50,000 sets in 1971 and to show rapid growth thereafter. Total lockset sales in Australia amounted to $4 million annually in the early 1970s. Techno had the important advantage of being capable of withstanding the hard Australian climate which, not unlike Florida's for example, was very humid, and had high salt-content air and high temperatures—factors which caused metal locks to corrode and fail rapidly and their finish to deteriorate easily.

Nevertheless, Australian sales in 1971 did not exceed 1,500 sets. Moreover, the Australian licensee surprised Pioneer in February 1972 by offering to sell its patent rights to an "improved" Techno lockset which the Australian firm had developed and registered in Australia recently. Apart from the question of whether or not the licensee's action was appropriate under the existing licensing agreement, Pioneer's inspection of a sample of the improved lockset convinced management that the improvements were of minor significance. A stalemate resulted, and the licensing agreement was terminated by mutual consent a few months later.

(c) **United Kingdom.** Another market which Techno wanted to enter as early as possible was the U.K. Initially, Mr. Corbin felt that a joint-venture arrangement would be preferable to other means of market entry. An import duty of 22½ % represented a high barrier to exports. And a licensing agreement was considered less attractive than a joint venture, partly in view of the disappointing Australian experience, and partly because a joint venture offered Pioneer greater control of the marketing effort—control that Mr. Corbin viewed as essential if Techno was to be successfully established in Britain.

The British market was quite large, with annual sales of $15 million in 1970-72. An acute housing shortage prevailed and the government was lending support to efforts aiming at expanding supply and reducing construction costs. Pioneer's management felt that some financial support for a joint venture might be obtained if it succeeded in convincing the government of the advantages which Techno offered, especially its lower costs and its durability. An additional encouragement to enter the British market was the fact that Mr. Corbin had gained many years' experience in it while he was the marketing manager of one of the largest Canadian metal lock companies prior to joining Pioneer in 1969. His preference for greater control of the marketing effort there was based on his view that many British firms tended to be too conservative in their approach and his belief that a carefully applied North American approach was needed to penetrate the British market.

However, several months of exploration failed to locate appropriate partners or attract government support, and the joint-venture alternative had to be abandoned. Instead, Pioneer was currently attempting to negotiate a licensing agreement with a British injection-moulding firm producing a wide variety of finished and intermediate products sold to several industries including the housing construction industry. In a tentative draft drawn by Pioneer's management, Pioneer proposed to grant the British firm exclusive sales rights in the U.K. and South Africa, provide the necessary technical know-how, and authorize it to use the Techno trade mark. Pioneer was also prepared to lend the licensee its moulds for a 12-week period to produce not more than 240,000 sets; afterwards, the licensee would acquire its own moulds. In exchange, Pioneer proposed to receive a royalty of 10% on net sales or 11c per set sold whichever was higher for subsequent sales. Finally, Pioneer asked for a guaranteed minimum royalty of $50,000 per annum for the first two years.

Although this was by no means the company's final offer, Mr. Corbin pointed out that major departures from the proposal were not likely to be acceptable to Pioneer. While awaiting the British firm's reaction, he was pondering what and how many concessions Pioneer should be prepared to make if necessary.

(d) **Japan.** Pioneer first came in contact with Ako & Co. of Japan during a 1972 trade fair in the United States at which the Techno lock was displayed. Ako was a national distributor for one of the largest paint manufacturers in Japan. It also handled a wide range of plastic materials used in construction and other industries, and generated a total sales volume of $10 million in 1972.

Ako expressed strong interest in the Techno lockset, and wanted to explore the prospects of becoming its sole distributor in the Far East. In addition, Ako itself was involved, jointly with one of the main construction firms in Japan, in a large modular housing project scheduled to build 16,000 houses per year for the next 5 years. The company was considering the adoption of Techno locksets for this project, pending the results of a market survey already under way which was using samples received from Pioneer earlier. As a distributor, Ako indicated that other builders were showing interest in Techno, and gave a tentative sales estimate of 20,000 to 30,000 sets per year to start with. Ako also stated that its representative would be in Canada in April 1973, at which time both companies could discuss the terms of an exclusive agency agreement or of a combined technical/agency agreement under which Techno would be assembled in Japan and sold exclusively by Ako in the Far East.

Encouraged by these prospects and by a favourable assessment of Ako as a distributor—an assessment he had just received from the Canadian Trade Commissioner's Office in Tokyo at his request—Mr. Corbin was now beginning to appraise various alternatives in preparation for his meeting with Ako's representative next month. He believed that the Japanese market could provide the sales volume which Pioneer badly needed, but was unable to estimate market potential at this stage, and did not know enough about Far Eastern Markets. He was convinced that success depended on the effectiveness with which Techno would be promoted by the Japanese distributor, and on effective protection of Pioneer's patent rights against possible infringements through unscrupulous copying of Techno by one or more firms in Japan. Meanwhile, the pros and cons of exporting assembled vs. unassembled locks to Japan had to be considered. If agreement was reached to export Techno unassembled, Pioneer could offer to sell the parts to Ako at around $1.10 per set f.o.b. Ako would pay a 10% import duty (instead of 17½% on assembled sets), incur about 20c-25c per set for freight, assembly and packaging, and could sell to builders for at least $1.95. If large orders could be generated and Pioneer was able to, say, double the size of present production runs, unit costs would drop by about 10%.

Mr. Corbin was also not sure whether to offer Ako exclusive agency in Japan only or in the Far East as a whole at present.

QUESTIONS

1. Appraise Pioneer's policies and attempts to establish Techno in foreign markets. What changes, if any, would you propose to make these policies more effective?
2. What terms would you advice Mr. Corbin to offer Ako? Why?

PLANNING AND EVALUATING THE MARKETING EFFORT

A MARKETING INFORMATION SYSTEM AND MARKETING RESEARCH

"Half the cost of running our economy is the cost of information. No other field offers such concentrated room for improvement as does information analysis."[1] This quotation highlights a fundamental point which has been stated or implied frequently throughout this book—namely, management's need for more, better, and current information for problem solving and decision making. Now that we have some background in marketing, perhaps we can better understand the function of managing information in a marketing system. The next three chapters relate to this subject. In this chapter we discuss a marketing information system and the related activity of marketing research. Chapter 28 is devoted to marketing planning and demand forecasting. In Chapter 29 we cover the managerial activity of performance evaluation, especially as related to a company's sales volume and its marketing costs.

NEED FOR A MARKETING INFORMATION SYSTEM

Today many environmental forces, plus changing conditions within a company, are making it imperative that a firm must develop the best possible arrangements

---

1 "Today's Office: Room for Improvement," *Dun's Review,* September, 1958, p. 50.

for managing its marketing information. Let's consider just a few of these external and internal factors and their relationship to information management. First, there is a *shortening of the time span allotted to an executive for decision making*. Product life cycles frequently are shorter than they used to be, and companies are being forced to shorten their entire new-product-development process. Also being shortened are test-marketing periods—periods during which a company runs a limited-market test of a price, a package, an ad, or some other feature in a marketing program before introducing it to the full market. In summary, the time available to an executive to gather and analyze information is less than it used to be.

Second, *marketing activity is becoming much more complex and broader in its scope,* thus putting further strain on information gathering and processing. Competition continues to intensify and firms engage more and more in nonprice competition. Companies are expanding their product offerings and their markets—even to the point of broadly engaging in multinational marketing. Our insights into buyer behavior and psychological and sociological market segmentation, while limited, are still sufficient to tell us there is a world of behavioral data we need to acquire and understand. *Shortages of energy and other raw materials* are calling for more efficient use of materials, resources and manpower. A company needs to know which of its products, territories, and customers are profitable, which ones need different treatment, and which ones should be eliminated.

Growing *consumer discontent* often is intensified because management lacks adequate information about some aspect of its marketing program. Maybe the firm does not realize its product is not up to consumer expectations, or its middlemen are not performing adequately, or its advertising is creating ill will. Finally, the knowledge explosion—*the information explosion*—itself is just fantastic. Management somehow must learn how to cope with the abundance of information. An executive must not be swamped by it. In effect, we have more than an adequate supply of information. We simply need to figure out what to do with it—how to control it—how to manage it.

Fortunately, computers and other data processing equipment continue to improve, thus providing management with fast, inexpensive means of processing masses of marketing information. In the same vein, mathematically oriented people are developing sophisticated models and other quantitative techniques for analyzing these data. At the same time, however, it is unfortunate that a sizable number of companies seem unaware of the importance of managing information in a more sophisticated fashion. In spite of what would seem to be an obvious need to develop a better system for managing information, even today a significant number of firms have no marketing research department. Another reasonably large segment of firms has only a small (sometimes one person) marketing research department whose scope of activity typically is limited to sporadic surveys, some sales-volume analysis, and other modest data-gathering efforts.

WHAT IS A MARKETING INFORMATION SYSTEM?

In firms that are conscious of the need for better information management, there is a shift from a fact-finding, information-gathering activity to a problem-solving and action-recommending function. In today's business setting, a company needs to add a new dimension to its information management, predicated on the systems approach to marketing management. A marketing information system would emphasize the continuing interaction and integration of information in the decision-making process.

A *marketing information system* (MkIS) may be defined as an interacting, continuing, future-oriented structure of people, equipment, and procedures designed to generate and process an information flow in order to aid managerial decision making in a company's marketing program.[2]

Implicit in this definition are several useful considerations. One point to note is the broad, systems concept of information handling. The system starts with the *determination* of what data are needed. Then it provides for the *generation* or gathering of this information. The information is then *processed*, with the aid of statistical analysis, model building, and other quantitative analytical techniques. Finally, there is provision for the *storage* of the data and the future *retrieval* of desired information. A second point is that the marketing information system is future-oriented. It is intended to anticipate and prevent problems, as well as to solve them. The system serves as a prognosis as well as a diagnosis; it is preventive as well as curative medicine for marketing. Third, the system operates on a continuing basis. It is not a sporadic, intermittent sort of thing. Finally, the emphasis is on the total system—the process—and not just on the analytical techniques or data processing equipment used in the process.

We are involved in a marketing intelligence operation. To some extent it resembles a military or diplomatic intelligence operation in that we are gathering, processing, and storing potentially useful information which currently exists in fragmented, unorganized—but open and available—fashion in several locations both inside and outside the company. In an MkIS, however, we are *not* suggesting the use of any undercover intelligence methods such as industrial espionage, bribery, hiring competitors' personnel to learn their secrets, etc. In most cases a company does not need to rely on such clandestine methods. Frequently they are valueless or even counterproductive. Moreover, all the information which a company needs usually is open and available by socially acceptable means if the firm will just establish a reasonably simple marketing information system.

A marketing information system is especially characterized by its involvement with the computer and with personnel possessing quantitative analytical capabilities. A modern MkIS would not be possible without a computer because of the masses of data to be handled. Essentially in an MkIS we are using the management scientist and his abilities to apply model building and other operations research techniques to the management of marketing information.

The typical informational input for a company's MkIS may be divided into four broad categories—two external and two internal. One area of external information relates to the economic, social, and political environment—general economic conditions, the labor market, social conditions, international situation, political considerations, etc. The other external area pertains to external aspects of a company's marketing system—its middlemen, competition, and all data pertaining to its customers. Internally a marketing information system depends upon input from the marketing department itself and from other functional areas—primarily accounting, but also the departments which are responsible for purchasing, inventory management, production scheduling, customer credit arrangements, and order filling.

---

2 Definition adapted from Samuel V. Smith, Richard H. Brien, and James E. Stafford, "Marketing Information Systems: An Introductory Overview," in Smith, Brien, and Stafford (eds.), *Readings in Marketing Information Systems*, Houghton Mifflin Company, Boston, 1968, p. 7.

BENEFITS AND USES OF AN MkIS

Unless management consciously establishes some communication system to process information gathered from within and outside the company, it is unlikely that the company is using its marketing information effectively. Unfortunately, experience has shown that information flowing from these primary sources is frequently lost, distorted, or delayed.

A marketing information system is of most obvious value in a large, multidivisional company where information is likely to get lost or distorted as it becomes widely dispersed. However, case experiences have shown that use of integrated information systems can also have beneficial effects on management's performance in small and medium-sized firms.[3]

For most small companies, however, a formal, computer-based system probably will not provide sufficient benefits to offset the costs of establishing and operating it. But a small firm can effectively adopt an arrangement which embodies the concept of systematized information handling. Only the small company will probably use less complex and less formal techniques in the various stages of its MkIS. The optimal arrangement probably is a noncomputer system which includes (1) coordinated efforts at information gathering and processing by various departments in a firm, (2) the use of data processing equipment other than a computer—mechanized accounting and billing equipment, office copiers, tape recorders, etc., and (3) the periodic, but frequent, use of outside marketing research firms to provide informational aid in problem solving and decision making.

Some of the possible benefits accruing from an effective marketing information system are as follows:[4]

1. It may provide more information within the firm's time constraints, thus leading to improved managerial performance.
2. Large, decentralized firms may gather information which is scattered in many places, and integrate it meaningfully.
3. Management may exploit the marketing concept more fully.
4. Users may retrieve information on a selective basis, taking only what they want or need.
5. Management may recognize developing trends more quickly.
6. A company may make far better use of information which is ordinarily collected in the course of its business operations; for example, sales by products, territories, or customer groups.
7. Management may be able to better control its marketing plan by receiving and heeding early warning signals.
8. It may prevent important information from being easily suppressed; for example, indications that a product should be withdrawn from the market.

The notion of a marketing information system is consistent with the philosophy of the marketing concept, which emphasizes the coordination and integration of all

---

3 For a report on the effects in small retailing firms, see Cyrus C. Wilson and Charles D. Greenidge, "The Effect of an Integrated Information System on Management Performance," in Reed Moyer (ed.), *Changing Marketing Systems*, American Marketing Association, Chicago, 1968, pp. 113-117. For a five-part case example illustrating in a medium-sized industrial company the development, organization, and implementation of an information system, see Richard L. Pinkerton, "How to Develop a Marketing Intelligence System," *Industrial Marketing*, in 1969, April, p. 41; May, p. 48; June, p. 60; July, p. 62; August, p. 54.

4 Conrad Berenson, "Marketing Information System," *Journal of Marketing*, October, 1969, pp. 17-18.

marketing activities in order to maximize the effectiveness of a company's marketing program. See Fig. 27-1.[5] A marketing information system might serve, for example, as a basis for *setting goals* and *formulating a marketing plan*. Research would be used to *predict* the results of alternative courses of action—e.g., reliance primarily on salespeople rather than advertising in promoting a product. (See the "A" feedbacks in Fig. 27-1.) Then later the information system would serve as the basis for *evaluating* the results of the marketing program ("B" feedbacks). Findings in the evaluation stage would then be the basis for reformulating goals and plans for the succeeding stage of the marketing program. "B" feedbacks (evaluative) from stage 1 would in effect become "A" feedbacks (formulative) for stage 2 in the ongoing marketing process.

In an earlier landmark study, Cox and Good pointed out that an effective MkIS has three operating sub systems related to (1) the control of marketing operations, (2) the planning of marketing activities, and (3) the basic research on particular marketing problem areas.[6] For each of these three subsystems, Fig. 27-2 illustrates some typical uses, benefits, and examples.

In another example Fig. 27-3 illustrates how the full information cycle can be used to improve marketing activities. In this figure we observe three marketing activities—sales forecasting, maintaining a central file on customers, and sales-force management. In sales forecasting the information system is being used to improve the accuracy of the annual sales forecast. In the sales-force-management project, the goal is to develop better quotas for a new compensation plan for salespeople. As the full information cycle is applied to each marketing project, we can see that the different projects each may emphasize some parts of the information cycle more than others.

As a company embraces the concept of a marketing information system, we can expect some changes in its organizational structure. The information system will become the nerve center of the entire marketing activity. Kotler envisions an organizational unit which will broaden the marketing research function and will improve the accuracy, timeliness, and comprehensiveness of marketing information services. This "Marketing Information and Analysis Center will function as the marketing nerve center for the company and will not only provide instantaneous information to meet a variety of executive needs but also will develop all kinds of analytical and decision aids for executives."[7] Of course, essential to the success of any marketing information system and any related organizational structure is the full support of top management.

RELATIONSHIP OF MARKETING INFORMATION SYSTEMS AND MARKETING RESEARCH

It may be a bit risky to generalize on this relationship, because it is perceived quite differently by various people. Some see an MkIS as simply a logical, computer-

---

5 The discussion of Fig. 26-1 is adapted from Brien and Stafford, "Marketing Information Systems: A New Dimension for Marketing Research," in Smith, Brien, and Stafford, *op. cit.,* pp. 19-21.

6 See Donald F. Cox and Robert E. Good, "How to Build a Marketing Information System," *Harvard Business Review,* May-June, 1967, pp. 145-154. For later reports on the status of MkIS, see The Conference Board, *Information Systems for Sales and Marketing Management,* report no. 591, New York, 1973; and Richard H. Brien, "Marketing Information Systems: The State of the Art," in B. W. Becker and H. Becker (eds.), 1972 *Combined Proceedings,* American Marketing Association, Chicago, series no. 34, 1973, pp. 19-27.

7 Philip Kotler, "A Design for the Firm's Marketing Nerve Center," *Business Horizons,* Fall, 1968, p. 70.

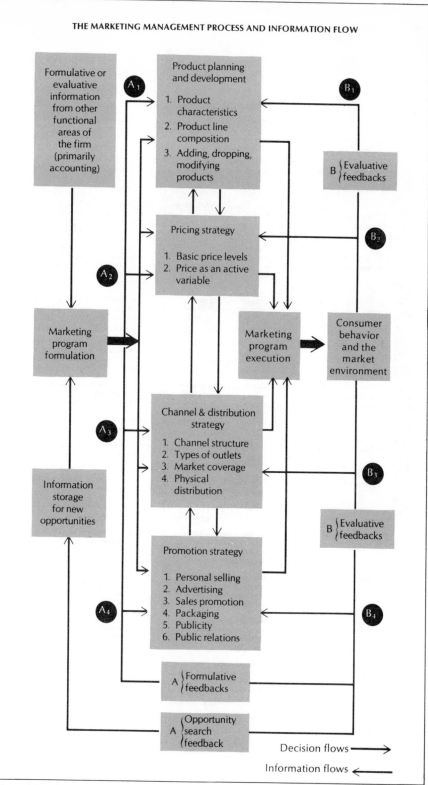

Figure 27-1. *Source:* Richard H. Brien and James E. Stafford, "Marketing Information Systems: A New Dimension in Marketing Research," *Journal of Marketing,* July, 1960, p. 20.

EXAMPLES OF BENEFITS AND USES OF A MARKETING INFORMATION SYSTEM

	Typical Applications	Benefits	Examples
Control Systems	1. Control of marketing costs	1. More timely computerized reports	1. Undesirable cost trends are spotted more quickly so that corrective action may be taken sooner
	2. Diagnosis of poor sales performance	2. Flexible on-line retrieval of data	2. Executives can ask supplementary questions of the computer to help pinpoint reasons for a sales decline and reach an action decision more quickly
	3. Management of fashion goods	3. Automatic spotting of problems and opportunities	3. Fast-moving fashion items are reported daily for quick reorder, and slow-moving items are also reported for fast price reductions
	4. Flexible promotion strategy	4. Cheaper, more detailed, and more frequent reports	4. On-going evaluation of a promotional campaign permits reallocation of funds to areas behind target
Planning Systems	1. Forecasting	1. Automatic translation of terms and classifications between departments	1. Survey-based forecasts of demand for complex industrial goods can be automatically translated into parts requirements and production schedules
	2. Promotional planning and corporate long-range planning	2. Systematic testing of alternative promotional plans and compatibility testing of various divisional plans	2. Complex simulation models both developed and operated with the help of data bank information can be used for promotional planning by product managers and for strategic planning by top management
	3. Credit management	3. Programmed executive decision rules can operate on data bank information	3. Credit decisions are automatically made as each order is processed
	4. Purchasing	4. Detailed sales reporting permits automation of management decisions	4. Computer automatically repurchases standard items on the basis of correlation of sales data with programmed decision rules
Basic-research-Systems	1. Advertising strategy	1. Additional manipulation of data is possible when stored for computers in an unaggregated file	1. Sales analysis is possible by new market segment breakdowns
	2. Pricing strategy	2. Improved storage and retrieval capability allows new types of data to be collected and used	2. Systematic recording of information about past R & D contract bidding situations allows improved bidding strategies
	3. Evaluation of advertising expenditures	3. Well-designed data banks permit integration and comparison of different sets of data	3. Advertising expenditures are compared to shipments by county to provide information about advertising effectiveness
	4. Continuous experiments	4. Comprehensive monitoring of input and performance variables yields information when changes are made	4. Changes in promotional strategy by type of customer are matched against sales results on a continuous basis

Figure 27-2. *Source:* Donald F. Cox and Robert E. Good, "How to Build a Marketing Information System," *Harvard Business Review,* May-June, 1967, p. 146

Marketing activity	Assessment of information needs	Data measurement and collection	Storage retrieval and transmission	Format, display, reporting	Analytical technologies and models	Data utilization: new concepts
1. Sales forecasting	More accurate annual sales forecasting	Customer industry information Salespeople probability estimates on contracts Competition product and marketing effort	More current updating of recent sales	Graphical display of actual sales vs. previous forecasts	Simulation model for evaluation of forecasts Statistical extrapolation methods	Relative product and marketing advantage; rating our firm relative to the prime competitor
2. Central file on customers	Learn which types of marketing efforts work most effectively with customers	Demographic, psychological, sociological, behavioral, and sales data on each customer	Creation of a new file		Experimental design Statistical evaluation	Measuring the impact of competitive actions on our sales
3. Sales-force management	Better quotas for new compensation program	Territory potential indicators Territory competitive pressure	New files	Computer reports	Computerized compensation formulas, sales-call routing Automated direct mail follow-up for efficient "holding" of customers	Optimal level of effort for both prospecting and holding Segmentation: match type of letter by type of customer

Figure 27-3. *Source:* Robert E. Good, "Managerial Design of Information Systems: The Full Information Cycle," in Jack L. Taylor, Jr., and James F. Robb (eds.), *Fundamentals of Marketing: Additional Dimensions,* 2d ed., McGraw-Hill Book Company, New York, 1975.

based extension of marketing research. The first marketing information systems were developed generally in the 1960s, while marketing research as a separately identified activity predates this by some 50 years. Other students of the situation see the two as distinctly different activities, related only to the extent that they both deal with the management of information. Firms without an MkIS will perceive a broader role for their marketing research group. If a company has formed MkIS, then the marketing research activity (whether departmentized or not) is probably treated as just one part of the information system.

The essence of what we mean by "marketing research" is contained in Richard Crisp's definition of the term. Crisp has called marketing research "the systematic, objective, and exhaustive search for and study of the facts relevant to any problem in the field of marketing."[8] This definition suggests a *systematic* activity, thus sounding like the essence of an MkIS. Yet, as traditionally practiced, marketing research has tended to be *unsystematic*. See Fig. 27-4 for a polarization of characteristics of the two activities.)

Marketing research tends to be conducted on a project-to-project basis, with each project having a starting point and an end. These projects often seem to deal with unrelated problems on an intermittent, almost "brush-fire" basis, as contrasted to the continuous information flow for decision making in a marketing information system. Marketing research tends to stress the collection of past data to solve problems. Information systems are future-oriented activities designed hopefully to prevent problems from arising. Marketing research is involved primarily with handling external data. Accounting departments and other nonmarketing areas in the firm typically gather and process internal marketing data, as when they analyze sales volume or marketing costs to evaluate performance in various sales territories or product lines.

CONTRASTING CHARACTERISTICS OF MARKETING RESEARCH AND A MARKETING INFORMATION SYSTEM

Marketing research	Marketing information system
1. Emphasis on handling external information	1. Handles both internal and external data
2. Concerned with solving problems	2. Concerned with preventing as well as solving problems
3. Operates in fragmented, intermittent fashion—on a project-to-project basis	3. Operates continuously—is a system
4. Tends to focus on past information	4. Tends to be future-oriented
5. Noncomputer-based	5. Is a computer-based process
6. Is one source of information input into a marketing information system	6. Includes other subsystems besides marketing research

Figure 27-4.

---

8 Richard D. Crisp, *Marketing Research,* McGraw-Hill Book Company, New York, 1957, p. 3.

Parenthetically we should recognize that many marketing research practitioners probably would not agree with the distinctions in the above paragraph and in Fig. 27-4. They would contend they already are doing much of what we have attributed to an MkIS. And they may be correct *if* the firm has no formal MkIS. Then the scope of the marketing research activity is likely to be much broader. It may well include some sales volume analysis, marketing cost analysis, demand forecasting, etc.

In firms that have an MkIS, the separate marketing research activity can be extremely valuable. Marketing research projects are a significant source of data entering an MkIS. Also the marketing researcher's contact with the external environment may provide an expertise which is a useful complement to the quantitatively oriented computer specialists so vital in a marketing information system.

Consequently, at this point we shall turn to the subject of marketing research and discuss its scope, the typical procedure in a marketing research investigation, the organizational structures typically used for marketing research, and the current status of the field.

SCOPE OF MARKETING RESEARCH ACTIVITIES

The scope and status of marketing research in Canada does not appear as well developed as in the United States. A Canadian study undertaken in 1969 indicated that although 57 per cent of Canadian firms had access to research data, only about 12 per cent of them had formally designated research departments.[9] The percentage of Canadian companies with Marketing Research departments is probably closer to 20 or 25 per cent today. While there has been a steady growth in marketing research activities in Canada, reflecting management's recognition of the importance of this activity, an American study conducted in 1973 by the American Marketing Association found that 60 per cent of the firms reporting had a formal marketing research department.[10]

The American Marketing Association's 1973 study found that the percentage of firms with marketing research departments ranged from 61 per cent in medium-sized firms to 81 percent among the large companies. The research departments were most commonly found among manufacturers of consumer products (70 percent), followed by publishing and broadcasting firms (66 percent), manufacturers of industrial goods (59 percent), and retailers, wholesalers, and advertising agencies (53-54 percent). Also, about half of these formal departments had been established just during the preceding decade. The most common activities were determination of market characteristics, measurement of market potentials, market-share analysis, and sales analysis.

The substantial difference between the Canadian and American organization for research can be attributed in large measure to the differences in market and firm size that exist between the two countries. In addition, the foreign parents of Cana-

---

9 W. H. Mahatoo and A. B. Blankenship, "The Status of Marketing Research in Canada—A Survey," *Canadian Marketer*, Winter 1971, pp. 25-28.

10 Dik Warren Twedt (ed.), *1973 Survey of Marketing Research*, American Marketing Association, Chicago, 1973, pp. 11-13, 21-23, 40-44. This survey covered 1,322 firms representing a diverse assortment including manufacturers, retailers, wholesalers, advertising agencies, publishers and broadcasters, banks, and public utilities.

dian companies are becoming more active in collecting research data on the Canadian market on behalf of their subsidiaries and affiliates. Canadian firms conduct essentially the same types of studies as do their American counterparts, but the percentage of firms participating in the various research activities would be lower in Canada. What is clear, however, is that companies on both sides of the border are continuing to broaden their marketing research activities. Moreover, marketing research is being linked—both by organization and by procedure—with planning and decision making.

PROCEDURE IN A MARKETING RESEARCH INVESTIGATION

In marketing research no two tasks are exactly alike, nor is there any single procedure that can be followed in all investigations. The general procedure illustrated in Fig. 27-5, however, is applicable to most projects. Some of the steps listed here are interrelated, some overlap, and some are not needed in every project.

DEFINE THE OBJECTIVE AND THE PROBLEM

A researcher should have a reasonably clear idea of what he is trying to do in a research job. Usually this means defining a problem. However, the objective of a research job is not always to *solve* a problem. Often the purpose of a sales analysis is to determine whether the company *has* a problem and, if so, in what territory, product, or class of customer it lies. To illustrate, a manufacturer of commercial airconditioning and refrigeration equipment had been enjoying a steady increase in sales volume over a period of years. Management decided to make a sales analysis, and this research project uncovered the fact that although the company's volume had been increasing, its share of the market had declined. In this instance, marketing research uncovered a problem which management did not know existed.

When marketing research ascertains that a problem does exist, the objective of the project is to determine exactly what the problem is and to attempt to solve it. Normally, a company starts with a broad, tentative statement of its problem. Through investigation it is able to pinpoint the problem precisely. In the case of the refrigeration equipment manufacturer, the broad problem was why this company's share of the market had decreased and how its position could be improved. To get this into manageable form, we can state the problem in parts. We can, for instance, ask: Have the company's product policies been the cause of its declining share of the market, or have weaknesses in the company's channel of distribution policies been the cause?

The case history of the Aurora Electronics Company (an actual company, but a fictitious name) may be used to illustrate the first three steps in a marketing research project, namely, problem definition, situation analysis, and informal investigation. The Aurora Company was a small electronics manufacturer with annual sales volume of $3 million, but with 90 percent of these sales coming from contracts with the federal government. The other 10 percent came almost entirely from sales of the electronic component part used in automatic garage-door openers. This component was sold directly to a large door manufacturer. Joseph Stacy, the president, was an engineer, and his company had an excellent reputation. The firm had no marketing department, no sales manager, and no salespeople. It had a fine engi-

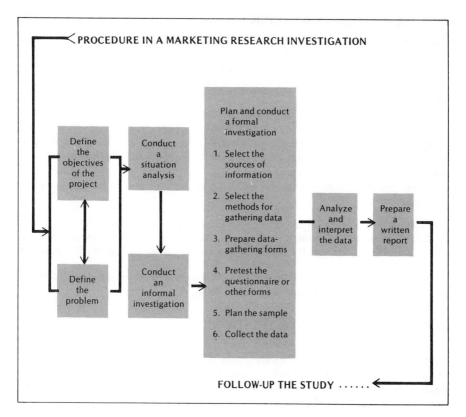

PROCEDURE IN A MARKETING RESEARCH INVESTIGATION

Define the objectives of the project

Conduct a situation analysis

Plan and conduct a formal investigation

1. Select the sources of information

2. Select the methods for gathering data

3. Prepare data-gathering forms

Analyze and interpret the data

Prepare a written report

Define the problem

Conduct an informal investigation

4. Pretest the questionnaire or other forms

5. Plan the sample

6. Collect the data

FOLLOW-UP THE STUDY ...... ⬅

Figure 27-5.

neering department; the entire company was heavily engineering-oriented. At the time of the case, the firm was interested in diversifying its product line and its market so as to reduce its heavy dependence on government contracts. The engineering department developed an FM auto radio—a tuner and amplifier unit which could be connected to the regular AM auto radio and could use the AM speaker.

The general problem, as presented to an outside marketing research firm, was to determine whether the company should add this product to its line. Breaking the problem down into parts which could be handled by research resulted in the following specific questions:

1. What is the market demand for such a product?
2. What product features are desired, such as push-button tuning or signal-seeking tuning?
3. What channels of distribution should be used for such a product?
4. What should its price be?
5. What changes or additions in the company's organizational structure would be required if the product were added?

With this tentative restatement of the problem, the researchers were ready for the next procedural step, the situation analysis.

CONDUCT SITUATION ANALYSIS

The situation analysis involves getting acquainted with the company and its business environment by means of library research and extensive interviewing of company officials. The researchers try to get a "feel" for the situation surrounding the problem. They analyze the company, its market, its competition, and the industry in general.

In the situation analysis the researchers also try to define the problem more clearly and develop hypotheses for further testing. In research, the establishment of hypotheses is a valuable step in problem solving. A *hypothesis* is a tentative supposition or a possible solution to a problem. It is something which is assumed or conceded merely for purposes of argument or action.

In the Aurora Company case, the situation analysis suggested the following hypotheses:

1. The company organization is inadequate to take on a consumer product.
2. The market for FM radios is limited geographically to a radius of 25 miles from FM stations. (This distance is the approximate sending or receiving limit for FM broadcasting.)
3. Marketing channels should be the same as those used for AM auto radios; distribution patterns for home radios are substantially different.

CONDUCT INFORMAL INVESTIGATION

Having gotten a feel for the problem, the researchers are now ready to conduct an informal investigation. To some extent this step overlaps the preceding one, which involves getting background information from *within* the company or from a library. The informal investigation consists of talking to people *outside* the company—middlemen, competitors, advertising agencies, customers, and people in the industry.

In the Aurora case, the researchers talked with many people. FM station owners and managers were of considerable help. Wholesalers and retailers of automobile radios were consulted, as were repairpeople for auto radios. Long interviews were held with automobile dealers handling German FM auto radios—the Blaupunkt and the Becker. Consumers who had purchased these imports were interviewed. Helpful information was derived from talks with sales representatives of the Motorola Company. (This source was extremely valuable since there were rumors in the trade that Motorola had already engineered and produced models of an FM auto radio. As it turned out, the rumors were true, and a year later Motorola introduced such a product to the market.) Advertising agencies were consulted regarding their possible future use of FM stations as an advertising medium—the idea being that an increase in their use of FM stations would in time increase the quantity of FM programming and thus make set ownership more attractive.

This important step in a research project will often determine whether further formal study is necessary. Decisions regarding the problem are frequently made after the informal investigation is completed. As a matter of fact, at this point Aurora executives decided *not* to market the FM auto radio.

PLAN AND CONDUCT FORMAL INVESTIGATION

After the problem is defined and the informal investigation shows that the project is economically feasible, the company determines what facts are needed. The next step for the researcher is to plan how and where to get the desired data.

Select the sources of information. First the investigator must determine what sources of information he will use. He may use primary data, secondary data, or both.

Primary data are original data gathered specifically for the project at hand. *Secondary data* are those already existing, having been collected originally for some other purpose. Thus when a researcher stands in a supermarket and observes whether people use shopping lists and in what order they go to the various departments, he is collecting primary data. When he gets information from Statistics Canada, a trade association report, or a library, he is using secondary data.

One of the biggest mistakes made by many people in marketing research is rushing out to get primary data before exhausting the information already available in secondary sources. Ordinarily, secondary information can be gathered much faster and at far less expense than can primary data.

At the same time, secondary sources of information must meet certain standards of accuracy in order to be of optimal usefulness. First, the information must be sufficiently *current*. If quotas for salespeople in Ontario and British Columbia in 1978 are set on the basis of data found in the 1971 Census, the quotas will be understated because these are areas of rapid growth in market potential. The information should be *classified in a manner useful* to the researcher. He may want to make a study of college students, but then find that his desired secondary source classifies the data by age groups of 10-19 and 20-29.

To be useful, the data must be *valid* (relevant). For instance, sales of ski equipment in Saskatchewan may not be a valid measure of the size of the Saskatchewan ski market, because many residents of that province who ski in Alberta or British Columbia will buy some equipment at the ski resort. Secondary information also must be *reliable*; that is, it must be based on a sampling procedure which is statistically sound. Finally, accuracy in the information implies that the original source generated the data in an *impartial* manner. In order to determine the validity, reliability, and impartiality of secondary information, the researcher may have to investigate the organization that collected the data and the methods it used in making its study.

Sources of secondary data. Several readily available, excellent sources of secondary information are at the disposal of a marketing researcher.[11]

1. Internal company records. Companies regularly maintain orderly records of salespeople's daily reports, call reports, sales orders, and customers' complaints. Companies also usually keep sales records for each territory, product, and class of customer. When a problem must be solved, the first place a company should go for information is to its own files. In many cases, this source may well be the only place where the needed information can be found.
2. Parent company records. Foreign parents of Canadian subsidiaries (mainly U.S. parents) are able to provide useful data on activities in the American market. If the parent is involved in multinational operations, experiences and data on worldwide market conditions and consumer reactions to marketing programs can be made available. In those cases where the Canadian company has a market posture which is similar to that of the parent and where Canadian strategy and market conditions is viewed as lagging the parent's by a number of years, then access to such data is an invaluable

---

11 For an excellent review of secondary sources of marketing research information, the reader is referred to: Ronald Rotenberg and Beth Hatton, "Sources of Marketing Information in Canada," *Canadian Marketer,* Spring 1974.

asset. The problem of comparability of data and situations is, however, a constant one.

3. Government. The Canadian government regularly furnishes more marketing data than any other single source in the nation. These data are available at very low prices even though there is a tremendous cost involved in collecting them. Also, the government has access under the law to types of information (company sales and profits, personal income, etc.) which it is impossible for a private company to obtain.

Statistics Canada (originally named the Dominion Bureau of Statistics) is the statistical arm of the Government of Canada. Statistics Canada was established in 1918 and regularly collects and publishes information on agriculture, construction and housing, education, fisheries, forestry, health and welfare, international commodity trade, employment, labor income, tourist travel, manufacturing, retail and wholesale trade, service trades, mining, national income and expenditure, prices and public finance, public utilities and transportation as well as the Census of Canada. Most government departments also publish both regular and incidental papers independently. The data published are both historical and on a forecast basis. The annual *Canadian Government Publications* lists all federal government publications according to the agency or department which prepared them. In addition, Statistics Canada publishes an annual catalogue.

Of the numerous reports published by Statistics Canada, one of the most useful to marketers is the *Market Research Handbook*. This publication appears annually (the most recent version, the 1976 edition, was published in March 1977—catalogue number 63-224) and contains a considerable amount of data under the following headings: selected economic indicators; merchandising and services; population characteristics; personal income and expenditure; housing, motor vehicles, and household facilities and equipment; Metropolitan area data; and Census Agglomeration data.

The *Canada Year Book* is an annual publication which contains somewhat less detailed historical data on many aspects of Canada's economy and population. In addition, much information of interest to marketers is contained in the decennial Census. Many volumes of data are published following each Census and Statistics Canada publishes a separate catalogue of Census publications. The marketer should be aware, however, that despite the availability and detail of Census data, these data should be used with caution since they are usually not published until three or four years after the Census is taken. For example, most of the reports on the 1971 Census did not appear until 1974 and 1975. Consequently, appropriate adjustments must be made in Census data before they can be used for marketing purposes.

A number of provinces also publish many reports and statistical summaries which are of interest. These provincial data are often not as well catalogued or easily located as are Government of Canada and Statistics Canada publications. However, many provinces do publish annual catalogues of their reports and publications and these are available from provincial government offices.

4. Trade, professional, and business associations. Associations are excellent sources of information for their members. They also supply data for outside groups. Through trade journals and periodic reports, members of associations can also keep up to date on activities in their given trades.

5. Private business firms. Private marketing research firms, advertising agencies, and individual manufacturers and middlemen may be able to provide information needed by a researcher. Companies such as the A. C. Nielsen Company, Canadian Facts, and Market Facts of Canada conduct various kinds of marketing research. In addition, the various management consulting firms such as Woods, Gordon and Company, Stevenson and Kellogg Limited, and Peat, Marwick and Partners regularly conduct marketing research projects on behalf of their clients. The types of reports prepared by these research companies are many and diverse. The Nielsen Company, for example, prepares a food-drug index giving information on a client's sales and on his competitors' sales for particular products. Data regarding inventories, retail prices, and promo-

tional activity at the retail level are also published. The Daniel Starch Company regularly measures readership of advertisements in various magazines and newspapers. Psychographics International of Canada prepares reports on consumer attitudes and shopping patterns in major Canadian markets for a large number of department store and discount store clients. A number of marketing research houses also operate consumer mail panels from which data are obtained regularly on purchase patterns.

6. Advertising media. Many magazines, newspapers, radio and television networks and stations, and outdoor advertising companies publish information that marketing researchers may not find available elsewhere. *Sales Management* annually publishes its "Survey of Buying Power" which covers population, retail sales, income, and effective buying power for all provinces, census metropolitan areas, and large cities. Many media publish circulation data, station reach and coverage maps, and statistics on their trading areas. Researchers should be aware that much of the data published by the media are produced for the purpose of attracting advertising revenue. For this reason, these data may not be appropriate in certain marketing research situations. Accurate data on circulation, reach and rates for all advertising media in Canada are published monthly in Maclean-Hunter's *Canadian Advertising Rates and Data*. Detailed data on all Canadian provincial and metropolitan markets appear in the annual Financial Post *Survey of Markets*.

7. University research organizations. Some of our universities operate research units and publish findings which are of value to the business community. Business research units play a leading role in this activity, although marketers may also obtain useful reports from a bureau of agricultural research or social research.

8. Foundations. Nonprofit research foundations and related groups carry out many kinds of research projects. Statistical analyses and reports on special topics of interest to Canadian business, or specifically Canadian in content, are published by such groups as the Conference Board in Canada, The American Management Association, the Committee for Economic Development and the C. D. Howe Institute. While Canada Council, Killam, Ford, Carnegie, Russell Sage, and similar foundations are not limited to business research, many of their reports are of interest to marketers.

9. Royal Commissions and the Economic Council. Many Federal and Provincial Royal Commissions conduct studies which are of direct interest to marketers. Royal Commission reports on Banking and Finance, Canada's Economic Prospects and Price Spreads of Food Products are examples of such studies. The Economic Council of Canada also issues annual reports as well as occasional studies on general economic prospects. The Canadian Consumer Council has also published a number of reports on consumer matters. A very valuable source of information on food prices and food retailing in general in Canada is the numerous reports of the Food Prices Review Board. These government reports are usually available in the Government Documents sections of most municipal and university libraries.

10. Libraries. For the marketing researcher and the student of marketing, a good library is probably the best, single, all-around source of secondary information. It will contain publications from practically all of the sources mentioned here. All researchers and students should be familiar with such resources as the *Business Periodicals Index*, the *Canadian Periodicals Index*, and the *Canadian Business Periodicals Index*. These indices contain references to articles which have appeared in various business publications. The *ProFile Index* contains references to provincial government publications and reports which are available on microfiche in many libraries. The ability to use bibliographies, card indices, and periodical indices is virtually a prerequisite for anyone hoping to do any kind of research.

Sources of primary data. After exhausting all reasonable secondary sources of information, the researcher may still lack sufficient data. Then he will turn to primary sources and gather the facts himself.

1. Company salespeople. Frequently a marketing analyst will interview salespeople in order to get pertinent market information, or he will ask the salespeople to interview middlemen, customers, or representatives from competitors. Salespeople can often supply quite current and detailed information from their territories and at a low marginal cost. These same data, if available at all from secondary sources, might come several months later. Management should not, however, use expensive sales personnel in research capacities if this diverts them from their primary job of selling. Also, salespeople are not trained field researchers, and the information they collect may be biased.

2. Middlemen, consumers, and others. Manufacturers can seek information from their wholesalers and retailers. Wholesalers, in turn, can use their retail customers as primary sources. Middlemen may be asked their opinion of a given product, company policy, or program. Sometimes middlemen can give a manufacturer a good indication of the feelings of the ultimate consumer or industrial user, but sellers may have to go directly to the household consumer or the industrial user to get the facts about attitudes, motives, and buying habits.

In some cases a firm's competitors may provide primary information. It may be gathered surreptitiously by having salespeople query the competitors' salespeople, or it may be gathered openly through the trade association. A firm may approach a competitor directly on matters of mutual interest. For instance, all supermarket operators or used-car dealers in a city may have a meeting to discuss the question of keeping their establishments open on Sundays.

Determine methods for gathering primary data. There are three widely used methods of generating primary data: survey, observation, and experimentation. Normally, not all three are used on one project. The choice of method will be influenced by the availability of time, money, personnel, and facilities.

Survey method. A *survey* consists of gathering data by interviewing a limited number of people (a sample) selected from a larger group. A survey has the advantage of getting to the original source of information. In fact, this may be the *only* way to find out the motives, opinions, or buying intentions of a group.

While the survey is still the most widely used method of collecting primary data, there may be a trend away from it. Not only have methods of observation and experimentation been improved and their value more fully realized, but the survey method contains certain inherent limitations. Surveys require careful planning, and there are opportunities for error in the construction of the questionnaire, in its editing, and in the interviewing process. Surveys may be very expensive, and they are time-consuming. Often the process is slow, and the researcher may need facts immediately. Another key weakness is that respondents often cannot or will not give correct answers. This is particularly destructive when a marketing analyst is searching for reasons underlying a respondent's behavior. There also are indications that researchers' access to one especially rich data base—business corporations—is declining and will continue to do so unless ways can be found to alleviate growing friction between businesspeople and researchers (particularly academicians).[12] Business respondents object to the sheer number and complexity of questionnaires received, as well as to the misuse of information.

---

12 Thomas L. Reuschling and Michael J. Etzel, "The Disappearing Data Source," *Business Horizons,* April, 1973, pp. 17-22; also see 'The Public Clams Up on Survey Takers," *Business Week,* Sept. 15, 1973, p. 216.

There has also been some recent debate on the subject of ethics in marketing research and a suggestion that consumers might become increasingly unwilling to participate in marketing research surveys.[13] Authors have pointed to the fact that consumers have, on occasion, been misled in the past in participating in surveys and may become "turned off" by the sheer volume of surveys being conducted.

The interviewing or data gathering in a survey may be done by the researcher in person, by telephone, or by mail. These three types of interviews may be evaluated on the following bases: (1) flexibility, (2) amount of information to be obtained, (3) accuracy, and (4) speed, cost, and administration.

Personal interviews are more flexible than the other two types because the interviewer can alter his questions to fit the situation as he sees it. He is able to probe more deeply if he is not satisfied with the answer. (Of course, there is a danger that a bias may be introduced into the survey if the original questions are altered.) Ordinarily, it is possible to obtain more information by personal interview than by telephone or mail. Virtually every subject lends itself to a personal interview. Also, the interviewer can by observation obtain data regarding a respondent's socioeconomic status—his home, neighborhood, and apparent standard of living. Finally, a statistically sound sample is more easily obtainable with personal interviews.

The major limitations of this method of interviewing are its relatively high cost, the length of time needed to plan and execute the survey, and the opportunity to introduce errors in the interviewing process. When the personal interview method is used on a broad geographic basis, as in a national survey of magazine readership or shaving habits, the advantage of flexibility pretty much disappears. Interviewers in these situations ordinarily must follow an exactly prescribed procedure. Probing becomes difficult, questions should not be reworded, and very little is left to the interviewer's discretion.

In a *telephone survey* the respondent is approached by telephone, and the interview is completed at that time. Telephone surveys can usually be conducted more rapidly and at less cost than either personal or mail surveys. Wide geographic areas can be covered without any traveling. Telephone surveys are less flexible than personal interviews but more flexible than mail surveys. Since a few interviewers can make any number of calls from a few central points, this method is quite easy to administer. Many of the problems involved in the management of interviewers in personal surveys are not present here. Another significant advantage is that a telephone survey may be timely. For instance, people may be asked whether they are watching television at the moment and, if so, the name of the program and the sponsor.

One limitation of the telephone survey is that interviews must be short. Normally, lengthy interviews cannot be conducted satisfactorily over the phone. Also, it is difficult to ascertain the socioeconomic characteristics of the respondents. It is virtually impossible to get a complete cross section of the public because some people do not have telephones, others have unlisted numbers, many are not at home

---

13 The following articles discuss the question of ethics in marketing research and the possibility of an increasing lack of consumer participation in surveys: Alice M. Tybout and Gerald Zaltman, "Ethics in Marketing Research: Their Practical Relevance," *Journal of Marketing Research,* November, 1974, pp. 357-368; George S. Day and Adrian B. Ryans, "The Changing Environment of Marketing Research in Canada," paper presented at the Second Triennial Canadian Marketing Workshop, held at York University, May, 1975; and George S. Day, "The Threats to Marketing Research," *Journal of Marketing Research,* November, 1975, pp. 462-467.

when the interviewer calls, and finally some refuse to respond in this type of survey.

Interviewing by mail involves mailing a questionnaire to potential respondents and having them return the completed form by mail. Since no interviewers are involved, this type of survey is not hampered by interviewer bias and problems connected with the management of interviewers. Mailed questionnaires are more economical than personal interviews and are particularly useful in broad, national surveys. Respondents may answer the questions at their leisure, so the replies may be carefully thought out. Also, if the respondent remains anonymous, he will probably give true answers because he does not feel the need to impress the interviewer. Finally, it is easier to reach some groups by mail than by either of the other two methods.

A major problem with mail questionnaires is the compilation of a good mailing list, especially in a broad-scale survey. If the sample can be drawn from a limited list, such as property taxpayers in certain counties or subscribers to a certain magazine, the list presents no problem. Another significant limitation concerns the sample reliability of the questionnaire returns, particularly when the returns are anonymous. If the respondents have characteristics which differentiate them from the nonrespondents, this factor would negate the validity of the survey results. A mail survey may lack timeliness; respondents are often slow in returning the questionnaire. Furthermore, the questionnaire must be reasonably short and the questions very simple; there is no way to elaborate or explain a puzzling question. There is also no opportunity to get additional data by observing the respondent. Often the representativeness of the sample is quite doubtful because the rate of returns on mail questionnaires is so low.

Observational method. In this research method the data are collected by observing some action of the respondent. No interviews are involved, although an interview may be used as a kind of follow-up to get additional information. For example, a customer may be observed buying beer in cans instead of bottles, and then he may be asked why he preferred one form of packaging to another. The consumer is unaware that he is being observed, so presumably he acts in his usual fashion. This is a valuable research tool, but unfortunately it is often underrated in favor of the interview technique.

Information may be gathered by personal or mechanical observation. In one form of personal observation, the researcher poses as a customer in a store. This technique is useful in getting information about the caliber of the salesperson or in determining what brands he pushes. In another situation, an observer may watch customers at a discreet distance and notice what may appear to motivate a purchase. Studies have been conducted to determine how customers buy products in self-service retail stores. To some, price is important—"what do you have on sale today?", "what is the quality of this low-priced brand?" Some have brand preferences—"give me a package of _____." Others need help in selecting a brand—"what brand do you recommend?" Surburban shopping centers have used the observation technique to determine where their customers come from. The investigators record the license numbers of cars in the parking lot, and the addresses of owners are then traced through license bureaus. Mechanical observation is illustrated by the use of an electric cord stretched across a highway to count the number of cars that pass during a certain time period. A mechanical recorder may be attached to a radio or television set. This device will record whether the set was on and to what station it was tuned. Hidden cameras are also useful in gathering data by observation.

The observation method has several merits. It can be highly accurate; often it removes all conjecture about what the consumer does in a given matter. If a researcher over a period of several weeks traces the license numbers of cars parked at a suburban shopping center, he has a pretty good idea of the area from which this center is drawing customers. The observation technique reduces interviewer bias, but the possibility of bias is not completely eliminated as long as field observers are used. Devices such as mechanical recorders or hidden cameras supply more detailed data than normally can be gathered by surveys.

A major drawback to the observation method, which has already been mentioned, is that field observer bias may creep in. However well trained an observer may be, mistakes are possible. A second disadvantage is that the technique is limited in its application. Observation tells *what* happened, but it cannot tell *why*. It cannot delve into motives, attitudes, or opinions. Finally, this technique may be expensive. Observers must be posted at a given location for a certain period of time. During part of the time, however, they may be just waiting for a consumer to perform the act to be observed.[14]

Experimental method. This method of gathering primary data involves the establishment of a scale model or a controlled experiment which simulates the real market situation as much as possible. The theory is that the small-scale experiment will furnish valuable information in designing a large-scale marketing program.

The experimental method may be used in several different ways and countless situations. In one instance, a firm may manufacture a few units of a product and give them to employees or consumers to try out. Probably the major application of the experimental method has been in market testing. This technique consists of establishing (1) a control market, in which all factors remain constant, and (2) one or more test markets, in which one factor is varied. A firm may be trying to determine whether to change the color of its package. In city A, the product is marketed in its traditional color; in each of cities B, C, and D, a different color is used. All other factors are presumably kept constant. Thus by measuring the sales in the four markets over a period of time, the manufacturer hopes to tell which color is best.

The outstanding merit of the experimental method is its realism. It is the only one of the three methods of gathering primary data which affords actual market tests and simulates an actual market situation. In testing the relative values of different advertisements or the value of an entire campaign, only the experimental method will tell which advertisement or campaign sold the most merchandise. Furthermore, this method holds great promise for the future as marketing research people improve their techniques. For instance, the method lends itself nicely to the use of mathematical models as a device for quantitative measurement.

Two big problems are encountered in market testing: selecting the control and test markets and controlling the variables. It is difficult—though necessary—to select markets that are identical in all significant socioeconomic factors. Experimental models, which have recently been developed, may be helpful in solving this problem. Some variables are really uncontrollable, and these may upset the comparability of results. Competitors may get wind of the test and try to confuse the picture

---

14 See Louis C. Wagner, "The Use of the Observational Method in Marketing Research," *University of Washington Business Review*, Autumn, 1968, pp. 18-24, for a more detailed review of some possible uses of this method, along with an analysis of its advantages and limitations.

by suddenly increasing their advertising, for example. Company salespeople or retail dealers may act abnormally if they find out that a test is being run. Furthermore, the experimental method is expensive; it requires long, careful planning and administration. Tests frequently cover six months—two months during which activity in the test and control centers is measured before anything new is introduced, two months during which the variable being tested (new color, new price, new advertising) is placed in the market, and two more months to allow for sales which may have been motivated by the test variable but were not made until sometime after it was removed.

Prepare data-gathering forms. Regardless of whether the interviewing or observation method is used to gather primary data, the researcher must prepare standard forms to record the information. The importance of the questionnaire, however, and the difficulty of designing it cannot be overemphasized. In fact, most of the problems in data collection, whether by personal, mail, or telephone survey, center around the preparation of the questionnaire. Marketing research textbooks devote whole chapters to this subject, and in at least one instance an entire book has been devoted to only part of the task.[15]

Ordinarily a questionnaire designed for a telephone survey will be short. A mail questionnaire typically can be longer. It may run one or two pages, or on rare occasions even longer. Personal interviewing provides an opportunity for flexibility in (1) the length of the questionnaire, (2) the degree to which it is structured (standardized), and (3) the use of projective techniques as in motivation research.[16]

Extreme care and skill are needed in designing questionnaires in order to minimize bias, misunderstanding, respondent anger, misleading answers, etc. Even in a carefully prepared questionnaire, mistakes are bound to occur. This is one good reason for pretesting a questionnaire. (See next section.) Some of the typical errors occurring in questionnaire design are as follows:

1. The respondent feels the information is none of your business: What is your family's income? How old are you? What percentage of your house mortgage remains to be paid?
2. Questions lack a standard of reference: Do you like a large kitchen? (What is meant by "large"?) Do you attend church regularly?
3. The respondent does not know the answer: What is your wife's favorite brand of lipstick?
4. The respondent cannot remember, so he guesses: How many calls did you (as a salesperson) make on office supply houses during the past year?

---

15 Stanley L. Payne, *The Art of Asking Questions*, Princeton University Press, Princeton, N.J., 1951. One procedure for questionnaire construction is set forth in Harper W. Boyd, Jr. and Ralph Westfall, *Marketing Research: Text and Cases*, 3rd. ed., Richard D. Irwin, Inc., Homewood, Ill., 1972, pp. 288-316, is as follows: (1) Determine what information is wanted, for example, quantitative market characteristics (number, age, sex, income, geographic location) of people visiting Alaska for a vacation only; (2) determine the type of questionnaire to be used (mail, telephone, or personal interview); (3) determine the content and necessity of each question and try to determine whether the respondents can and will answer it; (4) determine the type of question to use—open-ended, multiple-choice, or dichotomous, (5) decide on wording of questions; (6) decide on sequence of questions; (7) determine the physical form, layout, and method of reproduction; (8) prepare a preliminary draft and pretest it; (9) revise the questionnaire and prepare a final draft.

16 For an explanation and appraisal of the standardized (structured) versus the nonstandardized (nonstructured) types of questionnaires, both when the ojective of the questionnaire is clear to the respondent and when the objective is disguised, see Boyd and Westfall, *op. cit.*, pp. 136-143.

5. Questions are asked in improper sequence. Save the tough, embarrassing one for late in the interview. By then some rapport ordinarily has been established with the respondent. A "none-of-your-business" question asked too early may destroy the entire interview.

Pretest the questionnaire or other forms. No matter how good a researcher thinks his questionnaire is, it still should be pretested. This process is similar to field testing a product. Obviously, an engineer thinks a new model of his automobile is perfect; otherwise he would not have sent it away from the drawing board. But he knows from experience that the only way to test the automobile is to use it. The researcher must test in three areas. First, he wants to make sure that the questions are clear and are in the proper order. Second, he wants to find out whether the instructions to the interviewers are adequate. Finally, he wants to uncover any problems which may arise in the course of tabulating the questionnaires. The method used in pretesting consists simply in trying out the questionnaire on a small sample of people similar to those who will be interviewed. It is wise to let the research person do some interviewing. By observing the reaction of a few respondents, he may be able to catch a number of unforeseen problems.

Plan the sample. Normally it is unrealistic and unnecessary to survey or observe every possible person who could shed light on the research problem. Before the data can be gathered, therefore, the researcher must determine from whom he is going to seek the information. He must plan or establish a sample. As is true of research in general, sampling is no stranger to us because we employ it frequently in our everyday activities. We often base our opinion of a person on only one or two conversations with him. We often take a bite of food before ordering a larger quantity.

Actually, the fundamental idea of sampling is that "if a small number of items or parts (called a sample) are chosen at random from a larger number of items or a whole (called a universe, or population) the sample will tend to have the same characteristics, and to have them in approximately the same proportion, as the universe."[17] In marketing research, sampling is another procedural step whose importance is difficult to overestimate. Sampling is a source of errors in many survey results. In one study, an opinion on student government was derived from interviewing a sample of fraternity and sorority members. With no dormitory students, off-campus residents, or commuting students included, this was obviously a biased, nonrepresentative sample of student opinion.

One of the first questions asked regarding sampling is: How large should the sample be? To be statistically reliable, a sample must be large enough to be truly representative of the universe or population. There are other generalizations which a researcher should keep in mind, however. First, size is by no means the main source of sampling errors. Second, huge increases in sample size are needed to produce small increases in the statistical reliability of the sample. Third, in the mathematical determination of statistical reliability the size of the universe is *not* a factor to consider. Finally, the size of the sample is often determined by such practical factors as the time and money available and the amount of cross-classification of data desired.

To be statistically reliable a sample must be proportionate. That is, all types of units found in the universe must be represented in the sample. Also, these units

17 Richard D. Crisp, *op. cit.*, p. 95.

must appear in the sample in approximately the same proportion as they are found in the universe. Assume that a manufacturer of power lawn mowers wants to know what percentage of families in a certain metropolitan area own this product. Further assume that in this market one-half of the families live in the central city and the other half in the suburbs. Relatively more families in the suburbs have power mowers than in the city. Now, if 80 percent of the sample is made up of suburban dwellers, the percentage of families owning power mowers will be overstated because the sample lacks proportionality.

Innumerable sampling techniques may be used in marketing research. Many of these are quite similar, and many are used only infrequently. We should be able to get a basic understanding of sampling by considering three types: (1) simple random sample, (2) area samples, and (3) quota samples. The first two are probability samples, and the third is a nonprobability sample.

In *simple random sampling,* the sample is selected in such a way that every unit in the predetermined universe has a known and equal chance of being selected. Thus if we wished to use a random sample to determine department store preferences among people in Montreal, we would need an accurate and complete listing of all people within the city limits. If we wanted to use a random sample to determine feed and seed preferences among farmers in the Prairie Provinces, we would first decide what provinces to include and then get an up-to-date listing of all farmers in those provinces.

A variation of a simple random sample which is widely used is an *area sample.* Where it is not economically feasible to obtain a full list of the universe, an area sample may be used. In the above example of a study covering department store preferences among Montreal residents, one way to conduct an area sample would be to list all the blocks in the city and then select at random a sample of the blocks. Then every household or every other household in the sample blocks could be interviewed. In this sampling method, the researcher needs only a list of the city blocks, not a listing of all Montreal residents.

A *quota sample* is both a nonprobability sample and a stratified sample. Randomness is lost because proportionality is "forced." Every element in the universe does *not* have a known chance of being selected. To select a quota sample, the researcher must first decide which characteristics will serve as the basis of the quota and then determine in what proportion these characteristics occur in the universe. Thus in selecting a quota sample from among the people who went to Prince Edward Island for a vacation, the researcher may decide that the quota will be based upon the area of residence of the visitor. If a study found that 30 percent of the tourists visiting Prince Edward Island came from Nova Scotia, 30 percent from New Brunswick, 10 percent each from Quebec and Ontario, 15 percent from the northeastern United States, and 5 percent from the rest of Canada, the sample could then be forced to the extent that it is stratified on a nonprobability basis according to the area of residence of the tourists. Consequently, of the people included in the final sample, 30 percent would be from Nova Scotia, 30 percent from New Brunswick, and so on. In some studies, as many as four or five quota characteristics, such as age, sex, income, education level, geographic area, and city size, are established to delimit the sample.

Probability sampling has one big advantage: it is the only method that enables the reliability of the results to be measured with mathematical exactness. The mathematical theory of probability may be employed to estimate the size of the sampling error. Furthermore, it does not require a considerable fund of detailed information regarding the universe. On the other hand, probability sampling can be very expensive and time-consuming, particularly when there is wide geographic dispersion of the units in the sample. Adequate listings of units may not be available, and much skill in selecting the sample is required. In simple random sampling these limitations are accentuated.

In quota sampling much reliance is placed on the judgment of those designing and selecting the samples. There is no mathematical way of measuring the accuracy of the results.

Collect the data. The procedural stage during which the primary data are actually collected in the field—by interviewing, observation, or both—normally constitutes the weakest link in the entire research process. Ordinarily, in all other steps reasonably well-qualified people are working carefully to ensure the accuracy of the results. Great care goes into preparing the survey questionnaire and considerable planning underlies the selection of the sample. Then the fruits of these and earlier labors may be entirely lost if the fieldworkers (data gatherers) are poorly selected or inadequately trained and supervised. The management of fieldworkers is a difficult task because they are usually part-time workers with little job motivation and their work is done where it cannot be observed, often at many widely separated locations.

A myriad of errors may creep into a research project at this point, and poor interviewers only increase this possibility. Bias may be introduced because people in the sample are not at home or refuse to answer. Errors occur because the interviewers do not follow the prescribed sample. In some instances, fieldworkers are unable to establish rapport with respondents, or they revise the wording of a question and thus elicit untrue or inapplicable responses. Considerable error may be introduced by improper interpretation or recording of answers. Finally, some interviewers just plain cheat in one way or another.[18]

ANALYZE DATA AND PREPARE WRITTEN REPORT

The final steps in a marketing research project are to analyze the data, interpret the findings, and submit a written report. Today the availability of sophisticated electronic data-processing equipment enables a researcher to tabulate and statistically analyze masses of data quickly and relatively inexpensively.

The end product of the investigation is the researcher's conclusions and recommendations, supported by any necessary detailed analyses, and submitted in written form. It typically is helpful if an oral discussion can be held shortly after the written report has been submitted. Then the report can be expanded and explained as the recipients raise questions. Whatever form is used for transmitting the recommendations, suffice it to say that the researcher has "a message for Garcia," and he should put it in such a form that Garcia will be sure to read and understand it.

---

18 See Harper W. Boyd Jr., and Ralph Westfall, "Interviewers as a Source of Errors in Surveys," *Journal of Marketing*, April, 1955, pp. 311-324. Ten years later, and again fifteen years later, another survey of the subject was made by the same authors. They observed that some significant gains had been achieved in dealing with interviewer bias, but they also concluded that the same problems still existed to a major degree and that relatively little was being done to solve them; see Harper W. Boyd, Jr., and Ralph Westfall, "Interviewer Bias Once More Revisited," *Journal of Marketing Research*, May, 1970, pp. 249-253.

FOLLOW UP THE STUDY

For his own best interests, a researcher should follow up his study to determine whether his recommendations are being followed, and if not, then what are the reasons. So often the follow-up is omitted. Actually the analyst's future relations with the company can be influenced seriously by this step, whether he is in the firm's own marketing research department or working for an outside agency. Unless there is a follow-up, the company may not pay much real attention to the report; it may be filed and forgotten.

ORGANIZATIONAL STRUCTURE FOR MARKETING RESEARCH

When a firm wishes to carry out a project, there are two ways it can get the job done: by the company's own personnel or by an outside organization.

WITHIN THE COMPANY

Recent studies have indicated a strong trend toward companies having a separate marketing research department, with the manager of this department reporting either to the chief marketing executive or directly to top management. From an organizational standpoint, the separate marketing research department is usually a centralized unit. The field sales force and branch personnel may be involved in data gathering—as in the "sales-force-composite" method of sales forecasting—but typically the analysis and action determination are accomplished in the central department. A case may be built, however, for decentralizing the research function to the extent that field sales management and personnel may perform certain organized research tasks in their respective territories. Strategic and tactical benefits are to be gained when branch managers can analyze their markets, make on-the-spot decisions, and adjust quickly to changing market and competitive conditions.[19]

When marketing research is done within the company, the researchers are well versed in company policy and procedures and know what information is available. Also, the firm is more apt to use its research facilities fully. On many problems, executives might not bother to call in an outside agency, while they might—if the firm had a research department—present the same problems to it. Using company manpower and facilities can be expensive, however, and unless the company has adequately qualified full-time personnel, needed research projects may be unavoidably delayed.

OUTSIDE THE COMPANY

An interesting mark of maturity in marketing research is the fact that despite the comparative youth of the field, it has already developed many institutions from which a company may seek help in marketing research problems. One group of organizations, which is regularly available for hire in research projects, includes advertising agencies and marketing research or management consulting firms such as the A. C. Nielsen Company or Woods, Gordon and Company. A second group includes, for example, railroads, public utilities, and advertising firms which engage

---

19 Louis W. Stern and J. L. Heskett, "Grass Roots Market Research," *Harvard Business Review,* March-April, 1965, pp. 83-96.

in marketing research in order to promote the services they are selling. A third type of outside organization includes trade associations, university bureaus of business research, and government agencies which conduct marketing research on common problems faced by a group of companies.

Some companies have in their normal setup the nucleus of a marketing research department which can on occasion work with an outside agency on problems calling for a larger staff and more facilities than the companies themselves maintain.

These outside agencies employ highly qualified specialists in the marketing research field. Also, they have an objective; impartial approach. (Rarely does one hear of an actual case in which the agency seeks to retain its business by parroting what management wants to hear.) Finally, the agencies are experienced in their own right; they may bring to a given case the experiences of many other clients who had similar problems. Outside organizations do, of course, lack that intimate, continuing knowledge of a firm which can come only from a permanent employee relationship.

STATUS OF MARKETING RESEARCH

Business is just beginning to realize the full potential of marketing research. Many firms have long since passed beyond the nose-counting data-gathering stage—the stage where management was hindered by an insufficiency of information. Significant advances have been made in both quantitative and qualitative research methodology, to the point where researchers are making effective use of the behavioral sciences and mathematics. At the same time, however, we realize that far too many companies are still spending dollars on research for engineering and manufacturing their products, but only pennies, if anything, to determine the market opportunities for these products. In the studies which have been mentioned earlier, as many as seventy-five to eighty percent of Canadian firms do not have a formal marketing research department, and fifty percent or more do not have even one person formally assigned to the activity. These companies apparently are making very limited use of marketing research and are simply treating it as an information-gathering activity.

Several factors account for this less-than-universal acceptance of marketing research. Unlike the results of a chemical experiment, the results of marketing research cannot always be measured quantitatively. The research director cannot do a given job and then point to x percent increase in sales. Also, because management is not yet convinced of the value of marketing research, it will not always spend the amount of money necessary to do a good job. Good research costs money. Executives may not realize that they cannot always get half as good a job for half the amount of money.

Marketing research is far from perfect. We have noted several limitations of marketing research and several areas where major opportunities for error can occur—in sampling, field interviewing, etc. Even when marketing research is accurate, it is not a substitute for judgment. Research gathers, analyzes, and interprets facts, but the executive himself must make the decision.

Marketing research cannot predict future market behavior accurately in many cases, yet often that is what is expected of it. In fact, when dealing with consumer behavior, the researcher is hard pressed to get the truth regarding *present* attitudes or motives, much less those of next year. Predicting future market behavior obviously is loaded with risk. Can you imagine how many research projects predicated on estimates of the future were rendered invalid by the "energy crisis" of the mid-seventies? In that situation the energy crisis was so well publicized that inaccuracies in marketing research predictions probably were accepted by management. But consider the many other cases where future estimates (and thus the marketing research conclusions) proved to be innacurate, and management's reaction was likely that marketing research is just no good!

Even in firms with a sophisticated research capability and a good track record, the predictions of the future can be expensively inaccurate. Witness, for example, the multimillion dollar market failures of Ford's Edsel, Du Pont's Corfam (man-made substitute for leather), and RCA's venture into computers. In all three of these projects, the estimates of future market behavior proved to be inaccurate by the time the products were marketed. Ford's market predictions in connection with its later cars—Mustang, Maverick, and Pinto—proved to be quite good, however. The main point here is that when management is making decisions based on estimates of the future, these decisions must be based on executive opinions, assumptions, and judgment, and not on "hard data"—known facts.

Possibly a more fundamental reason for the modest status of marketing research has been the failure of researchers to communicate adequately with management. Admittedly, there is poor research and poor researchers. Moreover, sometimes the mentality of the direct, quick-acting, pragmatic, decision-making executive may be at odds with the cautious, complex, hedging-all-bets mentality of a marketing researcher. However, the researchers, like many manufacturers, are often product-oriented when they should be market-oriented. Thus, they concentrate on research methods and techniques, rather than on showing management how these methods can aid in making better marketing decisions. Executives are willing to invest heavily in technical research because they are convinced there is a "payout" in this activity. Management has not been similarly convinced of a return on its investment in marketing research.[20] To communicate more effectively, the marketing researcher must let management know what he is doing for the company. He must take the initiative in communicating with management, talk their language, and be willing to make recommendations rather than straddle the fence on issues.[21]

In management's relationship with marketing research today, another basic problem is the apparent reluctance of management (1) to treat marketing research as a continuing process and (2) to relate marketing research and decision making in a more systematic fashion. Too often marketing research seems to be viewed in a fragmented, one-project-at-a-time manner. It is used only when management realizes it has a marketing problem.

One reason why many executives have been unable to relate research and decision making more closely is their unfamiliarity with modern decision-making processes and the informational sources available from related business and nonbusi-

---

20 For a method of forecasting the return on investment of research dollars, see Lee Adler, "Profiting from Marketing Research," *Sales Management*, Nov. 10, 1970, p. 34. For some guidelines in evaluating research proposals, see A. B. Blankenship and Raymond F. Barker, "The Buyer's Side of Marketing Research," *Business Horizons*, August, 1973, pp. 73-80.

21 For a survey of marketing research directors in large corporations, reporting on the role and effectiveness of the marketing research department as perceived by the director, his immediate superior, and other executives who use the department's services, see James R. Krum, "Perceptions and Evaluations of the Role of the Corporate Marketing Research Department," *Journal of Marketing Research*, November, 1969, pp. 459-464. This study identified (1) some ambiguities in the role of marketing research and (2) the areas of disagreement between marketing research directors and other executives.

ness fields. Some executives resist the use of research because they fear it is a threat to their personal status. That is, research implies an evaluation of their effectiveness, and it may also invalidate many beliefs fondly held. Organizational defects such as the failure to identify clearly the company's goals and the lack of systematic marketing planning tend to limit the productive use of marketing research.

Regarding these basic problems, Newman observed:[22]

> Reflecting executives' lack of understanding of research and its potential contribution to decision making is the fact that research departments have tended to be technical job shops to which operating people could bring requests if they chose to do so. The weakness of this system is that it depends on the initiative of executives who are unfamiliar with research and who typically are unable to identify their problems well enough to ask for the help they need.
>
> Research departments which work only on requests brought to them tend to be occupied with routine, short-range operating problems. They are unlikely to be contributing to policy formulation, planning, and innovation. They cannot become an integral part of the decision-making process because line executives do not look to research for that sort of participation. Without a close relationship with the decision makers, research cannot play much of an educational role.

PRACTICAL CONSTRAINTS ON THE RESEARCH FUNCTION

Marketing research has developed more slowly in Canada than in the United States. Marketing research was not formally recognized in Canada until the late 1920s or early 1930s as opposed to around 1910 in the United States. This apparent lag in our formal recognition of research can be explained by a number of factors which serve to constrain our research practices, indeed, our marketing practices, when compared with American ones.

Three sets of factors can be viewed as helping to explain our practices compared with those prevalent in the U.S. These are interrelated but nonetheless can be viewed as somewhat distinct. The most apparent set of factors concerns the size, distribution and homogeneity of our market. We are well aware that most of our twenty-three million people are distributed in a hundred-mile wide by three-thousand-mile-long band placed against the American border. We are also well aware that this population, with its long and narrow distribution, lacks homogeneity. The most obvious population break is between French- and English-speaking Canadians. But following on the heels of this differentiation is the regional one. As far as marketers are concerned, the commonly used regional categories—The Atlantic Provinces, Quebec, Ontario, The Prairies, and British Columbia—connote differences in life style and thereby differences in wants, needs and reactions to marketing efforts. In addition, within the regions, distinctive cultural groups exist in large enough size to create some further differentiation. The American market contrasts with this situation not only in terms of scale of population and its regional distribution (though there are similarities in this regard) but also in its relative lack of distinctive linguistic and cultural variation. The effect of population size, distribution, and homogeneity makes research more expensive in Canada than in the United States. As Mahatoo puts it:[23]

---

22 Joseph W. Newman, "Put Research into Marketing Decisions," *Harvard Business Review*, March-April, 1962, pp. 109-110.

23 Winston H. Mahatoo, *Marketing Research in Canada*, Thomas Nelson & Sons Ltd., Toronto, 1968, p. 2.

Since according to current sampling theory, sample size is not related to population, for a given level of accuracy the same size of sample would be required in Canada as in the United States. Thus comparable surveys cost far more in Canada (in relation to gross sales) than in the United States. There are no short-cuts or reductions in the effort involved in selecting a probability sample or in conducting a market test.

In addition to the sample-size issue and the cost of sampling, the greater market differentiation in Canada relative to absolute size requires a more detailed knowledge of market segments and makes it more difficult for researchers in Canada than in the United States to use cluster sampling, to select interviewers who can communicate with diverse groups, and to understand the behavioral variables underlying the market responses of such groups.[24]

The nature of the market not only affects the practices of researchers in Canada in terms of generating data at relatively higher costs, but also it affects the sets of problems than can effectively be researched. The relevant problems in Canada differ somewhat from those in the United States because of what can be done about them. This raises the second set of factors—the mix of marketing variables available to Canadian firms and the amount of flexibility inherent in the mix. The presence of a market that is as distributed and differentiated as ours calls for the bringing into play of a large number of marketing variables in different combinations—but the relatively small size of the market prohibits this. Marketing managers are faced with the challenge of having a market that is in many ways richer in fabric than that existing in the United States. This richness raises more research problems. But at the same time, what we find is either an underdevelopment of, say, advertising media available to approach market segments or a cost structure (or both) which makes it difficult to cater to the market in terms of what its organization ideally calls for. Thus even though market diversity calls for more research, the size of market inhibits this. It also inhibits the development of controllable marketing mix variables which would allow the marketing manager to do something if he had the appropriate information. The usual statement heard is akin to: "Yes, that would be nice to know, but what could I do about it?"

The third set of factors which constrains our research efforts concerns the structure and control of our business organizations. From the standpoint of structure, within an industrial category or line of trade, one finds fewer firms in competition than is the American case—and of course this is to be expected as a result of smaller market size. This reduction in number of competitors in an industry or line of trade makes it much easier for competitors to emulate each other or, at least, to more easily see what marketing strategies are being used. The effect, though it is not a necessary one, appears to be to reduce the alternatives considered (whether product or promotion), because when they are researched and tested in markets, such activity is very visible and easily confounded by competitors. There is very little room to be as unobtrusive as a firm in the United States could be. In addition, unlike the United States where more variations can be tried, there is less about which to be obtrusive.

The control of firms raises another issue which affects the availability and scope of marketing research problems. Where Canadian firms are either strong or have a dominant position, they are usually to be found in primary industries and related lines of trade. Where the Canadian subsidiaries of foreign based parents, usually

24 *Ibid.*, pp. 2-3.

American, are either strong or have a dominant position, they are usually to be found in secondary manufacturing and related lines of trade. The former, being export oriented, are not concerned with research into the Canadian market. The latter, however, are, but here we face an interesting situation. In many cases, but certainly not all, the new-product marketing research or the new promotional strategy research has been conducted by the parent in its home market. The Canadian subsidiary has access to both the designs and results. In some cases one finds that the parent's data bank and analysis are generalized to the Canadian market extant; in some cases the parent's research is duplicated for Canada—which involves much less in the way of research problem solving and costs than the original research set-up; in some cases a research program is modified for the Canadian scene—still a task of lesser magnitude and cost than the original research. Many of the Canadian subsidiaries who can rely on their parents for what seems to be low-cost information dominate their industry or trade, or are the major competitors in it. Canadian firms that compete with them appear unable or unwilling to invest in marketing research to the same extent as the research those subsidiaries have at their disposal. The result in the past has been less research commissioned in Canada by the subsidiaries and, paradoxically, less by the Canadian firms in competition with them. The position of the Canadian firm is seemingly paradoxical because, given that it has a research disadvantage compared with a subsidiary, it could be expected to make this up. Rather, the option seems to have been to follow the lead of the subsidiaries in terms of product and strategy and trust that the subsidiaries did a thorough job. For these reasons the conduct of research in Canada has been a problem.

THE FUTURE: A MARKETING INFORMATION SYSTEM

The remarks in the preceding sections bring us full circle in marketing research and back to the need for a marketing information system. Today a mass of information flows from external sources and also from within a firm. That information must be gathered, processed, and the findings disseminated in a meaningful way to executives so they can manage their firms' marketing programs. To effectively manage this mass of information, a company needs more than the traditional marketing research actvity—a company needs an MkIS. A marketing information system is future-oriented, whereas traditional marketing research, with some exceptions, has been concerned largely with explaining why something in the past happened as it did. It is true that we can learn from the past. We should study the past, however, not for its sake alone but because it can guide us in the future. The expansion of temporal horizons focuses management's attention on forecasting and long-range planning. The importance of this future orientation is summed up well in the following statement: "To manage a business well is to manage its future; and to manage the future is to manage information."[25]

QUESTIONS AND PROBLEMS

1. Why does a company need a marketing information system?

---

25 Marion Harper, Jr., "A New Profession to Aid Management," *Journal of Marketing*, January, 1961, p. 1.

2. Give some practical examples showing how a firm might use a marketing information system.

3. *a.* What is a marketing information system?
   b. How does it differ from marketing research?

4. "The marketing information executive—rather than an operating, decision-making executive—should be the one to identify marketing problems, delineate the area to be studied, and design the research projects." Do you agree? Explain.

5. Should the director of marketing information report directly to the chief marketing executive or to the president?

6. A large wholesaler of electrical supplies and equipment located in Quebec wanted to learn as much as possible about the potential market for an electric milk cooler. This was essentially a chestlike container which could hold ten regular-sized farm milk cans.

   Many small farmers stored their cans of fresh milk in cool well water. Before the cans were collected by a local dairy, processor, or shipper, the temperature of the water—and the milk—might fluctuate considerably. Heat tended to raise the bacteria count in milk. In some cities and provinces milk having more than a certain level of bacteria count could not by law be processed for human consumption.

   The manufacturer of the electric cooler approached the wholesaler with the hope that he would add the product to his line. Before making a decision, the wholesaler wanted to do some informal investigating of the product's market possibilities. What should this informal investigation consist of?

7. A group of wealthy businessmen regularly spent some time each winter at a popular ski resort in the Laurentians. These men were intrigued with the possibility of forming a company to develop and operate a large ski resort in the Eastern Townships. It would be a complete resort with facilities appealing to middle- and upper-income markets. What types of information might they want to have before deciding whether to go ahead with the venture? What sources of information would be used?

8. Acquire the following information for the most recent year available, using secondary sources. In each case, cite your source of information and list alternative sources where the information is also available.
   a. Tons of iron ore mined in Newfoundland
   b. Wholesale sales in Manitoba
   c. Value of potatoes produced in Prince Edward Island
   d. Population of Orangeville, Ontario
   e. Total number of housing starts in the Atlantic Region
   f. Gross-margin as percentage of sales of Canada Packers Limited
   g. Labor force participation rates for women in Saskatchewan
   h. Number of shoe stores in New Brunswick
   i. Operating expense ratio for jewelry retailers
   j. Consumer expenditures for personal services and for durable goods
   k. Consumer price index—for any given month or the annual average

9. A manufacturer of a liquid glass cleaner competitive with Windex and Glass Wax wants to determine the amount of the product which he can expect to sell in various markets throughout the country. To help him in this project, prepare a report which shows the following information pertaining to your

home province and also, if possible, your home city. Carefully identify the source you use for this information and also state other sources which provide this information.

a. Number of households or families

b. Income or buying power per family or per household

c. Total retail sales in the most recent year for which you can find reliable data

d. Total annual sales of food stores, hardware stores, and drugstores

e. The number of food stores

10. A wholesaler of air-conditioning and refrigeration equipment for both domestic and commercial use wants to analyze his marketing costs in each territory to determine the relative profitability of each district. Specifically, what types of internal data would he use in this study?

11. Evaluate surveys, observational techniques, and experimentation as methods of gathering primary data in the following projects:

a. A sporting goods retailer wants to determine college students' brand preferences for skis, tennis rackets, and golf clubs.

b. A supermarket chain wants to determine women shoppers' preferences for the physical layout of fixtures and traffic patterns, particularly around check-out stands.

c. A manufacturer of conveyor belts wants to know who makes buying decisions for this product among present and prospective users.

12. Carefully evaluate the relative merits of personal, telephone, and mail surveys on the bases of flexibility, amount of information obtained, accuracy, speed, cost, and ease of administration.

13. What kind of a sample would you use in research projects designed to answer the following questions?

a. What brand of shoes is most popular among the female students on your campus?

b. Should the department stores in or near your hometown be open on Sundays?

c. What percentage of the business firms in the large city nearest your campus have automatic sprinkler systems?

14. What criteria should a manufacturing firm use or what questions should its executives ask in selecting an outside research organization to aid in marketing research work?

MARKETING PLANNING AND FORECASTING

We may recall from Chapter 2 that the management process involves developing a plan, operating (executing) it, and evaluating the results. Parts 3 to 6 were devoted to operating and directing a marketing program. This and the following chapter will emphasize planning and evaluation.

Three planning activities—marketing planning, sales forecasting, and budgeting—are closely interrelated. Marketing planning is the comprehensive activity. Forecasting demand then is the cornerstone of successful planning. One type of forecasting—sales forecasting—is the basis of all budgeting and operations (production as well as marketing) in a firm. Budgeting is the process of activating a marketing plan. That is, a budget is an operating plan expressed in dollars.

PLANNING IN THEORY AND PRACTICE

A careful student of marketing has referred to planning in marketing as "the exercise of analysis and foresight to increase the effectiveness of marketing activities."[1] Another writer states that "the purpose of planning is to manipulate the present

---

1 Wendell R. Smith, "The Role of Planning in Marketing," *Business Horizons*, Fall, 1959, p. 54.

systematically in order to be prepared for the future."[2] In simple language, planning is drawing from the past to decide in the present what to do in the future. Or, let's decide now what we're going to do later, when and how we are going to do it, and who will do it.

In Chapter 2, planning was discussed as a management function separate from that of establishing objectives. Actually, marketing planning, broadly viewed, starts with the determination of marketing goals. It then involves a determination of how the goals will be reached. Several alternative courses of action may be followed, and management must apply problem-solving processes to select the best of the alternatives. Thus planning is also concerned with the operating system—the strategies and tactics—through which the goals are reached, the quantity and quality of effort needed to attain the goals, and, finally, the firm's ability to generate this effort.

Planning may also be viewed as an extension of the input-output theory developed by Prof. Wassily Leontief of Harvard: "Most planning is the attempt to exercise such foresight with respect to the anticipated outputs of an organization so that the inputs can be utilized with maximum efficiency."[3] Once management forecasts its desired output—that is, sets a goal—then through careful planning it can determine what input factors will be needed to attain the output goal. To illustrate, assume that management wants to enter a new geographic market and attain a sales volume of $2 million in this market by the end of the second year. Through input-output analysis, management can estimate what inputs are necessary in the form of advertising, personal selling, production facilities, financing, and personnel to reach the goal. Management may find that the required inputs are beyond the firm's capacity. Then the output goal must be altered along more modest lines. Thus availability of inputs may actually set limits on output. In essence, planning involves a matching of means and ends, or inputs and outputs.

IMPORTANCE OF PLANNING

Planning may be done formally or informally—in a simple, crude fashion or in a scientific, sophisticated manner—but, nevertheless, planning is inevitable when a firm is confronted with alternative courses of action. The concept of planning is not new, but the growing importance of the marketing concept in our economy has resulted in an increased recognition of the value of formal, organized planning. As one writer said, "The hard core of the so-called marketing concept . . . is effective and scientific use of market planning."[4] Truly, any success which management has in increasing the profitability of marketing operations depends in large part upon the nature of the marketing planning. Formal marketing planning is one of the most effective *management tools* available for risk reduction.

The dynamic nature of our economy, the growing fierceness of competition, and the shrinking profit margins are forcing management to focus more attention on marketing planning. Careful, formal planning is essential for maximizing the chances of success: in new-product development, in setting up an international marketing program, in establishing a distribution system, and in countless other

---

2 Mark E. Stern, *Marketing Planning*, McGraw-Hill Book Company, New York, 1966, p. xi.

3 Wroe Alderson, *Marketing Behavior and Executive Action*, Richard D. Irwin, Inc., Homewood, Ill., 1957, p. 414.

4 Smith, *op. cit.*, p. 57.

aspects of a total marketing program. In this age, forward-looking competitors are adopting the systems approach to marketing. Computer technology is being employed to help management optimize its use of quantitative analytical techniques such as PERT, linear programming, input-output analysis, probability theory, etc. In such a competitive setting, a company may be committing economic suicide if it relies on haphazard, informal planning.

Many other advantages accrue from organized planning. It can save a considerable amount of executive time and effort. With a formal staff group assigned to planning tasks, line executives can be freed for other revenue-producing work. Also, internal coordination and communication can be improved, and executives can be provided with some framework for day-to-day decisions. Formal planning should also elicit disciplined thinking because executives must put their thoughts in writing before acting. Good planning forces a firm to do advance scheduling. As a result, management by crisis and expediency can be reduced to a minimum, and short-term disturbances can be placed in a proper perspective.

OBSTACLES TO SUCCESSFUL PLANNING

Despite the many benefits to be gained, most firms still do not employ formal marketing planning. Moreover, only "about 20 percent of the major industrial companies that are thought to be good marketing planners *are* good marketing planners."[5] This summary observation was based on a study (conducted by McKinsey & Company, a management consulting firm) which covered marketing planning in large industrial companies. The following four common administrative weaknesses in marketing planning were identified in this study:

1. Failure of the chief executive to establish and communicate major corporate goals
2. Inability to assess realistically the capabilities and probable strategies of competitors
3. Lack of internal coordination and communication with the firm
4. Overstructured planning process, generating unnecessary paper work and irrelevant details which obscure the critical problem areas

Other obstacles may be observed in the path leading to successful planning.[6] Often marketing strategies are based on goals which are unrealistic, conflicting, or too numerous. Many top-level executives claim they do not have time for formal planning activities. Yet these same administrators often seem reluctant to delegate authority to a staff planning group, pleading that staff people lack experience. Our limited abilities in interpreting consumers' attitudes and motivation also hinder successful marketing planning. Sometimes plans go awry because they are based on inadequate data. Another limitation has been the failure of marketing management to make effective use of the computer as an aid in developing marketing plans.

In a firm that has enjoyed a favorable rate of growth, the executives may see no need for organized planning. Planning is often absent also in a small firm where one man—frequently the founder—has dominated. Actually, if such a company is successful, often the guiding executive is fundamentally a good planner. He just does not recognize planning as a formal activity. In both of these nonplanning situ-

---

5 "Shortcomings Predominate in Marketing Planning," *Industrial Marketing*, July, 1967, p. 60.

6 "Long-range Planning: Séance or Science?" *Sales Management*, Jan. 15, 1969, p. 31.

ations, executives will claim that their operations change so frequently and so quickly that advance planning—especially long-range planning—is not feasible. Regardless of how substantial all the above difficulties may seem, they cannot negate the proved value of sound planning.

SCOPE OF PLANNING ACTIVITIES

The length of time for which planning is done serves as one basis for classifying planning. Long-range planning, for three, five, ten, or twenty-five years, is probably more important than short-range planning. Top management and special planning staffs are involved in long-range planning, and the resultant policy decisions cover broad, far-reaching topics, such as plant, market, or product expansion. Short-term planning usually covers periods of three months, six months, or a year. It is done at the operational level by lower- and middle-echelon executives and is concerned with such things as adjusting prices to meet current competition, buying for the coming season, handling the day-to-day problems of a sales force, and selecting middlemen in a new market.

For purposes of clarity we should distinguish among three planning concepts: (1) total company planning, (2) marketing planning, and (3) the annual marketing plan. *Total company planning* involves setting broad, but basic, company goals over the long run and then developing long-range strategies to achieve these goals. These long-range goals and strategies then become the framework within which departmental plans are developed. In company planning, attention is devoted to financial requirements, production goals, manpower needs, and research and development efforts as well as to the determination of market targets and the marketing programs needed to reach these targets.

The emphasis and starting point in company planning have shifted as firms have evolved from a production to a marketing orientation. In the past, company planning was concerned first with the production facilities and financial resources needed to generate what management estimated the company would sell. (Even today, financial planning dominates in industries such as oil, steel, and telephones where new production facilities require such huge capital investments.) As the marketing concept is implemented in a firm, however, marketing becomes the focal point in planning in that company. Now planning starts with (1) an identification of market objectives and opportunities, then (2) a determination of the marketing program needed to capitalize on those opportunities, and finally (3) the planning encompasses the plant and financial resources needed. As marketing influences both short-term and long-range company policies, total company planning and marketing planning tend to merge.

Short of that merger, however, we can identify long-range *marketing planning* as a distinct concept. This activity involves setting goals and strategies for the marketing effort in the firm. Marketing planning is done within the framework of the total company planning, and yet the marketing planning is recognized as being separate from similar activity in finance, production, and other major departments in a firm. Marketing planning would include the development of long-range programs for the major ingredients in the marketing mix—the product, the distribution system, the pricing structure, and the promotional activities. Separate planning might be done for subdivisions within these major ingredients—subdivisions such as product groups, market segments, or advertising, as separate from sales-force activities. In Parts 3 to 6 of this book, the major ingredients in the marketing mix were considered in consecutive order. Realistically, however, the planning in each of these areas must be done concurrently and be carefully coordinated because each element in the mix interacts with every other element.[7]

Whereas marketing planning is done on a continuing basis, the *annual marketing plan* reflects one time segment of the ongoing planning process. Thus management will develop a master plan covering a year's marketing operations. The overall plan will consist of several coordinated subplans in marketing. More attention can be devoted to tactical details in the annual plan than is feasible in longer-range planning. As an example, long-range marketing planning related to the product may set as a goal the introduction of truly innovative products. The marketing plan for 1978, however, may strive to correct an inventory imbalance by especially promoting the sales of one product which is in the declining stage of its life cycle. Long-range planning may speak in the role of personal salespeople in the promotional mix, while the annual plan for 1978 speaks of increased college recruiting as a source of salespeople.

THE PLANNING PROCESS

One series of steps which management can fruitfully follow in developing a marketing plan will be considered briefly at this point. A key point to remember in relation to the marketing planning process is that the final product—any marketing plan—should appear in detailed, *written* form. The first step in the planning process might be called the *situation analysis*. At this point management makes a thorough analysis of the company's existing situation—its markets, its competition, the product, the distribution channels, and the promotional programs. With this background management can set its *goals* in some detail. Recalling Chapter 2, we are reminded that these goals should be realistic, specific, and mutually consistent. Problems uncovered in the situation analysis should draw attention to the limitations and opportunities facing the company and thus should influence the goals. Next, the planning executives can examine alternative *strategies* and select the ones which, when implemented by an effective marketing mix, will offer the best potential for achieving the goals. The fourth step is to select the most appropriate *tactics*. These are the specific operational details which direct the plan in action. Finally, an effective planning process should provide for a periodic audit or *evaluation* of the operating results. In this way mistakes can be corrected, and the plan can be adjusted to its current environment.[8] See Figure 28-1.

FORECASTING MARKET DEMAND

The cornerstone of successful marketing planning is the measurement and forecasting of market demand. The key figure we need is the sales forecast because it is the basis for all budgeting and operations in the firm. A company can forecast its sales

---

7 For some findings from a five-year study on the accuracy of corporate planning in some 60 companies, see Richard F. Vancil, "The Accuracy of Long-Range Planning," *Harvard Business Review*, September-October, 1970, pp. 98-101.

8 For a review of some 30 publications on various aspects of planning, see Robert J. Mockler, "Theory and Practice of Planning," *Harvard Business Review*, March-April, 1970, pp. 148-150ff. The reviewed publications were selected on the basis of being most useful to executives in the management of their planning activities.

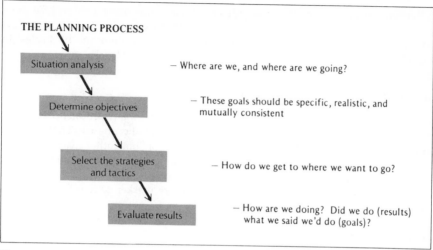

THE PLANNING PROCESS

Situation analysis — Where are we, and where are we going?

Determine objectives — These goals should be specific, realistic, and mutually consistent

Select the strategies and tactics — How do we get to where we want to go?

Evaluate results — How are we doing? Did we do (results) what we said we'd do (goals)?

Figure 28-1.

by using either of two basic procedures—a "top-down" or a "buildup" approach.

Using the "top-down (or "breakdown") approach, management generally would:

1. Start with a forecast of general economic conditions, as the basis to
2. Determine the industry's total market potential for a product. Then
3. Measure the share of this market the firm is getting. The measurements in items 2 and 3 form the basis for
4. Forecasting the sales of the product. The sales forecast, in turn, is the basis for all
5. Budgeting and other operational planning in the firm.

In the "buildup" technique, management estimates of future demand in various segments (territories or customer groups) of the market or from various organizational units (salespeople or branches) in the company. Then management simply accumulates the individual estimates into one total forecast.

As the need arises in this discussion, we shall define several terms—"market potential," "sales potential," "market share," and others—which often are used loosely in business. At this point we should understand the meaning of the terms "market factor" and "market index."

A *market factor* is an item or element which exists in a market, which may be measured quantitatively, and which is related to the demand for a product or service. To illustrate, the number of cars three years old and older is a market factor underlying the demand for replacement tires—that is, affecting the market potential for replacement tires. In Chapter 4 we spoke of population and income factors which affect the market for consumer projects. In Chapter 8 we mentioned some of the market factors which affect the demand for industrial goods.

A *market index* is simply a market factor expressed in percentages or in some other mathematical term. Sometimes more than one market factor is combined into a single index number. A market factor or market index may be developed for the entire national market or for any segment of it. To illustrate, say in 1978 the index representing expenditures for personal services was 165, with the year 1960 serving as the base period of 100. The index was computed in constant dollars, so increases in the price level did not affect the index numbers. Thus, from 1960 to 1978 there was a real increase of 65 percent in expenditures for services. If sales of our product are related directly to expenditures for personal services, then our 1978 sales (in constant dollars) should be about 65 percent above the 1960 level.

GENERAL ECONOMIC FORECAST

Forecasting sales or determining the market potential for many products frequently starts with a prediction of things to come in the national economy. Trends in the gross national product, disposable personal income, or some other macroeconomic measure may be the best indicator of future market demand for automobiles or other consumer products. The supply of money, interest rates, and rates of family formation are factors useful in estimating the future market demand for housing. Consequently, an early step in forecasting sales in many firms is a develop a forecast (or to study an already prepared forecast) of the relevant indicators of general economic conditions.

DETERMINATION OF MARKET POTENTIAL AND MARKET SHARE

The *market potential* for a product may be defined as the expected combined sales volume for all sellers of that product during a stated period of time in a stated market. Implicitly in this definition we assume the existence of a given set of environmental constraints such as technology, general economic conditions, a politico-legal situation, etc. *Market share* (synonymous with *sales potential* or *market penetration*) is "the ratio of a company's sales to the total industry sales on either an actual or potential basis."

Thus we may speak of the "market potential" for automatic washing machines, but the "market share" (or sales potential) for one company's brand. In the case of either market potential or market share, the market may encompass the entire country, or even the world, or it may be limited to some part segmented by income, by geographic area, or on some other basis. For example, we may speak of the *market potential* for washing machines on the West Coast or the *market share* for Canadian General Electric washers in homes with incomes of $7,000 to $10,000. The market potential and market share will be the same when a firm has a monopoly in its market, as in the case of a telephone company or some other public utility.

For some products the market potential can be derived from a national economic forecast because the market factors most predictive of future sales of these products are part of the forecast of the national economy and general business conditions. Thus, when a rise of 4 percent in the gross national product is forecasted for next year, the market potential for given products can be expected to increase at the same level. In determining the market potential for many other products, however, management can effectively bypass the step of preparing or studying a national economic forecast, because the key market factors most directly predictive of future sales of these products normally are not a part of the forecast of the national economy. For instance, the market potential for textbooks in a beginning marketing course is a function of the number of schools offering such a course and the total number of students enrolled.

Ordinarily a company will determine the market potential for its product in a given market, and then from this figure determine its market share (sales potential). If a company's sales are a minor segment of the industry total, it may start directly with a determination of sales potential and not compute the total industry market potential at all. In some industries the trade association gathers data from all member firms, and from this information a firm can rather easily determine the market potential or its market share. When a firm must compute these measures all by itself, several basic techniques are available. These will be explained briefly later in this chapter.

SALES FORECASTING

While a sales forecast ordinarily can be made more intelligently if the company first determines its market and/or sales potential, actually many firms start their marketing planning directly with the sales forecast.

The American Marketing Association defines a sales forecast as:[9] "An estimate of sales, in dollars or physical units for a specified future period under a proposed marketing plan or program and under an assumed set of economic and other forces outside the unit for which the forecast is made. The forecast may be for a specified item of merchandise or for an entire line."

The sales forecast and the marketing plan. We should note in the above definition that a sales forecast is influenced by a company's proposed marketing program. Unfortunately, the relationship between the sales forecast and the marketing plan in a firm is often misunderstood. Some executives speak of developing a marketing plan based on their annual sales forecast, for example. This is reversing the proper order of things. Perhaps the confusion arises because of the variety of demand forecasts we are dealing with. It is true that a forecast of the national economy or an estimate of market potential should precede the development of a marketing plan. However, the marketing goals and broad strategies—the core of a marketing plan—must be established before a sales forecast is made. That is, the sales forecast is dependent upon these predetermined goals and strategies. Certainly a different sales forecast will result, depending upon whether the goal is to liquidate an excess inventory of product A or to expand the firm's market share by aggressive advertising.

Now, once the sales forecast is prepared, it does become the key controlling factor in all *operational* planning throughout the company. The forecast is the basis of sound budgeting. Financial planning for working-capital requirements, plant expansion, and other needs is based on anticipated sales. Scheduling of all production resources and facilities, such as setting manpower needs, purchasing raw-materials, and determining the rate of production output, depends upon the sales forecast.

The sales forecast and sales potential. Because a sales forecast is dependent upon a company's marketing plan, it is not an estimate of sales under ideal conditions. This would be more like the calculation of sales potential. In some cases a sales forecast and a sales potential may be the same, but usually a sales forecast is less. The company's existing production facilities may limit its opportunity to sell more units during the coming year. Or the company might be able to bring its forecast nearer to its sales potential if funds were available to devote to sales-force expansion and a more intensive advertising campaign.

---

9 Committee on definitions, *Marketing Definitions: A Glossary of Marketing Terms,* American Marketing Associatin, Chicago, 1960, p. 20.

Sales-forecasting periods. One year is probably the most widely used period for sales forecasting, although many firms prepare forecasts for periods of three or six months. Also, many firms review their annual forecasts monthly or quarterly. Annual sales forecasts tie in with annual financial planning and reporting, and are often based on estimates of the coming year's general economic conditions.

Short-run forecasts of less than a year may be desirable when activity in the firm's industry is so volatile that it is not feasible to look ahead a full year. As a case in point, many firms engaged in fashion merchandising, producers and retailers alike, prepare a forecast which covers only one fashion season.[10]

In some instances, long-range forecasts (more than one year) are helpful in financial planning and in planning for long-term plant, equipment, and materials needs. These long-range estimates are really estimates of sales potentials rather than sales forecasts. They usually indicate maximum sales opportunity and are related to the firm's marketing program.

METHODS OF FORECASTING MARKET DEMAND

Predictions of future market demand—whether they are sales forecasts or estimates of market potential—may be based on techniques ranging from uninformed guesses to sophisticated statistical methods requiring the assistance of specialists. Marketing executives do not need to know how to do the statistical computations. However, these administrators should understand enough about a given technique to appreciate its merits and limitations, know when it is best used, and be able to ask intelligent questions regarding the assumptions underlying the method.[11]

Separate estimates should be prepared for each article or product line. Then each total product forecast should be subdivided in as much detail as possible. That is, a forecast should be prepared in dollars and/or units for each territory, customer group, or other meaningful sales unit. The itemized forecast can then be used in operational levels of planning, such as setting sales quotas or allocating the advertising appropriation.

Market-factor analysis. For most companies the analysis of market factors is probably the best forecasting method to use because it is the most reliable and valid. The fundamental thesis underlying this method is that the future sales of a given product depend upon the behavior of certain factors related to the market demand for the product. Thus if we can determine what these factors are and can measure their relationship to sales activity, we can forecast future sales simply by studying the behavior of the factors. If the market-factor behavior occurs prior to the period covered by the forecast, there is a lead-lag situation.

The key to the successful use of this method lies in the selection of the appropriate market factors. Management must be certain that a relationship does exist between the selected factor and the market for the product. It is also important that

---

10 As an example of short-run forecasting done by one such company—a manufacturer of seasonal, fashion sportswear—see Carl Vreeland, "The Jantzen Method of Short-range Forecasting," *Journal of Marketing*, April, 1963, pp. 66-70.

11 See Stanley J. PoKempner and Early L. Bailey, *Sales Forecasting Practices: An Appraisal*, The Conference Board, Experiences in Marketing Management, no. 25, New York, 1970; and John C. Chambers, Satinder K. Mullick, and Donald D. Smith, "How to Choose the Right Forecasting Technique," *Harvard Business Review*, July-August, 1971, pp. 45-74.

the researcher minimize the number of market factors used. The greater the number of factors, the greater the chance for erroneous estimates, and the more difficult it is to tell the extent to which each influences the demand for the article. The two procedures used to translate the market-factor behavior into an estimate of future sales are the direct-derivation method and the correlation analysis technique.

Direct derivation. As an illustration of the use of this method to estimate market potential, suppose that a manufacturer of automobile tires wants to know the market potential for replacement tires in Canada in 1978. The main market factor is the number of automobiles on the road. The first delimitation is the estimate of how many cars are likely prospects. Assume that the seller's studies show that the average passenger car is driven about 10,000 miles a year and that the average driver gets about 25,000 miles from a set of four tires. This means that all cars which become 2½ years old during 1978 can be considered a part of the potential market for replacement tires during that year. Reasonably detailed information regarding the number of cars sold between July 1, 1975 and June 30, 1976, is readily available from provincial and county licensing agencies and also has been compiled by private organizations. In addition, similar count must be established for cars reaching 5, 7½, and 10 years of age during 1978. These ages are multiples of 2½. That is, a 5-year-old car presumably would be ready for its second set of replacement tires. The number of cars in these age brackets times 4 should give a fair approximation of the market potential for replacement tires in 1978. We are, of course, dealing in averages. Not all drivers will get 25,000 miles from a set of tires, and not all cars will be driven exactly 10,000 miles a year.

The seller then must determine his share of this market. Here the analysis becomes more subjective. He must consider the quality of his product in relation to competitive products, the strength of his distribution system and promotional program, the extent of competition, his market share in past years, his plans for market expansion, and many other factors.

The market-factor-derivation method has much to recommend it. It is relatively simply and inexpensive to use, and it requires relatively little statistical analysis. It is reasonably easy to understand, so that non-statistics-oriented executives can follow the method and interpret the results. Usually the factors selected are those for which detailed, reliable data are available.

Correlation analysis. This technique is simply a mathematical refinement of the market-factor-derivation method. When correlation analysis is used, the variations in the potential sales of the product are mathematically correlated with the variations in the measurements of the market factor. In effect, correlation measures the variations in two series of historical data. Consequently, this method can be used only when a lengthy sales history of the industry or the firm is available, as well as a history of the market factor's measurement.

Probably the major advantage of correlation analysis is the exactness of the estimate of market demand, assuming, of course, that the elements in the statistical estimating equation are accurate. By placing the measure of the market factor into the estimating equation, the researcher can come up with an accurate estimate of the market or sales potential. This is a more precise measure than the one developed through direct derivation, where the correlation analysis is implicitly assumed to be a perfect + 1.00. Rarely does this perfect relationship exist between a market factor and the sales of a product. Also, correlation analysis allows a researcher to incorporate more than one factor into the formula.

There are at least two major limitations to this method. First, as suggested above, a lengthy sales history must be available. To do a really good job, a researcher needs about twenty periods of sales records. Also, he is assuming that approximately the same relationships have existed among the variables during this entire period and, furthermore, that this relationship will continue throughout the period for which potentials are being estimated. This may be a highly unrealistic assumption. The other major drawback is that some marketing executives do not understand correlation analysis nor can they do the necessary computations. Thus a statistical staff may be necessary. Even then, because of their lack of comprehension, the executives may suspect the results.

Survey of buyer intentions. Another commonly used method of forecasting is to survey a sample of potential customers, asking them how much of the stated product they would buy at a given price during a specified future time period. This technique is used for both consumer and industrial products. The sample of buyers may be ultimate users or middlemen. Some firms maintain consumer panels on a continuing basis to act as a sounding board for new-product ideas, prices, and other product features.

A major problem is that of selecting the sample of potential buyers. For many consumer products a very large, and thus very costly, sample would be needed. Aside from the extremely high cost and large amount of time that this method often entails, there is another very serious limitation. It is one thing for a consumer to say he *intends to buy* a product, but quite another for him *actually to buy it.* Surveys of buying intentions inevitably show an inflated measure of market potential. They are widely used, however, particularly where there are inadequate data for a market-factor derivation or a correlation analysis.

Surveys of buying intentions are probably most effective when there are relatively few buyers, when they are willing to express their buying intentions, and when their past record shows that their follow-up actions are consistent with their stated intentions.

Test marketing. In using this technique, a firm markets its product in a limited geographic area and, from this sample, projects the company's sales potential (market share) over a larger area. Test marketing is used frequently for new products in deciding whether sufficient profitable sales potential exists to warrant introducing the item. The technique also serves as a basis for evaluating various product features and alternative marketing strategies. The outstanding benefit of test marketing is that it can tell management how many people *actually buy* the product, instead of only how many *say they intend* to buy. If a company can afford the time and money for this method and can run a valid test, it will find that this is the best way of measuring the full potential for its particular product. Management estimates do not play as big a role here as they do in the other techniques for determining market potential.

These are big "ifs," however. Test marketing is expensive in time and money. Great care is needed to set up and control the test-marketing experiment and to arrange for informational feedback from these markets. Once a competitor learns you are test marketing, he usually is adept at "jamming" your experiment. That is, by unusual promotional or other marketing effort, he can create an artificial situation so that you test results are not meaningful.

Past sales and trend analysis. A favorite method of forecasting is to base the estimate *entirely* on past sales. This technique is used frequently by retailers whose main goal is to "beat last year's figures." The method consists simply in applying a flat percentage increase to the volume achieved last year or to the average volume of the past few years. The same rate of increase is anticipated for every product in the company's line.

This technique is simple, inexpensive, and easy to apply. For firms operating in a reasonably stable market situation, where their market shares have remained constant for a period of years, it is possible that past sales can be depended upon as the sole indicator of future volume. On balance, however, the method is highly unreliable. Most firms operate in a dynamic market. Also, it is unrealistic to assume that each article in the product mix will enjoy the same rate of growth. Finally, changes in the marketing program can have varying effects on future sales and destroy the relationship with past sales activity. In some of the other sales forecasting methods, management considers past sales to be one of several influencing factors.

Trend analysis is a variation of the forecasting method based on past sales, but it is a bit more complicated. It involves either a long-run projection of sales trends computed by the statistical technique known as the *least-squares method* or a short-run projection (forecasting for only a few months ahead) based upon a seasonal index of sales. Adding the statistical sophistication in long-run trend analysis does not really remove the inherent weakness of basing future estimates only on past sales activity. Short-run trend analysis may be acceptable if the firm's sales follow a reliable seasonal pattern. Thus if sales reach 10,000 units in the first quarter (January-March) and, historically, the second quarter is always about 50 percent better, we can forecast sales of 15,000 units in the April-June period.

Sales-force composite. This a buildup method which may be used to forecast sales or to estimate market potential. As used in sales forecasting, it consists of collecting from each salesperson or each middleman an estimate of sales of various products in his territory during the future period to be covered in the forecast. The total composite of these separate estimates is the company's sales forecast. This method may be used advantageously if the firm has competent, intelligent, high-caliber salespeople and if it is selling to a market composed of relatively few, but large, customers. Thus a sales forecast based on this method would be more applicable to large electrical generators than to small general use motors.

The sales-force-composite method has the merit of placing responsibility for forecasting upon the shoulders of those who must meet their own target. Also, it takes advantage of the salespeople's specialized knowledge of their own market, and it should make them more willing to accept their assigned sales quota. On the other hand, it takes salespeople away from their main task—selling. Furthermore, salespeople are not trained or qualified to do the research needed in forecasting. They are in no position to see the "big picture," that is, the total company operations and the socioeconomic conditions which influence future sales volume.

Executive judgment. This method covers a wide range of possibilities. Basically it consists of obtaining opinions regarding future sales volume from one or more executives. If these are really informed opinions, based on other valid factual measures such as market-factor analysis, then this type of executive judgment is desirable. Certainly all the previously discussed forecasting methods should be tempered with sound executive judgment. Forecasting should not be done solely by computer or mathematical model. On the other hand, forecasting by executive opinion alone is a risky technique. In some instances, it is simply intuition or guesswork.[12] See Fig. 28-2.

DETERMINING TERRITORIAL POTENTIALS

After a company has determined its sales potential or sales forecast for its entire market, management typically wants to establish these demand estimates for each territory assigned to its salespeople or its middlemen. Forecasts of territorial market demand may be used for several purposes, such as setting sales quotas, determining territorial boundaries, evaluating performance of sales units, or allocating advertising effort.

Once the potentials are calculated for the total market, it is ordinarily easy to compute territorial potentials. Management simply uses a pertinent market index which has been determined for small geographic areas such as counties or cities. For example, assume that a manufacturer of machine tools estimates his market share for a given year to be $12 million: the market factor he uses is the number of employees in manufacturing establishments. Referring to his information sources, he can get the number of manufacturing employees in each district. He determines that 9 percent of the total manufacturing employees are located in his western region and 6 percent in his eastern territory. The potentials in these territories are then calculated at $1,080,000 and $720,000, respectively.

QUESTIONS AND PROBLEMS

1. "Planning involves the matching of means and ends—of matching inputs and outputs." Explain how this concept may be applied in a practical fashion to the promotional program in a firm. To new-product development.
2. Explain some of the ways in which formal marketing planning serves as an effective form of risk management in marketing.
3. What are some of the reasons why some firms do no formal planning? Which of these obstacles are reflections of administrative weaknesses, and which ones are likely to occur even with good management?
4. Distinguish between marketing planning and an annual marketing plan.
5. What are the steps which usually should be followed in the process of writing a marketing plan?
6. Using examples of consumer or industrial products, carefully distinguish between market potential and sales forecast.
7. Why is the sales forecast usually smaller than the sales potential?
8. What companies—manufacturers or middlemen—might be interested in forecasting sales on a weekly or a monthly basis?

---

12 See Richard Staelin and Ronald E. Turner, "Error in Judgmental Sales Forecasts: Theory and Results," *Journal of Marketing Research*, February, 1973, pp. 10-16.

9. What effect would each of the following occurrences have on the market potential for furniture? For a manufactured grocery product?

   a. Establishment of an 18 percent federal sales tax accompanied by a major cut in federal income tax rates

   b. Increase in minimum wages to $3.50 per hour

10. What are some logical market factors which you might use in estimating the market potential for each of the following products?

    a. Home heating systems

    b. Milking machines   d. Sterling flatware

    c. Golf clubs   e. Safety goggles

11. How would you determine the market potential for a textbook in a beginning course in marketing?

12. What are some of the problems a researcher faces when using the test market method for determining market or sales potentials?

13. If a firm bases it sales forecasts on estimates compiled by its salespeople, should a salesperson be rewarded financially for correctly forecasting the sales in his territory during the coming year?

14. "No company should forecast its sales without making some use of the executive-judgment method, and yet this method never should be used to the exclusion of other methods." Discuss.

15. A grocery products manufacturer estimates that sales of his new cereal will reach $15 million next year. How much should he expect to sell in the province in which your school is located?

A WHIMSICAL VIEW OF SALES FORECASTING

Gather 'round children, and I shall tell you the story of the Sales Forecast. Like the fruit fly, the Forecast has a brief life and is usually abandoned by its parents the day after birth. Like us, the Forecast has one mother, and her name is Computer. But unlike us, the computer has a whole rookery of husbands who deny they're the father. Every Forecast has all its anonymous father's bad features and its mother's precise, beautiful profile.

Mating season is between September 15th and November 15th, give or take requested extensions. Gestation can be a matter of electronic seconds or several weeks depending on the skill of the obstetrician, the treasurer. Often the treasurer has difficulty decoding the seeds of wisdom ejaculated by the fathers, a rather ordinary breed called salesmen, district sales managers, regional sales managers, general sales managers, and perhaps even a marketing vice president (if he's not in a meeting).

Conception by the Computer takes place when the thousands of little numbers manufactured by the Fathers are inserted via interoffice memo into the Computer. You can tell when a Computer is ready for mating, because it does a fan dance with its blank punch cards and makes a whirring sound that sounds like "Shoot the data to me, Dada."

When a Forecast is born, it can be either black, which is beautiful, or red, which makes everybody sick just to look at it.

Treasurers always throw up when they see a red Forecast, especially if it looks like last year's annual report (which is really a Forecast that's grown up and thus become hopelessly out of date). A red Forecast has a very tough time being adopted by any nice family, especially families with names like Stockholder, Director, or President.

Usually, a red Forecast's birth results in the arrest, conviction, and execution of suspected fathers who haven't already slit their own throats.

Black Forecasts, on the other hand, create joy and merriment for all concerned. The treasurer especially beams with a grin implying that he is not only the obstetrician but perhaps even the father. When all the possible fathers enthusiastically invite a paternity suit, you *know* the Forecast was born black. It's ironic, but encouraging, that even companies in the South seem to love black Forecasts.

But, Forecasts, like children, don't always turn out so well. Though everybody knows a Forecast is just a promise when it's born, all hell breaks loose when it doesn't act like it said it would.

This sometimes happens. The Forecast is the only gambling device legalized in all 50 states with avid players even among bankers, but its principal characteristic is its vacillating personality. As a result, Forecasts are at the doctor's constantly having their insides altered and their columns straightened.

Every business should have a Forecast. It employs lots of people, puts iron in the blood, and self-destructs in 30 days.

Source: Jim Lavenson, "Meet Rosemary's Other Baby," *Sales Management,* Aug. 15, 1971, p. 26. Reprinted by permission of *Sales Management,* © 1971.

Figure 28-2.

ANALYSIS OF
SALES VOLUME AND
MARKETING COSTS

After a firm's plans have been set in operation, the results should be evaluated as promptly as possible. Without an evaluation, management is in no position to tell whether its plan worked, to what degree it was successful, and what the reasons were for success or failure. Planning and evaluation are interrelated activities. Evaluation logically follows planning in that planning sets forth what should be done, and evaluation shows what really was done. Sometimes a circular relationship exists: plans are made, the operational results are evaluated, and new plans are prepared on the basis of this appraisal.

Earlier in the book we discussed briefly the topic of evaluation as it related to separate parts of our marketing program—the product-planning process, the performance of our salespeople and middlemen, and the effectiveness of our advertising program, for instance. At this point, we want to make a study of the results of our total marketing effort in the form of an analysis of our sales volume and our marketing costs.

THE MARKETING AUDIT: A TOTAL EVALUATION PROGRAM

To appreciate fully the managerial activity of evaluation, we shall first consider the concept of a marketing audit as a total evaluation program.[1] Audits are not new to business management. Traditionally, they have carried the connotation of a review and evaluation of some business activity. They have long been used in accounting and financial operations, and we are also accustomed to personnel audits. Really all we are doing here is applying the concept of an audit to our marketing operations and the marketing program.

A *marketing audit* may be defined as *"a systematic, critical, and unbiased review and appraisal of the basic objectives and policies of the marketing function and of the organization, methods, procedures, and personnel employed to implement the policies and achieve the objectives."*[2] In this definition six areas in marketing are identified for appraisal—objectives, policies, organization, methods, procedures, and personnel. To qualify as a marketing audit, any appraisal must include all six, along with the underlying philosophies upon which the activities are based. A fragmented appraisal of some marketing activities may be useful, but it is only one part of an audit. To be classed as a marketing audit, the appraisal must be a coordinated study of the total marketing program, and it should be done at one time.

Although an audit suggests an after-the-fact review of a business structure, a marketing audit includes an evaluation of the effects of alternatives *before* a decision is reached. Thus the audit becomes an aid in decision making. In addition to identifying weaknesses in a company's program and suggesting means to eliminate them, marketing audits should include reviews of successful operations so that management may capitalize on its strong points. Furthermore, an audit should anticipate future situations. An audit is intended for "prognosis as well as diagnosis. . . . It is the practice of preventive as well as curative marketing medicine."[3]

SCOPE OF EVALUATION ACTIVITIES

A complete marketing audit is something of an ideal. Rarely does a firm conduct a full audit of its total marketing program because the cost and difficulty of the task are great. Instead, management usually appraises individual components of the marketing mix. Such an evaluation is desirable if a full-scale audit is impossible. A major shortcoming, however, is the possible lack of integration among the several areas studied. For instance, a recommendation stemming from a review of the distribution system may have serious implications in pricing or promotion.

The evaluation process is essentially the same three-stage task regardless of which area is being appraised. First, management must gather the facts and compare the actual results with the budgeted figures in order to determine the extent of the variations. Next, it must determine what specific factors in the marketing program are responsible for the program's results. Finally, it must develop plans and procedures with the intent of improving unsatisfactory conditions and capitalizing on favorable ones. To summarize, the administrator's job is to find out *what* happened, and *why* it happened, and then to decide *what to do* about it.

---

1 The "marketing audit" concept is presented in *Analyzing and Improving Marketing Performance: "Marketing Audits" in Theory and Practice,* American Management Association, Management Report no. 32, New York, 1959. Much of this section is based on this source. See especially Abe Shuchman, "The Marketing Audit: Its Nature, Purpose, and Problems," pp. 11-19; and Alfred R. Oxenfeldt, "The Marketing Audit as a Total Evaluation Program," pp. 25-36.

2 Oxenfeldt, *op. cit.,* p. 26.

3 Shuchman, *op. cit.,* p. 14.

MISDIRECTED MARKETING EFFORT

One of the primary benefits of evaluation activities is that they can help correct misdirected or misplaced marketing effort.[4]

THE "80-20" PRINCIPLE

A company does not enjoy the same rate of net profit on every individual sale. In most firms a large proportion of the orders, customers, territories, or products account for a small share of the profits. This relationship between selling units and profits has been characterized as the "80-20" principle. That is, 80 percent of the orders, customers, territories, or products contributes only 20 percent of the net sales, gross margin, or net profit. Conversely, 20 percent of these selling units account for 80 percent of the volume or profit. The 80-20 figure is used simply to epitomize the misplacement of marketing efforts. Actually, of course, the percentage split varies from one situation to another.

The basic reason for the 80-20 situation is that some misdirected or misplaced efforts are found in most marketing programs. Marketing efforts and costs follow the *number* of territories, customers, products, or other selling units rather than the actual or potential sales volume or profit. In a retail sale which is to be charged and delivered, approximately the same order-filling, billing, and delivery expenses are involved whether the sale is a mink coat or a necktie. Manufacturers may assign one salesperson to each territory, and yet there may be substantial differences in the volume and profit returns from various districts.

REASONS FOR MISDIRECTED MARKETING EFFORT

Many businesspeople are unaware of the misdirected marketing effort in their firms. They do not know what percentage of total sales and profits comes from a given product line or customer group. Ordinarily they do little or nothing about evaluating their marketing operations. They have relied upon sales volume as the sole criterion for measuring the success of a marketing program. The increasing acceptance of the marketing concept should blunt this emphasis on sales volume. It still exists, however, among manufacturers who set sales volume quotas for their salespeople, among wholesalers who pay their salespeople a commission on net sales, and among retailers who base their sales goals on the preceding year's sales volume figures.

Frequently executives cannot uncover their misdirection of effort because they lack sufficiently detailed information. The analogy of an iceberg in an open sea has been used to illustrate this situation. Only a small part of an iceberg is visible above the surface of the water, and the submerged 90 percent is the dangerous part. The figures representing total sales or total costs on an operating statement are like the visible part of an iceberg. The detailed figures representing sales, costs, and other performance measures for each territory, product, or salesperson correspond to the important submerged segment.

---

4 The term "misdirected marketing effort" was first noted in Charles H. Sevin's writings on distribution cost analysis. See Charles H. Sevin, *Distribution Cost Analysis,* U.S. Department of Commerce, Economic Series, no. 50, 1946; and Charles H. Sevin, *How Manufacturers Reduce Their Distribution Costs,* U.S. Department of Commerce, Economic Series, no. 72, 1948.

Total sales or costs on an operating statement, or other figures representing total performance, are too general for a marketing executive interested in evaluation. In fact, the total figures are often inconclusive and misleading. More than one company has shown satisfactory overall sales and profit figures, but when these totals were subdivided by territory, products, or some other basis, serious weaknesses were discovered. A manufacturer of rubber products showed an overall annual increase of 12 percent in sales and 9 percent in net profit on one of his product lines one year. But when he analyzed his figures more closely, he found that the sales change within each territory ranged from an increase of 19 percent to a decrease of 3 percent. In some territories, profits increased as much as 14 percent, and in others they were down 20 percent. This is a practical example of the "iceberg principle."

An even more important cause of misplaced marketing effort is that marketing executives must make decisions even though their knowledge of the exact nature of marketing costs is woefully inadequate. In other words, management lacks (1) knowledge of the disproportionate spread of marketing effort and (2) reliable standards for determining what should be spent on marketing and what results should be obtained from the expenditures.

As an illustration, a marketing executive really does not know how much to spend on advertising, marketing research, or sales training. Even more troublesome is the fact that, after the money is spent, there is no satisfactory yardstick to determine whether the results are satisfactory. If a company spends $250,000 more on advertising this year than last year, management ordinarily cannot state what the resultant increase in sales volume or profits should be. Nor do the executives know what the results would have been if an equivalent sum had been devoted to new-product development, management training institutes for middlemen, or some other aspect of the marketing program.[5]

ANALYSIS OF SALES VOLUME

An *analysis of sales volume* is a careful study of the internal records of a firm as they are summarized in the net sales section of the operating statement. A researcher studies the dollar and/or unit sales in total and analyzes these sales on the basis of such subdivisions as territories, product lines, time periods, customer groups, and order sizes. A sales volume analysis may be extended to include a study of the cost of goods sold and the resultant gross margin, also divided into various product and market bases. A *marketing cost analysis* is a detailed study of the operating expense section of the profit and loss statement in an attempt to determine the relative profitability of each product line and various market segments. A sales volume analysis and a marketing cost analysis are thus closely related activities. Together they constitute a detailed study of a company's operating statement.

LIMITATIONS OF VOLUME ANALYSIS

There are two major limitations to using a sales volume analysis as a basis for decision making. The first is that the necessary detailed data are usually not readily

---

5 For some contributions which accounting and financial management tools can make toward a more effective allocation of marketing effort, see V. H. Kirpalani and Stanley S. Shapiro, "Financial Dimensions of Marketing Management," *Journal of Marketing*, July, 1973, pp. 40-47.

available in a form useful to the analyst. Accumulating and processing these essential facts can be a tedious, expensive task. Fortunately, the advent of the computer and other electronic data processing equipment has greatly facilitated the information-gathering step and has opened tremendous new opportunities for management to analyze sales data.

The second limitation is that even a completely reliable sales volume analysis may, if used alone, be misleading. A volume analysis alone may show that sales of a certain product or sales in a given region are steadily increasing as a percentage of market potential. A study of gross margin or marketing costs, however, may show that the firm is enjoying a "profitless prosperity." Nevertheless, we hasten to point out that while a full marketing cost analysis is more desirable than a volume analysis alone, certainly a volume analysis is better than nothing.

BASES FOR ANALYZING VOLUME

There are many bases upon which a company may analyze its sales volume. These include total sales volume, territories, product lines, customer groups, and size of orders. To illustrate some aspects of a volume analysis and show what can be done with the results, we shall build our discussion around a hypothetical firm—the Dominion Office Furniture Company Ltd. This firm sells in all the provinces and its market is divided into four territories. The company's product mix is divided into four broad categories: desks, chairs, filing and safekeeping equipment, and accessories (wastebaskets, desk sets, desk pads, clothes trees). Some of these products are manufactured by Dominion, and others are purchased from outside sources but sold under the Dominion brand.

Total sales volume. There are two trend figures related to total sales volume that we should study. The first is the trend in the company's total sales volume over a period of years, and the second is the trend in the company's share of the market. As we know, a company's sales may increase steadily while its share of the market actually decreases.

An analysis of total sales volume is probably the easiest of all the usual types of marketing analyses made by management. Figures on the company's total volume ordinarily are readily available from the firm's accounting records. All an executive needs in addition is an accurate estimate of total industry sales in the geographic market covered by the company. Trade associations and government agencies are excellent sources for industry volume statistics in many fields.

Table 29-1 shows the information necessary to start an analysis of total sales volume in Dominion. The company's annual sales doubled (from $18 million to $36 million) during the ten-year period ending in 1976. Furthermore, they increased each year over the preceding year, with the exception of 1973. So far the company situation is very encouraging. When industry figures are introduced for comparison, however, the picture changes. During this decade, the industry's annual sales have increased from $120 million to $300 million (a 250 percent increase), with the result that the company's share of market declined from 15 to 12 percent. In summary, the company's annual sales increased 200 percent, but its market share declined 20 percent. We have now concluded the first of the three steps in the analytical procedure—we know *what* happened.

The next step is to determine *why* Dominion's market position declined. The number of possible causes is almost limitless, and this is what makes manage-

Table 29-1. Annual Sales Volume of Dominion Office Furniture Company Ltd. Industry Volume, and Company's Share in the Canadian Market.
This table gives the basic data needed for a sales volume analysis in a single firm. In this case, the company's volume doubled in ten years, but its share of the market declined from 15 to 12 percent. What factors might account for this decreasing market share? Is a sales volume analysis sufficient to detect situations characterized as "80-20" or "iceberg"?

Year	Company Volume, in millions of dollars	Industry Volume in Company's Market, in millions of dollars	Company's Percentage Share of Market
1976	36.0	300	12.0
1975	34.7	275	12.6
1974	33.1	255	13.0
1973	30.4	220	13.8
1972	31.7	235	13.5
1971	28.0	200	14.0
1970	24.5	170	14.4
1969	22.5	155	14.5
1968	21.8	150	14.8
1967	18.0	120	15.0

ment's task so difficult. A weakness in almost any aspect of Dominion's product line, distribution system, pricing structure, or promotional program may have contributed to the loss of market share. It may be that the real culprit is competition. There may be more strong competitors in the market, who were attracted by rapid growth rates in market potentials, or competitors' marketing programs may be more effective than Dominion's own excellent program.

Sales by territories. While a study of total sales volume may be a good place to start a sales analysis, it is usually insufficient because of the workings of the iceberg principle. To uncover activity in the submerged segments of the market, administrators will analyze sales volume by territories. This type of analysis may also bring to light the existence of the 80-20 principle in that a large share of volume may be coming from a small number of territories.

It may be helpful to explain briefly one four-step territorial sales analysis procedure which is reasonably simple and need not be expensive or time-consuming. The first step is to determine what share of the company's total sales volume should come from each territory. This involves selecting a market index which can be used to establish territorial potentials. (The use of market indices to determine territorial potentials was discussed in the preceding chapter.) For instance, one firm used an index of residential building permits issued. If 15 percent of the total residential building permits issued in the nation during one year were issued in the company's Manitoba region, then 15 percent of the company's sales volume should be obtained from that area. If the firm's total market covers only part of the country, then the total annual building permits issued in that limited area would be equated to

Table 29-2. Territorial Sales Volume in Four Territories of Dominion Office Furniture Company Ltd., 1976.

Here the iceberg principle is at work. Territory D is $2.4 million below its sales goal, while the performances in the other three regions are above par. How did management derive the figures in the market-index column?

Territory	Market Index, percent	Sales Goals, in millions of dollars	Actual Sales, in millions of dollars	Performance Percentage	Dollar Variation, in millions
A	30	10.8	12.5	116	+1.7
B	25	9.0	9.6	107	+ .6
C	21	7.6	7.7	101	+ .1
D	24	8.6	6.2	72	−2.4
Total	100	36.0	36.0		

100 percent. Thus if a company operated only in the four Atlantic provinces and if 28 percent of the building permits issued in that area were issued in Nova Scotia, then management should expect 28 percent of its total sales volume from that province.

The next step is to determine the actual total sales made during the period under the review. The third step is to multiply each territorial index by the actual *total* sales in order to establish the goal or par for each district. Finally, the actual sales figure in each territory is compared with the predetermined standard of performance for the region, and any variation is tabulated.

This procedure is illustrated in Table 29-2. Dominion has set up four sales territories to cover its market. By applying a pertinent market index chosen by management, we find that 30 percent of the total sales should have been obtained from territory A, 25 percent from territory B, etc. Applying these percentages to the total annual volume of $36 million, we find that the dollar *goal* was $10.8 million in region A, $9.0 million in region B, etc. The *actual* territorial sales are tabulated in column 4, and the dollar *variation* is listed in column 6.

The critical column is the one entitled Performance Percentage. The percentages are derived by dividing the actual sales by the territorial goal. A performance percentage of 100 means that the territory did exactly what was expected of it. Thus from the table we see that territories B and C did just a little better than was expected, territory A passed its goal by a wide margin, and territory D was quite a disappointment.

When management knows what has occurred in each territory, it must find the reasons for the performances and then take constructive action based upon the findings. Consequently, a careful study should be undertaken to find out why area D did so poorly. The fault may lie in one or more aspects of the marketing program in that area, or competition may be particularly strong there. An attempt should be made to determine what accounts for A's success and whether this information can be helpful in the other regions. Also, the executives should analyze territorial volume by products and customer groups. Even though Area A did well, the iceberg principle may be at work within the region. The fine total performance within A may be covering up weaknesses in separate product lines.

Sales by products. Management may use any of several types of volume analyses by product lines. One type is simply a tabulation of the annual sales by individual products or related groups of products for the past several years. This tabulation shows the percentage of total volume obtained from each line. From it, management can ascertain any trend in sales by products.

It is particularly helpful if industry figures are available for each product line. Then the executives can compare the firm's record of sales with industry figures, as was done in Table 29-1 for total sales. If the company's sales in one product line are decreasing, this is not so bad if industry sales for this article are also declining. If one product accounts for a very small part of the company volume, management can evaluate this situation better if industry figures are available for comparison.

Another type of product sales analysis is made by studying the sales of each product *in each territory* over a period of years. Through such a study, management can determine in what geographic market each product is relatively strong or weak. Dominion may find, for instance, that its total sales of desks increased 14 percent last year but that sales of this product declined 2 percent in territory B.

To study product sales in each territory, we can use the method illustrated in Table 29-2 in connection with the territorial analysis. That is, through the application of appropriate market indexes, management can establish sales goals for each product line in each territory. Then actual sales can be compared with these goals. In Table 29-2, we saw that territory A reached 116 percent of its goal, or an excess of $1.7 million; territory D was short of its goal by 28 percent, or $2.4 million. What actually occurred in these two districts is identified more specifically by the type of product sales analysis illustrated in Table 29-3. Selected market indexes were applied to each product line to establish product sales goals in each territory. Thus in A, the total goal was $10.8 million, with $4.5 million expected from sales of desks, $3.4 million from sales of chairs, etc. In district A, almost two-thirds of the $1.7 million excess over quota came from sales of desks, and one third was contributed by the line of filing equipment. While the region as a whole surpassed its goal by 16 percent, the sales of chairs declined about 3 percent ($100,000). In fact, sales of chairs were below par in both territories.

MARKETING COST ANALYSIS

An analysis of sales volume on the several bases discussed earlier in this chapter can be quite helpful in appraising a company's marketing efforts. A volume analysis, however, does not tell us anything about the *profitability* of a territory, product line, salesperson, or group of customers. In order to determine the relative profitability of the various selling units, management may conduct a marketing or distribution cost analysis.[6] In the literature, the term "distribution cost analysis" seems to be preferred. "*Marketing* cost analysis" is more representative of the full scope of the analytical activity and is more in line with the concept of marketing management. The two terms are used synonymously in this chapter.

---

6 Several fine books and journal articles cover the more technical phases of marketing cost analysis. For example, see Donald R. Longman and Michael Schiff, *Practical Distribution Cost Analysis*, Richard D. Irwin, Inc., Homewood, Ill., 1955; or J. Brooks Heckert and Robert B. Miner, *Distribution Costs*, 2d ed., The Ronald Press Company, New York 1955.

Table 29-3. Sales Volume in Two Territories of Dominion Office Furniture Company Ltd., 1976.

In Table 28-2, we saw that territory A exceeded its sales goal by $1.7 million (16 percent), while territory D was 28 percent below par. Now we can see more of our iceberg by determining which products accounted for these variations. Sales of desks were $1,150,000 above the goal in territory A and $1,400,000 below the forecast in territory D. Note also that A was well above its market target in filing equipment, while D fell off considerably in sales of chairs.

Product Line	Territory A ($000)			Territory D ($000)		
	Goal	Actual	Variation	Goal	Actual	Variation
Desks	$ 4,500	$ 5,650	+$1,150	$3,800	$2,400	−$1,400
Chairs	3,400	3,300	− 100	2,400	1,420	− 980
Filing equipment	2,100	2,700	+ 600	1,800	1,900	+ 100
Accessories	800	850	+ 50	600	480	− 120
Total	10,800	12,500	1,700	8,600	6,200	− 2,400

NATURE AND SCOPE OF MARKETING COST ANALYSIS

A marketing cost analysis is a detailed study of a firm's entire distribution cost structure. For the various cost items, management may establish a budgetary goal, and then analyze the cause of variations between the actual and the budgeted expenses.

Marketing cost analysis can be used by the individual business firms to determine the cost of performing marketing activities such as outside selling, billing, advertising, and warehousing. It can be used to determine the expenses and profits of the company's various products, customer classes, territories, and order sizes. Marketing cost analysis may also be used to establish and appraise various marketing policies and procedures.

Like a sales volume analysis, a marketing cost analysis is more concerned with analysis than with accounting practices. Furthermore, cost analysis is frequently performed on a sporadic or sampling basis, whereas the accounting system is maintained on a routine, continuing basis. We may analyze territorial costs in only half the districts or study the cost of selling various products for only a six-month period. The cost analysis, however, is closely related to the accounting system in one very important way. A detailed system of ledger accounts is a virtual necessity if management wishes to do a thorough cost analysis, because many of the raw data for a cost analysis come from the accounting records.

Some significant differences exist between marketing cost analysis and production cost accounting. First, their scope differs. In production cost accounting, management is interested in determining the costs per unit of product. In marketing cost analysis, the administrators are interested not only in marketing costs for each product but also in the marketing expenses attached to geographic market segments, separate customer classes, and various order sizes.

Most production expenses are related to the operation of machines or to men who are subject to constant personal supervision. Consequently, it is possible to measure rather accurately the cost of producing a unit of the product. On the other hand, marketing expenses are incurred by salespeople whose job is not completely repetitious and whose activities are not constantly observed by a supervisor. Therefore, usually it is not possible to determine the time, effort, and resultant costs related to individual marketing activities.

A third, and probably more important, difference exists. With respect to production activities, the costs are a function of volume $(C = fV)$. That is, the costs react to a change in volume. To illustrate, if the factory output is increased 15 percent, then as a *result* there is an accurately measurable change in costs. In marketing, on the other hand, volume is a function of costs $(V = fC)$. That is, the sales volume output reacts to a change in input cost factors. Volume will ordinarily increase, for example, as a *result* of adding more salespeople or spending money for advertising.

In these relationships, management can foretell quite accurately what will happen to production expenses when there is, say, an increase of 10 percent in the volume produced. A marketing executive is not in a correspondingly advantageous position. He cannot say, for instance, exactly how much increase in volume should be expected when the advertising budget is increased 10 percent or when two new salespeople are added in territory A.

PROBLEMS INVOLVED IN COST ANALYSIS

Management must realize the need for marketing costs studies, have some understanding of the techniques involved, and be able to interpret the results. A cost study will require a considerable amount of manpower, time, and money. Even if the company uses data processing equipment, the cost may still be high.

Classifying marketing expenses. Once management decides which of its costs can be categorized as marketing expenses, it must organize the costs into useful classifications. In the accounting systems of most companies, the operating expenses are classified according to the direct object of the expenditures. Thus we find ledger accounts for rent, salespeople's commissions, taxes, salaries, office supplies, etc. These are often called "natural" expenses. For purposes of a marketing cost analysis, administrators usually find it necessary to reclassify these expenses according to the marketing functions involved. Then all costs pertaining to one activity, such as advertising or warehousing, are grouped together.

To regroup the various natural (ledger) expenses, management should first determine which functional classifications will be most useful and then allocate the natural expenses to the appropriate function. There is no standard list of functional classifications. The following groupings, however, can apply to many firms:

1. Selling—direct costs (salespeople's compensation, travel, etc.)
2. Selling—indirect costs (sales training, marketing research, sales statistics, etc.)
3. Advertising and sales promotion
4. Warehousing
5. Transportation and shipping including order filing and packing
6. Credits and collection (bad-debt losses, credit office expenses)
7. Order processing and billing
8. Marketing administrative expenses

Allocating costs. Undoubtedly one of the most difficult problems in cost analysis, whether it is an analysis of marketing or of production expenses, is that of cost allocation. In marketing cost analysis, this problem occurs in two places. First, the ledger expenses must be allocated to appropriate activity cost groupings. Then these functional cost totals must be allocated to individual territories, products, or some other market segment. The choice of unreasonable cost allocation bases can distort the results and mislead management.

Operating expenses can be divided into direct and indirect expenses. (These are sometimes called "separable" and "common" expenses.) Direct, or separable, expenses are those which are incurred totally in connection with one market segment or one unit of the sales organization. Thus the salary, commission, and travel expenses of the salesperson in territory A are a direct expense for that territory. The cost of media time or space to advertise product C is a direct cost of marketing that product. The task of allocating direct expenses is easy. They can be apportioned in their entirety to the marketing unit, such as a product or territory, for which they were incurred.

The allocation problem really arises in connection with indirect, or common, costs. These are expenses which are incurred jointly by more than one marketing unit and therefore cannot be apportioned totally to one product, territory, or other market segment.

A given cost does not remain permanently in either the direct or the indirect category. Its classification depends upon the type of cost analysis being made. If a firm is analyzing costs by territories, then salesmen's salaries are direct expenses chargeable entirely to the territory in which they work. If the company conducts a cost analysis by products, however, and each salesman sells the entire line of products, then salaries are indirect expenses and should be prorated according to the estimated time salesmen devote to each product.

Within the category of indirect expenses, some costs are more indirect than others. That is, some of the activity cost groups are *directly* related, to some extent, to the territories, products, or other marketing units being studied. For instance, the total cost for advertising, order filling, or shipping would *decrease* if some of the products or territories were eliminated. By the same token, they would *increase* if some territories or product lines were added. These functional costs might be called *partially* indirect. On the other hand, activity groups covering marketing administrative expenses are *totally* indirect. Total expenses for maintaining the chief marketing executive, his staff, and his office would remain about the same, whether or not the number of territories or product lines was changed.

A study of business management today will disclose that different companies follow fundamentally different philosophies in allocating totally indirect costs such as administrative overhead expenses. One approach is to allocate these expenses equally among all territories, products, or other units being studied. This is an easy method but it is obviously inadequate and in no way related to actuality.

Another approach is to allocate these expenses in proportion to the sales volume obtained from each segment being analyzed. This method is also sometimes used to apportion partially indirect expenses, such as billing, shipping, and order filling. The philosophy is that the expense burden should be placed where it can best be borne. The large-volume territories or products are thus charged with the bulk of these expenses. Although this philosophy has some merit, it does not accurately reflect the real situation.

A third allocation system is simply to prorate the indirect costs in the same proportion as the direct expenses. If one territory has been charged with 20 percent of the total direct expenses, it is also assigned 20 percent of the indirect costs. Sometimes partially indirect expenses such as billing and shipping are allocated to the marketing unit on some reasonable basis. Then the totally indirect expenses of administrative overhead are prorated in the same proportion as the sum of the direct plus partially indirect costs.

In Table 29-5, which we shall discuss later, we shall see some of the better, more precise bases which are suggested for allocating a specific functional cost to various product groups or sales territories.

Full-cost versus contribution-margin controversy. One approach to the allocation of indirect costs is known as the *contribution-to-overhead* or the *contribution-margin* method. Under this system, management determines the gross margin of each marketing unit being studied. Then the direct expenses which have been allocated to each unit are deducted from the gross margin. These are the costs which presumably would be eliminated if the corresponding marketing unit were eliminated. After deducting these separable costs, the remainder is the amount which that unit is contributing to cover total overhead or indirect expenses.

There is a basic point of conflict between the contribution-margin approach and the full-cost approach to the allocation of costs. In the full-cost approach, all indirect expenses are allocated among the marketing units being analyzed. Proponents of the full-cost approach contend that the purpose of a marketing cost study is to determine the *net* profitability of the units being studied. They feel that the contribution-margin approach does not fulfill this purpose.

Under the contribution-margin system no attempt is made to allocate indirect costs, especially the *totally* indirect ones such as administrative expenses. Advocates of this approach contend that it is not reasonably possible to make an accurate apportionment of these items among organizational units or market segments. Furthermore, items such as administrative costs are not at all related to any one territory or product, and therefore the unit should not bear any of these costs. Contribution-margin supporters also state that management is not concerned with fixed, indirect costs when making decisions affecting short-run situations. They suggest that management is then concerned only with alternative courses of action where cost structures are variable. Finally, they point out that a full-cost analysis may show a product or territory with a net loss, whereas this unit may be contributing something to overhead. Some executives might recommend that the losing department be eliminated, overlooking the fact that the unit's contribution to overhead would then have to be borne by other units. Under the contribution-margin approach, there would be no question about keeping this unit as long as no better alternative could be discovered. On balance, it seems that both methods, contribution margin and full cost, are useful in marketing cost analysis.[7]

TYPES OF MARKETING COST ANALYSES

Three types of marketing cost analyses are commonly used by business. One is an analysis of costs as they appear in ledger accounts; another is a study of marketing

---

7 For more on this notion that either method may be appropriate, depending upon the situation, see John J. Wheatley, "The Allocation Controversy in Marketing Cost Analysis," *University of Washington Business Review,* Summer, 1971, pp. 61-70. See also Leland L. Beik and Stephen L. Buzby, "Profitability Analysis by Market Segments," *Journal of Marketing,* July, 1973, pp. 48-53; and W. J. E. Crissy, Paul Fischer, and Frank H. Mossman, "Segmental Analysis: Key to Marketing Profitability," *MSU Business Topics,* Spring, 1973, pp. 42-49.

expenses grouped into function classifications; and the third is an analysis of marketing costs after they have been allocated to territories, products, or other marketing units.

Analysis of ledger expenses. The simplest and least expensive way to make a marketing cost analysis is to study the object-of-expenditure costs as they appear in the accounting ledgers. The researcher simply lists expense totals for delivery salaries, salespeople's travel expenses, advertising salaries, telephone and telegraph, etc. These costs may be compared with similar totals for past years, and each expense may be expressed as a percentage of net sales. If at all possible, the company's expense ratios should be compared with industry figures. Many trade associations publish media figures and other measures of central tendency for the industry as a whole.

Analysis of functional expenses. When a marketing executive wants additional information in order to help him control the cost of various marketing functions, such as advertising or warehousing, he should make an analysis of marketing expenses classified into groups representing these activities.

The procedure in functional cost analysis is to decide what activity groups will be used and then allocate each ledger expense among the appropriate activities. An expense distribution sheet is often useful in this procedure (Table 29-4). The ledger expenses listed in the left-hand column are prorated among the appropriate columns which represent the functional groups. Some items such as the cost of advertising media space (newspapers) can be apportioned directly to one activity (advertising and sales promotion). For other expenses, the cost can be prorated only after management has established some reasonable basis for allocation. Rent or property taxes, for instance, may be allocated according to the proportionate amount of floor space occupied by each department. Thus, if the warehouse accounts for 30 percent of the total square feet of floor space in the firm, the warehousing function would be charged with 30 percent of the rent or property taxes. A columnar total represents the full cost of each function. In Dominion's case, advertising and sales promotion cost $169,750, and warehousing costs $200,000.

A functional cost analysis gives an executive more information than he can get from an analysis of ledger accounts alone. By comparing expense distribution sheets for several periods, management can ascertain which particular ledger expenses are responsible for significant changes in the cost of an activity. Finally, an analysis of activity expenses in total provides an excellent starting point for management to analyze costs by territories, products, or other marketing units.

Analysis of functional costs by market segments. The third and most beneficial type of marketing cost analysis is a study of the costs and profitability of each segment of the market. Common practice in this type of analysis is to divide the market by territories, products, customer groups, or order sizes. Cost analysis by market segment will enable management to pinpoint trouble spots or areas of satisfactory performance much more effectively than can be done with an analysis of either ledger-account expenses or activity costs.

The procedure for making a cost analysis by market segments is quite similar to the method used to analyze functional expenses. The total of each functional cost is prorated on some appropriate basis to each product or market segment being studied. By combining a sales volume analysis with a marketing cost study, a researcher

Table 29-4. Expense distribution sheet. Dominion Office Furniture Company Limited, 1976

The worksheet is a useful tool when allocating ledger-account expenses among the various groups of activity costs. Why is the salesperson's travel expense allocated entirely to direct selling, while the office expense is prorated among all activity groups? What is a good basis for allocating the property tax expense among the functional cost groups?

| Ledger expenses | Totals | Selling— direct costs | Selling— indirect costs | Advertising and sales promotion | Activity Cost Groups | | | | |
					Ware- housing	Transporta- tion and shipping	Credits and collections	Order processing and billing	Marketing adminis- trative
Salespeople's salaries	$2,500,000	$2,500,000							
Salespeople's travel	570,000	570,000							
Salespeople's commisions	2,400,000	2,400,000							
Media space	1,200,000			$1,200,000					
Dealer displays	200,000			200,000					
Advertising salaries	175,000			175,000					
Office supplies	180,000	25,000	18,500	25,500	$ 15,000	$ 19,500	$ 15,000	$ 52,500	$ 9,000
Telephone	90,000	42,000	9,000	6,750	1,500	5,250	9,000	6,000	10,500
Administrative salaries	615,000	150,000	100,000		55,000	40,000	60,000	110,000	100,000
Property taxes	240,000	8,000	20,500	12,500	128,500	18,000	13,500	23,500	15,500
Bad debts	30,000						30,000		
Freight out	1,500,000					1,500,000			
Total	$9,700,000	$5,695,000	$147,000	$1,619,750	$200,000	$1,583,750	$127,500	$192,000	$135,000

can, in effect, prepare a complete operating statement for each of the product or market segments. In a territorial analysis, for example, all he needs to do is classify sales by territories and then determine the cost of purchasing or making the merchandise which was sold in each region. The difference between the sales and cost figures is the territorial gross margin. The third step is to allocate each activity arrived at by subtracting expenses from gross margin is the territory's contribution to overhead. If all expenses are allocated and then subtracted from gross margin, the final result is the territory's net profit.

Table 29-5 presents examples of some reasonable bases for allocating groups of functional costs among sales territories and among product groups.

USE OF FINDINGS FROM COMBINED VOLUME AND COST ANALYSIS

The findings of a combined volume and cost analysis may be used by management in making decisions on many aspects of the marketing program.

Territorial decisions. Once marketing administrators know the net profit (or contribution to overhead) and the sales volume of the territories in relation to potential, they should throw their major effort into the weakest district because the greatest opportunity for improvement lies there.

Territorial boundaries may need adjustment to bring them into line with current potential. Often a company lets its territorial limits remain untouched long after shifts have occurred in market potential. As a result, some districts have more potential business than one salesperson can effectively develop, whereas others have insufficient potential to support a salesperson.

Territorial problems may stem from weaknesses in the distribution system, and changes in channels of distribution may be needed. Some firms which have been using manufacturers' agents may find it advisable to establish their own sales forces in growing markets. Other businesses may try to bypass wholesalers in some districts and sell directly to retailers or industrial users. Territorial problems may call for changes in selling methods. A company might use mail or telephone selling rather than personal salespeople in unprofitable districts. Intensive competition may be the cause of unprofitable volume in some districts, and changes in the promotional program may be advisable.

Of course, a losing territory might be abandoned completely. If an abandoned region has been contributing anything to overhead, however, even though a net loss was shown, management must recognize that this contribution must now be carried by the remaining districts.

Product decisions. When the relative profitability of each group of products is known, management may take action to improve the situation. A product line may be simplified by eliminating slow-moving, unprofitable styles, sizes, or colors. The salespeople's compensation plan may be altered to encourage the sale of high-margin items. Commissions may be reduced on low-margin items to deter the men from devoting an inordinate amount of effort to them. Channels of distribution may be altered. Instead of selling his complete group of products directly to industrial users, for example, a machine tools manufacturer shifted to industrial distributors for standard products of low unit value. Advertising appropriations may be altered in order to develop more effective advertising for some line of merchandise. Changes in product policies themselves may be effective. For instance, multiple

Table 29-5. Bases of allocating functional cost groups to sales territories and to product groups.
A given functional cost group may be distributed among territories or products on the basis of some measurable characteristic which bears a "causative" relationship to the total amount of that functional cost group. Explain, using numbers, how advertising media costs would be allocated to territories.

Functional cost group	Basis of Allocation	
	To sales territories	To product groups
1. Selling—direct costs: sales salaries, incentive compensation, travel, and other expenses	Direct	Selling time devoted to each product, as shown by special sales-call reports or other special studies
2. Selling—indirect costs: field sales-office expense, sales-administration expense, sales-personnel training, marketing research, new-product development, sales statistics	Equal charge for each salesperson	In proportion to direct selling time or time records by projects
3. Advertising, media costs such as TV, radio, billboards, newspapers, magazines, etc.; advertising production costs; advertising department salaries	Direct; or analysis of media circulation records	Direct; or analysis of space and time by media; other costs in proportion to media costs
4. Sales promotion: consumer promotions such as coupons, premiums, etc.; trade promotions such as price allowances, point-of-purchase displays, cooperative advertising, etc.	Direct; or analysis of source records	Direct: or analysis of source records
5. Transportation: railroad, truck, barge, etc.; payments to carriers for delivery of finished goods from plants to warehouses and from warehouses to customers; traffic department costs	Applicable rate times tonnages	Applicable rates times tonnages
6. Storage and shipping: rent or equivalent costs for storage of inventories in warehouses; insurance and taxes on finished goods inventories; labor and equipment for physical handling, loading, etc.	Number of shipping units	Warehouse space occupied by average inventory. Number of shipping units.
7. Order processing: preparation of customer invoices; freight accounting; credit and collection; handling cash receipts; provision for bad debts; salary, supplies, space and equipment costs	Number of order lines	Number of order lines

Source: Adapted from Charles H. Sevin, *Marketing Productivity Analysis*, McGraw-Hill Book Company, New York, 1965, pp. 13-15.

packaging may increase unit sales and thereby reduce the unit cost of order filling, billing, and shipping. Changes in physical distribution methods may enable a company to employ less expensive packaging materials and processes.

Pricing policies and practices with respect to each product should be reviewed carefully to determine whether price changes upward or downward may increase total revenue and net profit.

In the final analysis, management may decide to discontinue handling a product. Before this is done, however, consideration must be given to the effect this decision will have on other items in the line. Often a low-volume or unprofitable product must be carried simply to round out the line. Customers expect the seller to carry the article, and if he does not, he may lose business in his other products.

Decision on customer classes and order sizes. By combining a volume analysis with a cost study, the executives can determine the relative profitability of each group of customers. If a substandard rate of net profit is coming from one group, changes in the pricing structure used for these accounts may be required. The prices may be raised to cover costs more effectively. Or, if competition is severe and there is an elastic demand, the prices may be reduced. Perhaps accounts which have been approached directly should be turned over to middlemen.

Marketing cost analysis by *size of order* is often helpful in connection with customer-classification cost studies. Management can determine its break-even point with respect to order size and can ascertain the amount of sales volume and net profit obtained from each order-size classification. A common problem plaguing many firms today is that of the small order. Many orders are below the break-even point. The revenue from each of these is actually less than the allocated expenses because several costs, such as billing, accounting, or direct selling, are the same whether the order amounts to $10 or $10,000.

Small-order accounts create a difficult decision-making situation. Management's immediate reaction may be that no order below the break-even point should be accepted and that small-volume accounts should be dropped from the customer list. Actually, such a decision may be erroneous and harmful. Management should determine first *why* certain accounts are small-order problems and then adopt procedures to correct the situation. Proper handling can very often turn a losing account into a satisfactory one.

There are several reasons why a customer may be a small-order problem. He may be new and growing. (However, eventually he may become a profitable account.) He may be buying a sufficient total volume of merchandise, but on a hand-to-mouth basis. That is, he may send in many small orders instead of a few large ones. He may be spreading his purchases among many different suppliers, thus creating small-order problems for all of them. Sometimes the accounting method determines whether a customer or order is profitable. If a customer is charged only with the appropriate *marginal* costs required to do business with him, he may be a profitable customer, but if he is charged with his share of all costs—that is, if an average cost basis is used—his account may show up as a net loss.

A multitude of practical suggestions may be made to aid management in reducing the costs of small orders or increasing the size of the order. Management may initiate customer education, establish minimum order sizes, change the price structure, use multiple packaging, turn to direct-mail or telephone selling, or use wholesalers instead of direct selling.

FUTURE OF COST ANALYSIS

The use of marketing cost analysis has increased considerably in the past 30 years. Refinements in technique have come rapidly, and the future is highly promising. If there is any real problem in the area of cost analysis, it is the shortage of skilled personnel. This shortage will undoubtedly be alleviated as college instruction in the field is increased and as trade and professional associations in business administration place added emphasis on marketing cost studies. The situation will also be helped as marketing and accounting people come to realize that they have mutual problems in this area and can benefit from more closely coordinated efforts.

QUESTIONS AND PROBLEMS

1. The iceberg principle has been likened to a medical diagnosis where the patient's complaint is different from the real problem. Explain.
2. "A sales volume analysis is of very little value unless it is accompanied by a marketing cost analysis." Discuss.
3. A sales volume analysis by territories indicates that the sales of a manufacturer of roofing materials have increased 12 percent a year for the past three years in the territory comprising Manitoba, Saskatchewan and Alberta. Does this indicate conclusively that the company's sales volume performance is satisfactory in that region?
4. A manufacturer found that one of his products accounted for 35 to 45 percent of the company's total sales in all but two of the eighteen territories. In each of those two districts, this product accounted for only 15 percent of the company's volume. What factors might account for the relatively low sales of this article in the two districts?
5. Explain how the results of a territorial sales volume analysis may influence a firm's promotional program.
6. What effects may a sales analysis by products have on training, supervising, and compensating the salespeople?
7. "In production, costs are a function of volume; in marketing, volume is a function of costs." Explain.
8. Are the following expenses properly classified as marketing or production costs? Does the nature of the company or the nature of the product influence your decision?

   a. Credit
   b. Shipping
   c. Packaging
   d. Labeling

   e. Repair service
   f. Styling and designing
   g. Engineering
   h. Inventory control

9. What is an unprofitable sale? Explain carefully, keeping in mind the various kinds of costs such as total, marginal, average, etc. Should a company ever intentionally accept unprofitable business? Explain.
10. A national manufacturer of luggage and other leather products, such as briefcases, wallets, attache cases, and pocket notebooks, employs 30 salespeople. Each salesperson has a particular territory, and each one sells the entire group of products. The company calls directly on department stores and specialty luggage stores. The marketing department wishes to make a territorial cost analysis. What bases do you recommend they use for allocating each of the following costs?

   a. Salespeople's salaries
   b. Salespeople's commissions paid on net sales
   c. Sales training expenses
   d. Newspaper advertising
   e. National magazine advertising
   f. Marketing research
   g. Shipping
   h. Billing
   i. Manager of the sales force and his office expenses
   j. Marketing manager's salary and office expenses
11. Of what value is an analysis of ledger expenses? What are some marketing policies which might be based on this type of analysis?
12. "Firms should discontinue handling losing products." Discuss.
13. Do you agree with the following statements?
   a. "Customers whose annual purchases are large never present a small-order problem."
   b. "Small-order problems are always created by small-annual-volume customers."
14. Should a company discontinue selling to an unprofitable customer?

CONSUMERISM AND SOCIALLY ORIENTED MARKETING

In the first two chapters of this book we introduced the broader, societal dimension of marketing, and we examined briefly the role of marketing in the total economy. For the most part, however, we have used throughout the book a micro approach and a managerial orientation as we studied the problems facing an individual producer or middleman in the management of his marketing activities. Now in these two concluding chapters, once again we will step back and take a look at marketing from a broader societal perspective.

In the 1970s there is clearly emerging a social orientation in marketing which both broadens and complements managerial marketing. Since the 1960s our socio-economic goals and cultural values have been changing, thus leading to consumer discontent with the then-existing system. This discontent—labeled "consumerism"—in turn has led to a more socially oriented system of marketing (called "social marketing"). Now social marketing is resulting in management's awareness of its broadening social and ethical responsibilities.

CONSUMERISM

Before we consider the forces leading to consumerism, and the government and business responses to this phenomenon, let's first explain what consumerism means.

MEANING AND SCOPE OF CONSUMERISM

If social upheaval is too strong a term to describe consumerism, then at least it is a social movement—a social "happening"—of the 1960s and 1970s. Furthermore, this phenomenon shows every indication of growing stronger, rather than abating, in the years ahead.

Some definitions. We may define *consumerism* as the actions of individuals and organizations (consumer, government, and business) in response to consumers' dissatisfactions arising in exchange relationships. Consumerism is (1) a protest against perceived business injustices and (2) the efforts to remedy those injustices.[1]

In exchange relationships between buyers and sellers, the feeling clearly exists on the part of consumers that the balance of power lies with the sellers. Consumerism is an expression of this opinion and an attempt to achieve a more equal balance in the power of buyers and sellers.[2] In this context, consumerism may be seen as part of a more general concern for the quality of the environment, the rights of individuals, protection of privacy, the state of the economy, the impersonality of big business and big government, and other related social and economic issues.

Scope of consumerism. The accepted scope of consumerism today broadly envelopes three areas of consumer dissatisfaction and remedial efforts. The original, and still dominant, focus of consumerism involves the discontent generated in direct buyer-seller exchange relationships between consumers and business firms, especially in their marketing activities. Marketing is singled out as the main target of consumer discontent with business, because marketing is that part of a company's total program which is closest to the consumer, is most visible to him, and is the easiest for him to contact.

In the second of our perspectives on consumerism, we recognize that consumerism is *not* limited to discontent with business alone. Remembering the term "exchange relationship" in our prior definition of consumerism, we now see that

---

1 For a sample of other discussions of consumerism—its meaning, causes, actions, and prospects, see David W. Cravens and Gerald E. Hills, "Consumerism: A Perspective for Business," *Business Horizons*, August, 1970, pp. 21-28; Rom J. Markin, "Consumerism: Militant Consumer Behavior: A Social and Behavioral Analysis, "*Business and Society, Fall, 1971, pp. 5-17;* Robert O. Herrmann, "Consumerism: Its Goals, Organizations and Future." *Journal of Marketing*, October, 1970, pp. 55-60; Richard H. Buskirk and James T. Rothe, "Consumerism—An Interpretation," *Journal of Marketing*, October, 1970, pp. 61-65; John F. Willenborg, "The Emergence of Consumerism as a Social Force," *Business and Economic Review*, December, 1971, pp. 2-6; Boris W. Becker, "Consumerism: A Challenge or a Threat?" *Journal of Retailing*, Summer, 1972, pp. 16-28; and Philip Kotler, "What Consumerism Means for Marketers," *Harvard Business Review*, May-June, 1972, pp. 48-57.

For two good collections of articles on consumerism, see David A. Aaker and George S. Day (eds.), *Consumerism, Search for the Consumer Interest*, 2d ed., The Free Press, New York, 1974; and William T. Kelley (ed.), *New Consumerism*, Grid, Inc., Columbus, Ohio, 1973. A Canadian perspective on the growth of the consumer movement is contained in: David S. R. Leighton, "Consumerism in Canada," in Donald N. Thompson and David S. R. Leighton (eds.), *Canadian Marketing: Problems and Prospects.* Toronto: Wiley Publishers, 1973, pp. 3-12.

2 For the notion that both consumerism and environmentalism are on the brink of acquiring social power, see Charles G. Leathers, *"New Dimensions of Countervailing Power:* Consumerism and Environmentalism," *MSU Business Topics*, Winter, 1972, pp. 64-72.

consumerism is concerned with protecting consumers from *all* organizations with which there is an exchange relationship.[3] (Italics added.) Therefore, consumerism (dissatisfactions and remedial effort) may arise from a consumer's relations with such diverse organizations as hospitals, schools, athletic clubs, or government agencies (police department, trash collectors, tax assessors, street maintenance department, etc.). This broader concept of consumerism is in line with our societal definition of marketing (recall Chapter 1), where we recognized that the essence of marketing is an exchange transaction in any field of interpersonal endeavor, not just business alone.

Today the dimensions of consumerism have been expanded even further to include environmental matters affecting our quality of life. In this context consumerism is part of the broader social and political discontent of an activist generation. Perhaps basically consumerism falls in the same category as various group protests against a series of social crises such as "inadequate educational systems, hardcore unemployment, hazardous pollution of natural resources, antiquated transportation, shameful housing, insufficient and ineffective public facilities, lack of equal opportunity for all, and a highly dangerous failure of communication between young and old, black and white."[4] That is, people see things which they feel are wrong, and they are vocal and even active as they seek to change the situation.

The unusual feature of this third phase of consumerism is that we are dealing with an *indirect* impact on one social unit (person, business, etc.) stemming from an exchange relationship between two other people or organizations.[5] Consumer Jones buys steel from company A. But in producing the steel for that exchange, the mill pollutes the river used by Consumer Smith for fishing and swimming, so Smith protests. Or, one group of consumers buy drinks in throwaway containers and then litter the highway with them, thus reducing the quality of life for another group who enjoy driving through a litter-free countryside.

In other words, the exchange between two people or groups creates a problem for a third group. This problem situation is intensified by the fact that individuals have very little incentive to change their behavior, because the action of a single buyer or seller will have no observable impact on the environment. One person using a litter bag in his car, one firm hiring disadvantaged workers, one advertiser removing billboards, or one group using a car pool—each will have no noticeable effect on our total environment or quality of life. To get the concerted action on the part of enough individuals to produce the desired environmental change typically requires government action.

Consumerism yesterday and today. Consumerism really is not a new phenomenon. In the early 1900s and again in the 1930s there was a "consumer movement," in which efforts were made to protect the consumer from harmful products and from false and misleading advertising. Several laws were passed in connection with this movement.

There are three significant differences, however, between the earlier movements and that of today. First, the socioeconomic settings are vastly different. In the 1930s

---

3 Aaker and Day, *op. cit.*, p. xvii.

4 David Rockefeller, president of New York's Chase Manhattan Bank, as quoted in "The War that Business Must Win," *Business Week*, Nov. 1, 1969, p. 63.

5 Aaker and Day, *op. cit.*, pp. xv, xx.

there was a depression, incomes were very low, and we did not talk of an economy of abundance. Today's consumerism arose within an environment of high incomes, lower unemployment, and subsistence needs largely filled. It is an unfortunate paradox that, on the one hand, our advanced technology can provide us with so many mechanical marvels but that, on the other, it is the very complexity of these advancements which often creates service and quality-control problems. In a way, we are spoiled. We demand high levels of performance and are critical of imperfections, and yet the average level of performance is still far above what it was, say 10 or 20 years ago. In the same vein, on the one hand our high level of affluence enables us to buy products which were impossible to obtain with incomes of 30 or 40 years ago, and yet on the other hand, this very same affluence makes us choosier about what we buy and quicker to complain about these products when they do not perform as expected.

The second differentiating feature is the nature and purpose of the legislation related to the two consumer movements. In the 1930s the guiding political philosophy was to keep everyone in business and to protect small businesspeople from the giant companies, especially the corporate chain-store organizations. Legislative emphasis was placed primarily upon the protection of competition, and consumer protection (when there was any) occurred as a buy-product. (There were some exceptions—the Food and Drugs Act and various labeling laws, for example.) In today's political atmosphere the goal of consumer legislation is quite different—the laws first and foremost are intended to protect the consumer.

The third distinguishing aspect of today's consumerism is that it is much more likely to continue and to grow, because it has generated an institutional structure to support it. Not only have consumer-oriented laws been passed, but government agencies have been established at the federal, provincial, and local levels to administer these laws and to generally represent and protect consumer interests.

CONDITIONS LEADING TO CONSUMERISM

One may wonder why consumerism happened to occur in the 1960s when the factors of social and economic discontent (pollution, unsafe products, criticisms of advertising, urban decay, low-income consumers, etc.) had been with us for some time previously. In view of the cultural and economic changes taking place, a new consumer movement was inevitable—the time was ripe. It just so happened that a whole series of inflammable issues converged in the mid-1960s to touch off a real "social conflagration"—namely, consumerism.

Broad cultural changes. Four broad cultural changes have occurred in North America during the 1960s and early 1970s to provide a setting which was appropriate for the growth of the consumerism movement. The first was a dramatic *shift in the social and economic goals of consumers.* In the decades preceding the mid-1960s, consumers were primarily concerned with building an affluent society, a society of abundance. Following a number of years during the Depression and the Second World War, when consumers had to "do without," the 1950s and early 1960s were devoted to improving the consumer's material standard of living. The emphasis was on acquiring—consumers became very "things-oriented."

Having reached these material goals, we as consumers have begun to raise some serious questions concerning our materialistic society. Firstly, are the material things what we *really* want, and secondly, are the material things worth the price we are paying for them in terms of pollution, depleted natural resources, disadvantaged consumer groups in the midst of plenty, etc.?

Since the mid-1960s, our goals have been changing. Today we are seeking broader societal goals. We are concerned more with our physical environment and the quality of our life. We worry more about a *qualitative* standard of life, rather than a *quantative* material standard of living. Our orientation is shifting from things to people.

This change in goals can be viewed in terms of a hierarchy of human needs. After a person satisfies his subsistence needs, he moves up a hierarchy to social needs, and then on to self-esteem and self-fulfillment needs (Maslow's theory of a hierarchy of human needs). With some notable exceptions, consumers have achieved a measure of affluence and we have developed our product technology to an advanced stage. It is a natural evolution now to turn from individualistic, materialistic goals to social, quality-of-life goals. With their materialistic needs more or less taken for granted, consumers have time to be sensitive to social and environmental needs.[6]

The second broad change—a corollary of the first—is that we are *entering a more advanced stage of cultural-economic development.* One theory of economic growth holds that there are three observable stages of development: First a subsistence stage featuring agriculture, fishing, and hunting, then a secondary stage emphasizing manufacturing and product acquisition, and finally a tertiary stage where services (trade, education, transportation, government fields, communication, etc.) are paramount.[7] We are moving into the third stage. In this stage people are more willing to take the time, money, and effort to be concerned about other people and their physical environment. Manufacturing industries tend to decline in relative importance, and service-oriented industries (communication, knowledge, government) become more important. As a result, the balance of power in society tends to shift toward consumers, because service industries are a more people-type operation than are manufacturing industries.

The third cultural change underlying consumerism is the *active role of young people.* As as group, young people have probably always tended to be more idealistic and humanistic than older age groups, or at least it has seemed that way on the surface. And certainly the under-30 group in the 1960s was no exception. Compared with previous generations of young adults, however, today's young people definitely are different in that they are better educated, more articulate, and more inclined (less afraid) to speak out and take action.

The fourth cultural development has been the *growing visibility of, and concern for, environmental problem situations.* Canadians are gradually gaining some appreciation for the unique problems of consumers in the North and in the big cities, of low-income consumers, and of Native people and the aged. In terms of the natural environment, we are no longer willing to tolerate air and water pollution in the name of industry.

Consumer discontents and frustrations.[8] As we continue to trace the rise of consumerism, we shall use the analagous situation of building and lighting a fire.

---

6 For more on how the shift in consumer priorities and goals has invalidated products and procedures of the past, see W. Thomas Anderson, Jr., Louis K. Sharpe, and Robert J. Boewadt, "The Environmental Role for Marketing," *MSU Business Topics,* Summer, 1972, pp. 66-72.

7 Colin Clark, *The Conditions of Economic Progress,* 3d ed., Macmillan & Co., Ltd., London, 1957, p. 491.

8 The organizational structure in this and the next section is adapted from Philip Kotler, "What Consumerism Means for Marketers," *Harvard Business Review,* May-June, 1972, pp. 51-52.

Into the cultural setting just described came a series of highly inflammable issues which generated much consumer discontent and frustration. *Economic discontent* has been fostered by steadily rising inflation rates. *Social discontent* has been linked to the growing frustration on the part of certain groups of consumers and to general discontent with the performance of business in the marketplace. *Ecological discontent* was generated by hazardous pollution, traffic congestion, overcrowded cities, etc. *Political discontent* stemmed from the belief that political, legislative, and other governmental institutions were either unresponsive to consumer needs or unequipped to handle them.

In the business area, *discontent with the marketing system* was particularly strong and widespread. The marketing conditions which have fostered modern-day consumerism possibly can be summed up in this single observation: Consumers are frustrated, dissatisfied, and indignant because of unfulfilled promises, unrealized expectations, and unstated dangers in the products and services they have purchased. And nobody seemed willing to listen to the complaints or to do anything about them.

In the following section are presented a number of consumer complaints against marketing. These have been organized to parallel four basic consumer rights.

Right to safety: unsafe products; unstated dangers in products; unrealized expectations regarding product performance; inadequate repair service.

A consumer can't see, smell, touch, or taste the radiation emanating from his television set or the pesticide residue in his food. Power lawn mowers have injured countless people; dangerous toys and unsafe tires have been sold. Much attention has been directed to the benefits of contraceptive pills and some wonder drugs, but the advertising programs have had little to say about possible side effects of using these products. It was on this point of dangerous products that today's consumerism was launched when Ralph Nader started his crusade to increase the safety of automobiles.

While not directly related to product safety, a major product complaint is poor product quality backed up by confusing and worthless warranties. Moreover, consumers too often are led to expect higher performance levels than the product delivers. Parts fall off cars, zippers jam, meat products are adulterated, commuter trains run late, telephones do not work, wash-and-wear clothing really needs ironing, appliances do not perform as advertised, etc., etc. Probably the number of such occurrences is a small percentage of total units sold. Nevertheless, these occurrences are sufficiently frequent to arouse consumer wrath. Related to the problem of product quality is the poor repair service provided by many manufacturers and middlemen.

Right to be informed: inadequate and misleading information; deceptive advertising; deceptive packaging; misleading warranties; insufficient information on product contents, operating instructions, or care of product; deceptive personal selling tactics; deceptive pricing, deceptive credit terms.

Right to choose: confusing assortment of products, brands, and package sizes; lack of real competition; collusion among business firms; prices are fixed among "competing" sellers.

Right to be heard: business firms unresponsive to consumers' grievances; impersonal attitude in selling; we can't get past the computer and deal with real people.

The president of the Grocery Manufacturers of America observed: "The trend to self-service and super stores brought the consumer great dollar savings, but it also left her with no one to talk to about the weather, no one who could advise her on a product choice, and no one who would take responsibility if the product failed. The gulf between the consumer and the product manufacturer is even wider."[9] Did you ever try to get someone to listen to you when you want a company to correct the mistakes in a charge account messed up by a computerized accounting system, or when you want someone to straighten out an error in order filling and shipping?

Lighting the fires of consumerism. During the 1960s there was a growing belief—expressed in the writings of social critics, in some governmental activity, and in the efforts of consumer educational organizations—that something should, and could, be done to remedy the causes of consumer dissatisfaction. Developments in the field of consumerism in Canada closely paralleled similar developments in the United States. In both countries, the growing mass of consumer issues was ignited by a number of developments of the mid-1960s. The first of these developments centered around Ralph Nader, and General Motors' unsuccessful attempt to investigate and discredit him followed by Nader's successful attack on the unsafe aspects of GM's Corvair automobile. In Canada, the Federal Government provided the Economic Council of Canada with an assignment in 1966 to study and advise the government on several topics with respect to the Canadian economy, including such questions as consumer affairs, competition policy, and policy concerning trademarks, patents, copyrights, and industrial property. Also in this country, consumers, growing tired of rising food prices, began to boycott a number of food stores during the Fall of 1966. Such developments lent urgency to the study being conducted by the Economic Council of Canada, and in July, 1967 the Council presented its interim report on consumer affairs. One key recommendation of the Council was that a single organization be responsible for coordination of research and information activities, representation of the consumer interest, and the administration of a number of laws affecting both trade and financial matters.

In December, 1967, the Federal Government established the Department of Consumer and Corporate Affairs. Canada was the second country (after Norway) to appoint an individual of cabinet rank with the specific task of representing the consumer interest at the highest levels of government. This establishment of the Department of Consumer and Corporate Affairs marked the beginning of a new federal government thrust, administered by a growing consumer bureaucracy and resulting in a flood of revised and new legislation.[10]

Once lit, the fires of consumerism burned brightly with fuel from several sources. Mass media gave front-page and prime-time coverage to the activities of consumer advocates. Politicians in droves got on the consumer bandwagon. The social movement became increasingly institutionalized as new and existing organizations moved in the direction of consumer protection. Businesspeople inadvertently were a big help to consumerism, because so many of them ignored the movement or actively resisted it. In the early stages even the provincial and federal legislatures seemed slow to respond to expressed needs of the consumers.

ACTION RESPONSES TO CONSUMER DISCONTENT

Significant action-oriented efforts to remedy the conditions leading to consu-

---

9 "The U.S.'s Toughest Customer," *Time,* Dec. 12, 1969, p. 89.

10 Leighton, *op. cit.,* p. 7.

merism have come from the consumers themselves, from governmental activities, and from business organizations. The response from each of these three groups has, of course, been quite different, because of the differences in their attitudes and perceptions about consumerism.

Responses of consumers and consumer organizations. Consumers have reacted in a variety of ways to vent their frustrations and to correct what they consider to be injustices. These responses have been as individuals and in organized groups. They have ranged from refusing to buy a product or to shop at a certain store, to the writing of letters to Members of Parliament and to the local media. Many consumers are more active politically than ever before. They support consumer-oriented candidates. They write letters to editors, government officials, and business executives.

Consumers are becoming increasingly, and better, organized in their social and economic protests. In Canada, the major consumer organization is the Consumers' Association of Canada. This association had its origins in 1947 and its membership today numbers more than 100,000. The major objectives of the CAC involve representing the consumer viewpoint to governments. In recent years many other organizations such as church groups, labor unions, and student groups have become involved in consumer issues, whereas in previous years their efforts were in quite different directions.

While consumers have shown themselves to be much more interested today in becoming involved in consumer issues, it is not clear that all consumers have become so interested. A recent study has shown that consumers who join consumer organizations and who become involved in consumer issues tend to be non-representative of consumers in general. For the most part the consumer activists come from a higher social stratum, tend to be better educated, have higher incomes, and tend to be more cosmopolitan in their outlook on life.[11] Such results suggest that a large mass of consumers have been considerably slower in adopting a consumerist viewpoint. There can be no denying, however, that consumers in general are far more active than they have ever been before and the results of this activism are quite obvious in the amount of legislation which has been passed in recent years and in the growing strength of consumer organizations in this country.

Consumers are simply too heterogeneous a group to generate much uniform action. Conflicts and contradictions are bound to occur. We want clean air and no traffic congestion, but we also want unlimited use of our own auto. We want clean water, but we do not want to close the local factory and lose its jobs. Through all the heterogeneity, nevertheless, several common themes do emerge which give direction to the consumer movement, as witness some conclusions from one study:[12]

1. Most consumers recognize and value highly many aspects of the free enterprise system.
2. Many consumers are skeptical about certain business policies and are discontented with specific marketing activities such as advertising.
3. Many people concede that some of the imperfections in the marketing system result from consumer ineptness, carelessness, and apathy.

---

11 James G. Barnes and Jacques C. Bourgeois, "Is the Consumer Activist Really Different? A Profile and Implications for Marketing and Public Policy," in *Proceedings* of the Marketing Division of the Canadian Association of Administrative Sciences, Edmonton, 1975, pp. 325-332.

12 Hiram C. Barksdale and William R. Darden, "Consumer Attitudes toward Marketing and Consumerism," *Journal of Marketing*, October, 1972, pp. 28-35.

4. Respondents think that consumer problems are important and deserve more attention than they now receive.
5. Overwhelming support is voiced for additional government regulation as a means of solving consumer problems. This attitude is expressed by both liberals and conservatives.

Government responses. Consumerism is not likely to fade away; instead, it probably will grow stronger in the coming years. The main reason for this forecast is that today it is politically popular to support consumers. Politicians may have generally been unresponsive to consumer needs in the years prior to the mid-1960s. Since then, however, consumer-oriented activity at both the federal and provincial levels has been at an unprecedented rate. All the provinces and many cities have created some kind of office for consumer affairs. Provisions now exist in some provinces whereby a *group* of consumers allegedly injured in substantially the same manner can file a "class-action" suit against one firm or a group of companies. This provision is in response to the feeling that poor or even middle-class consumers, acting individually, do not have anything resembling an equal chance for justice in a court suit against a large business firm.

The scope of governmental activity in consumerism covers three areas—government support, legislation, and an expanded role for government regulatory agencies.

Government support. Beginning with the report of the Economic Council of Canada in 1967 and continuing through the years since then, the federal and provincial governments have provided strong and explicit support for consumer interests. Many legislative measures supporting consumers have been introduced by governments at both the federal and provincial levels. They have proposed new programs, established new agencies, and urged the strengthening of existing programs and agencies closely related to the consumer. The years since 1967 have seen a growing involvement of government in business affairs in the interest of consumers. Many new laws have been passed and programs introduced which restrict the scope of business in their dealings with the consumer. Governments have also given considerable support to consumer organizations such as the Consumers' Association of Canada and have been quite receptive to representations from such groups concerning the need for additional legislation and programs.

Legislation. Since the mid-1960s, federal and provincial legislatures have been passing for the first time laws whose primary purpose is to aid the consumer. In contrast, very often in the past marketing legislation was generally business-oriented, not consumer-oriented. As we have pointed out earlier, often the intent of such legislation was to protect competition or to benefit some segment of business, and any benefit or protection to the consumer occurred in an indirect manner, if it occurred at all. In contrast, recent years have seen the introduction of a large number of pieces of consumer-oriented legislation at both the federal and provincial levels in Canada.

A significant number of these laws are designed to protect the consumer's "right to safety"—especially in situations where the consumer cannot judge for himself the risk involved in the purchase and use of particular products. In Canada, we have such legislation as the Food and Drugs Act, which regulates and controls the manufacture, distribution, and sale of food, drug, and cosmetic products. A very important new piece of legislation in Canada which also protects the consumer's right to safety is the Hazardous Products Act. This law establishes standards for the manufacture of consumer products which are designed for household, garden, personal, recreation, or child use. Regulations under the Hazardous Products Act require that dangerous products be packaged as safely as possible and labeled with clear and adequate warnings. This law also makes provision for the removal of dangerous products from the marketplace.

One controversial area of product safety legislation is the paternalistic type of law that is intended to protect the consumer, whether or not he or she wants that protection. Thus, it is now mandatory to equip automobiles with seat belts and in the Provinces of Ontario and Quebec it is illegal to operate an automobile unless the seats belts are fastened. In effect, somebody else is forcing a consumer to accept what the other person feels is in the consumer's best interests—truly a new and broadening approach to consumer legislation.

Another series of laws and government programs supports the consumer's "right to be informed". These measures help in such areas as reducing the confusion and deception in packaging and labeling, identifying the ingredients and nutritional content in food products, advising consumers of the length of life of certain packaged food products, providing instructions and assistance in the care of various textile products, and determining the true rate of interest.

At the federal level, government has passed in recent years a number of pieces of legislation which are designed to provide consumers with more information. Possibly the most important of these is the Consumer Packaging and Labelling Act, which regulates the packaging, labeling, sale, and advertising of pre-packaged products. The Textile Labelling Act requires manufacturers of textile products to place labels on most articles made from fabrics. These labels must name the fibers, show the amount of each fiber in the product by percentage, and identify the dealer for whom or by whom the article was made. In addition, federal government programs assist the consumer in providing information on the care of textile products. For example, most textile products sold in Canada today carry care labels which provide instructions on the washing and ironing of textile products. Similarly, the Canada Standard Sizes program for children's clothing insures that all children's clothing manufactured in Canada by participating manufacturers is sized in a standard manner so that consumers can feel confident that sizes are standard across manufacturers.

At the provincial level, a number of programs exist which provide information to consumers. For example, all provinces have passed consumer protection legislation which requires that all consumer lending agencies and retail stores provide consumers with information concerning the true rate of interest that they are paying on borrowed money and on purchases made on credit.

Also at the provincial level there has been considerable interest in recent years in the passage of new consumer-oriented legislation. At the present time all provinces, for example, have on their books a number of laws which offer protection to the consumer. Each province has passed a general Consumer Protection Act, which deals primarily with the granting of credit. All provinces also have legislation which provides for a "cooling off" period during which the purchaser of goods or services in a door-to-door sale may cancel the contract, return any merchandise, and obtain a full refund. In addition, most provinces have legislation which provides for the disposal of unsolicited goods and credit cards received through the mail. And all provinces also administer legislation which regulates particular industries such as collection agencies, automobile dealerships and insurance agents.

The consumer is also protected at both the federal and provincial levels in Canada in the area of misleading and dishonest advertising. The federal Combines Investigation Act contains a number of provisions dealing with misleading advertising and these have been discussed in Chapter 24. Protection is also offered certain special interest consumer groups in a number of areas. For example, the Province of Quebec has recently passed a children's advertising code which regulates the advertising of products directed to the children's market.

A very recent development at the provincial level in Canada involves the passage of legislation in a number of provinces designed to protect the consumer against certain business practices which are not covered under existing legislation. This relatively new form of consumer law generally falls under the term "trade practices legislation," since it tends to prohibit certain unfair or deceptive trade practices.[13] Such legislation has recently been passed by the governments of Ontario, Alberta, and British Columbia, and is being planned in at least three other provinces. The passage of such trade practices legislation should provide additional protection for Canadian consumers in that these laws are designed to protect consumers against such illegal practices as advertising which claims that goods are new if in fact they have been reconditioned; representations on the part of service companies, that service, parts, replacement or repairs are needed if in fact this is not so; the sale of products at grossly excessive prices; practices which tend to take advantage of consumers who are unable to protect their own interests because of physical infirmity, ignorance, illiteracy, inability to understand the language of an agreement, or similar factors; and trade practices which tend to subject consumers to undue pressures to enter into the transaction.

These new trade practices laws have broken new ground in a number of areas. For example, the Alberta legislation provides, for the first time in Canada, for class action suits which may be brought against a supplier on behalf of all wronged consumers. The Alberta law also provides that a court may order corrective advertising by a supplier who has been convicted of an unfair trade practice, and further provides that the court may issue an interim injunction which restrains the company from carrying on certain acts or practices while court action is pending.

Effectiveness of government action. How effective have governmental efforts been in improving the consumer's position? The consumers' answer might start with that cigarette slogan, "You've come a long way, baby," and then would add, "but you still have a long way to go." Just as consumerism started with unrealized expectations from *business* performance, now the consumer is experiencing unrealized expectations from *government's* performance. Consumers expected much from the laws covering truth in packaging, credit practices, reduction of pollution, product safety, and many other topics. The results from these laws, however, have often been disappointing to consumer groups. Water and air pollution remain high and the energy crisis generated efforts to postpone or weaken the pollution-reduction legislation. Some consumer groups would appear to be of the opinion that government regulations pertaining to misleading advertising, hazardous products, and the establishment of quality standards, for example, have not gone far enough.[14]

---

13 Jacob S. Ziegel, "The New Trade Practices Legislation," *Canadian Consumer*, February, 1975, pp. 18-20.

14 See for example: James G. Barnes, "Consumer Protection Programs as Functional Aids to Risk Handling," working paper 75-6, School of Business, Queen's University at Kingston, 1975.

Certainly the consumers' position has been greatly improved, but the pace of improvement is still too slow to satisfy many consumer advocates. However, even with this criticism, consumers still have decidedly more confidence in government-enforced action than in voluntary business efforts. Consumers want more, not less, government intervention in the marketplace, according to various opinion polls and research studies.

Several factors account for the government's performance level being lower than consumers expected. One is that business lobbyists still are effective at getting amendments to a bill that will temper a strong antibusiness bias. A corollary factor is that compromise often is necessary to get any kind of consumer legislation passed. Often the strong consumer advocates fail to see all the long-run problems and implications contained in their requests. Then there are the interest conflicts within the body of consumers. They want the Department of the Environment to fight air pollution and they express concern over the depletion of energy resources, for example, yet they complain to their Members of Parliament when the government proposes an increased tax on the purchase of full-size automobiles which are heavy users of gasoline.

On balance it is becoming apparent that legislation and government agencies are not the total answer to consumer complaints about business and social conditions. While governmental action has helped considerably, it is not a cure-all. So let's see how business has responded to consumer discontent.

Business responses. As responses to consumerism, we know that business apathy, resistance, or token efforts simply increase the probability of more government regulation. It is as simple as this today—consumerism is a sufficiently entrenched, vocal, and well-organized force in the market place so that consumer complaints will be answered. The only question is: Answered by whom?—business or government? If business cannot or will not do the job, the only alternative is additional government intervention.

"The reaction of many businessmen who have been caught by consumerism, is like good old Charlie Brown's bafflement when his team lost its 43rd consecutive game: 'How can we lose when we're so sincere?' Good intentions don't impress anyone. The public wants good intentions translated into effective action, and they're going to get it, one way or another."

Source: Elisha Gray II, chairman of Whirlpool Corporation, as quoted in *Newsweek,* July 26, 1971, p. 44.

Yet, unfortunately, studies show that the business response "has tended to be superficial, negative, unplanned, and uncoordinated—even among the largest companies in the country.[15] These reactions are reflected in remarks such as, "Consumerism has nothing to do with us because we are industrial manufacturers," or "This consumerism is nothing new and anyway it doesn't apply to us because we've always been customer-oriented." These attitudes, held by a wide segment of business executives, simply overlook the facts that (1) the new consumerism is rooted in changing consumer goals, attitudes, and values, and (2) basic changes are occurring in the marketing environment as result of legislation, more powerful gov-

---

15 This paragraph is adapted from Frederick E. Webster, Jr., "Does Business Misunderstand Consumerism?" *Harvard Business Review,* September-October, 1973, pp. 89-97, especially pp. 89-92.

ernment involvement and the growing legitimacy earned by consumer advocates. Failure to understand the nature and scope of consumerism has the potential to cost industry untold sums of money (1) in actions forced by the government and (2) in lost sales to disenchanted customers.

Positive responses of individual firms. The above gloomy picture is offset some-what by a growing executive awareness of the dangers accompanying a negative response to consumerism. Consequently, we are seeing an increasing number of programs that are positive and substantive responses to consumer needs and prob-lems. Consumerism is forcing businesspeople to reexamine their social roles and to look at problems they previously ignored.

Perceptive businesspeople now see that the *long-run* net results from consu-merism can be social and economic gains for the consumers and businesspeople alike.[16] First, better-informed consumers normally are more efficient in their pur-chasing, and thus able to buy more goods and services in total. Second, if manufac-turers have to absorb the costs of reducing the pollution caused by their products, then the prices of these goods will rise and the demand will shift to low social-cost goods. This will mean lower government expenditures—and lower tax rates—to clean up the environment. Third, everybody wins when consumerism results in fewer unsafe products and thus more satisfied and healthy consumers. Finally, perhaps the most promising benefits to businesspeople are the unlimited market opportunities awaiting (1) the marketers of new products and services to satisfy en-vironmental demands and (2) the firms which reorient their marketing programs to reach the environmentally and socially conscious consumers.

More specifically in the short run, individual firms have developed responses to consumerism which relate to five areas in marketing. Some of these are voluntary efforts, and others are in response to legislation or rules set down by government departments. The first group of actions involves *better communication with consumers.* Many of the consumers' complaints can be summed up as failure to recognize the consumers' "right to be heard." Consumers often are frustrated simply because they cannot get anyone in the huge, impersonal, remote corporation to listen to them when they need some information, the product needs repairing, or some-thing else goes wrong. The individual consumer needs to be able to communicate with, and be answered by, a company.[17]

Many firms have responded to this need in a variety of ways. Appliance and in-surance companies have established 24-hour direct telephone lines which enable customers to call free of charge from anywhere in the country in order to register a complaint, ask about service, or get other information about products. Many com-panies, especially supermarket chains, have established consumer affairs officers whose responsibility it is to deal with customers, to answer their questions and to listen to and act upon their complaints. Most responsive companies have generally speeded up and otherwise improved their ability to respond to consumers' written inquiries or complaints.

In response to one of the major areas of consumer criticism, many companies today are generating *more and better information for consumers.* Point-of-sale informa-tion has been improved by a number of firms. Manufacturers are publishing in-

---

16 These points are developed in Kotler, *op. cit.,* pp. 53, 55.

17 See William G. Nickels and Noel B. Zabriskie, "Corporate Responsiveness and the Marketing Corre-spondence Function," *MSU Business Topics,* Summer, 1973, pp. 53-58.

structional booklets on the use and care of their products. Labeling is more informative than in the past in many instances. Several supermarkets, even where not required to do so by law, have instituted unit pricing. The ads run by several firms carry far more informational-type copy than in the past. One major automobile manufacturer produced a booklet containing advice on how to purchase a used car. Most companies in the energy industry, including the petroleum and gas companies and the electrical utilities, have published pamphlets containing information on how to insulate one's home in order to save on fuel bills.

In the area of *product improvements,* companies have introduced many product-safety changes and pollution-reduction measures. Warranties have been simplified and strengthened. Nutritional elements have been added to some foods, and lead removed from some gasolines. *Advertising* is being more carefully scrutinized than ever before. Many advertisers are extremely cautious in approving agency-prepared ads, in sharp contrast to past procedures for approval. Advertisers are involving their legal departments in the approval process. They are very sensitive to the fact that the Canadian Radio-Television and Telecommunications Commission may reject a commercial or the Advertising Standards Council may find an advertisement objectionable. The advertising industry and the media are doing a much more effective self-regulation job than ever before, especially through the Canadian Advertising Advisory Board and its Advertising Standards Councils.[18] Corporate leaders are working closely with advertising agency executives and the ad-creating people to develop some useful goals and guidelines. Advertisers are urged to "tell it like it is" and to "cool" the type of promotion which leads to exaggerated, and subsequently unrealized, expectations.[19]

Finally, many firms are *putting pressure on offenders or rewarding excellence in compliance.* Allstate Insurance Co. (Sears) offered premium discounts on cars that met certain safety standards. The company also offered discounts on collision insurance on cars that could withstand a 5-mile-per-hour crash into a test barrier without front- or rear-end damage. Some retailers refuse to handle products that are deceptively advertised or priced. Other retailers have rewarded ecologically desirable products with good shelf locations and in-store promotion.

Organizing for effective response. Many firms have made organizational changes to implement their response programs. Most of these moves have been to establish an "ombudsman" position—sometimes a high-level executive and sometimes a separate department of consumer affairs. The responsibilities of this department typically are (1) to serve as a listening post for consumer inquiries and complaints, and to see that they are answered, (2) to represent the consumers' interests when policies and programs are being formulated, and (3) to ensure that the firm maintains the necessary degree of societal orientation in its planning.

The ombudsman position or department must be an independent unit, preferably reporting directly to the chief executive. Placing consumer affairs in the marketing department is ordinarily a mistake, because when profit or competitive

---

18 See: R. E. Oliver, "Canada's Self-Regulation Sets World Model," *Financial Post Report on Advertising,* October 5, 1974, p. A-9; "Manual of General Guidelines for Advertising," Toronto: Canadian Advertising Advisory Board, 1975; and Mel S. Moyer and John C. Banks, "Self-Regulation in the Canadian Advertising Industry: An Analysis of the Advertising Standards Council," paper presented at the Second Triennial Canadian Marketing Workshop, York University, Toronto, May 29, 1975.

19 See Rolph E. Anderson and Marvin A. Jolson, "Consumer Expectations and the Communications Gap," *Business Horizons,* April, 1973, pp. 11-16.

crises arise, marketing executives too often are short-run oriented and do not place the consumer's interest foremost in their decision making.

A consumer affairs department that cannot act effectively in processing consumers' inquiries and representing consumers' interests in executive councils is probably worse than none at all. If the role of the ombudsman is only cosmetic—if the consumer affairs department is simply a public relations operation, then the company's position further deteriorates. Experience so far shows that consumers' reactions to consumer affairs representatives are mixed. Some programs get high ratings, and others are looked upon simply as "paper consumerism" and "corporate hypocrisy."[20]

Trade-association responses. Many trade associations have moved positively to respond to consumer dissatisfaction. From that position they can play a real leadership role in four basic areas:[21]

1. Coordinating and disseminating research among the association members.
2. Stimulating consumer and dealer education.
3. Developing (a) product standards for safety, quality, and performance, and (b) standards for advertising and promotion.
4. Establishing a system for processing consumer complaints.

Many trade associations have been active in one or more of the above areas. Of course, trade associations have not neglected the fact that their main purpose is to represent the interests of their members. Most large associations maintain offices in Ottawa, from which they interact with politicians and government officials in order to ensure that their viewpoint is understood. One trade association which represents its members' interests through a realization that illegal or unethical business practices lead to negative consumer attitudes toward business in general is the Better Business Bureau. In most cities, Better Business Bureaus have been operating for many years and they have generally met with the support of consumer groups. Where a Bureau member violates what may be acceptable business practices, the Bureau will take steps to encourage that member to cease such unacceptable practices. Where a member refuses, the Bureau can take more serious steps such as recommending to local media that advertising from the offending company no longer be accepted. Better Business Bureaus generally have little power to influence the activities of companies which are not members of the Bureau, although most Better Business Bureau offices will provide consumers with information on companies which are engaging in questionable business practices.

Limitations to business self-regulation.[22] Self-regulation is an obvious alternative to government regulation, and just as obviously, it is an alternative preferred by businesspeople. Generally speaking, unfortunately, the efforts at self-regulation have not been too successful, at least not in the eyes of consumer advocates. Many

---

20 "More Talk than Action on Consumer Complaints," *Business Week*, May 9, 1973, pp. 66. For an in-depth look at the consumer affairs executive, see Milton L. Blum, John B. Stewart, and Edward W. Wheatley, "Consumer Affairs: Viability of the Corporate Response," *Journal of Marketing*, April, 1974, pp. 13-19.

21 David A. Aaker and George S. Day, "Corporate Responses to Consumerism Pressures," *Harvard Business Review*, November-December, 1972, pp. 120-121.

22 For a fine analysis of the topic, see Louis L. Stern, "Consumer Protection via Self-Regulation," *Journal of Marketing*, July, 1971, pp. 47-53.

of the business responses already noted have come only as a result of government prodding by law or regulatory agency.

If an industry depends upon the *voluntary* compliance of its members toward meeting industry standards, the results are likely to be ineffective. For self-regulation to have any real chance of success, an industry must be able to *force* its members to comply with the industry standards. The problem is, however, that any enforcement measure strong enough to be effective (a boycott against an offender, for example), may be considered a violation of the restrictive trade practices provisions of the Combines Investigation Act. One reasonable solution to this problem might involve some form of joint business-government cooperation in the formulation of regulations. For example, the Canadian Code of Advertising Standards was formulated following consumer-government-industry consultation and is administered by the Advertising Standards Council. Similarly, this Council administers the Broadcast Code for Advertising to Children on behalf of the Canadian Association of Broadcasters. These and other codes of advertising standards apparently have the support of the federal government, since the government has not yet moved to impose legal regulations in those areas covered by the codes.

Two additional situations limit the effectiveness of self-regulation. The first is that often it is difficult to get a consensus among industry members regarding an acceptable set of product or promotion standards. The net result is that the industry settles for the least common denominator as the level for its standards. A second limitation is that executives often fail to see anything wrong in various business practices in their industry—practices which are highly criticized by outside observers. Thus the cause of self-regulation suffers when industry members openly condone questionable practices such as distorting a competitor's test market, deceptively advertising price savings "up to" some amount, unsubstantiated ad claims, deceptive consumer contests, etc.

Effective self-regulation by business can serve as a countervailing force in relation to consumer advocates and governmental action in setting and enforcing industry standards. For business to be effective in this respect, however, means that it must generate a much higher confidence level among the consumers than presently is the case.

Conclusion. It should be quite clear by now that consumerism is here to stay, and the negative business responses of the past are totally inadequate. No longer can business executives argue that a little puffery in advertising, a few bad products, a few crooks in marketing, and a little pollution here and there is really a small price to pay for the marketing system which has generated an affluent society in an economy of abundance.

Instead, business needs to develop strong, positive programs that will serve as a satisfactory response to consumerism.[23] These programs must generate (1) adequate consumer information, (2) safe products whose performance meets advertised expectations, (3) consumer satisfaction, and (4) a socially desirable environment. Striving for these goals may mean that some businesses will suffer *short-run*

---

23 For the contention that to formulate appropriate marketing policies we need a better understanding of the relationship between consumerism and consumer behavior, see Jerome E. Scott and Lawrence M. Lamont, "Consumerism: A Theoretical Framework for Analysis," in B. W. Becker and H. Becker (eds), *1972 Combined Proceedings,* American Marketing Association, Chicago, 1973, pp. 241-248; also see Cravens and Hills, "Consumerism: A Perspective for Business," *op. cit.;* and W. Heward Grafftey, "Two New Elements in Consumerism," *Canadian Business,* June 1974, pp. 60-61.

losses. Hopefully any opposition arising from these loss situations will not deter business from *(a)* its *long-run* goals of consumer interests, and *(b)* the emerging societal orientation in its marketing programs.

EMERGING SOCIAL ORIENTATION IN MARKETING

Out of consumerism and our changing consumer goals has emerged a new orientation in the practice and study of marketing—it is a social orientation. (This point was discussed briefly in the opening chapter.) This new approach—social marketing—is both a broadening and a logical extension of the managerial systems approach to marketing.[24]

SOCIAL MARKETING AND MANAGERIAL MARKETING

Social marketing is a broadening, but not a replacement, of managerial marketing. In social marketing we still have to develop a marketing program which will plan, price, promote, and distribute products and services to satisfy consumers' wants. But we also must go further and consider the social consequences of this marketing program. In managerial marketing we are concerned with marketing automobiles to people. In social marketing, in addition, we worry about the societal aspects of auto production and marketing—air pollution and traffic congestion, for example.

In managerial marketing the criteria for evaluating success are sales volume, costs, and profits. In social marketing we consider the social benefits and social costs. By means of a "social audit" we conceptually measure social products and the generating of social wealth. It is when the sales and profit criteria conflict with the social criteria that marketing management has a problem for which we somehow must find acceptable compromise solutions.[25]

CONFLICTS IN CONSUMER GOALS

The broadening of both consumer goals and a company's market targets creates some real problems for marketing management. The consumers' shift to societally oriented goals is not proving to be a simple or easy transition, because by no means

---

24 For some perspectives and viewpoints on social marketing—its meaning, the forces underlying it, government and business responses to it, and its relation to a managerial marketing mix—see William Lazer and Eugene J. Kelley, *Social Marketing*, Richard D. Irwin, Inc., Homewood Ill., 1973; and Leonard L. Berry and James S. Hensel (eds.), *Marketing and the Social Environment*, Petrocelli Books, New York, 1973. Also see Laurence P. Feldman, "Social Adaptation: A New Challenge for Marketing," *Journal of Marketing*, July, 1971, pp. 54-60; and W. T. Stanbury, "The Consumer Interest, Economic Welfare and Consumer Research," in *Proceedings* of the Marketing Division of the Canadian Association of Administrative Sciences, Edmonton, 1975, pp. 193-208.

25 For some ideas on developing and applying a set of "social indicators"—i.e., a data base of factors which would measure the social values in a firm's output, see Robert S. Raymond and Elizabeth Richards, "Social Indicators and Business Decisions," *MSU Business Topics*, Autumn, 1971, pp. 42-46; Polia Lerner Hamburger, *Social Indicators—A Marketing Perspective*, American Marketing Association, Chicago, 1974; and D. W. Henderson, *Social Indicators: A Rationale and Research Framework*. Ottawa: Information Canada, 1974.

For some suggestions as to what should be included in a social audit and who should do this job, see George A. Steiner, "Should Business Adopt the Social Audit?" *Conference Board Record*, May, 1972, pp. 7-10; and Raymond A. Bauer and Dan H. Fenn, Jr., "What *is* a Corporate Social Audit?" *Harvard Business Review*, January-February, 1973, pp. 37-48.

THE CHANGING PRIORITIES IN MARKETING EDUCATION

"The marketing graduate of 25 years ago learned, basically, to sell soap. The comparable graduate in recent years has learned to sell soap and to understand computer analyses of the soap market. Today's graduate in a growing number of schools completes a curriculum in which he examines both these areas of marketing. He also learns to evaluate the effect of that 'soap,' and the massive resources committed to its commercial success, on issues which lie beyond the traditional income statement."

Source: Betsy D. Gelb and Richard H. Brien, "Survival and Social Responsibility: Themes for Marketing Education and Management," *Journal of Marketing,* April, 1971, p. 3.

---

have we abandoned our desire for things—we have simply tempered this desire with a special concern.

Here is the difference, possibly oversimplified, between the pre-1960s goals and today's goals. Then, we wanted big cars that would go fast. We paid little attention to the air pollution, traffic congestion, depleting oil resources, polluted streams from mills making steel for autos, etc. Now today we still want autos, but we also want clean air, no traffic jams, clean water, and no dependence on foreign oil resources. Certainly the former goal—autos only—was much easier to achieve, because the element of conflict in goals was largely absent.

As a firm broadens its market targets (the publics it deals with), it becomes more difficult to satisfy them all, because often the goals and values of the different publics are in conflict. One group may want a mill closed because it pollutes the air and water. But another of the target markets wants it kept open because it provides jobs.

In trying to understand this problem of goal-conflict, perhaps a key point to keep in mind is that we are dealing with consumers—human beings—with all of their attendant contradictions, inconsistencies, and self-interests. Thus we criticize business for a lack of consumer information, but we often do not use the information when it is provided. We cry out for safer autos, but given the chance, a large percentage of people do not use their seat belts. We want more energy-generating facilities, but don't build an oil refinery or a power plant in our town. We criticize the rapid growth in federal spending and its contribution to inflation in the economy, yet we complain bitterly if the government decides to reduce spending by eliminating a project or closing an office in our city or province—those are necessary and beneficial. We want social benefits (clean air) until we find out the price we must pay (factory closed or auto use restricted). At that point we may have second thoughts on whether the benefit is worth its price.

Truly, there are no easy answers to the goal-conflict problems. And the situation often is further complicated when the groups involved seem to take an overly simplistic perspective. *However, there has been one significant accomplishment by business.* Today many marketing executives recognize that they have some social problems. Formerly they were concerned only with producing and marketing profitable products, and they never considered the social costs. Now these executives are awakening to the concept of social values, and the need for a societal orientation in their marketing programs.

ETHICAL AND SOCIAL RESPONSIBILITIES OF MARKETING MANAGEMENT

A recurring theme in this chapter has been the broadened perspectives in marketing. Continuing in this vein, we now want to focus on the ethical and social responsibilities of marketing executives, looking at both the conceptual and operational aspects of the subject. In so doing we shall repeat, and perhaps better tie together, some points mentioned earlier in the chapter.[26]

THE CONCEPT OF BUSINESS ETHICS

The dictionary defines "ethics" as the science of moral duty or the science of ideal human character. Ethics are moral principles or practices; they are professional standards of conduct. Thus, to act in an ethical fashion is to conform to some standard of moral behavior.

Importance of long-run viewpoint. At times, the pressures to follow an unethical course of action may seem almost irresistible to a marketing manager. If he feels that his personal interests or the success of his company is at stake, he may revert to the law of survival, and ethical considerations will be forgotten. It is easy to be ethical when no hardship is involved.

A key factor for an executive to remember when considering the ethics of a situation is to take a long-run point of view. He should understand that ethical behavior is not only morally right but, over the long run, also realistically sound. Too many administrators are shortsighted; they do not see the possible backlash from many of their activities. If the buyer was deceived or high-pressured, they seem to think this is unimportant, as long as the sale was made. These executives apparently do not realize that by continuing such practices, they can lose customers, invite public regulation, or both.

Problem of determining ethical standards. It is easy to say that a marketing executive should act in an ethical fashion, but it is far more difficult to put this axiom into practice. Each manager as an individual usually has his own standards of conduct, which he believes to be ethical, and he abides by them in the administration of his duties. It is doubtful that many people, marketing executives or otherwise, consciously engage in unethical practices. That is, most of us believe we are acting ethically *by our own standards*. However, ethical standards are set by a group—by society—and not by the individual. Thus the group evaluates the individual's judgment of what he thinks is ethical.

Now, the problem at this point is that the group (society) lacks commonly accepted standards of behavior. What is considered ethical conduct varies from one country to another, from industry to industry, and from one situation to another. The guidelines of personal conscience are also relative and individual, even among people with a common ethical tradition.

---

26 For an excellent "state of the art" assessment of social responsibility as it relates to marketing, see Thaddeus H. Spratlen, "Marketing: A Social Responsibility," in B. W. Becker and H. Becker (eds.), *1972 Combined Proceedings*, American Marketing Association, Chicago, 1973, pp. 65-75.

WHAT IS SOCIAL RESPONSIBILITY?

A marketing executive has a threefold responsibility—to his company, to his workers, and to his customers. For his company, his job is to provide a satisfactory net profit over the long run. To his employees, his responsibility is to provide a good working environment. For his customers, the executive's job is to maximize their standard of living by marketing want-satisfying goods and services at the lowest reasonable cost. In these relationships the marketing executive typically views any ethical considerations on a person-to-person basis.

The substance of social responsibility is much broader, however. It emphasizes an executive's institutional (company) actions and their effect on the entire social system. Without this broader viewpoint, personal and institutional acts tend to be separated. A marketing executive can lead a model personal life, but can continue to justify his company's pollution of a river because there is no direct personal involvement. To him, river pollution is a public problem to be solved by governmental action. The concept of social responsibility, however, requires him to consider his acts within the framework of the whole social system, and it holds him responsible for the effects these acts may have anywhere in that system:

> When a man's primary frame of reference is himself, he may be counted upon for antisocial behavior whenever his values conflict with those of society. If his values are limited primarily to a certain group or organization, he tends to become a partisan acting for that group. But, if he thinks in terms of a whole system, he begins to build societal values into his actions, even when they are for a certain organization. *This is the essence of social responsibility.* For the manager it means realizing that the business system does not exist alone and that a healthy business system cannot exist within a sick society.[27] [Italics Supplied]

Organizational location for social responsibility. To be effective, any program for social responsibility in a firm must start with top management—the chief executive officer and his board of directors. Unless the program has their wholehearted support in spirit and action, it is likely to be a token, lip-service type of effort.[28] However, the accountability for socially responsible actions also must permeate all executive echelons in a firm. Unfortunately, it does not always happen this way. Top management may have a strong commitment to this responsibility, while at the same time the executives at operational levels may be practising just the opposite. The advertising manager may have approved a price-comparison advertisement which is misleading; a purchasing agent may be pressuring a small supplier in order to get an especially low price; or a salesperson may offer a free trip to Europe to a government official if he will buy an expensive computer system from that salesperson.

REASONS FOR CONCERN ABOUT SOCIAL RESPONSIBILITY

The best reason why a marketing executive should have a high degree of social responsibility is simply that it is the morally right thing to do. We grant that this is an

---

27 Quotation and preceding paragraph from Keith Davis, "Understanding the Social Responsibility Puzzle," *Business Horizons*, Winter, 1967, p. 46.

28 See Kenneth R. Andrews, "Can the Best Corporations Be Made Moral?" *Harvard Business Review*, May-June, 1973, pp. 57-64.

easy reason to conceptualize, but far more difficult to put into operation. Now let's look at four points which have a more pragmatic flavor.[29]

Price of economic freedom and flexibility. Marketing executives must conduct their activities in a socially desirable manner in order to justify the privilege of operating in our relatively free economic system. No worthwhile privilege or freedom comes without a price. Our economic freedoms sometimes have a high price, just as our precious political freedoms do. Moreover, it is very much in management's self-interest to be concerned with social problems. A business cannot remain healthy if its social environment is sick. Also, a concern for the quality of life may very well lead to change, and this change may present opportunities for new business.

Minimize government intervention. When a marketing executive fails to act in a socially responsible manner, society's penalty typically is to restrict his freedom of operation. Indeed, most of the governmental limitations placed on marketing executives' activities throughout the years have been the result of management's failure to live up to its social responsibilities. Moreover, once some form of governmental control is established, it is rarely removed. So the wise course of action would seem to be to fulfill a social responsibility, thus minimizing additional government intervention.

The power-responsibility equation. Perhaps the concept that social power equals social responsibility helps to explain why business executives have a major responsibility to society. Marketing executives do have a great deal of social power as they influence markets and speak out on matters of economic policy. In business, we see many practical applications of the idea of reasonably balanced power and responsibility. Business executives urge labor leaders to be responsible; a management axiom holds that authority and responsibility should be matched. Now, if responsibility arises from power, then we may reason that the avoidance of social responsibility will lead to an erosion of social power. That is "those who do not take responsibility for their power, ultimately shall lose it."[30]

Marketing department represents company. Procter & Gamble put this point nicely in an annual report: "When a Procter & Gamble salesman walks into a customer's place of business—whether he is calling on an individual store or keeping an appointment at the headquarters of a large group of stores—he not only represents Procter & Gamble, but in a very real sense, he is Procter & Gamble." Therefore, as the public sees these people and their activities, so does the public judge the concern.

Ordinarily the public does not meet the production and office workers in a company. Consequently, a firm is rarely judged by the actions of these employee groups. In fact, the marketing department often is blamed for mistakes (such as a defective product or an incorrect bill) made by these other groups simply because

---

29 See Frederick E. Webster, Jr., *Social Aspects of Marketing*, Englewood Cliffs: Prentice-Hall, 1974.

30 Keith Davis, *op. cit.*, p. 49, as cited in Keith Davis and Robert L. Blomstrom, *Business and Its Environment*, McGraw-Hill Book Company, New York, 1966, p. 174. Also see Richard H. Brien, Betsy D. Gelb, and William D. Trammell, "The Challenge to Marketing Dominance: Will Social Responsibility Be Recognized?" *Business Horizons*, February, 1972, pp. 23-30.

the marketing personnel are the only employees who have contact with the public.

BUSINESS IS BEST QUALIFIED TO SOLVE SOCIAL PROBLEMS

In the past, the social responsibility of business executives was generally translated as the way they spent their companies' spare money and their own spare time. Direct dealings with social problems were considered outside the scope of business activity. Now there is the demand that the quality of life become the business of business.[31]

We might ask why business should be given this responsibility—why not the government or various local community groups, for example? (Drucker did note parenthetically that business is not the only institution with this responsibility; the same obligation is laid at the door of the government, educational institutions, labor unions, medical institutions, etc.) The chief executive of a large appliance corporation stated that business can and should be the catalyst to begin social reforms because it has the resources to get things done. That is, it can create jobs, it has the managerial skills to develop programs, and it can work at the local level.[32] A business executive with experience in constructing and marketing a low-income housing project said: "Government has been overly oriented toward *control*—not geared to results and achievement. Community leaders are—all too often—interested in personal power and pressing ideological points at the expense of genuine accomplishment."[33]

Within the business system, this same executive believes, marketing people are the logical management group to act as the catalyst for needed change. They are trained in persuasion and communication; they are people-oriented. As generalists, they relate effectively to other fields, and they have proved they can get things done—and on time. Most of all, as one advertising executive observed, a marketer is inherently a radical—a revolutionary—in that his real forte is the management of innovation, that is, the management of change.[34]

Role of profit in social action. We need to consider the profit factor, however, when stating that business is the best-qualified institution to tackle our social problems. It used to be that profit-making alone was sufficient justification for a firm's existence. Certainly profit making was the management's primary goal and the foundation for its strategic planning. Not so any more! Today society demands a broader outlook. However, let's make one point quite clear. Profit is still an absolutely essential element in a company's existence. It no longer is the *only* guide for management, but it still is a necessary one. A company with fine, socially responsible programs, but with no profits, will soon be out of business. In fact, one belief held by some people close to the scene is that business cannot solve our social prob-

---

31 Peter F. Drucker, "Business and the Quality of Life," *Sales Management*, Mar. 15, 1969, p. 31

32 Elisha Gray II, "Changing Values in the Business Society," *Business Horizons*, August, 1968, pp. 21-26.

33 Leonard Sucsy, as quoted in Roy Alexander, "The Marketer in the Ghetto," *Industrial Marketing*, October, 1969, pp. 57-72; quotation on p. 72. This article also lists a series of practical guidelines for business-social interaction.

34 Leo Bogart, "The Marketer as a Radical," *Conference Board Record*, October, 1968, pp. 20-25 and Bent Stidsen, "Marketing: Discipline or Skill?" in *Proceedings* of the Marketing Division of the Canadian Association of Administrative Sciences, Quebec City, 1976, pp. 30-38.

lems until we figure out some way to make these solutions a profitable venture for business managers.[35]

ACTION PROGRAMS REGARDING SOCIAL PROBLEMS

A marketing executive who wants to work toward solving major social problems will find many useful courses of action open to him, both within his firm and also in his company's dealings with the community. Just a sample of some possible actions within the firm's marketing program is listed below. Many firms, of course, have been active in these areas for some time with varying results.

1. Increase the efficiency of marketing operations, so as to lower distribution costs and selling prices, enabling consumers to maximize their purchasing power.
2. Properly interpret and anticipate consumer demand, whether it is an active or latent demand, thus better supplying want-satisfying goods and services.
3. Refuse to do business with unethical suppliers or customers.
4. Increase control over operating personnel—particularly salespeople and advertising people—to ensure higher social standards of operation.
5. Cooperate with trade associations, Better Business Bureaus, and other business groups interested in raising business standards.
6. Earlier we spoke of programs to (a) increase product safety, (b) minimize defective products, (c) repair those that need it, (d) improve warranties, and (e) develop more informative packaging and labeling.

In the community, marketing can play an active role in: hiring and training disadvantaged people; contributing to education and the arts; urban renewal; improving the physical environment; removing discrimination against women, old people, and minority groups; the marketing problems of low-income consumers. In a moment we shall discuss briefly some practical examples of marketing's involvement in two of these problem areas.

But first a reminder to marketing executives regarding the importance of communicating their social-action programs and accomplishments to the public. With all the criticism being heaped on business today, it is not enough just to *do* some good in the social arena. Business executives must start to *tell* people about it instead of hiding their light under a bushel. In the past, many presidents and other executives went out of their way to maintain a low profile. Now they are urged to be more visible in their community and in the public media. Let the public know what you are doing to improve the quality of life as well as the standard of living.[36]

Marketing problems of low-income consumers. In Canada, there has been less written on the economic problems of the poor than in other countries. In the United States, for example, considerable attention has been paid to the problem of the urban black population.[37] The problems of Canada's poor are somewhat different.

---

35 David B. McCall, "Profit: Spur for Solving Social Ills," *Harvard Business Review*, May-June, 1973, pp. 46-48 ff.

36 Some executives have resorted to taking lessons on how to handle themselves on television or in interviews with the press. See "Adjusting to a More Visible Role," *Business Week*, May 4, 1974, p. 49.

37 See, for example: Frederick P. Sturdivant (ed), *The Ghetto Marketplace*. New York: The Free Press, 1969; Leonard L. Berry, "The Low-Income Marketing System: An Overview," *Journal of Retailing*, Summer, 1972, pp. 43-63; and Donald E. Sexton, Jr., "Comparing the Cost of Food to Blacks and to Whites—A Survey," *Journal of Marketing*, July, 1972, pp. 40-46.

Low-income consumers are not as easily identified but tend to be scattered throughout the regions and subcultures of the country. We often hear discussion of the "poverty line," that level of family income below which consumers are considered to be "poor." There are a number of definitions of "poverty line,"[38] but in general large numbers of "poor" consumers are found among residents of the urban core of large cities, residents of certain parts of rural Canada, members of certain ethnic groups, native people, and the aged.

The Special Senate Committee on Poverty concluded that the complexities of the modern marketplace present problems for consumers in general, but especially so for the poor.[39] In their report on poverty, the Senate Committee made the following observations.

The poor are often handicapped with respect to purchasing power by lack of education, experience, information, training, and opportunity as well as by lack of ready cash. "Best-buy" decisions depend not only on information about quality and performance, but also on a comparison of prices in different kinds of stores in different locations. To get this information takes time, effort, and money. Because of transportation expenses or credit difficulties, the poor cannot shop around. As a result, they shop in small neighbourhood stores where prices are higher, and selection is limited—but where delivery service and credit are available.

The elderly poor, unable to walk far or carry bundles or afford a bus, would be an outstanding example of this group. They are truly trapped. . . . . The elderly poor find it difficult even to buy small portions of food suitable for one or two persons. Alarming numbers of the elderly are poor, and their problems are special. Some have always been poor, and advancing age magnifies their problems because they are less able to support themselves adequately. There is an increase in the need for such services as taxis, drugs, medical and dental care, and hospitalization or home nursing care. As consumers, the elderly are further crippled by these extra demands on their already inadequate incomes. With the cumulative downward spiral of poverty, it is unlikely that family members will be able to come to their rescue.

In order to spend wisely, the consumer must be well-informed about products. Here the poor are at a great disadvantage. Some may not be able to read well enough to understand the instructions or list of contents accompanying the container or the fabric or the appliance. The poor do not have easy access to the newspapers, magazines, paperbacks, and hardcover books which assess consumer products.

Buying food is the major difficulty faced by the poor. This is their largest and most regular outlay. The object should be to buy economical foods which will provide a reasonably balanced and nutritious diet. But, handicapped by a lack of information and mobility, the poor tend to concentrate too heavily on cheaper, starchy foods to the neglect of protein and vitamin-rich foods; or they may buy the more easily accessible, expensively processed and packaged foods.

In the furniture and appliance market, the poor are confronted with additional hazards. One of the problems arises from high-pressure selling. A glib and apparently sincere salesperson can often exert a hypnotic effect on his prospects. Susceptibility to a skilled salesperson is by no means confined to the poor, but paying for being gulled is much more serious for them than for the more prosperous.

The poor, if they buy a car, usually buy a used car. If they make a bad choice, they are saddled with the often-prohibitive costs of repair, in addition to the continuing instalment payments. Where the car is a necessity, this could mean the loss of a job. There is almost no limit to the amount that can be spent on repairing a used car; and finance charges are

---

38 David P. Ross, "Canadian Fact Book on Poverty," Ottawa: The Canadian Council on Social Development, 1975.

39 Special Senate Committee on Poverty, *Poverty in Canada,* Ottawa: Information Canada, 1971, p. 105.

considerably higher on used than on new cars and many used cars are re-possessed.

Almost all consumers, poor or not, face the fact that consumer credit plays an important role. The arithmetic used in consumer credit is not easy, and many people don't fully appreciate the extra burden of credit costs.[40]

Unfortunately, there is little evidence that business is taking action to solve some of the problems experienced by low-income consumers. While consumers in general benefit from the increased volume of consumer protection law and from the activities of organized consumer groups, and while governments play an important role in assisting the poor through Social Assistance, Old Age Assistance, Unemployment Insurance and similar plans, it is clear that much needs to be done. If business is truly consumer-oriented, then there can be no doubt that it has a role to play in alleviating the marketing problems of Canada's urban poor, of the aged, of native people, and of low-income consumers who encounter high prices in certain regions of the country.

Marketing and environmental pollution. One of the major social problems facing us today is the pollution of our physical environment. Our ecology—i.e., the relationship of people to their environment—is being disturbed, and in some cases seriously, by air, water, or noise pollution.

Who are the polluters? Marketing has contributed to the pollution problem. By stimulating a demand for products and by satisfying consumers' wants, marketing has helped to build mountains of solid wastes. Making and using these products pollutes our air and water. Promotional efforts in marketing have generated a "throwaway" society and have contributed to a "no-deposit, no-return" behavioral pattern.

However, we must understand this about our ecological problems—they are far more complex than many people realize. Marketing alone did not cause pollution. Production and engineering technology are responsible for air and water pollution from steel mills, chemical plants, paper mills, oil refineries, and utility power plants. Cattle feed lots and various mining operations contribute their share of wastes. Various government agencies have inadequate control over their own pollution-producing operations—and the critics of business want the government to control pollution. Selfish consumer behavior adds to the problem. We want clean air but we won't pay to tune up our auto engines. As a group, we demand highway beautification, but as individuals we toss stuff out of the car window and often leave some picnic grounds a shambles. We abandon old cars on city streets.

We are dealing with a complex assortment of technological, political, economic, and even cultural and psychological factors. Furthermore, contrary to the belief held by many critics, pollution is *not* the exclusive province of a capitalistic economy and big business. Pollution is a by-product of an industrialized urban society whether it is capitalistic, socialistic, or communistic.

The factor of goal conflict is certainly involved in ecological issues. We want to drive cars, and we also want clean air and no traffic jams. One reason we have an energy shortage is because our desire for a clean environment leads us to oppose the building of more energy-generating facilities in our city. We don't want mos-

---

40 Special Senate Committee on Poverty, *op. cit.*, pp. 106-107.

quitoes, but we also do not want the DDT residue (from insecticides) laced through our soil and water. Now if only someone would invent a *silent* snowmobile.

Marketing's contributions to pollution reduction. Because of the complexities in ecological problems, effective solutions will require cooperation from producers, marketers, and consumers, with the government serving as a coordinating and enforcement agency. The costs of pollution reduction and control are enormously high. Prices will have to be increased to pay for these efforts. To ensure that all companies comply, government regulation will be necessary. Otherwise, some firms will clean up their operation and have to raise prices, while others who do nothing will have an unfair competitive advantage.

Just as marketing alone did not cause pollution, so too marketing alone cannot cure it. But marketing can, should, and is contributing to the "solution of pollution." To do so is simply part of our social responsibility. We also can attract purely profit-oriented people to our cause, because there are many profitable business opportunities in pollution abatement. Pollution reduction is *not* limited to shut-down-the mill, don't-drive-your-car, and return-that-bottle type of negative alternatives. Some illustrations of positive efforts by marketers revolve around product planning, channels of distribution, and promotion.

The major polluting industries and many of the lesser culprits provide golden market opportunities for new pollution-control products. Marketing is also challenged to develop products which will *not* contribute to solid waste matter. The disposal of solid wastes is a monumental problem, and one way to cope with it is not to accumulate so much waste in the first place. Thus, biodegradable or recyclable products, and returnable or reusable containers, are desirable. In fact, it may be necessary at the national level to ban the sale of drinks in nonreturnable containers. A little innovative thinking also helps. As we run out of land for garbage dumps, some cities are generating electricity by using solid wastes for fuel.

Recycling—the reprocessing of waste products—is another area where marketing is reducing solid-waste pollution. The key to success in recycling is to develop an effective channel-of-distribution system which will move the waste products from consumer back to a producer who can use them as raw materials in manufacturing new products. Marketing's challenge is to find the incentive needed to stimulate the consumer to start this reverse channel movement.[41]

Marketers can use their skills in promotion and persuasion to urge consumers to conserve our natural resources by using them in a more efficient, less wasteful manner. Promotion also can be the tool to impress upon consumers the seriousness of our pollution and waste-disposal problems.

QUESTIONS AND PROBLEMS

1. Do you think that self-regulation by business will prevent, or correct, the abuses that led to consumer discontent?
2. In what ways is the consumerism phenomenon of the 1970s different from the consumer movement of the 1930s? What factors have led to the current movement?

---

41 See William G. Zikmund and William J. Stanton, "Recycling Solid Wastes: A Channels-of-Distribution Problem," *Journal of Marketing,* July 1971, pp. 34–39.

3. Why should consumers' right to information be preserved? How much information should consumers receive? Who should provide it?

4. What information do you think should be included in advertisements for each of the following products or services?

   a. Lipstick   d. Breakfast cereals
   b. Auto tires   e. Public accounting firm
   c. Typewriters   f. Personal loan (finance) company

5. How do you explain the success of the consumer movement in bringing about consumer legislation if, as some studies suggest, the leaders of the consumer movement are not representative of the mass of consumers?

6. What is the annual rate of interest charged by department stores and mail-order firms on their revolving credit accounts?

7. What suggestions do you have for a wife who wishes to minimize the cost of the following, and yet at the same time get want satisfaction in her purchases?

   a. Food for the family
   b. Clothes for herself
   c. Furniture for the house

8. How far should governments go to protect the consumer? To what extent is the concept of "caveat emptor" valid today?

9. What is the social and economic justification for the "paternalistic" types of laws—like the auto-seat-belt regulations—which require us to do something because the government says it is in our best interests?

10. What proposals do you have for resolving some of the consumer goal-conflict situations discussed in this chapter?

11. Discuss the relationship between illegal and unethical marketing practices. For instance, are illegal acts always unethical? Are unethical marketing activities always illegal? Give examples in each case.

12. Some salespeople in your company have increased their profitable sales volume considerably by employing slightly unethical practices. If you, as the sales manager, sanction these practices, you will meet your responsibility to your company and its stockholders. But you will be failing to meet your social responsibilities. What would you do in this case? Is management's social responsibility incompatible with its responsibility to its stockholders?

13. Does the fact that there has been a growth in consumer protection legislation in recent years mean that business has not effectively policed its own activities? How else might it be explained?

14. Why is it marketing's responsibility to reduce air, water, and noise pollution?

MARKETING: APPRAISAL AND PROSPECT

In this concluding chapter we shall develop in summary form a marriage of three topics—an appraisal of (1) marketing in the Canadian economy, (2) the government's role in marketing, and (3) the outlook for the future of marketing.

Our frame of reference is the present-day economic system of Canada: a free enterprise but *imperfect* economic system. Price is the prime determinant of resource allocation. We call our system imperfect, however, because the market is not composed of elements basic to the theoretical model of perfect competition—elements such as great numbers of well-informed buyers and sellers, always acting rationally, each so small that his individual activity has no appreciable influence on total supply, demand, or price. Another imperfection is the structural rigidity of our system. There is probably greater freedom of exit and entry in the retailing part of our market structure than in any other segment, but even here some rigidities exist. Also, in the interests of the general welfare, the various levels of government often act so as to affect the free play of market forces.

Another point to keep in mind is that the economic system contains many freedoms, but for every freedom—whether it is political, economic, religious, or social—we pay a price. For example, one economic privilege we have is freedom of choice; we are offered a wide variety of products and often a considerable number of brands of each product. The price we pay for this freedom is the burden of making up our minds—of making a marketing decision about which products and brands we will buy with our limited resources.

EVALUATION OF MARKETING SYSTEM

Anything so important and all-pervasive as marketing is bound to draw a share of censure. In some cases, criticism is leveled at marketing in the individual firms, while in other situations the target is the role of marketing in the economy. We can summarize the major charges at this point, but it will not be possible within the scope of this book to discuss them in detail.

In order to appraise our marketing system, we need some yardsticks for measurement. First, what is the objective of the system? Throughout this book we have stressed the philosophy of the marketing concept. The goal of the marketing concept is to develop a customer orientation on the part of management. In line with this philosophy, it seems reasonable to establish as a goal the satisfaction of consumers' wants, as they are expressed by the consumers themselves. Then marketing should be appraised on the basis of how well it achieves this goal, that is, how effectively it satisfies consumers' wants. We grant that this goal is a questionable one in the minds of many people. Some feel that the consumer does not know what is good for him—that some group (usually the government) should take over the responsibility for setting standards. Others believe that the social and economic goals should be to build a country's industrial strength, to promote the growth of its underdeveloped regions, or to perpetuate the great wealth and high social position of a favored few. Regardless of these other possible goals, however noteworthy some people think they are, *we shall evaluate marketing in light of its ability to satisfy consumers' wants, as the consumers themselves define or express these wants.*

Next we must try to establish objective, quantitative yardsticks for measuring the extent to which marketing has achieved this goal. In an *individual company* the effectiveness of marketing can be measured generally by the company's financial status. This is measured on the bases of operating costs, net profits, operating ratios, comparisons with similar firms, and so on. Tools have been developed to measure the profitability of various products, territories, channels, salespeople, and advertising media within a given firm.

A different situation prevails when we attempt to measure quantitatively marketing's contribution to consumer want satisfaction in *our economy.* Input-output analysis may be employed, although it is difficult to assign objective values to the various factors in input and output unless we use the market value of these factors. For instance, in the marketing system we can measure quantitatively the value of such inputs as newspaper space used in advertising, time and program costs for television advertising, freight carloadings, marketing research costs in developing the brand and package, salespeople's compensation and expenses, and others. The output factors may be summarized as consumer want satisfaction. But of course, so far no one has been able satisfactorily to impute objective values to this output. Market price indicates what consumers are willing to pay, but it does not accurately measure satisfaction received. Consequently, much of our evaluation of marketing's contribution to consumer want satisfaction in our economy must be done on a subjective basis.[1]

---

1 For a conceptual measurement of costs and benefits to producers, consumers, and society in marketing transactions, see Richard E. Homans and Ben M. Enis, "A Guide for Appraising Marketing Activities," *Business Horizons,* October, 1973, pp. 20-30.

For a conceptual framework to assess the contribution of the distribution system to our economic and social welfare, see Louis P. Bucklin, "Marketing Channels and Structures: A Macro View," in B. W. Becker

CRITICISMS OF MARKETING

Critics of our marketing system have raised many thought-provoking questions and generated many lively discussions. In order to summarize the major charges of the critics, we shall group them according to their relationships to the four components of the marketing mix—the product, the distribution structure, the price system, and promotional activities. Some of these complaints are a repeat of those noted in the discussion of consumerism in the preceding chapter.

With respect to the *product*, critics allege that many products are of poor quality; for the price the seller charges, the products and services should be better. Furthermore, heavily promoted product improvements are often trivial. Planned style obsolescence encourages consumers to get rid of products before they are physically worn out. Besides, there are too many different types of goods and too many different brands of each type. As a result, the buyer is confused; he is unable to make accurate buying decisions.

Probably the main objection to the *distribution structure* is that it is unnecessarily complex and includes too many middlemen. This is a two-part charge: there are too many different types of middlemen and too many of each type. Regarding the *price system*, we hear that prices are too high or too inflexible or that they are controlled by the large firms in an industry. Some people feel that price competition has been largely replaced by nonprice competition.

The strongest and most bitter indictments leveled against marketing are in the area of *promotional activities*—especially in personal selling and advertising. Most of the complaints about personal selling are at the retail level, where we find both consumers and businesspeople disenchanted with the poor quality of retail salesmanship. Objections are also voiced against the poor services offered by many retailers, even by stores whose high prices would seem to reflect a service-oriented policy.

The general criticisms against advertising may be divided into two groups—social and economic. From a *social* point of view, advertising is charged with overemphasizing our material standard of living and underemphasizing our cultural, spiritual, ethical, and moral values. Advertising also is charged with manipulating people—making them want to buy things they should not have, cannot afford, and do not need. Advertising, in effect, is being charged with being a major tool in the business system's management of consumer demand.[2]

A major social criticism of advertising today, and one that has some justification and should be considered by marketers throughout our economy, is that advertising is often false, misleading, deceptive, or in bad taste. Exaggerations, conflicting claims, overuse of sex and fear appeals, jarring commercials, inane claims, excessive numbers of commercials on radio and television, and poor choice of the placement of commercials are some examples of this general point of censure.[3] As with

---

and H. Becker (eds.), *1972 Combined Proceedings*, American Marketing Association, Chicago, 1973, pp. 28-40. This article also contains an extensive bibliography on the subject.

2 See Stephen A. Greyser, "Advertising: Attacks and Counters," *Harvard Business Review*, March-April, 1972, pp. 22 ff., for an adapted version of Greyser's testimony to the FTC concerning the social issues and social impact of advertising. Also see John A. Howard and Spencer F. Tinkham, "A Framework for Understanding Social Criticism of Advertising," *Journal of Marketing*, October, 1971, pp. 2-7.

3 For suggestions of five types of research to help reduce irritation in advertising, see Stephen A. Greyser, "Irritation in Advertising," *Journal of Advertising Research*, February, 1973, pp. 3-10; also see S. A. Greyser and Bonnie B. Reece, "Businessmen Look Hard at Advertising, *Harvard Business Review*, May-June, 1971, pp. 18ff.

most criticisms in marketing, this one applies to a small segment of advertising. The main offenders are advertisers of a limited number of consumer goods, and the advertising medium causing most of the furor is television. The charge of false, misleading, and offensive advertising is rarely made against advertisers of industrial products or companies which advertise consumer products in trade journals. Most of our retail department store display advertising is not subject to this charge, nor is most of the newspaper classified advertising.

Advertising is charged with causing a misallocation of our resources. This criticism is related to the assertion by John K. Galbraith and others that advertising has contributed significantly to an imbalance of expenditures between the private and public sectors of our economy, that advertising is so powerful that it causes consumers to overspend and to buy products which they really do not need. For instance, these people believe that business promotes frills on automobiles when it should be concerned with providing housing, improving our schools, and eliminating air and water pollution. Furthermore, these critics believe that more of our national output should be diverted from the private to the public sector.[4]

The *economic* criticisms of advertising have taken an interesting turn in recent years. We still hear that advertising costs too much—that it increases the cost of marketing and therefore raises the prices of products. In the past, much criticism was devoted to the competitive nature of advertising and the attendant economic waste which is claimed to result from generating imaginary brand differentials. Recently, however, the economic charge drawing the most interest is somewhat the opposite—namely, that advertising leads to restraint of competition, economic concentration, and monopoly.[5]

The main critical points in the argument on the anti-competitive effects of advertising are as follows:[6]

(a) the large company has the power of the large purse which enables it to spend substantial sums on advertising, particularly to implement product differentiation; (b) advertising thus creates a barrier to new firms entering industry; (c) the result is greater economic concentration; (d) because of their protected position, these firms charge monopolistic prices; and (e) high monopolistic prices in turn result in excessively larger profits.

The defenders of advertising counter with the following points to refute these arguments;

(a) the claim that advertising is a significant factor in industrial concentration has not been proven; (b) the suggestion that advertising contributes to raising prices and thus to inflation is not supported in overall terms by the postwar experience in North America; and (c) the point that industries with high advertising expenditures tend to earn considerably higher profits than industries making smaller advertising efforts appears to be not in accordance with the results obtained from research studies.

Undoubtedly the economic arguments will continue as long as respected professional researchers differ in their conclusions. Whatever approach may be used in

---

4 See John K. Galbraith, *The Affluent Society,* Houghton Mifflin Company, Boston, 1958; for a different point of view, see, for example, John W. Lowe, "An Economist Defends Advertising," *Journal of Marketing,* July, 1963, pp. 16-19; and V. E. Boyd, *Advertising and Public Service: Not-so-strange Bedfellows,* American Association of Advertising Agencies, No. 19, 1964.

5 The topic of the economic effects of advertising in Canada is dealt with in: O. J. Firestone, *The Economic Implications of Advertising,* Toronto: Methuen Publications, 1967.

6 *Ibid.,* pp. 184-185.

the future as we research the still unanswered questions, we can hope that it will (1) cease to evaluate advertising against the unrealistic backdrop of perfect competition and (2) consider advertising in terms of operational alternatives.[7]

IMPORTANCE OF UNDERSTANDING TRUE NATURE OF CRITICISMS

When evaluating charges against marketing, we should be careful to recognize the differences in the nature of the various points. We should understand what fundamentally is being criticized. In a company, is it the marketing department or some other department which is the cause of the complaints? In the economy, is it the marketing system or the general economic system which is being criticized? It is also helpful to sort out the points wherein the critics (1) are misinformed, (2) are unaware of the services performed by the marketing system, or (3) are trying to impose their own objective value judgments on consumers. That is, the critics do not agree that the goal of the marketing system should be consumer want satisfaction as the consumers *themselves* define and express their wants.

In some cases the criticisms of marketing are fully warranted; they point out weaknesses and inefficiencies in the system and call for improvement. By most people's standards, there are instances of deceptive packaging and of misleading and objectionable advertising. There are weaknesses in marketing, just as there are in any system developed and operated by human beings. The real key to the evaluation of our marketing system lies in the answers to two fundamental questions. First, is the present system of marketing achieving its goal (that is, satisfying consumers' wants as the consumers themselves express these wants) better than any other known alternative could? The answer is an unqualified "yes." Second, is constant effort being devoted to improving the system and increasing its productivity and efficiency? Generally speaking, the answer to this question is also a strong "yes."

Progress sometimes may seem slow. Companies that operate in a socially undesirable manner even over a short-run period of time are harmful. Price-fixing and objectionable advertising are intolerable and inexcusable. Instances of this nature, though widely publicized, are in a small minority, however, when the total picture of marketing is viewed. In essence, we are saying that weaknesses exist in marketing and that a continuing effort must be devoted to their elimination. However, at the same time, we should not overlook the improvements in marketing and consumer want satisfaction over the years. The way to correct existing weaknesses is not to destroy or seriously regulate the existing system.

DOES MARKETING COST TOO MUCH?

Many of the censures of marketing may be summarized in the general criticism that marketing costs too much. It is estimated that the total cost of marketing for all

---

7 The reader is referred to the following books and articles for more information on the economic effects of advertising:

L. G. Telser, "Some Aspects of the Economics of Advertising," *Journal of Business*, April, 1968, pp. 166-173.

J. J. Lambin, *Advertising, Competition and Market Conduct in Oligopoly Over Time*, Amsterdam: North-Holland Publishing Company, 1976.

R. Schmalensee, *The Economics of Advertising*, Amsterdam: North-Holland Publishing Company, 1972.

products is about 50 percent of the final price paid by ultimate consumers. Admittedly, total marketing costs are a substantial proportion of total sales value of all products. However, the question of whether marketing costs too much is in many respects somewhat academic because we do not have sufficient information to make comparisons. We do not know how the costs of marketing compare with the costs of manufacturing, mining, and other activities which create form utility. Even if we had accurate data on marketing costs, we would still have no objective criteria for determining whether these expenses are too high or not high enough. As we said in Chapter 29, we have not yet developed adequate tools for measuring the return (output) that is derived from a given marketing expenditure (input). To say that marketing costs are too high implies that one or more of the following situations prevail: marketing institutions are enjoying abnormally high profits; more services are being provided than consumers and businesspeople demand; marketing activities are performed in a grossly inefficient manner; consumption is declining; and total costs (production plus marketing) are increasing. Actually, there is no reasonable evidence that any of these conditions exist.

It is granted that total marketing costs have risen substantially both absolutely and relatively over the past 100 years. At the same time, careful studies indicate that these costs have been leveling off for the past three or four decades. Still, it is important that we understand the reasons for this increase in marketing expenses. Certainly it would be a mistake simply to jump to the conclusion that the cost increase indicates growing inefficiencies in marketing. Actually, the rise in marketing expense is traceable to several factors, some of which are external environmental influences. As an example, one reason for the increase in the number of people employed in marketing relative to the number employed in production is simply that the workweek in marketing has been shortened relative to that in production. In the latter part of the nineteenth century, people employed in wholesaling and retailing worked about 66 hours a week; those employed in production worked about 52. Today, both groups work about 40, and this shift toward equality has meant that relatively more employees were added in marketing.

Another reason why the number of workers and costs in marketing have increased is that consumers are demanding more services and more marketing refinements today than in the past. Consumers today demand credit, delivery, free parking, attractive stores, merchandise return privileges, and other services. A related point is the rise in consumer demand for products emphasizing style, and for merchandise assortments covering considerable breadth and depth. Certainly we could cut marketing costs and problems substantially if consumers would buy on a cash-and-carry, no-returns-permitted basis in stores displaying small quantities of standardized merchandise in pipe racks or in wooden boxes.

Sometimes the seeming increase in distribution costs is really the result of a more careful classification of business expenses. If a small businessperson or farmer produces his goods and sells them himself, all his operating expenses are classed as production expenses (creation of form utility) because he is classified as a producer. Once this businessperson or farmer employs the advantages of specialization of labor, however, or once his markets expand, he will probably use independent middlemen to help in the marketing process. Immediately the costs are separated into production and marketing classifications. Marketing expenses seem to have increased substantially, even though there may have been no real change in the total cost picture. In a large company which adopts the marketing concept, many expenses (such as new-product development, inventory control, transportation, and warehousing) which formerly were classified as production costs will now be shown as marketing expenses simply because the expense-generating activity is now the organizational responsibility of the marketing manager.

It is a mistake to study the trend in marketing costs alone. A total cost approach should be adopted. In many instances, a firm can reduce its total costs by increasing its marketing costs. To illustrate, an increase in advertising and personal selling expenditures may so expand a firm's market that the unit production cost can be reduced more than the marketing costs have increased. Thus the net effect is to reduce the total expenses. In another situation, production economies can result when a company locates near sources of raw materials or low-cost power; yet marketing costs (transportation) may be increased in the new location.

One approach to a better understanding of the role of marketing in the economy is to apply the concept of "value added by marketing" as a counterpart of the already-accepted concept of "value added by manufacturing." "Value added by marketing" is a much more accurate term than "cost of marketing" to describe the output or utilities created by marketing.

It is understandable that productivity in marketing may never match the level attained in manufacturing or agriculture. Marketing offers far fewer opportunities for mechanization. It is one thing to control the input and output value of machines, but it is quite another problem when the activity largely involves dealing with people. To the extent that the marketing system is not perfect and that marketing costs have not reached a theoretical minimum, we may say that marketing does cost too much. Until we can define this perfect system objectively, however, and until a better system for satisfying consumer wants is proposed, we shall continue with the existing system. Its benefits in both the private and public sectors of our economy are bounteous by almost any measure used. Canadian business must continue to improve the efficiency of marketing, to measure accurately its cost, and most important of all to explain to the Canadian public the essential role marketing plays in our economy.

GOVERNMENT'S ROLE IN MARKETING

In many situations the government probably rates second to the consumer in importance as an external environmental influence on marketing. Anything that is so much a part of our economic system as marketing is bound to be influenced directly by governmental action. Throughout this book, major legislation and other governmental actions were discussed when pertinent to particular areas of marketing. At this point we shall make a few summary observations regarding the role government plays in marketing.

At all times a marketing executive must be aware of the impact which his internal decisions have on the external environment of his firm. Particularly should he consider the political or governmental appraisal of his internal policy making? In most companies, the marketing department, more than any other, feels the intervention of the government—federal, provincial, or local. This in no way suggests that regulation of nonmarketing activities is unimportant.

Governmental intervention takes two forms. First, the government offers aid on a voluntary basis to businesses in an effort to foster competition and to increase business efficiency. Countless examples of such aid could be cited. Federal agencies such as the Federal Business Development Bank and departments such as Industry,

Trade and Commerce offer a number of programs and publish much information of considerable value to marketers. In addition, most provinces also offer marketing assistance through development agencies.

The second form of governmental intervention involves regulation and control. A study of our business history shows rather clearly that governmental regulations come about because (1) private industry is either unable or unwilling to accept its responsibility for acting in the public interest or (2) special-interest groups foster the legislation.

As examples of governmental action resulting from the inability or refusal of private business to accept its responsibilities, we have the various anticombines laws, laws prohibiting unfair competition, and the legal restrictions on advertising. In the late nineteenth century, society felt that monopolistic practices were contrary to the public interest, so the first anticombines legislation was passed. Later, when private industry did not accept its responsibilities in matters of labeling and selling food and drugs—when it sold adulterated products and used deceptive labels—food and drug legislation was brought in. In years following, shortsighted businesspeople found ways to circumvent the legislation, and it was strengthened further.

In some areas, government engages in business itself, directly competing with private enterprise. Often the original reason for such government activity was that private enterprise could not or would not meet consumer demand. This reason lies behind the government's development of water resources and its activity in financing home mortgages.

In some cases, a private business group seeks government intervention to support the group's self-interest. We see the results of this form of activity in such legislation as the provincial unfair-practices acts and ordinances regulating door-to-door selling. The stated purpose of these laws is to protect competition. In effect, however, they protect *competitors* rather than *competition*, and there is a substantial difference between the two. Some of these legal measures actually operated to penalize new forms of competition. In such cases these laws tend to injure competition.

Often a marketing executive who seeks legislation favoring his own special interest will profess to be an advocate of free competition, when in actual fact he is attempting to combat strong, but entirely fair, competition. Sometimes it seems that a marketer's only criterion of fair competition is whether it allows him to beat a competitor. Unfair competition is, of course, any situation in which he loses. Marketing management must realize that it is not possible to regulate one segment of the economy and let other parts go unrestrained. Regulation usually begets more regulation.

From the consumers' point of view, marketing legislation in the past has had two weaknesses. One is that in general it has been business-oriented rather than consumer-oriented. (There were some exceptions, of course, such as the Food and Drugs Act, the Consumer Packaging and Labelling Act, and the Hazardous Products Act.) The other weakness was the absence of federal "watchdogs." That is, under most laws a suit must be brought by an injured party, and not by an agency of the government. A corollary to that weakness is the absence of speedy, inexpensive means for the redress of consumer grievances.

Since the 1960s a dramatic shift has occurred relative to the first of those two weaknesses—namely, there has been a significant amount of consumer-oriented legislation. Regarding the second problem, the situation today is moderately improved. Some of the regulatory agencies—the CRTC, for example—are quite active in protecting consumers' interests. The problem of slow, expensive redress of grievances, however, still has not been noticeably improved.

BROADENING THE MARKETING CONCEPT

In the preceding chapter we developed the theme that changing cultural values led to consumerism, and subsequently to a societal orientation in the field of marketing. This emerging orientation, in turn, highlighted the ethical and social responsibilities of marketing executives. This sequence inevitably leads us to review the marketing concept which we have espoused throughout this book. We must analyze it critically to determine: (1) Is it an outmoded concept? or (2) Is it still viable? That is, is it workable in today's socioeconomic system—is it compatible with a socially oriented marketing perspective?[8]

In Chapter 1 we explained that the marketing concept is a three-part philosophy—namely, that a company should (1) develop an integrated marketing program (2) to generate profitable sales volume (3) by means of satisfying consumers' wants.

By virtue of the fact that the phenomenon of consumerism exists in Canada today, the marketing concept has to some extent failed. Peter Drucker (a professor, a management consultant, and certainly not an antagonist of business) referred to consumerism as "the shame of the total marketing concept." The customer-orientation theme in the marketing concept implies that business should look at the world from the buyer's end, find out what he wants, and then try to satisfy those wants in a profitable manner. Consequently, carried to their logical extremes, consumerism and the marketing concept are mutually exclusive; if one exists, the other does not. Yet most businesspeople probably would claim that they are consumer-oriented, and that they do try to satisfy their customers. They look on in wounded surprise at the wave of consumer discontent that is engulfing them.

Okay, then, what went wrong? Is it simply that the marketing concept has outlived its usefulness and is not compatible with today's social orientation in marketing? In these authors' opinion there is nothing wrong with the marketing concept that a broader interpretation won't cure. It is viable as it ever was. It is quite compatible with a societal orientation to marketing and with a marketing executive's social responsibility.

However, three things did occur which have hurt the credibility and acceptability of the marketing concept. The first is that too many marketing executives, while professing wholehearted agreement and support of the philosophy, were in actual practice giving it only token or lip-service implementation. In some cases these executives may have meant well, but they were simply too production- or engineering-oriented to fully comprehend the idea of customer orientation. To them, customer satisfaction was achieved by building a better mousetrap. In other cases the short-run crises forced line-operating executives to put their self-interest ahead of consumer satisfaction, even though top management may have been preaching consumer orientation. This point was discussed in the last chapter.

---

8 See Bent Stidsen and Thomas F. Schutte, "Marketing as a Communication System: The Marketing Concept Revisited," *Journal of Marketing*, October, 1972, pp. 22-27; Lynn J. Loudenback, "Social Responsibility and the Marketing Concept," *Atlanta Economic Review*, April, 1972, pp. 38-39; and E. Laird Landon, Jr., "The Invisible Backhand or the 'New Marketing Concept' Must Be Turning Adam Smith in His Grave," *Journal of the Academy of Marketing Science*, Fall, 1973, pp. 132-137.

Also see brief discussion of this subject in Chapter 1.

The two more fundamental factors affecting the full implementation of the marketing concept revolve around the narrow interpretation of consumer want satisfaction. Who is a consumer, and what is meant by want satisfaction? Answers to both of these questions have been too narrow and too short-run-oriented. Most of us as human beings—whether in our role as producer or consumer—tend to be short-run-oriented in most situations. We fail to see the boomerang effect—the long-run implications of our actions. Thus, I may want certain foods, and be satisfied when marketers cater to these wants. But these foods may be fattening or low in nutritional value, so there is a negative personal want-satisfaction effect on me in the long run. My wants for a TV set, or for some kind of medicine, or for cigarettes may be satisfied by companies. But the long-run effects may be radiation damage from the TV set, bad side effects from the medicine, and heart and lung damage from the cigarettes.

If the consumer-orientation goal of the marketing concept is defined as want satisfaction *in the long run*, then the marketing concept is more in line with the societal perspective of marketing. Of course, the problem of goal conflict (as discussed in the preceding chapter) crops up here again. To sell me the fattening foods is contrary to society's view of socially desirable want satisfaction. But to market nonfattening foods to me (while socially desirable and healthy for me) is just not what I want tonight, so the marketer loses my business. My short-run wants and long-run interests conflict.

Besides extending the *time* dimension in the marketing concept, we need to extend its *breadth* dimension. To view consumers as being only the direct buyers of a company's product—a view generally held in the past—is too narrow a dimension. We must broaden our definition of the markets to be satisfied to include groups affected by the direct buyer-seller exchange. Thus I may buy an auto and be satisfied with it. But the negative social effects of pollution and traffic congestion from my auto displease other groups. So in the broader context, we have not generated customer satisfaction and thus have not successfully implemented the marketing concept. A steel producer can sell a good product, reasonably priced—thus satisfying its direct customers. But if that mill is polluting the air and water when making that steel, then from the broader societal perspective, the marketing concept is not being implemented.

In conclusion, the marketing concept is compatible with a societal perspective of marketing when we define the marketing concept as a philosophy whereby a company strives (1) to develop an integrated marketing program (2) to generate long-run profitable sales volume (3) by means of satisfying the long-run wants of (a) product-buying customers and (b) the parts of society affected by the firm's activities.[9]

MARKETING IN AN ERA OF SHORTAGES

Seemingly all of a sudden, around 1973-1974, our economy of abundance developed several spots of scarcity. The oil shortage which triggered the so-called energy

---

9 For an excellent discussion of the application of a broadened application of the marketing concept to non-business entities, the reader is referred to: Philip Kotler and Sidney J. Levy, "Broadening the Concept of Marketing," *Journal of Marketing*, January, 1969, pp. 10-15; Philip Kotler, "A Generic Concept of Marketing," *Journal of Marketing*, April, 1972, pp. 46-54.

crisis generally epitomized the shortage situation. However, in the mid-1970s shortages seemed to occur suddenly not only in oil-based industries (plastics and other petrochemicals) but also in many other industries (wood, paper products, farm products, for example) where the shortages were not triggered by cutbacks in energy availability. This is not the place to argue the political and economic causes underlying the shortages, but we should recognize the impact they have on marketing in our economy.

To paraphrase an article title, marketing is not dead but it sure is going to be different in these shortage situations.[10] Because shortages could last for many years in some product categories, the face of marketing is likely to be different for a long time in these industries. In our discussion of the marketing implications in shortages, first we shall consider some "don'ts" for management and then some positive action proposals.

DON'T REDUCE MARKETING'S ROLE

Faced with a limited supply of its product and a situation where the company can sell all it can produce, the two biggest mistakes management can make are (1) to reduce the role of marketing in the firm and (2) to mistreat its customers.

It is bad enough, but perhaps understandable, when financial and production executives want to reduce the role of marketing during periods of shortages. Unfortunately, these executives seem to think that their functions are needed all the time, but that marketing is necessary only when supply exceeds demand. But what is really incomprehensible is when *marketing* executives talk about cutting sales forces, reducing advertising, and otherwise lessening their marketing effort.

These executive opinions reflect both a shortsighted point of view and a nonunderstanding of the role of marketing. Budget cuts and other reductions in marketing effort can hurt whether the scarcities are short-lived or long-lasting. If they end soon, management needs experienced people to maintain a competitive position in a market. As long as the shortages continue, experienced people in sales, advertising, and marketing research can play vital roles in solving problems and seeking new marketing opportunities.

Business executives need to recognize the true role of marketing in relation to demand. In the past, marketing's job was seen as finding customers for existing products, or developing new products for unmet wants. In either situation marketing was *stimulating* demand. A more useful perspective is to consider marketing's job as one of *managing* demand. Then excess demand becomes as much of a marketing problem as excess supply. "The tasks of coping with shrinking demand or deliberately discouraging segments of the market call for the use of all the major marketing tools. As such, marketing thinking is just as relevant to the problem of reducing demand as it is to the problem of increasing demand."[11]

DON'T MISTREAT CUSTOMERS

With the shift to excess demand and a seller's market, some companies may be tempted to abandon the customer-orientation keystone in the marketing concept. It

---

10 With apologies to Carl Rieser, "The Salesman Isn't Dead—He's Different," *Fortune*, November, 1962, p. 124, an article about the changing role of salesmen.

11 This paragraph is adapted from Philip Kotler and Sydney J. Levy, "Demarketing, Yes, Demarketing," *Harvard Business Review*, November-December, 1971, pp. 74-80, quote from p. 75.

probably would be only human for salespeople and sales executives to release their resentments and try to "get even" for the real and imagined mistreatment they have suffered at the hands of purchasing agents during the long periods of excess supply and a buyer's market.

Any such ideas are simply stupid at best and suicidal at worst, for several reasons. First, good customers—market franchises—are a major asset for any firm. They are harder to acquire than most assets, and you don't go around destroying customer relationships any more than you destroy the firm's plant or machinery. Second, the shortages in many areas may prove to be short-run, but ill-treated customers have long-run memories. Third, customer complaints today fall on receptive ears in Ottawa and in provincial legislatures, as we noted in the preceding chapter.

POSITIVE PROGRAMS FOR MARKETING MANAGEMENT DURING SHORTAGES

Far from being discouraged or abandoning a customer orientation, marketing executives should look upon this period as a time to rethink their marketing programs, adapt to changing priorities, and capitalize on the new opportunities generated by the scarcities. In a general marketing management sense, for example, executives can pursue alternative marketing strategies, depending upon their assessment of the demand for their product in relation to its supply. Increasing demand and adequate supply may call for a growth strategy, while increasing demand coupled with inadequate supply suggests a market retention strategy.[12]

One interesting development with major marketing implications is the emergence of a barter economy as a means of acquiring vital materials now in short supply. Company A will sell a scarce item to company B, if B can pay its bill, not in cash, but in another scarce item which A needs.[13]

More specifically, management can analyze its customer list and then consider actions pertaining to each of the four components of the marketing mix. A marketing cost analysis by customer groups, checking on present and potential profitability, will enable a seller to prune out marginal customers. If shipment priorities are to be set up, obviously the high-profit customers should get preferential treatment. However, a seller also has to consider the anticompetitive implications in these moves.

In product planning, companies have been slimming their product mix by eliminating low-margin products. Planned obsolescence may be de-emphasized in some firms. In planning new products, look for markets expanded by the shortages. Less building heat means more sweaters, and less gasoline means more bicycles, books, and home entertainment. Regarding pricing policies and strategies, the combination of shortages, price controls and inflation pose real challenges for marketing management.[14] Marketing cost analyses by channel of distribution may re-

---

12 For additional strategy-action guidelines, see David W. Cravens, "Marketing Management in an Era of Shortages," Business Horizons, February, 1974, pp. 79-85.

13 See "The Sultans of Swap," Time, Mar. 11, 1974, p. 87; and "Wanna Swap?" Wall Street Journal, Feb. 13, 1974, p. 1.

14 See "Pricing Strategy in an Inflation Economy," Business Week, Apr. 6, 1974, p. 43.

sult in eliminating some middlemen, employing a more selective distribution policy, or even restructuring the basic channels used by a firm.[15]

In the promotional areas of advertising and personal selling, several adjustments to shortages are being made. Advertising is shifting to more informational
ads. "Status" appeals are giving way to "utilitarian" appeals. (One interesting consumer backlash to current oil-company advertising is the query, "How come the
companies waited till now to tell us how to save gas, get better mileage, etc.?") Perhaps most important of all, from a societal viewpoint, is that advertising can play a
major role in stimulating economic and behavioral change in getting consumers to
husband rather than squander our resources.[16]

The role of the personal salespeople will change dramatically in shortage-ridden
companies, and there may be cutbacks in the size of some sales forces. The short-
age-era salesperson will work more on servicing good accounts, educating customers and middlemen, helping customers solve their shortage-induced problems, and
particularly on providing product and market information to customers.[17]

In conclusion, the forces of shortages and inflation are changing the lifestyle of
Canadian consumers in many instances. During the next decade, consumers may
decide to live more simply, cut back on their product acquisitions, and generally
conserve resources. These attitudes will have a significant impact on the marketing
programs in many companies.

ADDITIONAL PROSPECTS FOR THE FUTURE

What does the future hold for marketing? We just discussed two of the prospects—
a socially oriented marketing concept and marketing during shortages. Now to finish this book, let's briefly summarize some of the other broad forces which will re-
shape marketing in the final two decades of the twentieth century. The crystal ball
seems reasonably clear regarding many of these projections because they are a continuation of trends which have been in evidence for some years now. As we move
into the 1980s, perhaps the overriding feature we can expect is an accelerated rate of
change.

TOMORROW'S CONSUMERS WILL BE DIFFERENT

Perhaps the most significant prospect is that the markets of the 1980s will be quite
different from those of today. Consumers will be better educated and more critical.
Their goals will be more socially oriented, and they will expect marketers to play a
greater role in solving our environmental and social problems. Population growth
will slow down. The role of women will change dramatically with consequent effects on marketing. Family structures are changing toward smaller, less permanent
institutions (the divorce rate is rising). There will be further movement toward a

---

15 See M. Dale Beckman and Walter S. Good, "Physical Distribution Systems: A Method of Analysis," in
Proceedings of the 1975 Meetings of the Marketing Division of the Canadian Association of Administrative
Sciences, Edmonton, 1975, pp. 263-273.

16 See "Advertising: New Role in 'Unabundant' Economy," *Grey Matter*, February, 1974.

17 See Michael B. Rothfeld, "A New Kind of Challenge for Salesmen," *Fortune*, April, 1974, p. 156. *Sales
Management* magazine devoted an entire issue (Jan. 21. 1974) to a series of questions regarding how to keep
a sales force running in a crunch economy.

rental (rather than product ownership) economy and a growth in the services sector. Consumers will be less concerned with status, hard work, competition, and material success. Instead, their attention will swing more to personal fulfillment and achievement measured quite differently from past generations. These value differences are highlighted in the following comparison of attitudes held by (1) college graduates of today and (2) college graduates ten years after graduation. See Fig. 31-1. The authors of that study predicted that the value systems of today's graduates are permanent, not transitory. These values may be modified over time, but today's graduates are not going to settle down in the value mainstream as it has existed for the past 20 to 30 years.

USE OF SYSTEMS APPROACH AND MARKETING PLANNING

Throughout this book we have advocated the use of the systems approach in the philosophy and practice of marketing management. Even our definition of marketing back in Chapter 1 embodied the systems concept. We can anticipate a growing appreciation of the value of treating marketing as a total system, composed of several subsystems such as a marketing information system, a channel system, a physical distribution system, etc.

The acceptance of the systems approach to marketing implicitly carries with it several attendant trends. One is the recognition of the indispensable value of marketing planning, especially as firms become larger, more complex, and more decentralized. Second, the various marketing activities within a firm are becoming better integrated with one another, and marketing in total will be better coordinated with the other major functions (finance, production, etc.) in a company.

Third, we may expect the marketing programs in many firms to acquire an international perspective. Moreover, this international dimension will be integrated with the domestic arm, thus forming a global marketing enterprise. This trend will develop, if for no other reason, simply because in many companies the best opportunities for growth lie in foreign operations.[18] Finally, the adoption of a systems approach in marketing should facilitate the growth of vertical marketing channel systems as the dominant distribution network in our economy. This newer system will largely replace the traditional channel arrangement consisting of loosely aligned, independent, frequently conflicting assortments of manufacturers, wholesalers, and retailers. (For a review of major trends in retailing institutions, the final section of Chapter 17 could be reread profitably at this point.)

SCIENTIFIC MARKETING AND INTERDISCIPLINARY CONTRIBUTIONS

Enough groundwork has been laid to predict that marketing management in business is on the threshold of a new era in problem solving—an era which would abandon the heavy reliance on subjective executive judgment in favor of an approach based on knowledge from mathematics, the behavioral sciences, and other nonbusiness fields. Marketing executives traditionally have not been trained in the scientific approach, and they have resisted change in this area. For example, many of them have not made much effective use of a computer. But a new day is com-

---

18 J. R. G. Jenkins, "Cultural Dimensions of International Marketing," in *Proceedings* of the Second Annual Conference of the Canadian Association of Administrative Sciences, Toronto, 1974, p. 4-88.

THE CONTRASTING VALUES OF COLLEGE GRADUATES AND THE GRADUATES OF 10 YEARS EARLIER

10-year graduates	Current graduates
The system works, with reservations	The system does not work, but used to
Competition is a positive element	Competition is negative, "anti-humanist"
Hard work brings society's rewards	Hard work isn't worth the rewards it brings
Work itself is an important value	Work is a questionable value
Material success is desirable and attainable	Material success is questionable and no longer attainable for everyone
Success means accumulation	Conventionally defined success means accumulation
Material success and status go together	Material success and conventionally defined status are questionable values
Personal self-fulfillment comes with material success	Personal self-fulfillment may have no relation to material success
Freedom comes with money— the more money the more freedom	Freedom is a state of mind, it requires only minimum money. Hunting after money and success curtail freedom
Whatever cuts the incentive to work hard is dangerous for the system and its values	Working too hard and devoting too much attention to work is dangerous for the individual

Source: Scott Ward, Thomas S. Robertson, and William Capitman, " 'What Will Be Different about Tomorrow's Consumer?' " in Fred C. Allvine (ed.), *1971 Combined Proceedings,* American Marketing Association, Chicago, 1972, p. 373.

Figure 31-1.

ing—it may not come quickly, but it is coming. We can expect companies increasingly to implement the concept of a marketing information system as a continuing system of information management to aid in problem solving.

As a separate field of study, marketing evolved from the general discipline of economics. However, marketers now recognize that they can draw profitably from many other disciplines. The behavioral sciences—psychology, sociology, anthropology—have contributed much to an understanding of consumer behavior. Statistics and mathematics, as well, have contributed to quantitative measurement in marketing. Demography, geography, and ecology have contributed to an understanding of markets and market movements. Looking to the future, we can expect marketers to become better trained in the use of the tools of other disciplines and to be more cognizant of their value in marketing.

As part of this interdisciplinary approach, we are seeing a melding of the work of behavioral scientists and quantitative analysts. Unlike the separatism of the past, today we see psychologists and sociologists making extended use of quantitative techniques, while the mathematicians are trying to apply their theories to practical problems. This interdisciplinary activity is bearing fruit in many marketing areas, but especially in terms of broadening and deepening our understanding of buyer behavior.[19]

A major spur to scientific problem solving in marketing has been the developments in computer technology. The use of a computer can increase a firm's marketing efficiency tremendously because executives are able to analyze the marketing effort and conduct many other types of marketing research projects in greater detail, at less expense, and with more speed than has been possible heretofore. An obvious prediction is that as newer, more analytically trained people appear in marketing executive positions, companies will make substantial strides toward realizing the potential for computer use in marketing.[20]

GROWING SOCIETAL ORIENTATION IN MARKETING

Up to this point our crystal-ball gazing has centered largely on the role of marketing in the individual firm, that is, in the *private* sector of our economy. Now in shifting our attention to marketing's future role in the *public* sector, we should recall the discussion in the preceding chapter. Consumerism will probably loom larger, thus posing greater challenges for marketing to help consumers fulfill their expectations. Marketing must, and undoubtedly will, assume a key role in improving the economic situation for low-income consumers. After all, "creating and delivering a standard of living" is one definition of marketing. Marketing also will become increasingly involved in solving the problems of environmental pollution. We will increasingly question the value of continued economic growth when it is accompanied by the use of nonreplaceable natural resources. Marketing will play a major role in developing the effective use and conservation of these resources. The concept of demarketing will get more attention.

As societal values change, marketing may come under more criticism. In considering the marketability of a new product, rather than asking, "Can it be sold?" a marketing executive may be asking, "Should it be sold? Is it worth its cost to society?" In effect, we may see shift from the marketing concept to the human concept. Or perhaps these can be one and the same if business can interpret the marketing concept as being societally oriented over the long run.[21]

---

19 See John A. Howard, "Buyer Behavior and Related Technological Advances," *Journal of Marketing*, January, 1970, pp. 18-21.

20 See Philip Kotler, "The Future of the Computer in Marketing," *Journal of Marketing*, January, 1970, pp. 11-14; and Paul E. Green, "Measurement and Data Analysis," *Journal of Marketing*, January, 1970, pp. 15-17.

21 Leslie M. Dawson, "The Human Concept: New Philosophy for Business," *Business Horizons*, December, 1969, pp. 29-38.

QUESTIONS AND PROBLEMS

1. Some people feel that too much power is concentrated in big business in North America and that large firms should be broken up. Yet these same people will drive a General Motors car, buy groceries at a Loblaw's supermarket, buy home appliances made by General Electric, wash with a brand of Procter & Gamble soap and brush their teeth with Crest toothpaste. How do you reconcile the behavior of these people with their opinion concerning big business?

2. Name some products which you feel are marketed under too many different brand names. About how many should be eliminated? How should we go about the elimination process?

3. "Middlemen make unfairly high profits." Do you agree?

4. Some people believe that there are too many gasoline service stations in their communitites. Suggest a method for reducing the number of stations. Are there too many in your community? How many should be eliminated?

5. Evaluate the following criticisms of advertising:

   a. Advertising creates a false sense of values.

   b. Advertising costs too much.

   c. Advertising is in bad taste.

   d. Advertising is false, misleading, and deceptive.

   e. Advertising tends to create monopolies.

6. What proposals do you have for regulating advertising?

7. What specific recommendations do you have for reducing the costs of marketing?

8. List the major federal laws affecting marketing. Indicate in each case whether the law's principal purpose is to aid business or regulate it. Briefly describe the intent and provisions of each measure.

9. Besides the examples given in this chapter, can you name some fields of business which the government entered because private enterprise was unable to meet, or refused to meet, consumer demand?

10. Is the marketing concept compatible with a societal orientation in marketing?

11. "When a company can sell all it can produce (during periods of product shortages), management should cut expenses by reducing its sales force and advertising expenditures." Discuss.

12. Assume that a manufacturer's sales force is paid a salary plus a commission on sales volume. How can management motivate these people during periods of product shortages when they cannot get enough of the product to sell?

13. What can a manufacturer do to hold together his good retail distribution system when, because of shortages, he cannot supply these retailers with all the product quantities they order?

CASES FOR PART EIGHT

CASE 22: NEWFOUNDLAND TELEPHONE COMPANY*

Evaluation of research design

It was early in June and Mr. K. A. A. Marshall, Supervisor of Public Relations at Newfoundland Telephone Company in St. John's, was considering the possibility of preparing a corporate advertising program to be run as part of Newfoundland Telephone's annual advertising campaign to begin in October. The objectives of such a corporate advertising program would be, firstly, to improve the "corporate image" of Newfoundland Telephone particularly in the minds of its customers, both domestic and commercial, and in the minds of the public generally; and secondly, to expand the awareness of customers and the public of the many services offered by the company.

A logical first step in the preparation of such a corporate advertising campaign

---

*This case was prepared by James G. Barnes with the assistance of Mr. K. A. A. Marshall, Supervisor of Public Relations, Newfoundland Telephone Company, and is intended to stimulate class discussion concerning management problems rather than to illustrate either effective or ineffective handling of these problems.

would be to determine, as far as is possible, what image the general public has of the Newfoundland Telephone Company, and what degree of knowledge exists with regard to the services offered. Mr. Marshall felt that at the early stages of preparing the campaign he would have to focus his attention toward the company's existing image as seen by two distinct groups: domestic subscribers and commercial or business subscribers. By obtaining information on this subject, he would be better able to establish the direction which a corporate advertising campaign should take.

Research Project. In order to gather information on the existing "corporate image" of Newfoundland Telephone Company, Mr. Marshall decided to undertake a research study which would gather data from all areas of the Province of Newfoundland served by the company. The objectives of this research project were twofold:

(1) to determine the level of awareness among the business community of Newfoundland Telephone as a telecommunications company in general, and as a supplier of specific business hardware capability in particular;

(2) to ascertain the attitudes of residence subscribers toward many facets of "telephone service".

In order to determine the awareness of the business community of the ability of Newfoundland Telephone Company to supply a broad range of communications hardware and services, Mr. Marshall felt that he needed answers to the following questions:

(1) how aware is the business community that certain business services exist and that they are supplied by Newfoundland Telephone? These services include Data Communications Services; Teletypewriter Exchange Service (TWX); Foreign Exchange Service (FX); P.B.X.; Call Director; Intercom; Speakerphone; Code-a-phone; Bellboy; Electrowriter; and Communications Consultant Service. Short descriptions of these services are included as Exhibit I.

(2) What is the average businessperson's image of Newfoundland Telephone Company as a supplier of expertise in the area of telecommunications? What is this image compared with Canadian National Telecommunications?

(3) How aware is the average businessperson of the Trans-Canada Telephone System and its functions?

The Trans-Canada Telephone System is an association of the eight regional telephone companies in Canada, of which Newfoundland Telephone is one. These companies have joined forces to create a national communications network whereby voice or data may be transmitted throughout Canada. This association also gives the regional telephone companies a unified voice in their dealings with government and other bodies.

Mr. Marshall felt it was important that business subscribers realize that Newfoundland Telephone Company is more than a provincial organization and that it is a member of the Trans-Canada Telephone System.

It was also his opinion that Newfoundland Telephone should know the attitudes of average homeowners and domestic telephone users toward the service which they receive from their telephone company. In this regard, it was necessary to obtain the following information from domestic subscribers:

(1) what is their level of satisfaction with their present telephone service in terms of the actual operation of the telephone? How often do they experience trouble with their telephone?

Exhibit I
BUSINESS SERVICES OFFERED BY NEWFOUNDLAND
TELEPHONE COMPANY

1. Data Communications
Service — allows a business subscriber to transmit data from remote locations, branch plants, warehouses, retail outlets, offices, etc. to similar locations or to a centralized computer facility for immediate processing.

2. Teletypewriter Exchange
Service (TWX) — allows the subscriber to communicate with other TWX subscribers through a typewriter-like device linked through telephone lines, comparable to the competitive TELEX network.

3. Foreign Exchange
Service (FX) — enables a subscriber to have his telephone number listed in the telephone directory of a distant city, thereby allowing him to receive calls from the distant location direct, without the caller placing a long distance call.

4. PBX — is the conventional large switchboard system found in most large office buildings which allows an operator to receive calls and channel them to particular extension telephones.

5. Call Director — is a small desktop switchboard which allows one person to receive, hold and channel calls for up to thirty people in an office.

6. Intercom — is a service which permits interoffice communication without using regular business telephone lines.

7. Speakerphone — consists of a desk top microphone and loudspeaker which allows an individual or a group to carry on a telephone conversation without using the conventional telephone handset.

8. Code-a-phone — is an automatic answering service which enables a subscriber to record a message up to three minutes in length which is automatically activated and played when a caller dials the subscriber's telephone number. The caller is then able to record his own message which is available when the subscriber wishes to receive it.

9. Bellboy — is a paging device which is carried in a coat pocket by a doctor, businessperson or any individual who wishes to keep in touch with his office. By dialing a seven-digit number associated with the particular Bellboy instrument, a secretary can signal that a message has been received and that a call should be placed to the office immediately.

10. Electrowriter	—allows a subscriber to transmit handwritten messages over long-distance or within the same building through the telephone lines and have them received exactly as they are written.
11. Communications Consultant Service	—is a free consultant service offered by the telephone company to assess the telecommunications requirements of a particular business and to recommend the best system to meet such needs.

(2) when they have need for an installation of a new telephone, what is their evaluation of the courtesy and efficiency with which the installation is done?

(3) when they have need of repair service, how do they evaluate the performance of the company in terms of the efficiency of the repair work and the courtesy of the repair staff?

(4) how knowledgeable are home subscribers of the variety of telephone models available?

(5) what is their evaluation of the company's billing and account collection procedures?

(6) how much reliance do domestic subscribers place on "long distance" as a means of communication?

(7) what is the attitude of the average subscriber toward the rates charged by the telephone company?

In submitting his proposal to the management group at Newfoundland Telephone Company, Mr. Marshall suggested that the information needed by his office in order to formulate an effective corporate advertising campaign be collected through a research study carried out by three senior students in the Commerce program at Memorial University of Newfoundland. These students would visit telephone subscribers, both in the business and domestic sectors, and would interview them using an unstructured approach, guided by a questionnaire. Of the three students employed, only one had any previous experience in the conducting of marketing research projects, but all three were given special instruction on the products and services offered by the company before they actually interviewed any subscribers. In addition, a pre-test of the questionnaire and the interview method was conducted by the three interviewers before the actual study was begun.

Interview method. Mr. Marshall felt that since the purpose of the research was to discover the "below the surface" attitudes and awareness of the company's services on the part of business and domestic subscribers, the approach taken should rely on non-structured, non-disguised questioning. By using a "depth interview" approach, the interviewers used the questionnaires as a guide and directed the discussion toward specific problems and points raised by the interviewee. The interviewers were to use the questionnaire merely as a method of directing the discussion.

Sampling method. In the case of business subscribers, Mr. Marshall was interested in the opinions and levels of awareness of all businesspeople who are potential users of the many services offered by the company. The business sample was drawn solely from the St. John's market on the premise that many of the company's larger business subscribers are located in this area and that it would be possible to include a large variety of businesses in the sample. The business sample totalled thirty-five subscribers, and was selected on a non-profitability, judgment sampling basis so that the sample would include both large and small businesses, and businesses representing a variety of industries.

In obtaining the opinions and attitudes of domestic subscribers, it was decided to draw the sample from three different market areas: St. John's, Corner Brook and Grand Falls. These three areas represent the three largest urban areas of the Province and, in total, account for a very large percentage of the company's total subscribers. From each of the three areas a total of twenty-five subscribers were selected randomly to be interviewed.

Questionnaires. The questionnaires employed in the research study were designed mainly to serve as guides to the interviewers rather than to be answered exactly as they were presented.

The questionnaire used to elicit the opinions and levels of awareness of business subscribers is included as Exhibit II, and the domestic subscriber questionnaire is attached as Exhibit III.

Exhibit II
QUESTIONNAIRE EMPLOYED IN INTERVIEWING
BUSINESS SUBSCRIBERS:

Good morning, my name is ———
and I am a Memorial University student carrying out a Marketing Research Project for the summer on behalf of Newfoundland Telephone Company Limited. Our purpose is to ascertain customers' awareness of and reliance upon telecommunications services in the Province. I don't want to go over any set questionnaire, but rather discuss your own situation with you for a few minutes.

For instance ....
1. (a) What type of special phone equipment do you utilize in your business?
   (b) Have you ever had any trouble with it?
   (c) What do you think of your telephone service generally?
2. Are you aware of other services? List them. Has anybody ever come in to go over your business with you with a view to suggesting a system appropriate to your needs?
3. I would like to list several types of communications services available to business and have you tell me if you're aware of them.
   (Do not mention items respondent has already mentioned in Question 2.)
   Data Services
   TWX
   FX (Foreign Exchange)
   PBX and Call Director
   Intercom
   Speakerphone
   Code-a-phone

Bellboy
Electrowriter

4. (a) If you were ever in a position where you would like to transmit data over any distance, whom would you contact?
   (b) If you had a need for a TELEX or TWX Service, whom would you contact?
5. Have you ever heard of the Trans-Canada Telephone System? If yes, tell me what you know about it.
6. Clarify and list any general comments made by the respondent.
7. End interview.

Exhibit III
QUESTIONNAIRE EMPLOYED IN INTERVIEWING
DOMESTIC SUBSCRIBERS:

Good morning. My name is _____
and I'm a university student employed for the summer to carry out a Marketing Research Project on behalf of Newfoundland Telephone Company Limited. I don't want to go over a set list of questions, but I'd like to discuss some things about your telephone service generally for the next 10 minutes.

1. (a) Have you had any trouble with your telephone service recently?

                                                                    YES NO

   If yes, (b) obtain details
   Was repair done in reasonable period of time?
   Was repair man courteous?

2. (a) Have you had a new phone or extension put in your house over the last 3 years? If no, go to question 3. If yes, (b)
   (b) When?
   (c) What part of the house did you put it in?
   (d) (i) What kind of phone—i.e. model and colour?
       (ii) Did you have a good choice?
   (e) What kind of service did you get?   GOOD BAD
       —time to complete
       —quality of job
       —done when scheduled
       —courtesy
       —facilities available.

3. (a) What do you think of your telephone service generally?
   (b) What do you like best about your present phone service?

                          (For the Interviewer)

BEST	*LEAST*
Service (specify)	Billing
	Rates
Courtesy	Service (specify)
Progress	Courtesy
Other (specify)	Other (specify)

4. How often do you use Long Distance? Why?
5. Summarize any other general comment.
6. End Interview.

QUESTIONS

1. Evaluate the steps taken by Mr. Marshall in preparing for Newfoundland Telephone's corporate advertising campaign.
2. Evaluate the actual research project which was designed and executed in order to obtain information on which to base the advertising campaign?
3. Determine any areas of weakness on the design of the research project which could possibly bias the results obtained.
4. Do you feel that it will be possible for Mr. Marshall to prepare an effective corporate advertising campaign based on the data to be gathered from this research project?
5. What additional information might Mr. Marshall have collected during the course of this research project?

CASE 23: STARLING LIMITED

Marketing program for a new product

In answer to a market demand, Starling Limited developed a plastic attaché-type carrying case for its line of toy building blocks. The annual sales volume forecast for this carrying case, however, was too low to cover production costs, plus returning the rate of gross profit established as a company standard. Consequently, Mr. Arnold Ferris, the vice-president of sales in the toy division, proposed that this new carrying case also be added to the line of attaché cases now sold by the company's luggage division; he hoped that this would generate the additional sales volume necessary to make the new product a profitable venture.

Founded in 1910 in the East, Starling Limited's headquarters and sales offices were located in a large Eastern city, while manufacturing facilities were in Quebec and Ontario. Currently, Starling marketed in Canada and the U.S. Management was planning, however, to enter further into international markets and to establish production facilities overseas.

Generally, since its beginning the firm enjoyed a profitable growth rate. Sales in 1970 totalled $19 million, divided among three seemingly unrelated product lines—luggage, small home appliances, and toys. The luggage division accounted for about 75 percent of the annual volume, appliances generated 18 percent, and toys 5 percent.

Starling was one of the country's largest producers of carrying cases, especially men's and women's nonleather luggage. However, some of the units were constructed of injection-molded plastic, and in recent years the company had added a line of fiber glass cases. Shortly before World War II Starling acquired an appliance company producing toasters, irons, mixers, and other small electric appliances. In 1960 a line of plastic snap-together toys was added under the brand name of "Plato" (plastic-toy or play-toy).

Starling conducted an effective advertising, sales promotion, and publicity program. Television and full-color magazine advertising was used extensively. A public relations and publicity program was operated continuously. Starling also "merchandised" its national advertising and publicity programs by making available to retailers complete local advertising, point-of-sale, and other promotional materials.

Dealers were encouraged to promote and display Starling's products and to coordinate with Starling's national promotional program.

In the corporate organizational structure there were three vice presidents of sales and a vice president of marketing, all reporting to one of the two executive vice presidents. The marketing executive was responsible for advertising, sales promotion, marketing research, marketing planning, and other marketing services. Each of the sales vice presidents was responsible for sales of one of the three major product lines, and separate sales forces were used for each line.

It had come to the attention of Mr. Ferris that there was a definite need to improve the packaging of Starling's main toy product—Plato building blocks. These blocks were a system of precision-made, snap-together, colorful plastic units which originated in Denmark and were already one of the largest-selling toy items in Europe. With Starling's capabilities in the precision molding of plastic luggage, management recognized the potential of these building blocks in capturing a share of the North American toy market.

Starling began manufacturing Plato blocks in 1961 under a licensing aggreement with the Danish inventor. On the basis of successful results in ten test markets, Plato blocks were launched nationally in the Canadian market and the 1962 New York Toy Fair. Growth was rapid, and volume well exceeded the anticipated results. The company became one of the largest in the construction-building-block area of the toy market. Its main competition came from Samsonite's LEGO blocks, Mattel Company and others.

The toy products were sold to more than one hundred factory-franchised distributors and also directly to large specialty toy retailers. Retail prices ranged from $1.50 for a simple town plan of building blocks, through $4.95 to $9.95 for wheel toys, to $25 for an elaborate town plan. Retailer gross margins were typically 40 percent.

The need for improved packaging was indicated by an increasing number of letters from customers requesting a carrying case that would last for the life of the Plato blocks and would hold two or more sets of blocks. The original cardboard box wore out quickly and held only the set of blocks that came with it. These letters indicated some willingness to pay an additional price for a better case, but the amount was uncertain.

In response to this demand, Starling developed a plastic attaché-type carrying case, about 15 by 12 by 3 inches in size. The case was produced by the injection molding of polypropolene; thus the company could capitalize on its experience in manufacturing plastic luggage.

Upon the recommendation of a sample of toy dealers, a retail price of $9.95 was set for the new case. The wholesale selling price to Starling then would be $6. However, production costs at the expected sales volume would be $5.50, thus yielding a substantially lower gross margin than the 30 percent typically desired by Starling. Moreover, according to a limited survey, only 2 percent of the toy consumers would be willing to pay the $9.95 price. Expected sales at this price would be only about one-third to one-half of the dollar volume necessary to recover the fixed investment (molds, dyes, fixtures) and to meet established profit criteria within the next five years.

Mr. Ferris then conceived the idea that the additionally needed volume of sales might be generated if the toy carrying case were added as a low-priced unit to round out the line of attaché cases marketed by the luggage division. Mr. Ferris made this proposal to Mr. Richard Morris, the vice president of sales in the luggage division. The two men agreed to forward the proposal to the company's executive committee.

The luggage division marketed a wide assortment of carrying cases, including men's and women's luggage, attaché cases, and specialized cases for carrying almost anything, from musical instruments to sensitive electronic equipment. The luggage and attaché cases were sold under the Travelite brand, which enjoyed a fine reputation as a high-quality product. These products were distributed by the luggage division sales force directly to leading department stores and luggage stores on a highly selective basis and in the U.S. to trading-stamp firms, who offered the products as premiums in their redemption catalogues. A system of strongly suggested retail prices was used. A few retailers who sought to cut these prices soon lost their franchises on the grounds that they did not properly handle, display, or sell the product.

Starling had about a 35 percent share of the total attaché-case market in Canada and about 2 percent of the U.S. market. This product contributed $3.5 million of the luggage division's total sales of $16 million in 1970. The company's attaché products consisted of two lines: the Travelite *Executive* attaché cases, produced in three sizes and retailing for $25.95 to $29.95 and wholesaling for $14.25 to $16.50, and the Travelite *Signature* cases, manufactured in two sizes and retailing for $16.95 to $19.95 and wholesaling for $9.30 and $10.95.

In the total attaché-case market the price range was from $2.75 to $110. Travelite was a strong competitor in the middle to high price range. Investigation of the market made in response to the new-product proposal showed a total Canadian and U.S. market of approximately $14 million for attaché cases in the retail range of $2.75 to $12.74. Further delineation had shown a $9.5-million market in both countries for cases in the $7.75-to-$12.74 price range. The proposed attaché case was described as the third best case for the money in comparison testing with the six other cases expected to offer the strongest competition. Its disadvantages were that it looked cheaper and was less functional.

Management felt that Starling could capture a large share of the market potential in Canada and a reasonable share in the U.S. for the low-priced case. The executive committee was worried, however, by other considerations involved in adding this case to the existing line in the luggage division.

The case could be made in blue and red for the toy market and in more masculine colors such as brown, black, and olive green with an additional metal stripping for the attaché market per se. However, the case would still look cheap, especially as compared with the more expensive Travelite *Executive* and *Signature* lines.

If marketed as a Travelite case, management recognized that the weight of the brand name would enable Starling to distribute the proposed case through the existing selected outlets. This might preclude direct competition in these outlets from other cases in this price range. However, the Travelite quality image might be endangered. If another brand name were adopted, discount stores could be used in the channels of distribution. However, the proposed case then would not benefit from the presold Travelite name. Also, the consumer had more opportunity for comparison shopping in discount stores, so the product might not fare so well.

Mr. Ferris observed that while the attaché case might not be accepted by the consumer on its own merits as an adjunct to the luggage line, its importance to the toy department in fulfilling the demand for a carrying case might be reason for accepting the proposal as a whole.

QUESTIONS

1. Should the luggage division add the proposed product to its line of attaché cases?
2. If so:
   a. Should this case carry the Travelite brand?
   b. What should be its retail price?
   c. What channels of distribution should be used?
3. If not, what should the toy division do about a carrying case for its building blocks?

CASE 24: THE ARGENTINE DRUG CAPER*

Marketing cost analysis

Bill Cool, the general manager of the International Division of the Far Flung Drug Co., finds himself faced with an extremely difficult competitive situation in Argentina. A Japanese competitor is underpricing him on his major product ("super pill") in the Argentine market, and he is faced with total loss of all Argentine sales for this product. "Super pill" is manufactured in one of Far Flung Drug's United States plants from which the International Division purchases them.

Bill's problem, as he sees it, is a matter of meeting his competitor's price. "Super pill" and the Japanese competitive product are basically equal from the point of view of quality and performance. Delivery and credit terms are also similar. The basic financial facts are as follows:

Prices:
    Super pill $1.00 per gross
    Japanese pill $.60 per gross
Annual Volume:
    5,000,000 gross plus an estimated 5% annual growth factor
Manufacturing Cost:
    (Including transportation) $.70 per gross

In this situation Bill felt that he could not afford to meet the competitive price of $.60, since his division would then show a loss of $.10 per unit. He then remembered, somewhat vaguely, a discussion he got involved in while attending an executive development program. The discussion revolved around the idea that manufacturing costs were best thought of as consisting of two separate components, i.e., fixed and variable. The fixed costs were then described as a "kind of handicap" which a company tried to overcome by generating a sufficient profit contribution, i.e., the difference between sales and variable costs.

Bill wondered if these concepts might be applicable to his situation. As a result of a cable to his company's main office in Atlanta, Bill found that the accounting staff of Far Flung Drugs did not separate variable and fixed costs in its cost accounting system. However, they turned Bill's question over to a cost analyst who estimated that $.30 of the $.70 per unit manufacturing cost represented fixed costs.

---

*Case prepared by Prof. William L. Ferrara, Pennsylvania State University. Reproduced with permission.

Based on the above information, Bill calculated variable costs per gross as $.40 and a profit contribution of $.20 per gross if the competitive price was met. With these facts in hand Bill went to Atlanta to discuss his problem with the headquarters pricing policy staff.

In Atlanta, all agreed that the company's other products were covering the fixed costs and capacity was available for the foreseeable future to produce sufficient amounts of "super pill." All also agreed that the competitive price had to be met and could be met without any adverse effects and with a $.20 per gross profit contribution. Thus, Bill Cool went home satisfied that he could retain his Argentine "super pill" business at a price which would be profitable to Far Flung Drugs.

A few months later Bill noticed that reports concerning the profitability of South American sales were getting worse and worse. He could not understand this since everything seemed to be going well from a volume and cost point of view.

Bill decided that he had to uncover the causes of his poor showing, so he started to take apart the profit report for South America. To his surprise he found that the headquarters accounting staff was charging his Argentine sales of "super pill" with a manufacturing cost of $.70 rather than $.40. His anticipated profit contribution of $.20 per gross was in effect turned into a loss of $.10 per gross. An expected annual profit contribution of $1,000,000 (.20 × 5,000,000 gross) was being turned into a loss of $500,000 ($.10 × 5,000,000 gross) by a group of accountants.

Bill then tried to explain his poor South American showing to the company's executive committee at a special meeting called by the executive committee. They could not understand his explanation due to the fact that they were as concerned as the accountants with the "full cost" of manufacturing. Bill left the meeting, muttering to himself, "I make a sound and profitable decision and the accounting department makes me look like a bum. I guess they and the executive committee are really telling me to give up the Argentine market for 'super pill.' "

QUESTIONS

1. Assuming that "super pill" is a profitable product at the $.60 price, how would you adjust the profit report for South American sales to conform with Bill Cool's decision?

2. Was Bill Cool's decision really sound? That is, was there anything wrong with the analysis which preceded Bill's decision?

MARKETING ARITHMETIC

Marketing involves people—customers, middlemen, and producers. Much of the business activity of these people, however, is quantified in some manner. Consequently, mathematical figures are used as tools for the analysis of their quantitative relationships. Some knowledge of the rudiments of business arithmetic is essential for decision making in many areas of marketing. Since most students taking this course have already had a beginning course in accounting, this appendix is intended as a review. In marketing, we frequently use the following accounting or business arithmetic concepts: (1) the operating statement, (2) markups, and (3) analytical ratios. Another useful concept—discounts and terms of sale—was reviewed in Chapter 14 in connection with price policies.

THE OPERATING STATEMENT

An operating statement—often called a "profit and loss statement" or an "income and expense statement"—is one of the two main financial statements prepared by a company. The other is the balance sheet. An *operating statement* is s summary picture of the firm's income and expenses—its operations—over a period of time. In contrast, a *balance sheet* shows the assets, liabilities, and net worth of a company at a given time, for example, at the close of business on December 31, 1978.

The operating statement shows whether the business earned a net profit or suffered a net loss during the period covered. It arranges in orderly fashion a summary of the income and expense items which resulted in this net profit or loss. From the information in a profit and loss statement we also may compute several ratios useful in a financial analysis or a marketing analysis of the company's operations.

An operating statement may cover any selected period of time. Because of income tax requirements, virtually all firms prepare a statement covering operations during the calendar or fiscal year. In addition, it is common for businesses to prepare monthly, quarterly, or semiannual operating statements.

Figure A-1 is an example of an operating statement for a wholesaler or retailer. The main difference between the operating statement of a middleman and that of a manufacturer is in the cost-of-goods-sold section. A manufacturer shows a net figure for cost of goods *manufactured*, whereas the middleman's statement shows net *purchases*. If additional detail is desired, one can look to the accounting records and other supporting data upon which the operating statement was based.

MAJOR SECTIONS

From one point of view, the essence of business is very simple. A company buys or makes a product and then sells it for a higher price. Out of his sales revenue, the seller hopes to cover the cost of the merchandise and his own expenses and have something left over, which he calls "net profit." These relationships form the skeleton parts of an operating statement. Sales minus cost of goods sold equals gross margin; gross margin minus expenses equals net profit. An example based on Fig. A-1 is as follows:

Sales	$80,000
Cost of goods sold	48,000
Gross margin	32,000
Expenses	27,000
Net profit	$ 4,800

Sales. The first line in an operating statement records the gross sales—the total amount sold by the company. From this figure, the company deducts its sales returns and sales allowances. In virtually every firm at some time during an operating period, customers will want to return or exchange merchandise. In a sales return, the customer is refunded the full purchase price in cash or credit. In a sales allowance, the customer keeps the merchandise, but is given a reduction from selling because of some dissatisfaction. The income from the sale of returned merchandise is included in a company's gross sales.

After sales returns and allowances are deducted from gross sales, the resulting amount is net sales. This is the most important figure in the sales section of the statement. It represents the net amount of sales revenue out of which the company will pay for the products and all its expenses. The net sales figure is also the one upon which many operating ratios are based. It is set at 100 percent, and other items are then expressed as a percentage of net sales.

Cost of goods sold. From net sales, we must deduct the cost of the merchandise which was sold, as we work toward discovering the firm's final net profit. In deter-

Gross sales			$87,000
Less: Sales returns and allowances	$ 5,500		
Cash discounts allowed	1,500	7,000	
Net sales			$80,000
Cost of goods sold:			
Beginning inventory, January 1 (at cost)		18,000	
Gross purchases	49,300		
Less: Cash discounts taken on purchases	900		
Net purchases	48,400		
Plus: Freight in	1,600		
Net purchases (at delivered cost)		50,000	
Cost of goods available for sale		68,000	
Less: Ending inventory, December 31 (at cost)		20,000	
Cost of goods sold			48,000
Gross margin			32,000
Expenses:			
Salesmen's salaries and commissions		$11,000	
Advertising		2,400	
Office supplies		250	
Taxes (except income tax)		125	
Telephone and telegraph		250	
Delivery expenses		175	
Rent		800	
Heat, light, and power		300	
Depreciation		100	
Insurance		150	
Interest		150	
Bad debts		300	
Administrative salaries		7,500	
Office salaries		3,500	
Miscellaneous expenses		200	
Total expenses			27,200
Net profit			$ 4,800

Figure A-1. Alpha-Beta Company, operating statement, for year ending December 31, 1978.

mining cost of goods sold in a retail or wholesale operation, we start with the value of any merchandise on hand at the beginning of the period. To this we add the net cost of what was purchased during the period. From this total we deduct the value of whatever remains unsold at the end of the period. In Fig. A-1 the firm started with an inventory worth $18,000, and purchases were made which cost $50,000. Then the firm had a total of $68,000 worth of goods available for sale. If all were sold, the cost of goods sold would have been $68,000. At the end of the year, however, there is still $20,000 worth of merchandise on hand. Thus during the year, the company sold goods which cost $48,000.

In the preceding paragraph, we blithely spoke of merchandise "valued at" a certain figure or "worth" a stated amount. Actually, the problem of inventory valuation is complicated and sometimes controversial. The usual rule of thumb is to value inventories at cost or market, whichever is lower. The actual application of this rule may be difficult. Assume that a store buys six footballs at $2 each and the next week buys six more at $2.50 each and then places them, jumbled in a basket display for sale. Then one is sold, but there is no marking to indicate whether the cost of goods sold was $2 or $2.50, and the inventory value of the remaining eleven balls may be $27.50 or $28. If we multiply this situation by thousands of purchases and sales, we may begin to see the depth of the problem.

Another figure which deserves some comment is the net cost of delivered purchases. A company starts with its gross purchases at billed cost. Then it must deduct any purchases which were returned or any purchase allowances received. The company should also deduct any discounts taken for payment of the bill within a specified period of time. Deducting purchase returns and allowances and purchase discounts gives the net cost of the purchases. Then freight charges paid by the buyer (called "freight in") are added to net purchases to determine the net cost of *delivered* purchases. In some accounting systems, firms place their purchase discounts near the bottom of the operating statement in a section called "other income," thus treating these discounts as a reflection of financial ability to pay bills promptly. The preferred location of this income item in retail and wholesale operating statements today is in the cost-of-goods-sold section, so that management may see the net cost of its purchases.

In a manufacturing concern, the cost-of-goods-sold section takes on a slightly different form. Instead of determining the cost of goods *purchased,* the company determines the cost of goods *manufactured.* Cost of goods manufactured is added to the beginning inventory to ascertain the total goods available for sale. Then after the ending inventory of finished goods is deducted, the answer is cost of goods sold. To find the cost of goods *manufactured,* a company starts with the value of goods partially completed (beginning inventory of goods in process) and then adds the cost of raw materials and parts, direct and indirect labor, and factory overhead expenses incurred during the period. By deducting the value of goods still in process at the end of the period, management knows the cost of goods manufactured during that span of time.

Gross margin. Gross margin is determined simply by subtracting cost of goods sold from net sales. Gross margin, sometimes called "gross profit," is one of the key figures in the entire marketing program. When we say that a certain store has a "margin" of 30 percent or that a salesperson's compensation paid is set up to encourage the person to push the "high-margin" products, we are referring to the gross margin.

Expenses. Operating expenses are deducted from the gross margin to determine the net profit. The operating expense section includes marketing, administration, and possibly some miscellaneous expense items. It does not include cost of goods purchased or manufactured. These expenses have already been deducted. Expenses may be itemized in several different ways.

MARKUPS

It is common practice for retailers and wholesalers to use the concept of markup when determining the selling price of an article. Normally the selling price must exceed the cost of the merchandise by an amount sufficient to cover the operating expenses and still leave the desired profit. The difference between the selling price and the cost of the item is the markup. Sometimes it is termed the "mark-on."

The markup is closely related to the gross margin. It will be recalled that gross margin is equal to net sales minus cost of goods sold. Looking below the gross margin on an operating statement, we find that gross margin equals operating expenses plus net profit. Normally the initial markup in a company, department, or product line must be set a little higher than the overall gross margin desired for the selling unit because ordinarily some reductions will be incurred before all the articles are sold. For one reason or another, some items will not sell at the original price. They will have to be marked down, that is, reduced in price from the original level. Some pilferage and other shortages may also occur.

Typically, for convenience in computation and for other reasons, markups are expressed in percentages rather than dollars. The first problem is to determine the *base* for the percentage. That is, when we speak of a 40 percent markup, what do we mean—40 percent of what? Markups may be expressed as a percentage of either the cost price or the selling price. To determine markup percentage when it is based on cost, the formula is:

$$\text{Markup percentage} = \frac{\text{dollar markup}}{\text{cost}}$$

When the markup is based on selling price, the formula is:

$$\text{Markup percentage} = \frac{\text{dollar markup}}{\text{selling price}}$$

It is important that all interested parties understand which base is being used in a given situation. Otherwise the results can differ considerably. To illustrate, Mr. A runs a clothing store and claims he needs a 66-2/3 percent markup to make a small net profit. Mr. B, who runs a competitive store, says he needs only a 40 percent markup and that A must be inefficient or a big profiteer. Actually both merchants are using identical markups, but they are using different bases. Each man buys hats at $6 apiece and sets the selling price at $10. This is a markup of $4 per hat. Mr. A is expressing his markup as a percentage of cost—hence the 66-2/3 percent figure (4/6 = 66-2/3 percent). Mr. B, in quoting a 40 percent markup, bases his on the selling price (4/10 = 40 percent). It would be a mistake for Mr. A to try to get by on B's 40 percent markup, as long as A uses cost as his base. After buying hats at $6, Mr. A would end up with a selling price of $8.40 if he used B's markup but his own (A's) cost basis. That is, 40 percent over $6 equals $2.40. This $2.40 markup on the average over the entire hat department would *not* enable A to cover his usual expenses and make a profit. *Unless otherwise indicated, markup percentages are always stated as a percentage of the selling price.*

The computation of selling price is simple if we know dollar cost and the desired percentage markup. The following diagram, along with some examples, should help you understand the various relationships between selling price, cost, and markup, whether the markup is stated in percentages or dollars and whether the percentages are based on selling price or cost:

	$	%
Selling price		
−Cost		
Markup	$	%

In these examples, the markups are based on selling price. A merchant buys an article for $90 and knows he must get a markup of 40 percent. What is his selling price? By filling in the known information in the diagram, we see the following picture:

	$	
Selling price		100%
−Cost	90	
Markup	$	40%

It is easy to see that the percentage figure representing cost is 60 percent. Thus the $90 cost equals 60 percent of the selling price. The selling price is then $150. ($90 equals 60 percent times the selling price. Then $90 is divided by .6 or 60 percent to get the answer of $150.)

Another common situation facing a merchant is to have competition set a ceiling on selling price, or possibly he must buy an item to fit into one of his price lines. Then he wants to know the maximum amount he can pay for the item and still get his normal markup. For instance, assume that the selling price of an article is set at $60 (by competition or by the $59.95 price line). The retailer's normal markup is 35 percent. What is the most he should pay for this article? Again, let us fill in what we know in the diagram.

	$60	100%
Selling price		
−Cost		
Markup		35%

The dollar markup is $21 (35 percent of $60), so by a simple subtraction we find that the maximum cost the merchant will want to pay is $39.

It should be clearly understood that markups are figured on the selling price *at each level of business* in a channel of distribution. A manufacturer applies a markup to determine his selling price. The manufacturer's selling price then becomes the wholesaler's cost. Then the wholesaler must determine his own selling price by applying his usual markup percentage based on his—the wholesaler's—selling price. The same procedure is carried on by the retailer whose cost figure is the wholesaler's selling price. The following computations should illustrate this point:

Retailer's selling price	$20 }	Retailer's markup = $8 or 40 percent
Retailer's cost	$12 }	
Wholesaler's selling price	$12 }	Wholesaler's markup = $2, or 16-2/3 percent
Wholesaler's cost	$10 }	
Producer's selling price	$10 }	Producer's markup = $3, or 30 percent
Producer's cost	$7 }	

If a firm is used to dealing in markups based on cost—and sometimes this is done among wholesalers—the same diagrammatic approach may be employed that was used above in the examples of markup based on selling price. The only change is that cost will equal 100 percent, and the selling price will be 100 percent plus the markup based on cost. As an example, assume that a firm bought an article for $70 and wanted a 20 percent markup based on cost. The markup in dollars is $14 (20 percent of $70), and the selling price is $84 ($70 plus $14).

Even though it is customary to compute markups on the basis of selling price, a marketing executive should understand the relationships between markups on cost and markups on selling price. For instance, if a product costs $6 and sells for $10, there is a $4 markup. This is a 40 percent markup when based on selling price, but a 66-2/3 percent markup when based on cost. An executive should also be able to convert from one base to another. The following diagram may be helpful in understanding these relationships:

Selling price = 100%   Cost = 100%

$$40\%\left\{\begin{array}{c}\text{Markup} = \\ \$4.00\end{array}\right. \left.\begin{array}{c} \\ \end{array}\right\}66\text{-}2/3\%$$

$10 = 100% $10 = 166-2/3%

$$60\%\left\{\begin{array}{c}\text{Cost} = \\ \$6.00\end{array}\right. \left.\begin{array}{c} \\ \end{array}\right\}100\%$$

These convertible relationships may be expressed in the following formulas:

(1) Percentage markup on selling price = $\dfrac{\text{percentage markup on cost}}{100\% + \text{percentage markup on cost}}$

(2) Percentage markup on cost = $\dfrac{\text{percentage markup on selling price}}{100\% - \text{percentage markup on selling price}}$

To illustrate the use of these formulas, let us assume that a retailer has a markup of 25 percent on cost and wants to know what the corresponding figure is, based on selling price. In formula (1) we get

$$\frac{25\%}{100\% + 25\%} = \frac{25\%}{125\%} = 20\%$$

A markup of 33 1/3 percent based on selling price converts to 50 percent based on cost, by using formula (2) as follows:

$$\frac{33\ 1/3\%}{100\% - 33\ 1/3\%} = \frac{33\ 1/3\%}{66\ 2/3\%} = 50\%$$

ANALYTICAL RATIOS

From a study of the operating statement, management can develop several ratios which will be useful tools in evaluating the results of its marketing program. In most of these cases, net sales is used as the base of 100 percent. In fact, unless it is specifically mentioned to the contrary, all ratios reflecting gross margin, net profit, or any operating expense are stated as a percentage of net sales.

GROSS MARGIN PERCENTAGE

This is the ratio between gross margin and net sales. Referring to Fig. A-1, the gross margin percentage is $\dfrac{\$32,000}{\$80,000}$ or 40 percent.

NET PROFIT PERCENTAGE

This ratio is computed by dividing net profits by net sales. In Fig. A-1 the ratio is $\dfrac{\$4,800}{\$80,000}$ or 6 percent. This percentage may be computed either before or after federal income taxes are deducted, but the answer should be labeled adequately to reflect which it is.

OPERATING EXPENSE PERCENTAGE

When total operating expenses are divided by net sales, the result is the operating expense ratio or percentage. In Fig. A-1 the ratio is 34 percent $\dfrac{\$27,200}{\$80,000}$. In a similar fashion, we may determine the expense ratio for any given cost. Thus we note in Fig. A-1 that the rent expense was 1 percent, advertising was 3 percent, and salespeople's salaries and commissions were 13.75 percent. Frequently in its operating statement, a company will add a percentage column at the right. This column will start with net sales being 100 percent and will show for each item on the statement its percentage in relation to net sales.

RATE OF STOCKTURN

Management often measures the efficiency of its marketing operations by means of the stockturn ratio. This figure represents the number of times the average inventory is "turned over," or sold, during the period under study. The ratio is computed on either a cost or a selling-price basis. That is, both the numerator and the denominator of the ratio fraction must be expressed in the same terms, either cost or selling price.

On a cost basis, the formula is as follows:

$$\text{Rate of stockturn} = \frac{\text{cost of goods sold}}{\text{average inventory at cost}}$$

The average inventory is determined by adding the beginning and ending inventory and dividing this answer by 2. In Fig. A-1 the average inventory is $\dfrac{\$18,000 + \$20,000}{2} = \$19,000$. The stockturn rate is $\dfrac{\$48,000}{\$19,000}$ or 2.5. Because inventories usually are abnormally low at the first of the year in anticipation of taking physical inventory, this average may not be representative. Consequently, some companies add the book inventories at the beginning of each month and divide this sum by 12.

If the inventory is kept on a retail basis, as is done in most large retail organizations, the stockturn rate equals net sales divided by average inventory at selling price. Sometimes the stockturn rate is computed by dividing the number of *units* sold by the average inventory expressed in units.

Wholesale and retail trade associations in many types of businesses compile and publish figures showing the average rate of stockturn for their members. A firm with a low rate of stockturn is apt to be spending too much on storage and inventory expenses. Also, the company has a higher risk of obsolescence or spoilage. If the stockturn rate gets too high, this may indicate that the company maintains too low an average inventory. Often a firm in this situation is operating on a hand-to-mouth buying system. In addition to incurring high handling and billing costs per order, the company is apt to be out of stock on some items.

MARKDOWN PERCENTAGE

Sometimes a retailer is unable to sell an article at the originally posted price, and he reduces this price in order to move the goods. A *markdown* is the reduction from original selling price. Management frequently finds it very helpful to determine the markdown percentage and to analyze the size and number of markdowns and the reasons for them. Retailers, particularly, make extensive use of markdown analysis.

Markdowns are expressed as a percentage of net sales and *not* as a percentage of original selling price. To illustrate, assume that a retailer purchased a hat for $6 and marked it up 40 percent to sell for $10. The hat did not sell at that price, so he marked it down to $8. Now it is true that his advertisement or display sign may advertise a price cut of 20 percent. Yet in our calculations, his markdown is stated at $2, or 25 percent of the $8 selling price.

Markdowns in a department or in an entire company are computed for a given period of time by dividing total dollar markdowns by total net sales during that period. Two important points should be noted here. The markdown percentage is computed in this fashion, regardless of whether the markdown items were sold or are still in the store. Also, the percentage is computed with respect to total net sales and not only in connection with sales of marked-down articles. As an example, assume that a retailer buys ten hats at $6 each and prices them to sell at $10. He sells five hats at $10, marks the other five down to $8, and sells three at the lower price. His total sales are $74, and his markdowns are $10. He has a markdown ratio of 13.5 percent.

Markdowns do not appear on the profit and loss statement because they occur *before* an article is sold. The first item on an operating statement is gross sales. That figure reflects the actual selling price, which may be the selling price after a markdown has been taken.

A refinement in the computation of the markdown percentage involves sales allowances. Actually, these allowances are added to markdowns in determining the markdown percentage. The formula is:

$$\text{Markdown percentage} = \frac{\text{dollar markdown} + \text{dollar sales allowances}}{\text{total net sales in dollars}}$$

The reasoning here is that, in effect, an allowance is simply a markdown taken after the sale was made. In the hat example above, if the retailer saw that a hat was soiled, he would mark it down $2. Assume that he did not notice the defect and that he sold the hat for $10. The customer later saw that the hat was soiled and voiced his dissatisfaction. He kept the hat, but was given a $2 allowance. Allowances here should not be confused with sales returns where the customer returns the article and is refunded the full purchase price.

RETURN ON INVESTMENT

A commonly used measure of managerial performance and the operating success of a company is its rate of return on investment. We use both the balance sheet and the operating statement as sources of information. The appropriate formula for calculating return on investment (ROI) is as follows:

$$ROI = \frac{Net\ profit}{Sales} \times \frac{Sales}{Investment}$$

Two questions may quickly come to mind. First, what do we mean by "investment"? Second, why do we need two fractions? It would seem that the "sales" component in each fraction would cancel out, leaving net profit/investment as the meaningful ratio.

To answer the first query, consider a firm whose operating statement showed annual sales of $1,000,000 and a net profit of $50,000. At the end of the year the balance sheet reported:

Assets	$600,000	Liabilities		$200,000
		Capital stock	$300,000	
		Retained earnings	100,000	400,000
	$600,000			$600,000

Now, is the investment $400,000 or $600,000? Certainly the ROI will be different depending upon which figure we use. The answer depends upon whether we are talking to the stockholders or to the company executives. The stockholders are more interested in the return on what they have invested—in this case, $400,000. The ROI calculation then is:

$$\frac{Net\ profit\ \ \$50,000}{Sales\ \ \$1,000,000} \times \frac{Sales\ \ \$1,000,000}{Investment\ \ \$400,000} = 12\ 1/2\ \%$$

Management, on the other hand, is more concerned with the total investment, as represented by the total assets ($600,000). This is the factor which the executives must manage, regardless of whether the assets were acquired by stockholders' investment, retained earnings, or loans from outside sources.[1] Within this context the ROI computation becomes:

---

1 In fact, it has been suggested that the term "assets employed" or "assets managed" be used in the formula instead of "investment" when using the ROI concept as a measure of managerial performance. See Michael Schiff, "The Use of ROI in Sales Management," *Journal of Marketing*, July, 1963, pp. 70-73; and J. S. Schiff and Michael Schiff, "New Sales Management Tool: ROAM (Return on Assets Managed)," *Harvard Business Review*, July-August, 1967, pp. 59-66.

$$\frac{\text{Net profit} \quad \$50,000}{\text{Sales} \quad \$1,000,000} \times \frac{\text{Sales} \quad \$1,000,000}{\text{Investment} \$600,000} = 8 \ 1/3\%$$

Regarding the second question, we use two fractions because we are dealing with two separate elements—the rate of profit on sales and the rate of capital turnover. Management really should determine each rate separately and then multiply the two. The rate of profit on sales is influenced by marketing considerations—sales volume, price, product mix, advertising effort, etc. The capital turnover is a financial consideration not directly involved with costs or profits—only sales volume and assets managed.

To illustrate, assume that our company's profits doubled with the same sales volume and investment because management operated an excellent marketing program this year. In effect, we doubled our profit rate with the same capital turnover:

$$\frac{\text{Net profit} \ \$100,000}{\text{Sales} \ \$1,000,000} \times \frac{\text{Sales} \quad \$1,000,000}{\text{Investment} \ \$600,000} = 16 \ 2/3\%$$
$$10\% \quad \times \qquad\qquad 1.67 \quad = 16 \ 2/3\%$$

In another example let us assume that we earned our original profit of $50,000 but that we did it with an investment reduced to $500,000. We cut the size of our average inventory, and we closed some branch offices. By increasing our capital turnover from 1.67 to 2 we raise the ROI from 8 1/3 percent to 10 percent, even though sales volume and profit remain unchanged:

$$\frac{\$50,000}{\$1,000,000} \times \frac{\$1,000,000}{\$500,000} = 10\%$$
$$5\% \quad \times \quad 2 \quad = 10\%$$

Assume that we increase our sales volume—let us say we double it—but do not increase our profit or investment, the cost-profit squeeze is bringing us "profitless prosperity." The following interesting results occur:

$$\frac{\$50,000}{\$2,000,000} \times \frac{\$2,000,000}{\$600,000} = 8 \ 1/3\%$$
$$2 \ 1/2\% \quad \times \quad 3.33 \quad = 8 \ 1/3\%$$

The profit rate was cut in half, but this was offset by a doubling of the capital turnover rate, leaving the ROI unchanged.

QUESTIONS AND PROBLEMS

1. Construct an operating statement from the following data and compute the gross-margin percentage:

Purchases at billed cost	$15,000
Net sales	30,000
Sales returns and allowances	200
Cash discounts given	300

Cash discounts earned	100
Rent	1,500
Salaries	6,000
Opening inventory at cost	10,000
Advertising	600
Other expenses	2,000
Closing inventory at cost	7,500

2. Prepare a retail operating statement from the following data and compute the markdown percentage:

Rent	$ 9,000
Closing inventory at cost	28,000
Sales returns	6,500
Gross margin as percentage of sales	35%
Cash discounts allowed	2,000
Salaries	34,000
Markdowns	4,000
Other operating expenses	15,000
Opening inventory at cost	35,000
Gross sales	232,500
Advertising	5,500
Freight in	3,500

3. What are the percentages of markup on cost which correspond to the following percentages of markup on selling price?
   a. 20 percent   c. 50 percent
   b. 37 1/2 percent   d. 66 2/3 percent

4. What are the percentages of markup on selling price which correspond to the following percentages of markup on cost?
   a. 20 percent   c. 50 percent
   b. 33 1/3 percent   d. 300 percent

5. A hardware store bought a gross (twelve dozen) of hammers, paying $302.40 for the lot. The retailer estimated his operating expenses for this product to be 35 percent of sales, and he wanted a net profit of 5 percent of sales. He expected no markdowns. What retail selling price should he set for each hammer?

6. Competition in a certain line of sporting goods pretty well limits the selling price on a certain item to $25. If the store owner feels he needs a markup of 35 percent to cover his expenses and return a reasonable profit, what is the most he can pay for this item?

7. A retailer with annual net sales of $2 million maintains a markup of 66 2/3 percent based on cost. His expenses average 35 percent. What is his gross margin and net profit in dollars?

8. A company has a stockturn rate of five times a year, a sales volume of $600,000, and a gross margin of 25 percent. What is the average inventory at cost?

9. A store has an average inventory of $30,000 at retail and a stockturn rate of five times a year. If the company maintains a markup of 50 percent based on cost, what is the annual sales volume and cost of goods sold?

10. From the following data, compute the gross-margin percentage and the operating expense ratio:
    Stockturn rate = 9

Average inventory at selling price = 45,000
Net profit = $20,000
Cost of goods sold = $350,000

11. A ski shop sold 50 pairs of skis at $90 a pair, taking a 10 percent markdown in so doing. All the skis were originally purchased at the same price and had been marked up 60 percent on cost. What was the gross margin on the 50 pairs of skis?

12. A men's clothing store bought 200 suits at $90 each. The suits were marked up 40 percent. Eighty were sold at that price. The remaining suits were each marked down 20 percent from the original selling price, and then they were sold. Compute the sales volume and the markdown percentage.

13. An appliance retailer sold 60 radios at $30 each after taking markdowns equal to 20 percent of the actual selling price. Originally all the radios had been purchased at the same price and were marked up 50 percent on cost. What was the gross-margin percentage earned in this situation?

14. An appliance manufacturer produced a line of small appliances advertised to sell at $30. The manufacturer planned for wholesalers to receive a 20 percent markup, and retailers a 33 1/3 percent markup. Total manufacturing costs were $12 per unit. What did retailers pay for the product? What were the manufacturer's selling price and his percentage markup?

15. A housewares manufacturer produces an article at a full cost of $1.80. It is sold through a manufacturers' agent directly to large retailers. The agent receives a 20 percent commission on his sales, the retailers earn a margin of 30 percent, and the manufacturer plans a net profit of 10 percent on his selling price. What is the retail price of this article?

16. A manufacturer suggests a retail selling price of $400 on an item and grants a chain discount of 40-10-10. What is the manufacturer's selling price? (Chain discounts are discussed in Chapter 14.)

17. A building materials manufacturer sold a quantity of his product to a wholesaler for $350, and the wholesaler in turn sold to a lumberyard. The wholesaler's normal markup was 15 percent, and the retailer usually priced the item to include a 30 percent markup. What is the selling price to the consumer?

18. From the following data, calculate the return on investment, based on a definition of "investment" which is useful for evaluating managerial performance:

Net sales	$800,000	Markup	35%
Gross margin	$280,000	Average inventory	$ 75,000
Total assets	$200,000	Retained earnings	$ 60,000
Cost of goods sold	$520,000	Operating	$240,000
Liabilities	$40,000	expenses	

NAME INDEX

SUBJECT INDEX